HAMMOND NOVA WORLD ATLAS

HAMMOND INCORPORATED
MAPLEWOOD, NEW JERSEY 07040

Hammond Publications Advisory Board

ISBN 0-8437-1216-3

PRINTED IN THE UNITED STATES OF AMERICA

Library of Congress Cataloging-in-Publication Data

Hammond Incorporated.
Hammond nova world atlas.
p. cm.
Includes indexes.
ISBN 0-8437-1216-3
1. Atlases. I. Title. II. Title: Nova world atlas.
G1021.H27446 1991 [G&M]
912--dc20

CIP
MAP

CONTENTS

Introduction to the World Atlas IV
Introduction to the Maps and Indexes V
Gazetteer-Index VII

World and Polar Regions

World 1, 2
Arctic Ocean 4
Antarctica 5

Europe

Europe 6
United Kingdom and Ireland 8
Norway, Sweden, Finland, Denmark and Iceland 16
Germany 20
Netherlands, Belgium and Luxembourg 23
France 26
Spain and Portugal 29
Italy 32
Switzerland and Liechtenstein 35
Austria, Czechoslovakia and Hungary 38
Balkan States 41
Poland 44
Union of Soviet Socialist Republics 46

Africa

Africa 52
Northern Part 54
Southern Part 57

Asia

Asia 58
Near and Middle East 60
Turkey, Syria, Lebanon and Cyprus 63
Israel and Jordan 66
Iran and Iraq 68
Indian Subcontinent and Afghanistan 70
Japan and Korea 73
China and Mongolia 76
Burma, Thailand, Indochina and Malaya 79
Southeast Asia 82

Australia and Pacific Ocean

Australia and New Zealand 85
Pacific Ocean 88

South America

Northern Part 90
Southern Part 93

North America

North America 94
Canada 96
Newfoundland 99
Nova Scotia and Prince Edward Island 100
New Brunswick 102
Quebec 104
Ontario 107
Manitoba 110
Saskatchewan 112
Alberta 114
British Columbia 116
Mexico 118
Central America 121
West Indies 124

United States

United States 126
Alabama 129
Alaska 130
Arizona 131
Arkansas 132
California 133
Colorado 134
Connecticut 135
Delaware 146
Florida 136
Georgia 137
Hawaii 130
Idaho 138
Illinois 139
Indiana 140
Iowa 141
Kansas 142
Kentucky 143
Louisiana 144
Maine 145
Maryland 146
Massachusetts 147
Michigan 148
Minnesota 149
Mississippi 150
Missouri 151
Montana 152
Nebraska 153
Nevada 154
New Hampshire 155
New Jersey 156
New Mexico 157
New York 158
North Carolina 159
North Dakota 160
Ohio 161
Oklahoma 162
Oregon 163
Pennsylvania 164
Rhode Island 147
South Carolina 165
South Dakota 166
Tennessee 167
Texas 168
Utah 169
Vermont 155
Virginia 170
Washington 171
West Virginia 172
Wisconsin 173
Wyoming 174

The Fifty States 175

Introduction to the World Atlas

As in previous editions, the atlas is organized to make the retrieval of information as simple and quick as possible. The guiding principle in organizing the atlas material has been to present separate subjects on *separate* maps. In this way, each individual map topic is shown with the greatest degree of clarity, unencumbered with extraneous information that is best revealed on separate maps. Of equal importance from the standpoint of good atlas design is the treatment of all current information on a given country as a single atlas unit. Thus, the basic reference map of an area is accompanied on adjacent pages by all supplementary information pertaining to that area. For example, except for individual United States maps, the detailed index for a given map always appears on the same page as, or on the pages immediately following, the reference map. This same map index provides population data for the many cities, towns and villages shown on the map. Highlight information on the area, i.e., the total population and area, the capital, the highest point, is listed in the summary fact listings accompanying each unit. An adjacent locator map relates the subject area to the larger world beyond. A three-dimensional picture of the area is exhibited by means of the accompanying full-color topographic map. A separate economic map defines the vital agricultural, industrial and mineral resources of the area. In the case of the foreign maps, the flag of each independent nation appears on the appropriate page. Finally, certain country units contain special subject maps dealing with the history, climate, demography and vegetation of the area.

Of course, the maps have been thoroughly updated. These revisions echo the new nations, shifting boundaries and the fluid internal divisions of many countries. New communities generated by the opening up of resources in the developing nations are also noted. Up-to-date geographical information, both foreign and domestic, is received daily by the atlas editors. A worldwide correspondence and thorough research brings to the atlas user the latest geographical and demographic information obtainable.

In closing it may be said that the atlas has truly been designed for contemporary use. Just as the information presented on the following pages is as current and up to date as the editors and cartographers could issue it, so the design and organization has been as well planned as possible to create a work useful to present generations.

C. Dean Hammond III

President
HAMMOND INCORPORATED

Introduction to the Maps and Indexes

The following notes have been added to aid the reader in making the best use of this atlas. Though he may be familiar with maps and map indexes, the publisher believes that a quick review of the material below will add to his enjoyment of this reference work.

Arrangement — The Plan of the Atlas. The atlas has been designed with maximum convenience for the user as its objective. The first part of the atlas contains the general political reference maps, area by area. All geographically related information pertaining to a country or region appears on adjacent pages, eliminating the task of searching throughout the entire volume for data on a given area. Thus, the reader will find, conveniently assembled, political, topographic, economic and special maps of a political area or region, accompanied by detailed map indexes, statistical data, and illustrations of the national flags of the area.

The sequence of country units in this American-designed atlas in international in arrangement. Units on the world as a whole are followed by a section on the polar regions which, in turn, is followed by pages devoted to Europe and its countries. Following the maps of the European continent and its countries, the geographic sequence plan proceeds as follows: Africa, Asia, the Pacific and Australia, South America, North America, and ends with detailed coverage on the United States.

Political Maps — The Primary Reference Tool. The most detailed maps in each country unit are the *political maps.* It is our feeling that the reader is likely to refer to these maps more often than to any other in the book when confronted by such questions as — Where? How big? What is it near? Answering these common queries is the function of the political maps. Each political map stresses *political* phenomena — countries, internal political divisions, boundaries, cities and towns. The major political unit or units, shown on the map, are banded in distinctive colors for easy identification and delineation. First-order political subdivisions (states, provinces, counties on the state maps) are shown, scale permitting.

The reader is advised to make use of the *legend* appearing under the title on each political map. Map *symbols,* the special "language" of maps, are explained in the legend. Each variety of dot, circle, star or interrupted line has a special meaning which should be clearly understood by the user so that he may interpret the map data correctly.

Each country has been portrayed at a *scale* commensurate with its political, areal, economic or tourist importance. In certain cases, a whole map unit may be devoted to a single nation if that nation is considered to be of prime interest to most atlas users. In other cases, several nations will be shown on a single map if, as separate entities, they are of lesser relative importance. Areas of dense settlement and important significance within a country have been enlarged and portrayed in inset maps inserted on the margins of the main map. The reader is advised to refer to the linear or "bar" scale appearing on each map or map inset in order to determine the distance between points.

The *projection* system used for each map is noted near the title of the map. Map projections are the special graphic systems used by cartographers to render the curved three-dimensional surface of the globe on a flat surface. Optimum map projections determined by the attributes of the area have been used by the the publishers for each map in the atlas.

A word here as to the choice of place names on the maps. Throughout the atlas names appear, with a few exceptions, in their local official spellings. However, conventional Anglicized spellings are used for major geographical divisions and for towns and topographic features for which English forms exist; i.e., "Spain" instead of "España" or "Munich" instead of "München." Names of this type are normally followed by the local official spelling in parentheses. As an aid to the user the indexes are cross-referenced for all current and most former spellings of such names.

Names of cities and towns in the United States follow the forms listed in the *Post Office Directory* of the United States Postal Service. Domestic physical names follow the decisions of the Board on Geographic Names, U.S. Department of the Interior, and of various state geographic name boards.

It is the belief of the publishers that the boundaries shown in a general reference atlas should reflect current geographic and political realities. This policy has been followed consistently in the atlas. The presentation of *de facto* boundaries in cases of territorial dispute between various nations does not imply the political endorsement of such boundaries by the publisher, but simply the honest representation of boundaries as they exist at the time of the printing of the atlas maps.

Indexes — Pinpointing a Location. Each political map (except for individual United States maps) is accompanied by a comprehensive index of the place names appearing on the map. If you are unfamiliar with the location of a particular geographical place and wish to find its position within the confines of the subject area of the map, consult the map index as your first step. The name of the feature sought will be found in its proper alphabetical sequence with a key reference letter-number combination corresponding to its location on the map. After noting the key reference letter-number combination for the place name, turn to the map. The place name will be found within the square formed by the two lines of latitude and the two lines of longitude which enclose the co-ordinates — i.e., the marginal letters and numbers, the diagram below illustrates the system of indexing.

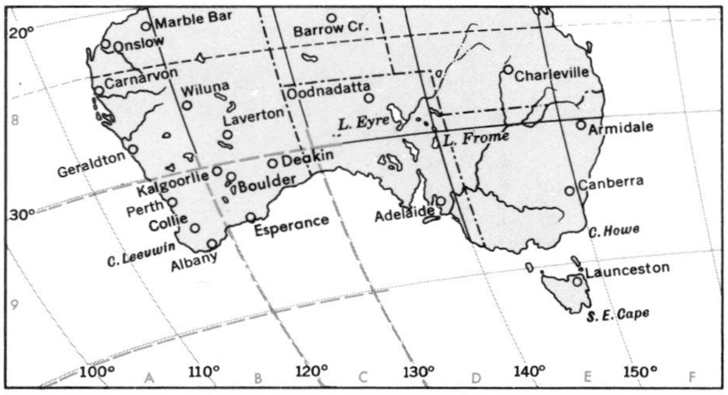

Where space on the map has not permitted giving the complete form of the place name, the complete form is shown in the index. Where a place is known by more than one name or by various spellings of the same name, the different forms have been included in the index. Physical features are listed under their proper names and not according to their generic terms; that is to say, Rio Negro will be found under Negro and not under Rio Negro. On the other hand, Rio Grande will be found under Rio Grande. Accompanying most index entries for cities and towns, and for other political units, are *population figures* for the particular entries. The large number of population figures in the atlas makes this work one of the most comprehensive statistical sources available to the public today. The population figures have been taken from the latest official censuses and estimates of the various nations.

Population and area figures for countries and major political units are listed in bold type *fact lists* on the margins of the indexes. In addition, the capital, largest city, highest point, monetary unit, principal languages and the prevailing religions of the country concerned are also listed. The Gazetteer-Index of the World on the following pages provides a quick reference index for countries and other important areas. Though population and area figures for each major unit are also found in the map section, the Gazetteer-Index provides a conveniently arranged statistical comparison contained in two pages.

Relief Maps. Accompanying each political map is a relief map of the area. The purpose of the relief map is to illustrate the surface configuration (TOPOGRAPHY) of the region. A shading technique in color simulates the relative ruggedness of the terrain — plains, plateaus, valleys, hills and mountains. Graded colors, ranging from greens for lowlands, yellows for intermediate elevations to browns in the highlands, indicate the height above sea level of each part of the land. A vertical scale at the margin of the map shows the approximate height in meters and feet represented by each color.

Economic Maps — Agriculture, Industry and Resources. One of the most interesting features that will be found in each country unit is the economic map. From this map one can determine the basic activities of a nation as expressed through its economy. A perusal of the map yields a full understanding of the area's economic geography and natural resources.

The agricultural economy is manifested in two ways: color bands and commodity names. The color bands express broad categories of *dominant land use*, such as cereal belts, forest lands, livestock range lands, nonagricultural wastes. The red commodity names, on the other hand, pinpoint the areas of production of *specific* crops; i.e., wheat, cotton, sugar beets, etc.

Major mineral occurrences are denoted by standard letter symbols appearing in blue. The relative size of the letter symbols signifies the relative importance of the deposit.

The manufacturing sector of the economy is presented by means of diagonal line patterns expressing the various *industrial* areas of consequence within a country.

The fishing industry is represented by names of commercial fish species appearing offshore in blue letters. Major waterpower sites are designated by blue symbols.

The publishers have tried to make this work the most comprehensive and useful atlas available, and it is hoped that it will prove a valuable reference work. Any constructive suggestions from the reader will be welcomed.

Sources and Acknowledgments

A multitude of sources goes into the making of a large-scale reference work such as this. To list them all would take many pages and would consume space better devoted to the maps and reference materials themselves. However, certain general sources were very useful in preparing this work and are listed below.

STATISTICAL OFFICE OF THE UNITED NATIONS.
Demographic Yearbook. New York. Issued annually.

STATISTICAL OFFICE OF THE UNITED NATIONS.
Statisical Yearbook. New York. Issued annually.

THE GEOGRAPHER, U.S. DEPARTMENT OF STATE
International Boundary Study papers. Washington. Various dates.

THE GEOGRAPHER, U.S. DEPARTMENT OF STATE.
Geographic Notes. Washington. Various dates.

UNITED STATES BOARD ON GEOGRAPHIC NAMES.
Decisions on Geographic Names in the United States. Washington. Various dates.

UNITED STATES BOARD ON GEOGRAPHIC NAMES.
Official Standard Names Gazetteers. Washington. Various dates.

CANADIAN PERMANENT COMMITTEE ON GEOGRAPHICAL NAMES.
Gazetteer of Canada series. Ottawa. Various dates.

UNITED STATES POSTAL SERVICE.
National Five Digit ZIP Code and Post Office Directory. Washington. Issued annually.

UNITED STATES POSTAL SERVICE.
Postal Bulletin. Washington. Issued weekly.

UNITED STATES DEPARTMENT OF THE INTERIOR. BUREAU OF MINES.
Minerals Yearbook. 4 vols. Washington. Various dates.

UNITED STATES GEOLOGICAL SURVEY.
Elevations and distances in the United States. Reston, Va. 1980.

CARTACTUAL.
Cartactual — Topical Map Service. Budapest. Issued bi-monthly.

AMERICAN GEOGRAPHICAL SOCIETY.
Focus. New York. Issued ten times a year.

THE AMERICAN UNIVERSITY.
Foreign Area Studies. Washington. Various dates.

CENTRAL INTELLIGENCE AGENCY.
General reference maps. Washington. Various dates.

A sample list of sources used for <u>specific</u> countries follows:

Afghanistan
CENTRAL STATISTICS OFFICE.
Preliminary Results of the First Afghan Population Census 1979. Kabul.

Albania
DREJTORIA E STATISTIKES.
1979 Census. Tiranë.

Argentina
INSTITUTO NACIONAL DE ESTADISTICA Y CENSOS.
Censo Nacional de Población y Vivienda 1980. Buenos Aires.

Australia
AUSTRALIAN BUREAU OF STATISTICS.
Census of Population and Housing 1981. Canberra.

Brazil
FUNDACAO INSTITUTO BRASILEIRO DE GEOGRAFIA E ESTATISTICA.
IX Recenseamento Geral do Brasil 1980. Rio de Janeiro.

Canada
STATISTICS CANADA.
1981 Census of Canada. Ottawa.

Cuba
COMITE ESTATAL DE ESTADISTICAS.
Censo de Población y Viviendas 1981. Havana.

Hungary
HUNGARIAN CENTRAL STATISTICAL OFFICE.
1980 Census. Budapest.

Indonesia
BIRO PUSAT STATISTIK.
Sensus Penduduk 1980. Jakarta.

Kuwait
CENTRAL OFFICE OF STATISTICS.
1980 Census. Al Kuwait.

New Zealand
DEPARTMENT OF STATISTICS.
New Zealand Census of Population and Dwellings 1981. Wellington.

Panama
DIRECCIÓN DE ESTADISTICA Y CENSO.
Censos Nacionales de 1980. Panamá.

Papua New Guinea
BUREAU OF STATISTICS.
National Population Census 1980. Port Moresby.

Philippines
NATIONAL CENSUS AND STATISTICS OFFICE.
1980 Census of Population. Manila.

Saint Lucia
CENSUS OFFICE.
1980 Population Census. Castries.

Singapore
DEPARTMENT OF STATISTICS.
Census of Population 1980. Singapore.

U.S.S.R.
CENTRAL STATISTICAL ADMINISTRATION.
1979 Census. Moscow.

United States
BUREAU OF THE CENSUS.
1980 Census of Population. Washington.

Vanuatu
CENSUS OFFICE.
1979 Population Census. Port Vila.

Zambia
CENTRAL STATISTICAL OFFICE.
1980 Census of Population and Housing. Lusaka.

Gazetteer—Index of the World

This alphabetical list of grand divisions, countries, states, colonial possessions, etc., gives page numbers and index references on which they are shown on the largest scale as well as area and population of each unit. The index reference shows the square on the respective map in which the name of the entry may be located.

Country	Page No.	Index Ref.	Area: Square Miles	Area: Square Kilometers	Population
*Afghanistan	70	A 2	250,775	649,507	15,540,000
Africa	54, 57	......	11,707,000	30,321,130	469,000,000
Alabama, U.S.A.	129	......	51,705	133,916	3,893,888
Alaska, U.S.A.	130	......	591,004	1,530,700	401,851
*Albania	43	E 5	11,100	28,749	2,590,600
Alberta, Canada	114	......	255,285	661,185	2,237,724
*Algeria	54	F 6	919,591	2,381,740	17,422,000
American Samoa	89	J 7	77	199	32,297
Andorra	31	G 1	188	487	31,000
*Angola	57	K14	481,351	1,246,700	7,078,000
Anguilla	124	F 3	35	91	6,519
Antarctica	5	......	5,500,000	14,245,000	......
*Antigua and Barbuda	124	G 3	171	443	72,000
*Argentina	93	H10	1,072,070	2,776,661	28,438,000
Arizona, U.S.A.	131	......	114,000	295,260	2,718,425
Arkansas, U.S.A.	132	......	53,187	137,754	2,286,435
Aruba	124	E 3	75	193	55,148
Ascension Island, St. Helena	1	......	34	88	719
Asia	58	......	17,128,500	44,362,815	2,633,000,000
*Australia	86	......	2,966,136	7,682,300	14,576,330
*Austria	38	B 3	32,375	83,851	7,507,000
*Bahamas	124	C 1	5,382	13,939	209,505
*Bahrain	60	F 4	240	622	358,857
*Bangladesh	70	F 3	55,126	142,776	87,052,024
*Barbados	125	G 4	166	430	248,983
*Belgium	25	E 7	11,781	30,513	9,855,110
*Belize	122	C 2	8,867	22,966	144,857
*Benin	54	G10	43,483	112,620	3,338,240
Bermuda	125	H 3	21	54	67,761
Bhutan	70	G 3	18,147	47,000	1,298,000
Bolivia	90	G 7	424,163	1,098,582	5,600,000
*Botswana	57	L16	224,764	582,139	819,000
*Brazil	90	K 6	3,284,426	8,506,663	119,098,992
British Columbia, Canada	117	......	366,253	948,596	2,744,467
British Indian Ocean Terr.	58	L10	29	75	2,000
Brunei	83	E 4	2,226	5,765	192,832
*Bulgaria	43	F 4	42,823	110,912	8,862,000
*Burkina Faso	54	F 9	105,869	274,200	6,908,000
*Burma (Myanmar)	81	B 2	261,789	678,034	32,913,000
*Burundi	57	M12	10,747	27,835	4,021,910
California, U.S.A.	133	......	158,706	411,049	23,667,565
*Cambodia (Kampuchea)	81	E 4	69,898	181,036	5,200,000
*Cameroon	54	J10	183,568	475,441	8,503,000
*Canada	96-97	......	3,851,787	9,976,139	24,343,181
*Cape Verde	1	......	1,557	4,033	324,000
Cayman Islands	124	B 3	100	259	16,677
*Central African Republic	54	K10	242,000	626,780	2,284,000
Central America	122-123	......	197,480	511,475	21,000,000
Ceylon, see Sri Lanka					
*Chad	54	K 8	495,752	1,283,998	4,309,000
Channel Islands	11	E 8	75	194	133,000
*Chile	93	F10	292,257	756,946	11,275,440
*China, People's Rep. of	77	......	3,691,000	9,559,690	958,090,000
China, Republic of (Taiwan)	77	K 7	13,971	36,185	16,609,961
*Colombia	90	F 3	439,513	1,138,339	27,520,000
Colorado, U.S.A.	134	......	104,091	269,596	2,889,735
*Comoros	57	P14	719	1,862	290,000
*Congo	57	J12	132,046	342,000	1,537,000
Connecticut, U.S.A.	135	......	5,018	12,997	3,107,576
Cook Islands	89	K 7	91	236	17,695
*Costa Rica	122	E 5	19,575	50,700	2,245,000
*Cuba	124	B 2	44,206	114,494	9,706,369
*Cyprus	64	E 5	3,473	8,995	629,000
*Czechoslovakia	39	C 2	49,373	127,876	15,276,799
Delaware, U.S.A.	146	R 3	2,044	5,294	594,317
*Denmark	19	......	16,629	43,069	5,124,000
District of Columbia, U.S.A.	146	F 5	69	179	638,432
*Djibouti	55	P 9	8,880	23,000	386,000
*Dominica	125	G 4	290	751	74,089
*Dominican Republic	124	D 3	18,704	48,443	5,647,977
*Ecuador	90	E 4	109,483	283,561	8,354,000
*Egypt	54	M 6	386,659	1,001,447	41,572,000
*El Salvador	122	C 4	8,260	21,393	4,813,000
England, U.K.	11	......	50,516	130,836	46,220,955
*Equatorial Guinea	57	H11	10,831	28,052	244,000
*Ethiopia	54-55	O 9	471,776	1,221,900	31,065,000
Europe	6	......	4,057,000	10,507,630	676,000,000

Country	Page No.	Index Ref.	Area: Square Miles	Area: Square Kilometers	Population
Faerøe Islands, Denmark	19	B 2	540	1,399	41,969
Falkland Islands & Dependencies	93	H14	6,198	16,053	1,812
*Fiji	89	H 8	7,055	18,272	588,068
*Finland	16	O 6	130,128	337,032	4,788,000
Florida, U.S.A.	136	......	58,664	151,940	9,746,342
*France	26	......	210,038	543,998	53,788,000
French Guiana	90	K 3	35,135	91,000	73,022
French Polynesia	89	L 8	1,544	4,000	137,382
*Gabon	57	J12	103,346	267,666	551,000
*Gambia	54	C 9	4,127	10,689	601,000
Georgia, U.S.A.	137	......	58,910	152,577	5,463,105
*Germany	20	......	137,753	356,780	78,278,587
*Ghana	54	F10	92,099	238,536	11,450,000
Gibraltar	31	D 4	2.28	5.91	29,760
*Great Britain & Northern Ireland (United Kingdom)	8	......	94,399	244,493	55,672,000
*Greece	43	F 6	50,944	131,945	9,599,000
Greenland	4	O 2	840,000	2,175,600	49,773
*Grenada	125	G 4	133	344	103,103
Guadeloupe & Dependencies	124	F 3	687	1,779	328,400
Guam	89	E 4	209	541	105,979
*Guatemala	122	B 3	42,042	108,889	7,262,419
*Guinea	54	D 9	94,925	245,856	5,143,284
*Guinea-Bissau	54	C 9	13,948	36,125	777,214
*Guyana	90	J 2	83,000	214,970	820,000
*Haiti	124	D 3	10,694	27,697	5,009,000
Hawaii, U.S.A.	130	......	6,471	16,760	964,691
Holland, see Netherlands					
*Honduras	122	D 3	43,277	112,087	3,691,000
Hong Kong	77	H 7	403	1,044	5,022,000
*Hungary	39	E 3	35,919	93,030	10,709,536
*Iceland	19	B 1	39,768	103,000	228,785
Idaho, U.S.A.	138	......	83,564	216,431	944,038
Illinois, U.S.A.	139	......	56,345	145,934	11,426,596
*India	70	D 4	1,269,339	3,287,588	683,810,051
*Indiana, U.S.A.	140	......	36,185	93,719	5,490,260
*Indonesia	83	D 7	788,430	2,042,034	147,490,298
Iowa, U.S.A.	141	......	56,275	145,752	2,913,808
*Iran	68	F 4	636,293	1,648,000	37,447,000
*Iraq	68	C 4	172,476	446,713	12,767,000
*Ireland	15	......	27,136	70,282	3,440,427
Ireland, Northern, U.K.	15	F 2	5,452	14,121	1,543,000
Isle of Man	11	C 3	227	588	64,000
*Israel	67	B 4	7,847	20,324	3,878,000
*Italy	32	......	116,303	301,225	57,140,000
*Ivory Coast (Côte d'Ivoire)	54	E10	124,504	322,465	7,920,000
*Jamaica	124	C 3	4,411	11,424	2,161,000
*Japan	75	......	145,730	377,441	117,057,485
*Jordan	67	D 3	35,000	90,650	2,152,273
*Kampuchea (Cambodia)	81	E 4	69,898	181,036	5,200,000
Kansas, U.S.A.	142	......	82,277	213,097	2,364,236
Kentucky, U.S.A.	143	......	40,409	104,659	3,660,257
*Kenya	57	O11	224,960	582,646	15,327,061
Kiribati	89	J 6	291	754	57,500
Korea, North	74	D 3	46,540	120,539	17,914,000
Korea, South	74	D 5	38,175	98,873	37,448,836
*Kuwait	60	E 4	6,532	16,918	1,355,827
*Laos	81	D 3	91,428	236,800	3,721,000
*Lebanon	64	F 6	4,015	10,399	3,161,000
*Lesotho	57	M17	11,720	30,355	1,339,000
*Liberia	54	E10	43,000	111,370	1,873,000
*Libya	54	J 6	679,358	1,759,537	2,856,000
*Liechtenstein	37	J 2	61	158	25,220
Louisiana, U.S.A.	144	......	47,752	123,678	4,206,312
*Luxembourg	25	J 9	999	2,587	364,000
Macau	77	H 7	6	16	271,000
*Madagascar	57	R16	226,657	587,041	8,742,000
Maine, U.S.A.	145	......	33,265	86,156	1,125,027
*Malawi	57	N14	45,747	118,485	5,968,000
Malaya, Malaysia	81	D 6	50,806	131,588	11,138,227

*Member of the United Nations

Country	Page No.	Index Ref.	Area Square Miles	Area Square Kilometers	Population
*Malaysia	81	D 6	128,308	332,318	13,435,588
	83	E 4			
*Maldives	58	L 9	115	298	143,046
*Mali	54	F 8	464,873	1,204,021	6,906,000
*Malta	32	E 7	122	316	343,970
Manitoba, Canada	110	......	250,999	650,087	1,026,241
Martinique	125	G 4	425	1,101	328,566
Maryland, U.S.A.	146	......	10,460	27,091	4,216,975
Massachusetts, U.S.A.	147	......	8,284	21,456	5,737,037
*Mauritania	54	D 8	419,229	1,085,803	1,634,000
*Mauritius	57	S19	790	2,046	959,000
Mayotte	119	P14	144	373	47,300
*Mexico	119	......	761,601	1,972,546	67,395,826
Michigan, U.S.A.	148	......	58,527	151,585	9,262,078
Midway Islands	154	A 5	1.9	4.9	453
Minnesota, U.S.A.	149	......	84,402	218,601	4,075,970
Mississippi, U.S.A.	150	......	47,689	123,515	2,520,638
Missouri, U.S.A.	151	......	69,697	180,515	4,916,759
Monaco	26	G 6	368 acres	149 hectares	25,029
*Mongolia	77	E 2	606,163	1,569,962	1,594,800
Montana, U.S.A.	152	......	147,046	380,849	786,690
Montserrat	125	G 3	40	104	12,073
*Morroco	54	E 5	172,414	446,550	20,242,000
*Mozambique	57	N16	303,769	786,762	12,130,000
*Namibia	57	K16	317,827	823,172	1,200,000
Nauru	89	G 6	7.7	20	7,254
Nebraska, U.S.A.	153	......	77,355	200,349	1,569,825
*Nepal	70	E 3	54,663	141,577	14,179,301
*Netherlands	25	F 5	15,892	41,160	14,227,000
Netherlands Antilles	124	F 3	390	1,010	246,000
Nevada, U.S.A.	154	......	110,561	286,353	800,493
New Brunswick, Canada	102	......	28,354	73,437	696,403
New Caledonia & Dependencies	89	G 8	7,335	18,998	133,233
Newfoundland, Canada	99	......	156,184	404,517	567,681
New Hampshire, U.S.A.	155	......	9,279	24,033	920,610
New Hebrides, see Vanuatu					
New Jersey, U.S.A.	156	......	7,787	20,168	7,364,823
New Mexico, U.S.A.	157	......	121,593	314,926	1,302,981
New York, U.S.A.	158	......	49,108	127,190	17,558,072
*New Zealand	87	......	103,736	268,676	3,175,737
*Nicaragua	122	D 4	45,698	118,358	2,703,000
*Niger	54	H 8	489,189	1,267,000	5,098,427
*Nigeria	54	H10	357,000	924,630	82,643,000
Niue	89	K 7	100	259	3,578
North America	94	......	9,363,000	24,250,170	370,000,000
North Carolina, U.S.A.	159	......	52,669	136,413	5,881,813
North Dakota, U.S.A.	160	......	70,702	183,118	652,717
Northern Ireland, U.K.	15	F 2	5,452	14,121	1,543,000
Northwest Territories, Canada	96	G 3	1,304,896	3,379,683	45,741
*Norway	16	F 7	125,053	323,887	4,092,000
Nova Scotia, Canada	100	......	21,425	55,491	847,442
Ohio, U.S.A.	161	......	41,330	107,045	10,797,624
Oklahoma, U.S.A.	162	......	69,956	181,186	3,025,290
*Oman	60	G 6	120,000	310,800	891,000
Ontario, Canada	107,108	......	412,580	1,068,582	8,625,107
Oregon, U.S.A.	163	......	97,073	251,419	2,633,149
*Pakistan	70	B 3	310,402	803,944	83,782,000
*Panama	122	G 6	29,761	77,082	1,830,175
*Papua New Guinea	82	B 7	183,540	475,369	3,010,727
	89	E 6			
*Paraguay	93	......	157,047	406,752	2,973,000
Pennsylvania, U.S.A.	164	......	45,308	117,348	11,863,895
Persia, see Iran					
*Peru	90	......	496,222	1,285,215	17,031,221
*Philippines	83	......	115,707	299,681	48,098,460
Pitcairn Islands	89	O 8	18	47	54
*Poland	45	......	120,725	312,678	35,815,000
*Portugal	30	B 3	35,549	92,072	9,933,000
Prince Edward Island, Canada	100	E 2	2,184	5,657	122,506
Puerto Rico	124-125	......	3,515	9,104	3,186,076
*Qatar	60	F 4	4,247	11,000	220,000
Quebec, Canada	105, 106	......	594,857	1,540,680	6,438,403
Reúnion	57	R20	969	2,510	491,000
Rhode Island, U.S.A.	147	H 5	1,212	3,139	947,154
Rhodesia, see Zimbabwe					
*Romania	45	F 3	91,699	237,500	22,048,305
*Rwanda	57	N12	10,169	26,337	4,819,317
Sabah, Malaysia	83	F 4	29,300	75,887	1,002,608
Saint Helena & Dependencies	1	......	162	420	5,147

Country	Page No.	Index Ref.	Area Square Miles	Area Square Kilometers	Population
*Saint Kitts and Nevis	124	F 3	104	269	44,404
*Saint Lucia	125	G 4	238	616	115,783
Saint Pierre & Miquelon	99	B 4	93.5	242	6,041
*Saint Vincent & the Grenadines	125	G 4	150	388	124,000
San Marino	32	D 3	23.4	60.6	19,149
*São Tomé and Príncipe	57	G11	372	963	85,000
Sarawak, Malaysia	83	E 5	48,202	124,843	1,294,753
Saskatchewan, Canada	113	......	251,699	651,900	968,313
*Saudi Arabia	60	D 4	829,995	2,149,687	8,367,000
Scotland, U.K.	13	......	30,414	78,772	5,117,146
*Senegal	54	D 9	75,954	196,720	5,508,000
*Seychelles	58	J10	145	375	63,000
Siam, see Thailand					
*Sierra Leone	54	C10	27,925	72,325	3,470,000
*Singapore	81	F 6	226	585	2,413,945
*Solomon Islands	89	G 6	11,500	29,785	221,000
*Somalia	55	R10	246,200	637,658	3,645,000
*South Africa	57	L18	455,318	1,179,274	23,771,970
South America	90	......	6,875,000	17,806,250	245,000,000
South Carolina, U.S.A.	165	......	31,113	80,583	3,121,833
South Dakota, U.S.A.	166	......	77,116	199,730	690,768
*Spain	31	......	194,881	504,742	37,430,000
*Sri Lanka	70	E 7	25,332	65,610	14,850,001
*Sudan	54	M 9	967,494	2,505,809	18,691,000
*Suriname	90	J 3	55,144	142,823	354,860
*Swaziland	57	N17	6,705	17,366	547,000
*Sweden	16	J 8	173,665	449,792	8,320,000
Switzerland	37	......	15,943	41,292	6,365,960
*Syria	64	G 5	71,498	185,180	8,979,000
Taiwan	77	K 7	13,971	36,185	16,609,961
*Tanzania	54	N13	363,708	942,003	17,527,560
Tennessee, U.S.A.	167	......	42,144	109,153	4,591,120
Texas, U.S.A.	168	......	266,807	691,030	14,229,288
*Thailand	81	D 3	198,455	513,998	46,455,000
*Togo	54	G10	21,622	56,000	2,472,000
Tokelau	89	J 6	3.9	10	1,575
Tonga	89	J 8	270	699	90,128
*Trinidad and Tobago	125	G 5	1,980	5,128	1,067,108
Tristan da Cunha, St. Helena	1	......	38	98	251
*Tunisia	54	H 5	63,378	164,149	6,637,000
*Turkey	64	D 3	300,946	779,450	45,217,556
Turks and Caicos Islands	124	D 2	166	430	7,436
Tuvalu	89	H 6	9.78	25.33	7,349
*Uganda	57	N11	91,076	235,887	12,630,076
*Ukrainian S.S.R., U.S.S.R.	50	D 5	233,089	603,700	49,755,000
*Union of Soviet Socialist Republics	46, 50	......	8,649,490	22,402,179	262,436,227
*United Arab Emirates	60	F 5	32,278	83,600	1,040,275
*United Kingdom	8	......	94,399	244,493	55,672,000
*United States of America	126-127	......	3,623,420	9,384,658	226,504,825
*Upper Volta (Burkina Faso)	54	F 9	105,869	274,200	6,908,000
*Uruguay	93	J10	72,172	186,925	2,899,000
Utah, U.S.A.	169	......	84,899	219,888	1,461,037
*Vanuatu	89	G 7	5,700	14,763	112,596
Vatican City	32	B 6	108.7 acres	44 hectares	728
*Venezuela	92	......	352,143	912,050	14,313,000
Vermont, U.S.A.	155	......	9,614	24,900	511,456
*Vietnam	81	E 3	128,405	332,569	52,741,766
Virginia, U.S.A.	170	......	40,767	105,587	5,346,818
Virgin Islands, British	125	H 1	59	153	11,006
Virgin Islands, U.S.A.	125	H 1	132	342	96,569
Wake Island	89	G 4	2.5	6.5	302
Wales, U.K.	11	D 5	8,017	20,764	2,790,462
Wallis and Futuna	89	J 7	106	275	9,192
Washington, U.S.A.	171	......	68,139	176,480	4,132,180
Western Sahara	54	D 6	102,703	266,000	76,425
*Western Samoa	89	J 7	1,133	2,934	158,130
West Virginia, U.S.A.	172	......	24,231	62,758	1,950,279
*White Russian S.S.R. (Byelo-russian S.S.R.), U.S.S.R.	50	C 4	80,154	207,600	9,560,000
Wisconsin, U.S.A.	173	......	56,153	145,436	4,705,521
World	5	......	57,970,000 (land)	150,142,300	4,415,00,000
Wyoming, U.S.A.	174	......	97,809	253,325	469,557
*Yemen	60	D 6	188,321	487,752	8,576,189
*Yugoslavia	43	C 3	98,766	255,804	22,471,000
Yukon Territory, Canada	96	C 3	207,075	536,324	23,153
*Zaire	57	L12	905,063	2,344,133	28,291,000
*Zambia	57	M14	290,586	752,618	5,679,808
*Zimbabwe	57	M15	150,803	390,580	7,360,000

This map has been prepared with the North Pole as the mathematical center. From it, distances to any part of the world may be measured. On Mercator's map of the world, the polar regions are so scattered that their relatively small area and availability for flight routes are disregarded. Today, with airplanes following great circle courses, often within the Arctic Circle, polar projection maps are indispensable to the people of this air-minded age.

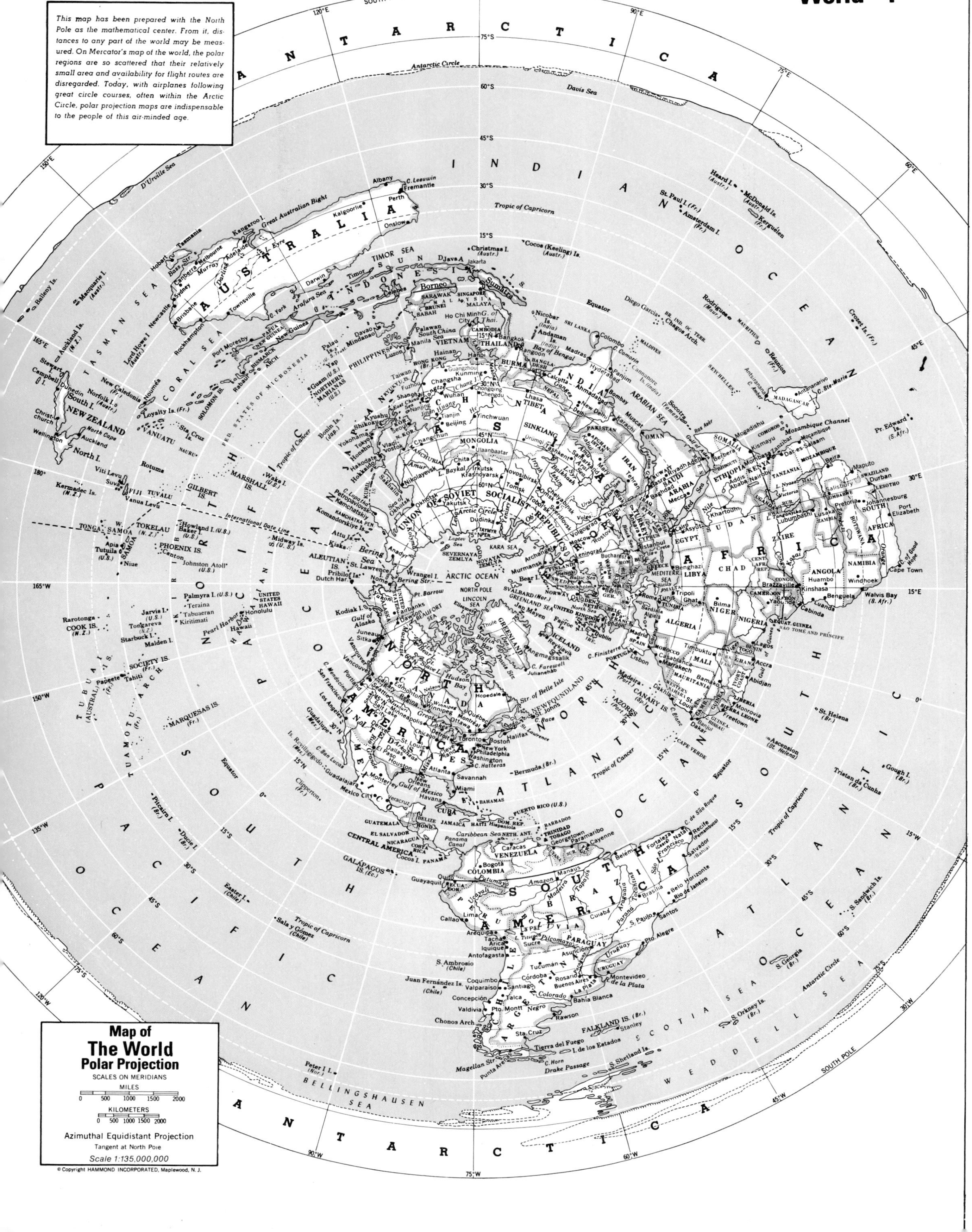

Map of
The World
Polar Projection
SCALES ON MERIDIANS
MILES 0 500 1000 1500 2000
KILOMETERS 0 500 1000 1500 2000
Azimuthal Equidistant Projection
Tangent at North Pole
Scale 1:135,000,000

The World

BRIESEMEISTER ELLIPTICAL
EQUAL-AREA PROJECTION

Capitals of Countries ⊛
Other Capitals ◉
International Boundaries - - -

Scale 1:80,000,000

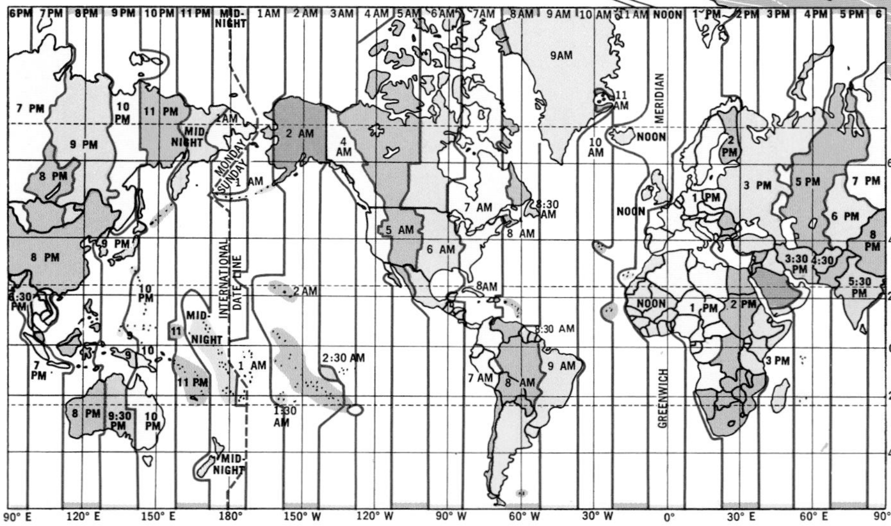

Time Zones

STANDARD TIME ZONES	Areas using half hour deviations.
	Areas not using zone system.

NOTE: Standard time zones in the U.S.S.R. are always advanced one hour.

World 3

LAND AREA 57,970,000 sq. mi.
(150,142,300 sq. km.)
WATER AREA 139,781,000 sq. mi.
(362,032,790 sq. km.)
TOTAL SURFACE AREA 197,751,000 sq.mi.
(512,175,090 sq. km.)
POPULATION 4,415,000,000

Antarctica
AZIMUTHAL EQUIDISTANT PROJECTION
Scale 1:62,000,000

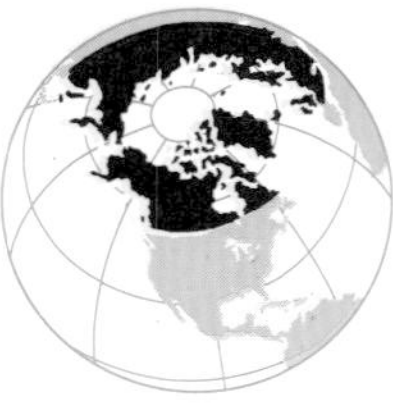

Alaska (gulf), U.S. D17
Alaska (pen.), U.S. D18
Alaska (range), U.S. C17
Alaska (reg.) C17
Aleutian (isls.), U.S. D18
Alexander (arch.), U.S. D16
Alexandra Land (isl.), U.S.S.R. A8
Amundsen (gulf), Canada B16
Anadyr' (gulf), U.S.S.R. C18
Anadyr' (riv.), U.S.S.R. C1
Arctic Ocean A15
Atlantic Ocean D11
Attu (isl.), U.S. D1
Axel Heiberg (isl.), Canada A14
Baffin (bay) B13
Baffin (isl.), Canada C13
Banks (isl)., Canada B16
Barents (sea) B8
Barrow (pt.), U.S. B18
Bathurst (isl.), Canada B14
Bear (isl.), Norway B9
Bear (isls.), U.S.S.R. B1
Beaufort (sea) B16
Belyy (isl.), U.S.S.R. B6
Bering (str.) C18
Bilibino, U.S.S.R. C1
Bol'shevik (isl.), U.S.S.R. A4
Boothia (gulf), Canada B14
Boothia (pen.), Canada B14
Borden (isl.), Canada B15
Bristol (bay), U.S. D18
Brodeur (pen.), Canada B14
Brooks (range), U.S. C17
Canada C13
Chelyuskin (cape), U.S.S.R. B4
Cherskiy, U.S.S.R. C1
Chukchi (pen.), U.S.S.R. C18
Chukchi (sea) C18
Columbia (cape), Canada A13
Cook (inlet), U.S. D17
Cumberland (sound), Canada C13
Davis (str.) C12
Denmark (strait) C11
Devon (isl.), Canada B14
Dezhnev (cape), U.S.S.R. C18
Disko (isl.), Greenl. C12
Dmitriya Lapteva (str.), U.S.S.R. B2
Dvina, Northern (riv.), U.S.S.R. C7
East (Dezhnev) (cape), U.S.S.R. C18
East Siberian (sea), U.S.S.R. B1
Edge (isl.), Norway B8
Ellef Ringnes (isl.), Canada B15
Ellesmere (isl.), Canada B14
Faddeyevskiy (isl.), U.S.S.R. B2
Farewell (cape), Greenl. D12
Finland C8
Foxe (basin), Canada C13
Franz Josef Land (isls.), U.S.S.R. A7
Frederikshåb, Greenl. C12
Garry (lake), Canada C14
George Land (isl.), U.S.S.R. B7
Godhavn, Greenl. C12
Godthåb (Nûk) (cap.), Greenl. C12
Graham Bell (isl.), U.S.S.R. A6
Great Bear (lake), Canada C16
Great Slave (lake), Canada C15
Greenland B12
Greenland (sea) B10
Grise Fiord, Canada B13
Grønnedal, Greenl. C12
Gunnbjørn (mt.), Greenl. C11
Gyda (pen.), U.S.S.R. C6
Hammerfest, Norway B9
Hayes (pen.), Greenl. B13
Hekla (mt.), Ice. C11
Holman Island, Canada B15
Holsteinsborg, Greenl. C12
Hope (isl.), Norway B8
Iceland C10
Igarka, U.S.S.R. C5
Igloolik, Canada B14
Indigirka (riv.), U.S.S.R. C2

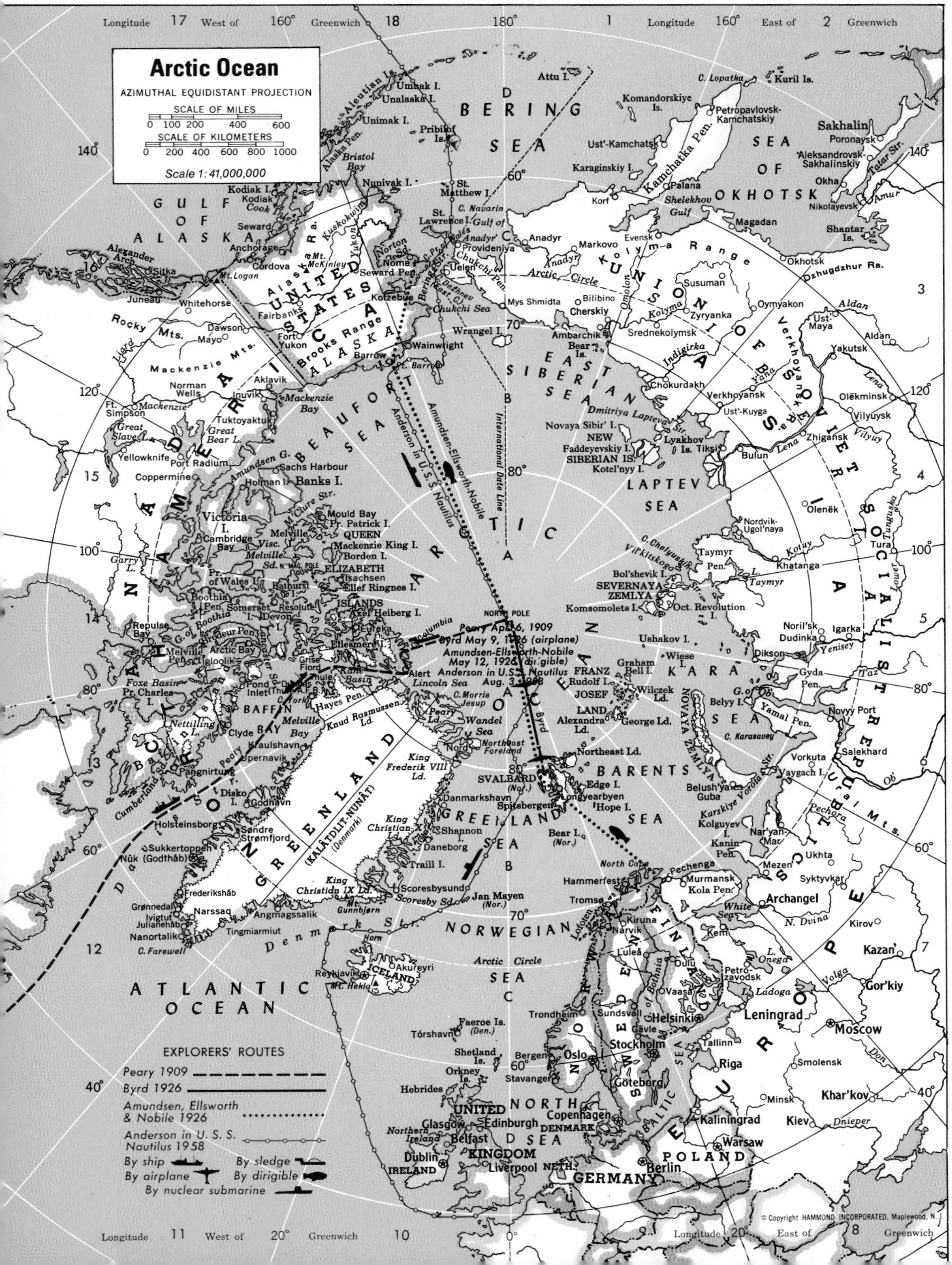

Inuvik, Canada C16
Ivigtut, Greenl. D12
Isachsen, Canada B15
Jan Mayen (isl.), Norway B10
Julianehåb, Greenl. D12
Juneau, U.S. D16
Kalâtdlit-Nunât (Greenland) B12
Kane (basin) B13
Kanin (pen.), U.S.S.R. C7
Kara (sea), U.S.S.R. B6
Karasavey (cape), U.S.S.R. B6
Karskiye Vorota (str.), U.S.S.R. B7
Kem', U.S.S.R. C8
Khatanga, U.S.S.R. B4
King Christian IX Land (reg.), Greenl. C11
King Christian X Land (reg.), Greenl. B11
King Frederik VIII Land (reg.), Greenl. B11
Kiruna, Sweden C8
Knud Rasmussen Land (reg.), Greenl. B12
Kodiak, U.S. D17
Kodiak (isl.), U.S. D17
Kola (pen.), U.S.S.R. C8
Kolguyev (isl.), U.S.S.R. B7
Kolyma (range), U.S.S.R. C1
Kolyma (riv.), U.S.S.R. C2
Komsomolets (isl.), U.S.S.R. A5
Korf, U.S.S.R. C1
Kotel'nyy (isl.), U.S.S.R. B2
Kotuy (riv.), U.S.S.R. B4
Kotzebue, U.S. C18
Kraulshavn, Greenl. B13
Kuskokwim (riv.), U.S. C17
Lancaster (sound), Canada B14
Laptev (sea), U.S.S.R. B3
Lena (riv.), U.S.S.R. C3
Lincoln (sea) A12
Lofoten (isls.), Norway C9
Logan (mt.), Canada C17
Longyearbyen, Norway B8
Lyakhov (isls.), U.S.S.R. B3
Mackenzie (bay), Canada B16
Mackenzie (mts.), Canada C16
Mackenzie (riv.), Canada C16
Mackenzie King (isl.), Canada B15
Markovo, U.S.S.R. C1
Mayo, Canada C16
M'Clure (str.), Canada B15
McKinley (mt.), U.S. C17
Melville (bay), Greenl. B13
Melville (isl.), Canada B15
Melville (pen.), Canada C14
Mezen', U.S.S.R. C7
Morris Jesup (cape), Greenl. A11
Mould Bay, Canada B16
Murmansk, U.S.S.R. C8
Mys Shmidta, U.S.S.R. C1
Nanortalik, Greenl. D12
Narssaq, Greenl. C12
Narvik, Norway C9
Nar'yan-Mar, U.S.S.R. C7
Navarin (cape), U.S.S.R. C18
Nettilling (lake), Canada C13
New Siberian (isls.), U.S.S.R. B2
Nikolayevsk, U.S.S.R. D2
Nome, U.S. C18
Nord, Greenl. A10
Nordvik-Ugol'naya, U.S.S.R. B4
Noril'sk, U.S.S.R. B5
Norman Wells, Canada C16
North (cape), Ice. C11
North (cape), Norway B8
Northeast Foreland (pen.), Greenl. A10
Northeast Land (isl.), Norway B8
North Magnetic Pole, Canada B15
North Pole A1
Norton (sound), U.S. C18
Norway C9
Norwegian (sea) C10
Novaya Sibir' (isl.), U.S.S.R. B2
Novaya Zemlya (isls.), U.S.S.R. B7
Novyy Port, U.S.S.R. C6
Nûk (cap.), Greenl. C12
Nunivak (isl.), U.S. D18
Ob' (gulf), U.S.S.R. B6
Ob' (riv.), U.S.S.R. C6
October Revolution (isl.), U.S.S.R. B5
Olenek, U.S.S.R. C4
Omolon (riv.), U.S.S.R. C1
Oymyakon, U.S.S.R. C2
Pangnirtung, Canada C13
Peary Land (reg.), Greenl. A11
Pechenga, U.S.S.R. C8
Pechora (riv.), U.S.S.R. C7
Pond Inlet, Canada B13
Port Radium, Canada C15
Pribilof (isls.), U.S. D18
Prince Charles (isl.), Canada C13
Prince of Wales (cape), U.S. C18
Prince of Wales (isl.), Canada B14
Prince Patrick (isl.), Canada B16
Provideniya, U.S.S.R. C18
Queen Elizabeth (isls.), Canada B15
Repulse Bay, Canada C14
Resolute, Canada B14
Reykjavík (cap.), Ice. C11
Rocky (mts.), Canada D16
Rudolf (isl.), U.S.S.R. A7
Sachs Harbour, Canada B16
Saint Lawrence (isl.), U.S. C18
Saint Matthew (isl.), U.S. C18
Salekhard, U.S.S.R. C6
Scoresby (sound), Greenl. B10
Scoresbysund, Greenl. B10
Severnaya Zemlya (isls.), U.S.S.R. A4
Seward, U.S. D17
Seward (pen.), U.S. C18
Shannon (isl.), Greenl. B10
Siberia (reg.), U.S.S.R. C2
Sitka, U.S. D16
Somerset (isl.), Canada B14
Søndre Strømfjord, Greenl. C12
Spitsbergen (isl.), Norway B9
Srednekolymsk, U.S.S.R. C2
Sukkertoppen, Greenl. C12
Susuman, U.S.S.R. C2
Svalbard (isls.), Norway B9
Sweden D9
Taymyr (lake), U.S.S.R. B5
Taymyr (pen.), U.S.S.R. B4
Taz (river), U.S.S.R. C5
Thule, Greenl. B13
Thule A.F.B. (Dundas), Greenl. B13
Tiksi, U.S.S.R. B3
Tingmiarmiut, Greenl. C12
Traill (isl.), Greenl. B10
Tromsø, Norway B9
Tuktoyaktuk, Canada C16
Uelen, U.S.S.R. C18
Umnak (isl.), U.S. D18
Unalaska (isl.), U.S. D18
Unimak (isl.), U.S. D18
Union of Soviet Socialist Republics C2
United States C17
Upernavik, Greenl. B12
Ural (mts.), U.S.S.R. C6
Ushakov (isl.), U.S.S.R. B5
Ust'-Kuyga, U.S.S.R. C3
Vaygach (isl.), U.S.S.R. C6
Verkhoyansk, U.S.S.R. C3
Verkhoyansk (range), U.S.S.R. C3
Victoria (isl.), Canada B15
Vil'kitskogo (str.), U.S.S.R. B4
Viscount Melville (sound), Canada B15
Vorkuta, U.S.S.R. C6
Wainwright, U.S. B18
Wandel (sea), Greenl. A10
White (sea), U.S.S.R. C8
Whitehorse, Canada C16
Wiese (isl.), U.S.S.R. B6
Wilczek Land (isl.), U.S.S.R. B6
Wrangel (isl.), U.S.S.R. B18
Yamal (pen.), U.S.S.R. B6
Yana (riv.), U.S.S.R. C3
Yellowknife, Canada C15
Yenisey (riv.), U.S.S.R. C5
York (cape), Greenl. B13
Yukon (riv.) C17
Zhigansk, U.S.S.R. C3
Zyryanka, U.S.S.R. C2

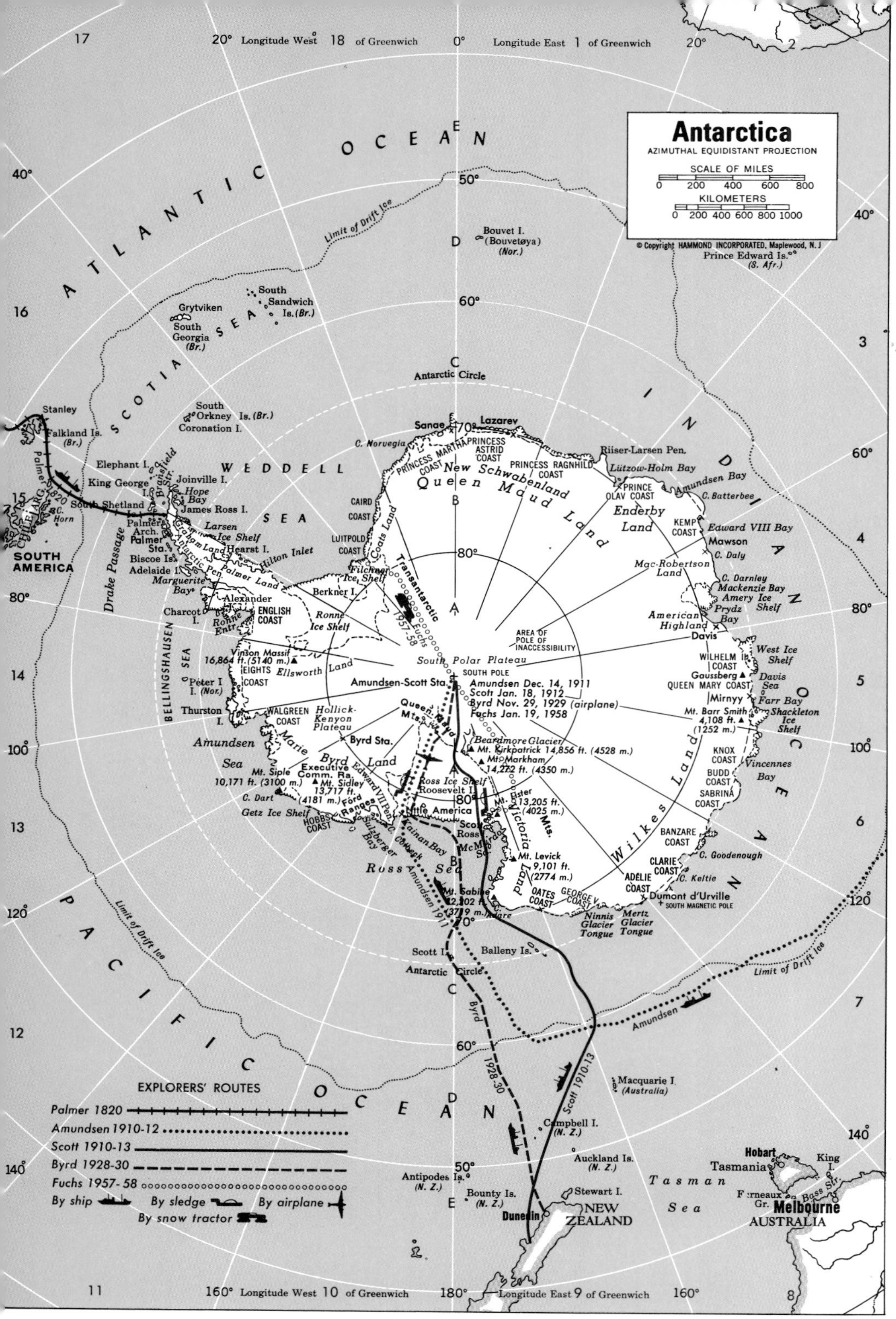

Adare (cape)	B9
Adelaide (isl.)	C15
Adélie Coast (reg.)	C7
Alexander (isl.)	B15
American Highland	B4
Amery Ice Shelf	C4
Amundsen (bay)	C3
Amundsen (sea)	B13
Amundsen-Scott Station	A14
Antarctic (pen.)	C15
Balleny (isls.)	C9
Banzare Coast (reg.)	C7
Barr Smith (mt.)	C5
Batterbee (cape)	C3
Beardmore (glac.)	A8
Bellingshausen (sea)	C14
Berkner (isl.)	B16
Biscoe (isls.)	C15
Bouvet (isl.)	D1
Bouvetøya (Bouvet) (isl.)	D1
Bransfield (str.)	C16
Budd Coast (reg.)	C6
Byrd Station	A12
Caird Coast (reg.)	B17
Charcot (isl.)	C15
Clarie Coast (reg.)	C7
Coats Land (reg.)	B17
Colbeck (cape)	B10
Coronation (isl.)	C16
Daly (cape)	C4
Darnley (cape)	C4
Dart (cape)	B12
Davis (sea)	C5
Davis Station	C4
Drake (passage)	C15
Dumont d'Urville Station	C7
Edward VII (pen.)	B11
Edward VIII (bay)	C4
Eights Coast (reg.)	B14
Elephant (isl.)	D16
Ellsworth Land (reg.)	B14
Enderby Land (reg.)	B3
English Coast (reg.)	B15
Executive Committee (range)	B12
Farr (bay)	C5
Filchner Ice Shelf	B16
Ford Ranges (mts.)	B11
Gaussberg (mt.)	C5
George V Coast (reg.)	C8
Getz Ice Shelf	B12
Goodenough (cape)	C7
Graham Land (reg.)	C15
Grytviken	D17
Hearst (isl.)	B16
Hilton (inlet)	B16
Hobbs Coast (reg.)	B12
Hollick-Kenyon (plat.)	B13
Hope (bay)	C16
Indian Ocean	C3
James Ross (isl.)	C16
Joinville (isl.)	C16
Kainan (bay)	B10
Keltie (cape)	C7
Kemp Coast (reg.)	C3
King George (isl.)	C16
Kirkpatrick (mt.)	A8
Knox Coast (reg.)	C6
Larsen Ice Shelf	C16
Lazarev Station	C1
Levick (mt.)	B8
Lister (mt.)	B8
Little America	B10
Luitpold Coast (reg.)	B17
Lützow-Holm (bay)	C3
Mackenzie (bay)	C4
Mac-Robertson Land (reg.)	B4
Marguerite (bay)	C15
Marie Byrd Land (reg.)	B13
Markham (mt.)	A8
Mawson	C4
McMurdo (sound)	B9
Mertz Glacier Tongue	C8
Mirnyy	C5
New Schwabenland (reg.)	B1
Ninnis Glacier Tongue	C8
Norvegia (cape)	B18
Oates Coast (reg.)	B8
Palmer (arch.)	C15
Palmer Land (reg.)	B15
Palmer Station	C15
Peter I (isl.)	B14
Prince Edward (isls.)	E2
Prince Olav Coast (reg.)	C3
Princess Astrid Coast (reg.)	B1
Princess Martha Coast (reg.)	B18
Princess Ragnhild Coast (reg.)	B2
Prydz (bay)	C4
Queen Mary Coast (reg.)	C5
Queen Maud (mts.)	A12
Queen Maud Land (reg.)	B1
Riiser-Larsen (pen.)	C2
Ronne Entrance (inlet)	B15
Ronne Ice Shelf	B15
Roosevelt (isl.)	A10
Ross (isl.)	B9
Ross (sea)	B10
Ross Ice Shelf	A10
Sabine (mt.)	B9
Sabrina Coast (reg.)	C6
Sanae Station	B18
Scotia (sea)	D16
Scott (isl.)	C10
Scott Station	B9
Shackleton Ice Shelf	C5
Sidley (mt.)	B12
Siple (mt.)	B12
South Georgia (isl.)	D17
South Magnetic Pole	C8
South Orkney (isls.)	C16
South Polar (plat.)	A1
South Pole	A4
South Sandwich (isls.)	D17
South Shetland (isls.)	C15
Sulzberger (bay)	B11
Thurston (isl.)	C14
Transantarctic (mts.)	B17
Victoria Land (reg.)	B8
Vincennes (bay)	C6
Vinson Massif (mt.)	B14
Walgreen Coast (reg.)	B13
Weddell (sea)	C16
West Ice Shelf	C5
Wilhelm II Coast (reg.)	C5
Wilkes Land (reg.)	B7

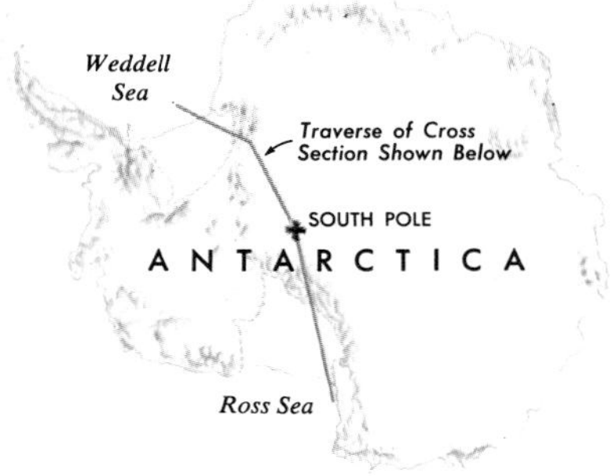

Antarctic Cross Section: Weddell Sea to Ross Sea

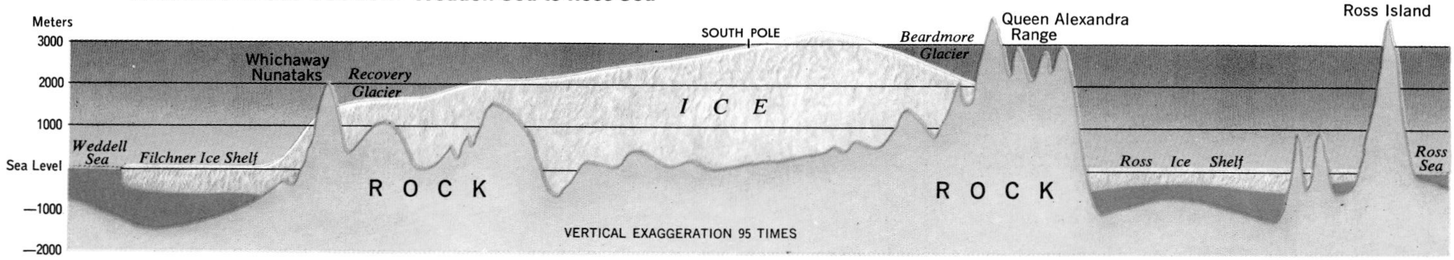

Information Based on American Geographical Society's "Antarctic Map Folio Series"

Aberdeen, Scotland . . . D 3
Adriatic (sea) . . . F 4
Aegean (sea) . . . G 5
Albania . . . G 4
Ålborg, Denmark . . . F 3
Alps (mts.) . . . E 4
Amsterdam (cap.), Netherlands . . . E 3
Andorra . . . E 4
Antwerp, Belgium . . . E 3
Arad, Romania . . . G 4
Araks (riv.), U.S.S.R. . . . J 5
Archangel, U.S.S.R. . . . J 2
Århus, Denmark . . . E 3
Armenian S.S.R., U.S.S.R. . . . J 4
Astrakhan', U.S.S.R. . . . J 4
Athens (cap.), Greece . . . G 5
Atlantic Ocean . . . C 4
Austria . . . F 4
Azerbaidzhan S.S.R., U.S.S.R. . . . J 4
Azov (sea), U.S.S.R. . . . H 4
Baku, U.S.S.R. . . . J 4
Balaton (lake), Hungary . . . F 4
Balearic (isls.), Spain . . . E 5
Balkan (mts.) . . . G 4
Baltic (sea) . . . F 3
Barcelona, Spain . . . E 4
Barents (sea) . . . J 1
Bari, Italy . . . F 4
Basel, Switzerland . . . E 4
Belfast (cap.), N. Ireland . . . D 3
Belgium . . . E 3
Belgrade (cap.), Yugoslavia . . . G 4
Bergen, Norway . . . E 2
Berlin (cap.), Germany . . . F 3
Bern (cap.), Switzerland . . . E 4
Bilbao, Spain . . . D 4
Birmingham, England . . . D 3
Biscay (bay) . . . D 4
Black (sea) . . . H 4
Bologna, Italy . . . F 4
Bonn, Germany . . . E 3
Bordeaux, France . . . D 4
Bornholm (isl.), Denmark . . . F 3
Bosporus (str.), Turkey . . . G 4
Bothnia (gulf) . . . G 2
Braşov, Romania . . . G 4
Bratislava, Czech. . . . F 4
Bremen, Germany . . . E 3
Brest, France . . . D 4
Bristol, England . . . D 3
Brno, Czech. . . . F 4
Brussels (cap.), Belgium . . . E 3
Bucharest (cap.), Romania . . . G 4
Budapest (cap.), Hungary . . . F 4
Bug (riv.) . . . G 3
Bulgaria . . . G 4
Burgas, Bulgaria . . . G 4
Burgos, Spain . . . D 4
Calais, France . . . E 3
Cardiff, Wales . . . D 3
Carpathian (mts.) . . . G 4
Cartagena, Spain . . . D 5
Caspian (sea), U.S.S.R. . . . J 4
Caucasus (mts.), U.S.S.R. . . . J 4
Channel (isls.), U.K. . . . D 4
Chemnitz, Germany . . . F 3
Cologne, Germany . . . E 3
Como, Italy . . . E 4
Constanţa, Romania . . . G 4
Copenhagen (cap.), Denmark . . . F 3
Córdoba, Spain . . . D 5
Cork, Ireland . . . D 3
Corsica (isl.), France . . . E 4
Cracow, Poland . . . F 3
Crete (isl.), Greece . . . G 5
Crimea (pen.), U.S.S.R. . . . H 4
Czechoslovakia . . . F 4
Danube (riv.) . . . G 4
Dardanelles (str.), Turkey . . . G 5
Debrecen, Hungary . . . G 4
Denmark . . . E 3
Denmark (str.) . . . B 2
Dnepropetrovsk, U.S.S.R. . . . H 4
Dnieper (riv.), U.S.S.R. . . . H 3
Dniester (riv.), U.S.S.R. . . . G 4
Don (riv.), U.S.S.R. . . . J 4
Donets (riv.), U.S.S.R. . . . H 4
Douro (riv.), Portugal . . . D 4
Dover, England . . . E 3
Drava (riv.) . . . F 4
Dresden, Germany . . . F 3
Dublin (cap.), Ireland . . . D 3
Dvina, Northern (riv.), U.S.S.R. . . . J 2
Ebro (riv.), Spain . . . D 4
Edinburgh (cap.), Scotland . . . D 3
Edirne, Turkey . . . G 4
Elba (isl.), Italy . . . E 4
Elbe (riv.) . . . F 3
El'brus (mt.), U.S.S.R. . . . J 4
England, U.K. . . . D 3
English (chan.) . . . D 4
Erfurt, Germany . . . F 3
Essen, Germany . . . E 3
Estonian S.S.R., U.S.S.R. . . . G 3
Etna (vol.), Italy . . . F 5
Faerøe (isls.), Denmark . . . D 2
Finisterre (cape), Spain . . . C 4
Finland . . . G 2
Finland (gulf) . . . G 3
Florence, Italy . . . F 4
France . . . E 4
Frankfurt, Germany . . . E 3
Frisian (isls.) . . . E 3
Gandzhe, U.S.S.R. . . . J 4
Garonne (riv.), France . . . D 4
Gdańsk, Poland . . . F 3
Geneva, Switzerland . . . E 4
Geneva (lake) . . . E 4
Genoa, Italy . . . E 4
Georgian S.S.R., U.S.S.R. . . . J 4
Germany . . . E-F 3
Gibraltar (U.K.) . . . D 5
Gibraltar (str.) . . . D 5
Glasgow, Scotland . . . D 3
Gor'kiy, U.S.S.R. . . . J 3
Göteborg, Sweden . . . F 3
Granada, Spain . . . D 5
Graz, Austria . . . F 4
Great Britain (isl.) . . . D 3
Greece . . . G 5
Guadalquivir (riv.), Spain . . . D 5
Guadiana (riv.) . . . D 5
Hague, The (cap.), Netherlands . . . E 3
Hamburg, Germany . . . F 3
Hammerfest, Norway . . . G 1
Helsinki (cap.), Finland . . . G 2
Hungary . . . F 4
Iceland . . . C 2
Ionian (sea) . . . F 5
Ireland . . . D 3
Irish (sea) . . . D 3
Istanbul, Turkey . . . G 4
Italy . . . F 4
Jan Mayen (isl.), Norway . . . D 1
Jönköping, Sweden . . . F 3
Kalinin, U.S.S.R. . . . H 3
Kaliningrad, U.S.S.R. . . . G 3
Kaluga, U.S.S.R. . . . H 3
Kama (riv.), U.S.S.R. . . . K 3
Karlsruhe, Germany . . . E 4
Karlstad, Sweden . . . F 3
Kassel, Germany . . . E 3
Katowice, Poland . . . F 3
Kattegat (str.) . . . F 3
Kaunas, U.S.S.R. . . . G 3
Kavála, Greece . . . G 4
Kazan', U.S.S.R. . . . J 3
Kecskemét, Hungary . . . F 4
Khar'kov, U.S.S.R. . . . H 4
Kherson, U.S.S.R. . . . H 4
Kiel, Germany . . . E 3
Kielce, Poland . . . E 3
Kiev, U.S.S.R. . . . H 3
Kirov, U.S.S.R. . . . J 3
Kirovograd, U.S.S.R. . . . H 4
Kishinev, U.S.S.R. . . . G 4
Kjölen (mts.) . . . F 2
Kola (pen.), U.S.S.R. . . . H 2
Krasnodar, U.S.S.R. . . . H 4
Kristiansand, Norway . . . E 3
Kristiansund, Norway . . . E 2
Krivoy Rog, U.S.S.R. . . . H 4
Kuopio, Finland . . . G 2
Kursk, U.S.S.R. . . . H 3
Kuybyshev, U.S.S.R. . . . K 3
La Coruña, Spain . . . D 4
Ladoga (lake), U.S.S.R. . . . H 2
Land's End (prom.), England . . . D 3
Lapland (reg.) . . . G 2
Latvian S.S.R., U.S.S.R. . . . G 3
Leeds, England . . . D 3
Leghorn, Italy . . . E 4
Le Havre, France . . . E 4
Leipzig, Germany . . . F 3
Leningrad, U.S.S.R. . . . H 3
León, Spain . . . D 4
Lésvos (isl.), Greece . . . G 5
Liechtenstein . . . F 4
Liège, Belgium . . . E 3
Lille, France . . . E 3
Limerick, Ireland . . . D 3
Limoges, France . . . E 4
Linköping, Sweden . . . F 3
Linz, Austria . . . F 4
Lions (gulf) . . . E 4
Lisbon (cap.), Portugal . . . D 5
Lithuanian S.S.R., U.S.S.R. . . . G 3
Liverpool, England . . . D 3
Ljubljana, Yugoslavia . . . F 4
Łódź, Poland . . . F 3
Lofoten (isls.), Norway . . . F 2
Loire (riv.), France . . . E 4
London (cap.), England . . . D 3
Luxembourg . . . E 4
Lyon, France . . . E 4
Madrid (cap.), Spain . . . D 4
Majorca (isl.), Spain . . . E 5
Málaga, Spain . . . D 5
Malta . . . F 5
Manchester, England . . . D 3
Mariupol, U.S.S.R. . . . H 4
Marmara (sea), Turkey . . . G 4
Marseille, France . . . E 4
Mediterranean (sea) . . . E 5
Minsk, U.S.S.R. . . . G 3
Moldavian S.S.R., U.S.S.R. . . . G 4
Monaco . . . E 4
Moscow (cap.), U.S.S.R. . . . H 3
Munich, Germany . . . F 4
Murcia, Spain . . . D 5
Murmansk, U.S.S.R. . . . H 2
Nantes, France . . . D 4
Naples, Italy . . . F 4
Netherlands . . . E 3
Nice, France . . . E 4
North (Nordkapp) (cape), Norway . . . G 1
North (sea) . . . E 3
Northern Ireland, U.K. . . . D 3
Norway . . . E 2
Norwegian (sea) . . . D 2
Nürnberg, Germany . . . F 4
Odense, Denmark . . . F 3
Oder (riv.) . . . F 3
Odessa, U.S.S.R. . . . H 4
Onega (lake), U.S.S.R. . . . H 2
Orenburg, U.S.S.R. . . . K 3
Orkney (isls.), Scotland . . . D 3
Orléans, France . . . E 4
Oslo (cap.), Norway . . . F 2
Palermo, Italy . . . F 5
Palma, Spain . . . E 5
Paris (cap.), France . . . E 4
Perm', U.S.S.R. . . . K 3
Piraiévs, Greece . . . G 5
Ploieşti, Romania . . . G 4
Plovdiv, Bulgaria . . . G 4
Plymouth, England . . . D 3
Po (riv.), Italy . . . E 4
Poland . . . F 3
Portugal . . . D 5
Poznań, Poland . . . F 3
Prague (cap.), Czech. . . . F 3
Pyrenees (mts.) . . . D 4
Reykjavík (cap.), Iceland . . . B 2
Rhine (riv.) . . . E 4

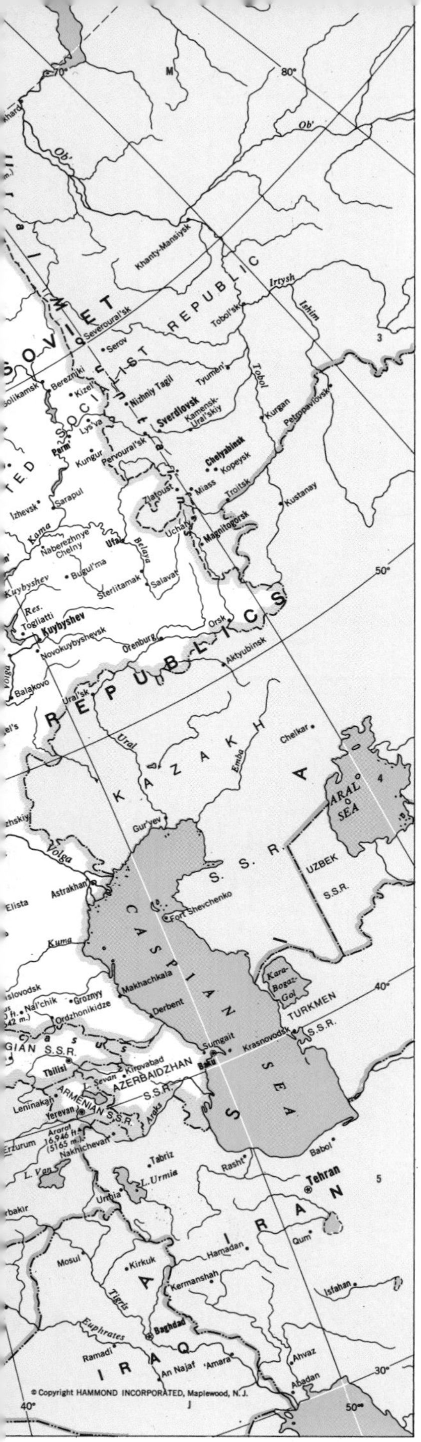

AREA 4,057,000 sq. mi.
(10,507,630 sq. km.)
POPULATION 676,000,000
LARGEST CITY Paris
HIGHEST POINT El'brus 18,510 ft.
(5,642 m.)
LOWEST POINT Caspian Sea -92 ft.
(-28 m.)

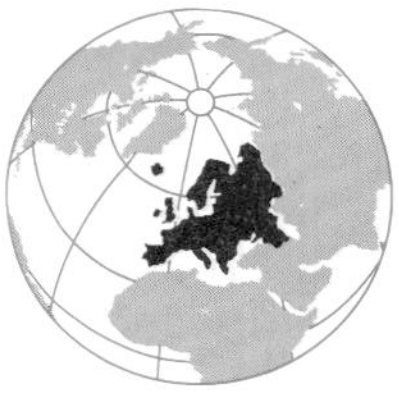

Population Distribution

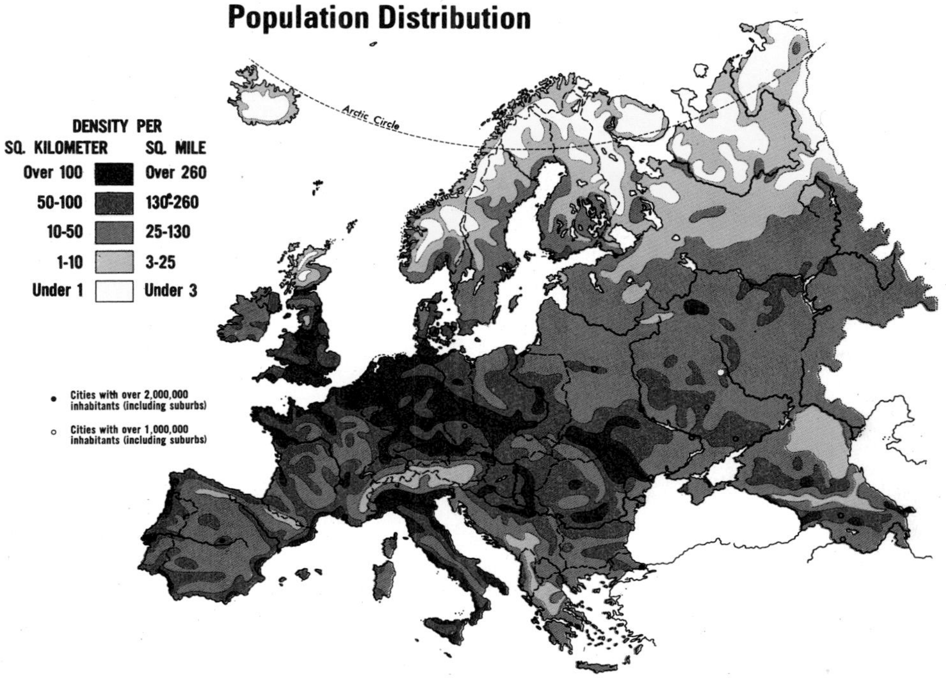

Vegetation

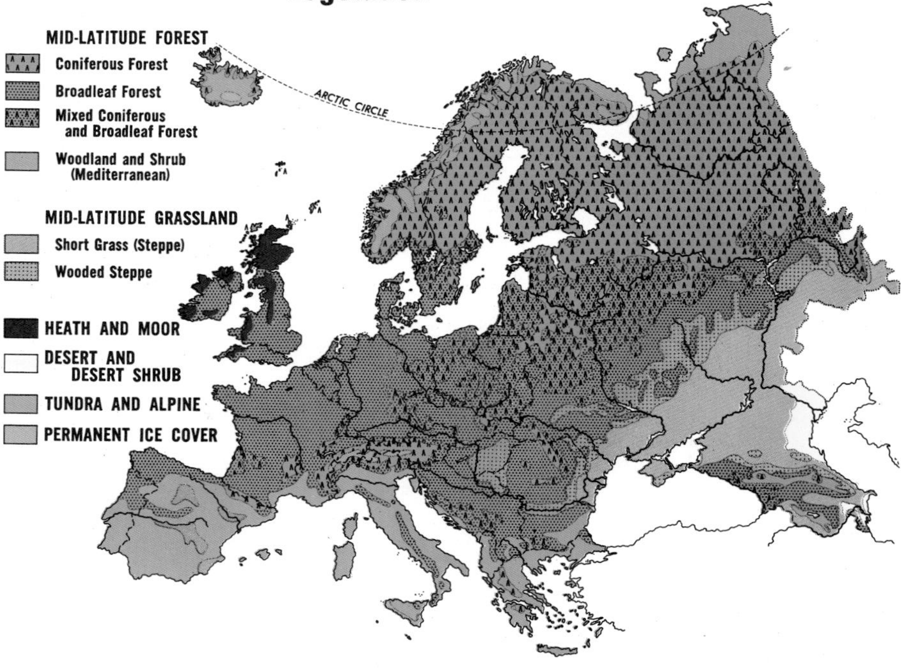

Rhône (riv.), France . . . E 4
Riga, U.S.S.R. . . . G 3
Romania . . . G 4
Rome (cap.), Italy . . . F 4
Rostov, U.S.S.R. . . . J 4
Rotterdam, Netherlands . . . E 3
Russian S.F.S.R., U.S.S.R. . . . H 3
Saarbrücken, Germany . . . E 4
Saint George's (chan.) . . . D 3
Salzburg, Austria . . . F 4
San Marino . . . F 4
Saragossa, Spain . . . D 4
Sarajevo, Yugoslavia . . . F 4
Saratov, U.S.S.R. . . . J 3
Sardinia (isl.), Italy . . . E 4
Sava (riv.) . . . F 4
Scotland, U.K. . . . D 3
Seine (riv.), France . . . E 4
Sevastopol', U.S.S.R. . . . H 4
Seville, Spain . . . D 5
Shetland (isls.), Scotland . . . D 2
Sicily (isl.), Italy . . . F 5
Skagerrak (str.) . . . E 3
Sofia (cap.), Bulgaria . . . G 4
Sognefjorden (fjord), Norway . . . E 2
Southampton, England . . . D 3
Spain . . . D 4
Stockholm (cap.), Sweden . . . F 3
Strasbourg, France . . . E 4
Stuttgart, Germany . . . E 4
Sweden . . . F 2
Switzerland . . . E 4
Szeged, Hungary . . . F 4
Tagus (riv.) . . . D 5
Tampere, Finland . . . G 2
Taranto (gulf), Italy . . . F 5
Tbilisi, U.S.S.R. . . . J 4
Tiber (riv.), Italy . . . F 4
Tiranë (cap.), Albania . . . F 4
Trieste, Italy . . . F 4
Trondheim, Norway . . . F 2
Turin, Italy . . . E 4
Turkey . . . H 5
Turku, Finland . . . G 2
Tyrrhenian (sea) . . . F 4
Ufa, U.S.S.R. . . . K 3
Ukrainian S.S.R., U.S.S.R. . . . G 4
Union of Soviet Socialist Republics . . . H 2
United Kingdom . . . D 3
Ural (mts.), U.S.S.R. . . . L 2
Valencia, Spain . . . D 5
Valletta (cap.), Malta . . . F 5
Varna, Bulgaria . . . G 4
Vatican City . . . F 4
Venice, Italy . . . F 4
Vienna (cap.), Austria . . . F 4
Vilnius, U.S.S.R. . . . G 3
Vistula (riv.), Poland . . . F 3
Volga (riv.), U.S.S.R. . . . J 4
Volgograd, U.S.S.R. . . . J 4
Wales, U.K. . . . D 3
Warsaw (cap.), Poland . . . G 3
Weser (riv.), Germany . . . E 3
White (sea), U.S.S.R. . . . H 2
White Russian S.S.R., U.S.S.R. . . . G 3
Wrocław, Poland . . . F 3
Yerevan, U.S.S.R. . . . J 4
Yugoslavia . . . F 4
Zagorsk, U.S.S.R. . . . H 3
Zagreb, Yugoslavia . . . F 4
Zaporozh'ye, U.S.S.R. . . . H 4
Zhitomir, U.S.S.R. . . . G 3
Zürich, Switzerland . . . E 4

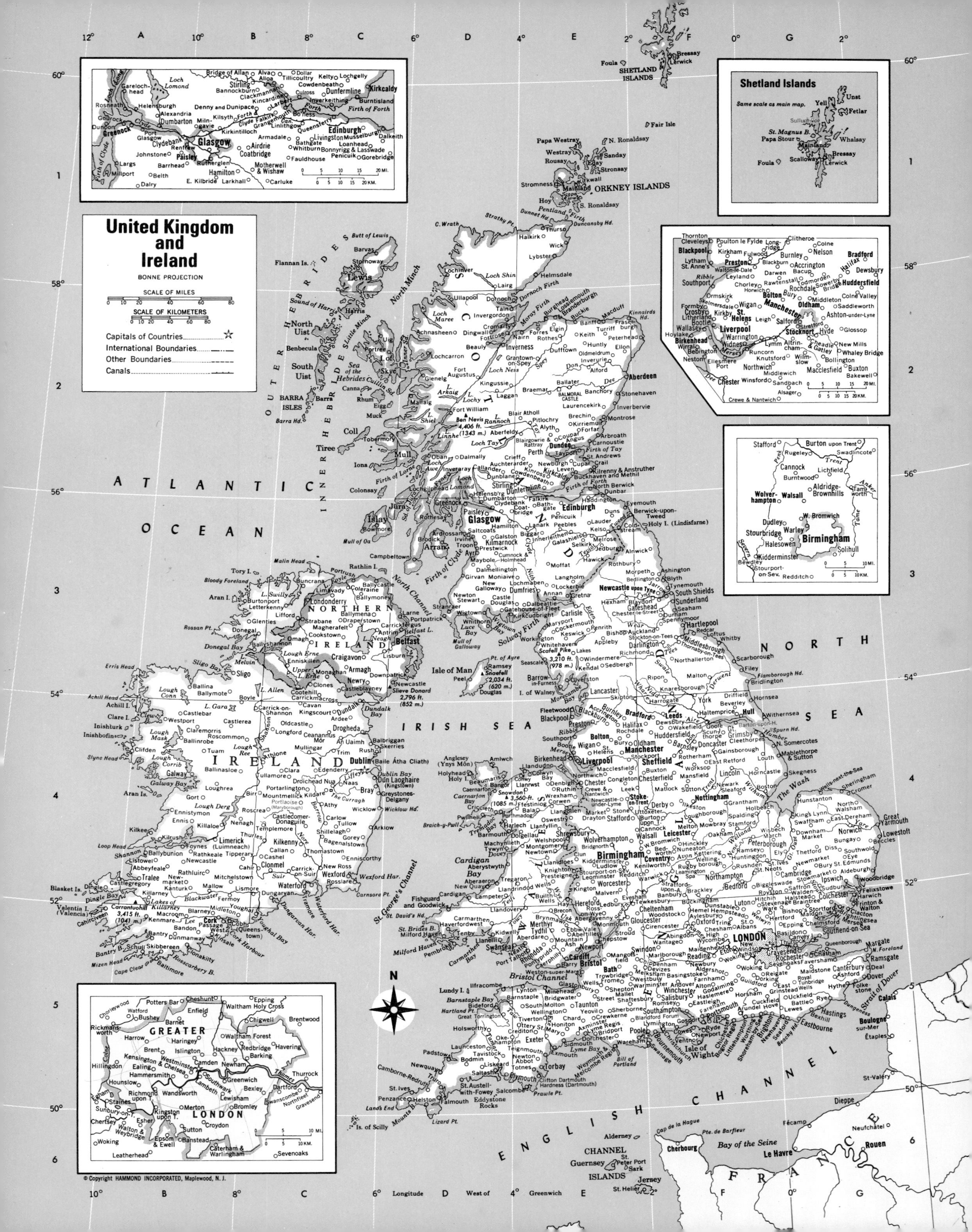

United Kingdom
and
Ireland
BONNE PROJECTION
SCALE OF MILES
0 10 20 40 60 80
SCALE OF KILOMETERS
0 10 20 40 60 80
Capitals of Countries
International Boundaries
Other Boundaries
Canals
Shetland Islands
Same scale as main map.
GREATER LONDON
ATLANTIC OCEAN
NORTH SEA
IRISH SEA
ENGLISH CHANNEL
NORTHERN IRELAND
IRELAND
SCOTLAND
ENGLAND
WALES
FRANCE
OUTER HEBRIDES
INNER HEBRIDES
ORKNEY ISLANDS
SHETLAND ISLANDS
CHANNEL ISLANDS
Isle of Man
LONDON
Dublin (Baile Átha Cliath)
Belfast
Edinburgh
Cardiff
Glasgow
Birmingham
Manchester
Liverpool
Longitude West of Greenwich

UNITED KINGDOM

AREA 94,399 sq. mi. (244,493 sq. km.)
POPULATION 55,672,000
CAPITAL London
LARGEST CITY London
HIGHEST POINT Ben Nevis 4,406 ft. (1,343 m.)
MONETARY UNIT pound sterling
MAJOR LANGUAGES English, Gaelic, Welsh
MAJOR RELIGIONS Protestantism, Roman Catholicism

IRELAND

AREA 27,136 sq. mi. (70,282 sq. km.)
POPULATION 3,440,427
CAPITAL Dublin
LARGEST CITY Dublin
HIGHEST POINT Carrantuohill 3,415 ft. (1,041 m.)
MONETARY UNIT Irish pound
MAJOR LANGUAGES English, Gaelic (Irish)
MAJOR RELIGION Roman Catholicism

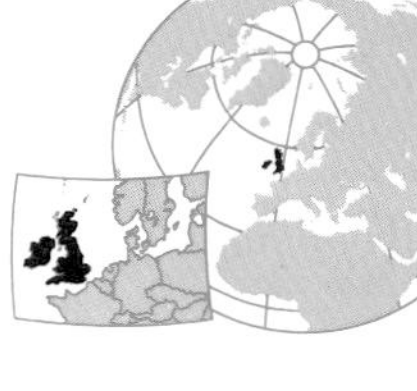

ENGLAND

COUNTIES

Avon, 920,200 . . . E 6
Bedfordshire, 491,700 . . . G 5
Berkshire, 659,000 . . . F 6
Buckinghamshire, 512,000 . . . G 6
Cambridgeshire, 563,000 . . . G 5
Cheshire, 916,400 . . . E 4
Cleveland, 567,900 . . . F 3
Cornwall, 405,200 . . . C 7
Cumbria, 473,600 . . . D 3
Derbyshire, 887,600 . . . F 5
Devon, 942,100 . . . D 7
Dorset, 575,800 . . . E 7
Durham, 610,400 . . . F 3
East Sussex, 655,600 . . . H 7
Essex, 1,426,200 . . . H 6
Gloucestershire, 491,500 . . . E 6
Greater London, 7,028,200 . . . H 8
Greater Manchester, 2,684,100 . . . H 2
Hampshire, 1,456,100 . . . F 6
Hereford and Worcester, 594,200 . . . E 5
Hertfordshire, 937,300 . . . G 6
Humberside, 848,600 . . . G 4
Isle of Wight, 111,300 . . . F 7
Isles of Scilly, 1,900 . . . A 7
Kent, 1,448,100 . . . H 6
Lancashire, 1,375,500 . . . E 4
Leicestershire, 837,900 . . . F 5
Lincolnshire, 524,500 . . . G 4
London, Greater, 7,028,200 . . . H 8
Manchester, Greater, 2,684,100 . . . H 2
Merseyside, 1,578,000 . . . G 2
Norfolk, 662,500 . . . H 5
Northamptonshire, 505,900 . . . G 5
Northumberland, 287,300 . . . E 2
North Yorkshire, 653,000 . . . F 3
Nottinghamshire, 977,500 . . . F 4
Oxfordshire 541,800 . . . F6
Shropshire (Salop) 359,000 . . . E5
Somerset 404,400 . . . E6
South Yorkshire 1,318,300 . . . F4
Staffordshire 997,600 . . . E5
Suffolk 577,600 . . . H5
Surrey 1,002,900 . . . G6
Sussex, East 655,600 . . . H7
Sussex, West 623,400 . . . G7
Tyne and Wear 1,182,900 . . . H3
Warwickshire 471,000 . . . F5
West Midlands 2,743,300 . . . F5
West Sussex 623,400 . . . G7
West Yorkshire 2,072,500 . . . J1
Wiltshire 512,800 . . . E6
Yorkshire, North 653,000 . . . F3
Yorkshire, South 1,318,300 . . . F4
Yorkshire, West 2,072,500 . . . J1

CITIES and TOWNS

Abingdon, 20,130 . . . F 6
Accrington, 36,470 . . . H 1
Adwick le Street, 17,650 . . . K 2
Aldeburgh, 2,750 . . . J 5
Aldershot, 33,750 . . . G 8
Aldridge Brownhills, 89,370 . . . E 5
Alfreton, 21,560 . . . F 4
Alnwick, 7,300 . . . F 2
Altrincham, 40,800 . . . H 2
Amersham, ⊙17,254 . . . G 7
Andover, 27,620 . . . F 6
Appleby, 2,240 . . . E 3
Arnold, 35,090 . . . F 4
Arundel, 2,390 . . . G 7
Ashford, 36,380 . . . H 6
Ashington, 24,720 . . . F 2
Ashton-under-Lyne, 48,500 . . . H 2
Axminster, ⊙4,515 . . . D 7
Aycliffe, ⊙20,203 . . . F 3
Aylesbury, 41,420 . . . G 7
Bacup, 14,990 . . . H 1
Bakewell, 4,100 . . . J 2
Banbury, 31,060 . . . F 5
Banstead, 44,100 . . . H 8
Barking, 153,800 . . . H 8
Barnet, 305,200 . . . H 7
Barnsley, 74,730 . . . J 2
Barnstaple, 17,820 . . . D 6
Barrow-in-Furness, 73,400 . . . D 3
Barton-upon-Humber, 7,750 . . . G 4
Basildon, 135,720 . . . J 8
Basingstoke, 60,910 . . . F 6
Bath, 83,100 . . . E 6
Batley, 41,630 . . . J 1
Battle, ⊙4,987 . . . H 7
Bebington, 62,500 . . . G 2
Bedford, 74,390 . . . G 5
Bedlington, 27,200 . . . F 2
Bedworth, 41,600 . . . F 5
Beeston and Stapleford, 65,360 . . . F 5
Benfleet, 49,180 . . . J 8
Bentley with Arksey, 22,320 . . . F 4
Berkhamsted, 15,920 . . . G 7
Beverley, 16,920 . . . G 4
Bexhill, 34,680 . . . H 7
Bexley, 213,500 . . . H 8
Biddulph, 18,720 . . . H 2
Birkenhead, 135,750 . . . G 2
Birmingham, 1,058,800 . . . F 5
Bishop Auckland, 32,940 . . . E 3
Bishop's Stortford, 21,720 . . . H 6
Blackburn, 101,670 . . . H 1
Blackpool, 149,000 . . . G 1
Blaydon, 31,940 . . . H 3
Blyth, 35,390 . . . F 2
Bodmin, 10,430 . . . C 7
Bognor Regis, 34,620 . . . G 7
Boldon, 24,430 . . . J 3
Bolton, 154,480 . . . H 2
Bootle 71,160 . . . G2
Boston 26,700 . . . G5
Bournemouth 144,100 . . . F7
Bracknell† 34,067 . . . G8
Bradford 458,900 . . . J1
Braintree and Bocking 26,300 . . . H6
Brent 256,500 . . . H8
Brentwood 58,690 . . . J8
Bridgwater 26,700 . . . E6
Bridlington 26,920 . . . G3
Bridport 6,660 . . . E7
Brigg 4,870 . . . G4
Brighouse 35,320 . . . J1
Brightlingsea 7,170 . . . J6
Brighton 156,500 . . . G7
Bristol 416,300 . . . E6
Broadstairs and Saint Peter's 21,670 . . . J6
Bromley 299,100 . . . H8
Bromsgrove 41,430 . . . E5
Buckfastleigh 2,870 . . . C7
Buckingham 5,290 . . . G6
Bude-Stratton 5,750 . . . C7
Bungay 4,120 . . . J5
Burgess Hill 20,030 . . . G7
Burnham-on-Crouch 4,920 . . . H6
Burnley 74,300 . . . H1
Burntwood† 23,088 . . . F5
Burton upon Trent 49,480 . . . F5
Bury 69,550 . . . H2
Bury Saint Edmunds 26,800 . . . H5
Bushey 24,500 . . . H7
Buxton 20,050 . . . J2
Caister-on-Sea† 6,287 . . . J5
Camborne-Redruth 43,970 . . . B7
Cambridge 106,400 . . . G5
Camden 185,800 . . . H8
Cannock 56,440 . . . E5
Canterbury 115,600 . . . H6
Canvey Island 29,550 . . . J8
Carlisle, 99,600 . . . D 3
Carlton, 46,690 . . . F 5
Caterham and Warlingham, 35,840 . . . H 8
Chatham, 59,550 . . . J 8
Cheadle and Gatley, 62,460 . . . H 2
Chelmsford, 58,320 . . . J 7
Cheltenham, 75,910 . . . E 6
Chertsey, 45,070 . . . G 8
Chesham, 20,830 . . . G 7
Cheshunt, 45,750 . . . H 7
Chester, 117,200 . . . G 2
Chesterfield, 69,480 . . . J 2
Chester-le-Street, 20,720 . . . J 3
Chichester, 20,940 . . . G 7
Chigwell, 54,220 . . . H 8
Chippenham, 18,550 . . . E 6
Chorley, 31,800 . . . G 2
Christchurch, 31,610 . . . F 7
Cirencester, 14,500 . . . E 6
Clacton, 39,380 . . . J 6
Clay Cross, 9,630 . . . J 2
Cleator Moor, ⊙7,686 . . . D 3
Cleethorpes, 37,200 . . . H 4
Clevedon, 15,140 . . . D 6
Clun, ⊙1,261 . . . D 6
Coalville, 28,740 . . . F 5
Cockermouth, 6,480 . . . D 3
Colchester, 79,600 . . . H 6
Colne, 19,030 . . . H 1
Colne Valley, 21,190 . . . J 2
Congleton, 21,500 . . . H 2
Consett, 35,080 . . . H 3
Corby, 48,850 . . . G 5
Coventry, 336,800 . . . F 5
Cowes, 19,190 . . . F 7
Crawley, 72,600 . . . G 6
Crewe and Nantwich, 98,100 . . . E 4
Cromer, 5,720 . . . J 5
Crook and Willington, 21,120 . . . E 3
Crosby, 56,750 . . . G 2
Croydon, 330,600 . . . H 8
Cuckfield, 26,500 . . . G 6
Darlington, 85,120 . . . F 3
Dartford, 44,130 . . . J 8
Darton, 15,710 . . . J 2
Darwen, 29,290 . . . H 1
Deal, 26,840 . . . J 6
Dearne, 24,780 . . . K 2
Denton, 38,110 . . . H 2
Derby, 213,700 . . . F 5
Dewsbury, 50,560 . . . J 1
Didcot, ⊙14,277 . . . F 6
Doncaster, 81,530 . . . F 4
Dorking, 22,410 . . . G 8
Dover, 34,160 . . . J 6
Downham Market, 4,120 . . . H 5
Droitwich, 13,950 . . . E 5
Dronfield, 20,000 . . . J 2
Dudley, 187,110 . . . E 5
Dunstable, 32,090 . . . G 6
Durham, 88,800 . . . J 3
Ealing, 293,800 . . . H 8
Eastbourne, 73,200 . . . H 7
East Grinstead, 19,420 . . . G 6
Eastleigh, 46,340 . . . F 7
East Retford, 18,260 . . . G 4
Egham, 30,320 . . . G 8
Egremont, ⊙7,253 . . . D 3
Eling, ⊙20,006 . . . F 7
Ellesmere, ⊙2,630 . . . E 5
Ellesmere Port, 63,870 . . . G 2
Enfield, 260,900 . . . H 7
Epsom and Ewell, 70,700 . . . G 8
Esher, 63,970 . . . H 8
Eston, ⊙46,219 . . . F 3
Eton, 4,950 . . . G 8
Evesham, 14,090 . . . F 5
Exeter, 93,300 . . . D 7
Exminster, ⊙3,181 . . . D 7
Exmouth, 26,840 . . . D 7
Falmouth, 17,530 . . . B 7
Fareham, 86,300 . . . F 7
Farnborough, 43,520 . . . G 8
Farnham, 33,140 . . . G 8
Farnworth, 26,110 . . . H 2
Faversham, 15,010 . . . H 6
Felixstowe, 19,460 . . . J 6
Felling, 38,990 . . . J 3
Filey, 5,660 . . . G 3
Fleet, 22,930 . . . G 8
Fleetwood, 30,070 . . . D 4
Folkestone, 45,610 . . . J 6
Formby, 24,850 . . . G 2
Framlingham, ⊙2,258 . . . J 5
Frimley and Camberley, 47,390 . . . G 8
Fulwood, 22,910 . . . G 1
Gainsborough, 17,440 . . . G 4
Gateshead, 91,230 . . . J 3
Gillingham, Dorset, ⊙4,050 . . . E 6
Gillingham, Kent, 93,900 . . . J 8
Glastonbury, 6,580 . . . E 6
Glossop, 24,820 . . . J 2
Gloucester, 91,600 . . . E 6
Godalming, 18,840 . . . G 8
Golborne, 28,720 . . . G 2
Goole, 17,920 . . . G 4
Gosport, 82,300 . . . F 7
Grange, 3,520 . . . E 3
Grantham 27,830 . . . G5
Gravesend 53,500 . . . J8
Great Grimsby 93,800 . . . G4
Great Torrington 3,430 . . . C7
Great Yarmouth 49,410 . . . J5
Greenwich 207,200 . . . H8
Guildford 58,470 . . . G8
Guisborough 14,860 . . . F3
Hackney 192,500 . . . H8
Hale 17,080 . . . H2
Halesowen 54,120 . . . E5
Halifax 88,580 . . . J1
Haltemprice 54,850 . . . G4
Haltwhistle† 3,511 . . . E2
Hammersmith 170,000 . . . H8
Haringey 228,200 . . . H8
Harlow 79,160 . . . H7
Harrogate 64,620 . . . F4
Harrow 200,200 . . . B5
Hartlepool 97,100 . . . F3
Harwich 15,280 . . . J6
Haslingden 15,140 . . . H1
Hastings 74,600 . . . H7
Hatfield† 25,359 . . . H7
Havant and Waterloo 112,430 . . . G7
Haverhill 14,550 . . . H5
Havering 239,200 . . . J8
Hayle† 5,378 . . . B7
Hazel Grove and Bramhall 40,400 . . . H2
Heanor 24,590 . . . F4
Hebburn 23,150 . . . J3
Hedon 3,010 . . . G4
Hemel Hempstead 71,150 . . . G7
Hereford 47,800 . . . E5
Hertford 20,760 . . . H7
Hetton 16,810 . . . J3
Hexham 9,820 . . . E3
Heywood 31,720 . . . H2
High Wycombe 61,190 . . . G8
Hillingdon 230,800 . . . G8
Hinckley 49,310 . . . F5
Hinderwell† 2,551 . . . G3
Hitchin 29,190 . . . G6
Hoddesdon 27,510 . . . H7
Holmfirth 19,790 . . . J2
Horley† 18,593 . . . H8
Hornsea 7,280 . . . G4
Horsham 26,770 . . . G6
Horwich 16,670 . . . G2
Houghton-le-Spring 33,150 . . . J3
Hounslow, 199,100 . . . G 8
Hove, 72,000 . . . G 7
Hoylake, 32,000 . . . G 2
Hoyland Nether, 15,500 . . . J 2
Hucknall, 27,110 . . . F 4
Huddersfield, 130,060 . . . J 2
Hugh Town, ⊙1,958 . . . A 8
Hull, 276,600 . . . G 4
Hunstanton, 4,140 . . . H 5
Huntingdon and Godmanchester, 17,200 . . . G 5
Huyton-with-Roby, 65,950 . . . G 2
Hyde, 37,040 . . . H 2
Ilfracombe, 9,350 . . . C 6
Ilkeston, 33,690 . . . F 5
Immingham, ⊙10,259 . . . G 4
Ipswich, 121,500 . . . J 5
Islington, 171,600 . . . H 8
Jarrow, 28,510 . . . J 3
Kendal, 22,440 . . . E 3
Kenilworth, 19,730 . . . F 5
Kensington and Chelsea, 161,400 . . . G 8
Keswick, 4,790 . . . D 3
Kettering, 44,480 . . . G 5
Keynsham, 18,970 . . . E 6
Kidderminster, 49,960 . . . E 5
Kidsgrove, 22,690 . . . E 4
King's Lynn, 29,990 . . . H 5
Kingston upon Thames, 135,600 . . . H 8
Kingswood, 30,450 . . . E 6
Kirkburton, 20,320 . . . J 2
Kirkby, 59,100 . . . G 2
Kirkby Lonsdale, ⊙1,506 . . . E 3
Kirkby Stephen, ⊙1,539 . . . E 3
Knutsford, 14,840 . . . H 2
Lambeth, 290,300 . . . H 8
Lancaster, 126,300 . . . E 3
Leatherhead, 40,830 . . . G 8
Leeds, 744,500 . . . J 1
Leek, 19,460 . . . H 2
Leicester, 289,400 . . . F 5
Leigh, 46,390 . . . H 2
Leighton-Linslade, 22,590 . . . F 7
Letchworth, 31,520 . . . G 6
Lewes, 14,170 . . . H 7
Lewisham, 237,300 . . . H 8
Leyland, 23,690 . . . G 1
Lichfield, 23,690 . . . F 5
Lincoln, 73,700 . . . G 4
Liskeard, 5,360 . . . C 7
Litherland, 23,530 . . . G 2
Littlehampton, 20,320 . . . G 7

(continued on following page)

UNITED KINGDOM

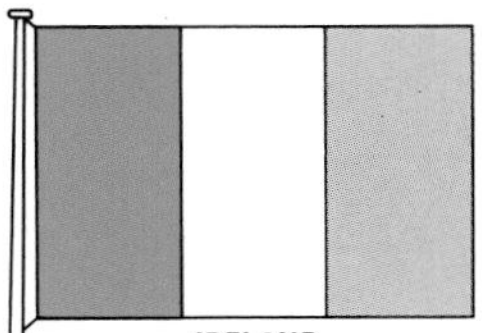

IRELAND

ENGLAND

AREA 50,516 sq. mi. (130,836 sq. km.)
POPULATION 46,220,955
CAPITAL London
LARGEST CITY London
HIGHEST POINT Scafell Pike 3,210 ft. (978 m.)

WALES

AREA 8,017 sq. mi. (20,764 sq. km.)
POPULATION 2,790,462
CAPITAL Cardiff
LARGEST CITY Cardiff
HIGHEST POINT Snowdon 3,560 ft. (1,085 m.)

SCOTLAND

AREA 30,414 sq. mi. (78,772 sq. km.)
POPULATION 5,117,146
CAPITAL Edinburgh
LARGEST CITY Glasgow
HIGHEST POINT Ben Nevis 4,406 ft. (1,343 m.)

NORTHERN IRELAND

AREA 5,452 sq. mi. (14,121 sq. km.)
POPULATION 1,543,000
CAPITAL Belfast
LARGEST CITY Belfast
HIGHEST POINT Slieve Donard 2,796 ft. (852 m.)

Topography

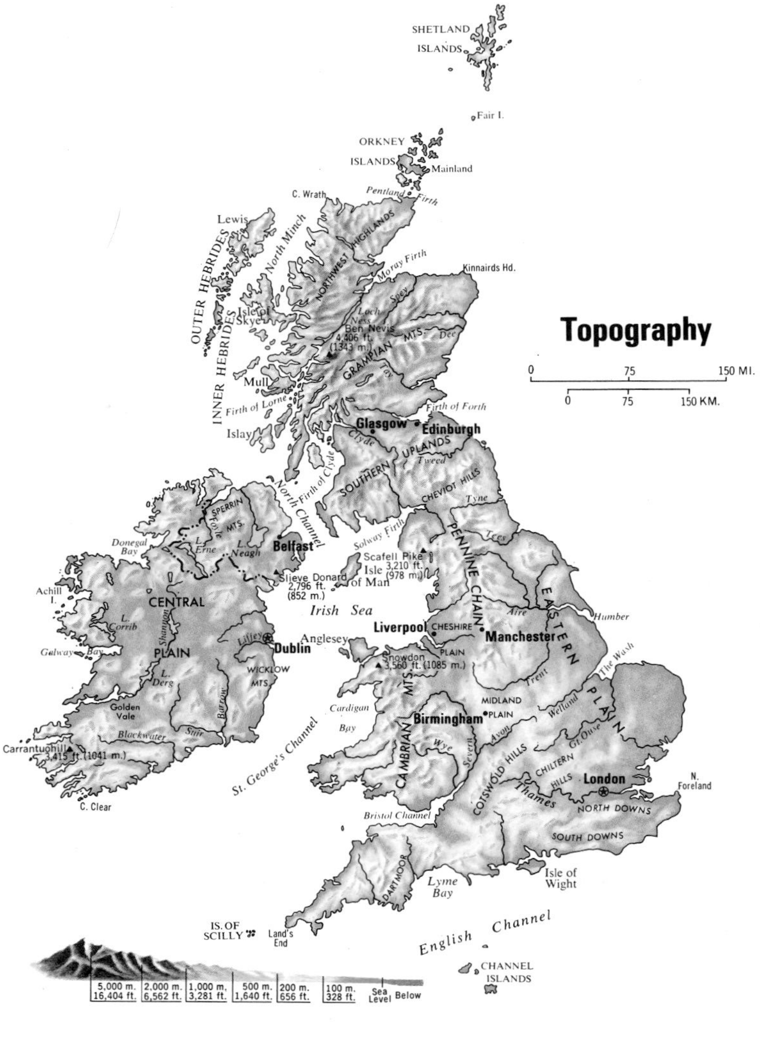

10 United Kingdom and Ireland

(continued)

Liverpool, 539,700 . . . G 2
Loftus, 7,850 . . . G 3
London (cap.), 7,028,200 . . . H 8
London, ★12,332,900 . . . H 8
Long Eaton, 33,560 . . . F 5
Longbenton, 50,120 . . . J 3
Looe, 4,060 . . . C 7
Loughborough, 49,010 . . . F 5
Lowestoft, 53,260 . . . J 5
Ludlow, ⊙7,466 . . . E 5
Luton, 164,500 . . . G 6
Lydd, 4,670 . . . H 7
Lyme Regis, 3,460 . . . E 7
Lymington, 36,780 . . . F 7
Lynton, 1,770 . . . D 6
Lytham Saint Anne's, 42,120 . . . G 1
Mablethorpe and Sutton, 6,750 . . . H 4
Macclesfield, 45,420 . . . H 2
Maidenhead, 48,210 . . . G 8
Maidstone, 72,110 . . . J 8
Maldon, 14,350 . . . H 6
Malmesbury, 2,550 . . . E 6
Malton, 4,010 . . . G 3
Malvern, 30,420 . . . E 5
Manchester, 490,000 . . . H 2
Mangotsfield, 23,000 . . . E 6
Mansfield, 58,450 . . . K 2
Mansfield Woodhouse, 25,400 . . . F 4
March, 14,560 . . . H 5
Margate, 50,290 . . . J 6
Market Harborough, 15,230 . . . G 5
Marlborough, 6,370 . . . F 6
Matlock, 20,300 . . . J 2
Melton Mowbray, 20,680 . . . G 5
Merton, 169,400 . . . H 8
Middlesbrough, 153,900 . . . F 3
Middleton, 53,340 . . . H 2
Middlewich, 7,600 . . . H 2
Mildenhall, ⊙9,269 . . . H 5
Millom, ⊙7,101 . . . D 3
Milton Keynes, 89,900 . . . F 5
Minehead, 8,230 . . . D 6
Moretonhampstead, ⊙1,440 . . . C 7
Morpeth, 14,450 . . . F 2
Mundesley, ⊙1,536 . . . J 5
Nelson, 31,220 . . . H 1
Neston, 18,210 . . . G 2
Newark, 24,760 . . . G 4
Newbury, 24,850 . . . F 6
Newcastle upon Tyne, 295,800 . . . H 3
Newcastle-under-Lyme, 75,940 . . . E 4
Newham, 228,900 . . . H 8
Newhaven, 9,970 . . . H 7
Newport, 22,430 . . . F 7
New Romney, 3,830 . . . J 7
Newton Abbot, 19,940 . . . D 7
Newton-le-Willows, 21,780 . . . H 2
New Windsor, 29,660 . . . G 8
Northallerton . . . F 3
Northam, 8,310 . . . C 6
Northampton, 128,290 . . . F 5
Northfleet, 27,150 . . . J 8
North Sunderland, ⊙1,725 . . . F 2
Northwich, 17,710 . . . H 2
Norton, 5,580 . . . G 3
Norton-Radstock, 15,900 . . . E 6
Norwich, 119,200 . . . J 5
Nottingham, 280,300 . . . F 5
Nuneaton, 69,210 . . . F 5
Oadby, 20,700 . . . F 5
Oakham, 7,280 . . . G 5
Okehampton, 4,000 . . . D 7
Oldham, 103,690 . . . H 2
Ormskirk, 28,860 . . . G 2
Oswaldtwistle, 14,270 . . . H 1
Oxford, 117,400 . . . F 6
Padstow, ⊙2,802 . . . B 7
Penryn, 5,660 . . . B 7
Penzance, 19,360 . . . B 7
Peterborough, 118,900 . . . G 5
Peterlee, ⊙21,846 . . . J 3
Plymouth, 259,100 . . . C 7
Polperro, ⊙1,491 . . . C 7
Poole, 110,600 . . . E 7
Porlock, ⊙1,290 . . . D 6
Portishead, 9,680 . . . E 6
Portland, 14,860 . . . E 7
Portslade-by-Sea, 18,040 . . . G 7
Portsmouth, 198,500 . . . F 7
Potters Bar, 24,670 . . . H 7
Poulton-le-Fylde, 16,340 . . . G 1
Preston, 94,760 . . . G 1
Prestwich, 32,850 . . . H 2
Queenborough, 31,550 . . . H 6
Radcliffe, 29,630 . . . H 2
Ramsbottom, 16,710 . . . H 2
Ramsgate, 40,090 . . . J 6
Rawtenstall, 20,950 . . . H 1
Rayleigh, 26,740 . . . J 8
Reading, 131,200 . . . G 8
Redbridge, 231,600 . . . H 8
Redcar, ⊙46,325 . . . F 3
Redditch, 44,750 . . . E 5
Reigate, 55,600 . . . H 8
Richmond upon Thames, 166,800 . . . H 8
Rickmansworth, 29,030 . . . G 8
Ripley, 18,060 . . . F 4
Rochdale, 93,780 . . . H 2
Rochester, 56,030 . . . J 8
Rothbury, ⊙1,818 . . . E 2
Rotherham, 84,770 . . . K 2
Royal Leamington Spa, 44,950 . . . F 5
Royal Tunbridge Wells, 44,800 . . . H 6
Rugby, 60,380 . . . F 5
Rugeley, 24,440 . . . E 5
Runcorn, 42,730 . . . G 2
Rushden, 21,840 . . . G 5
Ryde, 23,170 . . . F 7
Rye, 4,530 . . . H 7
Ryton, 15,170 . . . H 3
Saddleworth, 21,340 . . . J 2
Saint Agnes, ⊙4,747 . . . B 7
Saint Albans, 123,800 . . . H 7
Saint Austell-with-Fowey, 32,710 . . . C 7
Saint Columb Major, ⊙3,953 . . . B 7
Saint Helens, 104,890 . . . G 2
Saint Ives, Cornwall, 9,760 . . . B 7
Saint Neots, 17,940 . . . G 5
Salcombe, 2,370 . . . D 7
Sale, 59,060 . . . H 2
Salford, 261,100 . . . H 2
Salisbury, 35,460 . . . F 6
Saltburn and Marske-by-the-Sea, 21,170 . . . G 3
Sandbach, 14,280 . . . H 2
Sandown-Shanklin, 14,800 . . . F 7
Sandwich, 4,420 . . . J 6
Saxmundham, 1,820 . . . J 5
Scarborough, 43,300 . . . G 3
Scunthorpe, 68,100 . . . G 4
Seaford, 18,020 . . . H 7
Seaham, 22,470 . . . J 3
Seascale, ⊙2,106 . . . D 3
Seaton, 4,500 . . . D 7
Seaton Valley, 35,880 . . . J 3
Sedbergh, ⊙2,741 . . . E 3
Selsey, ⊙6,491 . . . G 7
Sevenoaks, 18,160 . . . J 8
Shaftesbury, 4,180 . . . E 7
Sheffield, 558,000 . . . J 2
Sherborne, 9,230 . . . E 7
Sheringham, 4,940 . . . J 5
Shildon, 15,360 . . . F 3
Shoreham-by-Sea, 19,620 . . . G 7
Shrewsbury, 56,120 . . . E 5
Silloth, ⊙2,662 . . . D 3
Sittingbourne and Milton, 32,830 . . . H 6
Skelmersdale, 35,850 . . . G 2
Skelton and Brotton, 15,930 . . . G 3
Sleaford, 8,050 . . . G 5
Slough, 89,060 . . . G 8
Solihull, 108,230 . . . F 5
Southampton, 213,700 . . . F 7
Southend-on-Sea, 159,300 . . . H 6
Southport, 86,030 . . . G 1
South Shields, 96,900 . . . J 3
Southwark, 224,900 . . . H 8
Southwold, 1,960 . . . J 5
Sowerby Bridge, 15,700 . . . H 1
Spalding, 17,040 . . . G 5
Spenborough, 41,460 . . . J 1
Spennymoor, 19,050 . . . F 3
Stafford, 54,860 . . . E 5
Staines, 56,380 . . . G 8
Stamford, 14,980 . . . G 5
Stanley, 42,280 . . . H 3
Staveley, 17,620 . . . K 2
Stevenage, 72,600 . . . G 6
Stockport, 138,350 . . . H 2
Stockton-on-Tees, 165,400 . . . F 3
Stoke-on-Trent, 256,200 . . . E 4
Stourbridge, 56,530 . . . E 5
Stourport-on-Severn, 19,430 . . . E 5
Stowmarket, 9,020 . . . J 5
Stratford-upon-Avon, 20,080 . . . F 5
Stretford, 52,450 . . . H 2
Stroud, 19,600 . . . E 6
Sudbury, 8,860 . . . H 5
Sunbury-on-Thames, 40,070 . . . G 8
Sunderland, 214,820 . . . J 3
Sutton, 166,700 . . . H 8
Sutton Bridge, ⊙3,113 . . . H 5
Sutton in Ashfield, 40,330 . . . K 2
Swadlincote, 21,060 . . . F 5
Swanage, 8,000 . . . E 7
Swindon, 90,680 . . . F 6
Tamworth, 46,960 . . . F 5
Taunton, 37,570 . . . D 6
Tavistock, ⊙7,620 . . . C 7
Telford, ⊙79,451 . . . E 5
Tenbury, ⊙2,151 . . . E 5
Tewkesbury, 9,210 . . . E 6
Thetford, 15,690 . . . H 5
Thirsk, ⊙2,884 . . . F 3
Thornaby-on-Tees, ⊙42,385 . . . F 3
Thorne, ⊙16,694 . . . F 4
Thornton Cleveleys, 27,090 . . . G 1
Thurrock, 127,700 . . . J 8
Tiverton, 16,190 . . . D 7
Todmorden, 14,540 . . . H 1
Tonbridge, 31,410 . . . H 8
Torbay, 109,900 . . . D 7
Torpoint, 6,840 . . . C 7
Tower Hamlets, 146,100 . . . H 8
Tow Law, 2,460 . . . H 4
Trowbridge, 20,120 . . . E 6
Truro, 15,690 . . . B 7
Turton, 22,800 . . . H 2
Tynemouth, 67,090 . . . J 3
Upton upon Severn, ⊙2,048 . . . E 5
Urmston, 44,130 . . . H 2
Uttoxeter, 9,100 . . . E 5
Ventnor, 6,980 . . . F 7
Wainfleet All Saints, ⊙1,116 . . . H 4
Wakefield, 306,500 . . . J 2
Wallasey, 94,520 . . . G 2
Wallsend, 45,490 . . . J 3
Walsall, 182,430 . . . E 5
Waltham Forest, 223,700 . . . H 8
Waltham Holy Cross, 14,810 . . . H 7
Walton and Weybridge, 51,270 . . . G 8
Walton-le-Dale, 27,660 . . . G 1
Wandsworth, 284,600 . . . H 8
Wantage, 8,490 . . . F 6
Ware, 14,900 . . . H 7
Wareham, 4,630 . . . E 7
Warley, 161,260 . . . E 5
Warminster, 14,440 . . . E 6
Warrington, 65,320 . . . G 2
Warwick, 17,870 . . . F 5
Washington, 27,720 . . . J 3
Watchet, 2,980 . . . D 6
Watford, 77,000 . . . H 7
Wellingborough, 39,570 . . . G 5
Wells, 8,960 . . . E 6
Wells-next-the-Sea, 2,450 . . . H 5
Welwyn, 39,900 . . . H 7
Wem, ⊙3,411 . . . E 5
West Bridgford, 28,340 . . . F 5
West Bromwich, 162,740 . . . F 5
West Mersea, 4,730 . . . H 6
Westminster, 216,100 . . . H 8
Weston-super-Mare, 51,960 . . . D 6
Weymouth and Melcombe Regis, 41,080 . . . E 7
Whickham, 29,710 . . . J 3
Whitchurch, ⊙7,142 . . . E 5
Whitehaven, 26,260 . . . D 3
Whitley Bay, 37,010 . . . J 3
Widnes, 58,330 . . . G 2
Wigan, 80,920 . . . G 2
Wigston, 31,650 . . . F 5
Wilmslow, 31,250 . . . H 2
Wilton, 4,090 . . . F 6
Winchester, 88,900 . . . F 6
Windermere, 7,860 . . . E 3
Winsford, 26,920 . . . G 2
Wirral, 27,510 . . . G 2
Wisbech, 16,990 . . . H 5
Witham, 19,730 . . . H 6
Withernsea, 6,300 . . . H 4
Wivenhoe, 5,630 . . . J 6
Woking, 79,300 . . . G 8
Wokingham, 22,390 . . . G 8
Wolverhampton, 266,400 . . . E 5
Wombwell, 17,850 . . . K 2
Woodhall Spa, 2,420 . . . G 4
Woodley and Sandford, ⊙24,581 . . . G 8
Woodstock, 2,070 . . . F 6
Wooler, ⊙1,833 . . . F 2
Worcester, 73,900 . . . E 5
Workington, 28,260 . . . D 3
Worksop, 36,590 . . . F 4
Worsbrough, 15,180 . . . J 2
Worsley, 49,530 . . . H 2
Worthing, 89,100 . . . G 7
Wymondham, 9,390 . . . J 5
Yateley, ⊙16,505 . . . G 8
Yeovil, 26,180 . . . E 7
York, 101,900 . . . F 4

OTHER FEATURES

Aire (riv.) . . . F 4
Atlantic Ocean . . . A 7
Avon (riv.) . . . F 5
Avon (riv.) . . . F 7
Axe Edge (mt.) . . . H 2
Barnstaple (bay) . . . C 6
Beachy (head) . . . H 7
Bigbury (bay) . . . C 7
Blackwater (riv.) . . . H 6
Bristol (chan.) . . . C 6
Brown Willy (mt.) . . . C 7
Cheviot (hills) . . . E 2
Cheviot, The (mt.) . . . E 2
Chiltern (hills) . . . G 6
Cleveland (hills) . . . F 3
Colne (riv.) . . . G 8
Cornwall (cape) . . . B 7
Cotswold (hills) . . . E 6
Cross Fell (mt.) . . . E 3
Cumbrian (mts.) . . . D 3
Dart (riv.) . . . D 7
Dartmoor National Park . . . C 7
Dee (riv.) . . . D 4
Derwent (riv.) . . . G 3
Derwent (riv.) . . . H 3
Don (riv.) . . . F 4
Dorset Heights (hills) . . . E 7
Dove (riv.) . . . J 2
Dover (str.) . . . J 7
Dungeness (prom.) . . . J 7
Dunkery (hill) . . . D 6
Eddystone (rocks) . . . C 7
Eden (riv.) . . . E 3
English (chan.) . . . D 8
Esk (riv.) . . . D 2
Exe (riv.) . . . D 7
Exmoor National Park . . . D 6
Fens, The (reg.) . . . G 5
Flamborough (head) . . . G 3
Formby (head) . . . G 2
Foulness Island (pen.) . . . J 6
Gibraltar (pt.) . . . H 4
Great Ouse (riv.) . . . H 5
Hartland (pt.) . . . C 6
High Willhays (mt.) . . . C 7
Hodder (riv.) . . . H 1
Holderness (pen.), 43,900 . . . G 4
Holy (isl.), 189 . . . F 2
Humber (riv.) . . . G 4
Irish (sea) . . . B 4
Kennet (riv.) . . . F 6
Lake District National Park . . . D 3
Land's End (prom.) . . . B 7
Lea (riv.) . . . G 6
Lincoln Wolds (hills) . . . G 4
Lindisfarne (Holy) (isl.), 189 . . . F 2
Liverpool (bay) . . . D 4
Lizard, The (pen.), 7,371 . . . B 8
Lundy (isl.), 49 . . . C 6
Lune (riv.) . . . E 3
Lyme (bay) . . . D 7
Manacle (pt.) . . . C 7
Medway (riv.) . . . H 6
Mendip (hills) . . . E 6
Mersea (isl.), 4,423 . . . J 6
Mersey (riv.) . . . G 2
Morecambe (bay) . . . D 3
Mounts (bay) . . . B 7
Naze, The (prom.) . . . J 6
Nene (riv.) . . . H 5
New (for.) . . . F 6
North (sea) . . . J 4
North Downs (hills) . . . G 6
North Foreland (prom.) . . . J 6
Northumberland National Park . . . E 2
North York Moors National Park . . . G 3
Orford Ness (prom.) . . . J 5
Ouse (riv.) . . . G 4
Ouse (riv.) . . . G 6
Parrett (riv.) . . . E 6
Peak District National Park . . . F 4
Peak, The (mt.) . . . J 2
Peel Fell (mt.) . . . E 2
Pennine Chain (range) . . . E 3
Plymouth (sound) . . . C 7
Portland, Bill of (pt.) . . . E 7
Prawle (pt.) . . . D 7
Purbeck, Isle of (pen.), 39,500 . . . F 7
Ribble (riv.) . . . E 4
Saint Alban's (head) . . . F 7
Saint Bees (head) . . . D 3
Saint Martin's (isl.), 106 . . . A 8
Saint Mary's (isl.), 1,958 . . . A 8
Scafell Pike (mt.) . . . D 3
Scilly (isls.), 1,900 . . . A 7
Selsey Bill (prom.) . . . G 7
Severn (riv.) . . . E 6
Sheppey (isl.), 31,550 . . . J 6
Sherwood (for.) . . . F 4
Skiddaw (mt.) . . . D 3
Solent (chan.) . . . F 7
Solway (firth) . . . D 3
South Downs (hills) . . . G 7
Spithead (chan.) . . . F 7
Spurn (head) . . . H 4
Stonehenge (ruins) . . . F 6
Stour (riv.) . . . E 7
Stour (riv.) . . . H 6
Stour (riv.) . . . J 6
Swale (riv.) . . . F 3
Tamar (riv.) . . . C 7
Taw (riv.) . . . D 7
Tees (riv.) . . . F 3
Test (riv.) . . . F 6
Thames (riv.) . . . H 6
Tintagel (head) . . . C 7
Torridge (riv.) . . . C 7
Trent (riv.) . . . G 4
Tresco (isl.), 246 . . . A 8
Tweed (riv.) . . . E 2
Tyne (riv.) . . . F 3
Ure (riv.) . . . F 3
Ver (riv.) . . . H 7
Walney, Isle of (isl.), 11,241 . . . D 3
Wash, The (bay) . . . H 5
Weald, The (reg.) . . . H 6
Wear (riv.) . . . F 3
Weaver (riv.) . . . G 2
Welland (riv.) . . . G 5
Wey (riv.) . . . G 6
Wharfe (riv.) . . . E 3
Wirral (pen.), 432,900 . . . G 2
Witham (riv.) . . . G 4
Wolds, The (hills) . . . G 4
Wye (riv.) . . . D 5
Wyre (riv.) . . . G 1
Yare (riv.) . . . J 5
Yorkshire Dales National Park . . . E 3

CHANNEL ISLANDS

CITIES and TOWNS

Saint Anne . . . E 8
Saint Helier (cap.), Jersey, ⊙28,135 . . . E 8
Saint Peter Port (cap.), Guernsey, ⊙16,303 . . . E 8
Saint Sampson's, ⊙6,534 . . . E 8

OTHER FEATURES

Alderney (isl.), 1,686 . . . E 8
Guernsey (isl.), 51,351 . . . E 8
Herm (isl.), 96 . . . E 8
Jersey (isl.), 72,629 . . . E 8
Sark (isl.), 590 . . . E 8

ISLE of MAN

CITIES and TOWNS

Castletown, 2,820 . . . C 3
Douglas (cap.), 20,389 . . . C 3
Laxey, 1,170 . . . C 3
Michael, 408 . . . C 3
Onchan, 4,807 . . . C 3
Peel, 3,081 . . . C 3
Port Erin, 1,714 . . . C 3
Port Saint Mary, 1,508 . . . C 3
Ramsey, 5,048 . . . C 3

OTHER FEATURES

Ayre (pt.) . . . C 3
Calf of Man (isl.) . . . C 3
Langness (prom.) . . . C 3
Snaefell (mt.) . . . C 3
Spanish (head) . . . C 3

WALES

COUNTIES

Clwyd, 376,000 . . . D 4
Dyfed, 323,100 . . . C 6
Gwent, 439,600 . . . D 6
Gwynedd, 225,100 . . . C 4
Mid Glamorgan, 540,400 . . . D 6
Powys, 101,500 . . . D 5
South Glamorgan, 389,200 . . . A 7
West Glamorgan, 371,900 . . . D 6

CITIES and TOWNS

Aberaeron, 1,340 . . . C 5
Abercarn, 18,370 . . . B 6
Aberdare, 38,030 . . . A 6
Abertillery, 20,550 . . . B 6
Amlwch, 3,630 . . . C 4
Bala, 1,650 . . . D 5
Bangor, 16,030 . . . C 4
Barmouth, 2,070 . . . C 5
Barry, 42,780 . . . B 7
Beaumaris, 2,090 . . . C 4
Bedwellty, 25,460 . . . B 6
Bethesda, 4,180 . . . D 4
Betws-y-Coed, 720 . . . D 4
Brecknock (Brecon), 6,460 . . . D 6
Brecon, 6,460 . . . D 6
Bridgend, 14,690 . . . A 7
Brynmawr, 5,970 . . . B 6
Builth Wells, 1,480 . . . D 5
Burry Port, 5,990 . . . C 6
Caernarfon, 8,840 . . . C 4
Caerphilly, 42,190 . . . B 6
Cardiff, 281,500 . . . B 7
Cardigan, 3,830 . . . C 5
Chepstow, 8,260 . . . E 6
Chirk, ⊙3,564 . . . D 5
Colwyn Bay, 25,370 . . . D 4
Criccieth, 1,590 . . . C 5
Cwmamman, 3,950 . . . D 6
Cwmbran, 32,980 . . . B 6
Denbigh, 8,420 . . . D 4
Dolgellau, 2,430 . . . D 5
Ebbw Vale, 25,670 . . . B 6
Ffestiniog, 5,510 . . . D 5
Fishguard and Goodwick, 5,020 . . . B 5
Flint, 15,070 . . . G 2
Gelligaer, 33,820 . . . A 6
Harlech, ⊙332 . . . C 5
Haverfordwest, 8,930 . . . B 6
Hawarden, ⊙20,389 . . . G 2
Hay, 1,200 . . . D 5
Holywell, 8,570 . . . G 2
Kidwelly, 3,090 . . . C 6
Knighton, 2,190 . . . D 5
Llandeilo, 1,780 . . . C 6
Llandovery, 2,040 . . . D 5
Llandrindod Wells, 3,460 . . . D 5
Llandudno, 17,700 . . . D 4
Llanelli, 25,870 . . . C 6
Llanfairfechan, 3,800 . . . D 4
Llangefni, 4,070 . . . C 4
Llangollen, 3,050 . . . D 5
Llanguicke, ⊙15,029 . . . D 6
Llanidloes, 2,390 . . . D 5
Llantrisant, ⊙27,490 . . . A 7
Llanwrtyd Wells, 460 . . . D 5
Llwchwr, 27,530 . . . D 6
Machynlleth, 1,830 . . . D 5
Maesteg, 21,100 . . . D 6
Menai Bridge, 2,730 . . . C 4
Merthyr Tydfil, 61,500 . . . A 6
Milford Haven, 13,960 . . . B 6
Mold, 8,700 . . . G 2
Montgomery, 1,000 . . . D 5
Mountain Ash, 27,710 . . . A 6
Mynyddislwyn, 15,590 . . . B 6
Narberth, 970 . . . C 6
Neath, 27,280 . . . D 6
Nefyn, ⊙2,086 . . . C 5
Newcastle Emlyn, 690 . . . C 5
Newport, Dyfed, ⊙1,062 . . . C 5
Newport, Gwent, 110,090 . . . B 6
New Quay, 760 . . . C 5
Newtown, 6,400 . . . D 5
Neyland, 2,690 . . . B 6
Ogmore and Garw, 19,680 . . . A 6
Pembroke, 14,570 . . . C 6
Penarth, 24,180 . . . B 7
Penmaenmawr, 4,050 . . . C 4
Pontypool, 36,710 . . . B 6
Pontypridd, 34,180 . . . A 6
Porthcawl, 14,980 . . . D 6
Porthmadog, 3,900 . . . C 5
Port Talbot, 58,200 . . . D 6
Prestatyn, 15,480 . . . D 4
Presteigne, 1,330 . . . D 5
Pwllheli, 4,020 . . . C 5
Rhondda, 85,400 . . . A 6
Rhyl, 22,150 . . . D 4
Risca, 15,780 . . . B 6
Ruthin, 4,780 . . . D 4
Saint David's, ⊙1,638 . . . B 6
Swansea, 190,800 . . . C 6
Tenby, 4,930 . . . C 6
Tredegar, 17,450 . . . B 6
Tywyn, 3,850 . . . C 5
Welshpool, 7,370 . . . D 5
Wrexham, 39,530 . . . E 4

OTHER FEATURES

Anglesey (isl.), 64,500 . . . C 4
Aran Fawddwy (mt.) . . . C 5
Bardsey (isl.), 9 . . . C 5
Berwyn (mts.) . . . D 5
Black (mts.) . . . D 6
Braich-y-Pwll (prom.) . . . C 5
Brecon Beacons (mt.) . . . D 6
Brecon Beacons National Park . . . D 6
Caldy (isl.), 70 . . . C 6
Cambrian (mts.) . . . D 5
Cardigan (bay) . . . C 5
Carmarthen (bay) . . . C 6
Cemmaes (head) . . . C 5
Dee (riv.) . . . D 4
Dovey (riv.) . . . D 5
Ely (riv.) . . . B 7
Gower (pen.), 17,220 . . . C 6
Great Ormes (head) . . . C 4
Holy (isl.), 13,715 . . . C 4
Lleyn (pen.), 25,800 . . . C 5
Menai (str.) . . . C 4
Milford Haven (inlet) . . . B 6
Pembrokeshire Coast National Park . . . C 6
Plynlimon (mt.) . . . D 5
Preseli (mts.) . . . C 6
Radnor (for.) . . . D 5
Rhymney (riv.) . . . B 6
Saint Brides (bay) . . . B 6
Saint David's (head) . . . B 6
Saint George's (chan.) . . . B 5
Saint Gowans (head) . . . C 6
Severn (riv.) . . . E 5
Snowdon (mt.) . . . D 4
Snowdonia National Park . . . D 4
Taff (riv.) . . . B 7
Teifi (riv.) . . . C 5
Towy (riv.) . . . D 6
Tremadoc (bay) . . . C 5
Usk (riv.) . . . B 6
Wye (riv.) . . . D 5
Ynys Môn (Anglesey) (isl.), 64,500 . . . C 4

★Population of met. area.
⊙Population of parish.

SCOTLAND

(map on page 13)

REGIONS

Borders, 99,409 . . . E 5
Central, 269,281 . . . D 4
Dumfries and Galloway, 143,667 . . . E 5
Fife, 336,339 . . . E 4
Grampian, 448,772 . . . F 3
Highland, 182,044 . . . D 3
Lothian, 754,008 . . . E 5
Orkney (islands area), 17,675 . . . E 1
Shetland (islands area), 18,494 . . . F 2
Strathclyde, 2,504,909 . . . C 4
Tayside, 401,987 . . . E 4
Western Isles (islands area), 29,615 . . . A 3

CITIES and TOWNS

Aberchirder, 877 . . . F 3
Aberdeen, 210,362 . . . F 3
Aberdour, 1,576 . . . D 1
Aberfeldy, 1,552 . . . E 4
Aberfoyle, 793 . . . D 4
Aberlady, 737 . . . F 4
Aberlour, 842 . . . E 3
Abernethy, 776 . . . E 4
Aboyne, 1,040 . . . F 3
Acharacle, ⊙764 . . . C 4
Achiltibuie, ⊙1,564 . . . C 3
Achnasheen, ⊙1,078 . . . C 3
Ae, 239 . . . E 5
Airdrie, 38,491 . . . C 2
Alexandria, 9,758 . . . A 1
Alford, 764 . . . F 3
Alloa, 13,558 . . . C 1
Alness, 2,560 . . . D 3
Altnaharra, ⊙1,227 . . . D 2
Alva, 4,593 . . . C 1
Alyth, 1,738 . . . E 4
Ancrum, 266 . . . F 5
Annan, 6,250 . . . E 6
Annat, ⊙550 . . . C 3
Annbank Station, 2,530 . . . D 5
Applecross, ⊙550 . . . C 3
Arbroath, 22,706 . . . F 4
Ardavasar, ⊙449 . . . B 3
Ardersier, 942 . . . E 3
Ardgay, 193 . . . D 3
Ardrishaig, 946 . . . C 4
Ardrossan, 11,072 . . . D 5
Armadale, 7,200 . . . C 2
Arrochar, 543 . . . D 4
Ascog, 230 . . . A 2
Auchenblae, 339 . . . F 4
Auchencairn, 215 . . . E 6
Auchinleck, 4,883 . . . D 5
Auchterarder, 1,738 . . . E 4
Auchtermuchty, 1,426 . . . E 4
Auldearn, 405 . . . E 3
Aviemore, 1,224 . . . E 3
Avoch, 776 . . . D 3
Ayr, 47,990 . . . D 5
Ayton, 410 . . . F 5
Bailivanish, 347 . . . A 3
Baillieston, 7,671 . . . B 2
Balallan, 283 . . . B 2
Balerno, 3,576 . . . D 2
Balfron, 1,149 . . . B 1
Ballantrae, 262 . . . C 5
Ballater, 981 . . . F 3
Ballingry, 4,332 . . . D 1
Ballinluig, 188 . . . E 4
Balloch, Highland, 572 . . . D 3
Balloch, Strathclyde, 1,484 . . . B 1
Baltasound, 246 . . . G 2
Banchory, 2,435 . . . F 3
Banff, 3,832 . . . F 3
Bankfoot, 868 . . . E 4
Bankhead, 1,492 . . . F 3
Bannockburn, 5,889 . . . C 1
Barrhead, 18,736 . . . B 2
Barrhill, 236 . . . D 5
Barvas, 279 . . . B 2
Bathgate, 14,038 . . . C 2
Bayble, 543 . . . B 2
Bearsden, 25,128 . . . B 2
Beattock, 309 . . . E 5
Beauly, 1,141 . . . D 3
Beith, 5,859 . . . D 5
Bellsbank, 3,066 . . . D 5
Bellshill, 18,166 . . . C 2
Berriedale, ⊙1,927 . . . E 2
Bieldside, 1,137 . . . F 3
Biggar, 1,718 . . . E 5
Birnam, 659 . . . E 4
Bishopbriggs, 21,570 . . . B 2
Bishopton, 2,931 . . . B 2
Blackburn, 7,636 . . . C 2
Blackford, 529 . . . E 4
Blair Atholl, 437 . . . E 4
Blairgowrie and Rattray, 5,681 . . . E 4
Blanefield, 835 . . . B 1
Blantyre, 13,992 . . . B 2
Blyth Bridge, ⊙441 . . . E 5
Bo'ness, 12,959 . . . C 1
Boat of Garten, 406 . . . E 3
Boddam, 1,429 . . . G 3
Bonar Bridge, 519 . . . D 3
Bonhill, 4,385 . . . B 1
Bonnybridge, 5,701 . . . C 1
Bonnyrigg and Lasswade, 7,429 . . . D 2
Bowmore, 947 . . . B 5
Braemar, 394 . . . E 3
Breasclete, 234 . . . B 2
Brechin, 6,759 . . . F 4
Bridge of Allan, 4,638 . . . C 1
Bridge of Don, 4,086 . . . F 3
Bridge of Weir, 4,724 . . . A 2
Brightons, 3,106 . . . C 1
Broadford, 310 . . . B 3
Brodick, 630 . . . C 5
Brora, 1,436 . . . E 2
Broxburn, 7,776 . . . D 1
Buchlyvie, 412 . . . B 1
Buckhaven and Methil, 17,930 . . . F 4
Buckie, 8,145 . . . E 3
Bucksburn, 6,567 . . . F 3
Bunessan, ⊙585 . . . B 4
Burghead, 1,321 . . . E 3
Burnmouth, 300 . . . F 5
Burntisland, 5,626 . . . D 1
Cairndow, ⊙874 . . . D 4
Cairnryan, 199 . . . D 6
Callander, 1,805 . . . D 4
Cambuslang, 14,607 . . . B 2
Campbeltown, 6,428 . . . C 5
Cannich, 203 . . . D 3
Canonbie, 234 . . . F 5
Caol, 3,719 . . . C 4
Carbost, ⊙772 . . . B 3
Cardenden, 6,802 . . . D 1
Carloway, 178 . . . B 2
Carluke, 8,864 . . . E 5
Carnoustie, 6,838 . . . F 4
Carnwath, 1,246 . . . E 5
Carradale, 262 . . . C 5
Carrbridge, 416 . . . E 3
Carron, 2,626 . . . C 1
Carsphairn, 186 . . . D 5
Castlebay, 284 . . . A 4
Castle Douglas, 3,384 . . . E 6
Castle Kennedy, 307 . . . D 6
Castletown, 902 . . . E 2
Catrine, 2,681 . . . D 5
Cawdor, 111 . . . E 3
Chirnside, 888 . . . F 5
Chryston, 8,322 . . . C 2
Clackmannan, 3,248 . . . C 1
Clarkston, 8,404 . . . B 2
Closeburn, 225 . . . E 5
Clovulin, ⊙315 . . . C 4
Clydebank, 47,538 . . . B 2
Coalburn, 1,460 . . . E 5
Coatbridge, 50,806 . . . C 2
Cockburnspath, 233 . . . F 5
Cockenzie and Port Seton, 3,539 . . . D 1
Coldingham, 423 . . . F 5
Coldstream, 1,393 . . . F 5
Coll, 305 . . . B 2
Colmonell, 218 . . . D 5
Comrie, 1,119 . . . E 4
Connel, 300 . . . C 4
Cononbridge, 914 . . . D 3
Corpach, 1,296 . . . C 4
Coupar Angus, 2,010 . . . E 4
Cove and Kilcreggan, 1,402 . . . A 1
Cove Bay, 765 . . . F 3
Cowdenbeath, 10,215 . . . D 1
Cowie, 2,751 . . . C 1
Craigellachie, 382 . . . E 3
Craignure, ⊙544 . . . C 4
Crail, 1,033 . . . F 4
Crawford, 384 . . . E 5
Creetown, 769 . . . D 6
Crieff, 5,718 . . . E 4
Crimond, 313 . . . G 3
Crinan, ⊙462 . . . C 4
Cromarty, 492 . . . E 3
Crosshill, 535 . . . D 5
Crossmichael, 317 . . . D 6
Cruden Bay, 528 . . . G 3
Cullen, 1,199 . . . F 3
Culross, 504 . . . C 1
Cults, 3,336 . . . F 3
Cumbernauld, 41,200 . . . C 1
Cumnock and Holmhead, 6,298 . . . D 5
Cupar, 6,607 . . . E 4
Currie, 6,764 . . . D 2
Dailly, 1,258 . . . D 5
Dalbeattie, 3,659 . . . E 6
Daliburgh, 261 . . . A 3
Dalkeith, 9,713 . . . D 2
Dalmally, 283 . . . D 4
Dalmellington, 1,949 . . . D 5
Dalry, 5,833 . . . D 5
Dalrymple, 1,336 . . . D 5
Darvel, 3,177 . . . D 5
Daviot, ⊙513 . . . D 3
Denholm, 581 . . . F 5
Denny and Dunipace, 10,424 . . . C 1
Dervaig, ⊙1,081 . . . B 4
Dingwall, 4,275 . . . D 3
Dollar, 2,573 . . . E 4
Dornoch, 880 . . . D 3
Douglas, 1,843 . . . E 5
Doune, 859 . . . D 4
Drongan, 3,609 . . . D 5
Drumbeg, ⊙833 . . . C 2
Drummore, 336 . . . D 6
Drumnadrochit, 359 . . . D 3
Drymen, 659 . . . B 1
Dufftown, 1,481 . . . E 3
Dumbarton, 25,469 . . . B 1
Dumfries, 29,259 . . . E 5
Dunbar, 4,609 . . . F 4
Dunbeath, 161 . . . E 2
Dunbeg, 939 . . . C 4
Dunblane, 5,222 . . . E 4
Dundee, 194,732 . . . F 4
Dundonald, 2,256 . . . D 5
Dunfermline, 52,098 . . . D 1
Dunkeld, 273 . . . E 4
Dunning, 564 . . . E 4
Dunoon, 8,759 . . . A 2
Dunragit, 323 . . . D 6
Duns, 1,812 . . . F 5
Duntochter, 3,532 . . . B 2
Dunure, 452 . . . D 5
Dunvegan, 301 . . . B 3
Dyce, 2,733 . . . F 3
Eaglesfield, 581 . . . E 5
Eaglesham, 2,788 . . . D 5
Earlston, 1,415 . . . F 5
East Calder, 2,690 . . . D 2
East Kilbride, 71,200 . . . B 2
East Linton, 882 . . . F 5
Eastriggs, 1,455 . . . E 5
Ecclefechan, 844 . . . E 5
Edinburgh (cap.), 470,085 . . . D 1
Edzell, 658 . . . F 4
Elderslie, 5,204 . . . B 2
Elgin, 17,042 . . . E 3
Elie and Earlsferry, 807 . . . F 4
Ellon, 2,855 . . . F 3
Embo, 260 . . . E 3
Errol, 762 . . . E 4
Evanton, 562 . . . D 3
Eyemouth, 2,704 . . . F 5
Fairlie, 1,029 . . . D 5
Falkirk, 36,901 . . . C 1
Falkland, 998 . . . E 4
Fallin, 3,159 . . . C 1
Fauldhouse, 5,247 . . . C 2
Ferness, ⊙287 . . . E 3
Ferryden, 740 . . . F 4
Findhorn, 664 . . . E 3
Findochty, 1,229 . . . E 3
Fintry, 296 . . . B 1
Fochabers, 1,238 . . . E 3
Forfar, 11,179 . . . F 4
Forres, 5,317 . . . E 3
Fort Augustus, 670 . . . D 3
Forth, 2,929 . . . C 2
Fortrose, 1,150 . . . D 3
Fort William, 4,370 . . . C 4
Foyers, 276 . . . D 3
Fraserburgh, 10,930 . . . G 3
Friockheim, 807 . . . F 4
Furnace, 220 . . . C 4
Fyvie, 405 . . . F 3
Gairloch, 125 . . . C 3
Galashiels, 12,808 . . . F 5
Galston, 4,256 . . . D 5
Gardenstown, 892 . . . F 3
Garelochhead, 1,552 . . . A 1
Gargunnock, 457 . . . B 1
Garlieston, 385 . . . D 6
Garmouth, 352 . . . E 3
Garrabost, 307 . . . B 2
Gartmore, 253 . . . B 1
Gatehouse-of-Fleet, 835 . . . D 6
Giffnock, 10,987 . . . B 2
Gifford, 575 . . . F 5
Girvan, 7,597 . . . D 5
Glamis, 190 . . . F 4
Glasgow, 880,617 . . . B 2
Glasgow, ★1,674,789 . . . B 2
Glenbarr, ⊙691 . . . C 5
Glencaple, 275 . . . E 5
Glencoe, 195 . . . C 4
Glenelg, ⊙1,468 . . . C 3
Glenluce, 725 . . . D 6
Glenrothes, 31,400 . . . E 4
Golspie, 1,374 . . . E 3
Gordon, 320 . . . F 5
Gorebridge, 3,426 . . . D 2
Gourock, 11,192 . . . A 1
Grangemouth, 24,430 . . . C 1
Grantown-on-Spey, 1,578 . . . E 3
Greenlaw, 574 . . . F 5
Greenock, 67,275 . . . A 2
Gretna, 1,907 . . . E 5
Gullane, 1,701 . . . F 4
Haddington, 6,767 . . . F 5
Halkirk, 679 . . . E 2
Hamilton, 45,495 . . . C 2
Hamnavoe, 307 . . . G 2
Harthill, 4,712 . . . C 2
Hatton, 315 . . . G 3
Hawick, 16,484 . . . F 5
Heathhall, 1,365 . . . E 5
Helensburgh, 13,327 . . . A 1
Helmsdale, 727 . . . E 2
Hill of Fearn, 233 . . . D 3
Hillside, 692 . . . F 4
Hillswick, ⊙696 . . . G 2
Hopeman, 1,248 . . . E 3
Huntly, 4,078 . . . F 3
Hurlford, 4,294 . . . D 5
Inchnadamph, ⊙833 . . . D 2
Innellan, 922 . . . A 2
Innerleithen, 2,293 . . . E 5
Insch, 881 . . . F 3
Inveraray, 473 . . . C 4
Inverbervie, 853 . . . F 4
Invercassley, ⊙1,067 . . . D 3
Invergordon, 2,385 . . . D 3
Invergowrie, 1,389 . . . E 4
Inverie, ⊙1,468 . . . C 3
Inverkeithing, 6,102 . . . D 1
Inverness, 35,801 . . . D 3
Inverurie, 5,534 . . . F 3
Irvine, 48,500 . . . D 5
Isle of Whithorn, 222 . . . D 6
Jedburgh, 3,953 . . . F 5
John O'Groats, 195 . . . E 2
Johnshaven, 544 . . . F 4
Johnstone, 23,251 . . . B 2
Kames, 230 . . . C 5
Keiss, 344 . . . E 2
Keith, 4,192 . . . F 3
Kelso, 4,934 . . . F 5
Kelty, 6,573 . . . D 1
Kemnay, 1,042 . . . F 3
Kenmore, 211 . . . E 4
Kilbarchan, 2,669 . . . A 2
Kilbirnie, 8,259 . . . A 2
Kilchoan, ⊙764 . . . B 4
Kildonan, ⊙1,105 . . . E 2
Killearn, 1,086 . . . B 1
Killin, 600 . . . D 4
Kilmacolm, 3,348 . . . A 2
Kilmarnock, 50,175 . . . D 5
Kilmaurs, 2,518 . . . D 5
Kilninver, ⊙247 . . . C 4
Kilrenny and Anstruther, 2,951 . . . F 4
Kilsyth, 10,210 . . . B 1
Kilwinning, 8,460 . . . D 5
Kinbrace, ⊙1,105 . . . E 2
Kincardine, 3,278 . . . C 1
Kinghorn, 2,163 . . . D 1
Kingussie, 1,036 . . . D 3
Kinlochewe, ⊙1,794 . . . C 3
Kinlochleven, 1,243 . . . D 4
Kinloch Rannoch, 241 . . . D 4
Kinloss, 2,378 . . . E 3
Kinross, 2,829 . . . E 4
Kintore, 970 . . . F 3
Kippen, 529 . . . B 1
Kirkcaldy, 50,207 . . . D 1
Kirkcolm, 346 . . . C 6
Kirkconnel, 3,318 . . . E 5
Kirkcowan, 354 . . . D 6
Kirkcudbright, 2,690 . . . E 6
Kirkhill, 210 . . . D 3
Kirkintilloch, 26,664 . . . B 2
Kirkmuirhill, 2,575 . . . E 5
Kirkton of Glenisla, ⊙331 . . . E 4
Kirkwall, 4,777 . . . E 2
Kirriemuir, 4,295 . . . E 4
Kyleakin, 268 . . . C 3
Kyle of Lochalsh, 687 . . . C 3
Kylestrome, ⊙745 . . . D 2
Ladybank, 1,216 . . . E 4
Laggan, 393 . . . D 3
Lairg, 572 . . . D 2
Lamlash, 613 . . . C 5
Lanark, 8,842 . . . E 5
Langholm, 2,509 . . . E 5
Larbert, 4,922 . . . C 1
Largs, 9,461 . . . A 2
Larkhall, 15,926 . . . E 5
Lauder, 639 . . . F 5
Laurencekirk, 1,416 . . . F 4

(continued)

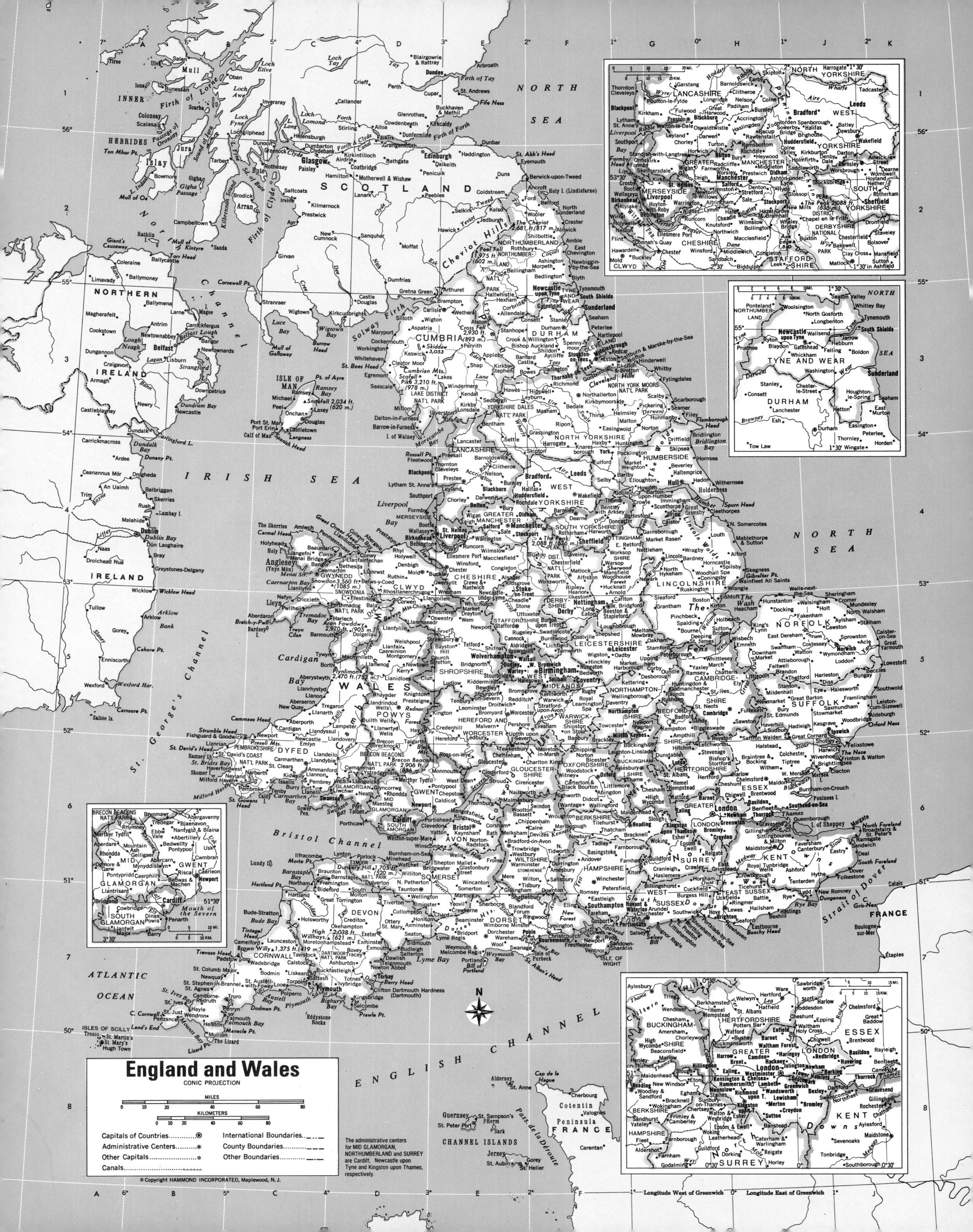
England and Wales
CONIC PROJECTION
MILES
0 10 20 40 60 80
KILOMETERS
0 10 20 40 60 80
Capitals of Countries
Administrative Centers
Other Capitals
Canals
International Boundaries
County Boundaries
Other Boundaries
The administrative centers for MID GLAMORGAN, NORTHUMBERLAND and SURREY are Cardiff, Newcastle upon Tyne and Kingston upon Thames, respectively.
© Copyright HAMMOND INCORPORATED, Maplewood, N. J.
Longitude West of Greenwich 0° Longitude East of Greenwich
SCOTLAND
WALES
NORTHERN IRELAND
IRELAND
FRANCE
NORTH SEA
IRISH SEA
ENGLISH CHANNEL
ATLANTIC OCEAN
Bristol Channel
St. George's Channel
North Channel
Strait of Dover
CHANNEL ISLANDS

Lennoxtown, 3,070 ... B 1
Lerwick, 6,195 ... G 2
Leslie, 3,303 ... E 4
Lesmahagow, 3,906 ... E 5
Leswalt, 237 ... C 6
Letham, 804 ... F 4
Leuchars, 2,482 ... F 4
Leurbost, 461 ... B 2
Leven, 9,507 ... F 4
Leverburgh, 223 ... B 3
Lhanbryde, 1,184 ... E 3
Lilliesleaf, 212 ... F 5
Limekilns, 812 ... D 1
Linlithgow, 6,098 ... C 1
Linwood, 10,510 ... B 2
Lionel, 187 ... B 2
Livingston, 21,900 ... C 2
Loanhead, 5,971 ... D 2
Lochailort, ⊙673 ... C 4
Lochaline, 213 ... C 4
Lochans, 355 ... D 6
Locharbriggs, 2,561 ... E 5
Lochawe, 200 ... C 4
Lochboisdale, 382 ... A 3
Lochcarron, 204 ... C 3
Lochgelly, 7,754 ... D 1
Lochgilphead, 1,217 ... C 4
Lochgoilhead, 216 ... D 4
Lochinver, 283 ... C 2
Lochmaben, 1,304 ... E 5
Lochmaddy, 307 ... A 3
Lochore, 2,994 ... D 1
Lochwinnoch, 2,064 ... A 2
Lockerbie, 3,135 ... E 5
Lossiemouth and Branderburgh, 5,817 ... E 3
Lumsden, 248 ... F 3
Luncarty, 584 ... E 4
Lybster, 554 ... E 2
Lyness, ⊙454 ... E 2
Macduff, 3,682 ... F 3
Machrihanish, 212 ... C 5
Maidens, 536 ... D 5
Mallaig, 903 ... C 4
Markinch, 2,366 ... E 4
Mauchline, 3,612 ... D 5
Maud, 634 ... F 3
Maybole, 4,703 ... D 5
Mayfield, 8,232 ... D 2
Meigle, 357 ... E 4
Melrose, 2,197 ... F 5
Melvaig, ⊙1,794 ... C 3
Methlick, 315 ... F 3
Methven, 806 ... E 4
Mid Yell, 220 ... G 2
Millport, 1,161 ... A 2
Milnathort, 1,099 ... E 4
Milngavie, 10,846 ... B 1
Minnigaff, 658 ... D 6
Mintlaw, 657 ... F 3
Moffat, 2,041 ... E 5
Moniaive, 342 ... E 5
Monifieth, 7,100 ... F 4
Montrose, 4,704 ... F 4
Morar, 184 ... C 4
Motherwell and Wishaw, 72,991 ... C 2
Muirkirk, 2,607 ... E 5
Muir of Ord, 1,339 ... D 3
Musselburgh, 17,045 ... D 2
Muthill, 672 ... E 4
Nairn, 5,821 ... E 3
Neilston, 4,358 ... B 2
Nethy Bridge, 431 ... E 3
New Abbey, 339 ... E 6
Newarthill, 7,003 ... C 2
Newburgh, Fife, 2,124 ... E 4
Newburgh, Grampian, 447 ... G 3
Newcastleton, 903 ... F 5
New Cumnock, 5,077 ... D 5
New Deer, 601 ... F 3
New Galloway, 337 ... D 5
Newmains, 6,847 ... C 2
Newmarket, 613 ... B 2
Newmill, 449 ... E 3
Newmilns and Greenholm, 3,509 ... D 5
New Pitsligo, 1,125 ... F 3
Newport-on-Tay, 3,762 ... F 4
New Scone, 3,830 ... E 4
Newtongrange, 4,555 ... D 2
Newton Mearns, 6,901 ... B 2
Newtonmore, 894 ... D 3
Newton Stewart, 1,983 ... D 6
Newtown Saint Boswells, 1,101 ... F 5
Newtyle, 664 ... E 4
North Berwick, 4,317 ... F 4
North Tolsta, 527 ... B 2
Oakley, 3,499 ... C 1
Oban, 6,515 ... C 4
Old Kilpatrick, 3,256 ... B 2
Oldmeldrum, 1,103 ... F 3
Oykel Bridge, ⊙742 ... D 3
Paisley, 94,833 ... B 2
Palnackie, 225 ... E 6
Patna, 2,867 ... D 5
Peebles, 6,049 ... E 5
Penicuik, 10,476 ... D 2
Penpont, 364 ... E 5
Perth, 43,098 ... E 4
Peterculter, 3,226 ... F 3
Peterhead, 14,846 ... G 3
Pierowall, ⊙735 ... E 1
Pitlochry, 2,468 ... E 4
Pitmedden, 313 ... F 3
Pittenweem, 1,548 ... F 4
Plockton, 288 ... C 3
Poolewe, ⊙1,794 ... C 3
Port Appin, ⊙2,172 ... C 4
Port Askaig, ⊙1,795 ... B 5
Port Bannatyne, 730 ... A 2
Port Charlotte, 240 ... B 5
Port Ellen, 932 ... B 5
Port Glasgow, 22,189 ... A 2
Portgordon, 814 ... F 3
Portknockie, 1,217 ... F 3
Portmahomack, 226 ... E 3
Portpatrick, 643 ... C 6
Portree, 1,374 ... B 3
Portsoy, 1,717 ... F 3
Port William, 517 ... D 6
Prestonpans, 3,272 ... D 1
Prestwick, 13,218 ... D 5
Queensferry, 5,339 ... D 1
Reay, 283 ... E 2
Renfrew, 18,880 ... B 2
Renton, 3,443 ... A 1
Rhu, 1,540 ... A 1
Rhynie, 333 ... F 3
Rigside, 1,195 ... E 5
Rosehearty, 1,220 ... F 3
Rosneath, 946 ... A 1
Rothes, 1,240 ... E 3
Rothesay, 6,285 ... A 2
Rutherglen, 24,091 ... B 2
Saint Abbs, 203 ... F 5
Saint Andrews, 12,837 ... F 4
Saint Combs, 738 ... G 3
Saint Cyrus, 340 ... F 4
Saint Margaret's Hope, 210 ... F 2
Saint Monance, 1,205 ... F 4
Saline, 831 ... C 1
Saltcoats, 14,861 ... D 5
Sandbank, 850 ... A 1
Sandhead, 248 ... D 6
Sandwick, 603 ... B 2
Sanquhar, 2,030 ... D 5
Sauchie, 6,082 ... C 1
Scalasaig, ⊙137 ... B 4
Scalloway, 896 ... G 2
Scarinish, ⊙875 ... B 4
Scourie, ⊙745 ... C 2
Scrabster, 273 ... E 2
Selkirk, 5,635 ... F 5
Shader, 258 ... B 2
Shawbost, 458 ... B 2
Shieldaig, ⊙550 ... C 3
Shotts, 9,512 ... C 2
Skateraw, 674 ... F 3
Skelmorlie, 1,535 ... A 2
Skipness, ⊙765 ... C 5
Slamannan, 1,584 ... C 2
Spean Bridge, 235 ... D 4
Springholm, 340 ... E 5
Stanley, 1,385 ... E 4
Stenhousemuir, 8,203 ... C 1
Stevenston, 11,786 ... D 5
Stewarton, 5,165 ... D 5
Stirling, 29,799 ... C 1
Stonehaven, 4,837 ... F 4
Stonehouse, 7,900 ... D 5
Stornoway, 5,371 ... B 2
Stow, 485 ... F 5
Strachan, ⊙390 ... F 3
Strachur Bay, ⊙678 ... C 4
Stranraer, 10,174 ... C 6
Strathaven, 5,464 ... D 5
Strathpeffer, 874 ... D 3
Strichen, 962 ... F 3
Stromeferry, ⊙1,724 ... C 3
Stromness, 1,680 ... E 2
Strontian, ⊙764 ... C 4
Struan, ⊙772 ... B 3
Swinton, 235 ... F 5
Tain, 2,057 ... D 3
Tarbert, Strathclyde, 1,391 ... C 5
Tarbert, W. Isles, 479 ... B 3
Tarbolton, 2,224 ... D 5
Tarland, 452 ... F 3
Tayport, 2,848 ... F 4
Thornhill, Central, 443 ... D 4
Thornhill, Dumf. & Gall., 1,510 ... E 5
Thurso, 9,113 ... E 2
Tillicoultry, 4,320 ... C 1
Tobermory, 652 ... B 4
Tolob, ⊙2,033 ... G 2
Tomatin, 214 ... D 3
Tomintoul, 306 ... E 3
Torphins, 499 ... F 3
Tradespark, 425 ... E 3
Tranent, 7,212 ... F 5
Troon, 11,656 ... D 5
Tullibody, 6,082 ... C 1
Turriff, 3,051 ... F 3
Tweedsmuir, ⊙105 ... E 5
Twynholm, 274 ... D 6
Tyndrum, ⊙1,153 ... D 4
Uddingston, 5,278 ... B 2
Uig, Highland, 103 ... B 3
Uig, W. Isles, ⊙1,948 ... A 2
Ullapool, 807 ... C 3
Uphall, 3,035 ... C 1
Viewpark, 9,812 ... C 2
Walkerburn, 842 ... F 5
Watten, 347 ... E 2
Wemyss Bay, 323 ... A 2
West Barns, 659 ... F 5
West Calder, 2,005 ... C 2
West Kilbride, 3,883 ... D 5
West Linton, 705 ... D 2
Whitburn, 11,647 ... C 2
Whitehills, 875 ... F 3
Whithorn, 990 ... D 6
Whiting Bay, 352 ... C 5
Wick, 7,804 ... E 2
Wigtown, 1,118 ... D 6
Winchburgh, 2,409 ... D 1
Yetholm, 435 ... F 5

OTHER FEATURES

A'Chralaig (mt.) ... C 3
Ailsa Craig (isl.), 3 ... C 5
Almond (riv.) ... E 4
Annan (riv.) ... E 5
Appin (dist.), 2,006 ... C 4
Ardgour (dist.), 315 ... C 4
Ardle (riv.) ... E 4
Ardnamurchan (pen.), 764 ... B 4
Argyll (dist.), 4,940 ... C 4
Arkaig, Loch (lake) ... C 4
Arran (isl.), 3,564 ... C 5
Askival (mt.) ... B 4
Assynt (dist.), 833 ... C 2
Athol (dist.), 1,082 ... D 4
Atlantic Ocean ... B 2
Avon (riv.) ... C 1
Avon (riv.) ... E 3
Awe, Loch (lake) ... C 4
Ayr (riv.) ... D 5
Ayr, Heads of (cape) ... D 5
Badenoch (dist.), 2,717 ... D 4
Baleshare (isl.), 64 ... A 3
Balmoral Castle ... E 3
Barra (sound) ... A 3
Barra (isl.), 1,005 ... A 4
Barra (head) ... A 4
Barra Isles (isls.), 1,092 ... A 4
Battock (mt.) ... F 4
Beauly (riv.) ... D 3
Beinn Dearg (mt.) ... D 3
Beinn a Ghlo (mt.) ... E 4
Bell Rock (isl.), 3 ... F 4
Ben Alder (mt.) ... D 4
Ben Avon (mt.) ... E 3
Benbecula (isl.), 1,355 ... A 3
Ben Cruachan (mt.) ... C 4
Ben Lawers (mt.) ... D 4
Ben Lui (mt.) ... D 4
Ben Macdhui (mt.) ... E 3
Ben Mhor (mt.) ... A 3
Ben More (mt.) ... B 4
Ben More (mt.) ... D 4
Ben More Assynt (mt.) ... D 2
Ben Nevis (mt.) ... D 4
Bernera (isl.), 276 ... B 2
Berneray (isl.), 131 ... A 3
Berneray (isl.), 6 ... A 4
Bidean nam Bian (mt.) ... D 4
Black Isle (pen.), 7,209 ... D 3
Blackwater (res.) ... D 4
Boisdale, Loch (inlet) ... A 3
Bracadale, Loch (inlet) ... B 3
Braemar (dist.), 7,624 ... E 3
Breadalbane (dist.), 3,649 ... D 4
Bressay (isl.), 248 ... G 2
Broad (bay) ... B 2
Broad Law (mt.) ... E 5
Broom, Loch (inlet) ... C 3
Brough Ness (prom.) ... F 2
Buchan (dist.), 40,089 ... F 3
Buddon Ness (prom.) ... F 4
Burray (isl.), 209 ... F 2
Burrow (head) ... D 6
Bute (isl.), 8,423 ... C 5
Bute (sound) ... C 5
Butt of Lewis (prom.) ... B 2
Cairn Gorm (mt.) ... E 3
Cairngorm (mts.) ... E 3
Cairn Toul (mt.) ... E 3
Caledonian (canal) ... D 3
Canna (isl.), 22 ... B 3
Carn Ban (mt.) ... D 3
Carn Eige (mt.) ... C 3
Carrick (dist.), 21,425 ... D 5
Carron (riv.) ... C 1
Carron (riv.) ... C 3
Cheviot (hills) ... F 5
Cheviot, The (mt.) ... F 5
Clisham (mt.) ... B 3
Clyde (riv.) ... D 5
Clyde (firth) ... D 5
Coll (isl.), 144 ... B 4
Colonsay (isl.), 137 ... B 4
Copinsay (isl.), 3 ... F 2
Cowal (dist.), 15,548 ... C 4
Creag Meagaidh (mt.) ... D 4
Cromarty (firth) ... D 3
Cuillin (hills) ... B 3
Cuillin (sound) ... B 3
Dee (riv.) ... D 5
Dee (riv.) ... F 3
Dennis (head) ... F 1
Deveron (riv.) ... F 3
Don (riv.) ... F 3
Doon (riv.) ... D 5
Dornoch (firth) ... E 3
Duirinish (dist.), 1,085 ... B 3
Duncansby (head) ... F 2
Dunnet (head) ... E 2
Earn (riv.) ... E 4
Earn, Loch (lake) ... D 4
Eday (isl.), 179 ... F 1
Eddrachillis (bay) ... C 2
Eden (riv.) ... F 4
Egilsay (isl.), 39 ... F 1
Eigg (isl.), 69 ... B 4
Eil, Loch (lake) ... C 4
Eishort, Loch (inlet) ... B 3
Enard (bay) ... C 2
Eriboll, Loch (inlet) ... D 2
Ericht, Loch (lake) ... D 4
Eriskay (isl.), 219 ... A 3
Erisort, Loch (inlet) ... B 2
Esk (riv.) ... F 5
Etive, Loch (inlet) ... C 4
Ewe, Loch (inlet) ... C 3
Eye (pen.), 850 ... B 2
Fair Isle (isl.), 65 ... F 3
Fetlar (isl.), 88 ... G 2
Fife Ness (prom.) ... F 4
Findhorn (riv.) ... E 3
Flannan (isls.), 3 ... A 2
Formartine (dist.), 10,768 ... F 3
Forth (riv.) ... B 1
Forth (firth) ... F 4
Forth and Clyde (canal) ... B 2
Foula (isl.), 33 ... F 2
Fyne, Loch (inlet) ... C 5
Galloway (dist.), 54,972 ... D 5
Galloway, Mull of (prom.) ... D 6
Gare Loch (inlet) ... A 1
Garioch (dist.), 6,863 ... F 3
Garry, Loch (lake) ... D 3
Gigha (isl.), 174 ... C 5
Girdle Ness (prom.) ... G 3
Glass (riv.) ... D 3
Glen More (dist.), 55,035 ... D 3
Goat Fell (mt.) ... C 5
Gometra (isl.), 10 ... B 4
Grampian (mts.) ... D 4
Great Cumbrae (isl.), 1,296 ... A 2
Gruinard (bay) ... C 3
Hallandale (riv.) ... E 2
Harris (sound) ... A 3
Harris (dist.), 2,175 ... B 3
Hebrides (sea) ... B 3
Hebrides, Inner (isls.), 14,881 ... B 4
Hebrides, Outer (isls.), 29,615 ... A 3
Helmsdale (riv.) ... E 2
Herma Ness (prom.) ... G 2
Holy (isl.), 10 ... C 5
Holy Loch (inlet) ... A 1
Hoy (isl.), 419 ... E 2
Inchcape (Bell Rock) (isl.), 3 ... F 4
Inchkeith (isl.), 3 ... D 1
Indaal, Loch (inlet) ... B 5
Inner (sound) ... C 3
Inner Hebrides (isls.), 14,881 ... B 4
Iona (isl.), 145 ... B 4
Isla (riv.) ... E 4
Islay (isl.), 3,816 ... B 5
Jura (isl.), 210 ... C 5
Jura (sound) ... C 5
Katrine, Loch (lake) ... D 4
Kerrera (isl.), 27 ... C 4
Kilbrannan (sound) ... C 5
Kinnairds (head) ... G 3
Kintyre (pen.), 10,077 ... C 5
Kintyre, Mull of (prom.) ... C 5
Knapdale (dist.), 4,082 ... C 5
Kyle of Tongue (inlet) ... D 2
Laggan (bay) ... B 5
Lammermuir (hills) ... F 5
Lennox (hills) ... B 1
Leven (lake) ... E 4
Leven, Loch (inlet) ... D 4
Lewis (dist.), 20,047 ... B 2
Liddel Water (riv.) ... F 5
Linnhe, Loch (inlet) ... C 4
Lismore (isl.), 166 ... C 4
Little Minch (sound) ... B 3
Lochaber (dist.), 13,813 ... D 4
Lochnagar (mt.) ... E 4
Lochy, Loch (lake) ... D 3
Lomond, Loch (lake) ... D 4
Long, Loch (inlet) ... D 4
Lorne (dist.), 12,162 ... C 4
Lorne (firth) ... C 4
Loyal, Loch (lake) ... D 2
Luce (bay) ... D 6
Luing (isl.), 151 ... C 4
Lyon (riv.) ... D 4
Machers, The (pen.), 6,192 ... D 6
Mainland (isl.), 12,747 ... E 1
Mainland (isl.), 12,944 ... G 2
Mar (dist.), 23,931 ... F 3
Maree, Loch (lake) ... C 3
May, Isle of (isl.), 10 ... F 4
Merrick (mt.) ... D 5
Minginish (dist.), 772 ... B 3
Moidart (dist.), 155 ... C 4
Monach (sound) ... A 3
Monadhliath (mts.) ... D 3
Moorfoot (hills) ... E 5
Moray (firth) ... E 3
Moriston (riv.) ... D 3
Morven (dist.), 398 ... C 4
Morven (mt.) ... E 2
Muck (isl.), 24 ... B 4
Muckle Flugga (isl.), 3 ... G 2
Mull (isl.), 2,024 ... C 4
Mull (head) ... F 1
Mull (sound) ... C 4
Nairn (riv.) ... D 3
na Keal, Loch (inlet) ... B 4
Naver (riv.) ... D 2
Ness, Loch (lake) ... D 3
Nevis, Loch (inlet) ... C 3
Nith (riv.) ... E 5
North (chan.) ... C 5
North (sound) ... F 1
North (sound) ... G 4
North Esk (riv.) ... F 4
North Minch (sound) ... B 3
North Ronaldsay (isl.), 134 ... F 1
North Uist (isl.), 1,469 ... A 3
Oa, Mull of (prom.) ... B 5
Ochil (hills) ... E 4
Oich (riv.) ... D 3
Orchy (riv.) ... D 4
Orkney (isls.), 17,675 ... F 1
Oronsay (isl.), 2 ... B 4
Outer Hebrides (isls.), 29,615 ... A 3
Oykel (riv.) ... D 3
Pabbay (isl.), 4 ... A 3
Papa Stour (isl.), 24 ... F 2
Papa Westray (isl.), 106 ... F 1
Paps of Jura (mt.) ... C 5
Park (dist.), 210 ... B 2
Peel Fell (mt.) ... F 5
Pentland (hills) ... D 2
Pentland (firth) ... E 2
Pladda (isl.), 2 ... C 5
Quoich, Loch (lake) ... C 3
Raasay (isl.), 163 ... C 3
Rannoch (dist.), 1,177 ... D 4
Rannoch, Loch (lake) ... D 4
Rhinns, The (pen.), 8,295 ... C 6
Roag, Loch (inlet) ... B 2
Rona (isl.), 3 ... B 3
Ross of Mull (pen.), 585 ... B 4
Rousay (isl.), 181 ... E 1
Rudha Hunish (cape) ... B 3
Rudh Re (cape) ... C 3
Rum (isl.), 40 ... B 3
Ryan, Loch (inlet) ... C 5
Saint Kilda (isl.), 65 ... A 2
Saint Magnus (bay) ... F 2
Sanda (isl.), 9 ... C 5
Sanday (isl.), 11 ... B 3
Sanday (isl.), 592 ... F 1
Scalpay (isl.), 483 ... B 3
Scalpay (isl.), 5 ... C 3
Scapa Flow (chan.) ... E 2
Scarp (isl.), 12 ... A 2
Scridain, Loch (inlet) ... B 4
Scurdie Ness (prom.) ... F 4
Seaforth, Loch (inlet) ... B 3
Seil (isl.), 326 ... C 4
Sgurr a Choire Ghlais (mt.) ... D 3
Sgurr Alasdair (mt.) ... B 3
Sgurr Mor (mt.) ... C 3
Sgurr na Lapaich (mt.) ... C 3
Shapinsay (isl.), 346 ... F 1
Shetland (isls.), 18,494 ... G 2
Shiant (sound) ... B 3
Shiel, Loch (lake) ... C 4
Shin (falls) ... D 3
Shin, Loch (lake) ... D 2
Shona (isl.), 17 ... C 4
Sidlaw (hills) ... E 4
Sinclair's (bay) ... E 2
Skye, Isle of (isl.), 7,183 ... B 3
Sleat (pt.) ... B 4
Sleat (dist.), 449 ... C 3
Small Isles (isls.), 171 ... B 4
Snizort, Loch (inlet) ... B 3
Soay (isl.), 5 ... B 3
Solway (firth) ... E 6
South Esk (riv.) ... F 4
South Ronaldsay (isl.), 776 ... F 2
South Uist (isl.), 2,281 ... A 3
Spean (riv.) ... D 4
Spey (riv.) ... E 3
Start (pt.) ... F 1
Stinchar (riv.) ... D 5
Strathbogie (dist.), 7,959 ... F 3
Strathmore (valley) ... E 4
Strathspey (dist.), 6,668 ... E 3
Strathy (pt.) ... E 2
Stroma (isl.), 8 ... E 2
Stronsay (isl.), 436 ... F 1
Sumburgh (head) ... G 2
Sunart, Loch (inlet) ... C 4
Swona (isl.), 3 ... E 2
Taransay (isl.), 5 ... A 3
Tarbat Ness (prom.) ... E 3
Tarbert, East Loch (inlet) ... B 3
Tarbert, Loch (inlet) ... B 5
Tarbert, West Loch (inlet) ... A 3
Tay (riv.) ... E 4
Tay (firth) ... F 4
Tay, Loch (lake) ... D 4
Teith (riv.) ... D 4
Teviot (riv.) ... F 5
Thurso (riv.) ... E 2
Tiree (isl.), 875 ... B 4
Tolsta (head) ... B 2
Tor Ness (prom.) ... E 2
Torridon, Loch (inlet) ... C 3
Trossachs, The (valley) ... D 4
Trotternish (dist.), 1,948 ... B 3
Tweed (riv.) ... F 5
Tyne (riv.) ... F 5
Ulva (isl.), 23 ... B 4
Unst (isl.), 1,124 ... G 2
Vaternish (dist.), 162 ... B 3
Vatersay (isl.), 77 ... A 4
West Burra (isl.), 501 ... G 2
Westray (firth) ... E 1
Westray (isl.), 735 ... E 1
Whalsay (isl.), 870 ... G 2
White Coomb (mt.) ... E 5
Wigtown (bay) ... D 6
Wrath (cape) ... C 2
Wyre (isl.), 36 ... F 1
Yarrow (riv.) ... E 5
Yell (isl.), 1,143 ... G 2
Ythan (riv.) ... F 3

★Population of met. area
⊙Population of parish.

Agriculture, Industry and Resources

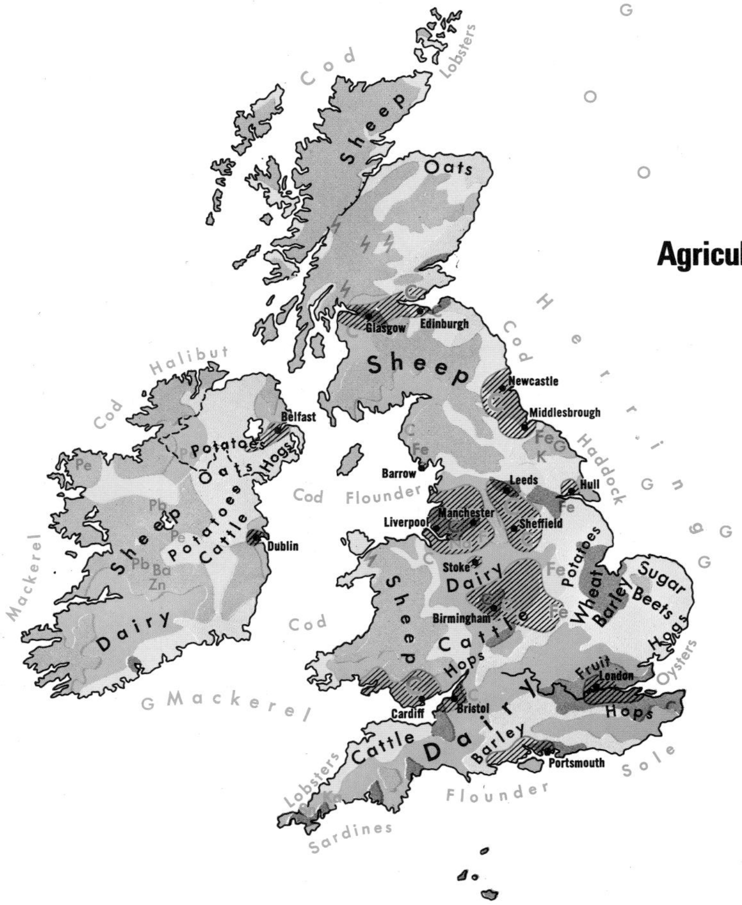

DOMINANT LAND USE

- Cereals (chiefly oats, barley)
- Truck Farming, Horticulture
- Dairy, Mixed Farming
- Livestock, Mixed Farming
- Pasture Livestock

MAJOR MINERAL OCCURRENCES

Ba	Barite	Na	Salt
C	Coal	O	Petroleum
F	Fluorspar	Pb	Lead
Fe	Iron Ore	Pe	Peat
G	Natural Gas	Sn	Tin
K	Potash	Zn	Zinc
Ka	Kaolin (china clay)		

Water Power

Major Industrial Areas

Scotland
CONIC PROJECTION
MILES
KILOMETERS
Capital
Regional Centers
Canals
International Boundaries
Regional Boundaries
Other Boundaries
© Copyright HAMMOND INCORPORATED, Maplewood, N. J.
Former Counties
Shetland Islands
Same scale as main map
ATLANTIC OCEAN
NORTH SEA
North Minch
Little Minch
North Channel
Sea of the Hebrides
OUTER HEBRIDES
INNER HEBRIDES
WESTERN ISLES
HIGHLAND
GRAMPIAN
TAYSIDE
STRATHCLYDE
CENTRAL
FIFE
LOTHIAN
BORDERS
DUMFRIES & GALLOWAY
ORKNEY ISLANDS
SHETLAND
ENGLAND
NORTHERN IRELAND
IRELAND
Edinburgh
Glasgow
Aberdeen
Dundee
Inverness
Longitude 5° West of Greenwich

IRELAND

Carlow 34,237 H6
Cavan 52,618 G4
Clare 75,008 D6
Cork 352,883 D7
Donegal 108,344 K2
Dublin 852,219 J5
Galway 149,223 D5
Kerry 112,772 B7
Kildare 71,977 H5
Kilkenny 61,473 G6
Laois 45,259 G6
Leitrim 28,360 E3
Leix (Laois) 45,259 G6
Limerick 140,459 D7
Longford 28,250 F4
Louth 74,951 J4
Mayo 109,525 C4
Meath 71,729 H4
Monaghan 46,242 H3
Offaly 51,829 F5
Roscommon 53,519 E4
Sligo 50,275 D3
Tipperary 123,565 F6
Waterford 77,315 F7
Westmeath 53,570 G5
Wexford 86,351 H7
Wicklow 66,295 J5

CITIES and TOWNS

Abbeydorney, 188 B7
Abbeyfeale, 1,337 C7
Abbeylara, ‡290 F4
Abbeyleix, 1,033 G6
Achill Sound, ‡1,163 B4
Aclare, ‡336 D3
Adare, 545 D6
Aghada-Farsid-Rostellan, 461 E8
Aghadoe, ‡497 B7
Aghagower, ‡693 C4
Ahascragh, 221 E5
Annagry, 201 E1
Annascaul, 236 B7
An Uaimh, 4,605 H4
An Uaimh, *6,665 H4
Ardagh, Limerick, 213 C7
Ardagh, Longford, ‡974 F4
Ardara, 683 E2
Ardee, *3,183 H4
Ardee, 3,096 H4
Ardfert, 286 B7
Ardfinnan, 510 F7
Ardmore, 233 F8
Ardrahan, ‡239 D5
Arklow, 6,948 J6
Arthurstown, 1,188 H7
Arva, 370 F4
Ashford, 341 J5
Askeaton, 844 D6
Athboy, 705 H4
Athea, 328 C7
Athenry, 1,240 D5
Athleague, ‡955 E4
Athlone, 9,825 F5
Athlone, *11,611 F5
Athy, 4,270 H6
Athy, *4,654 H6
Aughrim, 451 J6
Avoca, ‡620 J6
Bagenalstown (Muinebeag), 2,321 H6
Baile Átha Cliath (Dublin) (cap.), 567,866 K5
Bailieborough, 1,293 G4
Balbriggan, 3,741 J4
Balla, 293 C4
Ballaghaderreen, 1,121 E4
Ballina, Mayo, 6,063 C3
Ballina, *6,369 C3
Ballina, Tipperary, 336 E6
Ballinagh, 459 G4
Ballinakill, 300 G6
Ballineen D8
Ballinamore, 808 F3
Ballinasloe, 5,969 E5
Ballincollig-Carrigrohane, 2,110 D8
Ballindine, 232 C4
Ballingarry, Limerick, 422 D7
Ballingarry, Tipperary, ‡574 F6
Ballinlough, 242 D4
Ballinrobe, 1,272 C4
Ballintober, ‡867 E4
Ballintra, 197 E2
Ballisodare, 486 E3
Ballivor, 287 H4
Ballybay, 754 G3
Ballybay, *1,159 G3
Ballybofey-Stranorlar, 2,214 F2
Ballybunion, 1,287 B7
Ballycanew, ‡460 J6
Ballycarney, ‡294 J6
Ballycastle, ‡724 C3
Ballyconnell, 421 F3
Ballycotton, 389 F8
Ballydehob, 253 C8
Ballyduff, 406 B7
Ballygar, 359 E4
Ballygeary, 725 J7
Ballyhaise, 274 G3
Ballyhaunis, 1,093 D4
Ballyheigue, 450 B7
Ballyjamesduff, 673 G4
Ballylanders, 266 E7
Ballylongford, 504 B6
Ballymahon, 707 F4
Ballymakeery, 272 C8
Ballymore, ‡447 F5
Ballymore Eustace, 433 J5
Ballymote, 952 D3
Ballyporeen, ‡810 E7
Ballyragget, 519 G6
Ballyroan, ‡478 G6
Ballyshannon, 2,325 E3
Ballytore, ‡580 H5
Baltimore, 200 C9
Baltinglass, 909 H6
Baltray, 236 J4
Banagher, 1,052 F5
Bandon, 2,257 D8
Bandon, *4,071 D8
Bannow, ‡798 H7
Bansha, 184 E7
Bantry, 2,579 C8
Barna, ‡1,734 C5
Belmullet, 744 B3
Belturbet, 1,092 G3
Bennettsbridge, 367 G6
Birr, 3,319 F5
Birr, *3,881 F5
Blanchardstown, 3,279 H5
Blarney, 1,128 D8
Blessington, 637 J5
Boherbue, 372 C7
Borris, 430 H6
Borris-in-Ossory, 276 F6
Borrisokane, 769 E6
Borrisoleigh, 471 E6
Boyle, 1,727 E4
Boyle, *1,939 E4
Bray, 14,467 K5
Bray, *15,841 K5
Brí Chualann (Bray), 14,467 K5
Broadford, 226 C7
Brosna, 250 C7
Bruff, 547 D7
Bruree, 243 D7
Bunbeg-Derrybeg, 878 E1
Bunclody-Carrickduff, 929 H6
Buncrana, 2,955 G1
Buncrana, *3,334 G1
Bundoran, 1,337 E3
Burtonport, ‡1,288 E2
Buttevant, 1,045 D7
Cahir, 1,747 F7
Cahirciveen, 1,547 A8
Callan, 1,283 G7
Camolin, 306 J6
Campile, 231 H7
Cappamore, 567 E6
Cappawhite, 305 E6
Cappoquin, 872 F7
Carbury, ‡894 H5
Carlingford, 559 J3
Carlow, 9,588 H6
Carlow, *10,399 H6
Carndonagh, 1,146 G1
Carnew, 570 H6
Carrickmacross, 2,100 H4
Carrickmacross, *2,475 H4
Carrick-on-Shannon, 1,854 F4
Carrick-on-Suir, 5,006 F7
Carrigaholt, ‡493 B6
Carrigaline, 951 E8
Carrigallen, 230 F4
Carrigart, ‡753 F1
Carrigtwohill, 622 E8
Carrowkeel, ‡326 G1
Cashel, 2,692 F7
Castlebar, 5,979 C4
Castlebar, *6,476 C4
Castlebellingham, 407 J4
Castleblayney, 2,118 H3
Castleblayney, *2,395 H3
Castlecomer-Donaguile, 1,244 G6
Castledermot, 583 H6
Castlefin, 610 F2
Castlegregory, 216 A7
Castleisland, 1,929 B7
Castlemartyr, 491 E8
Castlepollard, 693 G4
Castlerea, 1,752 D4
Castletown, ‡504 F6
Castletownbere, 812 B8
Castletownroche, 399 D7
Castletownshend, 170 C9
Causeway, 215 B7
Cavan, 3,273 G3
Cavan, *4,312 G3
Ceanannus Mór, 2,391 G4
Ceanannus Mór, *2,653 G4
Celbridge, 1,568 H5
Charlestown-Bellahy, 677 D4
Charleville (Rathluirc), 2,232 D7
Clara, 2,156 F5
Claregalway, ‡594 D5
Claremorris, 1,718 C4
Clashmore, ‡379 F8
Clifden, 790 B5
Cloghan, 404 F5
Clogh-Chatsworth, 324 G6
Clogheen, 530 F7
Clogherhead, 649 J4
Clonakilty, 2,430 D8
Clonaslee, 285 F5
Clondalkin, 7,009 J5
Clonegal, 202 H6
Clones, 2,164 G3
Clonfert, ‡430 E5
Clonmany, ‡936 G1
Clonmel, 11,622 F7
Clonmel, *12,291 F7
Clonmellon, 328 H4
Clonroche, 222 H7
Clontuskert, 351 E4
Cloone, ‡460 F4
Cloughjordan, 480 E6
Cloyne, 654 E8
Coachford, 290 D8
Cóbh, 6,076 E8
Cóbh, *7,141 E8
Coill Dubh, 920 H5
Collon, 262 J4
Collooney, 546 E3
Cong, 233 C4
Convoy, 654 F2
Coolaney, ‡352 D3
Coolgreany, ‡603 J6
Cootehill, 1,415 G3
Cootehill, *1,542 G3
Cork, 128,645 E8
Cork, *134,430 E8
Corofin, 342 C6
Courtmacsherry, 210 D8
Courtown Harbour, 291 J6
Creeslough, 269 F1
Crookhaven, ‡400 B9
Croom, 756 D6
Crosshaven, 1,222 E8
Crossmolina, 1,077 C3
Crusheen, ‡405 D6
Culdaff, ‡621 G1
Daingean, 492 G5
Delvin, 223 G4
Dingle, 1,401 A7
Doaghbeg, ‡701 F1
Donabate, 426 J5
Donegal, 1,725 F2
Doneraile, 799 D7
Dooagh-Keel, 649 A4
Doon, 387 E6
Douglas, ‡4,448 D8
Drimoleague, 415 C8
Drishane, ‡1,548 C7
Drogheda, 19,762 J4
Drogheda, *20,095 J4
Droichead Nua, 5,053 H5
Droichead Nua, *6,444 H5
Dromahair, 177 E3
Drumcar, ‡1,215 J4
Drumconrath, ‡1,044 H4
Drumkeerin, ‡467 E3
Drumlish, 205 F4
Drumshanbo, 576 E3
Dublin (cap.), 567,866 K5
Dublin, *679,748 K5
Duleek, 658 J4
Duncannon, 228 H7
Dundalk, 21,672 H3
Dundalk, *23,816 H3
Dunfanaghy, 303 F1
Dungarvan, 5,583 F7
Dungloe, 940 E2
Dunkineely, 288 E2
Dún Laoghaire, 53,171 K5
Dún Laoghaire, *98,379 K5
Dunlavin, 423 H5
Dunleer 855 J4
Dunmanway 1,392 C8
Dunmore 522 D4
Dunmore East 656 G7
Dunshaughlin⊙ 283 H5
Durrow, Laois 596 G6
Durrow, Offaly⊙ 441 F5
Easky 184 D3
Edenderry 2,953 G5
Edenderry* 3,116 G5
Elphin 489 E4
Emyvale 281 G3
Ennis 5,972 D6
Ennis* 10,840 D6
Enniscorthy 5,704 J7
Enniscorthy* 6,642 J7
Enniskerry 772 J5
Ennistymon 1,013 C6
Eyrecourt 314 E5
Fahan⊙ 1,023 G1
Falcarragh 506 E1
Feakle⊙ 398 D6
Fenit 360 B7
Ferbane 1,064 F5
Fermoy 3,237 E7
Fermoy* 4,033 E7
Ferns 712 J6
Fethard, Tipperary 1,064 F7
Fethard, Wexford⊙ 637 H7
Foxford 868 C4
Foynes 624 C6
Frankford (Kilcormac) 1,089 F5
Frenchpark⊙ 693 E4
Freshford 585 G6
Galbally 258 E7
Galway 27,726 C5
Galway* 29,375 C5
Geashill⊙ 751 G5
Glandore⊙ 695 C8
Glanmire-Riverstown 1,113 E8
Glanworth 335 E7
Glenamaddy 315 D4
Glenbeigh 266 B7
Glencolumbkille⊙ 787 D2
Glengarriff 244 C8
Glenties 734 E2
Glenville⊙ 264 D7
Glin 623 C6
Golden⊙ 640 F7
Gorey 2,946 J6
Gorey* 3,024 J6
Gormanston⊙ 1,384 J4
Gort 975 D5
Gowran 402 G6
Graiguenamanagh-Tinnahinch 1,303 H6
Granard 1,054 F4
Greencastle 322 H1
Greenore 882 J4
Greystones-Delgany 4,517 K5
Gurteen 165 D3
Hacketstown 574 H6
Headford 673 C5
Holycross⊙ 902 F6
Hospital 525 E7
Inchigeelagh⊙ 516 C8
Inishannon 190 D8
Inistioge 179 G7
Inniscrone 582 C3
Johnstown 303 G6
Kanturk 2,063 D7
Keel-Dooagh 649 A4
Kells⊙ 423 G6
Kells (Ceanannus Mór) 2,391 G4
Kenmare 903 B8
Kilbaha⊙ 471 B6
Kilbeggan 635 G5
Kilcar 273 D2
Kilcock 827 H5
Kilconnell⊙ 629 E5
Kilcoole 679 K5
Kilcormac 1,089 F5
Kilcullen 880 H5
Kildare 3,137 H5
Kildysart 239 C6
Kilfenora⊙ 441 C6
Kilfinane 561 D7
Kilgarvan 228 B8
Kilkee 1,287 B6
Kilkelly 225 D4
Kilkenny 9,838 G6
Kilkenny* 13,306 G6
Killala 368 C3
Killaloe 871 D6
Killarney 7,184 C7
Killarney* 7,541 C7
Killavullen 221 D7
Killenaule 592 F6
Killeshandra 432 F3
Killimor 221 E5
Killinaboy⊙ 297 C6
Killorglin 1,150 B7
Killucan-Rathwire 290 G4
Killybegs 1,094 E2
Kilmacrennan 274 F1
Kilmacthomas 396 G7
Kilmallock 1,170 D7
Kilmeadan⊙ 262 G7
Kilmihill 284 C6
Kilmoganny 181 G7
Kilmore Quay 273 H7
Kilmurry⊙ 387 C6
Kilnaleck 273 G4
Kilronan 243 B5
Kilrush 2,671 C6
Kilsheelan⊙ 665 F7
Kiltimagh 978 C4
Kilworth 360 E7
Kingscourt 1,016 H4
Kingstown (Dún Laoghaire) 53,171 K5
Kinlough 160 E3
Kinnegad 362 G5
Kinnitty⊙ 420 F5
Kinsale 1,622 D8
Kinsale* 1,989 D8
Kinvara 293 D5
Knightstown 236 A8
Knock⊙ 1,202 D4
Knocklong 248 D7
Knocknagashel 168 C7
Labasheeda⊙ 468 C6
Laghy⊙ 625 E2
Lahinch 455 C6
Lanesborough-Ballyleague 906 E4
Laracor⊙ 404 H4
Laytown-Bettystown-Mornington 1,882 J4
Leenane⊙ 271 B4
Leighlindridge 379 H6
Leitrim⊙ 544 F3
Leixlip 2,402 H5
Letterkenny 4,930 F2
Letterkenny* 5,207 F2
Lifford 1,121 F2
Limerick 57,161 D6
Limerick* 63,002 D6
Liscarroll 231 D7
Lisdoonvarna 459 C5
Lismore 884 F7
Lismore⊙ 1,041 F7
Listowel 3,021 C7
Littleton 322 F6
Longford 3,876 F4
Longford* 4,791 F4
Lorrha⊙ 685 E5
Loughrea 3,075 E5
Louisburgh 310 B4
Louth 208 J4
Lucan-Doddsborough 4,245 J5
Luimneach (Limerick) 57,161 D6
Lusk 553 J4
Macroom 2,256 C8
Malahide 3,834 J5
Malin⊙ 552 G1
Mallow 5,901 D7
Mallow* 6,506 D7
Manorhamilton 858 E3
Manulla⊙ 660 C4
Maryborough (Portlaoise) 3,902 G5
Maynooth 1,296 H5
Meathas Truim 546 G4
Midleton 3,075 E8
Midleton* 4,666 E8
Milford 763 F1
Millstreet 1,319 D7
Milltown 260 A7
Miltown-Malbay 677 C6
Minard⊙ 397 A7
Mitchelstown 2,783 E7
Moate 1,378 F5
Mohill 868 F4
Monaghan 5,256 G3
Monasterevan 1,619 H5
Moneygall 282 F6
Monivea⊙ 405 D5
Mooncoin 413 G7
Mount Bellew 275 D5
Mountcharles 445 E2
Mountmellick 2,595 G5
Mountmellick* 2,864 G5
Mountrath 1,098 F5
Moville 1,089 G1
Moycullen⊙ 498 C5
Moynalty⊙ 583 H4
Muff 240 G1
Muinebeag 2,321 H6
Mullagh 293 H4
Mullaghmore⊙ 629 D3
Mullinahone 262 F7
Mullinavat 343 G7
Mullingar 6,790 G4
Mullingar* 9,245 G4
Naas 5,078 H5
Navan (An Uaimh) 4,605 H4
Nenagh 5,085 E6
Nenagh* 5,174 E6
Newbliss⊙ 547 G3
Newbridge (Droichead Nua) 5,053 H5
Newcastle 2,549 D7
Newcastle* 2,680 D7
Newmarket 886 C7
Newmarket-on-Fergus 1,052 D6
New Pallas⊙ 1,271 E6
Newport, Mayo 420 C4
Newport, Tipperary 582 E6
New Ross 4,775 H7
New Ross* 5,153 H7
Newtown Forbes⊙ 495 F4
Newtownmountkennedy 882 J5
Newtownsandes 268 C6
O'Briensbridge-Montpelier 237 D6
Oldcastle 759 G4
Old Leighlin⊙ 309 G6
Oola 348 E6
Oranmore 440 D5
Oughterard 628 C5
Passage East 408 G7
Passage West 2,709 E8
Patrickswell 415 D6
Pettigo 332 F2
Piltown 456 G7
Portarlington 3,117 G5
Portlaoise 3,902 G5
Portlaoise* 6,470 G5
Portlaw 1,166 G7
Portmarnock 1,726 J5
Portumna 913 E5
Queenstown (Cóbh) 6,076 E8
Rahan⊙ 531 F5
Ramelton 807 F1
Raphoe 945 F2
Rathangan 868 G5
Rathcoole 1,740 J5
Rathcormac 191 E7
Rathdowney 892 F6
Rathdrum 1,141 J6
Rathgormuck⊙ 231 F7
Rathkeale 1,543 D7
Rathluirc 2,232 D7
Rathmore 437 J5
Rathmullen 486 F1
Rathnew-Merrymeeting 954 J6
Rathowen⊙ 294 F4
Rathvilly 230 H6
Ratoath 300 J5
Riverstown 236 E3
Rockcorry 233 H3
Rosapenna⊙ 822 F1
Roscommon 1,556 E4
Roscommon* 2,821 E4
Roscrea 3,855 F6
Rosscarbery 309 C8
Rosses Point 464 D3
Rosslare 588 J7
Rosslare Harbour (Ballygeary) 725 J7
Roundstone 204 A5
Roundwood 260 J5
Rush 2,633 J4
Saint Johnston 463 F2
Scarriff 619 E6
Schull 457 B8
Scotstown 264 H3
Shanagolden 231 C6
Shannon Airport 3,657 D6
Shannon Bridge 188 F5
Shercock 313 G4
Shillelagh 246 J6
Shinrone 365 F5
Shrule 288 C4
Sixmilebridge 567 D6
Skerries 3,044 J4
Skibbereen 2,104 C8
Slane 483 H4
Sligo 14,080 E3
Sligo* 14,456 E3
Sneem 285 B8
Spiddal⊙ 819 C5
Stepaside 748 J5
Stradbally, Laois 891 G5
Stradbally, Waterford 158 F7
Strokestown 563 E4
Swanlinbar 257 F3
Swinford 1,105 C4
Swords 4,133 J5
Taghmon 369 H7
Tallaght 6,174 J5
Tallow, 883 F7
Tarbert, 485 C6
Teltown, ‡739 H4
Templemore, 2,174 F6
Templetuohy, 197 F6
Termonfeckin, 328 J4
Thomastown, 1,270 G7
Thurles, 6,840 F6
Thurles, *7,087 F6
Timoleague, 257 D8
Tinahely, 450 H6
Tipperary, 4,631 E7
Tipperary, *4,717 E7
Toomevara, 272 E6
Tralee, 12,287 B7
Tralee, *13,263 B7
Tramore, 3,792 G7
Trim, 1,700 H4
Trim, *2,255 H4
Tuam, 3,808 D4
Tuam, *4,952 D4
Tubbercurry, 959 D3
Tulla, 415 D6
Tullamore, 6,809 G5
Tullamore, *7,474 G5
Tullaroan, ‡301 G6
Tullow, 1,838 H6
Tullow, *1,945 H6
Tynagh, ‡452 E5
Tyrrellspass, 289 G5
Urlingford, 652 F6
Virginia, 583 G4
Waterford, 31,968 G7
Waterford, *33,676 G7
Waterville, 547 A8
Westport, 3,023 C4
Wexford, 11,849 H7
Wexford, *13,293 H7
Whitegate, 370 E8
Wicklow, 3,786 K6
Wicklow, *3,915 K6
Woodenbridge, ‡620 J6
Woodford, 198 E5
Youghal, 5,445 F8
Youghal, *5,626 F8

OTHER FEATURES

Achill (isl.), 3,129 A4
Allen (lake) E3
Allen, Bog of (marsh) H5
Aran (isl.), 773 D2
Aran (isls.), 1,499 B5
Arklow (bank) K6
Arrow (lake) E3
Awbeg (riv.) D7
Ballinskelligs (bay) A8
Ballycotton (bay) F8
Ballyheige (bay) B7
Ballyhoura (hills) E7
Ballyteige (bay) H7
Bandon (riv.) D8
Bann (riv.) J6
Bantry (bay) B8
Barrow (riv.) H7
Baurtregaum (mt.) A7
Bear (isl.), 288 B8
Blacksod (bay) A3
Blackstairs (mt.) H6
Blackwater (riv.) D7
Blackwater (riv.) H4
Blasket (isls.) A7
Bloody Foreland (prom.) E1
Blue Stack (mts.) E2
Boderg (lake) E4
Boggeragh (mts.) D7
Boyne (riv.) J4
Brandon (head) A7
Bride (riv.) E7
Broad Haven (harb.) B3
Brosna (riv.) F5
Bull, The (isl.), 5 A8
Caha (mts.) B8
Carlingford (inlet) J3
Carnsore (pt.) J7
Carrantuohill (mt.) B7
Clare (riv.) D5
Clare (isls.), 168 A4
Clear (cape) B9
Clear (isl.), 192 C9
Clew (bay) B4
Comeragh (mts.) F7
Conn (lake) C3
Connacht (prov.), 390,902 C4
Connemara (dist.), 7,599 B5
Cork (harb.) E8
Corrib (lake) C5
Courtmacsherry (bay) D8
Curragh, The H5
Dee (riv.) H4
Deel (riv.) D7
Deele (riv.) F2
Derg (lake) E6
Derravaragh (lake) G4
Derryveagh (mts.) E2
Dingle (bay) A7
Donegal (bay) D3
Drum (hills) F7
Dublin (bay) J5
Dundalk (bay) J4
Dunmanus (bay) B8
Dursey (isl.), 38 A8
Ennell (lake) G5
Erne (riv.) E3
Errigal (mt.) E1
Erris (head) A3
Fanad (head) F1
Fastnet Rock (isl.), 3 B9
Feale (riv.) C7
Fergus (riv.) D6
Finn (riv.) F2
Finn (riv.) G3
Flesk (riv.) C7
Foyle (inlet) G1
Foyle (riv.) G2
Galley (head) D9
Galtee (mts.) E7
Galtymore (mt.) E7
Galway (bay) C5
Gara (lake) D4
Garadice (lake) F3
Gill (lake) E3
Glyde (riv.) H4
Golden Vale (plain) E7
Gorumna (isl.), 1,108 B5
Gowna (lake) G4
Grand (canal) G5
Greenore (pt.) J7
Gweebarra (bay) D2
Hags (head) B6
Helvick (head) G7
Hook (head) H7
Horn (head) E1
Iar Connacht (dist.), 10,774 C5
Inishbofin (isl.), 236 A4
Inishbofin (isl.), 103 E1
Inisheer (isl.), 313 B5
Inishmaan (isl.), 319 C5
Inishmore (isl.), 864 B5
Inishowen (head) H1
Inishowen (pen.), 24,109 G1
Inishtrahull (isl.), 3 G1
Inishturk (isls.), 83 A4
Inny (riv.) A8
Inny (riv.) F4
Inver (bay) E2
Ireland's Eye (isl.) K5
Irish (sea) K4
Joyce's Country (dist.), 2,021 B4
Kenmare (riv.) A8
Kerry (head) A7
Key (lake) E3
Kilkieran (bay) B5
Killala (bay) C3
Killary (harb.) A4
Kinsale (harb.) E8
Kippure (mt.) J5
Knockboy (mt.) B8
Knockmealdown (mts.) F7
Lady's Island Lake (inlet) J7
Lambay (isl.), 24 K4
Laune (riv.) B7
Leane (lake) B7
Leane (lake) G4
Lee (riv.) D8
Leinster (mt.) H6
Leinster (prov.), 1,498,140 G5
Lettermullan (isl.), 221 B5
Liffey (riv.) H5
Liscannor (bay) B6
Long Island (bay) B9
Loop (head) A6
Lugnaquillia (mt.) J5
Macgillicuddy's Reeks (mts.) B7
Macnean (lake) F3
Maigue (riv.) D6
Maine (riv.) C7
Malin (head) F1
Mask (lake) C4
Maumturk (mts.) B5
Melvin (lake) E3
Mizen (head) B9
Moher (cliffs) B6
Monavullagh (mts.) F7
Moy (riv.) C3
Mulkear (riv.) E6
Mullaghareirk (mts.) C7
Mulroy (bay) F1
Munster (prov.), 882,002 D7
Mweelrea (mt.) B4
Mweenish (isl.), 198 B5
Nagles (mts.) E7
Nenagh (riv.) E6
Nephin (mt.) C3
Nore (riv.) G7
North (sound) B5
Omey (isl.), 34 A5
Oughter (lake) G3
Ovoca (riv.) J6
Owenmore (riv.) D3
Owey (isl.), 51 D1
Paps, The (mt.) C7
Partry (mts.) C4
Pollaphuca (res.) J5
Punchestown H5
Rathlin O'Birne (isl.), 3 C2
Ree (lake) F5
Roaringwater (bay) B9
Rosses (bay) D1
Rosskeeragh (pt.) D3
Royal (canal) G4
Saint Finan's (bay) A8
Saint George's (chan.) K7
Saint John's (pt.) D2
Saltee (isls.) H7
Seven (heads) D8
Seven Hogs, The (isls.) A7
Shannon (riv.) E6
Sheeffry (hills) B4
Sheelin (lake) G4
Sheep Haven (harb.) F1
Sheeps (head) B8
Sherkin (isl.), 82 C9
Silvermine (mts.) E6
Slaney (riv.) H7
Slieve Aughty (mts.) D5
Slieve Bloom (mts.) F5
Slieve Gamph (mts.) D3
Slievenaman (mt.) F7
Sligo (bay) D3
Slyne (head) A5
South (sound) C5
Stacks (mts.) B7
Suck (riv.) E5
Suir (riv.) G7
Swilly (inlet) F1
Tara (hill) H4
Tory (isl.), 273 E1
Tory (sound) E1
Tralee (bay) B7
Trawbreaga (bay) F1
Ulster (part) (prov.), 207,204 G2
Valencia (Valentia) (isl.), 770 A8
Valentia (isl.), 770 A8
Waterford (harb.) G7
Wexford (bay) J7
Wicklow (head) K6
Wicklow (mts.) J6
Youghal (bay) F8

NORTHERN IRELAND

DISTRICTS

Antrim, 37,600 J2
Ards, 52,100 K2
Armagh, 47,500 H3
Ballymena, 52,200 J2
Ballymoney, 22,700 J1
Bainbridge, 28,800 J3
Belfast, 368,200 J2
Carrickfergus, 27,500 K2
Castlereagh, 63,600 K2
Coleraine, 44,900 H1
Cookstown, 27,500 H2
Craigavon, 71,200 J3
Down, 48,800 K3
Dungannon, 43,000 H3
Fermanagh, 50,900 F3
Larne, 29,000 K2
Limavady, 25,000 H1
Lisburn, 80,800 J2
Londonderry, 86,600 G2
Magherafelt, 32,200 H2
Mourne (Newry and Mourne), 75,300 J3
Moyle, 13,400 J1
Newtownabbey, 71,500 J2
North Down, 59,600 K2
Omagh, 41,800 G2
Strabane, 35,500 G2

CITIES and TOWNS

Ahoghill, ‡1,929 J2
Annalong, 1,001 K3
Antrim, 8,351 J2
Ardglass, 1,052 K3
Armagh, 13,606 H3
Armoy, ‡1,051 J1
Augher, ‡1,986 G3
Aughnacloy, ‡1,885 H3
Ballycastle, 2,899 J1
Ballyclare, 5,155 J2
Ballygawley, ‡2,165 G3
Ballykelly, 1,116 G1
Ballymena, 23,386 J2
Ballymoney, 5,697 J1
Ballynahinch, 3,485 J3
Banbridge, 7,968 J3
Bangor, 35,260 K2
Belfast (cap.), 353,700 J2
Belfast, *551,940 J2
Bellaghy, ‡2,265 H2
Belleek, ‡2,487 E3
Beragh, ‡2,137 G2
Bessbrook, 2,619 J3
Brookeborough, ‡2,534 G3
Broughshane, 1,288 J2
Bushmills, 1,288 J1
Caledon, ‡1,828 H3
Carnlough, 1,416 J2
Carrickfergus, 16,603 K2
Carrowdore, 2,548 K2
Castledawson, 1,162 H2
Castlederg, 1,766 F2
Castlewellan, 1,488 K3
Claudy, ‡2,507 G2
Clogher, ‡1,888 G3
Coalisland, 3,614 H2
Coleraine, 16,354 H1
Comber, 5,575 K2
Cookstown, 6,965 H2
Craigavon, 12,740 J3
Crossgar, 1,098 K3
Crossmaglen, 1,085 H3
Crumlin, 1,450 J2
Cullybackey, 1,649 J2
Derrygonnelly, ‡2,539 F3
Dervock, ‡1,191 J1
Donaghadee, 4,008 K2
Downpatrick, 7,918 K3
Draperstown, ‡2,247 H2
Dromore, Bainbridge, 2,848 J3
Dromore, Omagh, ‡2,224 G3
Drumquin, ‡1,982 F2
Dundrum, ‡2,245 K3
Dungannon, 8,190 H3
Dungiven, 1,536 H2
Dunnamanagh, ‡2,242 G2
Ederny and Kesh, ‡2,497 F2
Enniskillen, 9,679 F3
Feeny, ‡1,459 H2
Fintona, 1,190 G3
Fivemiletown, ‡1,649 G3
Garvagh, ‡2,363 H2
Gilford, 1,592 J3
Glenarm, ‡1,728 J2
Glenavy, ‡2,360 J2
Glynn, ‡1,872 K2
Gortin, ‡2,033 G2
Greyabbey, ‡2,646 K2
Hillsborough, 1,021 J3
Holywood, 9,892 K2
Irvinestown, 1,457 F3
Keady, 2,145 H3
Kells, ‡2,560 J2
Kesh, ‡2,497 F3
Kilkeel, 4,090 K3
Killough, ‡3,295 K3
Killyleagh, 2,359 K3
Kilrea, 1,196 H2
Kircubbin, 1,075 K3
Larne, 18,482 K2
Limavady, 6,004 H1
Lisburn, 31,836 J2
Lisnaskea, 1,443 G3
Londonderry, 51,200 G2
Loughbrickland, ‡2,056 J3
Maghera, 2,085 H2
Magherafelt, 4,704 H2
Markethill, ‡2,352 H3
Millisle, 1,172 K2
Moneymore, 1,178 H2
Moy, ‡2,349 H3
Moygashel, 1,086 H3
Newcastle, 4,647 J3
Newry, 20,279 J3
Newtownabbey, 58,114 K2
Newtownards, 15,484 K2
Newtownbutler, ‡2,663 G3
Newtownhamilton, ‡1,936 H3
Newtownstewart, 1,433 G2
Omagh, 14,594 G2
Pomeroy, ‡1,786 H2
Portaferry, 1,730 K3
Portavogie, 1,310 K3
Portglenone, ‡2,061 H2
Portrush, 5,376 H1
Portstewart, 5,085 H1
Randalstown, 2,799 J2
Rathfriland, 1,886 J3
Rostrevor, 1,617 J3
Saintfield, ‡2,198 K3
Sion Mills, 1,588 G2
Sixmilecross, ‡1,980 G2
Stewartstown, ‡1,759 H2
Strabane, 9,413 G2
Strangford, ‡1,987 K3
Tandragee, 1,725 J3
Tempo, ‡2,282 G3
Trillick, ‡2,167 G3
Warrenpoint, 4,291 J3
Whitehead, 2,642 K2

OTHER FEATURES

Bann (riv.) H2
Belfast (inlet) K2
Blackwater (riv.) H3
Bush (riv.) H1
Derg (riv.) F2
Divis (mt.) J2
Dundrum (bay) K3
Erne (lake) F3
Foyle (inlet) G1
Foyle (riv.) G2
Giant's Causeway H1
Lagan (riv.) K2
Larne (inlet) K2
Magee, Island (pen.), 1,581 K2
Magilligan (pt.) H1
Main (riv.) J2
Mourne (mts.) J3
Mourne (riv.) G2
Neagh (lake) J2
North (chan.) K1
Rathlin (isl.), 109 J1
Red (bay) K1
Roe (riv.) H1
Saint John's (pt.) K3
Slieve Donard (mt.) K3
Sperrin (mts.) G2
Strangford (inlet) K3
Torr (head) K1
Ulster (part) (prov.), 1,537,200 G2
Upper Lough Erne (lake) F3

*City and suburbs.
‡Population of district.

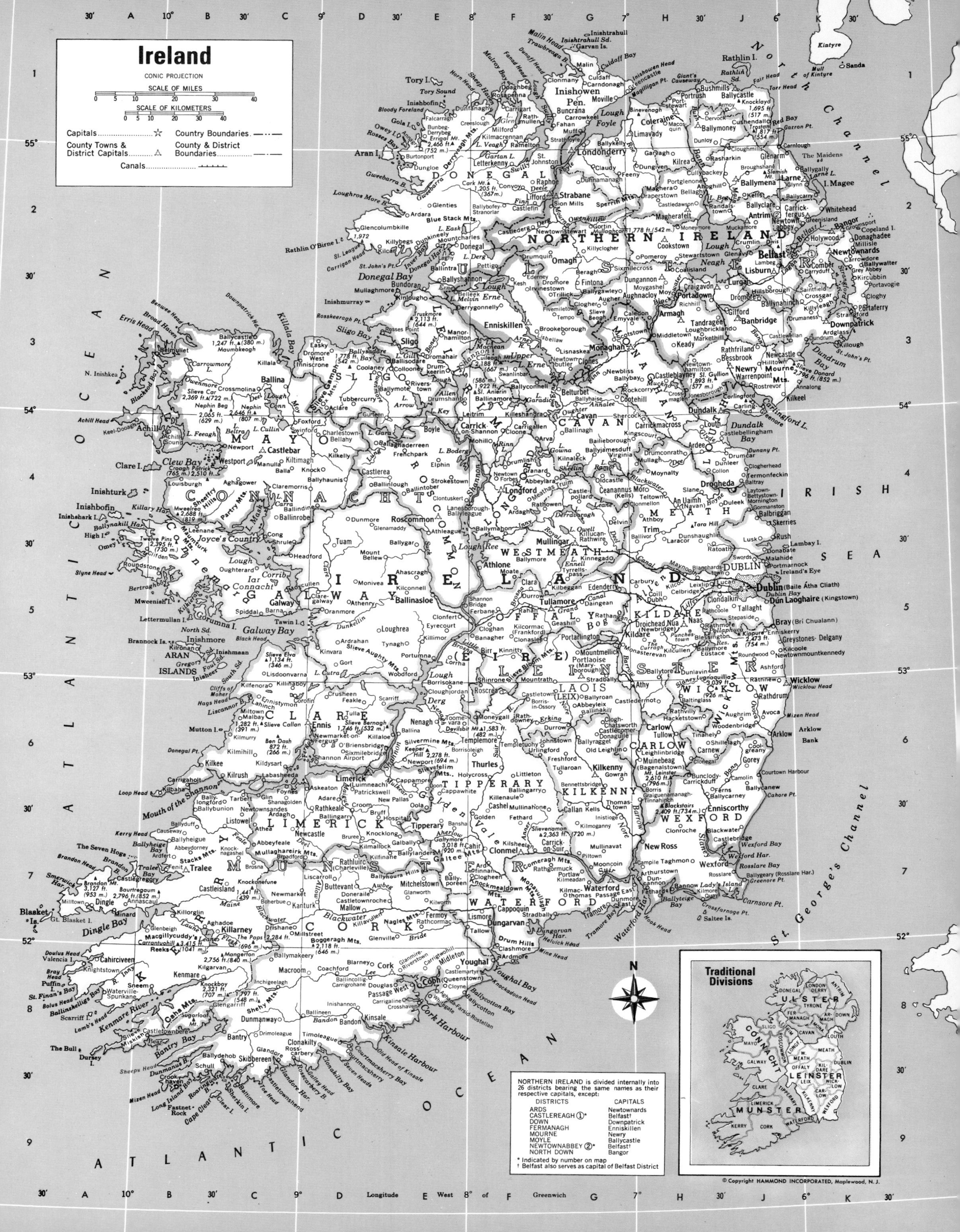
Ireland
CONIC PROJECTION
SCALE OF MILES
0 5 10 20 30 40
SCALE OF KILOMETERS
0 5 10 20 30 40
Capitals
Country Boundaries
County Towns & District Capitals
County & District Boundaries
Canals
NORTHERN IRELAND is divided internally into 26 districts bearing the same names as their respective capitals, except:
DISTRICTS — CAPITALS
ARDS — Newtownards
CASTLEREAGH ①* — Belfast†
DOWN — Downpatrick
FERMANAGH — Enniskillen
MOURNE — Newry
MOYLE — Ballycastle
NEWTOWNABBEY ②* — Belfast†
NORTH DOWN — Bangor
* Indicated by number on map
† Belfast also serves as capital of Belfast District
Traditional Divisions
ULSTER
CONNACHT
LEINSTER
MUNSTER
ATLANTIC OCEAN
IRISH SEA
North Channel
St. George's Channel
NORTHERN IRELAND
IRELAND (EIRE)
Longitude West 8° of Greenwich

Norway, Sweden, Finland and Denmark
CONIC PROJECTION
SCALE OF MILES
0 50 100 150
SCALE OF KILOMETERS
0 50 100 150 200
Capitals of Countries
Administrative Centers
International Boundaries
Internal Boundaries
Canals
SUBDIVISIONS
Indicated by Numbers
Counties in NORWAY
1 Akershus G 6
2 Vestfold G 7
3 Østfold G 7
4 Oslo G 7
Oslo is the administrative center for Akershus and Oslo County.
Counties in SWEDEN
5 Göteborg och Bohus G 7
6 Västmanland K 7
7 Södermanland K 7
8 Östergötland J 7
9 Malmöhus H 9
10 Kristianstad J 8
Svalbard
© Copyright HAMMOND INCORPORATED, Maplewood, N. J.

AREA 125,053 sq. mi.
(323,887 sq. km.)
POPULATION 4,092,000
CAPITAL Oslo
LARGEST CITY Oslo
HIGHEST POINT Glittertinden
8,110 ft. (2,472 m.)
MONETARY UNIT krone
MAJOR LANGUAGE Norwegian
MAJOR RELIGION Protestantism

AREA 173,665 sq. mi.
(449,792 sq. km.)
POPULATION 8,320,000
CAPITAL Stockholm
LARGEST CITY Stockholm
HIGHEST POINT Kebnekaise 6,946 ft.
(2,117 m.)
MONETARY UNIT krona
MAJOR LANGUAGE Swedish
MAJOR RELIGION Protestantism

AREA 130,128 sq. mi.
(337,032 sq. km.)
POPULATION 4,788,000
CAPITAL Helsinki
LARGEST CITY Helsinki
HIGHEST POINT Haltiatunturi
4,343 ft. (1,324 m.)
MONETARY UNIT markka
MAJOR LANGUAGES Finnish, Swedish
MAJOR RELIGION Protestantism

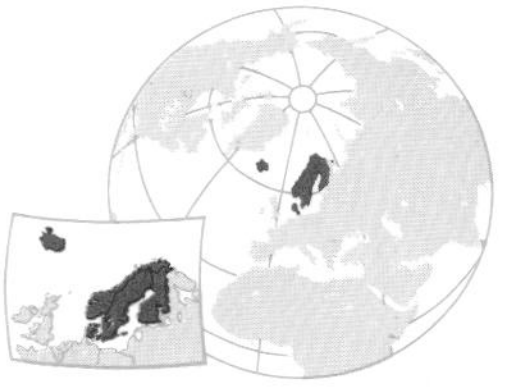

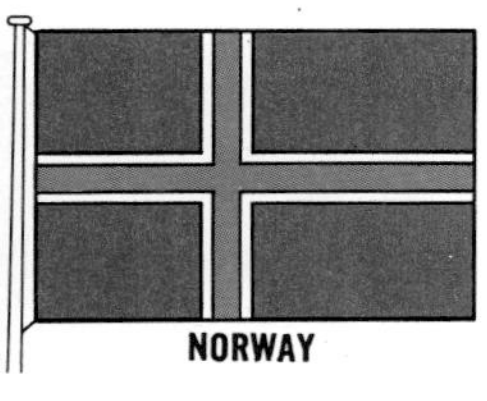

NORWAY

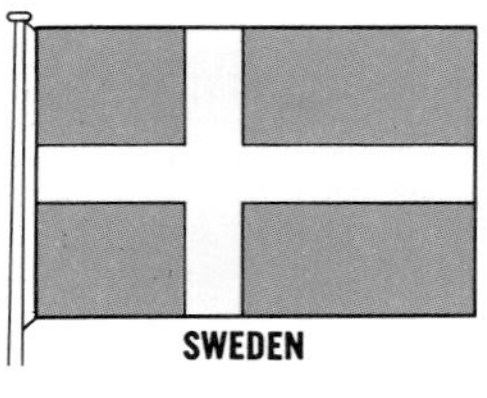

SWEDEN

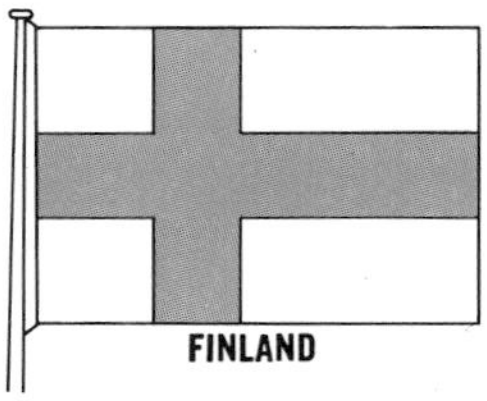

FINLAND

FINLAND

PROVINCES

Ahvenanmaa 22,380	L6
Åland (Ahvenanmaa) 22,380	L6
Häme 662,500	O6
Keski-Suomi 241,770	O5
Kuopio 252,023	P5
Kymi 346,478	Q6
Lappi 196,792	P3
Mikkeli 211,453	P6
Oulu 406,309	P4
Pohjois-Karjala 179,065	Q5
Turku ja Pori 697,988	N6
Uusimaa 1,085,625	O6
Vaasa 425,283	N5

CITIES and TOWNS

Äänekoski 10,725	O5
Åbo (Turku) 164,857	N6
Alavus 10,285	N5
Borgaå 18,740	O6
Ekenäs 7,391	N6
Espoo 117,090	O6
Forssa 18,442	N6
Haapajärvi 7,791	O5
Hämeenlinna 40,761	O6
Hamina 11,055	P6
Hangö 10,374	N7
Hanko (Hangö) 10,374	N7
Harjavalta 8,445	M6
Heinola 15,350	P6
Helsinki (cap.) 502,961	O6
Helsinki* 794,746	O6
Huutokoski† 6,458	P5
Hyvinkää 35,865	O6
Iisalmi 21,159	P5
Ikaalinen 8,364	N6
Imatra 35,590	Q6
Ivalo 2,661	P2
Jakobstad 20,397	N5
Jämsä 12,526	O6
Järvenpää 16,259	O6
Joensuu 41,429	R5
Jyväskylä 61,209	O5
Jyväskylä* 84,185	O5
Kajaani 20,583	P4
Kalajoki 3,624	N4
Kankaanpää 12,564	M6
Karhula 21,834	P6
Karis 8,152	N6
Karjaa (Karis) 8,152	N6
Karkkila 8,678	N6
Kauniainien 6,219	O6
Kauttua 3,297	M6
Kelloselkä† 8,200	Q3
Kemi 27,893	O4
Kemijärvi 12,951	P3
Kerava 19,966	O6
Kokemäki 10,188	N6
Kokkola 22,096	N5
Kotka 34,026	P6
Kotka* 60,235	P6
Kouvola 29,383	P6
Kouvola* 59,507	P6
Kristiinankaupunki (Kristinestad) 9,331	N5
Kristinestad 9,331	N5
Kuhmo 4,150	Q4
Kuopio 71,684	Q5
Kurikka 11,177	M5
Kuusamo 4,449	Q4
Kuusankoski 22,342	P6
Lahti 94,864	O6
Lahti* 112,129	O6
Lappeenranta 52,682	P6
Lapua 15,189	N5
Lieksa 20,274	R5
Loimaa 6,575	N6
Lovisa 8,674	P6
Maarianhamina (Mariehamn) 9,574	M7
Mänttä 7,910	O6
Mariehamn 9,574	M7
Mikkeli 27,112	P6
Naantali 7,814	M6
Nokia 22,308	N6
Nurmes 11,721	Q5
Nykarleby 7,408	N5
Oulainen 7,322	O4
Oulu 93,707	O4
Oulu* 103,044	O4
Outokumpu 10,736	Q5
Parainen 10,170	M6
Parkano 8,518	N6
Pieksämäki 12,923	P5
Pietarsaari (Jakobstad) 20,397	N5
Pori 80,343	M6
Pori* 86,635	M6
Posio† 6,205	Q3
Pudasjärvi† 12,594	P4
Raahe 15,379	O4
Raisio 14,271	M6
Rauma 29,081	M6
Riihimäki 24,106	O6
Rovaniemi 28,411	O3
Saarijärvi 2,714	O5
Salo 19,176	N6
Savonlinna 28,336	Q6
Seinäjoki 22,123	N5
Sodankylä 3,304	P3
Sotkamo 2,316	Q4
Suolahti 5,936	O5
Suonenjoki 9,286	P5
Tammisaari (Ekenäs) 7,391	N6
Tampere 168,118	N6
Tampere* 220,920	N6
Toijala 8,080	N6
Tornio 19,971	O4
Turku 164,857	N6
Turku* 217,423	N6
Turtola† 5,852	O3
Ulvila† 8,040	N6
Uusikaarlepyy (Nykarleby) 7,408	N5
Uusikaupunki 11,915	M6
Vaasa 54,402	M5
Vaasa* 58,224	M5
Valkeakoski 22,588	N6
Vammala 16,363	N6
Varkaus 24,450	Q5
Vasa (Vaasa) 54,402	M5
Vuotso† 10,186	P2
Ylivieska 10,827	O4

OTHER FEATURES

Åland (isls.)	L6
Baltic (sea)	K9
Bothnia (gulf)	M5
Finland (gulf)	P7
Hailuoto (isl.)	O4
Haltiatunturi (mt.)	M2
Hangöudd (prom.)	N7
Haukivesi (lake)	Q5
Iijoki (riv.)	O4
Inari (lake)	P2
Ivalojoki (riv.)	P2
Juojärvi (lake)	Q5
Kalajoki (riv.)	O4
Kallavesi (lake)	P5
Karlö (Hailuoto) (isl.)	O4
Keitele (lake)	O5
Kemijärvi (lake)	Q3
Kemijoki (riv.)	O3
Kiantajärvi (lake)	Q4
Kilpisjärvi (lake)	M2
Kitinen (riv.)	P3
Kivijärvi (lake)	O5
Koitere (lake)	R5
Kuusamojärvi (lake)	Q4
Längelmävesi (lake)	O6
Lapland (reg.)	O2
Lappajärvi (lake)	O5
Lapuanjoki (riv.)	N5
Lestijärvi (lake)	O5
Lokka (res.)	Q3
Muojärvi (lake)	R4
Muonio (riv.)	M2
Näsijärvi (lake)	O6
Onkivesi (lake)	P5
Orihvesi (lake)	Q5
Oulujärvi (lake)	P4
Oulujoki (riv.)	O4
Ounasjoki (riv.)	O3
Päijänne (lake)	O6
Pielinen (lake)	Q5
Puruvesi (lake)	Q6
Puulavesi (lake)	P5
Pyhäjärvi (lake)	O5
Pyhäjärvi (lake)	M6
Saimaa (lake)	Q6
Siikajoki (riv.)	O4
Simojärvi (lake)	P3
Simojoki (riv.)	O4
Tana (riv.)	P2
Tornio (riv.)	O3
Vallgrund (isl.)	M5
Ylikitka (lake)	Q3

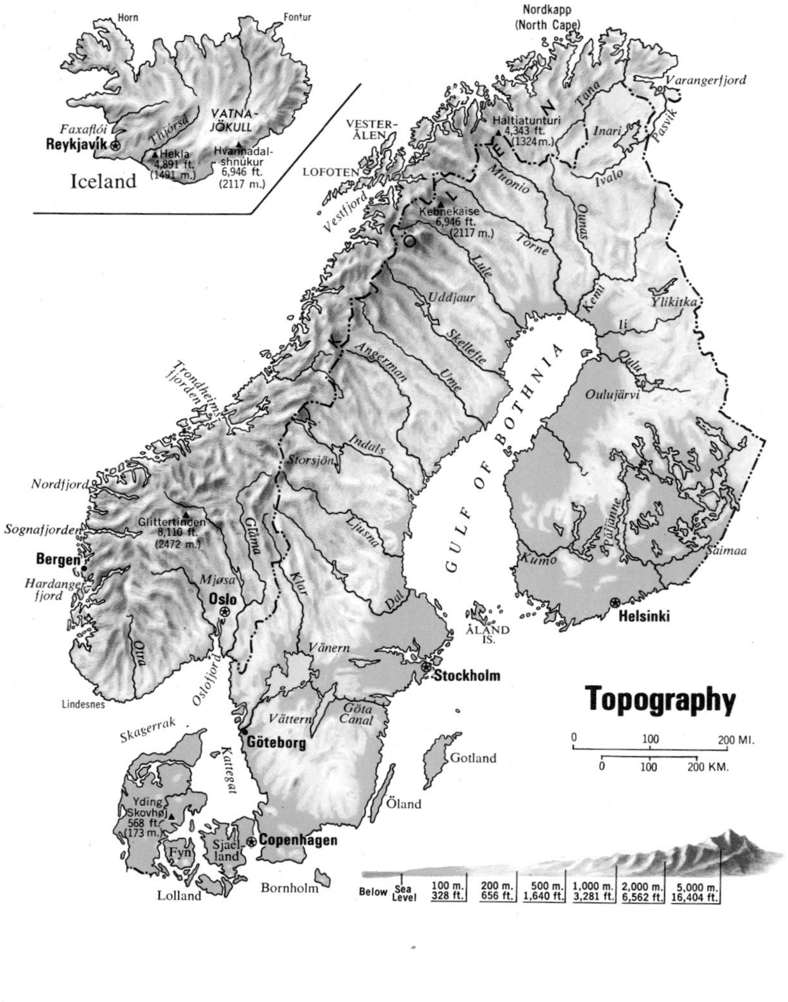

NORWAY

COUNTIES

Akershus 355,196	G6
Aust-Agder 86,216	E7
Buskerud 209,684	F6
Finnmark 79,373	O2
Hedmark 183,465	G6
Hordaland 386,492	E6
Møre og Romsdal 231,944	E5
Nordland 243,233	J3
Nord-Trøndelag 122,886	H4
Oppland 178,259	F6
Oslo (city) 462,732	D3
Østfold 228,546	G7
Rogaland 287,653	E7
Sogn og Fjordane 103,135	E6
Sør-Trøndelag 241,361	G5
Telemark 158,853	F7
Troms 144,111	L2
Vest-Agder 131,659	E7
Vestfold 182,433	G7

CITIES and TOWNS

Ålesund 40,868	D5
Ålgård 2,322	D7
Alta 5,582	N2
Åndalsnes 2,574	F5
Årdalstangen 2,360	F6
Arendal 11,701	F7
Arendal* 21,228	F7
Årnes 2,267	G6
Askim 8,413	E4
Bamble† 7,031	F7
Barentsburg	C2
Bergen 213,434	D6
Bodø 31,077	J3
Borge† 3,294	H2
Brønnøysund 3,130	G4
Dombås 1,114	F5
Drammen 50,777	C4
Drammen* 56,521	C4
Drøbak 4,538	D4
Eidsvoll 2,906	G6
Eigersund 11,379	D7
Elverum 7,391	G6
Farsund 8,908	E7
Flekkefjord 8,750	E7
Flora 8,822	D6
Fredrikstad 29,024	D4
Fredrikstad* 51,141	D4
Gjøvik 25,963	G6
Grimstad 13,091	F7
Halden 27,087	G7
Hamar 16,418	G6
Hamar* 25,138	G6
Hammerfest 7,610	N1
Hammerfest* 8,005	N1
Harstad 21,125	K2
Haugesund 27,386	D7
Haugesund* 29,277	D7
Hermansverk 706	E6
Holmestrand 8,246	C4
Holmsbu 273	D4
Honningsvag 3,780	O1
Horten 13,746	D4
Horten* 17,246	D4
Kirkenes 4,466	Q2
Kongsberg 19,854	F7
Kongsvinger 16,146	H6
Kopervik 4,221	D7
Kornsjø† 6,079	G7
Kragerø 5,249	F7
Kristiansand 59,488	F8
Kristiansund 18,847	E5
Kvinnherad† 2,898	E6
Larvik 9,097	C4
Larvik* 19,202	C4
Lenvik† 11,098	L2
Levanger 5,066	G5
Lillehammer 21,248	F6
Lillesand 3,028	F7
Lillestrøm† 11,550	E3
Longyearbyen	D2
Lysaker† 81,612	D3
Mandal 11,579	E7
Meråker† 2,907	G5
Mo 21,033	J3
Molde 20,334	E5
Mosjøen 9,341	H4
Moss 25,786	D4
Moss* 27,430	D4
Mysen 3,760	G7
Namsos 11,452	G4
Narvik 19,582	K2
Nesttun† 11,519	D6
Nittedal† 8,889	D3
Notodden 12,970	F7
Nøtterøy 11,944	D4
Ny-Ålesund	C2
Odda 7,401	E6
Oppdal 2,173	F5
Orkanger 3,685	F5
Oslo (cap.) 462,732	D3
Oslo* 645,413	D3
Porsgrunn 31,709	G7
Rakkestad 2,392	G7
Ringerike 30,156	C3
Risør 6,560	F7
Rjukan 5,334	F7
Røros 3,041	G5
Sandefjord 33,350	C4
Sandnes 33,934	D7
Sandvika† 34,337	C3
Sarpsborg 12,889	D4
Sarpsborg* 36,449	D4
Selje† 3,386	D5
Ski 9,081	D4
Skien 47,105	F7
Stavanger 86,639	D7
Stavern 2,604	D4
Steinkjer 20,553	G4
Stor-Elvdal† 2,993	G6
Sunndalsøra 5,114	F5
Sveagruva	D2
Svolvaer 3,942	J2
Tønsberg 9,964	D4
Tønsberg* 36,374	D4
Tromsø 43,830	L2
Trondheim 134,910	F5
Ullensvang† 2,326	E6
Vadsø 6,019	Q1
Vardø 3,875	R1
Vik 1,019	E6
Volda 3,511	E5
Voss 5,944	E6

OTHER FEATURES

Alsten (isl.)	H4
Andøya (isl.)	J2
Barduelv (riv.)	L2
Bellsund	C2
Bjørnafjorden (fjord)	D6
Bjornøya (isl.)	D3
Boknafjord (fjord)	D7
Bremanger (isl.)	D6
Dønna (isl.)	H3
Dovrefjell (hills)	F5
Edgeøya (isl.)	E2
Femundsjø (lake)	G5
Folda (fjord)	G4
Folda (fjord)	J3
Frohavet (bay)	F5
Frøya (isl.)	F5
Glittertinden (mt.)	F6
Hardangervidda (plat.)	E6
Hardangerfjord (fjord)	D7
Hinlopenstreten (str.)	C1
Hinnøya (isl.)	K2
Hitra (isl.)	F5
Hopen (isl.)	E2
Isfjorden (fjord)	C2
Jostedalsbreen (glac.)	E6
Kjölen (mts.)	K3
Kongsfjorden (fjord)	B2
Kvaløya (isl.)	O1
Lågen (riv.)	G6
Laksefjorden (fjord)	P1
Langøy (isl.)	J2
Lapland (reg.)	K2
Leka (isl.)	G4
Lindesnes (cape)	E8
Lista (pen.)	E7
Lofoten (isls.)	H2
Lopphavet (bay)	M1
Magerøya (isl.)	P1
Moskenesøya (isl.)	H3
Namsen (riv.)	H4
Nordaustlandet (isl.)	D1
Nordfjord (fjord)	E6
Nordkapp (pt.)	C1
Nordkinn (headland)	Q1
Nordkinn (pen.)	P1
North Cape (Nordkapp) (pt.)	P1
Norwegian (sea)	F3
Ofotfjorden (fjord)	K2
Oslofjord (fjord)	D4
Otra (riv.)	E7
Otterøya (isl.)	E5
Pasvikelv (riv.)	Q2
Platen, Kapp (pt.)	D1
Porsangen (fjord)	O1
Rana (fjord)	H3
Rauma (riv.)	F5
Ringvassøy (isl.)	L2
Romsdalsfjorden (fjord)	E5
Saltfjorden (fjord)	J3
Seiland (isl.)	N1
Senja (isl.)	K2
Skagerrak (str.)	F8
Smøla (isl.)	E5
Sognafjorden (fjord)	D6
Sørkapp (pt.)	C2
Sorøya (isl.)	N1
Spitsbergen (isl.)	C2
Storfjorden (fjord)	D2
Sulitjelma (mt.)	J3
Svalbard (isls.)	C3
Tana (riv.)	P1
Tanafjord (fjord)	Q1
Tokke (riv.)	F7
Trondheimsfjorden (fjord)	G5
Tyrifjord (lake)	C3
Vaerøy (isl.)	H3
Vagåvatn (lake)	F6
Vannøy (isl.)	L1
Varangerhalvøya (pen.)	Q1
Varangerfjord (fjord)	Q2
Vega (isl.)	G4
Vesterålen (isls.)	J2
Vestfjord (fjord)	H3
Vestvågøya (isl.)	H3
Vikna (isls.)	G4

SWEDEN

COUNTIES

Älvsborg 418,150	H7
Blekinge 155,391	J8
Gävleborg 294,595	K6
Göteborg och Bohus 714,660	G7
Gotland 54,447	L8
Halland 219,767	H8
Jämtland 133,559	J5
Jönköping 301,905	H8
Kalmar 240,768	K8
Kopparberg 281,082	J6
Kristianstad 272,090	J8

(continued on following page)

(continued)

Kronoberg 169,454 ... J8
Malmöhus 740,137 ... H9
Norrbotten 264,215 ... L3
Örebro 273,994 ... J7
Östergötland 387,104 ... J7
Skaraborg 263,382 ... H7
Södermanland 252,030 ... K7
Stockholm 1,493,052 ... L7
Uppsala 229,879 ... K7
Värmland 284,442 ... H7
Västerbotten 236,367 ... K4
Västernorrland 268,202 ... K5
Västmanland 259,872 ... K7

CITIES and TOWNS

Åhus 6,125 ... J9
Alingsås 18,892 ... H7
Älmhult 7,390 ... H8
Alvesta 7,261 ... J8
Älvsbyn 4,707 ... M4
Åmål 9,556 ... H7
Ånge 3,760 ... J5
Ängelholm 16,016 ... H8
Arboga 11,819 ... J7
Arbrå 2,734 ... K6
Årjäng† 2,596 ... H7
Arvidsjaur 4,194 ... L4
Arvika 13,934 ... H7
Åseda 2,465 ... J8
Askim 17,609 ... G8
Åtvidaberg 8,436 ... K7
Avesta 19,095 ... J6
Bålsta 8,243 ... G1
Båstad 2,452 ... H8
Bengtsfors 3,535 ... H7
Boden 19,590 ... M4
Bollnäs 13,305 ... K6
Bollstabruk 3,548 ... L5
Borås 67,537 ... H8
Borås* 187,710 ... H8
Borgholm 2,789 ... K8
Borlänge 40,158 ... J6
Brunflo 3,460 ... J5
Dalby† 4,013 ... H6
Danderyd† 36,596 ... H1
Dannemora 291 ... K6
Edsbyn 4,388 ... J6
Eksjö 9,686 ... J8
Emmaboda 5,652 ... J8
Enköping 18,541 ... G1
Eskilstuna 66,409 ... K7
Eslöv 13,629 ... H9
Fagersta† 14,778 ... J6
Falkenberg 14,148 ... H8
Falköping 15,126 ... H7
Falun 30,073 ... J6
Färjestaden 2,995 ... K8
Filipstad 7,835 ... H7
Finspång 16,346 ... J7
Flen 6,770 ... K7
Forshaga 6,000 ... H7
Frösö 10,274 ... J5
Frövi 2,583 ... J7
Gällivare 8,669 ... M3
Gamleby 3,666 ... J8
Gävle 67,454 ... K6
Gimo 3,154 ... K6
Gislaved 8,564 ... H8
Gnesta 3,835 ... G2
Göteborg 444,540 ... G8
Göteborg* 690,767 ... G8
Hagfors 8,060 ... H6
Hällefors 7,862 ... J7
Hallsberg 6,799 ... J7
Hallstahammar 13,583 ... K7
Hallstavik 5,162 ... L6
Halmstad 49,558 ... H8
Haparanda 5,031 ... N4
Härnösand 18,971 ... L5
Hässleholm 16,813 ... H8
Hedemora 7,039 ... K6
Helsingborg 80,986 ... H8
Helsingborg* 215,894 ... H8
Hjo 4,615 ... J7
Hofors 11,459 ... K6
Höganäs 10,866 ... H8
Holmsund 5,467 ... M5
Hörnefors 2,441 ... L5
Huddinge 48,339 ... H1
Hudiksvall 15,004 ... K6
Hultsfred 5,763 ... K8
Husum 2,517 ... L5
Hyltebruk 3,469 ... H8
Iggesund 4,448 ... K6
Järna 6,237 ... G2
Jokkmokk 3,186 ... L3
Jönköping 78,650 ... H8
Jönköping* 131,499 ... H8
Kalix 7,668 ... N4
Kalmar 32,049 ... K8
Karlshamn 17,447 ... J8
Karlskoga† 35,425 ... J7
Karlskrona 33,414 ... J8
Karlstad 51,243 ... H7
Katrineholm 22,884 ... K7
Kinna 13,676 ... H8
Kiruna 25,410 ... L3
Kisa 4,323 ... J7
Köping 20,059 ... J7
Kopparberg 3,942 ... J7
Kramfors 7,719 ... L5
Kristianstad 30,780 ... J9
Kristinehamn 21,146 ... H7
Kumla 11,451 ... J7
Kungälv† 12,764 ... G8
Kungsbacka† 11,986 ... G8
Kvissleby 3,413 ... K5
Laholm 3,898 ... H8
Landskrona 29,486 ... H9
Långshyttan 2,744 ... K6
Laxå 5,166 ... J7
Leksand 4,410 ... J6
Lessebo 2,991 ... J8
Lidingö 30,098 ... H1
Lidköping 21,001 ... H7
Lindesberg 8,247 ... J7
Linköping 80,274 ... K7
Linköping* 132,839 ... K7
Ljungby 12,969 ... J8
Ljusdal 7,075 ... J6
Ljusne 3,578 ... K6
Ludvika 18,217 ... J6
Luleå 42,139 ... N4
Lund 55,047 ... H9
Lycksele 8,586 ... L4
Lysekil 7,815 ... G7
Malmberget 10,239 ... M3
Malmö 241,191 ... H9
Malmö* 453,339 ... H9
Malung 6,211 ... H6
Mariefred 2,553 ... F1
Mariestad 16,454 ... H7
Markaryd 4,266 ... H8
Märsta 17,066 ... K7
Marstrand 1,168 ... G8
Mellerud 3,579 ... H7
Mjölby 12,488 ... J7
Mölndal† 47,248 ... H8
Mönsterås 5,005 ... K8
Mora 8,772 ... J6
Motala 29,454 ... J7
Nacka 19,708 ... H1
Nässjö 18,634 ... J8
Nora 5,515 ... J7
Norberg 5,438 ... K6
Norrköping 85,244 ... K7
Norrköping* 163,206 ... K7
Norrtälje 12,784 ... L7
Nybro 13,010 ... J8
Nyköping 30,352 ... K7
Nynäshamn 11,070 ... L7
Ockelbo 2,810 ... K6
Olofström 10,096 ... J8
Örebro 117,877 ... J7
Örebro* 171,440 ... J7
Örnsköldsvik 29,514 ... L5
Orrefors 919 ... J8
Orsa 5,099 ... J6
Oskarshamn 19,021 ... K8
Östersund 40,056 ... J5
Östhammar 1,783 ... L6
Oxelösund 13,862 ... K7
Piteå 16,169 ... M4
Rättvik 4,087 ... J6
Rimbo 3,404 ... L7
Ronneby 12,086 ... J8
Säffle 11,428 ... H7
Sala 11,216 ... K7
Saltsjöbaden 8,113 ... J1
Sandviken 27,994 ... K6
Säter 4,297 ... J6
Sävsjö 4,913 ... J8
Sigtuna 4,780 ... H1
Simrishamn 5,834 ... J9
Skanör med Falsterbo 4,909 ... H9
Skara 10,138 ... H7
Skellefteå 29,353 ... M4
Skövde 29,945 ... H7
Skutskär 7,174 ... K6
Smedjebacken 8,418 ... J6
Söderhamn 14,673 ... K6
Söderköping 5,310 ... K7
Södertälje 58,408 ... G1
Sollefteå 8,923 ... K5
Sollentuna† 40,905 ... H1
Solna† 53,992 ... H1
Sölvesborg 7,292 ... J9
Stenungsund 8,361 ... G7
Stockholm (cap.) 665,550 ... G1
Stockholm* 1,357,183 ... G1
Storuman 2,587 ... K4
Storvik 2,748 ... K6
Strängnäs 10,255 ... F1
Strömstad 4,735 ... G7
Strömsund 4,119 ... K5
Sundbyberg† 27,058 ... G1
Sundsvall 52,268 ... K5
Sunne 4,273 ... H7
Surahammar 6,509 ... J7
Sveg 2,608 ... J5
Svenljunga 3,189 ... H8
Täby† 41,285 ... H1
Tibro 8,476 ... J7
Tidaholm 8,039 ... J7
Tierp 5,005 ... K6
Timrå 11,416 ... K5
Tomelilla 5,371 ... J9
Torsby 3,632 ... H6
Torshälla 8,231 ... K7
Tranås 14,854 ... J7
Trelleborg 22,559 ... H9
Trollhättan 42,499 ... H7
Trosa 3,128 ... K7
Uddevalla 32,700 ... G7
Ulricehamn 7,827 ... H8
Umeå 49,715 ... M5
Uppsala 101,850 ... K7
Uppsala* 157,202 ... L7
Vadstena 5,294 ... J7
Vaggeryd 3,974 ... J8
Valdemarsvik 3,558 ... K7
Vallentuna 10,477 ... H1
Vänersborg 20,510 ... G7
Vännäs 3,876 ... L5
Vansbro 2,708 ... H6
Vara 3,049 ... H7
Varberg 19,467 ... G8
Värnamo 15,726 ... J8
Västerås 98,858 ... K7
Västerås* 147,508 ... K7
Västerhaninge 14,125 ... H1
Västervik 21,239 ... K8
Vaxholm† 3,744 ... J1
Växjö 40,328 ... J8
Vetlanda 12,358 ... J8
Vilhelmina 4,060 ... K4
Vimmerby 7,405 ... J8
Virserum 2,495 ... J8
Visby 19,886 ... L8
Ystad 14,286 ... H9

OTHER FEATURES

Ångermanälven (riv.) ... K5
Åsnen (lake) ... J8
Baltic (sea) ... K9
Bolmen (lake) ... H8
Bothnia (gulf) ... N4
Dalälven (riv.) ... K6
Fårö (isl.) ... L8
Göta (canal) ... J7
Göta (riv.) ... H7
Gotland (isl.) ... L8
Gräsö (isl.) ... L6
Hanöbukten (bay) ... J9
Hjälmaren (lake) ... J7
Hoburgen (cliff) ... L8
Hornslandet (pen.) ... K6
Indalsälven (riv.) ... H5
Kalixälv (riv.) ... N3
Kalmarsund (sound) ... K8
Kattegat (str.) ... G8
Kebnekaise (mt.) ... L3
Kölen (mts.) ... K3
Klarälv (riv.) ... H6
Lapland (reg.) ... M2
Ljusnan (riv.) ... H5
Luleälv (riv.) ... M4
Mälaren (lake) ... G1
Muonioälv (riv.) ... M2
Öland (isl.) ... K8
Öresund (sound) ... H9
Ornö (isl.) ... J2
Österdalälven (riv.) ... H6
Piteälv (riv.) ... M4
Siljan (lake) ... J6
Skagerrak (str.) ... F8
Sommen (lake) ... J8
Stora Lulevatten (lake) ... L3
Storsjön (lake) ... J5
Sulitelma (mt.) ... K3
Torneälv (riv.) ... M3
Uddjaur (lake) ... L4
Umeälv (riv.) ... L4
Vänern (lake) ... H7
Västerdalälven (riv.) ... H6
Vättern (lake) ... J7

*City and suburbs.
†Population of commune.
†Population of parish.

DENMARK

COUNTIES

Århus 534,333 ... D5
Bornholm 47,241 ... F9
Copenhagen (commune) 622,612 ... F6
Faerøe Islands 41,969 ... B2
Frederiksberg (commune) 101,874 ... F6
Frederiksborg 260,825 ... E5
Fyn 433,765 ... D7
København (Copenhagen) (commune) 622,612 ... F6
Københaven 616,571 ... F6
Nordjylland 457,165 ... D4
Ribe 198,153 ... B7
Ringkøbing 242,006 ... B5
Roskilde 154,314 ... E6
Sønderjylland 238,502 ... C7
Storstrøm 252,780 ... E7
Vejle 306,809 ... C6
Vestsjaelland 259,484 ... E6
Viborg 221,002 ... C4

CITIES and TOWNS

Åbenrå 15,196 ... C7
Åbybro 2,897 ... C3
Åkirkeby 2,001 ... F9
Ålborg 154,582 ... D4
Ålestrup 1,926 ... C4
Århus 245,941 ... D5
Års 4,266 ... C4
Årup 1,675 ... D7
AErøskøbing 1,223 ... D8
Agerbaek 935 ... B6
Allingaåbro 1,385 ... D5
Allinge-Sandvig 1,991 ... F8
Ansager 1,157 ... B6
Arden 1,303 ... C4
Asaå 1,344 ... D3
Askov 904 ... C7
Asnaes 1,413 ... E6
Assens, Århus 1,341 ... D4
Assens, Fyn 5,139 ... D7
Augustenborg 2,628 ... D8
Auning 1,516 ... D5
Avlum 1,729 ... B5
Baelum 1,169 ... D4
Bagenkop 776 ... D8
Ballerup 50,673 ... F6
Bandholm 693 ... E8
Bedsted 965 ... B4
Birkerød 13,663 ... F6
Bjerringbro 4,761 ... C5
Bogense 2,861 ... D6
Bolderslev 774 ... C8
Børkop 1,410 ... C6
Borup 1,591 ... E7
Braedstrup 2,163 ... C6
Bramming 3,678 ... B7
Brande 4,784 ... B6
Bredebro 1,173 ... B7
Broager 2,143 ... C8
Brønderslev 10,247 ... C3
Brørup 2,584 ... C7
Brovst 4,200 ... C3
Bryrup 579 ... C5
Christiansfeld 1,994 ... C7
Copenhagen (cap.) 603,368 ... F6
Copenhagen* 1,327,940 ... F6
Dronninglund 4,661 ... D3
Dybvad 805 ... D3
Ebeltoft 3,017 ... D5
Egernsund 1,323 ... C8
Egtved 1,311 ... C6
Ejby 1,372 ... C7
Esbjerg 68,097 ... B7
Faåborg 6,495 ... D7
Fakse 2,720 ... F7
Fakse Ladeplads 1,799 ... F7
Farsø 2,821 ... C4
Farum 9,936 ... F6
Fjerritslev 2,134 ... C3
Fredensborg 4,709 ... F6
Fredericia 36,157 ... C6
Frederiksberg 101,874 ... F6
Frederikshavn 24,846 ... D3
Frederikssund 11,272 ... E6
Frederiksvaerk 8,903 ... E6
Fuglebjerg 1,094 ... E7
Gedser 1,200 ... F8
Gedsted 1,006 ... C4
Gelsted 1,307 ... C7
Gentofte 77,744 ... F6
Gilleleje 2,943 ... F5
Give 2,366 ... C6
Glamsbjerg 2,226 ... D7
Glostrup 28,326 ... F6
Glumsø 1,027 ... E7
Glyngøre 1,071 ... C4
Gørding 1,261 ... B7
Gørlev 1,542 ... E7
Graested 1,654 ... F5
Gram 2,061 ... C7
Graåsten 2,947 ... C8
Grenaå 12,569 ... D5
Grindsted 7,558 ... B6
Haårby 1,506 ... D7
Haderslev 20,042 ... C7
Hadsten 3,914 ... C5
Hadsund 3,652 ... D4
Hals 1,654 ... D3
Hammel 3,247 ... C5
Hammerum 3,227 ... C5
Hanstholm 1,716 ... B3
Harboør 1,359 ... B4
Haårlev 1,228 ... F7
Hasle 18
Haslev 6,925 ... E7
Havdrup 1,833 ... F6
Hedensted 2,659 ... C6
Hellebaek 2,911 ... F5
Helsinge 3,613 ... F6
Helsingør 42,425 ... F6
Herning 32,973 ... B5
Hillerød 23,963 ... F6
Hinnerup 2,061 ... D5
Hirtshals 6,861 ... C2
Hjallerup 1,573 ... C3
Hjerm 647 ... B5
Hjørring 19,692 ... C3
Hobro 8,737 ... C4
Højer 1,416 ... B8
Højslev 1,641 ... C4
Holbaek 19,485 ... E6
Holeby 1,434 ... E8
Holstebro 25,006 ... B5
Holsted 1,390 ... B6
Høng 2,488 ... E7
Hornslet 2,561 ... D5
Horsens 44,120 ... C6
Hørsholm 19,346 ... F6
Hørve 1,139 ... E6
Hov 635 ... D6
Humlum 546 ... B4
Hundested 5,443 ... E6
Hurup 2,287 ... B4
Hvidbjerg 994 ... B4
Hvide Sande 2,129 ... A6
Ikast 9,222 ... C5
Jelling 1,540 ... C6
Jerslev 798 ... D3
Juelsminde 1,991 ... D6
Jyderup 2,901 ... E6
Kalundborg 12,248 ... D6
Karise 1,184 ... F7
Karup 1,694 ... C5
Kastrup† 17,391 ... F6
Kerteminde 5,007 ... D7
Kibaek 1,279 ... B5
Kjellerup 3,245 ... C5
Klitmøller 542 ... B3
København (Copenhagen) (cap.) 603,368 ... F6
Køge 18,608 ... F7
Kolding 41,602 ... C7
Kolind 1,036 ... D5
Korsør 15,502 ... E7
Kvaerndrup 891 ... D7
Langaå 2,320 ... C5
Lem 1,026 ... B5
Lemvig 6,448 ... B4
Løgstør 3,633 ... C4
Løgumkloster 2,091 ... B7
Lohals 580 ... D7
Løjt Kirkeby 1,203 ... C7
Løkken 1,345 ... C3
Løsning 1,967 ... C6
Lundby 747 ... E7
Lunderskov 1,494 ... C7
Lyngby 61,516 ... F6
Malling 1,584 ... D5
Mariager 1,692 ... D4
Maribo 5,287 ... E8
Marstal 4,124 ... D8
Middelfart 13,315 ... C7

Agriculture, Industry and Resources

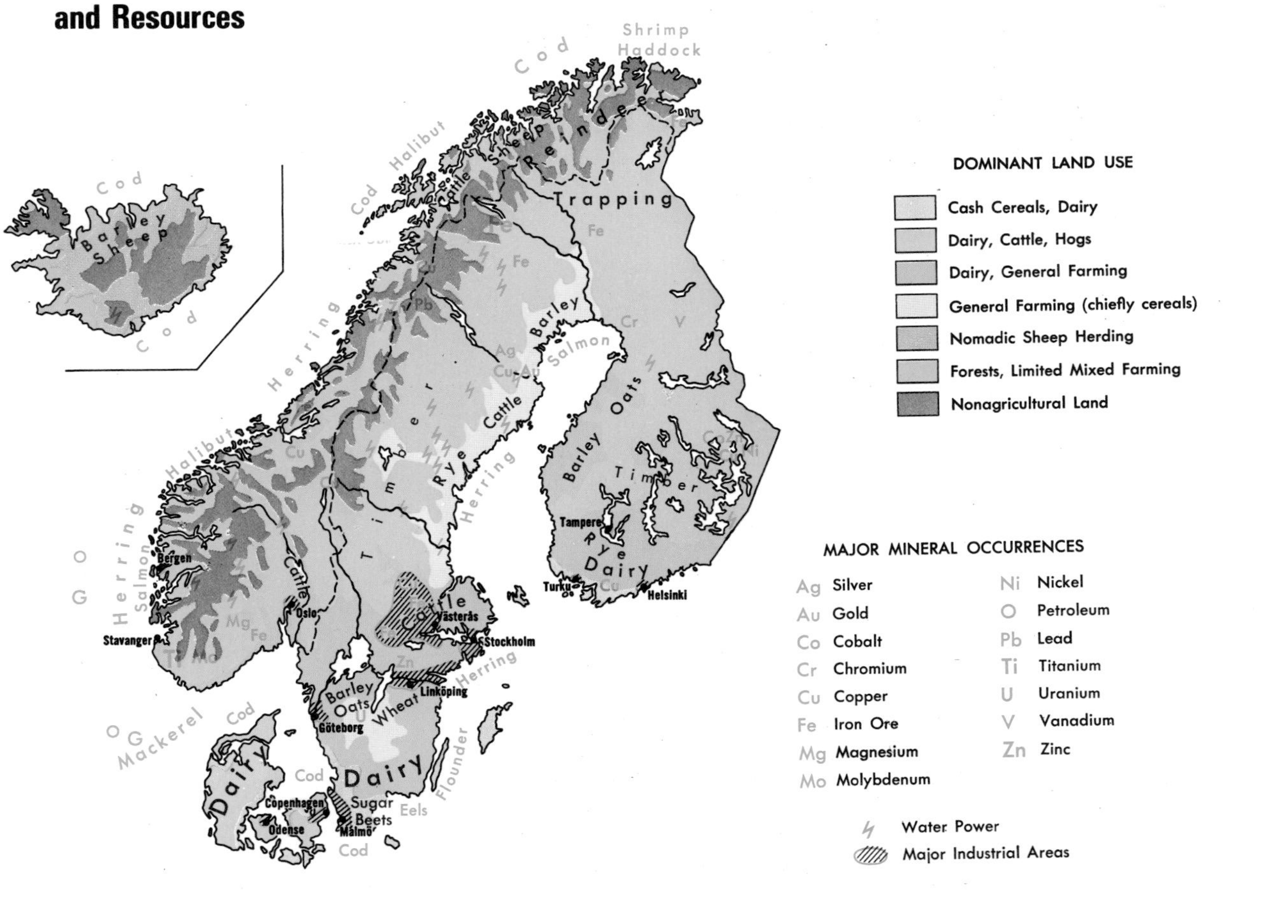

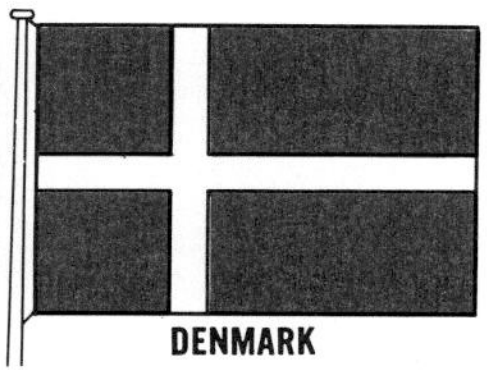

DENMARK

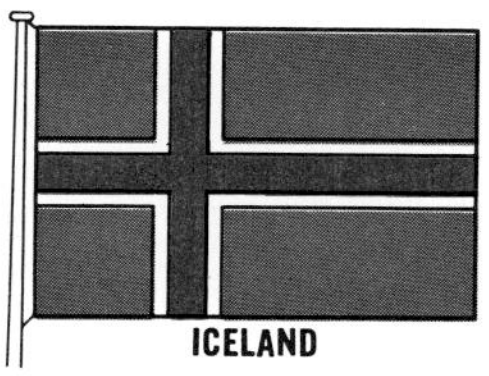

ICELAND

DENMARK

AREA 16,629 sq. mi. (43,069 sq. km.)
POPULATION 5,124,000
CAPITAL Copenhagen
LARGEST CITY Copenhagen
HIGHEST POINT Yding Skovhøj 568 ft. (173 m.)
MONETARY UNIT krone
MAJOR LANGUAGE Danish
MAJOR RELIGION Protestantism

ICELAND

AREA 39,768 sq. mi. (103,000 sq. km.)
POPULATION 228,785
CAPITAL Reykjavík
LARGEST CITY Reykjavík
HIGHEST POINT Hvannadalshnúkur 6,952 ft. (2,119 m.)
MONETARY UNIT króna
MAJOR LANGUAGE Icelandic
MAJOR RELIGION Protestantism

Møgeltønder 711 .... B8
Naestved 35,011 .... E7
Nakskov 16,393 .... E8
Neksø 3,527 .... F9
Nibe 2,796 .... C4
Nordborg 4,132 .... C7
Nordby, Ribe 2,084 .... B7
Nørre Åby 2,165 .... C7
Nørre Alslev 1,338 .... E8
Nørre Broby 904 .... D7
Nørre Nebel 901 .... B6
Nørre Snede 1,461 .... C6
Nørre Vorupør 644 .... B4
Nyborg 14,181 .... D7
Nykøbing, Storstrøm 20,059 .... F8
Nykøbing, Vestsjaelland 4,996 .... E6
Nykøbing, Viborg 9,066 .... B4
Nysted 1,229 .... E8
Odder 6,617 .... D6
Odense 168,178 .... D7
Ølgod 2,258 .... B6
Ørsted 1,093 .... D5
Øster Vrå 906 .... D3
Otterup 2,673 .... D7
Ovtrup 602 .... B6
Pandrup 1,525 .... C3
Praestø 2,789 .... F7
Ramme 506 .... B4
Randers 58,409 .... C5
Ranum 1,472 .... C4
Ribe 8,254 .... B7
Ringe 3,584 .... D7
Ringkøbing 6,298 .... A5
Ringsted 14,076 .... E7
Rødby 5,296 .... E8
Rødding 2,102 .... B7
Rødekro 2,246 .... C7
Rødkaersbro 1,098 .... C5
Rødvig 1,115 .... F7
Rømø 816 .... B7
Rønde 1,523 .... D5
Rønne 14,736 .... F9
Roskilde 44,248 .... E6
Roslev 1,058 .... B4
Rudkøbing 4,080 .... D8
Ruds Vedby 1,071 .... E7
Ry 2,699 .... C5
Ryomgård 1,000 .... D5
Saeby 5,430 .... D3
Sakskøbing 4,102 .... E8
Silkeborg 29,015 .... C5
Sindal 2,406 .... D3
Skaelskør 4,585 .... E7
Skaerbaek 2,483 .... B7
Skagen 11,620 .... D2
Skals 960 .... C4
Skanderborg 11,344 .... D5
Skårup 1,216 .... D7
Skibby 1,549 .... E6
Skive 17,015 .... B4
Skjern 6,056 .... B6
Skodborg 935 .... C7
Skørping 1,675 .... C4
Slagelse 26,851 .... E7
Slangerup 3,036 .... E6
Snedsted 1,105 .... B4
Søllested 960 .... E8
Sønderborg 24,526 .... C8
Sønder Omme 1,393 .... B6
Søndersø 885 .... D7
Sorø 8,683 .... E7
Stege 3,869 .... F8
Stenlille 1,014 .... E6
Stenstrup 1,245 .... D7
Stoholm 1,224 .... C5
Store Heddinge 2,630 .... F7
Støvring 2,366 .... C4
Strandby 1,017 .... D3
Struer 10,848 .... B5
Stubbekøbing 2,031 .... F8
Svaneke 1,193 .... F8
Svendborg 24,203 .... D7
Svinninge 1,797 .... E6
Tarm 3,150 .... B6
Tårnby 45,661 .... F6
Tåstrup 30,608 .... F6
Them 511 .... C5
Thisted 11,252 .... B4
Thyborøn 2,425 .... A4
Thyregod 1,001 .... C6
Tim 553 .... B5
Tinglev 1,531 .... C8
Tistrup 762 .... B6
Toftlund 2,147 .... B7
Tølløse 1,982 .... E6
Tommerup 1,439 .... D7
Tønder 7,469 .... B8
Tørring 1,537 .... C6
Tranebjerg 657 .... D6
Troense 771 .... D7
Trustrup 794 .... D5
Uldum 885 .... C6
Ulfborg 1,357 .... B5
Vamdrup 3,111 .... C7
Varde 11,615 .... B6
Vejen 6,213 .... C7
Vejle 43,976 .... C6
Vemb 989 .... B5
Vester Skerninge 603 .... D7
Vestervig 747 .... B4
Viborg 27,441 .... C5
Viby 1,549 .... F6
Videbaek 2,248 .... B5
Vig 1,037 .... E6
Vildbjerg 1,500 .... B5
Vinderup 2,284 .... B5
Vojens 5,595 .... C7
Vorbasse 791 .... B6
Vordingborg 11,639 .... E7
Vraå 2,652 .... C3

OTHER FEATURES

AErø (isl.) D8
Als (isl.) C8
Amager (isl.) F6
Anholt (isl.) E4
Årø (isl.) C7
Baågø (isl.) C7
Baltic (sea) E9
Bornholm (isl.) F9
Endelave (isl.) D6
Falster (isl.) F8
Fanø (isl.) B7
Fehmarn (str.) E8
Fejø (isl.) E8
Femø (isl.) E8
Frisian, North (isls.) B7
Fyn (isl.) D7
Gelsaå (riv.) C7
Gudenaå (riv.) C5
Isefjord (fjord) E6
Jutland (pen.) C5
Jylland (Jutland) (pen.) C5
Kattegat (str.) E4
Laesø (isl.) D3
Langeland (isl.) D8
Lille Baelt (chan.) C7
Limfjorden (fjord) A4
Løgstør Bredning (fjord) C4
Lolland (isl.) E8
Møn (isl.) F8
Mors (isl.) B4
North (sea) B9
North Frisian (isls.) B7
Omø (isl.) E7
Øresund (sound) F6
Rømø (isl.) B7
Samsø (isl.) D6
Sejerø (isl.) E6
Sjaelland (isl.) E6
Skagens Odde (cape) D2
Skagerrak (str.) C2
Skaw, The (Skagens Odde) (cape) D2
Storaå (riv.) B5
Store Baelt (chan.) D6
Susaå (riv.) E7
The Skaw (Skagens Odde) (cape) D2
Tranebjerg (mt.) C6
Yding Skovhøj (mt.) C6

FAEROE ISLANDS

CITIES and TOWNS

Klaksvík 4,536 .... B2
Tórshavn (cap.), Faerøe Is., 11,618 .... A3

OTHER FEATURES

Faerøe (isls.) B2
Sandoy (isl.) B3
Streymoy (isl.) B3
Sudhuroy (isl.) B3

ICELAND

CITIES and TOWNS

Akranes 4,253 .... B1
Akureyri 10,755 .... C1
Hafnarfjördhur 9,696 .... B2
Húsavík 1,993 .... C1
Ísafjördhur 2,680 .... B1
Keflavík 5,663 .... B1
Kópavogur 11,165 .... B1
Nes (Neskaupstadhur) 1,552 .... D1
Neskaupstadhur 1,552 .... D1
Ólafsfjördhur 1,086 .... C1
Reykjavík (cap.) 81,693 .... B1
Reykjavík* 98,521 70
Saudhárkrókur 1,600 .... B1
Seydhisfjördhur 884 .... D1
Siglufjördhur 2,161 .... C1
Vestmannaeyjar 5,186 .... B2

OTHER FEATURES

Bjargtangar (pt.) A1
Breidhafjördhur (fjord) B1
Faxaflói (bay) B1
Fontur (pt.) D1
Gerpir (cape) D1
Grímsey (isl.) C1
Hekla (vol.) B1
Horn (cape) B1
Húnaflói (bay) B1
Hvannadalshnúkur (mt.) C1
North (Horn) (cape) B1
Reykjanestá (cape) A2
Surtsey (isl.) B2
Thjórsá (riv.) C1
Vatnajökull (glac.) C1

*City and suburbs.

Germany
CONIC PROJECTION
SCALE OF MILES
0 20 40 60 80
SCALE OF KILOMETERS
0 20 40 60 80
Capitals of Countries
State Capitals
International Boundaries
State Boundaries
Canals
Scale 1:3,040,000
Longitude East 10° of Greenwich
DENMARK
BALTIC SEA
NORTH SEA
NORTH FRISIAN ISLANDS
EAST FRISIAN ISLANDS
WEST FRISIAN ISLANDS
NETHERLANDS
BELGIUM
LUXEMBOURG
FRANCE
SWITZERLAND
AUSTRIA
CZECHOSLOVAKIA
POLAND
SCHLESWIG-HOLSTEIN
MECKLENBURG
POMERANIA
LOWER SAXONY
BRANDENBURG
NORTH RHINE-WESTPHALIA
HESSE
THURINGIA
SAXONY
RHINELAND-PALATINATE
SAARLAND
BADEN-WÜRTTEMBERG
BAVARIA
BREMEN
HAMBURG
BERLIN
Kiel
Hamburg
Bremen
Hannover
Magdeburg
Potsdam
Schwerin
Rostock
Lübeck
Düsseldorf
Cologne
Bonn
Wiesbaden
Frankfurt
Mainz
Saarbrücken
Stuttgart
Munich (München)
Nürnberg
Dresden
Leipzig
Erfurt
Kassel
Regensburg
Augsburg
Berlin
Kiel Bay
Mecklenburg Bay
Pomeranian Bay
Helgoland Bay
Lüneburger Heide
Altmark
Harz
Thüringer Wald
Erzgebirge
Fichtelgebirge
Bohemian Forest
Bavarian Forest
Black Forest (Schwarzwald)
Swabian Jura
Franconian Jura
Bavarian Alps
Allgäu Alps
Oberpfälzer Wald
Spessart
Odenwald
Taunus
Westerwald
Hunsrück
Eifel
Teutoburger Wald
Sauerland
Spreewald
Rhön
Vogelsberg
L. of Constance (Bodensee)
Rhine
Elbe
Danube
Weser
Oder
Main
Zugspitze 9,718 ft. (2962 m.)
© Copyright HAMMOND INCORPORATED, Maplewood, N. J.

AREA 137,753 sq. mi. (356,780 sq. km.)
POPULATION 78,395,000
CAPITAL Berlin
LARGEST CITY Berlin
HIGHEST POINT Zugspitze 9,718 ft. (2,962 m.)
MONETARY UNIT Deutsche mark
MAJOR LANGUAGE German
MAJOR RELIGIONS Protestantism, Roman Catholicism

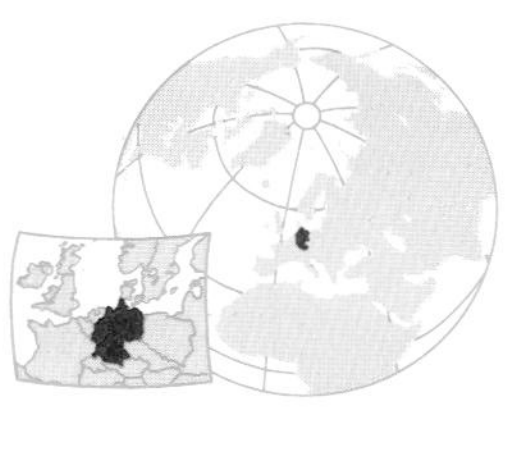

GERMANY

Topography

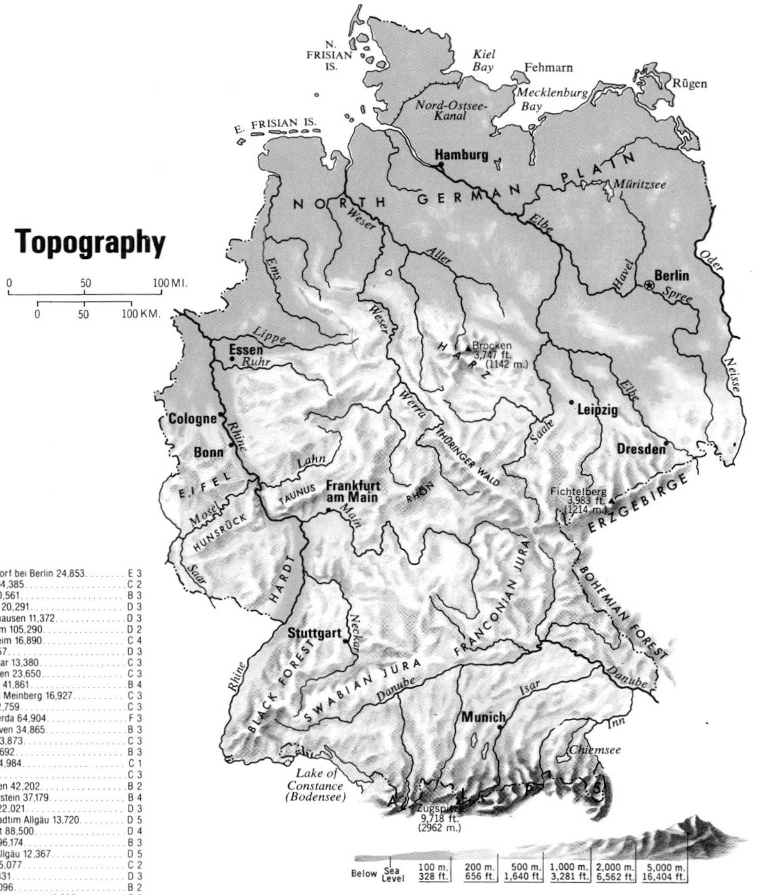

GERMANY

STATES

Baden-Württemberg 9,152,700 C 4
Bavaria 10,810,400 D 4
Berlin 3,078,984 E-F 4
Bremen 716,800 C 2
Hamburg 1,717,400 D 2
Hesse 5,549,800 C 3
Lower Saxony 7,238,500 C 2
North Rhine-Westphalia 17,129,600 B 3
Rhineland-Palatinate 3,665,800 B 4
Saarland 1,096,300 B 4
Schleswig-Holstein 2,582,400 C 1

East German States 15,611,488 D-E 2, 3

CITIES and TOWNS

Aachen 242,453 B 3
Aalen 64,735 D 4
Ahaus 27,126 B 2
Ahlen 54,214 B 3
Ahrensburg 24,964 D 2
Aken 11,742 D 3
Alfeld 24,273 C 2
Alsdorf 47,473 B 3
Alsfeld 18,091 C 3
Altena 26,753 B 3
Altenburg 51,193 E 3
Altona C 2
Alzey 15,190 C 4
Amberg 46,934 D 4
Andernach 27,132 B 3
Angermünde 11,786 E 2
Anklam 19,099 E 2
Annaberg-Buchholz 26,561 E 3
Ansbach 39,117 D 4
Apolda 28,649 D 3
Arnsberg 80,287 C 3
Arnstadt 29,462 D 3
Arolsen 15,619 C 3
Aschaffenburg 55,398 C 4
Aschersleben 36,674 D 3
Aue 32,622 E 3
Auerbach 18,168 E 3
Augsburg 249,943 D 4
Aurich 34,194 B 2
Backnang 29,614 C 4
Bad Berleburg 20,415 C 3
Bad Doberan 12,541 D 1
Bad Driburg 17,478 C 3
Bad Dürkheim 16,133 C 4
Bad Dürrenberg 15,192 D 3
Bad Ems 10,487 B 3
Baden-Baden 49,718 C 4
Badenweiler 3,720 B 5
Bad Gandersheim 11,614 D 3
Bad Harzburg 25,786 D 3
Bad Hersfeld 29,248 C 3
Bad Homburg vor der Höhe 51,196 C 3
Bad Honnef 20,903 B 3
Bad Kissingen 22,279 D 3
Bad Kreuznach 42,588 B 4
Bad Langensalza 166,282 D 3
Bad Lauterberg im Harz 14,715 D 3
Bad Mergentheim 19,895 C 4
Bad Münstereifel 14,340 B 3
Bad Nauheim 25,916 C 3
Bad Neuenahr-Ahrweiler 26,371 B 3
Bad Oldesloe 19,640 D 2
Bad Pyrmont 21,896 C 3
Bad Reichenhall 13,048 E 5
Bad Salzuflen 50,924 C 2
Bad Salzungen 17,277 C 3
Bad Schwartau 18,696 D 2
Bad Segeberg 13,320 D 2
Bad Tölz 12,458 D 5
Bad Vilbel 25,012 C 3
Bad Waldsee 14,296 C 5
Bad Wildungen 15,418 C 3
Bad Wimpfen 5,536 C 4
Baiersbronn 14,845 C 4
Balingen 29,310 C 4
Bamberg 74,236 D 4
Barsinghausen 32,873 C 2
Barth 12,069 E 1
Bassum 14,113 C 2
Bautzen 45,851 F 3
Bayreuth 67,035 D 4
Bayrischzell 1,639 E 5
Bebra 15,740 C 3
Bendorf 15,943 B 3
Bensheim 32,653 C 4
Bentheim 13,681 B 2
Berchtesgaden 8,558 E 5
Bergen 13,244 E 1
Bergisch Gladbach 99,517 B 3
Berleburg (Bad Berleburg) 20,415 C 3
Berlin (cap.) 3,078,984 E-F 4
Bernau bei Berlin 15,749 E 2
Bernburg 44,428 D 3
Biberach an der Riss 28,891 C 4
Bielefeld 316,058 C 2
Bietigheim-Bissingen 34,042 C 4
Bingen 24,541 B 4
Birkenfeld 5,883 B 4
Bischofswerda 11,540 F 3
Bitburg 10,591 B 4
Bitterfeld 27,062 E 3
Blankenburg am Harz 18,784 D 3
Blaubeuren 11,652 C 4
Böblingen 40,547 C 4
Bocholt 65,460 B 3
Bochum 414,842 B 3
Boizenburg an der Elbe 12,428 D 2
Bonn 283,711 B 3
Boppard 16,888 B 3
Borghorst 17,238 B 2
Borken 30,212 B 3
Borna 21,807 E 3
Bornheim 32,847 B 3
Bottrop 101,495 B 3
Brake 18,089 C 2
Bramsche 24,119 B 2
Brandenburg 94,071 E 2
Braunschweig 268,519 D 2
Breisach am Rhein 9,230 B 4
Bremen 572,969 C 2
Bremerhaven 143,836 C 2
Bremervörde 17,565 C 2
Bretten 22,140 C 4
Brilon 24,595 C 3
Brühl 44,305 B 3
Bruchsal 38,929 C 4
Brunsbüttel 11,451 C 2
Brunswick (Braunschweig) 268,519 D 2
Buchholz in der Nordheide 25,713 C 2
Bückeburg 21,393 C 2
Büdingen 16,845 C 3
Bühl 21,596 C 4
Bünde 40,021 C 2
Büren 17,352 C 3
Burg auf Fehmarn 5,874 D 1
Burg bei Magdeburg 29,027 D 2
Burghausen 16,892 E 4
Burgsteinfurt 31,367 B 2
Butzbach 20,592 C 3
Buxtehude 30,249 C 2
Calbe 15,976 D 3
Castrop-Rauxel 82,373 B 3
Celle 74,347 D 2
Cham 12,423 E 4
Charlottenburg E 4
Chemnitz 303,811 E 3
Clausthal-Zellerfeld 16,690 D 3
Cloppenburg 19,757 B 2
Coburg 46,244 D 3
Coesfeld 30,617 B 3
Cologne 1,013,771 B 3
Coswig, Dresden 22,149 E 3
Coswig, Halle 12,473 E 3
Cottbus 94,293 F 3
Crailsheim 24,506 D 4
Crimmitschau 28,845 E 3
Cuxhaven 60,353 C 2
Dachau 33,207 D 4
Dahlem E 4
Darmstadt 137,018 C 4
Deggendorf 25,188 E 4
Delitzsch 24,076 E 3
Delmenhorst 71,488 C 2
Demmin 17,270 E 2
Dessau 100,820 E 3
Detmold 65,629 C 3
Diepholz 14,201 C 2
Dillenburg 14,068 C 3
Dillingen 21,369 B 4
Dillingen an der Donau 11,601 D 4
Dingolfing 13,325 E 4
Dinkelsbühl 10,034 D 4
Döbeln 27,624 E 3
Donaueschingen 17,578 C 5
Donauwörth 17,077 D 4
Dorsten 65,718 B 3
Dortmund 630,609 B 3
Dresden 507,692 E 3
Duderstadt 23,255 D 3
Dudweiler B 4
Duisburg 591,635 B 3
Dülmen 37,013 B 3
Düren 87,774 B 3
Düsseldorf 664,336 B 3
Eberbach 15,834 C 4
Ebersbach 12,694 F 3
Eberswalde-Finow 47,141 E 2
Ebingen 22,594 C 4
Eckernförde 22,938 C 1
Ehingen 21,600 C 4
Eichstätt 13,080 D 4
Eilenburg 22,245 E 3
Einbeck 29,821 C 3
Eisenach 49,954 D 3
Eisenberg 13,450 D 3
Eisenhüttenstadt 46,455 F 2
Eiserfeld C 3
Eisleben 29,297 D 3
Ellwangen 21,994 D 4
Elmshorn 41,355 C 2
Emden 53,509 B 2
Emmendingen 24,722 B 4
Emmerich 29,113 B 3
Emsdetten 30,195 B 2
Erfurt 202,979 D 3
Erlangen 100,671 D 4
Eschwege 24,882 C 3
Eschweiler 53,603 B 3
Espelkamp 22,670 C 2
Essen 677,568 B 3
Esslingen am Neckar 95,298 C 4
Ettlingen 35,159 C 4
Euskirchen 43,558 B 3
Eutin 17,701 D 1
Falkensee 25,295 E 3
Falkenstein 14,367 E 3
Fellbach 42,501 C 4
Finsterwalde 22,466 E 3
Flensburg 93,213 C 1
Forchheim 23,430 D 4
Forst 28,084 F 3
Frankenberg-Eder 15,337 C 3
Frankenthal 43,684 C 4
Frankfurt am Main 636,157 C 3
Frankfurt an der Oder 70,817 F 2
Frechen 41,453 B 3
Freiberg 50,815 E 3
Freiburg im Breisgau 175,371 B 5
Freising 31,524 D 4
Freital 46,061 E 3
Freudenstadt 19,454 C 4
Friedberg 24,762 C 3
Friedland E 2
Friedrichshafen 51,544 C 5
Friedrichstadt 2,859 C 1
Fritzlar 15,079 C 3
Fulda 58,976 C 3
Fürstenfeldbruck 27,194 D 4
Fürstenwalde 31,065 F 2
Fürth 101,639 D 4
Füssen 10,506 D 5
Gadebusch D 2
Gaggenau 28,846 C 4
Garbsen 56,337 C 2
Gardelegen 12,987 D 2
Garmisch-Partenkirchen 26,831 D 5
Gatow E 4
Geesthacht 24,745 D 2
Geislingen an der Steige 28,693 C 4
Geldern 24,082 B 3
Gelnhausen 17,889 C 3
Gelsenkirchen 322,584 B 3
Genthin 15,916 E 2
Georgsmarienhütte 30,259 B 2
Gera 113,108 E 3
Geretsried 17,330 D 5
Germersheim 12,041 C 4
Gerolstein 6,857 B 3
Gifhorn 31,635 D 2
Glauchau 30,927 E 3
Glückstadt 12,159 C 2
Goch 28,213 B 3
Göggingen D 4
Göppingen 54,365 C 4
Görlitz 84,658 F 3
Goslar 53,957 D 3
Gotha 59,243 D 3
Göttingen 123,797 D 3
Greifswald 53,940 E 1
Greiz 37,612 E 3
Greven 27,479 B 2
Grevenbroich 56,392 B 3
Grevesmühlen 12,005 D 2
Griesheim 18,548 C 4
Grimma 17,100 E 3
Grimmen 14,571 E 1
Gronau 40,527 B 2
Grossenhain 18,712 E 3
Grossräschen 12,889 E 3
Guben (Wilhelm-Pieck-Stadt) 32,731 F 3
Gummersbach 49,316 B 3
Günzburg 13,528 D 4
Gunzenhausen 13,565 D 4
Güstrow 36,824 E 2
Gütersloh 77,128 C 3
Haar 18,824 D 4
Hagen 229,224 B 3
Halberstadt 46,669 D 3
Haldensleben 19,194 D 2
Halle 241,425 D 3
Halle-Neustadt 67,956 D 3
Haltern 29,750 B 3
Hamburg 1,717,383 D 2
Hameln 61,066 C 2
Hamm 172,210 B 3
Hammelburg 12,350 C 3
Hanau 86,676 C 3
Hannover 552,955 C 2
Harburg-Wilhelmsburg C 2
Hassloch 17,752 C 4
Haunstetten D 4
Havelberg D 2
Hechingen 15,926 C 4
Heide 21,918 C 1
Heidelberg 129,368 C 4
Heidenau 21,315 E 3
Heidenheim an der Brenz 49,943 D 4
Heilbronn 113,177 C 4
Heiligenstadt 13,931 D 3
Helmstedt 28,095 D 2
Hennef 27,815 B 3
Hennigsdorf bei Berlin 24,853 E 3
Herford 64,385 C 2
Herne 190,561 B 3
Hettstedt 20,291 D 3
Hildburghausen 11,372 D 3
Hildesheim 105,290 D 2
Hockenheim 16,890 C 4
Hof 54,357 D 3
Hofgeismar 13,380 C 3
Holzminden 23,650 C 3
Homburg 41,861 B 4
Horn-Bad Meinberg 16,927 C 3
Höxter 32,759 C 3
Hoyerswerda 64,904 F 3
Hückelhoven 34,865 B 3
Hünfeld 13,873 C 3
Hürth 51,692 B 3
Husum 24,984 C 1
Hüttental C 3
Ibbenbüren 42,202 B 2
Idar-Oberstein 37,179 B 4
Ilmenau 22,021 D 3
Immenstadtim Allgäu 13,720 D 5
Ingolstadt 88,500 D 4
Iserlohn 96,174 B 3
Isny im Allgäu 12,367 D 5
Itzehoe 35,077 C 2
Jena 99,431 D 3
Jever 12,096 B 2
Johanngeorgenstadt 10,328 E 3
Jülich 31,564 B 3
Jüterbog 13,477 E 3
Kaiserslautern 100,886 B 4
Kamenz 18,221 F 3
Karlsruhe 280,448 C 4
Kassel 205,534 C 3
Kaufbeuren 42,224 D 5
Kehl 29,861 B 4
Kelheim 11,996 D 4
Kempten 56,944 D 5
Kevelaer 20,971 B 3
Kiel 262,164 D 1
Kirchheim unter Teck 31,666 C 4
Kitzingen 19,116 C 4
Kleinmachnow 14,059 E 4
Klingenthal 13,614 E 3
Koblenz 118,394 B 3
Köln (Cologne) 1,013,771 B 3
Königs Wusterhausen 11,825 E 2
Königswinter 34,586 B 3
Konstanz 70,152 C 5
Köpenick 130,987 F 4
Korbach 22,998 C 3
Kornwestheim 27,771 C 4
Köthen 35,451 E 3
Krefeld 228,463 B 3
Kreuztal 30,473 C 3
Kronach 11,538 D 3
Kühlungsborn D 1
Kulmbach 25,711 D 3
Lage 31,724 C 3
Lahnstein 19,725 B 3
Lahr 35,570 B 4
Lampertheim 31,993 C 4
Landau in der Pfalz 37,661 C 4
Landsberg am Lech 15,862 D 4
Landshut 55,858 E 4
Langen 30,227 C 4
Langenhagen 47,092 C 2
Lauchhammer 26,939 E 3
Lauenburg an der Elbe 11,077 D 2
Lauf an der Pegnitz 19,443 D 4
Läuingen 8,778 D 4
Lauterbach 15,007 C 3
Leer 32,785 B 2
Lehrte 38,272 D 2
Leipzig 570,972 E 3
Lemgo 39,664 C 2
Lengerich 20,836 B 2
Leverkusen 165,947 B 3
Lichtenberg 192,063 F 4
Lichtenfels 13,719 D 3
Limbach-Oberfrohna 25,706 E 3
Limburg an der Lahn 28,606 C 3
Lindau 23,930 C 5
Lingen 43,785 B 2
Lippstadt 63,040 C 3
Löbau 18,077 F 3
Löhne 17,859 C 2
Lobenstein D 3
Lohr am Main 16,435 C 5
Lörrach 44,179 B 5
Lübben 14,224 E 3
Lübbenau 22,350 F 3
Lübeck 232,270 D 2
Luckau E 3
Luckenwalde 28,544 E 2
Lüdenscheid 76,213 B 3
Ludwigsburg 83,622 C 5
Ludwigshafen am Rhein 170,374 C 5
Ludwigslust 13,280 D 2
Lüneburg 64,586 D 2
Lünen 85,685 B 3
Magdeburg 276,089 D 2
Mainz 183,880 C 5
Mannheim 314,086 C 5
Marbach am Neckar 12,131 C 5
Marburg an der Lahn 72,458 C 3
Markkleeberg 22,380 E 3
Marktredwitz 16,404 E 5
Marl 91,930 B 3
Mayen 21,018 B 3
Mechernich 21,498 B 3
Meerane 25,037 E 3
Meiningen 26,134 D 3
Meissen 43,561 E 3
Melle 41,339 C 2
Melsungen 13,444 C 3
Memmingen 34,612 D 5
Meppen 27,308 B 2
Merseburg 54,269 D 3
Merzig 30,197 B 5
Meschede 32,472 C 3
Metzingen 19,224 C 5
Meuselwitz 13,585 E 3
Michelstadt 13,591 C 5
Minden 78,887 C 2
Mittenwald 8,831 D 5
Mittweida 19,259 E 3
Mölln 15,780 D 2
Mönchengladbach 261,367 B 3
Moosburg an der Isar 12,196 D 5
Mosbach 23,663 C 5
Mühldorf am Inn 12,638 E 5
Mülhausen (Thomas-Münzer-Stadt) 44,106 D 3
Mülheim an der Ruhr 189,259 B 3
Müllheim 12,183 B 5
München (Munich) 1,314,865 D 5
Münden 27,018 C 3
Munich 1,314,865 D 5
Münster 264,546 B 3
Nagold 19,047 C 5
Nauen 11,940 E 2
Naumburg 36,358 D 3
Neckarsulm 20,112 C 5
Neheim-Hüsten 36,373 C 3
Neubrandenburg 59,971 E 2
Neuburg an der Donau 19,400 D 5
Neuenhagen bei Berlin 12,603 F 5
Neu-Isenburg 35,631 C 3
Neumarkt in der Oberpfalz 29,713 D 5
Neumünster 84,777 C 1
Neunkirchen 54,992 B 5
Neuruppin 24,888 E 2
Neuss 148,198 B 3
Neustadt an der Weinstrasse 51,011 B 5
Neustadt bei Coburg 12,665 D 3
Neustadt in Holstein 15,333 D 1
Neustrelitz 27,074 E 2
Neu-Ulm 31,660 D 5
Neuwied 62,029 B 3
Nienburg 30,978 C 2
Norden 24,207 B 2
Nordenham 31,457 C 2
Norderstedt 61,553 D 2
Nordhausen 44,442 D 3
Nordhorn 49,598 B 2
Nördlingen 16,480 D 5
Northeim 32,665 C 3
Nuremberg 499,060 D 5
Nürnberg (Nuremberg) 499,060 D 5
Nürtingen 34,333 C 5
Oberammergau 4,704 D 5
Oberhausen 237,147 B 3
Oberstdorf 11,687 D 5
Oberursel 39,802 C 3
Oelsnitz 15,084 E 3
Oelsnitz im Erzgebirge 16,063 E 3
Offenbach am Main 115,251 C 3
Offenburg 51,553 B 5
Olbernhau 13,479 E 3
Oldenburg 134,706 C 2
Oldenburg in Holstein 9,201 D 1
Opladen B 3
Oranienburg 24,452 E 2
Oschatz 18,974 E 3
Oschersleben 17,377 D 2
Osnabrück 161,671 C 2
Osterholz-Scharmbeck 22,734 C 2
Osterode am Harz 29,668 D 3
Paderborn 103,705 C 3
Pankow 136,527 F 3
Papenburg 27,039 B 2
Parchim 22,927 D 2
Pasewalk 15,099 F 2
Passau 50,920 E 5
Peenemünde E 1
Peine 49,450 D 2
Perleberg 15,029 D 2
Pfaffenhofen an der Ilm 13,684 D 5
Pforzheim 108,635 C 5
Pinneberg 36,844 C 2
Pirmasens 53,651 B 5
Pirna 49,771 E 3
Plauen 80,353 E 3
Plettenberg 29,273 C 3
Pössneck 18,648 D 3
Porz am Rhein B 3
Potsdam 117,236 E 2
Preetz 15,305 D 1
Prenzlau 22,738 E 2
Pritzwalk 11,887 E 2
Puttgarden D 1
Quedlinburg 29,796 D 3
Radeberg 18,528 E 3
Radebeul 38,383 E 3
Radolfzell 23,274 C 5

(continued on following page)

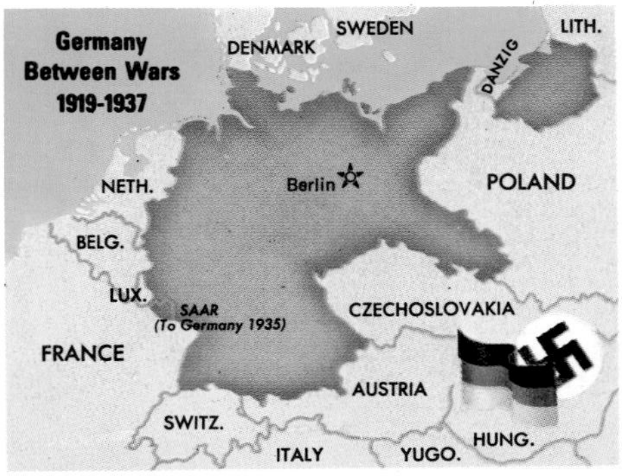

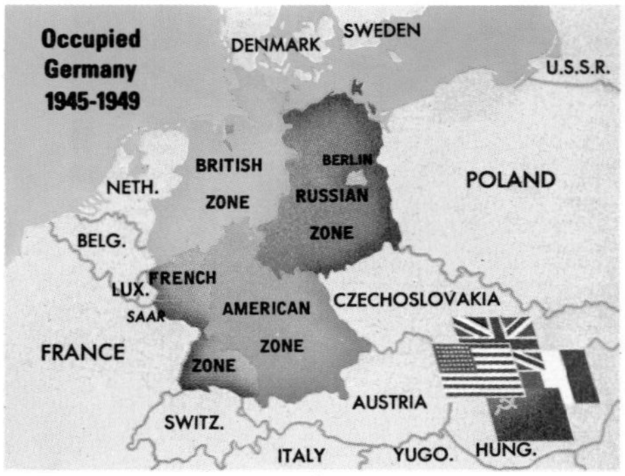

Rastatt 38,030 . . . . . C 4
Rastede 16,905 . . . . . C 2
Rathenow 32,011 . . . . . E 2
Ratingen 86,028 . . . . . B 3
Ratzeburg 12,189 . . . . . D 2
Ravensburg 42,725 . . . . . C 5
Recklinghausen 122,437 . . . . . B 3
Regensburg 131,886 . . . . . E 4
Reichenbach 27,440 . . . . . E 3
Remagen 14,627 . . . . . B 3
Remscheid 133,145 . . . . . B 3
Rendsburg 34,407 . . . . . C 1
Reutlingen 95,289 . . . . . C 4
Rheda-Wiedenbrück 37,371 . . . . . C 3
Rheine 71,539 . . . . . B 2
Rheinfelden 27,500 . . . . . B 5
Ribnitz-Damgarten 17,254 . . . . . E 1
Riesa 49,989 . . . . . E 3
Rietberg 22,421 . . . . . C 3
Rinteln 25,595 . . . . . C 2
Rosenheim 38,419 . . . . . D 5
Rosslau 16,520 . . . . . E 3
Rostock 210,167 . . . . . E 1
Rotenburg 19,155 . . . . . C 2
Rotenburg an der Fulda 14,438 . . . . . C 3
Roth bei Nürnberg 17,782 . . . . . D 4
Rothenburg ob der
Tauber 11,609 . . . . . D 4
Rottenburg am
Neckar 30,583 . . . . . C 4
Rottweil 24,534 . . . . . C 4
Rudolstadt 31,698 . . . . . D 3
Rüsselsheim 62,067 . . . . . C 4
Säckingen 13,956 . . . . . C 5
Saalfeld 33,648 . . . . . D 3
Saarbrücken 205,336 . . . . . B 4
Saarlouis 39,974 . . . . . B 4
Salzgitter 117,341 . . . . . D 2
Salzwedel 21,741 . . . . . D 2
Sangerhausen 32,721 . . . . . D 3
Sankt Goar 3,511 . . . . . B 3
Sankt Ingbert 43,263 . . . . . B 4
Sankt Wendel 27,558 . . . . . B 4
Sassnitz 13,857 . . . . . E 1
Saulgau 15,403 . . . . . C 5
Schkeuditz 15,585 . . . . . E 3
Schleswig 30,974 . . . . . C 1
Schlüchtern 13,801 . . . . . C 3
Schmalkalden 15,017 . . . . . D 3
Schmölln 13,406 . . . . . E 3
Schneeberg 20,376 . . . . . E 3
Schönebeck 45,197 . . . . . D 2
Schöneberg 169,835 . . . . . E 4
Schöningen 16,348 . . . . . D 2
Schramberg 19,677 . . . . . C 4
Schwabach 33,136 . . . . . D 4
Schwäbisch Gmünd 56,422 . . . . . C 4
Schwäbisch Hall 32,129 . . . . . C 4
Schwalmstadt 17,800 . . . . . C 3
Schwandorf im Bayern 22,547 . . . . . E 4
Schwedt 45,729 . . . . . F 2
Schweinfurt 56,164 . . . . . D 3
Schwelm 31,850 . . . . . B 3
Schwerin 104,984 . . . . . D 2
Schwetzingen 18,286 . . . . . C 4
Sebnitz 13,470 . . . . . F 3
Seesen 23,577 . . . . . D 3
Selb 16,723 . . . . . E 3
Senftenberg 29,953 . . . . . F 3
Sennestadt . . . . . C 3
Siegburg 34,943 . . . . . B 3
Siegen 116,552 . . . . . C 3
Sigmaringen 15,437 . . . . . C 4
Sindelfingen 54,134 . . . . . C 4
Singen 45,566 . . . . . C 5
Soest 40,308 . . . . . C 3
Solingen 171,810 . . . . . B 3
Soltau 19,949 . . . . . C 2
Sömmerda 20,712 . . . . . D.3
Sondershausen 23,383 . . . . . D 3
Sonneberg 29,193 . . . . . D 3
Sonthofen 17,821 . . . . . D 5
Spandau . . . . . E 3
Speyer 44,471 . . . . . C 4
Spremberg 22,862 . . . . . F 3
Springe 30,968 . . . . . C 2
Stade 42,097 . . . . . C 2
Stadthagen 23,003 . . . . . C 2
Stassfurt 26,225 . . . . . D 3
Stendal 39,647 . . . . . D 2
Stolberg 57,379 . . . . . B 3
Stralsund 72,167 . . . . . E 1
Straubing 43,774 . . . . . E 4
Strausberg 21,334 . . . . . F 2
Stuttgart 600,421 . . . . . C 4
Suhl 36,642 . . . . . D 3
Sulzbach 22,133 . . . . . B 4
Sulzbach-Rosenberg 18,596 . . . . . D 4
Tailfingen 17,278 . . . . . C 4
Tangermünde 12,898 . . . . . D 2
Tegel . . . . . E 3
Telgte 15,165 . . . . . B 3
Teltow 16,171 . . . . . E 4
Tempelhof . . . . . F 4
Templin 11,718 . . . . . E 2
Thale 17,248 . . . . . D 3
Thomas-Müntzer-Stadt 44,106 . . . . . D 3
Timmendorfer Strand 10,690 . . . . . D 1
Torgau 21,613 . . . . . E 3
Torgelow 14,320 . . . . . F 2
Traunstein 14,088 . . . . . E 5
Treptow 127,448 . . . . . F 4
Treuchtlingen 11,939 . . . . . D 4
Trier 100,338 . . . . . B 4
Troisdorf 56,402 . . . . . B 3
Tübingen 71,348 . . . . . C 4
Tuttlingen 32,342 . . . . . C 5
Übach-Palenberg 22,403 . . . . . B 3
Überlingen 17,735 . . . . . C 5
Ueckermünde 11,423 . . . . . F 2
Uelzen 37,550 . . . . . D 2
Uetersen 16,330 . . . . . C 2
Ulm 98,237 . . . . . C 4
Uslar 17,251 . . . . . C 3
Varel 24,435 . . . . . C 2
Vechta 21,786 . . . . . C 2
Verden 24,247 . . . . . C 2
Viersen 84,220 . . . . . B 3
Villingen-Schwenningen 80,646 . . . . . C 4
Vöklingen 47,271 . . . . . B 4
Waldheim 11,925 . . . . . E 3
Waldkirch 19,009 . . . . . B 4
Waldkraiburg 20,140 . . . . . E 4
Waldshut-Tiengen 22,046 . . . . . C 5
Walsrode 23,423 . . . . . C 2
Waltershausen 13,893 . . . . . D 3
Wangen im Allgäu 23,127 . . . . . C 5
Warburg 22,150 . . . . . C 3
Waren 22,921 . . . . . E 2
Warendorf 32,273 . . . . . B 3
Wedel 30,045 . . . . . C 2
Weida 11,816 . . . . . D 3
Weiden in der Oberpfalz 42,697 . . . . . D 4
Weilburg 12,652 . . . . . C 3
Weilheim im Oberbayern 15,347 . . . . . D 5
Weimar 63,144 . . . . . D 3
Weingarten 21,143 . . . . . C 5
Weinheim 41,005 . . . . . C 4
Weisenburg im Bayern 16,083 . . . . . D 4
Weissenfels 43,191 . . . . . D 3
Weissensee 78,451 . . . . . F 3
Weisswasser 25,910 . . . . . F 3
Werdau 22,249 . . . . . E 3
Wernigerode 34,658 . . . . . D 3
Wertheim 20,942 . . . . . C 4
Wesel 56,584 . . . . . B 3
Westerland 9,652 . . . . . C 1
Westerstede 16,977 . . . . . B 2
Wiehl 19,004 . . . . . B 3
Wiesbaden 250,592 . . . . . B 3
Wildbad im Schwarzwald 11,611 . . . . . C 4
Wildeshausen 12,055 . . . . . C 2
Wilhelm-Pieck-Stadt 32,731 . . . . . F 3
Wilhelmshaven 103,417 . . . . . B 2
Wismar 56,765 . . . . . D 2
Witten 108,771 . . . . . B 3
Wittenberg 51,364 . . . . . E 3
Wittenberge 32,907 . . . . . D 2
Wittingen 12,189 . . . . . D 2
Wittlich 15,321 . . . . . B 3
Witzenhausen 16,877 . . . . . C 3
Wolfen 27,570 . . . . . E 3
Wolfenbüttel 51,386 . . . . . D 2
Wolfsburg 126,298 . . . . . D 2
Wolgast 16,384 . . . . . E 1
Worms 75,732 . . . . . C 4
Wunstorf 36,795 . . . . . C 2
Wuppertal 405,369 . . . . . B 3
Würzburg 112,584 . . . . . C 4
Wurzen 20,501 . . . . . E 3
Xanten 15,688 . . . . . B 3
Zehdenick 12,651 . . . . . E 2
Zeitz 44,582 . . . . . E 3
Zella-Mehlis 16,301 . . . . . D 3
Zerbst 19,356 . . . . . E 3
Zeulenroda 13,452 . . . . . D 3
Zirndorf 13,661 . . . . . D 4
Zittau 42,298 . . . . . F 3
Zülpich 16,171 . . . . . B 3
Zweibrücken 35,978 . . . . . B 4
Zwickau 123,069 . . . . . E 3
Zwischenahn 22,581 . . . . . B 2

OTHER FEATURES

Aller (riv.) . . . . . C 2
Allgäu (reg.) . . . . . D 5
Altmark 267,229 (reg.) . . . . . D 2
Altmühl (riv.) . . . . . D 4
Ammersee (lake) . . . . . D 4
Amrum (isl.) . . . . . C 1
Arkona (cape) . . . . . E 1
Baltic (sea) . . . . . E 1
Baltrum 661 (isl.) . . . . . B 2
Bavarian (for.) . . . . . E 4
Bavarian Alps (range) . . . . . D 5
Bayerischer Wald Nat'l Park . . . . . E 4
Black (for.) . . . . . C 4
Black Elster (riv.) . . . . . E 3
Bodensee (Constance) (lake) . . . . . C 5
Bohemian (for.) . . . . . E 4
Borkum 8,495 (isl.) . . . . . B 2
Brandenburg 7,130,055 (reg.) . . . . . E 2
Breisgau (reg.) . . . . . B 5
Chiemsee (lake) . . . . . E 5
Constance (lake) . . . . . C 5
Danube (riv.) . . . . . C 4
Donau (Danube) (riv.) . . . . . C 4
East Friesland (reg.) . . . . . B 2
East Frisian (isls.) . . . . . B 2
Eder (res.) . . . . . C 3
Elbe (riv.) . . . . . C-D 2
Elde (riv.) . . . . . D 2
Elster, Black (riv.) . . . . . E 3
Elster, White (riv.) . . . . . E 3
Ems (riv.) . . . . . B 2
Erzgebirge (mts.) . . . . . E 3
Fehmarn 12,455 (isl.) . . . . . D 1
Feldberg (mt.) . . . . . C 5
Fichtelberg (mt.) . . . . . E 3
Fichtelgebirge (range) . . . . . D 3
Föhr (isl.) . . . . . C 1
Franconian Jura (range) . . . . . D 4
Frisian, East (isls.) . . . . . B 2
Frisian, North (isls.) . . . . . B 1
Grosser Arber (mt.) . . . . . E 4
Halligen (isls.) . . . . . C 1
Hardt (mts.) . . . . . C 4
Harz (mts.) . . . . . D 3
Hase (riv.) . . . . . B 2
Havel (riv.) . . . . . E 2
Hegau (reg.) . . . . . C 5
Helgoland (bay) . . . . . C 1
Helgoland 2,377 (isl.) . . . . . B 1
Hunsrück (mts.) . . . . . B 4
Hunte (riv.) . . . . . C 2
Iller (riv.) . . . . . D 4
Inn (riv.) . . . . . E 4
Isar (riv.) . . . . . E 4
Juist 2,228 (isl.) . . . . . B 2
Kaiserstuhl (mt.) . . . . . B 4
Kiel (bay) . . . . . D 1
Kiel (Nord-Ostsee) (canal) . . . . . C 1
Königssee (lake) . . . . . E 5
Lahn (riv.) . . . . . C 3
Langeoog 2,535 (isl.) . . . . . B 2
Lech (riv.) . . . . . D 4
Leine (riv.) . . . . . C 2
Lippe (riv.) . . . . . C 3
Lüneburger Heide (dist.) . . . . . C 2
Lusatia 594,784 (reg.) . . . . . F 3
Main (riv.) . . . . . C 4
Mecklenburg (bay) . . . . . D 1
Meckienburg 1,925,669 (reg.) . . . . . E 2
Mosel (riv.) . . . . . B 3
Mulde (riv.) . . . . . E 3
Naab (riv.) . . . . . E 4
Neckar (riv.) . . . . . C 4
Neisse (riv.) . . . . . F 3
Nord-Ostsee (canal) . . . . . C 1
Norderney 8,307 (isl.) . . . . . B 2
Nordstrand 2,729 (isl.) . . . . . C 1
North (sea) . . . . . B 2
North Friesland (reg.) . . . . . C 1
North Frisian (isls.) . . . . . B 1
Odenwald (for.) . . . . . C 4
Oder (riv.) . . . . . F 2
Oker (riv.) . . . . . D 2
Peene (riv.) . . . . . E 2
Pellworm 1,261 (isl.) . . . . . C 1
Pomerania 630,524 (reg.) . . . . . E 2
Pomeranian (bay) . . . . . F 1
Regen (riv.) . . . . . E 4
Regnitz (riv.) . . . . . D 4
Rhine (riv.) . . . . . B 3
Rhön (mts.) . . . . . D 3
Rügen 85,651 (isl.) . . . . . E 1
Ruhr (riv.) . . . . . B 3
Saale (riv.) . . . . . D 3
Saar (riv.) . . . . . B 4
Sauer (riv.) . . . . . B 4
Sauerland (reg.) . . . . . B 3
Saxony 5,148,714 (reg.) . . . . . E 3
Schneeberg (mt.) . . . . . D 3
Schwarzwald (Black) (for.) . . . . . C 4
Spessart (range) . . . . . C 4
Spiekeroog 732 (isl.) . . . . . B 2
Spree (riv.) . . . . . F 3
Spreewald (for.) . . . . . F 3
Starnbergersee (lake) . . . . . D 5
Swabian Jura (range) . . . . . C 4
Sylt 20,875 (isl.) . . . . . C 1
Tauber (riv.) . . . . . C 4
Taunus (range) . . . . . C 3
Tegernsee (lake) . . . . . D 5
Teutoburger Wald (for.) . . . . . C 2
Thüringer Wald (for.) . . . . . D 3
Thuringia (reg.) . . . . . D 3
Ücker (riv.) . . . . . E 2
Unstrut (riv.) . . . . . D 3
Usedom (isl.) . . . . . F 1
Vogelsberg (mts.) . . . . . C 3
Walchensee (lake) . . . . . D 5
Wangerooge 1,700 (isl.) . . . . . B 2
Warnow (riv.) . . . . . D 2
Watzmann (mt.) . . . . . E 5
Werra (riv.) . . . . . D 3
Weser (riv.) . . . . . C 2
Westerwald (for.) . . . . . B 3
White Elster (riv.) . . . . . E 3
Würmsee (Starnbergersee) (lake) . . . . . D 5
Zugspitze (mt.) . . . . . D 5

Agriculture, Industry and Resources

DOMINANT LAND USE

- Wheat, Sugar Beets
- Cereals (chiefly rye, oats, barley)
- Potatoes, Rye
- Dairy, Livestock
- Mixed Cereals, Dairy
- Truck Farming
- Grapes, Fruit
- Forests

MAJOR MINERAL OCCURRENCES

Ag	Silver	K	Potash
Ba	Barite	Lg	Lignite
C	Coal	Na	Salt
Cu	Copper	O	Petroleum
Fe	Iron Ore	Pb	Lead
G	Natural Gas	U	Uranium
Gr	Graphite	Zn	Zinc

Water Power

Major Industrial Areas

AREA 15,892 sq. mi. (41,160 sq. km.)
POPULATION 14,227,000
CAPITALS The Hague, Amsterdam
LARGEST CITY Amsterdam
HIGHEST POINT Vaalserberg 1,056 ft. (322 m.)
MONETARY UNIT guilder (florin)
MAJOR LANGUAGE Dutch
MAJOR RELIGIONS Protestantism, Roman Catholicism

AREA 11,781 sq. mi. (30,513 sq. km.)
POPULATION 9,855,110
CAPITAL Brussels
LARGEST CITY Brussels (greater)
HIGHEST POINT Botrange 2,277 ft. (694 m.)
MONETARY UNIT Belgian franc
MAJOR LANGUAGES French (Walloon), Flemish
MAJOR RELIGION Roman Catholicism

AREA 999 sq. mi. (2,587 sq. km.)
POPULATION 364,000
CAPITAL Luxembourg
LARGEST CITY Luxembourg
HIGHEST POINT Ardennes Plateau 1,825 ft. (556 m.)
MONETARY UNIT Luxembourg franc
MAJOR LANGUAGES Luxembourgeois (Letzeburgisch), French, German
MAJOR RELIGION Roman Catholicism

NETHERLANDS

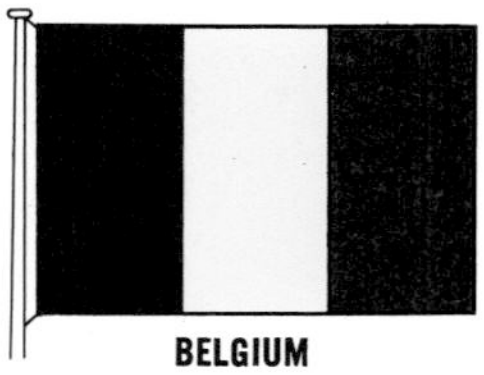

BELGIUM

LUXEMBOURG

BELGIUM

PROVINCES

Antwerp 1,533,249 F6
Brabant 2,176,373 F7
East Flanders 1,310,117 D7
Hainaut 1,317,453 D7
Liège 1,008,905 H7
Limburg 652,547 G7
Luxembourg 217,310 G9
Namur 380,561 F8
West Flanders 1,054,429 B7

CITIES and TOWNS†

Aalst 46,659 D7
Aalter 9,173 C6
Aarlen (Arlon) 13,745 H9
Aarschot 12,474 F7
Aat (Ath) 11,842 D7
Alken 8,677 G7
Alost (Aalst) 46,659 D7
Amay 7,617 G7
Andenne 8,091 G8
Anderlecht 103,796 B9
Anderlues 12,176 E8
Ans H7
Antoing 3,426 C7
Antwerp 224,543 E6
Antwerp* 928,000 E6
Antwerpen (Antwerp) 224,543 E6
Ardooie 7,081 C7
Arendonk 9,919 G6
Arlon 13,745 H9
As 5,496 H6
Asse 6,583 E7
Ath 11,842 D7
Attert H9
Aubange 3,761 H9
Audenarde (Oudenaarde) 26,615 D7
Auderghem 34,546 C9
Auvelais 8,287 F8
Aywaille 3,850 H8
Baerle-Hertog F6
Balen 15,110 G6
Basse-Sambre F8
Bastenaken (Bastogne) 6,816 H9
Bastogne 6,816 H9
Beernem C6
Beloeil D7
Berchem 50,241 F6
Berchem-Sainte-Agathe 19,087 B9
Bergen (Mons) 59,362 E8
Beringen G6
Bertogne H8
Bertrix 4,562 G9
Beveren 15,913 E6
Bilzen 7,178 G7
Binche 10,098 E8
Blankenberge 13,969 C6
Bocholt 6,497 H6
Boom 16,584 E6
Borgerhout 49,002 E6
Borgloon 3,412 G7
Borgworm (Waremme) 10,956 G7
Bourg-Léopold (Leopoldsburg) 9,593 G6
Boussu 11,474 D8
Braine-l'Alleud 18,531 E7
Braine-le-Comte 11,957 D7
Brecht F6
Bredene 9,244 B6
Bree 10,389 H6
Bruges 117,220 C6
Brugge (Bruges) 117,220 C6
Brussels (cap.)* 1,054,970 C9
Bruxelles (Brussels) (cap.)* 1,054,970 C9
Cerfontaine E8
Charleroi 23,689 E8
Charleroi* 458,000 E8
Chastre F7
Châtelet 14,752 F8
Chièvres 3,283 D7
Chimay 3,288 E8
Chiny G9
Ciney 7,536 G8
Comblain-au-Pont 3,582 G8
Comines 8,192 B7
Courcelles 17,015 E8
Courtrai (Kortrijk) 44,961 C7
Couvin 4,234 F8
Damme C6
De Haan C6
Deinze 16,711 C7
Denderleeuw 9,925 E7
Dendermonde 22,119 E6
De Panne 6,985 B6
Dessel 7,505 G6
Destelbergen D6
Deurne 80,766 F6
Diest 10,799 F7
Diksmuide 6,669 B6
Dilbeek 15,108 B9
Dilsen H6
Dinant 9,747 G8
Dison 8,466 H7
Dixmude (Diksmuide) 6,669 B6
Doische F8
Doornik (Tournai) 32,794 C7
Dour 10,059 D8
Drogenbos 4,840 B10
Duffel 13,802 F6
Durbuy H8
Ecaussinnes 6,630 E7
Edingen (Enghien) 4,115 D7
Eeklo 19,144 D6
Éghezée F7
Eigenbrakel (Braine-l'Alleud) 18,531 E7
Ekeren 27,648 E6
Ellezelles 3,556 D7
Enghien 4,115 D7
Érezée G8
Erquelinnes 4,471 E8
Esneux 6,183 H7
Essen 10,795 F6
Estampuis C7
Etterbeek 51,030 B9
Eupen 14,879 J7
Evere 26,957 C9
Evergem 12,886 D6
Farciennes E8
Fernelmont F7
Ferrières H8
Flémalle 8,135 G7
Fleurus 8,523 E8
Florennes 4,107 F8
Forest 55,135 B9
Fosses-La-Ville 3,972 F8
Frameries 11,224 D8
Froidchapelle E8
Furnes (Veurne) 9,496 B6
Ganshoren 21,147 B9
Geel 29,346 F6
Geldenaken (Jodoigne) 4,132 F7
Gembloux-sur-Orneau 11,249 F7
Genk 57,913 H7
Gent (Ghent) 148,860 D6
Geraardsbergen 17,533 D7
Gerpinnes F8
Ghent 148,860 D6
Ghent* 477,000 D6
Gistel B6
Gooik E7
Gouvy H8
Grammont (Geraardsbergen) 17,533 D7
Grez-Doiceau F7
Grimbergen E7
Haacht 4,436 F7
Habay H9
Hal (Halle) 20,017 E7
Halen 5,322 G7
Halle 20,017 E7
Hamme 17,559 E6
Hamois G8
Hamont-Achel 6,893 H6
Hannuit (Hannut) 7,232 G7
Hannut 7,232 G7
Harelbeke 18,498 C7
Hasselt 39,663 G7
Hastière F8
Heist-Knokke 27,582 C6
Heist-op-den-Berg 13,472 F6
Hensies D8
Herentals 18,639 F6
Herne E7
Herselt 7,412 F6
Herstal 29,600 H7
Herve 4,118 H7
Heuvelland B7
Hoboken 33,693 E6
Hoei (Huy) 12,736 G8
Hoeselt 6,884 G7
Honnelles D8
Hoogstraten 4,381 F6
Hotton G8
Huy 12,736 G8
Ichtegem B6
Ieper 20,825 B7
Ingelmunster 10,245 C7
Ittre E7
Ixelles 86,450 C9
Izegem 22,928 C7
Jabbeke C6
Jemappes 18,632 D8
Jette 40,013 B9
Jodoigne 4,132 F7
Kalmthout 12,724 F6
Kapellen 13,352 E6
Kasterlee F6
Kinrooi H6
Knokke-Heist 27,582 C6
Koekelare 7,807 B6
Koekelberg 17,570 B9
Koksijde B6
Kontich 14,432 E6
Kortemark 5,904 C6
Kortrijk 44,961 C7
Kraainem 11,390 C9
La Louvière 23,310 E8
La Louvière* 113,259 E8
Lanaken 8,659 H7
Landen 5,740 G7
Langemark-Poelkapelle 5,457 B7
Lasne F7
Lede 10,316 D7
Léglise H9
Leopoldsburg 9,593 G6
Le Roeulx E8
Lessen (Lessines) 8,906 D7
Lessines 8,906 D7
Leuven 30,623 F7
Leuze-en-Hainaut 7,185 D7
Libin G9
Libramont-Chevigny 2,975 G9
Lichtervelde 7,459 C6
Liedekerke 10,482 D7
Liège 145,573 H7
Liège* 622,000 H7
Lier 28,416 F6
Lierre (Lier) 28,416 F6
Limbourg 3,762 J7
Limburg (Limbourg) 3,762 J7
Linkebeek 4,265 C10
Linter G7
Lochristi D6
Lokeren 26,740 D6
Lommel 21,984 G6
Lontzen H9
Looz (Borgloon) 3,412 G7
Lo-Reninge B7
Louvain (Leuven) 30,623 F7
Luik (Liège) 145,573 H7
Lummen G7
Maaseik 8,622 H6
Maasmechelen H7
Machelen 7,057 C9
Maldegem 14,474 C6
Malines (Mechelen) 65,466 F6
Malmédy 6,464 J8
Manage E7
Manhay H8
Marche-en-Famenne 4,567 G8
Marchin 4,206 G8
Mechelen 65,466 F6
Meerhout 8,567 G6
Meise E7
Menen 22,037 C7
Menin (Menen) 22,037 C7
Merchtem 8,998 E7
Merelbeke 13,837 D7
Merksem 39,768 E6
Merksplas 5,065 F6
Messancy 3,150 H9
Mettet 3,372 F8
Meulebeke 10,458 C7
Middelkerke B6
Moeskroen (Mouscron) 37,311 C7
Mol 28,823 G6
Molenbeek-Saint-Jean 68,411 B9
Momignies E8
Mons 59,362 E8
Montigny-le-Tilleul E8
Moorslede B7
Mortsel 28,012 E6
Mouscron 37,311 C7
Namen (Namur) 32,269 F8
Namur 32,269 F8
Nassogne G8
Nazareth D7
Neerpelt 8,771 G6
Neufchâteau 2,670 G9
Nevele D6
Nieuport (Nieuwpoort) 8,273 B6
Nieuwpoort 8,273 B6
Nijvel (Nivelles) 16,126 E7
Ninove 12,428 D7
Nivelles 16,126 E7
Ohey G8
Onhaye F8
Oostende (Ostend) 71,227 B6
Oostkamp 8,999 C6
Opwijk 9,699 E7
Ostend 71,227 B6
Oudenaarde 26,615 D7
Oudenburg B6
Oud-Turnhout 9,245 F6
Oupeye H7
Overijse 16,181 F7
Overpelt 10,470 G6
Paliseul G9
Peer 7,201 G6
Péruwelz 7,878 D8
Philippeville 2,076 E8
Plombières F7
Pont-à-Celles E8
Poperinge 12,671 B7
Profondeville F8
Putte 6,953 F6
Quaregnon 17,688 D8
Quévy D8
Quiévrain 5,510 D8
Raeren 3,655 J7
Ravels G6
Rebecq 3,744 E7
Renaix (Ronse) 25,056 D7
Rendeux H8
Retie 6,619 G6
Rochefort 4,357 G8
Roeselare 40,428 C7
Ronse 25,056 D7
Roulers (Roeselare) 40,428 C7
Rouvroy G9
Ruislede C6
Sainte-Ode H8
Saint-Georges-sur-Meuse 6,003 G7
Saint-Gilles 55,055 B9
Saint-Hubert 3,091 G8
Saint-Josse-ten-Noode 23,633 C9
Saint-Nicolas G7
Saint-Trond (Sint-Truiden) 21,473 G7
Saint-Vith (Sankt Vith) 3,001 J8
Sankt Vith 3,001 J8
Schaerbeek 118,950 C9
Schoten 29,914 F6
Seraing 40,545 G7
's-Gravenbrakel (Braine-le-Comte) 11,957 D7
Sint-Laureins D6
Sint-Niklaas 49,214 E6

(continued on following page)

Agriculture, Industry and Resources

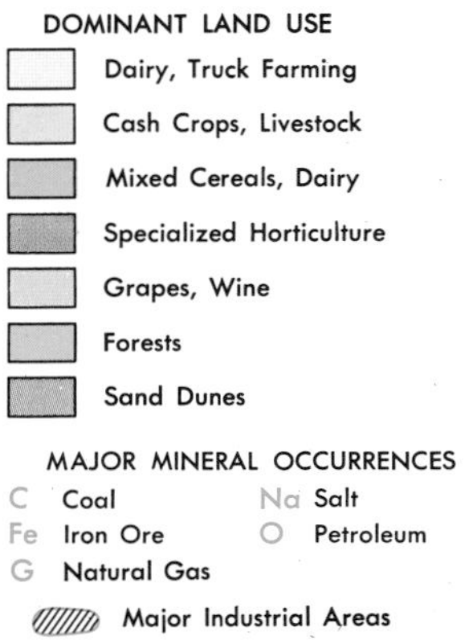

Sint-Pieters-Leeuw 16,856 .... B9
Sint-Truiden 21,473 .... G7
Soignies 12,006 .... D7
Somme-Leuze G8
Spa 9,504 .... H8
Sprimont H8
Staden 5,499 .... B7
Stavelot 4,723 .... H8
Steenokkerzeel 4,037 .... C9
Stekene E6
Stoumont H8
Tamise (Temse) 14,950 .... E6
Tellin G8
Temse 14,950 .... E6
Tenneville H8
Termonde (Dendermonde) 22,119 .... E6
Tessenderlo 11,778 .... G6
Theux 5,316 .... H8
Thuin 5,777 .... E8
Tielt 14,077 .... C7
Tielt-Winge 3,743 .... F7
Tienen 24,134 .... F7
Tintigny G9
Tirlemont (Tienen) 24,134 .... F7
Tongeren 20,136 .... G7
Tongres (Tongeren) 20,136 .... G7
Torhout 15,156 .... C6
Tournai 32,794 .... C7
Trois-Ponts H8
Tubeke (Tubize) 11,507 .... E7
Tubize 11,507 .... E7
Turnhout 38,007 .... F6
Uccle 78,909 .... B9
Ukkel (Uccle) 78,909 .... B9
Vaux-sur-Sûre H9
Verviers 33,587 .... H7
Veurne 9,496 .... B6
Vielsalm 3,587 .... H8
Vilvoorde 34,633 .... F7
Vilvorde (Vilvoorde) 34,633 .... F7
Viroinval F8
Virton 3,558 .... H9
Visé 6,880 .... H7
Vleteren B7
Vorst (Forest) 55,135 .... B9
Vresse-sur-Semois F9
Waarschoot 7,905 .... D6
Wachtebeke D6
Waregem 17,725 .... C7
Waremme 10,956 .... G7
Waterloo 17,764 .... E7
Watermaal-Bosvoorde
(Watermael-Boitsfort C9
Watermael-Boitsfort 25,123 .... C9
Waver (Wavre) 11,767 .... F7
Wavre 11,767 .... F7
Wellin G8
Wemmel 12,631 .... B9
Wervik 12,672 .... B7
Westerlo 14,173 .... F6
Westmalle F6
Wetteren 20,816 .... D7
Wezembeek-Oppem 10,899 .... D9
Wezet (Visé) 6,880 .... H7
Willebroek 15,726 .... E6
Wilrijk 43,485 .... E6
Wingene 7,140 .... C6
Woluwe-Saint-Lambert 47,360 .... C9
Woluwe-Saint-Pierre 40,884 .... C9
Ypres (Ieper) 20,825 .... B7
Zaventem 10,625 .... C9
Zedelgem C6
Zeebrugge C6
Zele 18,585 .... E6
Zelzate 12,785 .... D6
Zemst E7
Zinnik (Soignies) 12,006 .... D7
Zonhoven 13,484 .... G6
Zottegem 21,461 .... D7
Zuienkerke C6

OTHER FEATURES

Albert, (canal) F6
Ardennes, (for.) F9
Botrange, (mt.) J8
Dender, (riv.) D7
Deûle, (riv.) B7
Dyle, (riv.) F7
Hohe Venn, (plat.) H8
Lesse, (riv.) F8
Lys, (riv.) B7
Mark, (riv.) F6
Meuse, (riv.) F8
Nethe, (riv.) F6
North, (sea) D4
Ourthe, (riv.) G8
Rupel, (riv.) F7
Sambre, (riv.) D8
Schelde (Scheldt), (riv.) C7
Scheldt, (riv.) C7
Schnee Eifel, (plat.) J8
Semois, (riv.) G9
Senne, (riv.) E7
Vaalserberg, (mt.) J7
Vesdre, (riv.) H7
Weisserstein, (mt.) J8
Yser, (riv.) B7
Zitterwald, (plat.) J8

LUXEMBOURG

CITIES and TOWNS

Clervaux 916 .... J8
Diekirch† 5,059 .... J9
Differdange 9,287 .... H9
Dudelange† 14,615 .... J10
Echternach† 3,792 .... J9
Esch-sur-Alzette† 27,574 .... J9
Ettelbruck† 5,990 .... J9
Grevenmacher† 2,918 .... J9
Luxembourg (cap.) 78,272 .... J9
Mamer 3,123 .... H9
Mersch 1,869 .... J9
Pétange 6,234 .... H9
Remich† 12,138 .... J9
Viandent† 1,520 .... J9
Wiltz 1,601 .... H9

OTHER FEATURES

Alzette, (riv.) J9
Clerf, (riv.) J8
Eisling, (mts.) H9
Mosel, (riv.) J9
Our, (riv.) J9
Sauer, (riv.) J9

NETHERLANDS

PROVINCES

Drenthe 405,924 .... K3
Flevoland G4
Friesland 560,614 .... H2
Gelderland 1,639,997 .... H4
Groningen 540,062 .... K2
Limburg 1,051,620 .... H6
North Brabant 1,967,261 .... F5
North Holland 2,295,875 .... F3
Overijssel 985,569 .... J4
South Holland 3,048,648 .... E5
Utrecht 867,909 .... G4
Zeeland 332,286 .... D6

CITIES and TOWNS†

Aalsmeer 20,779 .... F4
Aalten 17,486 .... K5
Aardenburg 3,869 .... C6
Akkrum 5,044 .... H2
Alkmaar 65,199 .... F3
Almelo 62,634 .... K4
Alphen aan de Rijn 46,065 .... F4
Amersfoort 87,784 .... G4
Amstelveen 71,803 .... B5
Amsterdam (cap.) 751,156 .... B4
Amsterdam* 987,205 .... B4
Andijk 5,301 .... G3
Apeldoorn 134,055 .... H4
Apeldoorn* 237,231 .... H4
Appingedam 13,295 .... K2
Arnhem 126,051 .... H4
Arnhem* 281,126 .... H4
Assen 43,783 .... K3
Asten 12,295 .... H6
Axel 12,072 .... D6
Baarle-Nassau 5,583 .... F6
Baarn 25,045 .... G4
Barneveld 34,189 .... H4
Bath E6
Beilen 12,948 .... K3
Bemmel 14,218 .... H5
Bergeijk 9,009 .... G6
Bergen 14,306 .... F3
Bergen op Zoom 40,770 .... E5
Bergum 28,047 .... H2
Berkel 9,367 .... F5
Berkhout 5,167 .... F3
Beverwijk 37,551 .... F4
Blerick J6
Bloemendaal 17,940 .... E4
Blokzijl H3
Bodegraven 15,848 .... F4
Bolsward 9,934 .... H2
Borculo 9,859 .... J4
Borger 12,017 .... K3
Borne 18,216 .... K4
Boskoop 12,985 .... F4
Boxmeer 12,662 .... H5
Boxtel 22,465 .... G5
Breda 118,086 .... F5
Breda* 151,182 .... F5
Breezand F3
Breskens C6
Brielle 10,620 .... E5
Brouwershaven 3,263 .... D5
Brummen 20,460 .... J4
Brunssum 26,116 .... J7
Buiksloot C4
Bussum 37,848 .... G4
Capelle 35,696 .... F5
Coevorden 13,089 .... K3
Colijnsplaat D5
Culemborg 17,682 .... G5
Cuyk 15,366 .... H5
Dalen 5,084 .... K3
De Bilt 32,588 .... G4
Dedemsvaart 12,975 .... J3
De Koog F2
Delft 86,103 .... E4
Delfzijl 23,316 .... K2
Den Burg 12,132 .... F2
Denekamp 11,533 .... L4
Den Helder 60,421 .... F3
Deurne 26,539 .... H6
Deventer 65,557 .... J4
Didam 14,263 .... J5
De Wijk 4,631 .... J3
Diemen 13,704 .... C5
Dieren J4
Diever 3,162 .... J3
Dinxperlo 7,296 .... K5
Dirksland 6,495 .... E5
Doesburg 9,759 .... J4
Doetinchem 34,915 .... J5
Dokkum 11,203 .... H2
Domburg 3,874 .... C5
Dongen 19,219 .... F5
Doorn 11,966 .... G4
Dordrecht 101,840 .... F5
Dordrecht* 186,793 .... F5
Drachten 45,390 .... J2
Driebergen 17,022 .... G4
Dronten 16,544 .... H3
Druten 11,113 .... H5
Echt 17,035 .... H6
Edam-Volendam 21,507 .... G4
Ede 79,897 .... H4
Egmond aan Zee 5,734 .... E3
Eindhoven 192,562 .... G6
Eindhoven* 358,234 .... G6
Elburg 18,082 .... H4
Elst 16,686 .... H5
Emmeloord 34,467 .... H3
Emmen 86,700 .... K3
Enkhuizen 13,430 .... G3
Enschede 141,597 .... K4
Enschede* 239,015 .... K4
Epe 32,267 .... H4
Erica K3
Ermelo 23,835 .... H4
Etten-Leur 26,167 .... F5
Europoort E5
Flushing 43,806 .... C6
Franeker 11,415 .... H2
Geertruidenberg 6,185 .... F5
Geldermalsen 8,952 .... G5
Geldrop 25,879 .... H6
Geleen 35,910 .... H7
Gemert 15,267 .... H5
Gendringen 19,086 .... J5
Genemuiden 6,058 .... H3
Gennep 14,773 .... H5
Giessendam-Hardinxveld 15,523 .... F5
Giethoorn J3
Gilze 19,603 .... F5
Goes 28,505 .... D6
Goirle 13,447 .... G5
Goor 11,435 .... K4
Gorinchem 28,337 .... G5
Gorredijk J2
Gouda 56,403 .... F4
Graauw E6
Gramsbergen 5,866 .... K3
Grave 9,492 .... H5
Groenlo 8,693 .... K4
Groesbeek 18,094 .... H5
Groningen 163,357 .... K2
Groningen* 201,662 .... K2
Grouw 8,567 .... H2
Haamstede 4,575 .... D5
Haarlem 164,672 .... F4
Haarlem* 232,048 .... F4
Haarlemmermeer
(Hoofddorp) 72,046 .... F4
Hague, The (cap.) 479,369 .... E4
Hague, The* 682,452 .... E4
Halfweg 4,456 .... B4
Hallum H2
Hardenberg 28,489 .... J3
Harderwijk 28,508 .... H4
Hardinxveld-Giessendam 15,523 .... G5
Harlingen 14,533 .... G2
Hasselt 5,817 .... J3
Hattem 11,074 .... H4
Heemskert 31,728 .... F3
Heemstede 27,376 .... F4
Heer H7
Heerde 16,833 .... H4
Heerenveen 34,948 .... H3
Heerhugowaard 26,019 .... F3
Heerlen 71,500 .... J7
Heesch 8,659 .... G5
Heiloo 20,524 .... F3
Hellendoorn 32,068 .... J4
Hellevoetsluis 14,186 .... E5
Helmond 59,249 .... H6
Hengelo, Gelderland 8,015 .... J4
Hengelo, Overijssel 72,281 .... K4
Heusden 5,542 .... G5
Hillegom 17,489 .... E4
Hilvarenbeek 8,408 .... G6
Hilversum 94,041 .... G4
Hilversum* 110,498 .... G4
Hippolytushoef 7,847 .... G3
Hoek D6
Hoek van Holland (Hook of
Holland) D4
Hoensbroek 22,441 .... H7
Holijsloot C4
Hollum H2
Holwerd H2
Hoofddorp
(Haarlemmermeer) 72,046 .... F4
Hoogeveen 42,673 .... J3
Hoogezand-Sappemeer 33,860 .... K2
Hoogkarspel 5,112 .... G3
Hook of Holland D4
Hoorn 24,609 .... G3
Horst 16,242 .... H6
Huissen 11,049 .... H5
Huizen 25,603 .... G4
Hulst 17,283 .... E6
IJmuiden 6,633 .... E4
IJsselstein 15,450 .... F4
Ilpendam 3,310 .... C4
Joure 14,329 .... H3
Kampen 29,488 .... H3
Katwijk aan Zee 37,437 .... E4
Kerkdriel 7,584 .... G5
Kerkrade 46,609 .... J7
Kesteren 8,257 .... G5
Klazienaveen 9,520 .... L3
Kollum 11,887 .... J2
Krimpen aan den IJssel 26,396 .... F5
Landsmeer 8,082 .... C4
Laren 13,615 .... G4
Leek 15,713 .... J2
Leerdam 15,030 .... F5
Leeuwarden 85,074 .... H2
Leiden 99,891 .... E4
Leiden* 167,554 .... E4
Lelystad H3
Lemmer 10,013 .... H3
Lisse 19,182 .... F4
Lith 5,088 .... G5
Lochem 17,274 .... J4
Lonneker K4
Loon op Zand 18,000 .... G5
Losser 20,688 .... L4
Maarssen 18,346 .... F4
Maasbree 9,462 .... H6
Maassluis 28,170 .... E5
Maastricht 111,044 .... H7
Maastricht* 145,862 .... H7
Margraten 3,318 .... H7
Medemblik 6,432 .... G3
Meerssen 8,414 .... H7
Meppel 21,057 .... J3
Middelburg 36,372 .... C6
Middelharnis 14,245 .... E5
Middenmeer F3
Millingen aan den Rijn 5,035 .... J5
Moerdijk F5
Monnickendam 8,127 .... C4
Montfoort 3,442 .... G4
Muiden 6,567 .... G4
Muntendam 4,147 .... K2
Naaldwijk 24,117 .... E4
Naarden 17,319 .... G4
Nagele H3
Neede 10,842 .... K4
Nes 3,012 .... H2
Nieuwegein 22,648 .... G4
Nieuwe-Pekela 5,086 .... L2
Nieuwkoop 8,923 .... F4
Nieuw-Schoonebeek 7,556 .... L3
Nijkerk 21,615 .... H4
Nijmegen 148,493 .... H5
Nijmegen* 213,981 .... H5
Noordwijk 22,386 .... E4
Norg 6,041 .... J2
Numansdorp 7,072 .... E5
Nunspeet 21,340 .... H4
Odoorn 11,973 .... K3
Oisterwijk 16,263 .... G5
Oldenzaal 26,624 .... K4
Olst 8,480 .... J4
Ommen 16,136 .... J3
Onstwedde K2
Oostburg 18,461 .... C6
Oosterhout 40,077 .... F5
Ooosterwolde 5,845 .... J2
Oostmahorn J2
Oostzaan 6,336 .... C4
Ootmarsum 3,901 .... K4
Oss 45,643 .... H5
Otterlo H4
Oud-Beijerland 14,251 .... E5
Ouddorp 9,091 .... D5
Oudenbosch 11,061 .... E5
Oude-Pekela 8,067 .... K2
Oudewater 6,870 .... F4
Purmerend 32,614 .... F4
Putten 18,243 .... H4
Raalte 23,598 .... J4
Renkum 34,547 .... H5
Reusel 6,901 .... G6
Rheden 49,755 .... J4
Rhenen 16,893 .... H5
Ridderkerk 45,069 .... F5
Rijnsburg 10,698 .... F4
Rijssen 20,008 .... J4
Rijswijk 54,123 .... E4
Roden 16,437 .... J2
Roermond 36,695 .... J6
Roosendaal 51,685 .... F5
Rotterdam 614,767 .... E5
Rotterdam* 1,016,505 .... E5
Rutten H3
Ruurlo 7,557 .... J4
Sappemeer-Hoogezand 33,860 .... K2
Schagen 13,929 .... F3
Scheveningen E4
Schiedam 78,068 .... E5
Schijndel 18,658 .... G5
Schiphol B5
Schoonhoven 10,753 .... F5
's Gravendeel 7,242 .... E5
's Gravenhage (The Hague)
(cap.) 479,369 .... E4
's Gravenhage* 682,452 .... E4
's Gravenzande 15,833 .... E4
's Heerenberg 18,326 .... J5
's Hertogenbosch 86,184 .... G5
Simpelveld 6,783 .... H7
Sint Annaland E5
Sint Jacobiparochie H2
Sittard 34,278 .... H6
Sliedrecht 21,839 .... F5
Slochteren 13,447 .... K2
Sloten, North Holland B5
Sloterdijk B4
Sluis 3,140 .... C6
Smilde 8,247 .... K3
Sneek 28,123 .... H2
Soest 40,165 .... G4
Soesterberg G4
Stadskanaal 13,946 .... L3
Staphorst 11,608 .... J3
Steenbergen 12,930 .... E5
Steenwijk 20,721 .... J3
Stiens 7,711 .... H2
Swifterbant H3
Tegelen 18,386 .... J6
Ter Apel L3
Termunten 4,803 .... K2
Terneuzen 33,731 .... D6
Tholen 17,213 .... E5
Tiel 24,974 .... G5
Tilburg 151,513 .... G5
Tilburg* 212,510 .... G5
Twello 22,542 .... J4
Uden 28,946 .... H5
Uithoorn 22,812 .... F4
Uithuizen 5,194 .... K2
Ulrum 3,665 .... J2
Urk 9,397 .... H3
Utrecht 250,887 .... G4
Utrecht* 464,357 .... G4
Vaals 11,057 .... H7
Vaassen 7,225 .... H4
Valkenswaard 27,121 .... H6
Veendam 26,168 .... K2
Veenendaal 35,845 .... G4
Veenhuizen J2
Veere 4,252 .... D5
Veghel 22,308 .... H5
Veldhoven 30,030 .... G6
Velp J5
Velsen 64,035 .... F4
Venlo 61,659 .... J6
Venraij 31,526 .... H6
Vianen 12,821 .... G5
Vlaardingen 78,311 .... E5
Vlagtwedde 16,719 .... L3
Vlijmen 13,515 .... G5
Vlissingen (Flushing) 43,806 .... C6
Volendam-Edam 21,507 .... G4
Voorburg 45,209 .... E4
Voorst 22,542 .... J4
Vorden 7,276 .... J4
Vriezenveen 16,025 .... K4
Vught 23,261 .... G5
Waalre 13,219 .... G6
Waalwijk 25,977 .... F5
Wageningen 28,659 .... H5
Wamel 8,979 .... H5
Warmenhuizen 3,818 .... F3
Weert 36,850 .... H6
Weesp 17,037 .... C5
West-Terschelling 4,542 .... G2
Wierden 20,618 .... K4
Wijhe 6,888 .... J4
Wijk bij Duurstede 7,927 .... G5
Wijk en Aalburg 9,266 .... F5
Winschoten 19,760 .... L2
Winsum 5,007 .... K2
Winterswijk 27,413 .... K5
Woensdrecht 9,101 .... E6
Woerden 22,064 .... F4
Wolvega 22,812 .... J3
Workum 4,135 .... G3
Zaandam (Zaanstad) 124,795 .... B4
Zaandam (Zaanstad)* 137,371 .... B4
Zaltbommel 8,010 .... G5
Zandvoort 16,289 .... E4
Zeist 58,630 .... G4
Zevenaar 26,560 .... J5
Zevenbergen 13,307 .... E5
Zierikzee 8,816 .... D5
Zundert 12,444 .... F6
Zutphen 29,188 .... J4
Zwartsluis 4,391 .... H3
Zwijndrecht 38,271 .... E5
Zwolle 77,826 .... J3

OTHER FEATURES

Alkmaardermeer (lake) F3
Ameland (isl.) H2
Bergumermeer (lake) J2
Beulaker Wijde (lake) H3
Borndiep (chan.) H2
De Fluessen (lake) G3
De Honte (bay) D6
De Peel (reg.) H6
De Twente (reg.) K4
De Zaan (riv.) B4
Dollard (bay) L2
Dommel (riv.) H6
Duiveland (isl.) D5
Eastern Scheldt (est.) D5
Eems (riv.) K2
Eijerlandsche Gat (str.) F2
Flevoland Polders 35,618 .... G4
Friesche Gat (chan.) J2
Frisian, West (isls.) G2
Galgenberg (hill) H4
Goeree (isl.) D5
Grevelingen (str.) E5
Griend (isl.) G2
Groninger Wad (sound) J2
Groote IJ Polder B4
Haarlemmermeer Polder 72,046 .... B5
Haringvliet (str.) E5
Het IJ (est.) C4
Hoek van Holland (cape) D5
Hondsrug (hills) K3
Houtrak Polder A4
Hunse (riv.) K3
IJmeer (bay) C4
IJssel (riv.) J4
IJsselmeer (lake) G3
Lauwers (chan.) J1
Lauwers Zee (bay) J2
Lek (riv.) F5
Lemelerberg (hill) J4
Lower Rhine (riv.) H5
Maas (riv.) G5
Mark (riv.) F6
Marken (isl.) G4
Markerwaard Polder G3
Marsdiep (chan.) F3
North (sea) E3
North Beveland (isl.) D5
North East Polder 34,467 .... H3
North Holland (canal) C4
North Sea (canal) F4
Old Rhine (riv.) E4
Oostzaan Polder 6,336 .... B4
Orange (canal) K3
Overflakkee (isl.) E5
Pinke Gat (chan.) H2
Regge (riv.) K4
Rhine (riv.) J5
Roer (riv.) J6
Rottumeplaat (isl.) J1
Rottumeroog (isl.) J1
Schiermonnikoog (isl.) J1
Schouwen (isl.) D5
Slotermeer (lake) H3
Sneekermeer (lake) H2
South Beveland (isl.) D6
Terschelling (isl.) G2
Texel (isl.) F2
Tjeukemeer (lake) H3
Tjonger (riv.) J3
Vaalserberg (mt.) J7
Vecht (riv.) F4
Vechte (riv.) J3
Veersche Meer (lake) D5
Veluwe (reg.) H4
Vlieland (isl.) F2
Vliestroom (str.) G2
Voorne (isl.) D5
Waal (riv.) G5
Waddenzee (sound) G2
Walcheren (isl.) C5
Wester Eems (chan.) K1
Western Scheldt (De Honte)
(bay) D6
West Frisian (isls.) F2
Westgat (chan.) F3
Wieringermeer Polder 11,870 .... G3
Wilhelmina (canal) G6
Willems (canal) G5

*City and suburbs.
†Population of cities in Belgium & Netherlands are communes

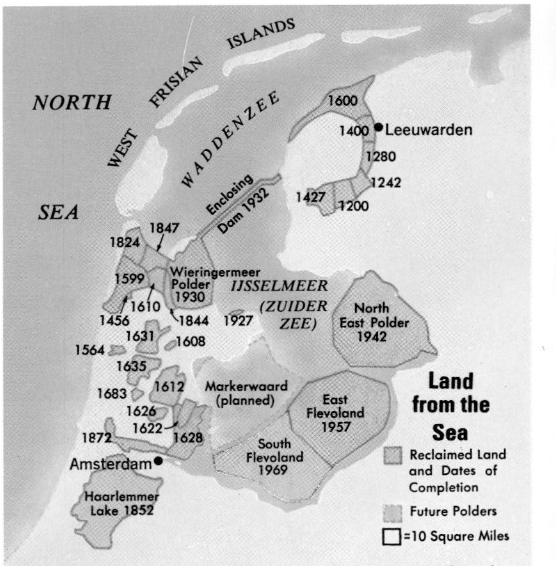

For centuries the Dutch have been renowned for the drainage of marshes and the construction of polders, i.e., arable land reclaimed from the sea. Future projects will convert much of the present IJsselmeer to agricultural land.

Topography

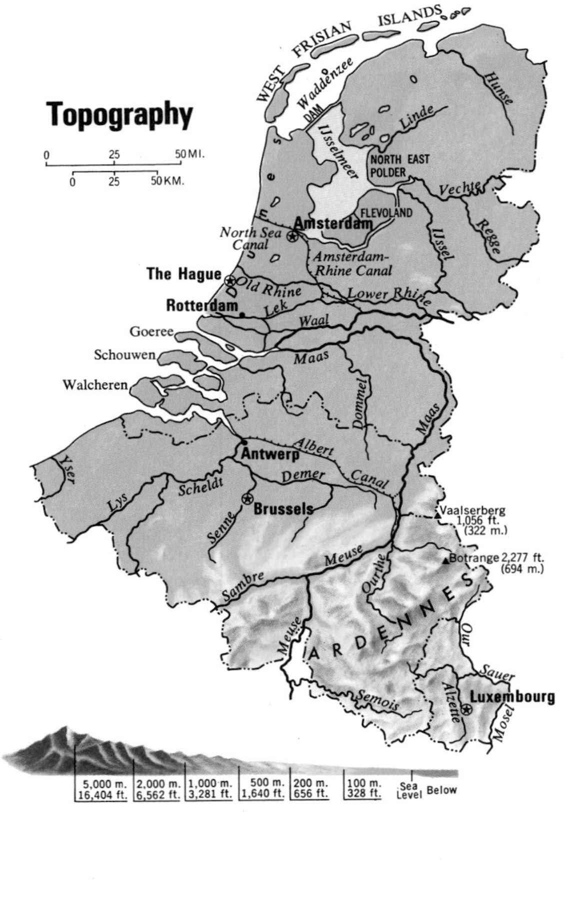

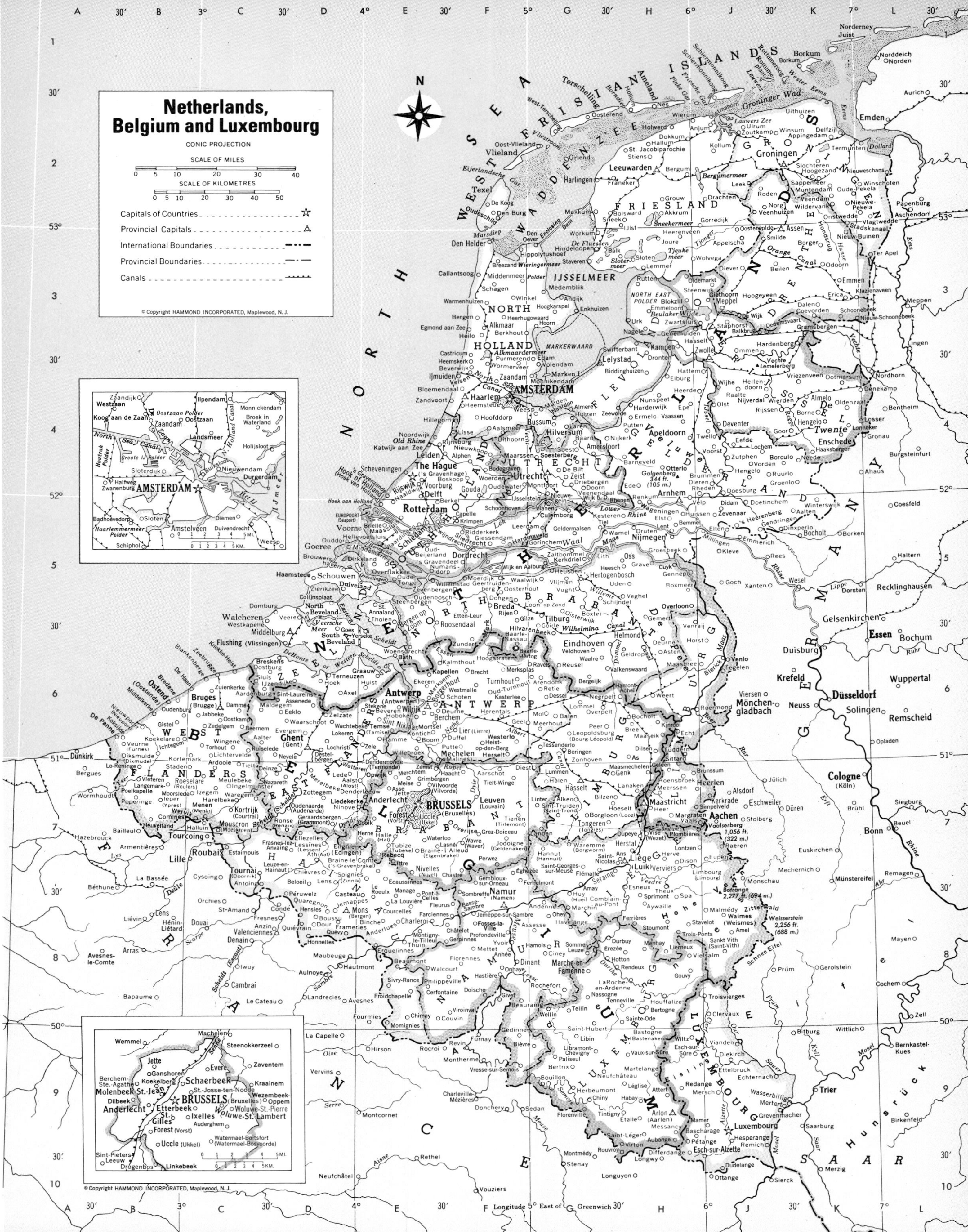
Netherlands, Belgium and Luxembourg
CONIC PROJECTION
SCALE OF MILES
0 5 10 20 30 40
SCALE OF KILOMETRES
0 5 10 20 30 40 50
Capitals of Countries
Provincial Capitals
International Boundaries
Provincial Boundaries
Canals
© Copyright HAMMOND INCORPORATED, Maplewood, N.J.
AMSTERDAM
BRUSSELS
© Copyright HAMMOND INCORPORATED, Maplewood, N.J.
Longitude 5° East of Greenwich
NORTH SEA
WEST FRISIAN ISLANDS
WADDENZEE
IJSSELMEER
GRONINGEN
FRIESLAND
DRENTHE
OVERIJSSEL
NORTH HOLLAND
SOUTH HOLLAND
UTRECHT
GELDERLAND
FLEVOLAND
ZEELAND
NORTH BRABANT
LIMBURG
ANTWERP
WEST FLANDERS
EAST FLANDERS
BRABANT
HAINAUT
NAMUR
LIÈGE
LUXEMBOURG
GERMANY
FRANCE
The Hague
Amsterdam
Rotterdam
Utrecht
Haarlem
Leiden
Delft
Groningen
Leeuwarden
Assen
Zwolle
Arnhem
Nijmegen
Eindhoven
Tilburg
Breda
Maastricht
Middelburg
Lelystad
Antwerp (Antwerpen)
Ghent (Gent)
Bruges (Brugge)
Mechelen
Leuven
Mons
Namur
Liège (Luik)
Hasselt
Arlon
Luxembourg
Esch-sur-Alzette
Ostend (Oostende)
Lille
Aachen
Cologne (Köln)
Düsseldorf
Essen
Trier
Emden
Vaalserberg 1,056 ft. (322 m.)
Botrange 2,277 ft. (694 m.)
Weisserstein 2,256 ft. (688 m.)
Galgenberg 344 ft. (105 m.)

France
CONIC PROJECTION
SCALE OF MILES
0 20 40 60 80 100
SCALE OF KILOMETERS
0 20 40 60 80 100
Capitals of Countries
Capitals of Departments
International Boundaries
Department Boundaries
Canals
Paris and Environs
Corsica
Same Scale as Main Map
UNITED KINGDOM
ENGLISH CHANNEL (La Manche)
BAY OF BISCAY
NORTH SEA
MEDITERRANEAN SEA
Gulf of Lions
SPAIN
ANDORRA
SWITZERLAND
GERMANY
BELGIUM
LUXEMBOURG
NETHERLANDS
ITALY
MONACO
CHANNEL ISLANDS
PARIS
LONDON
Longitude West of Greenwich
Longitude East of Greenwich

DEPARTMENTS

Ain 376,477 F4
Aisne 533,862 E3
Allier 378,406 E4
Alpes-de-Haute-Provence 112,178 G5
Alpes-Maritimes 816,681 G6
Ardèche 257,065 F5
Ardennes 309,306 F3
Ariège 137,857 D6
Aube 284,823 E3
Aude 272,366 E6
Aveyron 278,306 E5
Bas-Rhin 882,121 G3
Belfort (terr.) 128,125 G4
Bouches-du-Rhône 1,632,974 F6
Calvados 560,967 C3
Cantal 166,549 E5
Charente 337,064 D5
Charente-Maritime 497,859 C5
Cher 316,350 E4
Corrèze 240,363 D5
Corse du Sud 128,634 B6
Côte-d'Or 456,070 F4
Côtes-du-Nord 525,556 B3
Creuse 146,214 D4
Deux-Sèvres 335,829 C4
Dordogne 373,179 D5
Doubs 471,082 G4
Drôme 361,847 F5
Essonne 923,063 E3
Eure 422,952 D3
Eure-et-Loir 335,151 D3
Finistère 804,088 A3
Gard 494,575 F6
Gers 175,366 D6
Gironde 1,061,480 C5
Haute-Corse 161,208 B6
Haute-Garonne 777,431 D6
Haute-Loire 205,491 E5
Haute-Marne 212,304 F3
Hautes-Alpes 97,358 G5
Haute-Saône 222,254 G4
Haute-Savoie 447,795 G5
Hautes-Pyrénées 227,222 D6
Haute-Vienne 352,149 D5
Haut-Rhin 635,209 G4
Hauts-de-Seine 1,438,930 A2
Hérault 648,202 E6
Ille-et-Vilaine 702,199 C3
Indre 248,523 D4
Indre-et-Loire 478,601 D4
Isère 860,339 F5
Jura 238,856 F4
Landes 288,323 C5
Loire 742,396 F5
Loire-Atlantique 934,499 C4
Loiret 490,189 E4
Loir-et-Cher 283,686 D4
Lot 150,778 D5
Lot-et-Garonne 292,616 D5
Lozère 74,825 E5
Maine-et-Loire 629,849 C4
Manche 451,662 C3
Marne 530,399 F3
Mayenne 261,789 C3
Meurthe-et-Moselle 722,588 G3
Meuse 203,904 F3
Morbihan 563,588 B4
Moselle 1,006,373 G3
Nièvre 245,212 E4
Nord 2,510,738 E2
Oise 606,320 E3
Orne 293,523 C3
Paris (city) 2,299,830 B2
Pas-de-Calais 1,403,035 E2
Puy-de-Dôme 580,033 E5
Pyrénées-Atlantiques 534,748 C6
Pyrénées-Orientales 299,506 E6
Rhône 1,429,647 F5
Saône-et-Loire 569,810 F4
Sarthe 490,385 D3
Savoie 305,118 G5
Seine-et-Marne 755,762 E3
Seine-Saint-Denis 1,322,127 C1
Somme 538,462 E3
Tarn 338,024 E6
Tarn-et-Garonne 183,314 D5
Val-de-Marne 1,215,713 C1
Val-d'Oise 840,885 E3
Var 626,093 G6
Vaucluse 390,446 F6
Vendée 450,641 C4
Vienne 357,366 D4
Vosges 397,957 G3
Yonne 299,851 E4
Yvelines 1,082,255 D3

CITIES and TOWNS

Abbeville 25,252 D2
Agde 9,856 E6
Agen 33,763 D5
Aix-en-Provence 91,665 F6
Aix-les-Bains 21,884 G5
Ajaccio 47,065 B7
Albert 11,746 E2
Albertville 16,630 G5
Albi 43,942 E6
Alençon 32,917 D3
Alès 33,315 E5
Ambérieu-en-Bugey 9,294 F5
Amboise 10,498 D4
Amiens 129,453 D3
Ancenis 6,689 C4
Angers 136,603 C4
Angoulême 46,293 D5
Annecy 53,058 G5
Annonay 19,234 F5
Antibes 44,226 G6
Antony 57,450 B2
Apt 9,735 F6
Arcachon 13,856 C5
Argentan 16,063 D3
Argenteuil 101,542 A1
Arles 37,337 F6
Armentières 23,850 E2
Arras 45,804 E2
Asnières-sur-Seine 75,328 A1
Aubagne 26,145 F6
Aubenas 11,967 F5
Aubervilliers 72,859 B1
Auch 18,767 D6
Audincourt 18,570 G4
Aulnay-sous-Bois 77,982 B1
Auray 10,006 B4
Aurignac 744 D6
Aurillac 29,458 E5
Autun 19,441 F4
Auxerre 36,039 E4
Auxonne 6,414 F4
Avallon 8,518 E4
Avignon 73,482 F6
Avion 22,860 E2
Avranches 10,128 C3
Ax-les-Thermes 1,456 D6
Bagnères-de-Bigorre 9,080 D6
Bagnolet 35,858 B2
Bagnols-sur-Cèze 13,111 F5
Barbizon 1,189 E3
Barcelonnette 2,523 G5
Barfleur 701 C3
Bar-le-Duc 19,188 F3
Bar-sur-Aube 7,227 F3
Bastia 45,387 B6
Bayeux 13,381 C3
Bayonne 41,281 C6
Beaucaire 10,189 F6
Beaune 16,386 F4
Beauvais 53,493 E3
Belfort 54,469 G4
Belley 6,612 F5
Berck 14,104 D2
Bergerac 25,488 D5
Bernay 9,928 D3
Besançon 119,803 G4
Béthune 26,208 E2
Béziers 79,213 E6
Biarritz 27,453 C6
Blois 49,134 D4
Bobigny 43,041 B1
Bogny-sur-Meuse 6,845 F3
Bolbec 12,347 D3
Bondy 48,285 B1
Bonneville 6,717 G4
Bordeaux 220,830 C5
Boulogne-Billancourt 103,527 A2
Boulogne-sur-Mer 48,309 D2
Bourg-en-Bresse 40,052 F4
Bourges 75,200 E4
Bourgoin-Jallieu 18,504 F5
Bressuire 9,778 C4
Brest 163,940 A3
Briançon 8,523 G5

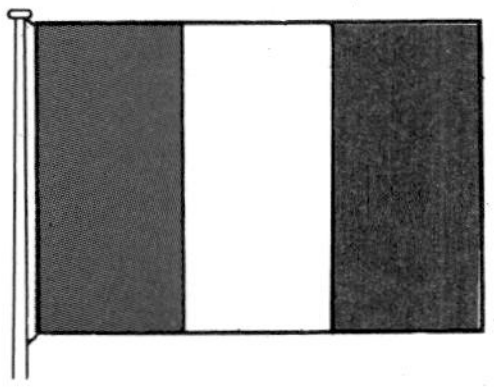

AREA 210,038 sq. mi. (543,998 sq. km.)
POPULATION 53,788,000
CAPITAL Paris
LARGEST CITY Paris
HIGHEST POINT Mont Blanc 15,771 ft. (4,807 m.)
MONETARY UNIT franc
MAJOR LANGUAGE French
MAJOR RELIGION Roman Catholicism

Brignoles 8,784 G6
Brioude 7,756 E5
Brive-la-Gaillarde 49,276 D5
Bruay-en-Artois 25,544 E2
Caen 116,987 C3
Cahors 19,288 D5
Calais 73,009 D2
Caluire-et-Cuire 43,024 F5
Cambrai 38,706 E2
Cannes 70,226 G6
Carcassonne 38,887 D6
Carmaux 11,970 E5
Carpentras 20,169 F5
Castelnaudary 8,947 E6
Castelsarrasin 6,562 D6
Castres 41,037 E6
Cavaillon 17,383 F6
Châlons-sur-Marne 50,870 F3
Chalon-sur-Saône 55,495 F4
Chambéry 52,286 F5
Chambord 166 D4
Chamonix-Mont-Blanc 6,246 G5
Champigny-sur-Marne 80,189 C2
Chantilly 10,517 E3
Charenton-le-Pont 20,383 B2
Charleville-Mézières 59,513 F3
Chartres 38,574 D3
Châteaubriant 12,417 C4
Château-du-Loir 5,598 D4
Châteaudun 14,634 D3
Château-Gontier 8,301 C4
Châteauroux 53,166 D4
Château-Thierry 13,379 E3
Châtellerault 33,811 D4
Châtillon 26,562 B2
Châtillon-sur-Seine 7,367 F4
Chatou 26,415 A1
Chaumont 26,568 F3
Chauny 14,324 E3
Chelles 24,192 C1
Cherbourg 31,333 C3
Chinon 5,378 D4
Choisy-le-Roi 38,629 B2
Cholet 49,887 C4
Clamart 52,881 A2
Clermont 7,834 E3
Clermont-Ferrand 153,379 E5
Clichy 47,731 B1
Cluny 4,335 F4
Cluses 12,713 G4
Cognac 21,567 C5
Colmar 58,585 G3
Colombes 83,241 A1
Commentry 8,074 E4
Commercy 6,918 F3
Compiègne 37,009 E3
Concarneau 15,096 A4
Cosne-Cours-sur-Loire 9,768 E4
Coudekerque-Branche 24,702 E2
Coulommiers 11,363 E3
Courbevoie 54,391 A1
Coutances 8,286 C3
Creil 31,893 E3
Crépy-en-Valois 10,661 E3
Créteil 58,665 B2
Cusset 13,672 E4
Dax 18,019 C6
Deauville 5,655 C3
Decazeville 9,318 E5
Decize 6,853 E4
Denain 26,096 E2
Dieppe 25,607 D3

Topography

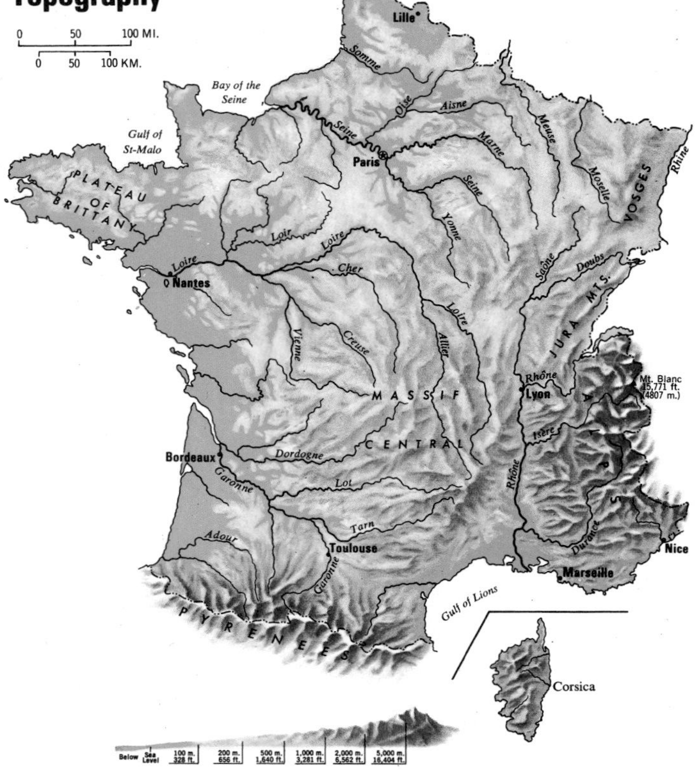

Historic Provinces

A resident of the city of Caen thinks of himself as a Norman rather than as a citizen of the modern department of Calvados. In spite of the passing of nearly two centuries, the historic provinces which existed before 1790 command the local patriotism of most Frenchmen.

Digne 13,140 G5
Digoin 10,449 F4
Dijon 149,899 F4
Dinan 13,303 B3
Dinard 9,211 B3
Dôle 28,109 F4
Domrémy-la-Pucelle 190 F3
Douai 43,954 E2
Douarnenez 17,851 A3
Doullens 6,806 E2
Draguignan 19,653 G6
Drancy 64,258 B1
Dreux 31,503 D3
Dunkirk (Dunkerque) 78,171 E2
Elbeuf 18,642 D3
Épernay 29,286 E3
Épinal 39,000 G3
Épinay-sur-Seine 46,458 B1
Erstein 6,494 G3
Étampes 18,810 E3
Étaples 10,423 D2
Eu 8,349 D3
Évreux 46,181 D3
Évry 15,300 E3
Falaise 8,133 C3
Fécamp 20,835 D3
Figeac 8,675 D5
Firminy 23,776 F5
Flers 18,590 C3
Foix 9,569 D6
Fontainebleau 16,436 E3
Fontenay-le-Comte 12,301 C4
Fontenay-sous-Bois 46,200 C2
Forbach 24,812 G3
Fougères 26,260 C3
Fourmies 15,318 F2
Fréjus 27,805 G6
Gagny 36,714 C1
Gaillac 7,653 D6
Gap 24,962 G5
Gardanne 8,175 F6
Gennevilliers 50,154 B1
Gentilly 16,843 B2
Gex 3,959 G4
Gien 13,817 E4
Gif 10,866 E3
Gisors 7,591 D3
Givet 7,787 F2
Givors 19,356 F5
Granville 12,869 C3
Grasse 24,260 G6
Graulhet 11,099 E6
Gray 8,718 F4
Grenoble 165,431 F5
Guebwiller 10,477 G4
Guéret 14,418 D4
Guingamp 9,269 B3
Guise 6,642 E3
Haguenau 23,023 G3
Harfleur 9,857 D3
Hautmont 19,130 F2
Hayange 8,479 F3
Hazebrouck 18,867 E2
Hendaye 9,404 C6
Hénin-Beaumont 26,296 E2
Hennebont 8,978 B4
Héricourt 8,481 G4
Hirson 11,909 F3
Honfleur 8,995 D3
Hyères 29,366 G6
Issoire 13,560 E5
Issoudun 15,065 D4
Issy-les-Moulineaux 47,355 A2
Istres 10,127 F6
Ivry-sur-Seine 62,804 B2
Joigny 10,825 E3
La Baule-Escoublac 13,854 B4
La Ciotat 29,290 F6
La Courneuve 37,917 B1
La Flèche 12,743 C4
La Grand-Combe 9,406 E5
L'Aigle 9,198 D3
Landerneau 13,983 B3
Langres 10,745 F4
Lannion 13,692 B3
Laon 27,420 E3
La Pallice C4
La Rochelle 72,936 C4
La Roche-sur-Yon 40,789 C4
La Seyne-sur-Mer 50,059 F6
Laval 50,734 C3
Lavelanet 9,278 E6
Le Blanc 7,431 D4
Le Blanc-Mesnil 49,062 B1
Le Bourget 10,520 B1
Le Cateau 8,680 E2
Le Chesnay 24,590 A2
Le Creusot 31,643 F4
Le Havre 216,917 C3
Le Mans 150,289 C3
Lens 39,973 E2
Le Puy 24,793 F5
Les Andelys 7,524 D3
Les Sables-d'Olonne 17,157 B4
Le Teil 7,993 F5
Le Tréport 6,463 D2
Levallois-Perret 52,460 A1
Lézignan-Corbières 6,929 E6
Libourne 21,265 C5
Liévin 33,040 E2
Lille 171,010 E2
Limoges 136,059 D5
Limoux 9,595 E6
Lisieux 24,972 D3
Livry-Gargan 32,879 C1
Lodève 7,131 E6
Longwy 20,107 F3
Lons-le-Saunier 20,897 F4
Lorient 68,655 B4
Loudéac 7,173 B3
Loudun 7,060 D4
Lourdes 17,685 C6
Louviers 17,919 D3
Luçon 8,834 C4
Lunel 12,392 E6
Lunéville 22,438 G3
Lure 8,538 G4
Luxeuil-les-Bains 10,061 G4
Lyon 454,265 F5
Mâcon 39,130 F4
Maisons-Alfort 53,963 B2
Maisons-Laffitte 23,465 A1
Malakoff 34,100 A2
Manosque 17,256 G6
Mantes-la-Jolie 42,403 D3
Marmande 13,223 C5
Marseille 901,421 F6
Martigues 26,850 F6
Maubeuge 34,152 F2
Mayenne 11,278 C3
Mazamet 13,148 E6
Meaux 41,831 E3
Mehun-sur-Yèvre 6,533 E4
Melun 36,913 E3
Mende 10,040 E5
Menton 24,736 G6
Metz 110,939 G3
Meudon 31,294 A2
Millau 20,401 E5
Mimizan 6,826 C5
Mirecourt 7,160 G3
Moissac 7,403 D5
Montargis 18,021 E3
Montauban 35,344 D5
Montbard 7,477 F4
Montbéliard 29,968 G4
Montbrison 9,945 E5
Montceau-les-Mines 28,093 F4
Mont-de-Marsan 24,812 C6
Mont-Dore 2,074 E5
Montélimar 25,422 F5
Montfort 2,701 C3
Montigny-les-Metz 24,208 G3
Montluçon 56,337 E4
Montmédy 1,859 F3
Montpellier 178,136 E6
Montreuil,
Seine-Saint-Denis 96,441 B2
Montrouge 40,189 B2
Mont-Saint-Michel 88 C3
Morlaix 15,919 B3
Morteau 6,515 G4
Moulins 25,856 E4
Moyeuvre-Grande 12,448 G3
Mulhouse 116,494 G4
Muret 13,041 D6
Nancy 106,906 G3
Nanterre 94,441 A1
Nantes 252,537 C4
Narbonne 36,525 E6
Nemours 11,159 E3
Neufchâteau 8,582 F3
Neuilly-sur-Seine 65,941 A1
Nevers 45,122 E4
Nice 331,002 G6
Nîmes 123,914 F6
Niort 59,297 C4
Nogent-le-Rotrou 12,284 D3
Noisy-le-Sec 37,674 B1
Noyon 13,784 E3
Oloron-Sainte-Marie 11,616 C6
Orange 19,847 F5
Orléans 88,503 D3
Orly 26,090 B2
Orthez 9,639 C6
Oullins 27,731 F5
Oyonnax 22,548 F4
Pamiers 12,906 D6
Pantin 42,651 B1
Paray-le-Monial 11,523 F4
Paris (cap.) 2,291,554 B2
Parthenay 12,549 C4
Pau 81,560 C6
Périgueux 34,779 D5
Péronne 8,358 E3
Perpignan 101,198 E6
Pessac 50,333 C5
Pézenas 6,768 E6
Pithiviers 9,976 E3
Poitiers 78,739 D4
Pont-à-Mousson 14,461 G3
Pontarlier 17,778 G4
Pontivy 9,478 B3
Pont-l'Abbe 6,618 A4
Pontoise 26,702 E3
Port-de-Bouc 20,448 F6
Port-Saint-Louis-du-Rhône 9,649 F6
Port-Vendres 5,448 E6
Privas 9,385 F5
Provins 12,281 E3
Puteau 35,366 A2
Quimper 50,856 A4
Quimperlé 9,783 B4
Rambouillet 18,446 D3
Redon 9,528 C4
Reims 177,320 E3
Remiremont 10,250 G3
Rennes 194,094 C3

(continued on following page)

(continued)

Rethel 8,189 .... F3
Révin 11,459 .... F3
Rezé 35,512 .... C4
Rive-de-Gier 17,369 .... F5
Roanne 54,999 .... E4
Rochechouart 2,953 .... D5
Rochefort 27,264 .... C4
Rodez 24,898 .... E5
Romans-sur-Isère 30,974 .... F5
Romilly-sur-Seine 17,276 .... F3
Romorantin-Lanthenay 15,727 .... D4
Roubaix 109,473 .... E2
Rouen 113,536 .... D3
Royan 17,978 .... C5
Rueil-Malmaison 62,504 .... A2
Sablé-sur-Sarthe 9,913 .... C4
Saint-Affrique 6,842 .... E6
Saint-Amand-Mont-Rond 11,896 .... E4
Saint-Brieuc 51,838 .... B3
Saint-Chamond 39,236 .... F5
Saint-Claude 12,651 .... F4
Saint-Cloud 28,052 .... A2
Saint-Denis 95,808 .... B1
Saint-Dié 22,834 .... G3
Saint-Dizier 36,377 .... F3
Sainte-Mère-Église 1,041 .... C3
Saintes 24,946 .... C5
Sainte-Savine 10,526 .... E3
Saint-Étienne 218,289 .... F5
Saint-Florent-sur-Cher 6,385 .... E4
Saint-Flour 6,900 .... E5
Saint-Gaudens 12,103 .... D6
Saint-Germain-en-Laye 35,351 .... D3
Saint-Gilles-Croix-de-Vie 6,569 .... B4
Saint-Girons 7,259 .... D6
Saint-Jean-d'Angély 8,801 .... C4
Saint-Jean-de-Luz 10,921 .... C6
Saint-Jean-de-Maurienne 9,525 .... G5
Saint-Jean-Pied-de-Port 1,725 .... C6
Saint-Junien 9,281 .... D5
Saint-Lô 21,670 .... C3
Saint-Malo 43,277 .... B3
Saint-Mandé 20,714 .... B2
Saint-Marcellin 6,768 .... F5
Saint-Maur-des-Fossés 80,797 .... B2
Saint-Mihiel 5,544 .... F3
Saint-Nazaire 65,228 .... B4
Saint-Omer 16,419 .... E2
Saint-Ouen 43,569 .... B1
Saint-Pol-de-Léon 6,571 .... A3
Saint-Quentin 69,956 .... E3
Saint-Raphaël 19,499 .... G6
Saint-Tropez 4,484 .... G6
Saint-Vallier 10,000 .... F5
Salon-de-Provence 31,783 .... F6
Sancerre 2,029 .... E4
Sarlat-La-Canéda 8,191 .... D5
Sarrebourg 12,442 .... G3
Sarreguemines 24,570 .... G3
Sartrouville 42,092 .... A1
Saumur 30,984 .... D4
Saverne 10,015 .... G3
Sceaux 19,651 .... A2
Sedan 23,867 .... F3
Sélestat 15,209 .... G3
Senlis 13,481 .... E3
Sens 25,621 .... E3
Sète 39,075 .... E6
Sèvres 21,100 .... A2
Sisteron 6,434 .... G5
Soissons 29,694 .... E3
Sotteville-les-Rouen 30,393 .... D3
Stiring-Wendel 12,665 .... G3
Strasbourg 251,520 .... H3
Suresnes 37,456 .... A2
Tarare 11,931 .... F5
Tarascon 8,522 .... F6
Tarbes 54,286 .... D6
Thann 8,508 .... G4
Thiers 14,534 .... E5
Thionville 37,943 .... G3
Thonon-les-Bains 24,673 .... G4
Thouars 11,835 .... C4
Tonneins 7,256 .... D5
Toul 16,141 .... F3
Toulon 180,508 .... F6
Toulouse 371,143 .... D6
Tourcoing 102,092 .... E2
Tournon 8,568 .... F5
Tournus 7,284 .... F4
Tours 139,560 .... D4
Troyes 71,600 .... F3
Tulle 18,375 .... D5
Uckange 11,552 .... G3
Ussel 9,816 .... E5
Uzès 6,470 .... F5
Valence 67,101 .... F5
Valenciennes 41,976 .... E2
Vannes 36,722 .... B4
Vence 7,332 .... G6
Vendôme 17,828 .... D4
Vénissieux 74,264 .... F5
Verdun-sur-Meuse 22,889 .... F3
Vernon 21,184 .... D3
Versailles 93,359 .... A2
Vesoul 17,883 .... F4
Vichy 32,107 .... E4
Vienne 25,981 .... F5
Vierzon 33,057 .... D4
Villefranche 6,600 .... G6
Villefranche-de-Rouergue 10,848 .... E5
Villefranche-sur-Saône 29,996 .... F4
Villejuif 53,884 .... B2
Villemomble 28,684 .... C1
Villeneuve-Saint-Georges 31,378 .... E3
Villeneuve-sur-Lot 17,818 .... D5
Villeurbanne 115,913 .... F5
Vincennes 44,256 .... B2
Vire 12,832 .... C3
Vitré 10,989 .... C3
Vitry-le-François 19,075 .... F3
Vitry-sur-Seine 87,119 .... B2
Vittel 6,791 .... F3
Vizille 6,810 .... F5
Voiron 17,879 .... F5
Wissembourg 6,679 .... G3
Yvetot 10,088 .... D3

OTHER FEATURES

Adour (riv.) C6
Ain (riv.) F4
Aisne (riv.) E3
Ajaccio (gulf) B7
Allier (riv.) E5
Aube (riv.) F3
Auvergne (mts.) E5
Belle-Île (isl.) B4
Biscay (bay) B5
Blanc (mt.) G5
Bonifacio (str.) B7
Calais (Dover) (str.) D2
Causses (reg.) D5
Cévennes (mts.) E5
Charente (riv.) C5
Cher (riv.) D4
Corse (cape) B6
Corsica (isl.) B6
Côte-d'Or (mts.) F4
Cotentin (pen.) C3
Cottian Alps (range) G5
Creuse (riv.) D4
Dordogne (riv.) D5
Dore Alps (mts.) E5
Doubs (riv.) G4
Drôme (riv.) F5
Dronne (riv.) D5
Durance (riv.) F6
English (chan.) B3
Eure (riv.) D3
Faucilles (mts.) G3
Forez (mts.) E5
Fréjus (pass) G5
Gard (riv.) F5
Garonne (riv.) C5
Gave de Pau (riv.) C6
Geneva (lake) G4
Gers (riv.) D6
Gironde (riv.) C5
Graian Alps (range) G5
Groix (isl.) B4
Hague (cape) C3
Hérault (riv.) E6
Hyères (isls.) G6
Indre (riv.) D4
Isère (riv.) F5
Isle (riv.) D5
Langres (plat.) F4
Limousin (reg.) D5
Lions (gulf) F6
Little Saint Bernard (pass) G5
Loir (riv.) D4
Loire (riv.) C4
Lot (riv.) D5
Manche, La (English) (chan.) B3
Maritime Alps (range) G5
Marne (riv.) C2
Mayenne (riv.) C4
Mediterranean (sea) E7
Médoc (reg.) C5
Meuse (riv.) F3
Mont Cenis (tunnel) G5
Morvan (plat.) F4
Moselle (riv.) G3
Noirmoutier (isl.) B4
North (sea) E1
Oise (riv.) E3
Oléron (isl.) C5
Omaha (beach) C3
Orb (riv.) E6
Orne (riv.) C3
Ouessant (isl.) A3
Penmarch (pt.) A4
Perche (reg.) D3
Puy-de-Dôme (mt.) E5
Pyrenees (range) C6
Ré (isl.) C4
Rhine (riv.) G3
Rhône (riv.) F5
Risle (riv.) D3
Riviera (reg.) G6
Saint-Florent (gulf) B6
Saint-Malo (gulf) B3
Saône (riv.) F4
Sarthe (riv.) D4
Sein (isl.) A3
Seine (bay) C3
Seine (riv.) D3
Sologne (reg.) E4
Somme (riv.) D2
Tarn (riv.) E6
Ushant (Ouessant) (isl.) A3
Utah (beach) C3
Vaccarès (lag.) F6
Vienne (riv.) D4
Vilaine (riv.) C4
Vosges (mts.) G3
Yonne (riv.) E3

MONACO

CITIES and TOWNS

Monte Carlo 11,599 .... G6

* City and suburbs

MONACO

AREA 368 acres (149 hectares)
POPULATION 25,029

Wine Regions

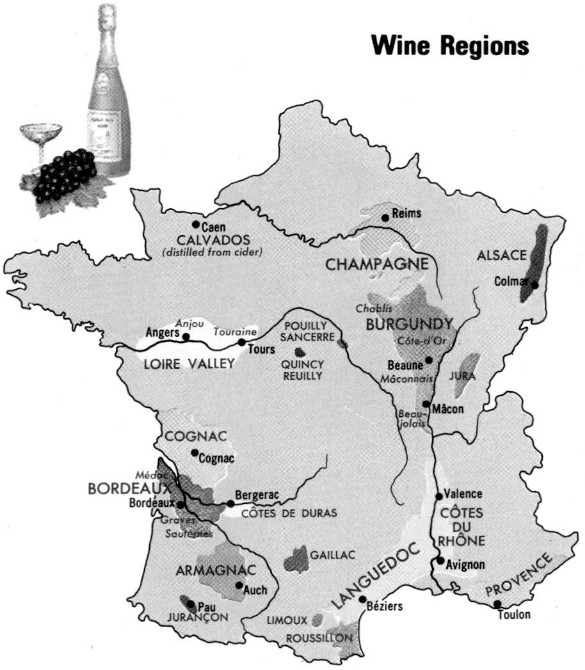

Climate, soil and variety of grape planted determine the quality of wine. Long, hot and fairly dry summers with cool, humid nights constitute an ideal climate. The nature of the soil is such a determining influence that identical grapes planted in Bordeaux, Burgundy and Champagne, will yield wines of widely different types.

Agriculture, Industry and Resources

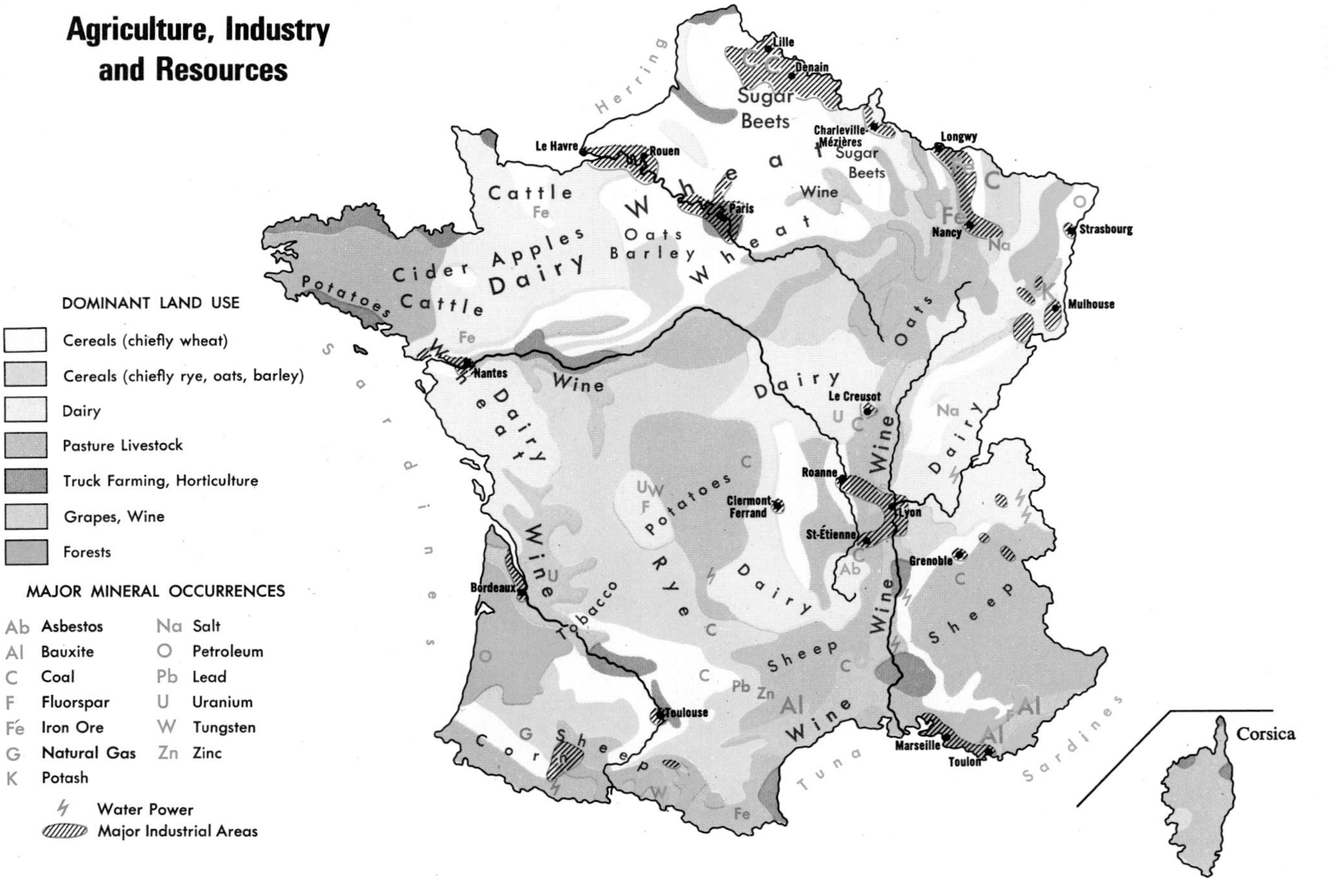

ANDORRA

SPAIN

PORTUGAL

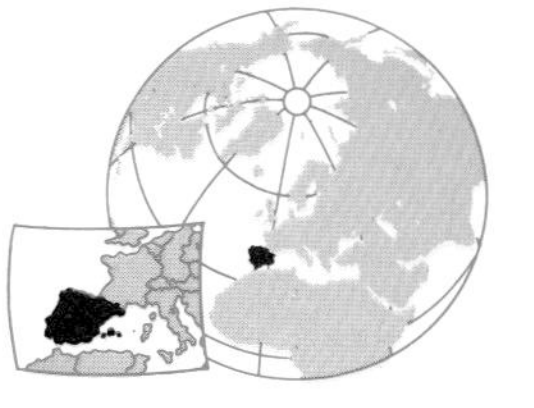

SPAIN

AREA 194,881 sq. mi. (504,742 sq. km.)
POPULATION 37,430,000
CAPITAL Madrid
LARGEST CITY Madrid
HIGHEST POINT Pico de Teide 12,172 ft. (3,710 m.) (Canary Is.); Mulhacén 11,411 ft. (3,478 m.) (mainland)
MONETARY UNIT peseta
MAJOR LANGUAGES Spanish, Catalan, Basque, Galician, Valencian
MAJOR RELIGION Roman Catholicism

PORTUGAL

AREA 35,549 sq. mi. (92,072 sq. km.)
POPULATION 9,933,000
CAPITAL Lisbon
LARGEST CITY Lisbon
HIGHEST POINT Malhão da Estrela 6,532 ft. (1,991 m.)
MONETARY UNIT escudo
MAJOR LANGUAGE Portuguese
MAJOR RELIGION Roman Catholicism

ANDORRA

AREA 188 sq. mi. (487 sq. km.)
POPULATION 31,000
CAPITAL Andorra la Vella
MONETARY UNITS French franc, Spanish peseta
MAJOR LANGUAGE Catalan
MAJOR RELIGION Roman Catholicism

GIBRALTAR

AREA 2.28 sq. mi. (5.91 sq. km.)
POPULATION 29,760
CAPITAL Gibraltar
MONETARY UNIT pound sterling
MAJOR LANGUAGES English, Spanish
MAJOR RELIGION Roman Catholicism

SPAIN

PROVINCES

Álava 204,323 ..... E1
Albacete 335,026 ..... E3
Alicante 920,105 ..... F3
Almería 375,004 ..... E4
Ávila 203,798 ..... D2
Badajoz 687,599 ..... C3
Baleares 558,287 ..... H3
Barcelona 3,929,194 ..... G2
Burgos 358,075 ..... E1
Cáceres 457,777 ..... C3
Cádiz 885,433 ..... D4
Castellón 385,823 ..... G2
Ciudad Real 507,650 ..... D3
Córdoba 724,116 ..... D3
Cuenca 247,158 ..... E2
Gerona 414,397 ..... H1
Granada 733,375 ..... E4
Guadalajara 147,732 ..... E2
Guipúzcoa 631,003 ..... E1
Huelva 397,683 ..... C4
Huesca 222,238 ..... F1
Jaén 661,146 ..... E4
La Coruña 1,004,188 ..... B1
Las Palmas 579,710 ..... C4
León 548,721 ..... C1
Lérida 347,015 ..... G2
Logroño 235,713 ..... E1
Lugo 415,052 ..... C1
Madrid 3,792,561 ..... E2
Málaga 867,330 ..... D4
Murcia 832,313 ..... F4
Navarra 464,867 ..... F1
Orense 413,733 ..... C1
Oviedo 1,045,635 ..... C1
Palencia 198,763 ..... D1
Pontevedra 750,701 ..... B1
Salamanca 371,607 ..... C2
Santa Cruz de Tenerife 590,514 ..... B5
Santander 467,138 ..... D1
Segovia 162,770 ..... D2
Sevilla 1,327,190 ..... D4
Soria 114,956 ..... E2
Tarragona 431,961 ..... G2
Teruel 170,284 ..... F2
Toledo 468,925 ..... D3
Valencia 1,767,327 ..... F3
Valladolid 412,572 ..... D2
Vizcaya 1,043,310 ..... E1
Zamora 251,934 ..... D2
Zaragoza 760,186 ..... F2

CITIES and TOWNS

Adra 10,851 ..... E4
Aguilar 12,893 ..... D4
Aguilas 15,525 ..... F4
Alagón 5,114 ..... F2
Alayor 5,124 ..... J3
Albacete 82,607 ..... F3
Albox 5,072 ..... E4
Alburquerque 7,530 ..... C3
Alcalá de Guadaira 28,781 ..... D4
Alcalá de Henares 59,783 ..... G4
Alcalá de los Gazules 5,262 ..... D4
Alcalá la Real 9,849 ..... E4
Alcanar 5,961 ..... G2
Alcañiz 10,229 ..... F2
Alcantarilla 19,895 ..... F4
Alcaudete 8,557 ..... E4
Alcázar de San Juan 24,620 ..... E3
Alcira 30,493 ..... F3
Alcora 6,711 ..... F2
Alcoy 61,371 ..... F3
Alfaro 8,766 ..... F1
Algeciras 74,754 ..... D4
Algemesí 21,158 ..... F3
Alhama de Granada 6,148 ..... E4
Alhama de Murcia 9,274 ..... F4
Alicante 177,918 ..... F3
Almadén 10,713 ..... D3
Almagro 9,066 ..... E3
Almansa 16,965 ..... F3
Almendralejo 21,929 ..... C3
Almería 104,008 ..... E4
Almodóvar del Campo 7,310 ..... D3
Almonte 9,960 ..... C4
Almuñécar 7,812 ..... E4
Álora 8,209 ..... D4
Altea 7,262 ..... G3
Amposta 11,767 ..... G2
Andorra 6,485 ..... F2
Andújar 25,962 ..... D3
Antequera 28,039 ..... D4
Aracena 5,390 ..... C4
Aranda de Duero 18,183 ..... E2
Aranjuez 28,559 ..... E2
Archena 7,118 ..... F3
Archidona 6,084 ..... D4
Arcos de la Frontera 16,217 ..... D4
Arenas de San Pedro 5,225 ..... D2
Arenys de Mar 8,325 ..... H2
Arévalo 5,807 ..... D2
Argamasilla de Alba 6,192 ..... E3
Arganda 11,876 ..... G4
Arnedo 9,809 ..... E1
Arrecife 21,310 ..... C4
Arroyo de la Luz 8,130 ..... C3
Artá 5,284 ..... H3
Arucas 9,095 ..... B5
Aspe 13,229 ..... F3
Astorga 11,794 ..... C1
Ávila de los Caballeros 30,958 ..... D2
Avilés 67,186 ..... C1
Ayamonte 9,897 ..... C4
Ayora 5,249 ..... F3
Azpeitia 7,835 ..... E1
Azuaga 10,719 ..... D3
Badajoz 80,793 ..... C3
Badalona 162,888 ..... H2
Baena 16,496 ..... D4
Baeza 12,607 ..... E4
Bailén 13,207 ..... E3
Balaguer 11,676 ..... G2
Bañolas 9,807 ..... H1
Baracaldo 108,757 ..... E1
Barbastro 13,243 ..... F1
Barcarrota 5,012 ..... C3
Barcelona 1,741,144 ..... H2
Barcelona‡ 2,000,000 ..... H2
Baza 14,290 ..... E4
Beas de Segura 6,592 ..... E3
Béjar 16,804 ..... D2
Bélmez 5,161 ..... D3
Benavente 11,779 ..... D1
Benicarló 12,831 ..... G2
Berga 11,163 ..... G1
Berja 7,081 ..... E4
Bermeo 16,714 ..... E1
Betanzos 7,283 ..... B1
Bilbao 393,179 ..... E1
Bilbao‡ 450,000 ..... E1
Binéfar 6,821 ..... G2
Blanes 15,810 ..... H2
Borjas Blancas 4,991 ..... G2
Bujalance 8,236 ..... D4
Bullas 8,131 ..... F4
Burgos 118,366 ..... E1
Burriana 21,298 ..... G3
Cabeza del Buey 8,704 ..... D3
Cabra 16,177 ..... D4
Cáceres 53,108 ..... C3
Cádiz 135,743 ..... C4
Calahorra 16,315 ..... E1
Calasparra 7,238 ..... F3
Calatayud 16,524 ..... F2
Calella 9,696 ..... H2
Callosa de Ensarriá 5,701 ..... G3
Calzada de Calatrava 5,751 ..... E3
Campanario 7,722 ..... D3
Campillos 7,014 ..... D4
Campo de Criptana 12,604 ..... E3
Candás 5,517 ..... D1
Candeleda 5,153 ..... D2
Cangas de Narcea 4,826 ..... C1
Caniles 5,099 ..... E4
Caravaca de le Cruz 10,411 ..... E3
Carballo 5,542 ..... B1
Carcagente 18,223 ..... F3
Carmona 22,832 ..... D4
Cartagena 52,312 ..... F4
Caspe 8,766 ..... G2
Cassá de la Selva 5,248 ..... H2
Castellón de la Plana 79,773 ..... G2
Castro del Río 10,087 ..... D4
Castro-Urdiales 8,369 ..... E1
Castuera 8,060 ..... D3
Caudete 7,332 ..... F3
Cazalla de la Sierra 5,382 ..... D4
Cazorla 6,938 ..... E4
Cehegín 9,661 ..... F3
Cervera 5,693 ..... G2
Ceuta 60,639 ..... D5
Chiclana de la Frontera 22,986 ..... C4
Chiva 5,394 ..... F3
Ciempozuelos 9,185 ..... F5
Cieza 22,929 ..... F3
Ciudadela 13,701 ..... H2
Ciudad Real 39,931 ..... D3
Ciudad-Rodrigo 11,694 ..... C2
Cocentaina 8,375 ..... F3
Coín 14,190 ..... D4
Colmenar de Oreja 4,930 ..... G5
Colmenar Viejo 12,886 ..... F4
Constantina 10,227 ..... D4
Consuegra 10,026 ..... E3
Córdoba 216,049 ..... D4
Corella 5,850 ..... F1
Coria 8,083 ..... C3
Coria del Río 18,085 ..... C4
Corral de Almaguer 8,006 ..... E3
Crevillente 15,749 ..... F3
Cuéllar 6,118 ..... D2
Cuenca 33,980 ..... E2
Cullera 15,128 ..... F3
Daimiel 17,710 ..... E3
Denia 14,514 ..... G3
Dolores 5,420 ..... F3
Don Benito 21,351 ..... C3
Dos Hermanas 36,921 ..... D4
Durango 20,403 ..... E1
Écija 27,295 ..... D4
Eibar 36,729 ..... E1
Ejea de los Caballeros 9,766 ..... F1
El Arahal 14,703 ..... D4
Elche 101,271 ..... F3
Elda 41,404 ..... F3
Elizondo 2,516 ..... F1
El Puerto de Santa María 36,451 ..... C4
Espejo 5,925 ..... D4
Estella 10,371 ..... E1
Estepa 9,376 ..... D4
Estepona 18,560 ..... D4
Felanitx 9,100 ..... H3
Ferrol del Caudillo 75,464 ..... B1
Figueras 22,087 ..... H1
Fraga 9,665 ..... G2
Fregenal de la Sierra 6,826 ..... C3
Fuengirola 20,597 ..... D4
Fuente de Cantos 5,967 ..... C3
Fuenterrabiá 2,350 ..... E1
Fuentes de Andalucía 8,257 ..... D4
Gandía 30,702 ..... F3
Gerona 37,095 ..... H2
Getafe 68,680 ..... F4
Gijón 159,806 ..... D1
Granada 185,799 ..... E4
Granollers 30,066 ..... H2
Guadalajara 30,924 ..... E2
Guadix 15,311 ..... E4
Guareña 7,706 ..... C3
Guernica y Luno 12,046 ..... E1
Haro 8,393 ..... E1
Hellín 15,934 ..... F3
Herencia 8,212 ..... E3
Hinojosa del Duque 9,873 ..... D3
Hortaleza G4
Hospitalet 241,978 ..... H2
Huelma 5,260 ..... E4
Huelva 96,689 ..... C4
Huercal-Overa 5,158 ..... F4
Huesca 33,076 ..... F1
Huéscar 6,384 ..... E4
Ibiza 16,943 ..... G3
Igualada 27,941 ..... G2
Inca 16,930 ..... H3
Irún 38,014 ..... F1
Iscar 5,192 ..... D2
Isla Cristina 11,402 ..... C4
Iznalloz 4,814 ..... E4
Jaca 9,936 ..... F1
Jaén 71,145 ..... E4
Jaraíz de la Vera 6,379 ..... D2
Játiva 20,934 ..... F3
Jávea 6,228 ..... G3
Jerez de la Frontera 112,411 ..... C4
Jerez de los Caballeros 8,607 ..... C3
Jijona 8,117 ..... F3
Jódar 11,973 ..... E4
Jumilla 16,407 ..... F3
La Almunia de Doña Godina 4,835 ..... F2
La Bañeza 8,480 ..... C1
La Bisbal 6,374 ..... H1
La Carolina 13,138 ..... E3
La Coruña 184,372 ..... B1
La Granja (San Ildefonso) 3,198 ..... E2
La Guardia 4,967 ..... B2
La Línea de la Concepción 51,021 ..... D4
La Orotava 8,246 ..... B4
La Palma del Condado 9,256 ..... C4
La Puebla 9,923 ..... H3
La Puebla de Montalbán 6,629 ..... D3
La Rambla 6,525 ..... D4
Laredo 9,114 ..... E1
La Roda 11,460 ..... E3
La Solana 13,894 ..... E3
Las Palmas de Gran Canaria 260,368 ..... B4
Las Pedroñeras 5,846 ..... E3
La Unión 9,998 ..... F4
Lebrija 15,081 ..... D4
Leganés 57,537 ..... F4
León 99,702 ..... D1
Lérida 73,148 ..... G2
Linares 45,330 ..... E3
Liria 11,323 ..... F3
Llerena 5,728 ..... C3
Llivia 801 ..... G1
Llodio 15,587 ..... E1
Lluctmayor 9,630 ..... H3
Logroño 83,117 ..... E1
Loja 11,549 ..... D4
Lora del Río 15,741 ..... D4
Lorca 25,208 ..... F4
Los Santos de Maimona 7,899 ..... C3
Los Yébenes 5,477 ..... E3
Lucena 21,527 ..... D4
Lugo 53,504 ..... C1
Madrid (cap.) 3,146,071 ..... F4
Madrid‡ 3,500,000 ..... F4
Madridejos 9,948 ..... E3
Madroñera 5,397 ..... D3
Mahón 17,802 ..... J3
Málaga 334,988 ..... D4
Málaga‡ 400,000 ..... D4
Malagón 7,732 ..... E3
Malpartida de Cáceres 5,054 ..... C3
Manacor 20,266 ..... H3
Mancha Real 7,547 ..... E4
Manlleu 13,169 ..... H1
Manresa 52,526 ..... G2
Manzanares 15,024 ..... E3
Marbella 19,648 ..... D4
Marchena 16,227 ..... D4
Marín 10,948 ..... B1
Martos 16,395 ..... E4
Mataró 73,129 ..... H2
Medina del Campo 16,345 ..... D2
Medina de Rioseco 4,874 ..... D2
Medina-Sidonia 7,523 ..... D4
Mérida 36,916 ..... C3
Miajadas 8,042 ..... D3
Mieres 22,790 ..... D1
Minas de Ríotinto 3,939 ..... C4
Miranda de Ebro 29,355 ..... E1
Moguer 7,629 ..... C4
Mollerusa 6,685 ..... G2
Monesterio 5,923 ..... C3
Monforte 14,002 ..... C1
Monóvar 9,071 ..... F3
Montehermoso 5,952 ..... C2
Montellano 6,658 ..... D4
Montijo 11,931 ..... C3
Montilla 18,670 ..... D4
Montoro 9,295 ..... D3
Monzón 14,089 ..... G2
Mora 10,523 ..... E3
Moratalla 5,101 ..... E3
Morón de la Frontera 25,662 ..... D4
Mota del Cuervo 5,130 ..... E3
Motril 25,121 ..... E4
Mula 9,168 ..... F3
Munera 5,003 ..... E3
Murcia 102,242 ..... F4
Navalcarnero 6,212 ..... F4
Navalmoral de la Mata 9,650 ..... D3
Nerja 7,413 ..... E4
Nerva 10,830 ..... C4
Novelda 16,867 ..... F3
Nules 9,027 ..... F3
Ocaña 5,603 ..... E3
Oliva 16,717 ..... F3
Oliva de la Frontera 8,560 ..... C3
Olivenza 7,616 ..... C3
Olot 18,062 ..... H1
Olvera 9,825 ..... D4
Onda 13,012 ..... F3
Onteniente 23,685 ..... F3
Orense 63,542 ..... C1
Orihuela 17,610 ..... F3
Osuna 17,384 ..... D4
Oviedo 130,021 ..... C1
Padul 6,377 ..... E4
Palafrugell 10,421 ..... H2
Palamós 7,679 ..... H2
Palencia 58,327 ..... D2
Palma 191,416 ..... H3
Palma del Río 15,075 ..... D4
Pamplona 142,686 ..... F1
Pego 8,861 ..... F3
Peñafiel 4,794 ..... E2
Peñaranda de Bracamonte 6,094 ..... D2
Peñarroya-Pueblonuevo 15,649 ..... D3
Pinos-Puente 7,634 ..... E4
Plasencia 26,897 ..... C2
Pola de Lena 5,760 ..... D1
Pollensa 7,625 ..... H3
Ponferrada 22,838 ..... C1
Pontevedra 27,118 ..... B1
Porcuna 8,169 ..... D4
Port-Bou 2,230 ..... H1
Portugalete 45,589 ..... E1
Posadas 7,245 ..... D4
Pozoblanco 13,280 ..... D3
Pozuelo de Alarcón 14,041 ..... D2
Priego de Córdoba 12,676 ..... D4
Puente-Genil 22,888 ..... D4
Puertollano 50,609 ..... D3
Puerto Real 13,993 ..... D4
Puigcerdá 4,418 ..... G1
Quesada 6,965 ..... E4
Quintana de la Serena 5,171 ..... D3
Quintanar de la Orden 7,764 ..... E3
Reinosa 10,863 ..... D1
Requena 9,836 ..... F3
Reus 47,240 ..... G2
Ripoll 9,283 ..... H1
Ronda 22,094 ..... D4
Roquetas 5,617 ..... G2
Rosas 5,448 ..... H1
Rota 20,021 ..... C4
Rute 8,294 ..... D4
Sabadell 148,223 ..... H2
Sagunto 17,052 ..... F3
Salamanca 125,132 ..... D2
Sallent 7,118 ..... H2
Salobreña 5,961 ..... E4
Salt 5,572 ..... H1
Sama 9,863 ..... D1
San Carlos de la Rápita 8,946 ..... G2
San Clemente 6,016 ..... E3
San Feliu de Guíxols 12,006 ..... H2
San Fernando 59,309 ..... C4
San Ildefonso 3,198 ..... E2

Agriculture, Industry and Resources

DOMINANT LAND USE

- Cereals (chiefly wheat)
- Livestock (chiefly sheep, goats)
- Mixed Cereals, Livestock
- Olives, Fruit
- Grapes, Fruit, Nuts, Mixed Cereals
- Forests
- Nonagricultural Land

MAJOR MINERAL OCCURRENCES

Ag	Silver	Na	Salt
C	Coal	O	Petroleum
Cu	Copper	Pb	Lead
Fe	Iron Ore	Py	Pyrites
G	Natural Gas	Sb	Antimony
Hg	Mercury	Sn	Tin
K	Potash	U	Uranium
Lg	Lignite	W	Tungsten
Mg	Magnesium	Zn	Zinc

Water Power
Major Industrial Areas

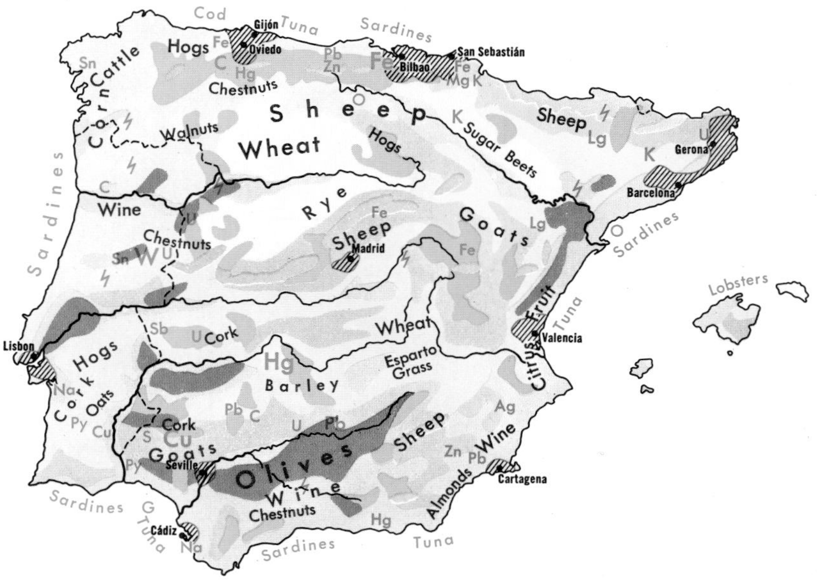

(continued on following page)

(continued)

San Lorenzo de El
  Escorial 8,098 ..... E2
Sanlúcar de Barrameda 29,483 ..... C4
Sanlúcar la Mayor 6,121 ..... C4
San Roque 8,224 ..... D4
San Sebastián 159,557 ..... E1
Santa Cruz de la Palma 10,393 ..... B4
Santa Cruz de Mudela 6,354 ..... E3
Santa Cruz de Tenerife 74,910 ..... B4
Santa Eugenia 5,946 ..... B1
Santa Fé 8,990 ..... E4
Santander 130,019 ..... D1
Santiago 51,620 ..... B1
Santo Domingo de la
  Calzada 5,638 ..... E1
Santoña 9,546 ..... E1
San Vicente de
  Alcántara 7,006 ..... C3
Saragossa 449,319 ..... F2
Saragossa‡ 500,000 ..... F2
Segorbe 6,962 ..... F3
Segovia 41,880 ..... D2
Seo de Urgel 6,604 ..... G1
Seville 511,447 ..... D4
Seville‡ 560,000 ..... D4
Sitges 8,906 ..... G2
Socuéllamos 12,610 ..... E3
Sóller 6,470 ..... H3
Solsona 5,346 ..... G2
Sonseca 6,594 ..... D3
Soria 24,744 ..... E2
Sotrondio 5,914 ..... D1
Sueca 20,019 ..... F3
Tabernes de Valldigna 13,962 ..... G3
Tafalla 8,858 ..... F1
Talavera de la Reina 39,889 ..... D2
Tarancón 8,238 ..... E3
Tarazona 11,067 ..... E2
Tarazona de la Mancha 5,952 ..... F3
Tarifa 9,201 ..... D4
Tarragona 53,548 ..... G2
Tarrasa 134,481 ..... G2
Tárrega 9,036 ..... G2
Tauste 6,832 ..... F2
Telde 13,257 ..... B5
Teruel 20,614 ..... F2
Tobarra 5,887 ..... F3
Toledo 43,905 ..... D3
Tolosa 15,164 ..... F1
Tomelloso 26,041 ..... E3
Tordesillas 5,815 ..... D2
Toro 8,455 ..... D2
Torredonjimeno 12,507 ..... D4
Torrejón de Ardoz 21,081 ..... G4
Torrelavega 19,933 ..... D1
Torremolinos 20,484 ..... D4
Torrente 38,397 ..... F3
Torrevieja 9,431 ..... F4
Torrijos 6,362 ..... D2
Torrox 5,583 ..... E4
Tortosa 20,030 ..... G2
Totana 12,714 ..... F4
Trigueros 6,280 ..... C4
Trujillo 9,024 ..... D3
Tudela 20,942 ..... F1
Úbeda 28,306 ..... E3
Ubrique 13,166 ..... D4
Utiel 9,168 ..... F3
Utrera 28,287 ..... D4
Valdemoro 6,263 ..... F4
Valdepeñas 24,018 ..... E3
Valencia 626,675 ..... F3
Valencia‡ 700,000 ..... F3
Valencia de Alcántara 5,963 ..... C3
Valladolid 227,511 ..... D2
Vall de Uxó 23,976 ..... F3
Vallecas G4
Valls 14,189 ..... G2
Valverde del Camino 10,566 ..... C4
Vejer de la Frontera 6,184 ..... C4
Vélez-Málaga 20,794 ..... E4
Vendrell 7,951 ..... G2
Vera 4,903 ..... F4
Vergara 11,541 ..... E1
Vicálvaro G4
Vich 23,449 ..... H2
Vigo 114,526 ..... B1
Vilafranca del
  Penedés 16,875 ..... G2
Villacañas 9,883 ..... E3
Villacarrillo 9,452 ..... E3
Villafranca de los
  Barros 12,610 ..... C3
Villagarcía 6,601 ..... B1
Villajoyosa 12,573 ..... F3
Villanueva de Córdoba 11,270 ..... D3
Villanueva del Arzobispo 8,076 ..... E3
Villanueva de la Serena 16,687 ..... D3
Villanueva de los
  Infantes 8,154 ..... E3
Villanueva y Geltrú 35,714 ..... G2
Villarreal de los
  Infantes 29,482 ..... G3
Villarrobledo 19,698 ..... E3
Villarrubia de los Ojos 9,144 ..... E3
Villaverde F4
Villena 23,483 ..... F3
Vinaroz 13,727 ..... G2
Vitoria 124,791 ..... E1
Yecla 19,352 ..... F3
Zafra 11,583 ..... C3
Zalamea de la Serena 6,017 ..... D3
Zamora 48,791 ..... D2
Zaragoza (Saragossa) 449,319 ..... F2

OTHER FEATURES

Alborán (isl.) E5
Alcaraz, Sierra de (range) E3
Alcudia (bay) H3
Almanzor (mt.) D2
Almanzora (riv.) F4
Andalusia (reg.) C4
Aneto (peak) G1
Aragón (reg.) F2
Arosa, Ria de (est.) B1
Asturias (reg.) C1
Balaitous (mt.) F1
Balearic (Baleares)
  (isls.) H3
Barbate (riv.) D4
Biscay (bay) E1
Cabrera (isl.) H3
Cádiz (gulf) C4
Cala Burras (pt.) D4
Canary (isls.) B4
Cantabrian (range) C1
Catalonia (reg.) G2
Cinca (riv.) G2
Columbretes (isls.) G3
Costa Brava (reg.) H2
Costa de Sola (Costa del Sol)
  (reg.) D4
Creus (cape) H1
Cuenca, Sierra de (range) F3
Demanda, Sierra de la (range) E1
Douro (riv.) C2
Duero (Douro) (riv.) C2
Ebro (riv.) G2
Eresma (riv.) D2
Esla (riv.) D2
Estats (peak) G1
Estremadura (reg.) C3
Finisterre (cape) B1
Formentera (isl.) G3
Formentor (cape) H2
Fuerteventura (isl.) C4
Galicia (reg.) B1
Gata (cape) F4
Gata (mts.) C2
Genil (riv.) D4
Gibraltar (str.) D5
Gomera (isl.) B5
Gran Canaria (isl.) B5
Gredos, Sierra de (range) D2
Guadalimar (riv.) E3
Guadalquivir (riv.) C4
Guadarrama, Sierra de (range) E2
Guadarrama (riv.) F4
Guadiana (riv.) D3
Gúdar, Sierra de (range) F2
Henares (riv.) G4
Hierro (isl.) A5
Ibiza (isl.) G3
Jalón (riv.) E2
Jarama (riv.) E2
Júcar (riv.) F3
Lanzarote (isl.) C4
La Palma (isl.) A4
León (reg.) C1
Llobregat (riv.) H2
Majorca (isl.) H3
Mallorca (Majorca)
  (isl.) H3
Mancha, La (reg.) E3
Manzanares (riv.) F4
Marismas, Las (marsh) C4
Mar Menor (lag.) F4
Mayor (cape) E1
Menorca (Minorca) (isl.) J2
Miño (riv.) B1
Minorca (isl.) J2
Moncayo, Sierra de (range) F2
Montserrat (mt.) G2
Morena, Sierra (range) E3
Mulhacén (mt.) E4
Murcia (reg.) F3
Nao (cape) G3
Navia (riv.) C1
Nevada, Sierra (mts.) E4
New Castile (reg.) E3
Odiel (riv.) C4
Old Castile (reg.) D2
Órbigo (riv.) D1
Palos (cape) F4
Peñalara (mt.) E2
Peñas (cape) D1
Peña Vieja (mt.) D1
Penibética, Sistema (range) E4
Perdido (mt.) G1
Pyrenees (range) F1
Rosas (gulf) H1
San Jorge (gulf) G2
Segre (riv.) G2
Segura (riv.) F3
Sil (riv.) C1
Tagus (riv.) D3
Tajo (Tagus) (riv.) D3
Teide, Pico de (peak) B5
Tenerife (isl.) B5
Ter (riv.) H1
Tinto (riv.) C4
Toledo (mts.) E3
Tortosa (cape) G2
Trafalgar (cape) C4
Turia (riv.) F3
Ulla (riv.) B1
Urgel, Llanos de (plain) G2
Valencia (gulf) G3
Valencia (reg.) F3
Valencia, Albufera de (lag.) G3
Vascongadas (reg.) E1

PORTUGAL

DISTRICTS

Aveiro 545,230 ..... B2
Beja 204,440 ..... C3
Braga 609,415 ..... B2
Bragança 180,395 ..... C2
Castelo Branco 254,355 ..... C3
Coimbra 399,380 ..... B2
Évora 178,475 ..... C3
Faro 268,040 ..... B4
Guarda 210,720 ..... C2
Leiria 376,940 ..... B3
Lisbon 1,568,020 ..... A1
Oporto (Porto)
  1,309,560 ..... B2
Portalegre 145,545 ..... C3
Porto 1,309,560 ..... B2
Santarém 427,995 ..... B3
Sétubal 469,555 ..... B3
Viano do Castelo
  250,510 ..... B2
Vila Real 265,605 ..... C2
Viseu 410,795 ..... C2

CITIES and TOWNS

Abrantes 11,775 ..... B3
Águeda 9,343 ..... B2
Albufeira 7,479 ..... B4
Alcácer do Sal 13,187 ..... B3
Alcântara 23,699 ..... A1

Topography

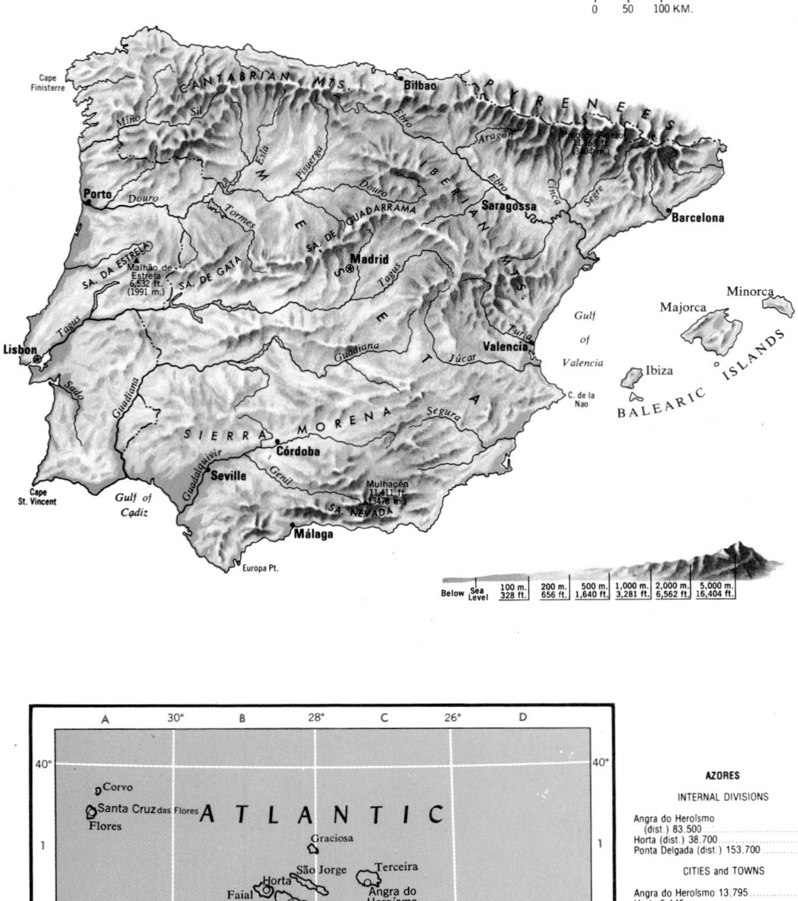

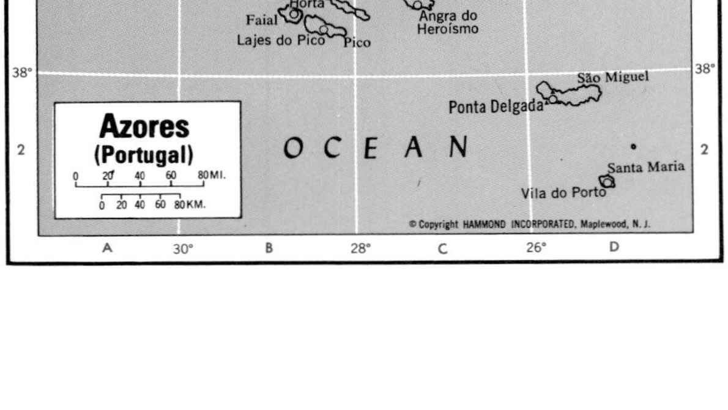

AZORES

INTERNAL DIVISIONS

Angra do Heroísmo
  (dist.) 83,500 ..... C1
Horta (dist.) 38,700 ..... A1
Ponta Delgada (dist.) 153,700 ..... D2

CITIES and TOWNS

Angra do Heroísmo 13,795 ..... C1
Horta 6,145 ..... B1
Lajes do Pico 2,147 ..... B1
Ponta Delgada 20,195 ..... C2
Santa Cruz das Flores 1,880 ..... A1
Vila do Porto 4,149 ..... D2

OTHER FEATURES

Azores (isls.) A2
Corvo (isl.) A1
Faial (isl.) B1
Flores (isl.) A1
Graciosa (isl.) C1
Pico (isl.) C1
Santa Maria (isl.) D2
São Jorge (isl.) B1
São Miguel (isl.) D2
Terceira (isl.) C1

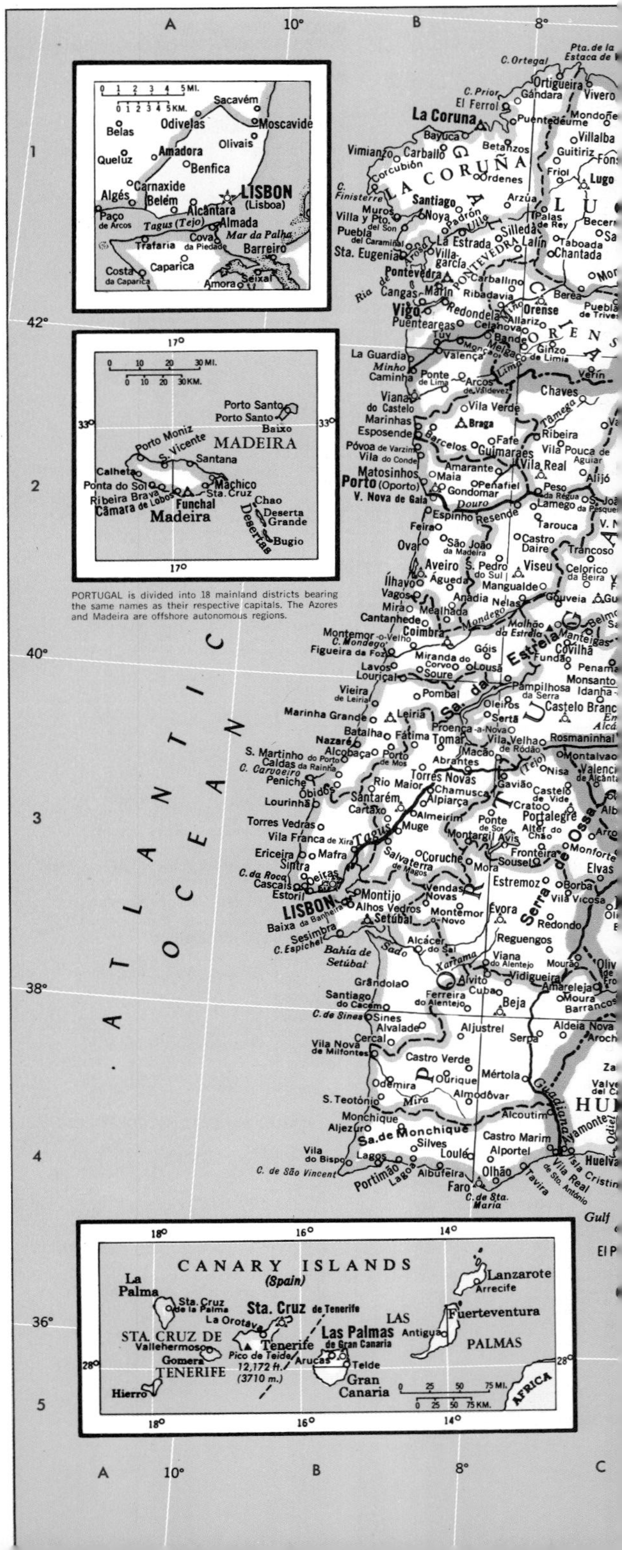

PORTUGAL is divided into 18 mainland districts bearing the same names as their respective capitals. The Azores and Madeira are offshore autonomous regions.

Alcobaça 4,799 B3
Aldeia Nova de São Bento 5,228 C4
Algés 18,010 A1
Alhos Vedros 7,915 B3
Aljustrel 7,473 B4
Almada 38,990 A1
Almeirim 8,780 B3
Alpiarça 7,623 B3
Alportel 7,632 C4
Amadora 65,870 A1
Amarante 6,067 B2
Amora 10,330 A1
Aveiro 19,905 B2
Avis 1,686 C3
Baixa da Banheira 18,550 B3
Barreiro 53,690 B1
Batalha 6,673 B3
Beja 14,760 C3
Belas 12,001 A1
Belém 19,043 A1
Benfica 39,459 A1
Borba 4,879 C3
Braga 48,735 B2
Bragança 9,310 C2
Caldas da Rainha 13,070 B3
Câmara de Lobos 14,068 A2
Campo Maior 7,405 C3
Cantanhede 6,734 B2
Caparica 13,315 A1
Carnaxide 38,309 A1
Cartaxo 6,628 B3
Cascais 14,925 B3
Castelo Branco 18,740 C3
Cercal 5,021 B4
Chaves 11,465 C2
Coimbra 55,985 B2
Coruche 17,461 B3
Cova da Piedade 21,000 A1
Covilhã 26,530 C2
Elvas 10,305 C3
Espinho 11,745 B2
Estoril 15,740 B3
Estremoz 9,565 C3
Évora 23,665 C3
Fafe 8,142 B2
Faro 20,470 B4
Fátima 6,433 B3
Feira 5,222 B2
Ferreira do Alentejo 6,153 B3
Figueira da Foz 10,485 B2
Funchal 38,340 A2
Fundão 5,081 C2
Gondomar 14,105 B2
Grândola 9,698 B3
Guarda 9,735 C2
Guimarães 24,280 B2
Ílhavo 11,083 B2
Lagoa 5,694 B4
Lagos 10,359 B4
Lamego 10,350 C2
Lavos 5,051 B2
Leiria 7,540 B3
Lisbon (Lisboa) (cap.) 769,410 A1
Lisbon‡ 1,100,000 A1
Loulé 12,777 B4
Louriçal 6,087 B3
Lourinhã 7,340 B3
Lousã 7,341 B2
Machico 10,905 A2
Mafra 7,149 B3
Mangualde 4,839 C2
Marinha Grande 18,548 B3
Matosinhos 22,505 B2
Mira 12,740 B2
Mirandela 5,203 C2
Monchique 8,155 B4
Montargil 5,070 B3
Montemor-o-Novo 9,284 B3
Montijo 26,730 B3
Moscavide 21,765 A1
Moura 9,351 C3
Nazaré 8,553 B3
Odemira 6,793 B4
Odivelas 26,020 A1
Oeiras 14,880 B3
Olhão 11,155 C4
Olivais 55,138 A1
Oporto (Porto) 300,925 B2
Ovar 16,004 B2
Paço de Arcos 11,791 A1
Penafiel 6,463 B2
Peniche 12,555 B3
Peso da Régua 5,376 C2
Pombal 12,508 B3
Ponta do Sol 5,599 A2
Ponte de Sor 9,951 C3
Portalegre 10,970 C3
Portimão 10,300 B4
Porto 300,925 B2
Póvoa de Varzim 17,415 B2
Proença-a-Nova 4,792 B3
Queluz 25,845 A1
Redondo 6,858 C3
Reguengos de Monsaraz 5,806 C3
Ribeira Brava 7,416 A2
Rio Maior 10,206 B3
Sacavém 12,625 A1
Salvaterra de Magos 6,265 B3
Santa Cruz 6,348 A2
Santarém 16,850 B3
Santiago do Cacem 5,887 B3
São Brás de Alportel (Alportel) 7,632 C4
São João da Madeira 14,225 B2
São Teotónio 6,146 B4
São Vicente 5,147 A2
Serpa 7,991 C4
Sertã 6,043 B3
Sesimbra 16,614 B3
Setúbal 49,670 B3
Silves 9,493 B4
Sines 6,996 B4
Sintra 15,994 B3
Soure 7,620 B2
Tavira 10,263 C4
Tomar 10,905 B3
Torres Novas 13,806 B3
Torres Vedras 14,833 B3
Trafaria 6,145 A1
Vagos 5,088 B2
Vendas Novas 8,979 B3
Viana do Castelo 12,510 B2
Vila do Conde 16,485 B2
Vila Franca de Xira 13,070 B3
Vila Nova de Gaia Gaia 50,805 B2
Vila Real Real 10,050 C2
Vila Real de Santo Antonio 10,320 C4
Viseu 16,140 C2

OTHER FEATURES

Atlantic Ocean A3
Carvoeiroeiro (cape) B3
Desertasrtas (isls.) A2
Douro (riv.) B2
Espichel (cape) B3
Estrela, Serra da (mts.) C2
Guadiana (riv.) C4
Lima (riv.) B2
Madeira (isl.)
Madeira (isls.) A2
Minho (riv.) B2
Mira (riv.) B4
Monchique, Serra de (mts.) B4
Mondego (riv.) B2
Monsanto (mt.) A1
Ossa, Serra da (mts.) C3
Palha, Mar da (bay) A1
Porto Santo (isl.) B2
Roca (cape) B3
Sado (riv.) B3
São Vincent (cape) B4
Santa María (cape) C4
Setúbal (bay) B3
Tagus (riv.) B3
Tâmega (riv.) C2
Tejo (Tagus) (riv.) B3
Xarrama (riv.) B3

ANDORRA

CITIES and TOWNS

Andorra la Vella (cap.) 12,000 G1

GIBRALTAR

Gibraltar 29,760 D4

PHYSICAL FEATURES

Europa (pt.) D4

‡Population of metropolitan area.

Italy
CONIC PROJECTION
SCALE OF MILES
0 20 40 60 80 100
SCALE OF KILOMETERS
0 20 40 60 80 100
Capitals of Countries
Regional Capitals
Provincial Capitals
International Boundaries
Regional Boundaries
The regions are subdivided into provinces bearing the same names as their respective capitals, except:
PROVINCE CAPITAL
MASSA-CARRARA Massa
PESARO-URBINO Pesaro
Vatican City
Rome and Environs
MEDITERRANEAN SEA
TYRRHENIAN SEA
ADRIATIC SEA
IONIAN SEA
LIGURIAN SEA
SWITZERLAND
AUSTRIA
YUGOSLAVIA
TUNISIA
GERMANY
CORSICA
SARDINIA
MALTA
ROME
MILAN
NAPLES
© Copyright HAMMOND INCORPORATED, Maplewood, N. J.
Longitude 12° East of Greenwich 14°

VATICAN CITY

AREA 108.7 acres
(44 hectares)
POPULATION 728

SAN MARINO

AREA 23.4 sq. mi.
(60.6 sq. km.)
POPULATION
19,149

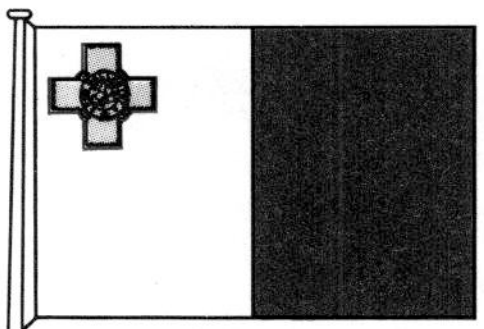

MALTA

AREA 122 sq. mi. (316 sq. km.)
POPULATION 343,970
CAPITAL Valletta
LARGEST CITY Sliema
HIGHEST POINT 787 ft. (240 m.)
MONETARY UNIT Maltese lira
MAJOR LANGUAGES Maltese, English
MAJOR RELIGION Roman Catholicism

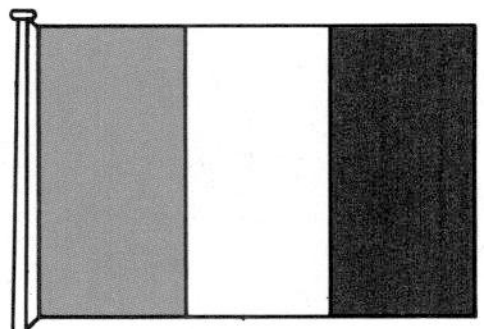

ITALY

AREA 116,303 sq. mi.
(301,225 sq. km.)
POPULATION 57,140,000
CAPITAL Rome
LARGEST CITY Rome
HIGHEST POINT Dufourspitze
(Mte. Rosa) 15,203 ft. (4,634 m.)
MONETARY UNIT lira
MAJOR LANGUAGE Italian
MAJOR RELIGION Roman Catholicism

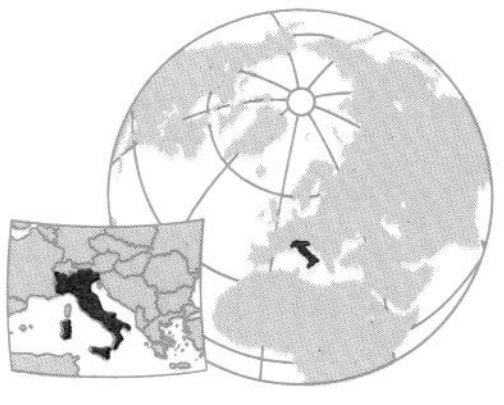

ITALY

REGIONS

Abruzzi 1,166,664 D3
Aosta 109,150 A2
Apulia (Puglia) 3,582,787 F4
Basilicata 603,064 F4
Calabria 1,988,051 F5
Campania 5,059,348 E4
Emilia-Romagna 3,846,755 C2
Friuli-Venezia Giulia 1,213,532 D1
Latium (Lazio) 4,689,482 D3
Liguria 1,853,578 B2
Lombardy 8,543,657 B2
Marche 1,359,907 D3
Molise 319,807 E4
Piedmont 4,432,313 A2
Sardinia 1,473,800 B4
Sicily 4,680,715 D6
Trentino-Alto Adige 841,886 C1
Tuscany 3,473,097 C3
Umbria 775,783 D3
Veneto 2,109,502 D3

PROVINCES

Agrigento 454,045 D6
Alessandria 483,183 B2
Ancona 416,611 D3
Aosta 109,150 A2
Arezzo 306,340 C3
Ascoli Piceno 340,758 D3
Asti 218,547 B2
Avellino 427,509 E4
Bari 1,351,288 F4
Belluno 221,155 D1
Benevento 286,499 E4
Bergamo 829,019 B2
Bologna 918,844 C2
Bolzano-Bozen 414,041 C1
Brescia 957,686 C2
Brindisi 366,027 G4
Cagliari 802,888 B5
Caltanissetta 282,069 D6
Campobasso 227,641 E4
Caserta 677,959 E4
Catania 938,273 E6
Catanzaro 718,069 F5
Chieti 351,567 E3
Como 720,463 B2
Cosenza 691,659 F5
Cremona 334,281 B2
Cuneo 540,504 A2
Enna 202,131 E6
Ferrara 383,639 C2
Florence 1,146,367 C3
Foggia 657,292 E4
Forlì 565,470 D2
Frosinone 422,630 D4
Genoa 1,087,973 B2
Gorizia 142,412 D2
Grosseto 216,315 C3
Imperia 225,127 B3
Isernia 92,166 E4
L'Aquila 293,066 D3
La Spezia 244,435 B2
Latina 376,238 D4
Lecce 696,503 G4
Leghorn 335,265 C3
Lucca 380,356 C3
Macerata 286,155 D3
Mantua 376,892 C2
Massa-Carrara 200,955 C2
Matera 194,629 F4
Messina 654,703 E5
Milan 3,903,685 B2
Modena 553,852 C2
Naples 2,709,929 E4
Novara 496,811 B2
Nuoro 273,021 B4
Padua 762,998 C2
Palermo 1,124,015 D5
Parma 395,497 C2
Pavia 526,389 B2
Perugia 552,936 D3
Pesaro e Urbino 316,383 D3
Pescara 264,981 E3
Piacenza 284,881 B2
Pisa 375,933 C3
Pistoia 254,335 C2
Pordenone 253,906 D2
Potenza 408,435 E4
Ragusa 255,047 E6
Ravenna 351,876 D2
Reggio di Calabria 578,323 E5
Reggio nell'Emilia 392,696 C2
Rieti 143,162 D3
Rome 3,490,377 F6
Rovigo 251,908 C2
Salerno 957,452 E4
Sassari 397,891 B4
Savona 296,043 B2
Siena 257,221 C3
Sondrio 169,149 B1
Syracuse 365,039 E6
Taranto 511,677 F4
Teramo 257,080 D3
Terni 222,847 D3
Trapani 405,393 D5
Trento 427,845 C1
Treviso 668,620 D2
Trieste 300,304 E2
Turin 2,287,016 A2
Udine 516,910 D1
Varese 725,823 B2
Venice 807,251 D2
Vercelli 406,252 B2
Verona 733,595 C2
Vicenza 677,884 C2
Viterbo 257,075 C3

CITIES and TOWNS

Acireale 34,081 E6
Acqui Terme 20,099 B2
Acri 8,150 F5
Adrano 31,988 E6
Adria 11,951 D2
Agira 11,262 E6
Agnone 3,965 E4
Agrigento 40,513 D6
Agropoli 9,413 E4
Alassio 13,512 A2
Alatri 5,710 D4
Alba 23,522 B2
Albano Laziale 15,561 F7
Albenga 13,397 B3
Albino 8,837 B2
Alcamo 41,448 D6
Alessandria 78,644 B2
Alghero 28,454 B4
Altamura 44,879 F4
Amalfi 4,205 E4
Amantea 6,132 E5
Amelia 4,331 D3
Ancona 88,427 D3
Andria 76,405 F4
Anguillara Sabazia 3,241 F6
Anzio 14,966 D4
Aosta 35,053 A2
Aprilia 18,412 D4
Aragona 11,213 D6
Arezzo 56,693 C3
Argenta 6,682 D2
Ariano Irpino 9,796 E4
Ariccia 7,287 F7
Artena 5,034 F7
Ascoli Piceno 43,041 D3
Assisi 4,630 D3
Asti 62,277 B2
Atessa 3,079 E3
Atri 4,686 D3
Augusta 32,501 E6
Avellino 44,750 E4
Aversa 46,536 E4
Avezzano 26,456 D3
Avigliano 5,400 E4
Avola 29,089 E6
Bagheria 32,465 D5
Barcellona Pozzo di Gotto 25,280 E5
Bari 339,110 F4
Barletta 75,116 F4
Bassano del Grappa 33,002 C2
Bellagio 3,258 B2
Belluno 22,180 D1
Benevento 48,523 E4
Bergamo 127,553 B2
Biancavilla 18,743 E6
Biella 46,453 B2
Bisceglie 45,014 F4
Bitonto 39,714 F4
Bitti 4,606 B4
Bologna 493,282 C2
Bolzano (Bolzen) 102,806 C1
Bondeno 7,451 C2
Bonorva 5,232 B4
Bordighera 8,994 A3
Borgo 4,013 C1
Borgomanero 16,655 B2
Bôrgo San Lorenzo 7,699 C2
Bosa 8,045 B4
Boves 3,896 A2
Bra 18,399 A2
Bracciano 7,681 C3
Brescia 189,092 C2
Bressanone 12,261 C1
Brindisi 76,612 G4
Bronte 17,823 E6
Brunico 5,175 D1
Budrio 5,635 C2
Busto Arsizio 72,400 B2
Cagli 4,356 D3
Cagliari 211,015 B5
Caltagirone 34,444 E6
Caltanissetta 52,838 D6
Camaiore 8,578 C3
Camerino 4,644 D3
Campobasso 35,551 E4
Campo Tures 1,325 C1
Canicatti 28,761 E6
Canosa di Puglia 30,263 E4
Cantù 28,617 B2
Capua 13,938 E4
Caravaggio 11,298 B2
Carbonia 23,031 B5
Carini 14,255 D5
Carloforte 6,671 B5
Carmagnola 16,469 A2
Carpi 41,789 C2
Carrara 56,236 C2
Casale Monferrato 35,156 B2
Casalmaggiore 6,374 C2
Cascina-Navacchio 28,263 C3
Caserta 51,621 E4
Cassano allo Ionio 9,661 F5
Cassino 14,747 D4
Castelfranco Veneto 16,042 D2
Castel Gandolfo 2,965 F7
Castellammare del Golfo 13,144 D5
Castellammare di Stabia 64,341 E4
Castel San Pietro Terme 6,985 C2
Castelvetrano 29,167 D6
Castiglion Fiorentino 3,797 C3
Castrovillari 15,207 F5
Catania 403,390 E6
Catanzaro 52,054 F5
Caulonia 3,402 F5
Cava de'Tirreni 33,868 E4
Cavarzere 7,917 D2
Cecina 19,415 C3
Cefalù 11,043 E5
Ceglie Messapico 17,512 F4
Celano 9,531 D3
Cerignola 44,648 E4
Cernobbio 8,026 B2
Cerveteri 5,239 E6
Cesano 2,883 F6
Cesena 49,915 D2
Cesenatico 12,805 D2
Chiari 12,017 C2
Chiavari 29,950 B2
Chieri 27,548 A2
Chieti 31,895 E3
Chioggia 24,044 D2
Chivasso 21,369 A2
Ciampino 36,728 F7
Cittadella 9,321 C2
Città di Castello 18,880 C3
Cittanova 11,045 F5
Cividale del Friuli 8,345 D1
Civitavecchia 41,305 C3
Clusone-Fiorine 6,428 C2
Codroipo 6,117 D2
Colle di Val d'Elsa 8,657 C3
Comacchio 10,437 D2
Comiso 24,508 E6
Como 73,257 B2
Conegliano 28,635 D2
Conversano 16,805 F4
Corato 38,163 F4
Cori 6,829 F7
Corigliano Calabro 14,518 F5
Corleone 11,057 D6
Correggio 11,415 C2
Cortina d'Ampezzo 7,285 D1
Cortona 3,482 C3
Cosenza 94,565 F5
Courmayeur 1,401 A2
Crema 26,061 B2
Cremona 75,988 B2
Crotone 44,081 F5
Cuneo 41,633 A2
Cuorgnè 6,752 A2
Desenzano del Garda 14,624 C2
Diano Marina 6,001 B3
Domodossola 18,562 A1
Dorgali 6,714 B4
Eboli 19,787 E4
Edolo 3,707 C1
Empoli 30,526 C3
Enna 27,351 E6
Este 12,992 C2
Fabriano 18,355 D3
Faenza 36,241 D2
Fano 31,238 D3
Fasano 21,247 F4
Favara 27,940 D6
Feltre 11,806 C1
Fermo 17,521 D3
Ferrandina 8,372 F4
Ferrara 97,507 C2
Fidenza 18,064 B2
Fiesole 3,772 C3
Finale Emilia 7,474 C2
Finale Ligure 11,461 B2
Firenze (Florence) 441,654 C3
Fiumicino 13,180 F7
Florence 441,654 C3
Floridia 16,562 E6
Foggia 136,436 E4
Foligno 26,887 D3
Fondi 16,472 D4
Forlì 83,303 D2
Formia 18,978 D4
Fossano 15,857 A2
Fossombrone 5,882 D3
Francavilla Fontana 30,347 F4
Frascati 14,217 F7
Frosinone 34,066 D4
Gaeta 21,973 D4
Galatina 22,137 G4
Galatone 13,880 F4
Gallarate 43,773 B2
Gallipoli 16,878 F4
Garessio 3,359 A2
Gela 66,845 E6
Gemona 6,863 D1
Genoa 787,011 B2
Genova (Genoa) 787,011 B2
Genzano di Roma 14,147 F7
Giarre 18,233 E6
Gioia del Colle 23,299 F4
Gioiosa Ionica 3,811 F5
Giovinazzo 17,768 F4
Giulianova 17,926 E3
Gorizia 35,912 D2
Gravina in Puglia 32,006 F4
Grosseto 48,309 C3
Grottaferrata 10,639 F7
Grottaglie 23,556 F4
Guardiagrele 4,122 E3
Guastalla 7,639 C2
Gubbio 12,371 D3
Guidonia 8,413 F6
Iglesias 24,472 B5
Imola 42,111 C2
Imperia 37,585 B3
Isernia 12,290 E4
Ivrea 26,530 B2
Jesi 33,011 D3
Ladispoli 6,625 E6
Lagonegro 5,613 E4
La Maddalena 10,405 B4
Lanciano 19,652 E3
Lanusei 5,508 B5
Lanuvio 2,970 F7
L'Aquila 36,233 D3
Larino 5,166 E4
La Spezia 121,254 B2
Latina 53,003 D4
Lauria 4,927 E4
Lavello 11,486 E4
Lecce 80,114 G4
Lecco 53,165 B2
Leghorn 170,369 C3
Legnago 15,534 C2
Lendinara 7,079 C2
Lentini 31,429 E6
Leonforte 16,317 E6
Lerici 5,407 B2
Licata 40,997 D6
Lido di Ostia 61,492 F7
Lido di Venezia 18,794 D2
Lipari 3,886 E5
Livigno 2,135 C1
Livorno (Leghorn) 170,369 C3
Lodi 42,489 B2
Lonigo 6,368 C2
Lucca 54,280 C3
Lucera 29,355 E4
Lugo 19,497 D2
Macerata 33,470 D3
Macomer 9,433 B4
Maglie 13,326 G4
Manduria 25,194 F4
Manfredonia 44,463 F4
Mantua 59,529 C2
Marino 12,135 F7
Marsala 34,150 D6
Marsciano 5,372 D3
Martina Franca 31,811 F4
Massa 56,591 C2
Massafra 22,610 F4
Massa Marittima 6,438 C3
Matera 43,026 F4
Mazara del Vallo 37,441 D6
Mazzarino 14,981 E6
Melfi 13,355 E4
Menfi 12,386 D6
Merano 30,951 C1
Mesagne 26,955 G4
Messina 203,937 E5
Mestre 184,818 D2
Milan 1,724,557 B2
Milazzo 18,576 E5
Minturno 2,428 D4
Mirandola 11,551 C2
Mira Taglio 10,194 D2
Mistretta 6,631 E6
Modena 149,029 C2
Modica 31,074 E6
Mola di Bari 23,778 F4
Molfetta 63,250 F4
Moncalieri 49,953 A2
Mondovì Breo 12,524 A2
Monfalcone 29,589 D2
Monopoli 29,776 F4
Monreale 19,348 D5
Monselice 9,047 C2
Montalto Uffugo 3,173 E5
Montebelluna 9,573 D2
Montefiascone 6,885 D3
Montepulciano 4,069 C3
Monterotondo 15,869 F6
Monte Sant'Angelo 17,756 F4
Montevarchi 16,849 C3
Monza 110,735 B2
Mortara 13,929 B2
Naples 1,214,775 E4
Nardò 24,142 F4
Narni 6,213 D3
Naro 13,171 D6
Nettuno 20,927 D4
Nicastro 27,206 F5
Nicosia 13,982 E6
Niscemi 23,925 E6
Nizza Monferrato 7,532 B2
Nocera Inferiore 44,415 E4
Noto 21,606 E6
Novara 92,634 B2
Novi Ligure 29,944 B2
Nuoro 30,551 B4
Olbia 20,998 B4
Oliena 7,030 B4
Orbetello 6,884 C3
Oristano 20,966 B5
Ortona 11,966 E3
Orvieto 8,813 D3
Osimo 12,034 D3
Ostia Antica 2,583 F7
Ostuni 27,241 F4
Otranto 3,707 G4
Ozieri 9,149 B4
Pachino 20,427 E6
Padua 210,950 C2
Palazzolo Acreide 8,981 E6
Palermo 556,374 D5
Palestrina 9,239 F7
Palma di Montechiaro 22,381 D6
Palmi 14,405 E5
Palombara Sabina 5,292 F6
Pantelleria 3,116 C6
Paola 11,330 E5
Parma 151,967 C2
Partanna 10,303 D6
Partinico 25,447 D6
Paterno 41,504 E6
Patti 7,500 E5
Pavia 80,639 B2
Pavullo nel Frignano 5,026 C2
Penne 5,889 D3
Pergine Valsugana 6,248 C1
Pergola 3,866 D3
Perugia 65,975 D3
Pesaro 72,104 D3
Pescara 125,391 E3
Pescia 9,918 C3
Piacenza 100,001 B2
Piazza Armerina 21,754 E6
Pietrasanta 6,620 B3
Pinerolo 33,935 A2
Piombino 35,641 C3
Piove di Sacco 7,035 C2
Pisa 91,156 C3
Pisticci 11,239 F4
Pistoia 55,403 C2
Poggibonsi 21,271 C3
Pomezia 11,915 F7
Pont Canavese 4,075 A2
Pontecorvo 5,986 D4
Pontinia 3,166 D4
Pontremoli 5,222 B2
Popoli 5,372 E3
Pordenone 43,230 D2
Portocivitanova 25,773 D3
Porto Empedocle 15,986 D6
Portoferraio 7,579 C3
Portofino 720 B2
Portogruaro 12,258 D2
Portomaggiore 6,343 C2
Porto Recanati 5,389 D3
Porto Torres 15,422 B4
Potenza 46,869 E4
Pozzallo 12,199 E6
Pozzuoli 53,546 D4
Prato 108,385 C3
Prima Porta 11,393 F6
Priverno 9,950 D4
Putignano 19,290 F4
Quartu Sant'Elena 29,715 B5
Ragusa 55,751 E6
Rapallo 22,272 B2
Ravenna 75,153 D2
Recanati 10,176 D3
Reggio di Calabria 110,291 E5
Reggio nell'Emilia 102,337 C2
Rho 39,206 B2
Riesi 15,855 E6
Rieti 26,775 D3
Rimini 101,579 D2
Rionero in Vulture 11,230 E4
Riva del Garda 8,513 C2
Roccastrada 2,629 C3
Rome (cap.) 2,535,018 F6
Ronciglione 5,900 C3
Rossano 12,119 F5
Rovereto 26,827 C2
Rovigo 31,124 C2
Ruvo di Puglia 23,133 F4

(continued on following page)

Topography

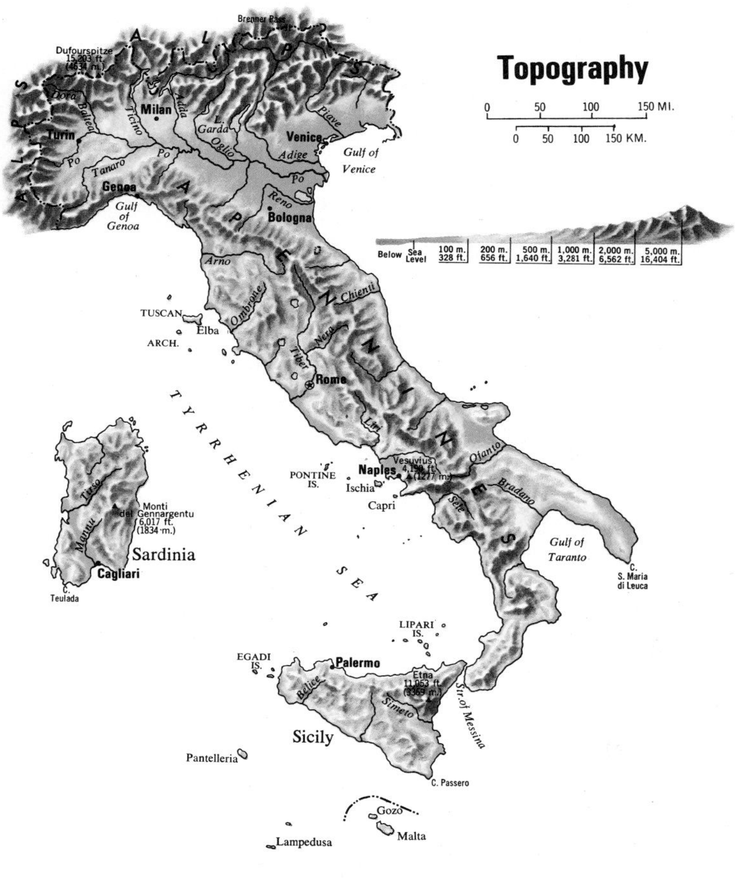

(continued)

Sabaudia 4,501 .... D4
Saint Vincent 3,737 .... A2
Sala Consilina 8,177 .... E4
Salemi 10,180 .... D6
Salerno 146,534 .... E4
Salsomaggiore Terme 13,677 .... B2
Saluzzo 13,929 .... A2
Sambiase 10,567 .... F5
San Bartolomeo in Galdo 6,943 .... E4
San Benedetto del
Tronto 40,108 .... E3
San Cataldo 19,609 .... D6
San Giovanni in Fiore 16,116 .... F5
San Giovanni in
Persiceto 12,151 .... C2
San Marco in Lamis 15,817 .... E4
San Miniato 3,245 .... C3
Sannicandro Garganico 17,939 .... E4
San Remo 47,684 .... A3
Sansepolcro 11,443 .... C3
San Severino Marche 6,447 .... D3
San Severo 49,622 .... E4
Santa Maria Capua
Vetere 31,077 .... E4
Sant'Elpidio a Mare 4,446 .... E3
Santeramo in Colle 19,758 .... F4
San Vito 3,901 .... B5
San Vito al Tagliamento 6,328 .... D2
San Vito dei Normanni 18,447 .... F4
San Vito Romano 3,256 .... F6
Saronno 32,477 .... B2
Sarroch 3,560 .... B5
Sassari 94,312 .... B4
Sassuolo 33,451 .... C2
Savigliano 14,036 .... A2
Savona 76,274 .... B2
Schio 27,890 .... C2
Sciacca 29,803 .... D6
Scicli 18,405 .... E6
Segni 7,193 .... F7
Senigallia 25,413 .... D3
Sesto Fiorentino 41,636 .... C3
Sestri Levante 18,331 .... B2
Settebagni 5,022 .... F6
Sezze 7,043 .... D4
Siderno 8,023 .... F5
Siena 56,539 .... C3
Siniscola 6,149 .... B4
Sinnai 8,499 .... B5
Siracusa (Syracuse) 93,006 .... E6
Sondrio 19,724 .... B1
Sora 14,031 .... D4
Soresina 9,300 .... C2
Sorrento 13,078 .... E4
Sorso 10,741 .... B4
Spoleto 18,013 .... D3
Squinzano 14,053 .... G4
Stresa 3,758 .... B2
Sulmona 18,221 .... D3
Susa 5,773 .... A2
Suzzara 12,013 .... C2
Syracuse 93,006 .... E6
Taormina 6,696 .... E6
Taranto 205,158 .... F4
Tarquinia 10,300 .... C3
Taurianova 12,198 .... E5
Tempio Pausania 10,382 .... B4
Teramo 31,163 .... D3
Termini Imerese 24,085 .... D6
Termoli 13,986 .... E3
Terni 75,873 .... D3
Terracina 24,092 .... D4
Terralba 8,551 .... B5
Tirano 7,413 .... C1
Tivoli 28,393 .... F6
Todi 5,705 .... D3
Tolentino 11,642 .... D3
Torino (Turin) 1,181,698 .... A2
Torre Annunziata 71,068 .... E4
Torre del Greco 74,752 .... E4
Torremaggiore 16,171 .... E4
Tortona 24,165 .... B2
Trani 40,508 .... F4
Trapani 90,305 .... D5
Trento 64,272 .... C1
Treviglio 21,920 .... B2
Treviso 87,447 .... D2
Tricase 10,481 .... G5
Trieste 257,259 .... E2
Trino 8,722 .... B2
Turin 1,181,698 .... A2
Udine 97,544 .... D2
Umbertide 6,640 .... D3
Urbino 7,725 .... D3
Valdagno 20,342 .... C2
Valenza 20,533 .... B2
Valmontone 6,543 .... F7
Varallo Pombia 3,118 .... B2
Varazze 11,676 .... B2
Varese 65,978 .... B2
Vasto 17,295 .... E3
Velletri 22,020 .... F7
Venairo 5,156 .... E4
Venezia (Venice) 108,082 .... D2
Venice 108,082 .... D2
Venosa 10,993 .... E4
Ventimiglia 20,343 .... A3
Verbania 29,894 .... B2
Vercelli 54,934 .... B2
Veroli 2,793 .... D4
Verona 227,032 .... C2
Viadana 6,667 .... C2
Viareggio 49,965 .... C3
Vibo Valentia 18,005 .... F5
Vicenza 99,451 .... C2
Vicovaro 3,005 .... F6
Vigevano 62,855 .... B2
Villacidro 12,651 .... B5
Villafranca di Verona 11,762 .... C2
Viterbo 39,291 .... C3
Vittoria 43,673 .... E6
Vittorio Veneto 25,476 .... D1
Vizzini 8,583 .... E6
Voghera 37,316 .... B2
Volterra 10,732 .... C3
Zagarolo 4,232 .... F7

OTHER FEATURES

Adda (riv.) B2
Adige (riv.) C2
Adriatic (sea) E3
Alicudi (isl.) E5
Apennines, Central (range) D3
Apennines, Northern (range) B2
Apennines, Southern (range) E4
Arno (riv.) C3
Asinara (isl.) B4
Bernina, Piz (peak) B1
Blanc (mt.) A2
Bolsena (lake) C3
Bonifacio (str.) B4
Bracciano (lake) D3
Brenner (pass) C1
Capraia (isl.) B3
Capri (isl.) E4
Carbonara (cape) B5
Carnic Alps (range) D1
Castellammare (gulf) D5
Circeo (cape) D4
Como (lake) B1
Cottian Alps (range) A2
Dolomite Alps (range) C1
Dora Baltea (riv.) A2
Dora Riparia (riv.) A2
Egadi (isls.) C6
Elba (isl.) C3
Etna (vol.) E6
Favignana (isl.) D6
Filicudi (isl.) E5
Gaeta (gulf) D4
Garda (lake) C2
Gennargentu, Monti del (mt.) B5
Genoa (gulf) B2
Giannutri (isl.) C3
Giglio (isl.) C3
Gorgona (isl.) B3
Graian Alps (range) A2
Gran Paradiso (mt.) A2
Great Saint Bernard (pass) A2
Ionian (sea) F6
Ischia (isl.) D4
Julian Alps (range) D1
Lampedusa (isl.) D7
Lepontine Alps (range) B1
Levanzo (isl.) D5
Ligurian (sea) B3
Linosa (isl.) D7
Lipari (isl.) E5
Lipari (isls.) E5
Maggiore (lake) B1
Manfredonia (gulf) F4
Marettimo (isl.) C6
Maritime Alps (range) A2
Marmolada (mt.) C1
Mediterranean (sea) B6
Messina (str.) E6
Metauro (riv.) D3
Mincio (riv.) C2
Montecristo (isl.) C3
Nera (riv.) D3
Oglio (riv.) C2
Ombrone (riv.) C3
Oristano (gulf) B5
Orosei (gulf) B4
Ortles (range) C1
Otranto (str.) G5
Ötztal Alps (range) C1
Panarea (isl.) E5
Panaro (riv.) C2
Pantelleria (isl.) D6
Pelagie (isls.) D7
Pennine Alps (range) A2
Pianosa (isl.) C3
Piave (riv.) D2
Po (riv.) C2
Pompeii (ruins) E4
Pontine (isls.) D4
Ponza (isl.) D4
Rosa (mt.) A1
Salina (isl.) E5
Salso (riv.) D6
San Pietro (isl.) B5
Santa Maria di Leuca (cape) G5
Sant'Antioco (pen.) B5
Sant'Eufemia (gulf) F5
Sardinia (isl.) B4
Sicily (isl.) E6
Sicily (str.) D6
Simplon (tunnel) A1
Spartivento (cape) B5
Spartivento (cape) F6
Squillace (gulf) F5
Stromboli (isl.) E5
Tagliamento (riv.) D1
Tanaro (riv.) B2
Taranto (gulf) F5
Testa del Gargano (cape) F4
Tiber (riv.) D3
Trasimeno (lake) D3
Tremiti (isls.) E3
Trieste (gulf) D2
Tuscan (arch.) B3
Tyrrhenian (sea) C4
Ustica (isl.) D5
Vaticano (cape) E5
Venice (gulf) D2
Ventotene (isl.) D4
Vesuvius (vol.) E4
Viso (mt.) A2
Volturno (riv.) E4
Vulcano (isl.) E5

MALTA

CITIES and TOWNS

Sliema 20,095 .... E7
Valletta (cap.) 14,042 .... E7
Victoria 5,249 .... E6

SAN MARINO

CITIES and TOWNS

San Marino (cap.) 4,628 .... D3
San Marino* 5,410 .... D3

VATICAN CITY

Vatican City 728 .... B6

*City and suburbs.

Agriculture, Industry and Resources

DOMINANT LAND USE

- Wheat, Rice, Dairy
- Pasture Livestock
- Cereals, Livestock
- Fruit, Truck and Mixed Farming
- Grapes, Wine
- Forests
- Nonagricultural Land

MAJOR MINERAL OCCURRENCES

Ab	Asbestos	K	Potash	Pb	Lead
Al	Bauxite	Lg	Lignite	Py	Pyrites
C	Coal	Mr	Marble	S	Sulfur
Fe	Iron Ore	Na	Salt	Sb	Antimony
G	Natural Gas	O	Petroleum	Zn	Zinc
Hg	Mercury				

Water Power

Major Industrial Areas

SWITZERLAND

AREA 15,943 sq. mi. (41,292 sq. km.)
POPULATION 6,365,960
CAPITAL Bern
LARGEST CITY Zürich
HIGHEST POINT Dufourspitze (Mte. Rosa) 15,203 ft. (4,634 m.)
MONETARY UNIT Swiss franc
MAJOR LANGUAGES German, French, Italian, Romansch
MAJOR RELIGIONS Protestantism, Roman Catholicism

LIECHTENSTEIN

AREA 61 sq. mi. (158 sq. km.)
POPULATION 25,220
CAPITAL Vaduz
LARGEST CITY Vaduz
HIGHEST POINT Grauspitze 8,527 ft. (2,599 m.)
MONETARY UNIT Swiss franc
MAJOR LANGUAGE German
MAJOR RELIGION Roman Catholicism

SWITZERLAND

LIECHTENSTEIN

Languages

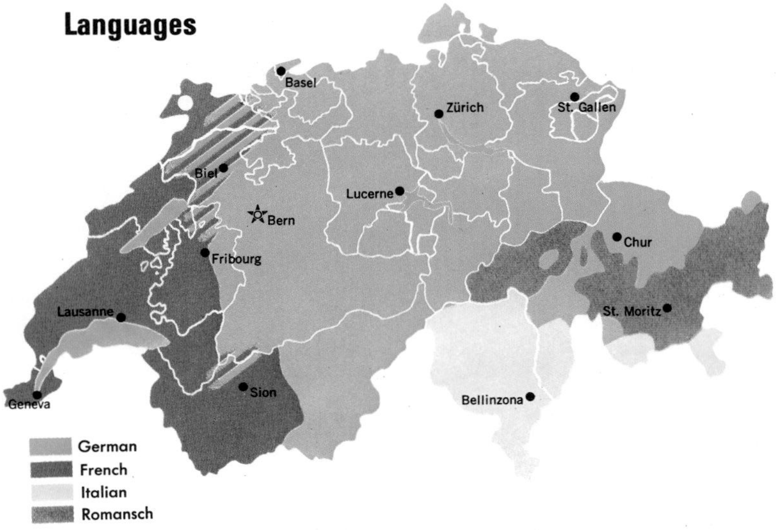

Switzerland is a multilingual nation with four official languages. 70% of the people speak German, 19% French, 10% Italian and 1% Romansch.

Agriculture, Industry and Resources

DOMINANT LAND USE

- Cereals, Dairy
- Pasture Livestock
- General Farming, Livestock
- Fruit, Truck, Mixed Farming
- Forests
- Nonagricultural Land

- Water Power
- Major Industrial Areas

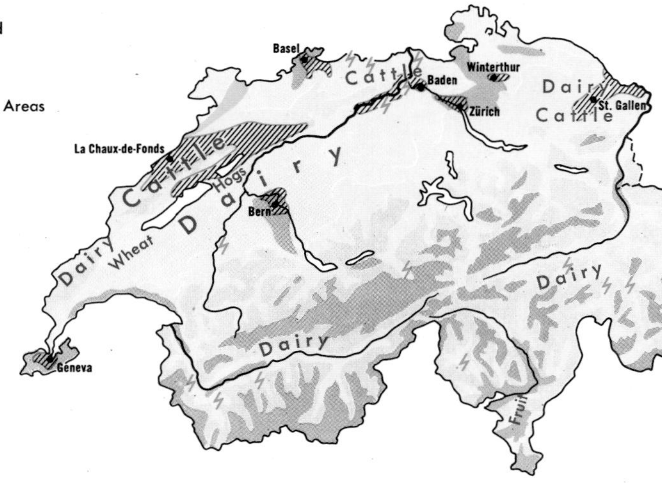

SWITZERLAND

CANTONS

Aargau 442,400	F2
Appenzell, Ausser Rhoden 46,700	H2
Appenzell, Inner Rhoden 13,500	H2
Baselland 219,500	E2
Baselstadt 209,700	E1
Bern 920,900	D2
Fribourg 181,600	D3
Geneva (Genève) 338,600	B4
Glarus 35,700	H3
Graubünden (Grisons) 164,300	H3
Grisons (Graubünden) 164,300	H3
Jura 67,200	D2
Lucerne (Luzern) 292,900	F2
Luzern 292,900	F2
Neuchâtel 162,200	C3
Nidwalden 26,900	F3
Obwalden 25,400	F3
Sankt Gallen 385,000	H2
Schaffhausen 69,300	G1
Schwyz 93,100	G2
Soleure (Solothurn) 221,800	E2
Solothurn 221,800	E2
Thurgau 183,500	H1
Ticino 264,400	G4
Uri 34,000	G3
Valais 214,000	D4
Vaud 523,500	B3
Zug 73,600	G2
Zürich 1,117,300	G2

CITIES and TOWNS

Aadorf 3,022	G2
Aarau 16,881	F2
Aarau* 51,800	F2
Aarberg 3,122	D2
Aarburg 5,943	E2
Adelboden 3,326	E3
Adliswil 15,920	F2
Aeschi bei Spiez 1,402	E3
Affoltern am Albis 7,363	F2
Affoltern im Emmental 1,223	E2
Aigle 6,532	C4
Airolo 2,140	G3
Alle 1,615	D2
Allschwil 17,638	D1
Alpnach 3,277	F3
Altdorf 8,647	G3
Altstätten 9,084	J2
Amriswil 7,601	H1
Andelfingen 1,453	G1
Andermatt 1,589	G3
Appenzell 5,217	H2
Arbedo-Castione 2,456	G4
Arbon 12,227	H1
Arbon* 15,400	H1
Ardon 1,498	D4
Arosa 2,717	J3
Arth 7,580	F2
Ascona 4,086	G4
Attalens 1,116	C3
Au 4,944	J2
Aubonne 1,983	B4
Avenches 2,235	D3
Baar 14,074	F2
Baden 14,115	F2
Baden* 66,800	F2
Bad Ragaz 3,713	H2
Balerna 3,885	G5
Balsthal 5,607	E2
Bäretswil 2,733	G2
Basel 199,600	E1
Basel* 379,700	E1
Bassecourt 2,985	D2
Bätterkinden 1,757	E2
Bauma 3,159	G2
Beatenberg 1,263	E3
Beinwil am See 2,520	F2
Belfaux 1,075	D3
Bellinzona 16,979	H4
Bellinzona* 31,000	H4
Belp 6,981	D3
Berg 1,039	H1
Bern (cap.) 154,700	D3
Bern* 285,300	D3
Beromünster 1,552	F2
Bettlach 4,046	D2
Bèx 5,069	D4
Biasca 4,696	H4
Biberist 7,769	D2
Biel 63,400	D2
Biel** 89,900	D2
Bière 1,252	B3
Binningen 15,344	D1
Bischofszell 4,233	H1
Blumenstein 1,049	E3
Bodio 1,425	G4
Bolligen 26,121	E3
Boltigen 1,519	D3
Bonaduz 1,289	H3
Boncourt 1,528	C2
Bönigen 1,738	E3
Boswil 1,904	F2
Boudry 4,372	C3
Bourg Saint-Pierre 236	D5
Breil-Brigels 1,215	H3
Breitenbach 2,455	E2
Bremgarten 4,873	F2
Brienz 2,796	F3
Brig 5,191	F4
Brissago 2,120	G4
Brittnau 2,888	E2
Broc 1,842	D3
Brugg 8,635	F2
Brusio 1,344	K4
Bubendorf 2,070	E2
Bubikon 3,244	G2
Buchs 8,454	H2
Bülach 11,043	G1
Bulle 7,556	D3
Buochs 3,232	F3
Büren an der Aare 3,085	D2
Burgdorf 15,888	E2
Burgdorf* 18,400	E2
Bürglen, Thurgau 1,920	H1
Bürglen, Uri 3,401	G3
Bussigny-près-Lausanne 4,509	B3
Bütschwil 3,270	H2
Carouge 14,055	B4
Castagnola 4,430	G4
Cazis 1,687	H3
Cernier 1,717	C2
Chalais 1,651	E4
Cham 8,209	F2
Chamoson 2,049	D4
Charmey 1,155	D3
Château-d'Oex 3,203	D4
Châtel-Saint-Denis 2,842	C3
Chêne-Bougeries 8,670	B4
Chavornay 1,521	C3
Chexbres 1,607	C3
Chiasso 8,868	G5
Chippis 1,561	E4
Chur 32,400	J3
Churwalden 1,052	J3
Claro 1,143	G4
Collombey-Muraz 2,279	C4
Collonge-Bellerive 3,541	B4
Conthey 4,259	D4
Coppet 1,097	B4
Corcelles-près-Payerne 1,256	C3
Corgémont 1,645	D2
Cossonay 1,529	B3
Courgenay 1,954	D2
Courrendlin 2,656	D2
Courroux 1,788	D2
Courtelary 1,462	C2
Courtételle 1,864	D2
Couvet 3,481	C3
Cully 1,535	C4
Davos 10,238	J3
Degersheim 3,400	H2
Delémont 11,797	D2
Derendingen 4,917	E2
Dielsdorf 2,691	F1
Diemtigen 1,913	D3
Diepoldsau 3,311	J2
Diessenhofen 2,532	G1
Dietikon 22,705	F2
Disentis-Mustér 2,319	G3
Domat-Ems 5,701	H3
Dombresson 1,109	C2
Dornach 5,258	E2
Döttingen 3,380	F1
Dübendorf 19,639	G2
Düdingen 4,932	D3
Dürnten 4,820	G2
Dürrenroth 1,084	E2
Ebnat-Kappel 5,131	H2
Echallens 1,643	C3
Ecublens 6,379	B3
Egg 5,250	G2
Eggiwil 2,391	E3
Eglisau 2,160	G1
Egnach 3,466	H1

(continued on following page)

Topography

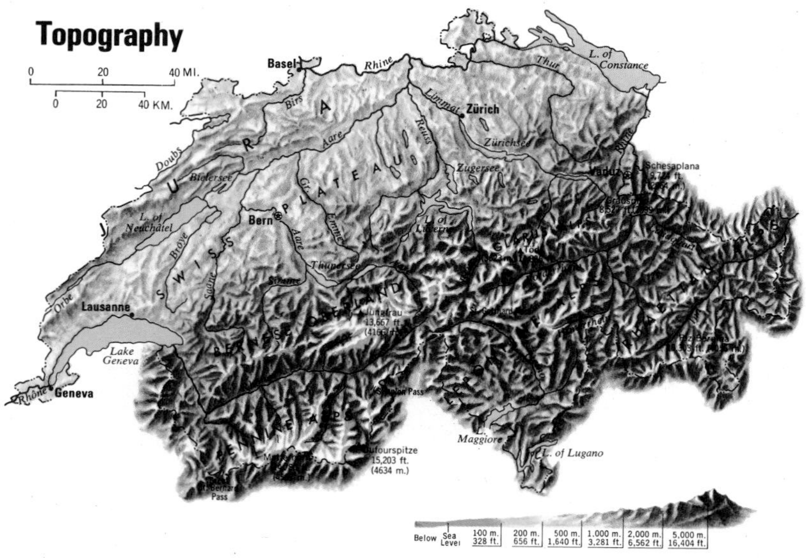

Einsiedeln 10,020 .... G2
Elgg 2,970 .... G2
Emmen 22,040 .... F2
Engelberg 2,841 .... F3
Ennenda 2,762 .... H2
Entlebuch 3,310 .... F3
Erlach 1,052 .... D2
Erlenbach im Simmental 1,436 .... E3
Ermatingen 1,787 .... H1
Erstfeld 4,516 .... G3
Eschenbach 3,387 .... G2
Escholzmatt 3,161 .... E3
Estavayer-le-Lac 3,439 .... C3
Evolène 1,403 .... D4
Faido 1,866 .... G4
Felsberg 1,321 .... H3
Feuerthalen 3,118 .... G1
Flawil 8,474 .... H2
Fleurier 4,124 .... C3
Flims 1,936 .... H3
Flüelen 1,731 .... G3
Flums 4,474 .... H2
Frauenfeld 17,576 .... G1
Freienbach 8,429 .... G2
Fribourg 41,600 .... D3
Fribourg* 53,500 .... D3
Frick 3,112 .... E1
Frutigen 5,796 .... E3
Fully 3,643 .... D4
Gais 2,344 .... H2
Gelterkinden 5,157 .... E2
Geneva (Genève) 163,100 .... B4
Geneva (Genève)* 320,200 .... B4
Gersau 1,753 .... G2
Gimel 1,205 .... B3
Giornico 1,389 .... G4
Giswil 2,760 .... F3
Giubiasco 5,796 .... H4
Gland 2,404 .... B4
Glarus 6,189 .... H2
Glattfelden 2,857 .... F1
Glis 3,389 .... E4
Gordola 2,586 .... G4
Gossau 12,793 .... H2
Grabs 4,245 .... H2
Grächen 1,063 .... E4
Grandson 2,135 .... C3
Grenchen 20,051 .... D2
Grenchen* 28,300 .... D2
Grindelwald 3,511 .... E3
Grosswangen 2,213 .... F2
Gruyères 1,234 .... D3
Gstaad D4
Gsteig 865 .... D4
Guggisberg 1,739 .... D3
Gurtnellen 1,048 .... G3
Guttingen 1,060 .... H1
Hallau 1,836 .... F1
Heiden 3,716 .... H2
Heimberg 3,046 .... E3
Hérémence 1,484 .... D4
Hergiswil 4,364 .... F3
Herisau 14,597 .... H2
Herzogenbuchsee 5,140 .... E2
Hilterfingen 3,647 .... E3
Hinwil 6,547 .... G2
Hitzkirch 1,468 .... F2
Hochdorf 5,222 .... F2
Horgen 15,691 .... G2
Huttwil 4,800 .... E2
Igis 5,283 .... J3
Ilanz 1,783 .... H3
Illnau 13,693 .... G2
Ingenbohl 5,111 .... G2
Innertkirchen 1,064 .... F3
Ins 2,435 .... D2
Interlaken 4,735 .... E3
Jegenstorf 2,858 .... D2
Jenaz 1,124 .... J3
Jona 9,286 .... G2
Jungfraujoch E3
Kaltbrunn 2,751 .... H2
Kandersteg 957 .... E4
Kerns 3,807 .... F3
Kerzers 2,688 .... D3
Kirchberg, Bern 3,595 .... E2
Kirchberg, St. Gallen 6,309 .... G2
Kleinlützel 1,271 .... D2
Klingnau 2,545 .... F1
Klosters Dorf 3,534 .... J3
Kloten 16,388 .... G2
Koblenz 1,439 .... F1
Kölliken 3,219 .... F2
Köniz 33,800 .... D3
Konolfingen 4,137 .... E3
Kreuzlingen 15,760 .... H1
Kriens 20,409 .... F2
Krummenau 1,904 .... H2
Küsnacht 12,193 .... G2
Küssnacht am Rigi 7,956 .... F2

Küttigen 4,181 .... F2
L'Abbaye 1,319 .... B3
La Chaux-de-Fonds 42,500 .... C2
Lachen 4,914 .... G2
Lancy 20,523 .... B4
La Neuveville 3,917 .... D2
Langenthal 13,077 .... E2
Langenthal* 22,100 .... E2
Langnau am Albis 4,879 .... G2
Langnau in Emmental 8,950 .... E3
La Roche 1,069 .... D3
La Sarraz 1,190 .... C3
La Tour-de-Peilz 8,864 .... C4
Läufelfingen 1,243 .... E2
Laufen 4,723 .... D2
Laufenburg 2,128 .... F1
Laupen 2,139 .... D3
Lauperswil 2,542 .... E3
Lausanne 136,100 .... C3
Lausanne* 228,700 .... C3
Lauterbrunnen 3,431 .... E3
Le Brassus 5,465 .... B3
Le Châble 4,541 .... D4
Le Chenit (Le Brassus) 5,465 .... B3
Le Landeron 2,768 .... C2
Le Locle 14,452 .... C2
Le Mont-sur-Lausanne 2,692 .... C3
Lengau 4,736 .... D2
Lenk 1,876 .... D4
Le Noirmont 1,516 .... C2
Lens 2,052 .... D4
Lenzburg 7,594 .... F2
Les Bois 1,110 .... C2
Les Ponts-de-Martel 1,327 .... C2
Leuk 2,796 .... E4
Leukerbad 1,056 .... E4
Leysin 2,752 .... C4
Liechtensteig 2,131 .... H2
Liestal 12,500 .... E2
Liestal-Sissach* 40,800 .... E2
Linthal 1,458 .... H3
Littau 13,495 .... F2
Locarno 14,143 .... G4
Locarno* 39,200 .... G4
Lodrino 1,075 .... G4
Lotzwil 2,323 .... E2
Lucens 2,144 .... C3
Lucerne 70,200 .... F2
Lucerne* 158,600 .... F2
Lugano 22,280 .... G4
Lugano* 64,200 .... G4
Lungern 1,813 .... F3
Luthern 1,706 .... E2
Lutry 4,994 .... C3
Lützelflüh 3,842 .... E3
Luzern (Lucerne) 70,200 .... F2
Lyss 8,131 .... D2
Maienfeld 1,542 .... J2
Malans 1,294 .... J3
Malleray 1,969 .... D2
Malters 5,100 .... F2
Malvaglia 1,099 .... H4
Männedorf 7,419 .... G2
Marbach 1,265 .... E3
Martigny 10,478 .... C4
Meilen 9,881 .... G2
Meiringen 3,759 .... F3
Melide 1,315 .... G5
Mellingen 3,211 .... F2
Mels 5,969 .... H2
Mendrisio 6,223 .... G5
Menzingen 3,483 .... G2
Menznau 2,185 .... E2
Mesocco 1,376 .... H4
Meyrin 14,255 .... B4
Minusio 5,027 .... G4
Möhlin 6,003 .... E1
Mollis 2,628 .... H2
Montana 1,725 .... D4
Monthey 10,114 .... C4
Montreux 20,421 .... C4
Morges 11,931 .... B3
Morges* 17,200 .... B3
Moudon 3,773 .... C3
Moutier 8,794 .... D2
Müllheim 1,620 .... G1
Mümliswil-Ramiswil 2,702 .... E2
Münchenbuchsee 6,459 .... E2
Münsingen 8,350 .... E3
Muotathal 2,763 .... G3
Muri 4,853 .... F2
Muri bei Bern 3,057 .... E3
Mürren E3
Murten 4,256 .... D3
Muttenz 15,518 .... E1
Näfels 3,739 .... H2
Naters 5,517 .... E4
Nebikon 1,378 .... F2
Nendaz 4,051 .... D4
Nesslau 1,934 .... H2

Netstal 2,771 .... H2
Neuchâtel 38,400 .... C3
Neuchâtel* 61,700 .... C3
Neuenegg 3,452 .... D3
Neuhausen am Rheinfall 12,103 .... G1
Neunkirch 1,239 .... F1
Nidau 7,962 .... D2
Niederbipp 3,293 .... E2
Niederurnen 3,354 .... G2
Nunningen 1,450 .... E2
Nyon 11,424 .... B4
Oberägeri 2,992 .... G2
Oberburg 3,015 .... E2
Oberdiessbach 2,145 .... E3
Oberdorf 1,953 .... E2
Oberriet 6,123 .... J2
Obersiggenthal 6,623 .... F1
Oberzwil 4,659 .... H2
Oensingen 3,387 .... E2
Oftringen 9,189 .... E2
Ollon 4,470 .... D4
Olten 21,209 .... E2
Olten* 49,000 .... E2
Opfikon 11,115 .... G2
Orbe 4,522 .... C3
Orsières 2,470 .... D4
Ouchy C4
Paradiso 3,101 .... G5
Payerne 6,899 .... C3
Penthalaz 1,701 .... C3
Péry 1,486 .... D2
Peseux 5,578 .... C3
Pfaffnau 2,584 .... E2
Pieterlen 3,485 .... D2
Plaffeien 1,448 .... D3
Pontresina 1,646 .... J3
Porrentruy 7,827 .... C2
Port-Valais 1,363 .... C4
Poschiavo 3,563 .... J4
Prangins 1,466 .... B4
Pratteln 15,127 .... E1
Pully 15,917 .... C4
Quinto 1,490 .... G3
Rafz 2,215 .... G1
Ramsen 1,217 .... G1
Rapperswil 8,713 .... G2
Raron 1,257 .... E4
Regensdorf 8,566 .... F2
Reichenbach im Kandertal 2,900 .... E3
Reiden 3,275 .... F2
Reinach in Aargau 5,862 .... F2
Reinach in Baselland 13,419 .... E2
Renan 1,094 .... C2
Renens 17,391 .... C3
Rheinau 2,075 .... G1
Rheineck 3,275 .... J2
Rheinfelden 6,866 .... E1
Richterswil 7,380 .... G2
Riehen 21,026 .... E1
Riggisberg 2,193 .... E3
Riva San Vitale 1,607 .... G5
Rivera 1,146 .... G4
Roggwil 3,403 .... E2
Rolle 3,658 .... B4
Romanshorn 8,329 .... H1
Romont 3,276 .... C3
Rorschach 11,963 .... H2
Rorschach* 24,200 .... H2
Rosenlaui F3
Rothrist 5,883 .... E2
Roveredo 2,037 .... H4
Rüeggisberg 1,857 .... E3
Rumlang 5,677 .... G2
Rüschegg 1,346 .... D3
Ruswil 4,756 .... F2
Rüthi 1,493 .... J2
Rüti, Zürich 9,546 .... G2
Saanen 5,840 .... D4
Sachseln 3,059 .... F3
Saignelégier 1,745 .... D2
Saint-Aubin-Sauges 2,058 .... C3
Saint-Blaise 2,586 .... D2
Sainte-Croix 6,240 .... B3
Saint-Imier 6,740 .... D2
Saint-Légier-La Chiésaz 2,230 .... C4
Saint-Martin 1,120 .... E4
Saint-Maurice 3,808 .... C4
Saint Moritz 5,699 .... J3
Saint Niklaus 2,043 .... E4
Saint-Prex 2,306 .... B4
Saint Stephan 1,213 .... D3
Saint-Ursanne 1,073 .... D2
Samedan 2,574 .... J3
Sankt Gallen 81,900 .... H2
Sankt Gallen* 90,400 .... H2
Sankt Margrethen 5,101 .... J2
Sargans 4,058 .... H2
Sarnen 6,952 .... F3
Satigny 1,877 .... A4

Savièse 3,585 .... D4
Saxon 2,409 .... D4
Schaffhausen 36,800 .... G1
Schaffhausen* 55,800 .... G1
Schänis 2,355 .... H2
Schattdorf 3,292 .... G3
Scherzingen 1,420 .... H1
Schiers 2,342 .... J3
Schinznach-Dorf 1,154 .... F2
Schleitheim 1,544 .... G1
Schlieren 11,869 .... F2
Schönenwerd 4,793 .... E2
Schübelbach 4,395 .... G2
Schüpfheim 3,773 .... F3
Schwanden 2,823 .... H2
Schwyz 12,194 .... G2
Scuol 1,686 .... K3
Sempach 1,619 .... F2
Seon 3,628 .... F2
Seuzach 3,258 .... G1
Sevelen 2,742 .... H2
Sierre 11,017 .... D4
Signau 2,642 .... E3
Sigriswil 3,540 .... E3
Silenen 2,338 .... G3
Sils im Domleschg 762 .... H3
Silvaplana 714 .... J4
Sins 2,435 .... F2
Sion 21,925 .... D4
Sirnach 3,706 .... G2
Sissach 4,938 .... E2
Solothurn (Soleure) 17,708 .... E2
Solothurn* 35,600 .... E2
Somvix 1,555 .... G3
Sonvico 1,129 .... G4
Spiez 9,911 .... E3
Stäfa 9,937 .... G2
Stalden 1,121 .... E4
Stans 5,180 .... F3
Steckborn 3,752 .... G1
Steffisburg 12,621 .... E3
Stein 1,763 .... E1
Stein am Rhein 2,751 .... G1
Suhr 7,223 .... F2
Sulgen 1,834 .... H1
Sumiswald 5,334 .... E2
Sursee 7,052 .... F2
Tafers 2,021 .... D3
Täuffelen 1,761 .... D2
Tavannes 3,869 .... D2
Tavetsch 1,273 .... G3
Teufen 5,300 .... H2
Thal 4,919 .... J2
Thalwil 13,591 .... G2
Thayngen 3,640 .... G1
Therwil 5,412 .... E1
Thun 37,000 .... E3
Thun* 63,600 .... E3
Thunstetten 2,483 .... E2
Thusis 2,381 .... H3
Trachselwald 1,199 .... E2
Tramelan 5,549 .... D2
Trimmis 1,109 .... J3
Troistorrents 2,208 .... C4
Trub 1,833 .... E3
Trun 1,607 .... G3
Turbenthal 2,939 .... G2
Uetendorf 3,132 .... E3
Unterägeri 4,671 .... G2
Unteriberg 1,344 .... G2
Unterkulm 2,596 .... F2
Unterseen 4,192 .... E3
Untervaz 1,230 .... H3
Urnäsch 2,313 .... H2
Uster 21,819 .... G2
Utzenstorf 3,193 .... E2
Uznach 3,984 .... H2
Uzwil 9,133 .... H2
Vallorbe 4,028 .... B3
Vaz-Obervaz 2,003 .... J3
Vechigen 3,595 .... E3
Vernayaz 1,356 .... D4
Versoix 5,627 .... B4
Vevey 17,957 .... C4
Vevey-Montreux* 62,300 .... C4
Villeneuve 3,705 .... C4
Visp 5,252 .... E4
Vouvry 1,851 .... C4
Vuadens 1,278 .... C3
Wädenswil 15,695 .... G2
Wahlern 4,832 .... D3
Wald 8,185 .... G2
Waldenburg 1,449 .... E2
Waldkirch 2,669 .... H2
Walenstadt 3,446 .... H2
Wallisellen 10,415 .... G2
Walzenhausen 2,082 .... J2
Wangen an der Aare 2,013 .... E2
Wängi 2,730 .... H1
Wartau 3,604 .... H2

Wattwil 8,566 .... H2
Weesen 1,308 .... H2
Weggis 2,517 .... F2
Weinfelden 8,621 .... H1
Wettingen 19,900 .... F2
Wetzikon 13,469 .... G2
Wil 14,646 .... H2
Wil* 20,500 .... H2
Wilchingen 1,066 .... F1
Wilderswil 1,666 .... E3
Wildhaus 1,104 .... H2
Willisau 2,728 .... F2
Wimmis 1,833 .... E3
Windisch 7,444 .... F1
Winterthur 93,500 .... G1
Winterthur* 110,100 .... G1
Wohlen 12,024 .... F2
Wohlen* 16,000 .... F2
Wohlen bei Bern 4,190 .... D3
Wolfenschiessen 1,470 .... F3
Wolhusen 3,556 .... F2
Worb 9,526 .... E3
Wünnewil 3,652 .... D3
Wynigen 1,986 .... E2
Yverdon 20,538 .... C3
Yvonand 1,321 .... C3

Zell, Luzern 1,590 .... E2
Zell, Zürich 4,008 .... G2
Zermatt 3,101 .... E4
Zizers 1,913 .... J3
Zofingen 9,292 .... E2
Zollikofen 9,069 .... E3
Zollikon 12,117 .... G2
Zug 22,972 .... G2
Zug* 51,300 .... G2
Zuoz 1,165 .... J3
Zürich 401,600 .... F2
Zürich* 718,100 .... F2
Zurzach 3,098 .... F1
Zweisimmen 2,738 .... D3

OTHER FEATURES

Aa (riv.) F3
Aare (riv.) E3
Ägerisee (lake) G2
Aiguille d'Argentière (mt.) C5
Aletschhorn (mt.) F4
Aroser Rothorn (mt.) J3
Ault (peak) H3
Balmhorn (mt.) E4
Bernese Oberland (reg.) E3
Bernina (peak) J4
Bernina (pass) K4
Bielersee (lake) D2
Bietschhorn (mt.) E4
Birs (riv.) D2
Blinnenhorn (mt.) F4
Blümlisalp (mt.) E3
Bodensee (Constance) (lake) H1
Borgne (riv.) D4
Breithorn (mt.) E5
Breithorn (mt.) E4
Brienzer Rothorn (mt.) F3
Brienzersee (lake) F3
Broye (riv.) C3
Buchegg (mts.) D2
Buin (peak) K3
Campo Tencia (peak) G4
Chasseron (mt.) C3
Churfirsten (mt.) H2
Clariden (mt.) G3
Constance (lake) H1
Cornettes de Bise (mts.) C4
Dammastock (mt.) F3
Davos (valley) J3
Dent Blanche (mt.) E4
Dent de Lys (mt.) D4

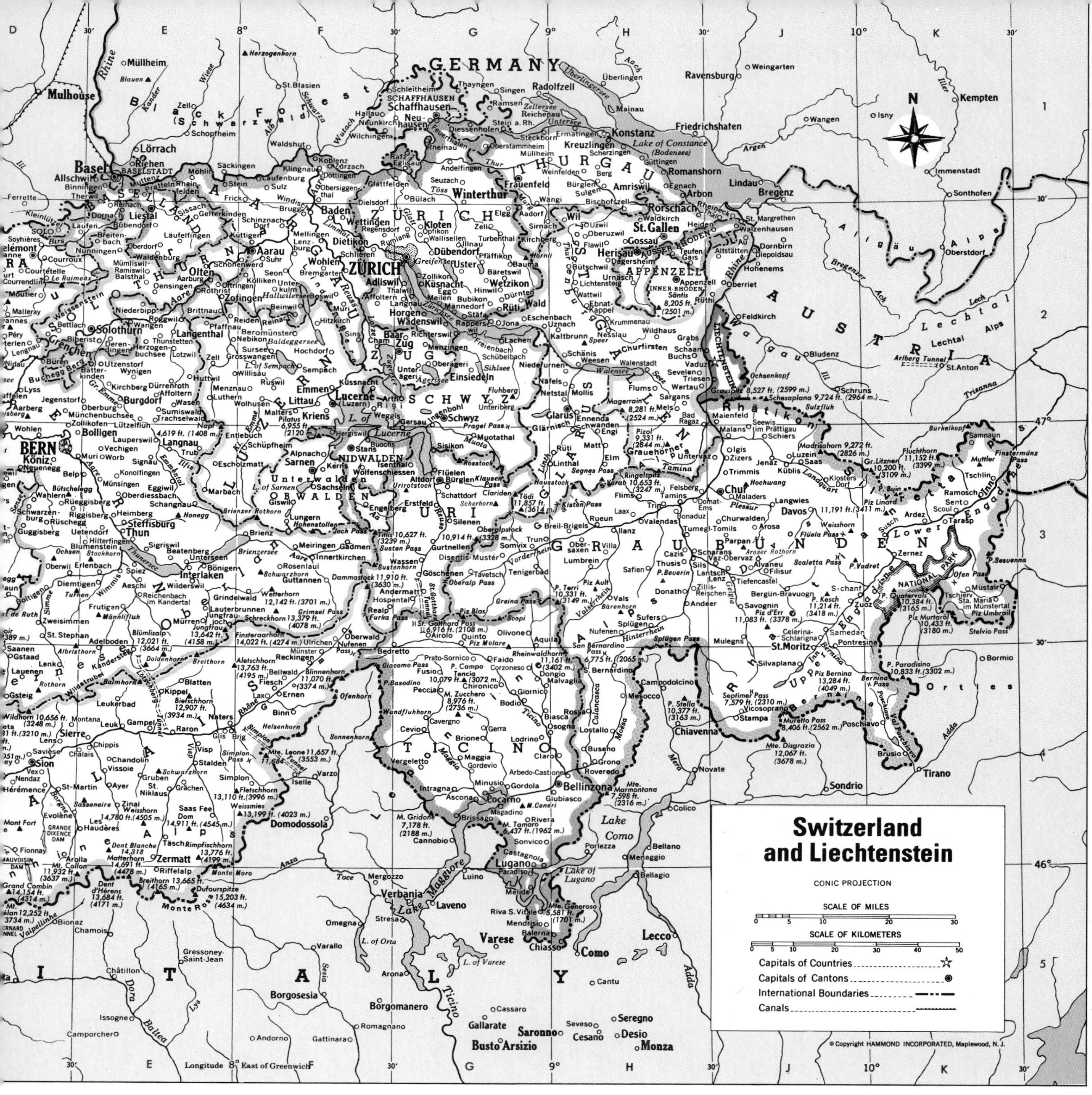

Dent de Ruth (mt.) D3
Dent d'Hérens (mt.) E5
Dents du Midi (mt.) C4
Diablerets (mt.) D4
Doldenhorn (mt.) E4
Dolent (mt.) C5
Dom (mt.) E4
Doubs (riv.) C2
Drance (riv.) D4
Dufourspitze (mt.) E5
Emmental (riv.) E3
Engadine (valley) K3
Err (peak) J3
Finsteraarhorn (mt.) F3
Finstermünz (pass) K3
Fletschhorn (mt.) F4
Fluchthorn (mt.) K3
Flüela (pass) J3
Furka (pass) F3
Generoso (mt.) H5
Geneva (lake) C4
Glärnisch (mt.) H2
Glarus Alps (mts.) H3
Grand Combin (mt.) D5
Grande Dixence (dam) D4
Grand Muveran (mt.) D4
Grauehörner (mts.) H3
Great Saint Bernard (mt.) D5
Great Saint Bernard (pass) D5
Greifensee (lake) G2
Greina (pass) G3
Grimsel (pass) F3
Gross Emme (riv.) E2
Gross Litzner (mt.) K3
Hinterrhein (riv.) H3
Hochwang (mt.) J3
Hohenstollen (mt.) F3
Hörnli (mt.) G2
Inn (riv.) K3
Jorat (mt.) C3
Jungfrau (mt.) E3
Jura (mts.) B3
Kaiseregg (mt.) D3
Kesch (peak) J3
La Dôle (mt.) B4
Landquart (riv.) J3
Le Chasseral (mt.) D2
Le Gros Crêt (mt.) B3
Léman (Geneva) (lake) C4
Leone (mt.) F4
Lepontine Alps (range) G4
Limmat (riv.) F2
Linard (peak) K3
Linden (mts.) F2
Linth (riv.) G3
Lötschberg (tunnel) E4
Lower Engadine (valley) K3
Lucerne (lake) F3
Lugano (lake) H5
Madrisahorn (mt.) J3
Maggia (riv.) G4
Maggiore (lake) G5
Männlifluh (mt.) E3
Marmontana (mt.) H4
Matterhorn (mt.) E4
Mauvoisin (dam) D4
Moësa (riv.) H4
Morat (lake) D3
Muota (riv.) G3
Murg (riv.) G1
Murtaröl (peak) K3
Muttler (mt.) K3
Naafkopf (mt.) J2
Napf (mt.) E3
National Park K3
Neuchâtel (lake) C3
Noirmont (mt.) B4
Oberalp (pass) G3
Oberalpstock (mt.) G3
Ochsen (mt.) D3
Ofen (pass) K3
Ofenhorn (mt.) F4
Orbe (riv.) C3
Pennine Alps (range) D5
Pilatus (mt.) F2
Plessur (riv.) J3
Poschiavo (valley) K4
Pragel (pass) G2
Quatervals (peak) K3
Reuss (riv.) F2
Rhaetian Alps (range) J3
Rhätikon (mts.) J2
Rheinwaldhorn (mt.) G4
Rhine (riv.) J2
Rhône (riv.) D4
Rigi (mt.) F2
Rimpfischhorn (mt.) E4
Ringelspitz (mt.) H3
Risoux (mt.) B3
Rosa (mt.) E5
Rosstock (mt.) G3
Rothorn (mt.) D4
Saane (Sarine) (riv.) D3
Saint Gotthard (pass) G3
Saint Gotthard (tunnel) G3
San Bernardino (pass) H3
Säntis (mt.) H2
Sarine (Saane) (riv.) D3
Sarnen (lake) F3
Schesaplana (mt.) J2
Scherhorn (mt.) G3
Schreckhorn (mt.) F3
Schwarzhorn (mt.) E4
Schwarzhorn (mt.) F3
Seez (riv.) H2
Sempach (lake) F2
Septimer (pass) J4
Sesvenna (peak) K3
Sihlsee (lake) G2
Silvretta (mts.) K3
Simme (riv.) D3
Simplon (pass) F4
Simplon (tunnel) F4
Sonnenhorn (mt.) F4
Splügen (pass) H3
Stockhorn (mt.) E3
Sulzflüh (mt.) J2
Susten (pass) G3
Sustenhorn (mt.) G3
Tamaro (mt.) G4
Tamina (riv.) H3
Tendre (peak) B3
Terri (peak) H3
Thunersee (lake) E3
Thur (riv.) G1
Ticino (riv.) G4
Titlis (mt.) F3
Tödi (mt.) G3
Toggenburg (dist.) H2
Töss (riv.) G1
Tour d'Ai (mt.) C4
Umbrail (peak) K3
Untersee (lake) H1
Unterwalden (reg.) F3
Upper Engadine (valley) J4
Urirotstock (mt.) G3
Vadret (peak) J3
Valserrhein (riv.) H3
Vanil Noir (mt.) D3
Vélan (mt.) D5
Visp (riv.) E4
Vorab (mt.) H3
Vorderrhein (riv.) G3
Wandfluhhorn (mt.) G4
Weissenstein (mts.) D2
Weisshorn (mt.) E4
Weisshorn (mt.) J3
Weissmies (mt.) F4
Wetterhorn (mt.) F3
Wildhorn (mt.) D4
Wildstrubel (mt.) E4
Zellersee (lake) G1
Zugersee (lake) F2
Zürichsee (lake) G2

LIECHTENSTEIN

CITIES and TOWNS

Schaan 4,552 H2
Triesen 2,971 H2
Vaduz (cap.) 4,614 H2

OTHER FEATURES

Grauspitz (mt.) J2
Ochsenkopf (mt.) J2
Rhätikon (mts.) J2
Rhine (riv.) J2

*City and suburbs.

AUSTRIA

PROVINCES

Burgenland 272,119 ... D3
Carinthia 525,728 ... B3
Lower Austria 1,414,161 ... C2
Salzburg 401,766 ... B3
Styria 1,192,442 ... C3
Tirol 540,771 ... A3
Upper Austria 1,223,444 ... B2
Vienna (city) 1,614,841 ... D2
Vorarlberg 271,473 ... A3

CITIES and TOWNS†

Admont 3,126 ... C3
Allentsteig 2,783 ... C2
Altheim 4,766 ... B2
Althofen 3,886 ... C3
Amstetten 13,330 ... C2
Andau 3,058 ... D3
Arnoldstein 6,740 ... B3
Aspang Markt 2,316 ... D3
Attnang-Puchheim 7,837 ... B2
Bad Aussee 5,039 ... B3
Baden 22,631 ... D2
Badgastein 5,228 ... B3
Bad Goisern 6,360 ... B3
Bad Hofgastein 5,525 ... B3
Bad Ischl 12,740 ... B3
Bad Leonfelden 2,712 ... C2
Bad Sankt-Leonhard im Lavanttal 4,882 ... C3
Berndorf 8,371 ... C3
Bischofshofen 9,417 ... B3
Bludenz 12,050 ... A3
Bramberg am Wildkogel 3,129 ... B3
Braunau am Inn 16,432 ... B2
Bregenz 22,839 ... A3
Bruck an der Leitha 7,506 ... D2
Bruck an der Mur 16,359 ... C3
Deutsch Feistritz 3,820 ... C3
Deutschkreutz 3,673 ... D3
Deutsch Landsberg 6,614 ... C3
Deutsch Wagram 4,481 ... D2
Dornbirn 33,810 ... A3
Ebenfurth 2,272 ... D3
Ebensee 9,413 ... B3
Eferding 3,014 ... B2
Eggenburg 3,730 ... C2
Ehrwald 2,198 ... A3
Horn 6,264 ... C2
Hüttenberg 3,251 ... C3
Imst 5,855 ... A3
Innsbruck 115,800 ... A3
Innsbruck* 167,200 ... A3
Jenbach 5,868 ... A3
Jennersdorf 4,210 ... C3
Judenburg 11,346 ... C3
Kapfenberg 26,001 ... C3
Kappl 2,156 ... A3
Kaprun 2,604 ... B3
Kindberg 6,128 ... C3
Kirchdorf an der Krems 3,471 ... C3
Kitzbühel 7,995 ... B3
Klagenfurt 74,326 ... C3
Klagenfurt* 112,600 ... C3
Klosterneuburg 21,912 ... D2
Knittelfeld 14,517 ... C3
Köflach 12,612 ... C3
Königswiesen 2,921 ... C2
Korneuburg 8,892 ... D2
Kössen 2,764 ... B3
Kötschach-Mauthen 3,740 ... B3
Krems an der Donau 21,733 ... C2
Kufstein 12,766 ... A3
Kundl 3,020 ... A3
Laa an der Thaya 5,455 ... D2
Laakirchen 7,664 ... B3
Lambach 3,301 ... C2
Landeck 7,388 ... A3
Längenfeld 2,838 ... A3
Langenlois 4,957 ... C2
Langenwang 4,071 ... C3
Lavamünd 4,120 ... C3
Leibnitz 6,646 ... C3
Lenzing 5,385 ... B3
Leoben 35,153 ... C3
Lienz 11,696 ... B3
Liezen 6,244 ... C3
Lilienfeld 3,126 ... C3
Linz 205,700 ... C2
Linz* 356,500 ... C2
Lustenau 15,239 ... A3
Mannersdorf am Leithagebirge 4,012 ... D3
Marchegg 2,678 ... D2
Mariazell 2,298 ... C3
Matrei in Osttirol 4,003 ... B3
Mattersburg 5,417 ... D3
Mattighofen 4,344 ... B2
Mauerkirchen 2,237 ... B2
Mautern in Steiermark 2,536 ... C3
Sankt Valentin 8,715 ... C2
Sankt Veit an der Glan 11,047 ... C3
Sankt Wolfgang im Salzkammergut 2,746 ... B3
Schärding 5,874 ... B2
Scheibbs 4,419 ... C2
Schladming 3,460 ... B3
Schrems 3,393 ... C2
Schruns 3,607 ... A3
Schwarzach im Pongau 3,616 ... B3
Schwaz 10,253 ... A3
Schwechat 14,997 ... D2
Schwertberg 3,881 ... C2
Sierning 8,162 ... C2
Sillian 1,988 ... B3
Solbad Hall in Tirol 12,335 ... A3
Spital am Pyhrn 2,315 ... C3
Spittal an der Drau 13,690 ... B3
Steinach 2,698 ... A3
Steyr 40,578 ... C2
Stockerau 12,634 ... D2
Strassburg 2,850 ... C3
Tamsweg 5,060 ... B3
Telfs 6,589 ... A3
Ternitz 10,287 ... D3
Traiskirchen 8,878 ... D2
Traun 20,843 ... C2
Trieben 4,639 ... C3
Trofaiach 8,731 ... C3
Tulln 7,705 ... D2
Velden am Wörthersee 7,306 ... C3
Vienna (cap.) 1,700,000 ... D2
Vienna* 1,858,700 ... D2
Villach 50,979 ... B3
Vöcklabruck 10,627 ... B2
Voitsberg 11,094 ... C3
Völkermarkt 10,772 ... C3
Vordernberg 2,508 ... C3
Waidhofen an der Thaya 4,200 ... C2
Waidhofen an der Ybbs 5,218 ... C3
Weitensfeld-Flattnitz 5,206 ... B3
Weitra 3,250 ... C2
Weiz 8,241 ... C3
Wels 47,279 ... C2
Weyer Markt 2,518 ... C3
Wien (Vienna) (cap.) 1,700,000 ... D2
Wiener Neustadt 34,774 ... D3
Wildon 2,002 ... C3
Wilhelmsburg 6,307 ... C2
Wolfsberg 31,176 ... C3
Wörgl 7,811 ... A3
Ybbs an der Donau 6,422 ... C2
Zams 3,120 ... A3
Zell am See 7,456 ... B3
Zell am Ziller 1,882 ... A3
Zeltweg 8,431 ... C3
Zirl 4,157 ... A3
Zistersdorf 3,412 ... D2
Zwettl-Niederösterreich 11,624 ... C2

OTHER FEATURES

AllgÄu Alps (mts.) ... A3
Bavarian Alps (mts.) ... A3
Bodensee (Constance) (lake) ... A3
Brenner (pass) ... A3
Carnic Alps (mts.) ... B3
Constance (lake) ... A3
Danube (riv.) ... C2
Donau (Danube) (riv.) ... D2
Drau (riv.) ... C3
Enns (riv.) ... C3
Grossglockner (mt.) ... B3
Hohe Tauern (range) ... B3
Inn (riv.) ... B2
Karawanken (range) ... C3
March (riv.) ... D2
Mühlviertel (reg.) ... C2
Mur (riv.) ... C3
Neusiedler See (lake) ... D3
Niedere Tauern (range) ... B3
Ötztal Alps (mts.) ... A3
Raab (riv.) ... C3
Rhine (riv.) ... A3
Salzach (riv.) ... B2
Salzkammergut (reg.) ... B3
Semmering (pass) ... C3
Thaya (riv.) ... C2
Traun (riv.) ... C2
Wildspitze (mt.) ... A3
Zugspitze (mt.) ... A3

CZECHOSLOVAKIA

REPUBLICS

Czech Socialist Rep. 9,964,338 ... B1
Slovak Socialist Rep. 4,670,409 ... E2

REGIONS

Bratislava (city) 333,000 ... D2
Jihočeský 662,002 ... C2
Jihomoravský 1,966,850 ... D2
Praha (city) 1,161,200 ... C1
Severočeský 1,122,035 ... C1
Severomoravský 1,849,286 ... D2
Středočeský 1,193,041 ... C2
Středoslovenský 1,436,351 ... E2
Východočeský 1,214,581 ... C1
Východoslovenský 1,298,481 ... F2
Západočeský 865,094 ... B2
Západoslovenský 1,610,542 ... D2

CITIES and TOWNS

Aš 120,000 ... B1
Austerlitz (Slavkov) ... D2
Bánovce nad Bebravou 11,400 ... E2
Banská Bystrica 53,000 ... E2
Banská štiavnica 7,486 ... E2
Bardejov 17,400 ... F2
Benešov 11,100 ... C2
Beroun 17,600 ... B2
Bílina 17,800 ... B1
Blansko 13,800 ... D2
Boskovice 8,531 ... D2
Brandýs nad Labem-Stará Boleslavv 333,000 ... C1
Bratislava 333,000 ... D2
Břeclav 21,100 ... D2
Brezno 14,800 ... E2
Brno 335,700 ... D2
Broumov 7,782 ... D1
Bruntál 12,300 ... D2
Bystřice nad Pernštejnem 6,471 ... D2
Bystřice pod Hostýnem 6,681 ... D2
Bytča 6,922 ... E2
Čadca 16,800 ... E2
Čalovo 6,591 ... D3
Čáslav 10,200 ... C2
Česká Lípa 18,600 ... C1
Česká Třebová 14,700 ... D2
České Budějovice 80,800 ... C2
Český Brod 6,640 ... C1
Český Krumlov 12,000 ... C2
Český Těšín 17,200 ... E2
Cheb 27,000 ... B1
Choceň 8,198 ... D1
Chodov 14,400 ... B1
Chomutov 44,200 ... B1
Chotěboř 6,692 ... C2
Chrudim 18,800 ... C2
Čierny Balog 6,435 ... E2
Děčín 46,500 ... C1
Detva 13,100 ... E2
Dobříš 6,378 ... C2
Dobruška 5,779 ... D1
Dolný Kubín 9,900 ... E2
Domažlice 9,100 ... B2
Dubnica nad Váhom 11,300 ... E2
Duchcov 9,712 ... B1
Dunajská Streda 13,000 ... D3
Dvory nad Žitavou 5,847 ... E3
Dvŭ Králové nad Labem 16,800 ... C1
Falknov (Sokolov) 23,900 ... B1
Fil'akovo 7,822 ... E2
Frenštát pod Radhoštěm 8,516 ... E2
Frýdek-Místek 43,800 ... E2
Frýdlant v. Čechách 5,948 ... C1
Frýdlant nad Ostravicí 6,250 ... E2
Galanta 12,300 ... D2
Gottwaldov 84,300 ... D2
Handlová 16,200 ... E2
Havířov 85,000 ... E2
Havlíčkŭv Brod 19,200 ... C2
Hlinsko 8,890 ... D2
Hlohovec 15,200 ... D2
Hlučín 15,300 ... E2
Hnúšt'a-Likier ... E2
Hodonín 22,600 ... D2
Holešov 9,091 ... D2
Holíč 7,602 ... D2
Holice 6,151 ... C1
Horažd'ovice ... B2
Hořice v Podkrkonoší 7,715 ... C1
Horná Štubňa ... E2
Horní Benešov ... D2
Horní Libina ... D2
Hořovice 5,665 ... C2
Horšovský Týn ... B2
Hostinné ... C1
Hradec Králové 85,600 ... C1
Hranice 13,300 ... D2
Hrinova 7,800 ... E2
Hronov 9,767 ... D1
Hrušovany ... D2
Humenné 22,200 ... G2
Humpolec 7,810 ... C2
Hurbanovo ... E3
Hustopeče ... D2
Ilava ... E2
Ivančice 7,314 ... D2

Topography

Eisenerz 11,563 ... C3
Eisenkappel-Vellach 3,761 ... C3
Eisenstadt 10,059 ... D3
Enns 9,622 ... C2
Feldbach 3,887 ... C3
Feldkirch 21,214 ... A3
Feldkirchen in Kärnten 11,188 ... B3
Ferlach 7,621 ... C3
Fieberbrunn 3,651 ... B3
Fohnsdorf 11,169 ... C3
Frankenmarkt 2,960 ... B3
Frauenkirchen 2,749 ... D3
Freistadt 5,956 ... C2
Freidberg 2,504 ... D3
Friesach 7,257 ... C3
Frohnleiten 5,081 ... C3
Fulpmes 2,553 ... A3
Fürstenfeld 6,054 ... C3
Gaming 4,181 ... C3
Gänserndorf 4,211 ... D2
Gleisdorf 4,921 ... C3
Gloggnitz 7,078 ... D3
Gmünd, Carinthia 2,267 ... B3
Gmünd, Lower Austria 6,323 ... C2
Gmunden 12,270 ... B3
Golling an der Salzach 3,089 ... B3
Götzis 7,931 ... A3
Gratwein 2,747 ... C3
Graz 251,900 ... C3
Graz* 314,200 ... C3
Grein 2,767 ... C2
Grieskirchen 4,519 ... B2
Grosssiegharts 3,288 ... C2
Grünburg 3,775 ... C3
Güssing 3,675 ... C3
Haag 5,060 ... C2
Hainburg an der Donau 6,009 ... D2
Hainfeld 3,897 ... C2
Hallein 14,371 ... B3
Hallstatt 1,303 ... B3
Hartberg 5,702 ... C3
Haslach an der Mühl 2,636 ... C2
Heidenreichstein 4,340 ... C2
Heiligenblut 1,324 ... B3
Hermagor-Preseggersee 7,531 ... B3
Herzogenburg 7,299 ... C2
Hohenau an der March 3,591 ... D2
Hohenberg 2,016 ... C3
Hohenems 11,487 ... A3
Hollabrunn 6,563 ... D2
Hopfgarten in Nordtirol 4,784 ... B3
Mauthausen 4,419 ... C2
Mauthen-Kötschach 3,750 ... B3
Mayrhofen 3,174 ... A3
Melk 5,108 ... C2
Mistelbach an der Zaya 6,306 ... D2
Mittersill 4,361 ... B3
Mödling 18,712 ... D2
Mondsee 2,141 ... B3
Murau 2,710 ... C3
Mürzzuschlag 11,564 ... C3
Neuberg an der Mürz 2,183 ... C3
Neumarkt am Wallersee 3,267 ... B3
Neunkirchen 10,922 ... C3
Neusiedl am See 3,999 ... D3
Neustift im Stubaital 2,789 ... A3
Ober Grafendorf 4,109 ... C2
Oberndorf bei Salzburg 3,293 ... B3
Obervellach 2,420 ... B3
Oberwart 5,661 ... D3
Paternion 5,805 ... B3
Perg 4,872 ... C2
Peuerbach 2,161 ... B2
Pfunds 2,043 ... A3
Pinkafeld 4,610 ... C3
Pöchlarn 3,199 ... C2
Pörtschach am Wörthersee 2,511 ... C3
Poysdorf 5,774 ... D2
Pregarten 3,249 ... C2
Raabs an der Thaya 4,194 ... C2
Radenthein 6,847 ... B3
Radkersburg 2,000 ... C3
Radstadt 3,585 ... B3
Rankweil 8,440 ... A3
Rechnitz 3,412 ... D3
Reichenau an der Rax 4,053 ... C3
Retz 4,780 ... D2
Ried im Innkreis 10,534 ... B2
Rottenmann 4,781 ... C3
Saalfelden am Steinernen Meer 10,172 ... B3
Salzburg 122,100 ... B3
Salzburg* 213,430 ... B3
Sankt Aegyd am Neuwalde 3,165 ... C3
Sankt Anton am Arlberg 2,086 ... A3
Sankt Johann in Tirol 5,942 ... B3
Sankt Michael im Lungau 2,839 ... B3
Sankt Michael in Obersteiermark 3,717 ... C3
Sankt Michael im Lungau 2,839 ... B3
Sankt Paul im Lavanttal 6,721 ... C3
Sankt Pölten 43,300 ... C2

AUSTRIA
AREA 32,375 sq. mi. (83,851 sq. km.)
POPULATION 7,507,000
CAPITAL Vienna
LARGEST CITY Vienna
HIGHEST POINT Grossglockner 12,457 ft. (3,797 m.)
MONETARY UNIT schilling
MAJOR LANGUAGE German
MAJOR RELIGION Roman Catholicism

CZECHOSLOVAKIA
AREA 49,373 sq. mi. (127,876 sq. km.)
POPULATION 15,276,799
CAPITAL Prague
LARGEST CITY Prague
HIGHEST POINT Gerlachovka 8,707 ft. (2,654 m.)
MONETARY UNIT koruna
MAJOR LANGUAGES Czech, Slovak
MAJOR RELIGIONS Roman Catholicism, Protestantism

HUNGARY
AREA 35,919 sq. mi. (93,030 sq. km.)
POPULATION 10,709,536
CAPITAL Budapest
LARGEST CITY Budapest
HIGHEST POINT Kékes 3,330 ft. (1,015 m.)
MONETARY UNIT forint
MAJOR LANGUAGE Hungarian
MAJOR RELIGIONS Roman Catholicism, Protestantism

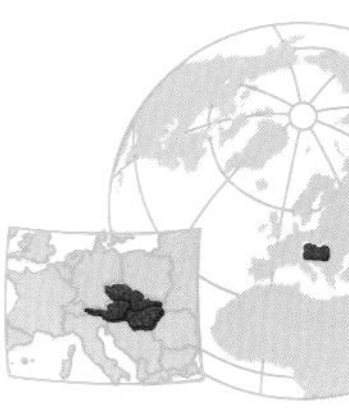

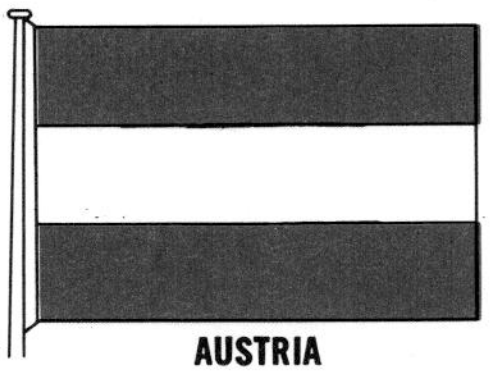
AUSTRIA

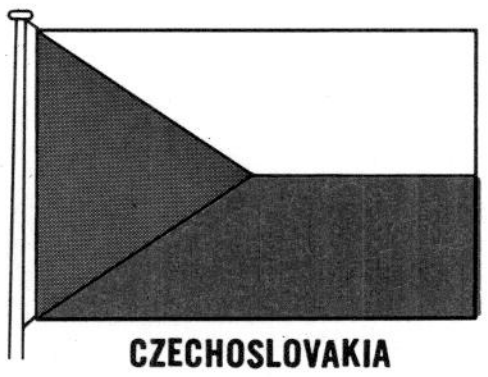
CZECHOSLOVAKIA

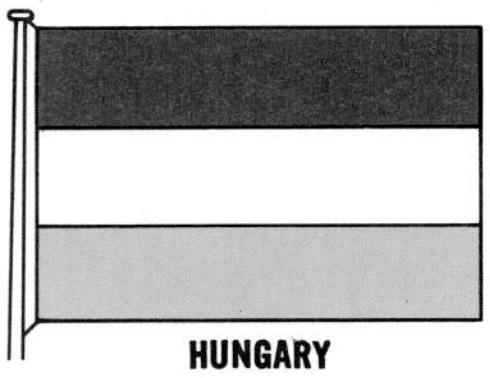
HUNGARY

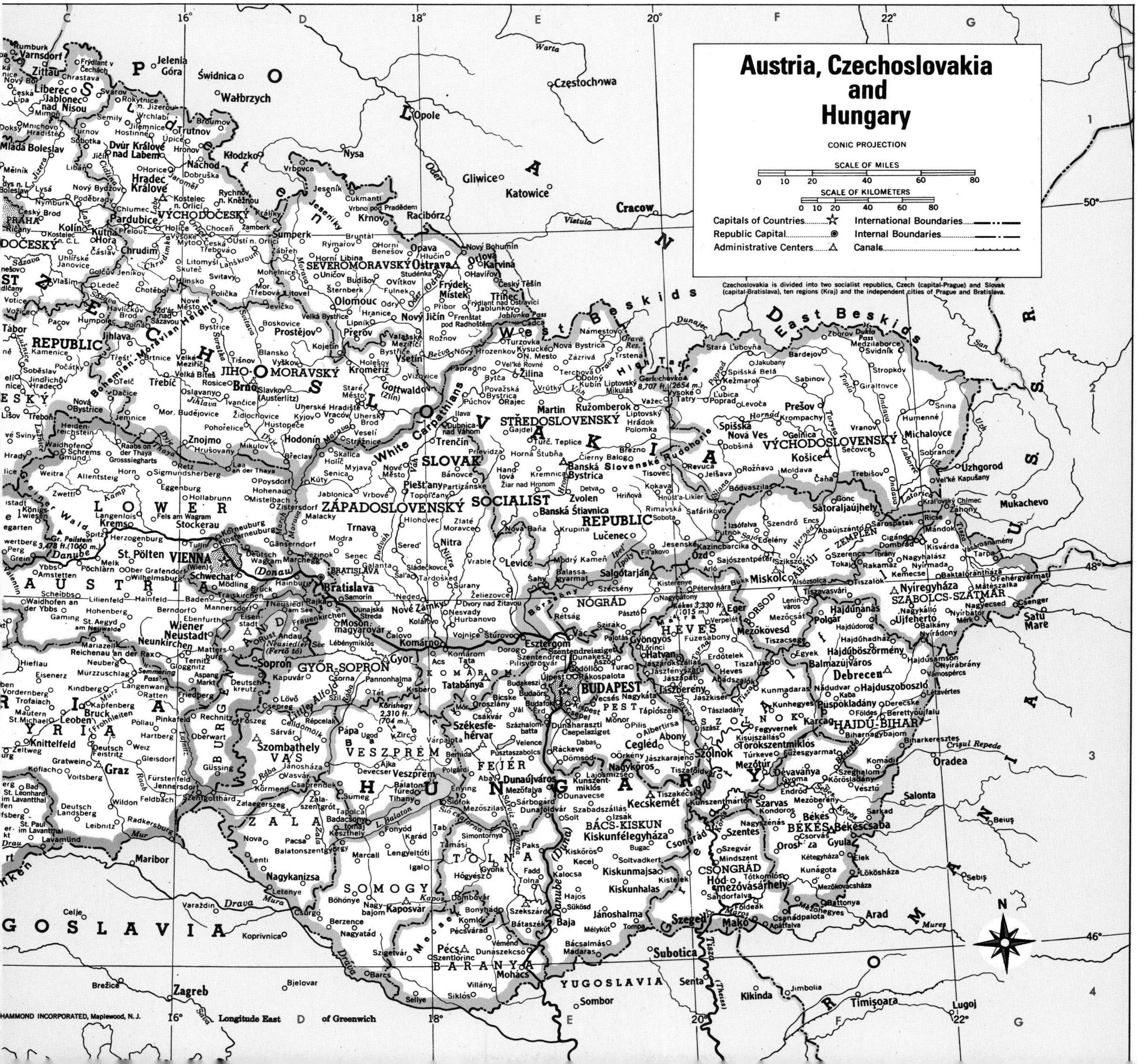

(continued)

Jablonec nad Nisou 36,300 ... C1
Jablonica ... D2
Jablunkov 9,405 ... E2
Jáchymov ... B1
Jakubany ... F2
Jaroměř 11,600 ... C1
Jelšava ... F2
Jemnice ... C2
Jeseník 10,900 ... D1
Jesenské ... F2
Jevíčko ... D2
Jičín 13,200 ... C1
Jihlava 44,500 ... C2
Jilemnice ... C1
Jindřichův Hradec 15,700 ... C2
Jiřkov 11,400 ... B1
Kadaň 18,100 ... B1
Kamenice ... C2
Kaplice ... C2
Karlovy Vary 43,300 ... B1
Karviná 79,100 ... E2
Kdyně ... B2
Kežmarok 11,000 ... F2
Kladno 61,200 ... B1
Klatovy 18,500 ... B2
Kojetín 5,852 ... D2
Kokava nad Rimavicou 5,391 ... E2
Kolárovo 10,500 ... D3
Kolín 29,100 ... C1
Komárno 28,200 ... D3
Košice 169,100 ... F2
Kostelec nad Orlicí 5,575 ... D1
Kráľovský Chlmec 5,329 ... G2
Kralupy nad Vltavou 16,900 ... C1
Kraslice 6,733 ... B1
Kremnica 5,941 ... E2
Krnov 25,000 ... D1
Kroměříž 23,200 ... D2
Krompachy 6,332 ... F2
Krupina 6,627 ... E2
Krupka 8,301 ... B1
Kutná Hora 19,200 ... C2
Kyjov 10,700 ... D2
Kynšperk 5,524 ... B1
Kysucké Nové Mesto 11,700 ... E2
Lanškroun 8,683 ... D2
Levice 19,000 ... E2
Levoča 10,100 ... F2
Libáň ... C1
Liberec 75,600 ... C1
Lidice ... C1
Lipník nad Bečvou 7,358 ... D2
Liptovský Mikuláš 19,400 ... E2
Litoměřice 19,700 ... C1
Litomyšl 8,112 ... D2
Litovel 5,805 ... D2
Litvínov 23,300 ... B1
Lomnice ... C2
Louny 15,200 ... B1
Lovosice 9,323 ... C1
L'ubica ... F2
Lučenec 23,300 ... E2
Lysá nad Labem 9,920 ... C1
Malacky 13,200 ... D2
Mariánské Lázně 14,600 ... B2
Martin 47,800 ... E2
Medzilaborce ... F2
Mělník 17,800 ... C1
Michalovce 23,600 ... G2
Mikulov 6,267 ... D2
Milevsko 7,091 ... C2
Mimoň 6,773 ... C1
Mladá Boleslav 36,900 ... C1
Mladá Vožice ... C2
Mnichovo Hradiště 5,239 ... C1
Modra 7,219 ... D2
Modrý Kameň 6,200 ... E2
Mohelnice 6,050 ... D2
Moldava nad Bodvou 5,397 ... F2
Moravská Třebová 9,052 ... D2
Moravské Budějovice 5,576 ... D2
Most 59,400 ... B1
Myjava 6,657 ... D2
Náchod 19,300 ... D1
Námestovo ... E2
Neded ... D2
Nejdek 8,187 ... B1
Nepomuk ... B2
Nesvady 5,453 ... E3
Netolice ... C2
Nitra 50,000 ... E2
Nová Baňa 6,218 ... E2
Nová Bystrica ... E2
Nová Bystřice ... C2
Nové Hrady ... C2
Nové Město na Moravě 6,581 ... D2
Nové Město nad Váhom 15,900 ... D2
Nové Strašecí ... B1
Nové Zámky 27,300 ... D3
Nový Bohumín 16,700 ... E2
Nový Bor 7,621 ... C1
Nový Bydžov 6,824 ... C1
Nový Hrozenkov ... E2
Nový Jičín 21,400 ... E2
Nymburk 13,600 ... C1
Nýřany 6,204 ... B2
Nýrsko ... B2
Odry ... D2
Olomouc 82,800 ... D2
Opava 53,800 ... E2
Orlová 25,500 ... E2
Ostrava 293,500 ... E2
Ostrov 18,200 ... B1
Pardubice 78,500 ... C1
Partizánske 15,100 ... E2
Pelhřimov 11,900 ... C2
Pezinok 13,100 ... D2
Piešťany 25,400 ... D2
Písek 25,100 ... C2
Plzeň 155,000 ... B2
Počátky ... C2
Podbořany ... B1
Poděbrady 13,400 ... C1
Pohořelice ... D2
Polička 6,529 ... D2
Polná ... C2
Polomka ... E2
Poprad 25,800 ... F2
Považská Bystrica 19,300 ... E2
Prachatice 7,900 ... B2
Prague (Praha) (cap.) 1,161,200 ... C1
Přelouč 6,251 ... C1
Přerov 43,500 ... D2
Prešov 61,000 ... F2
Přeštice ... B2
Příbor 7,726 ... E2
Příbram 31,300 ... B2
Prievidza 30,900 ... E2
Prostějov 44,200 ... D2
Protivín ... C2
Púchov 9,306 ... E2
Radnice ... B2
Rajec ... E2
Rakovník 14,200 ... B1
Revúca 5,901 ... F2
Říčany u Prahy 8,407 ... C2
Rimavská Sobota 5,800 ... E2
Rokycany 12,800 ... B2
Rokytnice nad Jizerou ... C1
Rosice ... D2
Roudnice nad Labem 11,800 ... C1
Rožňava 12,400 ... F2
Rožnov pod Radhoštěm 11,600 ... E2
Rumburk ... C1
Ružomberok 22,600 ... E2
Rychnov nad Kněžnou 7,500 ... D1
Rýmařov 7,522 ... D2
Sabinov 5,473 ... F2
Šafárikovo ... F2
Šahy 5,049 ... E2
Šal'a 15,200 ... D2
Samorín 8,287 ... D2
Sečovce 5,744 ... F2
Sedlčany ... C2
Semily 8,200 ... C1
Senec 8,544 ... D2
Senica 12,300 ... D2
Sereď 12,500 ... D2
Skalica 11,100 ... D2
Skuteč ... D2
Sládečkovce 5,598 ... D2
Slaný 13,200 ... C1
Slavkov ... D2
Snina 10,900 ... G2
Soběslav 6,140 ... C2
Sobotka ... C1
Sobrance ... G2
Sokolov 23,900 ... B1
Spišská Belá ... F2
Spišská Nová Ves 26,100 ... F2
Stará L'ubovňa 5,800 ... F2
Staré Město 6,293 ... D2
Šternberk 13,700 ... D2
Stod ... B2
Strakonice 19,000 ... B2
Strážnice 5,482 ... D2
Stříbro ... B2
Stropkov 5,645 ... F2
Studénka 9,744 ... D2
Štúrovo 8,287 ... E3
Šumperk 25,900 ... D1
Šurany 6,693 ... E2
Sušice 10,300 ... B2
Svárov ... C1
Svidník 4,600 ... F2
Svitavy 15,000 ... D2
Tábor 28,100 ... C2
Tachov 11,400 ... B2
Telč 5,285 ... C2
Teplice 52,300 ... B1
Tišnov 8,263 ... D2
Topol'čany 17,500 ... D2
Třebíč 23,900 ... C2
Trebišov 13,700 ... F2
Třeboň 6,068 ... C2
Trenčín 38,800 ... E2
Třešť 5,053 ... C2
Třinec 32,000 ... E2
Trnava 48,600 ... D2
Trutnov 24,500 ... D1
Turnov 13,600 ... C1
Turzovka 6,107 ... E2
Uherské Hradiště 32,100 ... D2
Uherský Brod 12,800 ... D2
Uničov 10,800 ... D2
Úpice 6,323 ... C1
Ústí nad Labem 74,900 ... C1
Ústí nad Orlicí 13,700 ... D2
Valašské Meziříčí 19,400 ... D2
Varnsdorf 14,700 ... C1
Važec ... E2
Vejprty ... B1
Velká Bíteš ... D2
Velká Bystřice ... D2
Vel'ké Kapušany ... G2
Velké Meziříčí 7,590 ... D2
Vel'ké Rovné ... E2
Veselí nad Lužnicí ... C2
Veselí nad Moravou 11,500 ... D2
Vimperk 5,749 ... B2
Vítkov 5,138 ... D2
Vizovice ... D2
Vlašim 8,873 ... C2
Vodňany 5,620 ... C2
Vojnice ... E3
Volary ... B2
Volyně ... B2
Votice ... C2
Vráble ... E2
Vracov ... D2
Vranov nad Teplou 14,700 ... F2
Vrbno pod Pradědem 5,594 ... D1
Vrbovce ... D1
Vrbové ... D2
Vrchlabí 11,700 ... C1
Vrútky 5,756 ... E2
Vsetín 24,100 ... D2
Vyškov 15,100 ... D2
Vysoké Mýto 8,830 ... D2
Vysoké Tatry ... F2
Vyšší Brod ... C2
Zábřeh 11,300 ... D2
Žamberk 5,040 ... D1
Žatec 17,400 ... B1
Zázrivá ... E2
Zbiroh ... B2
Zborov ... F2
Žďár nad Sázavou 17,800 ... C2
Želiezovce 5,478 ... E2
Žiar nad Hronom 14,800 ... E2
Židlochovice ... D2
Žilina 56,000 ... E2
Zlaté Moravce 10,300 ... E2
Zlín (Gottwaldov) 84,300 ... D2
Žlutice ... B1
Znojmo 28,500 ... D2
Zvolen 29,000 ... E2

OTHER FEATURES

Berounka (riv.) ... C2
Beskids, East (mts.) ... F1
Beskids, West (mts.) ... E2
Bohemian (for.) ... B2
Bohemian-Moravian Heights (hills) ... C2
Danube (riv.) ... C2
Dunajec (riv.) ... F2
Dyje (riv.) ... D2
Erzgebirge (mts.) ... B1
Gerlachovka (mt.) ... E2
Hornád (riv.) ... F2
Hron (riv.) ... E2
Ipel' (riv.) ... E2
Jablunka (pass) ... E2
Jeseníky (mts.) ... D1
Jihlava (riv.) ... D2
Krušné Hory (Erzgebirge) (mts.) ... B1
Labe (riv.) ... C1
Lipno (res.) ... C2
Lužnice (riv.) ... C2
Moldau (Vltava) (riv.) ... C2
Morava (riv.) ... D2
Nitra (riv.) ... E2
Oder (Odra) (riv.) ... D2
Ohře (riv.) ... B1
Ondava (riv.) ... F2
Orava (riv.) ... E2
Orlická (res.) ... C2
Sázava (riv.) ... C2
Slovenské Rudohorie (mts.) ... E2
Sudeten (mts.) ... C1
Svitava (riv.) ... D2
Svratka (riv.) ... D2
Tatra, High (mts.) ... E2
Torysa (riv.) ... F2
Úhlava (riv.) ... B2
Váh (riv.) ... D2
Vltava (riv.) ... C2
White Carpathians (mts.) ... E2

HUNGARY

COUNTIES

Bács-Kiskun 568,532 ... E3
Baranya 434,030 ... E4
Békés 436,987 ... F3
Borsod-Abaúj-Zemplén 808,924 ... F2
Budapest (city) 2,060,170 ... E3
Csongrád 456,862 ... F3
Fejér 421,568 ... E3
Győr-Sopron 428,476 ... D3
Hajdú-Bihar 552,417 ... F3
Heves 350,874 ... F3
Komárom 321,579 ... E3
Nógrád 239,907 ... E3
Pest 973,486 ... E3
Somogy 360,308 ... D3
Szabolcs-Szatmár 593,746 ... G3
Szolnok 446,379 ... F3
Tolna 266,414 ... E3
Vas 285,527 ... D3
Veszprém 386,740 ... D3
Zala 316,610 ... D3

CITIES and TOWNS

Aba 4,271 ... E3
Abádszalók 6,386 ... F3
Abaújszántó 4,209 ... F2
Abony 15,624 ... E3
Ács 8,423 ... E3
Ajka 29,601 ... D3
Albertirsa 11,252 ... E3
Alsózsolca 5,045 ... F2
Arló 4,203 ... F2
Aszód 6,218 ... E3
Bácsalmás 9,025 ... E3
Badacsonytomaj 2,933 ... D3
Baja 38,456 ... E3
Baktalórántháza 3,736 ... G2
Balassagyarmat 18,534 ... E2
Balatonfüred 12,599 ... D3
Balkány 7,667 ... G3
Balmazújváros 17,371 ... F3
Barcs 11,448 ... D4
Bátaszék 7,274 ... E3
Battonya 9,324 ... F3
Békés 22,287 ... F3
Békéscsaba 67,266 ... F3
Berettyóújfalu 16,406 ... F3
Berzence 3,406 ... D3
Bicske 10,720 ... E3
Biharkeresztes 4,788 ... F3
Biharnagybajom 4,093 ... F3
Böhönye 3,215 ... D3
Bonyhád 14,841 ... E3
Budafok 40,623 ... E3
Budaörs 13,958 ... E3
Budakeszi 10,429 ... E3
Budapest (cap.) 2,060,170 ... E3
Bugak 4,989 ... E3
Cegléd 40,567 ... E3
Celldömölk 12,533 ... D3
Cigánd 4,767 ... F2
Csabrendek 3,045 ... D3
Csákvár 5,238 ... E3
Csanádpalota 4,642 ... F3
Csenger 4,792 ... G3
Csepel 71,693 ... E3
Csepreg 4,079 ... D3
Csongrád 22,202 ... E3
Csorna 12,131 ... D3
Csorvás 6,826 ... F3
Csurgó 5,463 ... D3
Dabas 13,075 ... E3
Debrecen 192,484 ... F3
Derecske 9,579 ... F3
Dévaványa 11,208 ... F3
Devecser 5,482 ... D3
Dombóvár 19,917 ... E3
Dombrád 6,328 ... F2
Dömsöd 6,545 ... E3
Dorog 10,754 ... E3
Dunaföldvár 10,318 ... E3
Dunaharaszti 15,788 ... E3
Dunakeszi 25,187 ... E3
Dunaszekcső 2,999 ... E3
Dunaújváros 60,694 ... E3
Dunavecse 4,521 ... E3
Edelény 9,559 ... F2
Eger 61,283 ... F3
Egyek 7,956 ... F3
Elek 6,032 ... F3
Enes 2,565 ... F2
Endrőd 8,136 ... F3
Enying 7,518 ... E3
Érd 41,210 ... E3
Erdőtelek 4,250 ... F3
Esztergom 30,476 ... E3
Fadd 4,805 ... E3
Fegyvernek 8,421 ... F3
Fehérgyarmat 6,729 ... G3
Földeák 3,855 ... F3
Földes 5,293 ... F2
Fonyód 3,957 ... D3
Füzesabony 6,965 ... F3
Füzesgyarmat 7,097 ... F3
Gödöllő 28,057 ... E3
Gönc 2,875 ... F2
Gyoma 10,392 ... F3
Gyöngyös 36,927 ... E3
Gyönk 2,507 ... E3
Győr 123,618 ... D3
Gyula 34,514 ... F3
Hajdúböszörmény 32,145 ... F3
Hajdúdorog 10,118 ... F3
Hajdúhadház 13,626 ... F3
Hajdúnánás 18,146 ... F3
Hajdúsámson 7,492 ... F3
Hajdúszoboszló 23,374 ... F3
Hajós 5,113 ... E3
Hatvan 24,790 ... E3
Heves 10,943 ... F3
Hódmezővásárhely 54,481 ... F3
Hőgyész 3,534 ... E3
Ibrány 7,037 ... F2
Izsák 7,686 ... E3
Izsófalva 6,816 ... F2
Jánoshalma 12,534 ... E3
Jánosháza 3,274 ... D3
Jászapáti 10,424 ... E3
Jászárokszállás 10,139 ... E3
Jászberény 31,347 ... E3
Jászfényszaru 6,869 ... E3
Jászkarajenő 4,101 ... E3
Jászkisér 6,816 ... F3
Jászladány 7,823 ... F3
Kaba 6,654 ... F2
Kalocsa 18,613 ... E3
Kaposvár 72,330 ... D3
Kapuvár 11,243 ... D3
Karád 2,754 ... D3
Karcag 25,264 ... F3
Kazincbarcika 37,481 ... F2
Kecel 10,493 ... E3
Kecskemét 91,929 ... E3
Kemecse 4,583 ... F2
Keszthely 21,671 ... D3
Kétegyháza 4,728 ... F3
Kisbér 4,562 ... D3
Kiskőrös 15,499 ... E3
Kiskunfélegyháza 35,339 ... E3
Kiskunhalas 30,552 ... E3
Kiskunmajsa 14,439 ... E3
Kispest 65,106 ... E3
Kistelek 8,544 ... E3
Kisterenye 6,844 ... E2
Kisújszállás 13,699 ... F3
Kisvárda 17,828 ... G2
Komádi 8,765 ... F3
Komárom 19,955 ... E3
Komló 30,301 ... E3
Kondoros 7,319 ... F3
Körmend 11,787 ... D3
Körösladány 6,565 ... F3
Kőszeg 12,705 ... D3
Kunágota 4,622 ... F3
Kunhegyes 10,116 ... F3
Kunmadaras 7,343 ... F3
Kunszentmárton 11,103 ... F3
Kunszentmiklós 7,952 ... E3
Lajosmizse 12,872 ... E3
Lébénymiklós 6,190 ... D3
Lengyeltóti 3,389 ... D3
Leninváros 18,667 ... F3
Lenti 8,106 ... D3
Létavértes 9,106 ... G3
Letenye 4,395 ... D3
Lökösháza 2,514 ... F3
Lőrinci 10,679 ... E3
Madaras 4,519 ... E3
Makó 29,943 ... F3
Mándok 5,093 ... G2
Marcali 12,485 ... D3
Mátészalka 17,709 ... G3
Mélykút 7,640 ... E3
Mérk 3,211 ... G3
Mezőberény 12,702 ... F3
Mezőcsát 6,729 ... F3
Mezőfalva 5,008 ... E3
Mezőhegyes 8,631 ... F3
Mezőkovácsháza 7,473 ... F3
Mezőkövesd 18,435 ... F3
Mezőszilas 2,792 ... E3
Mezőtúr 22,018 ... F3
Mindszent 8,730 ... F3
Miskolc 206,727 ... F2
Mohács 21,385 ... E4
Monor 16,838 ... E3
Mór 12,066 ... E3
Mosonmagyaróvár 29,732 ... D3
Nádudvar 9,447 ... F3
Nagyatád 12,946 ... D3
Nagybajom 4,402 ... D3
Nagyecsed 8,225 ... G3
Nagyhalász 6,437 ... F2
Nagykálló 11,282 ... F3
Nagykanizsa 48,494 ... D3
Nagykáta 11,922 ... E3
Nagykőrös 27,900 ... E3
Nagyszénás 7,124 ... F3
Nyírábrány 4,509 ... G3
Nyíradony 7,146 ... G3
Nyírbátor 13,388 ... G3
Nyíregyháza 108,156 ... F3
Nyírmada 4,744 ... F2
Örkény 5,013 ... E3
Orosháza 36,243 ... F3
Oroszlány 20,604 ... E3
Ózd 48,521 ... F2
Pacsa 1,984 ... D3
Paks 19,514 ... E3
Pannonhalma 3,731 ... D3
Pápa 32,202 ... D3
Pásztó 7,962 ... E3
Pécs 168,788 ... E3
Pécsvárad 3,672 ... E3
Pétervására 2,753 ... F3
Pilis 9,055 ... E3
Pilisvörösvár 10,217 ... E3
Polgár 9,429 ... F3
Polgárdi 5,767 ... E3
Püspökladány 15,730 ... F3
Pusztaszabolcs 5,794 ... E3
Putnok 7,103 ... F2
Ráckeve 7,534 ... E3
Rajka 2,448 ... D3
Rakamaz 5,407 ... F2
Rákospalota 60,983 ... E3
Répcelak 1,997 ... D3
Ricse 2,992 ... G2
Sajószentpéter 13,992 ... F2
Salgótarján 49,320 ... E2
Sándorfalva 5,949 ... F3
Sárbogárd 11,178 ... E3
Sarkad 11,937 ... F3
Sárospatak 15,316 ... F2
Sárvár 15,126 ... D3
Sátoraljaújhely 19,252 ... F2
Sellye 2,804 ... D4
Siklós 10,567 ... E4
Simontornya 4,892 ... E3
Siófok 20,084 ... E3
Solt 6,911 ... E3
Soltvadkert 7,934 ... E3
Sopron 53,930 ... D3
Sükösd 4,430 ... E3
Sümeg 6,229 ... D3
Szabadszállás 8,223 ... E3
Szarvas 20,598 ... F3
Szécsény 5,690 ... E2
Százhalombatta 13,963 ... E3
Szeged 171,342 ... E3
Szeghalom 9,736 ... F3
Szegvár 6,395 ... F3
Székesfehérvár 103,197 ... E3
Szekszárd 34,592 ... E3
Szendrő 4,098 ... F2
Szentendre 16,844 ... E3
Szentes 35,326 ... F3
Szentgotthárd 5,837 ... D3
Szentlőrinc 3,926 ... E3
Szerencs 8,612 ... F2
Szigetvár 12,114 ... D3
Szikszó 6,419 ... F2
Szil 2,073 ... D3
Szolnok 75,203 ... F3
Szombathely 82,830 ... D3
Tab 3,922 ... E3
Tamási 7,602 ... E3
Tápiószele 5,575 ... E3
Tapolca 17,161 ... D3
Tarpa 3,436 ... G2
Tata 24,114 ... E3
Tatabánya 75,942 ... E3
Tét 4,441 ... D3
Tiszacsege 6,263 ... F3
Tiszaföldvár 12,560 ... F3
Tiszafüred 12,259 ... F3
Tiszakécske 12,378 ... E3
Tiszalök 6,230 ... F2
Tiszavasvári 13,292 ... F3
Tokaj 4,845 ... F2
Tolna 8,997 ... E3
Tompa 5,365 ... E3
Törökszentmiklós 25,551 ... F3
Tótkomlós 8,803 ... F3
Tura 8,235 ... E3
Túrkeve 11,393 ... F3
Újfehértó 14,412 ... F3
Újpest 80,384 ... E3
Újszász 7,098 ... F2
Vác 34,837 ... E3
Vál 2,488 ... E3
Vámospércs 5,213 ... F3
Várpalota 28,293 ... E3
Vásárosnamény 8,637 ... G2
Vasvár 4,275 ... D3
Vecsés 19,193 ... E3
Velence 3,463 ... E3
Vémend 2,293 ... E3
Verpelét 4,622 ... F2
Veszprém 54,898 ... D3
Vésztő 9,815 ... F3
Villány 2,764 ... E4
Záhony 3,049 ... G2
Zalaegerszeg 39,671 ... D3
Zalaszentgrót 5,346 ... D3
Zirc 5,980 ... D3

OTHER FEATURES

Bakony (mts.) ... D3
Balaton (lake) ... D3
Berettyó (riv.) ... F3
Bükk (mts.) ... F2
Csepelsziget (isl.) ... E3
Danube (riv.) ... E3
Dráva (riv.) ... D3
Duna (Danube) (riv.) ... E3
Fertő tó (Neusiedler See) (lake) ... D3
Great Alföld (plain) ... F3
Hernád (riv.) ... F2
Kapos (riv.) ... D3
Kékes (mt.) ... E3
Körös (riv.) ... F3
Maros (riv.) ... F3
Mátra (mts.) ... E3
Mecsek (mts.) ... D3
Mura (riv.) ... D3
Rába (riv.) ... D3
Sajó (riv.) ... F2
Sárviz csatorna (canal) ... E3
Sió csatorna (canal) ... E3
Szentendreisziget (isl.) ... E3
Tisza (riv.) ... F3
Zala (riv.) ... D3

*City and suburbs.
†Population of Austrian cities are communes.

Agriculture, Industry and Resources

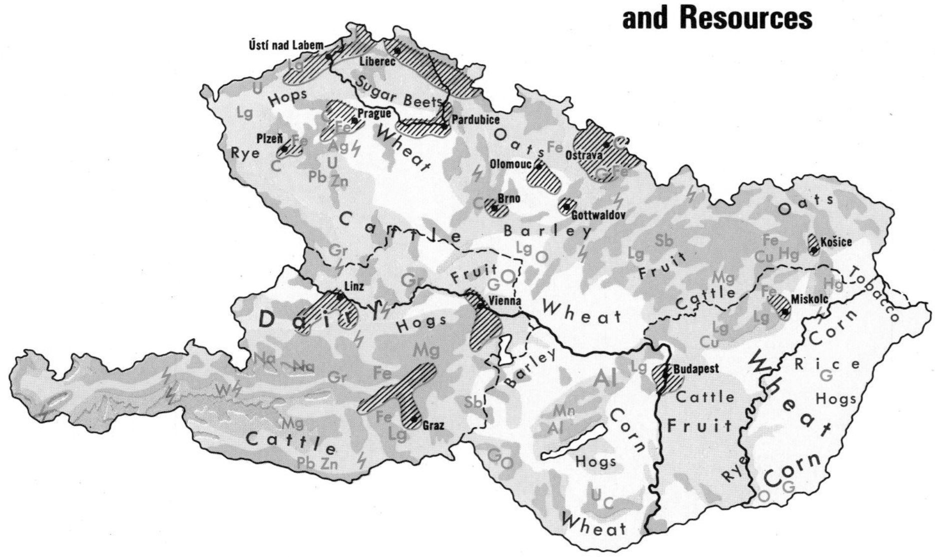

DOMINANT LAND USE

- Cereals (chiefly wheat, corn)
- Other Cereals, Livestock, Dairy
- General Farming, Livestock
- General Farming, Truck Farming
- Pasture Livestock
- Grapes, Wine
- Forests
- Nonagricultural Land

MAJOR MINERAL OCCURRENCES

Ag	Silver	Mg	Magnesium
Al	Bauxite	Mn	Manganese
C	Coal	Na	Salt
Cu	Copper	O	Petroleum
Fe	Iron Ore	Pb	Lead
G	Natural Gas	Sb	Antimony
Gr	Graphite	U	Uranium
Hg	Mercury	W	Tungsten
Lg	Lignite	Zn	Zinc

Water Power
Major Industrial Areas

YUGOSLAVIA

AREA 98,766 sq. mi. (255,804 sq. km.)
POPULATION 22,471,000
CAPITAL Belgrade
LARGEST CITY Belgrade
HIGHEST POINT Triglav 9,393 ft. (2,863 m.)
MONETARY UNIT Yugoslav dinar
MAJOR LANGUAGES Serbo-Croatian, Slovenian, Macedonian, Montenegrin, Albanian
MAJOR RELIGIONS Eastern Orthodoxy, Roman Catholicism, Islam

ALBANIA

AREA 11,100 sq. mi. (28,749 sq. km.)
POPULATION 2,590,600
CAPITAL Tiranë
LARGEST CITY Tiranë
HIGHEST POINT Korab 9,026 ft. (2,751 m.)
MONETARY UNIT lek
MAJOR LANGUAGE Albanian
MAJOR RELIGIONS Islam, Eastern Orthodoxy, Roman Catholicism

ROMANIA

AREA 91,699 sq. mi. (237,500 sq. km.)
POPULATION 22,048,305
CAPITAL Bucharest
LARGEST CITY Bucharest
HIGHEST POINT Moldoveanul 8,343 ft. (2,543 m.)
MONETARY UNIT leu
MAJOR LANGUAGES Romanian, Hungarian
MAJOR RELIGION Eastern Orthodoxy

BULGARIA

AREA 42,823 sq. mi. (110,912 sq. km.)
POPULATION 8,862,000
CAPITAL Sofia
LARGEST CITY Sofia
HIGHEST POINT Musala 9,597 ft. (2,925 m.)
MONETARY UNIT lev
MAJOR LANGUAGE Bulgarian
MAJOR RELIGION Eastern Orthodoxy

GREECE

AREA 50,944 sq. mi. (131,945 sq. km.)
POPULATION 9,599,000
CAPITAL Athens
LARGEST CITY Athens
HIGHEST POINT Olympus 9,570 ft. (2,917 m.)
MONETARY UNIT drachma
MAJOR LANGUAGE Greek
MAJOR RELIGION Eastern (Greek) Orthodoxy

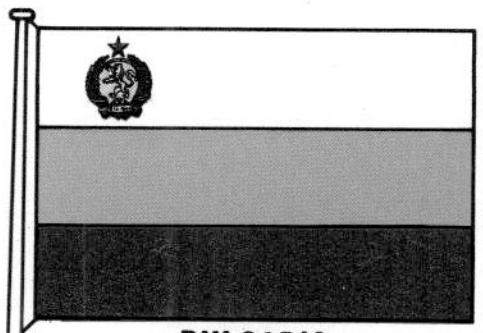
BULGARIA

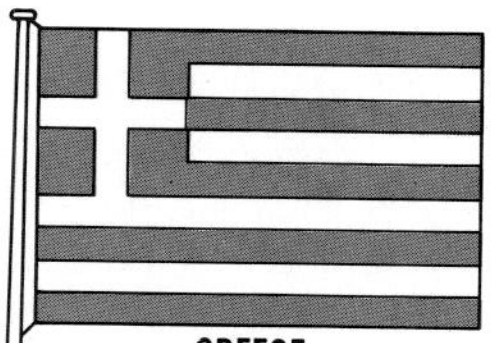
GREECE

YUGOSLAVIA

ALBANIA

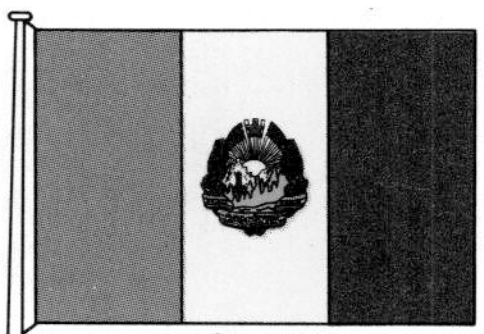
ROMANIA

Agriculture, Industry and Resources

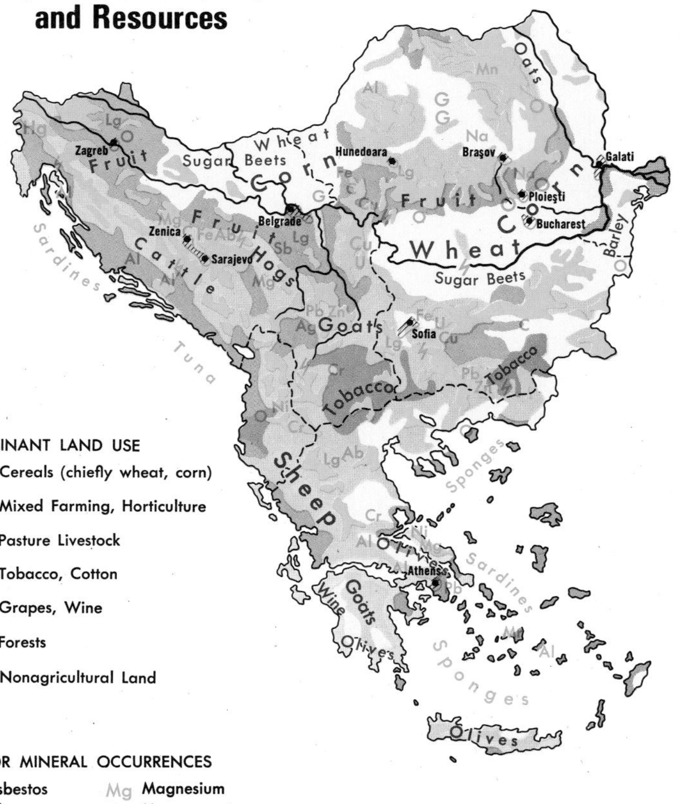

DOMINANT LAND USE

- Cereals (chiefly wheat, corn)
- Mixed Farming, Horticulture
- Pasture Livestock
- Tobacco, Cotton
- Grapes, Wine
- Forests
- Nonagricultural Land

MAJOR MINERAL OCCURRENCES

Ab	Asbestos	Mg	Magnesium
Ag	Silver	Mn	Manganese
Al	Bauxite	Mr	Marble
C	Coal	Na	Salt
Cr	Chromium	Ni	Nickel
Cu	Copper	O	Petroleum
Fe	Iron Ore	Pb	Lead
G	Natural Gas	Sb	Antimony
Hg	Mercury	U	Uranium
Lg	Lignite	Zn	Zinc

Water Power
Major Industrial Areas

ALBANIA

CITIES and TOWNS

Berat 25,700 .... D5
Çorovodë E5
Burrel D5
Delvinë 6,000 .... D6
Durrës (Durazzo) 53,800 .... D5
Elbasan 41,700 .... E5
Ersekë E5
Fier 23,000 .... D5
Gjirokastër 17,100 .... D5
Kavajë 18,700 .... D5
Korçë 47,300 .... E5
Krujë 7,900 .... D5
Kuçovë (Stalin) 14,000 .... D5
Kukës 6,100 .... E4
Leskovik E5
Lezhë D5
Lushnje 18,900 .... D5
Memaliaj D5
Peqin D5
Përmet E5
Peshkopi 6,600 .... E5
Pogradec 10,100 .... E5
Pukë E4
Sarandë 8,700 .... E6
Shëngjin D5
Shijak 6,200 .... D5
Shkodër 55,300 .... D5
Stalin 14,000 .... D5
Tepelenë D5
Tiranë (Tirana) (cap.) 171,300 .... E5
Vlorë 50,000 .... D5

OTHER FEATURES

Adriatic (sea) B4
Drin (riv.) E4
Korab (mt.) E5
Ohrid (lake) E5
Otranto (str.) D5
Prespa (lake) E5
Sazan (isl.) D5
Scutari (lake) D4
Vijosë (riv.) D5

BULGARIA

CITIES and TOWNS

Akhtopol 938 .... H4
Alfatar 3,249 .... H4
Ardino 5,080 .... G5
Asenovgrad 43,049 .... G5
Aytos 20,967 .... H4
Balchik 11,070 .... H4
Bansko 10,011 .... F5
Belogradchik 6,892 .... F4
Berkovitsa 16,253 .... F4
Blagoevgrad 50,043 .... F5
Botevgrad 17,789 .... F4
Bregovo 5,567 .... F3
Breznik 4,699 .... F4
Burgas 144,449 .... H4
Byala 10,564 .... G4
Byala Slatina 15,788 .... F4
Chirpan 20,595 .... G4
Devin 7,120 .... G5
Dimitrovgrad 45,596 .... G4
Dobrich (Tolbukhin) 86,184 .... H4
Dryanovo 9,804 .... G4
Elena 7,008 .... G4
Elin Pelin 5,499 .... F4
Elkhovo 12,397 .... H4
Gabrovo 75,034 .... G4
General-Toshevo 8,928 .... H4
Godech 5,225 .... F4
Gorna Oryakhovitsa 34,157 .... G4
Gotse Delchev 17,015 .... F5
Grudovo 9,871 .... H4
Ikhtiman 11,482 .... F4
Isperikh 10,500 .... H4
Ivaylovgrad 3,900 .... H5
Karapelit H4
Karlovo 25,472 .... G4
Karnobat 21,480 .... H4
Kavarna 10,872 .... J4
Kazanlŭk 53,607 .... G4
Kharmanli 19,240 .... H5
Khaskovo 75,031 .... G5
Kotel 8,229 .... H4
Krumovgrad 5,211 .... G5
Kubrat 9,826 .... H4
Kula 5,667 .... F4
Kŭrdzhali 47,757 .... G5
Kyustendil 48,239 .... F4
Lom 30,538 .... F4
Lovech 43,858 .... G4
Lukovit 10,400 .... G4
Malko Tŭrnovo 4,233 .... H4
Maritsa 8,664 .... H4
Michurin 4,434 .... H4
Mikhaylovgrad 40,064 .... F4
Momchilgrad 8,185 .... G5
Nesebŭr 6,768 .... H4
Nikopol 5,563 .... G4
Nova Zagora 21,872 .... H4
Novi Pazar 15,751 .... H4
Omurtag 9,067 .... H4
Oryakhovo 14,012 .... F4
Panagyurishte 20,649 .... F4
Pazardzhik 65,577 .... G4
Pernik 87,432 .... F4
Peshtera 16,882 .... G4
Petrich 24,381 .... F5
Pirdop 8,248 .... G4
Pleven 107,567 .... G4
Plovdiv 300,242 .... G4
Pomorie 11,960 .... H4
Popina H3
Popovo 19,428 .... H4
Provadiya 15,143 .... H4
Radomir 10,436 .... F4
Razgrad 42,486 .... H4
Råzlog 13,690 .... F5
Rositsa H4
Ruse 160,351 .... H4
Samokov 25,763 .... F4
Sandanski 19,003 .... F5
Sevlievo 24,421 .... G4
Shabla 4,471 .... J4
Shumen 83,525 .... H4
Silistra 58,270 .... H3
Simeonovgrad (Maritsa) 8,664 .... H4
Sliven 90,137 .... H4
Smolyan 29,032 .... G5
Smyadovo 5,020 .... H4
Sofia (cap.) 965,728 .... F4
Sozopol 3,877 .... H4
Stanke Dimitrov 42,034 .... F4
Stara Zagora 122,200 .... G4
Svilengrad 15,150 .... G5
Svishtov 29,412 .... G4
Teteven 12,555 .... G4
Tolbukhin 86,184 .... H4
Topolovgrad 7,230 .... H4
Troyan 23,692 .... G4
Trŭn 3,435 .... F4
Tŭrgovishte 38,796 .... H4
Tutrakan 11,447 .... H4
Varna 251,654 .... J4
Veliko Tŭrnovo 56,497 .... G4
Vidin 53,030 .... F4
Vratsa 61,265 .... F4
Yambol 75,861 .... H4
Zimnitsa H4
Zlatograd 7,732 .... G5

OTHER FEATURES

Balkan (mts.) G4
Black (sea) J4
Danube (riv.) H4
Dunav (Danube) (riv.) H4
Emine (cape) J4
Iskŭr (riv.) G4
Kaliakra (cape) J4
Maritsa (riv.) G4
Mesta (riv.) F5
Midzhur (mt.) F4
Musala (mt.) F4
Osŭm (riv.) G4
Rhodope (mts.) G5
Rujen (mt.) F4
Struma (riv.) F5
Timok (riv.) F3
Tundzha (riv.) G4
Vit (riv.) G4

GREECE

REGIONS

Aegean Islands 417,813 .... G6
Athens, Greater 2,566,775 .... F7
Áyion Óros (aut. dist.) 1,732 .... G5
Central Greece and Euboea 966,543 .... F6
Crete 456,642 .... G8
Epirus 310,334 .... E6
Ionian Islands 184,443 .... D6
Macedonia 1,888,952 .... E5
Pelopónnisos 986,912 .... F7
Thessaly 659,913 .... F6
Thrace 329,582 .... G5

CITIES and TOWNS

Agrínion 30,973 .... E6
Aíyina 5,704 .... F7
Aíyion 18,829 .... F6
Alexandroúpolis 22,995 .... H5
Alivérion 4,414 .... G6
Almirós 5,680 .... F6
Amaliás 14,177 .... E7
Amfilokhía 4,668 .... E6
Ámfissa 6,605 .... F6
Ándissa 1,762 .... H6
Andravídha 3,046 .... E6
Ándros 1,827 .... G7
Áno Viánnos 1,431 .... G8
Anóyia 2,750 .... G8
Ardhéa 3,555 .... F5
Areópolis 674 .... F7
Argalastí 1,621 .... F6
Árgos 18,890 .... F7
Argostólion 7,060 .... E6
Arkhángelos 3,016 .... J7
Arnaía 2,424 .... F5
Árta 19,498 .... E6
Astipálaia 787 .... H7
Atalándi 4,581 .... F6
Athens (cap.) 867,023 .... F7
Athens* 2,566,775 .... F7
Ayiá 3,241 .... F6
Áyios Kírikos 1,083 .... H7
Áyios Matthaíos 1,596 .... D6
Áyios Nikólaos 5,002 .... G8
Candia (Iráklion) 77,506 .... G8
Canea (Khaniá) 40,564 .... G8
Corinth 20,773 .... F7
Delfí 1,185 .... F6
Delvinákion 1,067 .... E6
Dhidhimótikhon 8,388 .... H5
Dhíkaia 1,222 .... H5
Dhimitsána 996 .... F7
Dhomokós 1,991 .... F6
Dráma 29,692 .... F5
Édhessa 13,967 .... F5
Elassón 7,200 .... F6
Elevtheroúpolis 4,888 .... G5
Ermoúpolis 13,502 .... G7
Fársala 6,967 .... F6
Filiátes 2,579 .... E6
Filiatrá 5,919 .... E7
Filippiás 3,248 .... E6
Flórina 11,164 .... E5
Gargaliánoi 5,888 .... E7
Grevená 8,106 .... E5
Ídhra 2,381 .... F7
Ierápetra 7,055 .... G8
Igoumenítsa 4,109 .... E6
Ioánnina 40,130 .... E6
Íos 1,270 .... G7
Iráklion 77,506 .... G8
Istiaía 4,059 .... F6
Itháki 2,293 .... E6
Kalámai 39,133 .... F7
Kalampáka 5,453 .... E6
Kalávrita 1,948 .... F6
Kálimnos 6,492 .... H7
Kándanos 403 .... F8
Kardhítsa 25,685 .... E6
Kariá 1,350 .... E6
Kariaí 301 .... G5
Káristos 3,550 .... G6
Kárpathos 1,363 .... H8
Karpenísion 4,414 .... E6
Kastéllion (Kíssamos) 2,996 .... F8
Kastéllion 1,152 .... G8
Kastoría 15,407 .... E5
Katákolon 690 .... E7
Kateríni 28,808 .... F5
Kavála 46,234 .... G5
Kéa 693 .... G7
Kérkira 28,630 .... D6
Khalkís 36,300 .... F6
Khaniá 40,564 .... G8
Khíos 24,084 .... G6
Khóra Sfakíon 246 .... G8
Kiáton 7,392 .... F6
Kilkís 10,538 .... F5
Kími 2,772 .... F6
Kiparissía 3,882 .... E7
Kíssamos 2,996 .... G8
Kíthira 349 .... F7
Komotiní 28,896 .... G5
Kónitsa 3,150 .... E5
Koropí 9,367 .... G7
Kos 7,828 .... H7
Kozáni 23,240 .... F5
Kranídhion 3,657 .... F7
Lagkadia 1,350 .... E7
Lamía 37,872 .... F6
Langadhás 6,707 .... F5
Langádhia F7
Lárisa 72,336 .... F6
Lávrion 8,283 .... G7
Leonídhion 3,181 .... F7
Levádhia 15,445 .... F6
Levkás 6,818 .... E6
Limenária 1,507 .... G5

(continued on following page)

(continued)

Topography

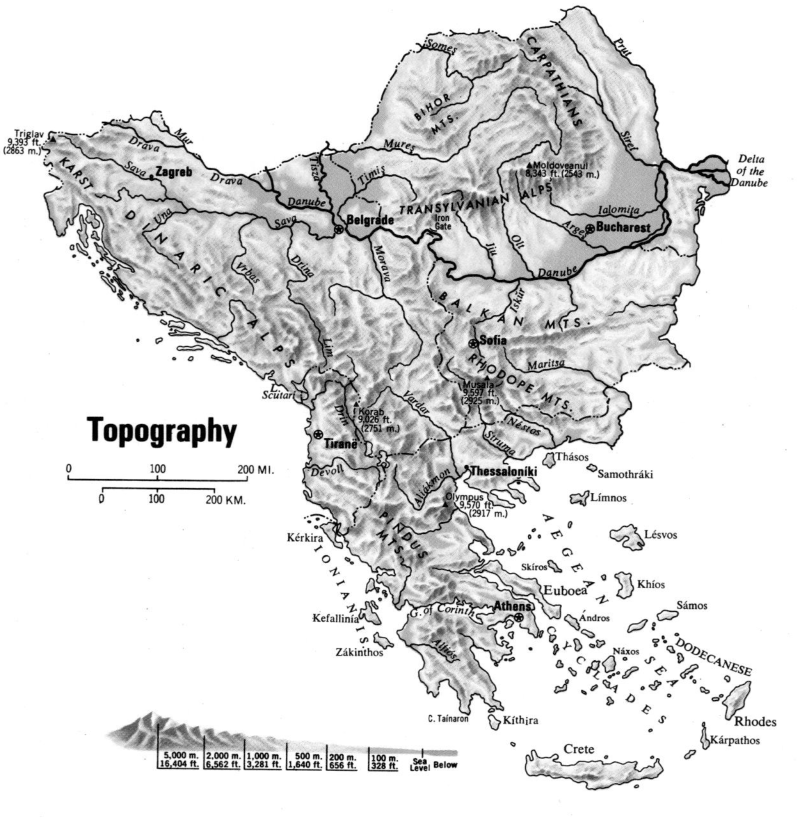

Límni 2,394 F6
Líndos 700 J7
Litókhoron 5,561 F5
Lixoúrion 3,364 E6
Loutrá Aidhipsoú 2,195 F6
Marathón 1,976 G6
Megalópolis 3,357 E7
Mégara 17,294 F6
Meligalá 1,724 F7
Mesolóngion 11,614 E6
Messíni 6,625 E7
Métsovon 2,823 E6
Mikínai 390 F7
Mílos 850 G7
Mírina 3,982 G6
Míthimna 1,414 G6
Mitilíni 23,426 H6
Moîrai 2,948 G8
Moláoi 2,484 F7
Monólithos 247 H7
Moúdhros 1,024 G6
Náousa 17,375 F5
Návpaktos 8,170 F6
Návplion 9,281 F7
Náxos 2,892 G7
Neápolis 3,070 F7
Neméa 4,356 F7
Néon Karlóvasi 4,401 H7
Nestórion 1,143 E5
Nigríta 7,301 F5
Oinói 188 F6
Orestías 10,727 H5
Paramithía 2,747 E6
Pátrai 111,607 E6
Pérdika 1,198 E6
Péta 2,116 E6
Pílos 2,258 E7
Piraiévs (Piraeus) 187,362 F7
Pírgos 20,599 E7
Píryi 1,455 G6
Píthion 1,047 H5
Plomárion 4,353 H6
Políkastron 5,279 F5
Políkhnitos 4,152 G6
Políyiros 3,707 F5
Póros 4,051 F7
Préveza 11,439 E6
Psakhná 4,650 F6
Psári 622 E7
Ptolemaís 16,588 E5
Réthimnon 14,969 G8
Rhodes (Ródhos) 32,092 J7
Salamís 18,256 F6
Salonika
(Thessaloníki) 345,799 F5
Sámi 957 E6
Sámos 5,146 H7
Samothráki 508 G5
Sápai 2,456 G5
Sérrai 39,897 F5
Sérvia 3,834 F5
Siátista 4,852 E5
Sidhirókastron 6,363 F5
Sími 2,344 H7
Sitía 6,167 H8
Skíathos 3,707 F6
Skíros 1,925 G6
Skópelos 2,545 F6
Souflíon 5,637 H5
Sparta 10,549 F7
Spétsai 3,427 F7
Spíli 789 G8
Stavrós 1,700 F5
Stílis 4,427 F6
Thásos 2,052 G5
Thessaloníki 345,799 F5
Thessaloníki* 482,361 F5
Thíra 1,322 G7
Thívai 15,971 F6
Timbákion 3,229 G8
Tínos 3,423 G7
Tírnavos 10,451 F6
Tríkkala 34,794 E6
Trípolis 20,209 F7
Vámos 652 F8
Vartholomión 3,015 E7
Vathí 2,491 H7
Velvendós 4,063 F5
Vérroia 29,528 F5
Vólos 51,290 F6
Vónitsa 3,324 E6
Vrondádhes 4,253 G6
Xánthi 24,867 G5
Yerolimín 73 F7
Yiannitsá 18,151 F5
Yíthion 4,915 F7
Zákinthos 9,339 E7
Zante (Zákinthos) 9,339 E7

OTHER FEATURES

Aegean (sea) G6
Akrítas (cape) E7
Aktí (pen.) G5
Amorgós (isl.) G7
Anáfi (isl.) G7
Andikíthira (isl.) F8
Ándros (isl.) G7
Árda (riv.) G5
Argolís (gulf) F7
Astipálaia (isl.) H7
Áthos (mt.) G5
Áyios Evstrátios
(isl.) G6
Áyios Yeóryios (cape) G5
Cephalonia (Kefallinía)
(isl.) E6
Corfu (Kérkira) (isl.) D6
Corinth (gulf) F6
Crete (isl.) G8
Crete (sea) G7
Cyclades (isls.) G7
Día (isl.) G8
Dodecanese (isls.) H8
Euboea (Évvoia)
(isl.) G6
Évros (riv.) H5
Évvoia (isl.) G6
Gávdhos (isl.) F8
Ídhi (mt.) G8
Ikaría (isl.) G7
Ionian (sea) D7
Íos (isl.) G7
Itháki (Ithaca) (isl.) E6
Kafirévs (cape) G6
Kálimnos (isl.) H7
Kárpathos (isl.) H8
Kásos (isl.) H8
Kassándra (pen.) F6
Kéa (isl.) G7
Kefallinía (isl.) E6
Kérkira (isl.) D6
Khálki (isl.) H7
Khaniá (gulf) G8
Khíos (isl.) G6
Kímolos (isl.) G7
Kiparissía (gulf) E7
Kíthira (isl.) F7
Kíthnos (isl.) G7
Kos (isl.) H7
Kriós (cape) F8
Kríti (Crete) (isl.) G8
Lakonía (gulf) F7
Léros (isl.) H7
Lésvos (isl.) G6
Levítha (isl.) H7
Levkás (isl.) E6
Límnos (isl.) G6
Maléa (cape) F7
Matapan (Taínaron) (cape) F7
Merabéllou (gulf) H8
Mesará (gulf) G8
Messíni (gulf) E7
Míkonos (isl.) G7
Mílos (isl.) G7
Mirtóön (sea) F7
Náxos (isl.) G7
Néstos (riv.) G5
Nísiros (isl.) H7
Northern Sporades (isls.) F6
Olympia (isls.) E7
Olympus (mt.) F5
Parnassus (mt.) F6
Páros (isl.) G7
Pátmos (isl.) H7
Paxoí (isl.) D6
Pindus (mts.) E6
Piniós (riv.) E6
Prespa (lake) E5
Psará (isl.) G6
Psevdhókavos (cape) G6
Rhodes (isl.) H7
Rhodope (mts.) G5
Salonika (Thermaic) (gulf) F6
Sámos (isl.) H7
Samothráki (isl.) G5
Saría (isl.) H8
Saronic (gulf) F7
Sérifos (isl.) G7
Sídheros (cape) H8
Sífnos (isl.) G7
Sími (isl.) H7
Síros (isl.) G7
Sithoniá (pen.) F5
Skíros (isl.) G6
Spátha (cape) F8
Strimón (gulf) G5
Strofádhes (isls.) E7
Taínaron (cape) F7
Thásos (isl.) G5
Thermaic (gulf) F6
Thíra (isl.) G7
Tílos (isl.) H7
Tínos (isl.) G7
Toronaic (gulf) F5
Vardar (riv.) E5
Voïvís (lake) F6
Vólvi (lake) F5
Voúxa (cape) F8
Zákinthos (Zante)
(isl.) E7

ROMANIA

CITIES and TOWNS

Aiud 25,173 F2
Alba Iulia 44,552 F2
Alexandria 38,296 G3
Anina 11,594 E3
Arad 161,568 E2
Babadag 8,423 J3
Bacău 131,413 H2
Baia de Aramă 5,065 F3
Baia Mare 112,893 F2
Băile Herculane 4,606 F3
Băileşti 21,246 F3
Balş 16,091 G3
Beiuş 9,992 F2
Bereşti Tîrg H2
Bicaz 9,490 G2
Bîrlad 59,059 H2
Bistriţa 47,562 G2
Bivolari H2
Blaj 21,678 F2
Borşa 25,287 G2
Botoşani 69,881 H2
Brad 18,391 F2
Brăila 203,983 H3
Braşov 259,108 G3
Bucharest (Bucureşti)
(cap.) 1,832,015 G3
Bucharest* 1,960,097 G3
Buhuşi 20,204 H2
Buzău 106,738 H3
Buziaş 8,310 E3
Calafat 16,421 F3
Călăraşi 58,960 H3
Caracal 31,159 G3
Caransebeş 27,429 F3
Carei 24,496 F2
Cernavodă 14,686 J3
Chişineu Criş 9,344 E2
Cîmpeni 7,722 F2
Cîmpia Turzii 23,745 F2
Cîmpina 33,259 H3
Cîmpulung 33,448 G3
Cîmpulung Moldovenesc 19,270 G2
Cisnădie 21,114 G3
Cluj-Napoca 274,095 F2
Cogealac J3
Comaneşti 18,177 H2
Constanţa 279,308 J3
Corabia 20,454 G4
Costeşti 10,446 G3
Craiova 220,893 F3
Cujmir F3
Curtea de Argeş 23,555 G3
Dăbuleni F4
Dăeni J3
Darabani 12,207 H1
Dej 35,396 F2
Deta 6,956 E3
Deva 68,290 F3
Dorohoi 23,121 H2
Drăgăneşti Olt 11,606 G3
Drăgăşani 16,290 F3
Drobeta-Turnu Severin 80,114 F3
Făgăraş 34,762 G3
Fălciu J2
Fălticeni 22,463 H2
Făurei 3,620 H3
Feteşti 28,730 H3
Focşani 62,275 H3
Folteşti H3
Găeşti 13,384 G3
Galaţi 252,884 H3
Gheorghe Gheorghiu-Dej 41,297 H2
Gheorghieni 20,592 G2
Gherla 19,303 G2
Giurgiu 53,241 G3
Haţeg 9,706 F3
Hîrlău 8,135 H2
Hîrşova 8,434 J3
Huedin 8,557 F2
Hunedoara 83,159 F3
Huşi 24,329 J2
Iaşi 262,493 H2
Ineu 10,414 E2
Isaccea 5,283 J3
Jibou F2
Jimbolia 15,325 E3
Lipova 12,427 E2
Luduş 15,771 G2
Lugoj 48,558 F3
Lupeni 28,251 F3
Mangalia 27,263 J4
Medgidia 43,691 J3
Mediaş 68,442 G2
Miercurea Ciuc 38,097 G2
Mizil 14,294 H3
Mociu G2
Moineşti 21,015 H2
Moldova Nouă 18,498 E3
Moreni 17,743 G3
Nădlac 8,407 E2
Năsăud 8,646 G2
Negreşti 7,435 H2
Ocna Mureş 16,381 G2
Odobeşti 8,440 H3
Odorheiu Secuiesc 33,392 G2
Olteniţa 25,536 H3
Oradea 175,400 E2
Orăştie 18,769 F3
Oraviţa 13,628 E3
Orşova 14,873 F3
Panciu 7,772 H3
Paşcani 26,937 H2
Pătulele F3
Pechea H3
Pecica E2
Periam E2
Petrila 25,087 F3
Petroşeni 42,316 F3
Piatra Neamţ 84,192 G2
Pincota 7,494 E2
Piteşti 125,029 G3
Pleniţa F3
Ploieşti 207,009 H3
Poenari Burchi G3
Poiana Mare F4
Pucioasa 14,056 G3
Rădăuţi 24,222 G2
Reghin 31,948 G2
Reşiţa 90,698 E3
Rîmnicu Sărat 29,815 H3
Rîmnicu Vîlcea 75,070 G3
Roman 56,466 H2
Roşiori de Vede 28,832 G3
Săcele 29,391 G3
Salonta 19,698 E2
Satu Mare 108,152 F2
Săveni 7,913 H1
Sebeş 27,448 F3
Sebiş 6,401 F2
Segarcea 8,783 F3
Sfîntu Gheorghe 51,210 G3
Sfîntu Gheorghe J3
Sibiu 156,854 G3
Sighetu Marmaţiei 38,879 F2
Sighişoara 32,296 G2
Şimleul Silvaniei 14,780 F2
Sinaia 14,215 G3
Sînnicolaul Mare 13,565 E2
Siret 6,677 G1
Slănic 8,017 G3
Slatina 54,954 G3
Slobozia 35,207 H3
Solca 4,835 G2
Sovata 10,745 G2
Ştefăneşti H2
Strehaia 11,431 F3
Suceava 66,857 G2
Sulina 5,240 J3
Tăşnad 10,441 F2
Techirghiol 11,228 J3
Tecuci 37,928 H3
Timişoara 281,320 E3
Tinca F2
Tîrgovişte 71,533 G3
Tîrgu Cărbuneşti 7,536 F3
Tîrgu Frumos 6,428 H2
Tîrgu Jiu 70,629 F3
Tîrgu Mureş 129,284 G2
Tîrgu Neamţ 15,756 G2
Tîrgu Ocna 12,960 H2
Tîrgu Secuiesc 18,265 H2
Tîrnăveni 27,799 F2
Topliţa 14,347 G2
Tulcea 67,091 J3
Turda 57,972 F2
Turnu Măgurele 30,003 G4
Urlaţa 10,900 H3
Urziceni 13,500 H3
Vasile Roaită J3
Vaslui 44,134 H2
Vatra Dornei 16,748 G2
Videle 11,323 G3
Vişeul de Sus 20,697 F2
Viziru H3
Zalău 36,158 F2
Zărneşti 23,378 G3
Zimnicea 15,111 G4

OTHER FEATURES

Argeş (riv.) G3
Bîrlad (riv.) H2
Black (sea) J4
Brăila (marshes) H3
Buzău (riv.) H3
Carpathian (mts.) G2
Crişul Alb (riv.) F2
Crişul Repede (riv.) F2
Danube (delta) J3
Danube (riv.) H4
Ialomiţa (marshes) J3
Ialomiţa (riv.) H3
Jijia (riv.) H2
Jiu (riv.) F3
Moldoveanul (mt.) G3
Mureş (riv.) E2
Olt (riv.) G3
Peleaga (mt.) F3
Pietrosul (mt.) G2
Prut (riv.) J2
Siret (riv.) H2
Someş (riv.) F2
Timiş (riv.) E3
Tîrnava Mare (riv.) G2
Transylvanian Alps (mts.) G3

YUGOSLAVIA

INTERNAL DIVISIONS

Bosnia and Hercegovina
(rep.) 3,710,965 C3
Croatia (rep.) 4,396,397 C3
Kosovo (aut. reg.) 1,240,919 E4
Macedonia (rep.) 1,623,598 E5
Montenegro (rep.) 527,207 D4
Serbia (rep.) 8,401,673 E3
Slovenia (rep.) 1,697,068 B2
Vojvodina (aut.
prov.) 1,953,980 D3

CITIES and TOWNS

Aleksinac 11,943 E4
Apatin 17,501 D3
Arendjelovac 15,659 E3
Bačka Topola 16,028 D3
Bakar B3
Banja Luka 85,786 C3
Bar 3,594 D4
Bečej 26,616 E3
Bela Crkva 11,137 E3
Belgrade (cap.) 727,945 E3
Beli Manastir 7,325 D3
Beograd (Belgrade)
(cap.) 727,945 E3
Berovo 5,053 F5
Bihać 24,155 B3
Bijeljina 24,888 D3
Bijelo Polje 9,298 D4
Bileća 4,083 D4
Biograd 3,595 B4
Bitola 64,467 E5
Bjelovar 21,019 C3
Blato 5,591 C4
Bled 4,710 A2
Bor 27,520 E3
Bosanska Dubica 9,191 C3
Bosanska Gradiška 9,742 C3
Bosanska Kostajnica 2,535 B3
Bosanska Krupa 8,947 C3
Bosanski Brod 10,113 D3
Bosanski Novi 9,861 C3
Bosanski Petrovac 4,113 C3
Bosanski Šamac 4,949 D3
Brčko 25,575 D3
Brežice 3,271 B3
Budva 2,483 D4
Bugojno 9,079 C3
Čačak 38,890 E4
Čakovec 11,766 C2
Čapljina 4,677 C4
Caribrod (Dimitrovgrad) 5,449 F4
Cazin 1,213 B3
Celje 30,827 B2
Cetinje 12,089 D4
Ćuprija 17,691 E4
Daruvar 8,478 C3
Debar 8,597 E5
Derventa 11,887 C3
Dimitrovgrad 5,449 F4
Djakovica 29,499 E4
Djakovo 15,833 D3
Doboj 18,073 C3
Donji Vakuf 4,928 C3
Drvar 6,237 C3
Dubrovnik 31,213 C4
Fiume (Rijeka) 128,883 B3
Foča 9,370 D4
Gacko 1,641 D4
Gevgelija 9,319 F5
Glamoč 2,627 C3
Gnjilane 21,359 E4
Gornji Milanovac 11,114 D3
Gornji Vakuf 2,429 C4
Gospić 8,238 B3
Gostivar 18,805 E5
Gračac 3,228 B3
Gračanica 9,302 D3
Gradačac 7,571 D3
Grubišno Polje 2,771 C3
Gusinje 2,616 D4
Herceg Novi 6,645 D4
Ivangrad 11,373 E4
Ivanjica 5,719 E4
Jajce 9,221 C3
Jesenice 16,163 A2
Kanjiža 11,348 D2
Karlovac 47,046 B3
Kavadarci 17,974 E5
Kičevo 14,189 E5
Kikinda 37,392 E3
Kladanj 3,255 D3
Ključ 3,466 C3
Knin 7,279 C3
Knjaževac 11,734 F4
Kočani 16,611 F5
Kočevje 7,277 B3
Kolašin 2,111 D4
Konjic 9,161 D4
Koper 16,683 A3
Koprivnica 16,398 C2
Kosovska Mitrovica 42,526 E4
Kostajnica 9,161 C3
Kotor 5,728 D4
Kragujevac 72,080 E3
Kraljevo 28,065 E4
Kranj 26,341 B2
Križevci 8,501 C2
Krk 1,500 B3
Krško 4,451 B3
Kruševac 29,902 E4
Kulen Vakuf 1,078 B3
Kumanovo 44,791 E4
Kutina 10,892 C3
Leskovac 46,050 E4
Livno 7,223 C4
Ljubinje 785 D4
Ljubljana 169,064 B3
Ljubuški 2,891 C4
Loznica 13,513 D3
Maglaj 5,869 D3
Makarska 6,589 C4
Maribor 94,976 B2
Modriča 7,406 D3
Mostar 47,821 D4
Murska Sobota 9,665 C2
Našice 5,836 C3
Negotin 11,325 F3
Nevesinje 3,077 D4
Nikšić 28,940 D4
Nin 1,782 B3
Niš 128,231 F4
Nova Gorizia A2
Nova Gradiška 11,765 C3
Novi 2,682 B3
Novi Pazar 28,696 E4
Novi Sad 143,591 D3
Novo Mesto 9,553 B3
Novska 5,168 C3
Ogulin 9,975 B3
Ohrid 26,352 E5
Omiš 3,515 C4
Opatija 9,238 A3
Osijek 94,989 D3
Pag 2,318 B3
Pančevo 53,979 E3
Paraćin 21,555 E4
Peć 41,783 E4
Petrinja 12,296 B3
Piran 5,485 A3
Pirot 29,658 F4
Plav 3,072 D4
Pljevlja 14,459 D4
Ploče 4,257 C4
Pola (Pula) 47,117 A3
Poreč 4,512 A3
Postojna 6,085 B3
Požarevac 33,336 E3
Preševo 7,634 E4
Priboj 12,556 D4
Prijedor 22,379 C3
Prijepolje 7,960 D4
Prilep 48,045 E5
Priština 71,264 E4
Prizren 41,875 E4
Prokuplje 20,617 E4
Prozor 1,420 C4
Ptuj 9,245 C2
Pula 47,117 A3
Rab 1,675 B3
Radoviš 9,373 F5
Ragusa (Dubrovnik) 31,213 C4
Raška 3,935 E4
Ravne na Koroškem 6,529 B2
Rijeka 128,883 B3
Rogatica 4,801 D4
Rovinj 8,998 A3
Rožaj E4
Ruma 24,180 D3
Šabac 43,539 D3
Samobor 7,821 B3
Sanski Most 8,718 C3
Sarajevo 245,058 D4
Senj 4,927 B3
Senta 24,694 D3
Šibenik 29,619 C4
Šid 11,867 D3
Sinj 4,705 C4
Sisak 37,215 C3
Sjenica 9,118 E4
Škofja Loka 4,971 A2
Skopje 308,117 E5
Skradin 893 B4
Slavonska Požega 18,160 C3
Slavonski Brod 38,829 D3
Smederevo 39,200 E3
Smederevska Palanka 18,837 E3
Sombor 44,210 D3
Split 150,739 C4
Srebrenica 3,101 D3
Sremska Mitrovica 32,569 D3
Štip 27,218 F5
Stolac 3,862 D4
Ston 407 C4
Struga 11,369 E5
Strumica 22,770 F5
Subotica 89,476 D2
Surdulica 7,048 F4
Svetozarevo 27,812 E4
Svilajnac 7,848 E3
Teslić 4,940 C3
Tetovo 35,293 E5
Titograd 54,639 D4
Titovo Užice 35,465 D4
Titov Veles 35,583 E5
Travnik 12,745 C3
Trbovlje 16,393 B2
Trebinje 3,553 D4
Trogir 6,162 C4
Trstenik 7,167 E4
Tržič 4,435 B2
Tuzla 53,836 D3
Ub 3,785 E3
Ulcinj 7,472 D5
Umag 3,228 A3
Uroševac E4
Valjevo 26,655 D3
Varaždin 34,662 B2
Vareš 7,632 D3
Velenje 11,225 B2
Velika Plana E3
Veliki Bečkerek
(Zrenjanin) 60,201 E3
Vinkovci 29,257 D3
Virovitica 16,389 C3
Višegrad 4,753 D4
Visoko 9,365 D4
Vlasenica 4,033 D3
Vranje 25,909 F4
Vrbas 22,502 D3
Vršac 33,573 E3
Vučitrn 11,701 E4
Vukovar 29,500 D3
Žabljak 1,023 D4
Zadar 43,588 B3
Zagreb 561,773 C3
Zaječar 27,724 E4
Zara (Zadar) 43,588 B3
Zenica 49,522 C3
Žepče 3,177 D3
Zrenjanin 60,201 E3
Zvornik 8,498 D3

OTHER FEATURES

Adriatic (sea) B4
Bobotov Kuk (mt.) D4
Bosna (riv.) D3
Brač (isl.) C4
Cazma (riv.) C3
Cres (isl.) B3
Čvrsnica (mt.) C4
Dalmatia (reg.) C4
Danube (riv.) E3
Dinaric Alps (mts.) B3
Drava (riv.) C3
Drina (riv.) D3
Dugi Otok (isl.) B3
Hvar (isl.) C4
Ibar (riv.) E4
Istria (pen.) A3
Kamenjak (cape) A3
Kladovo F3
Korab (mt.) E5
Korčula (isl.) C4
Kornat (isl.) B4
Krk (isl.) B3
Kupa (riv.) B3
Kvarner (gulf) B3
Lastovo (Lagosta) (isl.) C4
Lim (riv.) D4
Lošinj (isl.) B3
Midzhur (mt.) F4
Mljet (isl.) C4
Morava (riv.) E3
Mur (riv.) B2
Neretva (riv.) D4
Ohrid (lake) E5
Pag (isl.) B3
Palagruža (Pelagosa) (isl.) C4
Prespa (lake) E5
Rab (isl.) B3
Rujen (mt.) F4
Sava (riv.) D3
Scutari (lake) D4
Slavonia (reg.) C3
Šolta (isl.) C4
Tara (riv.) D4
Timok (riv.) F3
Tisa (riv.) E3
Triglav (mt.) A2
Una (riv.) C3
Vardar (riv.) E5
Vis (isl.) C4
Vrbas (riv.) C3
Žirje (isl.) B4

*City and suburbs.

The Balkan States
CONIC PROJECTION
SCALE OF MILES
0 25 50 75 100 125 150 175
SCALE OF KILOMETERS
0 25 50 75 100 125 150 175
Capitals of Countries
Administrative Centers
International Boundaries
Major Internal Boundaries
Minor Internal Boundaries
Canals
BULGARIA and GREECE are divided into counties and departments, respectively. Because of the scale no attempt has been made to delimit and name these subdivisions; their administrative centers have, however, been designated.
The larger divisions named in Greece are well-known geographical regions, without administrative function.
ROMANIA consists of thirty-nine counties and three cities of regional status, Bucharest, Constanţa and Petroşeni. Scale does not permit delimiting these counties.
ALBANIA is divided into twenty-seven districts. Scale does not permit the delimitation of these divisions.
YUGOSLAVIA is a federation of six republics. The Serbian republic includes an autonomous province (Vojvodina), and an autonomous region (Kosovo).
POLAND
CZECHOSLOVAKIA
GERMANY
AUSTRIA
HUNGARY
ROMANIA
U.S.S.R.
YUGOSLAVIA
SLOVENIA
CROATIA
BOSNIA AND HERCEGOVINA
MONTENEGRO
SERBIA
VOJVODINA
KOSOVO
MACEDONIA
ALBANIA
BULGARIA
GREECE
TURKEY
ITALY
Carpathian Mts.
Transylvanian Alps
Dinaric Alps
Balkan Mts.
Rhodope Mts.
Pindus Mts.
ADRIATIC SEA
BLACK SEA
TYRRHENIAN SEA
IONIAN SEA
AEGEAN SEA
SEA OF MARMARA
SEA OF CRETE
MEDITERRANEAN SEA
VIENNA (Wien)
BUDAPEST
BUCHAREST (Bucureşti)
Belgrade (Beograd)
Sofia
Tiranë
Athens
Zagreb
Ljubljana
Sarajevo
Skopje
Titograd
Novi Sad
Cluj-Napoca
Timişoara
Constanţa
Varna
Plovdiv
Thessaloníki (Salonika)
İSTANBUL
NAPLES (Napoli)
Crete (Kríti)
Rhodes
CYCLADES ISLANDS
DODECANESE IS.
THESSALY
EPIRUS
CENTRAL GREECE
EUBOEA
PELOPONNISOS
NORTHERN SPORADES
Longitude East of Greenwich

44 Poland

Topography

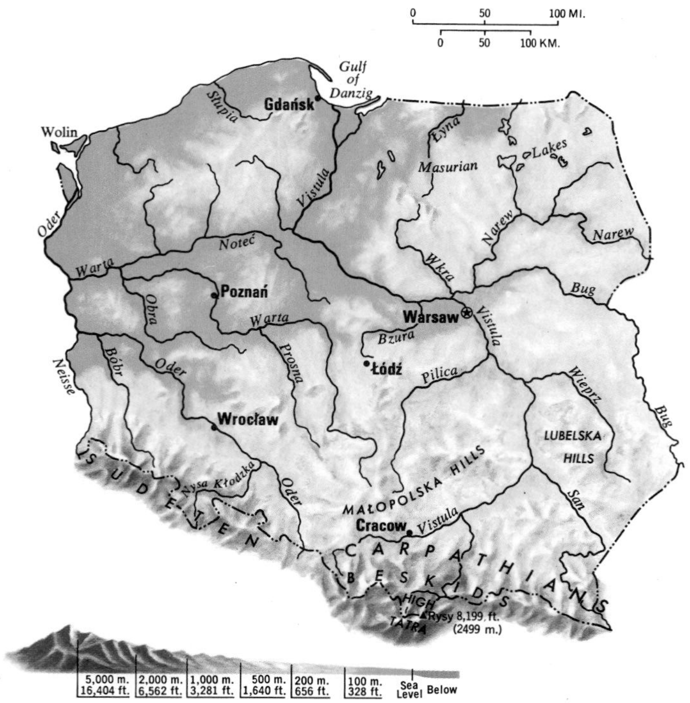

PROVINCES

Biata Podlaska 283,200	F3
Białystok 613,800	F2
Bielsko 765,500	D4
Bydgoszcz 982,100	C2
Chełm 221,000	F3
Ciechanów 398,500	E2
Cracow (Kraków) 1,097,600	E4
Cracow (city) 651,300	E4
Częstochowa 723,200	D3
Elbląg 419,800	D1
Gdańsk 1,312,300	D1
Gorzów 428,700	B2
Jelenia Góra 483,400	B3
Kalisz 640,300	D3
Katowice 3,439,700	D3
Kielce 1,030,400	E3
Konin 423,700	D2
Koszalin 428,500	C1
Krosno 418,000	E4
Legnica 405,600	C4
Leszno 340,600	C3
Łódź 1,063,700	D3
Łódź (city) 777,800	D3
Łomza 320,600	F2
Lublin 875,300	F3
Nowy Sącz 600,300	E4
Olsztyn 654,400	E2
Opole 961,600	C3
Ostrołęka 360,700	E2
Piła 414,000	C2
Piotrków 581,900	D3
Płock 479,700	D2
Poznań 1,156,500	C2
Przemyśl 373,100	F4
Radom 674,400	E3
Rzeszów 602,200	F4
Siedlce 602,100	F2
Sieradz 388,000	D3
Skierniewice 388,300	E3
Słupsk 352,900	C1
Suwałki 412,700	F1
Szczecin 841,400	B2
Tarnobrzeg 532,200	E3
Tarnów 573,900	E4
Torún 580,500	D2
Wałbrzych 709,600	C3
Warsaw 2,117,700	E2
Warsaw (city) 1,377,100	E2
Włocławek 402,000	D2
Wrocław 1,014,600	C3
Zamość 472,300	F3
Zielona Góra 575,000	B3

CITIES and TOWNS

Aleksandrów Kujawski 9,600	D2
Aleksandrów Łódzki 14,400	D3
Allenstein (Olsztyn) 94,119	E2
Andrespol 12,400	D3
Andrychów 14,300	D4
Augustów 19,784	F2
Auschwitz (Oświęcim) 39,600	D3
Bartoszyce 15,500	E1
Będzin 42,787	B3
Beuthen (Bytom) 186,993	A3
Biała Podlaska 26,100	F3
Białogard 20,500	C1
Białystok 166,619	F2
Bielawa 30,900	C3
Bielsk Podlaski 14,000	F2
Bielsko-Biała 105,601	D4
Biłgoraj 12,888	F3
Błonie 12,500	E2
Bochnia 14,500	E4
Bogatynia 11,800	B3
Boguszów-Gorce 11,900	B3
Bolesławiec 30,500	B3

Agriculture, Industry and Resources

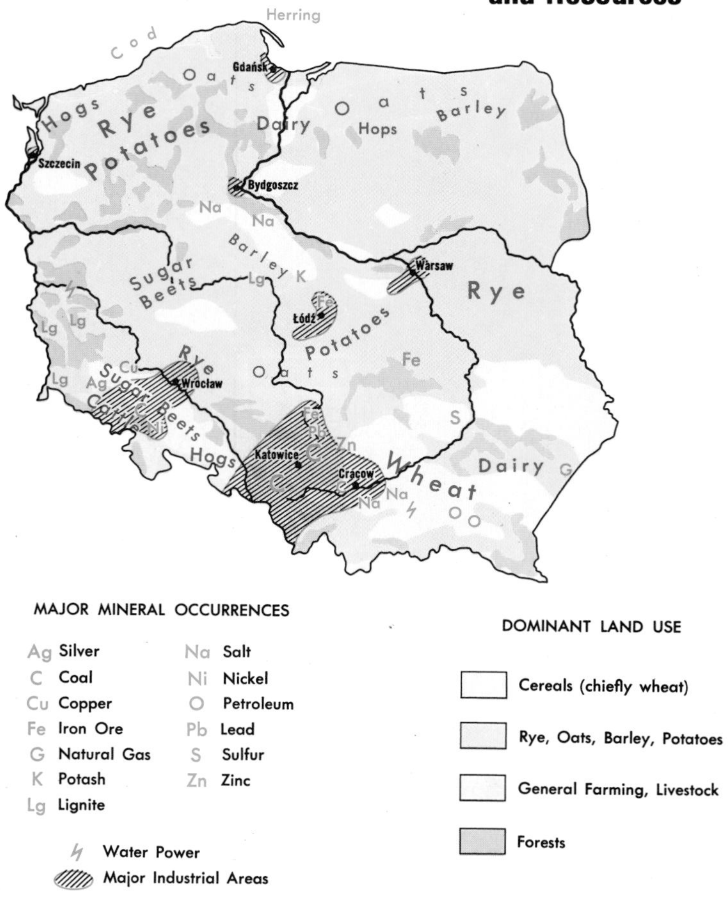

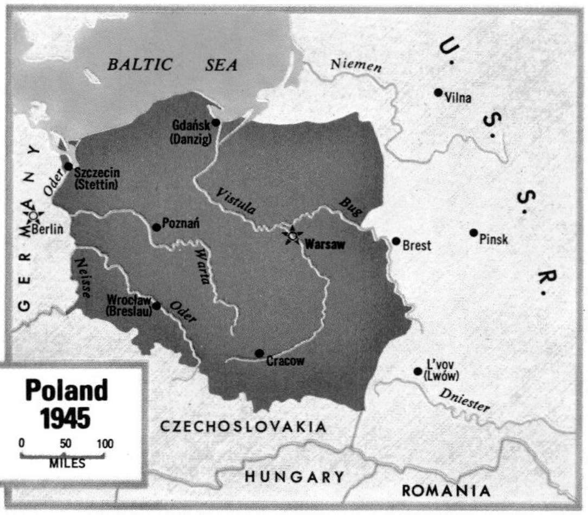

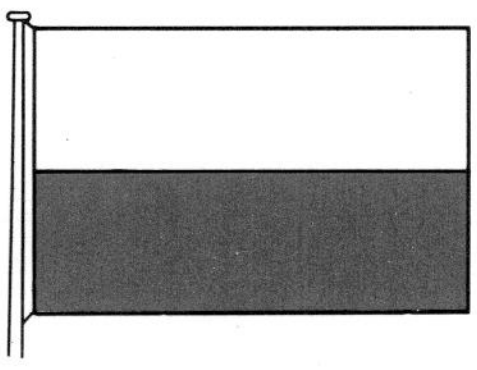

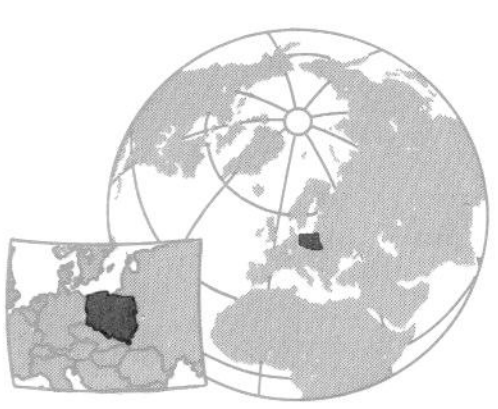

AREA 120,725 sq. mi. (312,678 sq. km.)
POPULATION 35,815,000
CAPITAL Warsaw
LARGEST CITY Warsaw
HIGHEST POINT Rysy 8,199 ft. (2,499 m.)
MONETARY UNIT zloty
MAJOR LANGUAGE Polish
MAJOR RELIGION Roman Catholicism

Braniewo 12,100 ..... D1
Breslau (Wrocław) 461,900 ..... C3
Brieg (Brzeg) 30,780 ..... C3
Brodnica 17,300 ..... D2
Brzeg 30,780 ..... C3
Brzeg Dolny 10,800 ..... C3
Brzesko 9,701 ..... E3
Busko Zdrój 11,100 ..... E3
Bydgoszcz 280,460 ..... C2
Bytom 186,993 ..... A3
Bytów 10,642 ..... C1
Chełm 38,789 ..... F3
Chełmno 17,906 ..... D2
Chełmza 14,200 ..... D2
Chodziez 14,100 ..... C2
Chojnice 23,500 ..... C2
Chojnów 11,000 ..... B3
Chorzów 151,338 ..... B4
Choszczno 9,800 ..... B2
Chrzanów 29,300 ..... B4
Ciechanów 28,500 ..... E2
Cieplice Śląskie-Zdrój 15,400 ..... B3
Cieszyn 25,234 ..... D4
Cracow 651,300 ..... E4
Czechowice-Dziedzice 25,400 ..... D4
Czeladź 31,843 ..... B4
Częstochowa 187,613 ..... D3
Dąbrowa Górnicza 61,660 ..... B3
Danzig (Gdańsk) 364,285 ..... D1
Darłowo 11,200 ..... C1
Dębica 22,900 ..... E3
Dęblin 14,600 ..... E3
Dębno 10,700 ..... B2
Działdowo 10,100 ..... E2
Dzierzoniów 32,800 ..... C3
Elbing (Elblag) 89,835 ..... D1
Ełk 27,188 ..... F2
Gdańsk 364,285 ..... D1
Gdynia 190,125 ..... D1
Gizycko 18,200 ..... E1
Gleiwitz (Gliwice) 170,912 ..... A4
Głogów (Glogau) 20,226 ..... C3
Głowno 12,800 ..... D2
Głubczyce 11,300 ..... C3
Głuchołazy 13,200 ..... C3
Gniezno 50,643 ..... C2
Goleniów 14,600 ..... B2
Gorlice 15,200 ..... E4
Gorzów Wielkopolski 74,267 ..... B2
Gostyń 13,000 ..... C3
Gostynin 12,000 ..... D2
Grajewo 11,200 ..... F2
Grodzisk Mazowiecki 20,400 ..... E2
Grójec 10,300 ..... E3
Grudziądz 75,511 ..... D2
Grünberg (Zielona Góra) 59,700 ..... B3
Gryfice 13,200 ..... B2
Guben (Gubin) 14,600 ..... B3
Hajnowka m4,345 ..... F2
Hindenburg (Zabrze) 199,400 ..... A4
Hirschberg (Jelenia Góra) 55,720 ..... B3
Hrubieszów 14,999 ..... F3
Iława 16,400 ..... D2
Inowrocław 54,817 ..... D2
Jarocin 18,100 ..... C3
Jarosław 29,000 ..... F4
Jasło 17,025 ..... E4
Jastrzębie Zdroj 34,400 ..... D3
Jaworzno 63,271 ..... B4
Jędrzejów 13,264 ..... E3
Jelenia Góra 55,720 ..... B3
Kalisz 81,227 ..... D3
Kamienna Góra 21,000 ..... B3
Kartuzy 10,558 ..... C1
Katowice 303,264 ..... B4
Kedzierzyn-Koźle 45,600 ..... C3
Kępno 10,151 ..... C3
Kętrzyn 19,300 ..... E1
Kielce 125,952 ..... E3
Kłobuck 12,600 ..... D3
Kłodzko 26,000 ..... C3
Kluczbork 18,000 ..... D3
Knurów 28,400 ..... A4
Kolberg (Kołobrzeg) 25,419 ..... B1
Koło 13,100 ..... D2
Kołobrzeg 25,419 ..... B1
Konin 40,600 ..... D2
Końskie 13,100 ..... E3
Konstantynów Łódzki 12,800 ..... D3
Kościan 18,700 ..... C2
Kościerzyna 18,914 ..... C1
Köslin (Koszalin) 64,414 ..... C1
Kostrzyń 11,200 ..... B2
Koszalin 64,414 ..... C1
Kraków (Cracow) 651,300 ..... E4
Krapkowice 13,800 ..... D3
Kraśnik Fabryczny 14,600 ..... F3
Krasnystaw 12,495 ..... F3
Krosno 26,500 ..... E4
Krotoszyn 21,900 ..... C3
Krynica 10,200 ..... E4
Küstrin 11,200 ..... B2
Kutno 30,000 ..... D2
Kwidzin 23,104 ..... D2
Łancut 12,049 ..... F3
Landsberg (Gorzów Wielkepolski) 74,267 ..... B2
Łaziska Górne 10,800 ..... A4
Lębork 25,000 ..... C1
Łęczyca 13,900 ..... D2
Legionowo 20,800 ..... E2
Legnica 75,843 ..... C3
Leszcyny 12,200 ..... A4
Leszno 33,890 ..... C3
Libiaz 10,600 ..... D3
Lidzbark Warmiński 12,900 ..... E1
Liegnitz (Legnica) 75,843 ..... C3
Lipno 10,900 ..... D2
Łódź 777,800 ..... D3
Łomza 25,500 ..... F2
Łowicz 20,400 ..... D2
Lubań 17,200 ..... B3
Lubartów 10,000 ..... F3
Lubin 28,400 ..... C3
Lublin 235,937 ..... F3
Lubliniec 19,800 ..... D3
Luboń 16,400 ..... C2
Lubsko 12,600 ..... B3
Łuków 15,500 ..... F3
Malbork (Marienburg) 30,900 ..... D1
Międzyrzec Podlaski 13,500 ..... F3
Międzyrzecz 14,900 ..... B2
Mielec 26,800 ..... E3
Mikłów 21,300 ..... B4
Mińsk Mazowiecki 24,200 ..... E2
Mława 20,007 ..... E2
Mońki 9,560 ..... F2
Morąg 9,681 ..... E2
Mrągowo 13,400 ..... E2
Myślenice 12,100 ..... E4
Mysłowice 44,737 ..... C4
Myszków 18,000 ..... D3
Nakło nad Notecia 16,800 ..... C2
Namysłów 11,076 ..... C3
Neisse (Nysa) 31,837 ..... C3
Nidzica 9,642 ..... E2
Nisko 10,000 ..... E3
Nowa Ruda 18,100 ..... C3
Nowa Sól 33,300 ..... B3
Nowy Dwór Mazowiecki 16,900 ..... E2
Nowy Sącz 41,103 ..... E4
Nowy Targ 21,900 ..... E4
Nysa 31,837 ..... C3
Oborniki 10,200 ..... C2
Oława 17,746 ..... C3
Oleśnica 27,500 ..... C3
Olkusz 15,800 ..... D3
Olsztyn 94,119 ..... E2
Opoczno 12,168 ..... E3
Opole 86,510 ..... C3
Oppeln 86,510 ..... C3
Orzesze 9,600 ..... A4
Ostróda 21,300 ..... D2
Ostrołęka 21,981 ..... E2
Ostrów Mazowiecka 15,000 ..... E2
Ostrów Wielkopolski 49,530 ..... C3
Ostrowiec Świętokrzyski 49,958 ..... E3
Oświęcim 39,600 ..... D3
Otwock 39,863 ..... E2
Ozorków 18,200 ..... D3
Pabianice 62,275 ..... D3
Piekary Śląskie 36,300 ..... B4
Piła 43,778 ..... C2
Pionki 13,600 ..... E3
Piotrków Trybunalski 59,683 ..... D3
Pisz 11,100 ..... E2
Pleszew 13,348 ..... C3
Płock 71,727 ..... D2
Płońsk 11,619 ..... E2
Police 12,700 ..... B2
Poznań 469,085 ..... C2
Prudnik 20,300 ..... C3
Pruszcz Gdanski 13,000 ..... D1
Pruszków 42,961 ..... E2
Przasnysz 11,100 ..... E2
Przemyśl 53,228 ..... F4
Puck 9,500 ..... D1
Puławy 34,800 ..... F3
Pułtusk 12,600 ..... E2
Rabka 10,700 ..... D4
Racibórz 40,418 ..... C3
Radom 158,640 ..... E3
Radomsko 31,179 ..... D3
Ratibor (Racibórz) 40,418 ..... C3
Rawa Mazowiecka 9,800 ..... E3
Rawicz 14,100 ..... C3
Ruda Śląska 142,407 ..... B4
Rumia 23,300 ..... D1
Rybnik 43,415 ..... D3
Rypin 10,029 ..... D2
Rzeszów 82,192 ..... F4
Sandomierz 16,800 ..... E3
Sanok 21,600 ..... F4
Schneidemühl (Piła) 36,600 ..... C2
Schweidnitz (Świdnica) 47,542 ..... C3
Siedlce 38,983 ..... F2
Siemianowice Śląskie 67,278 ..... B4
Sieradz 18,500 ..... D3
Sierpc 12,700 ..... D2
Skarzysko-Kamienna 39,194 ..... E3
Skawina 15,900 ..... D4
Skierniewice 25,590 ..... E2
Sławno 10,700 ..... C1
Słubice 12,000 ..... B2
Słupsk 68,311 ..... C1
Sochaczew 20,500 ..... E2
Sokółka 10,023 ..... F2
Sokołów Podlaski 9,569 ..... F2
Sopot 47,573 ..... D1
Sosnowiec 144,652 ..... B4
Śrem 15,600 ..... C2
Środa Śląska 10,259 ..... C3
Środa Wielkopolska 14,800 ..... C2
Stalowa Wola 29,768 ..... F3
Starachowice 42,807 ..... E3
Stargard Szeciński 44,400 ..... B2
Starogard Gdański 33,400 ..... D2
Stary Sacz 57,400 ..... E4
Stettin (Szczecin) 337,294 ..... B2
Stolp (Słupsk) 68,311 ..... C1
Strzegom 14,000 ..... C3
Strzelce Opolskie 14,700 ..... D3
Strzelin 9,800 ..... C3
Sulechów 10,200 ..... B2
Suwałki 25,360 ..... F1
Swarzędz 12,100 ..... C2
Świdnica 47,542 ..... C3
Świdnik 21,900 ..... F3
Świdwin 12,500 ..... B2
Świebodzice 18,500 ..... C3
Świebodzin 14,900 ..... B2
Świecie 17,900 ..... D2
Świętochłowice 57,633 ..... A4
Świnoujście (Swinemünde) 27,900 ..... B1
Szamotuły 14,600 ..... G2
Szczecin 337,204 ..... B2
Szczecinek 28,600 ..... C2
Szczytno 17,371 ..... E2
Szprotawa 11,200 ..... B3
Tarnobrzeg 18,800 ..... E3
Tarnów 85,514 ..... E4
Tarnowskie Góry 34,200 ..... A3
Tczew 40,794 ..... D1
Tomaszów Lubelski 12,329 ..... F3
Tomaszów Mazowiecki 54,911 ..... E3
Toruń 129,152 ..... D2
Trzcianka 10,900 ..... C2
Trzebinia-Siersza C4
Turek 18,500 ..... D2
Tychy 71,384 ..... B4
Ustka 9,900 ..... C1
Wąbrzeźno 11,800 ..... D2
Wadowice 11,700 ..... D4
Wągrowiec 15,600 ..... C2
Wałbrzych 125,048 ..... C3
Wałcz 18,900 ..... C2
Waldenburg (Wałbrzych) 125,048 ..... C3
Warsaw (Warszawa) (cap.) 1,377,100 ..... E2
Wejherowo 33,600 ..... D1
Wieliczka 13,600 ..... E3
Wieluń 14,300 ..... D3
Wisła 9,800 ..... D4
Włocławek 77,169 ..... D2
Wodzisław Śląski 25,600 ..... D4
Wolin 35,458 ..... B2
Wołomin 24,000 ..... E2
Wołów 10,500 ..... C3
Wrocław 523,318 ..... C3
Września 17,800 ..... C2
Wschowa 10,000 ..... C3
Wyszków E2
Ząbki 16,000 ..... E2
Ząbkowice Śląskie 13,800 ..... C3
Zabrze 197,214 ..... A4
Zagań 21,400 ..... B3
Zakopane 27,039 ..... D4
Zambrów 14,082 ..... E2
Zamość 34,734 ..... F3
Zary 28,300 ..... B3
Zawiercie 39,410 ..... D3
Zduńska Wola 29,066 ..... D3
Zgierz 42,838 ..... D3
Zgorzelec 28,400 ..... B3
Ziębice 9,700 ..... C3
Zielona Góra 73,156 ..... B3
Złocieniec 10,100 ..... C2
Złotoryja 12,200 ..... C3
Złotów 11,600 ..... C2
Znin 9,600 ..... C2
Zyrardów 33,196 ..... E2
Zywiec 22,400 ..... D4

OTHER FEATURES

Baltic (sea) B1
Beskids (range) D4
Brda (riv.) C2
Brynica (riv.) B4
Bug (riv.) F2
Danzig (Gdańsk) (gulf) D1
Dukla (pass) E4
Dunajec (riv.) E4
Gwda (riv.) C2
Hel (pen.) D1
High Tatra (range) D4
Kłodnica (riv.) A4
Łyna (riv.) E1
Mamry, Jezioro (lake) E1
Masurian (lkes) E2
Narew (riv.) E2
Neisse (riv.) B3
Noteć (riv.) B2
Nysa Kłodzka (riv.) C3
Nysa Łuzycka (Neisse) (riv.) B3
Oder (riv.) B2
Orava (res.) D4
Pilica (riv.) D3
Pomeranian (bay) B1
Prosna (riv.) C3
Przemsza (riv.) B4
Rysy (mt.) D4
San (riv.) F3
Słupia (riv.) C1
Śniardwy, Jezioro (lake) E2
Sudeten (range) B3
Uznam (Usedom) (isl.) B1
Vistula (riv.) D2
Warmia (reg.) D1
Warta (riv.) B2
Wieprz (riv.) F3
Wisła (Vistula) (riv.) D2
Wkra (riv.) E2
Wolin (Wollin) (isl.) B2

Union of Soviet Socialist Republics

UNION REPUBLICS

Armenian S.S.R. 3,031,000 ... E6
Azerbaidzhan S.S.R. 6,028,000 ... E5
Estonian S.S.R. 1,466,000 ... C4
Georgian S.S.R. 5,015,000 ... D5
Kazakh S.S.R. 14,684,000 ... G5
Kirgiz S.S.R. 3,529,000 ... H5
Latvian S.S.R. 2,521,000 ... C4
Lithuanian S.S.R. 3,398,000 ... C4
Moldavian S.S.R. 3,947,000 ... C5
Russian S.F.S.R. 137,551,000 ... D4
Tadzhik S.S.R. 3,801,000 ... H6
Turkmen S.S.R. 2,759,000 ... F6
Ukrainian S.S.R. 49,755,000 ... C5
Uzbek S.S.R. 15,391,000 ... G5
White Russian S.S.R. 9,560,000 ... C4

INTERNAL DIVISIONS

Abkhaz A.S.S.R. 505,000 ... E5
Adygey Aut. Obl. 405,000 ... D5
Adzhar A.S.S.R. 354,000 ... E5
Aginsk Buryat Aut. Okr. 69,000 ... M4
Bashkir A.S.S.R. 3,849,000 ... F4
Buryat A.S.S.R. 900,000 ... M4
Chechen-Ingush A.S.S.R. 1,154,000 ... E5
Chukchi Aut. Okr. 133,000 ... R3
Chuvash A.S.S.R. 1,292,000 ... E4
Dagestan A.S.S.R. 1,628,000 ... E5
Evenki Aut. Okr. 16,000 ... K3
Gorno-Altay Aut. Obl. 172,000 ... J4
Gorno-Badakhshan Aut. Obl. 127,000 ... H6
Jewish Aut. Obl. 190,000 ... O5
Kabardin-Balkar A.S.S.R. 674,000 ... E5
Kalmuck A.S.S.R. 294,000 ... E5
Karachay-Cherkess Aut. Obl. 368,000 ... E5
Karakalpak A.S.S.R. 904,000 ... G5
Karelian A.S.S.R. 736,000 ... D3
Khakass Aut. Obl. 500,000 ... J4
Khanty-Mansi Aut. Okr. 569,000 ... H3
Komi A.S.S.R. 1,119,000 ... F3
Komi-Permyak Aut. Okr. 173,000 ... F4
Koryak Aut. Okr. 34,000 ... R3
Mari A.S.S.R. 703,000 ... E4
Mordvinian A.S.S.R. 991,000 ... E4
Nagorno-Karabakh Aut. Obl. 161,000 ... E5
Nakhichevan' A.S.S.R. 239,000 ... E6
Nenets Aut. Okr. 47,000 ... F3
North Ossetian A.S.S.R. 597,000 ... E5
South Ossetian Aut. Obl. 98,000 ... E5
Tatar A.S.S.R. 3,436,000 ... F4
Taymyr Aut. Okr. 44,000 ... K2
Tuvinian A.S.S.R. 267,000 ... K4
Udmurt A.S.S.R. 1,494,000 ... F4
Ust'-Ordynskiy Buryat Aut. Okr. 133,000 ... L4
Yakut A.S.S.R. 839,000 ... N3
Yamal-Nenets Aut. Okr. 158,000 ... H3

CITIES and TOWNS

Abakan 128,000 ... K4
Abay 34,245 ... H5
Abaza 15,202 ... J4
Achinsk 117,000 ... K4
Agata ...
Aginskoye 7,922 ...
Akmolinsk (Tselinograd) 234,000 ...
Aksay 10,010 ...
Aktas ...
Aktash ...
Aktyubinsk 191,000 ...
Aldan 17,689 ...
Aleksandrovsk-Sakhalinskiy 20,342 ...
Alekseyevka 18,041 ...
Aleysk 32,487 ...
Alga 12,000 ...
Aliskerovo ...
Allakh-Yun' ...
Alma-Ata 910,000 ...
Almaznyy ...
Ambarchik ...
Amderma ...
Amursk 24,010 ...
Anadyr' 7,703 ...
Andizhan 230,000 ...
Angarsk 239,000 ...
Angren ...
Anzhero-Sudzhensk 105,000 ...
Aral'sk 37,722 ...
Archangel (Arkhangel'sk) 385,000 ...
Arkalyk 15,108 ...
Armavir 162,000 ...
Arsen'yev 60,000 ...
Artem 69,000 ...
Artemovskiy ...
Arys' 26,414 ...
Arzamas 93,000 ...
Asbest 79,000 ...
Ashkhabad 312,000 ... F6
Asino 29,395 ... J4
Astrakhan' 461,000 ... E5
Atbasar 37,228 ... G4
Atka ... Q3
Ayaguz 35,827 ... J5
Ayan ... O4
Aykhal ... M3
Bagdarin ... M4
Baku 1,022,000 ... F5
Baku* 1,550,000 ... F5
Balakovo 152,000 ... E4
Balashov 93,000 ... E4
Baley 27,215 ... M4
Balkhash 78,000 ... H5
Balykshi 22,397 ... F5
Bam ... N4
Barabinsk 37,274 ... H4
Baranovichi 131,000 ... C4
Barnaul 533,000 ... J4
Batagay 10,000 ... O3
Batumi 123,000 ... E5
Baykit ... K3
Baykonyr ... G5
Bayram-Ali 31,987 ... G6
Belgorod 240,000 ... D4
Belogorsk 63,000 ... N4
Belomorsk 16,595 ... D3
Beloretsk 71,000 ... F4
Belovo 112,000 ... J4
Berdichev 80,000 ... C5
Berdsk 67,000 ... J4
Berezniki 185,000 ... F4
Berezovo 6,000 ... G3
Beringovskiy ... T3
Bikin 17,473 ... O5
Bira ... O5
Birobidzhan 69,000 ... O5
Biruni ... G5
Biysk 212,000 ... J4
Blagoveshchensk 172,000 ... N4
Bobruysk 192,000 ... C4
Bodaybo 19,000 ... M4
Borisoglebsk 68,000 ... E4
Borzya 27,815 ... M4
Bratsk 214,000 ... L4
Brest 177,000 ... C4
Brindakit ... O4
Bryansk 394,000 ... D4
Bugul'ma 80,000 ... F4
Bukachacha 10,000 ... M4
Bukhara 185,000 ... G5
Bulun ... N2
Buzuluk 76,000 ... F4
Chadan ... K4
Chapayevsk 85,000 ... F4
Chara ... M4
Chardzhou 140,000 ... G6
Charsk 10,100 ... J5
Cheboksary 308,000 ... E4
Chegdomyn 16,499 ... O4
Chelkar 19,377 ... F5
Chelyabinsk 1,030,000 ... G4
Cheremkhovo 77,000 ... L4
Cherepovets 266,000 ... D4
Cherkessk 91,000 ... E5
Chernenko ... K4
Chernigov 238,000 ... D4
Chernogorsk 71,000 ... K4
Chernovtsy 219,000 ... C5
Chernyshevsk 10,000 ... M4
Cherskiy ... Q3
Chimbay 18,899 ... F5
Chimkent 322,000 ... H5
Chirchik 132,000 ... H5
Chita 303,000 ... M 4
Chokurdakh ... P 2
Chumikan ... O 4
Dal'negorsk 33,506 ... O 5
Dal'nerechensk 28,244 ... O 5
Daugavpils 116,000 ... C 4
Denau ... G 6
Dikson ... J 2
Dimitrovgrad 106,000 ... F 4
Dnepropetrovsk 1,066,000 ... D 5
Donetsk 1,021,000 ... D 5
Drogobych 66,000 ... C 5
Druzhba ... J 5
Druzhina ... P 3
Dudinka 19,701 ... J 3
Dushanbe 494,000 ... G 6
Dzerzhinsk 257,000 ... E 4
Dzhalal-Abad 55,000 ... H 5
Dzhalinda ... N 4
Dzhambul 264,000 ... H 5
Dzhelinda ... M 2
Dzhetygara 32,169 ... G 4
Dzhezkazgan 89,000 ... G 5
Dzhusaly 20,658 ... G 5
Egvekinot ... S 3
Ekibastuz 66,000 ... H 4
Ekimchan ... O 4
El'dikan ... O 3
Elista 70,000 ... E 5
Emba 17,820 ... F 5
Engel's 161,000 ... E 4
Evensk ... Q 3
Fergana 176,000 ... H 5
Fort-Shevchenko 12,000 ... F 5
Frolovo 33,398 ... E 5
Frunze 533,000 ... H 5
Gandzhe 232,000 ... E5
Gasan-Kuli ... F6
Gol'chikha ... J2
Gomel' 383,000 ... D4
Gor'kiy 1,344,000 ... E4
Gorno-Altaysk 34,413 ... J4
Gornyak 16,643 ... J4
Grodno 195,000 ... C4
Groznyy 375,000 ... E5
Gubakha 33,243 ... F4
Gulistan 30,879 ... G5
Gur'yev 131,000 ... F5
Gusinoozersk 10,000 ... L4
Gyda ... H2
Igarka 15,624 ... J3
Igrim ... G3
Ilanskiy 22,852 ... K4
Indiga ... E3
Inta 51,000 ... G3
Iolotan' 10,000 ... G6
Irkutsk 550,000 ... L4
Ishim 63,000 ... H4
Isil'kul' 25,958 ... H4
Iul'tin ... T3
Ivano-Frankovsk 150,000 ... C5
Ivanovo 465,000 ... E4
Ivdel 15,308 ... G3
Izhevsk 549,000 ... F4
Izmail 83,000 ... C5
Kachug ... L4
Kagan 34,117 ... G6
Kalachinsk 20,809 ... H4
Kalakan ... M4
Kalinin 412,000 ... D4
Kaliningrad 355,000 ... B4
Kalmykovo ... F5
Kaluga 265,000 ... D4
Kamen'-na-Obi 35,604 ... H4

AREA 8,649,490 sq. mi. (22,402,179 sq. km.)
POPULATION 262,436,227
CAPITAL Moscow
LARGEST CITY Moscow
HIGHEST POINT Communism Peak 24,599 ft. (7,498 m.)
MONETARY UNIT ruble
MAJOR LANGUAGES Russian, Ukrainian, White Russian, Uzbek, Azerbaidzhani, Tatar, Georgian, Lithuanian, Armenian, Yiddish, Latvian, Mordvinian, Kirgiz, Tadzhik, Estonian, Kazakh, Moldavian (Romanian), German, Chuvash, Turkmenian, Bashkir
MAJOR RELIGIONS Eastern (Russian) Orthodoxy, Islam, Judaism, Protestantism (Baltic States)

Kamenskoye R3
Kamensk-Ural'skiy 187,000 .... G4
Kamyshin 112,000 .... E4
Kandalaksha 42,656 .... C3
Kansk 101,000 .... K4
Kapchagay H5
Kara G3
Karaganda 572,000 .... H5
Karasuk 22,637 .... H4
Karatau 26,962 .... H5
Karazhal 17,702 .... H5
Kargasok J4
Karpinsk F4
Karshi 108,000 .... G6
Kartaly 42,801 .... G4
Katangli P4
Kattakurgan 53,000 .... G5
Kaunas 370,000 .... C4
Kavalerovo 16,415 .... O5
Kazan' 993,000 .... F4
Kem' 21,025 .... D3
Kemerovo 471,000 .... J4
Kentau 52,000 .... G5
Kerki 10,000 .... G6
Khabarovsk 528,000 .... O5
Khandyga O3
Khanty-Mansiysk 24,754 .... H3
Khar'kov 1,444,000 .... D4
Khatanga L2
Kherson 319,000 .... D5
Khilok 17,000 .... M4
Khiva 24,139 .... F5
Khodzheyli 36,435 .... F5
Kholmsk 37,412 .... P5
Khorog 12,295 .... H6
Kiev 2,144,000 .... D4

UNION REPUBLICS

	AREA (sq. mi.)	AREA (sq. km.)	POPULATION	CAPITAL and LARGEST CITY
RUSSIAN S.F.S.R.	6,592,812	17,075,400	137,551,000	Moscow 7,831,000
KAZAKH S.S.R.	1,048,300	2,715,100	14,684,000	Alma-Ata 910,000
UKRAINIAN S.S.R.	233,089	603,700	49,755,000	Kiev 2,144,000
TURKMEN S.S.R.	188,455	488,100	2,759,000	Ashkhabad 312,000
UZBEK S.S.R.	173,591	449,600	15,391,000	Tashkent 1,780,000
WHITE RUSSIAN S.S.R.	80,154	207,600	9,560,000	Minsk 1,262,000
KIRGIZ S.S.R.	76,641	198,500	3,529,000	Frunze 533,000
TADZHIK S.S.R.	55,251	143,100	3,801,000	Dushanbe 494,000
AZERBAIDZHAN S.S.R.	33,436	86,600	6,028,000	Baku 1,022,000
GEORGIAN S.S.R.	26,911	69,700	5,015,000	Tbilisi 1,066,000
LITHUANIAN S.S.R.	25,174	65,200	3,398,000	Vilnius 582,000
LATVIAN S.S.R.	24,595	63,700	2,521,000	Riga 835,000
ESTONIAN S.S.R.	17,413	45,100	1,466,000	Tallinn 430,000
MOLDAVIAN S.S.R.	13,012	33,700	3,947,000	Kishinev 503,000
ARMENIAN S.S.R.	11,506	29,800	3,031,000	Yerevan 1,019,000

Kirensk 10,000 .... L 4
Kirov 390,000 .... E 4
Kirovograd 237,000 .... D 5
Kirovskiy .... H 5
Kiselevsk 122,000 .... J 4
Kishinev 503,000 .... C 5
Kizel 46,264 .... F 4
Kizyl-Arvat 21,671 .... F 6
Klaipeda 176,000 .... B 4
Kokand 153,000 .... H 5
Kokchetav 103,000 .... H 4
Kolomna 147,000 .... D 4
Kolpashevo 24,911 .... J 4
Komsomol'sk 15,385 .... G 4
Komsomol'sk-na-Amure 264,000 .... O 4
Kondopoga 27,908 .... D 3
Kopeysk 146,000 .... G 4
Korf .... R 3
Korsakov 38,210 .... P 5
Koslan .... E 3
Kostroma 255,000 .... E 4
Kotlas 61,000 .... E 3
Kovel' 33,351 .... C 4
Kovrov 143,000 .... E 4
Kozhevnikovo .... L 2
Krasino .... F 2
Krasnodar 560,000 .... E 5
Krasnokamensk 51,000 .... M 4
Krasnokamsk 56,000 .... F 4
Krasnotur'insk 61,000 .... G 3
Krasnoural'sk 39,743 .... G 4
Krasnovodsk 53,000 .... F 5
Krasnoyarsk 796,000 .... K 4
Kremenchug 210,000 .... D 5
Krivoy Rog 650,000 .... D 5
Kudymkar 26,350 .... F 4
Kul'sary 16,427 .... F 5
Kulunda 15,264 .... H 4
Kulyab 55,000 .... H 6
Kum-Dag 10,000 .... F 6
Kungur 80,000 .... F 4
Kupino 20,799 .... H 4
Kurgan 310,000 .... G 4
Kurgan-Tyube 34,620 .... G 6
Kursk 375,000 .... D 4
Kushka .... G 6
Kustanay 165,000 .... G 4
Kutaisi 194,000 .... E 5
Kuybyshev 1,216,000 .... F 4
Kuybyshev 40,166 .... H 4
Kyakhta 15,316 .... L 4
Kyusyur .... N 2
Kyzyl 66,000 .... K 4
Kzyl-Orda 156,000 .... G 5
Labytnangi .... G 3
Lebedinyy .... N 4
Leninabad 130,000 .... G 5
Leninakan 207,000 .... E 5
Leningrad 4,073,000 .... D 4
Leningrad* 4,588,000 .... D 4
Leninogorsk 54,000 .... J 5
Leninsk .... G 5
Leninsk-Kuznetskiy 132,000 .... J 4
Leninskoye .... O 5
Lenkoran' 35,505 .... E 6
Lensk 16,758 .... M 3
Lesosibirsk .... K 4
Lesozavodsk 34,957 .... O 5
Liepāja 108,000 .... B 4
Lipetsk 396,000 .... E 4
Luga 31,905 .... D 4
Lutsk 137,000 .... C 4
L'vov 667,000 .... C 4
Lys'va 75,000 .... F 4
Magadan 121,000 .... P 4
Magdagachi 15,059 .... N 4
Magnitogorsk 406,000 .... G 4
Makhachkala 251,000 .... E 5
Makinsk 22,850 .... H 4
Mama .... M 4
Mariupol' 503,000 .... D 5
Markovo .... S 3
Mary (Merv) 74,000 .... G 6
Maykop 128,000 .... D 5
Mednogorsk 38,024 .... F 4
Medvezh'yegorsk 17,465 .... D 3
Mezen' .... E 3
Miass 150,000 .... G4
Michurinsk 101,000 .... E4
Millerovo 34,627 .... E5
Minsk 1,262,000 .... C4
Minsk* 1,276,000 .... C4
Minusinsk 56,000 .... K4
Mirnyy 23,826 .... M3
Mogilev 290,000 .... D4
Mogocha 17,884 .... N4
Molodechno 73,000 .... C4
Monchegorsk 51,000 .... C3
Moscow (cap.) 7,831,000 .... D4
Moscow* 8,011,000 .... D4
Motygino 10,000 .... K4
Mozyr' 73,000 .... C4
Murgab H6
Murmansk 381,000 .... D3
Muynak 12,000 .... F5
Mys Shmidta T3
Nadym H3
Nagornyy N4
Nakhichevan' 33,279 .... E6
Nakhodka 133,000 .... O5
Nal'chik 207,000 .... E5
Namangan 227,000 .... H5
Naminga M4
Nar'yan-Mar 16,864 .... F3
Naryn 21,098 .... H5
Navoi 84,000 .... G6
Nazyvayevsk 15,792 .... H4
Nebit-Dag 71,000 .... F6
Nefteyugansk 52,000 .... H3
Nel'kan O4
Nepa L4
Neryungri N4
Nevel'sk 20,726 .... P5
Nikolayev 440,000 .... D5
Nikolayevsk-na-Amure 30,082 .... P4
Nikol'skoye R4
Nizhneudinsk 39,743 .... K4
Nizhnevartovsk 109,000 .... H3
Nizhneyansk O3
Nizhniy Tagil 398,000 .... G4
Nordvik-Ugol'naya M2
Noril'sk 180,000 .... J3
Novaya Kazanka F5
Novgorod 186,000 .... D4
Novokazalinsk 34,815 .... G5
Novokuznetsk 541,000 .... J4
Novomoskovsk 147,000 .... E4
Novorossiysk 159,000 .... D5
Novosibirsk 1,312,000 .... J4
Novozybkov 34,433 .... D4
Novyy Port G3
Novyy Uzen' 18,073 .... F5
Novyy Urengoy H3
Nukus 109,000 .... G5

Topography

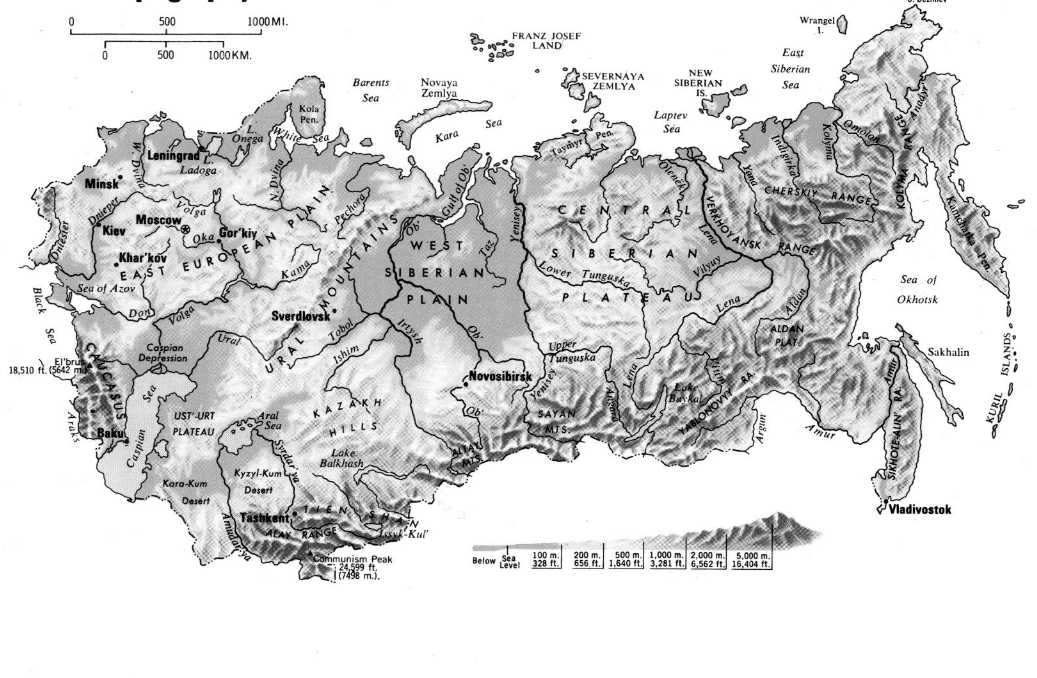

(continued)

Nyandoma 23,366 E3
Nyurba M3
Obluch'ye 17,000 N5
Odessa 1,046,000 D5
Okha 30,890 P4
Okhotsk P4
Olëkminsk N3
Olënek M3
Omsk 1,014,000 H4
Omsukchan Q3
Omutninsk 28,777 F4
Onega 25,047 D3
Ordzhonikidze 279,000 E5
Orel 305,000 D4
Orenburg 459,000 F4
Orotukan Q3
Orsk 247,000 F4
Osh 169,000 H5
Ostrogozhsk 29,921 D4
Oymyakon O3
Ozernovskiy Q4
Palana 2,735 R4
Panfilov 19,173 H5
Pärnu 51,000 C4
Partizansk 48,345 O5
Pavlodar 273,000 H4
Pechenga D2
Pechora 56,000 F3
Peleduy M4
Penza 483,000 E4
Perkatkin T2
Perm' 999,000 F4
Pervoural'sk 129,000 F4
Petropavlovsk 207,000 G4
Petropavlovsk-Kamchatskiy 215,000 R4
Petrovsk-Zabaykal'skiy 28,313 L4
Petrozavodsk 234,000 D3
Pevek S3
Pikol'skiy 32,862 G5
Pinsk 90,000 C4
Plastun O5
Podol'sk 202,000 D4
Pokrovsk N3
Poligus K3
Poltava 279,000 D5
Polyarnyy 15,321 D3
Ponoy E3
Poronaysk 23,610 P5
Prikumsk 35,768 E5
Progress 10,000 O5
Prokop'yevsk 266,000 J4
Provideniya T3
Przheval'sk 51,000 H5
Pskov 176,000 C4
Pushkin 90,000 C4
Raychikhinsk 25,157 N5
Riga 835,000 C4
Rostov-na-Donau 934,000 E5
Rovno 179,000 C4
Rubtsovsk 157,000 J4
Ruch'i E3
Rudnyy 110,000 G4
Ryazan' 453,000 E4
Rybach'ye H5
Rybinsk (Andropov) 239,000 D4
Rzhev 69,000 D4
Saksaul'sky F5
Salekhard 21,929 G3
Sal'sk 57,000 E5
Samagaltay K4
Samarkand 477,000 G6
Sangar N3
Saran' 55,000 H5
Saransk 263,000 E4
Sarapul 107,000 F4
Saratov 856,000 E4
Sarkand 18,296 J5
Segezha 28,810 D3
Semipalatinsk 283,000 H4
Serakhs G6
Serov 101,000 G4
Serpukhov 140,000 D4
Sevastopol' 301,000 D5
Severobaykal'sk M4
Severodvinsk 197,000 E3
Severo-Kuril'sk 8,000 Q4
Severoural'sk 29,880 G3
Severo-Yeniseysk K3
Shadrinsk 82,000 G4
Shakhtinsk 50,000 H5
Shakhty 209,000 E5
Shar'ya 25,788 E4
Shchuchinsk 40,432 H4
Shenkursk E3
Shevchenko 111,000 F5
Shilka 16,065 M4
Shimanovsk 16,880 N4
Shushenskoye 10,000 K4
Šiauliai 118,000 C4
Siktyakh N3
Simferopol' 302,000 D5
Skovorodino 10,000 N4
Slavgorod 32,908 H4
Slobodskoy 34,374 E4
Slyudyanka 20,639 L4
Smolensk 276,000 D4
Snezhnogorsk J3
Sochi 287,000 D5
Sokol 48,253 E4
Solikamsk 101,000 F3
Sortavala 22,188 C3
Sosnogorsk 24,688 F3
Sosnovo-Ozerskoye M4
Sovetskaya Gavan' 28,455 P5
Spassk-Dal'niy 53,000 O5
Srednekolymsk Q3
Sretensk 16,000 M4
Stalingrad (Volgograd) 929,000 E5
Stavropol' 258,000 E5
Stepanakert 30,293 E6
Sterlitamak 220,000 F4
Strezhevoy H3
Sukhana M3
Sukhumi 114,000 D5
Sumy 228,000 D4
Suntar M3
Surgut 107,000 H3
Susuman 12,000 P3
Sverdlovsk 1,211,000 F4
Svobodnyy 75,000 N4
Syktyvkar 171,000 F3
Syzran' 178,000 E4
Taganrog 276,000 D5
Takhiatash F5
Takhta-Bazar G6
Taksimo M4
Taldy-Kurgan 88,000 H5
Talgar 31,273 H5
Tallinn 430,000 C4
Tambey G2
Tambov 270,000 E4
Tara 22,358 H4
Tarko-Sale H3
Tartu 105,000 C4
Tashauz 84,000 F5
Tashkent 1,780,000 G5
Tatarsk 29,589 H4
Tavda G4
Tayshet 34,232 K4
Tazovskiy J3
Tbilisi 1,066,000 E5
Tedzhen 25,708 F6
Tekeli 29,846 H5
Temirtau 213,000 H4
Termez 57,000 G6
Ternopol' 144,000 C5
Tiksi N2
Tobol'sk 62,000 G4
Togliatti (Tol'yatti) 502,000 F4
Tokmak 59,000 H5
Tommot 8,000 N4
Tomsk 421,000 J4
Tot'ma E4
Troitsk 88,000 G4
Tselinograd 234,000 H4
Tskhinvali 30,311 E5
Tula 514,000 D4
Tulun 52,000 L4
Tura 3,528 L3
Turan K4
Turgay G5
Turkestan 67,000 G5
Tynda N4
Tyumen' 359,000 G4
Uelen T3
Ufa 969,000 F4
Uglegorsk 17,921 P5
Ukhta 87,000 F3
Ulan-Ude 300,000 L4
Ul'yanovsk 464,000 E4
Ural'sk 167,000 F4
Uray 17,385 G3
Urgench 100,000 G5
Ushtobe 24,484 H5
Usol'ye-Sibirskoye 103,000 L4
Ussuriysk 147,000 O5
Ust'-Ilimsk 69,000 L4
Ust'-Kamchatsk 10,000 R4
Ust'-Kamenogorsk 274,000 J5
Ust'-Kut 50,000 L4
Ust'-Kuyga O3
Ust'-Maya O3
Ust'-Nera P3
Ust'-Omchug P3
Ust'-Olenëk M2
Ust'-Ordynskiy 10,693 L4
Ust'-Port J2
Vanavara L3
Vanino 15,401 P5
Velikiye Luki 102,000 D4
Velikiy Ustyug 36,737 E3
Vel'sk 21,899 E3
Ventspils 40,467 B4
Verkhnevilyuysk N3
Verkniy At-Uryakh Q3
Verkhoyansk 2,000 N3
Vilnius (Vilna) 582,000 C4
Vilyuysk N3
Vinnitsa 314,000 C5
Vitebsk 297,000 D4
Vitimskiy M4
Vladimir 296,000 D4
Vladivostok 550,000 O5
Volgograd 929,000 E5
Volochanka K2
Vologda 237,000 E4
Vorkuta 100,000 G3
Voronezh 783,000 E4
Voroshilovgrad 463,000 E5
Vostochnyy O5
Votkinsk 90,000 F4
Voy-Vozh 10,000 F3
Vyazemskiy 18,365 O5
Vyborg 76,000 C3
Vyshniy Volochek 72,000 D4
Yakutsk 152,000 N3
Yalutorsk 25,426 G4
Yamsk Q4
Yaroslavl' 597,000 D4
Yartsevo J4
Yelets 112,000 D4
Yelizovo 10,000 Q4
Yeniseysk 19,880 K4
Yerevan 1,019,000 E6
Yermak 28,133 H4
Yermentau 15,276 H4
Yesil' 15,000 G4
Yessey L3
Yoshkar-Ola 201,000 E4
Yurga 78,000 J4
Yuzhno-Sakhalinsk 140,000 P5
Zabaykal'sk M5
Zakamensk 10,000 L4
Zaozernyy 27,216 K4
Zaporozh'ye 781,000 D5
Zarafshan G5
Zavitinsk 19,009 O4
Zaysan 10,000 J5
Zeya 16,684 N4
Zhatay O3
Zheleznogorsk-Ilimskiy 22,179 L4
Zhigalovo L4
Zhigansk N3
Zhitomir 244,000 C4
Zima 41,567 L4
Zlatoust 198,000 F4
Zyryanka Q3

OTHER FEATURES

Alakol' (lake) J5
Alazeya (riv.) Q3
Aldan (plat.) N4
Aldan (riv.) O3
Alexandra Land (isl.) E1
Altay (mts.) J5
Amga (riv.) O3
Amgun' (riv.) O4
Amudar'ya (riv.) G5
Amur (riv.) O4
Anabar (riv.) M2
Anadyr' (gulf) T3
Anadyr' (range) S3
Anadyr' (riv.) S3
Angara (riv.) K4
Aral (sea) F5
Arctic Ocean K1
Argun (riv.) M4
Arkticheskiy Institut (isls.) H2
Atrek (riv.) F6
Ayon (isl.) R2
Azov (sea) D5
Balkhash (lake) H5
Baltic (sea) B4
Barents (sea) D2
Baykal (lake) L4
Baykal (mts.) L4
Beloye (lake) D3
Belyy (isl.) G2
Bering (isl.) R4
Bering (sea) S4
Bering (strait) U3
Bet-Pak-Dala (des.) H5
Black (sea) D5
Bol'shevik (isl.) K2
Bol'shoy Lyakhovskiy (isl.) P2
Bolvanskiy Nos (cape) G2
Bratsk (res.) L4
Caspian (sea) F6
Caucasus (mts.) E5
Chelyuskin (cape) M2
Cherskiy (range) P3
Chu (riv.) H5
Chukchi (pen.) T3
Chukchi (sea) T2
Chulym (riv.) J4
Chuna (riv.) K4
Chunya (riv.) K3
Communism (peak) H6
Crimea (pen.) D5
Dezhnev (cape) T3
Dmitriya Lapteva (strait) O2
Dnieper (riv.) D5
Dniester (riv.) C5
Don (riv.) E5
Donets (riv.) D5
Dulgalakh (riv.) O3
Dvina, Northern (riv.) E3
Dvina, Western (riv.) C4
Dzhugdzhur (range) O4
East Siberian (sea) S2
Emba (riv.) F5
Etorofu (Iturup) (isl.) P5
Faddeyevskiy (isl.) P2
Finland (gulf) C4
Franz Josef Land (isls.) F1
George Land (isl.) E1
Gizhiga (bay) Q3
Govena (cape) R4
Graham Bell (isl.) G1
Gyda (pen.) H2
Gydan (Kolyma) (range) Q3
Hiiumaa (isl.) C4
Ili (riv.) H5
Imandra (lake) D3
Indigirka (riv.) P3
Irtysh (riv.) H4
Ishim (riv.) G4
Issyk-Kul' (lake) H5
Japan (sea) O6
Kakhovka (res.) D5
Kamchatka (pen.) Q4
Kanin (pen.) E3
Kanin Nos (cape) E3
Kara (sea) G2
Kara-Bogaz-Gol (gulf) F5
Karaginskiy (isl.) R4
Kara-Kum (canal) F6
Kara-Kum (des.) F5
Karskiye Vorota (strait) F2
Khanka (lake) O5
Kharasavey (cape) G2
Kheta (riv.) K2
Klyuchevskaya Sopka (vol.) Q4
Kola (pen.) D3
Kolguyev (isl.) E3
Kolyma (range) Q3
Kolyma (riv.) Q3
Komandorskiye (isls.) R4
Komsomolets (isl.) L1
Koni (pen.) Q4
Koryak (range) S3
Kotel'nyy (isl.) O2
Kotuy (riv.) L3
Kuma (riv.) E5
Kura (riv.) E6
Kuril (isls.) P5
Kuybyshev (res.) F4
Kyzyl-Kum (des.) G5
Ladoga (lake) D3
La Pérouse (str.) P5
Laptev (sea) N2
Lena (riv.) N3
Little Yenisey (riv.) K4
Long (str.) S2
Lopatka (cape) Q4
Lower Tunguska (riv.) K3
Lyatkhovskiye (isls.) O2
Mangyshlak (pen.) F5
Markha (riv.) M3
Matochkin Shar (str.) F2
Maya (riv.) O4
Mezen' (riv.) E3
Murgab (riv.) G6
Nadym (riv.) H3
Narodnaya (mt.) G3
Navarin (cape) T3
New Siberian (isls.) P2
Northern Dvina (riv.) E3
Novaya Sibir' (isl.) Q2
Novaya Zemlya (isls.) F2
Ob' (gulf) H3
Ob' (riv.) G3
October Revolution (isl.) L2
Oka (riv.) L4
Okhotsk (sea) P4
Olëkma (riv.) N4
Olënek (bay) N2
Olënek (riv.) M3
Oloy (range) R3
Olyutorskiy (cape) S4
Omolon (riv.) Q3
Omoloy (riv.) O3
Onega (lake) D3
Onega (riv.) D3
Ozernoy (cape) R4
Paramushir (isl.) Q4
Pechora (riv.) F3
Peipus (lake) C4
Penzhina (bay) R3
Pioner (isl.) J2
Pobeda (peak) J5
Pur (riv.) H3
Pyasina (riv.) J2
Riga (gulf) C4
Rybachiy (pen.) D2
Rybinsk (res.) D4
Saaremaa (isl.) B4
Sakhalin (gulf) P4
Sakhalin (isl.) P4
Sannikova (str.) O2
Sary Su (riv.) H5
Sayan (mts.) K4
Selemdzha (riv.) O4
Sergeya Kirova (isls.) J2
Severnaya Zemlya (isls.) L1
Shantar (isls.) O4
Shelagskiy (cape) R2
Shelekhov (gulf) Q4
Siberia (reg.) 38,524,000 M3
Sikhote-Alin' (range) O5
Stanovoy (range) N4
Stony Tunguska (riv.) K3
Syrdar'ya (riv.) G5
Tannu-Ola (range) K5
Tatar (str.) P4
Taymyr (lake) K2
Taymyr (pen.) L2
Taymyr (riv.) K2
Taz (riv.) J3
Tengiz (lake) G4
Terpeniye (cape) P5
Tobol (riv.) G4
Tsimlyansk (res.) E5
Tym (riv.) J3
Tyung (riv.) M3
Uda (riv.) Q4
Ulutau (mts.) G5
Ural (mts.) F4
Ural (riv.) F5
Urup (isl.) Q5
Ussuri (riv.) O5
Ust'-Urt (plat.) F5
Vakh (riv.) J3
Velikaya (riv.) S3
Verkhoyansk (range) N3
Vil'kitskogo (str.) L2
Vilyuy (range) M3
Vilyuy (res.) M3
Vilyuy (riv.) L3
Vitim (riv.) M4
Volga (riv.) E5
Western Dvina (riv.) C4
White (sea) D3
Wiese (isl.) H2
Wilczek Land (isl.) G1
Wrangel (isl.) T2
Yablonovyy (range) M4
Yamal (pen.) G2
Yana (riv.) O3
Yelizavety (cape) P4
Yenisey (riv.) J3
Zaysan (lake) J5
Zeya (riv.) N4
Zhelaniye (cape) H2

*City and suburbs.

Agriculture, Industry and Resources

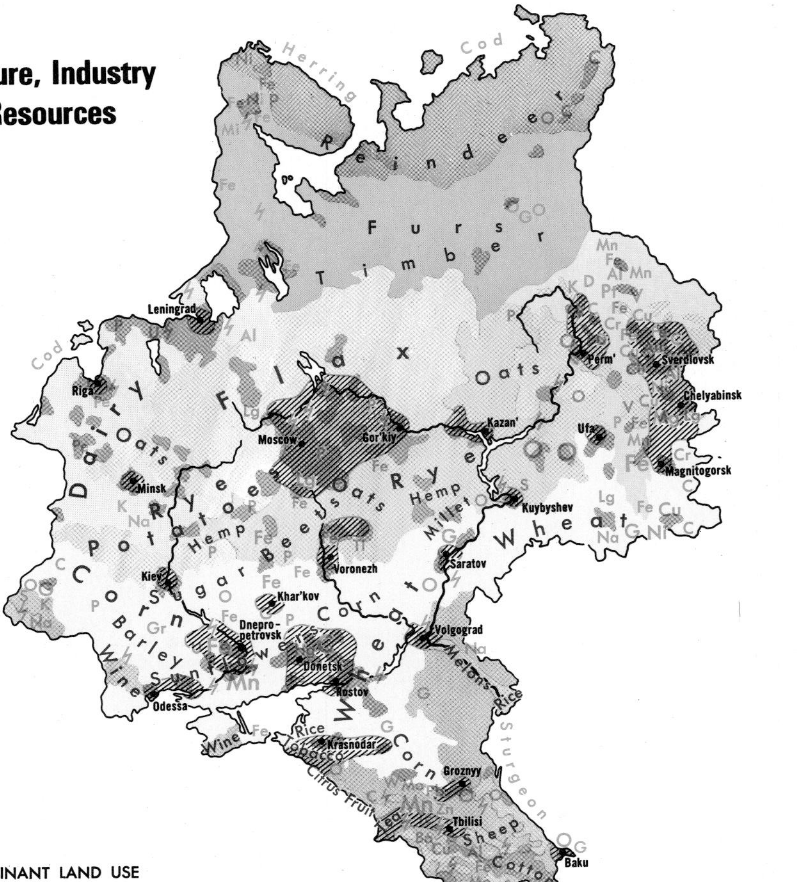

DOMINANT LAND USE

- Cereals (chiefly wheat, corn)
- Cereals (chiefly wheat, rye, oats)
- Dairy, Hogs, Livestock
- Livestock, Dairy
- Pasture Livestock
- Truck Farming, Potatoes, Vegetables, Dairy
- Flax, Dairy, Potatoes
- Cotton
- Vineyards, Orchards, Horticulture
- Sheep Herding, Limited Agriculture
- Forests
- Nonagricultural Land

MAJOR MINERAL OCCURRENCES

Ab	Asbestos	Hg	Mercury	Pb	Lead
Al	Bauxite	K	Potash	Pe	Peat
Au	Gold	Lg	Lignite	Pt	Platinum
Ba	Barite	Mg	Magnesium	S	Sulfur, Pyrites
C	Coal	Mi	Mica	Tc	Talc
Cr	Chromium	Mn	Manganese	Ti	Titanium
Cu	Copper	Mo	Molybdenum	U	Uranium
D	Diamonds	Na	Salt	V	Vanadium
Fe	Iron Ore	Ni	Nickel	W	Tungsten
G	Natural Gas	O	Petroleum	Zn	Zinc
Gr	Graphite	P	Phosphates		

Water Power — Major Industrial Areas

Agriculture, Industry and Resources

DOMINANT LAND USE

- Cereals (chiefly wheat, corn)
- Livestock, Dairy
- Truck Farming, Potatoes, Vegetables, Dairy
- Cotton
- Sheep Herding, Limited Agriculture
- Forests
- Nonagricultural Land

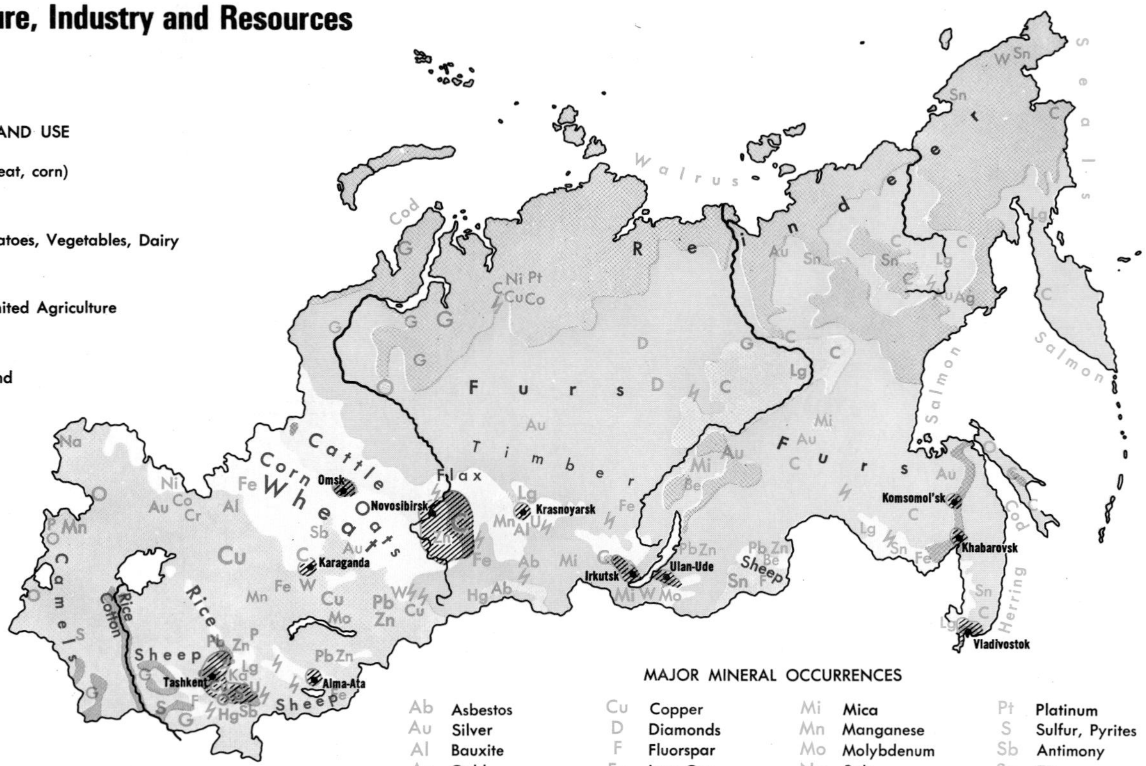

MAJOR MINERAL OCCURRENCES

Ab	Asbestos	Cu	Copper	Mi	Mica	Pt	Platinum
Au	Silver	D	Diamonds	Mn	Manganese	S	Sulfur, Pyrites
Al	Bauxite	F	Fluorspar	Mo	Molybdenum	Sb	Antimony
Au	Gold	Fe	Iron Ore	Na	Salt	Sn	Tin
Be	Beryl	G	Natural Gas	Ni	Nickel	U	Uranium
C	Coal	Hg	Mercury	O	Petroleum	W	Tungsten
Co	Cobalt	Ka	Kaolin	P	Phosphates	Zn	Zinc
Cr	Chromium	Lg	Lignite	Pb	Lead		

Water Power — Major Industrial Areas

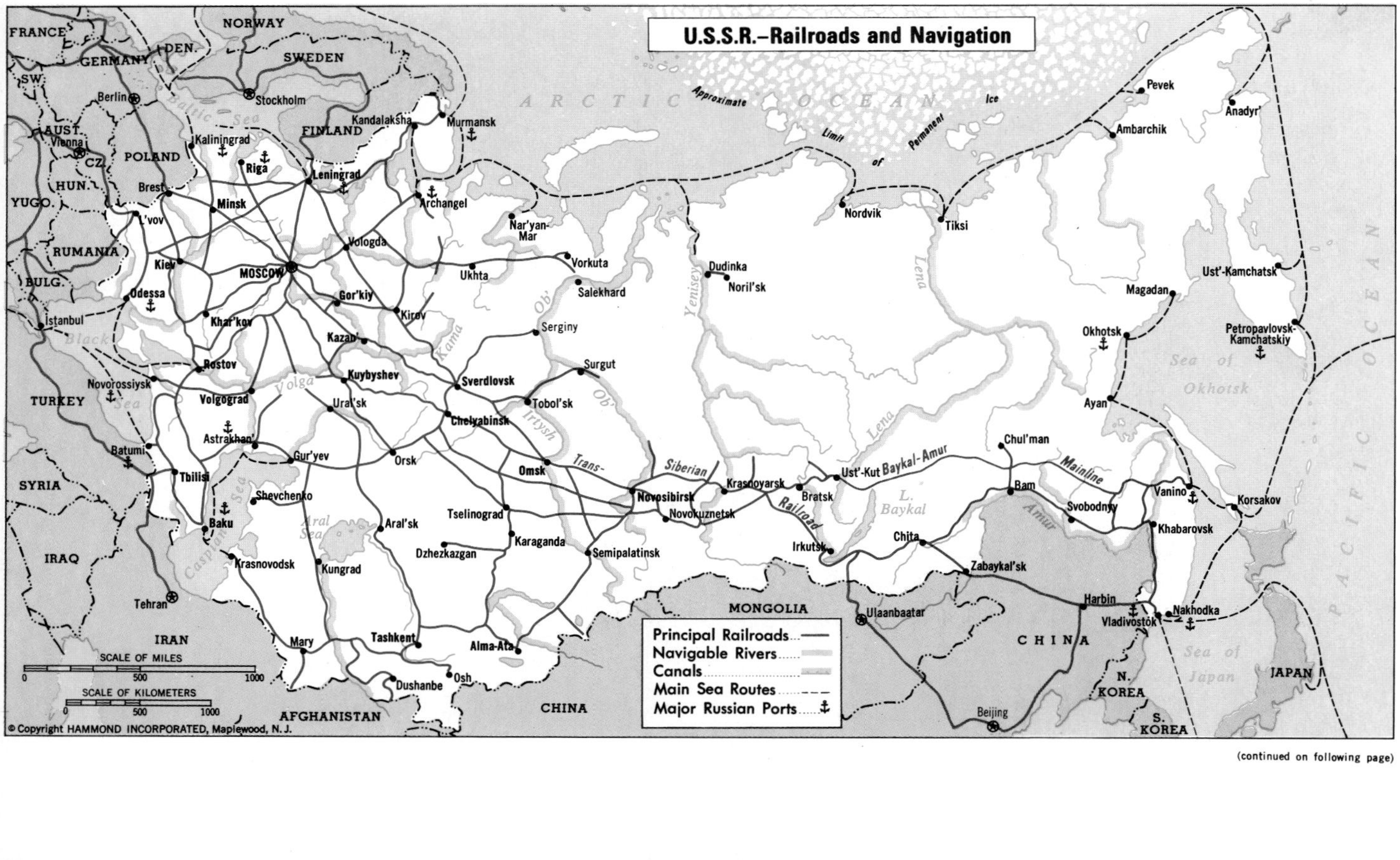

(continued on following page)

Union of Soviet Socialist Republics
European Part
CONIC PROJECTION
SCALE OF MILES
0 50 100 200 300
SCALE OF KILOMETERS
0 50 100 200 300
National Capitals
Capitals of Union Republics
Administrative Centers
International boundaries
Union Republic boundaries
A.S.S.R., Oblast, Kray boundaries
Autonomous Oblast boundaries
Autonomous Okrug boundaries
The government of the United States has not recognized the incorporation of Estonia, Latvia and Lithuania into the Soviet Union.
Administrative Divisions bear same names as their respective Capitals or Centers, except:
Abkhaz A.S.S.R. Sukhumi F6
Adygey Aut. Oblast Maykop F6
Adzhar A.S.S.R. Batumi F6
Bashkir A.S.S.R. Ufa J4
Chechen-Ingush A.S.S.R. Groznyy G6
Chuvash A.S.S.R. Cheboksary G3
Crimean Oblast Simferopol' D6
Dagestan A.S.S.R. Makhachkala G6
Kabardin-Balkar A.S.S.R. Nal'chik F6
Kalmuck A.S.S.R. Elista F5
Karachay-Cherkess Aut. Obl. Cherkessk F6
Karelian A.S.S.R. Petrozavodsk D2
Komi A.S.S.R. Syktyvkar H2
Komi-Permyak Aut. Okrug Kudymkar H3
Mari A.S.S.R. Yoshkar-Ola G3
Mordvinian A.S.S.R. Saransk G4
Nagorno-Karabakh Aut. Obl. Stepanakert G7
Nenets Aut. Okrug Nar'yan-Mar H1
North Ossetian A.S.S.R. Ordzhonikidze F6
South Ossetian Aut. Obl. Tskhinvali F6
Tatar A.S.S.R. Kazan' G3
Trans-Carpathian Oblast Uzhgorod B5
Udmurt A.S.S.R. Izhevsk H3
Volyn Oblast Lutsk C4
© Copyright HAMMOND INCORPORATED, Maplewood, N. J.

U.S.S.R. — EUROPEAN

UNION REPUBLICS

Armenian S.S.R. 3,031,000 F6
Azerbaidzhan S.S.R. 6,028,000 G6
Estonian S.S.R 1,466,000 C3
Georgian S.S.R. 5,015,000 F6
Latvian S.S.R 2,521,000 B3
Lithuanian S.S.R. 3,398,000 B3
Moldavian S.S.R. 3,947,000 C5
Russian S.F.S.R. 137,551,000 F3
Ukrainian S.S.R. 49,755,000 D5
White Russian S.S.R. 9,560,000 C4

INTERNAL DIVISIONS

Abkhaz A.S.S.R. 505,000 F6
Adygey Aut. Obl. 405,000 F6
Adzhar A.S.S.R. 354,000 F6
Bashkir A.S.S.R. 3,849,000 J4
Chechen-Ingush A.S.S.R. 1,154,000 G6
Chuvash A.S.S.R. 1,292,000 G3
Crimean Oblast 2,183,000 D6
Dagestan A.S.S.R. 1,628,000 G6
Kabardin-Balkar A.S.S.R. 674,000 F6
Kalmuck A.S.S.R. 294,000 F5
Karachay-Cherkess Aut. Obl. 368,000 F6
Karelian A.S.S.R. 736,000 D2
Komi A.S.S.R. 1,119,000 H2
Komi-Permyak Aut. Okr. 173,000 H3
Mari A.S.S.R. 703,000 G3
Mordvinian A.S.S.R. 991,000 G4
Nagorno-Karabakh Aut. Obl. 161,000 G7
Nakhichevan' A.S.S.R. 239,000 F7
Nenets Aut. Okr. 47,000 H1
North Ossetian A.S.S.R. 597,000 F6
South Ossetian Aut. Obl. 98,000 F6
Tatar A.S.S.R. 3,436,000 G3
Trans-Carpathian Oblast 1,155,000 B5
Udmurt A.S.S.R. 1,494,000 H3
Volyn Oblast 1,015,000 C4

CITIES and TOWNS

Abdulino 26,010 H4
Agdam 21,277 G6
Agryz 19,267 H3
Akhaltsikhe 18,972 F6
Akhtubinsk 43,466 G5
Akhty G6
Akhtyrka 41,354 E4
Akkerman (Belgorod-Dnestrovskiy) 32,928 D5
Alagir 18,161 F6
Alatyr' 43,499 G4
Alaverdi 21,311 F6
Aleksandriya 82,000 D5
Aleksandrovsk 18,286 J3
Alekseyevka 25,562 E4
Aleksin 67,000 E4
Ali-Bayramly 33,828 G7
Al'met'yevsk 110,000 H3
Alushta 22,016 D6
Amderma K1
Anapa 29,900 E6
Andropov 239,000 E3
Apatity 62,000 D1
Apsheronsk 32,867 F6
Archangel (Arkhangel'sk) 385,000 F2
Armavir 162,000 F5
Arzamas 93,000 F3
Astara G7
Astrakhan' 461,000 G5
Atkarsk 28,881 G4
Azov 75,000 E5
Bakhchisaray 15,912 D6
Baku 1,022,000 H6
Balakhna 36,542 F3
Balaklava D6
Balakovo 152,000 G4
Balashov 93,000 F4
Baltiysk 20,300 A4
Baranovichi 131,000 C4
Barysh 20,792 G4
Bataysk 90,000 E5
Batumi 123,000 F6
Belaya Tserkov' 151,000 C5
Belebey 32,460 H4
Belev 17,733 E4
Belgorod 240,000 E4
Belgorod-Dnestrovskiy 32,928 D5
Belomorsk 16,595 D2
Belorechensk 35,970 E6
Beloretsk 71,000 J4
Belozersk E3
Bel'tsy 125,000 C5
Belush'ya Guba H1
Bendery 101,000 C5
Berdichev 80,000 C5
Berdyansk 122,000 E5
Beregovo 27,308 B5
Berezniki 185,000 J3
Beslan 26,893 F6
Bezhetsk 30,030 E3
Birsk 29,607 J3
Bobrov 17,977 F4
Bobruysk 192,000 C4
Bologoye 33,949 D3
Bor 63,000 F3
Borislav 33,800 B5
Borisoglebsk 68,000 F4
Borisov 112,000 C4
Borovichi 60,000 D3
Brest 177,000 B4
Brezhnev 301,000 H3
Bryansk 394,000 D4
Bugul'ma 80,000 H4
Buguruslan 54,000 H4
Buturlinovka 21,643 F4
Buy 29,946 F3
Buynaksk 37,946 G6
Buzuluk 76,000 H4
Bykhov 17,371 C4
Cēsis 17,696 C3
Chadyr-Lunga 20,474 C5
Chapayevsk 85,000 G4
Chaykovskiy 48,034 H3
Cheboksary 308,000 G3
Cherepovets 266,000 E3
Cherkassy 228,000 D5
Cherkessk 91,000 F6
Chernigov 238,000 D4
Chernovtsy 219,000 C5
Chernushka 21,106 J3
Chervonograd 55,000 B4
Chiatura 25,474 F6
Chistopol' 64,000 H3
Chortkov 19,183 B5
Chudovo D3
Chusovoy 56,000 J3
Danilov 17,500 E3
Dankov 20,030 E4
Daugavpils 116,000 C3
Davlekanovo 20,123 H4
Derbent 70,000 G6
Dimitrovgrad 106,000 G4
Dneprodzerzhinsk 250,000 D5
Dnepropetrovsk 1,066,000 D5
Dobrush 16,809 D4
Dobryanka 18,349 J3
Donetsk 1,021,000 E5
Drogobych 66,000 B5
Dubna 55,000 E3
Dubna E4
Dubno 25,442 C4
Dvinsk (Daugavpils) 116,000 C3
Dyat'kovo 26,825 D4
Dzerzhinsk 257,000 F3
Dzhankoy 43,459 D5
Dzhul'fa G7
Echmiadzin 31,819 F6
Elektrostal' 139,000 E3
Elista 70,000 F5
El'ton G5
Engel's 161,000 G4
Fastov 51,000 C4
Feodosiya 76,000 D5
Frolovo 33,398 F5
Furmanov 40,155 F3
Gagra 23,025 E6
Galich 19,374 F3
Gandzhe 232,000 G6
Gatchina 75,000 C3
Gay 28,250 J4
Gaysin 23,741 C5
Gdov C3
Gelendzhik 29,086 E6
Genichesk 20,031 E5
Georgiu-Dezh 52,000 E4
Glazov 81,000 H3
Glubokoye C3
Glukhov 27,096 D4
Gomel' 383,000 D4
Gori 56,000 F6
Gorki 22,117 D4
Gor'kiy 1,344,000 F3
Gorlovka 336,000 E5
Gorodets 34,229 F3
Gremikha E1
Gremyachinsk 29,975 J3
Grodno 195,000 B4
Groznyy 375,000 G6
Gryazi 41,292 F4
Gubakha 33,243 J3
Gubkin 65,000 E4
Gudauta F6
Gudermes 32,445 G6
Gukovo 68,000 F5
Gus'-Khrustal'nyy 72,000 F3
Imishli 17,839 G7
Inta 51,000 K1
Inza 19,060 G4
Ishimbay 57,000 J4
Ivano-Frankovsk 150,000 B5
Ivanovo 465,000 E3
Izberbash 17,299 G6
Izhevsk 549,000 H3
Izmail 83,000 C5
Izyum 61,000 E5
Jēkabpils 22,440 C3
Jelgava 68,000 B3
Jurmala 61,000 B3
Kadiyevka (Stakhanov) 108,000 E5
Kafan 29,916 G7
Kagul 26,249 C5
Kakhovka 28,472 D5
Kalach 18,475 F4
Kalach-na-Donu 20,795 F5
Kalinin 412,000 E3
Kaliningrad, Kaliningrad 355,000 B4
Kaliningrad, Moscow Oblast 133,000 E3
Kalinkovichi 23,918 C4
Kaluga 265,000 E4
Kalush 60,000 B5
Kamenets-Podol'skiy 81,000 C5
Kamenka 30,067 F4
Kamensk-Shakhtinskiy 72,000 F5
Kamyshin 112,000 F4
Kanash 40,682 G3
Kandalaksha 42,656 D1
Kapsukas 28,763 B4
Karachayevsk F6
Karachev 15,972 E4
Kashin 17,678 E3
Kasimov 33,066 F4
Kaspiysk 38,990 G6
Kaunas 370,000 B4
Kazan' 993,000 G3
Kazatin 26,649 C5
Kem' 21,025 D2
Kerch' 157,000 E5
Keret' D1
Khachmas 22,313 G6
Khadyzhensk 17,856 E6
Khar'kov 1,444,000 E5
Khasavyurt 65,000 G6
Khashuri 24,469 F6
Kherson 319,000 D5
Khmel'nitskiy 172,000 C5
Khotin 10,319 C5
Khust 23,810 B5
Khvalynsk 16,249 G4
Kiev 2,144,000 D4
Kiliya 24,276 C5
Kimovsk 44,490 E4
Kimry 58,000 E3
Kinel' 39,373 H4
Kineshma 101,000 F3
Kirishi 27,252 D3
Kirov, Kaluga 29,355 D4
Kirov, Kirov 390,000 G3
Kirovakan 146,000 G6
Kirovo-Chepetsk 71,000 H3
Kirovograd 237,000 D5
Kirovsk 38,484 D1
Kirsanov 21,795 F4
Kishinev 503,000 C5
Kislovodsk 101,000 F6
Kizel 46,264 J3
Kizlyar 29,745 G6
Klaipeda 176,000 B3
Klintsy 67,000 D4
Kobrin 24,935 B4
Kobuleti 18,051 F6
Kohtla-Järve 73,000 C3
Kolomiya 52,000 B5
Kolomna 147,000 E4
Kolpino 114,000 D3
Kommunarsk 120,000 E5
Komrat 21,369 C5
Komsomol'skiy 17,078 K1
Kondopoga 27,908 D2
Königsberg (Kaliningrad) 355,000 B4
Konotop 82,000 D4
Konstantinovka 112,000 E5
Korenovsk 26,323 E5
Korosten' 65,000 C4
Korostyshev 21,153 C4
Koryazhma 33,230 G2
Kostopol' 17,548 C4
Kostroma 255,000 F3
Kotel'nich 29,196 G3
Kotel'nikovo 19,063 F5
Kotlas 61,000 G2
Kotovo 20,553 G4
Kotovsk, Odessa 36,463 C5
Kotovsk, Tambov 33,347 F4
Kovel' 33,351 C4
Kovrov 143,000 F3
Kovylkino 17,300 F4
Kramatorsk 178,000 E5
Krasnoarmeysk 60,000 G4
Krasnodar 560,000 E6
Krasnograd 18,386 E5
Krasnokamsk 56,000 H3
Krasnoslobodsk 17,749 G5
Krasnovishersk J2
Krasnyy Kut 17,087 G4

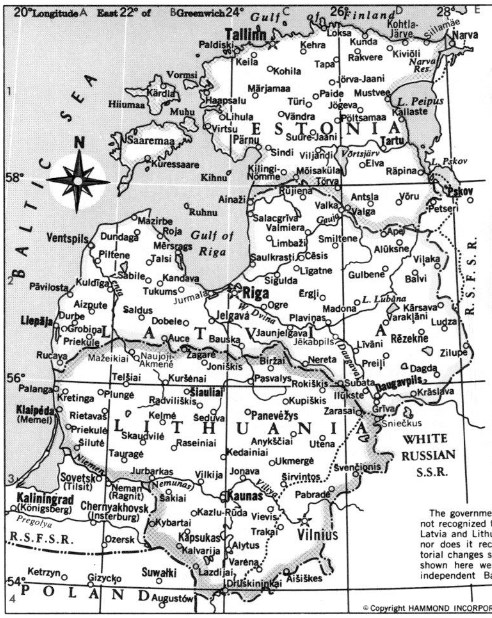

The government of the United States has not recognized the incorporation of Estonia, Latvia and Lithuania into the Soviet Union, nor does it recognize other post-war territorial changes shown on this map. The flags shown here were the official flags of the independent Baltic States prior to 1939.

The Baltic States

SCALE OF MILES 0 25 50 75 100
SCALE OF KILOMETERS 0 30 60 90 120 150 180

Capitals ☆
International Boundaries —·—
Union Republic Boundaries —·—
Prewar boundaries of the Baltic States where divergent from present boundaries ....

BALTIC STATES

Alytus 55,000 C 3
Biržai 11,400 C 2
Cēsis 17,696 C 2
Daugava (Western Dvina) (riv.) D 2
Daugavpils 127,000 D 3
Dobele 10,100 B 2
Druskininkai 11,200 C 3
Dvina, Western (riv.) C 2
Finland (gulf) D 1
Gauja (riv.) C 2
Haapsalu 11,483 B 1
Hiiumaa (isl.) B 1
Jēkabpils 22,440 C 2
Jelgava 68,000 B 2
Jonava 14,400 C 3
Jūrmala 61,000 B 2
Kapsukas 28,763 B 3
Kaunas 423,000 C 3
Kedainiai 19,677 C 3
Kihnu (isl.) B 1
Kingisepp (Kuressaare) 12,140 B 1
Kiviõli 11,153 D 1
Klaipeda 204,000 A 3
Kohtla-Järve 73,000 D 1
Kretinga 13,000 A 3
Kuldīga 12,300 A 2
Kuressaare 12,140 B 1
Kuršenai 11,500 B 2
Liepāja 114,000 A 2
Lubāna (lake) D 2
Mažeikiai 13,400 A 2
Memel (Klaipeda) 204,000 A 3
Muhu (isl.) B 1
Narva 73,000 E 1
Naujoji-Akmene 10,200 B 2
Niemen (riv.) A 3
Ogre 15,708 C 2
Panevežys 126,000 C 3
Pärnu 51,000 C 1
Peipus (lake) D 1
Plunge 13,600 B 3
Radviliškis 16,841 B 3
Rakvere 17,891 D 1
Rēzekne 30,803 D 2
Riga (cap.), Latvia 915,000 C 2
Riga (gulf) B 2
Saaremaa (isl.) B 1
Saldus 10,000 B 2
Šiauliai 145,000 B 3
Sillamäe 13,505 D 1
Šilute 12,400 A 3
Tallinn (cap.), Estonia 482,000 C 1
Tapa 10,037 C 1
Tartu 114,000 D 1
Taurage 19,461 B 3
Telšiai 20,220 B 2
Tukums 14,800 B 2
Ukmerge 21,663 C 3
Utena 13,300 C 3
Valga 16,795 D 2
Valmiera 20,331 C 2
Venta (riv.) B 2
Ventspils 40,467 A 2
Viliya (riv.) C 3
Viljandi 20,814 C 1
Vilnius (Vilna) (cap.), Lithuania 582,000 C 3
Vormsi (isl.) B 1
Võrtsjärv (lake) D 1
Võru 15,398 D 2
Western Dvina (riv.) C 2

Krasnyy Luch 106,000 E5
Krasnyy Sulin 41,684 F5
Kremenchug 210,000 D5
Krichev 25,682 D4
Krivoy Rog 650,000 D5
Krolevets 18,307 D4
Kronshtadt 39,477 C3
Kropotkin 70,000 F5
Krymsk 41,430 E5
Kuba 18,871 G6
Kudymkar 26,350 H3
Kulebaki 46,252 F3
Kumertau 52,000 J4
Kunda C3
Kungur 80,000 J3
Kupyansk 30,055 E5
Kuressaare 12,140 B3
Kursk 375,000 E4
Kutaisi 194,000 F6
Kuvandyk 22,914 J4
Kuybyshev 1,216,000 H4
Kuznetsk 94,000 G4
Kuzomen' E1
Labinsk 54,000 F6
Lakhdenpokh'ya C2
Lebedin 29,240 D4
Leninakan 207,000 F6
Leningrad 4,073,000 C3
Leningrad* 4,588,000 C3
Leninogorsk 54,000 H4
Lenkoran' 35,505 G7
L'gov 25,110 E4
Lida 66,000 C4
Liepāja 108,000 B3
Likhoslavl' E3
Lipetsk 396,000 E4
Lisichansk 119,000 E5
Livny 37,290 E4
Lodeynoye Pole 19,632 D2
Lozovaya 53,000 E5
Lubny 54,000 D4
Luga 31,905 C3
Lutsk 137,000 B4
L'vov (Lwów) 667,000 B5
Lys'va 75,000 J3
Lyubertsy 160,000 E3
Lyubotin 33,324 E4
Lyudinovo 33,871 D4
Makeyevka 436,000 E5
Makhachkala 251,000 G6
Makharadze 21,679 F6
Malaya Vishera 15,381 D3
Malgobek 20,548 F6
Manturovo 21,510 F3
Marganets 50,000 E5
Mariupol' 503,000 E5
Marks 17,132 G4
Maykop 128,000 F6
Mednogorsk 38,024 J4
Medvezh'yegorsk 17,465 D2
Melenki 18,545 F3
Meleuz 24,851 J4
Melitopol' 161,000 D5
Memel (Klaipeda) 176,000 B3
Merefa 29,985 E5
Mezen' F1
Michurinsk 101,000 F4
Mikhaylovka 58,000 F4
Millerovo 34,627 F5
Mineral'nye Vody 67,000 F6
Mingechaur 60,000 G6
Minsk 1,262,000 C4
Minsk* 1,276,000 C4
Mirgorod 28,407 D5
Mogilev 290,000 C4
Mogilev-Podol'skiy 26,051 C5
Molodechno 73,000 C4
Molotov (Perm') 999,000 J3
Monchegorsk 51,000 D1
Morshansk 44,245 F4
Moscow (Moskva) (cap.) 7,831,000 E3
Moscow* 8,011,000 E3
Mozhaysk 20,321 E3
Mozhga 38,930 H3
Mozyr' 73,000 C4
Mtsensk 27,833 E4
Mukachevo 72,000 B5
Murmansk 381,000 D1
Murom 114,000 F3
Mytishchi 141,000 E3
Nakhichevan' 33,279 F7
Nal'chik 207,000 F6
Narva 73,000 C3
Nar'yan-Mar 16,864 H1
Neftekamsk 70,000 J3
Nelidovo 29,813 D3
Nerekhta 25,722 F3
Nevel' 17,804 D3
Nevinnomyssk 104,000 F6
Nezhin 70,000 D4
Nikel' 21,299 C1
Nikolayev 440,000 D5
Nikol'sk 20,740 G4
Nikopol' 146,000 D5
Nizhnekamsk 134,000 H3
Nizhniy Lomov 17,460 F4
Nizhniy Novgorod (Gor'kiy) 1,344,000 F3
Nosovka 19,430 D4
Novaya Kakhovka 52,000 D5
Novgorod 186,000 D3
Novgorod-Severskiy D4
Novoanninskiy 20,461 F4
Novocherkassk 183,000 F5
Novograd-Volynskiy 41,194 C4
Novogrudok 19,374 C4
Novokuybyshevsk 109,000 G4
Novomoskovsk 147,000 E4
Novopolotsk 67,000 C3
Novorossiysk 159,000 E6
Novoshakhtinsk 104,000 E5
Novotroitsk 95,000 J4
Novoukrainka 19,554 D5
Novouzensk G4
Novovolynsk 41,187 B4
Novovyatsk 26,408 G3
Novozybkov 34,433 D4
Nurlat 17,533 H4
Nyandoma 23,366 F2
Nytva 17,491 H3
Nyuvchim H2
Obninsk 73,000 E3
Ochamchira 18,718 F6
Odessa 1,046,000 D5
Oktyabr'sk 33,981 G4
Oktyabr'skiy 88,000 H4
Okulovka 19,194 D3
Olenegorsk 21,485 D1
Olonets D2
Omutninsk 28,777 H3
Onega 25,047 E2
Ordzhonikidze 279,000 F6
Orel 305,000 E4
Orenburg 459,000 J4
Orgeyev 25,798 C5
Orsha 112,000 C4
Orsk 247,000 J4
Osa 15,038 J3
Osipenko (Berdyansk) 122,000 E5
Osipovichi 19,705 C4
Ostashkov 23,419 D3
Ostrogozhsk 29,921 E4
Ostrov 22,369 C3
Otradnyy 44,426 H4
Panevežys 102,000 B3
Pärnu 51,000 C3
Pavlograd 107,000 E5
Pavlovo 68,000 F3
Pechenga D1
Pechora 56,000 J1
Penza 483,000 G4
Perm' 999,000 J3
Pervomaysk 72,000 D5
Petrokrepost' D3
Petrovsk 30,953 G4
Petrozavodsk 234,000 D2
Petsamo (Pechenga) D1
Pinsk 90,000 C4
Podol'sk 202,000 E3
Podporozh'ye 21,545 D2
Pokhvistnevo 26,125 H4
Polonnoye 22,484 C4
Polotsk 71,000 C3
Poltava 279,000 D5
Polyarnyy 15,321 D1
Ponoy F1
Poti 45,979 F6
Povenets E2
Povorino 20,591 F4
Prikumsk 35,768 F6
Priluki 65,000 D4
Primorsk C2
Primorsko-Akhtarsk 25,981 E5
Priozersk 16,652 D2
Privolzhskiy 23,041 G4
Priyutovo 21,051 H4
Prokhladnyy 40,074 F6
Pskov 176,000 C3
Pugachev 33,963 G4
Pushkin 90,000 C3
Pyatigorsk 110,000 F6
Rabocheostrovsk D1
Rakhov B5
Rakvere 17,891 C3
Rasskazovo 40,038 F4
Razdan 26,833 G6
Rechitsa 60,000 C4
Reni 19,625 C5
Revel (Tallinn) 430,000 B3
Rēzekne 30,803 C3
Riga 835,000 B3
Romny 53,000 D4
Roslavl' 56,000 D4
Rossosh' 36,438 E4
Rostov 30,815 E3
Rostov-na-Donu 934,000 F5
Rovno 179,000 C4
Rtishchevo 37,146 F4
Rubezhnoye 66,000 E5
Rustavi 129,000 G6
Ruzayevka 41,084 F4
Ryazan' 453,000 E4
Ryazhsk 25,425 F4
Rybinsk (Andropov) 239,000 E3
Rybnitsa 32,266 C5
Rzhev 69,000 D3
Safonovo 53,000 D3
Saki 24,208 D5
Salavat 137,000 H4
Sal'sk 57,000 F5
Sal'yany 24,228 G7
Samara (Kuybyshev) 1,216,000 H4
Sambor 29,253 B5
Saransk 263,000 G4
Sarapul 107,000 H3
Saratov 856,000 G4
Sasovo 27,228 F4
Segezha 28,810 D2
Semenov 23,633 F3
Semiluki 18,221 E4
Sengiley G4
Serdobol (Sortavala) 22,188 D2
Serdobsk 33,783 F4
Sergach 22,509 F3
Serpukhov 140,000 E4
Sevastopol' 301,000 D6
Severodonetsk 113,000 E5
Severodvinsk 197,000 E2
Severomorsk 50,000 D1
Shakhty 209,000 F5
Shakhun'ya 20,009 G3
Shar'ya 25,788 G3
Shchekino 70,000 E4
Shchigry 17,133 E4
Sheki 43,158 G6
Shemakha 17,986 G6
Shepetovka 38,707 C4
Shostka 82,000 D4
Shpola 19,806 D5
Shumerlya 33,816 G3
Shuya 72,000 F3
Šiauliai 118,000 B3
Sibay 37,656 J4
Simferopol' 302,000 D6
Skadovsk D5
Skopin 24,429 F4
Slantsy 41,146 C3
Slavuta 25,573 C4
Slavyansk 140,000 E5
Slavyansk-na-Kubani 54,000 E5
Slobodskoy 34,374 H3
Slonim 30,279 B4
Slutsk 35,609 C4
Smela 62,000 D5
Smolensk 276,000 D4
Sochi 287,000 E6
Sokol 48,243 F3
Soligorsk 65,000 C4
Solikamsk 101,000 J3
Sol'-Iletsk 22,227 J4
Sorochinsk 23,235 H4
Soroki 21,924 C5
Sortavala 22,188 D2
Sosnogorsk 24,688 H2
Sovetsk (Tilsit) 38,456 B4
Sovetsk 17,027 G3
Stakhanov 108,000 E5
Stalingrad (Volgograd) 929,000 F5
Staraya Russa 34,577 D3
Staryy Oskol 115,000 E4
Stavropol' 258,000 F5
Stepanakert 30,293 G7
Sterlitamak 220,000 J4
Stupino 70,000 E4
Sudak E6
Sukhumi 114,000 F6
Sumgait 190,000 G6
Sumy 228,000 E4
Svetlogorsk 55,000 C4
Svetlograd 40,265 F5
Syktyvkar 171,000 H2
Syzran' 178,000 G4
Taganrog 276,000 E5
Tallinn 430,000 B3
Tambov 270,000 F4
Tartu 105,000 C3
Taurage 19,461 B3
Tbilisi 1,066,000 F6
Telavi 21,179 G6
Telšiai 20,220 B3
Temryuk 23,172 E5
Ternopol' 144,000 C5
Teykovo 41,607 E3
Tiflis (Tbilisi) 1,066,000 F6
Tighina (Bendery) 101,000 C5
Tikhoretsk 64,000 F5
Tikhvin 59,000 D3
Tilsit (Sovetsk) 38,456 B4
Timashevsk 29,055 E5
Tiraspol' 139,000 D5
Togliatti (Tol'yatti) 502,000 G4
Tokmak 59,000 E5
Toropets 16,863 D3
Torzhok 45,443 D3
Troitsko-Pechorsk J2
Tskhinvali 30,311 F6
Tuapse 60,000 E6
Tula 514,000 E4
Tutayev 16,839 E3
Tuymazy 37,021 H4
Tver (Kalinin) 412,000 E3
Tyrnyauz 18,253 F6
Uchaly 21,808 J4
Ufa 969,000 J4
Uglich 35,463 E3
Ukmerge 21,663 C3
Ul'yanovsk 464,000 G4
Uman' 79,000 D5
Unecha 21,749 D4
Ungeny 17,228 C5
Uryupinsk 38,192 F4
Usinsk J1
Usman' 20,150 E4
Uvarovo 24,946 F4
Uzhgorod 91,000 B5
Uzlovaya 65,000 E4
Valga 16,795 C3
Valmiera 20,331 C3
Valuyki 29,093 E4
Vasil'kov 26,741 D4
Velikiye Luki 102,000 D3
Velikiy Ustyug 36,737 F2
Vel'sk 21,899 F2
Ventspils 40,467 B3
Vereshchagino 23,585 H3
Vichuga 52,000 F3
Viipuri (Vyborg) 76,000 C2
Vileyka C4
Vilnius (Vilna) 582,000 C4
Vinnitsa 314,000 C5
Vinogradov 20,580 B5
Vitebsk 297,000 C3
Vladimir 296,000 F3
Vladimir-Volynskiy 28,412 B4
Volgodonsk 91,000 F5
Volgograd 929,000 F5
Volkhov 47,025 D3
Volkovysk 28,266 B4
Vologda 237,000 F3
Vol'sk 66,000 G4
Volzhsk 52,000 G3
Volzhskiy 209,000 G5
Vorkuta 100,000 K1
Voronezh 783,000 E4
Voroshilovgrad 463,000 E5
Voskresensk 76,000 E3
Votkinsk 90,000 H3
Voznesensk 36,457 D5
Vyatskiye Polyany 32,729 H3
Vyaz'ma 52,000 D3
Vyborg 76,000 C2
Vyksa 54,000 F3
Vyshniy Volochek 72,000 D3
Yalta 80,000 D6
Yanaul 20,115 J3
Yaroslavl' 597,000 E3
Yartsevo 36,662 D3
Yefremov 53,000 E4
Yelabuga 31,728 H3
Yelets 112,000 E4
Yenakiyevo 114,000 E5
Yerevan 1,019,000 F6
Yershov 21,731 G4
Yessentuki 78,000 F6
Yevlakh 29,462 G6
Yevpatoria 93,000 D5
Yeysk 71,000 E5
Yoshkar-Ola 201,000 G3
Yur'yevets 20,144 F3
Zagorsk 107,000 E3
Zapolyarnyy 22,084 D1
Zaporozh'ye 781,000 E5
Zelenodol'sk 85,000 G3
Zelenokumsk 29,691 F6
Zernograd 20,324 F5
Zheleznodorozhnyy 76,000 H2
Zheleznogorsk 65,000 E4
Zhigulevsk 52,130 G4
Zhitomir 244,000 C4
Zhlobin 25,359 D4
Zhmerinka 36,195 C5
Zhodino 22,083 C4
Zhovtnevoye 31,102 D5
Znamenka 27,393 D5
Zolotonosha 27,639 D5
Zugdidi 39,896 F6
Zuyevka 17,001 H3

OTHER FEATURES

Apsheron (pen.) H6
Araks (riv.) G7
Azov (sea) E5
Baltic (sea) B3
Barents (sea) E1
Belaya (riv.) H3
Beloye (lake) E2
Black (sea) D6
Bug (riv.) B4
Bug (riv.) D5
Caspian (sea) G6
Caucasus (mts.) F6
Crimea (pen.) D5
Desna (riv.) D4
Dnieper (riv.) D5
Dniester (riv.) C5
Don (riv.) F5
Donets (riv.) E5
Dvina (bay) E2
Dvina, Northern (riv.) F2
Dvina, Western (riv.) C3
Dykh-Tau (mt.) F6
El'brus (mt.) F6
Finland (gulf) C3
Hiiumaa (isl.) B3
Il'men' (lake) D3
Imandra (lake) D1
Kakhovka (res.) D5
Kama (riv.) H2
Kandalaksha (gulf) D1
Kanin (pen.) G1
Kara (sea) K1
Karskiye Vorota (str.) J1
Kazbek (mt.) F6
Khoper (riv.) F4
Kola (pen.) E1
Kolguyev (isl.) G1
Kuban' (riv.) E5
Kura (riv.) G6
Kuybyshev (res.) G4
Ladoga (lake) D2
Lapland (reg.) D1
Mezen' (riv.) G1
Moksha (riv.) F4
Narodnaya (mt.) J1
Niemen (riv.) B4
Novaya Zemlya (isls.) H1
Oka (riv.) F4
Onega (bay) E2
Onega (lake) E2
Onega (riv.) E2
Pechora (riv.) H1
Peipus (lake) C3
Pripet (marshes) C4
Pripyat' (riv.) C4
Prut (riv.) C5
Riga (gulf) B3
Rybachiy (pen.) D1
Rybinsk (res.) E3
Saaremaa (isl.) B3
Samara (riv.) H4
Sevan (lake) G6
Seym (riv.) D4
Sura (riv.) G4
Svir' (riv.) D2
Timan (ridge) G1
Tsil'ma (riv.) H1
Tsimlyansk (res.) F5
Tuloma (riv.) D1
Ural (mts.) J2
Ural (riv.) J4
Usa (riv.) K1
Valday (hills) D3
Vaygach (isl.) K1
Velikaya (riv.) C3
Volga (riv.) G5
Volga-Don (canal) F5
Volgograd (res.) G5
Volkhov (riv.) D3
Vorskla (riv.) E4
Vyatka (riv.) H3
Vychegda (riv.) G2
Vyg (lake) E2
White (sea) E1
Yamantau (mt.) J4
Yugorskiy (pen.) K1

*City and suburbs.

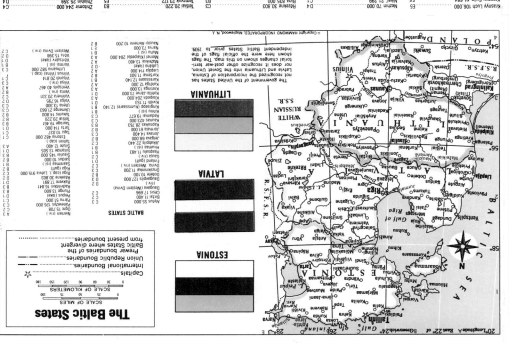

ALGERIA
AREA 919,591 sq. mi. (2,381,740 sq. km.)
POPULATION 17,422,000
CAPITAL Algiers
LARGEST CITY Algiers
HIGHEST POINT Tahat 9,852 ft. (3,003 m.)
MONETARY UNIT Algerian dinar
MAJOR LANGUAGES Arabic, Berber, French
MAJOR RELIGION Islam

ANGOLA
AREA 481,351 sq. mi. (1,246,700 sq. km.)
POPULATION 7,078,000
CAPITAL Luanda
LARGEST CITY Luanda
HIGHEST POINT Mt. Moco 8,593 ft. (2,620 m.)
MONETARY UNIT kwanza
MAJOR LANGUAGES Mbundu, Kongo, Lunda, Portuguese
MAJOR RELIGIONS Tribal religions, Roman Catholicism

BENIN
AREA 43,483 sq. mi. (112,620 sq. km.)
POPULATION 3,338,240
CAPITAL Porto-Novo
LARGEST CITY Cotonou
HIGHEST POINT Atakora Mts. 2,083 ft. (635 m.)
MONETARY UNIT CFA franc
MAJOR LANGUAGES Fon, Somba, Yoruba, Bariba, French, Mina, Dendi
MAJOR RELIGIONS Tribal religions, Islam, Roman Catholicism

BOTSWANA
AREA 224,764 sq. mi. (582,139 sq. km.)
POPULATION 819,000
CAPITAL Gaborone
LARGEST CITY Francistown
HIGHEST POINT Tsodilo Hill 5,922 ft. (1,805 m.)
MONETARY UNIT pula
MAJOR LANGUAGES Setswana, Shona, Bushman, English, Afrikaans
MAJOR RELIGIONS Tribal religions, Protestantism

BURKINA FASO
AREA 105,869 sq. mi. (274,200 sq. km.)
POPULATION 6,908,000
CAPITAL Ouagadougou
LARGEST CITY Ouagadougou
HIGHEST POINT 2,352 ft. (717 m.)
MONETARY UNIT CFA franc
MAJOR LANGUAGES Mossi, Lobi, French, Samo, Gourounsi
MAJOR RELIGIONS Islam, tribal religions, Roman Catholicism

BURUNDI
AREA 10,747 sq. mi. (27,835 sq. km.)
POPULATION 4,021,910
CAPITAL Bujumbura
LARGEST CITY Bujumbura
HIGHEST POINT 8,858 ft. (2,700 m.)
MONETARY UNIT Burundi franc
MAJOR LANGUAGES Kirundi, French, Swahili
MAJOR RELIGIONS Tribal religions, Roman Catholicism, Islam

CAMEROON
AREA 183,568 sq. mi. (475,441 sq. km.)
POPULATION 8,503,000
CAPITAL Yaoundé
LARGEST CITY Douala
HIGHEST POINT Cameroon 13,350 ft. (4,069 m.)
MONETARY UNIT CFA franc
MAJOR LANGUAGES Fang, Bamileke, Fulani, Duala, French, English
MAJOR RELIGIONS Tribal religions, Christianity, Islam

CAPE VERDE
AREA 1,557 sq. mi. (4,033 sq. km.)
POPULATION 324,000
CAPITAL Praia
LARGEST CITY Praia
HIGHEST POINT 9,281 ft. (2,829 m.)
MONETARY UNIT Cape Verde escudo
MAJOR LANGUAGE Portuguese
MAJOR RELIGION Roman Catholicism

CENTRAL AFRICAN REPUBLIC
AREA 242,000 sq. mi. (626,780 sq. km.)
POPULATION 2,284,000
CAPITAL Bangui
LARGEST CITY Bangui
HIGHEST POINT Gao 4,659 ft. (1,420 m.)
MONETARY UNIT CFA franc
MAJOR LANGUAGES Banda, Gbaya, Sangho, French
MAJOR RELIGIONS Tribal religions, Christianity, Islam

CHAD
AREA 495,752 sq. mi. (1,283,998 sq. km.)
POPULATION 4,309,000
CAPITAL N'Djamena
LARGEST CITY N'Djamena
HIGHEST POINT Emi Koussi 11,204 ft. (3,415 m.)
MONETARY UNIT CFA franc
MAJOR LANGUAGES Arabic, Bagirmi, French, Sara, Massa, Moudang
MAJOR RELIGIONS Islam, tribal religions

COMOROS
AREA 719 sq. mi. (1,862 sq. km.)
POPULATION 290,000
CAPITAL Moroni
LARGEST CITY Moroni
HIGHEST POINT Karthala 7,746 ft. (2,361 m.)
MONETARY UNIT CFA franc
MAJOR LANGUAGES Arabic, French, Swahili
MAJOR RELIGION Islam

CONGO
AREA 132,046 sq. mi. (342,000 sq. km.)
POPULATION 1,537,000
CAPITAL Brazzaville
LARGEST CITY Brazzaville
HIGHEST POINT Leketi Mts. 3,412 ft. (1,040 m.)
MONETARY UNIT CFA franc
MAJOR LANGUAGES Kikongo, Bateke, Lingala, French
MAJOR RELIGIONS Christianity, tribal religions, Islam

DJIBOUTI
AREA 8,880 sq. mi. (23,000 sq. km.)
POPULATION 386,000
CAPITAL Djibouti
LARGEST CITY Djibouti
HIGHEST POINT Moussa Ali 6,768 ft. (2,063 m.)
MONETARY UNIT Djibouti franc
MAJOR LANGUAGES Arabic, Somali, Afar, French
MAJOR RELIGIONS Islam, Roman Catholicism

EGYPT
AREA 386,659 sq. mi. (1,001,447 sq. km.)
POPULATION 41,572,000
CAPITAL Cairo
LARGEST CITY Cairo
HIGHEST POINT Jeb. Katherina 8,651 ft. (2,637 m.)
MONETARY UNIT Egyptian pound
MAJOR LANGUAGE Arabic
MAJOR RELIGIONS Islam, Coptic Christianity

EQUATORIAL GUINEA
AREA 10,831 sq. mi. (28,052 sq. km.)
POPULATION 244,000
CAPITAL Malabo
LARGEST CITY Malabo
HIGHEST POINT 9,868 ft. (3,008 m.)
MONETARY UNIT CFA franc
MAJOR LANGUAGES Fang, Bubi, Spanish
MAJOR RELIGIONS Tribal religions, Christianity

ETHIOPIA
AREA 471,776 sq. mi. (1,221,900 sq. km.)
POPULATION 31,065,000
CAPITAL Addis Ababa
LARGEST CITY Addis Ababa
HIGHEST POINT Ras Dashan 15,157 ft. (4,620 m.)
MONETARY UNIT birr
MAJOR LANGUAGES Amharic, Gallinya, Tigrinya, Somali, Sidamo, Arabic, Ge'ez
MAJOR RELIGIONS Coptic Christianity, Islam

GABON
AREA 103,346 sq. mi. (267,666 sq. km.)
POPULATION 551,000
CAPITAL Libreville
LARGEST CITY Libreville
HIGHEST POINT Ibounzi 5,165 ft. (1,574 m.)
MONETARY UNIT CFA franc
MAJOR LANGUAGES Fang and other Bantu languages, French
MAJOR RELIGIONS Tribal religions, Christianity, Islam

GAMBIA
AREA 4,127 sq. mi. (10,689 sq. km.)
POPULATION 601,000
CAPITAL Banjul
LARGEST CITY Banjul
HIGHEST POINT 100 ft. (30 m.)
MONETARY UNIT dalasi
MAJOR LANGUAGES Mandingo, Fulani, Wolof, English, Malinke
MAJOR RELIGIONS Islam, tribal religions, Christianity

GHANA
AREA 92,099 sq. mi. (238,536 sq. km.)
POPULATION 11,450,000
CAPITAL Accra
LARGEST CITY Accra
HIGHEST POINT Togo Hills 2,900 ft. (884 m.)
MONETARY UNIT cedi
MAJOR LANGUAGES Twi, Fante, Dagbani, Ewe, Ga, English, Hausa, Akan
MAJOR RELIGIONS Tribal religions, Christianity, Islam

GUINEA
AREA 94,925 sq. mi. (245,856 sq. km.)
POPULATION 5,143,284
CAPITAL Conakry
LARGEST CITY Conakry
HIGHEST POINT Nimba Mts. 6,070 ft. (1,850 m.)
MONETARY UNIT syli
MAJOR LANGUAGES Fulani, Mandingo, Susu, French
MAJOR RELIGIONS Islam, tribal religions

GUINEA-BISSAU
AREA 13,948 sq. mi. (36,125 sq. km.)
POPULATION 777,214
CAPITAL Bissau
LARGEST CITY Bissau
HIGHEST POINT 689 ft. (210 m.)
MONETARY UNIT Guinea-Bissau escudo
MAJOR LANGUAGES Balante, Fulani, Crioulo, Mandingo, Portuguese
MAJOR RELIGIONS Islam, tribal religions, Roman Catholicism

IVORY COAST
AREA 124,504 sq. mi. (322,465 sq. km.)
POPULATION 7,920,000
CAPITAL Yamoussoukro
LARGEST CITY Abidjan
HIGHEST POINT 5,745 ft. (1,751 m.)
MONETARY UNIT CFA franc
MAJOR LANGUAGES Bale, Bete, Senufu, French, Dioula
MAJOR RELIGIONS Tribal religions, Islam

KENYA
AREA 224,960 sq. mi. (582,646 sq. km.)
POPULATION 15,327,061
CAPITAL Nairobi
LARGEST CITY Nairobi
HIGHEST POINT Kenya 17,058 ft. (5,199 m.)
MONETARY UNIT Kenya shilling
MAJOR LANGUAGES Kikuyu, Luo, Kavirondo, Kamba, Swahili, English
MAJOR RELIGIONS Tribal religions, Christianity, Hinduism, Islam

LESOTHO
AREA 11,720 sq. mi. (30,355 sq. km.)
POPULATION 1,339,000
CAPITAL Maseru
LARGEST CITY Maseru
HIGHEST POINT 11,425 ft. (3,482 m.)
MONETARY UNIT loti
MAJOR LANGUAGES Sesotho, English
MAJOR RELIGIONS Tribal religions, Christianity

LIBERIA
AREA 43,000 sq. mi. (111,370 sq. km.)
POPULATION 1,873,000
CAPITAL Monrovia
LARGEST CITY Monrovia
HIGHEST POINT Wutivi 5,584 ft. (1,702 m.)
MONETARY UNIT Liberian dollar
MAJOR LANGUAGES Kru, Kpelle, Bassa, Vai, English
MAJOR RELIGIONS Christianity, tribal religions, Islam

LIBYA
AREA 679,358 sq. mi. (1,759,537 sq. km.)
POPULATION 2,856,000
CAPITAL Tripoli
LARGEST CITY Tripoli
HIGHEST POINT Bette Pk. 7,500 ft. (2,286 m.)
MONETARY UNIT Libyan dinar
MAJOR LANGUAGES Arabic, Berber
MAJOR RELIGION Islam

MADAGASCAR
AREA 226,657 sq. mi. (587,041 sq. km.)
POPULATION 8,742,000
CAPITAL Antananarivo
LARGEST CITY Antananarivo
HIGHEST POINT Maromokotro 9,436 ft. (2,876 m.)
MONETARY UNIT Madagascar franc
MAJOR LANGUAGES Malagasy, French
MAJOR RELIGIONS Tribal religions, Roman Catholicism, Protestantism

MALAWI
AREA 45,747 sq. mi. (118,485 sq. km.)
POPULATION 5,968,000
CAPITAL Lilongwe
LARGEST CITY Blantyre
HIGHEST POINT Mulanje 9,843 ft. (3,000 m.)
MONETARY UNIT Malawi kwacha
MAJOR LANGUAGES Chichewa, Yao, English, Nyanja, Tumbuka, Tonga, Ngoni
MAJOR RELIGIONS Tribal religions, Islam, Christianity

MALI

AREA 464,873 sq. mi. (1,204,021 sq. km.)
POPULATION 6,906,000
CAPITAL Bamako
LARGEST CITY Bamako
HIGHEST POINT Hombori Mts. 3,789 ft. (1,155 m.)
MONETARY UNIT Mali franc
MAJOR LANGUAGES Bambara, Senufu, Fulani, Soninke, French
MAJOR RELIGIONS Islam, tribal religions

MAURITANIA

AREA 419,229 sq. mi. (1,085,803 sq. km.)
POPULATION 1,634,000
CAPITAL Nouakchott
LARGEST CITY Nouakchott
HIGHEST POINT 2,972 ft. (906 m.)
MONETARY UNIT ouguiya
MAJOR LANGUAGES Arabic, Wolof, Tukolor, French
MAJOR RELIGION Islam

AFRICA

AREA 11,707,000 sq. mi. (30,321,130 sq. km.)
POPULATION 469,000,000
LARGEST CITY Cairo
HIGHEST POINT Kilimanjaro 19,340 ft. (5,895 m.)
LOWEST POINT Lake Assal, Djibouti -512 ft. (-156 m.)

MAURITIUS

AREA 790 sq. mi. (2,046 sq. km.)
POPULATION 959,000
CAPITAL Port Louis
LARGEST CITY Port Louis
HIGHEST POINT 2,711 ft. (826 m.)
MONETARY UNIT Mauritian rupee
MAJOR LANGUAGES English, French, French Creole, Hindi, Urdu
MAJOR RELIGIONS Hinduism, Christianity, Islam

MAYOTTE

AREA 144 sq. mi. (373 sq. km.)
POPULATION 47,300
CAPITAL Dzaoudzi

RÉUNION

AREA 969 sq. mi. (2,510 sq. km.)
POPULATION 491,000
CAPITAL St-Denis

MOROCCO

AREA 172,414 sq. mi. (446,550 sq. km.)
POPULATION 20,242,000
CAPITAL Rabat
LARGEST CITY Casablanca
HIGHEST POINT Jeb. Toubkal 13,665 ft. (4,165 m.)
MONETARY UNIT dirham
MAJOR LANGUAGES Arabic, Berber, French
MAJOR RELIGIONS Islam, Judaism, Christianity

MOZAMBIQUE

AREA 303,769 sq. mi. (786,762 sq. km.)
POPULATION 12,130,000
CAPITAL Maputo
LARGEST CITY Maputo
HIGHEST POINT Mt. Binga 7,992 ft. (2,436 m.)
MONETARY UNIT metical
MAJOR LANGUAGES Makua, Thonga, Shona, Portuguese
MAJOR RELIGIONS Tribal religions, Roman Catholicism, Islam

NAMIBIA

AREA 317,827 sq. mi. (823,172 sq. km.)
POPULATION 1,200,000
CAPITAL Windhoek
LARGEST CITY Windhoek
HIGHEST POINT Brandberg 8,550 ft. (2,606 m.)
MONETARY UNIT rand
MAJOR LANGUAGES Ovambo, Hottentot, Herero, Afrikaans, English
MAJOR RELIGIONS Tribal religions, Protestantism

NIGER

AREA 489,189 sq. mi. (1,267,000 sq. km.)
POPULATION 5,098,427
CAPITAL Niamey
LARGEST CITY Niamey
HIGHEST POINT Banguezane 6,234 ft. (1,900 m.)
MONETARY UNIT CFA franc
MAJOR LANGUAGES Hausa, Songhai, Fulani, French, Tamashek, Djerma
MAJOR RELIGIONS Islam, tribal religions

NIGERIA

AREA 357,000 sq. mi. (924,630 sq. km.)
POPULATION 82,643,000
CAPITAL Lagos
LARGEST CITY Lagos
HIGHEST POINT Dimlang 6,700 ft. (2,042 m.)
MONETARY UNIT naira
MAJOR LANGUAGES Hausa, Yoruba, Ibo, Ijaw, Fulani, Tiv, Kanuri, Ibibio, English, Edo
MAJOR RELIGIONS Islam, Christianity, tribal religions

RWANDA

AREA 10,169 sq. mi. (26,337 sq. km.)
POPULATION 4,819,317
CAPITAL Kigali
LARGEST CITY Kigali
HIGHEST POINT Karisimbi 14,780 ft. (4,505 m.)
MONETARY UNIT Rwanda franc
MAJOR LANGUAGES Kinyarwanda, French, Swahili
MAJOR RELIGIONS Tribal religions, Roman Catholicism, Islam

SÃO TOMÉ AND PRÍNCIPE

AREA 372 sq. mi. (963 sq. km.)
POPULATION 85,000
CAPITAL São Tomé
LARGEST CITY São Tomé
HIGHEST POINT Pico 6,640 ft. (2,024 m.)
MONETARY UNIT dobra
MAJOR LANGUAGES Bantu languages, Portuguese
MAJOR RELIGIONS Tribal religions, Roman Catholicism

SENEGAL

AREA 75,954 sq. mi. (196,720 sq. km.)
POPULATION 5,508,000
CAPITAL Dakar
LARGEST CITY Dakar
HIGHEST POINT Futa Jallon 1,640 ft. (500 m.)
MONETARY UNIT CFA franc
MAJOR LANGUAGES Wolof, Peul (Fulani), French, Mende, Mandingo, Dida
MAJOR RELIGIONS Islam, tribal religions, Roman Catholicism

SEYCHELLES

AREA 145 sq. mi. (375 sq. km.)
POPULATION 63,000
CAPITAL Victoria
LARGEST CITY Victoria
HIGHEST POINT Morne Seychellois 2,993 ft. (912 m.)
MONETARY UNIT Seychellois rupee
MAJOR LANGUAGES English, French, Creole
MAJOR RELIGION Roman Catholicism

SIERRA LEONE

AREA 27,925 sq. mi. (72,325 sq. km.)
POPULATION 3,470,000
CAPITAL Freetown
LARGEST CITY Freetown
HIGHEST POINT Loma Mts. 6,390 ft. (1,947 m.)
MONETARY UNIT leone
MAJOR LANGUAGES Mende, Temne, Vai, English, Krio (pidgin)
MAJOR RELIGIONS Tribal religions, Islam, Christianity

SOMALIA

AREA 246,200 sq. mi. (637,658 sq. km.)
POPULATION 3,645,000
CAPITAL Mogadishu
LARGEST CITY Mogadishu
HIGHEST POINT Surud Ad 7,900 ft. (2,408 m.)
MONETARY UNIT Somali shilling
MAJOR LANGUAGES Somali, Arabic, Italian, English
MAJOR RELIGION Islam

SOUTH AFRICA

AREA 455,318 sq. mi. (1,179,274 sq. km.)
POPULATION 23,771,970
CAPITALS Cape Town, Pretoria
LARGEST CITY Johannesburg
HIGHEST POINT Injasuti 11,182 ft. (3,408 m.)
MONETARY UNIT rand
MAJOR LANGUAGES Afrikaans, English, Xhosa, Zulu, Sesotho
MAJOR RELIGIONS Protestantism, Roman Catholicism, Islam, Hinduism, tribal religions

SUDAN

AREA 967,494 sq. mi. (2,505,809 sq. km.)
POPULATION 18,691,000
CAPITAL Khartoum
LARGEST CITY Khartoum
HIGHEST POINT Jeb. Marra 10,073 ft. (3,070 m.)
MONETARY UNIT Sudanese pound
MAJOR LANGUAGES Arabic, Dinka, Nubian, Beja, Nuer
MAJOR RELIGIONS Islam, tribal religions

SWAZILAND

AREA 6,705 sq. mi. (17,366 sq. km.)
POPULATION 547,000
CAPITAL Mbabane
LARGEST CITY Manzini
HIGHEST POINT Emlembe 6,109 ft. (1,862 m.)
MONETARY UNIT lilangeni
MAJOR LANGUAGES siSwati, English
MAJOR RELIGIONS Tribal religions, Christianity

TANZANIA

AREA 363,708 sq. mi. (942,003 sq. km.)
POPULATION 17,527,560
CAPITAL Dar es Salaam
LARGEST CITY Dar es Salaam
HIGHEST POINT Kilimanjaro 19,340 ft. (5,895 m.)
MONETARY UNIT Tanzanian shilling
MAJOR LANGUAGES Nyamwezi-Sukuma, Swahili, English
MAJOR RELIGIONS Tribal religions, Christianity, Islam

TOGO

AREA 21,622 sq. mi. (56,000 sq. km.)
POPULATION 2,472,000
CAPITAL Lomé
LARGEST CITY Lomé
HIGHEST POINT Agou 3,445 ft. (1,050 m.)
MONETARY UNIT CFA franc
MAJOR LANGUAGES Ewe, French, Twi, Hausa
MAJOR RELIGIONS Tribal religions, Roman Catholicism, Islam

TUNISIA

AREA 63,378 sq. mi. (164,149 sq. km.)
POPULATION 6,367,000
CAPITAL Tunis
LARGEST CITY Tunis
HIGHEST POINT Jeb. Chambi 5,066 ft. (1,544 m.)
MONETARY UNIT Tunisian dinar
MAJOR LANGUAGES Arabic, French
MAJOR RELIGION Islam

UGANDA

AREA 91,076 sq. mi. (235,887 sq. km.)
POPULATION 12,630,076
CAPITAL Kampala
LARGEST CITY Kampala
HIGHEST POINT Margherita 16,795 ft. (5,119 m.)
MONETARY UNIT Ugandan shilling
MAJOR LANGUAGES Luganda, Acholi, Teso, Nyoro, Soga, Nkole, English, Swahili
MAJOR RELIGIONS Tribal religions, Christianity, Islam

WESTERN SAHARA

AREA 102,703 sq. mi. (266,000 sq. km.)
POPULATION 76,425
HIGHEST POINT 2,700 ft. (823 m.)
MAJOR LANGUAGE Arabic
MAJOR RELIGION Islam

ZAIRE

AREA 905,063 sq. mi. (2,344,113 sq. km.)
POPULATION 28,291,000
CAPITAL Kinshasa
LARGEST CITY Kinshasa
HIGHEST POINT Margherita 16,795 ft. (5,119 m.)
MONETARY UNIT zaire
MAJOR LANGUAGES Tshiluba, Mongo, Kikongo, Kingwana, Zande, Lingala, Swahili, French
MAJOR RELIGIONS Tribal religions, Christianity

ZAMBIA

AREA 290,586 sq. mi. (752,618 sq. km.)
POPULATION 5,679,808
CAPITAL Lusaka
LARGEST CITY Lusaka
HIGHEST POINT Sunzu 6,782 ft. (2,067 m.)
MONETARY UNIT Zambian kwacha
MAJOR LANGUAGES Bemba, Tonga, Lozi, Luvale, Nyanja, English
MAJOR RELIGIONS Tribal religions

ZIMBABWE

AREA 150,803 sq. mi. (390,580 sq. km.)
POPULATION 7,360,000
CAPITAL Harare
LARGEST CITY Harare
HIGHEST POINT Mt. Inyangani 8,517 ft. (2,596 m.)
MONETARY UNIT Zimbabwe dollar
MAJOR LANGUAGES English, Shona, Ndebele
MAJOR RELIGIONS Tribal religions, Protestantism

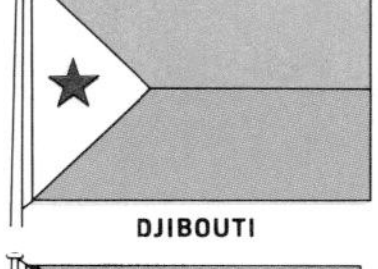

ALGERIA

CITIES and TOWNS

Ain Sefra 22,400 .... G5
Algiers (cap.) 1,365,400 .... G4
Annaba 255,900 .... H4
Béchar 72,800 .... F5
Bejaïa 89,500 .... G4
Biskra 90,500 .... H5
Blida 160,900 .... G4
Bou Saâda 50,000 .... G5
Constantine 335,100 .... H4
Djelfa 51,000 .... G5
Ech Cheliff 106,100 .... G4
El Bayadh 38,500 .... G5
El Oued 72,100 .... H5
Ghardaïa 70,500 .... G5
Jijel 49,800 .... H4
Laghouat 59,200 .... G5
Mascara 62,300 .... G4
Mostaganem 101,600 .... F4
Oran 491,900 .... F4
Ouargla 77,400 .... G5
Saïda 62,100 .... G4
Sétif 144,200 .... H4
Sidi Bel Abbès 116,000 .... F4
Skikda 107,700 .... H4
Tamanrasset 23,200 .... H7
Tébessa 67,200 .... H4
Tiaret 62,900 .... G4
Tizi Ouzou 73,100 .... G4
Tlemcen 109,400 .... F5
Touggourt 75,600 .... G5

OTHER FEATURES

Ahaggar (range) H7
Grand Erg Occidental (des.) G5
Grand Erg Oriental (des.) H5
Sahara (des.) EM7
Tanezrouft (des.) G7

ANGOLA

CITIES and TOWNS

Benguela 40,996 .... J14
Cabinda 21,124 .... J13
Lobito 59,528 .... J14
Luanda (cap.) 475,328 .... J13
Lubango 31,674 .... J14
Malange 31,599 .... K13
Namibe (Moçâmedes) 12,076 .. J15
Saurimo 12,901 .... L13

OTHER FEATURES

Cubango (riv.) K14
Cunene (riv.) J15

BENIN

CITIES and TOWNS

Abomey 38,000 .... G10
Cotonou 178,000 .... G10
Parakou 21,000 .... G10
Porto-Novo (cap.) 104,000 ... G10

BOTSWANA

CITIES and TOWNS

Francistown 22,000 .... M16
Gaborone (cap.) 21,000 .... M16
Kayne 10,664 .... L6
Mahalapye 12,056 .... M16
Serowe 15,723 .... M16

OTHER FEATURES

Kalahari (des.) L16
Makgadikgadi (salt pan) L16
Ngami (lake) L16
Okovanggo (swamps) L14

BURUNDI

CITIES and TOWNS

Bujumbura (cap.) 141,040 .... N12
Gitega 19,500 .... N12

CAMEROON

CITIES and TOWNS

Buea 24,584 .... H11
Douala 458,426 .... J11
Ebolowa 24,000 .... J11
Foumban 33,944 .... J10
Garoua 63,900 .... J10
Maroua 67,187 .... J9
Ngaoundéré 38,992 .... J10
N'Kongsamba 71,298 .... J11
Yaoundé (cap.) 313,706 .... J11

OTHER FEATURES

Biafra (bight) H11
Cameroon (mt.) H11
Sanaga (riv.) J11

CENTRAL AFRICAN REPUBLIC

CITIES and TOWNS

Bambari 31,285 .... L10
Bangassou 21,773 .... L10
Bangui (cap.) 279,792 .... K10
Berberati 27,285 .... K11
Bossangoa 25,150 .... K10
Bouar 29,528 .... K10

OTHER FEATURES

Lobaye (riv.) K10
Shinko (riv.) L10

CHAD

CITIES and TOWNS

Abéché 28,100 .... L9
Bongor 14,300 .... K9
Faya-Largeau 6,800 .... K8
Moundou 39,600 .... K10
N'Djamena (cap.) 179,000 .... K9

OTHER FEATURES

Baguirmi (reg.) K9
Chad (lake) K9
Emi Koussi (mt.) K8
Ennedi (plat.) L8
Sahara (des.) EM7
Shari (riv.) K9
Sudan (reg.) EM9
Tibesti (mts.) K7
Wadai (reg.) L9

COMOROS

CITIES and TOWNS

Moroni (cap.) 12,000 .... P14

OTHER FEATURES

Mwali (isl.) P14
Njazidja (isl.) P14
Nzwani (isl.) P14

CONGO

CITIES and TOWNS

Brazzaville (cap.) 298,967 .... J12
Impfondo K11
Ouesso K11

FLAGS OF AFRICA

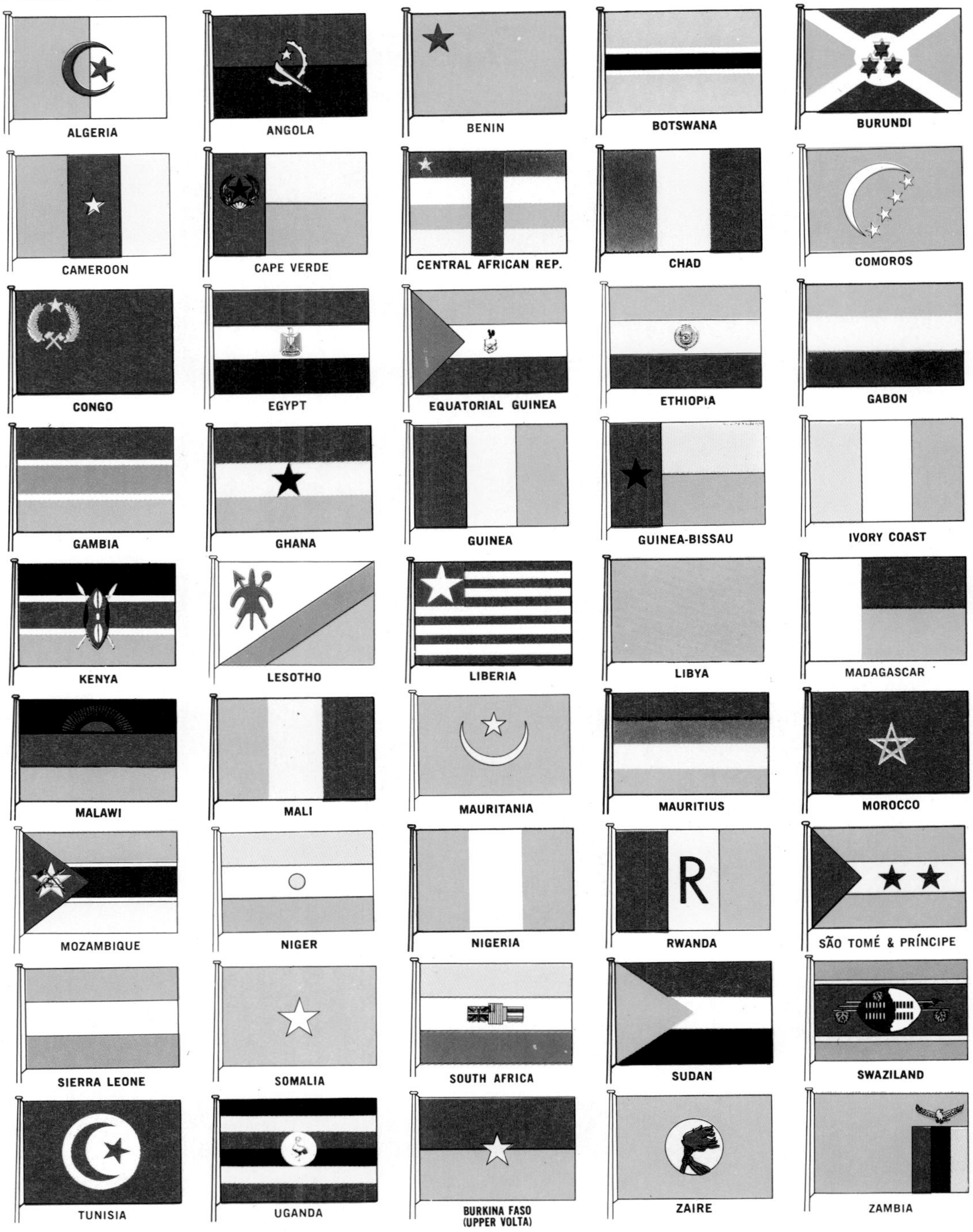

Pointe-Noire 141,700 .... J12

OTHER FEATURES

Congo (riv.) K12
Ubangi (riv.) K11

DJIBOUTI

CITIES and TOWNS

Djibouti (cap.) 96,000 .... P9
Obock P9

EGYPT

CITIES and TOWNS

Alexandria 2,318,655 .... M5
Aswân 144,377 .... N7
Asyût 213,983 .... N6
Beni Suef 118,148 .... N6
Cairo (cap.) 5,084,463 .... N5
Damietta (Dumyat) 93,546 ...... N5
El A'lamein M5
El Faiyûm 167,081 .... M6
El Khârga 26,375 .... N6
El Minya 146,423 .... M6
Ismailia 145,978 .... N5
Luxor 92,748 .... N6
Mersá Matrûh 27,857 .... M5
Port Said 262,620 .... N5
Qena 94,013 .... N6
Sidi Barrani 1,574 .... M5
Suez 194,001 .... N6
Tanta 284,636 .... N5

OTHER FEATURES

Aqaba (gulf) O6
Arabian (des.) N6
Aswân (dam) N7
Banas (cape) O7
Farâfra (oasis) M6
Khârga (oasis) N6
Libyan (des.) M6
Nasser (lake) N7
Nile (riv.) N7
Qattara (depr.) M5
Sahara (des.) .... E M7
Sinai (pen.) N6
Siwa (oasis) M6
Suez (canal) N5
Suez (gulf) N6

EQUATORIAL GUINEA

CITIES and TOWNS

Bata 270,241 .... H11
Malabo (cap.) 37,237 .... A3

OTHER FEATURES

Annobón (isl.) G12
Bioko (Fernando Po) (isl.) H11
Elobey (isl.) H11
Río Muni (terr.) 203,000 .... J11

ETHIOPIA

CITIES and TOWNS

Addis Ababa (cap.) 1,196,300 .... O10
Adwa 16,400 .... O9
Aksum 12,800 .... O9
Asmara 393,800 .... O9
Assab 16,000 .... P9
Debra Markos 30,260 .... O9
Dessye 49,750 .... O9
Dire Dawa 63,700 .... P10
Gondar 38,600 .... O9
Harar 48,440 .... P10
Jimma 47,360 .... O10
Makale 30,780 .... P9
Massawa 19,800 .... O8
Soddu 11,900 .... O10
Yirga-Alam 14,500 .... O10

OTHER FEATURES

Abay (Blue Nile) (riv.) O9
Dahlak (arch.) P8
Danakil (reg.) P9
Dashan, Ras (mt.) O9
Eritrea (reg.) O8
Mandeb, Bab el (str.) R9
Ogaden (reg.) P10
Tana (lake) O9

GABON

CITIES and TOWNS

Franceville 9,345 .... J12
Lambaréné 17,770 .... H12
Libreville (cap.) 105,080 .... H11
Mouila 15,016 .... J12
Oyem 12,455 .... J11
Port-Gentil 48,190 .... H12
Tchibanga 14,001 .... J12

OTHER FEATURES

Lopez (cape) H12
Ogooué (riv.) J12

GAMBIA

CITIES and TOWNS

Banjul (Bathurst) (cap.) 39,476 .... C9
Georgetown 2,510 .... C9

GHANA

CITIES and TOWNS

Accra (cap.) 564,194 .... G11
Axim 8,107 .... F11
Cape Coast 51,653 .... F11
Ho 24,199 .... G10
Keta 14,446 .... G10
Koforidua 46,235 .... F10
Kumasi 260,286 .... F10
Obuasi 31,005 .... F10
Oda 20,957 .... F10
Sekondi 33,713 .... F11
Sekondi-Takoradi* 160,868 .... F11
Takoradi 58,161 .... F11
Tamale 83,653 .... F10
Tarkwa 14,702 .... F10
Tema 60,767 .... G10
Wa 21,374 .... F9
Winneba 30,778 .... F11
Yendi 22,072 .... F10

OTHER FEATURES

Ashanti (reg.) F10
Volta (riv.) F10

GUINEA

CITIES and TOWNS

Beyla E10
Conakry (cap.)* 525,671 .... D10
Dabola D9
Kankan 85,310 .... E9
Kindia 79,861 .... D9
Labé 79,670 .... D9
N'Zérékoré 23,000 .... E10
Siguiri E9

GUINEA-BISSAU

CITIES and TOWNS

Bissau (cap.) 109,486 .... D9
Bolama○ 9,133 .... D9
Cacheu○ 15,194 .... C9

IVORY COAST

CITIES and TOWNS

Abidjan 685,828 .... E10
Agboville 27,192 .... F10
Bingerville 18,218 .... F10
Bondoukou 19,111 .... F10
Bouaké 173,248 .... F10
Dabou 23,870 .... F11
Daloa 60,958 .... E10
Dimbokro 30,986 .... F10
Ferkessédougou 25,307 .... E10
Gagnoa 42,362 .... E10
Grand-Bassam 25,808 .... F11
Katiola 21,559 .... E10
Korhogo 47,657 .... E10
Man 50,315 .... E10
Port-Bouet 72,616 .... F11
Sassandra 9,404 .... E11
Yamoussoukro (cap) 50,000 ...... E10

OTHER FEATURES

Cavally (riv.) E10
Sassandra (riv.) E10

KENYA

CITIES and TOWNS

Eldoret 18,196 .... O11
Kisumu 32,431 .... N12
Lamu 7,403 .... P12
Malindi 10,757 .... P12
Mombasa 247,073 .... P12
Nairobi (cap.) 509,286 .... O12
Nakuru 47,151 .... O11
Nanyuki 11,624 .... O11

OTHER FEATURES

Elgon (mt.) N11
Kenya (mt.) O12
Turkana (Rudolf) (lake) O11

LESOTHO

CITIES and TOWNS

Maseru (cap.) 71,500 .... M17

LIBERIA

CITIES and TOWNS

Buchanan 23,999 .... D10
Greenville 8,462 .... E11
Harper 10,627 .... E11
Marshall D10

(continued on following page)

Agriculture, Industry and Resources

DOMINANT LAND USE

- Cereals, Horticulture, Livestock
- Cash Crops, Mixed Cereals
- Cotton, Cereals
- Diversified Tropical Crops
- Plantation Agriculture
- Oases
- Pasture Livestock
- Nomadic Livestock Herding
- Forests
- Nonagricultural Land

MAJOR MINERAL OCCURRENCES

Ab	Asbestos	Mi	Mica
Ag	Silver	Mn	Manganese
Al	Bauxite	Na	Salt
Au	Gold	O	Petroleum
Be	Beryl	P	Phosphates
C	Coal	Pb	Lead
Co	Cobalt	Pt	Platinum
Cr	Chromium	Sb	Antimony
Cu	Copper	Sn	Tin
D	Diamonds	So	Soda Ash
Fe	Iron Ore	Ti	Titanium
G	Natural Gas	U	Uranium
Gp	Gypsum	V	Vanadium
Gr	Graphite	W	Tungsten
K	Potash	Zn	Zinc

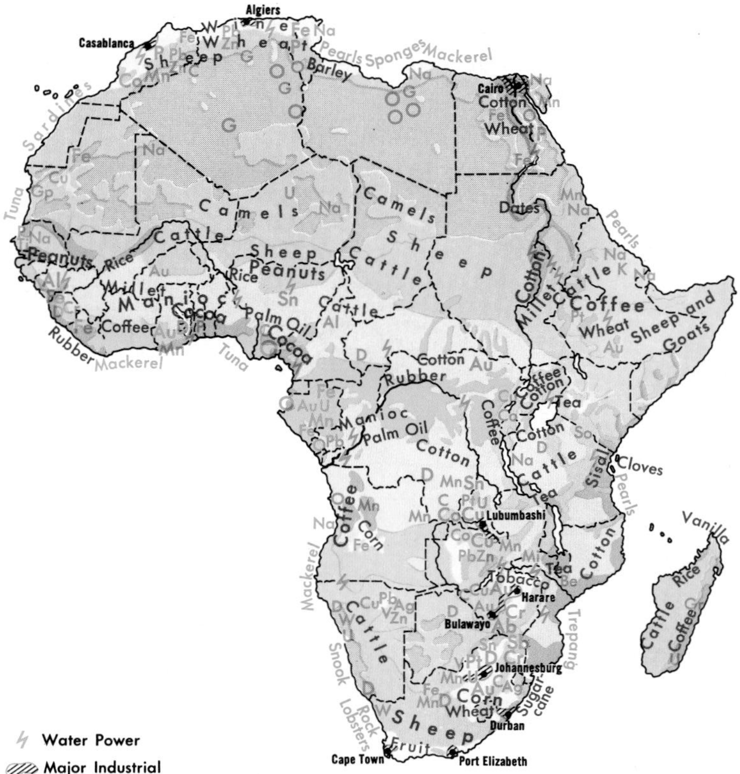

Water Power

Major Industrial Areas

Monrovia (cap.) 166,507 ...... D10

OTHER FEATURES

Palmas (cape) E11

LIBYA

CITIES and TOWNS

Ajedabia○ 53,170 ...... L5
Baida○ 59,765 ...... L5
Benghazi○ 286,943 ...... K5
Brak○ 12,507 ...... J6
Derna○ 44,145 ...... L5
El Azizia○ 34,077 ...... J5
El Jauf○ 6,481 ...... L7
El Marj (Barce)○ 55,444 ...... L5
Ghadames○ 6,172 ...... J6
Gharian○ 65,224 ...... J5
Ghat○ 6,924 ...... J6
Homs○ 66,890 ...... J5
Misurata○ 102,439 ...... K5
Murzuk○ 22,185 ...... J6
Nalut○ 23,535 ...... J5
Sebha○ 35,879 ...... K6
Shahat○ 17,157 ...... L5
Syrte○ 22,797 ...... K5
Tobruk○ 58,384 ...... L5
Tripoli (cap.)○ 550,438 ...... J5
Ubari○ 19,132 ...... J6
Waddan○ 5,347 ...... K6
Zella○ 72,092 ...... K6
Zliten○ 58,981 ...... K5
Zwara○ 15,078 ...... J5

OTHER FEATURES

Cyrenaica (reg.) L6
Fezzan (reg.) J6
Idehan (des.) J6
Kufra (oasis) L7
Sahara (des.) EM7
Sidra (gulf) L5
Tripolitania (reg.) J5

MADAGASCAR

CITIES and TOWNS

Ambanja 12,258 ...... R14
Ambatondrazaka 18,044 ...... R15
Ambilobe 9,415 ...... R14
Ambositra 16,780 ...... R16
Antalaha 17,541 ...... S14
Antananarivo 451,808 ...... R15
Antsirabe 32,979 ...... R16
Antsiranana (Diego-Suarez) 40,443 ...... R14
Arivonimamo 8,497 ...... R15
Faradofay (Fort-Dauphin) 13,805 ...... R17
Farafangana 10,817 ...... R16
Fenoarivo 7,696 ...... R16
Fianarantsoa 68,054 ...... R16
Maevatanana 7,197 ...... R15
Maintirano 6,375 ...... P15
Majunga 65,864 ...... R15
Manakara 19,768 ...... R16
Mananjary 14,638 ...... R16
Marovoay 20,253 ...... R15
Moramanga 10,806 ...... R15
Morondava 19,061 ...... P16
Sambava 6,215 ...... S14
Tamatave 77,395 ...... S15
Toliara 45,676 ...... P16

OTHER FEATURES

Bobaomby (Amber) (cape) S15
Mozambique (chan.) O16
Nossi-Bé (isl.) R14
Tsiafajavona (mt.) R15
Vohimena (Ste Marie) (cape) P17

MALAWI

CITIES and TOWNS

Blantyre 222,153 ...... N15
Karonga 11,873 ...... N13
Lilongwe (cap.) 102,924 ...... N14
Nkhotakota 10,312 ...... N14
Zomba 21,000 ...... N15

OTHER FEATURES

Nyasa (lake) N14
Shire (riv.) N15

MALI

CITIES and TOWNS

Bamako (cap.) 404,022 ...... E9
Bougouni 17,246 ...... E9
Djenné 10,251 ...... F9
Gao 30,714 ...... G8
Goundam 10,262 ...... F8
Kati 24,991 ...... E9
Kayes 44,736 ...... D9
Kita 17,538 ...... E9
Koulikoro 16,376 ...... E9
Koutiala 27,497 ...... F9
Mopti 53,885 ...... F9
Nioro 11,617 ...... E8
San 22,962 ...... F9
Ségou 64,890 ...... E9
Sikasso 47,030 ...... E9
Timbuktu 20,483 ...... F8

OTHER FEATURES

Adrar des Iforas (plat.) G7
Niger (riv.) G9
Sahara (des.) EM7

MAURITANIA

CITIES and TOWNS

Atar 16,326 ...... D7
Bir Mogreïn D6
Bogué 8,056 ...... D8
Boutilimit 7,261 ...... D8
Fdérik 2,160 ...... D7
Kaédi 20,248 ...... D8
Kiffa 10,629 ...... D8
Néma 8,232 ...... E8
Nouadhibou 21,961 ...... C7
Nouakchott (cap.) 134,986 ...... C8
Rosso 16,466 ...... C8
Tidjikja 7,870 ...... D8

OTHER FEATURES

Adrar (reg.) D7
Blanc (cape) C7
Hodh (reg.) E8
Sahara (des.) EM7
Senegal (riv.) D8
Tagant (reg.) D8

MAURITIUS

CITIES and TOWNS

Curepipe 52,709 ...... S19
Mahébourg 15,463 ...... T19
Port Louis (cap.) 141,022 ...... S19

MAYOTTE

CITIES AND TOWNS

Mamoutzou (cap.) 196 ...... R14

MOROCCO

CITIES and TOWNS

Agadir 61,192 ...... D5
Al Hoceima 18,686 ...... F4
Casablanca 1,506,373 ...... E5
El Jadida 55,501 ...... E5
Essaouira 30,061 ...... D5
Fès 325,327 ...... F5
Kenitra 139,206 ...... E5
Khenifra 25,526 ...... F5
Larache 45,710 ...... E4
Marrakech 332,741 ...... E5
Meknès 248,369 ...... E5
Ouezzane 33,267 ...... E5
Oujda 175,532 ...... F5
Rabat (cap.) 367,620 ...... E5
Safi 129,113 ...... E5
Salé 155,557 ...... E5
Settat 42,325 ...... E5
Tangier (Tanger) 187,894 ...... E4
Taroudant 22,272 ...... E5
Taza 55,157 ...... F5
Tétouan 139,105 ...... F4

OTHER FEATURES

Atlas (mts.) E5
Beddouza, Ras el (cape) E5
Draa, Wadi (dry riv.) E6
Juby (cape) D5

MOZAMBIQUE

CITIES and TOWNS

Bartolomeu Dias○ 6,102 ...... O16
Beira 46,293 ...... O15
Caia 1,363 ...... N15
Chibuto 23,763 ...... N16
Chimoio 4,507 ...... N15
Homoíne 1,122 ...... O16
Ibo 1,015 ...... P14
Inhambane 4,975 ...... O16
Magude 1,502 ...... N16
Maniamba 7,634 ...... O14
Maputo (cap.) 755,300 ...... N17
Marromeu 1,330 ...... O15
Massangena○ 3,301 ...... N16
Meconta 1,051 ...... O14
Moçambique 1,730 ...... P15
Mocímboa da Praia 935 ...... P14
Mocuba 2,293 ...... O15
Nacala 4,601 ...... P14
Nampula 23,072 ...... P15
Pemba 3,629 ...... P14
Quelimane 10,522 ...... O15
Songo 1,350 ...... N15
Tete 4,549 ...... N15
Vila de Sena○ 21,074 ...... N15
Xai-Xai 5,234 ...... N16

OTHER FEATURES

Angoche (isl.) O16
Delagoa (bay) N17
Delgado (cape) P14
Mozambique (chan.) O16
Nyasa (chan.) N14
Rovuma (riv.) O14
Save (riv.) N16

NAMIBIA

CITIES and TOWNS

Bethanie 1,207 ...... K17
Gobabis 4,428 ...... K16
Grootfontein 4,627 ...... K15
Karasburg 2,693 ...... K17
Karibib 1,653 ...... K16
Keetmanshoop 10,297 ...... K17
Lüderitz 6,642 ...... J17
Mariental 4,629 ...... K16
Omaruru 2,783 ...... K16
Oranjemund 2,594 ...... K17
Otjiwarongo 8,018 ...... K16
Outjo 2,545 ...... K15
Rehoboth 5,363 ...... K16
Swakopmund 5,681 ...... J16
Tsumeb 12,338 ...... K15
Usakos 2,334 ...... K16
Windhoek (cap.) 61,369 ...... K16

OTHER FEATURES

Caprivi Strip (reg.) L15
Cubango (riv.) K15
Cunene (riv.) J15
Damaraland (reg.) K16
Etosha Pan (salt pan) J15
Fish (riv.) K17
Fria (cape) J15
Great Namaland (reg.) K17
Kalahari (des.) L16
Namib (des.) J16
Okovanggo (riv.) K15
Orange (riv.) K17
Ovamboland (reg.) K15

NIGER

CITIES and TOWNS

Agadès 11,000 ...... H8
Bilma J8
Birni-N'Konni 10,000 ...... H9
Gaya 5,000 ...... G9
Iférouane H8
Maradi 45,852 ...... H9
N'Guigmi J9
Niamey (cap.) 225,314 ...... G9
Tahoua 31,265 ...... H9
Zinder 58,436 ...... H9

OTHER FEATURES

Aïr (mts.) H8
Djado (plat.) J7
Niger (riv.) G9
Sahara (des.) EM7
Ténéré (des.) J8

NIGERIA

CITIES and TOWNS

Aba 177,000 ...... H10
Abeokuta 253,000 ...... G10
Benin City 136,000 ...... H10
Bonny H11
Calabar 103,000 ...... H10
Enugu 187,000 ...... H10
Ibadan 847,000 ...... G10
Ife 176,000 ...... G10
Ilorin 282,000 ...... G10
Kaduna 202,000 ...... H9
Kano 399,000 ...... H9
Katsina 109,424 ...... H9
Lagos (cap.) 1,060,848 ...... G10
Maiduguri 189,000 ...... J9
Ogbomosho 432,000 ...... H10
Onitsha 220,000 ...... H10
Oshogbo 282,000 ...... H10
Oyo 152,000 ...... G10
Port Harcourt 242,000 ...... H11
Sokoto H9
Yola J10
Zaria 224,000 ...... H9

OTHER FEATURES

Adamawa (reg.) J10
Benin (bight) G11
Benue (riv.) H10
Chad (lake) K9
Gongola (riv.) J9
Kaduna (riv.) H9
Niger (riv.) G9

RÉUNION

CITIES and TOWNS

Le Port 21,564 ...... P20
Le Tampon 17,089 ...... P20
Saint-Denis (cap.) 80,075 ...... P19
Saint-Louis 10,252 ...... P20
Saint-Pierre 21,817 ...... P20

OTHER FEATURES

Bassas da India (isl.) O16
Europa (isl.) P16
Glorioso (isls.) R14
Juan de Nova (isl.) P15
Piton des Neiges (mt.) P20

RWANDA

CITIES and TOWNS

Kigali (cap.) 117,749 ...... N12

SÃO TOMÉ AND PRÍNCIPE

CITIES and TOWNS

São Tomé (cap.) 7,681 ...... H11

OTHER FEATURES

Príncipe (isl.) H11
São Tomé (isl.) H11

SENEGAL

CITIES and TOWNS

Dagana 10,506 ...... D8
Dakar (cap.) 798,792 ...... C9
Diourbel 50,618 ...... C9
Kaolack 106,899 ...... C9
Louga 35,063 ...... C8
Matam 10,002 ...... D8
M'Bour 37,663 ...... C9
Saint-Louis 88,404 ...... C8
Tambacounda 25,147 ...... D9
Thiès 117,333 ...... C9
Ziguinchor 72,726 ...... C9

OTHER FEATURES

Senegal (riv.) D8
Verde (cape) C9

SEYCHELLES

OTHER FEATURES

Aldabra (isls.) P13
Assumption (isl.) R14
Cerf (isl.) S13
Cosmoledo (isls.) R13
Farquhar (isl.) S14
Providence (isl.) S13
Saint Pierre 47 ......

SIERRA LEONE

CITIES and TOWNS

Bo 42,216 ...... D10
Bonthe 6,230 ...... D10
Freetown (cap.) 274,000 ...... D10
Makeni 28,684 ...... D10

OTHER FEATURES

Sherbro (isl.) D10

SOMALIA

CITIES and TOWNS

Afmadu 2,580 ...... P11
Barawa (Brava) 6,167 ...... P11
Baydhabo 14,962 ...... P11
Belet Weyne 11,426 ...... P11
Berbera 12,219 ...... R9
Borama 3,244 ...... P9
Bosaso R9
Brava 6,167 ...... P11
Bulo Burti 5,247 ...... P11
Burao 12,617 ...... R10
Chisimayu 17,872 ...... P12
Eil S10
Erigabo 4,279 ...... R9
Galcaio R10
Giohar 13,156 ...... R11
Hargeysa 40,254 ...... P10
Jilib 3,232 ...... P11
Las Anod 2,441 ...... R10
Marka 17,708 ...... R11
Mogadishu (cap.) 371,000 ...... R11
Oddur P11
Zeila 1,226 ...... P9

OTHER FEATURES

Asèr, Ras (cape) S9
Chiambone, Ras (cape) P12
Giuba (Juba) (riv.) P11
Mijirtein (reg.) R10
Mudugh (reg.) R10
Wabi Shabelle (riv.) R11

SOUTH AFRICA

INTERNAL DIVISIONS

Bophuthatswana (aut. rep.) 1,200,000 ...... L17
Cape (prov.) 5,543,506 ...... L18
Ciskei (aut. rep.) M18
Natal (prov.) 5,722,215 ...... N17
Orange Free State (prov.) 1,833,216 ...... M17
Transkei (aut. rep.) 2,000,000 ...... M18
Transvaal (prov.) 10,673,033 ...... M16
Venda (aut. rep.) 450,000 ...... N16

CITIES and TOWNS

Aliwal North 12,311 ...... M18
Beaufort West 17,862 ...... L18
Bellville 49,026 ...... G19
Benoni□ 164,543 ...... M17
Bethlehem 29,918 ...... M17
Bisho M18
Bloemfontein□ 182,329 ...... L17
Calvinia 6,386 ...... K18
Cape Town (cap.)□ 833,731 ...... F19
Ceres 9,230 ...... H18
Cradock 20,822 ...... M18
De Aar 18,057 ...... L18
Durban□ 975,494 ...... N18
East London□ 126,671 ...... M18
George 24,625 ...... L18
Germiston□ 293,257 ...... M17
Goodwood 31,592 ...... G19
Graaff-Reinet 22,392 ...... L18
Grahamstown 41,302 ...... M18
Johannesburg□ 1,417,818 ...... M17
Kimberley 105,258 ...... L17
King William's Town 15,798 ...... M18
Knysna 13,479 ...... L18
Kraaifontein 10,286 ...... G19
Kroonstad 51,988 ...... M17
Ladysmith 28,920 ...... N17
Louis Trichardt 8,906 ...... M16
Malmesbury 9,314 ...... G18
Messina 21,121 ...... M16
Middelburg, C. of G.H. 11,121 ...... M18
Middelburg, Transv. 26,942 ...... N17
Mmabatho L17
Moorreesburg 4,945 ...... K18
Mossel Bay 17,574 ...... L18
Newcastle 14,407 ...... N17
Oudtshoorn 26,907 ...... L18
Paarl 49,244 ...... H19
Parow 60,768 ...... G19
Pietermaritzburg□ 174,179 ...... N17
Pietersburg 27,174 ...... N16
Pinelands 11,769 ...... G19
Port Elizabeth□ 413,961 ...... M18
Port Nolloth 2,893 ...... K17
Port Shepstone 5,581 ...... N18
Potchefstroom 57,443 ...... M17
Pretoria (cap.)□ 573,283 ...... M17
Prieska 8,521 ...... L17
Queenstown 39,304 ...... M18
Richards Bay 598 ...... N17
Saldanha 4,994 ...... K18
Simonstown 12,137 ...... F19
Somerset West 11,828 ...... G19
Stellenbosch 29,955 ...... G19
Strand 24,503 ...... G19
Thohoyandou N16
Uitenhage 70,517 ...... M18
Umtata 25,216 ...... M18
Upington 28,632 ...... L17
Vryburg 16,916 ...... L17
Walvis Bay 21,725 ...... J16
Wellington 17,092 ...... H18
Worcester 41,198 ...... H18

OTHER FEATURES

Agulhas (cape) K19
Algoa (bay) M18
Cape (pt.) F20
False (bay) G20
Good Hope (cape) F20
Hangklip (cape) G20
Kalahari (des.) L16
Limpopo (riv.) N16
Maclear (cape) F20
Molopo (riv.) L17
Nossob (riv.) L17
Orange (riv.) K17

Robben (isl.) F19
Saint Helena (bay) K18
Sandown (bay) G20
Table (bay) F19
Table (mt.) F19
Vaal (riv.) M17
Zululand□ 756,707 N17

SUDAN

CITIES and TOWNS

Atbara 66,000 N8
Dongola 6,000 M8
Ed Damazin 12,000 N9
Ed Dueim 27,000 N9
El Fasher 52,000 M9
El Geneina 33,000 L9
El Obeid 90,000 N9
En Nahud 23,000 M9
Gedaref 92,000 O9
Juba 57,000 N10
Kadugli 18,000 M9
Kassala 99,000 O8
Khartoum (cap.) 334,000 N8
Khartoum North 151,000 N8
Kosti 57,000 N9
Malakal 35,000 N10
Nyala 60,000 L9
Omdurman 299,000 N8
Port Sudan 133,000 O8
Wadi Halfa N7
Wad Medani 107,000 N9
Wau 53,000 N10

OTHER FEATURES

Arab, Bahr el (riv.) M10
Atbara (riv.) O8
Blue Nile (riv.) N9
Gezira, El (reg.) N9
Meroe (ruin) N8
Nasser (lake) N7
Nile (riv.) N7
Nubian (des.) N7
Sahara (des.) EM7
Sobat (riv.) N10
Sudan (reg.) FM9
White Nile (riv.) N10

SWAZILAND

CITIES and TOWNS

Mbabane (cap.) 23,109 N17

TANZANIA

CITIES and TOWNS

Arusha 55,281 O12
Bagamoyo 5,112 O13
Bukoba 20,430 N12
Chake Chake 4,862 P13
Dar es Salaam (cap.) 757,346 P1
Dodoma 45,703 N13
Geita 3,066 N12
Iringa 57,182 O13
Kigoma-Ujiji 50,044 N12
Kilosa 4,458 O13
Kilwa Kivinje 2,790 P13
Kondoa 4,514 O12
Lindi 27,308 O14
Lushoto 1,803 O12
Mbeya 76,606 N13
Morogoro 61,890 O13
Moshi 52,223 O12
Mtwara-Mikindani 48,510 P14
Musoma 32,658 N12
Mwadui 7,383 N12
Mwanza 110,611 N12
Nachingwea 3,751 O14
Pangani 2,955 O13
Shinyanga 21,703 N12
Singida 29,252 N12
Songea 17,954 O14
Tabora 67,392 N12
Tanga 103,409 O12
Zanzibar 110,669 P13

OTHER FEATURES

Great Ruaha (riv.) O13
Kilimanjaro (mt.) O12
Mafia (isl.) P13
Natron (lake) O12
Nyasa (lake) N14
Pangani (riv.) O12
Pemba (isl.) P13
Rufiji (riv.) O13
Rukwa (lake) N13

Tanganyika (lake) N13
Victoria (lake) N12
Zanzibar (isl.) P13

TOGO

CITIES and TOWNS

Anécho 10,889 G10
Kpalimé 19,801 G10
Lomé (cap.) 148,443 G10
Sokodé 29,623 G10

TUNISIA

CITIES and TOWNS

Bizerte 62,856 J4
Gabès 40,585 H5
Gafsa 42,225 H5
Kairouan 54,546 H4
Mahdia 25,711 J4
Menzel Bourguiba 42,111 H4
Moknine 26,035 J4
Sfax 171,297 J5
Sousse 69,530 J4
Tunis (cap.) 550,404 J4

OTHER FEATURES

Bon (cape) J4
Djerba (isl.) J5
Djerid, Shott el (salt lake) H5
Gabès (gulf) J5

UGANDA

CITIES and TOWNS

Arua 10,837 N11
Entebbe 21,096 N12
Jinja 52,509 N11
Kabale 8,234 N12
Kampala (cap.) 478,895 N11
Mbarara 16,078 N12
Soroti 8,130 N11

OTHER FEATURES

Albert (lake) M11
Edward (lake) M12
Kioga (lake) N11
Ruwenzori (range) N11
Victoria (lake) N12

BURKINA FASO (UPPER VOLTA)

CITIES and TOWNS

Bobo Dioulasso 115,063 F9
Koudougou 36,838 F9
Ouagadougou (cap.) 172,661 F9
Ouahigouya 25,690 F9

OTHER FEATURES

Black Volta (riv.) F9
Red Volta (riv.) F9

Sudan (reg.) FM9
White Volta (riv.) F9

WESTERN SAHARA

CITIES and TOWNS

Dakhla C7
Laayoune 24,519 D6

OTHER FEATURES

Blanc (cape) C7
Bojador (cape) C6

ZAIRE

CITIES and TOWNS

Aketi 17,200 L11
Bandundu□ K12
Beni 22,800 M11
Boma 61,100 J13
Bukavu 134,861 M12
Bumba 34,700 L11
Bunia 28,800 N11
Butembo 27,800 M11
Demba 22,000 L13
Dilolo 14,000 L13
Gemena 37,300 L11
Goma 48,600 M12
Ilebo 32,200 L12
Isiro 49,300 M11
Kalemie 62,300 M13
Kamina 56,300 L13
Kananga 428,960 L13
Kasongo 37,800 M12
Kikwit 111,960 K13
Kinshasa (cap.) 1,323,039 K12
Kisangani 229,596 M11
Kolwezi 81,600 L14
Lubumbashi 318,000 M14
Luebo 21,800 L13
Manono 44,500 M13
Matadi 110,436 J13
Mbandaka 107,910 K11
Mbanza-Ngungu 55,800 K13
Mbuji-Mayi 256,154 L13
Mwene Ditu 71,200 L13
Panda-Likasi 146,394 M14
Port Kindu 42,800 L12
Tshikapa 38,900 L13
Virunga 21,900 M13
Watsa 21,300 M11
Yangambi 22,600 L11

OTHER FEATURES

Albert (lake) M11
Aruwimi (riv.) M11
Bomu (riv.) L11
Boyoma (Stanley) (falls) M11
Congo (riv.) K12
Edward (lake) M12
Kasai (riv.) K12
Kivu (reg.) M12
Lualaba (riv.) M13
Luapula (riv.) M14
Lulua (riv.) L13
Mweru (lake) M13
Ruwenzori (range) N11
Stanley (falls) M11
Stanley Pool (lake) K12
Tanganyika (lake) N13
Ubangi (riv.) K11
Uele (riv.) L11
Zaire (Congo) (riv.) K12

ZAMBIA

CITIES and TOWNS

Broken Hill (Kabwe) 143,635 M14
Choma 17,943 M15
Kabwe 143,635 M14
Kasama 38,093 N13
Livingstone 71,987 M15
Lusaka (cap.) 538,469 M15
Mazabuka 29,602 M15
Mongu 24,919 L15
Mpika 25,880 N14
Ndola 282,439 M14
Senanga 7,204 L15
Solwezi 15,032 M14

OTHER FEATURES

Bangweulu (lake) N14
Kafue (riv.) M15
Kariba (lake) M15
Mweru (lake) M13
Victoria (falls) M15

Zambezi (riv.) M15

ZIMBABWE

CITIES and TOWNS

Bulawayo 359,000 M16
Chegutu 12,000 M15
Chinhoyi 25,000 M15
Gwaai○ 2,710 M15
Gwelo 68,000 M15
Harare (cap.) 601,000 N15
Hwange 33,000 M15
Kadoma 32,000 M15
Kariba 3,943 M15
Matopos○ 11,330 M16
Mutare 61,000 N15
Nyanda 22,000 N15
Salisbury (Harare) (cap.) 601,000 N15
Shurugwi 8,387 M15

OTHER FEATURES

Kariba (lake) M15
Limpopo (riv.) N16
Victoria (falls) M15
Zambezi (riv.) M15

*City and suburbs.
○Population of sub-district or division.
□Population of urban area.

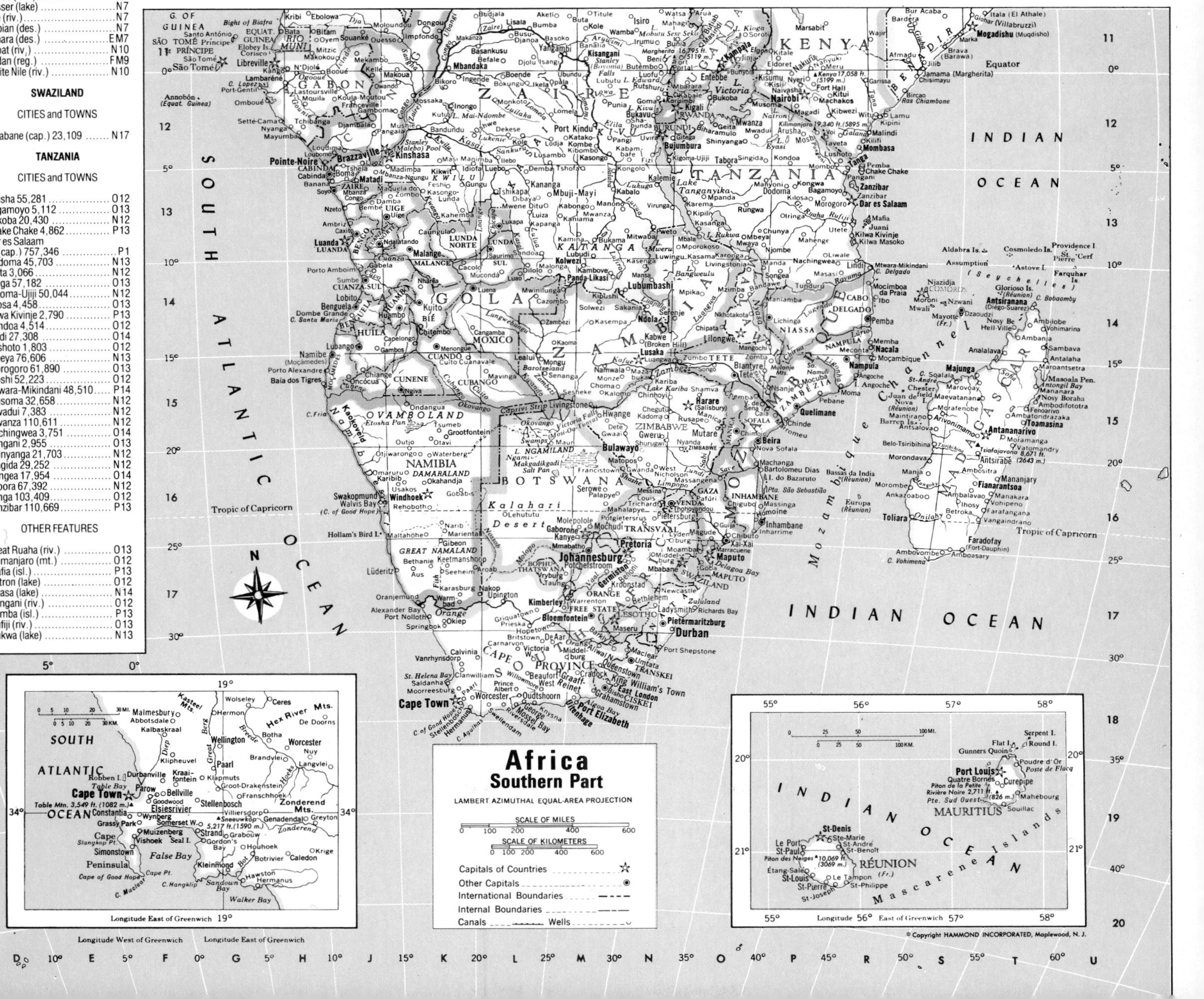

Asia
LAMBERT AZIMUTHAL EQUAL-AREA PROJECTION
SCALE OF MILES
0 100 200 400 600 800 1000 1200
SCALE OF KILOMETERS
0 200 400 600 800 1000 1200
Capitals of Countries
Other Capitals
International Boundaries
Other Boundaries
Canals
Scale 1:46,500,000
© Copyright HAMMOND INCORPORATED, Maplewood, N. J.
Longitude 90° East of Greenwich 100°
ARCTIC OCEAN
ATLANTIC OCEAN
NORWEGIAN SEA
BARENTS SEA
KARA SEA
LAPTEV SEA
EAST SIBERIAN SEA
CHUKCHI SEA
BERING SEA
SEA OF OKHOTSK
SEA OF JAPAN
EAST CHINA SEA
SOUTH CHINA SEA
PHILIPPINE SEA
PACIFIC OCEAN
INDIAN OCEAN
ARABIAN SEA
BAY OF BENGAL
MEDITERRANEAN SEA
BLACK SEA
CASPIAN SEA
RED SEA
UNION OF SOVIET SOCIALIST REPUBLICS
RUSSIAN SOVIET FEDERATED SOCIALIST REPUBLIC
KAZAKH S.S.R.
MONGOLIA
CHINA
INDIA
PAKISTAN
AFGHANISTAN
IRAN
SAUDI ARABIA
TURKEY
IRAQ
SYRIA
YEMEN
OMAN
BURMA
THAILAND
VIETNAM
CAMBODIA
MALAYSIA
SINGAPORE
INDONESIA
PHILIPPINES
JAPAN
N. KOREA
S. KOREA
TAIWAN
HONG KONG
SRI LANKA (CEYLON)
MALDIVES
NEPAL
BHUTAN
BANGLADESH
AUSTRALIA
ALASKA
NORTH AMERICA
UNITED STATES
MADAGASCAR
SOMALIA
ETHIOPIA
EGYPT
SUDAN

Population Distribution

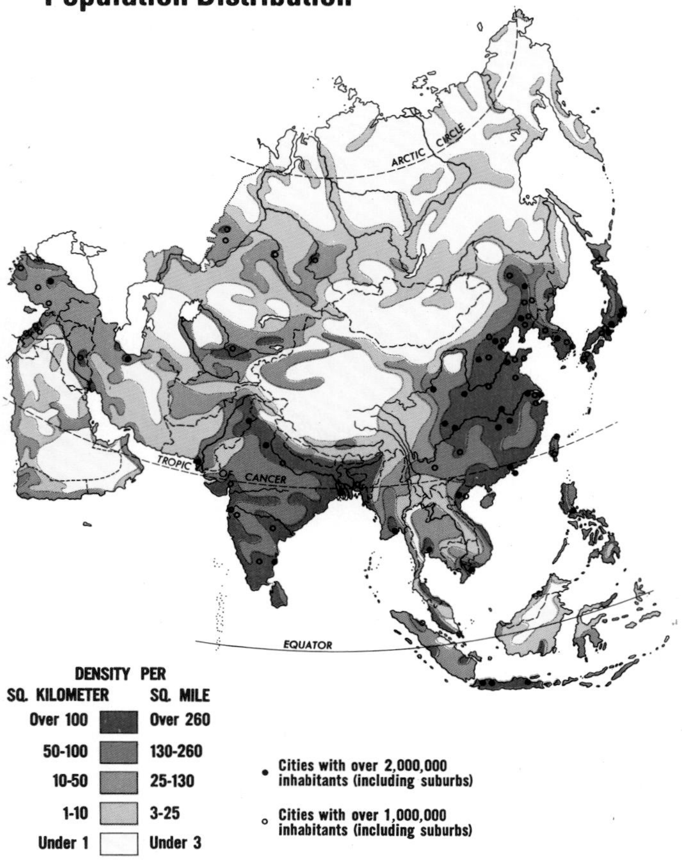

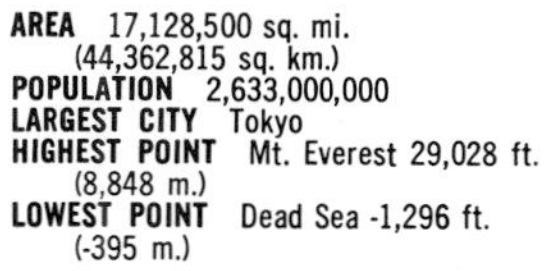

Vegetation

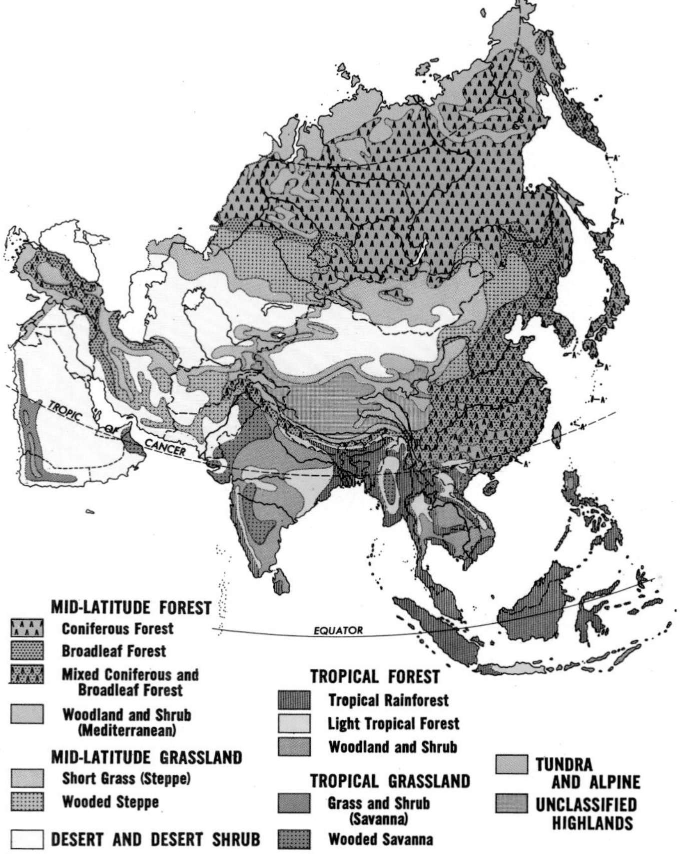

Abadan, Iran F 6
Abu Dhabi (cap.), U.A.E. G 7
Adana, Turkey E 6
Aden, Yemen F 8
Aden (gulf) F 8
Afghanistan H 6
Agra, India J 7
Ahmadabad, India J 7
Aleppo, Syria E 6
Al Kuwait (cap.), Kuwait F 7
Alma-Ata, U.S.S.R. J 5
Altai (mts.) K 5
Altun Shan (range), China K 6
Amman (cap.), Jordan E 6
Amudar'ya (riv.), U.S.S.R. H 5
Amur (riv.) P 5
Andaman (isls.), India L 8
Ankara (cap.), Turkey E 5
Aqaba (gulf) E 7
Arabian (sea) H 8
Araks (riv.) F 6
Aral (sea), U.S.S.R. G 5
Ararat (mt.), Turkey F 6
Arctic (ocean) C 1
Asahikawa, Japan P 5
Ashkhabad, U.S.S.R. G 6
Baghdad (cap.), Iraq F 6
Bahawalpur, Pakistan J 7
Bahrain G 7
Bali (isl.), Indonesia N 10
Balkhash (lake), U.S.S.R. J 5
Bandar Seri Begawan (cap.), Brunei N 9
Bandung, Indonesia M10
Bangalore, India J 8
Bangkok (cap.), Thailand M 8
Bangladesh L 7
Basra, Iraq F 6
Baykal (lake), U.S.S.R. N 4
Beijing (Peking) (cap.), China N 5
Beirut (cap.), Lebanon E 6
Bengal (bay) K 8
Bering (sea) V 4
Bering (strait) W 3
Bhutan L 7
Black (sea) E 5
Blagoveshchensk, U.S.S.R. O 4
Bombay, India J 8
Bonin (isls.), Japan E 7
Borneo (isl.) N 9
Brahmaputra (riv.) L 7
British Indian Ocean Territory J10
Brunei N 9
Bukhara, U.S.S.R. H 5
Burma L 7
Calcutta, India K 7
Cambodia M 8
Cannanore (isls.), India H 8
Caspian (sea) G 5
Celebes (isl.), Indonesia N10
Chang Jiang (Yangtze) (riv.), China N 6
Chelyabinsk, U.S.S.R. H 4
Chengdu, China M 6
China L 6
Chittagong, Bangladesh L 7
Chongqing, China M 7
Christmas (isl.), Australia M11
Chukchi (pen.), U.S.S.R. V 3
Cocos (isls.), Australia L11
Colombo (cap.), Sri Lanka J 9
Comorin (cape), India J 9
Cyprus E 6
Dalian, China O 6
Damascus (cap.), Syria E 6
Da Nang, Vietnam M 8
Delhi, India J 7
Dhahran, Saudi Arabia F 7
Dhaka (cap.), Bangladesh L7
Diego Garcia (isl.), Br. Ind. Ocean Terr. J10
Doha (cap.), Qatar G 7
Dushanbe, U.S.S.R. H 6
East China (sea) O 7
Euphrates (riv.) F 6
Everest (mt.) K 7
Frunze, U.S.S.R. J 5
Fukuoka, Japan O 6
Ganges (riv.) K 7
George Town, Malaysia M 9
Gobi (des.) M 5
Great Khingan (range), China O 5
Great Wall (ruins), China N 5
Guangzhou (Canton), China N 7
Hadhramaut (reg.), Yemen F 8
Hainan (isl.), China N 8
Haiphong, Vietnam M 7
Hakodate, Japan R 5
Halmahera (isl.), Indonesia O 9
Hangzhou, China N 6
Hanoi (cap.), Vietnam M 7
Harbin, China O 5
Herat, Afghanistan H 6
Himalaya (mts.) L 7
Hindu Kush (mts.) J 6
Hiroshima, Japan P 6
Ho Chi Minh City, Vietnam M 8
Hokkaido (isl.), Japan R 5
Hong Kong N 7
Honshu (isl.), Japan P 6
Huang He (Hwang Ho) (riv.), China N 6
Hue, Vietnam M 8
Hyderabad, India J 8
Hyderabad, Pakistan H 7
Inch'on, S. Korea O 6
India J 7
Indian (ocean) H10
Indonesia M10
Indus (riv.) H 7
Inner Mongolia (reg.), China N 5
Iran G 7
Iraq F 6
Irkutsk, U.S.S.R. M 4
Irrawaddy (riv.), Burma L 7
Irtysh (riv.), U.S.S.R. J 4
Isfahan, Iran G 6
Islamabad (cap.), Pakistah J 6
Israel E 6
Izmir, Turkey D 6
Jaipur, India J 7
Jakarta (cap.), Indonesia M10
Japan R 6
Japan (sea) P 6
Java (isl.), Indonesia M10
Jerusalem (cap.), Israel E 6
Jidda, Saudi Arabia E 7
Jordan E 6
Kabul (cap.), Afghanistan H 6
Kamchatka (pen.), U.S.S.R. S 4
Kanpur, India K 7
Kara (sea), U.S.S.R. H 2
Karachi, Pakistan H 7
Karakorum (ruins), Mongolia M 5
Kathmandu (cap.), Nepal K 7
Kazakh, S.S.R., U.S.S.R. H 5
Kerman, Iran G 6
Khabarovsk, U.S.S.R. P 5
Khyber (pass) J 6
Kirgiz S.S.R., U.S.S.R. J 5
Kistna (riv.), India J 8
Kitakyushu, Japan P 6
Kobe, Japan P 6
Kolyma (range), U.S.S.R. S 3
Krasnoyarsk, U.S.S.R. L 4
Kuala Lumpur (cap.), Malaysia M 9
Kunlun (range), China K 6
Kunming, China M 7
Kuril (isls.), U.S.S.R. R 5
Kuwait F 7
Kyoto, Japan P 6
Kyushu (isl.), Japan P 6
Lahore, Pakistan J 6
Lanzhou, China M 6
Laos M 8
Laptev (sea), U.S.S.R. O 2
Latakia, Syria E 6
Lebanon E 6
Lena (riv.), U.S.S.R. O 3
Leyte (isl.), Philippines O 8
Lhasa, China L 7
Lucknow, India K 7
Luzon (isl.), Philippines O 8
Macau N 7
Madras, India K 8
Magnitogorsk, U.S.S.R. H 4
Makassar (str.), Indonesia N10
Malacca (str.) M 9
Malaya (reg.), Malaysia M 9
Malaysia M 9
Maldives J 9
Male (cap.), Maldives J 9
Mandalay, Burma L 7
Manila (cap.), Philippines N 8
Mecca (cap.), Saudi Arabia F 7
Medan, Indonesia L 9
Medina, Saudi Arabia F 7
Mekong (riv.) M 8
Mindanao (isl.), Philippines O 9
Molucca (isls.), Indonesia O10
Mongolia M 5
Mosul, Iraq F 6
Muscat (cap.), Oman G 7
Mysore, India J 8
Nagasaki, Japan O 6
Nagoya, Japan P 6
Naha, Japan O 7
Nanjing, China N 6
Nepal K 7
New Delhi, India J 7
New Guinea (isl.) P10
Nicosia (cap.), Cyprus E 6
North Korea O 5
Novosibirsk, U.S.S.R. J 4
Ob' (riv.), U.S.S.R. H 3
Okhotsk (sea), U.S.S.R. R 4
Okinawa (isls.), Japan O 7
Oman G 8
Omsk, U.S.S.R. J 4
Osaka, Japan P 6
Pacific (ocean) T 5
Pakistan H 7
Pamir (plat.) J 6
Peking (cap.), China N 5
Persian (gulf) G 7
Philippines O 8
Phnom Penh (cap.), Cambodia M 8
Poona, India J 8
Pusan, S. Korea O 6
P'yongyang (cap.), N. Korea O 6
Qatar G 7
Rangoon (cap.), Burma L 8
Rawalpindi, Pakistan J 6
Red (sea) E 7
Riyadh (cap.), Saudi Arabia F 7
Russian Soviet Federated Socialist Republic, U.S.S.R. L3
Ryukyu (isls.), Japan O 7
Sabah (reg.), Malaysia N 9
Saigon (Ho Chi Minh City), Vietnam M 8
Sakhalin (isl.), U.S.S.R. R 4
Salween (riv.) L 8
Samarkand, U.S.S.R. H 6
San'a (cap.), Yemen F 8
Sapporo, Japan P 5
Sarawak (reg.), Malaysia N 9
Saudi Arabia F 7
Seoul (cap.), S. Korea O 8
Severnaya Zemlya (isls.), U.S.S.R. M 1
Shanghai, China O 6
Shikoku, Japan P 6
Siberia (reg.), U.S.S.R. M 4
Singapore M 9
Sinkiang (reg.), China K 5
Socotra (isl.), Yemen G 8
South China (sea) N 8
South Korea O 6
Sri Lanka K 9
Sulu (sea), Philippines N 9
Sumatra (isl.), Indonesia L 9
Sunda (str.), Indonesia M 10
Surabaya, Indonesia N 10
Sverdlovsk, U.S.S.R. H 4
Syrdar'ya (riv.), U.S.S.R. H 5
Syria E 6
Tabriz, Iran F 6
Tadzhik S.S.R., U.S.S.R. H 6
Taipei (cap.), Taiwan O 7
Taiwan (isl.) N 7
Ta'izz, Yemen F 8
Takla Makan (des.), China K 6
Tashkent, U.S.S.R. H 5
Taymyr (pen.), U.S.S.R. L 2
Tehran (cap.), Iran G 6
Tel Aviv-Jaffa, Israel E 6
Thailand M 8
Tianjin, China N 6
Tibet (reg.), China K 6
Tien Shan (range) K 5
Tigris (riv.) F 6
Timor (isl.), Indonesia O 10
Tokyo (cap.), Japan R 6
Tonkin (gulf) M 8
Turkey E 6
Turkmen S.S.R., U.S.S.R. G 6
Ulaanbaatar (cap.), Mongolia M 5
Union of Soviet Socialist Republics L 3
United Arab Emirates G 7
Ural (mts.), U.S.S.R. G 4
Urmia (lake), Iran F 6
Ürümqi, China K 5
Uzbek S.S.R., U.S.S.R. H 5
Varanasi, India K 7
Verkhoyansk, U.S.S.R. P 3
Vientiane (cap.), Laos M 8
Vietnam M 8
Vladivostok, U.S.S.R. P 5
Wŏnsan, N. Korea O 6
Wuhan, China N 6
Xi'an, China M 6
Yakutsk, U.S.S.R. O 3
Yalu (riv.) O 5
Yangtze (riv.), China N 6
Yellow (sea) O 6
Yemen F 8
Yenisey (riv.), U.S.S.R. K 3
Yogyakarta, Indonesia M 10
Yokohama, Japan R 6
Zhengzhou, China S 3

Near and Middle East

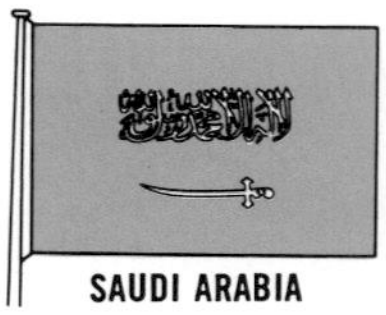

SAUDI ARABIA

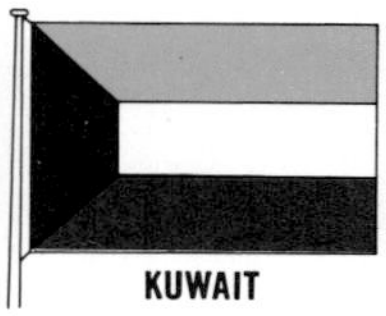

KUWAIT

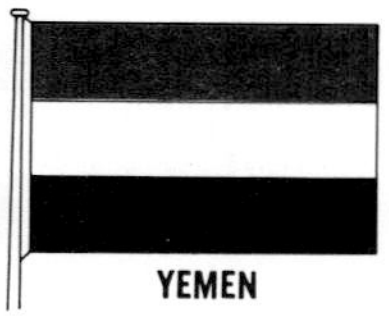

YEMEN

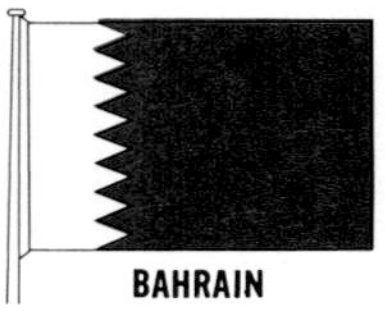

BAHRAIN

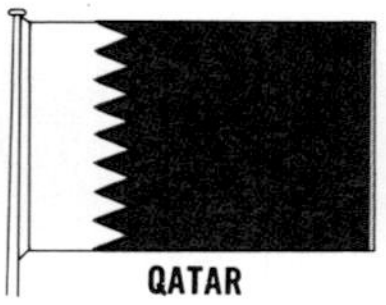

QATAR

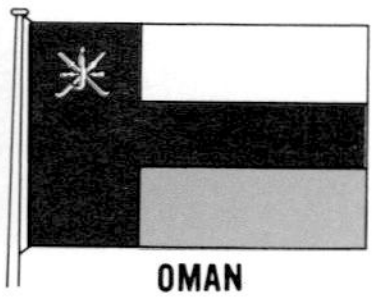

OMAN

AFGHANISTAN

CITIES and TOWNS

Anar Darreh	H3
Andkhvoy	H2
Aqcheh	J2
Aybak 33.016	J2
Baghlan 75.130	J2
Balkh	J2
Bamian 7.355	J3
Baraki Barak	J3
Belcheragh	J2
Chahar Borjak	H3
Charikar 25.093	J2
Dowlat Yar	J3
Dowlatabad	H3
Dowshi	J2
Farah 18.797	H3
Farsi	H3
Feyzabad 10.142	K2
Gardez 11.415	J3
Gereshk	H3
Ghazni 30.425	J3
Ghurian	H3
Gizab	J3
Hazar Qadam	J3
Herat 163.960	H3
Jalalabad 56.384	K3
Jorm	K2
Kabul (cap.) 905.108	J3
Kalat (Qalat) 5.946	J3
Kandahar (Qandahar) 178.409	J3
Khanabad	J2
Khugiani	J3
Kowst	J3
Kuhestan	H3
Landay	H3
Lash-e Joveyn	H3
Lashkar Gah 26.646	H3
Mar'uf	J3
Mazar-e Sharif 122.567	J2
Meymaneh 54.954	H2
Mirabad	H3
Moqor	J3
Now Zad	H3
Owbeh	H3
Panjab	J3
Pol-e Khomri	J2
Qalat 5.946	J3
Qale'h-ye Now 5.340	H3
Qale'h-ye Panjeh	K2
Qandahar 178.409	J3
Qonduz 107.191	J2
Rostaq	J2
Rudbar	H3
Sakhar	J3
Sar-e Pol	J2
Shah Juy	J3
Sheberghan 54.870	H2
Shindand	H3
Spin Buldak	J3
Tagab	J3
Taloqan 46.202	J2
Teyvareh	H3
Tulak	H3
Zaranj 6.477	H3
Zibak	K2

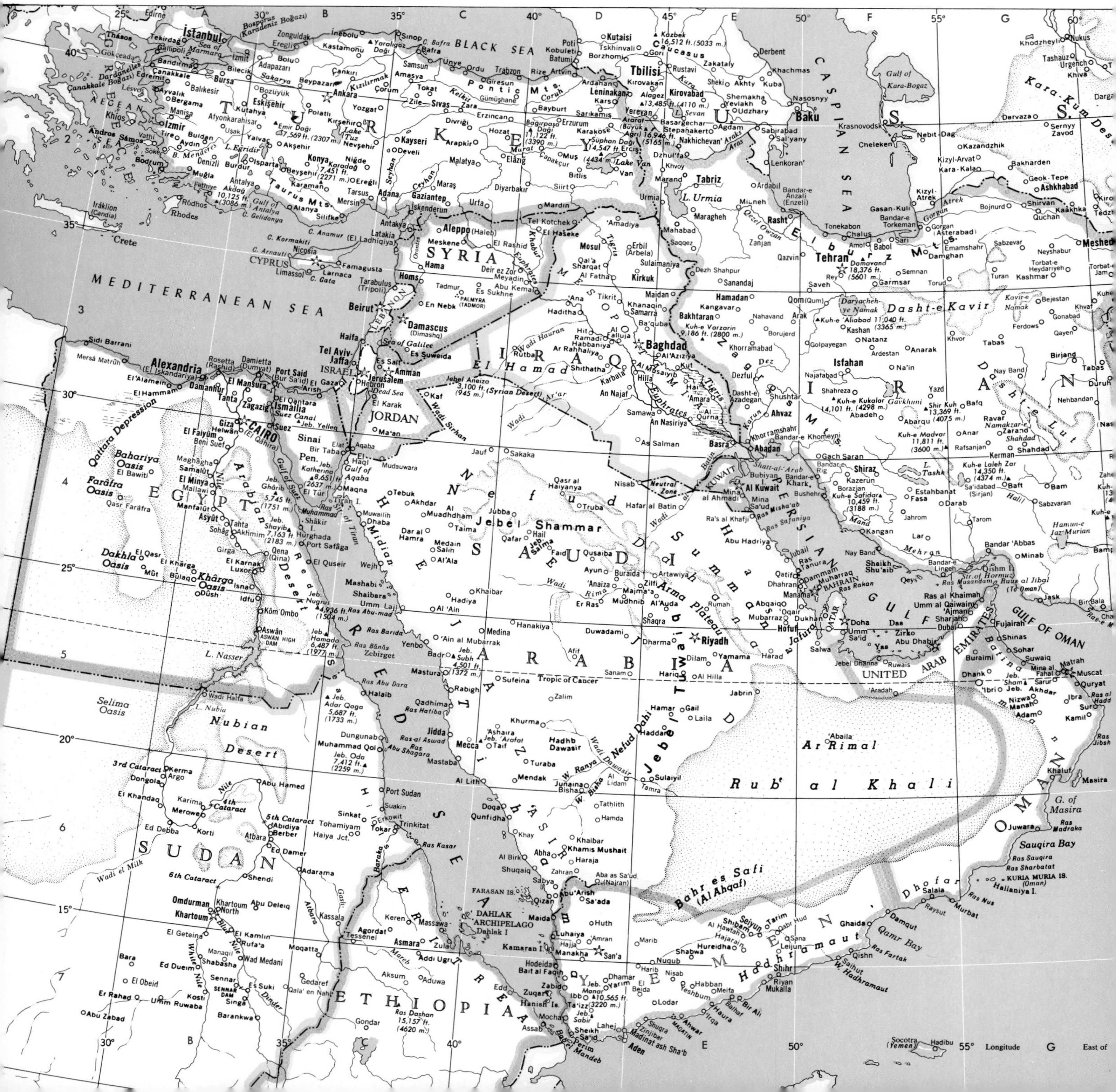

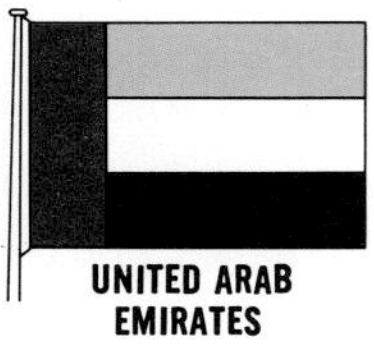

UNITED ARAB EMIRATES

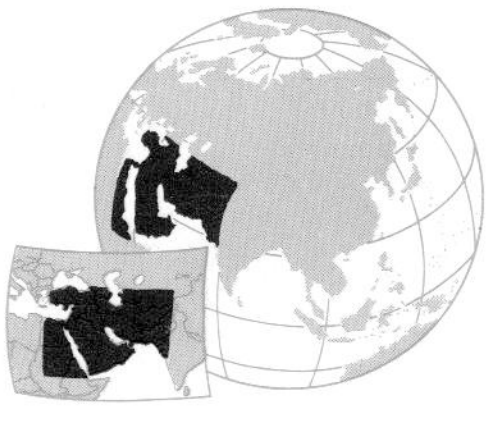

OTHER FEATURES

Farah Rud (riv.) H3
Gowd-e Zerreh (depr.) H4
Harirud (riv.) H3
Helmand (riv.) J3
Hindu Kush (mts.) J2
Kabul (riv.) K3
Konar (riv.) K2
Lurah (riv.) J3
Margow, Dasht-e (des.) H3
Murghab (riv.) H2
Namaksar (salt lake) H3
Paropamisus (mts.) H3
Rigestan (reg.) H3

BAHRAIN

CITIES and TOWNS

Manama (cap.) 88,785 .... F4
Muharraq 37,732 .... F4

GAZA STRIP

CITIES and TOWNS

Gaza* 118,272 .... B3

IRAN

CITIES and TOWNS

Abadan 296,081 .... E3
Abadeh 16,000 .... F3
Abarqu 8,000 .... F3
Ahvaz 329,006 .... E3
Amol 68,782 .... F2
Anar 463 .... G3
Anarak 2,038 .... F3
Arak 114,507 .... E3
Ardabil 147,404 .... E2
Ardestan 5,868 .... F3
Asterabad (Gorgan) 88,348 .... F2
Babol 67,790 .... F2
Bafq 5,000 .... G3
Baft 6,000 .... G4

(continued on following page)

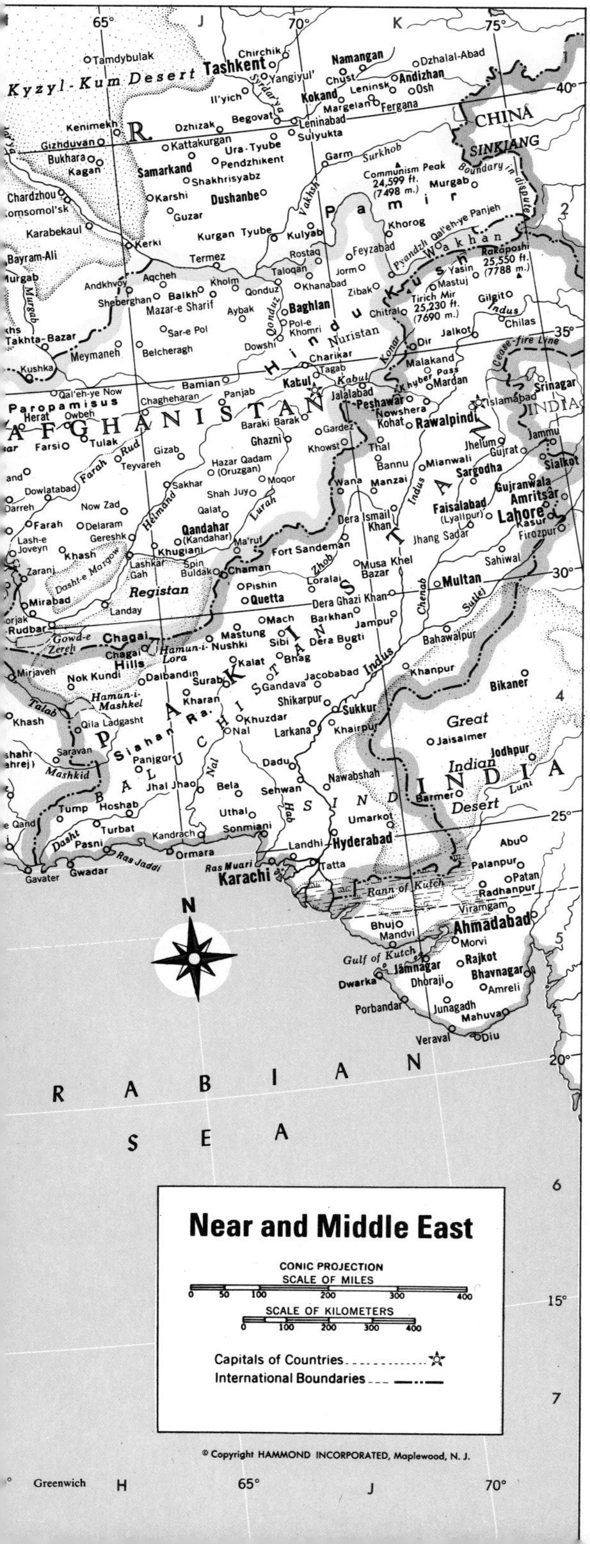

SAUDI ARABIA

AREA 829,995 sq. mi. (2,149,687 sq. km.)
POPULATION 8,367,000
CAPITAL Riyadh
MONETARY UNIT Saudi riyal
MAJOR LANGUAGE Arabic
MAJOR RELIGION Islam

YEMEN

AREA 188,321 sq. mi. (487,792 sq. km.)
POPULATION 8,425,189
CAPITAL San'a
MONETARY UNIT Yemeni rial
MAJOR LANGUAGE Arabic
MAJOR RELIGION Islam

QATAR

AREA 4,247 sq. mi. (11,000 sq. km.)
POPULATION 220,000
CAPITAL Doha
MONETARY UNIT Qatari riyal
MAJOR LANGUAGE Arabic
MAJOR RELIGION Islam

KUWAIT

AREA 6,532 sq. mi. (16,918 sq. km.)
POPULATION 1,355,827
CAPITAL Al Kuwait
MONETARY UNIT Kuwaiti dinar
MAJOR LANGUAGE Arabic
MAJOR RELIGION Islam

BAHRAIN

AREA 240 sq. mi. (622 sq. km.)
POPULATION 358,857
CAPITAL Manama
MONETARY UNIT Bahraini dinar
MAJOR LANGUAGE Arabic
MAJOR RELIGION Islam

OMAN

AREA 120,000 sq. mi. (310,800 sq. km.)
POPULATION 891,000
CAPITAL Muscat
MONETARY UNIT Omani rial
MAJOR LANGUAGE Arabic
MAJOR RELIGION Islam

UNITED ARAB EMIRATES

AREA 32,278 sq. mi. (83,600 sq. km.)
POPULATION 1,040,275
CAPITAL Abu Dhabi
MONETARY UNIT dirham
MAJOR LANGUAGE Arabic
MAJOR RELIGION Islam

Topography

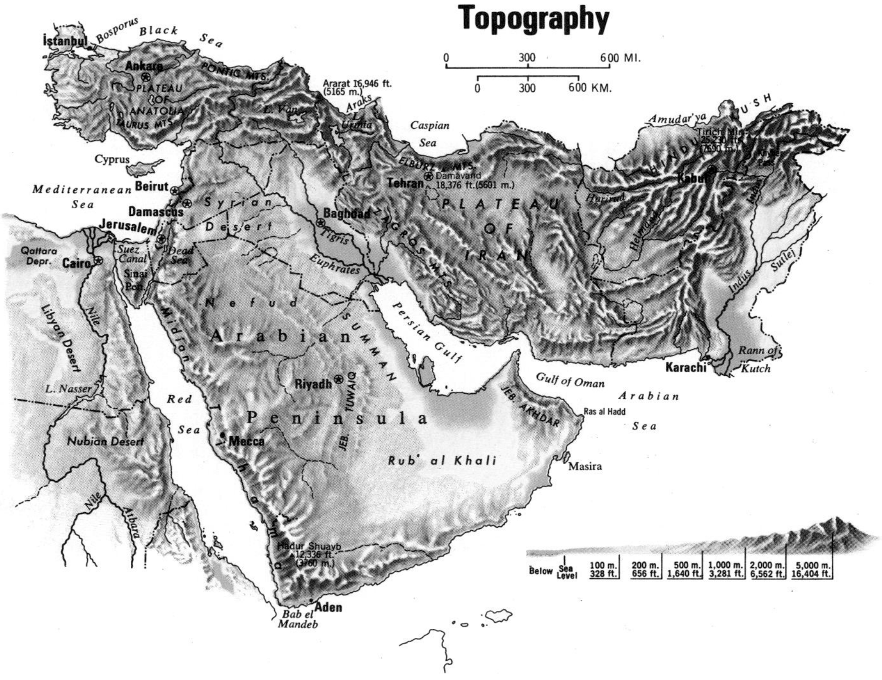

(continued)

Bakhtaran 290,861 ... E3
Bam 22,000 ... G4
Bampur 1,585 ... H4
Bandar 'Abbas 89,103 ... G4
Bandar-e Anzali (Enzeli) 55,978 ... E2
Bandar-e Khomeyni 6,000 ... E3
Bandar-e Lengeh 4,920 ... F4
Bandar-e Rig 1,889 ... F4
Bandar-e Torkeman 13,000 ... F2
Bejestan 3,823 ... G3
Birjand 25,854 ... G3
Bojnurd 31,248 ... G2
Borazjan 20,000 ... F4
Borujerd 100,103 ... E3
Bushehr 57,681 ... F4
Chah Bahar 1,800 ... H4
Chalus 15,000 ... F2
Damghan 13,000 ... F2
Darab 13,000 ... G4
Dasht-e Azadegan 21,000 ... E3
Dashtiari ... H4
Dezful 110,287 ... E3
Dezh Shahpur 1,384 ... E2
Emamshahr 30,767 ... G2
Enzeli 55,978 ... E2
Estahbanat 18,187 ... F4
Fahrej (Iranshahr) 5,000 ... H4
Fasa 19,000 ... F4
Ferdows 11,000 ... G3
Gach Saran ... F3
Garmsar 4,723 ... F2
Golpayegan 20,515 ... F3
Gonabad 8,000 ... G3
Gorgan 88,348 ... F2
Hamadan 155,846 ... E3
Iranshahr 5,000 ... H4
Isfahan 671,825 ... F3
Jahrom 38,236 ... F4
Kangan 2,682 ... F4
Kangavar 9,414 ... E3
Kashan 84,545 ... F3
Kashmar 17,000 ... G2
Kazerun 51,309 ... F4
Kerman 140,309 ... G3
Khash 7,439 ... H4
Khorramabad 104,928 ... E3
Khorramshahr 146,709 ... E3
Khvoy 70,040 ... E2
Lar 22,000 ... F4
Mahabad 28,610 ... E2
Maragheh 60,820 ... E2
Marand 24,000 ... E2
Meshed 670,180 ... H2
Mianeh 28,447 ... E2
Minab 4,228 ... G2
Mirjaveh 11,000 ... H4
Nahavand 24,000 ... E3
Na'in 5,925 ... F3
Najafabad 76,236 ... F3
Nasratabad (Zabol) 20,000 ... H3
Natanz 4,370 ... F3
Nehbandan 2,130 ... G3
Neyshabur 59,101 ... G2
Nikshahr ... H4
Pahlevi (Enzeli) 55,978 ... E2
Qasr-e Qand 1,879 ... H4
Qayen 6,000 ... G3
Qazvin 138,527 ... E2
Qom 246,831 ... F3
Quchan 29,133 ... G2
Qum (Qom) 246,831 ... F3
Rafsanjan 21,000 ... G3
Rasht 187,203 ... E2
Ravar 5,074 ... G3
Rey 102,825 ... F2
Reza'iyeh (Urmia) 163,991 ... D2
Sabzevar 69,174 ... G2
Sabzvaran 7,000 ... G4
Sai'dabad 20,000 ... G4
Sanandaj 95,834 ... E2
Saqqez 17,000 ... E2
Saravan ... H4
Sari 70,936 ... F2
Saveh 17,565 ... F2
Semnan 31,058 ... F2
Shahdad 2,777 ... G3
Shahreza 34,220 ... F3
Shiraz 416,408 ... F4
Shirvan 11,000 ... G2
Shustar 24,000 ... E3
Sirjan (Sai'dabad) 20,000 ... G4
Tabas 10,000 ... G3
Tabas-Masina (Tabas) 466 ... H3
Tabriz 598,576 ... E2
Tarom 394 ... G4
Tehran (cap.) 4,496,159 ... F2
Tonekabon 12,000 ... F2
Torbat-e Heydariyeh 30,106 ... G2
Torbat-e Jam 13,000 ... H2
Torud 721 ... F2
Turan ... G2
Turbat-i-Shaikh Jam 13,000 ... H2
Urmia 163,991 ... D2
Yazd 135,978 ... F3
Yazdan ... H3
Zabol 20,000 ... H3
Zahedan 92,628 ... H4
Zanjan 99,967 ... E2
Zarand 5,000 ... G3

OTHER FEATURES

Araks (riv.) ... E2
Atrek (riv.) ... G2
Bazman, Kuh-e (mt.) ... H4
Damavand (mt.) ... F2
Dez (riv.) ... E3
Elburz (mts.) ... F2
Gavkhuni (lake) ... F3
Gorgan (riv.) ... F2
Halil (riv.) ... G4
Jaz Murian, Hamun-e (marsh) ... G4
Karun (riv.) ... E3
Kavir, Dasht-e (salt des.) ... G3
Kavir-e Namak (salt des.) ... G3
Lut, Dasht-e (des.) ... G3
Maidani, Ras (cape) ... G4
Mand Rud (riv.) ... F4
Mashkid (riv.) ... H4
Mehran (riv.) ... F4
Namak, Daryacheh-ye (salt lake) ... F3
Namaksar (salt lake) ... H3
Namakzar-e Shahdad (salt lake) ... G3
Oman (gulf) ... G5
Persian (gulf) ... F4
Qeys (isl.) ... F4
Qezel Owzan (riv.) ... E2
Qeshm (isl.) ... G4
Safidar, Kuh-e (mt.) ... F4
Shaikh Shua'ib (isl.) ... F4
Shir Kuh (mt.) ... F3
Taftan, Kuh-e (mt.) ... H4
Talab (riv.) ... H4
Tashk (lake) ... F4
Urmia (lake) ... E2
Zagros (mts.) ... E3

IRAQ

CITIES and TOWNS

Al 'Aziziya 7,450 ... E3
Al Falluja 38,072 ... D3
Al Fatha† 15,329 ... D2
Al Musaiyib 15,955 ... D3
Al Qurna 5,638 ... E3
'Amadiya 2,578 ... D2
'Amara 64,847 ... E3
'Ana 15,729 ... D3
An Najaf 128,096 ... D3
An Nasiriya 60,405 ... E3
Arbela (Erbil) 90,320 ... D2
Ar Rahhaliya 1,579 ... D3
As Salman 3,584 ... E3
Baghdad (cap.) 502,503 ... E3
Baghdad* 1,745,328 ... E3
Baq'uba 34,575 ... D3
Basra 313,327 ... E3
Erbil 90,320 ... D2
Habbaniya 14,405 ... D3
Haditha 6,870 ... D3
Hai 16,988 ... E3
Hilla 84,717 ... D3
Hit 9,131 ... D3
Karbal'a 83,301 ... D3
Khanaqin 23,522 ... D3
Kirkuk 167,413 ... D2
Kirkuk* 176,794 ... D2
Kut 42,116 ... E3
Maidan 354 ... E3
Mosul 315,157 ... D2
Qala' Sharqat 2,434 ... D2
Ramadi 28,723 ... D3
Rutba 5,091 ... D3
Samarra 24,746 ... D3
Samawa 33,473 ... D3
Shithatha 2,326 ... D3
Sulaimaniya 86,822 ... E2
Tikrit 9,921 ... D3

OTHER FEATURES

'Aneiza, Jebel (mt.) ... C3
'Ara'r, Wadi (dry riv.) ... D3
Batin, Wadi al (dry riv.) ... E4
Euphrates (riv.) ... E3
Hauran, Wadi (dry riv.) ... D3
Mesopotamia (reg.) ... D3
Syrian (El Hamad) (des.) ... D3
Tigris (riv.) ... E3

KUWAIT

CITIES and TOWNS

Al Kuwait (cap.) 181,774 ... E4
Mina al Ahmadi ... E4
Mina Saud ... E4

OTHER FEATURES

Bubiyan (isl.) ... E4
Persian (gulf) ... F4

OMAN

CITIES and TOWNS

Adam ... G5
Buraimi ... G5
Dhank ... G5
Ibra ... G5
I'bri ... G5
Juwara ... G6
Kamil ... G5
Khaluf ... G5
Khasab ... G4
Manah ... G5
Masqat (Muscat) (cap.) 7,500 ... G5
Matrah 15,000 ... G5
Mina al Fahal ... G5
Murbat ... G6
Muscat (cap.) 7,500 ... G5
Nizwa ... G5
Quryat ... G5
Raysut (Risut) ... F6
Salala 4,000 ... F6
Sarur ... G5
Shinas ... G5
Sohar ... G5
Sur ... G5
Suwaiq ... G5

OTHER FEATURES

Akhdar, Jebel (range) ... G5
Batina (reg.) ... G5
Dhofar (reg.) ... F6
Hadd, Ras al (cape) ... G5
Jibsh, Ras (cape) ... G5
Kuria Muria (isls.) ... G6
Madraka, Ras (cape) ... G6
Masira (gulf) ... G6
Masira (isl.) ... G5
Musandam, Ras (cape) ... G4
Nus, Ras (cape) ... G6
Oman (gulf) ... G5
Oman (reg.) ... G5
Ruus al Jibal (dist.) ... G4
Sauqira (bay) ... G6
Sauqira, Ras (cape) ... G6
Sham, Jebel (mt.) ... G5
Sharbatat, Ras (cape) ... G6

QATAR

CITIES and TOWNS

Doha (cap.) 150,000 ... F4
Dukhan ... F4
Umm Sai'd ... F5

OTHER FEATURES

Persian (gulf) ... F4
Rakan, Ras (cape) ... F4

SAUDI ARABIA

CITIES and TOWNS

Aba as Sau'd 47,501 ... D6
'Abaila ... F5
Abha 30,150 ... D6
Abqaiq ... E4
Abu 'Arish ... D6
Abu Hadriya ... E4
'Ain al Mubarrak ... C5
Al 'Ain ... C4
Al 'Ala ... C4
Al 'Auda ... E4
Al Birk ... D6
Al Hilla ... E5
Al Lidam ... D5
Al Lith ... C5
Al Muadhdam ... C4
'Anaiza ... D4
Artawiya ... E4
'Ashaira ... D5
Ayun ... D4
Badr ... C5
Buraida 69,940 ... D4
Dam ... D5
Dammam 127,844 ... F4
Dar al Hamra ... C4
Dhaba ... C4
Dhahran ... E4
Dharma ... E5
Dilam ... E5
Doqa ... D6
Duwadami ... D5
Er Ras ... D4
Faid ... D4
Gail ... E5
Haddar ... E5
Hadiya ... C4
Hafar al Batin ... E4
Hail 40,502 ... D4
Hamar ... E5
Hamda ... D6
Hanakiya ... D5
Haql ... C4
Harad ... E5
Haraja ... D6
Hariq ... E5
Hofuf 101,271 ... E4
Jabrin ... E5
Jauf ... C4
Jidda 561,104 ... C5
Jizan (Qizan) 32,812 ... D6
Jubail ... F4
Jubba ... D4
Junaina ... D5
Kaf ... C3
Khaibar, 'Asir ... D5
Khaibar, Hejaz ... C4
Khamis Mushait 49,581 ... D6
Khay ... D6
Khurma ... D5
Laila ... E5
Majmaa' ... D4
Maqna ... C4
Marib ... E6
Mastaba ... C5
Mastura ... C5
Mecca 366,801 ... C5
Medain Salih ... C4
Medina 198,186 ... D5
Mendak ... D5
Mina Sau'd ... E4
Mubarraz 54,325 ... E4
Mudhnib ... D4
Muwailih ... C4
Najran (Aba as Sau'd) 47,501 ... D6
Nisab ... D4
O'qair ... E4
Qadhima ... C5
Qafar ... D4
Qasr al Haiyanya ... D4
Qatif ... E4
Qizan 32,812 ... D6
Qunfidha ... D6
Qusaiba ... D4
Rabigh ... C5
Ra's al Khafji ... E4
Ras Tanura ... F4
Riyadh (cap.) 666,840 ... E5
Rumah ... E4
Sabya ... D6
Sakaka ... D4
Salwa ... F5
Shaqra ... D4
Shuqaiq ... D6
Sufeina ... D5
Sulaiyil ... E5
Taif 204,857 ... D5
Taima ... C4
Tamra ... E5
Tathlith ... D6
Tebuk (Tabuk) 74,825 ... C4
Truba ... D4
Turaba ... D5
Umm Lajj ... C4
Wejh ... C4
Yamama ... E5
Yenbo ... C5
Zahran ... D6
Zalim ... D5
Zilfi ... E4

OTHER FEATURES

Abu-Mad, Ras (cape) ... C5
'Aneiza, Jebel (mt.) ... C3
Aqaba (gulf) ... C4
Arafat, Jebel (mt.) ... D5
'Ara'r, Wadi (dry riv.) ... D3
Arma (plat.) ... E4
Aswad, Ras al (cape) ... C5
Bahr es Safi (des.) ... E6
Barida, Ras (cape) ... C5
Bisha, Wadi (dry riv.) ... D5
Dahana (des.) ... E4
Dawasir, Wadi (dry riv.) ... E5
Dawasir, Hadhb (range) ... D5
Farasan (isls.) ... D6
Hatiba, Ras (cape) ... C5
Jafura (des.) ... F5
Mashabi (isl.) ... C4
Midian (dist.) ... C4
Mishaa'b, Ras (cape) ... E4
Nefud (des.) ... D4
Nefud Dahi (des.) ... D5
Persian (gulf) ... F4
Ranya, Wadi (dry riv.) ... D5
Red (sea) ... C5
Rima, Wadi (dry riv.) ... D4
Rimal, Ar (des.) ... F5
Rub al Khali (des.) ... F5
Safaniya, Ras (cape) ... E4
Salma, Jebel (mts.) ... D4
Shaibara (isl.) ... C4
Shammar, Jebel (plat.) ... D4
Sirhan, Wadi (dry riv.) ... C3
Subh, Jebel (mt.) ... C5
Summan (plat.) ... E4
Tihama (reg.) ... C5
Tiran (isl.) ... C4
Tiran (str.) ... C4
Tuwaiq, Jebel (range) ... E5

UNITED ARAB EMIRATES

CITIES and TOWNS

Abu Dhabi (cap.) 347,000 ... F5
'AJman ... G4
'Aradah ... F5
Buraimi ... G5
Dubai ... F4
Fujairah ... G4
Jebel Dhanna ... F5
Ras al Khaimah ... G4
Ruwais ... F5
Sharjah ... F4
Umm al Qaiwain ... G4

OTHER FEATURES

Das (isl.) ... F4
Oman (gulf) ... G5
Yas (isl.) ... F5
Zirko (isl.) ... F5

WEST BANK

CITIES and TOWNS

Hebron 38,309 ... C3

OTHER FEATURES

Dead (sea) ... C3

YEMEN

CITIES and TOWNS

Aden 240,370 ... E7
Ahwar ... E7
'Amran ... D6
Bait al Faqih ... D7
Balhaf ... E7
Bir 'Ali ... E7
Damqut ... F6
Dhamar 19,467 ... D7
El Beida 5,975 ... E7
Ghaida ... F6
Habban ... E7
Hadibu ... F7
Hajarain ... E6
Hajja 5,814 ... D6
Harib ... E7
Haura ... E7
Hodeida 80,314 ... D7
Hureidha ... E6
Huth ... D6
Ibb 19,066 ... D7
'Irqa ... E7
Lahej ... D7
Leijun ... E6
Lodar ... E7
Luhaiya ... D6
Madinat ash Sha'b ... E7
Marib 292 ... E6
Meifa ... E7
Mocha ... D7
Mukalla 45,000 ... E7
Nisab ... E7
Nuqub ... E6
Qishn ... F6
Riyan ... E7
Sa'ada 4,252 ... D6
Saihut ... F6
San'a (cap.) 134,588 ... D6
Seiyun 20,000 ... E6
Shabwa ... E6
Sheikh Sa'id ... D7
Shibam ... E6
Shihr ... E7
Shuqra ... E7
Ta'izz 78,642 ... D7
Tarim ... E6
Yarim ... D7
Yeshbum ... E7
Zabid ... D7
Zinjibar ... E7

OTHER FEATURES

Bab el Mandeb (str.) ... D7
Fartak, Ras (cape) ... F6
Hadhramaut (dist.) ... E7
Hadhramaut, Wadi (dry riv.) ... F7
Hanish (isls.) ... D7
Jebel Manar (mt.) ... D7
Jebel Sabir (mt.) ... D7
Kamaran (isl.) ... D6
Manar, Jebel (mt.) ... D7
Mandeb, Bab el (str.) ... D7
Perim (isl.) ... D7
Ras Fartak (cape) ... F6
Red (sea) ... C5
Sabir, Jebel (mt.) ... D7
Socotra (isl.) ... F7
Tihama (reg.) ... C5
Wadi Hadhramaut (dry riv.) ... F7
Zuqar (isl.) ... D7

*City and suburbs.

Agriculture, Industry and Resources

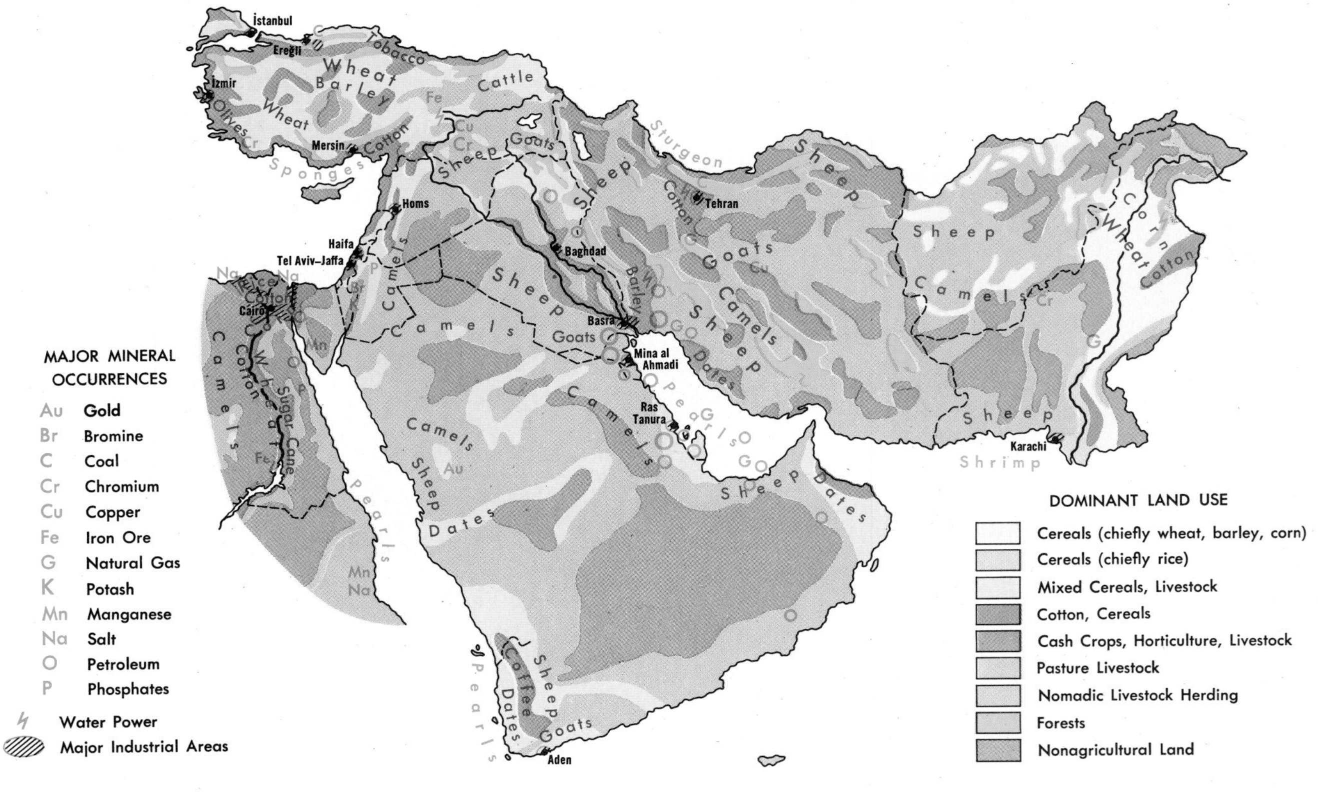

TURKEY

SYRIA

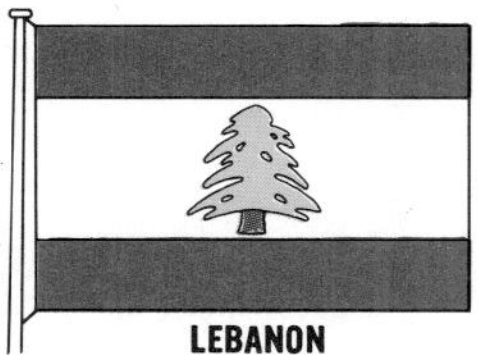

LEBANON

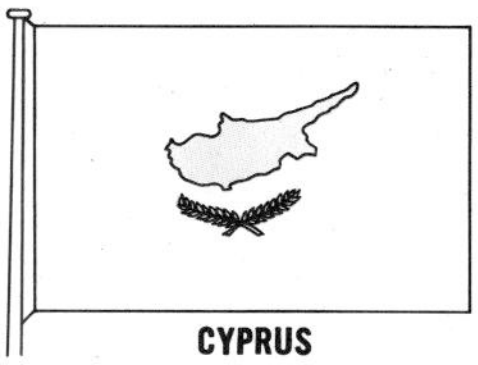

CYPRUS

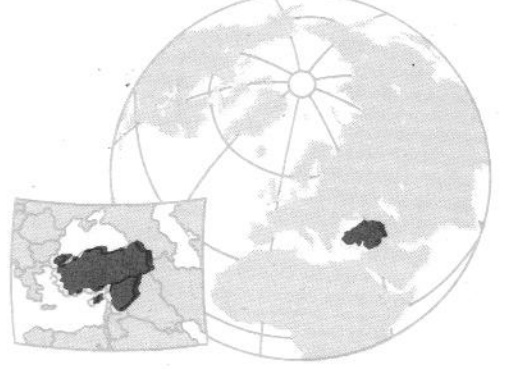

AREA 300,946 sq. mi. (779,450 sq. km.)
POPULATION 45,217,556
CAPITAL Ankara
LARGEST CITY Istanbul
HIGHEST POINT Ararat 16,946 ft. (5,165 m.)
MONETARY UNIT Turkish lira
MAJOR LANGUAGE Turkish
MAJOR RELIGION Islam

AREA 71,498 sq. mi. (185,180 sq. km.)
POPULATION 8,979,000
CAPITAL Damascus
LARGEST CITY Damascus
HIGHEST POINT Hermon 9,232 ft. (2,814 m.)
MONETARY UNIT Syrian pound
MAJOR LANGUAGES Arabic, French, Kurdish, Armenian
MAJOR RELIGIONS Islam, Christianity

AREA 4,015 sq. mi. (10,399 sq. km.)
POPULATION 3,161,000
CAPITAL Beirut
LARGEST CITY Beirut
HIGHEST POINT Qurnet es Sauda 10,131 ft. (3,088 m.)
MONETARY UNIT Lebanese pound
MAJOR LANGUAGES Arabic, French
MAJOR RELIGIONS Christianity, Islam

AREA 3,473 sq. mi. (8,995 sq. km.)
POPULATION 629,000
CAPITAL Nicosia
LARGEST CITY Nicosia
HIGHEST POINT Troödos 6,406 ft. (1,953 m.)
MONETARY UNIT Cypriot pound
MAJOR LANGUAGES Greek, Turkish, English
MAJOR RELIGIONS Eastern (Greek) Orthodoxy, Islam

CYPRUS

CITIES and TOWNS

- Dhali 2,970 ... E5
- Episkopi 2,150 ... E5
- Famagusta 38,960 ... F5
- Ktima ... E5
- Kyrenia 3,892 ... E5
- Kythrea 3,400 ... E5
- Lapithos 3,600 ... E5
- Larnaca 19,608 ... E5
- Lefka 3,650 ... E5
- Limassol 79,641 ... E5
- Morphou 9,040 ... E5
- Nicosia (cap.) 115,718 ... E5
- Paphos 8,984 ... E5
- Polis 2,200 ... E5
- Rizokarpasso 3,600 ... F5
- Yialousa 2,750 ... E5

OTHER FEATURES

- Andreas (cape) ... F5
- Arnauti (cape) ... E5
- Gata (cape) ... E5
- Greco (cape) ... F5
- Kormakiti (cape) ... E5
- Troodos (mt.) ... E5

LEBANON

CITIES and TOWNS

- A'leih 18,630 ... F6
- Amyun 7,926 ... F5
- Baa'lbek 15,560 ... G5
- Batrun 5,976 ... F5
- Beirut (cap.) 474,870 ... F6
- Beirut* 938,940 ... F6
- Hermil 2,652 ... G5
- Merj U'yun 9,318 ... F6
- Rasheiya 6,731 ... F6
- Rayak 1,480 ... G6
- Saida 32,200 ... F6
- Sidon (Saida) 32,200 ... F6
- Sur 16,483 ... F6
- Tripoli (Tarabulus) 127,611 ... F5
- Tyre (Sur) 16,483 ... F6
- Zahle 53,121 ... F6
- Zegharta 18,210 ... G5

OTHER FEATURES

- Lebanon (mts.) ... F6
- Leontes (Litani) (riv.) ... F6
- Litani (riv.) ... F6
- Sauda, Qurnet es (mt.) ... G5

SYRIA

PROVINCES

- Aleppo 1,316,872 ... G4
- Damascus 1,457,934 ... G6
- Deir ez Zor 292,780 ... H5
- Dera' 230,481 ... G6
- El Quneitra 16,490 ... F6
- Es Suweida 139,650 ... G6
- Hama 514,748 ... G5
- Haseke 468,506 ... J4
- Homs 546,176 ... G5
- Idlib 383,695 ... G5
- Latakia 389,552 ... G5
- Rashid 243,736 ... H5
- Tartus 302,065 ... G5

CITIES and TOWNS

- Abu Kemal 6,907 ... J5
- A'in el A'rab 4,529 ... H4
- Aleppo 639,428 ... G4
- Azaz 13,923 ... G4
- Baniyas 8,537 ... F5
- Busra ... G6
- Damascus (cap.) 836,668 ... G6
- Damascus* 923,253 ... G6
- Deir ez Zor 66,164 ... H5
- Dera' 27,651 ... G6
- Dimashq (Damascus) (cap.) 836,668 ... G6
- Duma 30,050 ... G6
- El Bab 27,366 ... G4
- El Haseke 32,746 ... J4
- El Ladhiqiya (Latakia) 125,716 ... F5
- El Quryatein ... G5
- El Quneitra 17,752 ... F6
- El Rashid 37,151 ... H5
- En Nebk 16,334 ... G5
- Es Suweide 29,524 ... G6
- Et Tell el Abyad ... H4
- Haffe 4,656 ... G5
- Haleb (Aleppo) 639,428 ... G4
- Hama 137,421 ... G5
- Harim 6,837 ... G4
- Homs 215,423 ... G5
- Idlib 34,515 ... G5
- Izra 3,226 ... G6
- Jeble 15,715 ... F5
- Jerablus 8,610 ... G4
- Jisr esh Shughur 13,131 ... G5
- Khan Sheikhun ... G5
- Latakia 125,716 ... F5
- Masyaf 7,058 ... G5
- Membij 13,796 ... G4
- Meskene ... H5
- Meyadin 12,515 ... J5
- Qala't es Salihiye ... J5
- Qamishliye 31,448 ... J4
- Quteife 4,993 ... G6
- Raqqa (El Rashid) 37,151 ... H5
- Sabkha 3,375 ... H5
- Safita 9,650 ... G5
- Selemiya 21,677 ... G5
- Tadmur 10,670 ... H5
- Tartus 29,842 ... F5
- Telkalakh 6,242 ... F5
- Zebdani 10,010 ... G6

OTHER FEATURES

- A'mrit (ruins) ... F5
- Arwad (Ruad) (isl.) ... F5
- A'si (Orontes) (riv.) ... G5
- Druz, Jebel ed (mts.) ... G6
- El Furat (riv.) ... H4
- Euphrates (El Furat) (riv.) ... H4
- Hermon (mt.) ... F6
- Khabur (riv.) ... J5
- Orontes (riv.) ... G5
- Palmyra (Tadmor) (ruins) ... H5
- Ruwaq, Jebel er (mts.) ... G5

TURKEY

PROVINCES

- Adana 1,240,475 ... F4
- Adiyaman 346,892 ... H4
- Afyonkarahisar 579,171 ... D3
- Ağri 330,201 ... K3
- Amasya 322,806 ... F2
- Ankara 2,585,293 ... E3
- Antalya 669,357 ... D4
- Artvin 228,026 ... J2
- Aydin 609,869 ... B4
- Balikesir 789,255 ... B3
- Bilecik 137,120 ... D2
- Bingöl 210,804 ... J3
- Bitlis 218,305 ... J3
- Bolu 428,704 ... D2
- Burdur 222,896 ... D4
- Bursa 961,639 ... C2
- Çanakkale 369,385 ... B2
- Çankiri 265,468 ... E2
- Çorum 547,580 ... F2
- Denizli 560,916 ... C4
- Diyarbakir 651,233 ... H4
- Edirne 340,732 ... B2
- Elâziğ 417,924 ... H3
- Erzincan 283,683 ... H3
- Erzurum 746,666 ... J3
- Eskişehir 495,097 ... D3
- Gaziantep 715,939 ... G4
- Giresun 463,587 ... H2
- Gümüşhane 293,673 ... H2
- Hakkâri 126,036 ... K4
- Hatay 744,113 ... G4
- Içel 714,817 ... F4
- Isparta 322,685 ... D4
- Istanbul 3,904,588 ... C2
- Izmir 1,673,966 ... B3
- Kahramanmaraş 641,480 ... G4
- Kars 707,398 ... K2
- Kastamonu 438,243 ... E2
- Kayseri 676,809 ... F3
- Kirklareli 268,399 ... B2
- Kirşehir 232,853 ... F3
- Kocaeli 477,736 ... C2
- Konya 1,422,461 ... E4
- Kütahya 470,423 ... C3
- Malatya 574,558 ... H3
- Manisa 872,375 ... B3
- Mardin 519,687 ... J4
- Muğla 400,796 ... C4
- Muş 267,203 ... J3
- Nevşehir 249,308 ... F3
- Niğde 463,121 ... F4
- Ordu 664,290 ... G2
- Rize 336,278 ... J2
- Sakarya 495,649 ... D2
- Samsun 906,381 ... F2
- Siirt 381,503 ... J4
- Sinop 267,605 ... F2
- Sivas 741,713 ... G3
- Tekirdağ 319,987 ... B2
- Tokat 599,166 ... G2
- Trabzon 719,008 ... H2
- Tunceli 164,591 ... H3
- Urfa 597,277 ... H4
- Uşak 229,679 ... C3
- Van 386,314 ... K3
- Yozgat 500,371 ... F3
- Zonguldak 836,156 ... D2

CITIES and TOWNS

- Acigöl 3,934 ... F3
- Acipayam 5,046 ... C4
- Adalia (Antalya) 130,774 ... D4
- Adana 475,384 ... F4
- Adapazari 114,130 ... D2
- Adilcevaz 9,022 ... K3
- Adiyaman 43,782 ... H4
- Afşin 18,231 ... G3
- Afyonkarahisar 60,150 ... D3
- Ağlasun 4,288 ... D4
- Ağli 3,399 ... E2
- Ağri (Karaköse) 35,284 ... K3
- Ahlat 7,995 ... K3
- Akçaabat 10,756 ... H2
- Akçadağ 7,366 ... G3
- Akçakoca 9,066 ... D2
- Akdağmadeni 7,909 ... F3
- Akhisar 53,357 ... B3
- Aksaray 45,564 ... F3
- Akşehir 35,544 ... D3
- Akseki 5,141 ... D4
- Akviran 3,799 ... E4
- Akyazi 12,438 ... D2
- Alaca 12,552 ... F2
- Alacahan 2,321 ... G3
- Alaçam 10,013 ... F2
- Alanya 18,520 ... D4
- Alaşehir 23,243 ... C3
- Alexandretta (Iskenderun) 107,437 ... G4
- Aliağa 5,727 ... B3
- Alibeyköyü 33,387 ... D6
- Almus 4,225 ... G2
- Alpu 3,718 ... D3
- Altindağ 512,392 ... E2
- Altinova 6,980 ... B3
- Altintaş 3,386 ... C3
- Altinözü 5,158 ... G4
- Alucra 7,070 ... H2
- Amasra 4,369 ... E2
- Amasya 41,496 ... G2
- Anamur 21,475 ... E4
- Andirin 5,018 ... G4
- Ankara (cap.) 1,701,004 ... E3
- Antakya 77,518 ... G4
- Antalya 130,774 ... D4
- Antioch (Antakya) 77,518 ... G4
- Araç 3,594 ... E2
- Aralik 4,155 ... L3
- Arapkir 8,436 ... H3
- Ardahan 16,285 ... K2
- Ardeşen 7,980 ... J2
- Ardanuç 2,942 ... K2
- Arguvan 2,461 ... H3
- Arhavi 6,311 ... J2
- Arpaçay 2,651 ... K2
- Arsin 6,557 ... H2
- Artova 2,813 ... G2
- Artvin 13,390 ... J2
- Aşkale 10,817 ... J3
- Avanos 8,635 ... F3
- Ayancik 7,202 ... F1
- Ayaş 4,575 ... E2
- Aybasti 13,180 ... G2
- Aydin 59,579 ... B4
- Aydincik 6,739 ... E4
- Ayranci 2,664 ... E4
- Ayvacik 3,120 ... B3
- Ayvalik 18,041 ... B3
- Babadağ 5,890 ... C4
- Babaeski 17,090 ... B2
- Bafra 34,288 ... F2
- Bahçe 10,212 ... G4
- Bakirköy 200,942 ... D6
- Baklan 3,327 ... C4
- Balâ 4,107 ... E3
- Balikesir 99,443 ... B3
- Balya 2,362 ... B3
- Banaz 6,264 ... C3
- Bandirma 45,752 ... B2
- Bartin 18,409 ... E2
- Başkale 8,558 ... K3
- Başmakçi 5,925 ... C4
- Batman 64,384 ... J4
- Bayat 4,671 ... F2
- Bayburt 20,156 ... J2
- Bayindir 14,078 ... B3
- Baykan 2,690 ... J3
- Bayramiç 6,385 ... B3
- Bergama 29,749 ... B3
- Beşiktaş 174,931 ... D6
- Beşiri 4,165 ... J4
- Besni 16,313 ... G4
- Beykoz 76,804 ... D5
- Beyoğlu 230,532 ... D6
- Beypazari 14,963 ... D2
- Beyşehir 15,060 ... D4
- Beytüşşebap 2,766 ... K4
- Biga 15,188 ... B2
- Bigadiç 7,535 ... C3
- Bilecik 11,269 ... D2
- Bingöl (Çapakçur) 22,047 ... J3
- Birecik 20,104 ... H4
- Bismil 12,775 ... J4
- Bitlis 25,054 ... J3
- Bodrum 7,858 ... B4
- Boğazliyan 10,329 ... F3
- Bolu 32,812 ... D2
- Bolvadin 29,218 ... D3
- Bor 16,560 ... F4
- Borçka 4,636 ... J2
- Bornova 45,096 ... B3
- Boyabat 13,139 ... F2
- Bozdoğan 7,218 ... C4
- Bozkir 5,294 ... E4
- Bozkurt 2,948 ... F2
- Bozova 5,462 ... H4
- Bozüyük 15,197 ... C3
- Bucak 15,090 ... D4
- Bulancak 14,153 ... H2
- Bulanik 8,296 ... K3
- Buldan 11,115 ... C3
- Bünyan 12,277 ... G3
- Burdur 36,633 ... D4
- Burhaniye 12,800 ... B3
- Bursa 346,103 ... C2
- Büyükada ... D6
- Büyükdere ... D5
- Çal 3,274 ... C3
- Çala 2,450 ... K2
- Caldiran 3,366 ... K3

(continued on following page)

Agriculture, Industry and Resources

DOMINANT LAND USE

- Cereals (chiefly wheat, barley), Livestock
- Cash Crops, Horticulture, Livestock
- Pasture Livestock
- Nomadic Livestock Herding
- Forests
- Nonagricultural Land

MAJOR MINERAL OCCURRENCES

- Ab Asbestos
- Al Bauxite
- C Coal
- Cr Chromium
- Cu Copper
- Fe Iron Ore
- Hg Mercury
- Mg Magnesium
- Na Salt
- O Petroleum
- P Phosphates
- Pb Lead
- Py Pyrites
- Sb Antimony
- Zn Zinc

- Water Power
- Major Industrial Areas

64 Turkey, Syria, Lebanon and Cyprus

(continued)

Çalköy 3,002 .... C3
Çamardi 2,419 .... F4
Çameli 2,502 .... C4
Çamlidere 4,386 .... E2
Çan 11,797 .... B2
Çanakkale 30,788 .... B6
Çandir 6,986 .... F3
Çankaya 895,005 .... E3
Çankiri 28,512 .... E2
Çapakçur 22,047 .... J3
Çardak 4,232 .... C6
Çarşamba 23,973 .... G2
Çatak 2,366 .... K4
Çatalca 7,693 .... C2
Çatalzeytin 2,271 .... F1
Çay 12,200 .... D3
Çaycuma 8,118 .... E2
Çayeli 13,480 .... J2
Çayiralan 8,071 .... F3
Çayirli 4,580 .... J3
Çekerek 3,796 .... F2
Çelikhan 5,066 .... H3
Çemişkezek 3,048 .... H3
Çerkeş 3,780 .... E2
Çerkezköy 8,428 .... C2
Çermik 9,749 .... H3
Çeşme 5,284 .... B3
Çetinkaya 3,616 .... G3
Ceyhan 62,909 .... F4
Ceylânpinar 20,171 .... H4
Çiçekdagi 3,203 .... F3
Cide 3,520 .... E2
Çifteler 8,163 .... D3
Cihanbeyli 10,079 .... E3
Çildir 2,260 .... K2
Cimin 5,341 .... H3
Çine 11,308 .... B4
Çivril 7,721 .... C3
Cizre 15,557 .... K4
Çölemerik 11,735 .... K4
Çorlu 40,134 .... B2
Çorum 64,852 .... F2
Çubuk 13,793 .... E2
Çukur 5,479 .... F3
Çukurca 3,019 .... K4
Çumra 19,225 .... E4
Çüngüş 2,616 .... H3
Daday 2,528 .... E2
Darende 8,055 .... G3
Dazkiri 3,912 .... D4
Delice 3,462 .... E3
Demirci 15,016 .... C3
Demirkent 4,204 .... E4
Demirköy 4,257 .... B2
Denizli 106,902 .... C4
Dereli 4,188 .... H2
Derik 13,292 .... J4
Derinkuyu 5,618 .... F3
Develi 17,323 .... F3
Devrek 9,164 .... D2
Devrekâni 4,014 .... E2
Dicle 5,247 .... J3
Dikili 6,916 .... B3
Dinar 19,873 .... D3
Dirmil 3,476 .... C4
Divriği 12,302 .... H3
Diyadin 5,094 .... K3
Diyarbakir 169,535 .... H4
Doğanbey 3,077 .... D4
Doğanhisar 9,487 .... D3
Doğanşehir 10,280 .... G3
Döger 3,478 .... D3
Doğubeyazit 17,612 .... K3
Domaniç 2,729 .... C3
Dörtyol 19,390 .... F4
Dumlu 4,206 .... J2
Durağan 3,259 .... F2
Dursunbey 8,615 .... C3
Düzce 32,129 .... D2
Eceabat 3,642 .... B6
Edirne 63,001 .... B2
Edremit 26,110 .... B3
Eflâni 3,793 .... E2
Eğridir 9,799 .... D4
Elâziğ 131,415 .... H3
Elbistan 26,048 .... G3
Eldivan 3,302 .... E2
Eleşkirt 8,202 .... K3
Elmali 10,184 .... C4
Emet 6,239 .... C3
Emirdağ 13,184 .... D3
Emirgazi 5,244 .... E4
Enez 2,486 .... B2
Erbaa 20,315 .... G2
Erciş 22,351 .... K3
Erdek 8,685 .... B2
Erdemli 19,936 .... F4
Ereğli 45,992 .... D2
Ereğli 50,354 .... F4
Ergani 21,936 .... H3
Erkilet 3,924 .... F3
Ermenak 13,464 .... E4
Eruh 5,340 .... K4
Erzin 15,314 .... G4
Erzincan 60,351 .... H3
Erzurum 162,973 .... J3
Eskimalatya 10,182 .... H3
Eskipazar 2,865 .... E2
Eskişehir 259,952 .... D3
Eşme 7,828 .... C3
Espiye 8,168 .... H2
Eynesil 6,081 .... H2
Eyüp 95,486 .... D6
Ezibider 3,631 .... H2
Ezine 9,359 .... B3
Fakili 4,173 .... F3
Fatih 504,127 .... D6
Fatsa 19,758 .... G2
Feke 5,576 .... G4
Fethiye 12,700 .... C4
Fevzipaşa 5,495 .... G4
Findikli 5,008 .... J2
Finike 4,200 .... D4
Foça 4,829 .... B3
Gallipoli 13,466 .... C5
Gaziantep 300,882 .... G4
Gazipaşa 6,696 .... E4
Gebze 33,110 .... C2
Gediz 10,649 .... C3
Gelibolu (Gallipoli) 13,466 .... C5
Gemerek 5,769 .... G3
Gemlik 20,704 .... C2
Genç 7,671 .... J3
Genezin 4,925 .... F3
Gercüş 4,393 .... J4
Gerede 8,259 .... E2
Gerger 2,773 .... H3
Germencik 10,558 .... B4
Gerze 7,313 .... F2
Gevaş 6,333 .... K3
Geyve 7,806 .... D2
Giresun 38,236 .... H2
Gökçe 4,470 .... B2
Göksun 10,481 .... G3
Gölbaşi 15,103 .... G4
Gölcük 33,279 .... C2
Göle 7,680 .... K2
Gölhisar 7,095 .... C4
Gölköy 10,022 .... G2
Gölmarmara 11,982 .... C3
Gölpazari 5,002 .... D2
Gönen 16,091 .... B2
Gördes 7,909 .... C3
Görele 8,079 .... H2
Göynücek 2,600 .... F2
Göynük 2,519 .... D2
Güdül 4,746 .... E2
Gülnar 6,344 .... E4
Gülşehir 6,188 .... F3
Gümüş 3,066 .... F2
Gümüşhaciköy 12,789 .... F2
Gümüşhane 11,166 .... H2
Güney 7,154 .... C3
Gürün 9,138 .... G3
Hacibektaş 5,032 .... F3
Hacilar 15,622 .... F3
Hadim 10,467 .... E4
Hafik 5,398 .... G3
Hakkâri
(Çöelemerik) 11,735 .... K4
Halfeti 3,689 .... H4
Hamur 2,267 .... K3
Hanac 2,581 .... K2
Hani 7,559 .... J3
Harput 3,231 .... H3
Haruniye 12,837 .... G4
Hassa 10,926 .... G4
Hatay (Antakya) 77,518 .... G4
Havran 7,552 .... B3
Havsa 4,298 .... B2
Havza 15,341 .... F2
Haymana 6,123 .... E3

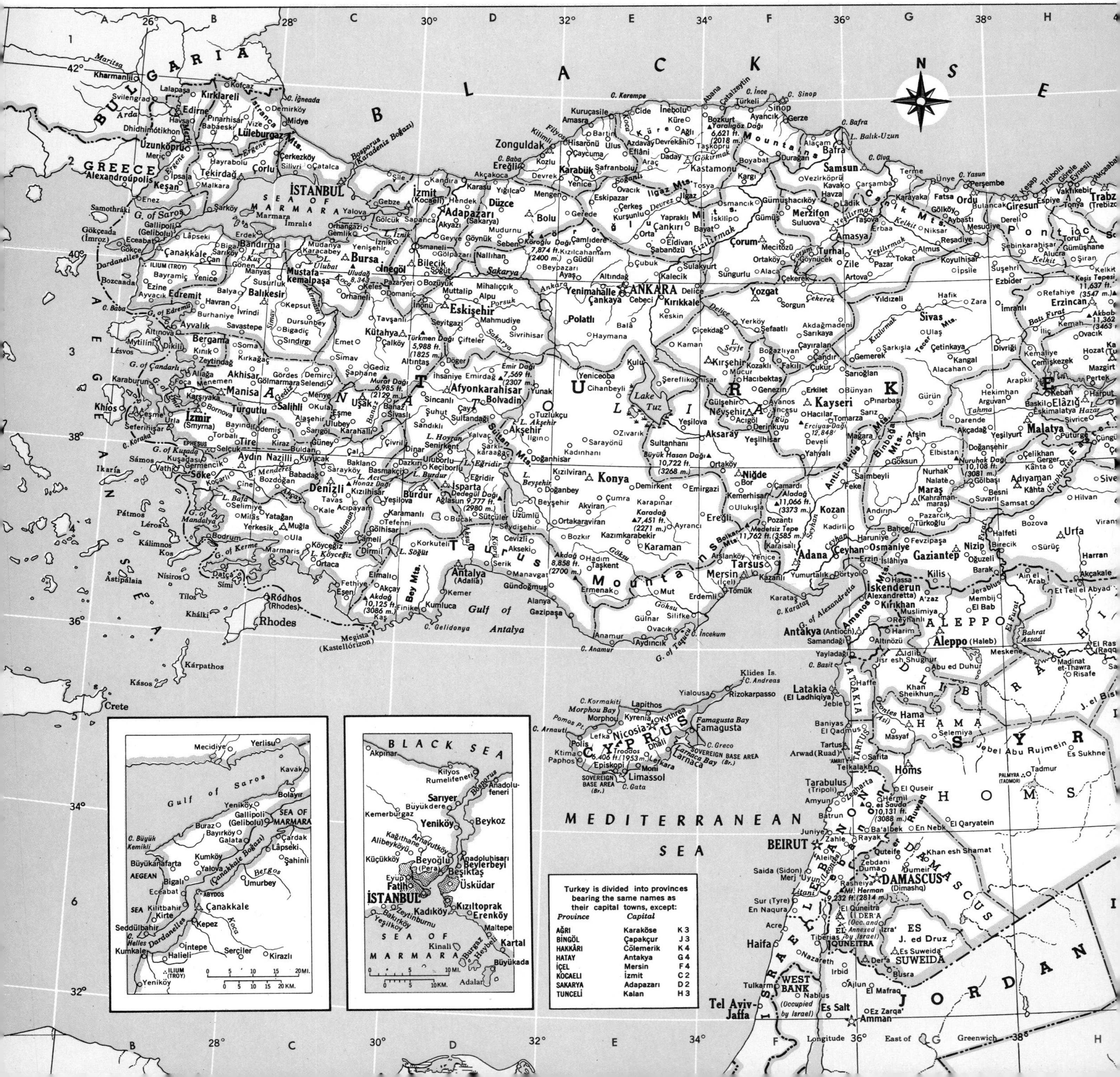

Hayrabolu 12,331 B2
Hazro 4,896 J3
Hekimhan 11,818 G3
Hendek 15,291 D2
Hilvan 6,473 H4
Hinis 10,226 J3
Hisarönü 4,485 E2
Hizan 2,545 K3
Hopa 9,089 J2
Horasan 7,724 K2
Hozat 5,796 H3
Içel (Mersin) 152,236 F4
Idil 4,862 J4
Iğdir 29,542 K3
Ilgaz 6,624 E2
Ilgin 11,830 D3
Ilica 8,947 J3
Imranli 5,667 H2
Incesu 7,089 F3
Inebolu 6,824 E2
Inegöl 37,805 C2
Inönü 4,152 D3
Ipsala 6,829 B2
Ipsile 2,328 G2
Iskenderun 107,437 G4
Iskilip 16,588 F2
Islâhiye 20,683 G4
Isparta 62,870 D4
Ispir 3,929 J2
Istanbul 2,547,364 D6
Ivrindi 3,730 B3
Izmir 636,834 B3
Izmit 165,483 D2
Iznik 11,614 C2
Kadiköy 354,957 D6
Kadinhani 11,802 E3
Kadirli 34,779 F4
Kağithane 164,448 D6
Kağizman 11,517 K2
Kâhta 15,602 H4
Kalan 11,637 H3
Kale 3,399 C4
Kalecik 4,707 E2
Kaman 16,516 E3
Kandira 10,187 D2
Kangal 5,937 G3
Karabük 69,182 E2
Karacabey 21,648 C2
Karahalli 5,539 C3
Karaisali 2,316 F4
Karakoçan 5,604 H3
Karaköse (Ağri) 35,284 K3

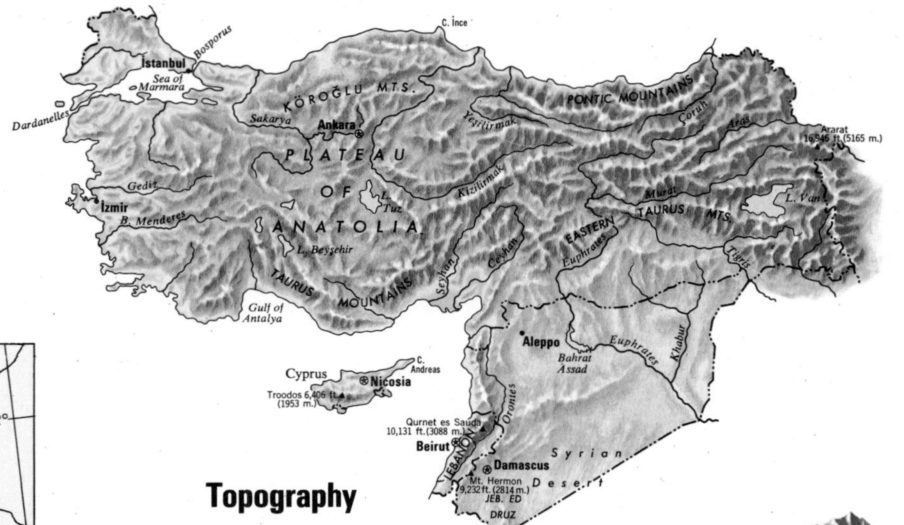

Topography

0 100 200 MI.

0 100 200 KM.

Below Sea Level | 100 m. 328 ft. | 200 m. 656 ft. | 500 m. 1,640 ft. | 1,000 m. 3,281 ft. | 2,000 m. 6,562 ft. | 5,000 m. 16,404 ft.

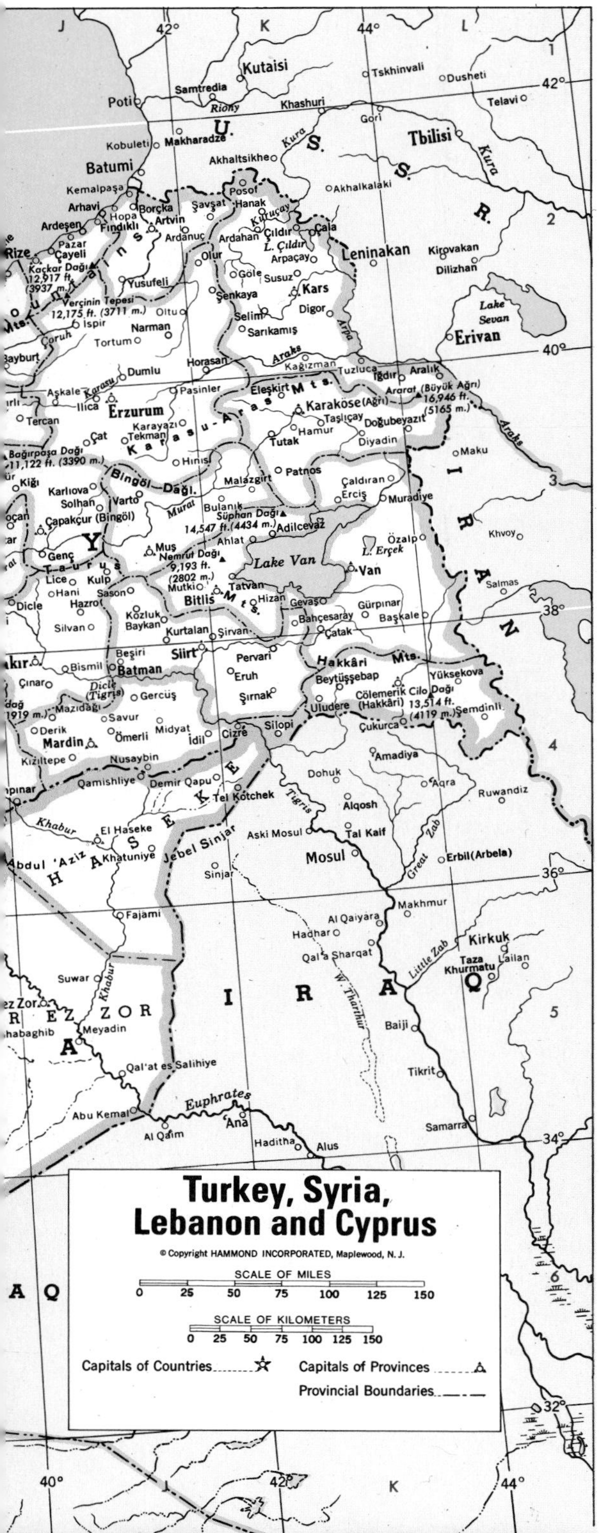

Karaman 43,759 E4
Karamanli 5,904 C4
Karapinar 19,589 E4
Karasu 11,600 D2
Karataş 5,598 F4
Karayaka 4,242 G2
Karayazi 3,595 J3
Kargi 5,021 F2
Karliova 3,631 J3
Kars 54,892 K2
Karşiyaka 171,600 B3
Kartal 53,073 D6
Kaş 2,493 C4
Kastamonu 29,993 F2
Kavak, Çanakkale 3,932 C5
Kavak, Samsun 3,964 F2
Kayseri 207,037 F3
Kazanli 4,461 F4
Kazimkarabekir 4,086 E4
Keban 5,800 H3
Keçiborlu 7,096 D4
Keles 2,423 C3
Kelkit 6,928 H2
Kemah 3,038 H3
Kemaliye 3,014 H3
Kemalpaşa 7,572 J2
Kemerburgaz 7,234 D5
Kemirhisar 6,205 F4
Kepsut 4,704 C3
Keşan 27,088 B2
Keşap 5,264 H2
Keskin 10,540 E3
Kiği 5,598 J3
Kilimli 26,649 D2
Kilis 54,055 G4
Kinik 11,785 B3
Kiraz 5,284 C3
Kirikhan 38,118 G4
Kirikkale 137,874 E3
Kirkağaç 15,078 B3
Kirklareli 33,265 B2
Kirşehir 41,415 F3
Kizilcahamam 7,050 E2
Kizilhisar 11,119 C4
Kiziltepe 21,531 J4
Kizilviran 3,260 E4
Kocaeli (Izmit) 165,483 D2
Koçarli 5,182 B4
Konya 246,727 E4
Korkuteli 10,334 D4
Köyceğiz 4,612 C4
Koyulhisar 3,861 G2
Kozakli 6,200 F3
Kozan 32,045 F4
Kozlu 27,322 D2
Kozluk 6,197 J3
Küçükköy 56,411 C6
Kula 10,807 C3
Kulp 4,474 J3
Kulu 11,707 E3
Kumkale 1,752 B6
Kumluca 7,704 D4
Küre 2,378 E2
Kurşunlu 6,562 E2
Kurtalan 7,001 J3
Kuşadasi 10,269 B4
Kütahya 82,442 C3
Kuyucak 6,039 C4
Lâdik 6,785 G2
Lâpseki 3,727 C6
Lice 8,625 J3
Lüleburgaz 32,401 B2
Maden 15,151 H3
Mağara 4,314 G3
Mahmudiye 5,240 D3
Malatya 154,505 H3
Malazgirt 13,094 K3
Malkara 14,399 B2
Maltepe 66,343 D6
Manavgat 10,804 D4
Manisa 78,114 B3
Manyas 4,410 B3
Maraş (Kahramanmaraş) 135,782 G4
Mardin 36,629 J4
Marmaris 5,596 C4
Mazgirt 3,141 H3
Mazidaği 4,842 J4
Mecitözü 6,066 F2
Menemen 18,464 B3
Mengen 2,459 D2
Meriç 3,922 B2
Mersin 152,236 F4
Merzifon 30,801 F2
Mesudiye 4,294 F4
Midyat 16,905 J4
Midye 2,003 C2
Mihaliçcik 4,004 D3
Milâs 17,929 B4
Mucur 9,398 F3
Mudanya 8,399 C2
Mudurnu 3,905 D2
Muğla 24,178 C4
Muradiye 6,334 K3
Muş 27,761 J3
Mustafakemalpaşa 27,706 C3
Mut 11,466 E4
Mutki 2,815 J3
Muttalip 3,917 D3
Nallihan 7,883 D2
Narman 4,607 J2
Nazilli 52,176 C4
Nevşehir 30,203 F3
Niğde 31,844 F4
Niksar 19,156 G2
Nizip 36,190 G4
Nurhak 5,330 G4
Nusaybin 23,684 J4
Ödemiş 37,364 C3
Of 10,376 J2
Oğuzeli 7,194 G4
Oltu 10,093 J2
Ömerli 4,738 J4
Ordu 47,481 G2
Orhaneli 3,335 C3
Orhangazi 12,181 C2
Orta 3,596 E2
Ortaca 8,604 C4
Ortakaraviran 3,856 E4
Ortaköy, Çorum 2,657 F2
Ortaköy, Niğde 6,371 F3
Osmancik 11,921 F2
Osmaneli 4,789 D2
Osmaniye 61,581 G4
Ovacik, Tunceli 2,248 H3
Özalp 4,188 K3
Palu 5,489 H3
Pasinler 14,267 J3
Patnos 15,918 K3
Pazar, Rize 8,856 J2
Pazar, Tokat 4,337 G2
Pazarcik 15,943 G4
Pazaryeri 5,633 C3
Pera (Beyoğlu) 230,532 D6
Perşembe 6,701 G2
Pertek 4,176 H3
Pervari 4,126 K4
Pinarbaşi 9,503 G3
Pinarhisar 10,523 B2
Polatli 35,267 E3
Posof 2,209 K2
Pozanti 5,408 F4
Pülümür 3,442 H3
Pütürge 4,878 H3
Refahiye 6,570 H3
Reşadiye 9,022 G2
Reyhanli 25,749 G4
Rize 36,044 J2
Şabanözü 3,442 E2
Safranbolu 14,793 E2
Saimbeyli 3,622 G4
Sakarya (Adapazari) 114,130 D2
Salihli 45,514 C3
Samandaği 22,540 F4
Samsat 2,083 H4
Samsun 168,478 F2
Sandikli 13,181 D3
Sapanca 9,040 D2
Şaphane 3,919 C3
Sarayköy 10,513 C4
Sarayönü 8,946 E3
Sarigöl 6,979 C3
Sarikamiş 21,262 K2
Sarikaya 5,160 F3
Sariköy 4,695 B2
Sarioğlan 3,245 G3
Sariyer 79,329 D5
Sariz 3,591 G3
Şarkikaraağaç 4,772 D3
Şarkişla 12,763 G3
Şarköy 5,396 B2
Sason 3,211 J3
Savaştepe 7,179 B3
Şavşat 3,078 K2
Savur 4,983 J4
Seben 2,471 D2
Şebinkarahisar 10,214 H2
Şefaatli 6,769 F3
Seferihisar 6,484 B3
Selçuk 12,251 B3
Selendi 4,457 C3
Selim 3,569 K2
Selimiye 2,989 B4
Senirkent 8,247 D3
Şenkaya 3,190 K2
Şereflikoçhisar 20,523 E3
Serik 14,161 D4
Seydişehir 25,651 D4
Seyitgazi 2,819 D3
Siirt 35,654 J4
Şile 4,062 C2
Silifke 19,257 E4
Silivri 8,525 C2
Silopi 4,460 K4
Silvan 29,599 J3
Simav 11,601 C3
Sincanli 3,847 D3
Sindirgi 7,818 C3
Sinop 16,098 F2
Şiran 5,048 H2
Şirnak 10,587 K4
Şirvan 5,166 K3
Sivas 149,201 G3
Sivasli 4,394 C3
Siverek 40,990 H4
Sivrihisar 8,713 D3
Smyrna (Izmir) 636,834 B3
Söğüt 5,329 D3
Söke 35,407 B4
Solhan 7,014 J3
Soma 23,713 B3
Sorgun 14,081 F3
Şuhut 8,154 D3
Sulakyurt 4,311 E2
Sultandaği 4,017 D3
Sultanhani 5,112 E3
Suluova 21,278 F2
Sungurlu 21,641 F2
Sürmene 8,096 J2
Sürüç 20,395 H4
Suşehri 10,863 H2
Susurluk 14,000 C3
Susuz 5,006 K2
Sütçüler 2,721 D4
Tarsus 102,186 F4
Taşkent 7,098 E4
Taşköprü 8,146 F2
Taşliçay 3,684 K3
Taşova 6,516 F4
Tatvan 29,271 K3
Tavas 9,728 C4
Tavşanli 19,575 C3
Tefenni 4,280 C4
Tekirdağ 41,257 B2
Tércan 6,068 J3
Terme 15,660 G2
Tire 30,694 B3
Tirebolu 7,385 H2
Tokat 48,588 G2
Tomarza 6,548 F3
Tömük 7,660 F4
Tonya 10,544 H2
Torbali 17,237 B3
Tortum 4,110 J2
Torul 3,221 H2
Tosya 17,515 F2
Trabzon 97,210 H2
Trebizond (Trabzon) 97,210 H2
Tunceli (Kalan) 11,637 H3
Turgutlu 47,009 B3
Turhal 39,170 F2
Türkeli 2,194 F2
Türkoğlu 9,207 G4
Tutak 4,325 K3
Tuzluca 5,209 K3
Tuzlukçu 4,613 D3
Ula 5,117 C4
Ulaş 2,469 G3
Ulubey 4,214 C3
Uluborlu 10,016 D3
Uludere 4,050 K4
Ulukişla 6,336 F4
Umurbey 2,754 C6
Ünye 23,366 G2
Urfa 132,934 H4
Ürgüp 6,758 F3
Urla 13,903 B3
Uşak 58,578 C3
Üsküdar 202,957 D6
Üzümlü 4,365 D4
Uzunköprü 27,005 B2
Vakfikebir 12,556 H2
Van 63,663 K3
Varto 5,572 J3
Vezirköprü 11,705 F2
Viranşehir 26,244 H4
Vize 8,203 B2
Yahyali 13,738 F3
Yalova, Istanbul 27,289 C2
Yalvaç 18,305 D3
Yaprakli 3,020 E2
Yatağan 4,903 C4
Yayladaği 4,471 F5
Yenice, Çanakkale 4,004 B3
Yenice, Içel 4,106 F4
Yenice, Zonguldak 5,791 E2
Yeniceoba 5,740 E3
Yeniköy, Istanbul D6
Yenimahalle 198,643 E3
Yenişehir 15,188 C2
Yerkesik 2,381 C4
Yerköy 19,927 F3
Yeşilhisar 10,409 F3
Yeşilköy D6
Yeşilova, Burdur 3,685 C4
Yeşilova, Niğde 5,237 E3
Yeşilyurt 7,451 H3
Yildizeli 7,043 G3
Yozgat 32,501 F3
Yüksekova 7,329 L4
Yumurtalik 2,442 F4
Yunak 6,187 D3
Yusufeli 3,050 J2
Zara 10,376 G3
Zeytinburnu 123,548 D6
Zeytindağ 3,517 B3
Zile 32,157 G2
Zivarik 2,703 E3
Zonguldak 90,221 D2

OTHER FEATURES

Abydos (ruins) B6
Aci (lake) C4
Adalar (isl.) D6
Aegean (sea) A3
Ağri, Büyük (Ararat) (mt.) L3
Akdağ (mt.) C4
Aladağ (mt.) F4
Alexandretta (gulf) F4
Amanos (mts.) G4
Anamur (cape) E5
Anatolia (reg.) D3
Ankara (riv.) D3
Antalya (gulf) D4
Anti-Taurus (mts.) G3
Araks (riv.) K2
Ararat (mt.) L3
Arpa (riv.) K2
Baba (cape) A3
Bati Firat (riv.) H3
Beyşehir (lake) D4
Black (sea) E1
Bosporus (str.) C2
Bozcaada (isl.) A3
Burgaz (isl.) D6
Büyük Ağri (Ararat) (mt.) L3
Çanakkale Boğazi (Dardanelles) (str.) B6
Çandarli (gulf) B3
Canik (mts.) G2
Ceyhan (riv.) F4
Cilo Daği (mt.) K4
Çoruh (riv.) J2
Dardanelles (str.) B6
Dicle (riv.) J4
Eastern Taurus (mts.) J3
Ephesus (ruins) B3
Erciyas Daği (mt.) F3
Ergene (riv.) B2
Euphrates (Firat) (riv.) G4
Firat (riv.) G4
Gediz (riv.) C3
Gelidonya (cape) D4
Gökçeada (isl.) A2
Göksu (riv.) E4
Helles (cape) B6
Heybeli (isl.) D6
Ilium (ruins) B6
Imroz (Gökçeada) (isl.) A2
Ince (cape) F1
Istranca (mts.) B2
Kaçkar Daği (mt.) J2
Karadeniz Boğazi (Bosporus) (str.) C2
Karasu-Aras (mts.) J3
Kelkit (riv.) G2
Kerme (gulf) B4
Keşiş Tepesi (mt.) H3
Kizilirmak (riv.) F2
Koca (riv.) C3
Köroğlu (mts.) E2
Küre (mts.) E2
Mandalya (gulf) B4
Marmara (isl.) B2
Marmara (sea) C2
Menderes, Büyük (riv.) C4
Meriç (riv.) B2
Murat (riv.) H3
Pontic (mts.) H2
Porsuk (riv.) D3
Prinkipo (Adalar) (isl.) D6
Sakarya (riv.) D2
Saros (gulf) B2
Seyhan (riv.) F4
Simav (riv.) C3
Sinop (cape) F1
Sultan (mts.) D3
Süphan Daği (mt.) K3
Taurus (mts.) D4
Tigris (Dicle) J4
Troy (Ilium) (ruins) B6
Tuz (lake) E3
Van (lake) K3
Yeşilirmak (riv.) G2

* City and suburbs

Topography

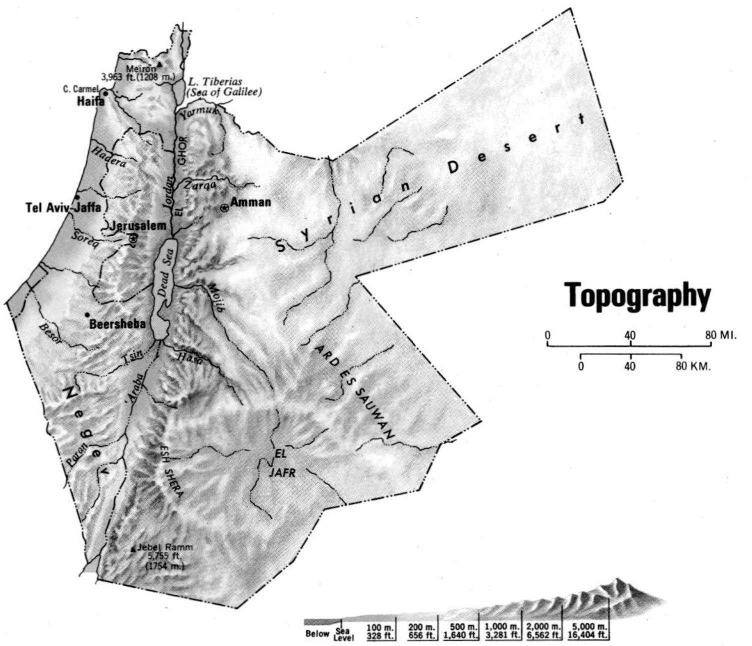

ISRAEL

DISTRICTS

Central 572,300 .... B3
Haifa 480,800 .... C2
Jerusalem 338,600 .... B4
Northern 473,700 .... C2
Southern 351,300 .... B5
Tel Aviv 905,100 .... B3

CITIES and TOWNS

Acre 34,400 .... C2
Afiqim 1,243 .... D2
'Afula 17,400 .... C2
Ahuzzam 407 .... B4
Akko (Acre) 34,400 .... C2
Arad 5,400 .... C5
'Arrabe 6,000 .... C2
Ashdod 40,500 .... B4
Ashdot Yaa'qov 1,197 .... D2
Ashqelon 43,100 .... A4
Atlit 1,516 .... B2
Avihayil 579 .... B3
Bat Shelomo 218 .... B2
Bat Yam 124,100 .... B3
Be'eri 390 .... A5
Be'er Menuha D5
Beersheba (Be'er Sheva) 101,000 .... B5
Be'er Tuveya 602 .... B4
Beit Guvrin B4
Bene Beraq 74,100 .... B3
Bet Qama 228 .... B5
Bet She'an 11,300 .... D3
Bet Shemesh 10,100 .... B4
Binyamina 2,701 .... B2
Carmiel C2
Dafna 577 .... D1
Dalyat al-Karmel 6,200 .... B2
Dan 498 .... D1
Dimona 23,700 .... D4
Dor 195 .... B2
E'in Gedi C5
E'in Harod 1,372 .... C2
Elat D6
Elath (Elat) 12,800 .... D6
El 'Auja D5
Elyakim 568 .... C2
Elyashiv 435 .... B3
Even Yehuda 3,464 .... B3
Gal'on 356 .... B4
Gat 430 .... B4
Gedera 5,400 .... B4
Gerofit D5
Gesher 360 .... C2
Gesher Haziv 238 .... C1
Gevara'm 283 .... B4
Gilat 561 .... B5
Ginnosar 473 .... D2
Giv'atayim 48,500 .... B3
Giva't Brenner 1,505 .... B4
Giv'at Hayyim 1,360 .... B3
Habonim 189 .... B2
Hadera 31,900 .... B3
Haifa 227,800 .... B2
Haifa* 367,400 .... B2
Hatseva D5
Hazerim 127 .... B5
Hazor Hagelilit D2
Helez 466 .... B4
Herzeliyya 41,200 .... B3
Hod Hasharon 13,500 .... B3
Hodiyya 400 .... B4
Holon 121,200 .... B3
Iksal 2,156 .... C2
Jerusalem (cap.) 376,000 .... C4
Jish 1,498 .... C1
Kafar Kanna 5,200 .... C2
Kafr Yasif 2,975 .... C2
Karkur-Pardes Hanna 13,600 .... C3
Kefar Blum 565 .... D1
Kefar Gila'di 701 .... C1
Kefar Ruppin 306 .... D3
Kefar Sava 26,500 .... B3
Kefar Vitkin 808 .... B3
Kefar Zekhariya 420 .... B4
Kinneret 909 .... D2
Lod (Lydda) 30,500 .... B4
Lydda 30,500 .... B4
Magen 149 .... A5
Maa'lot-Tarshiha C1
Malkiya D1
Mash 'Abbe Sade 238 .... B6
Mavqii'm 177 .... B4
Megiddo C2
Metula 261 .... D1
Migdal 688 .... C2
Migdal Ha E'meq C2
Mikhmoret 608 .... B3
Mishmar Hanegev 336 .... B5
Mishmar Hayarden D1
Mivtahim 398 .... A5
Mizpe Ramon 331 .... D5
Moza Illit 219 .... C4
Mughar 4,010 .... C2
Muqeible 459 .... C2
Nahariyya 24,000 .... C1
Nazareth 33,300 .... C2
Nazerat I'llit C2
Negba 453 .... B4
Nes Ziyyona 11,700 .... B4
Netanya 70,700 .... B3
Netivot B5
Nevatim 436 .... B5
Newe Yam 211 .... B2
Newe Zohar C5
Nir Yitzhaq 209 .... A5
Nizzanim 479 .... B4
Ofaqim B5
O'mer B5
Oron C6
Or Yehuda B4
Pardes Hanna-Karkur 13,600 .... B2
Peduyim 361 .... B5
Petah Tiqwa 112,000 .... B3
Qadima 2,937 .... B3
Qalansuwa B3
Qedma 157 .... B4
Qiryat Atta C2
Qiryat Bialik 18,000 .... C2
Qiryat Gat 19,200 .... B4
Qiryat Mal'akhi B4
Qiryat Motzkin 17,600 .... C2
Qiryat Shemona 15,200 .... C1
Qiryat Tivo'n 9,800 .... C2
Qiryat Yam 19,800 .... C2
Raa'nana 14,900 .... B3
Ramat Gan 120,900 .... B3
Ramat Hasharon 20,100 .... B3
Rame 2,986 .... C2
Ramla 34,100 .... B4
Rehovot 39,200 .... B4
Rei'm 155 .... A5
Revadim 175 .... B4
Revivim 258 .... D5
Rishon Le Ziyyon 51,900 .... B4
Rosh Ha 'Ayin B3
Rosh Pinna 700 .... D2
Ruhama 497 .... B4
Saa'd 418 .... B5
Safad (Zefat) 13,600 .... C2
Sakhnin 8,400 .... C2
Sede Boqer D5
Sederot B4
Sedom D5
Sedot Yam 511 .... B3
Shave Ziyyon 269 .... B2
Shefara'm 11,800 .... C2
Shefayim 614 .... B3
Shoval 393 .... B5
Tayibe 11,700 .... C3
Tel Aviv-Jaffa 343,300 .... B3
Tel Aviv-Jaffa* 1,219,900 .... B3
Tiberias 23,800 .... C2
Tirat Hakarmel 14,400 .... B2
Tirat Zevi 353 .... D3
Tur'an 2,304 .... C2
Umm el Fahm 13,300 .... C2
Urim 203 .... B5
Uzza 487 .... B4
Yad Mordekhai 416 .... A4
Yagur 1,266 .... C2
Yahav D5
Yavne 10,100 .... B4
Yavne'el 1,580 .... D2
Yehud 8,900 .... B3
Yeroham 5,800 .... B6
Yesodot 293 .... B4
Yesud Hamaa'la 428 .... D1
Yiftah D1
Yirka 2,715 .... C2
Yotvata D5
Zavdi'el 396 .... B4
Ze'elim 148 .... A5
Zefat 13,600 .... C2
Zikhron Yaa'qov 6,500 .... B2
Zippori 241 .... C2

OTHER FEATURES

Aqaba (gulf) D6
'Araba, Wadi (valley) D5
Beer Sheva' (dry riv.) B5
Besor (riv.) B5
Carmel (cape) B2
Carmel (mt.) C2
Dead (sea) C4
Galilee, Sea of (Tiberias) (lake) D2
Galilee (reg.) C2
Gerar (dry riv.) B5
Hadera (dry riv.) B3
Haniqra, Rosh (cape) C1
Jordan (riv.) D3
Judaea (reg.) B5
Lakhish (dry riv.) B4
Meiron (mt.) C1
Negev (reg.) D5

Agriculture, Industry and Resources

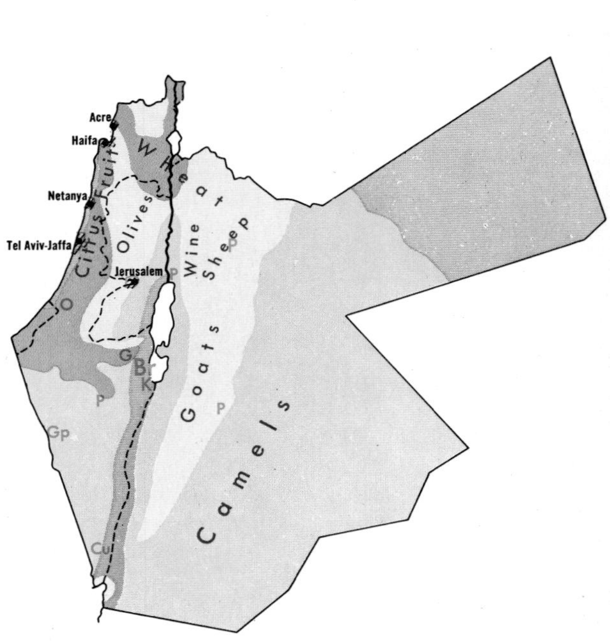

DOMINANT LAND USE

- Cereals, Livestock
- Cash Crops, Horticulture
- Nomadic Livestock Herding
- Nonagricultural Land

MAJOR MINERAL OCCURRENCES

- Br Bromine
- Cu Copper
- G Natural Gas
- Gp Gypsum
- K Potash
- O Petroleum
- P Phosphates
- Major Industrial Areas

ISRAEL

JORDAN

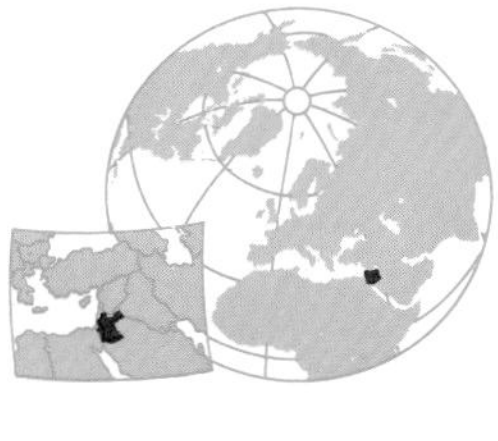

ISRAEL

AREA 7,847 sq. mi. (20,324 sq. km.)
POPULATION 3,878,000
CAPITAL Jerusalem
LARGEST CITY Tel Aviv-Jaffa
HIGHEST POINT Meiran 3,963 ft. (1,208 m.)
MONETARY UNIT shekel
MAJOR LANGUAGES Hebrew, Arabic
MAJOR RELIGIONS Judaism, Islam, Christianity

JORDAN

AREA 35,000 sq. mi. (90,650 sq. km.)
POPULATION 2,152,273
CAPITAL Amman
LARGEST CITY Amman
HIGHEST POINT Jeb. Ramm 5,755 ft. (1,754 m.)
MONETARY UNIT Jordanian dinar
MAJOR LANGUAGE Arabic
MAJOR RELIGION Islam

Qishon (riv.)	C2
Ramon (mt.)	D5
Rubin (dry riv.)	B4
Tabor (mt.)	C2
Tiberias (lake)	D2
Yarmuk (riv.)	D2
Yarqon (riv.)	B3

GAZA STRIP

CITIES and TOWNS

'Abasan 1,481	A5
Bani Suheila 7,561	A5
Beit Hanun 4,756	A4
Deir el Balah 10,854	A5
Deir el Balah* 18,118	A5
Gaza 87,793	A5
Gaza* 118,272	A5
Jabaliya 10,508	A4
Jabaliya* 43,604	A4
Khan Yunis 29,522	A5
Khan Yunis* 52,997	A5
Rafah 10,812	A5
Rafah* 49,812	A5

WEST BANK

CITIES AND TOWNS

'Ajja 1,322	C3
'Anabta 3,426	C3
Anin 914	C2
'Anza 807	C3
'Aqqaba 1,127	C3
'Aqraba 2,501	C3
Ariha (Jericho) 5,312	C4
'Arraba 4,231	C3
'Arura 849	C3
'Attil 3,808	C3
Beit Fajjar 2,474	C4
Beit Hanina 1,177	C4
Beit Jala 6,041	C4
Beit Lahm (Bethlehem) 14,439	C4
Beit Nuba 1,350	C4
Beit Sahur 5,380	C4
Bethlehem 14,439	C4
Biddu 1,259	C4
Birqin 2,036	C3
Bir Zeit 2,311	C4
Burqa 2,477	C3
Deir Ballut 1,058	C3
Deir Sharaf 973	C3
Dhahiriya 4,875	B5
Duma 524	C3
Dura 4,954	C4
El Bira 9,674	C4
El Bira* 13,037	C4
El Khalil (Hebron) 38,309	C4
Er Rihiya 679	C5
Ez Zababida 1,474	C3
Falama 162	C3
Halhul 6,041	C4
Haris 641	C3
Hebron 38,309	C4
Idna 3,713	B4
I'mwas 1,955	B4
Jaba 2,817	C3
Jalama 784	C3
Jalbun 914	C3
Jalud 221	C3
Jenin 8,346	C3
Jenin* 13,365	C3
Jericho 5,312	C4
Jericho* 6,931	C4
Jifna 655	C4
Kharas 1,364	C4
Nablus (Nabulus) 41,799	C3
Nahhalin 1,109	C4
Nil'in 1,227	C4
Qabalan 1,970	C3
Qabatiya 6,005	C3
Qaffin 2,480	C3
Qalqiliya 8,926	C3
Qibya 926	C4
Rafidiya 1,123	C3
Ramallah 12,134	C4
Rammun 1,198	C4
Rantis 897	C3
Salfit 3,201	C3
Samu 3,784	C5
Shuf'at 14,000	C4
Shuweika 2,332	C3
Silat Dhahr 2,104	C3
Sinjil 1,823	C3
Siris 1,285	C3
Tammun 2,952	C3
Tarqumiya 2,412	C4
Tubas 5,262	C3
Tulkarm 10,255	C3
Tulkarm* 15,275	C3
Tur 12,200	C4
Yab'ad 4,857	C3
Yabrud 277	C4
Yamun 4,384	C3
Yatta 7,281	C5
Zububa 633	C2

OTHER FEATURES

Golan Heights	D1
West Bank	C3

JORDAN

GOVERNORATES

El Asima 1,000,000	D4
El Balqa 113,000	D4
El Karak 93,000	E5
Irbid 506,000	D3
Ma'an 62,000	D5

CITIES and TOWNS

'Ajlun⊙ 42,000	D3
Amman (cap.) 711,850	D4
'Anjara 3,163	D3
'Aqaba 15,000	D6
Bala'ma 769	E3
Baqura 3,042	D2
Damiya 483	D3
Dana 844	E5
Deir Abu Sai'd 1,927	D3
Dhira'	D5
El 'Al 492	D4
El Husn 3,728	D3
El Karak 10,000	E4
El Kitta 987	D3
El Madwar 164	E3
El Mafraq 15,500	E3
El Majdal 259	D3
El Quweira 268	E5
El Yaduda 251	D4
Er Rafid 787	D2
Er Ramtha 19,000	E2
Er Rumman 293	D3
Er Ruseifa 6,200	E3
Esh Shaubak 01	D5
Es Sahab 2,580	E4
Es Salt 24,000	D3
Es Sukhna 649	E3
Et Tafila⊙ 17,000	E5
Et Taiyiba 2,606	D2
Ez Zarqa' 263,400	E3
Harima 635	D2
Hawara 2,342	D2
Hisban 718	D4
I'bbin 1,364	D3
Irbid 136,770	D2
Jabir 132	E2
Jarash⊙ 29,000	D3
Kitim 1,026	D3
Kufrinja 3,922	D3
Kuraiyima	D3
Maa'd 125	D2
Maa'n 9,500	E5
Ma'daba 22,600	D4
Mai'n 1,271	D4
Manja 353	D4
Mazra'	C5
Nau'r 2,382	D4
Nitil 348	D4
Qumeim 955	D2
Ra's en Naqb 225	E5
Safi	E5
Safut 4,210	D3
Samar 716	D2
Sarih 3,390	D2
Shunat Nimrin 109	D4
Subeihi 514	D3
Suf	D3
Suweilih 3,457	D3
Suweima 315	D4
Um Jauza 582	D3
Wadi es Sir 4,455	D4
Wadi Musa 654	E5
Waqqas 2,321	D2
Zuweiza 126	D4

OTHER FEATURES

'Ajlun (range)	D3
Aqaba (gulf)	D6
'Araba, Wadi (valley)	D5
Dead (sea)	C4
Ebal (mt.)	C3
El Ghor (reg.)	C6
El Lisan (pen.)	C5
Hasa, Wadi el (dry riv.)	E5
Jordan (riv.)	D3
Judaea (reg.)	C4
Khirbet Qumran (site)	D4
Mashash, Wadi (dry riv.)	C4
Nebo (mt.)	D4
Petra (ruins)	D5
Ramm, Jebel (mt.)	D5
Samaria (reg.)	C3
Shallala, Wadi esh (dry riv.)	D2
Shu'eib, Wadi (dry riv.)	D4
Tell 'Asur (mt.)	C4
Yabis, Wadi el (dry riv.)	D3
Zarqa (riv.)	D3

*City and suburbs.
⊙Population of subdivision.

IRAN

INTERNAL DIVISIONS

Azerbaijan, East
(prov.) 3,194,543 . . . . . E1
Azerbaijan, West
(prov.) 1,404,875 . . . . . D1
Bakhtaran (prov.) 1,016,199 . . . . . E3
Bakhtiari
(governorate) 394,300 . . . . . F4
Boyer Ahmediyeh and Kohkiluyeh
(governorate) 244,750 . . . . . G5
Bushehr (prov.) 345,427 . . . . . G6
Central (Markazi)
(prov.) 6,921,283 . . . . . G3
Esfahan (Isfahan)
(prov.) 1,974,938 . . . . . H4
Fars (prov.) 2,020,947 . . . . . H6
Gilan (prov.) 1,577,800 . . . . . F2
Hamadan (governorate) 1,086,512 . . . . . F3
Hormozgan (prov.) 463,419 . . . . . J7
Ilam (governorate) 244,222 . . . . . E4
Isfahan (prov.) 1,974,938 . . . . . H4
Kerman (prov.) 1,088,045 . . . . . K6
Khorasan (prov.) 3,266,650 . . . . . K3
Khuzestan (prov.) 2,176,612 . . . . . F5
Kordestan (Kurdistan)
(prov.) 781,889 . . . . . E3
Lorestan (Luristan)
(governorate) 924,848 . . . . . F4
Mazandaran (prov.) 2,384,226 . . . . . H2
Semnan (governorate) 485,875 . . . . . J3
Sistan and Baluchestan
(prov.) 659,297 . . . . . M6
Yazd (governorate) 356,218 . . . . . J5
Zanjan (governorate) 579,000 . . . . . F2

CITIES and TOWNS

Abadan 296,081 . . . . . F5
Abadeh 16,000 . . . . . H5
Abarqu 8,000 . . . . . H5
Abhar 24,000 . . . . . F2
Agha Jari 24,195 . . . . . F5
Ahar 24,000 . . . . . E1
Ahvaz (Ahwaz) 329,006 . . . . . F5
Amol 68,782 . . . . . H2
Anarak 2,038 . . . . . H4
Andimeshk 16,000 . . . . . F4
Aradan 8,978 . . . . . H3
Arak 114,507 . . . . . F3
Ardabil 147,404 . . . . . F1
Ardestan 5,868 . . . . . H4
Asadabad 7,000 . . . . . F3
Asterabad (Gorgan) 88,348 . . . . . J2
Babol 67,790 . . . . . H2
Babol Sar 7,237 . . . . . H2
Baft 6,000 . . . . . K6
Bakhtaran 290,861 . . . . . E3
Bam 22,000 . . . . . L6
Bandar 'Abbas 89,103 . . . . . J7
Bandar-e Anzali
(Enzeli) 55,978 . . . . . F2
Bandar-e Deylam 3,691 . . . . . G5
Bandar-e Khomeyni 6,000 . . . . . F5
Bandar-e Lengeh 4,920 . . . . . J7
Bandar-e Mas hur 17,000 . . . . . F5
Bandar-e Rig 1,889 . . . . . G6
Bandar-e Torkeman 13,000 . . . . . H2
Bandar Shahpur 6,000 . . . . . F5
Bastak 2,473 . . . . . J7
Bastam 3,296 . . . . . J2
Behbehan 39,874 . . . . . G5
Behshahr 26,032 . . . . . H2
Bejestan 3,823 . . . . . K3
Bijar 12,000 . . . . . E3
Birjand 25,854 . . . . . L4
Bojnurd 31,248 . . . . . K2
Borazjan 20,000 . . . . . G6
Borujerd 100,103 . . . . . F4
Bostan 4,619 . . . . . F5
Bowkan 9,000 . . . . . E2
Bushehr (Bushire) 57,681 . . . . . G6
Chalus 15,000 . . . . . G2
Damavand 5,319 . . . . . H3
Damghan 13,000 . . . . . J2
Darab 13,000 . . . . . J6
Daran 4,609 . . . . . G4
Darreh Gaz 11,000 . . . . . L2
Dasht-e Azadegan 21,000 . . . . . F5
Dehkhvareqan 6,000 . . . . . D2
Delijan 6,000 . . . . . G4
Dezful 110,287 . . . . . F4
Dizful (Dezful) 110,287 . . . . . F4
Duzdab (Zahedan) 92,628 . . . . . M6
Emamshahr 30,767 . . . . . J2
Enzeli 55,978 . . . . . F2
Esfahan (Isfahan) 671,820 . . . . . G4
Eslamabad 12,000 . . . . . E3
Estahbanat 18,187 . . . . . J6
Evaz 6,064 . . . . . J7
Ezna 5,000 . . . . . F4
Fahrej (Iranshahr) 5,000 . . . . . M7
Fariman 8,000 . . . . . L3
Farrashband 3,532 . . . . . G6
Fasa 19,000 . . . . . H6
Ferdows 11,000 . . . . . K3
Firuzabad 8,718 . . . . . H6
Firuzkuh 4,684 . . . . . H3
Fowman 9,000 . . . . . F2
Gach Saran G5
Ganaveh 9,000 . . . . . G6
Garmsar 4,723 . . . . . H3
Gavater M8
Ghaemshahr 63,289 . . . . . H2
Golpayegan 20,515 . . . . . G4
Golshan (Tabas) 10,000 . . . . . K4
Gomishan 6,000 . . . . . J2
Gonabad 8,000 . . . . . L3
Gonbad-e Kavus 59,868 . . . . . J2
Gonbadli 531 . . . . . M2
Gorgan (Gurgan) 88,348 . . . . . J2
Haft Gel 10,000 . . . . . F5
Hamadan 155,846 . . . . . F3
Hashtpar 5,000 . . . . . F2
Hormoz 2,569 . . . . . J7
Huzgan 4,722 . . . . . F5
Ilam 15,000 . . . . . E4
Iranshahr 5,000 . . . . . M7
Isfahan 671,825 . . . . . G4
Jahrom 38,236 . . . . . H6
Jajarm 3,641 . . . . . K2
Jask 1,078 . . . . . K8
Kakhk 4,043 . . . . . L3
Kangan 2,682 . . . . . G7
Kangavar 9,414 . . . . . F3
Karaj 138,774 . . . . . G3
Kashan 84,545 . . . . . G3
Kashmar 17,000 . . . . . L3
Kazerun 51,309 . . . . . G6
Kazvin (Qazvin) 138,527 . . . . . F2
Kerman 140,309 . . . . . K5
Khaf 5,000 . . . . . L3
Khalkhal 5,422 . . . . . F2
Khash 7,439 . . . . . M6
Khiyav 9,000 . . . . . E1
Khoman 3,054 . . . . . F2
Khomeinishar 46,836 . . . . . G4
Khorramabad 104,928 . . . . . F4
Khorramshahr 146,709 . . . . . F5
Khvaf 5,000 . . . . . L3
Khvonsar 10,947 . . . . . F4
Khvor 2,912 . . . . . J4
Khvoy (Khoi) 70,040 . . . . . D1
Kord Kuy 9,855 . . . . . J2
Lahijan 25,725 . . . . . G2
Lar 22,000 . . . . . J7
Mahabad 28,610 . . . . . D2
Mahallat 12,000 . . . . . G4
Mahan 8,000 . . . . . K5
Maku 7,000 . . . . . D1
Malamir (Izeh) 1,983 . . . . . F5
Malayer 28,434 . . . . . F3
Maragheh 60,820 . . . . . E2
Marand 24,000 . . . . . D1
Marv Dasht 25,498 . . . . . H6
Mashhad (Meshed) 670,180 . . . . . L2
Masjed Soleyman 77,161 . . . . . F5
Medishahr 9,000 . . . . . H3
Mehran 664 . . . . . E4
Meshed 670,180 . . . . . L2
Meshed-i-Sar (Babol
Sar) 12,000 . . . . . H2
Meybod 15,000 . . . . . J4
Miandowab 19,000 . . . . . E2
Mianeh 28,447 . . . . . E2
Minab 4,228 . . . . . K7
Mirjaveh 11,000 . . . . . M6
Naft-e Shah 3,043 . . . . . D4
Nahavand 24,000 . . . . . F3
Na'in 5,925 . . . . . H4
Najafabad 76,236 . . . . . G4
Naraq 2,725 . . . . . G3
Nasratabad (Zabol) 20,000 . . . . . M5
Natanz 4,370 . . . . . H4
Neyriz 16,114 . . . . . J6
Neyshabur 59,101 . . . . . L2
Nishapur (Neyshabur) 59,101 . . . . . L2
Nosratabad 20,000 . . . . . L6
Now Shahr 8,000 . . . . . G2
Orumiyeh (Urmia) 163,991 . . . . . D2
Oshnoviyeh 5,000 . . . . . D2
Pahlevi (Enzeli) 55,978 . . . . . F2
Pazanan 81 . . . . . F5
Qasr-e-Shirin 15,094 . . . . . E3
Qayen 6,000 . . . . . L4
Qazvin 138,527 . . . . . F2
Qom 246,831 . . . . . G3
Qorveh 2,929 . . . . . E3
Quchan 29,133 . . . . . L2
Qum (Qom) 246,831 . . . . . G3
Rafsanjan 21,000 . . . . . K5
Ramhormoz 9,000 . . . . . F5
Rasht 187,203 . . . . . F2
Ravar 5,074 . . . . . K5
Resht (Rasht) 187,203 . . . . . F2
Rey 102,825 . . . . . G3
Reza'iyeh (Urmia) 163,991 . . . . . D2
Rigan 8,255 . . . . . L6
Rud Sar 7,460 . . . . . G2
Sabzevar 69,174 . . . . . K2
Sabzvaran 7,000 . . . . . K6
Saeendey 4,195 . . . . . E2
Sai'dabad 20,000 . . . . . J6
Sakht-Sar 12,000 . . . . . G2
Salmas 13,161 . . . . . D1
Sanandaj 95,834 . . . . . E3
Saqqez 17,000 . . . . . E2
Sarab 16,000 . . . . . E2
Sarakhs 3,461 . . . . . M2
Saravan 4,012 . . . . . N7
Sar Dasht 6,000 . . . . . D2
Sari 70,936 . . . . . H2
Savanat (Estahbanat) 18,187 . . . . . J6
Saveh 17,565 . . . . . G3
Semnan 31,058 . . . . . H3
Shadegan 6,000 . . . . . F5
Shahdad 2,777 . . . . . K5
Shahistan (Saravan) 4,012 . . . . . N7
Shahreza 34,220 . . . . . H4
Shahr Kord 24,000 . . . . . G4
Shahrud (Emamshahr) 30,767 . . . . . J2
Sharafkhaneh 1,260 . . . . . D1
Shiraz 416,408 . . . . . H6
Shirvan 11,000 . . . . . K2
Shush 1,433 . . . . . F4
Shushtar 24,000 . . . . . F4
Sinneh (Sanandaj) 95,834 . . . . . E3
Sirjan (Sai'dabad) 20,000 . . . . . J6
Sivand 1,811 . . . . . H5
Sonqor 10,433 . . . . . E3
Sufian 2,914 . . . . . E1
Sultanabad (Kashmar) 17,000 . . . . . L3
Tabas 10,000 . . . . . K4
Tabriz 598,576 . . . . . D2
Taft 7,000 . . . . . J5
Tajrish 157,486 . . . . . G3
Takestan 13,485 . . . . . F2
Tehran (cap.) 4,496,159 . . . . . G3
Tonekabon 12,000 . . . . . G2
Torbat-e-Heydariyeh 30,106 . . . . . L3
Torbat-e Jam 13,000 . . . . . M3
Tun (Ferdows) 11,000 . . . . . K3
Turbat-i-Shaikh Jam 13,000 . . . . . M3
Tuysarkan 12,000 . . . . . F3
Urmia 163,991 . . . . . D2
Varamin 11,183 . . . . . G3
Yazd (Yezd) 135,978 . . . . . J5
Yazd-e Khvasat 3,544 . . . . . H5
Zabol 20,000 . . . . . M5
Zahedan 92,628 . . . . . M6
Zanjan 99,967 . . . . . K5
Zarand 5,000 . . . . . H6
Zarqam 7,000 . . . . . H6
Zenjan (Zanjan) 99,967 . . . . . F2

OTHER FEATURES

Aji Chai (riv.)	E1
A'rabi (isl.)	G7
Araks (Aras) (riv.)	E1
Atrak (Atrek) (riv.)	J2
Bakhtegan (lake)	J6
Baluchistan (reg.)	M7
Bampur (riv.)	M7
Behistun (ruins)	E3
Caspian (sea)	G1
Damavand (Demavend) (mt.)	H3
Dez (riv.)	F4
Elburz (mts.)	G2
Farsi (isl.)	G7
Gorgan (riv.)	J2
Hari Rud (riv.)	M3
Karkheh (riv.)	E4
Karun (riv.)	F5
Kashaf Rud (riv.)	M2
Khark (Kharg) (isl.)	G6
Kuh (cape)	K8
Kurang (riv.)	G4
Laristan (reg.)	J7
Makran (reg.)	M8
Mand Rud (riv.)	G6
Mehran (riv.)	J7
Namaksar (lake)	M4
Nezwar (mt.)	H3
Oman (gulf)	M8
Pasargadae (ruins)	H5
Persepolis (ruins)	H6
Persian (gulf)	F6
Qareh Su (riv.)	E1
Qareh Su (riv.)	G3
Qeshm (isl.)	J7
Qezel Owzam (riv.)	F2
Safid Rud (riv.)	F2
Shaikh Shua'ib (isl.)	H7
Shelagh (riv.)	M5
Shirvan (riv.)	E3
Shur (riv.)	J7
Siah Kuh (mt.)	L3
Silup (riv.)	M8
Susa (ruins)	F4
Talab (riv.)	N6
Tashk (lake)	J6
Urmia (lake)	D2
Zagros (mts.)	E4
Zarineh (riv.)	E2
Zilbir (riv.)	D1
Zohreh (riv.)	F5

IRAQ

GOVERNORATES

Anbar	B4
An Najaf	C5
Babil	D4
Baghdad	D4
Basra	E5
Dhi Qar	E5
Diyala	D4
Dohuk	C2
Erbil	C3
Karbala	B4
Maysan	E5
Muthanna	D5
Ninawa	B3
Qadisiya	D4
Salahuddin	C3
Sulaimaniya	D3
Tamin	D3
Wasit	D4

CITIES and TOWNS

Ad Diwaniya 60,553	D5
A'faq 5,390	D4
Al A'ziziya 7,450	D4
Al Falluja 38,072	C4
Al Fatha† 15,329	C3
A'li Gharbi 15,456	E4
A'li Sharqi 8,398	E4
Al Kufa 30,862	D4
Al Musaiyib 15,955	D4
Al Q'aim 3,372	B3
Al Qaiyara 3,060	C3
Al Qosh 3,863	C2
Al Qurna 5,638	E5
A'madiya 2,578	C2
A'mara 64,847	E5
A'na 15,729	B3
An Najaf 128,096	D5
An Nasiriya 60,405	D5
A'qra 8,659	D2
Arbela (Erbil) 90,320	D2
Aski Mosul 643	C2
As Salman 1,789	D5
Az Zubair 41,408	E5
Badra 3,564	D4
Baghdad (cap.) 502,503	D4
Baghdad* 1,745,328	D4
Baiji 6,785	C3
Baq'uba 34,575	D4
Basra 313,327	E5
Dohuk 16,998	C2
Erbil 90,320	D2
Fao 15,399	F6
Habbaniya 14,405	C4
Haditha 6,870	C3
Hai 16,988	E4
Halabja 11,206	D3
Hilla 84,717	D4
Hindiya 16,436	C4
Hit 9,131	C4
Karbal'a 83,301	C4
Khanaqin 23,522	D3
Kifri 8,500	D3
Kirkuk 167,413	D3
Kirkuk* 176,794	D3
Kubaisa 4,023	C4
Kut 42,116	D4
Makhmur 2,556	C3
Mandali 11,262	D4
Mosul 315,157	C2
Muqdadiyah 12,181	D4
Naft Kaneh	D3
Na'maniya 11,943	D4
Qal'at Diza 6,250	D2
Ramadi 28,723	C4
Rania 4,090	D2
Refai' 7,681	E5
Rumaitha 10,222	D5
Rutba 5,091	B4
Ruwandiz 5,801	D2
Sad'iya 5,285	D3
Samarra 24,746	C3
Samawa 33,473	D5
Shaikh Saa'd 2,958	E4
Shaqlawa 6,814	D2
Shatra 18,822	E5
Sinjar 7,942	B2
Sulaimaniya 86,822	D3
Tal Kaif 7,482	C2
Taza Khurmatu 2,681	D3
Tikrit 9,921	C3
Tuz Khurmatu 13,860	D3
Zakho 14,790	C2

OTHER FEATURES

Adhaim (riv.)	D3
Aneiza, Jebel (mt.)	A4
A'rab, Shatt-al- (riv.)	F5
A'ra'r, Wadi (dry riv.)	B5
Babylon (ruins)	D4
Batin, Wadi al (dry riv.)	E6
Ctesiphon (ruins)	D4
Darbandikhan (dam)	D3
Euphrates (riv.)	D4
Great Zab (riv.)	C2
Hauran, Wadi (dry riv.)	B4
Little Zab (riv.)	C3
Mesopotamia (reg.)	B3
Nineveh (ruins)	C2
Sad'iya, Hor (lake)	E4
Saniya, Hor (lake)	E5
Shai'b Hisb, Wadi (dry riv.)	C5
Sinjar, Jebel (mts.)	B2
Siyah Kuh (mt.)	D2
Syrian (des.)	B4
Tigris (riv.)	E4
Ubaiyidh, Wadi (dry riv.)	B5
Ur (ruins)	E5

*City and suburbs.
†Population of commune.

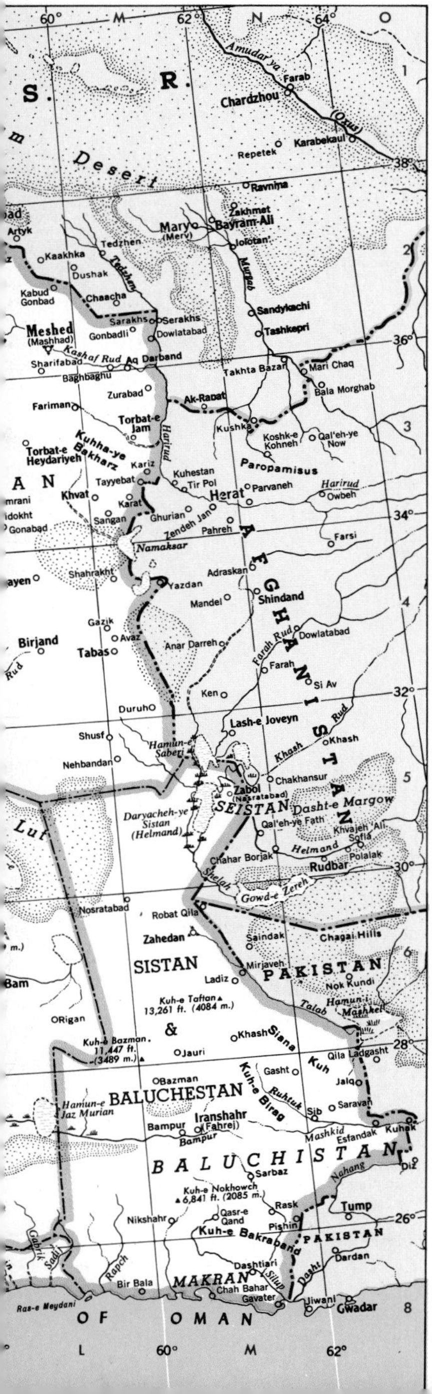

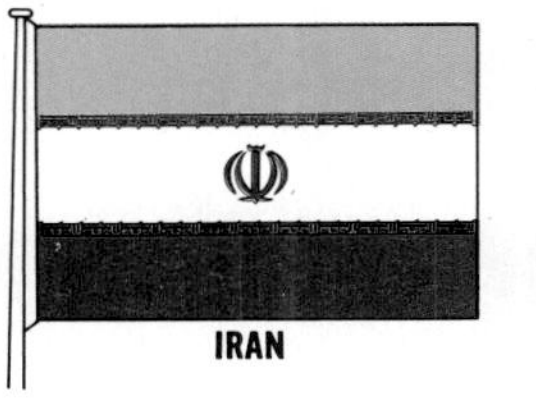

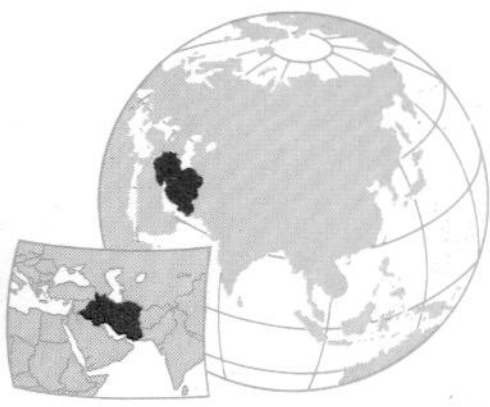

AREA 636,293 sq. mi. (1,648,000 sq. km.)
POPULATION 37,447,000
CAPITAL Tehran
LARGEST CITY Tehran
HIGHEST POINT Damavand 18,376 ft. (5,601 m.)
MONETARY UNIT Iranian rial
MAJOR LANGUAGES Persian, Azerbaijani, Kurdish
MAJOR RELIGION Islam

AREA 172,476 sq. mi. (446,713 sq. km.)
POPULATION 12,767,000
CAPITAL Baghdad
LARGEST CITY Baghdad
HIGHEST POINT Haji Ibrahim 11,811 ft. (3,600 m.)
MONETARY UNIT Iraqi dinar
MAJOR LANGUAGES Arabic, Kurdish
MAJOR RELIGION Islam

Topography

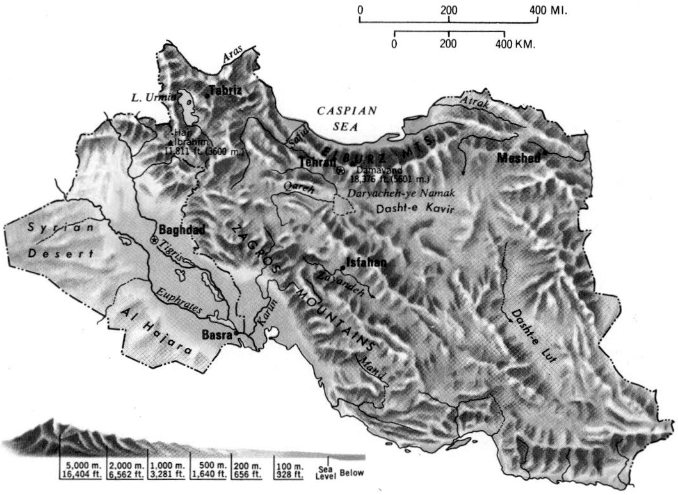

Agriculture, Industry and Resources

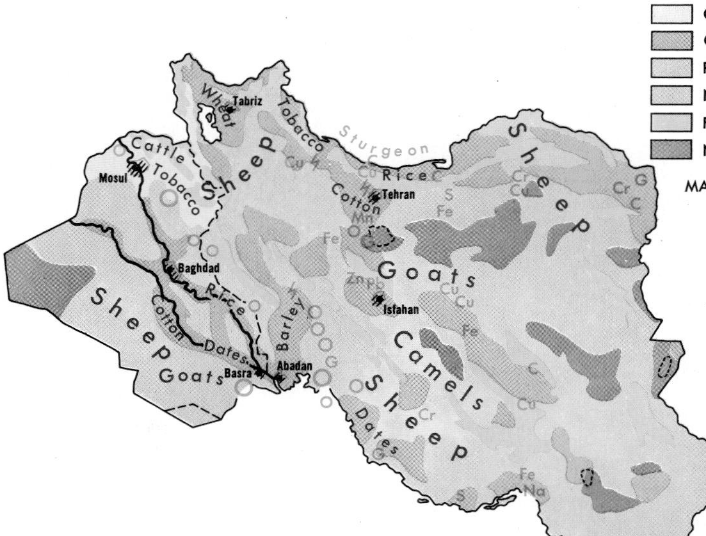

DOMINANT LAND USE

- Cereals, Livestock
- Cash Crops, Horticulture, Livestock
- Pasture Livestock
- Nomadic Livestock Herding
- Forests
- Nonagricultural Land

MAJOR MINERAL OCCURRENCES

- C Coal
- Cr Chromium
- Cu Copper
- Fe Iron Ore
- G Natural Gas
- Mn Manganese
- Na Salt
- O Petroleum
- Pb Lead
- S Sulfur, Pyrites
- Zn Zinc

- Water Power
- Major Industrial Areas

Indian Subcontinent and Afghanistan
CONIC PROJECTION
SCALE OF MILES
0 50 100 200 300
KILOMETERS
0 50 100 200 300
Capitals of Countries
Provincial and State Capitals
International Boundaries
Provincial and State Boundaries
Canals
© Copyright HAMMOND INCORPORATED, Maplewood, N. J.
Longitude East 85° of Greenwich
ARABIAN SEA
BAY OF BENGAL
INDIAN OCEAN
AFGHANISTAN
U. S. S. R.
SINKIANG
SRI LANKA (CEYLON)
MALDIVES
LAKSHADWEEP (India)
ANDAMAN AND NICOBAR ISLANDS (India)
BHUTAN
BANGLADESH
Tropic of Cancer
BOMBAY
CALCUTTA
KARACHI
DELHI
New Delhi
MADRAS
Kabul
Colombo
Kathmandu

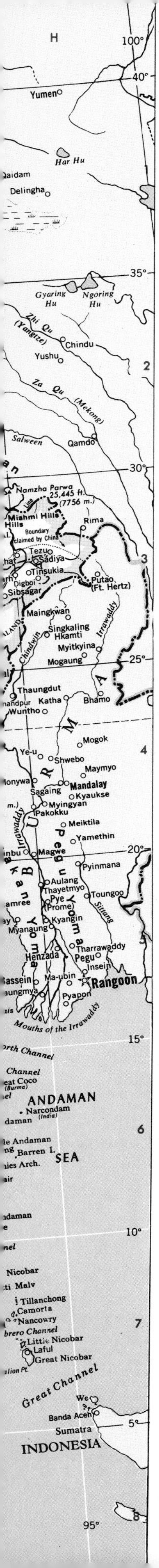

INDIA

AREA 1,269,339 sq. mi. (3,287,588 sq. km.)
POPULATION 683,810,051
CAPITAL New Delhi
LARGEST CITY Calcutta (greater)
HIGHEST POINT Nanda Devi 25,645 ft. (7,817 m.)
MONETARY UNIT Indian rupee
MAJOR LANGUAGES Hindi, English, Bihari, Telugu, Marathi, Bengali, Tamil, Gujarati, Rajasthani, Kanarese, Malayalam, Oriya, Punjabi, Assamese, Kashmiri, Urdu
MAJOR RELIGIONS Hinduism, Islam, Christianity, Sikhism, Buddhism, Jainism, Zoroastrianism, Animism

PAKISTAN

AREA 310,403 sq. mi. (803,944 sq. km.)
POPULATION 83,782,000
CAPITAL Islamabad
LARGEST CITY Karachi
HIGHEST POINT K2 (Godwin Austen) 28,250 ft. (8,611 m.)
MONETARY UNIT Pakistani rupee
MAJOR LANGUAGES Urdu, English, Punjabi, Pushtu, Sindhi, Baluchi, Brahui
MAJOR RELIGIONS Islam, Hinduism, Sikhism, Christianity, Buddhism

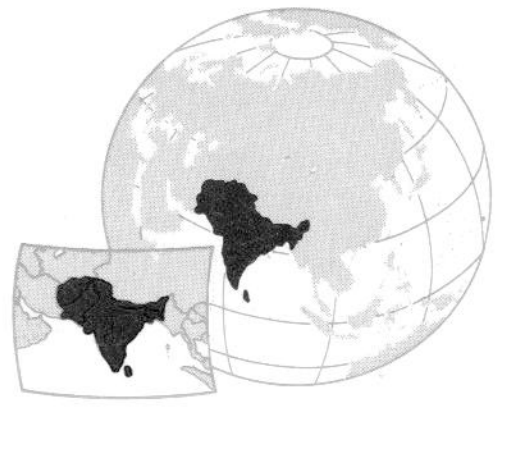

SRI LANKA (CEYLON)

AREA 25,332 sq. mi. (65,610 sq. km.)
POPULATION 14,850,001
CAPITAL Colombo
LARGEST CITY Colombo
HIGHEST POINT Pidurutalagala 8,281 ft. (2,524 m.)
MONETARY UNIT Sri Lanka rupee
MAJOR LANGUAGES Sinhala, Tamil, English
MAJOR RELIGIONS Buddhism, Hinduism, Christianity, Islam

AFGHANISTAN

AREA 250,775 sq. mi. (649,507 sq. km.)
POPULATION 15,540,000
CAPITAL Kabul
LARGEST CITY Kabul
HIGHEST POINT Nowshak 24,557 ft. (7,485 m.)
MONETARY UNIT afghani
MAJOR LANGUAGES Pushtu, Dari, Uzbek
MAJOR RELIGION Islam

NEPAL

AREA 54,663 sq. mi. (141,577 sq. km.)
POPULATION 14,179,301
CAPITAL Kathmandu
LARGEST CITY Kathmandu
HIGHEST POINT Mt. Everest 29,028 ft. (8,848 m.)
MONETARY UNIT Nepalese rupee
MAJOR LANGUAGES Nepali, Maithili, Tamang, Newari, Tharu
MAJOR RELIGIONS Hinduism, Buddhism

MALDIVES

AREA 115 sq. mi. (298 sq. km.)
POPULATION 143,046
CAPITAL Male
LARGEST CITY Male
HIGHEST POINT 20 ft. (6 m.)
MONETARY UNIT Maldivian rufiyaa
MAJOR LANGUAGE Divehi
MAJOR RELIGION Islam

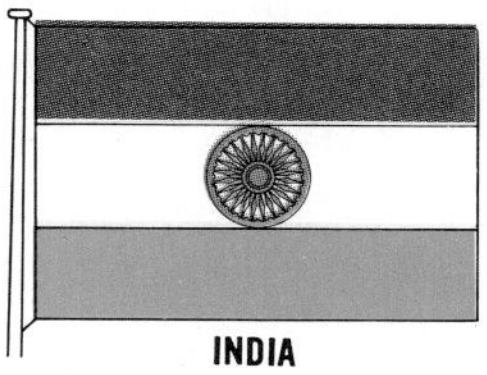
INDIA

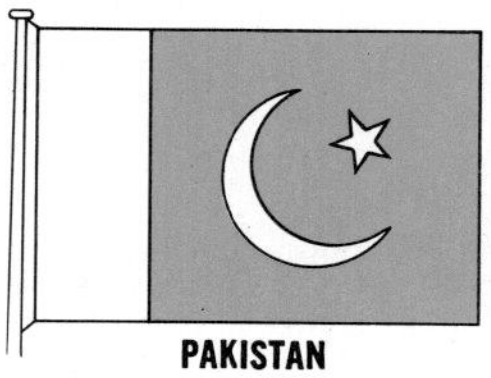
PAKISTAN

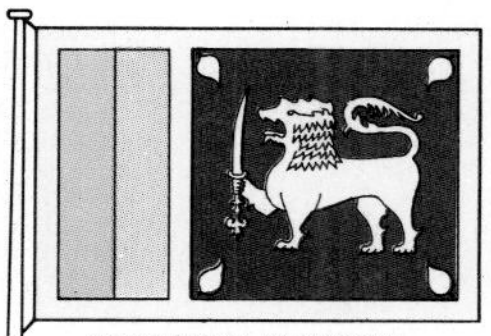
SRI LANKA (CEYLON)

BHUTAN

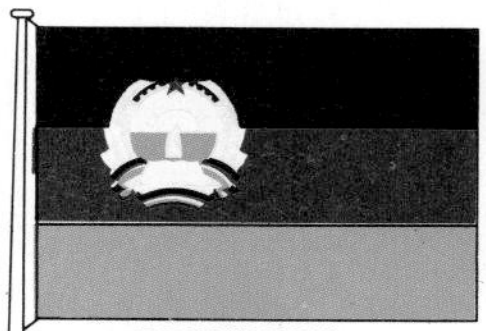
AFGHANISTAN

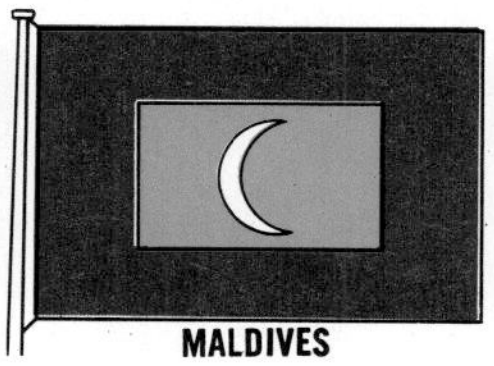
MALDIVES

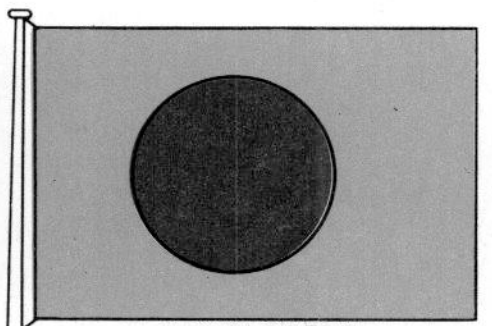
BANGLADESH

NEPAL

BHUTAN

AREA 18,147 sq. mi. (47,000 sq. km.)
POPULATION 1,298,000
CAPITAL Thimphu
LARGEST CITY Thimphu
HIGHEST POINT Kula Kangri 24,784 ft. (7,554 m.)
MONETARY UNIT ngultrum
MAJOR LANGUAGES Dzongka, Nepali
MAJOR RELIGIONS Buddhism, Hinduism

BANGLADESH

AREA 55,126 sq. mi. (142,776 sq. km.)
POPULATION 87,052,024
CAPITAL Dhaka
LARGEST CITY Dhaka
HIGHEST POINT Keokradong 4,034 ft. (1,230 m.)
MONETARY UNIT taka
MAJOR LANGUAGES Bengali, English
MAJOR RELIGIONS Islam, Hinduism, Christianity

AFGHANISTAN

CITIES and TOWNS

Bala Murghab 10,000 .... A1
Balkh 15,000 .... B1
Chahardeh B2
Girishk 10,000 .... A2
Kabul (cap.) 318,094 .... B2
Kabul* 534,350 .... B2
Kuhsan A2
Kushk 10,000 .... A1
Landi Muhammad Amin Khan 1,000 .... A2
Panjao 3,000 .... B2
Qaleh-i-Kang 17,400 .... A2
Sabzawar 5,000 .... A2
Shindand (Sabzawar) 5,000 .... A2
Taiwara 5,000 .... A2

OTHER FEATURES

Farah Rud (riv.) A2
Hari Rud (riv.) A1
Helmand (riv.) B2
Hindu Kush (mts.) B1
Jam (mt.) A2
Kabul (riv.) C2
Kunar (riv.) C1
Kunduz (riv.) B1
Lora (riv.) B2
Margo, Dasht-i- (des.) A2
Namaksar (salt lake) A2
Paropamisus (range) A2
Registan (reg.) B2

BANGLADESH

CITIES and TOWNS

Chittagong 416,733 .... G4
Cox's Bazar (Maheshkhali) ... G4
Dhaka (Dacca) (cap.) 1,310,976 .... G4
Dhaka (Dacca)□ 2,539,991 . G4
Habiganj G4
Jamalpur F4
Khulna 436,000 .... F4
Kishorganj G4
Madaripur G4
Maheshkhali G4
Narayanganj 176,879 .... G4
Nawabganj F4
Noakhali 19,874 .... G4
Rangamati 6,416 .... G4

OTHER FEATURES

Bengal, Bay of (sea) F5
Brahmaputra (riv.) G3
Ganges (riv.) F3
Sundarbans (reg.) F4

BHUTAN

CITIES and TOWNS

Bumthang 10,000 .... G3
Punakha 12,000 .... G3
Taga Dzong 18,000 .... G3
Tongsa Dzong 2,500 .... G3

OTHER FEATURES

Chomo Lhari (mt.) F3
Himalaya (mts.) E2
Kula Kangri (mt.) G3

INDIA

INTERNAL DIVISIONS

Andaman and Nicobar Isls. (terr.) 115,133 .... G6
Andhra Pradesh (state) 43,502,708 .... D5
Arunachal Pradesh (terr.) 467,511 .... G3
Assam (state) 14,625,152 .. G3
Bihar (state) 56,353,369 .... F4
Chandigarh (terr.) 257,251 .... D2
Dadra and Nagar Haveli (terr.) 74,170 .... C4
Daman and Diu (terr.) 857,771 .... C4
Delhi (terr.) 4,065,698 ...... D3
Gujarat (state) 26,697,475 .. C4
Haryana (state) 10,036,808 . D3
Himachal Pradesh (state) 3,460,434 .... D2
Jammu and Kashmir (state) 4,616,632 .... D2
Karnataka (state) 29,299,014 .... D6
Kerala (state) 21,347,375 ... D6
Lakshadweep (terr.) 31,810 .... C6
Madhya Pradesh (state) 41,654,119 .... D4
Maharashtra (state) 50,412,235 .... C5
Manipur (state) 1,072,753 .. G4
Meghalaya (state) 1,011,699 .... G3
Mizoram (terr.) 332,390 .... G4
Nagaland (state) 516,449 .... G3

(continued on following page)

Topography

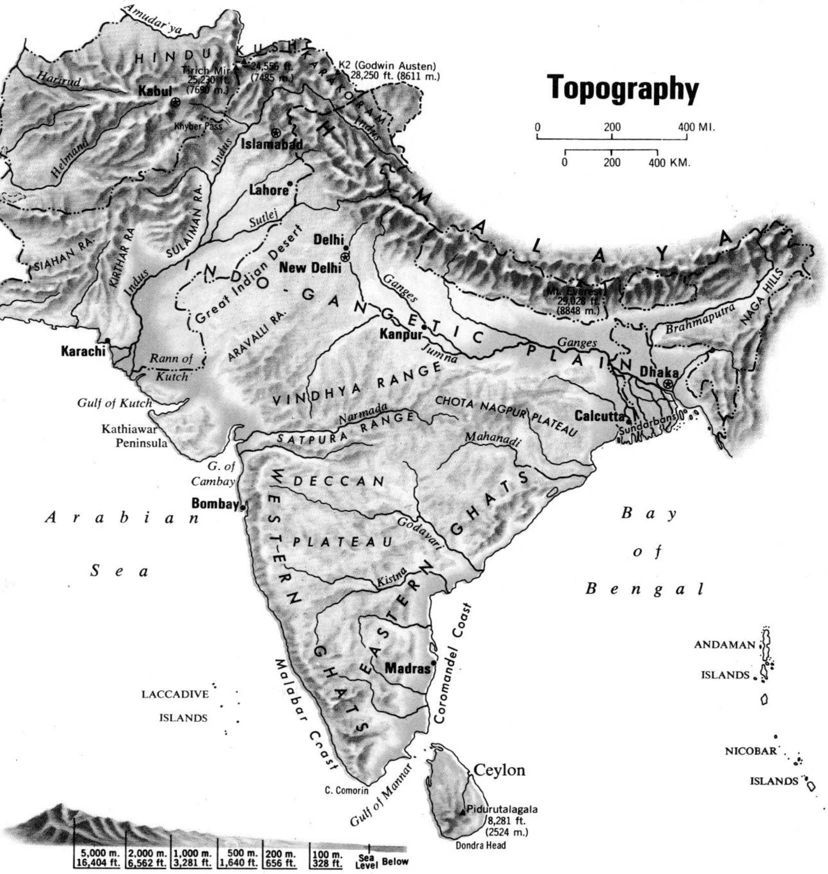

Orissa (state) 21,944,615 E5
Pondicherry (terr.) 471,707 E6
Punjab (state) 13,551,060 D2
Rajasthan (state) 25,765,806 C3
Sikkim (state) 209,843 F3
Tamil Nadu (state) 41,199,168 D6
Tripura (state) 1,556,342 G4
Uttar Pradesh (state) 88,341,144 D3
West Bengal (state) 44,312,011 F4

CITIES and TOWNS

Abu 9,840 C4
Agra 591,917 D3
Agra□ 634,622 D3
Ahmadabad 1,591,832 C4
Ahmadabad□ 1,741,522 C4
Ajanta D4
Ajmer 262,851 C3
Akola 168,438 D4
Alibag 11,913 C5
Aligarh 252,314 D3
Allahabad 490,622 E3
Allahabad□ 513,036 E3
Alleppey 160,166 D7
Almora 19,671 D3
Ambikapur 23,087 E4
Amravati 193,800 D4
Amritsar 407,628 C2
Amritsar□ 458,029 C2
Asansol 155,968 F4
Aurangabad, Maharashtra 150,483 D5
Baltit C1
Bandra B7
Bangalore 1,540,741 D6
Bangalore□ 1,653,779 D6
Bareilly 296,248 D3
Baroda 466,696 C4
Baroda□ 467,487 C4
Barwani 22,099 D4
Belgaum 192,427 C5
Benares (Varanasi) 583,856 E3
Bhagalpur 172,202 F4
Bhatpara 204,750 F1
Bhavnagar 225,358 C4
Bhawanipatna 22,808 E5
Bhilai 157,173 E4
Bhopal 298,022 D4
Bikaner 188,518 C3
Bombay (Greater)* 5,970,575 B7
Bunji C1
Calcutta 3,148,746 F2
Calcutta□ 7,031,382 F2
Calicut (Kozhikode) 333,979 D6
Cawnpore (Kanpur) 1,154,388 E3
Chamba 11,814 D2
Chanderi 10,294 D4
Chandigarh 218,743 D2
Chembur B7
Chilas C1
Chushul D2
Cocanada (Kakinada) 164,200 E5
Cochin 439,066 D6
Coimbatore 356,368 D6
Coimbatore□ 736,203 D6
Colachel 18,819 D7
Cuttack 194,068 F4
Dehra Dun 166,073 D2
Delhi 3,287,883 D3
Delhi□ 3,647,023 D3
Dhanbad□ 434,031 F4
Dharmsala 10,939 D2
Dharwar-Hubli 379,166 C5
Diphu 10,200 G3
Dispur 1,725 G3
Dungarpur 19,773 C4
Durgapur 206,638 F4
Dwarka 17,801 B4
Gangtok 12,000 F3
Garden Reach 154,913 F2
Gaya 179,884 F4
Gilgit C1
Gorakhpur 230,911 E3
Goregaon B7
Guntur 269,991 D5
Gwalior 384,772 D3
Gwalior□ 406,140 D3
Haflong 5,197 G3
Honavar 12,444 C6
Howrah 737,877 F2
Hubli-Dharwar 379,166 C5
Hunza (Baltit) C1
Hyderabad 1,607,396 D5
Hyderabad□ 1,796,339 D5
Ichchapuram 15,850 F5
Indore 543,381 D4
Indore□ 560,936 D4
Itanagar⊙ 18,787 G3
Jabalpur 426,224 D4
Jabalpur□ 534,845 D4
Jaipur 615,258 D3
Jaipur□ 636,768 D3
Jaisalmer 16,578 C3
Jajpur 16,707 F4
Jalor 15,478 C3
Jammu 155,338 D2
Jamnagar 214,816 B4
Jamnagar□ 227,640 B4
Jamshedpur 341,576 F4
Jamshedpur□ 456,146 F4
Jhansi 173,292 D3
Jodhpur 317,612 C3
Jubbulpore (Jabalpur) 426,224 D4
Juhu B7
Jullundur 296,106 D2
Kakinada 164,200 E5
Kamarhati 169,404 F1
Kandla 17,995 C4
Kanpur 1,154,388 E3
Kanpur□ 1,275,242 E3
Kargil 2,390 D2
Katarnian Ghat E3
Kavaratti 4,420 C6
Kendrapara 20,079 F4
Kohima 21,545 G3
Kolhapur 259,050 C5
Koraput 21,505 E5
Kota 212,991 D3
Kozhikode 333,979 D6
Kumta 19,112 C6
Kurla B7
Leh 5,519 D2
Lucknow 749,239 E3
Lucknow□ 813,982 E3
Ludhiana 397,850 D2
Ludhiana□ 401,176 D2
Madras 2,469,449 E6
Madras□ 3,169,930 E6
Madurai 549,114 D7
Madurai□ 711,501 D7
Mahabaleshwar 7,318 C5
Mahe 8,972 D6
Malad B6
Malegaon 191,847 C4
Malvan 17,579 C5
Mandi 16,849 D2
Mandla 24,406 E4
Mangalore 165,174 C6
Meerut 270,993 D3
Mercara 19,357 D6
Mirpur C2
Moradabad 258,590 D3
Mulund B6
Muzaffarabad C2
Mysore 355,685 D6
Nagar D1
Nagpur 866,076 D4
Nagpur□ 930,459 D4
Nahan 16,017 D2
Naini Tal 23,986 D3
Nasik 176,091 C5
New Delhi (cap.) 301,801 D3
Okha Port 10,687 B4
Pachmarhi 1,212 D4
Panna 22,316 E4
Pasighat 5,116 G3
Patna 473,001 F3
Patna□ 491,217 F3
Poona 856,105 C5
Poona□ 1,135,034 C5
Porto Novo 17,412 E6
Raipur 174,518 E4
Rajahmundry 165,912 E5
Rajapur 9,017 C5
Rajkot 300,612 C4
Rameswaram 16,755 D7
Rampur, Uttar Pradesh 161,417 D3
Ranchi 175,934 F4
Raxaul 12,064 E3
Sadiya⊙ 64,252 H3
Saharanpur 225,396 D3
Salem 308,716 D6
Salem□ 416,440 D6
Santa Cruz B7
Sarnath E3
Secunderabad 250,636 D5
Seringapatam 14,100 D6
Sholapur 398,361 D5
Sidhi 8,341 E4
Silvassa C4
Sirohi 18,774 C4
Skardu D1
South Suburban 272,600 F2
Srinagar 403,413 D2
Srinagar□ 423,253 D2
Sundargarh 17,244 E4
Surat 471,656 C4
Surat□ 493,001 C4
Tehri 5,480 D2
Thana 170,675 B6
Tiruchchirappalli 307,400 D6
Tiruchchirappalli□ 464,624 D6
Tiruchendur 18,126 D7
Tollygunge F2
Tranquebar 17,318 E6
Trivandrum 409,627 D7
Trombay B7
Tura 15,489 G3
Tuticorin 155,310 D7
Udaypur 161,278 C4
Udhampur 16,392 D2
Ujjain 203,278 D4
Ulhasnagar 168,462 C5
Varanasi 583,856 E3
Varanasi□ 606,721 E3
Vellore□ 178,554 D6
Vengurla 11,805 C5
Vijayawada 317,258 D5
Visakhapatnam 352,504 E5
Vizagapatam (Visakhapatnam) 352,504 E5
Warangal 207,520 D5
Yanam 8,291 E5
Yasin C1

OTHER FEATURES

Abor (hills) G3
Adam's Bridge (sound) D7
Agatti (isl.) C6
Amindiri (isl.) C6
Amindivi (isls.) C6
Amini (Amindiri) (isl.) C6
Andaman (isls.) G6
Andaman (sea) G6
Androth (isl.) C6
Anjidiv (Angedeva) (isl.) C6
Arabian (sea) B5
Back (bay) B7
Baltistan (reg.) D1
Bengal, Bay of (sea) F5
Berar (reg.) D4
Brahmaputra (riv.) G3
Butcher (isl.) B7
Cambay (gulf) C4
Cannanore (isls.) C6
Car Nicobar (isl.) G7
Chambal (riv.) D3
Chenab (riv.) C2
Chetlat (isl.) C6
Chilka (lake) F5
Coco (chan.) G6
Colaba (pt.) B7
Comorin (cape) D7
Coromandel Coast (reg.) E6
Daman (dist.) C4
Damodar (riv.) F4
Deccan (plat.) D6
Diu (dist.) C4
Eastern Ghats (mts.) D6
Elephanta (isl.) B7
Ganga (Ganges) (riv.) F3
Ganges, Mouths of the (delta) F4
Ganges (riv.) F3
Ghaghra (riv.) E3
Goa (dist.) C5
Godavari (riv.) D5
Godwin Austen (K2) (mt.) D1
Golconda (ruins) D5
Great (chan.) G7
Great Indian (des.) C3
Great Nicobar (isl.) G7
Himalaya (mts.) D2
Hindu Kush (mts.) C1
Hooghly (riv.) F2
Indus (riv.) B3
Jhelum (riv.) C2
Jumna (riv.) E3
K2 (mt.) D1
Kachchh (gulf) B4
Kachchh (Kutch), Rann of (salt marsh) B4
Kadmat (isl.) C6
Kalpeni (isl.) C7
Kamet (mt.) D2
Kanchenjunga (mt.) F3
Karakoram (mts.) D1
Kaveri (riv.) D6
Khasi (hills) G3
Kiltan (isl.) C6
Kistna (Krishna) (riv.) D5
Krishna (Kistna) (riv.) D5
Kunlun (range) D1
Kutch (Kachchh) (gulf) B4
Kutch, Rann of (salt marsh) B4
Laccadive (Cannanore) (isls.) C6
Ladakh (reg.) D2
Little Andaman (isl.) G6
Little Nicobar (isl.) G7
Mahanadi (riv.) E4
Malabar (hill) B7
Malabar Coast (reg.) C6
Mannar (gulf) D7
Middle Andaman (isl.) G6
Minicoy (isl.) C7
Miri (hills) G3
Mishmi (hills) H3
Nancowry (isl.) G7
Nanda Devi (mt.) D2
Nanga Parbat (mt.) D1
Narmada (riv.) D4
Nicobar (isls.) G7
North Andaman (isl.) G6
Palk (strait) D7
Penganga (riv.) D5
Periyar (lake) D7
Pitti (isl.) C6
Pulicat (lake) E6
Rakaposhi (mt.) C1
Salsette (isl.) B7
Sambhar (lake) C3
Satpura (range) D4
Shipki (pass) D2
South Andaman (isl.) G6
Sundarbans (reg.) F4
Sutlej (riv.) C3
Ten Degree (chan.) G7
Towers of Silence B7
Travancore (reg.) D7
Tungabhadra (riv.) D5
Vindhya (range) D4
Western Ghats (mts.) C5
Zaskar (mts.) D2

MALDIVES

Maldives 136,000 C7

NEPAL

CITIES and TOWNS

Dhangarhi E3
Jumla⊙ 122,753 E3
Kathmandu⊙ 353,752 E3
Lalitpur⊙ 154,998 E3
Mukhtinath E3
Mustang⊙ 26,944 E3
Nepalganj 23,523 E3
Pokhara 20,611 E3
Pyuthan⊙ 137,338 E3
Ridi E3
Sallyana⊙ 141,457 E3

OTHER FEATURES

Annapurna (mt.) E3
Bheri (riv.) E3
Dhaulagiri (mt.) E3
Everest (mt.) F3
Himalaya (mts.) D2
Kanchenjunga (mt.) F3

PAKISTAN

PROVINCES

Azad Kashmir C2
Baluchistan 2,409,000 B3
Federal Administrated Tribal Areas C2
Islamabad District 235,000 C2
Northern Areas D1
North-West Frontier 10,909,000 C2
Punjab 37,374,000 C2
Sind 13,965,000 B3

CITIES and TOWNS

Abbottabad 47,011 C2
Bahawalpur 133,956 C3
Bahawalpur* 181,000 C3
Baltit C1
Campbellpore 19,041 C2
Chiniot 69,124 C2
Dera Ghazi Khan 71,429 C3
Dera Ismail Khan 59,892 C2
Faisalabad 822,263 C2
Gujranwala 360,419 C2
Gujrat 100,581 C2
Hunza (Baltit) C1
Hyderabad 628,310 B3
Islamabad (cap.) 77,318 C2
Jacobabad 57,292 B3
Jhang Sadar 135,722 C2
Jhelum 63,653 C2
Karachi 3,498,634 B4
Karachi* 3,650,000 B4
Khanewal 67,617 C2
Kohat 64,634 C2
Lahore 2,165,372 C2
Larkana 71,943 B3
Lyallpur (Faisalabad) 822,263 C2
Mardan 115,218 C2
Mardan* 131,000 C2
Multan 542,195 C2
Multan* 723,000 C2
Nagar D1
Nal B3
Nawabshah 80,779 B3
Nowshera 56,117 C2
Peshawar 268,366 C2
Peshawar* 331,000 C2
Quetta 156,000 B2
Rahimyar Khan 74,407 C3
Rahimyar Khan* 130,000 C3
Rawalpindi 615,392 C2
Sahiwal 106,213 C2
Sargodha 201,407 C2
Sargodha* 225,000 C2
Shikarpur 70,301 B3
Sialkot 203,779 C2
Sukkur 158,876 B3
Tando Adam 31,246 B3

OTHER FEATURES

Arabian (sea) B5
Bolan (pass) B3
Chagai (hills) A3
Chenab (riv.) C2
Hindu Kush (mts.) B1
Indus (riv.) B3
Jhelum (riv.) C2
Khyber (pass) C2
Kunar (riv.) C1
Kutch, Rann of (salt marsh) B4
Mashkel (riv.) A3
Mohenjo Daro (ruins) B3
Muari, Ras (cape) B4
Ravi (riv.) C2
Siahan (range) A3
Sulaiman (range) C3
Sutlej (riv.) C3
Talab (riv.) A3
Taxila (ruins) C2
Tirich Mir (mt.) C1
Zhob (riv.) B2

SRI LANKA (CEYLON)

CITIES and TOWNS

Colombo (cap.) 618,000 D7
Colombo* 852,098 D7
Hambantota 6,908 E7
Kalmunai 19,176 E7
Mannar 11,157 E7
Mullaittivu 4,930 E7
Nuwara Eliya 16,347 E7
Polonnaruwa 9,551 E7
Puttalam 17,982 D7
Sigiriya 1,446 E7
Vavuniya 15,639 E7

OTHER FEATURES

Adam's (peak) E7
Adam's Bridge (shoals) D7
Dondra (head) E7
Kirigalpota (mt.) E7
Mannar (gulf) D7
Palk (str.) D7
Pedro (pt.) E6
Pidurutalagala (mt.) E7

*City and suburbs.
⊙Population of district.
□Population of urban areas.

Agriculture, Industry and Resources

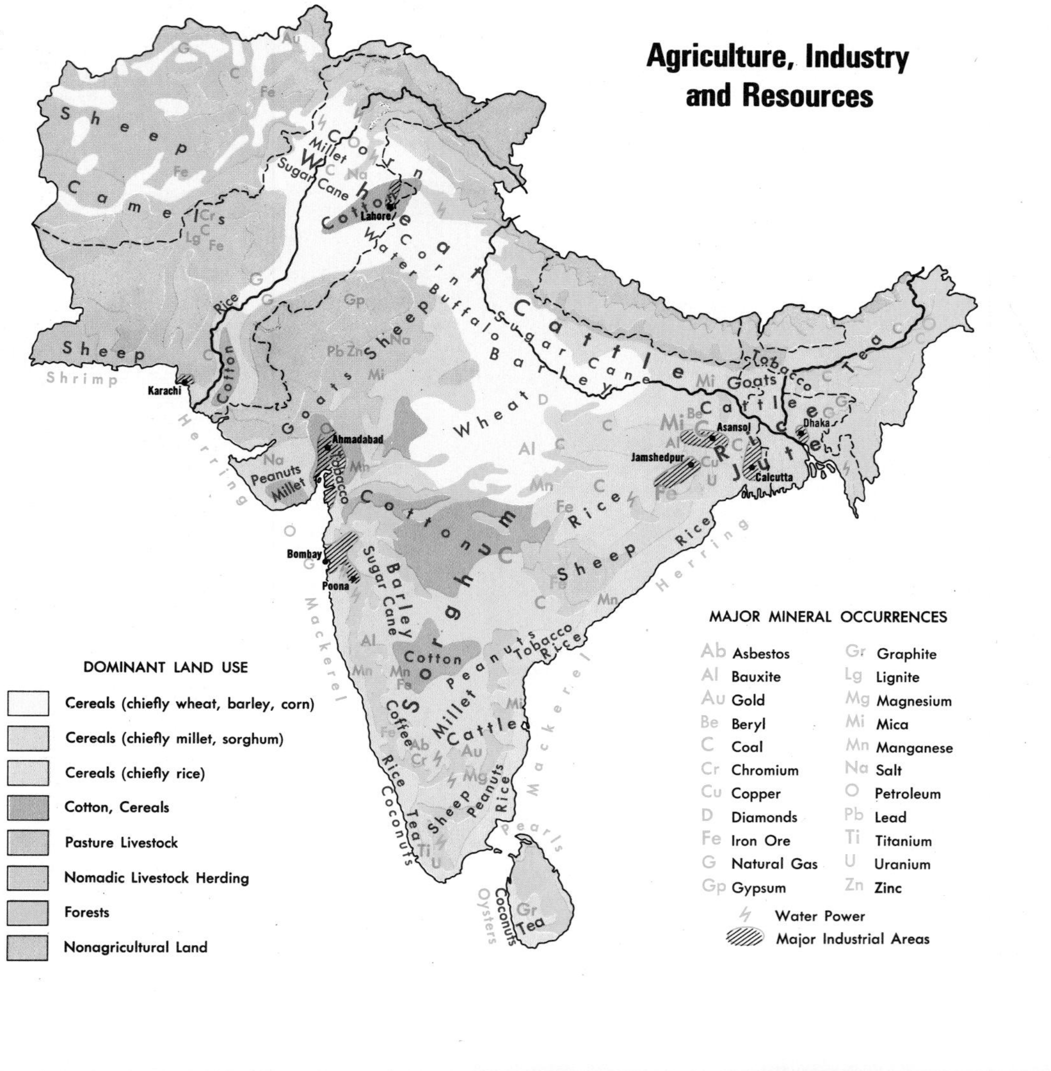

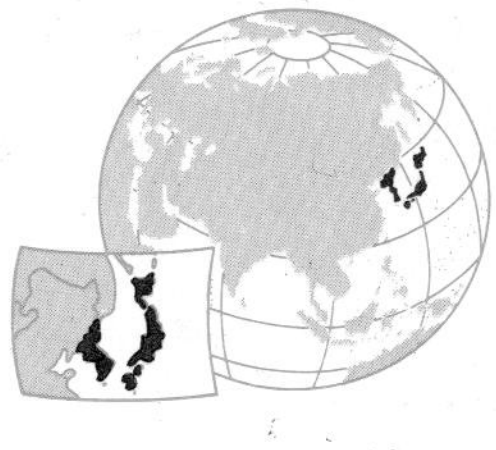

AREA 145,730 sq. mi. (377,441 sq. km.)
POPULATION 117,057,485
CAPITAL Tokyo
LARGEST CITY Tokyo
HIGHEST POINT Fuji 12,389 ft. (3,776 m.)
MONETARY UNIT yen
MAJOR LANGUAGE Japanese
MAJOR RELIGIONS Buddhism, Shintoism

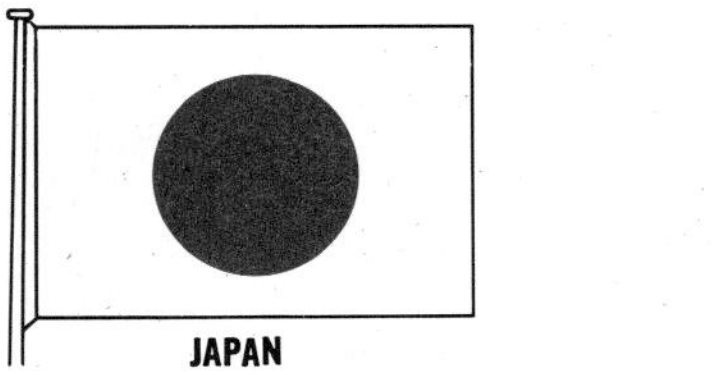

JAPAN

AREA 46,540 sq. mi. (120,539 sq. km.)
POPULATION 17,914,000
CAPITAL P'yŏngyang
LARGEST CITY P'yŏngyang
HIGHEST POINT Paektu 9,003 ft. (2,744 m.)
MONETARY UNIT won
MAJOR LANGUAGE Korean
MAJOR RELIGIONS Confucianism, Buddhism, Ch'ondogyo

NORTH KOREA

AREA 38,175 sq. mi. (98,873 sq. km.)
POPULATION 37,448,836
CAPITAL Seoul
LARGEST CITY Seoul
HIGHEST POINT Halla 6,398 ft. (1,950 m.)
MONETARY UNIT won
MAJOR LANGUAGE Korean
MAJOR RELIGIONS Confucianism, Buddhism, Ch'ondogyo, Christianity

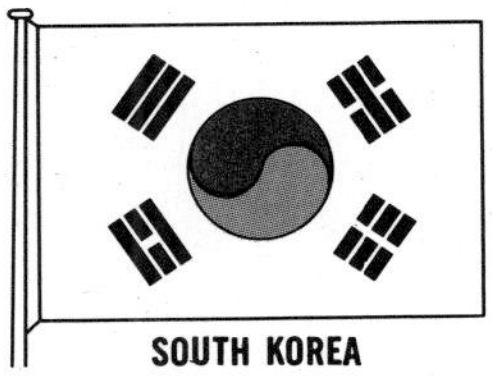

SOUTH KOREA

JAPAN

PREFECTURES

Aichi 5,923,569 ..... H6
Akita 1,232,481 ..... J4
Aomori 1,468,646 ..... K3
Chiba 4,149,147 ..... P2
Ehime 1,465,215 ..... F7
Fukui 773,599 ..... G5
Fukuoka 4,292,963 ..... D7
Fukushima 1,970,616 ..... K5
Gifu 1,867,978 ..... H6
Gumma 1,756,480 ..... J5
Hiroshima 2,646,324 ..... E6
Hokkaido 5,338,206 ..... K2
Hyogo 4,992,140 ..... H7
Ibaraki 2,342,198 ..... K5
Ishikawa 1,069,872 ..... H5
Iwate 1,385,563 ..... K4
Kagawa 961,292 ..... G6
Kagoshima 1,723,902 ..... E8
Kanagawa 6,397,748 ..... O2
Kochi 808,397 ..... F7
Kumamoto 1,715,273 ..... E7
Kyoto 2,424,856 ..... J7
Mie 1,626,002 ..... H6
Miyagi 1,955,267 ..... K4
Miyazaki 1,085,055 ..... E8
Nagano 2,017,564 ..... J5
Nagasaki 1,571,912 ..... D7
Nara 1,077,491 ..... J8
Niigata 2,391,938 ..... J5
Oita 1,190,314 ..... E7
Okayama 1,814,305 ..... F6
Okinawa 1,042,572 ..... N6
Osaka 8,278,925 ..... J8
Saga 837,674 ..... E7
Saitama 4,821,340 ..... O2
Shiga 985,621 ..... J7
Shimane 768,886 ..... F6
Shizuoka 3,308,799 ..... H6
Tochigi 1,698,003 ..... K5
Tokushima 805,166 ..... G7
Tokyo 11,673,554 ..... O2
Tottori 581,311 ..... G6
Toyama 1,070,791 ..... H5
Wakayama 1,072,118 ..... G6
Yamagata 1,220,302 ..... K4
Yamaguchi 1,555,218 ..... E6
Yamanashi 783,050 ..... J6

CITIES and TOWNS

Abashiri 43,825 ..... M1
Ageo 146,358 ..... O2
Aikawa 13,546 ..... H4
Aizuwakamatsu 108,650 ..... J5
Ajigasawa 18,086 ..... J3
Akashi 234,905 ..... H8
Aki 24,480 ..... F7
Akita 261,246 ..... J4
Akkeshi 16,778 ..... M2
Akune 30,295 ..... E7
Amagasaki 545,783 ..... H8
Amagi 42,725 ..... E7
Anan 60,439 ..... G7
Aomori 264,222 ..... K3
Asahi 34,028 ..... K6
Asahikawa 320,526 ..... L2
Ashibetsu 36,520 ..... L2
Ashikaga 162,359 ..... J5
Ashiya 76,211 ..... H8
Atami 51,437 ..... J6
Atsugi 108,955 ..... O2
Awaji 9,623 ..... H8
Ayabe 43,490 ..... G6
Beppu 133,894 ..... E7
Bibai 38,416 ..... L2
Biratori 9,331 ..... L2
Chiba 659,356 ..... P2
Chichibu 61,798 ..... J5
Chigasaki 152,023 ..... O3
Chitose 61,031 ..... K2
Chofu 175,924 ..... O2
Choshi 90,374 ..... K6
Daito 110,829 ..... J8
Ebetsu 77,624 ..... K2
Eniwa 39,884 ..... K2
Esashi, Hokkaido 10,172 ..... L1
Esashi, Hokkaido 14,409 ..... J3
Esashi, Iwate 36,336 ..... K4
Fuchu, Hiroshima 50,217 ..... F6
Fuchu, Tokyo 182,474 ..... O2
Fuji 199,195 ..... J6
Fujieda 90,358 ..... J6
Fujisawa 265,975 ..... O3
Fukagawa 36,000 ..... L2
Fukuchiyama 60,003 ..... G6
Fukue 32,018 ..... D7
Fukui 231,364 ..... G5
Fukuoka 1,002,201 ..... D7
Fukushima 246,531 ..... K5
Fukuyama 329,714 ..... F6
Funabashi 423,101 ..... P2
Furukawa 54,356 ..... K4
Gifu 408,707 ..... H6
Gobo 30,272 ..... G7
Gose 37,554 ..... J8
Gosen 39,376 ..... J5
Goshogawara 49,040 ..... K3
Gotsu 27,992 ..... F6
Habikino 94,160 ..... J8
Haboro 13,624 ..... K1
Hachinohe 224,366 ..... K3
Hachioji 322,580 ..... O2
Hadano 103,663 ..... O3
Hagi 52,724 ..... E6
Hakodate 307,453 ..... K3
Hakui 28,726 ..... H5
Hamada 50,316 ..... E6
Hamamatsu 468,884 ..... H6
Hanamaki 65,826 ..... K4
Hanno 55,926 ..... O2
Haramachi 43,483 ..... K5
Hayama 24,026 ..... O3
Higashiosaka 524,750 ..... J8
Hikone 85,066 ..... H6
Himeji 436,086 ..... G6
Himi 61,789 ..... H5
Hino 126,847 ..... O2
Hirakata 297,618 ..... J7
Hirara 29,301 ..... L7
Hirata 30,942 ..... F6
Hiratsuka 195,635 ..... O3
Hiroo 11,399 ..... L2
Hirosaki 164,911 ..... K3
Hiroshima 852,611 ..... E6
Hitachi 202,383 ..... K5
Hitachiota 35,322 ..... K5
Hitoyoshi 41,118 ..... E7
Hofu 105,540 ..... E6
Hondo 40,432 ..... E7
Honjo 40,488 ..... J4
Hyuga 53,448 ..... E7
Ibaraki 210,286 ..... J7
Ibusuki 32,339 ..... E8
Ichihara 194,068 ..... P3
Ichikawa 319,291 ..... P2
Ichinohe 21,433 ..... K3
Ichinomiya 238,463 ..... H6
Ichinoseki 59,122 ..... K4
Ide 9,112 ..... J7
Iida 77,112 ..... H6
Iizuka 75,417 ..... E7
Ikeda, Hokkaido 12,306 ..... L2
Ikeda, Osaka 100,268 ..... H7
Ikoma 48,848 ..... J8
Ikuno 6,658 ..... G6
Imabari 119,726 ..... F6
Imari 60,913 ..... D7
Imazu 11,519 ..... G6
Ina 54,468 ..... H6
Isahaya 73,341 ..... D7
Ise 104,957 ..... H6
Ishigaki 34,657 ..... L7
Ishige 19,220 ..... P2
Ishinomaki 115,085 ..... K4
Ishioka 43,679 ..... K5
Itami 171,978 ..... H7
Ito 68,072 ..... J6
Itoigawa 36,646 ..... H5
Itoman 39,363 ..... N6
Iwaizumi 20,219 ..... K4
Iwaki 330,213 ..... K5
Iwakuni 111,069 ..... E6
Iwami 16,063 ..... G6
Iwamizawa 72,305 ..... L2
Iwanai 25,823 ..... K2
Iwasaki 4,437 ..... J3
Iwata 67,665 ..... H6
Iwatsuki 83,825 ..... O2
Iyo 27,805 ..... F7
Izuhara 18,460 ..... D6
Izumi 118,237 ..... J8
Izumiotsu 66,250 ..... J8
Izumisano 86,139 ..... G6
Izumo 71,568 ..... F6
Joetsu 123,418 ..... H5
Joyo 58,923 ..... J7
Kadoma 143,238 ..... J7
Kaga 61,599 ..... H5
Kagoshima 456,827 ..... E8
Kaizuka 79,506 ..... H8
Kakogawa 169,293 ..... G6
Kamaishi 68,981 ..... L4
Kamakura 165,552 ..... O3
Kameoka 58,184 ..... J7
Kamiisco 27,229 ..... K3
Kaminoyama 37,858 ..... J4
Kamiyaku 8,668 ..... E8
Kamo 8,953 ..... J7
Kanazawa 395,263 ..... H5
Kanonji 44,131 ..... F6
Kanoya 67,951 ..... E8
Kanuma 81,799 ..... J5
Karatsu 75,224 ..... D7
Kaseda 24,969 ..... D8
Kashihara 95,701 ..... J8
Kashiwa 203,065 ..... P2
Kashiwara 63,586 ..... J8
Kashiwazaki 80,351 ..... J5
Kasugai 213,857 ..... H6
Kasukabe 121,639 ..... O2
Katsuta 79,996 ..... K5
Katsuura 26,755 ..... K6
Kawachinagano 66,936 ..... J8
Kawagoe 225,465 ..... O2
Kawaguchi 345,538 ..... J6
Kawanishi 115,773 ..... H7
Kawasaki 1,014,951 ..... O2
Kesennuma 66,616 ..... K4
Kikonai 10,034 ..... K3
Kimitsu 76,016 ..... O3
Kiryu 134,239 ..... J5
Kisarazu 96,840 ..... P3
Kishiwada 174,952 ..... J8
Kitaibaraki 44,332 ..... K5
Kitakami 48,759 ..... K4
Kitakata 37,471 ..... J5
Kitakyushu 1,058,058 ..... E6
Kitami 91,519 ..... L2
Kizu 11,890 ..... J7
Kobayashi 38,325 ..... E8
Kobe 1,360,605 ..... H7
Kochi 280,962 ..... F7
Kodaira 156,181 ..... O2
Kofu 193,879 ..... J6
Koga 55,973 ..... J5
Koganei 102,714 ..... O2
Kokubu 31,660 ..... E8
Komagane 30,318 ..... H6
Komatsu 100,273 ..... H5
Koriyama 264,628 ..... K5
Koshigaya 195,917 ..... P2
Koyama 16,394 ..... E8
Kubohama 17,817 ..... F7
Kuji 38,122 ..... K3
Kuki 45,797 ..... O2
Kumagaya 131,485 ..... J5
Kumamoto 488,166 ..... E7
Kumano 27,026 ..... G7
Kumiyama 11,540 ..... J7
Kurashiki 392,755 ..... F6
Kurayoshi 50,785 ..... F6
Kure 242,655 ..... F6
Kuroiso 42,349 ..... K5
Kurume 204,474 ..... E7
Kushikino 30,456 ..... E8
Kushima 30,038 ..... E8
Kushimoto 18,997 ..... G7
Kushiro 206,840 ..... M2
Kyonan 13,067 ..... O3
Kyoto 1,461,059 ..... J7
Machida 255,305 ..... O2
Maebashi 250,241 ..... J5
Maihara 12,845 ..... G6
Maizuru 97,780 ..... G6
Makubetsu 18,444 ..... L2
Makurazaki 29,685 ..... O3
Mashike 9,312 ..... K2
Masuda 50,734 ..... E6
Matsubara 132,662 ..... H8
Matsue 127,440 ..... F6
Matsumae 18,307 ..... J3
Matsumoto 185,595 ..... H5
Matsusaka 108,893 ..... H6
Matsuto 36,170 ..... H5
Matsuyama 367,323 ..... F7
Mihara 83,679 ..... F6
Miki 53,731 ..... H7
Mikuni 21,602 ..... G5
Minamata 36,782 ..... E7
Minobu 10,345 ..... J6
Minoo 79,621 ..... J7
Misawa 37,437 ..... K3
Mitaka 164,950 ..... O2
Mito 197,953 ..... K5
Mitsukaido 38,820 ..... P2
Miura 47,888 ..... O3
Miyako 61,912 ..... L4
Miyakonojo 118,289 ..... E8
Miyazaki 234,347 ..... E8
Miyazu 30,194 ..... G6
Miyoshi 37,193 ..... F6
Mizusawa 52,266 ..... K4
Mobara 64,942 ..... K6
Mombetsu 32,825 ..... L1
Monbetsu 15,029 ..... L2
Mooka 47,345 ..... K5
Mori 17,030 ..... K2
Moriguchi 178,383 ..... J7
Morioka 216,223 ..... K4
Motobu 17,823 ..... N6
Muko 45,886 ..... J7
Murakami 32,939 ..... J4
Muroran 158,715 ..... K2
Muroto 26,660 ..... G7
Musashino 139,508 ..... O2
Mutsu 44,646 ..... K3
Nachikatsuura 23,596 ..... H7
Nagahama, Ehime 13,144 ..... F7
Nagahama, Shiga 54,064 ..... H6
Nagano 306,637 ..... J5
Nagaoka, Kyoto 65,557 ..... J7
Nagaoka, Niigata 171,742 ..... J5
Nagaokakyo 65,557 ..... J7
Nagasaki 450,194 ..... D7
Nagato 27,327 ..... E6
Nago 45,210 ..... N6
Nagoya 2,079,740 ..... H6
Naha 295,006 ..... N6
Nakaminato 33,147 ..... K5
Nakamura 34,437 ..... F7
Nakasato 14,248 ..... K3
Nakatsu 59,111 ..... E7
Nanao 49,493 ..... H5
Nankoku 42,832 ..... F7
Nara 257,538 ..... J8
Narashino 117,852 ..... P2
Nayoro 35,145 ..... L1
Naze 46,359 ..... O5
Nemuro 45,817 ..... M2
Neyagawa 254,311 ..... J7
Nichinan 52,171 ..... E8
Niigata 423,188 ..... J5
Niihama 131,712 ..... F6
Niimi 30,014 ..... F6
Niitsu 58,970 ..... J5
Nishinomiya 400,622 ..... H8

(continued on following page)

Agriculture, Industry and Resources

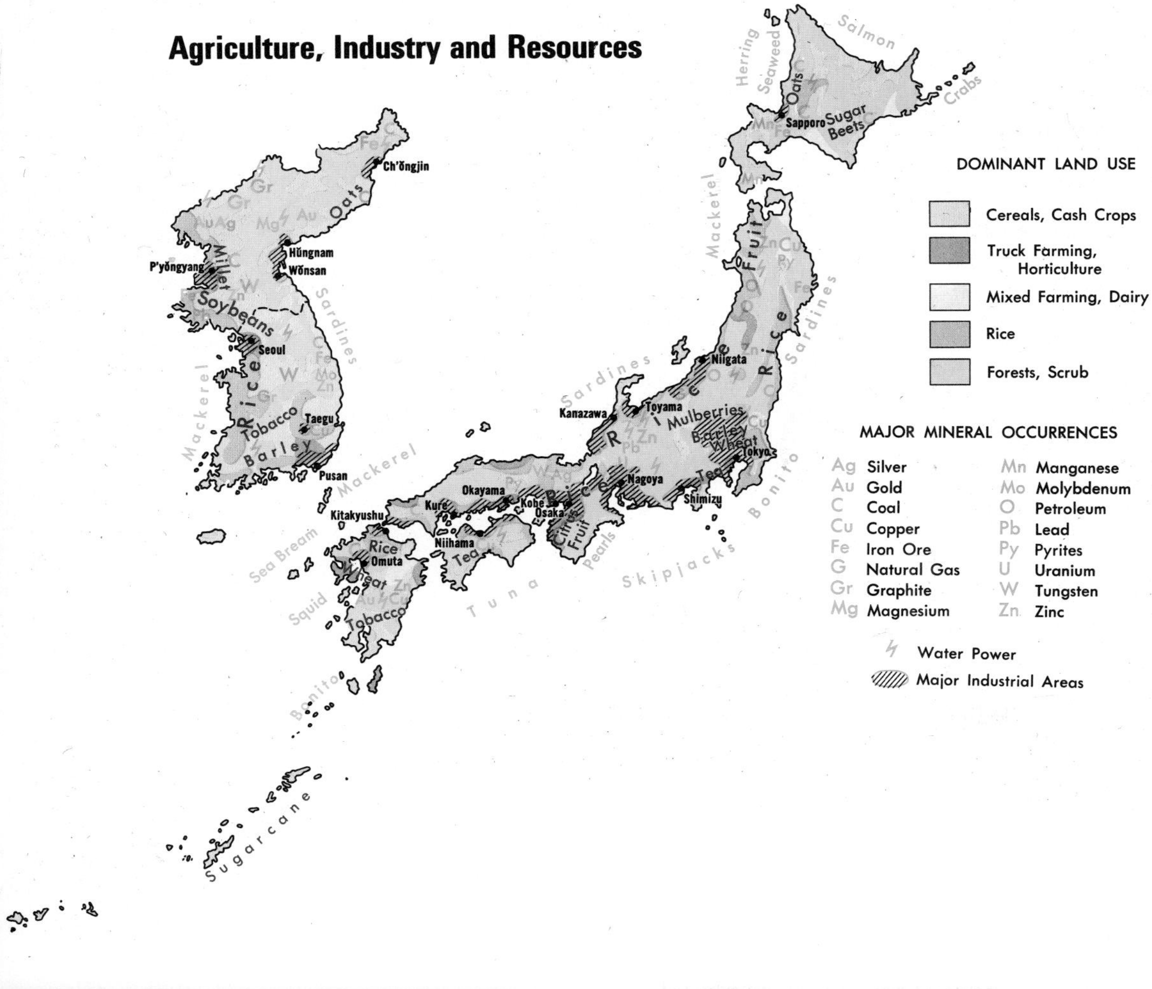

(continued)

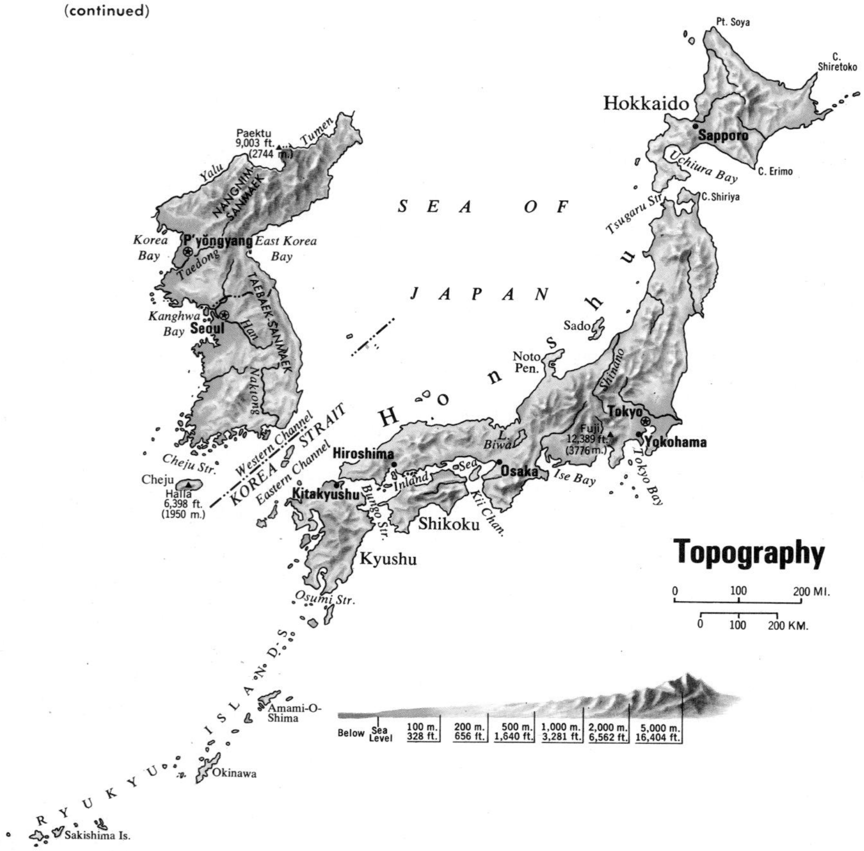

Topography

Nishinoomote 24,266 .... E8
Nobeoka 134,521 .... E7
Noboribetsu 50,885 .... K2
Noda 78,193 .... P2
Nogata 58,551 .... E7
Nose 9,749 .... J7
Noshiro 59,215 .... J3
Noto 15,815 .... H5
Numata 45,255 .... J5
Numazu 199,325 .... J6
Obama 33,890 .... G6
Obihiro 141,774 .... L2
Oda 37,449 .... F6
Odate 71,828 .... K3
Odawara 173,519 .... J6
Ofunato 39,632 .... K4
Oga 39,619 .... J4
Ogaki 140,424 .... H6
Ogi 4,717 .... J5
Ohata 12,632 .... K3
Oita 320,237 .... E7
Ojiya 44,375 .... J5
Okawa 50,395 .... E7
Okaya 61,776 .... H5
Okayama 513,471 .... F6
Okazaki 234,510 .... H6
Omagari 40,581 .... K4
Omiya 327,698 .... O2
Omu 7,407 .... L1
Omura, Bonin Is. 1,507 .... M3
Omura, Nagasaki 60,919 .... E7
Omuta 165,969 .... E7
Onagawa 16,945 .... K4
Ono 41,918 .... H6
Onoda 43,804 .... E6
Onomichi 102,951 .... F6
Osaka 2,778,987 .... J8
Ota 110,723 .... J5
Otaru 184,406 .... K2
Otawara 42,332 .... K5
Otofuke 26,933 .... L2
Otsu 191,481 .... J7
Owase 31,797 .... H6
Oyabe 35,791 .... H5
Oyama 120,264 .... J5
Ozu 37,294 .... F7
Rausu 8,249 .... M1
Rikuzentakata 29,439 .... K4
Rumoi 36,882 .... K2
Ryotsu 22,110 .... J4
Ryugasaki 40,565 .... P2
Sabae 57,252 .... H5
Saga 152,258 .... E7
Sagamihara 377,398 .... O2
Saigo 14,409 .... F5
Saiki 52,863 .... E7
Saito 37,054 .... E7
Sakado 51,232 .... O2
Sakai, Ibaraki 24,347 .... P1
Sakai, Osaka 750,688 .... J8
Sakaide 67,624 .... G6
Sakaiminato 35,821 .... F6
Sakata 97,723 .... J4
Saku 56,143 .... J5
Sakurai 54,314 .... J8
Sanda 35,261 .... H7
Sanjo 81,806 .... J5
Sapporo 1,240,613 .... K2
Sarufutsu 3,552 .... L1
Sasebo 250,729 .... D7
Satte 43,083 .... O1
Sawara 48,670 .... K6
Sayama 98,548 .... O2
Sendai, Kagoshima 61,788 .... E8
Sendai, Miyagi 615,473 .... K4
Setouchi 15,290 .... O5
Settsu 76,704 .... J8
Shari 15,996 .... M2
Shibata 74,025 .... J5
Shibetsu 30,028 .... M2
Shimabara 45,179 .... E7
Shimamoto 22,404 .... J7
Shimizu 243,049 .... J6
Shimoda 31,700 .... J6
Shimonoseki 266,593 .... E6
Shingu 39,023 .... H7
Shinjo 42,227 .... K4
Shiogama 59,235 .... K4
Shirakawa 42,685 .... K5
Shiranuka 14,897 .... M2
Shiroishi 40,862 .... K4
Shizunai 24,833 .... L2
Shizuoka 446,952 .... H6
Shobara 23,867 .... F6
Soka 167,177 .... O2
Soma 37,551 .... K5
Sonobe 14,827 .... J7
Suita 300,956 .... J7
Sukagawa 54,922 .... K5
Sukumo 25,340 .... F7
Sumoto 44,137 .... G6
Sunagawa 26,023 .... K2
Susaki 31,019 .... F7
Suttsu 6,511 .... J2
Suwa 49,594 .... H6
Suzu 28,238 .... H5
Suzuka 141,829 .... H6
Tachikawa 138,129 .... O2
Tagawa 61,464 .... E7
Tajimi 68,901 .... H6
Takaishi 66,824 .... H8
Takamatsu 298,999 .... F6
Takaoka 169,621 .... H5
Takarazuka 162,624 .... H7
Takasaki 211,348 .... J5
Takatsuki 330,570 .... J7
Takayama 60,504 .... H5
Takefu 65,012 .... G6
Takikawa 50,090 .... K2
Tanabe, Kyoto 30,022 .... J7
Tanabe, Wakayama 66,999 .... G7
Tateyama 56,139 .... K6
Tendo 48,082 .... K4
Tenri 62,909 .... J8
Teshio 6,509 .... K1
Toba 29,346 .... H6
Tobetsu 17,351 .... K2
Togane 33,406 .... K6
Toi 6,983 .... J6
Tojo 13,796 .... F6
Tokamachi 50,211 .... J5
Tokorozawa 196,870 .... O2
Tokunoshima 35,391 .... O5
Tokushima 239,281 .... G7
Tokuyama 106,967 .... F6
Tokyo (cap.) 8,646,520 .... O2
Tokyo* 11,673,554 .... O2
Tomakomai 132,477 .... K2
Tomiyama 7,389 .... O3
Tondabayashi 91,393 .... J8
Tosa 30,679 .... F7
Tosashimizu 24,856 .... F7
Tosu 50,733 .... E7
Tottori 122,312 .... G6
Towada 54,365 .... K3
Toyama 290,143 .... H5
Toyohashi 284,585 .... H6
Toyonaka 398,384 .... J7
Toyooka 46,210 .... G6
Toyota 248,774 .... H6
Tsu 139,538 .... H6
Tsubame 43,265 .... J5
Tsuchiura 104,028 .... J5
Tsuruga 60,205 .... G6
Tsuruoka 95,932 .... J4
Tsuyama 79,907 .... F6
Ube 161,969 .... E6
Ueda 105,151 .... J5
Ugo 21,956 .... K4
Uji 133,405 .... J7
Uozu 48,419 .... H5
Urakawa 20,213 .... L2
Urawa 331,145 .... O2
Ushibuka 24,250 .... D7
Usuki 39,163 .... F7
Utsunomiya 344,420 .... K5
Uwajima 70,428 .... F7
Wajima 33,234 .... H5
Wakasa 6,989 .... G6
Wakayama 389,717 .... G6
Wakkanai 55,464 .... K1
Warabi 76,311 .... O2
Yaizu 94,102 .... J6
Yakumo 19,260 .... J2
Yamagata 219,773 .... K4
Yamaguchi 106,099 .... E6
Yamato 145,881 .... O2
Yamatokoriyama 71,001 .... J8
Yamatotakada 58,637 .... J8
Yao 261,639 .... J8
Yatabe 22,225 .... P2
Yatsushiro 103,691 .... E7
Yawata 50,132 .... J7
Yawatahama 45,259 .... F7
Yoichi 25,816 .... K2
Yokawa 8,015 .... H7
Yokkaichi 247,001 .... H6
Yokohama 2,621,771 .... O3
Yokosuka 389,557 .... O3
Yokote 43,030 .... K4
Yonago 118,332 .... F6
Yonezawa 91,974 .... K5
Yono 71,044 .... O2
Yubari 50,131 .... L2
Yubetsu 6,693 .... L1
Yukuhashi 53,750 .... E7
Yuzawa 38,005 .... K4
Zushi 56,298 .... O3

OTHER FEATURES

Abashiri (riv.) M1
Agano (riv.) J4
Akan National Park M2
Amakusa (isls.) D7
Amami (isls.) N5
Amami-O-Shima (isl.) N5
Ara (riv.) O2
Asahi (mt.) J4
Asama (mt.) J5
Ashizuri (cape) F7
Aso (mt.) E7
Aso National Park E7
Atsumi (bay) H6
Awa (isl.) J4
Awaji (isl.) H8
Bandai (mt.) K5
Bandai-Asahi National Park J4
Biwa (lake) H6
Bonin (isls.) M3
Boso (pen.) K6
Bungo (strait) F7
Chichi (isl.) M3
Chichibu-Tama National Park J6
Chokai (mt.) J4
Chubu-Sangaku National Park H5
Dai (mt.) F6
Daimanji (mt.) F5
Daio (cape) H6
Daisen-Oki National Park F6
Daisetsu (mt.) L2
Daisetsu-Zan National Park L2
Dogo (isl.) F5
Dozen (isls.) F5
East China (sea) C8
Edo (riv.) P2
Erimo (cape) L3
Esan (pt.) K3
Etorofu (isl.) N1
Fuji (mt.) J6
Fuji (riv.) J6
Fuji-Hakone-Izu National Park H6
Gassan (mt.) J4
Goto (isls.) D7
Habomai (isls.) N2
Hachiro (lag.) J3
Haha (isl.) M3
Hakken (mt.) H6
Haku (mt.) H5
Hakusan National Park H5
Harima (sea) G6
Hida (riv.) H6
Hodaka (mt.) H5
Hokkaido (isl.) L2
Honshu (isl.) J5
Ie (isl.) N6
Iheya (isl.) N6
Iki (isl.) D7
Ina (riv.) H7
Inawashiro (lake) K5
Inubo (cape) K6
Iriomote (isl.) K7
Iro (cape) J6
Ise (bay) H6
Ise-Shima National Park H6
Ishigaki (isl.) L7
Ishikari (bay) K2
Ishikari (riv.) L2
Ishizuchi (mt.) F7
Iwaki (mt.) K3
Iwate (mt.) K4
Iwo (isl.) M4
Iyo (sea) E7
Izu (isls.) J6
Izu (pen.) J6
Japan (sea) G4
Joshinetsu-Kogen National Park J5
Kagoshima (bay) E8
Kamui (cape) K2
Kariba (mt.) K2
Kasumiga (lag.) K5
Kazan-retto (Volcano) (isls.) M4
Kerama (isls.) M6
Kii (chan.) G7
Kikai (isl.) O5
Kino (riv.) G6
Kirishima-Yaku National Park E7
Kita Iwo (isl.) M4
Kitakami (riv.) K4
Komaga (mt.) K2
Koshiki (isls.) D8
Kuchino (isl.) O4
Kuju (mt.) E7
Kume (isl.) M6
Kunashiri (isl.) N1
Kutcharo (lake) M2
Kyushu (isl.) E7
Meakan (mt.) L2
Minami Iwo (isl.) M5
Miura (pen.) O3
Miyako (isl.) L7
Miyako (isls.) L7
Mogami (riv.) K4
Motsuta (cape) J2
Muko (isl.) M3
Muko (riv.) H7
Muroto (pt.) G7
Mutsu (bay) K3
Naka (riv.) K5
Nampo-Shoto (isls.) M3
Nansei Shoto (Ryukyu) (isls.) M6
Nantai (mt.) J5
Nasu (mt.) J5
Nemuro (strait) M1
Nii (isl.) J6
Nikko National Park J5
Nishino (isl.) M3
Nojima (cape) K6
Nosappu (pt.) N2
Noto (pen.) H5
Nyudo (cape) J4
Oani (riv.) K3
Obitsu (riv.) P3
Oga (pen.) J4
Ogasawara-gunto (Bonin) (isls.) M3
Okhotsk (sea) M1
Oki (isls.) F5
Okinawa (isl.) N6
Okinawa (isls.) N6
Okinoerabu (isl.) N5
Okushiri (isl.) J2
Oma (cape) K3
Omono (riv.) J4
Ono (riv.) E7
Ontake (mt.) H6
Osaka (bay) H8
O-Shima (isl.) J6
Osumi (isls.) E8
Osumi (pen.) E8
Osumi (str.) E8
Otakine (mt.) K5
Rikuchu-Kaigan National Park L4
Rishiri (isl.) K1
Ryukyu (isls.) L7
Sado (isl.) J4
Sagami (bay) O3
Sagami (riv.) O2
Sagami (sea) J6
Saikai National Park D7
Sakishima (isls.) K7
San'in Kaigan National Park G6
Sata (cape) E8
Setonaikai National Park H7
Shikoku (isl.) F7
Shikotan (isl.) N2
Shikotsu (lake) K2
Shikotsu-Toya National Park K2
Shimane (pen.) F6
Shimokita (pen.) K3
Shinano (riv.) J5
Shiono (cape) H7
Shiragami (cape) J3
Shirane (mt.) J5
Shirane (mt.) H6
Shiretoko (cape) M1
Shiriya (cape) K3
Soya (pt.) L1
Suo (sea) E7
Suruga (bay) J6
Suwanose (isl.) O4
Suzu (pt.) H5
Takeshima (isls.) F5
Tama (riv.) O2
Tanega (isl.) E8
Tappi (cape) K3

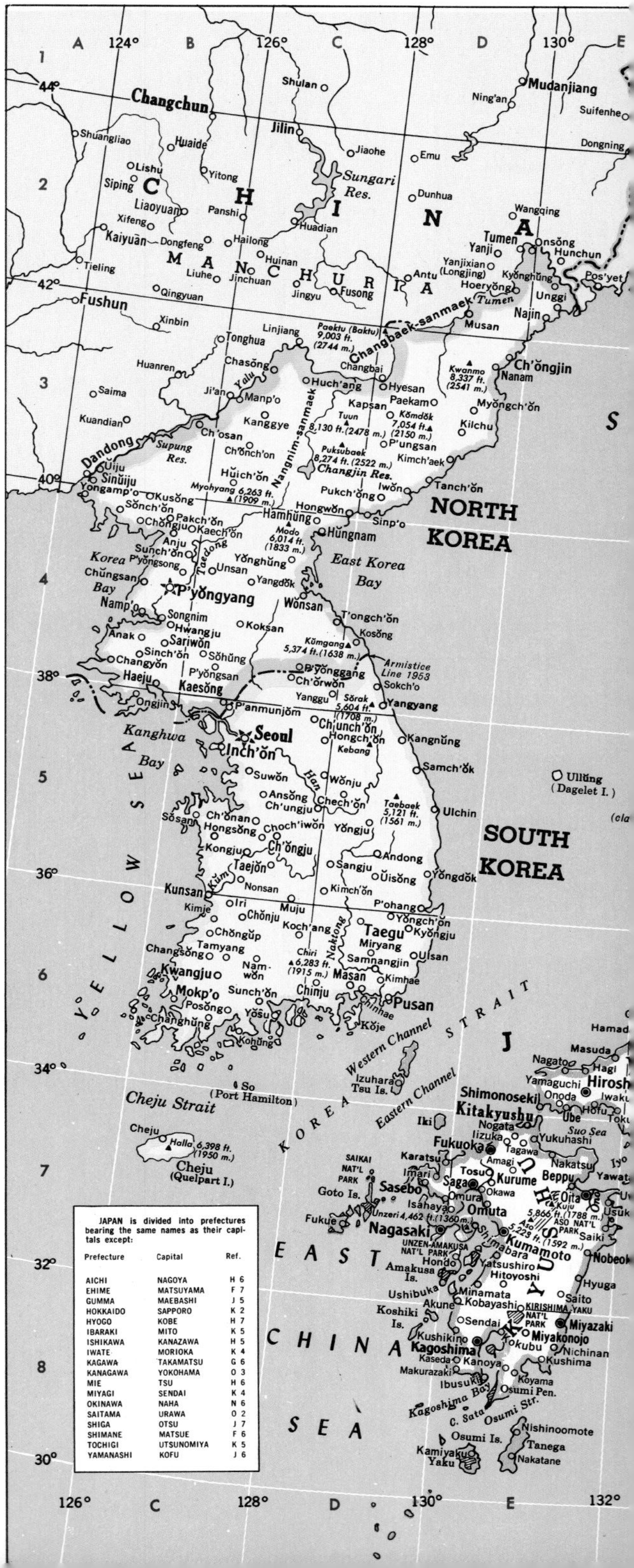

JAPAN is divided into prefectures bearing the same names as their capitals except:

Prefecture	Capital	Ref.
AICHI	NAGOYA	H 6
EHIME	MATSUYAMA	F 7
GUMMA	MAEBASHI	J 5
HOKKAIDO	SAPPORO	K 2
HYOGO	KOBE	H 7
IBARAKI	MITO	K 5
ISHIKAWA	KANAZAWA	H 5
IWATE	MORIOKA	K 4
KAGAWA	TAKAMATSU	G 6
KANAGAWA	YOKOHAMA	O 3
MIE	TSU	H 6
MIYAGI	SENDAI	K 4
OKINAWA	NAHA	N 6
SAITAMA	URAWA	O 2
SHIGA	OTSU	J 7
SHIMANE	MATSUE	F 6
TOCHIGI	UTSUNOMIYA	K 5
YAMANASHI	KOFU	J 6

Tarama (isl.) L7
Tazawa (lake) K4
Teshio (mt.) L1
Teshio (riv.) L1
Tobi (isl.) J4
Tokachi (mt.) L2
Tokachi (riv.) L2
Tokara (isls.) O5
Tokuno (isl.) O5
Tokyo (bay) O2
Tone (riv.) K6
Tosa (bay) F7
Towada (lake) K3
Towada-Hachimantai National Park K3
Toya (lake) K2
Toyama (bay) H5
Tsu (isls.) D6
Tsugaru (str.) K3
Tsurugi (mt.) G7
Uchiura (bay) K2
Unzen (mt.) D7
Unzen-Amakusa National Park D7
Volcano (isls.) M4
Wakasa (bay) G6
Yaeyama (isls.) K7
Yaku (isl.) E8
Yodo (riv.) J7
Yonaguni (isl.) K7
Yoron (isl.) N6
Yoshino (riv.) G6
Yoshino-Kumano National Park H7
Zao (mt.) K5

KOREA (NORTH)

CITIES and TOWNS

Ch'ŏngjin 306,000 ..... E3
Chŏngju B4
Haeju 140,000 ..... B4
Hamhŭng 484,000 ..... C4
Heijo (P'yŏngyang) (cap.) 1,250,000 ..... C4
Hongwŏn C3
Huch'ang C3
Hŭich'ŏn C3
Hyesan D3
Iwŏn D3
Kaech'ŏn B4
Kaesŏng 175,000 ..... C4
Kanggye C3
Kapsan C3
Kilchu D3
Kimch'aek 100,000 ..... D3
Najin E2
Namp'o 140,000 ..... B4
Onsŏng E2
P'anmunjŏm C5
P'yŏngyang (cap.) 1,250,000 ..... C4
Sariwŏn B4
Sinŭiju 300,000 ..... B3
Songnim B4
Wŏnsan 275,000 ..... C4

OTHER FEATURES

Baktu (Paektu) (mt.) C3
Changjin (res.) C3
East Korea (bay) D4
Japan (sea) G4
Kanghwa (bay) B5
Kŏmdŏk (mt.) D3
Kŭmgang (mt.) D4
Kwanmo (mt.) D3
Myohyang (mt.) C3
Nangnim-sanmaek (range) C3
Paektu (mt.) C3
Puksubaek (mt.) C3
Sasu (mt.) C4
Supung (res.) B3
Taedong (riv.) C4
Tumen (riv.) D2
Tuun (mt.) C3
Yalu (riv.) C3
Yellow (sea) B6

KOREA (SOUTH)

CITIES and TOWNS

Andong 95,364 ..... D5
Ansŏng 27,723 ..... C5
Changhŭng 22,227 ..... C6
Changsŏng 26,266 ..... C6
Chech'ŏn 74,239 ..... D5
Cheju 135,081 ..... C7
Chinhae 103,640 ..... D6
Chinju 154,646 ..... D6
Choch'iwŏn 29,198 ..... C5
Ch'ŏnan 96,766 ..... C5
Ch'ŏngju 192,707 ..... C5
Chŏngŭp 54,864 ..... C6
Chŏnju 311,393 ..... C6
Ch'ŏrwŏn 8,180 ..... C4
Ch'unch'ŏn 140,530 ..... D5
Ch'ungju 105,274 ..... C5
Hongch'ŏn 29,499 ..... D5
Hongsŏng 26,995 ..... C5
Inch'ŏn 800,007 ..... C5
Iri 117,155 ..... C6
Kangnŭng 84,981 ..... D5
Kimch'ŏn 67,078 ..... D5
Kimje 221,414 ..... C6
Kimhae 203,428 ..... D6
Koch'ang 23,721 ..... C6
Kohŭng 217,446 ..... C6
Kongju 39,756 ..... C5
Kunsan 154,780 ..... C6
Kwangju 607,011 ..... C6
Kyŏngju 108,431 ..... D6
Masan 371,917 ..... D6
Miryang 42,951 ..... D6
Mokp'o 192,958 ..... C6
Muju 18,130 ..... C6
Namwŏn 50,857 ..... C6
Nonsan 226,429 ..... C5
P'anmunjŏm C5
P'ohang 134,418 ..... D5
Posŏng 20,256 ..... C6
Pusan 2,453,173 ..... D6
Samch'ŏk 42,526 ..... D5
Samnangjin 19,374 ..... D6
Sangju 52,839 ..... D5
Seoul (cap.) 6,889,502 ..... C5
Sokch'o 71,387 ..... D4
Sŏsan 38,081 ..... C5
Sunch'ŏn 108,063 ..... C6
Suwŏn 224,145 ..... C5
Taegu 1,310,768 ..... D6
Taejŏn 506,708 ..... C5
Tamyang 15,494 ..... C6
Ŭisŏng 26,480 ..... D5
Ulchin 27,607 ..... D5
Ulsan 252,570 ..... D6
Wŏnju 120,276 ..... D5
Yanggu 277,986 ..... C4
Yangyang 10,819 ..... D4
Yŏngch'on 50,765 ..... D6
Yŏngdŏk 18,671 ..... D5
Yŏngju 70,793 ..... D5
Yŏsu 130,623 ..... C6

OTHER FEATURES

Cheju (isl.) C7
Cheju (str.) C7
Chiri (mt.) C6
Dagelet (Ullŭng) (isl.) E5
East China (sea) C8
Halla (mt.) C7
Han (riv.) C5
Japan (sea) G4
Kanghwa (bay) B5
Kebang (mt.) D5
Kŏje (isl.) D6
Korea (str.) D6
Kŭm (riv.) C5
Naktong (riv.) D6
Port Hamilton (So) (isl.) C6
Quelpart (Cheju) (isl.) C7
So (isl.) C6

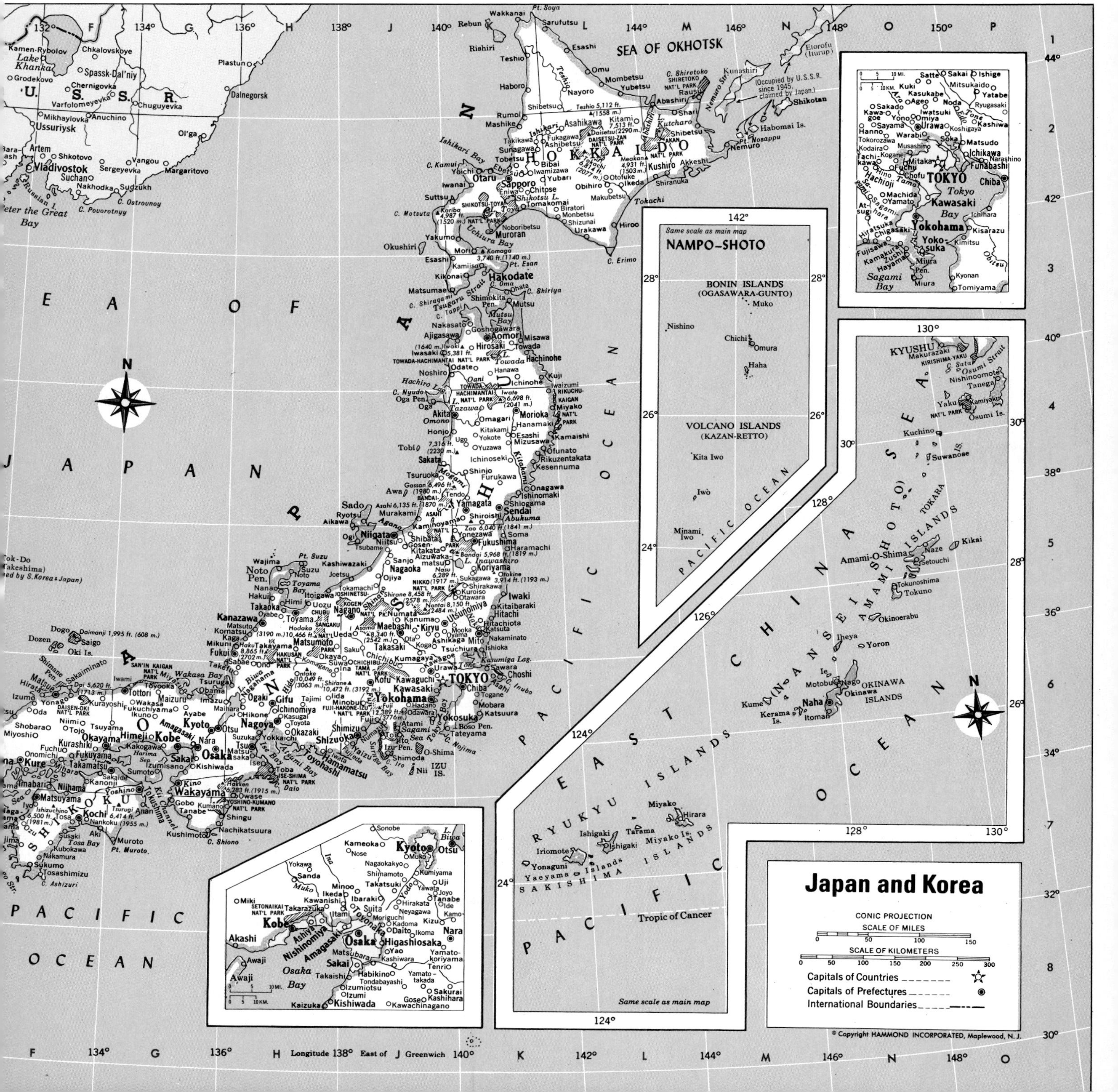

CHINA (MAINLAND)

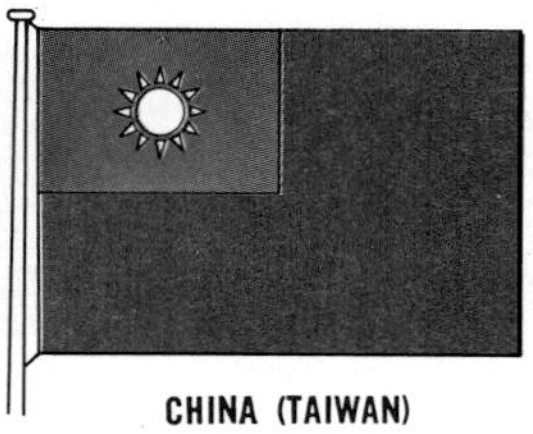

CHINA (TAIWAN)

MONGOLIA

CHINA (MAINLAND)

AREA 3,691,000 sq. mi. (9,559,690 sq. km.)
POPULATION 958,090,000
CAPITAL Beijing
LARGEST CITY Shanghai
HIGHEST POINT Mt. Everest 29,028 ft. (8,848 m.)
MONETARY UNIT yuan
MAJOR LANGUAGES Chinese, Chuang, Uigur, Yi, Tibetan, Miao, Mongol, Kazakh
MAJOR RELIGIONS Confucianism, Buddhism, Taoism, Islam

Topography

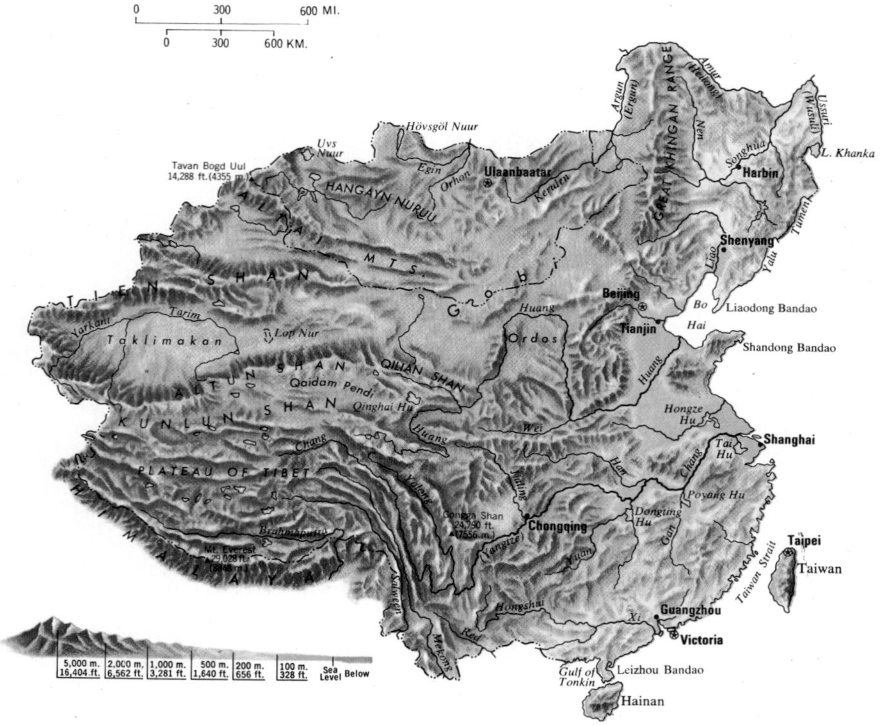

CHINA†

PROVINCES

Anhui (Anhwei) 47,130,000	J5
Fujian (Fukien) 24,500,000	J6
Gansu (Kansu) 18,730,000	E3
Guangdong (Kwangtung) 55,930,000	H7
Guangxi Zhuangzu (Kwangsi Chuang Autonomous Reg. 34,020,000	G7
Guizhou (Kweichow) 26,860,000	G6
Heilongjiang (Heilungkiang) 33,760,000	K2
Hebei (Hopei) 50,570,000	J4
Henan (Honan) 70,660,000	H5
Hubei (Hupei) 45,750,000	H5
Hunan 51,660,000	H6
Jiangsu (Kiangsu) 58,340,000	K5
Jiangxi (Kiangsi) 31,830,000	J6
Jilin (Kirin) 24,740,000	L3
Liaoning 37,430,000	K3
Nei Monggol (Inner Mongolian Aut. Reg.) 8,900,000	H3
Ningxia Huizu (Ningsia Hui Aut. Reg.) 3,660,000	F3
Qinghai (Tsinghai) 3,650,000	E4
Shaanxi (Shensi) 27,790,000	G5
Shanxi (Shansi) 24,340,000	H4
Shandong (Shantung) 71,600,000	J4
Sichuan (Szechwan) 97,070,000	F5
Taiwan 16,609,961	K7
Xinjiang Uygur (Sinkiang-Uigur Aut. Reg.) 12,330,000	B3
Xizang (Tibet Aut. Reg.) 1,790,000	B5
Yunnan 30,920,000	F7
Zhejiang (Chekiang) 37,510,000	K6

CITIES AND TOWNS

Aihui (Aigun) (Heihe)	L1
Amoy (Xiamen) 400,000	J7
Anqing (Anking) 160,000	J5
Anshan 1,500,000	K3
Anyang 225,000	H4
Aqsu (Aksu)	B3
Baoding (Paoting) 350,000	J4
Baoji (Paoki) 275,000	G5
Baoshan	E7
Baotou (Paotow) 800,000	G3
Bei'an (Pehan) 130,000	L2
Beihai (Pakhoi) 175,000	G7
Beijing (Peking) (cap.) ○8,500,000	J3
Bengbu (Pengpu) 400,000	J5
Benxi (Penki) 750,000	K3
Canton (Guangzhou) 2,300,000	H7
Chamdo (Qamdo)	E5
Changchun 1,500,000	K3
Changde (Changteh) 225,000	H6
Changhua 137,236	K7
Changsha 850,000	H6
Changzhi (Changchih)	H4
Changzhou (Changchow) 400,000	K5
Chankiang (Zhanjiang) 220,000	H7
Chao'an (Chaochow)	J7
Charkhlia (Ruoqiang)	C4
Chefoo (Yantai) 180,000	K4
Chengchow (Zhengzhou) 1,500,000	H5
Chengde (Chengteh) 200,000	J3
Chengdu (Chengtu) 2,000,000	F5
Cherchen (Qiemo)	C4
Chiai 238,713	K7
Chinchow (Jinzhou) 750,000	K3
Chinkiang (Zhenjiang) 250,000	J5
Chinwangtao (Qinhuangdao) 400,000	K4
Chongqing (Chungking) 3,500,000	G6
Chüanchow (Quanzhou) 130,000	J7
Chuchow (Zhuzhou) 350,000	H6
Chuguchak (Tacheng)	B2
Chungshan (Zhongshan) 135,000	H7
Dali	E6
Dalian 1,480,240	K4
Dandong (Tantung) 450,000	K3
Datong (Tatung) 300,000	H3
Erenhot	H3
Foshan (Fatshan)	H7
Fushun 1,700,000	K3
Fuxin (Fusin) 350,000	K3
Fuzhou (Foochow) 900,000	J6
Ganzhou (Kanchow) 135,000	H6
Garyarsa (Gartok)	B5
Gejiu (Kokiu) 250,000	F7
Golmud (Golmo)	D4
Guangzhou (Canton) 2,300,000	H7
Guilin (Kweilin) 225,000	G6
Guiyang (Kweiyang) 1,500,000	G6
Gulja (Yining) 160,000	B3
Gyangzê	C6
Haikou (Hoihow) 500,000	H7
Hailar	J2
Hami (Kumul)	D3
Handan (Hantan) 500,000	H4
Hangzhou (Hangchow) 1,100,000	J5
Hanzhong (Hanchung) 120,000	G5
Harbin 2,750,000	L2
Hefei (Hofei) 400,000	J5
Hegang (Hokang) 3,530,000	L2
Heihe (Aihui) (Aigun)	L1
Hengyang 310,000	H6
Hohhot (Huhehot) 700,000	H3
Horqin Youyi Qianqi (Ulanhot) 110,000	K2
Hotan	B4
Huainan 350,000	J5
Huangshi 200,000	J5
Ichang (Yichang) 150,000	H5
Ichun (Yichun) 200,000	L2
Ipin (Yibin) 275,000	F6
Jiamusi (Kiamusze) 275,000	M2
Ji'an (Kian) 100,000	J6
Jiangmen (Kongmoon) 150,000	H7
Jiaozuo (Tsiaotso) 300,000	H4
Jilin (Kirin) 1,200,000	L3
Jinan (Tsinan) 1,500,000	J4
Jingdezhen (Kingtehchen) 300,000	J6
Jining (Tsining) 160,000	H3
Jinshi (Tsingshih) 100,000	H6
Jinzhou (Chinchow) 750,000	K3
Jiujiang (Kiukiang) 120,000	J6
Jixi (Kisi) 350,000	M2
Juichin (Ruijin)	J6
Kaifeng 330,000	H5
Kalgan (Zhangjiakou) 1,000,000	J3
Kanchow (Ganzhou) 135,000	H6
Kaohsiung 1,028,334	J7
Karakax (Kara Kash) (Moyu)	A4
Karghalik (Yecheng)	A4
Kashi (Kashgar) 175,000	A4
Kaxgar (Kashi) 175,000	A4
Keelung 342,604	K6
Keriya (Yutian)	B4
Khotan (Hotan)	B4
Kiamusze (Jiamusi) 275,000	M2
Kian (Ji'an) 100,000	J6
Kingtehchen (Jingdezhen) 300,000	J6
Kirin (Jilin) 1,200,000	L3
Kisi (Jixi) 350,000	M2
Kiukiang (Jiujiang) 120,000	J6
Kokiu (Gejiu) 250,000	F7
Kongmoon (Jiangmen) 150,000	H7
Kuldja (Yining) 160,000	B3
Kunming 1,700,000	F6
Kwangchow (Canton) 2,300,000	H7
Kweilin (Guilin) 225,000	G6
Kweisui (Hohhot) 700,000	H3
Kweiyang (Guiyang) 1,500,000	G6
Lanzhou (Lanchow) 1,500,000	F4
Leshan (Loshan) 250,000	F6
Lhasa 175,000	D6
Lhazê (Lhatse)	C6
Lianyungang (Lienyünkang) 300,000	J5
Liaoyang 250,000	K3
Liaoyuan 300,000	K3
Linqing (Lintsing)	J4
Liuzhou (Liuchow) 250,000	G7
Lopnur (Yuli)	C3
Lüda (Dalian) 1,480,240	K4

(continued on following page)

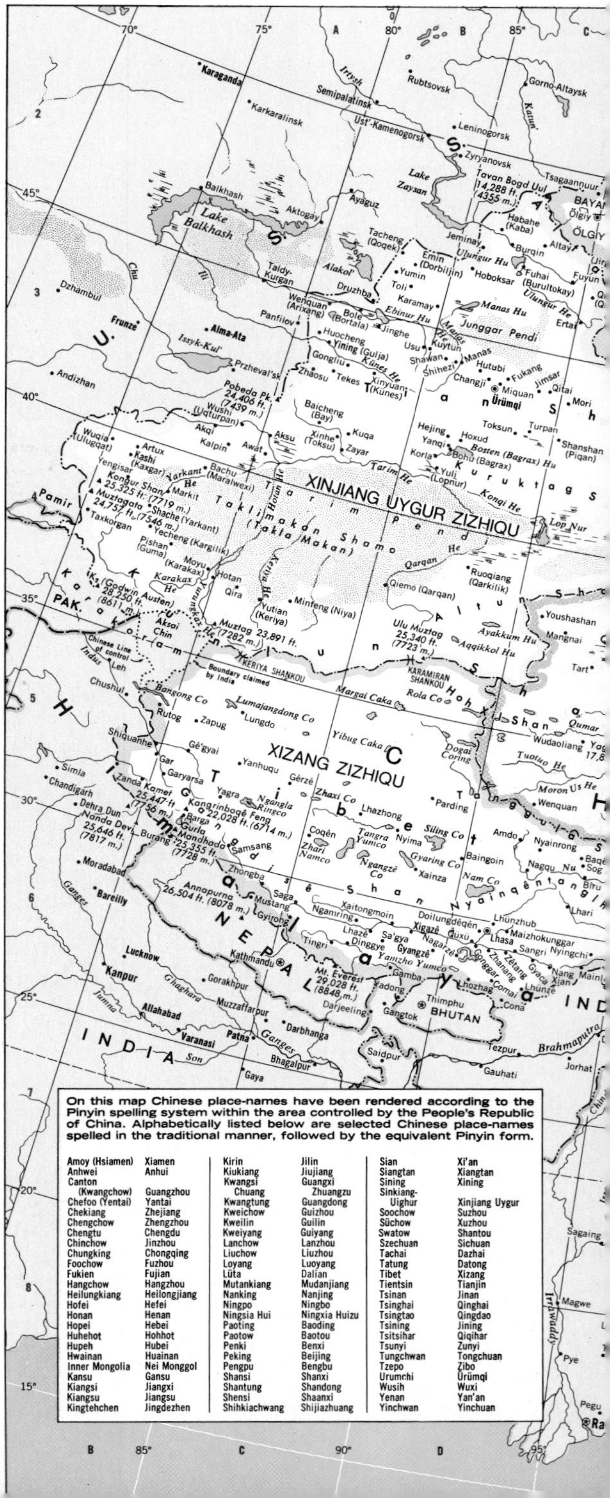

On this map Chinese place-names have been rendered according to the Pinyin spelling system within the area controlled by the People's Republic of China. Alphabetically listed below are selected Chinese place-names spelled in the traditional manner, followed by the equivalent Pinyin form.

Amoy (Hsiamen)	Xiamen	Kirin	Jilin	Sian	Xi'an
Anhwei	Anhui	Kiukiang	Jiujiang	Siangtan	Xiangtan
Canton (Kwangchow)	Guangzhou	Kwangsi Chuang	Guangxi Zhuangzu	Sining	Xining
Chefoo (Yentai)	Yantai	Kwangtung	Guangdong	Sinkiang-Uighur	Xinjiang Uygur
Chekiang	Zhejiang	Kweichow	Guizhou	Soochow	Suzhou
Chengchow	Zhengzhou	Kweilin	Guilin	Süchow	Xuzhou
Chengtu	Chengdu	Kweiyang	Guiyang	Swatow	Shantou
Chinchow	Jinzhou	Lanchow	Lanzhou	Szechuan	Sichuan
Chungking	Chongqing	Liuchow	Liuzhou	Tachai	Dazhai
Foochow	Fuzhou	Loyang	Luoyang	Tatung	Datong
Fukien	Fujian	Lüta	Dalian	Tibet	Xizang
Hangchow	Hangzhou	Mutankiang	Mudanjiang	Tientsin	Tianjin
Heilungkiang	Heilongjiang	Nanking	Nanjing	Tsinan	Jinan
Hofei	Hefei	Ningpo	Ningbo	Tsinghai	Qinghai
Honan	Henan	Ningsia Hui	Ningxia Huizu	Tsingtao	Qingdao
Hopei	Hebei	Paoting	Baoding	Tsining	Jining
Huhehot	Hohhot	Paotow	Baotou	Tsitsihar	Qiqihar
Hupeh	Hubei	Penki	Benxi	Tsunyi	Zunyi
Hwainan	Huainan	Peking	Beijing	Tungchwan	Tongchuan
Inner Mongolia	Nei Monggol	Pengpu	Bengbu	Tzepo	Zibo
Kansu	Gansu	Shansi	Shanxi	Urumchi	Ürümqi
Kiangsi	Jiangxi	Shantung	Shandong	Wusih	Wuxi
Kiangsu	Jiangsu	Shensi	Shaanxi	Yenan	Yan'an
Kingtehchen	Jingdezhen	Shihkiachwang	Shijiazhuang	Yinchwan	Yinchuan

CHINA (TAIWAN)

AREA 13,971 sq. mi. (36,185 sq. km.)
POPULATION 16,609,961
CAPITAL Taipei
LARGEST CITY Taipei
HIGHEST POINT Yü Shan 13,113 ft. (3,997 m.)
MONETARY UNIT new Taiwan yüan (dollar)
MAJOR LANGUAGES Chinese, Formosan
MAJOR RELIGIONS Confucianism, Buddhism, Taoism, Christianity, tribal religions

MONGOLIA

AREA 606,163 sq. mi. (1,569,962 sq. km.)
POPULATION 1,594,800
CAPITAL Ulaanbaatar
LARGEST CITY Ulaanbaatar
HIGHEST POINT Tabun Bogdo 14,288 ft. (4,355 m.)
MONETARY UNIT tughrik
MAJOR LANGUAGES Khalkha Mongolian, Kazakh (Turkic)
MAJOR RELIGION Buddhism

HONG KONG

AREA 403 sq. mi. (1,044 sq. km.)
POPULATION 5,022,000
CAPITAL Victoria
MONETARY UNIT Hong Kong dollar
MAJOR LANGUAGES Chinese, English
MAJOR RELIGIONS Confucianism, Buddhism, Christianity

MACAU

AREA 6 sq. mi. (16 sq. km.)
POPULATION 271,000
CAPITAL Macau
MONETARY UNIT pataca
MAJOR LANGUAGES Chinese, Portuguese
MAJOR RELIGIONS Confucianism, Buddhism, Taoism, Christianity

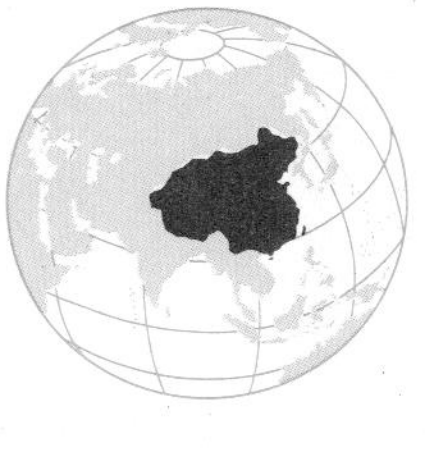

(continued)

Luoyang (Loyang) 750,000 ..... H5
Lüshun K4
Luzhou (Luchol) 225,000 .... G6
Ma'anshan J5
Manzhouli (Manchouli) J2
Maoming (Mowming) H7
Mengzi F7
Mianyang G5
Minfeng (Niya) B4
Moyu (Karakax) A4
Mudanjiang
(Mutankiang) 400,000 ...... M3
Mukden (Shenyang) 3,750,000 K3
Nanchang 900,000 .... J6
Nanchong (Nanchung) 275,000 G5
Nanjing (Nanking) 2,000,000 ... J5
Nanning 375,000 .... G7
Nanping J6
Nantong 300,000 .... K5
Nanyang H5
Neijiang (Neikiang) 240,000 .... G6
Nenjiang L2
Ningbo (Ningpo) 350,000 .... K6
Ningsia (Yinchuan,
Yinchwan) 175,000 .... G4
Paicheng (Baicheng) K2
Pakhoi (Beihai) 175,000 .... G7
Paoki (Baoji) 275,000 .... G5
Paoting (Baoding) 350,000 ..... J4
Paotow (Baotou) 800,000 .... G3
Pehan (Bei'an) 130,000 .... L2
Peking (Beijing)
(cap.)○ 8,500,000 .... J3
Pengpu (Bengbu) 400,000 ...... J5
Penki (Benxi) 750,000 .... K3
Pingdingshan H5
Pingliang G4
Pingtung 165,360 .... K7
Pingxiang, Guangxi
Zhuangzu G7
Pingxiang, Jiangxi H6
Piqan (Shanshan) D3
Qamdo E5
Qarkilik (Ruoqiang) C4
Qiemo (Qarqan) C4
Qingdao (Tsingtao) 1,900,000 . K4
Qingjiang 110,000 .... J5
Qinhuangdao
(Chinwangtao) 400,000 ...... K4
Qiqihar
(Tsitsihar) 1,500,000 .... K2
Qitai C3

Qoqek (Tacheng) B2
Quanzhou
(Chüanchow) 130,000 .... J7
Ruijin (Juichin) J6
Ruoqiang (Qarkilik) C4
Shache (Yarkand) A4
Shanghai○ 10,980,000 .... K5
Shangqui (Shangkiu) 250,000 .. J5
Shangrao (Shangjao) 100,000 . J6
Shangshui 100,000 .... J5
Shanshan (Piqan) D3
Shantou (Swatow) 400,000 ..... J7
Shaoguan (Shiukwan) 125,000 H7
Shaoxing (Shaohing) 225,000 .. K5
Shaoyang 275,000 .... H6
Shashi 125,000 .... H5
Shenyang (Mukden) 3,750,000 K3
Shigatse (Xigazê) C6
Shihezi (Shihhotzu) C3
Shijiazhuang
(Shihkiachwang) 1,500,000 . J4
Shiyan H5
Shizuishan (Shihsuishan) G4
Shuangcheng L2
Shuangyashan 150,000 .... M2
Siakwan (Xiaguan) E6
Sian (Xi'an) 1,900,000 .... G5
Siangfan (Xiangfan) 150,000 ... H5
Siangtan (Xiangtan) 300,000 ... H6
Sienyang (Xianyang) 125,000 .. G5
Simao (Fusingchen) F7
Sinchu 208,038 .... K7
Singtai (Xingtai) H4
Sining (Xining) 250,000 .... F4
Sinsiang (Xinxiang) 300,000 .... H4
Sinyang (Xinyang) 125,000 ..... H5
Siping (Szeping) 180,000 .... K3
Soche (Shache) A4
Suao K7
Süchow (Xuzhou) 1,500,000 ... J5
Suifenhe M3
Suihua L2
Suining G5
Suzhou (Soochow) 1,300,000 . K5
Swatow (Shantou) 400,000 ..... J7
Tacheng (Qoqek) B2
Tai'an J4
Taichung 565,255 .... K7
Tainan 541,390 .... J7
Taipei 2,108,193 .... K7
Taitung K7
Taiyuan 2,725,000 .... H4

Taizhou (Taichow) 275,000 ..... K5
Tali (Dali) E6
Tangshan 1,200,000 .... J4
Tantung (Dandong) 450,000 ... K3
Tao'an K2
Taoyuan 105,841 .... K6
Tatung (Datong) 300,000 .... H3
Tehchow (Dezhou) J4
Tianjin (Tientsin)○ 7,210,000 ... J4
Tianshui 100,000 .... F5
Tieling K3
Tientsin (Tianjin)○ 7,210,000 ... J4
Tongchuan (Tungchwan) G5
Tonghua (Tunghwa) 275,000 ... L3
Tongjiang (Tungkiang) M2
Tongliao K3
Tongling J5
Tsiaotso (Jiaozuo) 300,000 ..... H4
Tsinan (Jinan) 1,500,000 .... J4
Tsingkiang
(Qingjiang) 110,000 .... J5
Tsingshih (Jinshi) 100,000 ...... H6
Tsingtao (Qingdao) 1,900,000 . K4
Tsining (Jining) 160,000 .... H3
Tsitsihar
(Qiqihar) 1,500,000 .... K2
Tsunyi (Zunyi) 275,000 .... G6
Tumen M3
Tunxi (Tunki) J6
Turpan (Turfan) C3
Tzekung (Zigong) 350,000 ...... F6
Tzepo (Zibo) 1,750,000 .... J4
Uch Turfan (Wushi) A3
Ulanhot (Horquin Youyi
Qianqi) 100,000 .... K2
Ulughchat (Wuqia) A4
Ürümqi
(Urumchi) 500,000 .... C3
Usu B3
Wanxian (Wanhsien) 175,000 .. G5
Weifang 260,000 .... J4
Weihai (Weihaiwei) K4
Wenzhou 250,000 .... J6
Wuda G4
Wuhan 4,250,000 .... H5
Wuhu 300,000 .... J5
Wuqi G4
Wuqia A4
Wushi A3
Wuxi (Wusih) 900,000 .... K5
Wuxing (Wuhing) 160,000 .... K5
Wuzhong (Wuchung) G4

Wuzhou (Wuchow) 150,000 .... H7
Xiaguan (Siakwan) E6
Xiamen (Amoy) 400,000 .... J7
Xi'an (Sian) 1,900,000 .... G5
Xiangfan (Siangfan) 150,000 ... H5
Xiangtan (Siangtan) 300,000 ... H6
Xianyang (Sienyang) 125,000 .. G5
Xiapu (Siapu) K6
Xichang (Sichang) F6
Xigazê (Shigatse) C6
Xingtai (Singtai) H4
Xining (Sining) 250,000 .... F4
Xinxiang (Sinsiang) 300,000 .... H4
Xinyang (Sinyang) 125,000 ..... H5
Xuzhou (Süchow) 1,500,000 ... J5
Ya'an 100,000 .... F6
Yadong C6
Yan'an (Yenan) G4
Yanji (Yenki) 130,000 .... L3
Yangquan
(Yangchüan) 350,000 .... H4
Yangzhou (Yangchow)
210,000 .... J5
Yantai (Chefoo) 180,000 .... K4
Yarkand (Shache) A4
Ya Xian G8
Yecheng A4
Yenan (Yan'an) G4
Yibin (Ipin) 275,000 .... F6
Yichang (Ichang) 150,000 ...... H5
Yichun 200,000 .... L2
Yinchuan (Ningsia) 175,000 .... G4
Yingkou 215,000 .... K3
Yining 160,000 .... B3
Yiyang H6
Yuci (Yütze) H4
Yuli (Lopnur) C3
Yumen 325,000 .... E4
Yungkia (Wenzhou) 250,000 ... J6
Yutian B4
Zhangjiakou
(Kalgan) 1,000,000 .... J3
Zhangzhou (Changchow) J7
Zhanjiang
(Chankiang) 220,000 .... H7
Zhaoqing H7
Zhengzhou
(Chengchow) 1,500,000 ..... H5
Zhenjiang
(Chinkiang) 250,000 .... J5
Zhongshan
(Chungshan) 135,000 .... H7

Zhuzhou (Chuchow) 350,000 ... H6
Zibo (Tzepo) 1,750,000 .... J4
Zigong (Tzekung) 350,000 ...... F6
Zunyi (Tsunyi) 275,000 .... G6

OTHER FEATURES

Altun Shan (range) C4
Alxa Shamo (des.) F4
Amur (Heilong Jiang) (riv.) L2
A'nyêmaqên Shan (mts.) E5
Argun' (Ergun He) (riv.) K1
Bashi (chan.) K7
Bayan Har Shan (range) E5
Bo Hai (gulf) J4
Bosten (Bagrax) Hu (lake) C3
Chang Jiang (Yangtze) (riv.) K5
Da Hingan Ling (range) J3
Dian Chi (lake) F7
Dongsha (isl.) J7
Dongting Hu (riv.) H6
East China (sea) L6
Ergun He (Argun') (riv.) K1
Er Hai (lake) F6
Everest (mt.) C6
Formosa (Taiwan) (str.) J7
Gangdisê Shan (range) B5
Ghenghis Khan Wall (ruin) H2
Gobi (des.) G3
Grand (canal) J4
Great Wall (ruins) G4,J
Gurla Mandhada (mt.) B5
Hainan (isl.) H8
Hangzhou Wan (bay) K5
Heilong Jiang (Amur) (riv.) L2
Himalaya (mts.) C6
Hotan He (riv.) B4
Huang He (Yellow) (riv.) J4
Hulun Nur (lake) J2
Inner Mongolia (reg.) H3
Jinmen (Quemoy) (isl.) J7
Jinsha Jiang (Yangtze) (riv.) E5
Junggar Pendi (desert
basin) C2
Karakhoto (ruins) F3
Karamiran Shankou (pass) C4
Keriya Shankou (pass) B4
Khanka (lake) M3
Kongur Shan (mt.) A4
Künes He (riv.) B3
Kunlun Shan (range) B4
Kuruktag Shan (range) C3

Lancang Jiang (riv.) F7
Leizhau Bandao (pen.) G7
Liaodong Bandao (pen.) K3
Liao He (riv.) K3
Lop Nor (Lop Nur) (lake) D3
Manas He (riv.) C3
Mazu (Matsu) (isl.) K6
Mekong (Lancang Jiang)
(riv.) F7
Muztag (mt.) B4
Muztagata (mt.) A4
Nam Co (lake) D5
Namzha Parwa (mt.) E6
Nan Ling (mts.) H6
Nu Jiang (riv.) E6
Nyainqêntanglha Shan
(range) D5
Olwampi (cape) K7
Ordos (reg.) G4
Penghu (Pescadores) (isls.) J7
Pobeda (peak) A3
Poyang Hu (lake) J6
Pratas (Dongsha) (isl.) J7
Qaidam Pendi (basin)
(swamp) D4
Qarqan He (riv.) C4
Qilian Shan (range) E4
Qinghai Hu (lake) E4
Qiongzhou Haixia (str.) G7
Quemoy (Jinmen) (isl.) J7
Salween (Nu Jiang) (riv.) E6
Siling Co (lake) C5
Songhua Jiang (Sungari)
(riv.) M2
South China (sea) J7
Tai Hu (lake) J5
Taiwan (Formosa) (str.) J7
Taizhou (Tachen) (isls.) K6
Takla Makan (Taklimakan Shamo)
(des.) B4
Tanggula Shan (range) D5
Tangra Yumco (lake) C5
Tarim Pendi (basin) B4
Tian Shan (range) C3
Tibet (reg.) B5
Tongtian He (Zhi Qu) (riv.) E5
Tonkin (gulf) G7
Tumen (riv.) L3
Ulu Muztag (mt.) C4
Ussuri (Wusuli Jiang) (riv.) M2
Wei He (riv.) G5
Wusuli Jiang (Ussuri) (riv.) M2

Xiang Jiang (riv.) H6
Xi Jiang (riv.) H7
Yalong Jiang (riv.) F6
Yalu (riv.) L3
Yangtze (Chang Jiang) (riv.) K5
Yarkant He (riv.) A4
Yellow (Huang He) (riv.) J4
Yellow (sea) K4
Yü Shan (mt.) K7

HONG KONG

CITIES and TOWNS

Kowloon* 2,378,480 .... H7
Victoria (cap.)* 1,026,870 ...... H7

MACAU (MACAO)

CITIES and TOWNS

Macau (Macao (cap.) 226,880 . H7

MONGOLIA

CITIES and TOWNS

Tamsagbulag J2
Ulaanbaatar (Ulan Bator)
(cap.) 345,000 .... G2

OTHER FEATURES

Altai (mts.) C2
Dzavhan Gol (riv.) D2
Hangayn Nuruu (mts.) E2
Har Us Nuur (lake) D2
Herlen Gol (Kerulen)
(riv.) H2
Hovd Gol (riv.) D2
Hövsgöl Nuur (lake) F1
Hyargas Nuur (lake) D2
Karakorum (ruins) F2
Kerulen (riv.) H2
Munku-Sardyk (mt.) F1
Orhon Gol (riv.) F2
Selenge Mörön (riv.) G2
Tannu-Ola (range) D1
Tavan Bogd Uul (mt.) C2
Uvs Nuur (lake) D1

○Population of municipality. *City and suburbs †Populations of mainland cities excluding Peking (Beijing), Shanghai and Tianjin (Tientsin), courtesy of Kingsley Davis, Office of Int'l Population and Urban Research, Institute of Int'l Studies, Univ. of California.

Agriculture, Industry and Resources

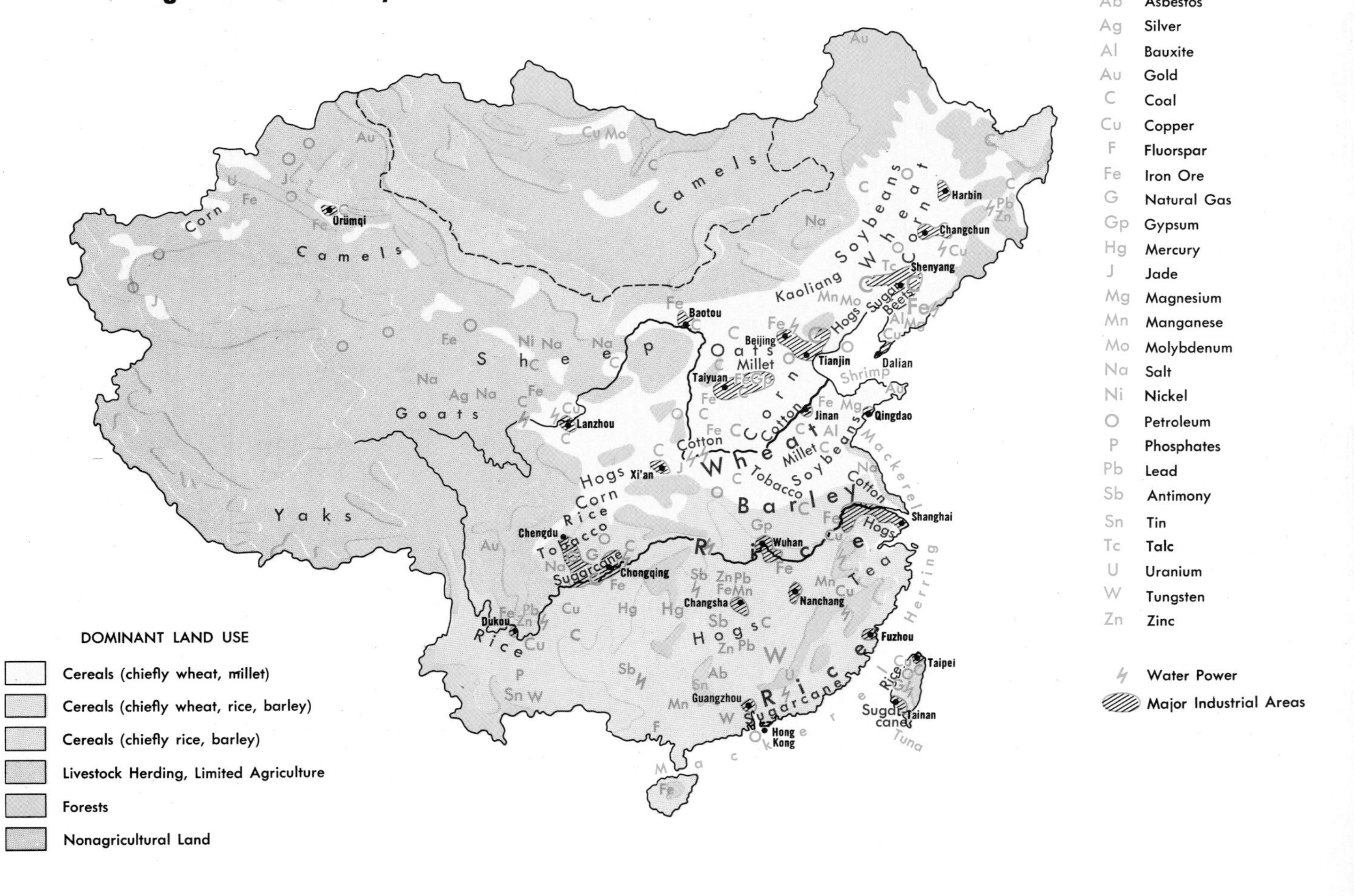

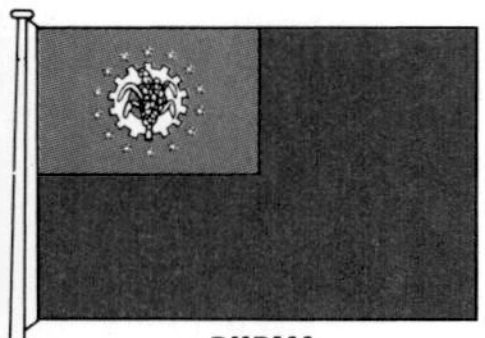

BURMA

THAILAND

LAOS

CAMBODIA

VIETNAM

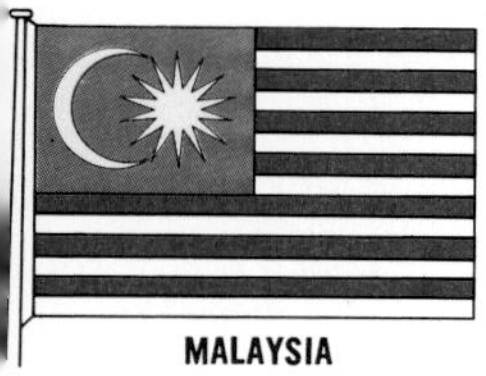

MALAYSIA

SINGAPORE

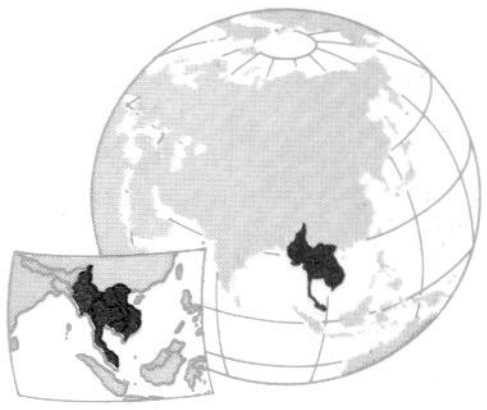

BURMA

AREA 261,789 sq. mi. (678,034 sq. km.)
POPULATION 32,913,000
CAPITAL Rangoon
LARGEST CITY Rangoon
HIGHEST POINT Hkakabo Razi 19,296 ft. (5,881 m.)
MONETARY UNIT kyat
MAJOR LANGUAGES Burmese, Karen, Shan, Kachin, Chin, Kayah, English
MAJOR RELIGIONS Buddhism, tribal religions

THAILAND

AREA 198,455 sq. mi. (513,998 sq. km.)
POPULATION 46,455,000
CAPITAL Bangkok
LARGEST CITY Bangkok
HIGHEST POINT Doi Inthanon 8,452 ft. (2,576 m.)
MONETARY UNIT baht
MAJOR LANGUAGES Thai, Lao, Chinese, Khmer, Malay
MAJOR RELIGIONS Buddhism, tribal religions

LAOS

AREA 91,428 sq. mi. (236,800 sq. km.)
POPULATION 3,721,000
CAPITAL Vientiane
LARGEST CITY Vientiane
HIGHEST POINT Phou Bia 9,252 ft. (2,820 m.)
MONETARY UNIT kip
MAJOR LANGUAGE Lao
MAJOR RELIGIONS Buddhism, tribal religions

CAMBODIA

AREA 69,898 sq. mi. (181,036 sq. km.)
POPULATION 5,200,000
CAPITAL Phnom Penh
LARGEST CITY Phnom Penh
HIGHEST POINT 5,948 ft. (1,813 m.)
MONETARY UNIT riel
MAJOR LANGUAGE Khmer (Cambodian)
MAJOR RELIGION Buddhism

VIETNAM

AREA 128,405 sq. mi. (332,569 sq. km.)
POPULATION 52,741,766
CAPITAL Hanoi
LARGEST CITY Ho Chi Minh City (Saigon)
HIGHEST POINT Fan Si Pan 10,308 ft. (3,142 m.)
MONETARY UNIT dong
MAJOR LANGUAGES Vietnamese, Thai, Muong, Meo, Yao, Khmer, French, Chinese, Cham
MAJOR RELIGIONS Buddhism, Taoism, Confucianism, Roman Catholicism, Cao-Dai

MALAYSIA

AREA 128,308 sq. mi. (332,318 sq. km.)
POPULATION 13,435,588
CAPITAL Kuala Lumpur
LARGEST CITY Kuala Lumpur
HIGHEST POINT Mt. Kinabalu 13,455 ft. (4,101 m.)
MONETARY UNIT ringgit
MAJOR LANGUAGES Malay, Chinese, English, Tamil, Dayak, Kadazan
MAJOR RELIGIONS Islam, Confucianism, Buddhism, tribal religions, Hinduism, Taoism, Christianity, Sikhism

SINGAPORE

AREA 226 sq. mi. (585 sq. km.)
POPULATION 2,413,945
CAPITAL Singapore
LARGEST CITY Singapore
HIGHEST POINT Bukit Timah 581 ft. (177 m.)
MONETARY UNIT Singapore dollar
MAJOR LANGUAGES Chinese, Malay, Tamil, English, Hindi
MAJOR RELIGIONS Confucianism, Buddhism, Taoism, Hinduism, Islam, Christianity

Topography

BURMA

INTERNAL DIVISIONS

Arakan (state) 1,710,913 .... B3
Chin (state) 323,094 .... B2
Irrawaddy (div.) 4,152,521 .... B3
Kachin (state) 735,144 .... C1
Karen (state) 865,218 .... C3
Kayah (state) 126,492 .... C3
Magwe (div.) 2,632,144 .... B2
Mandalay (div.) 3,662,312 .... B2
Mon (state) 1,313,111 .... C3
Pegu (div.) 3,174,109 .... C3
Rangoon (div.) 3,186,886 .... C3
Sagaing (div.) 3,115,502 .... B1
Shan (state) 3,178,214 .... C2
Tenasserim (div.) 717,607 .... C4

CITIES and TOWNS

Akyab (Sittwe) 42,329 .... B2
Allanmyo 15,580 .... B3
Amarapura 11,268 .... B2
Amherst 6,000 .... C3
An B3
Anin C4
Bassein 126,045 .... B3
Bhamo 9,821 .... C1
Chauk 24,466 .... B2
Danubyu B3
Falam B2
Fort Hertz (Putao) C1
Gawai C1
Gokteik C2
Gwa B3
Gyobingauk 9,922 .... C3
Haka B2
Henzada 61,972 .... B3
Hmawbi 23,032 .... C3
Homalin B1
Hsenwi C2
Hsipaw C2
Htawgaw C1
Insein 143,625 .... C3
Kamaing C1
Karathuri C5
Katha 7,648 .... C1
Kawludo C3
Kawthaung 1,520 .... C5
Keng Hkam C2
Keng Tung C2
Koma C4
Kunlong C2
Kyaikto 13,154 .... C3
Kya-in Seikkyi C3
Kyangin 6,073 .... B3
Kyaukme C2
Kyaukpadaung 5,480 .... B2
Kyaukpyu 7,335 .... B3
Kyaukse 8,659 .... C2
Labutta 12,982 .... B3
Lai-hka C2
Lamu B3
Lashio C2
Lenya C5
Letpadan 15,896 .... C3
Lewe B3
Loi-kaw C3
Lonton B1
Magwe 13,270 .... B2
Maingkwan C1
Maliwun C5
Mandalay 418,008 .... C2
Man Hpang C2
Martaban 5,661 .... C3
Ma-ubin 23,362 .... B3
Maungdaw 3,772 .... B2
Mawkmai C2
Mawlaik 2,993 .... B2
Mawlu C1
Maymyo 22,287 .... C2
Meiktila 19,474 .... B2
Mergui 33,697 .... C4
Minbu 9,096 .... B2
Minhla 6,470 .... B3
Mogaung 2,920 .... C1
Mogok 8,334 .... C2
Mohnyin C1
Möng Hsat C2
Möng Maü C3
Möng Mit C2
Möng Pan C2
Möng Si C2
Möng Tön C2
Möng Tung C2
Monywa 26,279 .... B2
Moulmein 171,977 .... C3
Mudon 20,136 .... C3
Myanaung 11,155 .... B3
Myaungmya 24,532 .... B3
Myingyan 36,439 .... B2
Myitkyina 12,382 .... C1
Myohaung 6,534 .... B2
Naba B1
Namhkam C2
Namlan C2
Namtu C2
Natmauk B2
Okkan 14,443 .... B3
Okpo 12,155 .... C3
Pakokku 30,943 .... B2
Palaw 5,596 .... C4
Paletwa B2
Pantha B2
Papun C3
Pasawng C3
Paungde 17,286 .... B3
Pegu 47,378 .... C3
Prome (Pye) 36,997 .... B3
Putao C1
Pyapon 19,174 .... B3
Pye 36,997 .... B3
Pyinmana 22,025 .... C3
Pyu 10,443 .... C3
Rangoon (cap.) 1,586,422 .... C3
Rangoon* 2,055,365 .... C3
Rathedaung 2,969 .... B2
Sadon C1
Sagaing 15,382 .... B2
Samka C2
Sandoway 5,172 .... B3
Shingbwiyang B1
Shwebo 17,827 .... B2
Shwenyaung C2
Singkaling Hkamti B1
Singu 4,027 .... C2
Sinlumkaba C1
Sittwe 42,329 .... B2
Sumprabum C1
Syriam 15,296 .... C3
Taungdwingyi 16,233 .... C2
Taunggyi C2
Tavoy 40,312 .... C4
Tharrawaddy 8,977 .... C3
Thaton 38,047 .... C3
Thaungdut B1
Thayetmyo 11,649 .... B3
Thazi 7,531 .... C2
Thongwa 10,829 .... C3
Toungoo 31,589 .... C3
Wakema 20,716 .... B3
Yamethin 11,167 .... C2
Yandoon 15,245 .... B3
Ye 12,852 .... C4
Yenangyaung 24,416 .... B2
Yesagyo 7,880 .... B2
Ye-u 5,307 .... B2
Ywathit C3
Zadi C4
Zalun 899 .... B3

OTHER FEATURES

Amya (pass) C4
Andaman (sea) B4
Arakan Yoma (mts.) B3
Ataran (riv.) C4
Bengal, Bay of (sea) B3
Bentinck (isl.) C5

(continued on following page)

80 Burma, Thailand, Indochina and Malaya

(continued)

Bilauktaung (range) C4
Chaukan (pass) C1
Cheduba (isl.) B3
Chin (hills) B2
Chindwin (riv.) B2
Coco (chan.) B4
Combermere (bay) B3
Daung Kyun (isl.) C4
Dawna (range) C3
Great Coco (isl.) B4
Great Tenasserim (riv.) C4
Heinze Chaung (bay) C4
Heywood (chan.) B3
Hka, Nam (riv.) C2
Hkakabo Razi (mt.) C1
Indawgyi (lake) C1
Inle (lake) C2
Irrawaddy (riv.) B3
Irrawaddy, Mouths of the (delta) B4
Kadan Kyun (isl.) C4
Kaladan (riv.) B2
Kalegauk (isl.) C4
Khao Luang (mt.) C5
Lanbi Kyun (isl.) C5
Launglon Bok (isls.) C4
Loi Leng (mt.) C2
Manipur (riv.) B2
Martaban (gulf) C4
Mekong (riv.) D2
Mergui (arch.) C5
Mon (riv.) B2
Mu (riv.) B2
Negrais (cape) B3
Pakchan (riv.) C5
Pangsau (pass) C1
Pawn, Nam (riv.) C2
Pegu Yoma (mts.) B3
Preparis (isl.) B4
Ramree (isl.) B3
Salween (riv.) C3
Shan (plat.) C2
Sittang (riv.) C3
Taungthonton (mt.) B1
Tavoy (pt.) C4
Tenasserim (isl.) C4
Teng, Nam (riv.) C2
Three Pagodas (pass) C4
Victoria (mt.) B2

CAMBODIA (KAMPUCHEA)

CITIES and TOWNS

Batdambang (Battambang) D4
Choam Khsant E4
Kampong Cham E4
Kampong Chhnang D4
Kampong Khleang E4
Kampong Saom D5
Kampong Spoe E5
Kampong Thum E4
Kampong Trabek E5
Kampot E5
Kaoh Nhek E4
Kracheh E4
Krong Kaoh Kong D4
Krong Keb E5
Kulen E4
Lumphat E4
Moung Roessei D4
Pailin D4
Paoy Pet D4
Phnom Penh (cap.) c. 300,000 E5
Phnum Tbeng Meanchey E4
Phsar Ream D5
Phumi Banam E5
Phumi Phsar E4
Phumi Prek Kak E4
Phumi Samraong D4
Pouthisat D4
Prek Pouthi E5
Prey Veng E5
Pursat (Pouthisat) D4
Rovieng Tbong E4
Sambor E4
Senmonoron E4
Siempang E4
Siemreab D4
Sisophon D4
Sre Ambel D5
Sre Khtum E4
Stoeng Treng E4
Suong E5
Svay Rieng E5
Takev E5
Virochey E4

OTHER FEATURES

Angkor Wat (ruins) E4
Dangrek (mts.) D4
Drang, Ia (riv.) E4
Joncs (plain) E5
Khong, Se (riv.) E4
Kong, Kaoh (isl.) D5
Mekong (riv.) E4
Rung, Kaoh (isl.) D5
San, Se (riv.) E4
Sen, Stoeng (riv.) E4
Srepok (riv.) E4
Tang, Kaoh (isl.) D5
Thailand (gulf) D5
Tonle Sap (lake) D4
Wai, Poulo (isls.) D5

LAOS

CITIES and TOWNS

Attapu 2,750 E4
Ban Khon E4
Ban Lahanam E3
Borikan D3
Champasak 3,500 E4
Dônghén E3
Khamkeut⊙ 31,206 E3
Louang Namtha 1,459 D2
Louangphrabang 7,596 D3
Muang Hinboun 1,750 E3
Muang Kènthao D3
Muang Khammoun 5,500 E3
Muang Không 1,750 E4
Muang Khôngxédôn 2,000 E4
Muang Khoua D2
Muang May E4
Muang Ou Tai D2
Muang Paktha D2
Muang Phin E3
Muang Tahoi E3
Muang Vapi E4
Muang Xaignabouri (Sayaboury) 2,500 D3
Mounlapamôk E4
Napè E3
Nong Het E3
Pakxé 8,000 E4
Phiafai⊙ 17,216 E4
Phôngsali 2,500 D2
San Nua (Sam Neua) 3,000 E2
Saravan 2,350 E4
Savannakhét 8,500 E3
Sayaboury (Muang Xaignabouri) 2,500 D3
Thakhek (Muang Khammouan) 5,500 E3
Tourakom D3
Viangchan (Vientiane) 132,253 D3
Vientiane (cap.) 132,253 D3
Xiangkhoang 3,500 D3

OTHER FEATURES

Bolovens (plat.) E4
Hou, Nam (riv.) D2
Jars (plain) D3
Mekong (riv.) D3
Ou, Nam (riv.) D2
Phou Bia (mt.) D3
Phou Cô Pi (mt.) E3
Phou Loi (mt.) D2
Rao Co (mt.) E3
Se Khong (riv.) E4
Tha, Nam (riv.) D2
Xianghoang (plat.) D3

MALAYA, MALAYSIA*

STATES

Federal Territory 937,875 D7
Johor (Johore) 1,601,504 D7
Kedah 1,102,200 D6
Kelantan 877,575 D6
Melaka 453,153 D7
Negeri Sembilan 563,955 D7
Pahang 770,644 D7
Perak 1,762,288 D6
Perlis 147,726 D6
Pinang (Penang) 911,586 D6
Selangor 1,467,441 D7
Terengganu 542,280 D6

CITIES and TOWNS

Alor Gajah 2,222 D7
Alor Setar 66,260 D6
Bandar Maharani (Muar) 61,218 D7
Bandar Penggaram (Batu Pahat) 53,291 D7
Batu Gajah 10,692 D6
Batu Pahat 53,291 D7
Bentong 22,683 D7
Butterworth 61,187 D6
Chukai 12,514 D6
Gemas 5,214 D7
George Town (Pinang) 269,603 C6
Ipoh 247,953 D6
Johor Baharu (Johore Bharu) 136,234 F5
Kampar 26,591 D6
Kangar 8,758 D6
Kelang 113,611 D7
Keluang 43,272 D7
Kota Baharu 55,124 D6
Kota Tinggi 8,725 F5
Kuala Dungun 17,560 D6
Kuala Lipis 9,270 D6
Kuala Lumpur (cap.) 451,977 D7
Kuala Lumpur* 937,875 D7
Kuala Pilah 12,508 D7
Kuala Rompin 1,384 D7
Kuala Selangor 3,132 D7
Kuala Terengganu 53,320 D6
Kuantan 43,358 D7
Kulai 11,841 F5
Lumut 3,255 D6
Malacca (Melaka) 87,160 D7
Mawai F5
Melaka 87,160 D7
Mersing 18,246 E7
Muar 61,218 D7
Pekan 4,682 D7
Pekan Nanas 9,003 E5
Pinang (George Town) 269,603 C6
Pontian Kechil 8,349 E5
Port Dickson 10,300 D7
Port Kelang D7
Port Weld 3,233 D6
Raub 18,433 D7
Segamat 17,796 D7
Seremban 80,921 D7
Sungai Petani 35,959 C6
Taiping 54,645 D6
Tanah Merah 7,012 D6
Telok Anson 44,524 D6
Tumpat 10,673 D6

OTHER FEATURES

Aur, Pulau (isl.) E7
Belumut, Gunong (mt.) D7
Gelang, Tanjong (pt.) D6
Johor, Sungai (riv.) F5
Johore (str.) E6
Kelantan, Sungai (riv.) D6
Langkawi, Pulau (isl.) C6
Ledang, Gunong (mt.) D7
Lima, Pulau (isl.) F6
Malacca (str.) D7
Malay (pen.) D6
Pahang, Sungai (riv.) D7
Pangkor, Pulau (isl.) D6
Perak, Gunong (mt.) D6
Perhentian, Kepulauan (isls.) D6
Pulai, Sungai (riv.) E5
Ramunia, Tanjong (pt.) F6
Redang, Pulau (isl.) D6
Sedili Kechil, Tanjong (pt.) F5
Tahan, Gunong (mt.) D6
Temiang, Bukit (mt.) D6
Tenggol, Pulau (isl.) D6
Tinggi, Pulau (isl.) E7

SINGAPORE

CITIES and TOWNS

Jurong 50,974 E6
Nee Soon 37,641 F6
Serangoon 89,558 F6
Singapore (cap.) 2,413,945 F6

OTHER FEATURES

Keppel (harb.) F6
Main (str.) F6
Singapore (str.) F6
Tekong Besar, Pulau (isl.) F6

THAILAND (SIAM)

CITIES and TOWNS

Ang Thong 7,267 C4
Ayutthaya (Phra Nakhon Si Ayutthaya) 37,213 D4
Ban Aranyaprathet 12,276 D4
Bangkok (cap.) 1,867,297 D4
Bangkok* 2,495,312 D4
Bang Lamung D4
Bang Saphan C5
Ban Kantang 9,247 C6
Ban Kapong C5
Ban Khlong Yai D5
Ban Kui Nua D4
Ban Ngon D3
Ban Pak Phanang 13,590 D5
Banphot Phisai C3
Ban Pua D3
Ban Sattahip D4
Ban Tha Uthen D3
Bua Chum D4
Buriram 16,431 D4
Chachoengsao 22,106 D4
Chai Badan D4
Chai Buri D3
Chainat 9,944 D4
Chaiya C5
Chaiyaphum 12,540 D4
Chang Khoeng C3
Chanthaburi 15,479 D4
Chiang Dao C3
Chiang Khan D3
Chiang Mai 83,729 C3
Chiang Rai 13,927 C3
Chiang Saen C2
Chon Buri 39,367 D4
Chumphon 11,643 C5
Den Chai C3
Hat Yai 47,953 C6
Hot C3
Hua Hin 21,426 D4
Kalasin 14,960 D3
Kamphaeng Phet 12,378 C3
Kanchanaburi 16,397 C4
Khanu C3
Khemmarat E4
Khon Kaen 29,431 D3
Khorat (Nakhon Ratchasima) 66,071 D4
Krabi 8,764 C5
Krung Thep (Bangkok) (cap.) 1,867,297 D4
Kumphawapi D3
Lae D3
Lampang 40,100 C3
Lamphun 11,309 C3
Lang Suan 4,020 C5
Loei 10,137 D3
Lom Sak 10,597 D3
Lop Buri 23,112 D4
Mae Hong Son 3,981 C3
Maha Sarakham 19,707 D3
Mukdahan E3
Nakhon Nayok 8,185 D4
Nakhon Pathom 34,300 C4
Nakhon Phanom 20,385 D3
Nakhon Ratchasima 66,071 D4
Nakhon Sawan 46,853 D4
Nakhon Si Thammarat 40,671 D5
Nan 17,738 D3
Nang Rong D4
Narathiwat 21,256 D6
Ngao D3
Nong Khai 21,150 D3
Pattani 21,938 D6
Phanat Nikhom 10,514 D4
Phangnga 5,738 C5
Phatthalung 13,336 D6
Phayao 20,346 C3
Phet Buri 27,755 C4
Phetchabun 6,240 D3
Phichai D3
Phichit 10,814 D3
Phitsanulok 33,883 D3
Phon Phisai D3
Phrae 17,555 D3
Phra Nakhon Si Ayutthaya 37,213 D4
Phuket 34,362 C6
Phutthaisong D4
Prachin Buri 14,167 D4
Prachuap Khiri Khan 9,075 D5
Pran Buri D4
Rahaeng (Tak) 16,317 C3
Ranong 10,301 C5
Rat Buri 32,271 C4
Rayong 14,846 D4
Roi Et 20,242 D4
Rong Kwang D3
Sakon Nakhon 18,943 E3
Samut Prakan 46,632 D4
Samut Sakhon 33,619 D4
Samut Songkhram 23,574 C4
Sara Buri 25,025 D4
Satun 7,315 C6
Sawankhalok 8,387 C3
Selaphum E3
Sing Buri 9,050 D4
Singora (Songkhla) 41,193 D6
Sisaket 13,662 E4
Songkhla 41,193 D6
Sukhothai 15,488 D3
Suphan Buri 18,768 C4
Surat Thani 24,923 C5
Surin 16,342 D4
Suwannaphum D4
Tak 16,317 C3
Takua Pa 7,825 C5
Thoen C3
Thon Buri 628,015 D4
To Mo D6
Trang 32,985 C6
Trat 7,917 D4
Ubon 40,650 E4
Udon Thani 56,218 D3
Uthai Thani 10,525 C4
Uttaradit 12,022 D3
Warin Chamrap 21,520 E4
Yala 30,051 D6
Yasothon 12,079 D4

OTHER FEATURES

Amya (pass) C4
Bilauktaung (range) C4
Chang, Ko (isl.) D4
Chao Phraya, Mae Nam (riv.) D4
Chi, Mae Nam (riv.) D3
Dangrek (Dong Rak) (mts.) D4
Doi Inthanon (mt.) C3
Doi Pha Hom Pok (mt.) C2
Doi Pia Fai (mt.) D4
Kao Prawa (mt.) C3
Khao Luang (mt.) C5
Khwae Noi, Mae Nam (riv.) C4
Kra (isth.) C5
Kut, Ko (isl.) D5
Laem Pho (cape) D6
Laem Talumphuk (cape) D5
Lanta, Ko (isl.) C6
Luang (mt.) C5
Mae Klong, Mae Nam (riv.) C4
Mekong (riv.) E3
Mun, Mae Nam (riv.) D4
Nan, Mae Nam (riv.) D3
Nong Lahan (lake) D3
Pakchan (riv.) C5
Pa Sak, Mae Nam (riv.) D4
Phangan, Ko (isl.) D5
Phuket, Ko (isl.) C5

Agriculture, Industry and Resources

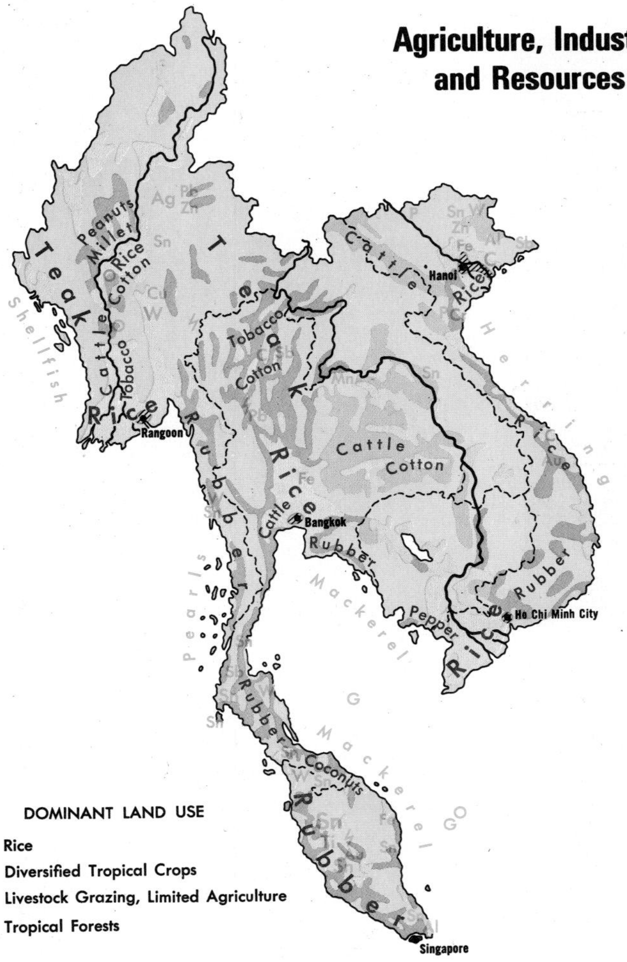

DOMINANT LAND USE

- Rice
- Diversified Tropical Crops
- Livestock Grazing, Limited Agriculture
- Tropical Forests

MAJOR MINERAL OCCURRENCES

Ag Silver	Cu Copper	O Petroleum	Sn Tin
Al Bauxite	Fe Iron Ore	P Phosphates	Ti Titanium
Au Gold	G Natural Gas	Pb Lead	W Tungsten
C Coal	Mn Manganese	Sb Antimony	Zn Zinc
Cr Chromium			

Water Power

Major Industrial Areas

Ping, Mae Nam (riv.) C3
Samui (str.) D5
Samui, Ko (isl.) D5
Siam (Thailand) (gulf) D5
Tao, Ko (isl.) C5
Tapi, Mae Nam (riv.) C5
Terutao, Ko (isl.) C6
Tha Chin, Mae Nam (riv.) C4
Thale Luang (lag.) D6
Thalu, Ko (isls.) C5
Three Pagodas (pass) C4
Wang, Mae Nam (riv.) C3

VIETNAM

CITIES and TOWNS

An Loc (Binh Long) 15,276 E5
An Nhon F4
An Tuc (An Khe) F4
Ap Long Ha F5
Ap Vinh Hao F5
Bac Can E2
Bac Giang E2
Bac Lieu 53,841 E5
Bac Ninh 22,560 E2
Ba Don E3
Bai Thuong E3
Ban Me Thuot 68,771 F4
Bao Ha D2
Bao Lac E2
Bien Hoa 87,135 E5
Binh Long (An Loc) 15,276 E5
Binh Son F4
Bo Duc E4
Bong Son (Hoai Nhon) F4
Cam Ranh 118,111 F5
Can Tho 182,424 E5
Cao Bang E2
Cao Lanh 16,482 E5
Chau Phu 37,175 E5
Chu Lai F4
Con Cuong E3
Cua Rao E3
Da Lat 105,072 F5
Dam Doi E5
Da Nang 492,194 E3
Dien Bien Phu D2
Dong Hoi E3
Duong Dong D5
Gia Dinh E5
Go Cong 33,191 E5
Ha Giang E2
Haiphong* 1,279,067 E2
Hanoi (cap.)* 2,570,905 E2
Ha Tien E5
Ha Tinh E3
Hau Bon E4
Hoa Binh E2
Hoa Da F5
Hoai Nhon F4
Ho Chi Minh City (Saigon)* 3,419,678 E5
Hoi An 45,059 F4
Hoi Xuan E2
Hon Chong E5
Hon Gai 100,000 E2
Hue 209,043 E3
Huong Khe E3
Ke Bao E2
Khanh Hoa F4
Khanh Hung 59,015 E5
Khe Sanh E3
Kien Hung E5
Kontum 33,554 E4
Lac Giao (Ban Me Thuot) 68,771 E4
Lai Chau D2
Lang Son 15,071 E2
Lao Cai E2
Loc Ninh E5
Long Xuyen 72,658 E5
Mo Duc F4
Mong Cai E2
Muong Khuong E2
My Tho 119,892 E5
Nam Dinh E2
Nghia Lo D2
Nha Trang 216,227 F4
Ninh Binh E3
Phan Rang 33,377 F5
Phan Thiet 80,122 F5
Phu Cuong 28,267 E5
Phu Lang Thuong (Bac Giang) E2
Phuc Loi E3
Phu Dien E3
Phu Ly E2
Phu My F4
Phu Qui E3
Phu Rieng E5
Phu Tho 10,888 E2
Phu Vinh 48,485 E5
Pleiku 23,720 E4
Quang Nam E4
Quang Ngai 14,119 F4
Quang Tri 15,874 E3
Quang Yen E2
Quan Long 59,331 E5
Qui Nhon 213,757 F4
Rach Gia 104,161 E5
Ron E3
Sa Dec 51,867 E5
Saigon (Ho Chi Minh City)* 3,419,678 E5
Song Cau F4
Son Ha F4
Son La D2
Son Tay 19,213 E2
Tam Ky 38,532 F4
Tam Quan F4
Tan An 38,082 E5
Tay Ninh 22,957 E5
Thai Binh 14,739 E2
Thai Nguyen E2
Thanh Hoa 31,211 E3
Thanh Tri E5
That Khe E2
Tien Yen E2
Tra Vinh (Phu Vinh) 48,485 E5
Truc Giang 68,629 E5
Trung Khanh Phu E2
Tuyen Quang E2
Tuy Hoa 63,552 F4
Van Hoa E2
Van Ninh F4
Van Yen E2
Vinh 43,954 E3
Vinh Long 30,667 E5
Vinh Yen E2
Vu Liet E3
Vung Tau 108,436 E5
Xuan Loc E5
Yen Bai E2

OTHER FEATURES

Bach Long Vi, Dao (isl.) F2
Ba Den, Nui (mt.) E5
Bai Bung, Mui (Ca Mau) (pt.) E5
Black (riv.) D2
Ca Mau (Mui Bai Bung) (pt.) E5
Cam Ranh, Vinh (bay) F5
Cat Ba, Dao (isl.) E2
Chon May, Vung (bay) F3
Cu Lao, Hon (isls.) F5
Deux Frères, Les (isls.) E5
Dinh, Mui (cape) F5
Fan Si Pan (mt.) D2
Ia Drang (riv.) E4
Joncs (plain) E5
Kontum (plat.) E4
Khoai, Hon (isl.) E5
Lang Bian, Nui (mts.) E4
Lay, Mui (cape) E3
Mekong, Mouths of the (delta) E5
Nam Tram, Mui (cape) F4
Nightingale (Bach Long Vi) (isl.) F2
Panjang, Hon (Hon Tho Chau) (isl.) D5
Phu Quoc, Dao (isl.) D5
Rao Co (mt.) E3
Red (riv.) E2
Se San (riv.) E4
Sip Song Chau Thai (mts.) D2
Song Ba (riv.) F4
Song Ca (riv.) E3
Song Cai (riv.) E4
South China (sea) F4
Tonkin (gulf) E3
Varella, Mui (cape) F4
Wai, Poulo (isls.) E4
Yang Sin, Chu (mt.) F4

*See Southeast Asia, p. 84 for other part of Malaysia.

*City and suburbs.

⊙Population of district.

Burma, Thailand, Indochina and Malaya
CONIC PROJECTION
SCALE OF MILES
0 50 100 150 200
SCALE OF KILOMETERS
0 50 100 200 300
International Boundaries
Division and State Boundaries
Capitals of Countries
Division and State Capitals
© Copyright HAMMOND INCORPORATED, Maplewood, N. J.
Longitude East 96° of Greenwich
BHUTAN
INDIA
BANGLADESH
CHINA
BURMA
THAILAND
CAMBODIA
LAOS
VIETNAM
MALAYSIA
MALAYA
SUMATRA
INDONESIA
SINGAPORE
BAY OF BENGAL
ANDAMAN SEA
GULF OF THAILAND
GULF OF TONKIN
SOUTH CHINA SEA
Gulf of Martaban
Strait of Malacca
ANDAMAN IS. (India)
NICOBAR IS. (India)
HAINAN
Paracel Is.
KACHIN STATE
SHAN STATE
CHIN STATE
KAYAH STATE
KAREN STATE
MON STATE
SAGAING
MANDALAY
MAGWE
PEGU
IRRAWADDY
RANGOON
TENASSERIM
RAKHINE
JOHOR
Tropic of Cancer
RANGOON
BANGKOK
Phnom Penh
HO CHI MINH CITY
Hanoi
Vientiane
Kuala Lumpur
Singapore
Mandalay
Moulmein
Kunming
Nanning
Da Nang
Hue
Haiphong
George Town
Ipoh
Chiang Mai
N

PHILIPPINES

AREA 115,707 sq. mi. (299,681 sq. km.)
POPULATION 48,098,460
CAPITAL Manila
LARGEST CITY Manila
HIGHEST POINT Apo 9,692 ft. (2,954 m.)
MONETARY UNIT peso
MAJOR LANGUAGES Pilipino (Tagalog), English, Spanish, Bisayan, Ilocano, Bikol
MAJOR RELIGIONS Roman Catholicism, Islam, Protestantism, tribal religions

Topography

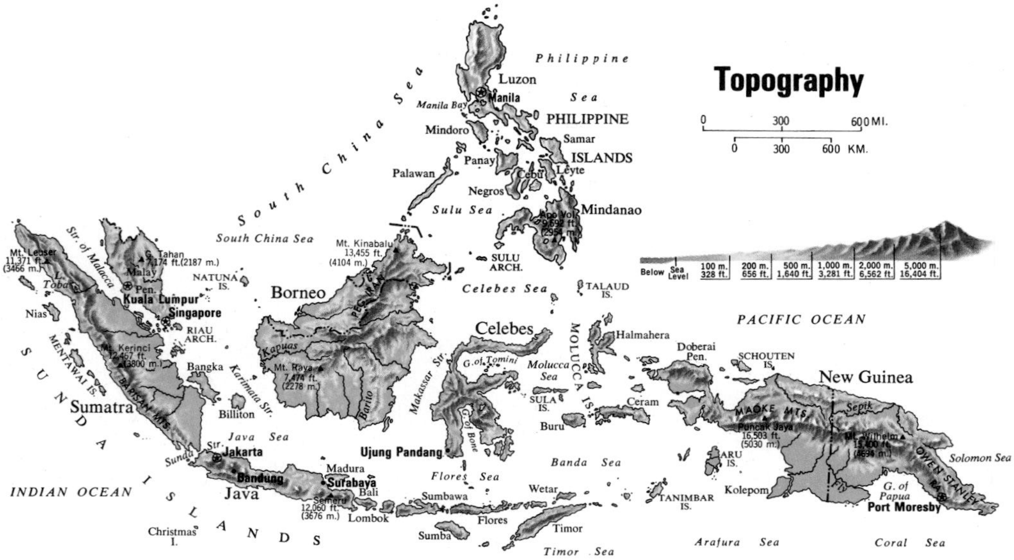

Agriculture, Industry and Resources

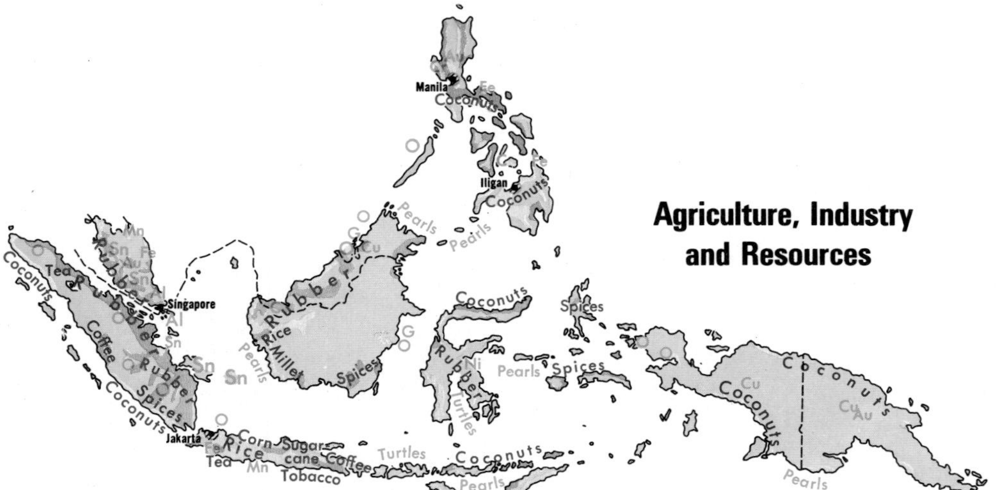

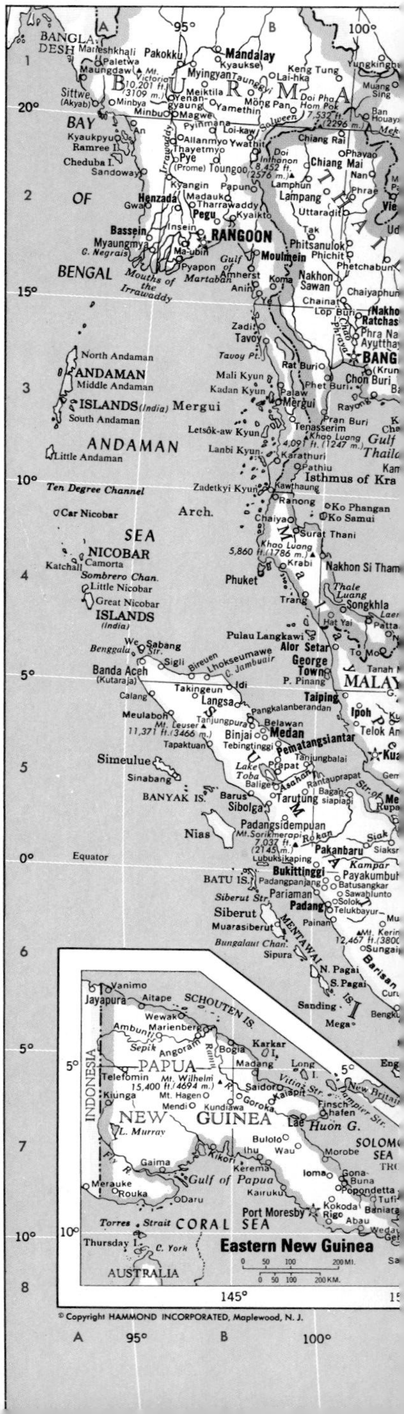

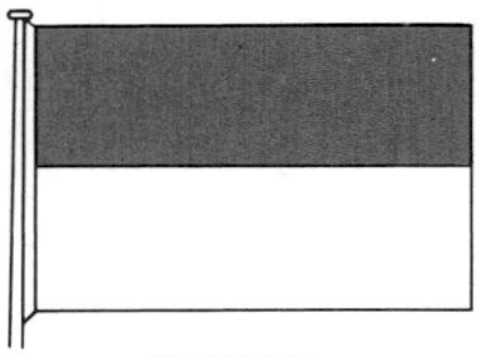

INDONESIA

AREA 788,430 sq. mi. (2,042,034 sq. km.)
POPULATION 147,490,298
CAPITAL Jakarta
LARGEST CITY Jakarta
HIGHEST POINT Puncak Jaya 16,503 ft. (5,030 m.)
MONETARY UNIT rupiah
MAJOR LANGUAGES Bahasa Indonesia, Indonesian and Papuan languages, English
MAJOR RELIGIONS Islam, tribal religions, Christianity, Hinduism

BRUNEI

AREA 2,226 sq. mi. (5,765 sq. km.)
POPULATION 192,832
CAPITAL Bandar Seri Begawan
LARGEST CITY Bandar Seri Begawan
HIGHEST POINT Pagon 6,070 ft. (1,850 m.)
MONETARY UNIT Brunei Dollar
MAJOR LANGUAGES Malay, English, Chinese
MAJOR RELIGIONS Islam, Buddhism, Christianity, tribal religions

PAPUA NEW GUINEA

AREA 183,540 sq. mi. (475,369 sq. km.)
POPULATION 3,010,727
CAPITAL Port Moresby
LARGEST CITY Port Moresby
HIGHEST POINT Mt. Wilhelm 15,400 ft. (4,694 m.)
MONETARY UNIT kina
MAJOR LANGUAGES pidgin English, Hiri Motu, English
MAJOR RELIGIONS Tribal religions, Christianity

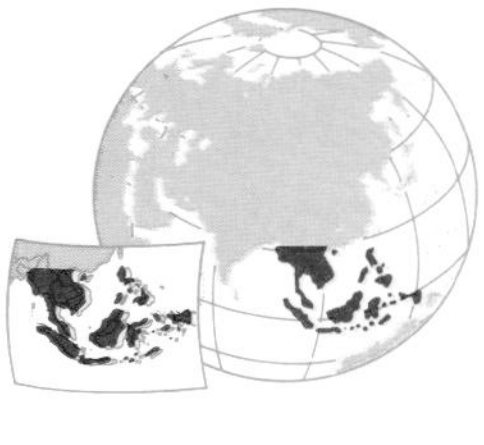

BRUNEI

CITIES and TOWNS

Bandar Seri Begawan 63,868 . E 4
Seria 23,511 . E 5

CHINA

OTHER FEATURES

Amphitrite (isls.) . E 2
Crescent (isls.) . E 2
Duncan (isls.) . E 2
Lincoln (isl.) . E 2
Money (isl.) . E 2
Paracel (isls.) . E 2
Robert (isl.) . E 2
Triton (isl.) . E 2
Xisha (isls.) . E 2
Woody (isl.) . E 2

INDONESIA

CITIES AND TOWNS

Agats . K 7
Amahai . H 6
Ambon (Amboina) 208,898 . H 6
Ampana . G 6
Amurang . G 5
Atambua . G 7
Auba . H 7
Baa . G 8
Babo . K 7
Bagansiapiapi . C 5
Balige . B 5
Balikpapan 280,675 . F 6
Banda Aceh 72,090 . A 4
Bandanaira . H 6
Bandung 1,462,637 . H 2
Banggai . G 6
Bangil •49,438 . K 2
Bangkalan •41,639 . K 2
Banjarmasin 381,286 . E 6
Bantul •40,585 . J 2
Banyumas . J 2
Banyuwangi •76,596 . L 2
Barabai •33,688 . F 6
Barus •46,120 . B 5
Batang •69,577 . J 2
Batavia (Jakarta) (cap.) 6,503,449 . H 1
Baturaja •48,350 . C 6
Batusangkar . C 6
Baubau . G 7
Baukau . H 7
Bekasi •123,264 . H 2
Belawan . B 5
Bengkalis •14,072 . C 5
Bengkayang •15,404 . E 5
Bengkulu 64,783 . C 6
Benteng . F 7
Beo . H 5
Biak . K 6
Binjai 76,464 . B 5
Bintuhan . C 6
Bireuen . B 4
Bitung •59,507 . H 5
Blitar 78,503 . K 2
Blora •67,853 . K 2
Bogor 247,409 . H 2
Bojonegoro •74,241 . J 2
Bondowoso •50,317 . L 2
Bonthain •30,377 . F 7
Brebes •87,918 . H 2
Bukittinggi 70,771 . B 6
Bula . J 6
Buli . H 5
Bulukumba •63,932 . G 7
Bumiayu •65,403 . H 2
Buntok . F 6
Buol . G 5
Calang . B 5
Ciamis •105,434 . H 2
Cianjur •132,058 . H 2
Cijulang •44,487 . H 2
Cilacap •118,815 . H 2
Cimahi •157,222 . H 2
Cirebon 223,776 . H 2
Curup •71,965 . C 6
Demak •57,676 . J 2
Demta . L 6
Denpasar •98,005 . E 7
Dili . H 7
Djambi (Jambi) 230,373 . C 6
Djokjakarta (Yogyakarta) 398,727 . J 2
Dobo . J 7
Dompu •14,103 . F 7
Donggala . F 6
Ende . G 7
Fakfak . J 6
Galela •11,554 . H 5
Garut •93,340 . H 2
Genting . D 5
Gorontalo 97,628 . G 5
Gresik •48,561 . K 2
Hollandia (Jayapura) •45,786 . K 6
Indramayu •69,441 . H 2
Isimu . G 5
Jailolo •17,243 . H 5
Jakarta (cap.) 6,503,449 . H 1
Jambi 230,373 . C 6
Jayapura •45,786 . L 6
Jember •115,201 . K 2
Jeneponto •6,883 . F 7
Jepara •75,124 . J 2
Jogjakarta (Yogyakarta) 398,727 . J 2
Jombang •80,643 . K 2
Kaimana . J 6
Kayuagung •37,319 . D 6
Kalianda •42,609 . D 7
Kampung Baru (Tolitoli) •10,071 . G 5
Karangasem •15,177 . F 7
Karosa . F 6
Kau . H 5
Kebumen •81,571 . J 2
Kediri 221,830 . K 2
Kendal •32,544 . J 2
Kendari •28,628 . G 6
Kepi . K 7
Ketapang . E 6
Klaten •58,870 . J 2
Kokonau . K 6
Kolaka •10,384 . G 6
Kolonodale . G 6
Kotaagung •20,154 . C 7
Kotabaharu . E 6
Kotabaru •23,443 . F 6
Kotabumi . C 7
Kotawaringin . E 6
Kragan •33,389 . K 2
Krawang •99,552 . H 2
Kualakapuas . E 6
Kudus •79,186 . J 2
Kumai . E 6
Kumai •13,564 . E 6
Kuningan •105,255 . H 2
Kupang •49,354 . G 8
Kutaraja (Banda Aceh) 72,090 . A 4
Kutoarjo •52,989 . J 2
Labuha . H 6
Labuhan •34,274 . G 2
Laham . F 5
Lahat •48,136 . C 6
Laiwui . H 6
Lamongan •38,897 . K 2
Langsa •58,060 . B 5
Larantuka . G 7
Lawang •59,071 . K 2
Lekitobi . G 6
Letong . D 5
Longiram . F 5
Longnawan . F 5
Lubuklinggau •43,011 . C 6
Lubuksikaping •24,244 . B 5
Lumajang •79,641 . K 2
Madiun 150,562 . K 2
Majalengka •80,999 . H 2
Magelang 123,484 . J 2
Magetan •59,507 . K 2
Makassar (Ujung Pandang) 709,038 . F 7
Malang 511,780 . K 2
Malili . G 6
Malinau •14,130 . F 5
Mamuju •17,345 . F 6
Manado 217,159 . G 5
Manokwari . J 6
Maros . F 6
Martapura •55,011 . F 6
Masamba •16,571 . G 6
Mataram •46,846 . F 7
Maumere . G 7
Medan 1,378,955 . B 5
Menggala •20,878 . D 6
Merauke •21,366 . K 7
Mindiptana . L 7
Mojokerto 68,849 . K 2
Muarabungo •26,304 . C 6
Muarasiberut . B 6
Muaratewe . F 6
Muntok •31,719 . D 6
Nabire . K 6
Nangapinoh •19,983 . E 6
Nangatayap . E 6
Negara •65,762 . E 7
Ngabang •33,190 . D 5
Ngawi . K 2
Okaba . K 7
Pacitan •51,993 . J 2
Padang 480,922 . B 6
Padangpanjang 34,517 . B 6
Padangsidempuan •134,611 . B 5
Painan . C 6
Pakanbaru 186,262 . C 5
Palangkaraya 60,447 . E 6
Palaumerak •58,655 . G 1
Paleleh •7,603 . G 5
Palembang 787,187 . D 6
Palopo . F 6
Pamangkat •62,402 . D 5
Pamekasan •55,409 . L 2
Pameungpeuk •41,449 . H 2
Panarukan •37,482 . K 2
Pandeglang •35,550 . G 1
Pangkalanberandan •60,299 . B 5
Pangkalanbuun . E 6
Pangkalpinang 90,096 . D 6
Pare •107,806 . K 2
Parepare 86,450 . F 6
Pariaman •44,428 . B 6
Pasangkayu . F 6
Pasuruan 95,864 . K 2
Pati •75,397 . J 2
Payakumbuh 78,836 . C 6
Pekalongan 132,558 . J 2
Pemalang •110,206 . J 2
Pematangsiantar 150,376 . B 5
Perabumulih •88,031 . C 6
Pinrang . F 6
Piru . H 6
Plaju . D 6
Ponorogo •58,321 . J 2
Pontianak 304,778 . D 6
Poso . G 6
Prapat •7,723 . B 5
Praya •89,266 . F 7
Probolinggo 100,296 . K 2
Purbolinggo •41,031 . J 2
Purwakarta •93,016 . H 2
Purwodadi •75,713 . J 2
Purwokerto •125,464 . H 2
Purworejo •28,663 . J 2
Putussibau •12,408 . E 5
Raha . G 6
Rangkasbitung •78,685 . G 2
Ransiki . J 6
Rantauprapat . C 5
Rembang •33,610 . K 2
Rengat •33,559 . C 6
Ruteng •12,294 . G 7
Sabang, Celebes . F 5
Sabang, Weh 23,821 . B 4
Salatiga 85,849 . J 2
Samarinda 264,718 . F 6
Sambas •48,253 . D 5
Samboja . F 6
Sampang •60,136 . K 2
Sampit . E 6
Sanggau •7040 . E 5
Sangkulirang •8,769 . F 5
Saparua . H 6
Sarmi . K 6
Saumlaki . J 7
Sawahlunto 13,561 . C 6
Seba . G 8
Semarang 1,026,671 . J 2
Semitau •7,165 . E 5
Serang •79,675 . G 1
Serui . K 6
Siaksriinderapura . C 5
Sibolga 59,897 . B 5
Sidoharjo •59,942 . K 2
Sigli •10,623 . B 4
Sinabang . B 5
Sindangbarang •70,603 . D 7
Singaraja . F 7
Singkawang •93,650 . D 5
Sinjai . G 7
Sintang •24,842 . E 5
Situbondo •36,094 . L 2
Soe . G 7
Solo (Surakarta) 469,888 . J 2
Solok 31,724 . C 6
Sorong •23,763 . J 6
Sragen •50,515 . J 2
Subang •35,077 . H 2
Sukabumi 109,994 . H 2
Sukadana •9,741 . E 6
Sumbawa Besar . F 7
Sumedang . H 2
Sumenep •46,659 . L 2
Surabaya 2,027,913 . K 2
Surakarta 469,888 . J 2
Takalar . F 7
Takingeun . B 5
Talangbetutu . C 6
Tanahgrogot . F 6
Tanahmerah . K 7
Tangerang . G 1
Tanjungbalai 41,894 . C 5
Tanjungkarang 284,275 . D 7
Tanjungpandan •61,225 . D 6
Tanjungpinang . C 5
Tanjungpriok •147,824 . H 1
Tanjungpura •30,992 . B 5
Tanjungredeb . F 5
Tanjungselor . F 5
Tapaktuan . B 5
Tarakan •31,118 . F 5
Tarutung . B 5
Tasikmalaya •135,919 . H 2
Tebingtinggi 92,087 . B 5
Tegal 131,728 . J 2
Telukbayur . C 6
Temanggung •85,492 . J 2
Tenggarong •15,081 . F 6
Tepa . H 7
Terempa . D 5
Ternate •34,539 . H 5
Tjilatjap (Cilacap) •118,815 . H 2
Tjirebon (Cirebon) 223,776 . H 2
Tobelo . H 5
Tolitoli •10,071 . G 5
Tondano •35,978 . H 5
Trenggalek •49,065 . K 2
Tual . J 7
Tuban •54,212 . K 2
Tulungagung •53,880 . K 2
Turen •76,018 . K 2
Ujung Pandang 709,038 . F 7
Vikeke . H 7
Wahai . H 6
Waikabubak . F 7
Waingapu . G 7
Wajabula . H 5
Waren . K 6
Wasior . K 6
Watampone . G 6
Weda . H 5
Wonogiri •56,435 . J 2
Wonosobo •47,650 . J 2
Wonreli . H 7
Yogyakarta 398,727 . J 2

OTHER FEATURES

Adi (isl.) . J 6
Adonara (isl.) 71,462 . G 7
Alas (str.) . F 7
Alor (isl.) 86,136 . G 7
Ambelau (isl.) . H 6
Anambas (isls.) 29,572 . D 5
Arafura (sea) . J 8
Aru (isls.) 34,195 . K 7
Asahan (riv.) . B 5
Asia (isls.) . J 5
Ayu (isls.) . J 5
Babar (isl.) . H 7
Babar (isls.) 28,636 . H 7
Bacan (isls.) 29,137 . H 6
Balabalagan (isls.) . F 6
Bali (isl.) 2,074,438 . F 7
Bali (sea) . F 7
Bali (str.) . E 7
Banda (isls.) 13,638 . H 6
Banda (sea) . H 7
Banggai (arch.) 169,025 . G 6
Bangka (isl.) 298,017 . D 6
Bangka (str.) . C 6
Banyak (isls.) 1,980 . B 5
Barbar (isls.) . J 7
Barisan (mts.) . C 6
Barito (riv.) . E 6
Batu (isls.) 16,390 . B 6
Bawean (isl.) 64,551 . K 1
Belitung (Billiton) (isl.) 128,694 . D 6
Benggala (str.) . A 4
Berau (bay) . J 6
Berhala (str.) . C 6
Biak (isl.) . K 6
Billiton (isl.) 128,694 . D 6
Binongko (isl.) 11,549 . G 7
Bintan (isl.) 102,644 . C 5
Blackwood (Ngundju) (cape) . F 8
Boano (isl.) . H 6
Bone (gulf) . G 7
Borneo (isl.) . E 5
Bosch, van den (cape) . J 6
Bungalaut (chan.) . B 6
Bunguran (Great Natuna) (isl.) . D 5
Bunguran (Natuna) (isls.) . D 5
Bunyu (isl.) . F 5
Buru (isl.) 23,034 . H 6
Buru (sea) . H 6
Butung (isl.) 188,173 . G 6
Celebes (Sulawesi) (isl.) 7,732,383 . G 5
Celebes (sea) . G 5
Cenderawasih (bay) . K 6
Ceram (isl.) 158,591 . H 6
Ciremay (mt.) . H 2
Damar (isl.) . H 7
Damar (isls.) . H 7
Dampier (str.) . J 6
Dempo (mt.) . C 6
Digul (riv.) . K 7
Doberai (pen.) . J 6
Enggano (isl.) 1,082 . C 7
Ewab (Kai) (isls.) 108,328 . J 7
Fatagar Tuting (cape) . J 6
Flores (isl.) 860,328 . G 7
Flores (sea) . F 7
Frederik Hendrik (Kolepom) (isl.) . K 7
Gebe (isl.) 8,607 . H 6
Gede (mt.) . H 2
Geelvink (Cenderawasih) (bay) . K 6
Gorong (isl.) . J 6
Gorong (isls.) . J 6
Great Kai (isl.) 38,748 . J 7
Great Natuna (isl.) . D 5
Gunungapi (isl.) . H 7
Halmahera (isl.) 122,521 . H 5
Halmahera (sea) . H 5
Hari (riv.) . C 6
Indian Ocean . E 8
Indramayu (pt.) . H 1
Irian Jaya (reg.) 923,440 . J 6
Jambuair (cape) . B 4
Jamursba (cape) . J 5
Java (head) . C 7
Java (isl.) 73,712,411 . J 2
Java (sea) . D 6
Jaya, Puncak (mt.) . K 6
Jayawijaya (range) . K 6
Jemaja (isl.) 5,628 . D 5
Kabaena (isl.) . G 7
Kahayan (riv.) . E 6
Kai (isls.) 108,328 . J 7
Kalao (issl.) . G 7
Kalaotoa (isl.) . G 5
Kalimantan (reg.) 4,956,865 . E 5
Kampar (riv.) . C 5
Kangean (isl.) . F 7
Kangean (isls.) 89,060 . F 7
Kapuas (riv.) . D 6
Karakelong (isl.) . H 5
Karimata (arch.) 9,398 . D 6
Karimata (isl.) . D 6
Karimata (str.) . D 6
Karimunjawa (isls.) 5,025 . J 1
Kawi (mt.) . K 2
Kawio (isls.) . G 5
Kayan (riv.) . F 5
Kelasa (str.) . D 6
Kengah (isls.) . F 7
Kerinci (mt.) . C 6
Kisar (isl.) . H 7
Kobroor (isl.) . K 7
Kolepom (isl.) . K 7
Komodo (isl.) 30,407 . F 7
Komoran (isl.) . K 7
Krakatau (Rakata) (isl.) . C 7
Kur (isl.) . J 7
Lakor (isl.) . H 7
Larat (isl.) . J 7
Laurot (Laut Kecil) (isls.) . E 7
Laut (isl.) 55,711 . F 6
Laut (North Natuna) (isl.) . D 5
Laut Kecil (isls.) . E 7
Lawu (mt.) . J 2
Leti (isls.) . H 7
Leuser (mt.) . B 5
Lima (isls.) . F 7
Lingga (arch.) 46,658 . D 5
Lingga (isl.) 18,027 . D 6
Little Kai (isl.) . J 7
Liukang Tenggaja (isls.) . F 7
Lomblen (isl.) 62,572 . G 7
Lombok (isl.) 1,581,193 . F 7
Lombok (str.) . E 7
Macan (isls.) . G 7
Madura (isl.) 1,509,774 . K 2
Madura (str.) . K 2
Maffin (bay) . K 6
Mahakam (riv.) . F 6
Makassar (str.) . F 6
Malacca (str.) . C 5
Malangka (cape) . G 5
Mamberamo (riv.) . K 6
Mandar (cape) . F 6
Mangkalihat (cape) . F 5
Mangole (isl.) . H 6
Manipa (str.) . H 6
Manui (isl.) . G 6
Maoke (mts.) . K 6
Mapia (isls.) . J 5
Maras (mt.) . D 6
Maratua (isl.) . F 5
Masela (isl.) . H 7
Mega (isl.) . C 6
Mentawai (isls.) 30,107 . B 6
Misool (isl.) . J 6
Moa (isl.) . H 7
Molucca (sea) . H 6
Moluccas (isls.) 944,240 . H 6
Morotai (isl.) 27,333 . H 5
Muli (str.) . K 7
Müller (mts.) . E 5
Muna (isl.) 156,186 . G 7
Muryo (mt.) . J 2
Musi (riv.) . C 6
Natuna (isls.) 23,893 . D 5
Ngunju (cape) . F 8
Nias (isl.) 356,093 . B 5
Nila (isl.) . H 7
North Natuna (isl.) . D 4
North Pagai ((isl.) . C 6
Numfoor (isl.) . J 6
Nusa Barung (isl.) . K 3
Obi (isl.) . H 6
Obi (isls.) 12,437 . H 6
Ombai (str.) . H 7
Panaitan (isl.) . C 7
Pantar (isl.) 28,259 . G 7
Patuha (mt.) . H 2
Pegun (isl.) . J 5
Pelabuhan Ratu (bay) . G 2
Peleng (isl.) . G 6
Pembuang (riv.) . E 6
Penyu (isls.) . H 7
Perkam (cape) . K 6
Pujut (pt.) . G 1
Puting, Borneo (cape) . E 6
Puting, Sumatra (cape) . C 7
Raja Ampat Group (isls.) . H 6
Rakata (isl.) . C 7
Rangasa (cape) . F 6
Rantekombola (mt.) . F 6
Raung (mt.) . L 2
Raya (mt.) . E 6
Rewataya (reef) . F 7
Riau (arch.) 483,230 . C 5
Rokan (riv.) . C 5
Romang (isl.) . H 7
Roti (isl.) 76,270 . G 8
Rupat (isl.) 17,672 . C 5
Sabra (cape) . J 6
Salabangka (isls.) . G 6
Salawati (isl.) . J 6
Sandalwood (Sumba) (isl.) 291,190 . F 7
Sanding (isl.) . C 6
Sangeang (isl.) . F 7
Sanggabuwana (mt.) . G 2
Sangihe (isl.) . H 5
Sangihe (isls.) 183,000 . G 5
Saweba (cape) . J 6
Sawu (isl.) . G 8
Sawu (isls.) 51,002 . G 8
Sawu (sea) . G 7
Schouten (isls.) 110,148 . K 6
Schwaner (mts.) . E 6
Sebatik (isl.) . F 5
Sebuku (bay) . F 5
Selaru (isl.) . J 7
Selatan (cape) . E 6
Selayar (isl.) 92,342 . G 7
Semeru (mt.) . K 2
Sera (isl.) . J 7
Serasan (isl.) 5,024 . D 5
Sermata (isl.) . H 7
Serua (isl.) . H 7
Siak (riv.) . C 5
Siau (isl.) 46,801 . H 5
Siberut (isl.) 14,732 . B 6
Siberut (str.) . B 6
Simeulue (isl.) 29,147 . A 5
Singkep (isl.) 28,631 . D 6
Sipura (isl.) 6,051 . B 6
Sisi (cape) . F 6
Slamet (mt.) . J 2
Solor (isl.) 24,586 . G 7
Sopi (cape) . H 5
Sorikmerapi (mt.) . B 5
South China (sea) . D 4
South Natuna (isls.) . D 5
South Pagai (isl.) . C 6
Subi Besar (isl.) . D 5
Sudirman (range) . K 6
Sula (isls.) 36,922 . H 6
Sulawesi (isl.) 7,732,383 . G 6
Sumatra (isl.) 19,360,400 . B 5
Sumba (isl.) 291,190 . F 7
Sumba (str.) . F 7
Sumbawa (isl.) 621,140 . F 7
Sumbing (mt.) . J 2
Sunda (str.) . C 7
Supiori (isl.) . K 6
Tahulandang (isl.) 21,493 . H 5
Talaud (isls.) 46,395 . H 5
Taliabu (isl.) 18,303 . G 6
Tambelan (isls.) 4,032 . D 5
Tanimbar (isls.) 55,405 . J 7
Tariku (riv.) . K 6
Taritatu (riv.) . K 6
Tidore (isl.) 28,655 . H 5
Tiger (Macan) (isls.) . G 7
Timor (reg.) 1,435,527 . H 7
Timor (sea) . H 7
Toba (lake) . B 5
Togian (isls.) 13,913 . G 6
Tolo (gulf) . G 6
Tomini (gulf) . G 6
Torawitan (cape) . G 5
Towuti (lake) . G 6
Trangan (isl.) . J 7
Tukangbesi (isls.) 73,106 . G 7
Turtle (Penju) (isls.) . H 7
Vals (cape) . K 7
Vogelkop (Doberai) (pen.) . J 6
Waigeo (isl.) . J 5
Wakde (isl.) . K 6
Wangiwangi (isl.) 28,469 . G 7
Watubela (isls.) . J 6
We (isl.) . B 4
Wetar (isl.) . H 7
Wokam (isl.) . K 7
Workai (isl.) . K 7
Wowoni (isl.) . G 6
Yamdena (isl.) . J 7
Yapen (isl.) 50,888 . K 6
Yapen (str.) . K 6

MALAYSIA

STATES

Labuan 26,453 . F 4
(North Borneo) Sabah 1,002,608 . F 3
Sarawak 1,294,753 . E 5

CITIES and TOWNS

Beaufort 2,709 . F 4
Bintulu 4,424 . E 5
Kabong . E 5
Kampong Sibuti . E 5
Kapit 1,929 . E 5
Keningau 2,037 . F 4
Kota Kinabalu 40,939 . F 4
Kuching 63,535 . E 5
Kudat 5,089 . F 4
Labuan 7,216 . E 4
Lahad Datu 5,169 . F 5
Lamag . F 4
Marudi 4,700 . E 5
Miri 35,702 . E 5
Mukah 1,717 . E 5
Papar 1,855 . F 4
Ranau 2,024 . F 4
Sandakan 42,413 . F 4
Sematan . D 5
Semporna 3,371 . F 5
Serian 2,209 . E 5
Sibu 50,635 . E 5
Simanggang 8,445 . E 5
Suai . E 5
Tawau 24,247 . F 5
Weston . F 4

OTHER FEATURES

Balambangan (isl.) . F 4
Banggi (isl.) . F 4
Barut, Tanjong (cape) . E 5
Borneo (isl.) . E 5
Iran (mts.) . E 5
Kinabalu (mt.) . F 4
Labuan (isl.) 17,189 . E 4
Labuk (bay) . F 4
Malay (pen.) . B 4
Rajang (riv.) . E 5
Sebatik (isl.) . F 5
Sirik (cape) . E 5
South China (sea) . D 4

PAPUA NEW GUINEA

CITIES and TOWNS

Abau . C 7
Aitape 3,368 . B 6
Ambunti 1,035 . B 6
Angoram 1,846 . B 6
Baniara . C 7
Bogia 755 . B 6
Bulolo 6,730 . B 7
Buna . C 7
Daru 7,127 . B 7
Finschhafen 756 . C 7
Gaima . B 7
Gehua . C 8
Gona . C 7
Goroka 18,511 . B 7
Ihu 541 . B 7
Ioma . C 7
Kaiapit 515 . B 7
Kairuku . B 7
Kerema 3,389 . B 7
Kikori 763 . B 7
Kiunga 1,407 . B 7
Kokoda . C 7
Kundiawa 4,299 . B 7
Lae 61,617 . B 7
Madang 21,335 . B 7
Marienberg . B 6
Mendi 4,130 . B 7
Morobe . C 7
Mount Hagen 13,441 . B 7
Popondetta 6,429 . C 7
Port Moresby (cap.) 123,624 . B 7
Rigo . C 7
Rouka . B 7
Saidor 500 . B 7
Samarai 864 . C 8
Telefomin . B 7
Tufi . C 7
Vanimo 3,071 . B 6
Wau 2,349 . B 7
Wedau . C 7
Wewak 19,890 . B 6

OTHER FEATURES

Coral (sea) . B 7
Dampier (str.) . C 7
D'Entrecasteaux (isls.) . C 7
Fly (riv.) . A 7
Huon (gulf) . C 7
Karkar (isl.) . B 6
Kiriwina (isl.) . C 7
Long (isl.) . B 7
Louisiade (arch.) . D 8
Milne (bay) . C 8
Misima (isl.) . C 8
Murray (lake) . B 7
New Britain (isl.) 148,773 . C 7
Ramu (riv.) . B 7
Rossel (isl.) . D 8
Schouten (isls.) . B 6
Sepik (riv.) . B 6
Solomon (sea) . C 7
Tagula (isl.) . C 8
Torres (str.) . A 7
Trobriand (isls.) . C 7
Vitiaz (str.) . B 7
Wilhelm (mt.) . B 7
Woodlark (isl.) . C 7

PHILIPPINES

CITIES and TOWNS

Aparri 45,070 . G 2
Bacolod 262,415 . G 3
Baguio 119,009 . G 2
Bangued 28,666 . G 2
Bangui 11,122 . G 2
Batangas 143,570 . G 3
Baybay 74,640 . H 3
Bayombong 32,066 . G 2
Bislig 81,615 . H 4
Bontoc 17,091 . G 2
Butuan 172,489 . H 4
Cabanatuan 138,298 . G 2
Cagayan de Oro 227,312 . G 4
Calapan 67,370 . G 3
Catbalogan 58,737 . H 3
Cateel 20,084 . H 4
Cavite 87,666 . G 3
Cebu 490,281 . G 3
Cotabato 83,871 . G 4
Daet 54,785 . G 3
Davao 610,375 . H 4
Dumaguete 63,411 . G 4
Glan 48,882 . G 4
Iba 22,791 . F 2
Iloilo 244,827 . G 3
Laoag 69,648 . F 2
Legazpi 99,766 . G 3
Lingayen 65,187 . F 2
Lucena 107,880 . G 3
Manila (cap.) 1,630,485 . G 3
Marawi 53,812 . G 4
Mati 78,178 . H 4
Mondragon 20,423 . H 3
Naga 90,712 . G 3
Oroquieta 47,328 . G 4
Palanan 10,295 . G 2
Puerto Princesa 60,234 . F 4
Roxas 81,183 . G 3
San Jose 66,262 . G 3
Siocon (Siokun) 29,515 . G 4
Sorsogon 60,574 . G 3
Surigao 79,745 . H 4
Tacloban 102,523 . H 3
Tarlac 175,691 . G 2
Taytay 22,980 . F 3
Tuguegarao 73,507 . G 2
Vigan 33,483 . F 2
Zamboanga 343,722 . G 4

OTHER FEATURES

Babuyan (isls.) . G 2
Balabac (isl.) . F 4
Balabac (str.) . F 4
Basilan (isl.) . G 4
Batan (isls.) . G 1
Bohol (isl.) . G 4
Bugsuk (isl.) . F 4
Builuyan (cape) . F 4
Busuanga (isl.) . F 3
Cagayan (isls.) . F 4
Cagayan Sulu (isl.) . F 4
Calamian Group (isls.) . F 3
Catanduanes (isl.) . H 3
Cebu (isl.) . G 3
Cuyo (isls.) . G 3
Davao (gulf) . H 4
Dinagat (isl.) . H 3
Dumaran (isl.) . G 3
Espiritu Santo (cape) . H 3
Jolo (isl.) . G 4
Leyte (isl.) . H 3
Lubang (isls.) . G 3
Luzon (isl.) . G 2
Masbate (isl.) . G 3
Matutum (mt.) . G 4
Mindanao (isl.) . H 4
Mindanao (sea) . G 4
Mindoro (isl.) . G 3
Mindoro (str.) . F 3
Moro (gulf) . G 4
Negros (isl.) . G 4
Olutanga (isl.) . G 4
Palawan (isl.) . F 4
Palawan (passg.) . F 4
Panay (isl.) . G 3
Pangutaran Group (isls.) . G 4
Philippine (sea) . G 2
Polillo (isl.) . G 3
Samar (isl.) . H 3
San Agustin (cape) . H 4
San Miguel (isls.) . F 4
Sarangani (isls.) . G 4
Siargao (isl.) . H 4
Sibutu (passg.) . F 4
Sibuyan (isl.) . G 3
Sibuyan (sea) . G 3
South China (sea) . D 4
Sulu (arch.) . G 4
Sulu (sea) . G 4
Tagolo (pt.) . G 4
Tapul Group (isls.) . G 4
Tawitawi Group (isls.) . G 4
Tinaca (pt.) . H 4
Tubbataha (reefs) . G 4
Visayan (sea) . G 3

•Population of district, sub-district or division.

AUSTRALIA

AREA 2,966,136 sq. mi. (7,682,300 sq. km.)
POPULATION 14,576,330
CAPITAL Canberra
LARGEST CITY Sydney
HIGHEST POINT Mt. Kosciusko 7,310 ft. (2,228 m.)
LOWEST POINT Lake Eyre -39 ft. (-12 m.)
MONETARY UNIT Australian dollar
MAJOR LANGUAGE English
MAJOR RELIGIONS Protestantism, Roman Catholicism

NEW ZEALAND

AREA 103,736 sq. mi. (268,676 sq. km.)
POPULATION 3,175,737
CAPITAL Wellington
LARGEST CITY Auckland
HIGHEST POINT Mt. Cook 12,349 ft. (3,764 m.)
MONETARY UNIT New Zealand dollar
MAJOR LANGUAGES English, Maori
MAJOR RELIGIONS Protestantism, Roman Catholicism

AUSTRALIA

NEW ZEALAND

AUSTRALIA

STATES and TERRITORIES

Ashmore and Cartier Is., Terr. of . . . C 2
Australian Capital Territory 221,609 . . . H 7
Coral Sea Islands Territory . . . H 2
New South Wales 5,126,217 . . H 6
Norfolk Island 2,175 . . . L 5
Northern Territory 123,324 . . . E 3
Queensland 2,295,123 . . . G 4
South Australia 1,285,033 . . . F 6
Tasmania 418,957 . . . H 8
Victoria 3,832,443 . . . G 7
Western Australia 1,273,624 . . B 5

CITIES and TOWNS

Adelaide (cap.), S. Aust. 882,520 . . . D 8
Albany, W. Aust. 15,222 . . . B 6
Albury, N.S.W. 35,072 . . . H 7
Alice Springs, N. Terr. 18,395 . E 4
Altona, Vic. 30,909 . . . J 3
Ararat, Vic. 8,336 . . . G 7
Armidale, N.S.W. 18,922 . . . J 6
Ashfield, N.S.W. 41,253 . . . K 4
Auburn, N.S.W. 46,622 . . . K 4
Ayr, Queens. 8,787 . . . H 3
Bairnsdale, Vic. 9,459 . . . H 7
Ballarat, Vic. 35,681 . . . G 7
Bankstown, N.S.W. 152,636 . . K 4
Bathurst, N.S.W. 19,640 . . . H 6
Bega, N.S.W. 4,388 . . . J 7
Bendigo, Vic. 31,841 . . . G 7
Blackall, Queens. 1,609 . . . H 4
Blacktown, N.S.W. 181,139 . . . K 4
Blue Mountains, N.S.W. 55,877 . . . J 6
Bordertown, S. Aust. 2,138 . . . F 7
Botany, N.S.W. 34,703 . . . L 4
Boulder-Kalgoorlie, W. Aust. 19,848 . . . C 6
Bourke, N.S.W. 3,326 . . . H 6
Bowen, Queens. 7,663 . . . H 3
Box Hill, Vic. 47,579 . . . K 2
Brighton, S. Aust. 19,441 . . . D 8
Brighton, Vic. 33,697 . . . K 3
Brisbane (cap.), Queens. 942,836 . . . K 3
Brisbane Water, N.S.W. 71,984 . . . J 6
Broadmeadows, Vic. 103,540 . J 2
Broken Hill, N.S.W. 26,913 . . . G 6
Broome, W. Aust. 3,666 . . . C 3
Brunswick, Vic. 44,464 . . . K 2
Bunbury, W. Aust. 21,749 . . . B 6
Bundaberg, Queens. 32,560 . . J 4
Burnie-Somerset, Tas. 19,994 . . . H 8
Burnside, S. Aust. 37,593 . . . E 8
Burwood, N.S.W. 28,896 . . . K 4
Busselton, W. Aust. 6,463 . . . A 6
Cairns, Queens. 48,557 . . . H 3
Camberwell, Vic. 85,883 . . . K 2
Campbelltown, S. Aust. 43,084 . . . E 8
Canberra (cap.), A.C.T. *220,822 . . . H 7
Canterbury, N.S.W. 126,741 . . K 4
Carnarvon, W. Aust. 5,053 . . . A 4
Casino, N.S.W. 9,743 . . . J 5
Caulfield, Vic. 69,922 . . . K 2
Ceduna, S. Aust. 2,794 . . . E 6
Cessnock-Bellbird, N.S.W. 16,916 . . . J 6
Charleville, Queens. 3,523 . . . H 5
Charters Towers, Queens. 6,823 . . . H 4
Chelsea, Vic. 26,034 . . . K 3
Clermont, Queens. 1,659 . . . H 4
Cloncurry, Queens. 1,961 . . . G 4
Cobar, N.S.W. 3,583 . . . H 6
Coburg, Vic. 55,035 . . . K 2
Coffs Harbour, N.S.W. 16,020 . J 6
Collie, W. Aust. 2,667 . . . B 6
Collinsville, Queens. 2,756 . . . H 4
Concord, N.S.W. 23,926 . . . K 4
Condobolin, N.S.W. 3,355 . . . H 6
Coober Pedy, S. Aust. 2,078 . . E 5
Cooma, N.S.W. 7,978 . . . H 7
Coonamble, N.S.W. 3,090 . . . H 6
Cootamundra, N.S.W. 6,540 . . H 6
Cowra, N.S.W. 7,900 . . . H 6
Croydon, Vic. 36,210 . . . L 2
Cunnamulla, Queens. 1,627 . . H 5
Dalby, Queens. 8,784 . . . J 5
Dandenong, Vic. 54,962 . . . L 3
Darwin (cap.), N. Terr. 56,482 . E 2
Deniliquin, N.S.W. 7,354 . . . G 7
Derby, W. Aust. 2,933 . . . C 3
Devonport, Tas. 21,424 . . . H 8
Doncaster and Templestowe, Vic. 90,660 . . . K 2
Drummoyne, N.S.W. 30,961 . . K 4
Dubbo, N.S.W. 23,986 . . . H 6
Echuca, Vic. 7,943 . . . G 7
Elizabeth, S. Aust. 32,608 . . . E 7
Eltham, Vic. 34,648 . . . K 2
Enfield, S. Aust. 66,797 . . . D 7
Esperance, W. Aust. 6,375 . . . C 6
Essendon, Vic. 56,380 . . . J 2
Fairfield, N.S.W. 129,557 . . . K 4
Footscray, Vic. 49,756 . . . J 2
Forbes, N.S.W. 8,029 . . . H 6
Fremantle, W. Aust. 22,484 . . . B 6
Gawler, S. Aust. 9,433 . . . F 6
Geelong, Vic. 14,471 . . . G 7
Geraldton, W. Aust. 20,895 . . . A 5
Gladstone, Queens. 22,083 . . J 4
Glen Innes, N.S.W. 6,052 . . . J 5
Glenorchy, Tas. 41,019 . . . H 8
Gold Coast, Queens. 135,437 . . . J 5
Goondiwindi, Queens. 3,576 . H 5
Goulburn, N.S.W. 21,755 . . . J 6
Grafton, N.S.W. 17,005 . . . J 5
Griffith, N.S.W. 13,187 . . . H 6
Gunnedah, N.S.W. 8,909 . . . H 6
Gympie, Queens. 10,768 . . . J 5
Hamilton, Vic. 9,751 . . . G 7
Hawthorne, Vic. 30,689 . . . K 2
Hay, N.S.W. 2,958 . . . H 6
Heidelberg, Vic. 64,757 . . . K 2
Hindmarsh, S. Aust. 7,593 . . . D 8
Hobart (cap.), Tas. 128,603 . . . H 8
Holyroyd, N.S.W. 80,116 . . . K 4
Home Hill, Queens. 3,138 . . . H 3
Hornsby, N.S.W. 111,081 . . . K 3
Horsham, Vic. 12,034 . . . G 7
Hughenden, Queens. 1,657 . . G 4
Hurstville, N.S.W. 64,910 . . . K 4
Ingham, Queens. 5,598 . . . H 3
Innisfail, Queens. 7,933 . . . H 3
Inverell, N.S.W. 9,734 . . . J 5
Kadina, S. Aust. 2,943 . . . F 6
Kalgoorlie, W. Aust. 9,145 . . . C 6
Katanning, W. Aust. 4,413 . . . B 6
Katherine, N. Terr. 3,737 . . . E 2
Keilor, Vic. 81,762 . . . J 2
Kempsey, N.S.W. 9,037 . . . J 6
Kensington and Norwood, S. Aust. 8,950 . . . E 8
Kew, Vic. 28,870 . . . K 2
Kingaroy, Queens. 5,134 . . . J 5
Knox, Vic. 88,902 . . . L 2
Kogarah, N.S.W. 46,322 . . . K 4
Kwinana-Newtown, W. Aust. 12,355 . . . B 2
Lane Cove, N.S.W. 29,113 . . . L 4
Launceston, Tas. 31,273 . . . H 8
Leichhardt, N.S.W. 57,332 . . . L 4
Leigh Creek, S. Aust. 1,635 . . . F 6
Leonora, W. Aust. 524 . . . C 5
Lismore, N.S.W. 24,033 . . . J 5
Lithgow, N.S.W. 12,793 . . . J 6
Liverpool, N.S.W. 92,715 . . . K 4
Longreach, Queens. 2,971 . . . G 4
Mackay, Queens. 35,361 . . . H 4
Maitland, N.S.W. 38,865 . . . J 6
Malvern, Vic. 43,211 . . . K 2
Mandurah, W. Aust. 10,978 . . . B 3
Maralinga, S. Aust. . . . E 6
Mareeba, Queens. 6,309 . . . G 3
Marion, S. Aust. 66,580 . . . D 8
Maroochydore-Mooloolaba, Queens. 17,460 . . . J 5
Marrickville, N.S.W. 83,448 . . . L 4
Maryborough, Queens. 20,111 . . . J 5
Maryborough, Vic. 7,858 . . . G 7
Meekatharra, W. Aust. 989 . . . B 5
Melbourne (cap.), Vic. 2,578,759 . . . K 2
Merredin, W. Aust. 3,520 . . . B 6
Mildura, Vic. 15,763 . . . G 6
Mingenew, W. Aust. 368 . . . B 5
Mitcham, S. Aust. 60,309 . . . D 8
Moora, W. Aust. 1,677 . . . B 6
Moorabbin, Vic. 97,810 . . . K 3
Mordialloc, Vic. 27,869 . . . K 3
Moree, N.S.W. 10,459 . . . H 5
Mossman, Queens. 1,614 . . . G 3
Mount Gambier, S. Aust. 18,193 . . . G 7
Mount Isa, Queens. 23,679 . . . F 4
Mount Morgan, Queens. 2,974 . . . J 4
Mudgee, N.S.W. 6,015 . . . J 6
Murray Bridge, S. Aust. 8,664 . F 7
Murwillumbah, N.S.W. 7,807 . . J 5
Muswellbrook, N.S.W. 8,548 . . J 6
Naracoorte, S. Aust. 4,758 . . . F 7
Narrabri, N.S.W. 7,296 . . . J 6
Narrandera, N.S.W. 5,813 . . . H 6
Narrogin, W. Aust. 4,969 . . . B 6
Narromine, N.S.W. 2,994 . . . H 6
Nedlands, W. Aust. 20,257 . . . B 2
Newcastle, N.S.W. 135,207 . . . J 6
New Norfolk, Tas. 6,243 . . . H 8
Northam, W. Aust. 6,791 . . . B 6
Northampton, W. Aust. 750 . . . A 5
Northcote, Vic. 51,235 . . . K 2
North Sydney, N.S.W. 48,500 . L 4
Nowra-Bomaderry, N.S.W. 17,887 . . . J 6
Nunawading, Vic. 97,052 . . . K 2
Nyngan, N.S.W. 2,485 . . . H 6
Oakleigh, Vic. 55,612 . . . K 2
Orange, N.S.W. 27,626 . . . H 6
Orbost, Vic. 2,586 . . . H 7
Parkes, N.S.W. 9,047 . . . H 6
Parramatta, N.S.W. 130,943 . . K 4
Penrith, N.S.W. 108,720 . . . J 6
Perth (cap.), W. Aust. 809,035 B 2
Peterborough, S. Aust. 2,575 . F 6
Port Adelaide, S. Aust. 35,407 . . . D 7
Port Augusta, S. Aust. 15,566 F 6
Port Hedland, W. Aust. 12,948 . . . B 3
Portland, Vic. 9,353 . . . G 7
Port Lincoln, S. Aust. 9,846 . . . E 6
Port Melbourne, Vic. 8,585 . . . K 2
Port Macquarie, N.S.W. 19,581 . . . J 6
Port Pirie, S. Aust. 14,695 . . . F 6
Prahan, Vic. 45,018 . . . K 2
Preston, Vic. 84,519 . . . K 2
Proserpine, Queens. 3,058 . . . H 4
Queenstown, Tas. 3,714 . . . H 8
Randwick, N.S.W. 116,202 . . . L 4
Red Cliffe, Queens. 42,223 . . . J 5
Renmark, S. Aust. 3,475 . . . G 6
Richmond, Vic. 24,506 . . . K 2
Ringwood, Vic. 38,665 . . . K 2
Rockdale, N.S.W. 83,719 . . . K 4
Rockhampton, Queens. 50,146 . . . H 4
Rockingham, W. Aust. 24,932 . B 2
Roebourne, W. Aust. 1,688 . . . B 4
Roma, Queens. 5,706 . . . H 5
Ryde, N.S.W. 88,948 . . . K 4
Saint George, Queens. 2,204 . H 5
Saint Kilda, Vic. 49,366 . . . K 2
Sale, Vic. 12,968 . . . H 7
Salisbury, S. Aust. 86,451 . . . E 7
Sandringham, Vic. 31,175 . . . K 3
Sarina, Queens. 2,815 . . . H 4
Seymour, Vic. 6,494 . . . H 7
Shepparton-Maroopna, Vic. †27,373 . . . G 7
South Sydney, N.S.W. 30,776 . L 4
Springvale, Vic. 80,186 . . . K 3
Stanthorpe, Queens. 3,966 . . . J 5
Stirling, W. Aust. 161,858 . . . B 2
Strathfield, N.S.W. 25,882 . . . K 4
Sunshine, Vic. 94,419 . . . J 2
Sutherland, N.S.W. 165,336 . . K 5
Swan Hill, Vic. 8,398 . . . G 7
Sydney (cap.), N.S.W. 2,876,508 . . . L 4
Tamworth, N.S.W. 29,657 . . . J 6
Taree, N.S.W. 14,697 . . . J 6
Tea Tree Gully, S. Aust. 67,237 . . . E 7

(continued on following page)

Agriculture, Industry and Resources

DOMINANT LAND USE

- Cereals (chiefly wheat), Livestock
- Dairy, Truck Farming
- Cash Crops, Horticulture, Fruit
- Pasture Livestock
- Range Livestock
- Forests
- Nonagricultural Land

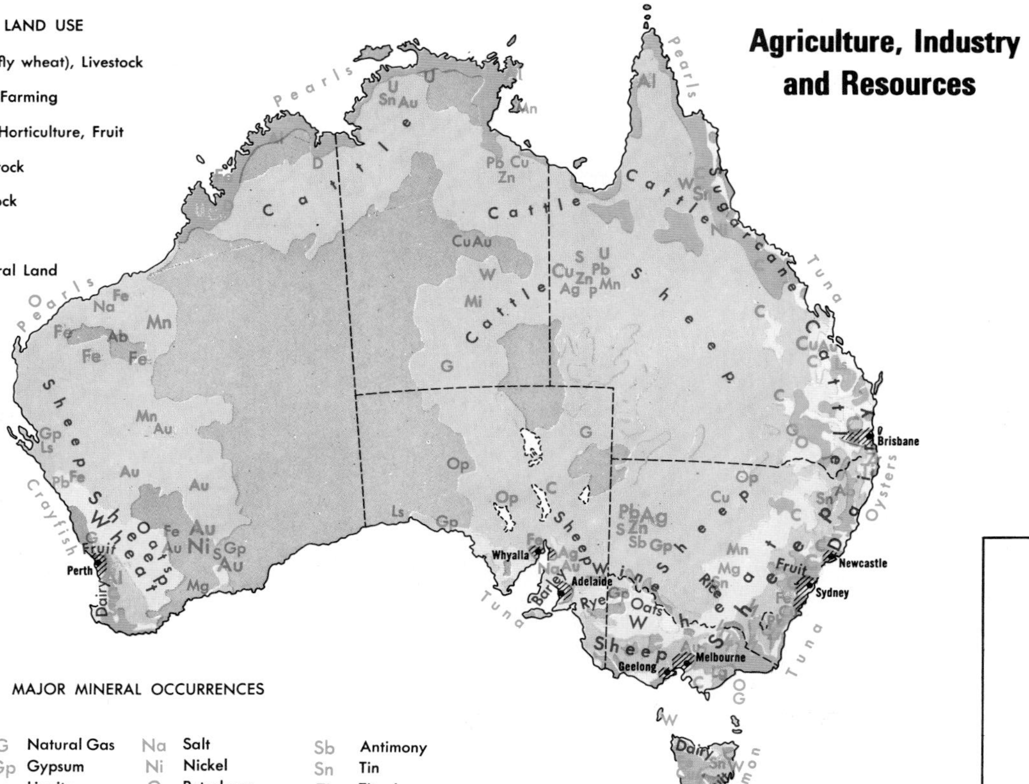

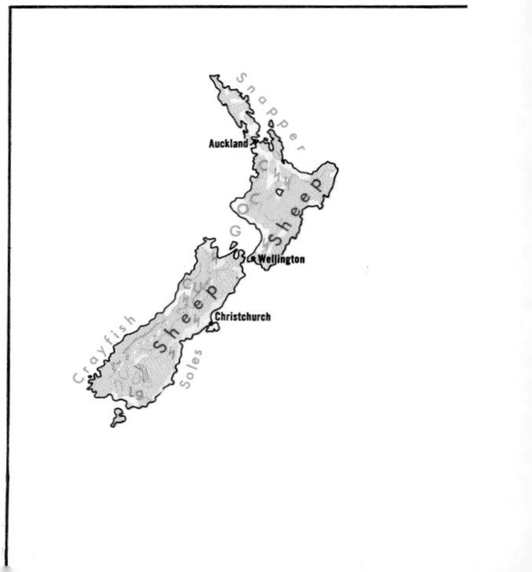

MAJOR MINERAL OCCURRENCES

Ab	Asbestos	G	Natural Gas	Na	Salt	Sb	Antimony
Ag	Silver	Gp	Gypsum	Ni	Nickel	Sn	Tin
Al	Bauxite	Lg	Lignite	O	Petroleum	Ti	Titanium
Au	Gold	Ls	Limestone	Op	Opals	U	Uranium
C	Coal	Mg	Magnesium	P	Phosphates	W	Tungsten
Cu	Copper	Mi	Mica	Pb	Lead	Zn	Zinc
D	Diamonds	Mn	Manganese	S	Sulfur, Pyrites	Zr	Zirconium
Fe	Iron Ore						

Water Power
Major Industrial Areas

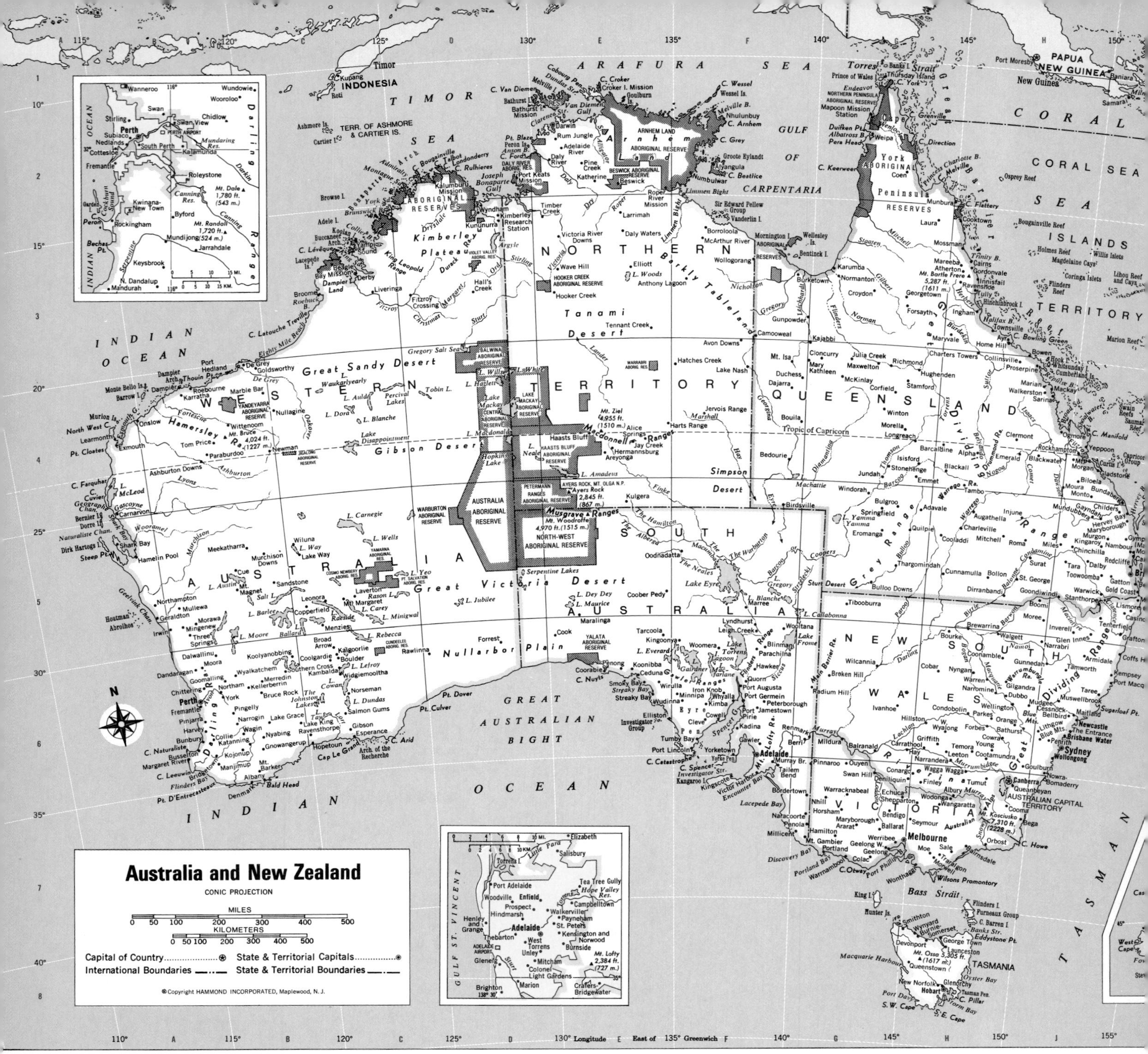

Temora, N.S.W. 4,350 .... H 6
Tennant Creek, N. Terr. 3,118 . E 3
Tenterfield, N.S.W. 3,402 ..... J 5
Thursday Island, Queens. 2,283 .... G 2
Toowoomba, Queens. 63,401 . J 5
Townsville, Queens. 86,112 .. H 3
Tully, Queens. 2,728 .... H 3
Tumut, N.S.W. 5,816 .... H 7
Unley, S. Aust. 35,844 .... D 8
Victor Harbor, S. Aust. 4,522 . F 7
Wagga Wagga, N.S.W. 36,837 .... H 7
Wagin, W. Aust. 1,488 .... B 6
Walgett, N.S.W. 2,157 .... H 6
Wangaratta, Vic. 16,202 ...... H 7
Warren, N.S.W. 2,153 .... H 6
Warrnambool, Vic. 21,414 ..... G 7
Warwick, Queens. 8,853 .... J 5
Waverley, N.S.W. 61,575 ...... L 4
Waverley, Vic. 122,471 .... K 2
Werribee, Vic. .... G 7
West Torrens, S. Aust. 45,099 D 8
Williamstown, Vic. 25,554 .... J 2
Willoughby, N.S.W. 52,120 .... K 3
Wollongong, N.S.W. 169,381 . J 6
Wonthaggi, Vic. 4,797 .... G 7
Woodville, S. Aust. 77,634 ... D 7
Woollahra, N.S.W. 51,659 ..... L 4
Woomera, S. Aust. 1,658 ...... F 6
Wyndham, W. Aust. 1,509 ..... D 3
Wynyard, Tas. 4,582 .... H 8
Young, N.S.W. 6,906 .... H 6

OTHER FEATURES

Adele (isl.), W. Aust. .... C 3
Admiralty (gulf), W. Aust. ..... D 2
Albatross (bay), Queens. ...... G 2
Alberga, The (riv.), S. Aust. ... E 5
Altona (bay), Vic. .... J 3
Amadeus (lake), N. Terr. ...... E 4
Anson (bay), N. Terr. .... D 2
Arafura (sea) .... E 2
Arid (cape), W. Aust. .... C 6
Arnhem (cape), N. Terr. ...... F 2
Arnhem Land (reg.), N. Terr. .. E 2
Ashburton (riv.), W. Aust. ..... B 4
Australian Alps (mts.), Vic. .... H 7
Avon (riv.), W. Aust. .... B 6
Ayers Rock (mt.), N. Terr. ..... E 5
Bald (head), W. Aust. .... B 7
Balonne (riv.), Queens. .... H 5
Banks (str.), Tas. .... H 8
Barcoo (creek), S. Aust. ...... F 5
Barkly Tableland, N. Terr. .... F 3
Barlee (lake), W. Aust. .... B 5
Barrow (isl.), W. Aust. .... A 4
Barwon (riv.) .... H 5
Bass (str.) .... H 7
Bathurst (isl.), N. Terr. ...... D 2
Beatrice (cape), N. Terr. ..... F 2
Bentinck (isl.), Queens. ...... F 3
Blanche (lake), S. Aust. ...... F 5
Blue (mts.), N.S.W. .... H 6
Botany (bay), N.S.W. .... L 4
Bougainville (cape), W. Aust. . D 2
Bougainville (reef), Coral Sea Is. Terr. .... H 3
Bowling Green (cape), Queens. .... H 3
Broad (sound), Queens. .... H 4
Bruce (mt.), W. Aust. .... B 4
Brunswick (bay), W. Aust. .... C 3
Buccaneer (arch.), W. Aust. ... C 3
Bulloo (riv.), Queens. .... G 5
Burdekin (riv.), Queens. ...... H 3
Cape Barren (isl.), Tas. .... H 8
Capricorn Group (isls.), Queens. .... J 4
Carey (lake), W. Aust. .... C 5
Carnegie (lake), W. Aust. ..... C 5
Carpentaria (gulf) .... F 2
Cartier (isl.) .... C 2
Clarence (str.), N. Terr. ...... E 2
Cobourg (pen.), N. Terr. ...... E 2
Collier (bay), W. Aust. .... C 3
Comet (riv.), Queens. .... H 4
Coopers (Barcoo) (creek), S. Aust. .... G 5
Coral (sea) .... H 2
Coringa (isls.), Coral Sea Is. Terr. .... H 3
Cowan (lake), W. Aust. .... C 6
Croker (cape), N. Terr. .... E 2
Dale (mt.), W. Aust. .... B 2
Daly (riv.), N. Terr. .... E 2
Dampier (arch.), W. Aust. ..... B 4
Dampier Land (reg.), W. Aust. . C 3
Darkin (riv.), W. Aust. .... B 2
Darling (range), W. Aust. ..... B 6
Darling (riv.), N.S.W. .... G 6
Dawson (riv.), Queens. .... H 4
De Grey (riv.), W. Aust. ...... C 4
D'Entrecasteaux (pt.), W. Aust. .... B 7
Diamantina (riv.), Queens. .... G 4
Direction (cape), Queens. ..... G 2
Dirk Hartogs (isl.), W. Aust. ... A 5
Disappointment (lake), W. Aust. .... C 4
Discovery (bay) .... E 7
Dorre (isl.), W. Aust. .... A 5
Dover (pt.), W. Aust. .... D 6
Drysdale (riv.), W. Aust. ..... D 3
Duifken (pt.), Queens. .... G 2
Dundas (str.), N. Terr. .... E 2
Durack (range), W. Aust. ..... D 3
Eddystone (pt.), Tas. .... H 8
Encounter (bay), S. Aust. ..... F 7
Endeavor (str.), Queens. ..... G 2
Everard (lake), S. Aust. ...... E 6
Exmouth (gulf), W. Aust. ..... A 4
Eyre (lake), S. Aust. .... F 5
Eyre (pen.), S. Aust. .... F 6
Fitzroy (riv.), Queens. .... J 4
Fitzroy (riv.), W. Aust. .... C 3
Flattery (cape), Queens. ..... H 2
Flinders (bay), W. Aust. ...... A 6
Flinders (isl.), Tas. .... H 7
Flinders (range), S. Aust. .... F 6
Flinders (riv.), Queens. ...... G 3
Ford (cape), N. Terr. .... D 2
Fortescue (riv.), W. Aust. .... B 4
Fraser (isl.), Queens. .... J 4
Frome (lake), S. Aust. .... G 6
Furneaux Group (isls.), Tas. 1,039 .... H 8
Gairdner (lake), S. Aust. ..... F 6
Garden (isl.), W. Aust. .... A 2
Gascoyne (riv.), W. Aust. ..... A 4
Gawler (ranges), S. Aust. ..... F 6
Geelvink (chan.), W. Aust. .... A 5
Geographe (chan.), W. Aust. ... A 4
Georges (riv.), N.S.W. .... K 4
Georgina (riv.), Queens. ...... F 4
Gibson (des.), W. Aust. ...... C 4
Gilbert (riv.), Queens. .... G 3
Goulburn (isls.), N. Terr. ..... E 2
Great Australian (bight) ...... D 6
Great Barrier (reef) .... H 2
Great Dividing (range), N.S.W. J 6
Great Sandy (des.), W. Aust. .. C 4
Great Sandy (Fraser) (isl.), Queens. .... J 5
Great Victoria (des.) .... D 5
Gregory (lake), S. Aust. ...... F 5
Gregory (riv.), Queens. ...... F 3
Grenville (cape), Queens. ..... G 2
Groote (isl.), N. Terr. 2,230 ... F 2
Hamersley (range), W. Aust. .. B 4
Hay (dry riv.), N. Terr. .... F 4
Hervey (bay), Queens. .... J 4
Hinchinbrook (isl.), Queens. ... H 3
Holmes (reef), Coral Sea Is. Terr. .... H 3
Hook (isl.), Queens. .... H 4
Hope Valley (res.), S. Aust. ... E 7
Houtman Abrolhos (isls.), W. Aust. .... A 5
Howe (cape) .... J 7
Investigator (str.), S. Aust. .... F 7
Isaacs (riv.), Queens. .... H 4
Joseph Bonaparte (gulf) ...... D 2
Kangaroo (isl.), S. Aust. 3,515 F 7
Kimberley (plat.), W. Aust. .... D 3
King (isl.), Tas. 2,592 .... G 7
King (sound), W. Aust. .... C 3
King Leopold (range), W. Aust. .... D 3
Kosciusko (mt.), N.S.W. ...... H 7
Lacepede (range), W. Aust. ... D 3
Lachlan (riv.), N.S.W. .... G 6
Latouche Treville (cape), W. Aust. .... C 3
Leeuwin (cape), W. Aust. ..... A 6
Lefroy (lake), W. Aust. .... C 6
Leichhardt (riv.), Queens. ..... F 3
Lévêque (cape), W. Aust. ..... C 3

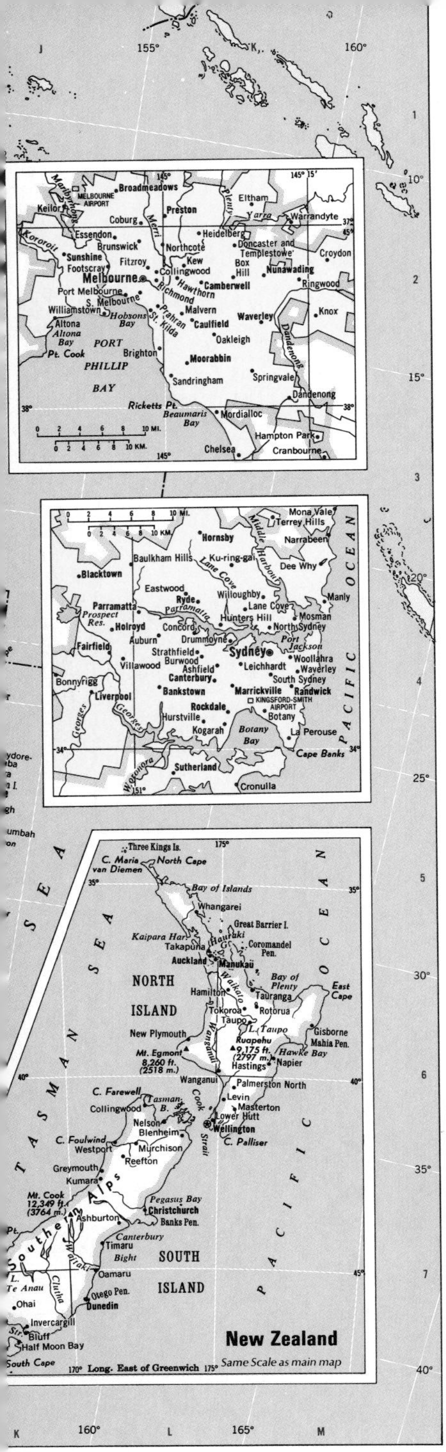

Population Distribution

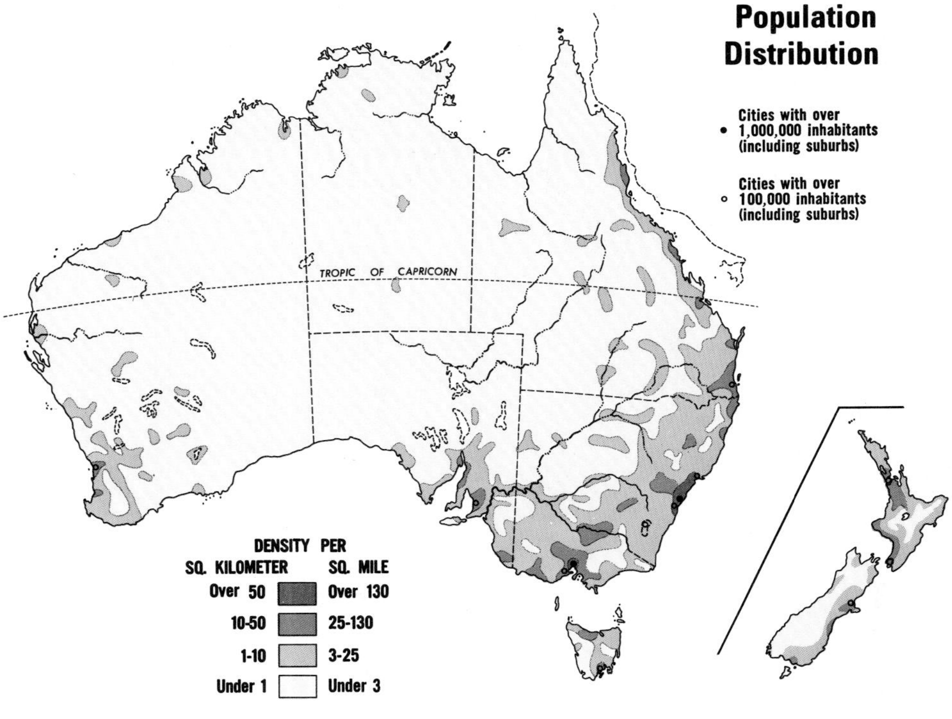

Topography

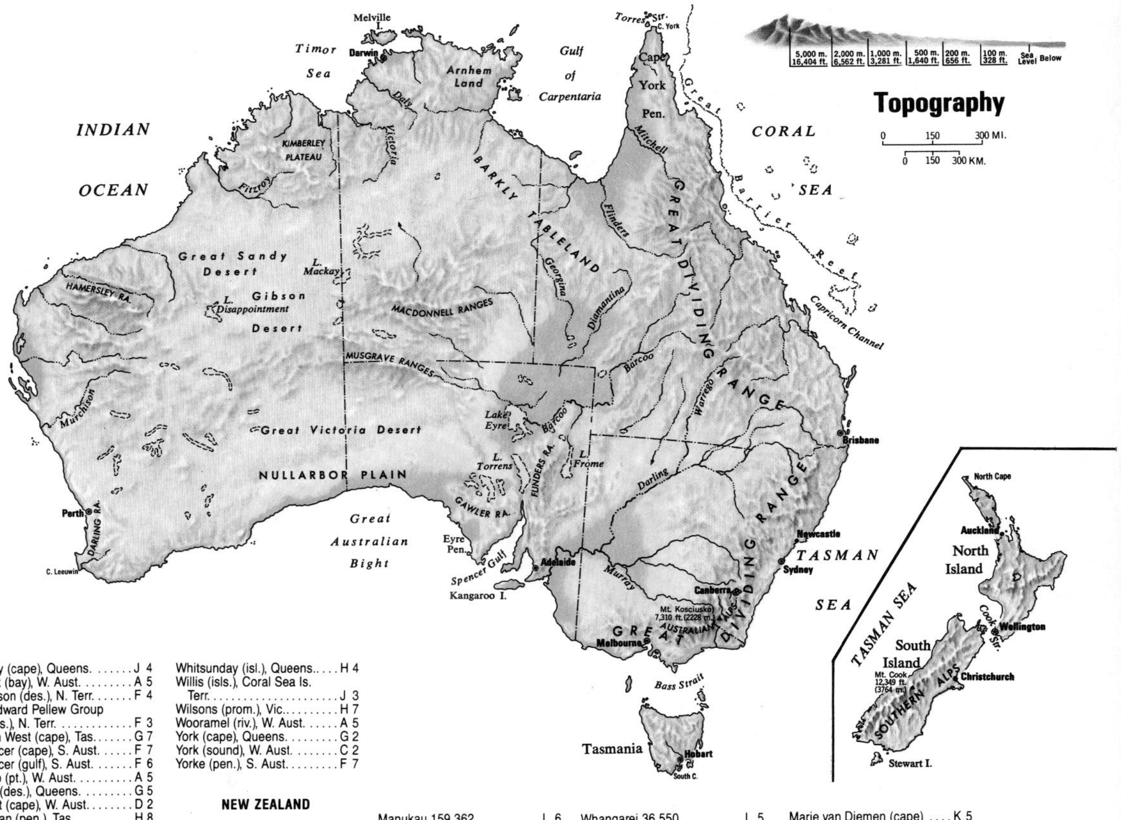

Lihou (cays), Coral Sea Is. Terr. .... J 3
Limmen Bight (riv.), N. Terr. ... F 3
Little Para (riv.), S. Aust. .... D 7
Lofty (mt.), S. Aust. .... E 8
Londonderry (cape), W. Aust. . D 2
Macdonald (lake), W. Aust. ... D 4
Macdonnell (ranges), N. Terr. . E 4
Mackay (lake), N. Terr. .... D 4
Macquarie (harb.), Tas. .... G 8
Macumba (riv.), S. Aust. .... F 5
Magdelaine (cays), Coral Sea Is. Terr. .... H 3
Main Barrier (range), N.S.W. .. G 6
Manifold (cape), Queens. ..... J 4
Margaret (riv.), W. Aust. ...... D 3
Maurice (lake), S. Aust. ...... E 5
Melville (bay), N. Terr. .... F 2
Melville (cape), Queens. ...... G 2
Melville (isl.), N. Terr. .... E 2
Mitchell (riv.), Queens. .... G 3
Montague (sound), W. Aust. ... C 2
Monte Bello (isls.), W. Aust. ... A 4
Moore (lake), W. Aust. .... B 5
Moreton (isl.), Queens. .... J 5
Mornington (isl.), Queens. ..... F 3
Murchison (riv.), W. Aust. ..... B 5
Murray (riv.) .... G 6
Murrumbidgee (riv.), N.S.W. .. H 6
Musgrave (range), S. Aust. ... E 5
Naturaliste (cape), W. Aust. ... A 6
Naturaliste (chan.), W. Aust. .. A 5
Norman (riv.), Queens. .... G 3
North West (cape), W. Aust. .. A 4
Nullarbor (plain) .... D 6
Onkaparinga (riv.), S. Aust. ... D 8
Ord (riv.), W. Aust. .... D 3
Ossa (mt.), Tas. .... H 8
Oyster (bay), Tas. .... H 8
Paroo (riv.), N.S.W. .... G 5
Pera (head), Queens. .... G 2
Peron (cape), W. Aust. .... A 2
Pillar (cape), Tas. .... H 8
Plenty (riv.), Vic. .... K 2
Port Davey (inlet), Tas. ...... G 8
Port Phillip (bay), Vic. .... K 3
Prince of Wales (isl.), Queens. G 2
Princess Charlotte (bay), Queens. .... G 2
Recherche (arch.), W. Aust. ... C 6
Roebuck (bay), W. Aust. ...... C 3
Roper (riv.), N. Terr. .... E 3
Rulhieres (cape), W. Aust. .... D 2
Saint Vincent (gulf), S. Aust. .. D 8
Sandy (cape), Queens. .... J 4
Shark (bay), W. Aust. .... A 5
Simpson (des.), N. Terr. ...... F 4
Sir Edward Pellew Group (isls.), N. Terr. .... F 3
South West (cape), Tas. ...... G 7
Spencer (cape), S. Aust. ..... F 7
Spencer (gulf), S. Aust. ...... F 6
Steep (pt.), W. Aust. .... A 5
Sturt (des.), Queens. .... G 5
Talbot (cape), W. Aust. ...... D 2
Tasman (pen.), Tas. .... H 8
Tasman (sea) .... J 7
Thomson (riv.), Queens. ...... G 4
Timor (sea) .... D 2
Torrens (lake), S. Aust. ...... F 6
Torrens (riv.) .... E 7
Torres (str.), Queens. .... G 2
Trinity (bay), Queens. .... H 3
Van Diemen (cape), N. Terr. .. D 2
Van Diemen (gulf), N. Terr. ... E 2
Victoria (riv.), N. Terr. .... E 3
Warrego (riv.), Queens. ...... H 5
Wellesley (isls.), Queens. .... F 3
Wells (lake), W. Aust. .... C 5
Wessel (cape), N. Terr. ...... F 2
Wessel (isls.), N. Terr. ...... F 2
Whitsunday (isl.), Queens. .... H 4
Willis (isls.), Coral Sea Is. Terr. .... J 3
Wilsons (prom.), Vic. .... H 7
Wooramel (riv.), W. Aust. ..... A 5
York (cape), Queens. .... G 2
York (sound), W. Aust. .... C 2
Yorke (pen.), S. Aust. .... F 7

NEW ZEALAND

CITIES and TOWNS

Ashburton 14,151 .... K 7
Auckland 144,963 .... L 6
Blenheim 17,849 .... L 7
Bluff 2,720 .... K 8
Christchurch 164,680 .... L 7
Dunedin 77,176 .... K 8
Gisborne 29,986 .... L 6
Greymouth 8,103 .... K 7
Hamilton 91,109 .... L 6
Hastings 36,083 .... L 6
Invercargill 49,446 .... K 8
Levin 14,652 .... L 6
Lower Hutt 63,245 .... L 6
Manukau 159,362 .... L 6
Masterton 18,785 .... L 6
Napier 48,314 .... L 6
Nelson 33,304 .... L 7
New Plymouth 44,095 .... L 6
Oamaru 13,043 .... K 8
Palmerston North 60,105 .... L 6
Rotorua 38,157 .... L 6
Takapuna 64,844 .... L 6
Taupo 13,651 .... L 6
Tauranga 37,099 .... L 6
Timaru 28,412 .... K 7
Tokoroa 18,713 .... L 6
Wanganui 37,012 .... L 6
Wellington (cap.) 135,688 .... L 7
Westport 4,686 .... K 7
Whangarei 36,550 .... L 5

OTHER FEATURES

Alps, Southern (mts.) .... K 7
Canterbury (bight) .... L 7
Clutha (riv.) .... K 8
Cook (str.) .... L 6
East (cape) .... L 6
Egmont (mt.) .... L 6
Foveaux (str.) .... K 8
Great Barrier (isl.) .... L 5
Hauraki (gulf) .... L 6
Hawke (bay) .... L 6
Islands (bay) .... L 5
Marie van Diemen (cape) ..... K 5
North (isl.) 2,322,989 .... K 6
Otego (pen.) .... K 8
Pegasus (bay) .... L 7
Plenty (bay) .... L 6
Ruapehu (mt.) .... L 6
South (cape) .... K 8
South (isl.) 3,175,737 .... L 7
Stewart (isl.) .... K 8
Tasman (bay) .... L 6
Three Kings (isl.) .... K 5
Waikato (riv.) .... L 6
West (cape) .... K 8

*Population of metropolitan area.
†Population of urban area.

FIJI

AREA 7,055 sq. mi. (18,272 sq. km.)
POPULATION 588,068
CAPITAL Suva
LARGEST CITY Suva
HIGHEST POINT Tomaniivi 4,341 ft. (1,323 m.)
MONETARY UNIT Fijian dollar
MAJOR LANGUAGES Fijian, Hindi, English
MAJOR RELIGIONS Protestantism, Hinduism

SOLOMON ISLANDS

AREA 11,500 sq. mi. (29,785 sq. km.)
POPULATION 221,000
CAPITAL Honiara
HIGHEST POINT Mount Popomanatseu 7,647 ft. (2,331 m.)
MONETARY UNIT Solomon Islands dollar
MAJOR LANGUAGES English, pidgin English, Melanesian dialects
MAJOR RELIGIONS Tribal religions, Protestantism, Roman Catholicism

KIRIBATI

AREA 291 sq. mi. (754 sq. km.)
POPULATION 56,213
CAPITAL Bairiki (Tarawa)
HIGHEST POINT (on Banaba I.) 285 ft. (87 m.)
MONETARY UNIT Australian dollar
MAJOR LANGUAGES I-Kiribati, English
MAJOR RELIGIONS Protestantism, Roman Catholicism

TONGA

AREA 270 sq. mi. (699 sq. km.)
POPULATION 90,128
CAPITAL Nuku'alofa
LARGEST CITY Nuku'alofa
HIGHEST POINT 3,389 ft. (1,033 m.)
MONETARY UNIT pa'anga
MAJOR LANGUAGES Tongan, English
MAJOR RELIGION Protestantism

NAURU

AREA 7.7 sq. mi. (20 sq. km.)
POPULATION 7,254
CAPITAL Yaren (district)
MONETARY UNIT Australian dollar
MAJOR LANGUAGES Nauruan, English
MAJOR RELIGION Protestantism

TUVALU

AREA 9.78 sq. mi. (25.33 sq. km.)
POPULATION 7,349
CAPITAL Fongafale (Funafuti)
HIGHEST POINT 15 ft. (4.6 m.)
MONETARY UNIT Australian dollar
MAJOR LANGUAGES English, Tuvaluan
MAJOR RELIGION Protestantism

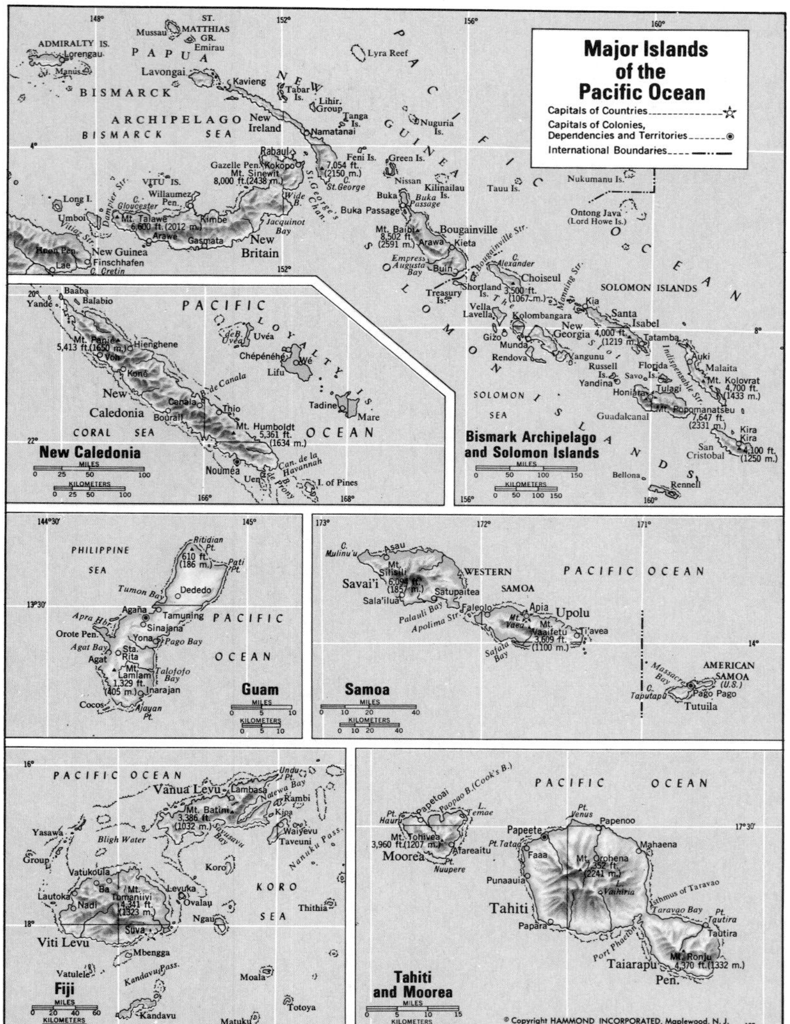

Abaiang (atoll) 3,296 .... H 5
Abemama (atoll) 2,300 ...... H 5
Adamstown (cap.), Pitcairn Is. 54 .... N 8
Admiralty (isls.) .... E 6
Agaña (cap.), Guam 896 ..... E 4
Agrihan (isl.) .... E 4
Ailinglapalap (atoll) 1,385 .... G 5
Ailuk (atoll) 413 .... H 4
Aitutaki (atoll) 2,348 .... K 7
Alofi (cap.), Niue 960 .... K 7
Alotau 4,310 .... E 7
Ambrym (isl.) 6,324 .... G 7
American Samoa 32,297 ..... J 7
Anaa (atoll) 444 .... M 7
Angaur (isl.) 243 .... D 5
Apataki (atoll) .... M 7
Apia (cap.), W. Samoa 33,100. J 7
Arno (atoll) 1,487 .... H 5
Arorae (atoll) 1,626 .... H 6
Atafu (atoll) 577 .... J 6
Atiu (isl.) 1,225 .... L 8
Austral (isls.) 5,208 .... L 8
Avarua (cap.), Cook Is. .... L 8
Babelthuap (isl.) 10,391 ...... D 5
Bairiki (cap.), Kiribati 1,777 ... H 5
Baker (isl.) .... J 5
Banaba (isl.) 2,314 .... G 6
Banks (isls.) 3,158 .... G 7
Belau 12,116 .... D 5
Belep (isls.) 624 .... G 7
Bellona (reefs) .... G 8
Beru (atoll) 2,318 .... H 6
Bikini (atoll) .... G 4
Bismarck (arch.) 218,339 .... E 6
Bonin (isls.) 1,879 .... E 3
Bora-Bora (isl.) 2,572 .... L 7
Bougainville (isl.) 71,761 ..... F 6
Bounty (isls.) .... H 10
Bourail 3,149 .... G 8
Butaritari (atoll) 2,971 .... H 5
Capitol Hill (cap.), No. Marianas 592 .... E 4
Caroline (isl.) .... M 7
Caroline (isls.) .... E 5
Chichi (isl.) 1,879 .... E 3
Choiseul (isl.) 10,349 .... F 6
Christmas (Kiritimati) (isl.) 674 .... L 5
Cook (isls.) 17,695 .... K 7
Coral (sea) .... F 7
Danger (Pukapuka) (atoll) 797 .... K 7
Daru 7,127 .... E 6
Disappointment (isls.) 373.... N 7
Ducie (isl.) .... O 8
Easter (isl.) 1,598 .... Q 8
Ebon (atoll) 887 .... G 5
Efate (isl.) 18,038 .... G 7
Enderbury (isl.) .... J 6
Enewetak (Eniwetok) (atoll) 542 .... G 4
Erromanga (isl.) 945 .... H 7
Espiritu Santo (isl.) 16,220 ... G 7
Fais (isl.) 207 .... E 5
Fakaofo (atoll) 654 .... J 6
Fanning (Tabuaeran) (isl.) 340 L 5
Faraulep (atoll) 132 .... E 5
Fatuhiva (isl.) 386 .... N 7
Fiji 588,068 .... H 8
Flint (isl.) .... L 7
Fly (riv.) .... E 6
Fongafale (cap.), Tuvalu ...... H 6
French Polynesia 137,382.... L 8
Funafuti (atoll) 2,120 .... H 6
Futuna (Hoorn) (isls.) 3,173 .. J 7
Gambier (isls.) 556 .... N 8
Gardner (Nukumaroro)(isl.)... J 6
Gilbert (isls.) 47,711 .... H 6
Greenwich (Kapingamarangi) (atoll) 508 .... F 5
Guadalcanal (isl.) 46,619 .... F 7
Guam (isl.) 105,979 .... E 4
Hall (isls.) 647 .... F 5
Hawaiian (isls.) 964,691 ...... J 3
Henderson (isl.) .... O 8
Hivaoa (isl.) 1,159 .... N 6
Honiara (cap.), Solomon Is. 14,942 .... F 6
Hoorn (isls.) 3,173 .... J 7
Howland (isl.) .... J 5
Huahine (isl.) 3,140 .... L 7
Hull (Orona)(isl.) .... J 6
Huon (gulf) .... E 6
Ifalik (atoll) 389 .... E 5
Iwo (isl.) .... E 3
Jaluit (atoll) 1,450 .... G 5
Jarvis (isl.) .... K 6
Johnston (atoll) 327 .... K 4
Kadavu (Kandavu) (isl.) 8,699 H 7
Kanton (isl.) .... J 6
Kapingamarangi (atoll) 508... F 5
Kavieng 4,633 .... E 6
Kermadec (isls.) 5 .... J 9
Kieta 3,491 .... F 6
Kimbe 4,662 .... F 6
Kingman (reef) .... K 5
Kiribati 57,500 .... J 6
Kiritimati (isl.) 674 .... L 5
Kolonia (cap.), Micronesia 5,549 .... F 5
Koror (cap.), Belau 6,222 ..... D 5
Kosrae (isl.) 5,491 .... G 5
Kwajalein (atoll) 6,624 .... G 5
Lae 61,617 .... E 6
Lau Group (isls.) 14,452 ..... J 7
Lavongai (isl.) .... F 6
Lifu (isl.) 7,585 .... G 8
Line (isls.) .... K 5
Little Makin (atoll) 1,445 ..... H 5
Lord Howe (Ontong Java) (isl.) 1,082 .... G 6
Lord Howe (isl.) 287 .... G 9
Lorengau 3,986 .... E 6
Louisiade (arch.) .... F 7
Loyalty (isls.) 14,518 .... G 8
Luganville 4,935 .... G 7
Madang 21,335 .... E 6
Majuro (atoll) (cap.), Marshall Is. 8,583 .... H 5
Makin (Butaritari) (atoll) 2,971 H 5
Malaita (isl.) 50,912 .... G 6
Malden (isl.) .... L 6
Malekula (isl.) 15,931 .... G 7
Maloelap (atoll) 763 .... H 5
Mangaia (isl.) 1,364 .... L 8
Mangareva (isl.) 556 .... N 8
Manihiki (atoll) 405 .... K 7
Manra (isl.) .... K 6
Manua (isls.), 1,459 .... K 7
Manus (isl.) 25,844 .... E 6
Marcus (isl.) .... F 3
Maré (isl.) 4,156 .... G 8
Marianas, Northern 16,780 ... E 4
Mariana Trench .... E 4
Marquesas (isls.) 5,419 ...... N 6
Marshall Islands 30,873 ...... G 4
Marutea (atoll) .... N 8
Mata Utu (cap.), Wallis and Futuna 558 .... J 7
Mauke (isl.) 684 .... L 8
Melanesia (reg.) .... E 5
Micronesia (reg.) .... E 4
Micronesia, Federated States of 73,160 .... F 5
Midway (isls.) 453 .... J 3
Mili (atoll) 763 .... H 5
Moen (isl.) 10,351 .... F 5
Moorea (isl.) 5,788 .... L 7
Mururoa (isl.) .... M 8
Nadi 6,938 .... H 7
Namonuito (atoll) 783 .... E 5
Namorik (atoll) 617 .... G 5
Nanumea (atoll) 844 .... H 6
Nauru 7,254 .... G 6
Ndeni (isl.) 4,854 .... G 7
New Britain (isl.) 148,773 .... F 6
New Caledonia 133,233 ..... G 8
New Caledonia (isl.) 118,715 .... G 8
New Georgia (isl.) 16,472 .... F 6
New Guinea (isl.) .... E 6
New Ireland (isl.) 65,657 ..... F 6
Ngatik (atoll) 560 .... F 5
Ngulu (atoll) 21 .... D 5
Niuatoputapu (isl.) 1,650 ..... J 7
Niue (isl.) 3,578 .... K 7
Niutao (atoll) 866 .... H 6
Nomoi (isls.) 1,879 .... F 5
Nonouti (atoll) 2,223 .... H 6
Norfolk Island (terr.) 2,175.... G 8
Northern Marianas 116,780 .. E 4
Nouméa (cap.), New Caled. 56,078 .... G 8
Nui (atoll) 603 .... H 6
Nuku'alofa (cap.), Tonga 18,356 .... J 8
Nukuhiva (isl.) 1,484 .... M 6

Nukumaroro (isl.) J 6
Ocean (Banaba) (isl.) 2,314 G 6
Oeno (isl.) O 8
Onotoa (atoll) 1,997 H 6
Ontong Java (isl.) 1,082 G 6
Orona (isl.) J 6
Pacific Islands, Terr. of the 132,929 F 5
Pagan (isl.) E 4
Pago Pago (cap.), Amer. Samoa 3,075 J 7
Palmyra (atoll) K 5
Papeete (cap.), Fr. Poly. 22,967 M 7
Papua (gulf) E 6
Papua New Guinea 3,010,727 E 6
Peleliu (isl.) 609 D 5
Penrhyn (Tongareva) (atoll) 608 L 6
Phoenix (isls.) J 6
Pines (isl.) 1,095 G 8
Pitcairn (isl.) 54 O 8
Polynesia (reg.) K 7
Pohnpei (Ponape)(isl.) 19,935 F 5
Popondetta 6,429 E 6
Port Moresby (cap.), Papua N.G. 123,624 E 6
Pukapuka (atoll) 797 K 7
Pulap (atoll) 427 E 5
Puluwat (atoll) 441 E 5
Rabaul 14,954 F 6
Raiatea (isl.) 2,517 L 7
Raivavae (isl.) 1,023 M 8
Rakahanga (atoll) 269 K 7
Ralik Chain (isls.) G 5
Rangiroa (atoll) M 7
Rapa (isl.) 398 M 8
Rarotonga (isl.) 9,477 K 8
Ratak Chain (isls.) G 5
Reao (atoll) 424 N 7
Rennell (isl.) 1,132 F 7
Rikitea N 8
Rimatara (isl.) 813 L 8
Rongelap (atoll) 235 G 4
Rota (isl.) 1,261 E 4
Rotuma (isl.) 2,805 H 7
Rurutu (isl.) 1,555 L 8
Saipan (isl.) 14,549 E 4
Sala y Gómez (isl.) P 8
Samarai 869 E 7
Samoa (isls.) J 7
San Cristobal (isl.) 11,212 G 7
Santa Cruz (isls.) 5,421 G 6
Santa Isabel (isl.) 10,420 G 6
Savai'i (isl.) 43,150 J 7
Senyavin (isls.) 20,035 F 5
Society (isls.) 117,703 L 7
Solomon (isls.) F 6
Solomon (sea) F 6
Solomon Islands 221,000 G 6
Starbuck (isl.) L 6
Suva (cap.), Fiji 63,628 H 7
Swains (isl.) 27 K 7
Sydney (Manra)(isl.) K 6
Tabiteuea (atoll) 3,942 H 6
Tabuaeran (isl.) 340 L 5
Tahaa (isl.) 3,513 L 7
Tahiti (isl.) 95,604 L 7
Takaroa (atoll) 337 M 7
Tanna (isl.) 15,715 H 7
Tarawa (atoll) 17,129 H 5
Tasman (sea) G 9
Teraina (isl.) 458 L 5
Tinian (isl.) 866 E 4
Tokelau (isls.) 1,575 J 6
Tonga 90,128 J 8
Tongareva (atoll) 608 L 6
Tongatapu (isls.) 57,130 J 8
Torres (isls.) 325 G 7
Torres (strait) E 7
Trobriand (isls.) F 6
Truk (isls.) 37,488 F 5
Tuamotu (arch.) 9,052 M 7
Tubuai (Austral) (isls.) 5,208 M 8
Tubuai (isl.) 1,419 M 8
Tutuila (isl.) 30,538 J 7
Tuvalu 7,349 H 6

VANUATU

AREA 5,700 sq. mi. (14,763 sq. km.)
POPULATION 112,596
CAPITAL Vila
HIGHEST POINT Mt. Tabwemasana 6,165 ft. (1,879 m.)
MONETARY UNIT vatu
MAJOR LANGUAGES Bislama, English, French
MAJOR RELIGIONS Christian, animist

WESTERN SAMOA

AREA 1,133 sq. mi. (2,934 sq. km.)
POPULATION 158,130
CAPITAL Apia
LARGEST CITY Apia
HIGHEST POINT Mt. Silisili 6,094 ft. (1,857 m.)
MONETARY UNIT tala
MAJOR LANGUAGES Samoan, English
MAJOR RELIGIONS Protestantism, Roman Catholicism

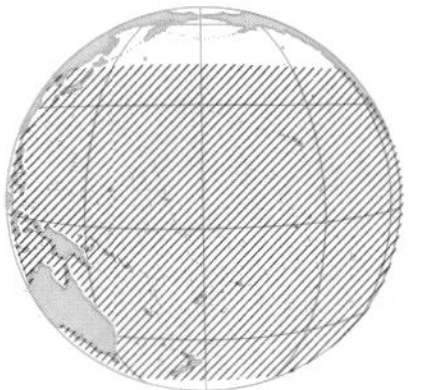

Uapou (isl.) 1,563 M 6
Ujelang (atoll) 309 F 5
Ulithi (atoll) 710 D 4
Upolu (isl.) 114,620 J 7
Uturoa 2,517 L 7
Uvéa (isl.) 2,777 G 7
Vaitupu (atoll) 1,273 H 6
Vanikoro (isl.) 267 G 7
Vanimo 3,071 E 6
Vanua Levu (isl.) 103,122 H 7
Vanuatu 112,596 G 7
Vila (cap.), Vanuatu 4,729 G 7
Viti Levu (isl.) 445,422 H 7
Volcano (isls.) E 3
Vostok (isl.) L 7
Wake (isl.) 302 G 4
Wallis (isls.) 6,019 J 7
Wallis and Futuna 9,192 J 7
Washington (Teraina) (isl.) 458 L 5
Wau 2,349 E 6
Western Samoa 158,130 J 7
Wewak 19,890 E 6
Woleai (isl.) 638 E 5
Wotje (atoll) 535 H 5
Yap (isl.) 6,670 D 5

°City and suburbs.
•Population of urban area.

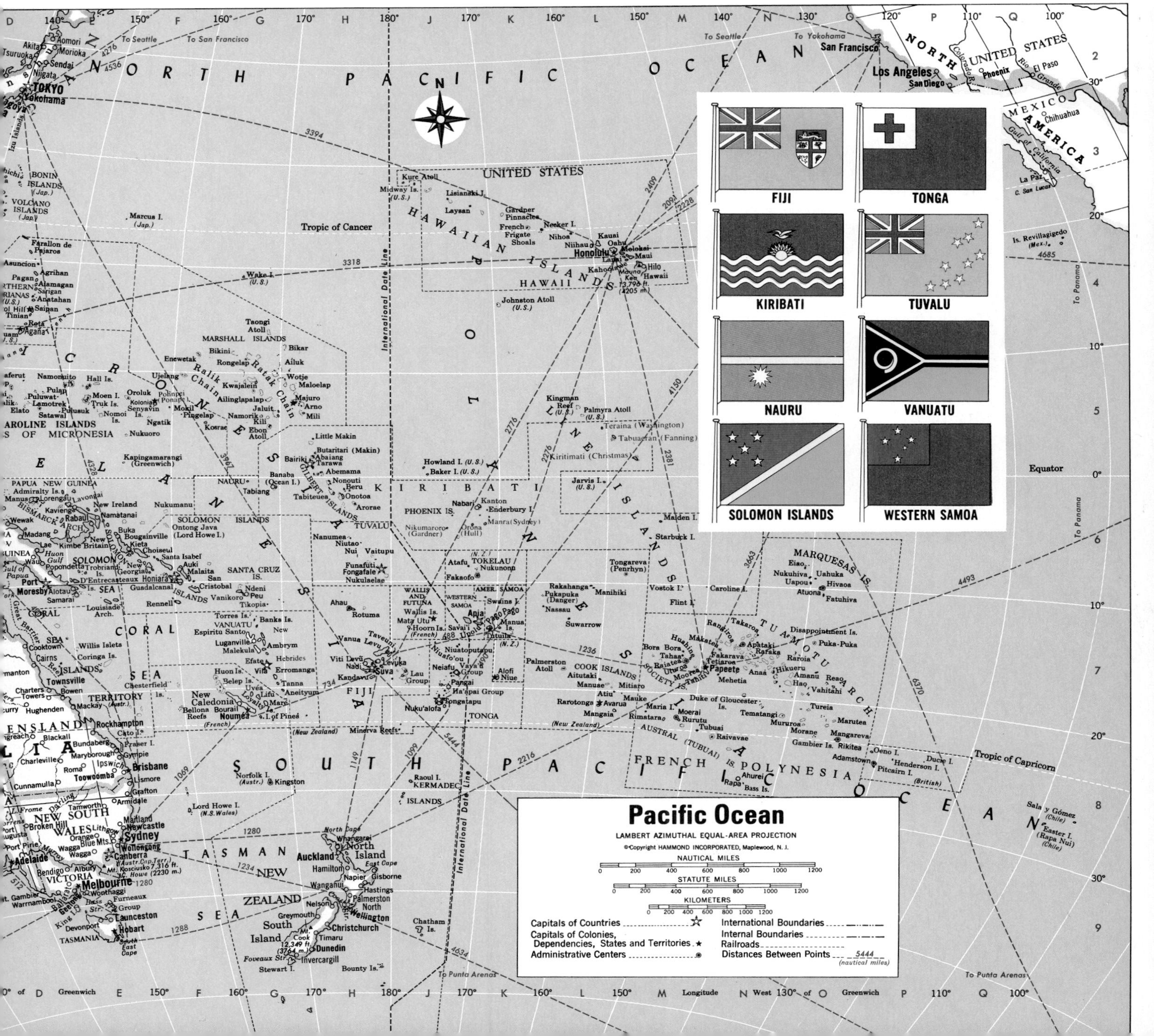

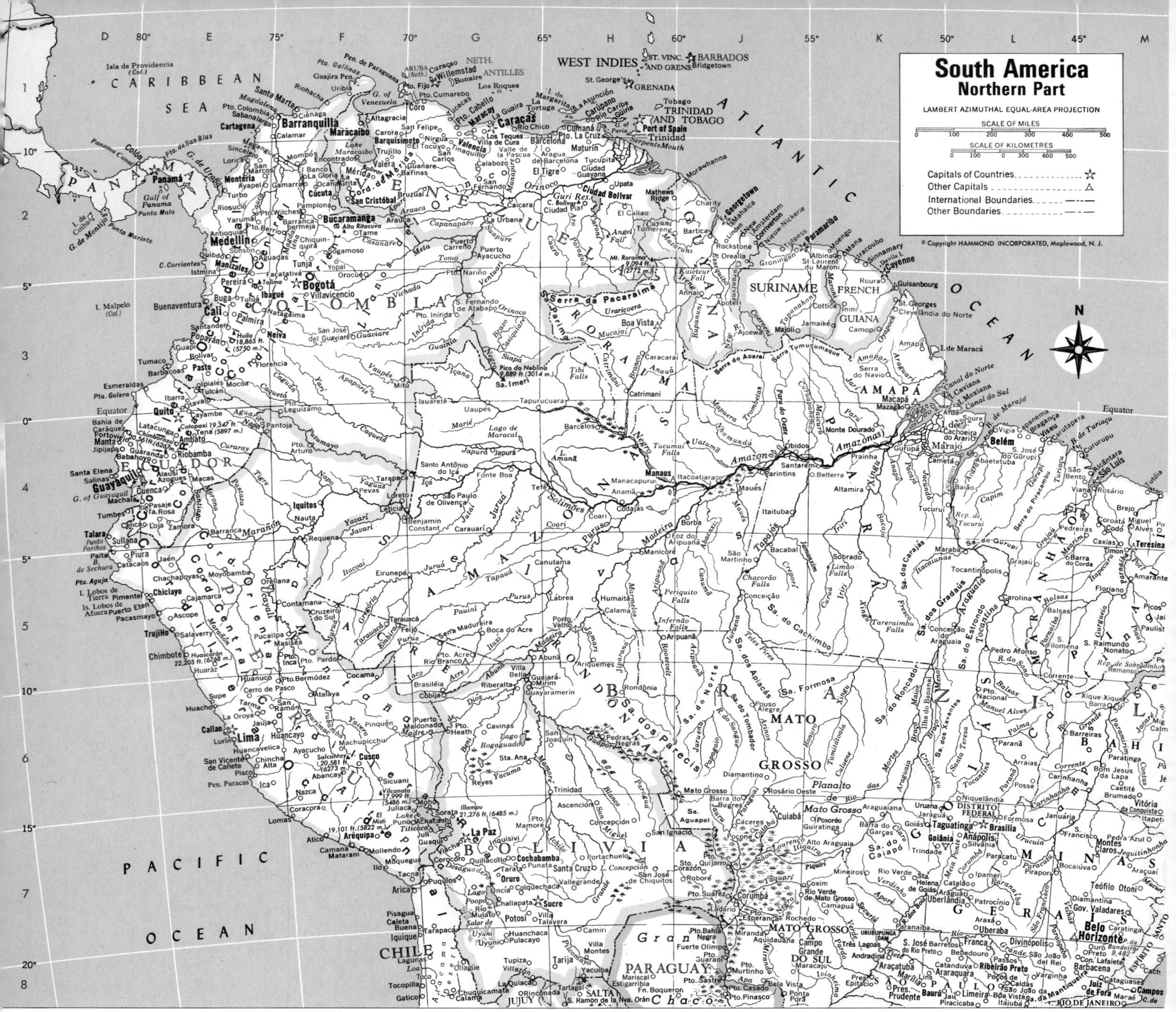

ARGENTINA

PROVINCES

Buenos Aires 10,796,036 H 11
Catamarca 206,204 G 9
Chaco 692,410 H 9
Chubut 262,196 G 12
Córdoba 2,407,135 H 10
Corrientes 657,716 J 9
Distrito Federal 2,908,001 J 10
Entre Ríos 902,241 J 10
Formosa 292,479 H 8
Jujuy 408,514 G 8
La Pampa 207,132 G 11
La Rioja 163,342 G 9
Mendoza 1,187,305 G 10
Misiones 579,579 K 9
Neuquén 241,904 G 11
Río Negro 383,896 G 12
Salta 662,369 G 8
San Juan 469,973 G 10
San Luis 212,837 G 10
Santa Cruz 114,479 G 13
Santa Fe 2,457,188 H 9
Santiago del Estero 652,318 H 9
Tierra del Fuego, Antártida, e Islas del Atlántico Sur 29,451 G 14
Tucumán 968,066 G 9

CITIES and TOWNS

Azul 43,582 J 11
Bahía Blanca *220,765 H 11
Balcarce 28,985 J 11
Bell Ville 26,559 H 10
Bolívar 16,382 H 11
Buenos Aires (cap.) *9,927,404 H 10
Campana 51,498 H 10
Catamarca *88,432 H 9
Chivilcoy 43,779 H 11
Comodoro Rivadavia 96,865 G 13
Concepción del Uruguay 46,065 J 10
Concordia 93,618 J 10
Córdoba *982,018 G 10
Corrientes 179,590 J 9
Cruz del Eje 23,473 H 10
Curuzú Cuatiá 24,955 J 9
Embarcación 9,016 G 8
Esperanza 22,838 H 10
Formosa 95,067 J 9
Gaimán 2,651 G 12
Gastre G 12
General Alvear 21,250 G 11
General Pico 30,180 H 11
General Roca 38,296 G 11
Godoy Cruz 141,553 G 10
Goya 47,357 J 9
Jachal 8,832 G 10
Jujuy 124,487 G 8
La Plata *560,341 J 11
La Rioja 66,826 G 9
Liberador General San Martín 30,814 H 8
Lincoln 19,009 H 10
Maquinchao 1,295 G 12
Mar del Plata 407,024 J 11
Mendoza *596,796 G 10
Mercedes 50,856 G 10
Miramar 15,473 J 11
Necochea 50,939 J 11
Neuquén 90,037 G 11
Olavarría 63,686 H 11
Paraná 159,581 J 10
Pehuajó 25,613 H 11
Pergamino 68,989 H 10
Plaza Huincul 7,988 G 11
Posadas 139,941 J 9
Presidencia Roque Sáenz Peña 49,261 J 9
Puerto Madryn 20,709 G 12
Punta Alta 54,375 H 11
Rafaela 53,152 H 10
Rawson 12,981 H 12
Reconquista 32,442 H 9
Resistencia *218,438 J 9
Rinconada G 8
Río Cuarto 110,148 H 10
Río Gallegos 43,479 G 14
Río Grande 13,271 G 14
Rivadavia H 8
Rosario *954,606 H 10
Rosario de la Frontera 13,531 H 9
Salta 260,323 G 8
San Antonio de los Cobres 2,357 G 8
San Carlos de Bariloche 48,222 F 12
San Francisco *58,616 H 10
San Juan *290,479 G 10
San Julián 4,278 G 13
San Luis 70,632 G 10
San Miguel de Tucumán *496,914 H 9
San Nicolás 96,313 J 10
San Rafael 7,047 G 10
Santa Cruz 2,353 G 14
Sante Fe 287,240 H 10
Santa Rosa 51,689 H 11
Santiago del Estero 148,357 H 9
Tandil 78,821 J 11
Tartagal 31,367 H 8
Trelew 52,073 G 12
Trenque Lauquen 22,504 H 11
Tres Arroyos 42,118 J 11
Ushuaia 10,988 G 14
Valcheta 2,994 G 12
Venado Tuerto 46,775 H 10
Viedma 24,338 H 12
Villa Dolores 21,508 G 10
Villa María *67,490 H 10

OTHER FEATURES

Aconcagua (mt.) G 10
Andes de Patagonia (mts.) F 14
Argentino (lake) G 14
Bermejo (riv.) H 9
Colorado (riv.) H 11
Estados, Los (isl.) H 14
Gran Chaco (reg.) H 8
Iguassú (falls) K 9
Magellan (str.) G 14
Maipo (mt.) G 10
Nahuel Huapi (lake) F 12
Negro (riv.) H 11
Ojos del Salado (mt.) G 9
Pampas (plain) H 11
Patagonia (reg.) F 12
Plata, Río de la (est.) J 11
Salado (riv.) G 11
Salado (riv.) H 9
San Antonio (cape) J 11
San Martín (lake) F 13
San Matías (gulf) H 12
Staten (Los Estados) (isl.) H 14
Tierra del Fuego (isl.) G 14
Tres Puntas (cape) H 13
Uruguay (riv.) J 9
Valdés (pen.) H 12

BOLIVIA

CITIES and TOWNS

Cochabamba 204,684 G 7
Guaqui 2,266 G 7
Guayamerín 1,470 G 6
Huanchaca G 8
La Paz (cap.) 635,283 G 7
Oruro 124,213 G 7
Potosí 77,397 G 7
Puerto Suárez 1,159 J 7
Santa Cruz 254,682 H 7
Sucre (cap.) 63,625 H 7
Tarija 38,916 H 8

OTHER FEATURES

Abuná (riv.) G 6
Beni (riv.) G 6
Desaguadero (riv.) G 7
Grande (riv.) H 7
Guaporé (riv.) H 6
Illampu (mt.) G 7
Mamoré (riv.) H 6
Poopó (lake) G 7
Real, Cordillera (mts.) G 7
Titicaca (lake) F 7

BRAZIL

STATES

Acre 301,605 F 5
Alagoas 1,987,581 N 5
Amapá (terr.) 175,634 K 3
Amazonas 1,432,066 G 5
Bahia 9,474,263 M 6
Ceará 5,294,876 N 5
Distrito Federal 1,177,393 L 7
Espírito Santo 2,023,821 M 8
Goiás 3,865,482 L 6
Maranhão 4,002,599 L 5
Mato Grosso 1,141,661 J 6
Mato Grosso do Sul 1,370,333 J 8
Minas Gerais 13,390,805 M 7
Pará 3,411,868 K 4
Paraíba 2,772,600 N 5
Paraná 7,630,466 K 8
Pernambuco 6,147,102 N 5
Piauí 2,140,066 M 5
Rio de Janeiro 11,297,327 M 8
Rio Grande do Norte 1,899,720 N 5
Rio Grande do Sul 7,777,212 K 9
Rondônia 492,810 H 6
Roraima (terr.) 79,153 H 3
Santa Catarina 3,628,751 K 9
São Paulo 25,040,698 L 8
Sergipe 1,141,834 N 6

CITIES and TOWNS

Alagoinhas 76,377 N 6
Alcobaça 3,430 N 7
Alegrete 54,786 J 9
Amapá 2,676 J 3
Amarante 6,848 M 5
Anápolis 160,520 L 7
Andradina 42,036 K 8
Aracaju 288,106 N 6
Araçatuba 1,113,486 K 8
Araguari 73,302 L 7
Arapiraca 84,133 N 5
Araraquara 77,202 L 8
Araxá 51,339 L 7
Bacabal 43,229 J 5
Bagé 66,743 K 10
Bahia (Salvador) 1,496,276 N 6
Barbacena 69,675 M 8
Barcelos 1,846 H 4
Barra do Garças 65,294 K 7
Barretos 65,294 L 8
Baurú 178,861 L 8
Bebedouro 39,070 L 8
Belém 758,117 L 4
Belo Horizonte †2,541,788 M 7
Benjamin Constant 6,563 G 4
Blumenau 144,819 L 9
Boa Vista 43,131 H 3
Borba 5,366 J 4
Botucatu 56,316 L 8
Bragança 1,208 L 4
Brasiléia 4,835 G 6
Brasília (cap.) 411,305 L 7
Brejo 5,859 M 4
Brumado 24,663 M 6

(continued on following page)

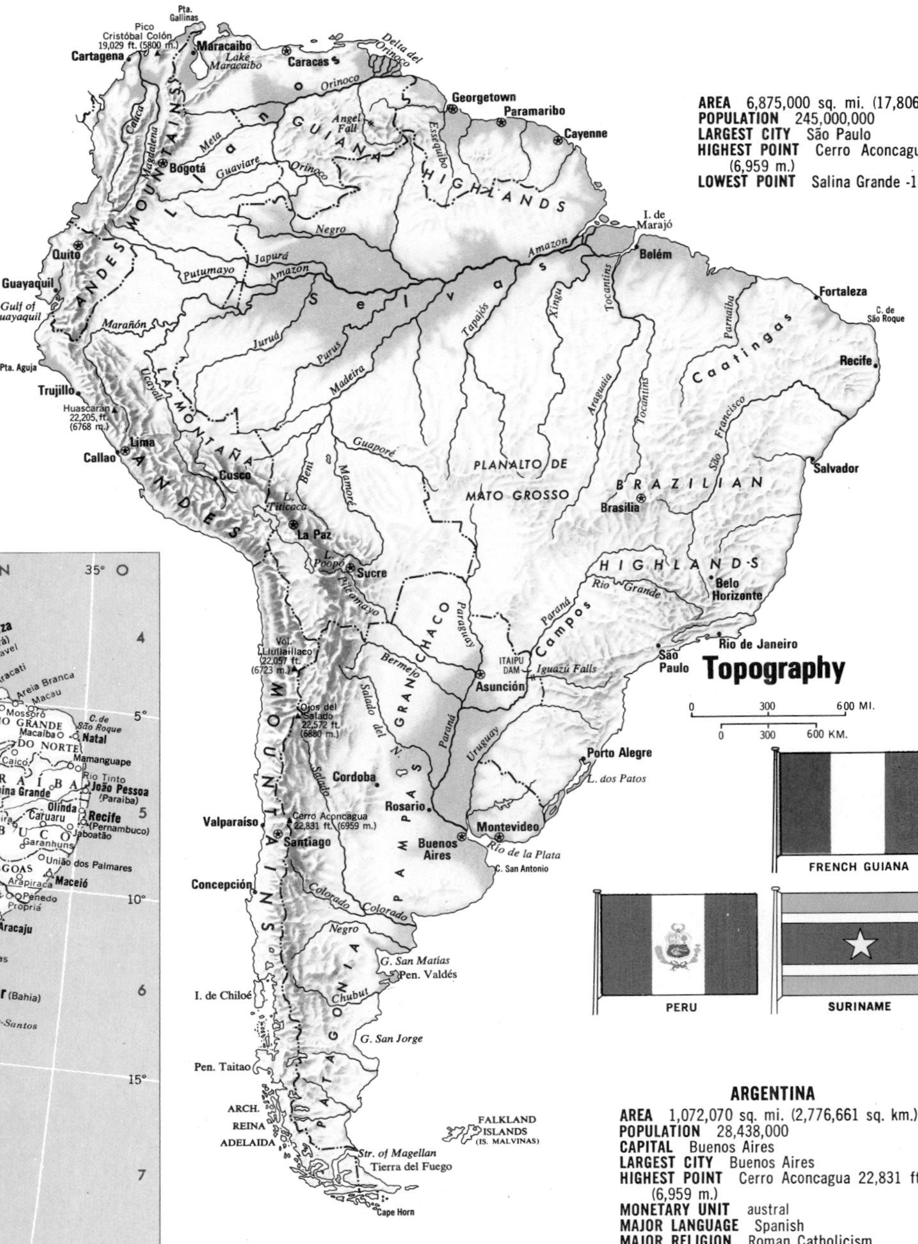

AREA 6,875,000 sq. mi. (17,806,250 sq. km.)
POPULATION 245,000,000
LARGEST CITY São Paulo
HIGHEST POINT Cerro Aconcagua 22,831 ft. (6,959 m.)
LOWEST POINT Salina Grande -131 ft. (-40 m.)

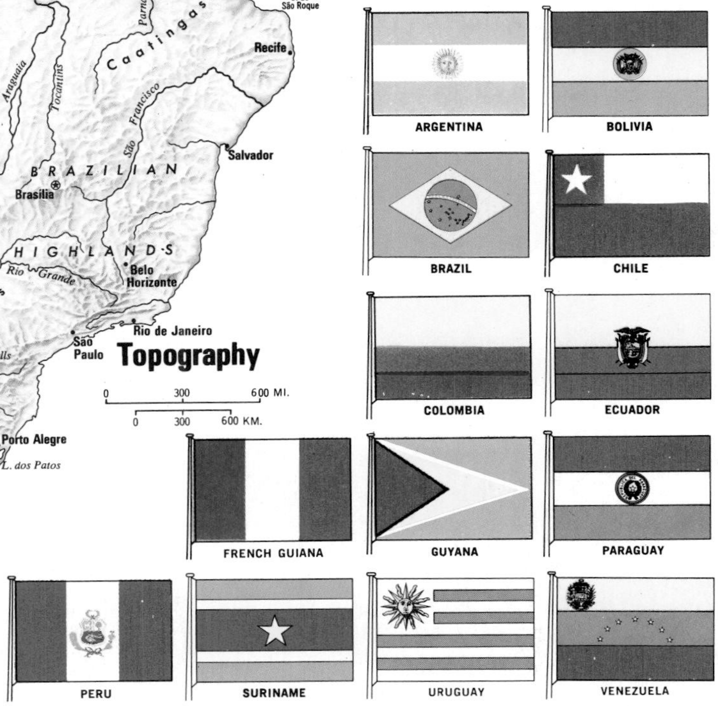

ARGENTINA

AREA 1,072,070 sq. mi. (2,776,661 sq. km.)
POPULATION 28,438,000
CAPITAL Buenos Aires
LARGEST CITY Buenos Aires
HIGHEST POINT Cerro Aconcagua 22,831 ft. (6,959 m.)
MONETARY UNIT austral
MAJOR LANGUAGE Spanish
MAJOR RELIGION Roman Catholicism

BOLIVIA

AREA 424,163 sq. mi. (1,098,582 sq. km.)
POPULATION 5,600,000
CAPITALS La Paz, Sucre
LARGEST CITY La Paz
HIGHEST POINT Nevada Ancohuma 21,489 ft. (6,550 m.)
MONETARY UNIT Bolivian peso
MAJOR LANGUAGES Spanish, Quechua, Aymara
MAJOR RELIGION Roman Catholicism

BRAZIL

AREA 3,284,426 sq. mi. (8,506,663 sq. km.)
POPULATION 119,098,992
CAPITAL Brasília
LARGEST CITY São Paulo (greater)
HIGHEST POINT Pico da Neblina 9,889 ft. (3,014 m.)
MONETARY UNIT cruzeiro
MAJOR LANGUAGE Portuguese
MAJOR RELIGION Roman Catholicism

CHILE

AREA 292,257 sq. mi. (756,946 sq. km.)
POPULATION 11,275,440
CAPITAL Santiago
LARGEST CITY Santiago
HIGHEST POINT Ojos del Salado 22,572 ft. (6,880 m.)
MONETARY UNIT Chilean escudo
MAJOR LANGUAGE Spanish
MAJOR RELIGION Roman Catholicism

COLOMBIA

AREA 439,513 sq. mi. (1,138,339 sq. km.)
POPULATION 27,520,000
CAPITAL Bogotá
LARGEST CITY Bogotá
HIGHEST POINT Pico Cristóbal Colón 19,029 ft. (5,800 m.)
MONETARY UNIT Colombian peso
MAJOR LANGUAGE Spanish
MAJOR RELIGION Roman Catholicism

ECUADOR

AREA 109,483 sq. mi. (283,561 sq. km.)
POPULATION 8,354,000
CAPITAL Quito
LARGEST CITY Guayaquil
HIGHEST POINT Chimborazo 20,561 ft. (6,267 m.)
MONETARY UNIT sucre
MAJOR LANGUAGES Spanish, Quechua
MAJOR RELIGION Roman Catholicism

FRENCH GUIANA

AREA 35,135 sq. mi. (91,000 sq. km.)
POPULATION 73,022
CAPITAL Cayenne
LARGEST CITY Cayenne
HIGHEST POINT 2,723 ft. (830 m.)
MONETARY UNIT French franc
MAJOR LANGUAGE French
MAJOR RELIGIONS Roman Catholicism, Protestantism

GUYANA

AREA 83,000 sq. mi. (214,970 sq. km.)
POPULATION 820,000
CAPITAL Georgetown
LARGEST CITY Georgetown
HIGHEST POINT Mt. Roraima 9,094 ft. (2,772 m.)
MONETARY UNIT Guyana dollar
MAJOR LANGUAGES English, Hindi
MAJOR RELIGIONS Christianity, Hinduism, Islam

PARAGUAY

AREA 157,047 sq. mi. (406,752 sq. km.)
POPULATION 2,973,000
CAPITAL Asunción
LARGEST CITY Asunción
HIGHEST POINT Amambay Range 2,264 ft. (690 m.)
MONETARY UNIT guaraní
MAJOR LANGUAGES Spanish, Guaraní
MAJOR RELIGION Roman Catholicism

PERU

AREA 496,222 sq. mi. (1,285,215 sq. km.)
POPULATION 17,031,221
CAPITAL Lima
LARGEST CITY Lima
HIGHEST POINT Huascarán 22,205 ft. (6,768 m.)
MONETARY UNIT sol
MAJOR LANGUAGES Spanish, Quechua, Aymara
MAJOR RELIGION Roman Catholicism

SURINAME

AREA 55,144 sq. mi. (142,823 sq. km.)
POPULATION 354,860
CAPITAL Paramaribo
LARGEST CITY Paramaribo
HIGHEST POINT Julianatop 4,200 ft. (1,280 m.)
MONETARY UNIT Suriname guilder
MAJOR LANGUAGES Dutch, Hindi, Indonesian
MAJOR RELIGIONS Christianity, Islam, Hinduism

URUGUAY

AREA 72,172 sq. mi. (186,925 sq. km.)
POPULATION 2,899,000
CAPITAL Montevideo
LARGEST CITY Montevideo
HIGHEST POINT Mirador Nacional 1,644 ft. (501 m.)
MONETARY UNIT Uruguayan peso
MAJOR LANGUAGE Spanish
MAJOR RELIGION Roman Catholicism

VENEZUELA

AREA 352,143 sq. mi. (912,050 sq. km.)
POPULATION 14,313,000
CAPITAL Caracas
LARGEST CITY Caracas
HIGHEST POINT Pico Bolívar 16,427 ft. (5,007 m.)
MONETARY UNIT Bolívar
MAJOR LANGUAGE Spanish
MAJOR RELIGION Roman Catholicism

Cáceres 33,472 . . . . . J 7
Cachoeira do Sul 59,967 . . . . K 10
Cachoeiro de Itapemirim 84,994 . . . . . N 8
Caicó 30,777 . . . . . N 5
Cajazeiras 30,834 . . . . . N 5
Campina Grande 222,229 . . . . N 5
Campinas 566,517 . . . . . L 8
Campo Grande 282,844 . . . . . K 8
Campos 174,218 . . . . . M 8
Cananéia 5,581 . . . . . L 8
Caratinga 39,621 . . . . . M 7
Caravelas 3,704 . . . . . N 7
Caruaru 137,636 . . . . . N 5
Cataguases 40,659 . . . . . M 8
Catalão 30,516 . . . . . L 7
Catanduva 64,813 . . . . . L 8
Caxias 56,755 . . . . . M 4
Caxias do Sul 198,824 . . . . . K 9
Ceará (Fortaleza) 648,815 . . . N 4
Codajás 4,923 . . . . . H 4
Codó 11,593 . . . . . M 4
Colatina 61,057 . . . . . N 7
Conceição . . . . . J 5
Conselheiro Lafaiete 66,262 . . M 8
Corumbá 66,014 . . . . . J 7
Crateús 29,905 . . . . . M 5
Crato 49,244 . . . . . N 5
Cruz Alta 53,315 . . . . . K 9
Cruzeiro do Sul 11,189 . . . . . F 5
Cuiabá 167,894 . . . . . J 7
Curitiba †843,733 . . . . . K 9
Diamantina 20,197 . . . . . M 7
Divinópolis 108,344 . . . . . L 8
Erexim 46,927 . . . . . K 9
Feira de Santana 225,003 . . . . N 6
Floriano 35,761 . . . . . M 5
Florianópolis 153,547 . . . . . L 9
Fonte Boa 3,278 . . . . . G 4
Fortaleza 648,815 . . . . . N 4
Foz do Iguaçú 93,619 . . . . . K 9
Franca 143,630 . . . . . L 8
Garanhuns 64,854 . . . . . N 5
Goiânia 703,263 . . . . . L 7
Governador Valadares 173,699 . . . . . M 7
Guarapuava 17,189 . . . . . K 9
Humaitá . . . . . H 5
Iguatu 39,611 . . . . . N 5
Ilhéus 71,240 . . . . . N 6
Ipiaú 27,384 . . . . . N 6
Itabuna 129,938 . . . . . M 6
Itajaí 78,867 . . . . . L 9
Itajubá 53,506 . . . . . L 8
Itapetinga 36,897 . . . . . M 7
Itaqui 23,136 . . . . . J 9
Jaboatão 67,120 . . . . . O 5
Jacarèzinho 92,364 . . . . . K 8
Jacobina 26,723 . . . . . N 6
Januária 20,484 . . . . . M 6
Jaú 59,522 . . . . . L 8
Jequié 84,792 . . . . . M 6
João Pessoa 290,424 . . . . . O 5
Joinvile 217,074 . . . . . L 9
Juazeiro 60,940 . . . . . M 5
Juazeiro do Norte 125,248 . . . M 5
Juiz de Fora 299,728 . . . . . M 8
Jundiaí 210,015 . . . . . L 8
Limeira 137,812 . . . . . L 8
Lins 44,633 . . . . . L 8
Londrina 258,054 . . . . . K 8
Macapá 89,081 . . . . . K 3
Macau 17,543 . . . . . N 4
Maceió 376,479 . . . . . N 5
Manaus 613,068 . . . . . H 4
Manicoré 9,532 . . . . . H 5
Maracaju 9,699 . . . . . K 8
Marília 103,904 . . . . . K 8
Maringa 158,047 . . . . . K 8
Mato Grosso . . . . . J 6
Montes Claros 151,881 . . . . . M 7
Mossoró 118,007 . . . . . N 5
Natal 376,552 . . . . . O 5
Niterói 386,185 . . . . . M 8
Olinda 266,392 . . . . . N 5
Ourinhos 52,698 . . . . . K 8
Ouro Preto 27,821 . . . . . M 8
Paracatu 29,911 . . . . . L 7
Paraíba (João Pessoa) 290,424 . . . . . O 5
Paranaguá 68,366 . . . . . L 9
Parnaíba 21,305 . . . . . M 4
Passo Fundo 103,121 . . . . . K 9
Passos 56,998 . . . . . L 8
Patrocínio 29,520 . . . . . L 7
Paulo Afonso 62,066 . . . . . N 5
Pedreiras 30,843 . . . . . L 4
Pelotas 197,092 . . . . . K 10
Penedo 27,064 . . . . . N 6
Pernambuco (Recife) 1,184,215 . . . . . O 5
Pesqueira 27,864 . . . . . N 5
Petrolina 73,436 . . . . . M 5
Petrópolis 149,427 . . . . . M 8
Picos 33,098 . . . . . M 5
Piracicaba 179,395 . . . . . L 8
Pirapora 31,533 . . . . . L 7
Piripiri 29,497 . . . . . M 4
Poços de Caldas 81,448 . . . . . L 8
Ponta Grossa 171,111 . . . . . K 9
Porto Alegre 1,108,883 . . . . . K 10
Pôrto Esperança 410 . . . . . J 7
Pôrto Nacional 19,052 . . . . . L 6
Porto Seguro 5,007 . . . . . N 7
Porto Velho 101,644 . . . . . H 5
Presidente Epitacio 23,406 . . . K 8
Presidente Prudente 127,623 . K 8
Propriá 19,034 . . . . . N 6
Recife 1,184,215 . . . . . O 5
Ribeirão Preto 300,704 . . . . . L 8
Rio Branco 87,462 . . . . . G 5
Rio de Janeiro †9,018,637 . . . M 8
Rio Grande 124,706 . . . . . K 10
Rio Pardo 18,370 . . . . . K 9
Rio Verde 47,639 . . . . . K 7
Salgueiro 25,915 . . . . . N 5
Salvador 1,496,276 . . . . . N 6
Santa Maria 151,202 . . . . . K 9
Santana do Livramento 58,165 . . . . . K 10
Santarém 101,534 . . . . . J 4
Santo Amaro 29,627 . . . . . N 6
Santo Ângelo 50,161 . . . . . K 9
Santo Antônio do Platina 21,284 . . . . . K 8
Santos 411,023 . . . . . L 8
São Bernardo do Campo 381,261 . . . . . L 8
São Borja 41,598 . . . . . J 9
São Gonçalo 221,278 . . . . . P 13
São João da Bôa Vista 45,712 . . . . . L 8
São João del Rei 53,401 . . . . . M 8
São José do Rio Preto 171,982 . . . . . K 8
São Leopoldo 94,864 . . . . . K 9
São Luís 182,466 . . . . . M 4
São Martinho . . . . . J 5
São Mateus 22,522 . . . . . N 7
São Paulo 7,033,529 . . . . . L 8
Sena Madureira 6,668 . . . . . G 5
Senhor do Bonfim 33,811 . . . . N 6
Serra do Navio 415 . . . . . K 3
Sobral 69,072 . . . . . M 4
Sorocaba 254,718 . . . . . L 8
Taguatinga 480,109 . . . . . L 7
Taubaté 155,371 . . . . . L 8
Tefé 14,670 . . . . . G 4
Teófilo Otoni 83,108 . . . . . M 7
Teresina 339,264 . . . . . M 4
Tocantinópolis 8,427 . . . . . L 5
Três Lagoas 45,171 . . . . . K 8
Tubarão 64,585 . . . . . L 9
Tutóia 4,766 . . . . . M 4
Uaupés . . . . . G 4
Uberaba 180,296 . . . . . L 7
Uberlândia 230,400 . . . . . L 7
União da Vitória 22,682 . . . . . K 9
Uruguaiana 79,059 . . . . . J 9
Vacaria 37,370 . . . . . K 9
Valença 29,904 . . . . . N 6
Varginha 57,448 . . . . . M 8
Vila Velha Argolas 74,166 . . . . N 8
Vitória 144,143 . . . . . N 8
Vitória da Conquista 125,717 . M 6
Volta Redonda 177,772 . . . . . M 8
Xique-Xique 17,625 . . . . . M 6

OTHER FEATURES

Abuná (riv.) . . . . . G 6
Acaraí, Serra do (mts.) . . . . . J 3
Acre (riv.) . . . . . G 6
Amazon (Amazonas) (riv.) . . . . J 4
Apiacas, Serra dos (mts.) . . . . J 6
Araguaia (riv.) . . . . . L 5
Aripuanã (riv.) . . . . . H 5
Bandeira, Pico de (mt.) . . . . . M 8
Braço Maior do Araguaia (riv.) K 6
Braço Menor do Araguaia (riv.) . . . . . K 6
Branco (riv.) . . . . . H 3
Caatingas (for.) . . . . . M 5
Campos (plain) . . . . . M 6
Carajás, Serra dos (mts.) . . . . K 5
Carinhanha (riv.) . . . . . L 6
Caviana (isl.) . . . . . L 3
Corcovado (mt.) . . . . . O 14
Frio (cape) . . . . . M 8
Gradaús, Serra dos (mts.) . . . . L 5
Grande, Rio (riv.) . . . . . L 8
Gurupi, Serra do (mts.) . . . . . L 5
Iguassú (falls) . . . . . K 9
Itaipu (res.) . . . . . K 8
Itapecuru (riv.) . . . . . M 5
Japurá (riv.) . . . . . G 4
Javari (riv.) . . . . . F 4
Jequitinhonha (riv.) . . . . . M 7
Juruá (riv.) . . . . . G 4
Madeira (riv.) . . . . . H 5
Mantiqueira, Serra da (mts.) . . M 8
Mar, Serra de (mts.) . . . . . L 9
Marajó (isl.) . . . . . L 4
Mato Grosso, Planalto de (plat.) . . . . . K 7
Neblina, Pico da (peak) . . . . . G 3
Negro (riv.) . . . . . J 7
Nhamundá (riv.) . . . . . J 4
Oyapock (riv.) . . . . . K 3
Pacaraimã, Serra (mts.) . . . . . H 3
Paraguai (riv.) . . . . . J 7
Parecis, Serra dos (mts.) . . . . . H 6
Parnaíba (riv.) . . . . . M 5
Patos (lag.) . . . . . K 10
Roncador, Serra do (mts.) . . . . K 6
Roosevelt (riv.) . . . . . H 5
Santa Catarina (isl.) . . . . . L 9
São Francisco (riv.) . . . . . N 5
São João de Merití (riv.) . . . . . N 13
São Roque (cape) . . . . . O 5
São Sebastião (isl.) . . . . . M 8
São Tomé (cape) . . . . . M 8
Selvas (for.) . . . . . F-J 5
Sertao (reg.) . . . . . M 5
Solimões (riv.) . . . . . H 4
Tapajós (riv.) . . . . . J 5
Teles Pires (riv.) . . . . . J 5
Tocantins (riv.) . . . . . L 5
Todos-os-Santos (bay) . . . . . N 6
Tumucumaque, Serra (mts.) . . K 3
Urubupunga (dam) . . . . . K 8
Uruguai (riv.) . . . . . K 9
Xingu (riv.) . . . . . K 4

CHILE

CITIES and TOWNS

Antofagasta 125,100 . . . . . F 8
Arauco 5,400 . . . . . F 11
Arica 87,700 . . . . . F 7
Calama 45,900 . . . . . G 8
Calbuco △21,673 . . . . . F 12
Cauquenes 20,200 . . . . . F 11
Cerro Manantiales . . . . . G 14
Chañaral △36,949 . . . . . F 9
Chillán 128,515 . . . . . F 11
Chuquicamata 22,100 . . . . . G 8
Concepción 206,226 . . . . . F 11
Copiapó 45,200 . . . . . F 9
Coquimbo 73,953 . . . . . F 9
Corral △5,533 . . . . . F 11
Curepto △13,020 . . . . . F 11
Illapel 12,200 . . . . . F 10
Iquique 645,000 . . . . . F 8
La Serena 99,908 . . . . . F 9
La Unión 15,200 . . . . . F 12
Linares 37,900 . . . . . F 11
Los Ángeles 49,500 . . . . . F 11
Los Vilos △10,453 . . . . . F 10
Lota 48,100 . . . . . F 11
Maullín △14,544 . . . . . F 12
Mulchén 13,700 . . . . . F 11
Ollagüe . . . . . G 8
Osorno 68,800 . . . . . F 12
Ovalle 31,700 . . . . . F 10
Parral 17,000 . . . . . F 11
Puerto Montt 119,059 . . . . . F 12
Punta Arenas 2,140 . . . . . F 14
Quirihue △11,178 . . . . . F 11
San Fernando 23,600 . . . . . F 10
Santiago (cap.) 3,614,947 . . . F 10
Talca 133,160 . . . . . F 11
Talcahuano 148,300 . . . . . F 11
Tarapacá . . . . . G 7
Temuco 197,232 . . . . . F 11
Tocopilla 22,000 . . . . . F 8
Valdivia 115,536 . . . . . F 11
Vallenar 26,800 . . . . . F 9
Valparaíso 271,580 . . . . . F 10
Villarrica 25,091 . . . . . F 11
Viña del Mar 281,361 . . . . . F 10

OTHER FEATURES

Andes (mts.) . . . . . F 10
Atacama (des.) . . . . . G 8
Chiloé (isl.) 119,286 . . . . . E 12
Corcovado (gulf) . . . . . F 12
Coronados (gulf) . . . . . F 12
Horn (cape) . . . . . G 15
Llullaillaco (vol.) . . . . . G 8

Agriculture, Industry and Resources

MAJOR MINERAL OCCURRENCES

- Al Bauxite
- Ag Silver
- Au Gold
- Be Beryl
- C Coal
- Cr Chromium
- Cu Copper
- D Diamonds
- Em Emeralds
- Fe Iron Ore
- G Natural Gas
- Hg Mercury
- Id Iodine
- Mi Mica
- Mn Manganese
- Mo Molybdenum
- N Nitrates
- Na Salt
- Ni Nickel
- O Petroleum
- P Phosphates
- Pb Lead
- Pt Platinum
- Q Quartz Crystal
- S Sulfur
- Sb Antimony
- Sn Tin
- U Uranium
- V Vanadium
- W Tungsten
- Zn Zinc

- Water Power
- Major Industrial Areas

DOMINANT LAND USE

- Wheat, Livestock
- Wheat, Corn, Livestock
- Cereals, Livestock
- Diversified Tropical Crops (chiefly plantation agriculture)
- Truck Farming, Horticulture, Special Crops
- Upland Cultivated Areas
- Intensive Livestock Ranching
- Upland Livestock Grazing, Limited Agriculture
- Extensive Livestock Ranching
- Forests
- Nonagricultural Land

Loa (riv.) . . . F 8
Magellan (str.) . . . E 14
Maipo (mt.) . . . O 10
Navarino (isl.) . . . G 14
O'Higgins (lake) . . . F 13
Ojos del Salado (mt.) . . . G 9
Penas (gulf) . . . E 13
Taitao (pen.) . . . E 13
Tierra del Fuego (isl.) . . . G 14

COLOMBIA

CITIES and TOWNS

Arauca 7,613 . . . F 2
Barrancabermeja 87,191 . . . F 2
Barranquilla 661,009 . . . F 1
Bogotá (cap.) 2,696,270 . . . F 3
Bolívar . . . E 3
Bucaramanga 291,661 . . . F 2
Buenaventura 115,770 . . . E 3
Buga 71,016 . . . E 3
Cali 898,253 . . . E 3
Cartagena 292,512 . . . E 1
Chiquinquirá 21,727 . . . F 2
Ciénaga 42,546 . . . F 1
Cúcuta 219,772 . . . F 2
El Banco 20,756 . . . F 2
Facatativá 27,892 . . . F 3
Florencia 31,817 . . . E 3
Ibagué 176,223 . . . E 3
Ipiales 30,871 . . . E 3
Leticia 6,285 . . . F 4
Magangué 34,396 . . . E 2
Manizales 199,904 . . . E 2
Medellín 1,070,924 . . . E 2
Mitú 1,637 . . . F 3
Mocoa 6,221 . . . E 3
Montería 89,583 . . . E 2
Neiva 105,476 . . . F 3
Ocaña 38,352 . . . F 2
Palmira 140,481 . . . E 3
Pamplona 31,817 . . . F 2
Pasto 119,339 . . . E 3
Pereira 174,128 . . . E 3
Popayán 77,669 . . . E 3
Puerto Carreño 2,172 . . . G 2
Puerto Wilches 5,282 . . . F 2
Quibdó 28,040 . . . E 2
San Marcos 26,542 . . . E 2
Santa Marta 102,484 . . . F 1
Sincelejo 68,797 . . . E 2
Sogamoso 48,891 . . . F 2
Tuluá 86,736 . . . E 3
Tumaco 38,742 . . . E 3
Tunja 51,620 . . . F 2
Villavicencio 82,869 . . . F 3
Yarumal 21,333 . . . E 2

OTHER FEATURES

Alto Ritacuva (mt.) . . . F 2
Apaporis (riv.) . . . F 3
Arauca (riv.) . . . G 2
Caquetá (riv.) . . . F 4
Casanare (riv.) . . . F 2
Cauca (riv.) . . . E 2
Central, Cordillera (mts.) . . . E 2
Guainía (riv.) . . . G 3
Guajira (pen.) . . . F 1
Guaviare (riv.) . . . F 3
Huila (mt.) . . . E 3
Inírida (riv.) . . . G 3
Magdalena (riv.) . . . F 2
Meta (riv.) . . . G 2
Occidental, Cordillera (mts.) . . . E 3
Oriental, Cordillera (mts.) . . . F 2
Orinoco (riv.) . . . G 2
Putumayo (riv.) . . . F 3
Tolima (mt.) . . . E 3
Vaupés (riv.) . . . F 3
Vichada (riv.) . . . F 3

ECUADOR

CITIES and TOWNS

Ambato 77,955 . . . E 4
Babahoyo 28,914 . . . D 4
Baquerizo Moreno 1,311 . . . D 7
Cuenca 104,470 . . . E 4
Esmeraldas 60,364 . . . D 3
Guayaquil 823,219 . . . D 4
Ibarra 41,335 . . . E 3
Jipijapa 19,996 . . . D 4
Latacunga 21,921 . . . E 4
Loja 47,697 . . . E 4
Macas 1,934 . . . E 4
Machala 69,170 . . . D 4
Manta 64,519 . . . D 4
Pasaje 20,790 . . . E 4
Portoviejo 59,550 . . . D 4
Puerto Villamil . . . D 7
Quito (cap.) 599,828 . . . E 4
Riobamba 58,087 . . . E 4
Santa Elena 7,687 . . . D 4
Santa Rosa 19,696 . . . E 4
Tena . . . E 4
Tulcán 24,398 . . . E 3

OTHER FEATURES

Chimborazo (mt.) . . . E 4
Cotopaxi (mt.) . . . E 4
Guayaquil (gulf) . . . D 4
Morona (riv.) . . . E 4
Napo (riv.) . . . F 4
Occidental, Cordillera (mts.) . . . E 4
Pastaza (riv.) . . . E 4
Real, Cordillera (mts.) . . . E 4
Santiago (riv.) . . . E 4

FALKLAND ISLANDS

CITIES and TOWNS

Stanley (cap.) . . . J 14

OTHER FEATURES

East Falkland (isl.) . . . J 14
Falkland (sound) . . . H 14
West Falkland (isl.) . . . H 14

FRENCH GUIANA

CITIES and TOWNS

Cayenne (cap.) 37,097 . . . K 2
Guisanbourg . . . K 3
Iracoubo 483 . . . K 2
Mana 623 . . . K 2
Saint-Georges 921 . . . K 3
St-Laurent du Maroni 5,042 . . . K 2

OTHER FEATURES

Devils (isl.) . . . K 2
Maroni (riv.) . . . K 3
Oyapock (riv.) . . . K 3

GUYANA

CITIES and TOWNS

Corriverton ●10,502 . . . J 2
Georgetown (cap.) 63,184 . . . J 2
Morawhanna ●292 . . . J 2
New Amsterdam 17,782 . . . J 2

OTHER FEATURES

Courantyne (riv.) . . . J 3
Cuyuni (riv.) . . . H 2
Essequibo (riv.) . . . J 2
Kaieteur (falls) . . . J 3
Mazaruni (riv.) . . . H 2
Roraima (mt.) . . . H 2
Rupununi (riv.) . . . J 3

PARAGUAY

CITIES and TOWNS

Asunción (cap.) 387,676 . . . J 9
Concepción 19,392 . . . J 8
Encarnación 23,343 . . . J 9
Fuerte Olimpo 3,063 . . . J 8
Mariscal Estigarribia 3,150 . . . H 8
Puerto Casado 4,078 . . . J 8
Puerto Guaraní 302 . . . J 8
Puerto Sastre 160 . . . J 8
Villarrica 17,687 . . . J 9

OTHER FEATURES

Gran Chaco (reg.) . . . H 8
Itaipu (res.) . . . K 8
Paraguay (riv.) . . . J 8
Paraná (riv.) . . . K 9
Pilcomayo (riv.) . . . H 8

PERU

CITIES and TOWNS

Arequipa 447,431 . . . F 7
Ayacucho 68,535 . . . F 6
Cajamarca 60,280 . . . E 5
Callao 441,374 . . . E 6
Cañete 15,277 . . . E 6
Catacaos 30,927 . . . D 5
Cerro de Pasco 71,558 . . . E 6
Chiclayo 280,244 . . . E 5
Chimbote 216,406 . . . E 5
Chincha Alta 37,475 . . . E 6
Coracora 4,598 . . . F 7
Cusco 181,604 . . . F 6
Huacho 43,402 . . . E 6
Huancavelica 20,889 . . . E 6
Huancayo 165,132 . . . F 6
Huánuco 52,628 . . . E 6
Huaráz 45,116 . . . E 5
Ica 111,087 . . . E 6
Ilo 31,549 . . . F 7
Iquitos 173,629 . . . F 4
Jauja 14,630 . . . E 6
Juliaca 77,976 . . . F 7
La Oroya 33,305 . . . E 6
Lima (cap.) 375,957 . . . E 6
Machupicchu 544 . . . F 6
Matarani . . . F 7
Mollendo 21,206 . . . F 7
Moquegua 21,488 . . . F 7
Nazca 22,756 . . . F 6
Pacasmayo 17,588 . . . D 5
Paita 18,749 . . . D 5
Pisco 53,414 . . . E 6
Piura 186,354 . . . D 5
Pucallpa 91,953 . . . E 5
Puerto Maldonado 12,609 . . . G 6
Puno 66,477 . . . F 7
Sullana 80,947 . . . D 4
Supe 10,061 . . . E 6
Tacna 92,862 . . . F 7
Talara 55,122 . . . D 4
Tarma 34,369 . . . E 6
Trujillo 354,557 . . . E 5
Tumbes 48,187 . . . D 4

OTHER FEATURES

Aguja (pt.) . . . D 5
Altiplano (plat.) . . . F 7
Apurímac (riv.) . . . F 6
Central, Cordillera (mts.) . . . E 5
Huascarán (mt.) . . . E 5
Madre de Dios (riv.) . . . G 6
Marañón (riv.) . . . E 4
Misti, El (mt.) . . . F 7
Montaña, La (reg.) . . . F 5
Napo (riv.) . . . F 4
Occidental, Cordillera (mts.) . . . F 6
Oriental, Cordillera (mts.) . . . E 5
Paracas (pen.) . . . E 6
Putumayo (riv.) . . . F 4
Real, Cordillera (mts.) . . . F 6
Sechura (bay) . . . D 5
Titicaca (lake) . . . F 7
Ucayali (riv.) . . . E 5
Urubamba (riv.) . . . F 6
Vilcanota (mt.) . . . F 6

SURINAME

CITIES and TOWNS

Albina 1,000 . . . K 3
Groningen 600 . . . J 2
Moengo 2,100 . . . K 3
Nieuw-Nickerie 7,400 . . . J 2
Paramaribo (cap.) ●67,905 . . . K 2
Totness 1,300 . . . J 2

OTHER FEATURES

Coeroeni (riv.) . . . J 3
Tapanahoni (riv.) . . . J 3

URUGUAY

CITIES and TOWNS

Artigas 29,256 . . . J 10
Canelones 15,938 . . . J 10
Colonia 16,895 . . . J 10
Durazno 25,811 . . . J 10
Florida 25,030 . . . J 10
Fray Bentos 19,569 . . . J 10
Maldonado 22,159 . . . K 11
Melo 38,260 . . . K 10
Mercedes 34,667 . . . J 10
Minas 35,433 . . . K 10
Montevideo (cap.) 1,173,254 . . . J 11
Paysandú 62,412 . . . J 10
Rivera 49,013 . . . J 10
Rocha 21,612 . . . K 10
Salto 72,948 . . . J 10
San José 28,427 . . . J 10
Tacuarembó 34,152 . . . J 10
Treinta y Tres 25,757 . . . K 10
Trinidad 17,598 . . . J 10

OTHER FEATURES

Mirim (lag.) . . . K 10
Negro (riv.) . . . J 10
Plata, Río de la (est.) . . . J 11
Uruguay (riv.) . . . J 9

VENEZUELA

CITIES and TOWNS

Barcelona 78,201 . . . H 2
Barinas 56,329 . . . G 2
Barquisimeto 330,815 . . . F 2
Bruzual 941 . . . G 2
Calabozo 37,282 . . . G 2
Caracas (cap.) 1,035,499 . . . G 1
Carora 36,115 . . . F 1
Carúpano 50,935 . . . H 1
Ciudad Bolívar 103,728 . . . H 2
Ciudad Piar 3,965 . . . H 2
Coro 68,701 . . . G 1
Cumaná 119,751 . . . H 1
El Tigre 49,801 . . . H 2
El Tocuyo 19,351 . . . G 2
Guanare 34,148 . . . G 2
La Guaira 20,344 . . . G 1
Los Teques 63,106 . . . G 1
Maracaibo 651,574 . . . F 1
Maracay 255,134 . . . G 1
Maturín 98,188 . . . H 2
Mérida 74,214 . . . F 2
Puerto Ayacucho 10,417 . . . G 2
Puerto Cabello 72,103 . . . G 1
Puerto La Cruz 63,276 . . . H 1
San Carlos 21,029 . . . G 2
San Cristóbal 151,717 . . . F 2
San Felipe 43,801 . . . G 1
San Fernando 38,960 . . . G 2
Trujillo 25,921 . . . F 2
Tucacas 4,780 . . . G 1
Tucupita 21,417 . . . H 2
Valencia 367,171 . . . G 2
Valera 76,740 . . . F 2
Valle de la Pascua 36,809 . . . G 2
Villa de Cura 27,832 . . . G 2

OTHER FEATURES

Angel (fall) . . . H 2
Arauca (riv.) . . . G 2
Apure (riv.) . . . F 2
Bolívar (mt.) . . . F 2
Caroní (riv.) . . . H 3
Casiquiare, Brazo (riv.) . . . G 3
Maracaibo (lake) . . . F 2
Margarita (isl.) . . . H 1
Mérida (mts.) . . . F 2
Orinoco (riv.) . . . G 2
Paraguana (pen.) . . . F 1
Paria (gulf) . . . H 1
Serpents Mouth (str.) . . . H 2
Tortuga, La (isl.) . . . G 1
Venezuela (gulf) . . . F 1

*City and suburb.
†Population of metropolitan area.
△Population of commune.
●Population of district, sub-district or division.

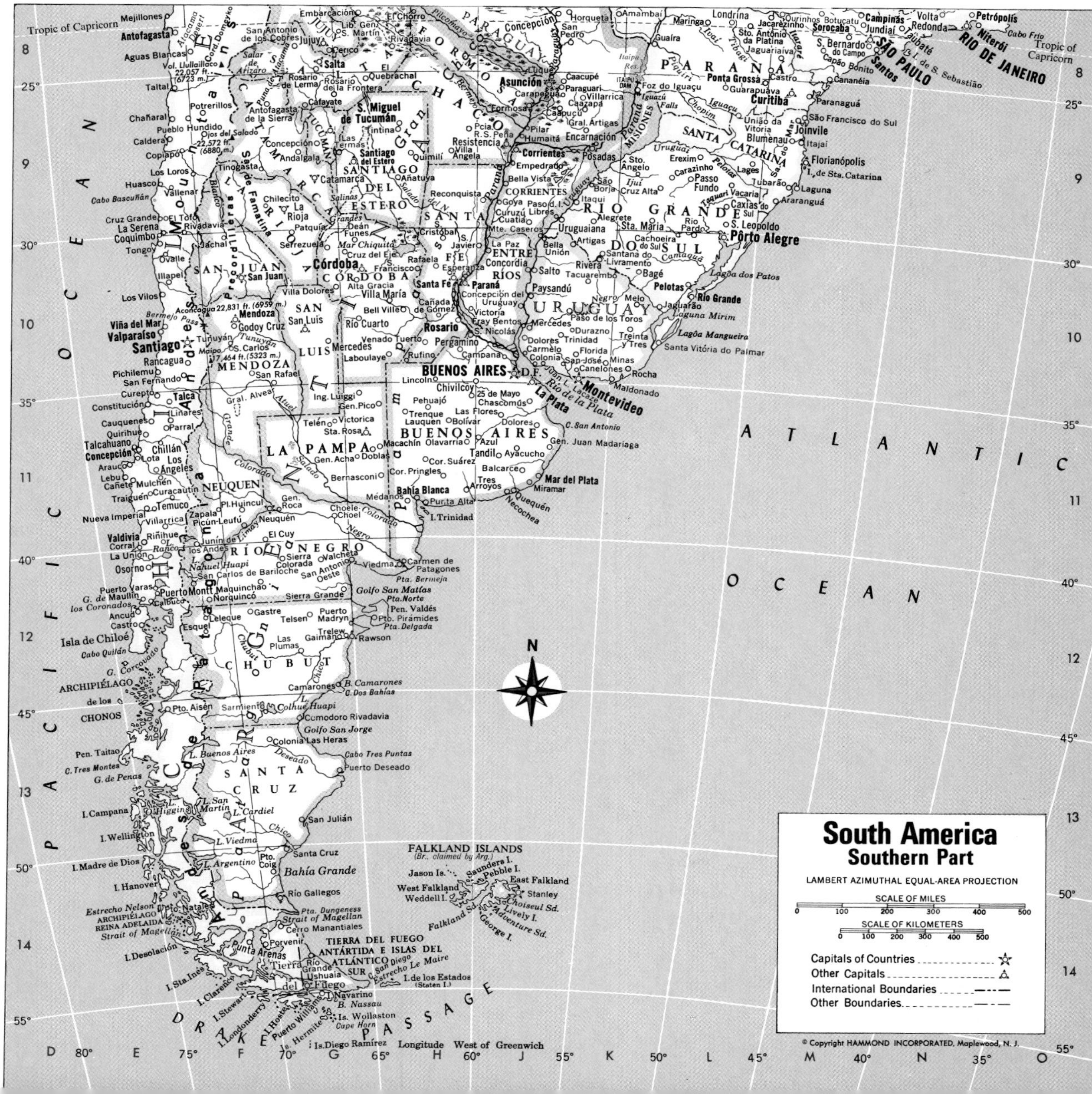

North America
LAMBERT AZIMUTHAL EQUAL-AREA PROJECTION
MILES
0 100 200 400 600 800
KILOMETERS
0 100 200 400 600 800
Capitals of Countries
Other Capitals
International Boundaries
Other Boundaries
© Copyright HAMMOND INCORPORATED, Maplewood, N. J.
Longitude West 90° of Greenwich
ARCTIC OCEAN
ATLANTIC OCEAN
PACIFIC OCEAN
NORTH POLE
GREENLAND SEA
NORWEGIAN SEA
EAST SIBERIAN SEA
CHUKCHI SEA
BERING SEA
BEAUFORT SEA
LABRADOR SEA
CARIBBEAN SEA
Gulf of Mexico
Gulf of Alaska
Hudson Bay
Baffin Bay
ASIA
U.S.S.R.
EUROPE
NORWAY
UNITED KINGDOM
SCOTLAND
ICELAND
GREENLAND
(KALAALLIT NUNAAT)
(Den.)
CANADA
NORTHWEST TERRITORIES
YUKON TERRITORY
BRITISH COLUMBIA
ALBERTA
SASKATCHEWAN
MANITOBA
ONTARIO
QUEBEC
NEWFOUNDLAND
UNITED STATES
ALASKA
MEXICO
WEST INDIES
BAHAMAS
CUBA
JAMAICA
HAITI
DOMINICAN REP.
PUERTO RICO
BELIZE
GUATEMALA
HONDURAS
EL SALVADOR
NICARAGUA
COSTA RICA
PANAMA
SOUTH AMERICA
COLOMBIA
VENEZUELA
ECUADOR
PERU
BRAZIL
BOLIVIA
Tropic of Cancer
Arctic Circle
Equator

Population Distribution

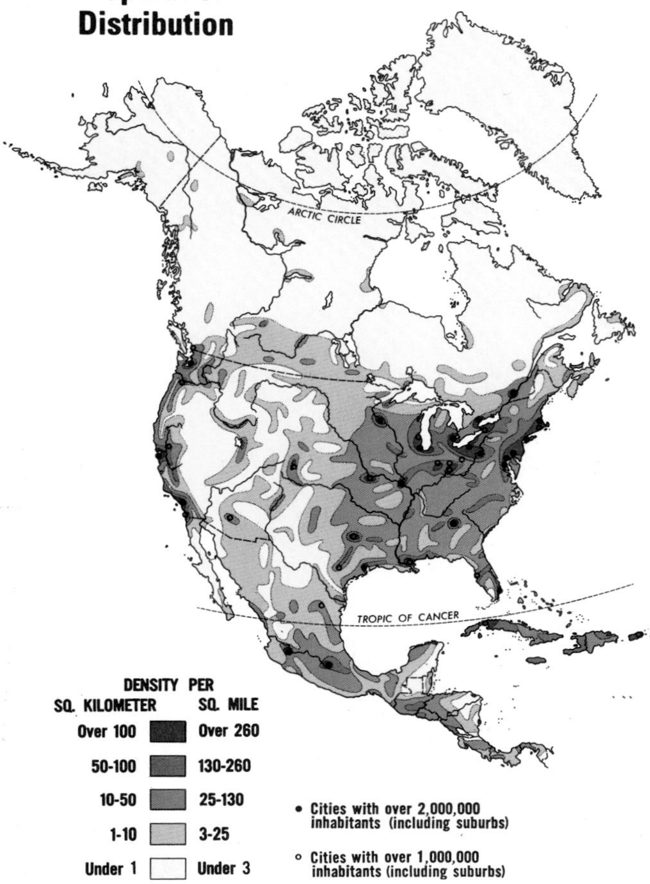

AREA 9,363,000 sq. mi.
(24,250,170 sq. km.)
POPULATION 370,000,000
LARGEST CITY New York
HIGHEST POINT Mt. McKinley 20,320 ft.
(6,194 m.)
LOWEST POINT Death Valley -282 ft.
(-86 m.)

Vegetation

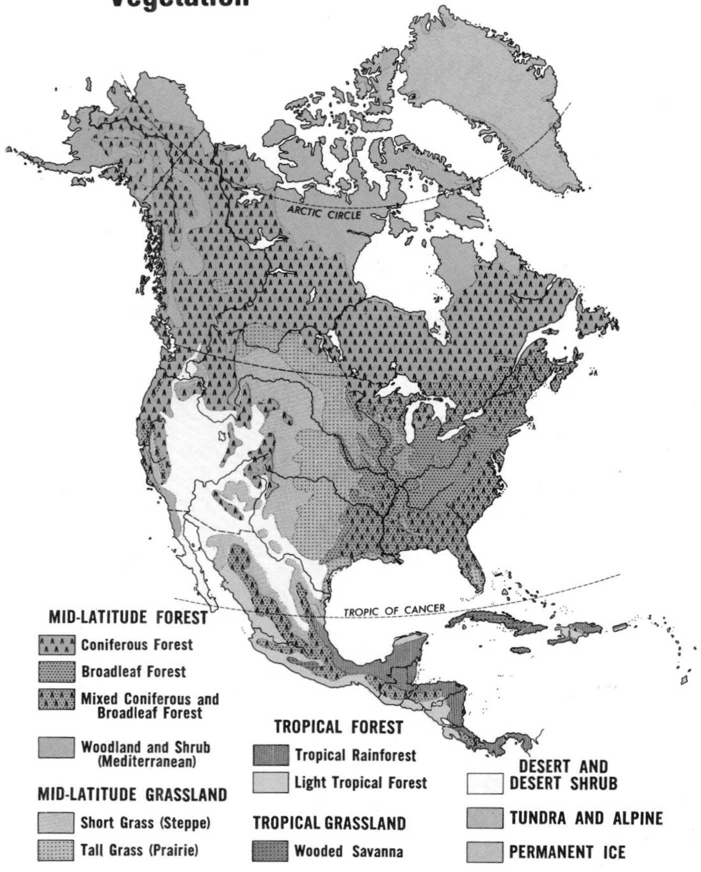

Acapulco de Juárez, Mex. H 8
Alaska (pen.), Alaska C 4
Albany (cap.), N.Y. L 5
Albuquerque, N. Mex. H 6
Amarillo, Texas H 6
Anchorage, Alaska D 3
Antigua (isl.) M 8
Arctic (ocean) B 2
Arkansas (riv.), U.S. J 6
Athabasca (lake), Can. H 4
Atlanta (cap.), Ga. K 6
Augusta (cap.), Maine M 5
Austin (cap.), Texas J 6
Baffin (isl.), N.W.T. L 2
Bahamas L 7
Baltimore, Md. L 6
Barbados N 8
Barrow (pt.), Alaska C 2
Baton Rouge (cap.), La. J 6
Beaufort (sea) D 2
Belize K 8
Belmopan (cap.), Belize K 8
Bering (str.) B 3
Bermuda (isls.) M 6
Birmingham, Ala. K 6
Bismarck (cap.), N. Dak. H 5
Boise (cap.), Idaho G 5
Boston (cap.), Mass. L 5
Buffalo, N.Y. L 5
Calgary (cap.), Alta. G 4
California (gulf), Mex. G 7
Canada G 4
Canaveral (cape), Fla. L 7
Caribbean (sea) K 8
Carson City (cap.), Nev. G 6
Cascade (range), U.S. F 5
Charleston, S.C. L 6
Charleston (cap.), W. Va. K 6
Charlotte, N.C. K 6
Charlottetown (cap.), P.E.I. M 5
Chattanooga, Tenn. K 6
Cheyenne (cap.), Wyo. H 5
Chicago, Ill. K 5
Chihuahua, Mex. H 7
Cincinnati, Ohio K 6
Ciudad Juárez, Mex. H 6
Cleveland, Ohio K 5
Clipperton (isl.) H 8
Coast (ranges), U.S. F 5
Cocos (isl.), C. Rica K 9
Cod (cape), Mass. M 5
Colorado (riv.), U.S. G 6
Columbia (cap.), S.C. K 6
Columbia (riv.), U.S. F 5
Columbus (cap.), Ohio K 6
Concord (cap.), N.H. L 5
Costa Rica K 8
Cuba L 7
Dallas, Texas J 6
Denver (cap.), Colo. H 6
Des Moines (cap.), Iowa J 5
Detroit, Mich. K 5
Dominica M 8
Dominican Republic L 8
Dover (cap.), Del. L 6
Duluth, Minn. J 5
Edmonton, Alta. G 4
Ellesmere (isl.), N.W.T. K 1
El Paso, Texas H 6
El Salvador J 8
Erie (lake) K 5
Fairbanks, Alaska D 3
Farewell (cape), Greenl. P 4
Florida (strs.) K 7
Fort Worth, Texas J 6
Frankfort (cap.), Ky. K 6
Fraser (riv.), Br. Col. F 4
Fredericton, N. Br. M 5
Fresno, Calif. G 6
Godthåb (Nuuk) (cap.), Greenl. N 3
Grand Bahama (isl.), Bahamas L 7
Grand Rapids, Mich. K 5
Great Bear (lake), N.W.T. F 3
Greater Antilles (isls.) K 7
Great Falls, Mont. G 5
Great Salt (lake), Utah G 6
Great Slave (lake), N.W.T. H 3
Greenland P 2
Greenland (sea) T 2
Grenada M 8
Guadalajara, Mex. H 7
Guadeloupe (isl.) M 8
Guantánamo, Cuba L 7
Guatemala J 8
Guatemala (cap.), Guat. J 8
Haiti L 8
Halifax (cap.), N.S. M 5
Hamilton, Ont. K 5
Harrisburg (cap.), Pa. L 5
Hartford (cap.), Conn. L 5
Hatteras (cape), N.C. L 6
Havana (cap.), Cuba K 7
Helena (cap.), Mont. G 5
Hispaniola (isl.) L 7
Honduras K 8
Houston, Texas J 7
Hudson (bay), Can. K 3
Huron (lake) K 5
Indianapolis (cap.), Ind. K 5
Inuvik, N.W.T. E 3
Jackson (cap.), Miss. K 6
Jacksonville, Fla. K 6
Jamaica L 8
James (bay), Can. K 4
Jefferson City (cap.), Mo. J 6
Juan de Fuca (str.) F 5
Julianehåb (Qaqortoq), Greenl. P 3
Juneau, Alaska E 4
Kansas City, Mo. J 6
Ketchikan, Alaska E 4
Key West, Fla. K 7
Kingston (cap.), Jamaica L 8
Knoxville, Tenn. K 6
Kodiak (isl.), Alaska C 4
Labrador (reg.), Newf. M 4
Lansing (cap.), Mich. K 5
Lesser Antilles (isls.) M 8
Lincoln (cap.), Nebr. J 5
Little Rock (cap.), Ark. J 6
London, Ont. K 5
Los Angeles, Calif. G 6
Louisville, Ky. K 6
Lower California (pen.), Mex. G 7
Mackenzie (riv.), N.W.T. F 3
Macon, Ga. K 6
Madison (cap.), Wis. K 5
Managua (cap.), Nic. K 8
Manitoba (lake), Man. H 4
Martinique (isl.) M 8
Mazatlán, Mex. H 7
McKinley (mt.), Alaska C 3
Mead (lake), U.S. G 6
Medicine Hat, Alta. H 4
Memphis, Tenn. K 6
Mendocino (cape), Calif. F 5
Mérida, Mex. J 7
Mexico H 7
Mexico (gulf) K 7
Mexico City (cap.), Mex. J 7
Miami, Fla. K 7
Michigan (lake), U.S. K 5
Milwaukee, Wis. K 5
Minneapolis, Wis. J 5
Mississippi (riv.), U.S. J 6
Missouri (riv.) J 5
Mobile, Ala. K 6
Monterrey, Mex. J 7
Montgomery (cap.), Ala. K 6
Montpelier (cap.), Vt. L 5
Montréal, Que. L 5
Moose Jaw, Sask. H 4
Nares (str.) L 2
Nashville (cap.), Tenn. K 6
Nassau (cap.), Bahamas L 7
Nelson (riv.), Man. J 4
Netherlands Antilles M 8
Newfoundland (isl.), Can. M 4
New Orleans, La. K 7
New York, N.Y. L 5
Nicaragua K 8
Nome, Alaska B 3
Norfolk, Va. L 6
North Bay, Ont. L 5
North Saskatchewan (riv.), Can. G 4
Nuuk (cap.), Greenl. N 3
Oakland, Calif. F 6
Oaxaca, Mex. J 8
Ohio (riv.), U.S. K 6
Oklahoma City (cap.), Okla. J 6
Olympia (cap.), Wash. F 5
Omaha, Nebr. J 5
Ontario (lake) L 5
Ottawa (cap.), Can. L 5
Panama K 9
Panama (canal), Pan. L 8
Panamá (cap.), Pan. L 9
Parry (chan.), N.W.T. G 2
Peace (riv.), Can. G 4
Pensacola, Fla. K 6
Philadelphia, Pa. L 6
Phoenix (cap.), Ariz. G 6
Pierre (cap.), S. Dak. J 5
Pittsburgh, Pa. K 5
Port-au-Prince (cap.), Haiti L 8
Portland, Maine M 5
Portland, Oreg. F 5
Providence (cap.), R.I. L 5
Prudhoe (bay), Alaska D 2
Puebla, Mex. J 8
Puerto Rico M 8
Qaanaaq, Greenl. M 2
Quebec (cap.), Que. L 5
Queen Charlotte (isls.), Br. Col. E 4
Queen Elizabeth (isls.), N.W.T. G 2
Raleigh (cap.), N.C. L 6
Red (riv.) J 5
Red (riv.), U.S. J 6
Regina (cap.), Sask. H 4
Reno, Nev. G 6
Richmond (cap.), Va. L 6
Rio Grande (riv.) H 7
Rochester, N.Y. L 5
Rocky (mts.) F 4
Sable (cape), N.S. M 5
Sacramento (cap.), Calif. F 6
Saint Augustine, Fla. K 7
Saint John (cap.), N. Br. M 5
St. John's (cap.), Newf. N 5
Saint Kitts and Nevis M8
Saint Lawrence (gulf) M 5
Saint Lawrence (riv.) L 5
Saint Louis, Mo. K 6
Saint Lucia M 8
Saint Paul (cap.), Minn. J 5
Saint Pierre and Miquelon (isls.) N 5
Saint Vincent and The Grenadines M 8
Salem (cap.), Oreg. F 5
Salt Lake City (cap.), Utah G 6
Saltillo, Mex. H 7
San Antonio, Texas J 7
San Diego, Calif. G 6
San Francisco, Calif. F 6
San José (cap.), C. Rica K 9
San Juan (cap.), P. Rico M 8
San Salvador (cap.), El Salv. J 8
Santa Fe (cap.), N. Mex. H 6
Santiago de Cuba, Cuba L 8
Santo Domingo (cap.), Dom. Rep. L 8
Saskatoon, Sask. H 4
Sault Ste. Marie, Ont. K 5
Savannah, Ga. K 6
Seattle, Wash. F 5
Shreveport, La. J 6
Sierra Madre Occidental (mts.), Mex. H 7
Sierra Nevada (range), Calif. F 6
Sioux City, Iowa J 5
Sioux Falls, S. Dak. J 5
Snake (riv.), U.S. G 5
South Platte (riv.), U.S. H 6
South Saskatchewan (riv.), Can. G 4
Springfield (cap.), Ill. J 6
Sudbury, Ont. K 5
Superior (lake) K 5
Sverdrup (isls.), N.W.T. J 2
Tacoma, Wash. F 5
Tallahassee (cap.), Fla. K 6
Tampa, Fla. K 7
Tampico, Mex. J 7
Tegucigalpa (cap.), Hond. K 8
Thule (Qaanaaq), Greenl. M 2
Thunder Bay, Ont. K 5
Toledo, Ohio K 5
Topeka (cap.), Kansas J 6
Toronto (cap.), Ont. K 5
Trenton (cap.), N.J. L 5
Trinidad and Tobago N 8
Tucson, Ariz. G 6
Tulsa, Okla. J 6
United States H 5
Vancouver, Br. Col. F 4
Vancouver (isl.), Br. Col. F 5
Veracruz, Mex. J 8
Victoria (cap.), Br. Col. F 5
Victoria (isl.), N.W.T. G 2
Virgin Islands (isls.) M 8
Washington, D.C. (cap.), U.S. L 6
West Indies (isls.) M 7
Whitehorse (cap.), Yukon E 3
Wichita, Kansas J 6
Windward (passg.) L 8
Winnipeg (cap.), Man. J 5
Woods (lake) J 5
Yellowknife, N.W.T. G 3
Yucatán (pen.), Mex. K 7
Yukon (riv.) C 3

Abitibi (lake), Ont. H 6
Aklavik, N.W.T. 721 C 2
Albany (riv.), Ont. H 5
Alberta (prov.) 2,237,724 E 5
Amherst, N.S. 9,684 K 6
Amos, Que. 9,421 J 6
Anticosti (isl.), Que. K 6
Athabasca (lake) F 4
Athabasca (riv.), Alta. E 4
Axel Heiburg (isl.), N.W.T. N 3
Baffin (reg.), N.W.T. 8,300 G 1
Baffin (bay), N.W.T. J 1
Baffin (isl.), N.W.T. J 1
Baker Lake, N.W.T. 954 G 3
Banff Nat'l Park, Alta. E 5
Banks (isl.), N.W.T. D 1
Bathurst, N. Br. 15,705 K 6
Belle Isle (str.), Newf. L 5
Bonavista, Newf. 4,460 L 6
Boothia (pen.), N.W.T. G 1
Brandon, Man. 36,242 F 6
British Columbia (prov.) 2,744,467 D 4
Cabot (str.) K 6
Calgary, Alta. 592,743 E 5
Cambridge Bay, N.W.T. 815 F 2
Campbellton, N. Br. 9,818 K 6
Camrose, Alta. 12,570 E 5
Cape Breton (isl.), N.S. K 6
Cartwright, Newf. 658 L 5
Channel-Port aux Basques, Newf. 5,988 L 6
Charlottetown (cap.), P.E.I. 15,282 K 6
Chatham, N. Br. 6,779 K 6
Chesterfield Inlet, N.W.T. 249 G 3
Chibougamau, Que. 10,732 J 6
Chicoutimi, Que. 60,064 J 6
Chidley (cape), Newf. K 3
Chilliwack, Br. Col. ○40,642 D 6
Churchill, Man. 1,186 G 4
Coast (mts.) C 4
Coppermine, N.W.T. 809 E 2
Corner Brook, Newf. 24,339 K 6
Cornwall, Ont. 46,144 J 7
Cranbrook, Br. Col. 15,915 E 6
Cree (lake), Sask. F 4
Dartmouth, N.S. 62,277 K 7
Dauphin, Man. 8,971 F 5
Davis (str.), N.W.T. K 1
Dawson, Yukon 697 C 3
Devon (isl.), N.W.T. M 3
Drumheller, Alta. 6,508 E 5
Edmonton (cap.), Alta. 532,246 E 5
Edmundston, N. Br. 12,044 K 6
Ellesmere (isl.), N.W.T. N 3
Eskimo Point, N.W.T. 1,022 G 3
Estevan, Sask. 9,174 F 6
Finlay (riv.), Br. Col. D 4
Flin Flon, Man.-Sask. 8,261 F 4
Fogo (isl.), Newf. L 6
Fort-Chimo, Que. K 4
Fort Frances, Ont. 8,906 G 6
Fort Franklin, N.W.T. 521 D 3
Fort-George, Que. 2,222 J 5
Fort McMurray, Alta. 31,000 E 4
Fort McPherson, N.W.T. 632 C 2
Fort Nelson, Br. Col. 3,724 D 4
Fort Providence, N.W.T. 605 E 3
Fort Saskatchewan, Alta. 12,169 E 5
Fort Simpson, N.W.T. 980 D 3
Fort Smith (reg.), N.W.T. 22,384 E 3
Fort Smith, N.W.T. 2,298 E 3
Foxe (basin), N.W.T. J 2
Franklin (dist.), N.W.T. H 1
Fraser (riv.), Br. Col. D 5
Fredericton, N. Br. 43,723 K 6
Frobisher Bay, N.W.T. 2,333 K 3
Fundy (bay) K 7
Gander, Newf. 10,404 L 6
Gaspé, Que. 17,261 K 6
Georgian (bay), Ont. H 6
Geraldton, Ont. 2,956 H 6
Glace Bay, N.S. 21,466 L 6
Goose Bay, Newf. 7,103 K 5
Gouin (res.), Que. J 6
Grand Falls, Newf. 8,765 L 6
Grande Prairie, Alta. 24,263 E 4
Great Bear (lake), N.W.T. D 2
Great Slave (lake), N.W.T. E 3
Guelph, Ont. 71,207 H 7
Halifax (cap.), N.S. 114,594 K 7
Hamilton, Ont. 306,434 H 7
Harbour Grace, Newf. 2,988 L 6
Havre-St-Pierre, Que. 3,200 K 5
Hay River, N.W.T. 2,863 E 3
Hearst, Ont. 5,533 H 6
Hecate (str.), Br. Col. C 5
Hull, Que. 56,225 J 6
Inuvik (reg.), N.W.T. 7,485 D 2
Inuvik, N.W.T. 3,147 C 2
Iroquois Falls, Ont. 6,339 H 6
Jasper Nat'l Park, Alta. E 5
Jonquière, Que. 60,354 J 6
Juan de Fuca (str.), Br. Col. D 6
Kamloops, Br. Col. 64,048 D 5
Kane (basin), N.W.T. N 3
Kapuskasing, Ont. 12,014 H 6
Keewatin (reg.), N.W.T. 4,327 G 2
Kelowna, Br. Col. 59,196 E 6
Kenora, Ont. 9,817 G 5
Kingston, Ont. 52,616 J 7
Kirkland Lake, Ont. 12,219 H 6
Kitikmeot (reg.), N.W.T. 3,245 F 1
Kitimat, Br. Col. 12,462 D 5
Kluane (lake), Yukon C 3
Kootenay (lake), Br. Col. E 5
Labrador (reg.), Newf. K 4
Lacombe, Alta. 5,591 E 5
Lake Harbour, N.W.T. 252 J 3
Lake Louise, Alta. 355 E 5
Lancaster (sound), N.W.T. H 1
Leduc, Alta. 12,471 E 5
Lesser Slave (lake), Alta. E 4
Lethbridge, Alta. 54,072 E 6
Liard (riv.) D 3
Lloydminster, Alta.-Sask. 15,031 E 5
Logan (mt.), Yukon B 3
London, Ont. 254,280 H 7
Lunenburg, N.S. 3,014 K 7
Mackenzie (dist.), N.W.T. E 3
Mackenzie (riv.), N.W.T. C 2
Magdalen (isls.), Que. K 6
Manicouagan (riv.), Que. K 5
Manitoba (lake), Man. G 5
Manitoba (prov.) 1,026,241 G 5
Manitoulin (isl.), Ont. H 6
Maple Creek, Sask. 2,470 F 6
Marathon, Ont. 2,271 H 6
Mayo, Yukon 398 C 3
M'Clintock (chan.), N.W.T. F 1
Medicine Hat, Alta. 40,380 E 5
Melville, Sask. 5,092 F 5
Melville (isl.), N.W.T. E 1
Merritt, Br. Col. 6,110 D 5
Minto (lake), Que. J 4
Mistassibi (riv.), Que. J 5
Mistassini (lake), Que. J 5
Moncton, N. Br. 54,743 K 6
Mont-Joli, Que. 6,359 K 6
Mont-Laurier, Que. 8,405 J 6
Montréal, Que. 980,354 J 7
Moose Jaw, Sask. 33,941 F 6
Moosomin, Sask. 2,579 F 5
Moosonee, Ont. 1,433 H 5
Morden, Man. 4,579 G 6
Nain, Newf. 938 K 4
Nanaimo, Br. Col. 47,069 D 6
Nares (str.), N.W.T. N 3
Nelson, Br. Col. 9,143 E 6
Nelson (riv.), Man. G 4
New Brunswick (prov.) 696,423 K
Newfoundland (isl.) L 6
Newfoundland (prov.) 567,681 L 5
New Westminster, Br. Col. 38,550 D 6
Niagara Falls, Ont. 70,960 J 7
Norman Wells, N.W.T. 420 D 2
North Battleford, Sask. 14,030 F 5
North Bay, Ont. 51,268 J 6
North Magnetic Pole F 1
North Saskatchewan (riv.) E 5
N. Vancouver, Br. Col. 33,952 D 6
Northwest Territories 45,741 E 2
Nova Scotia (prov.) 847,422 K 7
Okanagan (lake), Br. Col. D 6
Ontario (prov.) 8,625,107 H 5
Ottawa (cap.), Canada 295,163 J 6
Ottawa (riv.) J 6
Owen Sound, Ont. 19,883 H 7
Pangnirtung, N.W.T. 839 K 2
Parry (chan.), N.W.T. E-H 1
Parry Sound, Ont. 6,124 J 6
Peace (riv.), Alta. E 4
Peace River, Alta. 5,907 E 4
Peel (riv.) C 2
Pelly (riv.), Yukon C 3
Pembroke, Ont. 14,026 J 6
Péribonca (riv.), Que. J 5
Peterborough, Ont. 60,620 J 7
Pond Inlet, N.W.T. 705 J 1
Portage la Prairie, Man. 13,086 G 5
Port Radium, N.W.T. 56 E 2
Poste-de-la-Baleine, Que. 435 J 4
Povungnituk, Que. J 3
Prince Albert, Sask. 31,380 F 5
Prince Albert Nat'l Park, Sask. F 5
Prince Edward Island (prov.) 122,506 K 6
Prince George, Br. Col. 67,559 D 5
Prince Patrick (isl.), N.W.T. M 3
Prince Rupert, Br. Col. 16,197 C 5
Québec (prov.) 6,438,403 J 5
Québec (cap.), Que. 166,474 J 6
Queen Charlotte (isls.), Br. Col. C 5
Queen Elizabeth (isls.), N.W.T. M 3
Quesnel, Br. Col. 8,240 D 5
Race (cape), Newf. L 6
Rainy (lake), Ont. G 6
Rainy River, Ont. 1,061 G 6
Rankin Inlet, N.W.T. 1,109 G 3
Ray (cape), Newf. K 6
Red Deer, Alta. 46,393 E 5
Regina (cap.), Sask. 162,613 F 5
Reindeer (lake) F 4
Revelstoke, Br. Col. 5,544 E 5
Riding Mountain Nat'l Park, Man. F 5
Rimouski, Que. 29,120 K 6
Rivière-du-Loup, Que. 13,459 K 6
Roberval, Que. 11,429 J 6
Robson (mt.), Br. Col. D 5
Rocky (mts.) D 4
Rocky Mountain House, Alta. 4,698 E 5
Rouyn, Que. 17,224 J 6
Sable (cape), N.S. K 7
Sable (isl.), N.S. L 7
Saint Elias (mt.), Yukon B 3
Saint John, N. Br. 80,521 K 6
St. John's (cap.), Newf. 83,770 L 6
Saint Lawrence (riv.) K 6

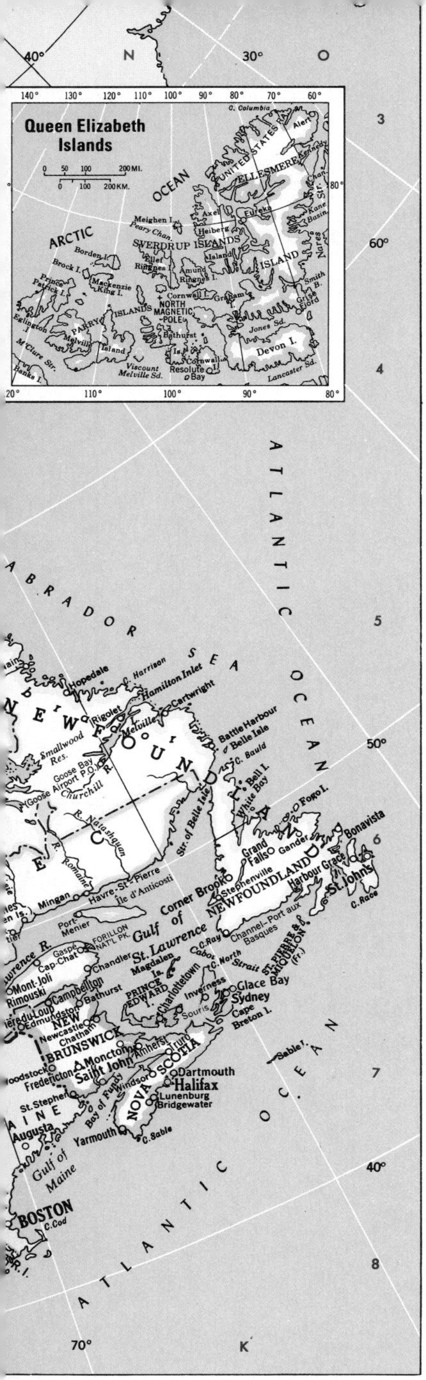

AREA 3,851,787 sq. mi. (9,976,139 sq. km.)
POPULATION 24,343,181
CAPITAL Ottawa
LARGEST CITY Montréal
HIGHEST POINT Mt. Logan 19,524 ft. (5,951 m.)
MONETARY UNIT Canadian dollar
MAJOR LANGUAGES English, French
MAJOR RELIGIONS Protestantism, Roman Catholicism

Population Distribution

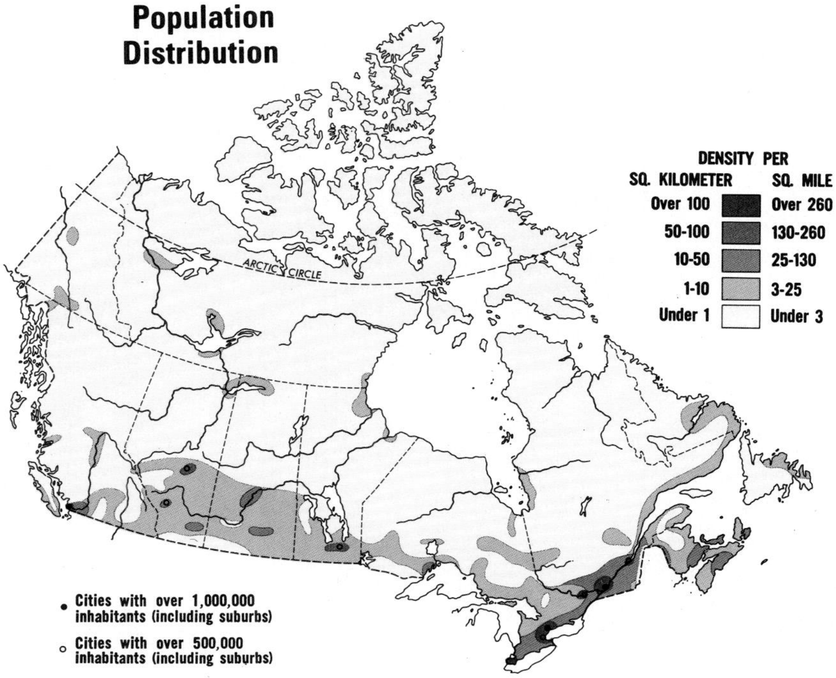

Vegetation

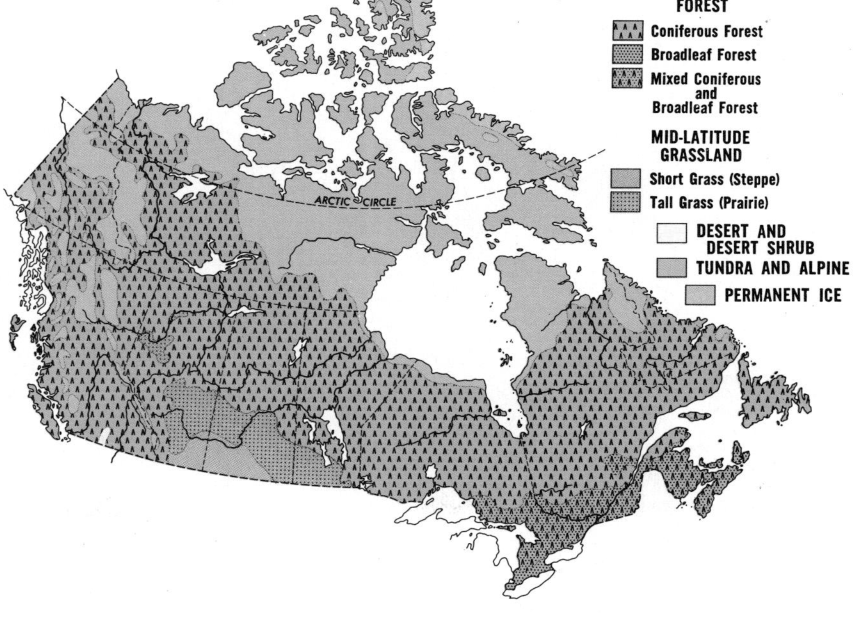

Saint Pierre & Miquelon (isls.) 6,041 .... L 6
Sarnia, Ont. 50,892 .... H 7
Saskatchewan (prov.) 968,313 F 5
Saskatchewan (riv.) .... F 5
Saskatoon, Sask. 154,210 .... F 5
Sault Sainte Marie, Ont. 82,697 .... H 6
Schefferville, Que. 1,997 .... K 5
Selkirk, Man. 10,037 .... G 5
Sept-Îles (Seven Is.), Que. 29,262 .... K 5
Shawinigan, Que. 23,011 .... J 6
Sherbrooke, Que. 74,075 .... J 7
Sioux Lookout, Ont. 3,074 .... G 5
Skeena (riv.), Br. Col. .... D 5
Slave (riv.) .... E 3
Smallwood (res.), Newf. .... K 5
Southampton (isl.), N.W.T. .... H 2
Stettler, Alta. 5,136 .... E 5
Stewart (riv.), Yukon .... C 3
Stikine (riv.), Br. Col. .... C 4
Sudbury, Ont. 91,829 .... H 6
Swift Current, Sask. 14,747 .. F 5
Sydney, N.S. 29,444 .... K 6
Terrace, Br. Col. ○10,914 .... D 5
The Pas, Man. 6,390 .... F 5
Thompson, Man. 14,288 .... G 4
Thunder Bay, Ont. 112,486 .... H 6
Timmins, Ont. 46,114 .... H 6
Toronto (cap.), Ont. 599,217 .. H 7
Trail, Br. Col. 9,599 .... E 6
Trois-Rivières, Que. 50,466 .... J 6
Truro, N.S. 12,552 .... K 6
Tuktoyaktuk, N.W.T. 772 .... C 2
Val-d'Or, Que. 21,371 .... J 6
Vancouver, Br. Col. 414,281 .. D 6
Vancouver (isl.), Br. Col. .... D 6
Vanderhoof, Br. Col. 2,323 .... D 5
Vègreville, Alta. 5,251 .... E 5
Vernon, Br. Col. 19,987 .... E 5
Victoria (cap.), Br. Col. 64,379 D 6
Victoria (isl.), N.W.T. .... E 1
Wabush, Newf. 3,155 .... K 5
Waterton-Glacier International Peace Park, Alta. .... E 6
Wetaskiwin, Alta. 9,597 .... E 5
Weyburn, Sask. 9,523 .... F 6
Whitehorse (cap.), Yukon 14,814 .... C 3
Williams Lake, Br. Col. 8,362 . D 5
Williston (lake), Br. Col. .... D 4
Windsor, N.S. 3,646 .... K 7
Windsor, Ont. 192,083 .... H 7
Winnipeg (cap.), Man. 564,473 .... G 6
Winnipeg (lake), Man. .... G 5
Winnipegosis (lake), Man. .... F 5
Wood Buffalo Nat'l Park, Alta. . E 4
Woods (lake) .... G 6
Wrigley, N.W.T. 137 .... D 3
Yarmouth, N.S. 7,475 .... K 7
Yellowknife (cap.), N.W.T. 9,483 .... E 3
Yoho Nat'l Park, Br. Col. .... E 5
York Factory, Man. .... G 4
Yorkton, Sask. 15,339 .... F 5
Yukon Territory 23,153 .... C 3

○Population of municipality.

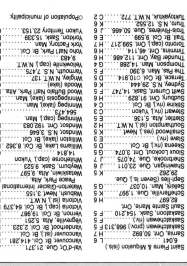

Topography

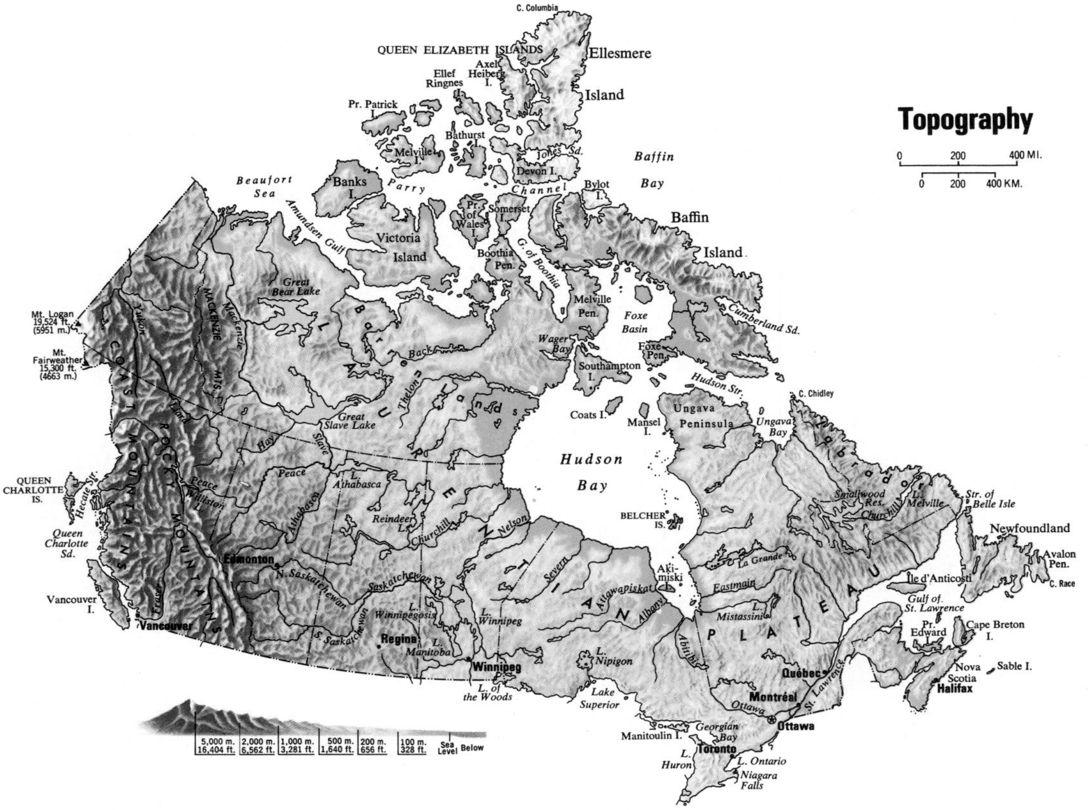

Agriculture, Industry and Resources

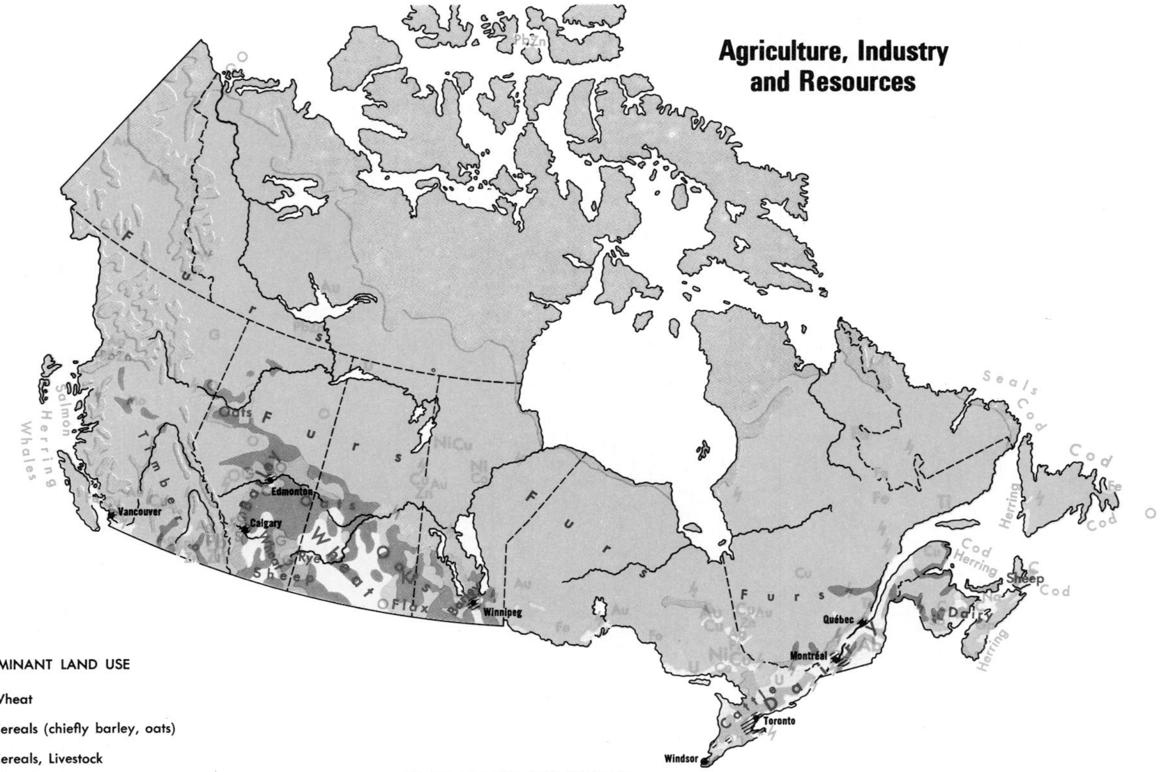

DOMINANT LAND USE

- Wheat
- Cereals (chiefly barley, oats)
- Cereals, Livestock
- General Farming, Livestock
- Dairy
- Fruit, Vegetables
- Pasture Livestock
- Range Livestock
- Forests
- Nonagricultural Land

MAJOR MINERAL OCCURRENCES

Ab Asbestos	Fe Iron Ore	Ni Nickel	Sb Antimony
Ag Silver	G Natural Gas	O Petroleum	Ti Titanium
Au Gold	Gp Gypsum	Pb Lead	U Uranium
C Coal	K Potash	Pt Platinum	W Tungsten
Co Cobalt	Mo Molybdenum	S Sulfur	Zn Zinc
Cu Copper	Na Salt		

Water Power

Major Industrial Areas

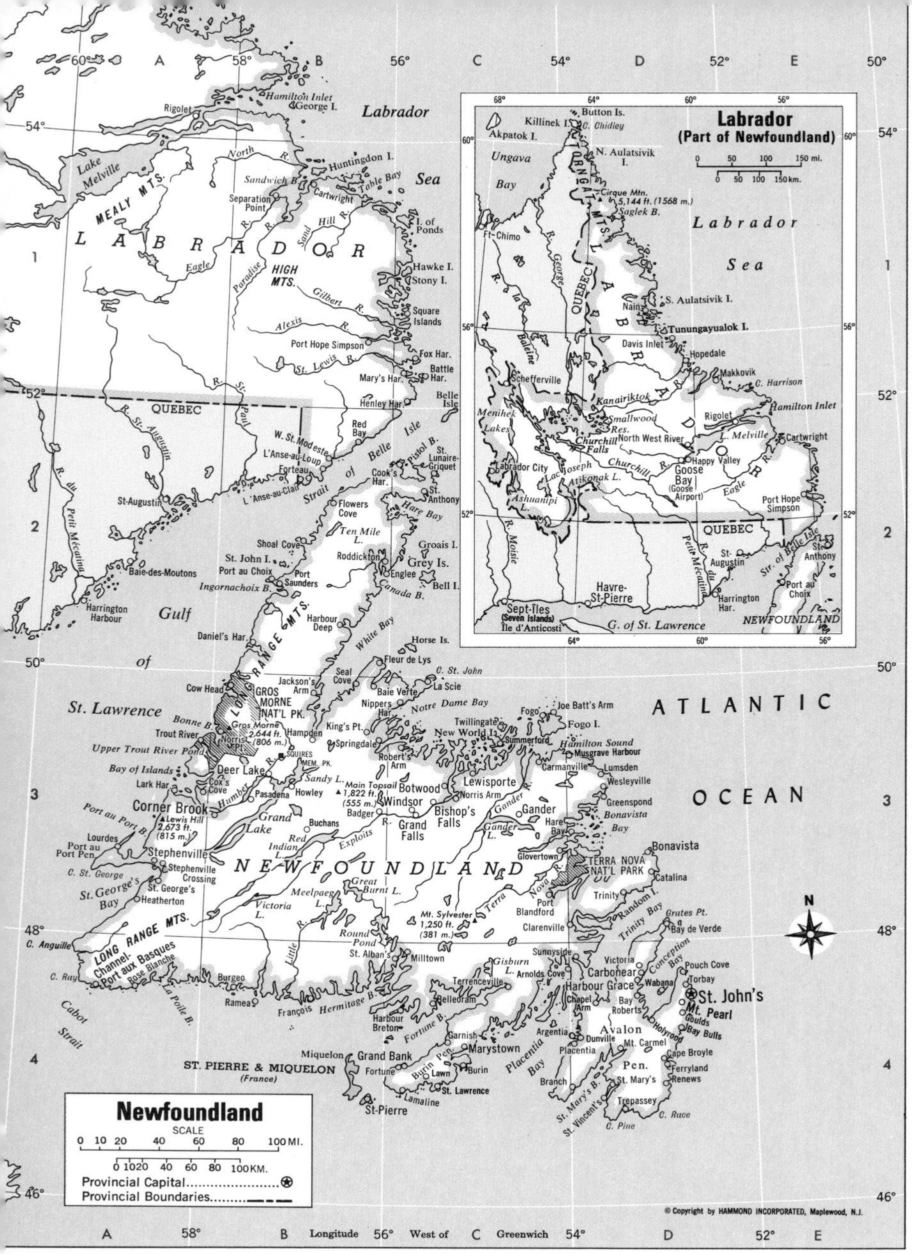

AREA 156,184 sq. mi. (404,517 sq. km.)
POPULATION 567,681
CAPITAL St. John's
LARGEST CITY St. John's
HIGHEST POINT in Torngat Mountains 5,420 ft. (1,652 m.)
SETTLED IN 1610
ADMITTED TO CONFEDERATION 1949
PROVINCIAL FLOWER Pitcher Plant

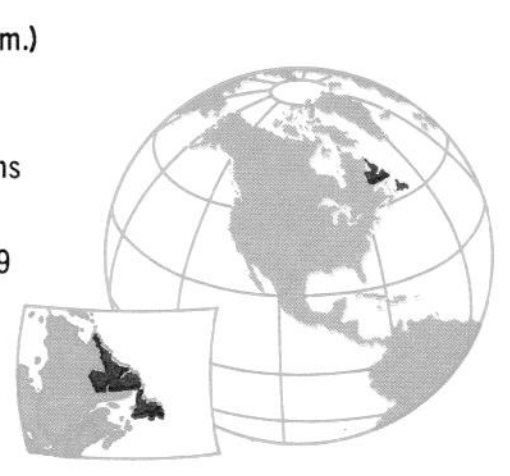

Topography

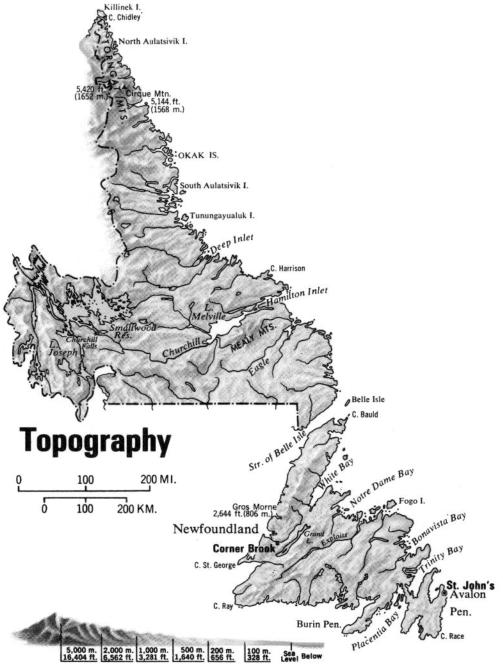

CITIES and TOWNS

Arnold's Cove 1,124 ..... C 4
Badger 1,090 ..... B 3
Baie Verte 2,491 ..... B 3
Battle Harbour ..... C 1
Bay Bulls 1,081 ..... D 4
Bay de Verde 786 ..... D 3
Bay Roberts 4,512 ..... D 4
Belleoram 565 ..... C 4
Bishop's Falls 4,395 ..... C 3
Bonavista 4,460 ..... D 3
Botwood 4,074 ..... C 3
Buchans 1,655 ..... B 3
Burgeo 2,504 ..... B 4
Burin 2,904 ..... C 4
Carbonear 5,335 ..... D 4
Carmanville 966 ..... C 3
Cartwright 658 ..... E 2
Catalina 1,162 ..... D 3
Channel-Port aux Basques 5,988 ..... A 4
Clarenville 2,878 ..... C 3
Corner Brook 24,339 ..... A 3
Cow Head 695 ..... A 3
Cox's Cove 980 ..... B 3
Deer Lake 4,348 ..... B 3
Dunville 1,817 ..... D 4
Englee 998 ..... C 2
Ferryland 795 ..... D 4
Fleur de Lys 616 ..... C 2
Fogo 1,105 ..... C 3
Fortune 2,473 ..... B 4
Gander 10,404 ..... C 3
Garnish 761 ..... C 4
Glovertown 2,165 ..... C 3
Goose Bay-Happy Valley (Goose Airport) 7,103 ..... D 2
Goulds 4,242 ..... D 4
Grand Bank 3,901 ..... B 4
Grand Falls 8,765 ..... C 3
Hampden 838 ..... B 3
Harbour Breton 2,461 ..... B 4
Harbour Grace 2,988 ..... D 4
Hare Bay 1,520 ..... C 3
Holyrood 1,789 ..... D 4
Joe Batt's Arm-Barr'd Islands 1,155 ..... D 3
King's Point 825 ..... B 3
Labrador City 11,538 ..... C 2
Lamaline 548 ..... C 4
Lark Harbour 783 ..... A 3
La Scie 1,422 ..... C 3
Lawn 999 ..... C 4
Lewisporte 3,963 ..... C 3
Lourdes 932 ..... A 3
Lumsden 645 ..... D 3
Marystown 6,299 ..... C 4
Milltown-Head of Bay d'Espoir 1,376 ..... C 4
Mount Pearl 11,543 ..... D 4
Nain 938 ..... D 1
Norris Arm 1,216 ..... C 3
Norris Point 1,033 ..... B 3
Pasadena 2,685 ..... B 3
Placentia 2,204 ..... D 4
Port au Choix 1,311 ..... B 2
Port Blandford 702 ..... C 3
Port Hope Simpson 581 ..... E 2
Port Saunders 769 ..... B 2
Pouch Cove 1,522 ..... D 4
Ramea 1,386 ..... B 4
Rigolet 271 ..... D 2
Robert's Arm 1,005 ..... C 3
Roddickton 1,142 ..... B 2
Rose Blanche-Harbour le Cou 975 ..... A 4
Saint Alban's 1,968 ..... B 4
Saint Anthony 3,017 ..... C 2
Saint George's 1,756 ..... A 3
St. John's (cap.) 83,770 ..... D 4
St. John's *154,820 ..... D 4
Saint Lawrence 2,012 ..... C 4
Saint Lunaire-Griquet 1,010 ..... C 2
Saint Vincent's-St. Stephens-Peter's River 796 ..... D 4
Seal Cove 751 ..... B 2
Shoal Cove 223 ..... B 2
Springdale 3,501 ..... B 3
Stephenville 8,876 ..... A 3
Stephenville Crossing 2,172 ..... A 3
Summerford 1,198 ..... C 3
Sunnyside 703 ..... C 4
Terrenceville 796 ..... C 4
Torbay 3,394 ..... D 4
Trepassey 1,473 ..... D 4
Trout River 759 ..... A 3
Twillingate 1,506 ..... C 3
Victoria 1,870 ..... D 4
Wabana 4,254 ..... D 4
Wesleyville 1,225 ..... D 3
Windsor 5,747 ..... C 3

OTHER FEATURES

Ashuanipi (lake) ..... C 2
Atikonak (lake) ..... D 2
Avalon (pen.) ..... D 4
Bell (isl.) ..... C 2
Belle (isl.) ..... C 1
Belle Isle (str.) ..... B 2
Bonavista (bay) ..... D 3
Bonne (bay) ..... A 3
Cabot (str.) ..... A 4
Chidley (cape) ..... D 1
Churchill (riv.) ..... D 2
Conception (bay) ..... D 4
Exploits (riv.) ..... B 3
Fogo (isl.) ..... D 3
Fortune (bay) ..... C 4
Grand (lake) ..... B 3
Grey (isls.) ..... C 2
Gros Morne Nat'l Park ..... B 3
Hamilton (inlet) ..... E 2
Hamilton (sound) ..... D 3
Hare (bay) ..... C 2
Hermitage (bay) ..... B 4
Humber (riv.) ..... B 3
Ingornachoix (bay) ..... A 2
Killinek (isl.) ..... C 1
Labrador (reg.) ..... D 1
Long Range (mts.) ..... A 4
Mealy (mts.) ..... A 1
Meelpaeg (lake) ..... B 3
Melville (lake) ..... E 2
Menihek (lakes) ..... C 2
Newfoundland (isl.) ..... B 2
New World (isl.) ..... C 3
North Aulatsivik (isl.) ..... D 1
Notre Dame (bay) ..... C 3
Pistolet (bay) ..... C 2
Placentia (bay) ..... C 4
Ponds (isl.) ..... C 1
Port au Port (pen.) ..... A 3
Race (cape) ..... D 4
Random (isl.) ..... D 3
Ray (cape) ..... A 4
Red Indian (lake) ..... B 3
Saint George's (bay) ..... A 3
Saint John (cape) ..... C 2
Saint Lawrence (gulf) ..... A 3
Saint Mary's (bay) ..... D 4
Sandy (lake) ..... B 3
Smallwood (res.) ..... D 2
South Aulatsivik (isl.) ..... D 1
Terra Nova Nat'l Park ..... D 3
Torngat (mts.) ..... D 1
Trinity (bay) ..... D 3
White (bay) ..... B 2

*Population of metropolitan area.

Agriculture, Industry and Resources

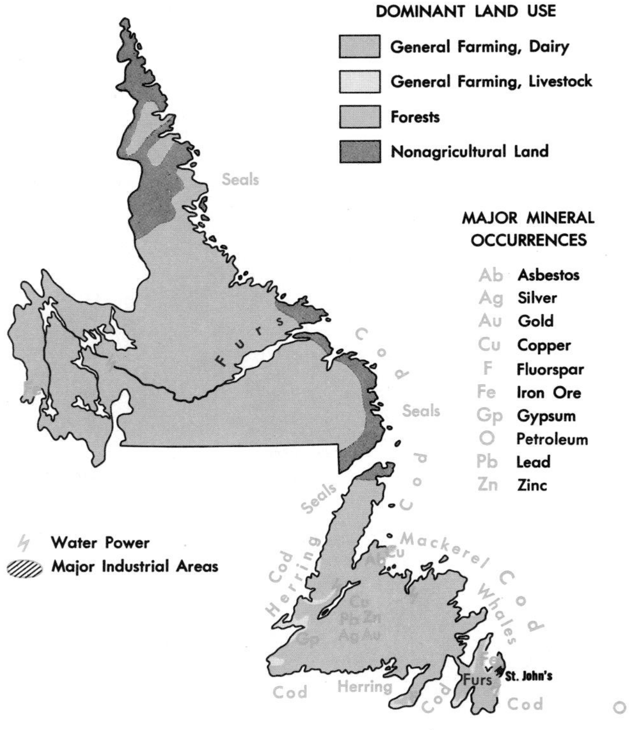

NOVA SCOTIA

COUNTIES

Annapolis 22,522 .... C 4
Antigonish 18,110 .... F 3
Cape Breton 127,035 .... H 3
Colchester 43,224 .... E 3
Cumberland 35,231 .... D 3
Digby 21,689 .... C 4
Guysborough 12,752 .... F 3
Halifax 288,126 .... E 4
Hants 33,121 .... D 4
Inverness 22,337 .... G 2
Kings 49,739 .... D 4
Lunenburg 45,746 .... D 4
Pictou 50,350 .... F 3
Queens 13,126 .... C 4
Richmond 12,284 .... H 3
Shelburne 17,328 .... C 5
Victoria 8,432 .... H 2
Yarmouth 26,290 .... C 5

CITIES and TOWNS

Alder Point 651 .... H 2
Aldershot .... D 3
Amherst⊙ 9,684 .... D 3
Annapolis Royal⊙ 631 .... C 4
Antigonish⊙ 5,205 .... F 3
Arichat 824 .... H 3
Aylesford 744 .... D 3
Baddeck⊙ 972 .... H 2
Barrington Passage 722 .... C 5
Bear River-Sissiboo 854 .... C 4
Beaverbank 1,322 .... E 4
Berwick 1,699 .... D 4
Bridgetown 1,047 .... C 4
Bridgewater 6,669 .... D 4
Brookfield 619 .... E 3
Brooklyn 1,269 .... D 4
Cambridge Station 799 .... D 3
Canning 763 .... D 3
Canso 1,255 .... H 3
Centreville 765 .... D 3
Chéticamp 1,022 .... G 2
Chester 1,131 .... D 4
Chester Basin 639 .... D 4
Church Point 318 .... B 4
Clark's Harbour 1,059 .... C 5
Coldbrook Station 617 .... D 3
Cow Bay 670 .... E 4
Dartmouth 62,277 .... E 4
Debert 618 .... E 3
Digby⊙ 2,558 .... C 4
Dominion 2,856 .... J 2
Donkin 873 .... J 2
Ellershouse-Hartville 662 .... D 4
Elmsdale 1,172 .... E 4
Enfield 1,510 .... E 4
Fall River 1,897 .... E 4
Falmouth 1,110 .... D 3
Glace Bay 21,466 .... J 2
Guysborough⊙ 496 .... G 3
Halifax (cap.)⊙ 114,594 .... E 4
Halifax *277,727 .... E 4
Hantsport 1,395 .... D 3
Herring Cove 1,323 .... E 4
Hilden 1,262 .... E 3
Ingonish 471 .... H 2
Inverness 2,013 .... G 2
Judique 925 .... G 3
Kentville⊙ 4,974 .... D 3
Kingston 1,612 .... D 4
Lakeside 936 .... E 4
Lantz 1,172 .... E 4
Liverpool⊙ 3,304 .... D 4
Lockeport 929 .... C 5
Louisbourg 1,410 .... J 3
Louisdale 979 .... G 3
Lower West Pubnico 790 .... C 5
Lunenburg⊙ 3,014 .... D 4
Mahone Bay 1,228 .... D 4
Meteghan 890 .... B 4
Middleton 1,834 .... C 4
Milford Station 748 .... E 3
Milton 1,678 .... D 4
Mount Uniacke 1,145 .... E 4
Mulgrave 1,099 .... G 3
Musquodoboit Harbour 936 .... E 4
New Glasgow 10,464 .... F 3
New Victoria 1,374 .... H 2
New Waterford 8,808 .... J 2
North Sydney 7,820 .... H 2
Oxford 1,470 .... E 3
Parrsboro 1,799 .... D 3
Pictou⊙ 4,628 .... F 3
Porters Lake 893 .... E 4
Port Hastings 312 .... G 3
Port Hawkesbury 3,850 .... G 3
Port Hood⊙ 701 .... G 2
Port Morien 717 .... J 2
Port Williams 1,227 .... D 3
Prospect 693 .... E 4
Pugwash 648 .... E 3
Reserve Mines 2,472 .... H 2
River Hébert 835 .... D 3
Saint Peters 669 .... H 3
Sandy Point 691 .... C 5
Scotchtown 2,037 .... H 2
Sheet Harbour 819 .... F 4
Shelburne⊙ 2,303 .... C 5
Shubenacadie 984 .... E 3
Springhill 4,896 .... E 3
Stellarton 5,435 .... F 3
Stewiacke 1,174 .... E 3
Sydney⊙ 29,444 .... H 2
Sydney Mines 8,501 .... H 2
Terence Bay 960 .... E 4
Thorburn 1,014 .... F 3
Three Mile Plains 1,355 .... D 4
Timberlea 1,159 .... E 4
Trenton 3,154 .... F 3
Truro⊙ 12,552 .... E 3
Waterville 687 .... D 3
Waverley 1,699 .... E 4
Wedgeport 827 .... C 5
Western Shore 1,712 .... D 4
Westmount 3,097 .... H 2
Westville 4,522 .... F 3
Wileville 746 .... D 4
Windsor⊙ 3,646 .... D 3
Wolfville 3,235 .... D 3
Yarmouth⊙ 7,475 .... B 5

OTHER FEATURES

Advocate (bay) .... D 3
Ainslie (lake) .... G 2
Amet (sound) .... E 3
Andrew (isl.) .... H 3
Annapolis (basin) .... C 4
Annapolis (riv.) .... C 4
Antigonish (harb.) .... G 3
Argos (cape) .... G 3
Aspy (bay) .... H 2
Avon (riv.) .... D 4
Baccaro (pt.) .... C 5
Baddeck (riv.) .... H 2
Barachois (pt.) .... G 4
Barren (isl.) .... G 4
Barrington (bay) .... C 5
Bedford (basin) .... E 4
Berry (head) .... G 3
Boularderie (isl.) .... H 2
Bras d'Or (lake) .... H 3
Breton (cape) .... J 3
Brier (isl.) .... B 4
Canso (cape) .... H 3
Canso (str.) .... G 3
Cap d'Or (cape) .... D 3

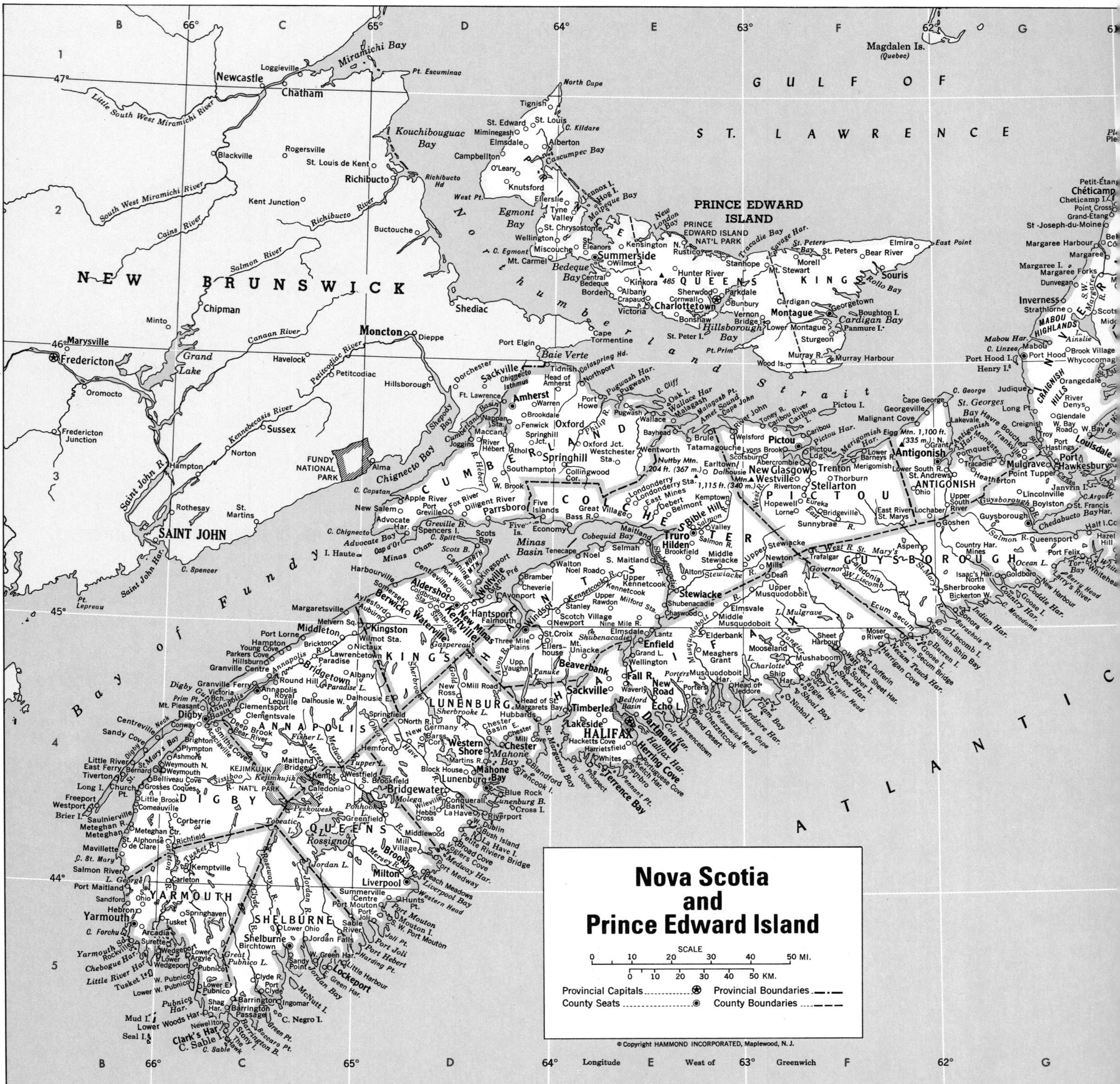

Cape Breton (isl.) J 2
Cape Breton Highlands Nat'l Park H 2
Cape Negro (isl.) C 5
Cape Sable (isl.) C 5
Capstan (cape) D 3
Caribou (isl.) F 3
Carleton (riv.) C 4
Charlotte (lake) F 4
Chebogue (harb.) B 5
Chedabucto (bay) G 3
Chéticamp (isl.) G 2
Chignecto (bay) D 3
Chignecto (cape) C 3
Chignecto (isth.) D 3
Clam (bay) F 4
Cliff (cape) E 3
Clyde (riv.) C 5
Cobequid (bay) E 3
Coddle (harb.) G 3
Coldspring (head) E 3
Cole (harb.) E 4
Country (harb.) G 3
Craignish (hills) G 3
Cross (isl.) D 4
Cumberland (basin) D 3
Dalhousie (mt.) E 3
Dauphin (cape) H 2
Digby Gut (chan.) C 4
Digby Neck (pen.) B 4
East (bay) H 3
East (riv.) F 3
East Bay (hills) H 3
Egmont (cape) H 2
Eigg (mt.) F 3
Fisher (lake) C 4
Five (isls.) D 3
Forchu (bay) H 3
Forchu (cape) B 5
Framboise Cove (bay) H 3
Fundy (bay) C 3
Gabarus (bay) H 3
Gabarus (cape) J 3
Gaspereau (lake) D 4
George (cape) G 3
George (lake) B 5

PRINCE EDWARD ISLAND

AREA 2,184 sq. mi. (5,657 sq. km.)
POPULATION 122,506
CAPITAL Charlottetown
LARGEST CITY Charlottetown
HIGHEST POINT 465 ft. (142 m.)
SETTLED IN 1720
ADMITTED TO CONFEDERATION 1873
PROVINCIAL FLOWER Lady's Slipper

NOVA SCOTIA

AREA 21,425 sq. mi. (55,491 sq. km.)
POPULATION 847,442
CAPITAL Halifax
LARGEST CITY Halifax
HIGHEST POINT Cape Breton Highlands 1,747 ft. (532 m.)
SETTLED IN 1605
ADMITTED TO CONFEDERATION 1867
PROVINCIAL FLOWER Trailing Arbutus or Mayflower

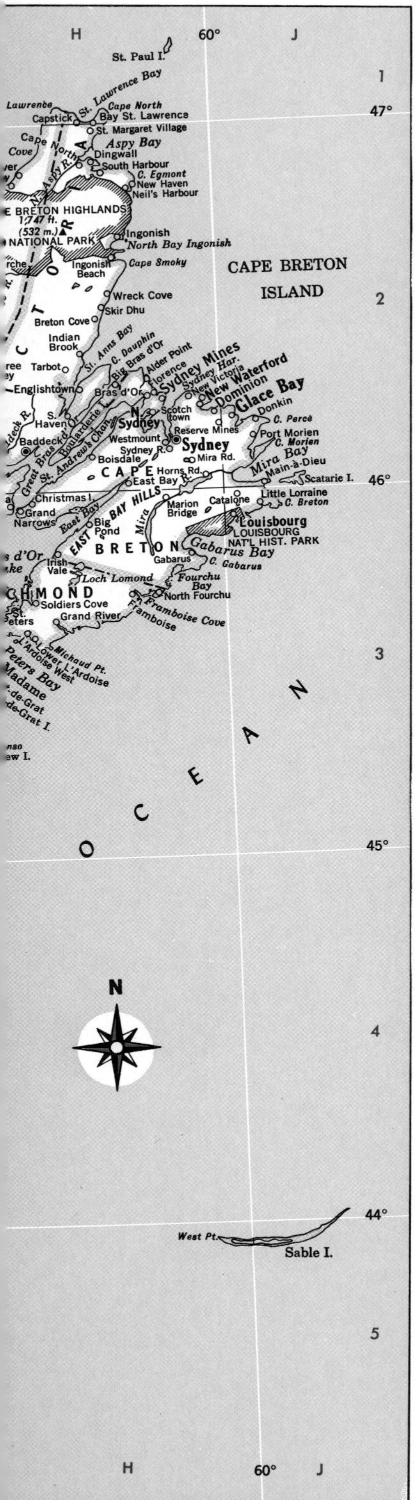

Gold (riv.) D 4
Goose (isl.) F 4
Goose (isl.) G 3
Governor (lake) F 3
Great Bras d'Or (chan.) H 2
Great Pubnico (lake) C 5
Green (pt.) C 5
Greville (bay) D 3
Guysborough (riv.) G 3
Halifax (harb.) E 4
Harding (pt.) D 5
Haute (isl.) C 3
Hébert (riv.) D 3
Henry (isl.) G 3
Indian (harb.) G 3
Ingonish North (bay) H 2
Janvrin (isl.) G 3
Jeddore (harb.) F 4
John (cape) E 3
Joli (pt.) D 5
Jordan (bay) C 5
Jordan (lake) C 4
Jordan (riv.) C 5
Kejimkujik (lake) C 4
Kejimkujik Nat'l Park C 4
Kennetcook (riv.) E 3
La Have (isl.) D 4
La Have (riv.) D 4
Linzee (cape) G 2
Liscomb (isl.) G 4
Little River (harb.) B 5
Liverpool (bay) D 5
Lomond, Loch (lake) H 3
Long (isl.) B 4
Louisbourg Nat'l Hist. Park J 3
Lunenburg (bay) D 4
Mabou (harb.) G 2
Mabou Highlands (hills) G 2
Madame (isl.) H 3
Mahone (bay) D 4
Malagash (pt.) E 3
Margaree (isl.) F 4
McNutt (isl.) C 5
Medway (harb.) D 4
Medway (riv.) C 4
Merigomish (harb.) F 3
Mersey (riv.) C 4
Michaud (pt.) H 3
Minas (basin) D 3
Minas (chan.) D 3
Mira (bay) J 2
Mira (riv.) H 3
Mocodome (cape) G 3
Molega (lake) D 4
Morien (cape) J 2
Mouton (isl.) D 5
Mud (isl.) B 5
Mulgrave (lake) F 3
Musquodoboit (riv.) E 4
Necum Teuch (harb.) F 4
Nichol (isl.) F 4
North (cape) H 1
North (mt.) D 3
North Aspy (riv.) H 2
North Bay Ingonish (bay) H 2
North East Margaree (riv.) H 2
Northumberland (str.) E 2
Nuttby (mt.) E 3
Oak (isl.) E 3
Ocean (lake) G 3
Ohio (riv.) D 4
Panuke (lake) D 4
Paradise (lake) C 4
Pennant (pt.) E 4
Percé (cape) J 2
Peskowesk (lake) C 4
Petit-de-Grat (isl.) H 3
Petpeswick (head) E 4
Philip (riv.) E 3
Pictou (harb.) F 3
Pictou (isl.) F 3
Pleasant (bay) H 2
Ponhook (lake) D 4
Porters (lake) E 4
Port Hebert (harb.) D 5
Port Hood (isl.) G 2
Port Joli (harb.) D 5
Port Mouton (harb.) D 5
Poulet Cove (bay) H 2
Prim (pt.) C 4
Pubnico (harb.) C 5
Pugwash (harb.) E 3
Roseway (riv.) C 4
Rossignol (lake) C 4
Sable (cape) C 5
Sable (isl.) J 5
Saint Andrews (chan.) H 2
Saint Anns (bay) H 2
Saint Georges (bay) G 3
Saint Lawrence (bay) H 1
Saint Lawrence (cape) H 1
Saint Margarets (bay) E 4
Saint Mary (cape) B 4
Saint Marys (bay) B 4
Saint Mary's (riv.) F 3
Saint Patrick (chan.) G 3
Saint Paul (isl.) H 1
Saint Peters (bay) H 3

Topography

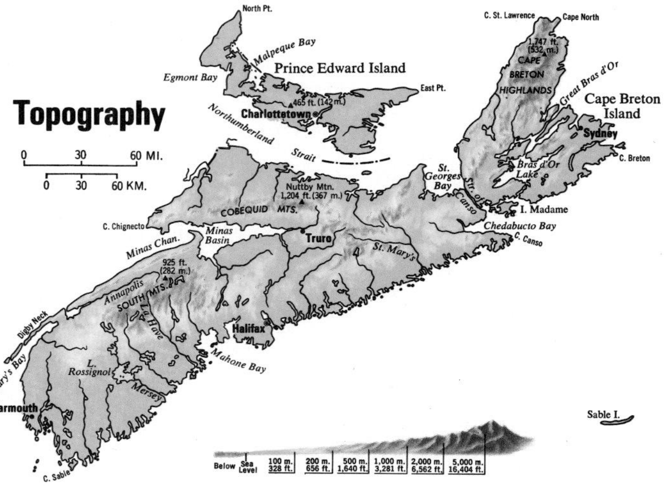

Salmon (riv.) E 3
Salmon (riv.) G 3
Scatarie (isl.) J 2
Scots (bay) D 3
Seall (isl.) B 5
Sheet (harb.) F 4
Sherbrooke (lake) D 4
Sherbrooke (riv.) D 4
Shoal (bay) F 4
Shubenacadie (lake) E 4
Shubenacadie (riv.) E 3
Sissiboo (riv.) C 4
Smoky (cape) H 2
Sober (isl.) F 4
South West Margaree (riv.) G 2
Split (cape) D 3
Spry (harb.) F 4
Stewiacke (riv.) E 3
Sydney (harb.) H 2
Tangier (riv.) F 4
Taylor (head) F 4
Tobeatic (lake) C 4
Tor (bay) G 3
Tupper (lake) D 4
Tusket (isl.) B 5
Tusket (riv.) C 4
Verte (bay) D 2
Wallace (harb.) E 3
West (bay) G 3
West (pt.) H 5
West (riv.) F 3
Western (head) D 5
West Liscomb (riv.) F 3
West Saint Mary's (riv.) F 3
Whitehaven (harb.) G 3
Yarmouth (sound) B 5

PRINCE EDWARD ISLAND

COUNTIES

Kings 19,215 F 2
Prince 42,821 D 2
Queens 60,470 E 2

CITIES and TOWNS

Alberton 1,020 E 2
Bunbury 1,024 F 2
Charlottetown (cap.)⊙ 15,282 E 2
Cornwall 1,838 E 2
Georgetown⊙ 737 F 2
Kensington 1,143 E 2
Miscouche 752 D 2
Montague 1,957 F 2
Murray Harbour 443 F 2
North Rustico 688 E 2
O'Leary 736 D 2
Parkdale 2,018 E 2
Saint Edward 650 D 2
Saint Eleanors 2,716 E 2
Sherwood 5,681 E 2
Souris 1,413 F 2
Summerside⊙ 7,828 E 2
Tignish 982 D 2
Wilmot 1,563 E 2

OTHER FEATURES

Bedeque (bay) E 2
Boughton (isl.) F 2
Cardigan (bay) F 2
Cascumpeque (bay) E 2
East (pt.) G 2
Egmont (bay) D 2
Egmont (cape) D 2
Hillsborough (bay) E 2
Hog (isl.) E 2
Kildare (cape) E 2
Lennox (isl.) E 2
Malpeque (bay) E 2
New London (bay) E 2
North (pt.) E 1
Northumberland (str.) D 2
Panmure (isl.) F 2
Prim (pt.) E 2
Prince Edward Island Nat'l Park E 2
Rollo (bay) F 2
Saint Lawrence (gulf) F 2
Saint Peters (bay) F 2
Saint Peters (isl.) E 2
Savage (harb.) F 2
Tracadie (bay) F 2
West (pt.) D 2
Wood (isls.) F 3

⊙County seat.
*Population of metropolitan area.

Agriculture, Industry and Resources

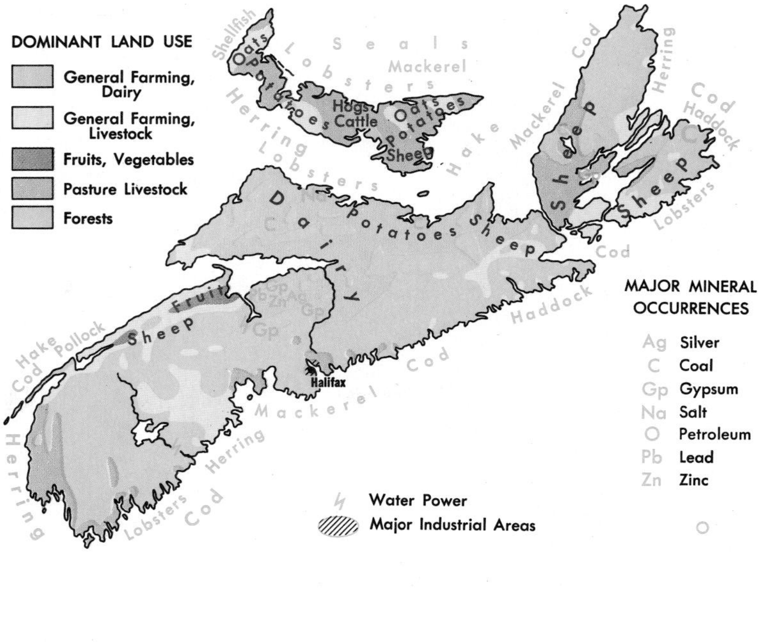

COUNTIES

Albert 23,632 . . . . F 3
Carleton 24,659 . . . . C 2
Charlotte 26,571 . . . . C 3
Gloucester 86,156 . . . . E 1
Kent 30,799 . . . . E 2
King's 51,114 . . . . E 3
Madawaska 34,892 . . . . B 1
Northumberland 54,134 . . . . D 2
Queen's 12,485 . . . . D 3
Restigouche 40,593 . . . . C 1
Saint John 86,148 . . . . E 3
Sunbury 21,012 . . . . D 3
Victoria 20,815 . . . . C 1
Westmorland 107,640 . . . . F 2
York 74,213 . . . . C 3

CITIES and TOWNS

Acadie Siding 64 . . . . E 2
Acadieville 176 . . . . E 2
Adamsville 94 . . . . E 2
Albert Mines 120 . . . . F 3
Alcida 174 . . . . E 1
Aldouane 64 . . . . E 2
Allardville 478 . . . . E 1
Alma 329 . . . . F 3
Anagance 114 . . . . E 3
Anse-Bleue 562 . . . . E 1
Apohaqui 341 . . . . E 3
Argyle 63 . . . . C 2
Armstrong Brook 191 . . . . E 1
Aroostook 403 . . . . C 2
Arthurette 178 . . . . C 2
Astle 201 . . . . D 2
Atholville 1,694 . . . . D 1
Aulac 113 . . . . F 3
Back Bay 455 . . . . D 3
Baie-Sainte-Anne 709 . . . . F 1
Baie-Verte 175 . . . . F 2
Bairdsville 81 . . . . C 2
Baker Brook 527 . . . . B 1
Balmoral 1,823 . . . . D 1
Barachois 686 . . . . F 2
Barnaby River 38 . . . . E 2
Barnettville 117 . . . . E 2
Bartibog Bridge 122 . . . . E 1
Bas-Caraquet 1,859 . . . . F 1
Bass River 112 . . . . E 2
Bath 794 . . . . C 2
Bathurst⊙ 15,705 . . . . E 1
Bayfield 81 . . . . G 2
Bayside . . . . C 3
Beaubois 211 . . . . E 1
Beaver Brook Station 95 . . . . E 1
Beaver Harbour 316 . . . . D 3
Beechwood 111 . . . . C 2
Beersville 52 . . . . E 2
Belledune 690 . . . . E 1
Bellefleur 83 . . . . C 1
Bellefond 243 . . . . E 1
Belleisle Creek 145 . . . . E 3
Benjamin River 171 . . . . D 1
Ben Lomond . . . . E 3
Benton 101 . . . . C 3
Beresford 3,652 . . . . E 1
Berry Mills 238 . . . . E 2
Bertrand 1,268 . . . . E 1
Berwick 129 . . . . E 3
Black Point 131 . . . . D 1
Black River 150 . . . . E 3
Blacks Harbour 1,356 . . . . D 3
Blackville 892 . . . . E 2
Blissfield 119 . . . . D 2
Bloomfield Ridge 153 . . . . D 2
Bloomfield Station 62 . . . . E 3
Bocabec 34 . . . . C 3
Boiestown 299 . . . . D 2
Bonny River 153 . . . . D 3
Bossé 193 . . . . B 1
Bourgeois 215 . . . . F 2
Brantville 1,066 . . . . E 1
Breau-Village 293 . . . . F 2
Brest 94 . . . . E 2
Brewers Mills 199 . . . . C 2
Briggs Corner 89 . . . . E 2
Bristol 824 . . . . C 2
Brockway (Lower Brockway-Brockway) 97 . . . . C 3
Browns Flat 295 . . . . D 3
Buctouche 2,476 . . . . F 2
Burnsville 156 . . . . E 1
Burton⊙ 291 . . . . D 3
Burtts Corner 484 . . . . D 2
Cambridge-Narrows 433 . . . . E 3
Campbellton 9,818 . . . . D 1
Canaan 115 . . . . E 2
Canaan Forks 78 . . . . E 2
Canaan Road 86 . . . . E 2
Canterbury 474 . . . . C 3
Cap-Bateau 417 . . . . F 1
Cape Tormentine 229 . . . . G 2
Cap Lumière 262 . . . . F 2
Cap-Pelé 2,199 . . . . F 2
Caraquet 4,315 . . . . E 1
Carlingford 229 . . . . C 2
Carlisle 75 . . . . C 2
Caron Brook 171 . . . . B 1
Carrolls Crossing 119 . . . . D 2
Castalia 145 . . . . D 4
Central Blissville 155 . . . . D 3
Centre-Saint-Simon (St. Simon) 991 . . . . E 1
Centreville 577 . . . . C 2
Chance Harbour 63 . . . . D 3
Charlo 1,603 . . . . D 1
Chatham 6,779 . . . . E 1
Chatham Head . . . . E 2
Chipman 1,829 . . . . E 2
Clair 915 . . . . B 1
Clarendon 80 . . . . D 3
Cliffordvale (Limestone-Cliffordvale) 69 . . . . C 2
Clifton 194 . . . . E 1
Coal Branch 90 . . . . E 2
Coal Creek 61 . . . . E 2
Cocagne Cape 278 . . . . F 2
Cocagne-Cocagne Sud 600 . . . . F 2
Codys 125 . . . . E 3
Coldstream 217 . . . . C 2
Coles Island 160 . . . . E 3
College Bridge 536 . . . . F 3
Collette 198 . . . . E 2
Connell 58 . . . . C 2
Connors 96 . . . . B 1
Cork 54 . . . . D 3
Cornhill 111 . . . . E 3
Coughlan 181 . . . . E 2
Cross Creek 192 . . . . D 2
Cumberland Bay 231 . . . . E 2
Dalhousie⊙ 4,958 . . . . D 1
Dalhousie Junction 105 . . . . D 1
Darlington 749 . . . . D 1
Daulnay 398 . . . . E 1
Dawsonville 278 . . . . C 1
Debec 200 . . . . C 2
Dieppe 8,511 . . . . F 2
Dipper Harbour 166 . . . . D 3
Doaktown 1,009 . . . . D 2
Dorchester⊙ 1,101 . . . . F 3
Dorchester Crossing 605 . . . . F 2
Douglastown 1,091 . . . . E 1
Drummond 849 . . . . C 1
Duguayville 337 . . . . E 1
Dumfries 150 . . . . C 3
Dupuis Corner 303 . . . . F 2
Durham Bridge 255 . . . . D 2
East Riverside-Kingshurst 989 . . . . E 3
Edmundston⊙ 12,044 . . . . B 1
Eel River Bridge 377 . . . . F 1
Eel River Crossing 1,431 . . . . D 1
Elgin 301 . . . . E 3
Enniskillen 63 . . . . D 3
Escuminac 194 . . . . F 1
Evandale 58 . . . . D 3
Evangeline 356 . . . . F 1
Everett 48 . . . . C 1
Fairfield 250 . . . . E 3
Fairhaven 142 . . . . C 4
Fairisle 415 . . . . E 1
Fairvale 3,960 . . . . E 3
Ferry Road 325 . . . . E 1
Fielding 197 . . . . C 2
Five Fingers 189 . . . . C 1
Flatlands 249 . . . . D 1
Florenceville 709 . . . . C 2
Forest City 25 . . . . C 3
Fosterville 58 . . . . C 3
Four Falls 69 . . . . C 2
Fredericton (cap.)⊙ 43,723 . . . . D 3
Fredericton Junction 711 . . . . D 3
Gagetown⊙ 618 . . . . D 3
Gardner Creek 56 . . . . E 3
Geary 654 . . . . D 3
Germantown 62 . . . . F 3
Gillespie 96 . . . . C 2
Glassville 147 . . . . C 2
Glencoe 147 . . . . D 1
Glenlivet 284 . . . . D 1
Gloucester Junction 36 . . . . E 1
Gondola Point 3,076 . . . . D 3
Grafton 385 . . . . C 2
Grand Bay 3,173 . . . . D 3
Grande-Anse 817 . . . . E 1
Grand Falls 6,203 . . . . C 1
Grand Falls Hill 152 . . . . C 1
Grand Harbour 614 . . . . D 4
Gray Rapids 266 . . . . E 2
Hammondvale 72 . . . . E 3
Hampstead 87 . . . . D 3
Hampton⊙ 3,141 . . . . E 3
Harcourt 127 . . . . E 2
Hardwicke 114 . . . . E 1
Hardwood Ridge 191 . . . . D 2
Hartland 846 . . . . C 2
Harvey, Albert 58 . . . . F 3
Harvey, York 356 . . . . D 3
Hatfield Point 176 . . . . E 3

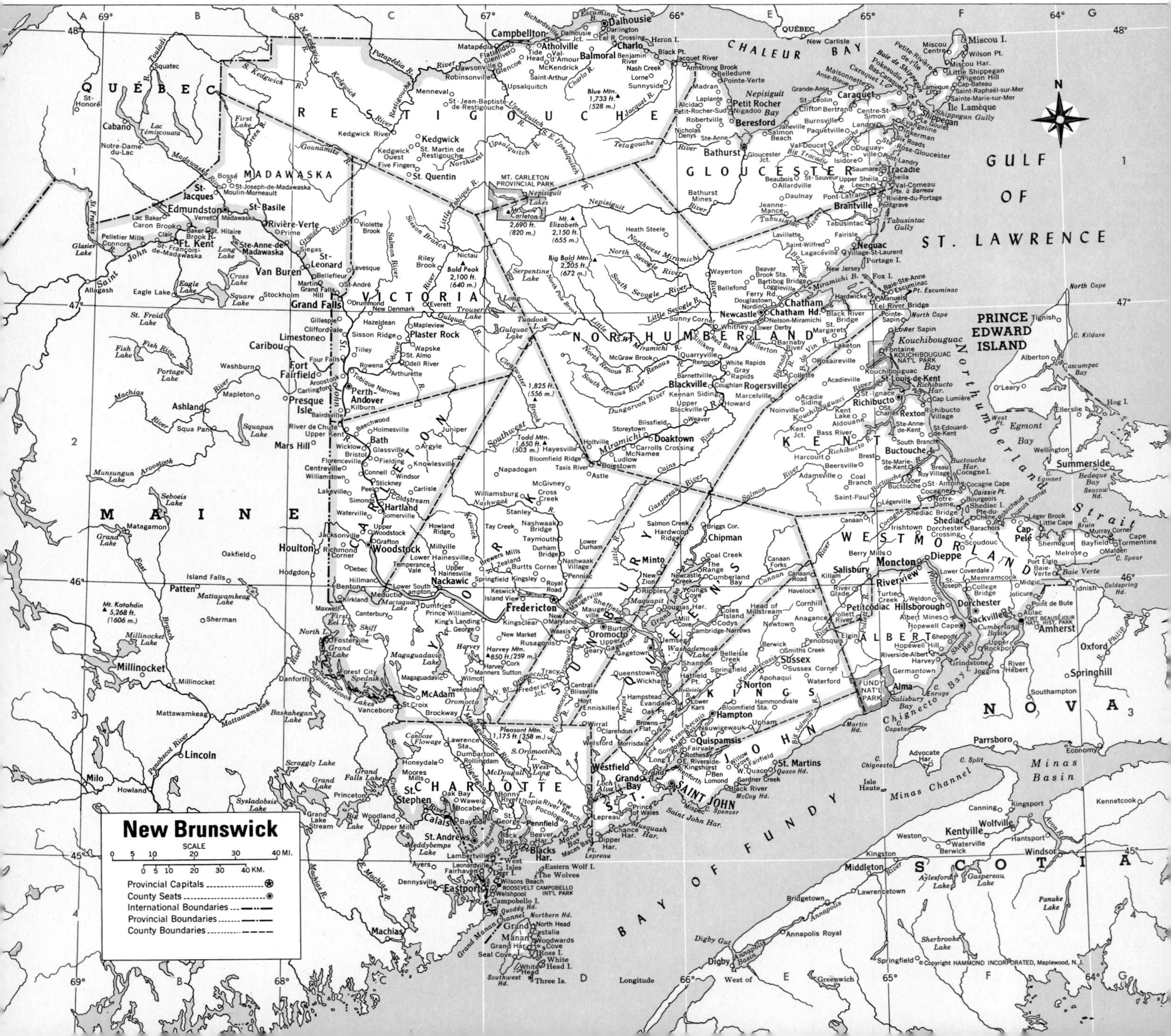

Havelock 439 E 3
Hayesville 107 D 2
Hazeldean 108 C 2
Head of Millstream 61 E 3
Hillman 69 C 2
Hillsborough 1,239 F 3
Holmesville 146 C 2
Holtville 222 D 2
Honeydale 77 C 3
Hopewell Cape⊙ 144 F 3
Hopewell Hill 172 F 3
Howard 77 E 2
Howland Ridge 55 C 2
Hoyt 114 D 3
Inkerman 396 F 1
Irishtown 605 F 2
Island View 240 D 3
Jacksonville 363 C 2
Jacquet River 778 E 1
Janeville 204 E 1
Jeanne Mance 89 E 1
Jemseg 228 D 3
Jolicure 96 F 3
Juniper 525 C 2
Kedgwick 1,222 C 1
Keenan Siding 86 E 2
Kent Junction 112 E 2
Kent Lake 57 E 2
Keswick 260 D 3
Kilburn 134 C 2
Killam 60 E 2
Kingsclear 250 D 3
Kingsley 145 D 2
Kirkland 69 C 3
Knowlesville 82 C 2
Kouchibouguac 213 F 2
Lac Baker 292 B 1
Lagacéville 227 E 1
Lake George 170 C 3
Laketon 81 E 2
Lakeville 201 C 2
Lambertville 109 C 3
Lamèque 1,571 F 1
Landry 281 E 1
Laplante 197 E 1
Lavillette 576 E 1
Lawrence Station 229 C 3
Leech 584 E 1
Léger Brook F 2
Légerville 184 F 2
Le Goulet 1,173 F 1
Leonardville 158 C 4
Lepreau 208 D 3
Levesque 77 C 1
Little Cape 513 F 2
Little Shippegan 131 F 1
Loggieville 781 E 1
Lorne 937 D 1
Lower Coverdale 616 F 2
Lower Derby 206 E 2
Lower Durham 52 D 2
Lower Hainesville 66 C 2
Lower Kars 30 E 3
Lower Millstream 184 E 3
Lower Sapin F 2
Lower Southampton C 3
Ludlow 100 D 2
Maces Bay 182 D 3
Madran 247 E 1
Magaguadavic 126 C 3
Maisonnette 757 E 1
Malden 93 G 2
Manners Sutton 159 D 3
Manuels 332 F 1
Mapleview 65 C 2
Marcelville 61 E 2
Martin 104 C 1
Maugerville 249 D 3
Maxwell 64 C 3
McAdam 1,837 C 3
McGivney 156 D 2
McKendrick 608 D 1
McNamee 147 D 2
Meductic 234 C 3
Melrose 121 F 2
Memramcook 276 F 2
Menneval 110 C 1
Midgic Station 208 F 3
Mill Cove 253 D 3
Millerton 130 E 2
Millville 309 C 2
Minto 3,399 D 2
Miscou Centre 554 F 1
Miscou Harbour 106 F 1
Mispec 180 E 3
Moncton 54,743 F 2
Moores Mills 117 C 3
Morrisdale 202 D 3
Moulin-Morneault 459 B 1
Murray Corner 233 G 2
Nackawic 1,357 C 2
Napadogan 103 D 2
Nash Creek 235 D 1
Nashwaak Bridge 142 D 2
Nashwaak Village 258 D 2
Nauwigewauk 139 E 3
Neguac 1,755 E 1
Nelson-Miramichi 1,452 E 2
Newcastle⊙ 6,284 E 2
Newcastle Creek 210 D 2
New Denmark 112 C 1
New Jersey 65 E 1
New Market 143 D 3
New Maryland 485 D 3
New River Beach 33 D 3
Newtown 154 E 3
New Zion 171 D 2
Nicholas Denys 170 D 1
Nictau 30 C 1
Nigadoo 1,075 E 1
Noinville 50 E 2
Nordin 393 E 1
North Head 661 D 4
Norton 1,372 E 3
Notre-Dame 344 F 2
Oak Bay 183 C 3
Oak Point 83 D 3
Oromocto 9,064 D 3
Paquetville 626 E 1
Peel 117 C 2
Pelletier Mills 88 B 1
Pennfield D 3
Penniac 179 D 2
Penobsquis 259 E 3
Perth-Andover⊙ 1,872 C 2
Petitcodiac 1,401 E 3
Petite-Rivière-de-l'Île 549 F 1
Petit Rocher 1,860 E 1
Petit Rocher Sud E 1
Pigeon Hill 595 F 1
Plaster Rock 1,222 C 2
Pocologan 150 D 3
Point de Bute 155 F 3
Pointe-du-Chêne 482 F 2
Pointe-Sapin 331 F 2
Pointe-Verte 1,335 E 1
Pollett River 73 E 3
Pontgrave 229 F 1
Pont-Lafrance 875 E 1
Pont-Landry 444 F 1
Port Elgin 504 F 2
Prime 89 B 1
Prince of Wales 138 D 3
Prince William 225 C 3
Quarryville 205 E 2
Queenstown 112 D 3
Quispamsis 6,022 E 3
Red Bank 141 E 2
Renforth 1,490 E 3
Renous 192 E 2
Rexton 928 F 2
Richardsville D 1
Richibucto⊙ 1,722 E 2
Richibucto Village 442 F 2
Richmond Corner 84 C 2
Riley Brook 126 C 1
Ripples 233 D 3
River de Chute 22 C 2
River Glade 268 E 3
Riverside-Albert 478 F 3
Riverview 14,907 F 2
Rivière-du-Portage 661 F 1
Rivière Verte 1,054 B 1
Robertville 733 E 1
Robichaud 485 F 2
Robinsonville 206 C 1
Rogersville 1,237 E 2
Rollingdam 65 C 3
Rosaireville 86 E 2
Rothesay 1,764 E 3
Rowena 73 C 2
Roy 173 F 2
Royal Road 41 D 2
Rusagonis 231 D 3
Sackville 5,654 F 3
Saint Almo 17 C 2
Saint-André 385 C 1
Saint Andrews⊙ 1,760 C 3
Saint-Antoine 1,217 F 2
Saint Arthur 369 D 1
Saint-Basile 3,214 B 1
Saint-Charles 355 F 2
Saint Croix 86 C 3
Sainte-Anne 329 E 1
Sainte-Anne-de-Kent 337 F 2
Sainte-Anne-de-Madawaska 1,332 B 1
Saint-Édouard-de-Kent 157 F 2
Sainte-Marie-de-Kent 283 F 2
Sainte-Marie-sur-Mer 539 F 1
Sainte-Rose-Gloucester 410 F 1
Saint-François-de-Madawaska 753 B 1
Saint George 1,163 D 3
Saint Hilaire 244 B 1
Saint-Ignace 96 F 2
Saint-Isidore 794 E 1
Saint-Jacques 2,297 B 1
Saint-Jean-Baptiste-de-Restigouche 228 C 1
Saint John⊙ 80,521 E 3
Saint-Joseph 630 F 3
Saint-Joseph-de-Madawaska 173 B 1
Saint-Léolin 799 E 1
Saint Leonard 1,566 C 1
Saint-Louis-de-Kent 1,166 F 2
Saint Margarets 63 E 2
Saint Martin de Restigouche 124 C 1
Saint Martins 530 E 3
Saint-Paul 365 E 2
Saint Quentin 2,334 C 1
Saint-Raphaël-sur-Mer 562 F 1
Saint Sauveur 252 E 1
Saint Stephen 5,120 C 3
Saint Wilfred E 1
Salisbury 1,672 E 2
Salmon Beach 277 E 1
Salmon Creek 38 E 2
Saumarez 690 E 1
Scoudouc 207 F 2
Seal Cove 548 D 4
Shannon 39 E 3
Shediac 4,285 F 2
Shediac Bridge 441 F 2
Sheffield 112 D 3
Sheila 1,172 F 1
Shemogue 199 F 2
Shepody 86 F 3
Shippegan 2,471 F 1
Siegas 227 C 1
Sillikers 292 E 2
Simonds 221 C 2
Sisson Ridge 170 C 2
Six Roads 239 F 1
Smiths Creek 163 E 3
Somerville 326 C 2
South Branch 86 F 2
Springfield, King's 116 E 3
Springfield, York 130 C 2
Stanley 432 D 2
Stickney 232 C 2
Storeytown 140 D 2
Sunny Corner 405 E 2
Sunnyside 87 D 1
Sussex 3,972 E 3
Sussex Corner 1,023 E 3
Tabusintac 231 E 1

AREA 28,354 sq. mi. (73,437 sq. km.)
POPULATION 696,403
CAPITAL Fredericton
LARGEST CITY Saint John
HIGHEST POINT Mt. Carleton 2,690 ft. (820 m.)
SETTLED IN 1611
ADMITTED TO CONFEDERATION 1867
PROVINCIAL FLOWER Purple Violet

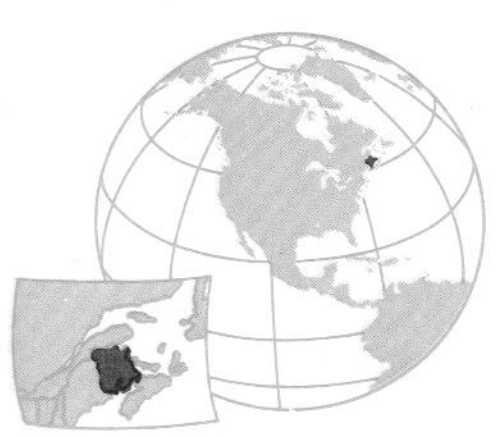

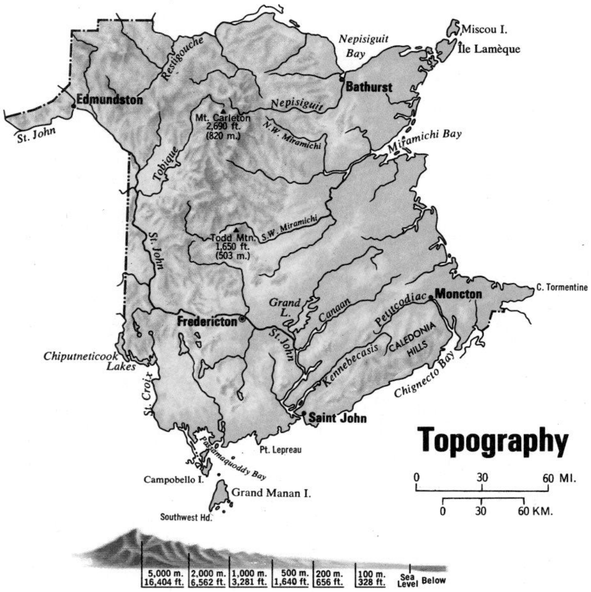

Topography

Agriculture, Industry and Resources

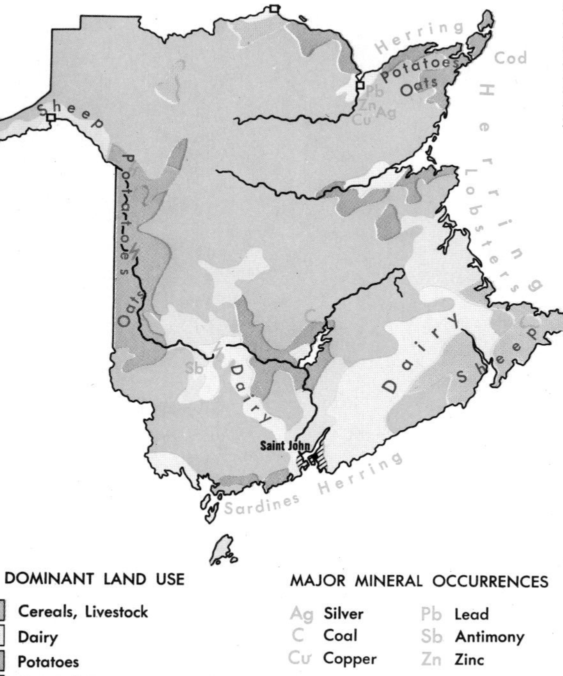

DOMINANT LAND USE

- Cereals, Livestock
- Dairy
- Potatoes
- General Farming, Livestock
- Pasture Livestock
- Forests

MAJOR MINERAL OCCURRENCES

- Ag Silver
- C Coal
- Cu Copper
- Pb Lead
- Sb Antimony
- Zn Zinc
- Water Power
- Major Industrial Areas

Taxis River 118 D 2
Tay Creek 161 D 2
Taymouth 301 D 2
Temperance Vale 357 C 2
The Range 58 E 2
Thibault 306 C 1
Tide Head 952 D 1
Tilley 95 C 2
Tobique Narrows 140 C 2
Tracadie 2,452 F 1
Tracy 636 D 3
Turtle Creek 81 F 3
Tweedside 87 C 3
Upham 107 E 3
Upper Blackville 60 E 2
Upper Buctouche 158 F 2
Upper Gagetown 236 D 3
Upper Hainesville 189 C 2
Upper Kent 203 C 2
Upper Maugerville 543 D 3
Upper Mills 153 C 3
Upper Rockport 18 F 3
Upper Sheila 706 E 1
Upper Woodstock 257 C 2
Upsalquitch 112 D 1
Val-Comeau 534 F 1
Val d'Amour 462 D 1
Val Doucet 505 E 1
Verret 637 B 1
Village-Saint-Laurent 187 E 1
Waasis 264 D 3
Wapske 195 C 2
Waterford 120 E 3
Waterville 181 C 2
Waweig C 3
Wayerton 188 E 1
Weaver 86 E 2
Weldon 227 F 3
Welsford 230 D 3
Welshpool 260 D 4
Westfield 1,100 D 3
West Quaco 48 E 3
White Head 185 D 4
White Rapids 238 E 2
Whitney 216 E 2
Wickham 72 D 3
Wicklow 143 C 2
Williamsburg 258 D 2
Williamstown 156 C 2
Willow Grove 509 E 3
Wilmot 57 C 3
Wilson Point 45 F 1
Wilsons Beach 844 D 4
Windsor 43 C 2
Wirral 110 D 3
Woodstock⊙ 4,649 C 2
Woodwards Cove 146 D 4
Youngs Cove 65 E 3
Zealand 458 D 2

OTHER FEATURES

Bald (mt.) C 1
Bartibog (riv.) E 1
Bay du Vin (riv.) E 2
Big Tracadie (riv.) E 1
Buctouche (harb.) F 2
Buctouche (riv.) F 2
Campobello (isl.) D 4
Canaan (riv.) E 2
Carleton (mt.) D 1
Chaleur (bay) E 1
Chignecto (bay) F 3
Chiputneticook (lakes) C 3
Cocagne (isl.) F 2
Cumberland (basin) F 3
Deer (isl.) D 4
Digdeguash (riv.) C 3
Escuminac (bay) D 1
Escuminac (pt.) F 1
Fundy (bay) E 3
Fundy Nat'l Park E 3
Gaspereau (riv.) D 2
Grand (bay) D 3
Grand (lake) C 3
Grand (lake) D 3
Grand Manan (chan.) C 4
Grand Manan (isl.) D 4
Grande (riv.) C 1
Green (riv.) B 1
Hammond (riv.) E 3
Harvey (lake) C 3
Heron (isl.) D 1
Kedgwick (riv.) C 1
Kennebecasis (riv.) E 3
Keswick (riv.) C 2
Kouchibouguac (bay) F 2
Kouchibouguacis (riv.) E 2
Kouchibouguac Nat'l Park F 2
Lamèque (isl.) F 1
Lepreau (riv.) D 3
Little (riv.) D 2
Long (isl.) D 3
Long Reach (inlet) D 3
Maces (bay) D 3
Mactaquac (lake) C 3
Madawaska (riv.) B 1
Magaguadavic (lake) C 3
Magaguadavic (riv.) C 3
Miramichi (bay) E 1
Miscou (isl.) F 1
Miscou (pt.) F 1
Mount Carleton Prov. Park D 1
Musquash (harb.) D 3
Nashwaak (riv.) D 2
Nepisiguit (bay) E 1
Nepisiguit (riv.) D 1
Nerepis (riv.) D 3
Northern (head) D 4
North Sevogle (riv.) D 1
Northumberland (str.) F 2
Northwest Miramichi (riv.) D 1
Oromocto (lake) C 3
Oromocto (riv.) D 3
Passamaquoddy (bay) C 3
Patapédia (riv.) C 1
Petitcodiac (riv.) F 3
Pokemouche (riv.) E 1
Pokesudie (isl.) F 1
Pollett (riv.) E 3
Quaco (head) E 3
Renous (riv.) D 2
Restigouche (riv.) C 1
Richibucto (harb.) F 2
Richibucto (riv.) E 2
Roosevelt Campobello Int'l Park D 4
Saint Croix (riv.) C 3
Saint Francis (riv.) A 1
Saint John (harb.) E 3
Saint John (riv.) C 2
Saint Lawrence (gulf) F 1
Salisbury (bay) F 3
Salmon (riv.) C 1
Salmon (riv.) E 2
Shediac (isl.) F 2
Shepody (bay) F 3
Shippegan (bay) E 1
Shippegan Gully (str.) F 1
South Sevogle (riv.) D 1
Southwest (head) D 4
Southwest Miramichi (riv.) D 2
Spear (cape) G 2
Spednik (lake) C 3
Spencer (cape) E 3
Tabusintac (riv.) E 1
Tabusintac Gully (str.) F 1
Tetagouche (riv.) D 1
Tobique (riv.) C 2
Upsalquitch (riv.) D 1
Utopia (lake) D 3
Verte (bay) G 2
Washademoak (lake) E 3
West (isls.) D 4
White Head (isl.) D 4

⊙County seat.

Topography

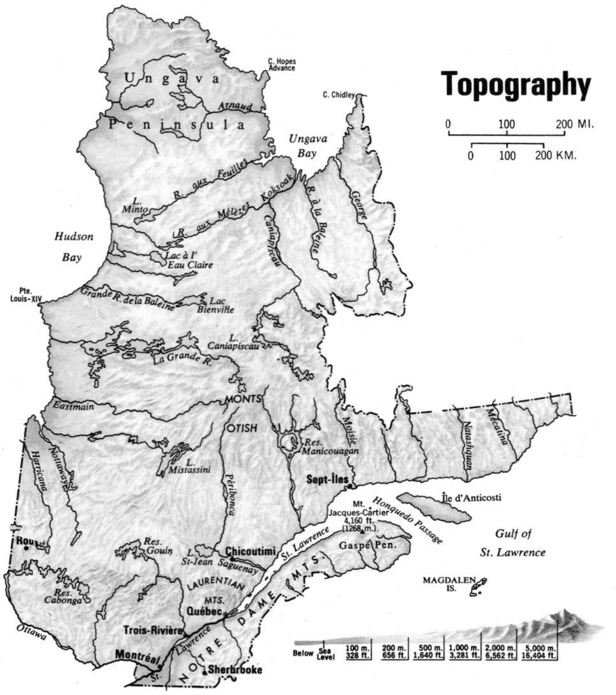

COUNTIES

Argenteuil 32,454 . . . . C 4
Arthabaska 59,277 . . . . E 4
Bagot 26,840 . . . . E 4
Beauce 73,427 . . . . G 3
Beauharnois 54,034 . . . . C 4
Bellechasse 23,559 . . . . G 3
Berthier 31,096 . . . . C 3
Bonaventure 40,487 . . . . C 2
Brome 17,436 . . . . E 4
Chambly 307,090 . . . . J 4
Champlain 119,595 . . . . E 2
Charlevoix-Est 17,448 . . . . . . G 2
Charlevoix-Ouest 14,172 . . . . G 2
Châteauguay 59,968 . . . . D 4
Chicoutimi 174,441 . . . . G 1
Compton 20,536 . . . . F 4
Deux-Montagnes 71,252 . . . . C 4
Dorchester 33,949 . . . . C 3
Drummond 69,770 . . . . E 4
Frontenac 26,814 . . . . G 4
Gaspé-Est 41,173 . . . . D 1
Gaspé-Ouest 18,943 . . . . C 1
Gatineau 54,229 . . . . B 3
Hull 131,213 . . . . B 4
Huntingdon 16,953 . . . . C 4
Iberville 23,180 . . . . D 4
Île-de-Montréal 1,760,122 . . . . H 4
Île-Jésus 268,335 . . . . H 4
Joliette 60,384 . . . . C 3
Kamouraska 28,642 . . . . H 2
Labelle 34,395 . . . . B 3
Lac-Saint-Jean-Est 47,891 . . . F 1
Lac-Saint-Jean-Ouest 62,952 . E 1
Laprairie 105,962 . . . . H 4
L'Assomption 109,705 . . . . D 4
Lévis 94,104 . . . . J 3
L'Islet 22,062 . . . . G 2
Lotbinière 29,653 . . . . F 3
Maskinongé 20,763 . . . . D 3
Matane 29,955 . . . . B 1
Matapédia 23,715 . . . . B 2
Mégantic 57,892 . . . . F 3
Missisquoi 36,161 . . . . D 4
Montcalm 27,557 . . . . C 3
Montmagny 25,622 . . . . G 3
Montmorency No. 1 23,048 . . . F 2
Montmorency No. 2 6,436 . . . . G 3
Napierville 13,562 . . . . D 4
Nicolet 33,513 . . . . E 3
Papineau 37,975 . . . . B 4
Pontiac 20,283 . . . . A 3
Portneuf 58,843 . . . . E 3
Québec 458,980 . . . . F 3
Richelieu 53,058 . . . . D 4
Richmond 40,871 . . . . E 4
Rimouski 69,099 . . . . J 1
Rivière-du-Loup 41,250 . . . . . . H 2
Rouville 42,391 . . . . D 4
Saguenay 115,881 . . . . H 1
Saint-Hyacinthe 55,888 . . . . . . D 4
Saint-Jean 55,576 . . . . D 4
Saint-Maurice 107,703 . . . . D 3
Shefford 70,733 . . . . E 4
Sherbrooke 115,983 . . . . E 4
Soulanges 15,429 . . . . C 4
Stanstead 38,186 . . . . F 4
Témiscouata 52,570 . . . . J 2
Terrebonne 193,865 . . . . H 4
Vaudreuil 50,043 . . . . C 4
Verchères 63,353 . . . . J 4
Wolfe 15,635 . . . . F 4
Yamaska 14,797 . . . . E 3

CITIES and TOWNS

Acton Vale 4,371 . . . . E 4
Albanel 992 . . . . E 1
Alma® 26,322 . . . . F 1
Amqui® 4,048 . . . . B 2
Ancienne-Lorette 12,935 . . . . . H 3
Angers . . . . B 4
Anjou 37,346 . . . . H 4
Annaville 712 . . . . E 3
Armagh 878 . . . . G 3
Arthabaska® 6,827 . . . . F 3
Arvida . . . . F 1
Asbestos 7,967 . . . . F 4
Ascot Corner 847 . . . . F 4
Audet 760 . . . . G 4
Ayer's Cliff® 810 . . . . E 4
Aylmer 26,695 . . . . B 4
Baie-Comeau 12,866 . . . . A 1
Baie-d'Urfé 3,674 . . . . G 4
Baie-Saint-Paul® 3,961 . . . . . . G 2
Baie-Trinité 749 . . . . B 1
Beaconsfield 19,613 . . . . H 4
Beauceville 4,302 . . . . G 3
Beauharnois® 7,025 . . . . D 4
Beaumont 791 . . . . F 3
Beauport 60,447 . . . . J 3
Beaupré 2,740 . . . . G 2
Bécancour® 10,247 . . . . E 3
Bedford® 2,832 . . . . E 4
Beebe Plain 1,072 . . . . E 4
Bélair (Val-Bélair) 12,695 . . . . H 3
Beloeil 17,540 . . . . D 4
Bernierville 2,120 . . . . F 3
Berthier-en-Bas 562 . . . . G 3
Berthierville® 4,049 . . . . D 3
Bic 2,994 . . . . J 1
Biencourt 824 . . . . J 2
Black Lake 5,148 . . . . F 3
Blainville 14,682 . . . . H 4
Boischatel 3,345 . . . . J 3
Bois-des-Filion 4,943 . . . . H 4
Bolduc 1,565 . . . . G 4
Bonaventure 1,371 . . . . C 2
Boucherville 29,704 . . . . J 4
Bromont 2,731 . . . . E 4
Bromptonville 3,035 . . . . F 4
Brossard 52,232 . . . . H 4
Brownsburg 2,875 . . . . C 4
Buckingham 7,992 . . . . B 4
Cabano 3,291 . . . . J 2
Cacouna 1,160 . . . . H 2
Calumet 729 . . . . C 4
Candiac 8,502 . . . . J 4
Cap-à-l'Aigle 819 . . . . G 2
Cap-Chat 3,464 . . . . B 1
Cap-de-la-Madeleine 32,626 . E 3
Caplan-Rivière Caplan 1,139 . C 2
Cap-Saint-Ignace 1,485 . . . . . G 2
Cap-Santé® 671 . . . . F 3
Carignan 4,544 . . . . J 4
Carleton 2,710 . . . . C 2
Causapscal 2,501 . . . . B 2
Chambly 12,190 . . . . J 4
Chambord 961 . . . . E 1
Chandler 3,946 . . . . D 2
Charlemagne 4,827 . . . . H 4
Charlesbourg 68,326 . . . . J 3
Charny 8,240 . . . . J 3
Châteauguay 36,928 . . . . H 4
Château-Richer® 3,628 . . . . . . F 3
Chénéville 633 . . . . B 4
Chicoutimi® 60,064 . . . . G 1
Chicoutimi-Jonquière *135,172 . . . . G 1
Chute-aux-Outardes 2,280 . . . A 1
Clermont 3,621 . . . . G 2
Coaticook 6,271 . . . . F 4
Coleraine 1,660 . . . . F 4
Compton 728 . . . . F 4
Contrecoeur 5,449 . . . . D 4
Cookshire® 1,480 . . . . F 4
Coteau-du-Lac 1,247 . . . . C 4
Coteau-Landing® 1,386 . . . . . . C 4
Côte-Saint-Luc 27,531 . . . . H 4
Courcelles 608 . . . . G 4
Courville . . . . J 3
Cowansville 12,240 . . . . E 4
Crabtree 1,950 . . . . D 4
Danville 2,200 . . . . E 4
Daveluyville 1,257 . . . . E 3
Deauville 942 . . . . E 4
Dégelis 3,477 . . . . J 2
Delisle 4,011 . . . . F 1
Delson 4,935 . . . . H 4
Desbiens 1,541 . . . . E 1
Deschaillons-sur-Saint-Laurent 950 . . . . E 3
Deschambault 977 . . . . E 3
Deschênes . . . . B 4
Deux-Montagnes 9,944 . . . . . . H 4
Didyme 667 . . . . E 1
Disraëli 3,181 . . . . F 4
Dolbeau 8,766 . . . . E 1
Dollard-des-Ormeaux 39,940 . H 4
Donnacona 5,731 . . . . F 3
Dorion 5,749 . . . . C 4
Dorval 17,727 . . . . H 4
Dosquet 703 . . . . F 3
Douville . . . . D 4
Drummondville® 27,347 . . . . . E 4
Drummondville-Sud 9,220 . . . . E 4
Dunham 2,887 . . . . E 4
Durham-Sud 1,045 . . . . E 4
East Angus 4,016 . . . . F 4
East Broughton 1,397 . . . . F 3
East Broughton Station 1,302 . F 3
Eastman 612 . . . . E 4
Entrelacs 1,735 . . . . C 3
Farnham 6,498 . . . . E 4
Ferme-Neuve 2,266 . . . . B 3
Forestville 4,271 . . . . H 1
Frampton 684 . . . . G 3
Francoeur 1,422 . . . . F 3
Gaspé 17,261 . . . . D 1
Gatineau 74,988 . . . . B 4
Giffard . . . . J 3
Girardville 1,128 . . . . E 1
Gracefield 869 . . . . A 3
Granby 38,069 . . . . E 4
Grand'Mère 15,442 . . . . E 3
Grande-Rivière 4,420 . . . . D 2
Grandes-Bergeronnes 748 . . . H 1
Grande-Vallée 700 . . . . D 1
Greenfield Park 18,527 . . . . . . J 4
Grenville 1,417 . . . . C 4
Gros-Morne 672 . . . . C 1
Hampstead 7,598 . . . . H 4
Ham-Sud® 62 . . . . F 4
Hauterive 13,995 . . . . A 1
Hébertville 2,515 . . . . F 1
Hébertville-Station 1,442 . . . . F 1
Hemmingford 737 . . . . D 4
Henryville 595 . . . . D 4
Howick 639 . . . . D 4
Hudson 4,414 . . . . C 4
Hull® 56,225 . . . . B 4
Huntingdon® 3,018 . . . . C 4
Île-Perrot 5,945 . . . . G 4
Iberville® 8,587 . . . . D 4
Inverness® 329 . . . . F 3
Joliette® 16,987 . . . . D 3
Jonquière 60,354 . . . . F 1
Jonquière-Chicoutimi *135,172 . . . . F 1
Kingsey Falls 818 . . . . E 4
Kirkland 10,476 . . . . H 4
Knowlton (Lac-Brome)® 4,316 . . . . E 4
La Baie 20,935 . . . . G 1
Labelle 1,534 . . . . C 3
Lac-à-la-Croix 1,017 . . . . F 1
Lac-Alouette-Lac-Brière 1,356 D 4
Lac-au-Saumon 1,332 . . . . B 2
Lac-aux-Sables 838 . . . . E 3
Lac-Beaufort . . . . F 3
Lac-Bouchette 1,703 . . . . E 1
Lac-Carré 717 . . . . C 3
Lac-des-Écorces 766 . . . . B 3
Lac-Drolet 1,120 . . . . G 4
Lac-Etchemin 2,729 . . . . G 3
Lachenaie 8,631 . . . . D 4
Lachine 37,521 . . . . H 4
Lachute® 11,729 . . . . C 4
Lac-Mégantic® 6,119 . . . . G 4
Lacolle 1,319 . . . . D 4
Lac-Saint-Charles 5,837 . . . . . H 3
Lafontaine 4,799 . . . . C 4
La Guadeloupe 1,692 . . . . F 4
La Malbaie® 4,030 . . . . G 2
Lambton 1,559 . . . . F 4
L'Annonciation 2,384 . . . . C 3
Lanoraie (Lanoraie-d'Autry) 1,613 . . . . D 4
La Pêche 4,977 . . . . B 4
La Pérade 1,039 . . . . E 3
La Pocatière 4,560 . . . . H 2
La Prairie® 10,627 . . . . J 4
La Providence . . . . E 4
Larouche 662 . . . . F 1
La Salle 76,299 . . . . H 4
L'Ascension 1,287 . . . . F 1
L'Assomption® 4,844 . . . . D 4
La Station-du-Coteau 892 . . . . C 4
Laterrière 788 . . . . F 1
La Tuque 11,556 . . . . E 2
Laurentides 1,947 . . . . D 4
Laurier-Station 1,123 . . . . F 3
Laurierville 939 . . . . F 3
Lauzon 13,362 . . . . J 3
Laval 268,335 . . . . H 4
Lavaltrie 2,053 . . . . D 4
L'Avenir 1,116 . . . . E 4
Lawrenceville 562 . . . . E 4
Le Moyne 6,137 . . . . J 4
L'Épiphanie 2,971 . . . . D 4
Léry 2,239 . . . . H 4
Lévis 17,895 . . . . J 3
Lennoxville 3,922 . . . . F 4
Les Méchins 803 . . . . B 1
Linière 1,168 . . . . G 3
L'Islet 1,070 . . . . G 2
L'Islet-sur-Mer 774 . . . . G 2
L'Isle-Verte 1,142 . . . . G 1
Longueuil® 124,320 . . . . J 4
Loretteville® 15,060 . . . . H 3
Lorraine 6,881 . . . . H 4
Louiseville® 3,735 . . . . E 3
Luceville 1,524 . . . . J 1
Lyster 830 . . . . F 3
Magog 13,604 . . . . E 4
Maniwaki® 5,424 . . . . B 3
Manseau 626 . . . . E 3
Maple Grove 2,009 . . . . H 4
Maria 1,178 . . . . C 2
Marieville® 4,877 . . . . D 4
Mascouche 20,345 . . . . H 4
Maskinongé 1,005 . . . . E 3
Masson 4,264 . . . . B 4
Massueville 671 . . . . E 4
Matane® 13,612 . . . . B 1
Matapédia 586 . . . . B 2
Melocheville 1,892 . . . . C 4
Mercier 6,352 . . . . H 4
Metabetchouan 3,406 . . . . F 1
Mirabel® 14,080 . . . . H 4
Mistassini 6,682 . . . . E 1
Montauban 557 . . . . E 3
Mont-Carmel 807 . . . . H 2
Montcerf 570 . . . . A 3
Montebello 1,229 . . . . B 4
Mont-Joli 6,359 . . . . J 1
Mont-Laurier® 8,405 . . . . B 3
Mont-Louis 756 . . . . C 1
Montmagny® 12,405 . . . . G 3
Montréal® 980,354 . . . . H 4
Montréal *2,828,349 . . . . H 4
Montréal-Est 3,778 . . . . J 4
Montréal-Nord 94,914 . . . . H 4
Mont-Rolland 1,517 . . . . C 4
Mont-Royal 19,247 . . . . H 4
Mont-Saint-Hilaire 10,066 . . . . D 4
Morin Heights 592 . . . . C 4
Murdochville 3,396 . . . . C 1
Nantes 1,167 . . . . F 4

Agriculture, Industry and Resources

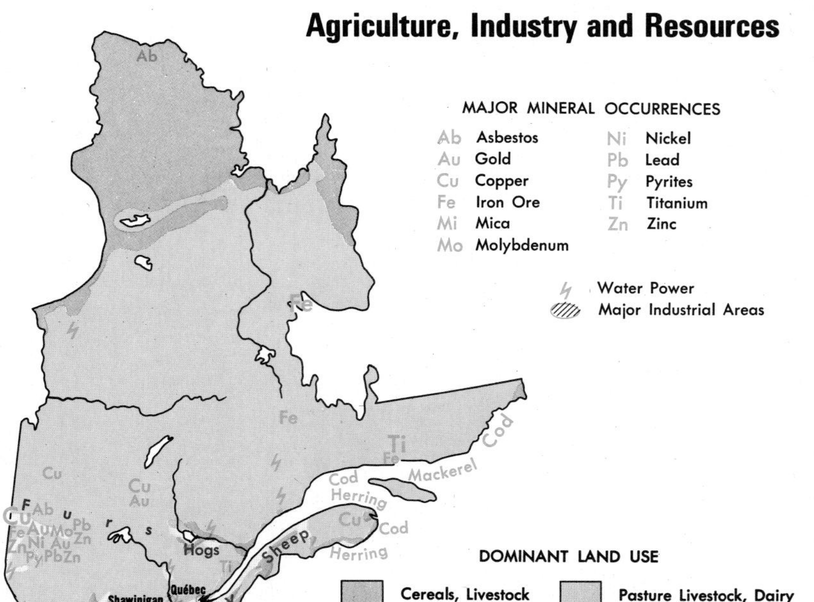

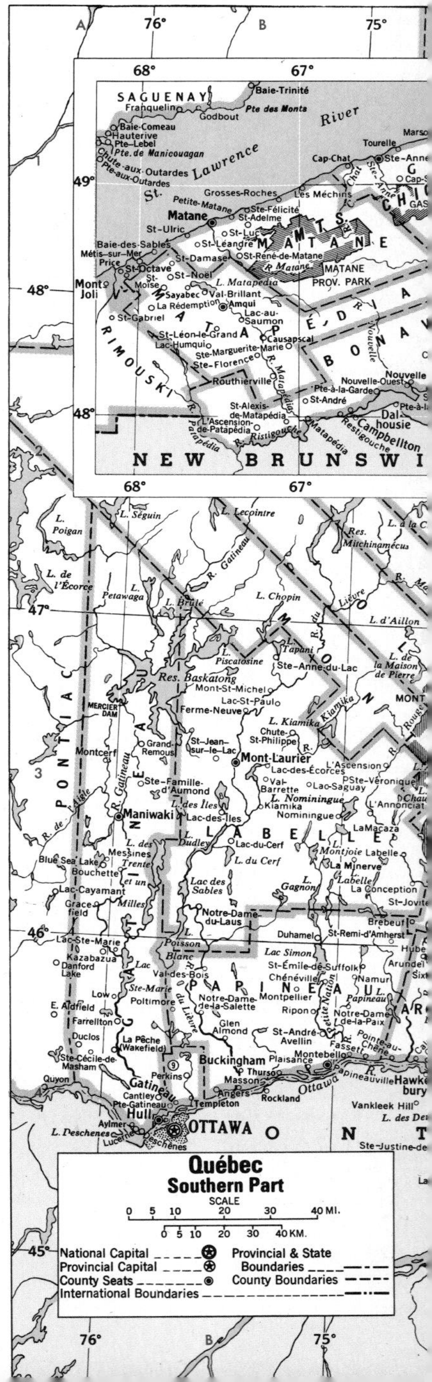

Napierville◎ 2,343 .... D 4
Neuville 996.............. F 3
New Carlisle◎ 1,292......... D 2
New Richmond 4,257......... C 2
Nicolet 4,880 .... E 3
Nominingue 881 .... B 3
Normandin 4,041 .... E 1
North Hatley 689............ F 4
Notre-Dame-de-la-Doré 1,064 E 1
Notre-Dame-des-Laurentides . H 3
Notre-Dame-des-Prairies
6,150 .... D 3
Notre-Dame-du-Bon-Conseil
1,089 .... E 4
Notre-Dame-du-Lac◎ 2,258 .. J 2
Nouvelle 669 .... C 2
Oka 1,538................. C 4
Omerville 1,398............ E 4
Ormstown 1,659 .... D 4
Orsainville .... H 3
Otis 673 .... G 1
Otterburn Park 4,268 .... D 4
Outremont 24,338........... H 4
Pabos 1,295............... D 2
Pabos-Mills 1,565 .... D 2
Papineauville◎ 1,481 .... C 4
Paspébiac 1,914 .... D 2
Percé◎ 4,839.............. D 1
Petit-Cap 1,023 .... D 1
Petite-Matane 1,065......... B 1
Petit-Saguenay (Saint-
François-d'Assise) 804 .... G 1
Pierrefonds 38,390 .... H 4
Pierreville 1,212 .... E 3

Pincourt 8,750.............. D 4
Pintendre 1,849............. J 3
Plaisance 748 .... B 4
Plessisville 7,249 .... F 3
Pohénégamooke 3,702 ...... H 2
Pointe-à-la-Croix 1,481 ...... C 2
Pointe-au-Père 796.......... J 1
Pointe-au-Pic 1,054 .... G 2
Pointe-aux-Outardes 1,056... A 1
Pointe-aux-Trembles 36,270 .. J 4
Pointe-Calumet 2,935 .... G 4
Pointe-Claire 24,571......... H 4
Pointe-du-Lac 5,359......... E 3
Pointe-Gatineau .... B 4
Pointe-Lebel 1,573 .... A 1
Pont-Rouge 3,580........... F 3
Port-Alfred 8,621 .... G 1
Portneuf 1,333.............. F 3
Portneuf-sur-Mer (Rivière-
Portneuf-sur-Mer) 1,255 ... H 1
Price 2,273................. A 1
Princeville 4,023 .... F 3
Proulxville 588............. E 3
Québec (cap.) 166,474 ...... H 3
Québec *576,075 .... H 3
Quyon 744 .... A 4
Rawdon 2,958 .... D 3
Repentigny 34,419 .... J 4
Richelieu 1,832............. D 4
Richmond◎ 3,568........... E 4
Rigaud 2,268............... C 4
Rimouski◎ 29,120 .... J 1
Rimouski-Est 2,506 .... J 1
Ripon 620.................. B 4

Rivière-à-Pierre 615 .... E 3
Rivière-au-Renard 2,211 ..... D 1
Rivière-Bleue 1,690 .... J 2
Rivière-Bois-Clair 604 .... F 3
Rivière-du-Loup◎ 13,459..... H 2
Rivière-du-Moulin .... G 1
Rivière-Éternité 659 .... G 1
Rivière-Portneuf-Portneuf-sur-
Mer 1,255 .... H 1
Robertsonville 1,987 .... F 3
Roberval◎ 11,429........... E 1
Rock Island 1,179........... E 4
Rosemère 7,778 .... H 4
Rougemont 972............. D 4
Roxboro 6,292.............. H 4
Roxton Falls 1,245 .... E 4
Sacré-Coeur-de-Saguenay
1,678 .... H 1
Saint-Adelme 618........... B 1
Saint-Adelphe 1,159......... E 3
Saint-Adolphe-d'Howard
1,686.................... C 4
Saint-Adrien 597............ F 4
Saint-Agapitville 2,954....... F 3
Saint-Aimé-des-Lacs 861 .... G 2
Saint-Alban 673............. E 3
Saint-Alexandre-de-
Kamouraska 1,048........ H 2
Saint-Alexis-des-Monts 1,984. D 3
Saint-Amable 2,424 .... J 4
Saint-Ambroise 3,606......... F 1
Saint-Anaclet 1,377 .... J 1
Saint-André-Avellin 1,312 .... B 4
Saint-André-Est 1,293 .... C 4

Saint-Anselme 1,808 .... F 3
Saint-Antoine 7,012 .... H 4
Saint-Antonin 941........... H 2
Saint-Aubert 884............ G 2
Saint-Augustin-de-Québec
2,475 .... E 3
Saint-Basile-Sud 1,719 ...... F 3
Saint-Basile-le-Grand 7,658 .. J 4
Saint-Benjamin 1,027........ G 3
Saint-Bernard 585 .... F 3
Saint-Bernard-sur-Mer 711 ... G 2
Saint-Boniface-de-Shawinigan
3,164 .... D 3
Saint-Bruno 2,580........... F 1
Saint-Bruno-de-Montarville
22,880 .... J 4
Saint-Camille-de-Bellechasse
1,744 .... G 3
Saint-Casimir 1,133 .... E 3
Saint-Césaire 2,935 .... D 4
Saint-Charles 1,019 .... G 3
Saint-Charles-de-Mandeville
1,392 .... D 3
Saint-Chrysostome 1,018 .... D 4
Saint-Côme 660 .... D 3
Saint-Constant 9,938........ H 4
Saint-Cyprien 860........... J 2
Saint-Cyrille 1,041 .... E 4
Saint-Damien-de-Buckland
1,522 .... G 3
Saint-David 5,380........... J 3
Saint-David-de-Falardeau
1,876 .... F 1
Saint-Denis 861 .... D 4

AREA 594,857 sq. mi. (1,540,680 sq. km.)
POPULATION 6,438,403
CAPITAL Québec
LARGEST CITY Montréal
HIGHEST POINT Mont D'Iberville 5,420 ft. (1,652 m.)
SETTLED IN 1608
ADMITTED TO CONFEDERATION 1867
PROVINCIAL FLOWER White Garden Lily

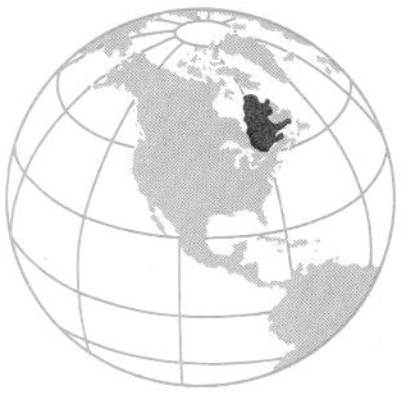

Saint-Dominique 2,068 ...... E 4
Saint-Donat-de-Montcalm
1,521 .... C 3
Sainte-Adèle 4,675.......... C 4
Sainte-Agathe 709 .... F 3
Sainte-Agathe-des-Monts
5,641 .... C 3
Sainte-Anne-de-Beaupré
3,292 .... F 2
Sainte-Anne-de-Bellevue
3,981 .... H 4
Sainte-Anne-des-Monts◎
6,062 .... C 1
Sainte-Anne-des-Plaines
4,258 .... H 4
Sainte-Anne-du-Lac 686 ..... B 3
Sainte-Aurélie 1,045......... G 3
Sainte-Blandine 849......... J 1

Sainte-Catherine 1,474 ...... F 3
Sainte-Claire 1,566.......... G 3
Sainte-Croix◎ 1,814......... F 3
Sainte-Félicité 711 .... B 1
Sainte-Foy 68,883 .... H 3
Sainte-Geneviève 2,573 ..... H 4
Sainte-Genevièe-de-
Batiscan◎ 356 .... E 3
Sainte-Hélène-de-Bagot
1,328.................... E 4
Sainte-Hénédine◎ 639....... F 3
Sainte-Julie-de-Verchères
14,243 .... J 4
Sainte-Julienne◎ 750........ D 4
Sainte-Justine 1,080 .... G 3
Saint-Élie 639 .... E 3
Saint-Elzéar 743 .... F 3
Sainte-Marie 8,937.......... G 3

Sainte-Martine◎ 2,196....... D 4
Saint-Émile 5,216........... H 3
Sainte-Monique 705......... F 1
Sainte-Pétronille 982 .... J 3
Sainte-Perpétue-de-L'Islet
1,232 .... H 2
Saint-Éphrem-de-Tring 973 ... G 3
Saint-Épiphane 647 .... H 2
Sainte-Pudentienne 866 ..... E 4
Sainte-Rosalie 2,862 .... E 4
Saint-Esprit 1,068........... D 4
Sainte-Thérèse 18,750....... H 4
Sainte-Thérèse-Ouest
(Boisbriand) 13,471 .... H 4
Sainte-Thècle 1,703 .... E 3
Saint-Étienne-de-Grès 845 ... E 3
Saint-Étienne-de-Lauzon
1,218 .... J 3

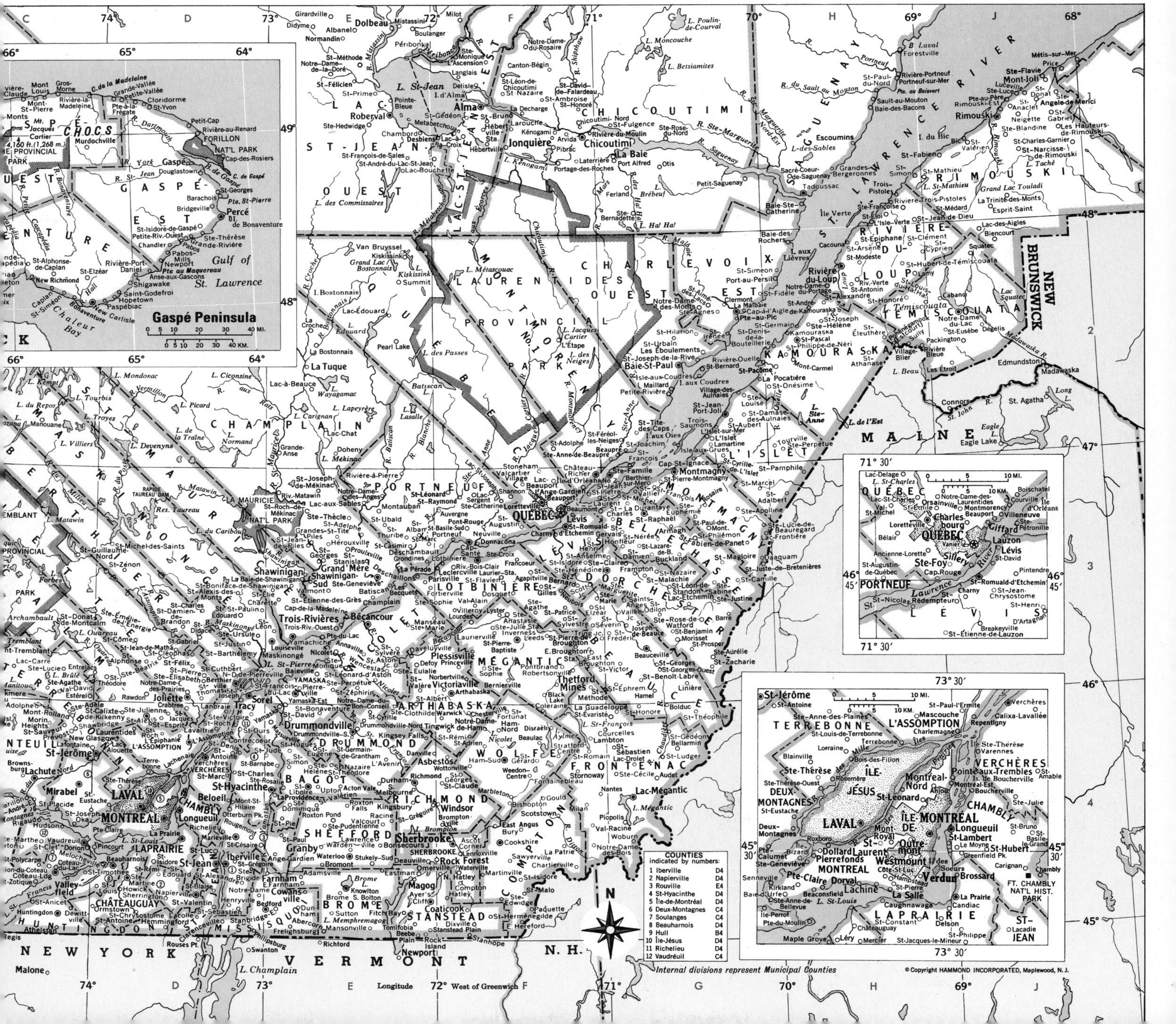

(continued)

Saint-Eustache 29,716 H 4
Saint-Fabien 1,361 J 1
Saint-Félicien 9,058 E 1
Saint-Félix-de-Valois 1,462 D 3
Saint-Ferréol-les-Neiges 1,758 G 2
Saint-Flavien 734 F 3
Saint-François-de-Sales 831 E 1
Saint-François-du-Lac⊙ 942 E 3
Saint-Fulgence 950 G 1
Saint-Gabriel 3,161 D 3
Saint-Gabriel-de-Rimouski 779 J 1
Saint-Gédéon, Frontenac 1,569 G 4
Saint-Gédéon, Lac-St-Jean-E. 1,000 F 1
Saint-Georges, Beauce 10,342 G 3
Saint-Georges, Champlain 3,344 E 3
Saint-Georges-Ouest 6,378 G 3
Saint-Germain-de-Grantham 1,373 E 4
Saint-Gervais 973 G 3
Saint-Gilles 912 F 3
Saint-Grégoire (Mont-St-Grégoire) 740 D 4
Saint-Henri 1,970 J 3
Saint-Honoré, Beauce 1,116 G 4
Saint-Honoré, Chicoutimi 1,790 F 1
Saint-Hubert 60,573 J 4
Saint-Hubert-de-Témiscouata 871 J 2
Saint-Hyacinthe⊙ 38,246 D 4
Saint-Isidore 811 F 3
Saint-Isidore-de-Laprairie 769 D 4
Saint-Jacques 2,152 D 4
Saint-Jacques-le-Mineur 1,203 H 4
Saint-Jean-Chrysostome 6,930 J 3
Saint-Jean-de-Dieu 1,377 J 1
Saint-Jean-de-Matha 931 D 3
Saint-Jean-Port-Joli⊙ 1,813 G 2
Saint-Jean-sur-Richelieu⊙ 35,640 D 4
Saint-Jérôme 25,123 H 4
Saint-Joachim 1,139 G 2
Saint-Joseph-de-Beauce 3,216 G 3
Saint-Joseph-de-Sorel 2,545 D 3
Saint-Jovite 3,841 C 3
Saint-Lambert 20,557 J 4
Saint-Laurent 65,900 H 4
Saint-Lazare 731 G 3
Saint-Léonard 79,429 H 4
Saint-Léonard-d'Aston 992 E 3
Saint-Léon-de-Chicoutimi 749 F 1
Saint-Léon-de-Standon 816 G 3
Saint-Léon-le-Grand 722 B 2
Saint-Liboire⊙ 746 E 4
Saint-Louis-de-Gonzague 615 D 4
Saint-Louis-de-Terrebonne 14,172 H 4
Saint-Louis-du-Ha! Ha! 809 H 2
Saint-Luc 8,815 D 4
Saint-Luc-de-Matane 598 B 1
Saint-Marc-des-Carrières 2,822 E 3
Saint-Méthode-de-Frontenac 925 F 3
Saint-Michel-de-Bellechasse 963 G 3
Saint-Michel-des-Saints 1,584 D 3
Saint-Nazaire-de-Chicoutimi 962 F 1
Saint-Nérée 970 G 3
Saint-Nicolas 5,074 H 3
Saint-Noël 666 B 1
Saint-Odilon 580 G 3
Saint-Omer 718 C 2
Saint-Ours 625 D 4
Saint-Pacôme 1,996 G 2
Saint-Pamphile 3,428 H 3
Saint-Pascal⊙ 2,763 H 2
Saint-Paul-de-Montminy 602 G 3
Saint-Paulin 663 D 3
Saint-Paul-l'Ermite (Le Gardeur) 8,312 J 4
Saint-Philippe-de-Néri 715 H 2
Saint-Pie 1,725 E 4
Saint-Pierre 5,305 H 4
Saint-Pierre-d'Orléans 880 G 3
Saint-Polycarpe 602 C 4
Saint-Prime 2,522 E 1
Saint-Prosper-de-Dorchester 2,150 G 3
Saint-Raphaël⊙ 1,346 G 3
Saint-Raymond 3,605 F 3
Saint-Rédempteur 4,463 J 3
Saint-Régis 1,370 C 4
Saint-Rémi 5,146 D 4
Saint-Roch-de-l'Achigan 1,160 D 4
Saint-Roch-de-Richelieu 1,650 D 4
Saint-Romuald-d'Etchemin⊙ 9,849 J 3
Saint-Sauveur-des-Monts 2,348 C 4
Saint-Siméon 1,152 G 2
Saint-Simon 602 H 1
Saint-Stanislas 1,443 E 3
Saint-Sylvère 1,006 E 3
Saint-Timothée 2,113 D 4
Saint-Tite 3,031 E 3
Saint-Tite-des-Caps 626 G 2
Saint-Ubald 1,605 E 3
Saint-Ulric 792 B 1
Saint-Urbain-de-Charlevoix 1,079 G 2
Saint-Victor 1,104 G 3
Saint-Zacharie 1,284 G 3
Saint-Zotique 1,774 C 4
Sault-au-Mouton 828 H 1
Sawyerville 939 F 4
Sayabec 1,721 B 2
Scotstown 762 F 4
Senneville 1,221 G 4
Shannon 3,488 F 3
Shawbridge 942 C 4
Shawinigan 23,011 E 3
Shawinigan-Sud 11,325 E 3
Shawville 1,608 A 4
Sherbrooke⊙ 74,075 E 4
Sherrington 614 D 4
Sillery 12,825 J 3
Sorel⊙ 20,347 D 4
Squatec 1,000 J 2
Stanstead Plain 1,093 F 4
Sutton 1,599 E 4
Tadoussac⊙ 900 H 1
Templeton B 4
Terrebonne 11,769 H 4
Thetford Mines 19,965 F 3
Thurso 2,780 B 4
Tourelle (Tourelle-Grand-Tourelle) 942 C 1
Tourville 659 H 2
Tracy 12,843 D 3
Tring-Jonction 1,315 F 3
Trois-Pistoles 4,445 H 1
Trois-Rivières 50,466 E 3
Trois-Rivières *111,453 E 3
Trois-Rivières-Ouest 13,107 E 3
Upton 926 E 4
Val-Barrette 609 B 3
Val-Brillant 687 B 1
Valcourt 2,601 E 4
Val-David 2,336 C 3
Vallée-Jonction 1,200 G 3
Valleyfield (Salaberry-de-Valleyfield) 29,574 C 4
Vanier 10,725 J 3
Varennes 8,764 J 4
Vaudreuil⊙ 7,608 C 4
Verchères⊙ 4,473 J 4
Verdun 61,287 H 4
Victoriaville 21,838 F 3
Villeneuve J 3
Warwick 2,847 F 4
Waterloo⊙ 4,664 E 4
Waterville 1,397 F 4
Weedon-Centre 1,263 F 4
Westmount 20,480 H 4
Wickham 2,043 E 4
Windsor 5,233 F 4
Wottonville 673 F 4
Yamachiche⊙ 1,258 E 3

OTHER FEATURES

Alma (isl.) F 1
Aylmer (lake) F 4
Baskatong (res.) B 3
Batiscan (riv.) E 2
Bécancour (riv.) F 3
Bonaventure (isl.) D 1
Bonaventure (riv.) C 1
Brome (lake) E 4
Brompton (lake) E 4
Cascapédia (riv.) C 1
Chaleur (bay) C 2
Champlain (lake) D 4
Chaudière (riv.) G 4
Chic-Chocs (mts.) C 1
Chicoutimi (riv.) F 2
Coudres (isl.) G 2
Deschênes (lake) A 4
Deux Montagnes (lake) C 4
Ditton (riv.) F 4
Forillon Nat'l Park D 1
Fort Chambly Nat'l Hist. Park J 4
Gaspé (bay) D 1
Gaspé (cape) D 1
Gaspé (pen.) D 2
Gaspésie Prov. Park C 1
Gatineau (riv.) B 3
Îles (lake) B 3
Jacques-Cartier (mt.) C 1
Jacques-Cartier (riv.) F 2
Kénogami (lake) F 1
Kiamika (lake) B 3
La Maurice Nat'l Park D 3
Laurentides Prov. Park F 2
Lièvre (riv.) B 4
Lièvres (isl.) H 2
Maskinongé (riv.) D 3
Matane (riv.) B 1
Matane Prov. Park B 1
Matapédia (riv.) B 2
Mégantic (lake) G 4
Memphremagog (lake) E 4
Mercier (dam) A 3
Métabetchouane (riv.) F 1
Mille Îles (riv.) H 4
Montmorency (riv.) F 2
Mont-Tremblant Prov. Park C 3
Nicolet (riv.) E 3
Nominingue (lake) B 3
Nord (riv.) C 4
Orléans (isl.) F 3
Ottawa (riv.) B 4
Ouareau (riv.) D 3
Ouelle (riv.) H 2
Patapédia (riv.) B 2
Péribonca (riv.) F 1
Petite Nation (riv.) B 4
Prairies (riv.) H 4
Rimouski (riv.) J 1
Ristigouche (riv.) B 2
Saguenay (riv.) G 1
Sainte-Anne (riv.) F 3
Sainte-Anne (riv.) G 2
Saint-François (lake) F 4
Saint-François (riv.) E 4
Saint-Jean (lake) E 1
Saint Lawrence (gulf) D 2
Saint Lawrence (riv.) H 1
Saint-Louis (lake) H 4
Saint-Maurice (riv.) E 2
Saint-Pierre (lake) E 3
Shawinigan (riv.) E 3
Shipshaw (riv.) F 1
Soeurs (isl.) H 4
Témiscouata (lake) H 2
Tremblant (lake) C 3
Trente et un Milles (lake) B 3
Verte (isl.) H 1
Yamaska (riv.) E 4
York (riv.) D 1

⊙County seat.
*Population of metropolitan area.

QUÉBEC, NORTHERN

INTERNAL DIVISIONS

Abitibi (county) 93,529 B 2
Abitibi (terr.) B 3
Berthier (county) 31,096 B 3
Bonaventure (county) 40,487 D 3
Champlain (county) 119,595 C 3
Charlevoix-Est (co.) 17,448 C 3
Charlevoix-Ouest (county) 14,172 C 3
Chicoutimi (county) 174,441 C 2
Gaspé-Est (county) 41,173 E 3
Gaspé-Ouest (county) 18,943 D 3
Gatineau (county) 54,229 B 3
Joliette (county) 60,384 B 3
Lac-Saint-Jean-Est (county) 47,891 C 3
Lac-Saint-Jean-Ouest (county) 62,952 C 2
Maskinongé (county) 20,763 C 3
Matane (county) 29,955 D 3
Matapédia (county) 23,715 D 3
Mistassini (terr.) B 2
Montcalm (county) 27,557 B 3
Montmorency No. I (county) 23,048 C 3
Nouveau-Québec (terr.) E 1
Pontiac (county) 20,283 B 3
Portneuf (county) 58,843 C 3
Québec (county) 458,980 C 3
Rimouski (county) 69,099 D 3
Saguenay (county) 115,881 D 2
Saint-Maurice (co.) 107,703 C 3
Témiscamingue (co.) 52,570 B 3

CITIES and TOWNS

Alma⊙ 26,322 C 3
Amos⊙ 9,421 B 3
Baie-Comeau 12,866 D 3
Baie-du-Poste 1,690 C 2
Chicoutimi⊙ 60,064 C 3
Gaspé 17,261 E 3
Hauterive 13,995 D 3
Jonquière 60,354 C 3
Lévis 17,895 C 3
La Tuque 11,556 C 3
Manicouagan D 2
Maniwaki⊙ 5,424 B 3
Matane⊙ 13,612 D 3
Mistassini (Baie-du-Poste) 1,690 C 2
Mont-Laurier⊙ 8,405 B 3
Montmagny⊙ 12,405 C 3
New Carlisle⊙ 781 E 3
Nouveau-Comptoir B 2
Percé⊙ 4,839 E 3
Port-Cartier-Ouest D 3
Port-Menier⊙ 275 E 3
Povungnituk 745 E 1
Québec (cap.)⊙ 166,474 C 3
Rimouski⊙ 29,120 D 3
Rivière-au-Tonnerre 480 D 2
Rivière-du-Loup 13,459 D 3
Rouyn 17,224 B 3
Sept-Îles 29,262 D 2
Seven Islands (Sept-Îles) 29,262 D 2
Shawinigan 23,011 C 3
Tadoussac 900 C 3
Val d'Or 21,371 B 3
Ville-Marie 2,651 B 3

OTHER FEATURES

Allard (lake) E 2
Anticosti (isl.) E 3
Baleine, Grand Rivière de la (riv.) B 1
Bell (riv.) B 3
Betsiamites (riv.) C 2
Bienville (lake) C 2
Broadback (riv.) B 2
Cabonga (res.) B 3
Caniapiscau (riv.) D 1
Eastmain (riv.) B 2
Eau Claire (lake) C 1
Feuilles (riv.) C 1
Gaspésie Prov. Park D 3
George (riv.) F 2
Gouin (res.) C 3
Grande Rivière, La (riv.) B 2
Honguedo (passage) E 3
Hudson (bay) A 1
Hudson (str.) F 1
Jacques-Cartier (passage) E 3
James (bay) A 2
Koksoak (riv.) D 1
Laurentides Prov. Park C 3
Louis-XIV (pt.) B 2
Manicouagan (res.) D 2
Minto (lake) E 2
Mistassibi (riv.) C 3
Mistassini (lake) C 2
Moisie (riv.) D 2
Natashquan (riv.) E 2
Nottaway (riv.) B 2
Nouveau-Québec (crater) F 1
Otish (mts.) C 2
Ottawa (riv.) B 3
Péribonca (riv.) C 3
Plétipi (lake) C 2
Saguenay (riv.) C 3
Saint-Jean (lake) C 3
Saint Lawrence (gulf) E 3
Saint Lawrence (riv.) D 3
Ungava (pen.) E 1

⊙County seat.
*Population of metropolitan area.

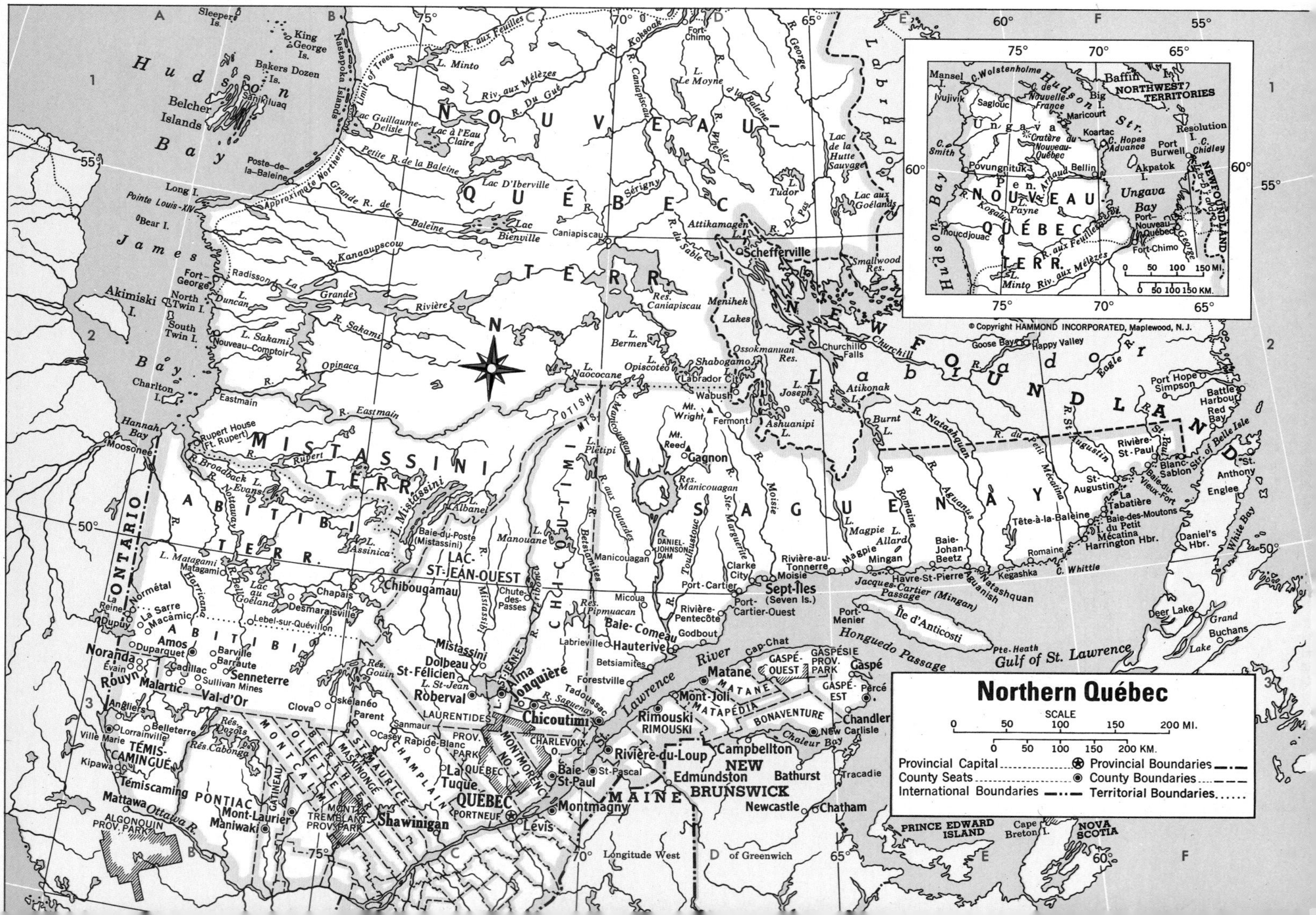

ONTARIO, NORTHERN

INTERNAL DIVISIONS

Algoma (terr. dist.) 133,553 . . . D 3
Cochrane (terr. dist.) 96,875 . . D 2
Kenora (terr. dist.) 59,421 . . . . C 2
Manitoulin (terr. dist.) 11,001 . D 3
Nipissing (terr. dist.) 80,268 . . E 3
Parry Sound (terr. dist.)
33,528 . . . . E 3
Rainy River (terr. dist.) 22,798 B 3
Renfrew (county) 87,484 . . . . . E 3
Sudbury (reg. munic.)
159,779 . . . . D 3
Sudbury (terr. dist.) 27,068 . . . D 3
Thunder Bay (terr. dist.)
153,997 . . . . C 3
Timiskaming (terr. dist.)
41,288 . . . . D 3

CITIES and TOWNS

Chalk River 1,010 . . . . E 3
Elliot Lake 16,723 . . . . D 3
Fort Albany 482 . . . . D 2
Fort Frances⊙ 8,906 . . . . B 3
Kapuskasing 12,014 . . . . D 3
Kenora⊙ 9,817 . . . . B 3
Kirkland Lake 12,219 . . . . D 3
Moose Factory 1,452 . . . . D 2
Moosonee 1,433 . . . . D 2
Nickel Centre 12,318 . . . . D 3
North Bay⊙ 51,268 . . . . E 3
Pembroke⊙ 14,026 . . . . E 3
Sault Sainte Marie⊙ 82,697 . . D 3
Sudbury 91,829 . . . . D 3
Thunder Bay⊙ 112,486 . . . . . . C 3
Timmins 46,114 . . . . D 3
Valley East 20,433 . . . . D 3

OTHER FEATURES

Abitibi (lake) . . . . E 3
Abitibi (riv.) . . . . D 2
Albany (riv.) . . . . C 2
Algonquin Prov. Park . . . . E 3
Asheweig (riv.) . . . . C 2
Attawapiskat (lake) . . . . C 2
Attawapiskat (riv.) . . . . C 2
Basswood (lake) . . . . B 3
Berens (riv.) . . . . A 2
Big Trout (lake) . . . . B 2
Black Duck (riv.) . . . . C 1
Bloodvein (riv.) . . . . A 2
Caribou (isl.) . . . . C 3
Cobham (riv.) . . . . A 2
Eabamet (lake) . . . . C 2
Ekwan (riv.) . . . . C 2
English (riv.) . . . . B 2
Fawn (riv.) . . . . C 2
Finger (lake) . . . . B 2
Georgian (bay) . . . . D 3
Hannah (bay) . . . . D 2
Henrietta Maria (cape) . . . . . . D 1
Hudson (bay) . . . . D 1
Huron (lake) . . . . D 3
James (bay) . . . . D 2
Kapiskau (riv.) . . . . D 2
Kapuskasing (riv.) . . . . D 3
Kenogami (riv.) . . . . C 2
Kesagami (riv.) . . . . E 2
Lake of the Woods (lake) . . . . . B 3
Lake Superior Prov. Park . . . . . D 3
Little Current (riv.) . . . . C 2
Long (lake) . . . . C 3
Manitoulin (isl.) . . . . D 3
Mattagami (riv.) . . . . D 3
Michipicoten (isl.) . . . . C 3
Mille Lacs (lake) . . . . B 3
Missinaibi (lake) . . . . D 3
Missinaibi (riv.) . . . . D 2
Missisa (lake) . . . . C 2
Nipigon (lake) . . . . C 3
Nipissing (lake) . . . . E 3
North (chan.) . . . . D 3
North Caribou (lake) . . . . B 2
Nungesser (lake) . . . . B 2
Ogidaki (mt.) . . . . D 3
Ogoki (riv.) . . . . C 2
Opazatika (riv.) . . . . D 3
Opinnagau (riv.) . . . . D 2
Otoskwin (riv.) . . . . B 2
Ottawa (riv.) . . . . E 3
Pipestone (riv.) . . . . B 2
Polar Bear Prov. Park . . . . D 2
Pukaskwa Prov. Park . . . . C 3
Quetico Prov. Park . . . . B 3
Rainy (lake) . . . . B 3
Red (lake) . . . . B 2
Sachigo (riv.) . . . . B 2
Saganaga (lake) . . . . B 3
Saint Ignace (isl.) . . . . C 3
Saint Joseph (lake) . . . . B 2
Sandy (lake) . . . . B 2
Savant (lake) . . . . B 2
Seine (riv.) . . . . B 3
Seul (lake) . . . . B 2
Severn (lake) . . . . B 2
Severn (riv.) . . . . B 2
Shamattawa (riv.) . . . . C 2
Shibogama (lake) . . . . C 2
Sibley Prov. Park . . . . C 3
Slate (isls.) . . . . C 3
Stout (lake) . . . . B 2
Superior (lake) . . . . C 3
Sutton (lake) . . . . D 2
Sutton (riv.) . . . . D 2
Timagami (lake) . . . . D 3
Timiskaming (lake) . . . . E 3
Trout (lake) . . . . B 2
Wabuk (pt.) . . . . D 1
Winisk (lake) . . . . C 2
Winisk (riv.) . . . . C 2
Winnipeg (riv.) . . . . A 2
Woods (lake) . . . . B 3

ONTARIO

INTERNAL DIVISIONS

Algoma (terr. dist.) 133,553 . . . J 5
Brant (county) 104,427 . . . . . . D 4
Bruce (county) 60,020 . . . . C 3
Cochrane (terr. dist.) 96,875 . . J 4
Dufferin (county) 31,145 . . . . . D 3
Dundas (county) 18,946 . . . . . . J 2
Durham (reg. munic.) 283,639 F 3
Elgin (county) 69,707 . . . . C 5
Essex (county) 312,467 . . . . . . B 5
Frontenac (county) 108,133 . . H 3
Glengarry (county) 20,254 . . . K 2
Grenville (county) 27,176 . . . . J 3
Grey (county) 73,824 . . . . D 3
Haldimand-Norfolk (reg.
munic.) 89,456 . . . . E 5
Haliburton (county) 11,361 . . F 2
Halton (reg. munic.) 253,883 . E 4
Hamilton-Wentworth (reg.
munic.) 411,445 . . . . D 4
Hastings (county) 106,883 . . . G 3
Huron (county) 56,127 . . . . . . C 4
Kenora (terr. dist.) 59,421 . . . . G 5
Kent (county) 107,022 . . . . B 5
Lambton (county) 123,445 . . . B 5
Lanark (county) 45,676 . . . . . . H 3
Leeds (county) 53,765 . . . . H 3
Lennox and Addington
(county) 33,040 . . . . G 3
Manitoulin (terr. dist.) 11,001 . B 2
Middlesex (county) 318,184 . . C 4
Muskoka (dist. munic.)
38,370 . . . . E 3
Niagara (reg. munic.) 368,288 E 4
Nipissing (terr. dist.) 80,268 . . F 2
Northumberland (county)
64,966 . . . . G 3
Ottawa-Carleton (reg. munic.)
546,849 . . . . J 2
Oxford (county) 85,920 . . . . . . D 4
Parry Sound (terr. dist.)
33,528 . . . . D 2
Peel (reg. munic.) 490,731 . . . E 4
Perth (county) 66,096 . . . . C 4
Peterborough (county)
102,452 . . . . F 3
Prescott (county) 30,365 . . . . . K 2
Prince Edward (county)
22,336 . . . . G 3
Rainy River (terr. dist.) 22,798 G 5
Renfrew (county) 87,484 . . . . . G 2
Russell (county) 22,412 . . . . . . J 2
Simcoe (county) 225,071 . . . . . E 3
Stormont (county) 61,927 . . . . K 2
Sudbury (reg. munic.)
159,779 . . . . K 6
Sudbury (terr. dist.) 27,068 . . . J 5
Thunder Bay (terr. dist.)
153,997 . . . . H 5
Timiskaming (terr. dist.)
41,288 . . . . K 5
Toronto (metro. munic.)
2,137,395 . . . . K 4
Victoria (county) 47,854 . . . . . . F 3
Waterloo (reg. munic.)
305,496 . . . . D 4
Wellington (county) 129,432 . . D 4
York (reg. munic.) 252,053 . . . E 4

CITIES and TOWNS

Ailsa Craig 765 . . . . C 4
Ajax 25,475 . . . . E 4
Alban 342 . . . . D 1
Alexandria 3,271 . . . . K 2
Alfred 1,057 . . . . K 2
Alliston 4,712 . . . . E 3
Almonte 3,855 . . . . H 2
Alvinston 736 . . . . B 5
Amherstburg 5,685 . . . . A 5
Amherst View 6,110 . . . . H 3
Ancaster 14,428 . . . . D 4
Angus 3,085 . . . . E 3
Apsley 264 . . . . F 3
Arkona 473 . . . . C 4
Armstrong 378 . . . . H 4
Arnprior 5,828 . . . . H 2
Aroland 291 . . . . H 4
Arthur 1,700 . . . . D 4
Astorville 340 . . . . E 1
Athens 948 . . . . J 3
Atherley 366 . . . . E 3
Atikokan 4,452 . . . . G 5
Atwood 723 . . . . D 4
Aurora 16,267 . . . . J 3
Avonmore 273 . . . . K 2
Aylmer 5,254 . . . . C 5
Ayr 1,295 . . . . D 4
Ayton 424 . . . . D 3
Baden 945 . . . . D 4
Bala 577 . . . . E 2
Bancroft 2,329 . . . . G 2
Barrie⊙ 38,423 . . . . E 3
Barry's Bay 1,216 . . . . G 2
Batawa 430 . . . . G 3
Bath 1,071 . . . . H 3
Bayfield 649 . . . . C 4
Beachburg 682 . . . . H 2
Beachville 917 . . . . D 4
Beardmore 583 . . . . H 5
Beaverton 1,952 . . . . E 3
Beeton 1,989 . . . . E 3
Belle River 3,568 . . . . B 5
Belleville⊙ 34,881 . . . . G 3
Belmont 831 . . . . C 5
Bethany 365 . . . . F 3
Bewdley 508 . . . . F 3
Binbrook 306 . . . . E 4
Blackstock 720 . . . . F 3
Blenheim 4,044 . . . . C 5
Blind River 3,444 . . . . J 5
Bloomfield 718 . . . . G 4
Blyth 926 . . . . C 4
Bobcaygeon 1,625 . . . . F 3
Bonfield 540 . . . . E 1
Bothwell 915 . . . . C 5
Bourget 1,057 . . . . J 2
Bracebridge⊙ 9,063 . . . . E 2
Bradford 7,370 . . . . E 3
Braeside 492 . . . . H 2
Brampton⊙ 149,030 . . . . J 4
Brantford⊙ 74,315 . . . . D 4
Bridgenorth 1,633 . . . . F 3
Brigden 635 . . . . B 5
Brighton 3,147 . . . . G 3
Britt 419 . . . . D 2
Brockville⊙ 19,896 . . . . J 3
Bruce Mines 635 . . . . J 5
Brussels 962 . . . . C 4
Burford 1,461 . . . . D 4
Burgessville 302 . . . . D 4
Burk's Falls 922 . . . . E 2
Burlington 114,853 . . . . E 4
Cache Bay 665 . . . . D 1
Caesarea 551 . . . . F 3
Calabogie 256 . . . . H 2
Caledon 26,645 . . . . E 4
Callander 1,158 . . . . E 1
Cambridge 77,183 . . . . D 4
Campbellford 3,409 . . . . G 3
Cannington 1,623 . . . . E 3
Capreol 3,845 . . . . K 5
Caramat 265 . . . . H 5
Cardinal 1,753 . . . . J 3
Carleton Place 5,626 . . . . H 2
Carlisle 781 . . . . D 4
Carlsbad Springs 616 . . . . J 2
Carp 707 . . . . H 2
Cartier 590 . . . . J 5
Casselman 1,675 . . . . J 2
Castleton 346 . . . . F 3
Chalk River 1,010 . . . . G 1
Chapleau 3,243 . . . . J 5
Charing Cross 443 . . . . B 5
Chatham⊙ 40,952 . . . . B 5
Chatsworth 383 . . . . D 3
Cherry Valley 289 . . . . G 4
Chesley 1,840 . . . . C 3
Chesterville 1,430 . . . . J 2
Chute-à-Blondeau 365 . . . . K 2
City View . . . . J 2
Clarence Creek 796 . . . . J 2
Clarksburg 508 . . . . D 3
Clifford 645 . . . . D 4
Clinton 3,081 . . . . C 4
Cobalt 1,759 . . . . K 5
Cobden 997 . . . . H 2
Coboconk 426 . . . . F 3
Cobourg⊙ 11,385 . . . . F 4
Cochrane⊙ 4,848 . . . . K 5
Colborne 1,796 . . . . G 4
Colchester 711 . . . . B 6
Coldwater 964 . . . . E 3
Collingwood 12,064 . . . . D 3
Comber 667 . . . . B 5
Consecon 295 . . . . G 3
Cookstown 918 . . . . E 3
Cornwall⊙ 46,144 . . . . K 2
Cottam 404 . . . . B 5
Courtland 647 . . . . D 5
Courtright 1,024 . . . . B 5
Crediton 370 . . . . C 4
Creemore 1,182 . . . . D 3
Crysler 540 . . . . J 2
Cumberland 518 . . . . J 2
Cumberland Beach-Bramshot-
Buena Vista 679 . . . . E 3
Dashwood 426 . . . . C 4
Deep River 5,095 . . . . G 1
Delaware 481 . . . . C 5
Delhi 4,043 . . . . D 5
Delta 360 . . . . H 3
Deseronto 1,740 . . . . G 3
Douglas 303 . . . . H 2
Drayton 809 . . . . D 4
Dresden 2,550 . . . . B 5
Drumbo 476 . . . . D 4
Dryden 6,640 . . . . G 4
Dublin 295 . . . . C 4
Dubreuilville △988 . . . . J 5
Dundalk 1,250 . . . . D 3
Dundas 19,586 . . . . D 4
Dungannon 284 . . . . C 4
Dunnville 11,353 . . . . E 5
Durham 2,458 . . . . D 3
Dutton 1,115 . . . . C 5
Earlton 1,028 . . . . K 5
East York 101,974 . . . . J 4
Echo Bay 786 . . . . J 5
Eden Mills 318 . . . . D 4
Eganville 1,245 . . . . G 2
Egmondville 465 . . . . C 4
Elgin 327 . . . . H 3
Elk Lake 526 . . . . K 5
Elliot Lake 16,723 . . . . B 1
Elmira 7,063 . . . . D 4
Elmvale 1,183 . . . . E 3
Elmwood 364 . . . . C 3
Elora 2,666 . . . . D 4
Embro 727 . . . . C 4
Embrun 1,883 . . . . J 2
Emeryville-Puce 1,611 . . . . B 5
Emo 762 . . . . F 5
Englehart 1,689 . . . . K 5
Enterprise 357 . . . . H 3
Erieau 430 . . . . C 5
Erin 2,313 . . . . D 4
Espanola 5,836 . . . . J 5
Essex 6,295 . . . . B 5
Etobicoke 298,713 . . . . J 4
Everett 570 . . . . E 3
Exeter 3,732 . . . . C 4
Fauquier 561 . . . . J 5
Fenelon Falls 1,701 . . . . F 3
Fergus 6,064 . . . . D 4
Field 462 . . . . E 1
Finch 353 . . . . J 2
Fingal 380 . . . . C 5
Fitzroy Harbour 446 . . . . H 2
Flesherton 565 . . . . D 3
Foleyet 484 . . . . J 5
Fordwich 365 . . . . C 4
Forest 2,671 . . . . C 4
Formosa 393 . . . . C 3
Fort Erie 24,096 . . . . E 5
Fort Frances⊙ 8,906 . . . . F 5
Foxboro 597 . . . . G 3
Frankford 1,919 . . . . G 3
Fraserdale 303 . . . . J 5
Freelton 307 . . . . D 4
Gananoque 4,863 . . . . H 3
Garden Village 270 . . . . E 1
Geraldton 2,956 . . . . H 5
Glencoe 1,694 . . . . C 5
Glen Miller 639 . . . . G 3
Glen Robertson 378 . . . . K 2
Glen Walter 710 . . . . K 2
Goderich⊙ 7,322 . . . . C 4
Gogama 652 . . . . J 5
Goodwood 335 . . . . E 3
Gore Bay⊙ 777 . . . . B 2
Gorrie 468 . . . . C 4
Grafton 409 . . . . G 4
Grand Bend 680 . . . . C 4
Grand Valley 1,226 . . . . D 4
Granton 315 . . . . C 4
Gravenhurst 8,532 . . . . E 3
Greely 567 . . . . J 2
Green Valley 459 . . . . K 2
Grimsby 15,797 . . . . E 4
Guelph⊙ 71,207 . . . . D 4

(continued on following page)

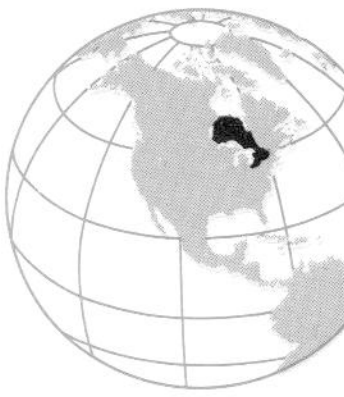

AREA 412,580 sq. mi. (1,068,582 sq. km.)
POPULATION 8,625,107
CAPITAL Toronto
LARGEST CITY Toronto
HIGHEST POINT in Timiskaming Dist. 2,275 ft. (693 m.)
SETTLED IN 1749
ADMITTED TO CONFEDERATION 1867
PROVINCIAL FLOWER White Trillium

(continued)

Haileybury⊙ 4,925	K 5
Haldimand 16,866	E 5
Haliburton 1,443	F 2
Halton Hills 35,190	E 4
Hamilton⊙ 306,434	E 4
Hamilton *542,095	E 4
Hanover 6,316	C 3
Harriston 1,954	D 4
Harrow 2,274	B 5
Harrowsmith 599	H 3
Harwood 332	F 3
Hastings 975	G 3
Havelock 1,385	G 3
Hawkesbury 9,877	K 2
Hawkestone 275	E 3
Hawk Junction 349	J 5
Hearst 5,533	J 5
Hensall 973	C 4
Hepworth 393	C 3
Hickson 263	D 4
Highgate 435	C 5
Hillsburgh 1,065	D 4
Hillsdale 370	E 3
Holland Landing 2,771	E 3
Honey Harbour 505	E 3
Hornepayne 1,848	J 5
Hudson 515	G 4
Huntsville 11,467	E 2
Huron Park 1,104	C 4
Ignace 2,499	G 5
Ilderton 301	C 4
Ingersoll 8,494	C 4
Ingleside 1,400	J 2
Innerkip 715	D 4
Inverhuron 438	C 3
Iron Bridge 821	A 1
Iroquois 1,211	J 3
Iroquois Falls 6,339	J 5
Johnstown 789	J 3
Kakabeka Falls 300	G 5
Kanata 19,728	J 2
Kapuskasing 12,014	J 5
Kars 449	J 2
Kearney 538	E 2
Keene 353	F 3
Keewatin 1,863	F 5
Kemptville 2,362	J 2
Kenora⊙ 9,817	F 4
Killaloe Station 634	G 2
Killarney 433	C 2
Kincardine 5,778	C 3
Kingston⊙ 52,616	H 3
Kingsville 5,134	B 6
Kinmount 262	F 3
Kirkland Lake 12,219	K 5
Kitchener⊙ 139,734	D 4
Kitchener *287,801	D 4
Komoka 1,152	C 5
Lakefield 2,374	F 3
Lanark 753	H 2
Lancaster 637	K 2
Langton 348	D 5
Lansdowne 540	H 3
Larder Lake 1,084	K 5
Latchford 397	K 5
Leamington 12,528	B 5
Limoges 930	J 2
Lincoln 14,196	E 4
Linden Beach 579	B 6
Lindsay⊙ 13,596	F 3
Linwood 450	D 4
Lion's Head 467	C 2
Lisle 265	E 3
Listowel 5,026	D 4
Little Britain 265	E 3
Little Current 1,507	B 2
London⊙ 254,280	C 5
London *283,668	C 5
Longlac 2,431	H 5
Long Sault 1,227	K 2
L'Orignal⊙ 1,819	K 2
Lucan 1,616	C 4
Lucknow 1,088	C 4
Lyn 518	J 3
Lynden 451	D 4
Lynhurst 685	C 5
MacGregor's Bay 861	G 2
MacTier 647	E 2
Madawaska 264	F 2
Madoc 1,249	G 3
Maitland 667	J 3
Mallorytown 368	J 3
Manitouwadge 3,155	H 5
Manitowaning 518	C 2
Manotick-Hillside Gardens 2,694	J 2
Marathon 2,271	H 5
Markdale 1,289	D 3
Markham 77,037	K 4
Markstay 444	D 1
Marmora 1,304	G 3
Martintown 388	K 2
Massey 1,274	C 1
Matachewan 444	J 5
Matheson 966	K 5
Mattawa 2,652	F 1
Mattice 803	J 5
Maxville 836	K 2
Maynooth 277	G 2
McGregor 1,145	B 5
McKerrow 260	C 1
Meaford 4,367	D 3
Melbourne 346	C 5
Merlin 745	B 5
Merrickville 984	J 3
Metcalfe 687	J 2
Midhurst 1,457	E 3
Midland 12,132	D 3
Mildmay 928	C 3
Milford Bay 401	E 2
Millbank 337	D 4
Millbrook 927	F 3
Milton⊙ 28,067	E 4
Milverton 1,463	D 4
Minaki 319	F 4
Mindemoya 376	B 2
Minden⊙ 838	F 3
Mississauga 315,056	J 4
Mitchell 2,777	C 4
Monkton 520	C 4
Moonbeam 838	J 5
Moorefield 308	D 4
Mooretown 344	B 5
Moose Creek 393	K 2
Morewood 264	J 2
Morpeth 284	C 5
Morrisburg 2,308	J 3
Mount Albert 1,165	E 3
Mount Brydges 1,557	C 5
Mount Forest 3,474	D 4
Mount Hope 557	E 4
Munster 1,531	J 2
Nakina 936	H 4
Nanticoke⊙ 19,816	E 5
Napanee 4,803	G 3
Navan 419	J 2
Neustadt 511	D 3
Newboro 260	H 3
Newburgh 617	H 3
Newbury 441	C 5
Newcastle 32,229	F 4
New Hamburg 3,923	D 4
New Liskeard 5,551	K 5
Newmarket⊙ 29,753	E 3
Niagara Falls 70,960	E 4
Niagara-on-the-Lake 12,186	E 4
Nickel Centre 12,318	D 1
Nipigon 2,377	H 5
Nobel 386	D 2
Nobleton 1,861	J 3
Noelville 702	D 1
North Bay⊙ 51,268	E 1
North Gower 818	J 2
North York 559,521	J 4
Norwich 2,117	D 5
Norwood 1,278	F 3
Nottawa 360	D 3
Oakville 75,773	E 4
Oakwood 404	F 3
Odessa 849	H 3
Oil City 266	B 5
Oil Springs 627	B 5
Omemee 819	F 3
Onaping Falls 6,198	J 5
Opasatika 413	J 5
Orangeville⊙ 13,740	D 4
Orillia 23,955	E 3
Osgoode 1,138	J 2
Oshawa 117,519	F 4
Oshawa *154,217	F 4
Ottawa⊙ (cap.), Canada 295,163	J 2
Ottawa-Hull *717,978	J 2
Otterville 776	D 5
Owen Sound⊙ 19,883	D 3
Paincourt 414	B 5
Paisley 1,039	C 3
Pakenham 367	H 2
Palmerston 1,989	D 4
Paris 7,485	D 4
Parkhill 1,358	C 4
Parry Sound⊙ 6,124	E 2
Pefferlaw 857	E 3
Pelham 11,104	E 4
Pembroke⊙ 14,026	G 2
Penetanguishene 5,315	D 3
Perth⊙ 5,655	H 3
Petawawa 5,520	G 2
Peterborough⊙ 60,620	F 3
Petrolia 4,234	B 5
Pickering 37,754	K 4
Picton⊙ 4,361	G 3
Plantagenet 870	K 2
Plattsville 495	D 4
Point Edward 2,383	B 4
Pontypool 759	F 3
Port Burwell 655	D 5
Port Carling 629	E 2
Port Colborne 19,225	E 5
Port Elgin 6,131	C 3
Port Franks 547	C 4
Port Hope 9,992	F 4
Port Lambton 921	B 5
Portland 271	H 3
Port McNicoll 1,883	E 3
Port Perry 4,712	E 3
Port Rowan 811	D 5
Port Stanley 1,891	C 5
Pottageville 286	J 3
Powassan 1,169	E 1
Prescott⊙ 4,670	J 3
Princeton 462	D 4
Puce-Emeryville 1,611	B 5
Rainy River 1,061	F 5
Ramore 382	K 5
Rayside-Balfour 15,017	K 5
Red Rock 1,260	H 5
Renfrew 8,283	H 2
Richards Landing 405	J 5
Richmond 2,880	J 2
Richmond Hill 37,778	J 4
Ridgetown 3,062	C 5
Ripley 591	C 3
River Valley 275	D 1
Rockcliffe Park 1,869	J 2
Rockland 3,961	J 2
Rockwood 1,068	D 4
Rodney 1,007	C 5
Rosslyn Village 362	G 5
Round Lake Centre 255	G 2
Russell 1,099	J 2
Ruthven 649	B 6
Saint Albert 254	J 2
Saint Catharines⊙ 124,018	E 4
Saint Catharines-Niagara *304,353	E 4
Saint Charles 382	D 1
Saint Clair Beach 2,845	B 5
Saint Clements 890	D 4
Saint-Eugène 470	K 2
Saint George 865	D 4
Saint Isidore de Prescott 746	K 2

Saint Jacobs 1,189 .... D 4
Saint Mary's 4,883 .... C 4
Saint Thomas⊚ 28,165 ...... C 5
Saint Williams 442 .... D 5
Salem 825 .... D 4
Sarnia⊚ 50,892 .... B 5
Sauble Beach 729 .... C 3
Sault Sainte Marie⊚ 82,697 . J 5
Scarborough 443,353 .... K 4
Schomberg 923 .... J 3
Schreiber 1,968 .... H 5
Scotland 600 .... D 4
Seaforth 2,114 .... C 4
Searchmont 384 .... J 5
Sebringville 579 .... C 4
Seeleys Bay 503 .... H 3
Shakespeare 602 .... D 4
Shallow Lake 418 .... C 3
Shannonville 314 .... G 3
Shanty Bay 358 .... E 3
Sharbot Lake 495 .... H 3
Shedden 292 .... C 5
Shelburne 2,862 .... D 3
Simcoe⊚ 14,326 .... D 5
Sioux Lookout 3,074 .... G 4
Sioux Narrows 394 .... F 5
Smithfield 349 .... G 3
Smiths Falls 8,831 .... H 3
Smithville 1,936 .... E 4
Smooth Rock Falls 2,352 .... J 5
Sombra 420 .... B 5
Southampton 2,830 .... C 3
South Mountain 285 .... J 3
South River 1,109 .... E 2
Spanish 1,063 .... J 5
Sparta 283 .... C 5
Spencerville 438 .... J 3
Springfield 555 .... C 5
Springford 309 .... D 5
Stayner 2,530 .... E 3
Stirling 1,638 .... G 3
Stittsville 2,652 .... J 2
Stoney Creek 36,762 .... E 4
Stoney Point 1,090 .... B 5
Straffordville 752 .... D 5
Stratford⊚ 26,262 .... C 4
Strathroy 8,748 .... C 5
Sturgeon Falls 6,045 .... E 1
Sudbury⊚ 91,829 .... K 5
Sudbury *149,923 .... K 5
Sunderland 703 .... E 3
Sundridge 734 .... E 2
Sydenham 595 .... H 3
Tamworth 402 .... H 3
Tara 687 .... C 3
Tavistock 1,885 .... D 4
Tecumseh 6,364 .... B 5
Teeswater 1,026 .... C 3
Terrace Bay 2,639 .... H 5
Thamesford 1,920 .... C 4
Thamesville 961 .... C 5
Thedford 694 .... C 4
Thessalon 1,620 .... J 5
Thornbury 1,435 .... D 3
Thorndale 581 .... C 4
Thornton 414 .... E 3
Thorold 15,412 .... E 4
Thunder Bay⊚ 112,486 ...... H 5
Thunder Bay *121,379 .... H 5
Tilbury 4,298 .... B 5
Tillsonburg 10,487 .... D 5
Timmins 46,114 .... J 5
Tiverton 806 .... C 3
Tobermory 282 .... C 2
Toronto (cap.)⊚ 599,217 ..... K 4
Toronto *2,998,947 .... K 4
Tottenham 3,022 .... E 3
Trenton 15,085 .... G 3
Trout Creek 652 .... E 2
Turkey Point 407 .... D 5
Tweed 1,574 .... G 3
Udora 375 .... E 3
Union 485 .... C 5
Uxbridge 4,209 .... E 3
Valley East 20,433 .... J 5
Vanier 18,792 .... J 2
Vankleek Hill 1,774 .... K 2
Vars 527 .... J 2
Vaughan 29,674 .... J 4
Vermilion Bay 505 .... G 4
Verner 1,076 .... D 1
Vernon 303 .... J 2
Verona 754 .... H 3
Victoria Harbour 1,125 .... E 3
Vienna 369 .... D 5
Virginiatown 1,010 .... K 5
Vittoria 420 .... D 5
Wabigoon 268 .... G 5
Walden 10,139 .... J 5
Waikerton⊚ 4,682 .... C 3
Wallaceburg 11,506 .... B 5
Wardsville 450 .... C 5
Warkworth 618 .... G 3
Warren 579 .... D 1
Warsaw 314 .... F 3
Wasaga Beach 4,705 .... D 3
Washago 569 .... E 3
Waterloo 49,428 .... D 4
Watford 1,402 .... C 5
Waubaushene 878 .... E 3
Wawa 4,206 .... J 5
Webbwood 519 .... C 1
Welcome 293 .... F 4
Welland 454,448 .... E 5
Wellesley 997 .... D 4
Wellington 1,082 .... G 4
Wendover 326 .... J 2
West Lorne 1,258 .... C 5
Westmeath 262 .... H 2
Westport 621 .... H 3
Wheatley 1,638 .... B 5
Whitby⊚ 36,698 .... F 4
Whitchurch-Stouffville 13,557 . J 3
White River △1,006 .... J 5
Whitney 766 .... F 2
Wiarton 2,074 .... C 3
Wikwemikong 1,030 .... C 2
Williamsburg 407 .... J 3
Williamsford 256 .... D 3
Williamstown 328 .... K 2
Winchester 2,001 .... J 2
Windsor⊚ 192,083 .... B 5
Windsor *246,110 .... B 5
Wingham 2,897 .... C 4
Wolfe Island 271 .... H 3
Woodstock⊚ 26,603 .... D 4
Woodville 575 .... F 3
Wroxeter 350 .... C 4
Wyoming 1,682 .... B 5
Yarker 319 .... H 3
York 134,617 .... J 4
Zephyr 330 .... E 3
Zurich 795 .... C 4

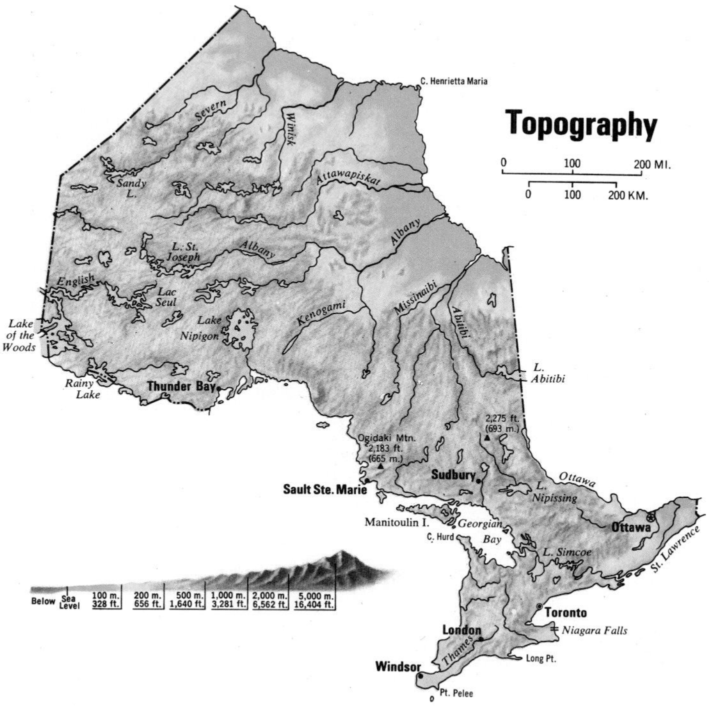

OTHER FEATURES

Abitibi (riv.) .... J 5
Algonquin Prov. Park .... F 2
Amherst (isl.) .... H 3
Balsam (lake) .... F 3
Barrie (isl.) .... B 1
Bays (lake) .... F 2
Big Rideau (lake) .... H 3
Black (riv.) .... E 3
Bruce (pen.) .... C 2
Buckhorn (lake) .... F 3
Cabot (head) .... C 2
Charleston (lake) .... J 3
Christian (isl.) .... D 3
Clear (lake) .... F 3
Cockburn (isl.) .... A 2
Couchiching (lake) .... E 3
Croker (cape) .... D 3
Don (riv.) .... J 4
Doré (lake) .... G 2
Douglas (pt.) .... C 3
Erie (lake) .... E 5
Flowerpot (isl.) .... C 2
French (riv.) .... D 1
Georgian (bay) .... D 2
Georgian Bay Is. Nat'l Park .... C 2, D 3
Georgina (isl.) .... E 3
Grand (riv.) .... D 4
Humber (riv.) .... J 3
Hurd (cape) .... C 2
Huron (lake) .... B 3
Ipperwash Prov. Park .... C 4
Joseph (lake) .... E 2
Killarney Prov. Park .... C 1
Killbear Point Prov. Park ..... D 2
Lake of the Woods (lake) ..... F 5
Lake Superior Prov. Park ..... J 5
Lonely (isl.) .... C 2
Long (pt.) .... D 5
Long Point (bay) .... D 5
Madawaska (riv.) .... G 2
Magnetawan (riv.) .... D 2
Main (chan.) .... C 2
Manitou (lake) .... C 2
Manitoulin (isl.) .... B 2
Mattagami (riv.) .... J 5
Michipicoten (isl.) .... H 5
Missinaibi (riv.) .... J 5
Mississagi (riv.) .... A 1
Mississippi (lake) .... H 2
Muskoka (lake) .... E 2
Niagara (riv.) .... E 4
Nipigon (lake) .... H 5
Nipissing (lake) .... E 1
North (chan.) .... A 1
Nottawasaga (bay) .... D 3
Ogidaki (mt.) .... J 5
Ontario (lake) .... G 4
Opeongo (lake) .... F 2
Ottawa (riv.) .... H 2
Owen (sound) .... D 3
Panache (lake) .... C 1
Parry (isl.) .... D 2
Parry (sound) .... D 2
Pelee (pt.) .... B 6
Petre (pt.) .... G 4
Point Pelee Nat'l Park .... B 5
Presqu'ile Prov. Park .... G 4
Pukaskwa Prov. Park .... H 5
Quetico Prov. Park .... G 5
Rainy (lake) .... G 5
Rice (lake) .... F 3
Rideau (lake) .... H 3
Rondeau Prov. Park .... C 5
Rosseau (lake) .... E 2
Saint Clair (lake) .... B 5
Saint Clair (riv.) .... B 5
Saint Lawrence (lake) .... K 3
Saint Lawrence (riv.) .... J 3
Saint Lawrence Is. Nat'l Park . J 3
Saugeen (riv.) .... C 3
Scugog (lake) .... F 3
Seul (lake) .... G 4
Severn (riv.) .... E 3
Sibley Prov. Park .... H 5
Simcoe (lake) .... E 3
South (bay) .... C 2
Spanish (riv.) .... C 1
Stony (lake) .... G 3
Superior (lake) .... H 5
Sydenham (riv.) .... B 5
Thames (riv.) .... B 5
Theano (pt.) .... J 5
Thousand (isls.) .... H 3
Timagami (lake) .... K 5
Trout (lake) .... E 1
Vernon (lake) .... E 2
Walpole (isl.) .... B 5
Welland (canal) .... E 5
Woods (lake) .... F 5

⊚County seat.
*Population of metropolitan area.
△Population of town or township.

Agriculture, Industry and Resources

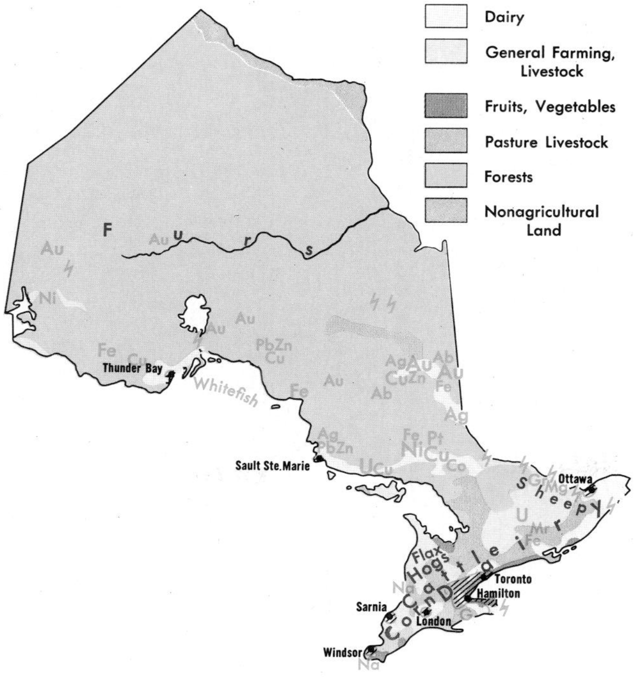

DOMINANT LAND USE

- Cereals, Cash Crops, Livestock
- Dairy
- General Farming, Livestock
- Fruits, Vegetables
- Pasture Livestock
- Forests
- Nonagricultural Land

MAJOR MINERAL OCCURRENCES

Ab	Asbestos	Mg	Magnesium
Ag	Silver	Mr	Marble
Au	Gold	Na	Salt
Co	Cobalt	Ni	Nickel
Cu	Copper	Pb	Lead
Fe	Iron Ore	Pt	Platinum
G	Natural Gas	U	Uranium
Gr	Graphite	Zn	Zinc

Water Power
Major Industrial Areas

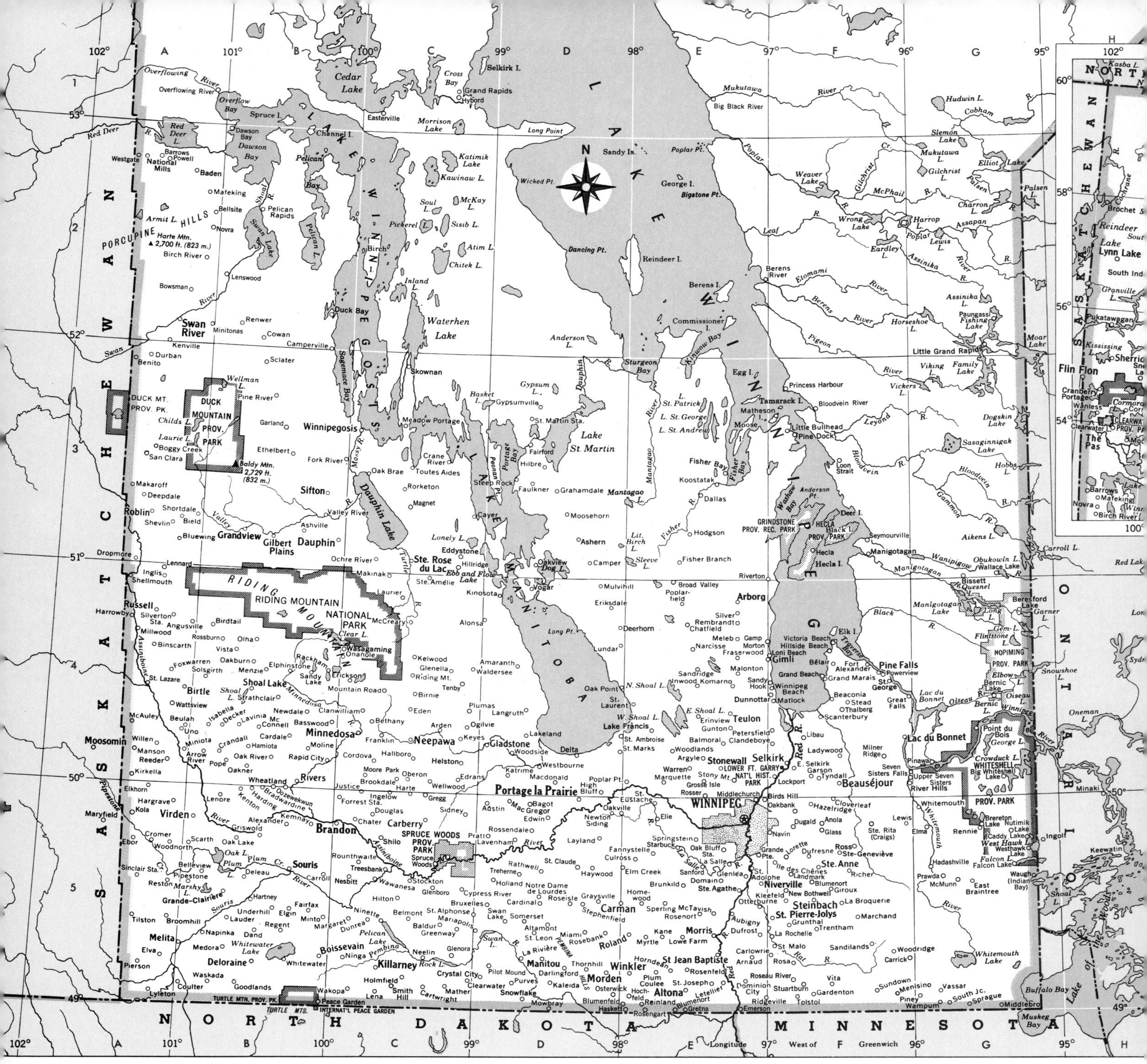

CITIES and TOWNS

Alexander 244 . . . . . B 5
Altona 2,757 . . . . . E 5
Amaranth 257 . . . . . D 4
Arborg 964 . . . . . E 4
Arden 192 . . . . . C 4
Ashern 570 . . . . . D 3
Austin 416 . . . . . D 5
Baldur 344 . . . . . C 5
Barrows 199 . . . . . A 2
Beauséjour 2,462 . . . . . F 4
Belmont 314 . . . . . C 5
Benito 441 . . . . . A 3
Berens River 681 . . . . . F 2
Binscarth 472 . . . . . A 4
Birch River 597 . . . . . A 2
Birds Hill 711 . . . . . F 4
Birtle 887 . . . . . B 4
Bloodvein River 413 . . . . . F 3
Blumenort 533 . . . . . F 5
Boissevain 1,660 . . . . . C 5
Bowsman 454 . . . . . A 2
Brandon 36,242 . . . . . C 5
Brochet 215 . . . . . H 2
Camperville 586 . . . . . B 2
Carberry 1,510 . . . . . C 5
Carman 2,408 . . . . . D 5
Cartwright 384 . . . . . C 5
Churchill 1,186 . . . . . K 2
Cormorant 445 . . . . . H 3
Cranberry Portage 948 . . . . . H 3
Crane River 336 . . . . . C 3
Cross Lake 510 . . . . . J 3
Crystal City 489 . . . . . C 5
Cypress River 260 . . . . . C 5
Darlingford 170 . . . . . D 5
Dauphin 8,971 . . . . . B 3
Deloraine 1,136 . . . . . B 5
Dominion City 437 . . . . . E 5
Douglas 170 . . . . . C 5
Duck Bay 594 . . . . . B 2
Dugald 410 . . . . . F 5
Dunnottar 287 . . . . . E 4
Easterville 589 . . . . . C 1
East Selkirk 985 . . . . . F 4
Elgin 172 . . . . . B 5
Elie 450 . . . . . E 5
Elkhorn 509 . . . . . A 5
Elm Creek 293 . . . . . E 5
Elphinstone 201 . . . . . B 4
Emerson 762 . . . . . E 5
Erickson 540 . . . . . C 4
Eriksdale 339 . . . . . D 4
Ethelbert 474 . . . . . B 3
Fairford 668 . . . . . D 3
Falcon Lake 220 . . . . . G 5
Fisher Branch 511 . . . . . E 3
Flin Flon 7,894 . . . . . H 3
Fort Alexander 1,425 . . . . . F 4
Garson 318 . . . . . F 4
Gilbert Plains 812 . . . . . B 3
Gillam 1,427 . . . . . K 2
Gimli 1,550 . . . . . F 4
Gladstone 964 . . . . . D 4
Glenboro 741 . . . . . C 5
Grand Marais 207 . . . . . F 4
Grand Rapids 567 . . . . . C 1
Grandview 1,013 . . . . . B 3
Great Falls 272 . . . . . F 4
Gretna 545 . . . . . E 5
Grosse Isle 171 . . . . . E 4
Grunthal 572 . . . . . F 5
Hamiota 728 . . . . . B 4
Hartney 490 . . . . . B 5
Haywood 240 . . . . . D 5
Hillridge 201 . . . . . C 3
Hochfeld 187 . . . . . E 5
Holland 418 . . . . . D 5
Île des Chênes 814 . . . . . F 5
Inglis 209 . . . . . A 4
Inwood 197 . . . . . E 4
Island Lake 2,664 . . . . . J 3
Kelwood 199 . . . . . C 4
Killarney 2,342 . . . . . C 5
Kleefeld 335 . . . . . F 5
La Broquerie 429 . . . . . F 5
Lac du Bonnet 985 . . . . . G 4
Landmark 433 . . . . . F 5
La Rivière 251 . . . . . D 5
La Salle 345 . . . . . E 5
Laurier 241 . . . . . C 4
Letellier 178 . . . . . E 5
Little Grand Rapids 559 . . . . . G 2
Lockport 212 . . . . . F 4
Lorette 1,092 . . . . . F 5
Lowe Farm 241 . . . . . E 5
Lundar 634 . . . . . D 4
Lynn Lake 2,087 . . . . . H 2
MacGregor 795 . . . . . D 5
Mafeking 266 . . . . . B 2
Manigotagan 216 . . . . . F 3
Manitou 861 . . . . . D 5
McCreary 618 . . . . . C 4
Melita 1,156 . . . . . A 5
Miami 401 . . . . . D 5
Middlechurch 342 . . . . . E 4
Miniota 247 . . . . . B 4
Minitonas 628 . . . . . B 2
Minnedosa 2,637 . . . . . B 4
Moosehorn 216 . . . . . D 3
Moose Lake 557 . . . . . H 3
Morden 4,579 . . . . . D 5
Morris 1,570 . . . . . E 5
Neepawa 3,425 . . . . . C 4
New Bothwell 233 . . . . . F 5
Newdale 238 . . . . . B 4
Ninette 287 . . . . . C 5
Niverville 1,329 . . . . . F 5
Norway House 441 . . . . . J 3
Notre Dame de Lourdes 627 . . . . . D 5
Oakbank 1,277 . . . . . F 5
Oakburn 255 . . . . . B 4
Oak Lake 369 . . . . . B 5
Oak River 179 . . . . . B 4
Oakville 383 . . . . . D 5
Ochre River 284 . . . . . C 3
Onanole 386 . . . . . C 4
Oozewekwun 453 . . . . . B 5
Paungassi 296 . . . . . G 2
Pelican Rapids 178 . . . . . B 2
Petersfield 170 . . . . . E 4
Pierson 238 . . . . . A 5
Pikwitonei 175 . . . . . J 3
Pilot Mound 838 . . . . . D 5
Pinawa 2,006 . . . . . G 4
Pine Falls 885 . . . . . F 4
Pine River 314 . . . . . B 3
Pipestone 173 . . . . . B 5
Plumas 269 . . . . . D 4
Plum Coulee 592 . . . . . E 5
Point du Bois 182 . . . . . G 4
Poplar Point 264 . . . . . D 4
Portage la Prairie 13,086 . . . . . D 4
Powerview 691 . . . . . F 4
Rapid City 431 . . . . . B 4
Red Sucker Lake 312 . . . . . K 3
Reinland 198 . . . . . E 5
Reston 589 . . . . . A 5
Richer 288 . . . . . F 5
Riding Mountain 168 . . . . . C 4
Rivers 1,107 . . . . . B 4
Riverton 657 . . . . . E 3
Roblin 1,953 . . . . . A 3
Roland 301 . . . . . D 5
Rorketon 229 . . . . . C 3
Rosenfeld 263 . . . . . E 5
Rossburn 696 . . . . . B 4
Russell 1,660 . . . . . A 4
Saint Adolphe 928 . . . . . E 5
Saint Ambroise 263 . . . . . E 4
Saint Claude 592 . . . . . D 5
Sainte Agathe 326 . . . . . E 5
Sainte Anne 1,338 . . . . . F 5
Sainte Rose du Lac 1,090 . . . . . C 3
Saint Eustache 285 . . . . . E 5
Saint George 303 . . . . . F 4
Saint Jean Baptiste 584 . . . . . E 5
Saint Laurent 312 . . . . . D 4
Saint Lazare 414 . . . . . A 4
Saint Leon 197 . . . . . D 5
Saint Malo 672 . . . . . F 5
Saint Pierre-Jolys 919 . . . . . F 5
Sandy Lake 301 . . . . . B 4
Sanford 385 . . . . . E 5
Selkirk 10,037 . . . . . F 4
Sherridon 138 . . . . . H 3
Shoal Lake 835 . . . . . B 4
Sifton 210 . . . . . B 3
Somerset 596 . . . . . D 5
Snow Lake 1,853 . . . . . H 3
Souris 1,731 . . . . . B 5
South Indian Lake 770 . . . . . H 2
Split Lake 985 . . . . . J 2
Sprague 199 . . . . . G 5
Starbuck 224 . . . . . E 5
Steinbach 6,676 . . . . . F 5
Stonewall 2,210 . . . . . E 4
Stony Mountain 1,313 . . . . . E 4
Strathclair 390 . . . . . B 4
Swan Lake 367 . . . . . D 5
Swan River 3,782 . . . . . A 2
Teulon 925 . . . . . E 4

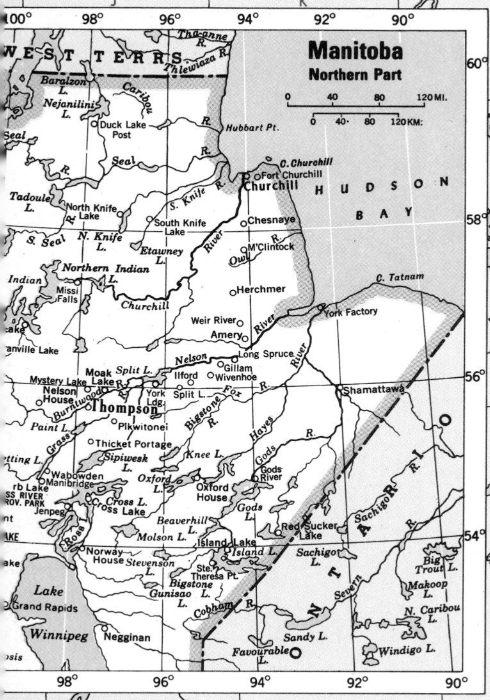

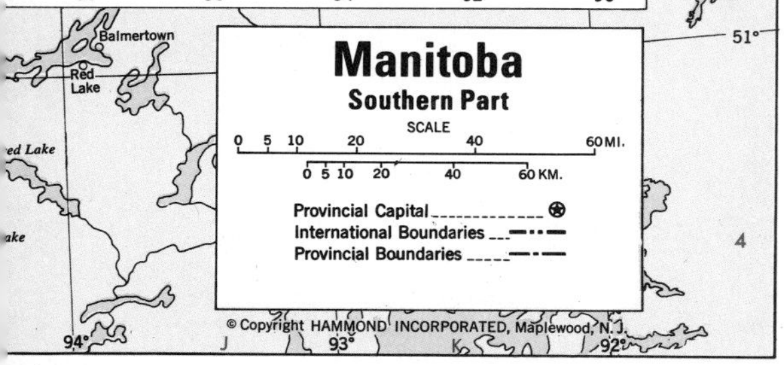

Manitoba
Southern Part

SCALE
0 5 10 20 40 60 MI.
0 5 10 20 40 60 KM.

Provincial Capital ⊛
International Boundaries
Provincial Boundaries

The Pas 6,390 . . . . . H 3
Thicket Portage 195 . . . . . J 3
Thompson 14,288 . . . . . J 2
Treherne 743 . . . . . D 5
Tyndall 421 . . . . . F 4
Virden 2,940 . . . . . A 5
Vita 364 . . . . . F 5
Wabowden 655 . . . . . J 3
Wallace Lake •2,044 . . . . . G 3
Wanless 193 . . . . . H 3
Warren 459 . . . . . E 4
Waskada 239 . . . . . B 5
Wawanesa 492 . . . . . C 5
Whitemouth 320 . . . . . G 5
Whitewater •856 . . . . . B 5
Winkler 5,046 . . . . . E 5
Winnipeg (cap.) 564,473 . . . . . E 5
Winnipeg *584,842 . . . . . E 5
Winnipeg Beach 565 . . . . . F 4
Winnipegosis 855 . . . . . B 3
Woodlands 185 . . . . . E 4
Wooodridge 170 . . . . . G 5
York Landing 229 . . . . . J 2

AREA 250,999 sq. mi. (650,087 sq. km.)
POPULATION 1,026,241
CAPITAL Winnipeg
LARGEST CITY Winnipeg
HIGHEST POINT Baldy Mtn. 2,729 ft. (832 m.)
SETTLED IN 1812
ADMITTED TO CONFEDERATION 1870
PROVINCIAL FLOWER Prairie Crocus

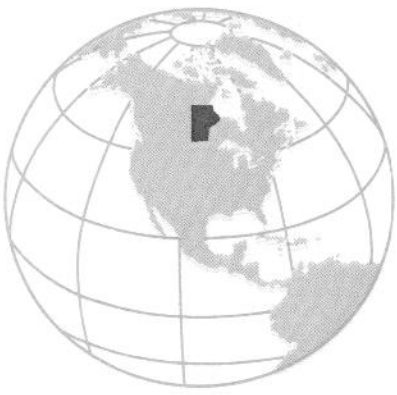

OTHER FEATURES

Aikens (lake) . . . . . G 3
Anderson (lake) . . . . . D 2
Anderson (pt.) . . . . . F 3
Armit (lake) . . . . . A 2
Assapan (riv.) . . . . . G 2
Assiniboine (riv.) . . . . . C 5
Assinika (lake) . . . . . G 2
Assinika (riv.) . . . . . G 2
Atim (lake) . . . . . C 2
Baldy (mt.) . . . . . B 3
Basket (lake) . . . . . C 3
Beaverhill (lake) . . . . . J 3
Berens (isl.) . . . . . E 2
Berens (riv.) . . . . . F 2
Bernic (lake) . . . . . G 4
Big Sand (lake) . . . . . H 2
Bigstone (lake) . . . . . J 3
Bigstone (pt.) . . . . . E 2
Bigstone (riv.) . . . . . J 3
Birch (isl.) . . . . . C 2
Black (isl.) . . . . . F 3
Black (riv.) . . . . . F 4
Bloodvein (riv.) . . . . . F 3
Bonnet (lake) . . . . . G 4
Buffalo (bay) . . . . . G 5
Burntwood (riv.) . . . . . J 2
Caribou (riv.) . . . . . J 1
Carroll (lake) . . . . . G 3
Cedar (lake) . . . . . B 1
Channel (isl.) . . . . . B 2
Charron (lake) . . . . . G 2
Childs (lake) . . . . . A 3
Chitek (lake) . . . . . C 2
Churchill (cape) . . . . . K 2
Churchill (riv.) . . . . . J 2
Clear (lake) . . . . . C 4
Clearwater Lake Prov. Park . . . H 3
Cobham (riv.) . . . . . G 1
Cochrane (riv.) . . . . . H 2
Commissioner (isl.) . . . . . E 2
Cormorant (lake) . . . . . H 3
Cross (bay) . . . . . C 1
Cross (lake) . . . . . J 3
Crowduck (lake) . . . . . G 4
Dancing (pt.) . . . . . D 2
Dauphin (lake) . . . . . C 3
Dauphin (riv.) . . . . . D 3
Dawson (bay) . . . . . B 2
Dog (lake) . . . . . D 3
Dogskin (lake) . . . . . G 3
Duck Mountain Prov. Park . . . . B 3
Eardley (lake) . . . . . F 2
East Shoal (lake) . . . . . E 4
Ebb and Flow (lake) . . . . . C 3
Egg (isl.) . . . . . E 3
Elbow (lake) . . . . . G 4
Elk (isl.) . . . . . F 4
Elliot (lake) . . . . . G 2
Etawney (lake) . . . . . J 2
Etomami (riv.) . . . . . F 2
Falcon (lake) . . . . . G 5
Family (lake) . . . . . G 3
Fisher (bay) . . . . . E 3
Fisher (riv.) . . . . . E 3
Fishing (lake) . . . . . G 2
Flintstone (lake) . . . . . G 4
Fox (riv.) . . . . . K 2
Gammon (riv.) . . . . . G 3
Garner (lake) . . . . . G 4
Gem (lake) . . . . . G 4
George (isl.) . . . . . E 2
George (lake) . . . . . G 4
Gilchrist (creek) . . . . . F 2
Gilchrist (lake) . . . . . G 2
Gods (lake) . . . . . K 3
Gods (riv.) . . . . . K 3
Granville (lake) . . . . . H 2
Grass (riv.) . . . . . J 3
Grass River Prov. Park . . . . . H 3
Grindstone Prov. Rec. Park . . . F 3
Gunisao (lake) . . . . . J 3
Gypsum (lake) . . . . . D 3
Harrop (lake) . . . . . G 2
Harte (mt.) . . . . . A 2
Hayes (riv.) . . . . . K 3
Hecla (isl.) . . . . . F 3
Hecla Prov. Park . . . . . F 3
Hobbs (lake) . . . . . G 3
Horseshoe (lake) . . . . . G 2
Hubbart (pt.) . . . . . K 2
Hudson (bay) . . . . . K 2
Hudwin (lake) . . . . . G 1
Inland (lake) . . . . . C 2
International Peace Garden . . B 5
Island (lake) . . . . . K 3
Katimik (lake) . . . . . C 2
Kawinaw (lake) . . . . . C 2
Kinwow (bay) . . . . . E 2
Kississing (lake) . . . . . H 2
Knee (lake) . . . . . J 3
Lake of the Woods (lake) . . . . . H 5
La Salle (riv.) . . . . . E 5
Laurie (lake) . . . . . A 3
Leaf (riv.) . . . . . F 2
Lewis (lake) . . . . . G 2
Leyond (riv.) . . . . . F 3
Little Birch (lake) . . . . . E 3
Lonely (lake) . . . . . C 3
Long (lake) . . . . . G 4
Long (pt.) . . . . . D 1
Long (pt.) . . . . . D 4
Manigotagan (lake) . . . . . G 4
Manigotagan (riv.) . . . . . G 3
Manitoba (lake) . . . . . D 4
Mantagao (riv.) . . . . . E 3
Marshy (lake) . . . . . B 5
McKay (lake) . . . . . C 2
McPhail (riv.) . . . . . F 2
Minnedosa (riv.) . . . . . B 4
Moar (lake) . . . . . G 2
Molson (lake) . . . . . J 3
Moose (isl.) . . . . . E 3
Morrison (lake) . . . . . C 1
Mossy (riv.) . . . . . C 3
Mukutawa (lake) . . . . . G 2
Mukutawa (riv.) . . . . . E 1
Muskeg (bay) . . . . . G 6
Nejanilini (lake) . . . . . J 1
Nelson (riv.) . . . . . J 2
Nopiming Prov. Park . . . . . G 4
Northern Indian (lake) . . . . . J 2
North Knife (lake) . . . . . J 2
North Seal (riv.) . . . . . H 2
North Shoal (lake) . . . . . E 4
Nueltin (lake) . . . . . H 1
Oak (lake) . . . . . B 5
Obukowin (lake) . . . . . G 3
Oiseau (lake) . . . . . G 4
Oiseau (riv.) . . . . . G 4
Overflow (bay) . . . . . A 1
Overflowing (riv.) . . . . . A 1
Owl (riv.) . . . . . K 2
Oxford (lake) . . . . . J 3
Paint (lake) . . . . . J 2
Palsen (riv.) . . . . . G 2
Pelican (bay) . . . . . B 2
Pelican (lake) . . . . . B 2
Pelican (lake) . . . . . C 5
Pembina (hills) . . . . . D 5
Pembina (riv.) . . . . . C 5
Peonan (pt.) . . . . . D 3
Pickerel (lake) . . . . . C 2
Pigeon (riv.) . . . . . F 2
Pipestone (creek) . . . . . A 5
Plum (creek) . . . . . B 5
Plum (lake) . . . . . B 5
Poplar (riv.) . . . . . E 2
Porcupine (hills) . . . . . A 2
Portage (bay) . . . . . D 3
Punk (isl.) . . . . . F 3
Quesnel (lake) . . . . . G 4
Rat (riv.) . . . . . F 5
Red (riv.) . . . . . F 4
Red Deer (lake) . . . . . A 2
Red Deer (riv.) . . . . . A 2
Reindeer (isl.) . . . . . E 2
Reindeer (lake) . . . . . H 2
Riding (mt.) . . . . . B 4
Riding Mountain Nat'l Park . . . B 4
Rock (lake) . . . . . C 5
Ross (isl.) . . . . . J 3
Sagemace (bay) . . . . . B 3
Saint Andrew (lake) . . . . . E 3
Saint George (lake) . . . . . E 3
Saint Martin (lake) . . . . . D 3
Saint Patrick (lake) . . . . . E 3
Sale (riv.) . . . . . E 5
Sandy (isls.) . . . . . D 2
Sasaginnigak (lake) . . . . . G 3
Seal (riv.) . . . . . J 2
Selkirk (isl.) . . . . . C 1
Setting (lake) . . . . . H 3
Shoal (lake) . . . . . G 5
Shoal (riv.) . . . . . B 2
Sipiwesk (lake) . . . . . J 3
Sisib (lake) . . . . . C 2
Sleeve (lake) . . . . . E 3
Slemon (lake) . . . . . G 1
Snowshoe (lake) . . . . . G 4
Soul (lake) . . . . . C 2
Souris (riv.) . . . . . B 5
Southern Indian (lake) . . . . . H 2
South Knife (riv.) . . . . . J 2
South Seal (riv.) . . . . . J 2
Split (lake) . . . . . J 2
Spruce (isl.) . . . . . B 1
Spruce Woods Prov. Park . . . . C 5
Stevenson (lake) . . . . . J 3
Sturgeon (bay) . . . . . E 3
Swan (lake) . . . . . B 2
Swan (lake) . . . . . D 5
Swan (riv.) . . . . . A 3
Tadoule (lake) . . . . . J 2
Tamarack (isl.) . . . . . F 3
Tatnam (cape) . . . . . K 2
Traverse (bay) . . . . . F 4
Turtle (mts.) . . . . . B 5
Turtle (riv.) . . . . . C 3
Turtle Mountain Prov. Park . . . . B 5
Valley (riv.) . . . . . B 3
Vickers (lake) . . . . . F 3
Viking (lake) . . . . . G 3
Wanipigow (riv.) . . . . . G 3
Washow (bay) . . . . . F 3
Waterhen (lake) . . . . . C 2
Weaver (lake) . . . . . F 2
Wellman (lake) . . . . . B 3
West Hawk (lake) . . . . . G 5
West Shoal (lake) . . . . . E 4
Whitemouth (lake) . . . . . G 5
Whitemouth (riv.) . . . . . G 5
Whiteshell Prov. Park . . . . . G 4
Whitewater (lake) . . . . . B 5
Wicked (pt.) . . . . . D 2
Winnipeg (lake) . . . . . E 2
Winnipeg (riv.) . . . . . G 4
Winnipegosis (lake) . . . . . C 2
Woods (lake) . . . . . H 5
Wrong (lake) . . . . . F 2

*Population of metropolitan area.
•Population of rural municipality.

Topography

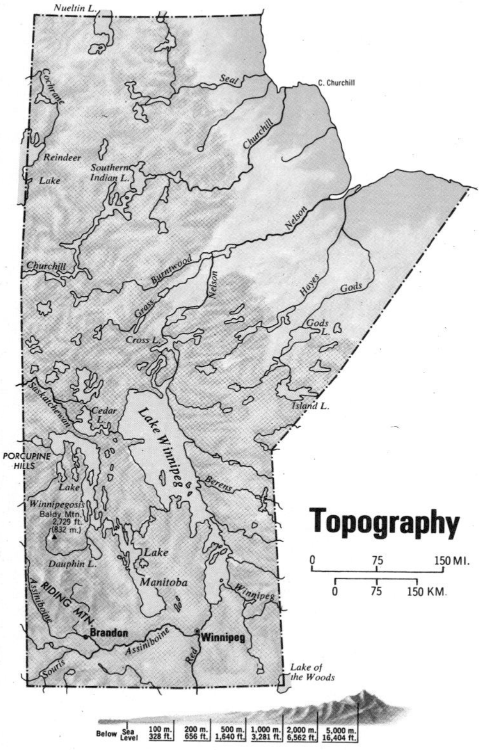

0 75 150 MI.
0 75 150 KM.

Agriculture, Industry and Resources

DOMINANT LAND USE

- Cereals (chiefly barley, oats)
- Cereals, Livestock
- Dairy
- Livestock
- Forests
- Nonagricultural Land

MAJOR MINERAL OCCURRENCES

Au	Gold	Ni	Nickel
Co	Cobalt	O	Petroleum
Cu	Copper	Pb	Lead
Na	Salt	Pt	Platinum
		Zn	Zinc

Water Power
Major Industrial Areas

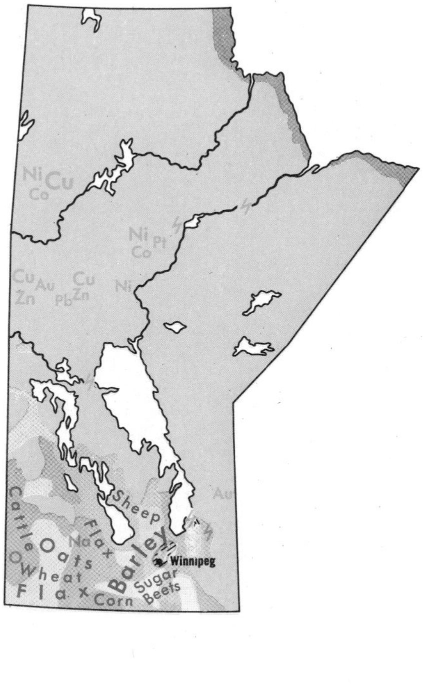

Topography

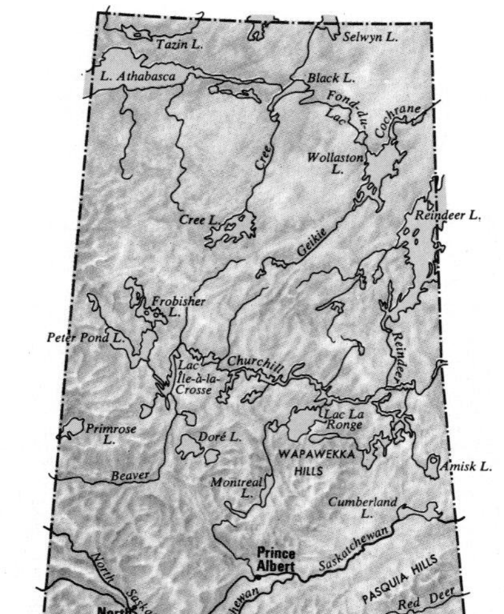

CITIES and TOWNS

Abbey 218 .... C 5
Aberdeen 496 .... E 3
Abernethy 300 .... H 5
Air Ronge 557 .... M 3
Alameda 318 .... J 6
Alida 169 .... K 6
Allan 871 .... E 4
Alsask 652 .... B 4
Annaheim 209 .... G 3
Antelope •231 .... C 5
Arborfield 439 .... H 2
Archerwill 286 .... H 3
Arcola 493 .... J 6
Arlington Beach •432 .... F 4
Asquith 507 .... D 3
Assiniboia 2,924 .... E 6
Avonlea 442 .... G 5
Baildon •799 .... F 5
Balcarres 739 .... H 5
Balgonie 777 .... G 5
Batoche .... E 3
Battleford 3,565 .... C 3
Beauval 606 .... L 3
Beechy 279 .... D 5
Bengough 536 .... F 6
Bethune 369 .... F 5
Bienfait 835 .... J 6
Biggar 2,561 .... C 3
Big River 819 .... D 2
Birch Hills 957 .... F 3
Bjorkdale 269 .... H 3
Blaine Lake 653 .... D 3
Borden 197 .... D 3
Brabant Lake 245 .... M 3
Bradwell 168 .... E 4
Bredenbury 467 .... K 5
Briercrest 151 .... F 5
Broadview 840 .... J 5
Brock 184 .... C 4
Browning •687 .... J 6
Bruno 772 .... F 3
Buchanan 392 .... J 4
Buffalo Gap •598 .... F 6
Buffalo Narrows 1,088 .... L 3
Burstall 550 .... B 5
Cabri 632 .... C 5
Cadillac 173 .... D 6
Calder 164 .... K 4
Cana •1,238 .... J 5
Candle Lake 219 .... F 2
Cando 163 .... C 3
Canoe Lake 182 .... L 3
Canora 2,667 .... J 4
Canwood 340 .... E 2
Carievale 246 .... K 6
Carlyle 1,074 .... J 6
Carnduff 1,043 .... K 6
Carrot River 1,169 .... H 2
Central Butte 548 .... E 5
Ceylon 184 .... G 6
Chaplin 389 .... E 5
Chitek Lake 170 .... D 2
Choiceland 543 .... G 2
Christopher Lake 227 .... F 2
Churchbridge 972 .... J 5
Clavet 234 .... E 4
Climax 293 .... C 6
Cochin 221 .... C 2
Codette 236 .... H 2
Coleville 383 .... B 4
Colonsay 594 .... F 4
Connaught Heights •982 .... G 3
Conquest 256 .... D 4
Consul 153 .... B 6
Coronach 1,032 .... F 6
Craik 565 .... F 4
Craven 206 .... G 5
Creelman 184 .... H 6
Creighton 1,636 .... N 4
Cudworth 947 .... F 3
Cumberland House 831 .... J 2
Cupar 669 .... G 5
Cut Knife 624 .... B 3
Dalmeny 1,064 .... E 3
Davidson 1,166 .... E 4
Debden 403 .... E 2
Delisle 980 .... D 4
Denare Beach 592 .... M 4
Denzil 199 .... B 3
Deschambault Lake 386 .... M 3
Dinsmore 398 .... D 4
Dodsland 272 .... C 4
Domremy 209 .... F 3
Drake 211 .... G 4
Duck Lake 699 .... E 3
Dundurn 531 .... E 4
Dysart 275 .... H 5
Earl Grey 303 .... G 5
Eastend 723 .... C 6
Eatonia 528 .... B 4
Ebenezer 164 .... J 4
Edam 384 .... C 2
Edenwold 143 .... G 5
Elbow 313 .... E 4
Eldorado 229 .... L 2
Elfros 199 .... H 4
Elrose 624 .... D 4
Elstow 143 .... E 4
Endeavour 199 .... J 3
Englefeld 271 .... G 3
Erwood 149 .... J 3
Esterhazy 3,065 .... K 5
Estevan 9,174 .... J 6
Eston 1,413 .... C 4
Eyebrow 168 .... E 5
Fillmore 396 .... H 6
Fleming 141 .... K 5
Flin Flon 367 .... N 4
Foam Lake 1,452 .... H 4
Fond du Lac 494 .... L 2
Fort Qu'Appelle 1,827 .... H 5
Fox Valley 380 .... B 5
Francis 182 .... H 5
Frobisher 166 .... J 6
Frontier 619 .... C 6
Gainsborough 308 .... K 6
Gerald 197 .... K 5
Glaslyn 430 .... C 2
Glenavon 284 .... J 5
Glen Ewen 168 .... K 6
Goodsoil 263 .... L 4
Govan 394 .... G 4
Grand Coulee 208 .... G 5
Gravelbourg 1,338 .... E 6
Grayson 264 .... J 5
Green Acres 139 .... F 2
Green Lake 634 .... L 4
Grenfell 1,307 .... J 5
Guernsey 198 .... F 4
Gull Lake 1,095 .... C 5
Hafford 557 .... D 3
Hague 625 .... E 3
Hanley 484 .... E 4
Harris 259 .... D 4
Hawarden 137 .... E 4
Hearts Hill •552 .... B 3
Hepburn 411 .... E 3
Herbert 1,019 .... D 5
Hodgeville 329 .... E 5
Holdfast 297 .... F 5
Hudson Bay 2,361 .... J 3
Humboldt 4,705 .... F 3
Hyas 165 .... J 4
Île-à-la-Crosse 1,035 .... L 3
Imperial 501 .... F 4
Indian Head 1,889 .... H 5
Invermay 353 .... J 4
Ituna 870 .... H 4
Jansen 223 .... G 4
Jasmin •14 .... H 4
Kamsack 2,688 .... K 4
Kelliher 397 .... H 4
Kelvington 1,054 .... H 3
Kenaston 345 .... E 4
Kennedy 275 .... J 5
Kerrobert 1,141 .... C 4
Kincaid 256 .... D 6
Kindersley 3,969 .... B 4
Kinistino 783 .... F 3
Kipling 1,016 .... J 5
Kisbey 228 .... J 6
Kronau 154 .... G 5
Kyle 516 .... C 5
Lac Pelletier •586 .... C 6
Lafleche 583 .... E 6
Laird 233 .... E 3
Lake Lenore 361 .... G 3
La Loche 1,632 .... L 3
Lampman 651 .... J 6
Lancer 156 .... C 5
Landis 277 .... C 3
Lang 219 .... G 6
Langenburg 1,324 .... K 5
Langham 1,151 .... E 3
Lanigan 1,732 .... F 4
La Ronge 2,579 .... L 3
Lashburn 813 .... B 2
Leader 1,108 .... B 5
Leask 478 .... E 2
Lebret 274 .... H 5
Lemberg 414 .... H 5
Leoville 393 .... D 2
Leroy 504 .... G 4
Lestock 402 .... G 4
Limerick 164 .... E 6
Lintlaw 234 .... H 3
Lipton 364 .... H 5
Lloydminster 6,034 .... A 2
Loon Lake 369 .... B 1
Loreburn 201 .... E 4
Lucky Lake 333 .... D 5
Lumsden 1,303 .... G 5
Luseland 704 .... B 3
Macdowall 171 .... E 2
Macklin 976 .... A 3
Macoun 190 .... H 6
Maidstone 1,001 .... B 2
Mankota 375 .... D 6
Manor 368 .... K 6
Maple Creek 2,470 .... B 6
Marcelin 238 .... E 3
Margo 153 .... H 4
Marriott •627 .... D 4
Marsden 229 .... B 3
Marshall 453 .... B 2
Martensville 1,966 .... E 3
Maryfield 431 .... K 6
Maymont 212 .... D 3
McLean 189 .... G 5
Meacham 178 .... F 3
Meadow Lake 3,857 .... C 1
Meath Park 262 .... F 2
Medstead 163 .... C 2
Melfort 6,010 .... G 3
Melville 5,092 .... J 5
Meota 235 .... C 2
Mervin 155 .... C 2
Midale 564 .... H 6
Middle Lake 275 .... F 3
Milden 251 .... D 4
Milestone 602 .... G 5
Montmartre 544 .... H 5
Montreal Lake 448 .... F 1
Moose Jaw 33,941 .... F 5
Moose Range •679 .... H 2
Moosomin 2,579 .... K 5
Morse 416 .... D 5
Mortlach 293 .... E 5
Mossbank 464 .... E 6
Muenster 385 .... F 3
Naicam 886 .... G 3
Neilburg 354 .... B 3
Neuanlage 144 .... E 3
Neudorf 425 .... J 5
Neuhorst 146 .... E 3
Nipawin 4,376 .... H 2
Nokomis 524 .... F 4
Norquay 552 .... J 4
North Battleford 14,030 .... C 3
North Portal 164 .... J 6
Odessa 232 .... H 5
Ogema 441 .... G 6
Osler 527 .... E 3
Outlook 1,976 .... E 4
Oxbow 1,191 .... J 6
Paddockwood 211 .... F 2
Pangman 227 .... G 6
Paradise Hill 421 .... B 2
Patuanak 173 .... L 3
Paynton 210 .... B 2
Pelican Narrows 331 .... N 3
Pelly 391 .... K 4
Pennant 202 .... C 5
Pense 472 .... G 5
Perdue 407 .... D 3
Pierceland 425 .... K 4
Pilger 150 .... F 3
Pilot Butte 1,255 .... G 5
Pine House 612 .... M 3
Plenty 175 .... C 4
Plunkett 150 .... F 4
Ponteix 769 .... D 6
Porcupine Plain 937 .... H 3
Preeceville 1,243 .... J 4
Prelate 317 .... B 5
Prince Albert 31,380 .... F 2
Prud'homme 222 .... F 3
Punnichy 394 .... G 4
Qu'Appelle 653 .... H 5
Quill Lake 514 .... G 3
Quinton 169 .... G 4
Rabbit Lake 159 .... D 2
Radisson 439 .... D 3
Radville 1,012 .... G 6
Rama 133 .... H 4
Raymore 635 .... G 4
Redvers 859 .... K 6
Regina (cap.) 162,613 .... G 5
Regina *164,313 .... G 5
Regina Beach 603 .... F 5
Rhein 271 .... J 4
Richmound 188 .... B 5
Riverhurst 193 .... E 5
Rocanville 934 .... K 5
Roche Percé 142 .... J 6
Rockglen 511 .... F 6
Rosetown 2,664 .... D 4
Rose Valley 538 .... H 3
Rosthern 1,609 .... E 3
Rouleau 443 .... G 5
Saint Benedict 157 .... F 3
Saint Brieux 401 .... G 3
Saint Louis 448 .... F 3
Saint Philips •538 .... K 4
Saint Walburg 802 .... B 2
Saltcoats 549 .... J 4
Sandy Bay 756 .... N 3
Saskatoon 154,210 .... E 3
Saskatoon *154,210 .... E 3
Sceptre 169 .... B 5
Scott 203 .... C 3
Sedley 373 .... H 5
Semans 344 .... G 4
Shaunavon 2,112 .... C 6
Sheho 285 .... H 4
Shell Lake 220 .... D 2
Shellbrook 1,228 .... E 2
Simpson 231 .... F 4
Sintaluta 215 .... H 5
Smeaton 246 .... G 2
Southey 697 .... G 5
Spalding 337 .... G 3
Spiritwood 926 .... D 2
Springside 533 .... J 4
Spy Hill 354 .... K 5
Star City 527 .... G 3
Stenen 143 .... J 4
Stockholm 391 .... J 5
Stonehenge •701 .... F 6
Storthoaks 142 .... K 6
Stoughton 716 .... J 6
Strasbourg 842 .... G 4
Sturgis 789 .... J 4
Swift Current 14,747 .... D 5
Tantallon 196 .... K 5
Theodore 473 .... J 4
Timber Bay 152 .... F 1
Tisdale 3,107 .... H 3
Togo 181 .... K 4
Tompkins 275 .... C 5
Torch River •2,440 .... G 2
Torquay 311 .... H 6
Tramping Lake 178 .... B 3
Tugaske 175 .... E 5
Turnor Lake 166 .... L 3
Turtleford 505 .... B 2
Unity 2,408 .... B 3
Uranium City 2,507 .... L 2
Val Marie 236 .... D 6
Vanguard 292 .... D 6
Vanscoy 298 .... D 4
Vibank 369 .... H 5
Viscount 386 .... F 4
Vonda 313 .... F 3
Wadena 1,495 .... H 4
Wakaw 1,030 .... F 3
Waldeck 292 .... D 5
Waldheim 758 .... E 3
Walpole •711 .... K 6
Wapella 487 .... K 5
Warman 2,076 .... E 3
Waseca 169 .... B 2
Waskesiu Lake 176 .... E 2
Watrous 1,830 .... F 4
Watson 901 .... G 3
Wawota 622 .... J 6
Weldon 279 .... F 2
Welwyn 170 .... K 5
Weyburn 9,523 .... H 6
White City 602 .... G 5
White Fox 394 .... H 2
Whitewood 1,003 .... J 5
Wilcox 202 .... G 5
Wilkie 1,501 .... C 3
Willow Bunch 494 .... F 6
Willow Creek •1,218 .... B 6
Windthorst 254 .... J 5
Wiseton 195 .... D 4
Wishart 212 .... H 4
Wollaston Lake 248 .... N 2
Wolseley 904 .... H 5
Wymark 162 .... D 5
Wynyard 2,147 .... G 4
Yarbo 158 .... K 5
Yellow Grass 477 .... H 6
Yorkton 15,339 .... J 4
Young 456 .... F 4
Zenon Park 273 .... H 2

OTHER FEATURES

Allan (hills) .... E 4
Amisk (lake) .... M 4
Antelope (lake) .... C 5
Antler (riv.) .... K 6
Arm (riv.) .... F 5
Assiniboine (riv.) .... J 3
Athabasca (lake) .... L 2
Bad (lake) .... C 4
Bad (hills) .... C 4
Basin (lake) .... F 3
Batoche Nat'l Hist. Site .... E 3
Battle (creek) .... B 6
Battle (riv.) .... B 3
Bear (hills) .... C 4
Beaver (hills) .... H 4
Beaver (riv.) .... L 4
Beaverlodge (lake) .... L 2
Big Muddy (lake) .... G 6
Bigstick (lake) .... B 5
Birch (lake) .... C 2
Bitter (lake) .... B 5
Black (lake) .... M 2
Boundary (plat.) .... B 6
Brightsand (lake) .... B 2
Bronson (lake) .... B 2

Agriculture, Industry and Resources

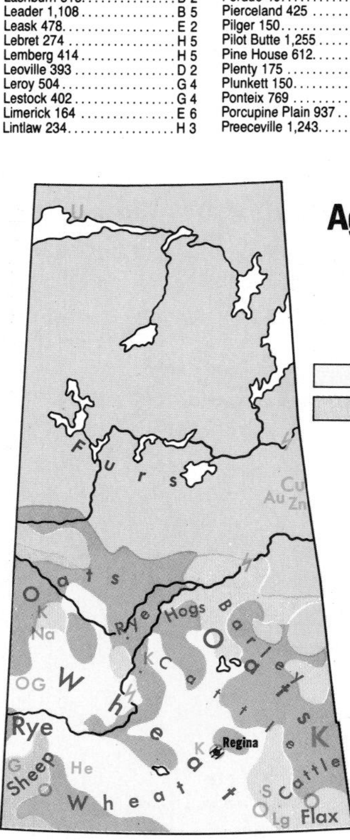

DOMINANT LAND USE

- Wheat
- Cereals (chiefly barley, oats)
- Cereals, Livestock
- Livestock
- Forests

MAJOR MINERAL OCCURRENCES

- Au Gold
- Cu Copper
- G Natural Gas
- He Helium
- K Potash
- Lg Lignite
- Na Salt
- O Petroleum
- S Sulfur
- U Uranium
- Zn Zinc
- Water Power
- Major Industrial Areas

Buffalo Pound Prov. Park F 5
Cabri (lake) B 4
Cactus (hills) F 5
Candle (lake) F 2
Cannington Manon Hist. Park J 6
Canoe (lake) L 3
Carrot (riv.) J 2
Chaplin (lake) E 5
Chipman (riv.) M 2
Chitek (lake) D 2
Churchill (riv.) M 3
Clearwater (riv.) L 3
Cochrane (riv.) N 2
Coteau (hills) D 4
Cowan (lake) D 2
Crane (lake) B 5
Crean (lake) E 1
Cree (lake) L 3
Cree (riv.) M 2
Cumberland (lake) J 1
Cypress (hills) B 6
Cypress (lake) B 6
Cypress Hills Prov. Park B 6
Danielson Prov. Park E 4
Delaronde (lake) E 1
Diefenbaker (lake) E 4
Doré (lake) L 3
Douglas Prov. Park E 4
Duck Lake Hist. Park E 3
Duck Mountain Prov. Park K 4
Eagle (hills) C 3
Eaglehill (creek) D 4
Ear (lake) B 3
Echo Valley Prov. Park G 5
Etomami (riv.) J 3
Eyebrow (lake) E 5
Eyehill (creek) B 3
Fife (lake) E 6
File (hills) H 5
Fir (riv.) J 2
Fond du Lac (riv.) M 2
Forrest (lake) L 3
Fort Battleford Nat'l Hist. Park C 3
Fort Carlton Hist. Park E 3
Fort Pitt Hist. Park B 2
Fort Walsh Nat'l Hist. Park A 6
Foster (riv.) M 3
Frenchman (riv.) C 6
Frobisher (lake) L 3
Gap (creek) B 6
Gardiner (dam) D 4
Geikie (riv.) M 3
Good Spirit (lake) J 4
Goodspirit Lake Prov. Park J 4
Great Sand (hills) B 5
Green (lake) D 1
Greenwater Lake Prov. Park H 3
Haultain (riv.) L 3
Île-à-la-Crosse (lake) L 3
Ironspring (creek) G 3
Jackfish (lake) C 2
Katepwa Prov. Park H 5
Kingsmere (lake) E 1
Kiyiu (lake) C 4
Lac La Ronge Prov. Park M 3
Lanigan (creek) F 4
Last Mountain (lake) F 4
Leaf (lake) J 2
Leech (lake) J 4
Lenore (lake) G 3
Little Manitou (lake) F 4
Lodge (creek) B 6
Long (creek) H 6
Loon (creek) G 4
Makwa (lake) B 1
Makwa (riv.) B 1
Manito (lake) B 3
Maple (creek) B 5
McFarlane (riv.) L 2
Meadow (lake) C 1
Meadow Lake Prov. Park K 4
Meeting (lake) D 2
Midnight (lake) C 2
Ministikwan (lake) B 1
Missouri Coteau (hills) F 5
Montreal (lake) F 1
Moose (mt.) J 6
Moose Jaw (riv.) G 5
Moose Mountain (creek) J 6
Moose Mountain Prov. Park J 6
Mossy (riv.) H 1
Muddy (lake) B 3
Mudjatik (riv.) L 3
Nipawin Prov. Park G 1
North Saskatchewan (riv.) D 3
Notukeu (creek) D 6
Oldman (riv.) L 2
Old Wives (lake) E 5
Opuntia (lake) C 4
Overflowing (riv.) K 2
Pasquia (hills) J 2
Pasquia (riv.) K 2
Pelican (lake) E 5
Peter Pond (lake) L 3
Pheasant (hills) J 5
Pine Lake Prov. Park E 4
Pinto (creek) D 6
Pipestone (creek) K 6
Pipestone (riv.) L 2
Ponass (lakes) H 3
Poplar (riv.) E 6
Porcupine (hills) K 3
Primrose (lake) L 3
Primrose Lake Air Weapons Range L 3
Prince Albert Nat'l Park E 1
Qu'Appelle (riv.) J 5
Quill (lakes) G 4
Red Deer (riv.) A 5
Red Deer (riv.) K 3
Reindeer (lake) N 3
Reindeer (riv.) M 3
Riou (lake) M 2
Rivers (lake) F 6
Ronge, La (lake) M 3
Rowans Ravine Prov. Park F 4
St. Victor Petroglyphs Hist. Park E 6
Saskatchewan (riv.) H 2
Saskatchewan Landing Prov. Park C 5
Saskeram (riv.) K 2
Scott (lake) M 2
Selwyn (lake) M 2
Souris (riv.) H 6
South Saskatchewan (riv.) C 5
Steele Narrows Hist. Park B 2
Stripe (lake) C 4
Sturgeon (riv.) E 2
Swan (riv.) J 3
Swift Current (creek) D 5
Tazin (lake) L 2
The Battlefords Prov. Park C 2
Thickwood (hills) D 2
Thunder (hills) L 4
Tobin (lake) H 2
Torch (riv.) H 2
Touchwood (hills) G 4
Tramping (lake) C 3
Trout (riv.) L 2
Turtle (lake) C 2
Twelvemile (lake) E 6
Vermilion (hills) E 5
Wapawekka (hills) M 4
Waskana (creek) G 5
Waskesiu (lake) E 2
Wathaman (riv.) M 3
Weed (hills) J 5
White Fox (riv.) G 2
White Gull (creek) G 2
Whiteshore (lake) C 3
Whiteswan (lakes) F 1
William (riv.) L 2
Willow Bunch (lake) F 6
Witchekan (lake) D 2
Wollaston (lake) N 2
Wood (mt.) E 6
Wood (riv.) E 6
Wood Mountain Hist. Park E 6

AREA 251,699 sq. mi. (651,900 sq. km.)
POPULATION 968,313
CAPITAL Regina
LARGEST CITY Regina
HIGHEST POINT Cypress Hills 4,567 ft. (1,392 m.)
SETTLED IN 1774
ADMITTED TO CONFEDERATION 1905
PROVINCIAL FLOWER Prairie Lily

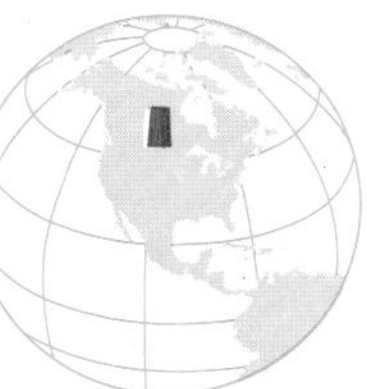

*Population of metropolitan area.
•Population of rural municipality.

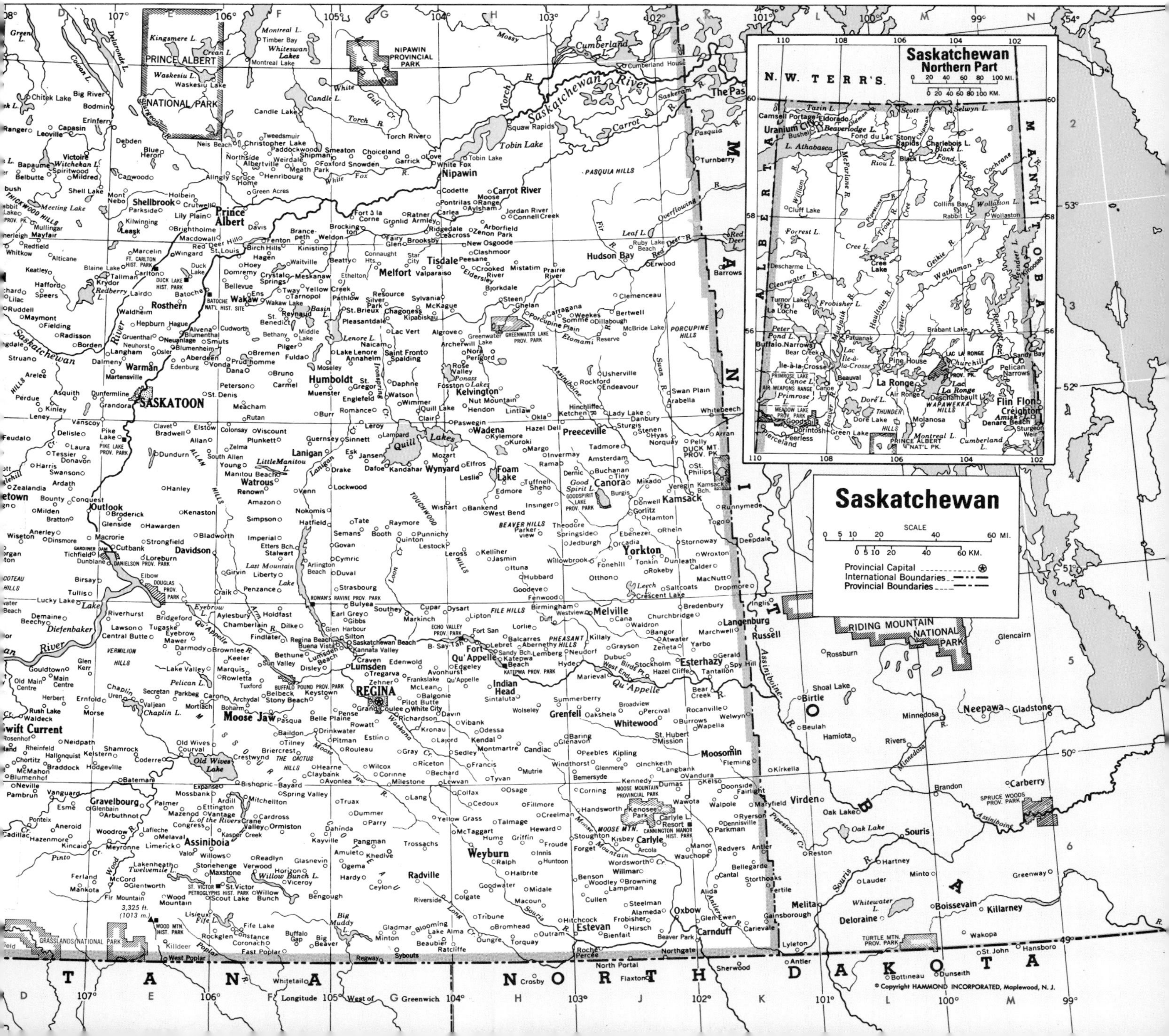

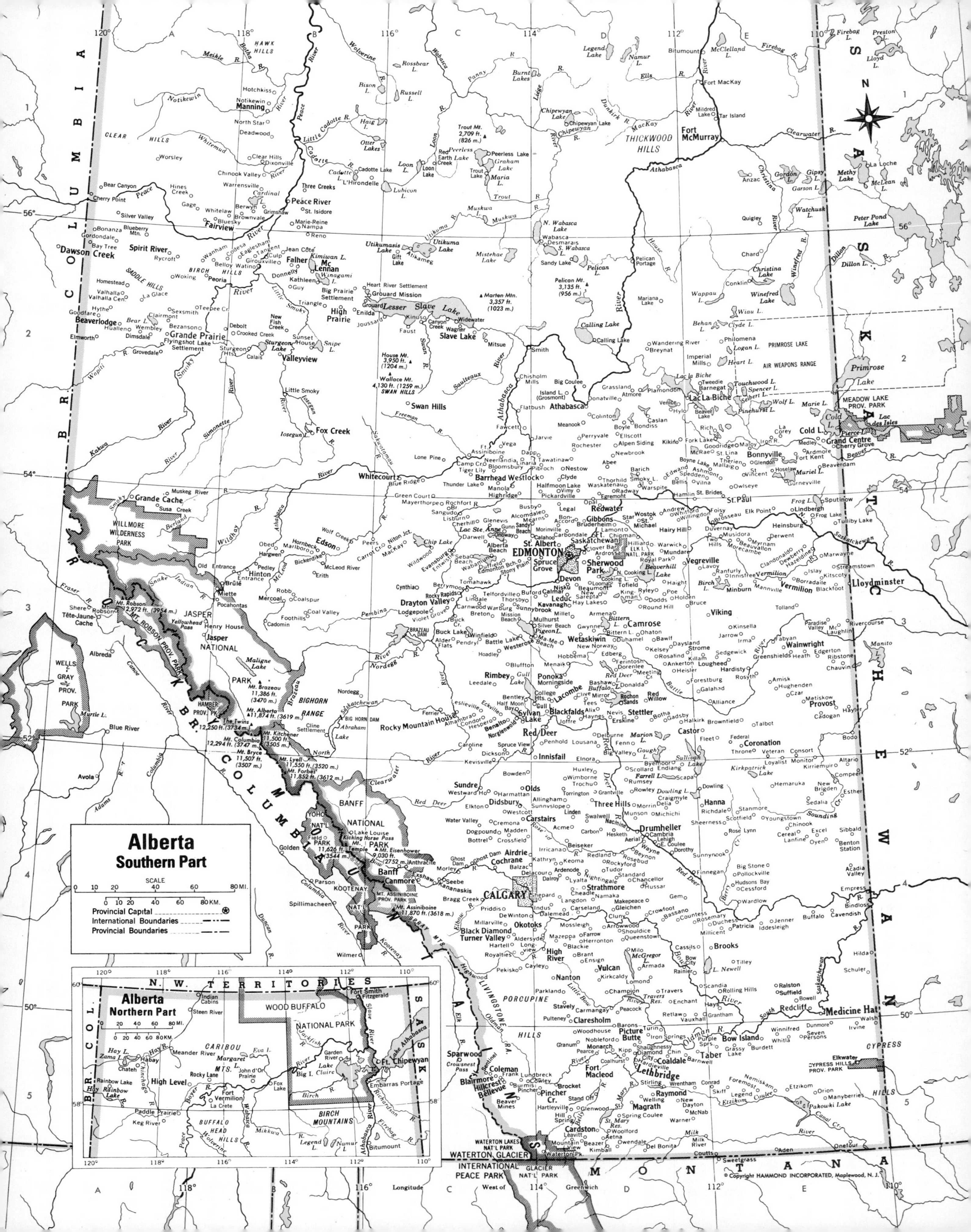
Alberta
Southern Part
SCALE
0 10 20 40 60 80 MI.
0 10 20 40 60 80 KM.
Provincial Capital
International Boundaries
Provincial Boundaries
Alberta
Northern Part
0 20 40 60 80 MI.
N. W. TERRITORIES
WOOD BUFFALO
NATIONAL PARK
BIRCH MOUNTAINS
CARIBOU MTS.
BUFFALO HEAD HILLS
High Level
Ft. Chipewyan
Fort Smith
B R. C O L U M B I A
S A S K A T C H E W A N
M O N T A N A
© Copyright HAMMOND INCORPORATED, Maplewood, N. J.
Longitude
West of
Greenwich
EDMONTON
CALGARY
Red Deer
Lethbridge
Medicine Hat
Fort McMurray
Grande Prairie
Peace River
Lloydminster
Jasper
Banff
JASPER NATIONAL PARK
BANFF NATIONAL PARK
WATERTON LAKES NAT'L PARK
WATERTON GLACIER INTERNATIONAL PEACE PARK
WILLMORE WILDERNESS PARK
PRIMROSE LAKE AIR WEAPONS RANGE
Lesser Slave Lake
THICKWOOD HILLS
SWAN HILLS
CLEAR HILLS
BIRCH HILLS
SADDLE HILLS
PORCUPINE HILLS
CYPRESS HILLS PROV. PARK
MEADOW LAKE PROV. PARK
WELLS GRAY PROV. PARK
MT. ROBSON PROV. PARK
HAMBER PROV. PK.
MT. ASSINIBOINE PROV. PARK
KOOTENAY NAT'L PARK
YOHO NAT'L PARK
Mt. Robson 12,972 ft. (3954 m.)
Mt. Columbia 12,294 ft. (3747 m.)
Mt. Alberta 11,874 ft. (3619 m.)
Mt. Assiniboine 11,870 ft. (3618 m.)

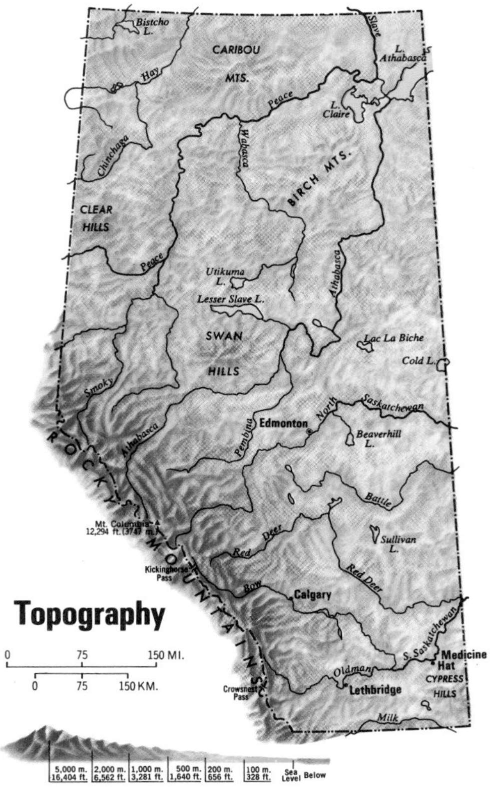

Topography

0 75 150 MI.
0 75 150 KM.

CITIES and TOWNS

Acme 457 . . . . D 4
Airdrie 8,414 . . . . C 4
Alberta Beach 485 . . . . C 3
Alix 837 . . . . D 3
Andrew 548 . . . . D 3
Antler Lake 334 . . . . D 3
Ardmore 224 . . . . E 2
Arrowwood 156 . . . . D 4
Athabasca 1,731 . . . . D 2
Banff 4,208 . . . . C 4
Barnwell 359 . . . . D 5
Barons 315 . . . . D 4
Barrhead 3,736 . . . . C 2
Bashaw 875 . . . . D 3
Bassano 1,200 . . . . D 4
Bawlf 350 . . . . D 3
Beaumont 2,638 . . . . D 3
Beaverlodge 1,937 . . . . A 2
Beiseker 580 . . . . D 4
Bentley 823 . . . . C 3
Berwyn 557 . . . . B 1
Big Valley 360 . . . . D 3
Black Diamond 1,444 . . . . C 4
Blackfalds 1,488 . . . . D 3
Blackfoot 220 . . . . E 3
Blackie 298 . . . . D 4
Bon Accord 1,376 . . . . D 3
Bonnyville 4,454 . . . . E 2
Bowden 989 . . . . C 4
Bow Island 1,491 . . . . E 5
Boyle 638 . . . . D 2
Bragg Creek 505 . . . . C 4
Breton 552 . . . . C 3
Brooks 9,421 . . . . E 4
Bruce 88 . . . . E 3
Bruderheim 1,136 . . . . D 3
Burdett 220 . . . . E 5
Calgary 592,743 . . . . C 4
Calgary *592,743 . . . . C 4
Calmar 1,003 . . . . D 3
Camrose 12,570 . . . . D 3
Canmore 3,484 . . . . C 4
Carbon 434 . . . . D 4
Cardston 3,267 . . . . D 5
Carmangay 266 . . . . D 4
Caroline 436 . . . . C 3
Carseland 484 . . . . D 4
Carstairs 1,587 . . . . D 4
Castor 1,123 . . . . D 3
Cereal 249 . . . . E 4
Champion 339 . . . . D 4
Chauvin 298 . . . . E 3
Chipman 266 . . . . D 3
Clairmont 469 . . . . A 2
Claresholm 3,493 . . . . D 4
Clive 364 . . . . D 3
Clyde 364 . . . . D 2
Coaldale 4,579 . . . . D 5
Coalhurst 882 . . . . D 5
Cochrane 3,544 . . . . C 4
Cold Lake 2,110 . . . . E 2
College Heights 267 . . . . D 3
Consort 632 . . . . E 3
Cooking Lake 218 . . . . D 3
Coronation 1,309 . . . . E 3
Coutts 400 . . . . D 5
Cowley 304 . . . . D 5
Cremona 382 . . . . C 4
Crossfield 1,217 . . . . C 4
Daysland 679 . . . . D 3
Delburne 574 . . . . D 3
Desmarais 260 . . . . D 2
Devon 3,885 . . . . D 3
Didsbury 3,095 . . . . C 4
Donalda 280 . . . . D 3
Donnelly 336 . . . . B 2
Drayton Valley 5,042 . . . . C 3
Drumheller 6,508 . . . . D 4
Duchess 429 . . . . E 4
East Coulee 218 . . . . D 4
Eckville 870 . . . . C 3
Edgerton 387 . . . . E 3
Edmonton (cap.) 532,246 . . . . D 3
Edmonton *657,057 . . . . D 3
Edmonton Beach 280 . . . . C 3
Edson 5,835 . . . . B 3
Elk Point 1,022 . . . . E 3
Elnora 249 . . . . D 3
Entwistle 462 . . . . C 3
Erskine 259 . . . . D 3
Evansburg 779 . . . . C 3
Exshaw 353 . . . . C 4
Fairview 2,869 . . . . A 1
Falher 1,102 . . . . B 2
Faust 399 . . . . C 2
Foremost 568 . . . . E 5
Forestburg 924 . . . . E 3
Fort Assiniboine 207 . . . . C 2
Fort Chipewyan 944 . . . . C 5
Fort Macleod 3,139 . . . . D 5
Fort McKay 267 . . . . E 1
Fort McMurray 31,000 . . . . E 1
Fort Saskatchewan 12,169 . . . . D 3
Fort Vermilion 752 . . . . B 5
Fox Creek 1,978 . . . . B 2
Fox Lake 634 . . . . B 5
Gibbons 2,276 . . . . D 3
Gift Lake 428 . . . . C 2
Girouxville 325 . . . . B 2
Gleichen 381 . . . . D 4
Glendon 430 . . . . E 2
Glenwood 259 . . . . D 5
Grand Centre 3,146 . . . . E 2
Grande Cache 4,523 . . . . A 3
Grande Prairie 24,263 . . . . A 2
Granum 399 . . . . D 5
Grimshaw 2,316 . . . . B 1
Grouard Mission 221 . . . . C 2
Hanna 2,806 . . . . E 4
Hardisty 641 . . . . E 3
Hay Lakes 302 . . . . D 3
Heisler 212 . . . . D 3
High Level 2,194 . . . . A 5
High Prairie 2,506 . . . . B 2
High River 4,792 . . . . D 4
Hines Creek 575 . . . . A 1
Hinton 8,342 . . . . B 3
Holden 430 . . . . D 3
Hughenden 267 . . . . E 3
Hythe 639 . . . . A 2
Innisfail 5,247 . . . . D 3
Innisfree 255 . . . . E 3
Irma 474 . . . . E 3
Irricana 558 . . . . D 4
Irvine 360 . . . . E 5
Jasper 3,269 . . . . B 3
John d'Or Prairie 437 . . . . B 5
Joussard 330 . . . . B 2
Killam 1,005 . . . . E 3
Kinuso 285 . . . . C 2
Kitscoty 497 . . . . E 3
Lac La Biche 2,007 . . . . E 2
Lacombe 5,591 . . . . D 3
La Crete 479 . . . . B 5
Lake Louise 355 . . . . B 4
Lamont 1,563 . . . . D 3
Leduc 12,471 . . . . D 3
Legal 1,022 . . . . D 3
Lethbridge 54,072 . . . . D 5
Linden 407 . . . . D 4
Little Buffalo Lake 253 . . . . B 1
Lloydminster 8,997 . . . . E 3
Longview 301 . . . . C 4
Lougheed 226 . . . . E 3
Lundbreck 244 . . . . C 5
Magrath 1,576 . . . . D 5
Manning 1,173 . . . . B 1
Mannville 788 . . . . E 3
Marlboro 211 . . . . B 3
Marwayne 500 . . . . E 3
Mayerthorpe 1,475 . . . . C 3
McLennan 1,125 . . . . B 2
Medicine Hat 40,380 . . . . E 4
Milk River 894 . . . . D 5
Millet 1,120 . . . . D 3
Mirror 507 . . . . D 3
Monarch 212 . . . . D 5
Morinville 4,657 . . . . D 3
Morrin 244 . . . . D 4
Mundare 604 . . . . D 3
Myrnam 397 . . . . E 3
Nacmine 369 . . . . D 4
Nampa 334 . . . . B 1
Nanton 1,641 . . . . D 4
New Norway 291 . . . . D 3
New Sarepta 417 . . . . D 3
Nobleford 534 . . . . D 5
North Calling Lake 234 . . . . D 2
Okotoks 3,847 . . . . C 4
Olds 4,813 . . . . D 4
Onoway 621 . . . . C 3
Oyen 975 . . . . E 4
Peace River 5,907 . . . . B 1
Penhold 1,531 . . . . D 3
Picture Butte 1,404 . . . . D 5
Pincher Creek 3,757 . . . . D 5
Plamondon 259 . . . . D 2
Pollockville 19 . . . . E 4
Ponoka 5,221 . . . . D 3
Provost 1,645 . . . . E 3
Rainbow Lake 504 . . . . A 5
Ralston 357 . . . . E 4
Raymond 2,837 . . . . D 5
Redcliff 3,876 . . . . E 4
Red Deer 46,393 . . . . D 3
Redwater 1,932 . . . . D 3
Rimbey 1,685 . . . . C 3
Robb 230 . . . . B 3
Rockyford 329 . . . . D 4
Rocky Mountain House 4,698 . C 3
Rosemary 328 . . . . E 4
Rycroft 649 . . . . A 2
Ryley 483 . . . . D 3
Saint Albert 31,996 . . . . D 3
Saint Paul 4,884 . . . . E 3
Sangudo 398 . . . . C 3
Sedgewick 879 . . . . E 3
Sexsmith 1,180 . . . . A 2
Shaughnessy 270 . . . . D 5
Sherwood Park 29,285 . . . . D 3
Slave Lake 4,506 . . . . C 2
Smith 216 . . . . D 2
Smoky Lake 1,074 . . . . D 2
Spirit River 1,104 . . . . A 2
Spruce Grove 10,326 . . . . D 3
Standard 379 . . . . D 4
Stavely 504 . . . . D 4
Stettler 5,136 . . . . D 3
Stirling 688 . . . . D 5
Stony Plain 4,839 . . . . C 3
Strathmore 2,986 . . . . D 4
Strome 281 . . . . E 3
Sundre 1,742 . . . . C 4
Swan Hills 2,497 . . . . C 2
Sylvan Lake 3,779 . . . . C 3
Taber 5,988 . . . . E 5
Thorhild 576 . . . . D 2
Thorsby 737 . . . . C 3
Three Hills 1,787 . . . . D 4
Tilley 345 . . . . E 4
Tofield 1,504 . . . . D 3
Trochu 880 . . . . D 4
Turner Valley 1,311 . . . . C 4
Two Hills 1,193 . . . . E 3
Valleyview 2,061 . . . . B 2
Vauxhall 1,049 . . . . D 4
Vegreville 5,251 . . . . E 3
Vermilion 3,766 . . . . E 3
Veteran 314 . . . . E 3
Viking 1,232 . . . . E 3
Vilna 345 . . . . E 2
Vulcan 1,489 . . . . D 4
Wabamun 662 . . . . C 3
Wabasca 701 . . . . D 2
Wainwright 4,266 . . . . E 3
Warburg 501 . . . . C 3
Warner 477 . . . . D 5
Waskatenau 290 . . . . D 2
Wembley 1,169 . . . . A 2
Westlock 4,424 . . . . C 2
Wetaskiwin 9,597 . . . . D 3
Whitecourt 5,585 . . . . C 2
Wildwood 441 . . . . C 3
Willingdon 366 . . . . E 3
Youngstown 297 . . . . E 4

OTHER FEATURES

Abraham (lake) . . . . B 3
Alberta (mt.) . . . . B 3
Assiniboine (mt.) . . . . C 4
Athabasca (lake) . . . . C 5
Athabasca (riv.) . . . . D 1
Banff Nat'l Park . . . . B 4
Battle (riv.) . . . . D 3
Bear (lake) . . . . A 2
Beaver (riv.) . . . . E 2
Beaverhill (lake) . . . . D 3
Behan (lake) . . . . E 2
Belly (riv.) . . . . D 5
Berland (riv.) . . . . A 3
Berry (creek) . . . . E 4
Biche (lake) . . . . E 2
Big (isl.) . . . . B 5
Big Horn (dam) . . . . B 3
Bighorn (range) . . . . B 3
Birch (hills) . . . . A 2
Birch (lake) . . . . E 3
Birch (mts.) . . . . B 5
Birch (riv.) . . . . B 5
Bison (lake) . . . . B 1
Bittern (lake) . . . . D 3
Botha (riv.) . . . . B 1
Bow (riv.) . . . . D 4
Boyer (riv.) . . . . A 5
Brazeau (mt.) . . . . B 3
Brazeau (riv.) . . . . B 3
Buffalo (lake) . . . . D 3
Buffalo Head (hills) . . . . B 5
Burnt (lakes) . . . . C 1
Cadotte (lake) . . . . B 1
Cadotte (riv.) . . . . B 1
Calling (lake) . . . . D 2
Canal (creek) . . . . E 5
Cardinal (lake) . . . . B 1
Caribou (mts.) . . . . B 5
Chinchaga (riv.) . . . . A 5
Chip (lake) . . . . C 3
Chipewyan (lake) . . . . D 1
Chipewyan (riv.) . . . . D 1
Christina (lake) . . . . E 2
Christina (riv.) . . . . E 1
Claire (lake) . . . . B 5
Clear (hills) . . . . A 1
Clearwater (riv.) . . . . C 4
Clearwater (riv.) . . . . E 1
Clyde (lake) . . . . E 2
Cold (lake) . . . . E 2
Columbia (mt.) . . . . B 3
Crowsnest (pass) . . . . C 5
Cypress (hills) . . . . E 5
Cypress Hills Prov. Park . . . . E 5
Dillon (riv.) . . . . E 2
Dowling (lake) . . . . D 4
Dunkirk (riv.) . . . . D 1
Eisenhower (mt.) . . . . C 4
Elbow (riv.) . . . . C 4
Elk Island Nat'l Park . . . . D 3
Ells (riv.) . . . . D 1
Etzikom Coulee (riv.) . . . . E 5
Eva (lake) . . . . B 5
Farrell (lake) . . . . D 4
Firebag (riv.) . . . . E 1
Forbes (mt.) . . . . B 4
Freeman (riv.) . . . . C 2
Frog (lake) . . . . E 3
Garson (lake) . . . . E 1
Gipsy (lake) . . . . E 1
Gordon (lake) . . . . E 1
Gough (lake) . . . . D 3
Graham (lake) . . . . C 1
Gull (lake) . . . . C 3
Haig (lake) . . . . B 1
Hawk (hills) . . . . B 1
Hay (lake) . . . . A 5
Hay (riv.) . . . . A 5
Heart (lake) . . . . E 2
Highwood (riv.) . . . . C 4
House (mt.) . . . . C 2
House (riv.) . . . . D 2
Iosegun (lake) . . . . B 2
Iosegun (riv.) . . . . B 2
Jackfish (riv.) . . . . B 5
Jasper Nat'l Park . . . . A 3
Kakwa (riv.) . . . . A 2
Kickinghorse (pass) . . . . B 4
Kimiwan (lake) . . . . B 2
Kirkpatrick (lake) . . . . E 4
Kitchener (mt.) . . . . B 3
Legend (lake) . . . . D 1
Lesser Slave (lake) . . . . C 2
Liége (riv.) . . . . D 1
Little Bow (riv.) . . . . D 4
Little Cadotte (riv.) . . . . B 1
Little Smoky (riv.) . . . . B 2
Livingstone (range) . . . . C 4
Logan (lake) . . . . E 2
Loon (lake) . . . . C 1
Loon (riv.) . . . . C 1
Lubicon (lake) . . . . C 1
Lyell (mt.) . . . . B 4
MacKay (riv.) . . . . D 1
Maligne (lake) . . . . B 3
Margaret (lake) . . . . B 5
Marie (lake) . . . . E 2
Marion (lake) . . . . D 3
Marten (mt.) . . . . C 2
McClelland (lake) . . . . E 1
McGregor (lake) . . . . D 4
McLeod (riv.) . . . . B 3
Meikle (riv.) . . . . A 1
Mikkwa (riv.) . . . . B 5
Milk (riv.) . . . . D 5
Mistehae (lake) . . . . C 2
Muriel (lake) . . . . E 2
Muskwa (lake) . . . . C 1
Muskwa (riv.) . . . . C 1
Namur (lake) . . . . D 1
Newell (lake) . . . . E 4
Nordegg (riv.) . . . . C 3
North Saskatchewan (riv.) . . . . E 3
North Wabasca (lake) . . . . D 1
Notikewin (riv.) . . . . A 1
Oldman (riv.) . . . . D 5
Otter (lakes) . . . . B 1
Pakowki (lake) . . . . E 5
Panny (riv.) . . . . C 1
Peace (riv.) . . . . B 1
Peerless (lake) . . . . C 1
Pelican (lake) . . . . D 2
Pelican (mts.) . . . . D 2
Pembina (riv.) . . . . C 3
Pigeon (lake) . . . . D 3
Pinehurst (lake) . . . . E 2
Porcupine (hills) . . . . C 4
Primrose (lake) . . . . E 2
Rainbow (lake) . . . . A 5
Red Deer (lake) . . . . D 3
Red Deer (riv.) . . . . D 4
Richardson (riv.) . . . . C 5
Rocky (mts.) . . . . B-C 4
Rosebud (riv.) . . . . D 4
Russell (lake) . . . . C 1
Saddle (hills) . . . . A 2
Sainte Anne (lake) . . . . C 3
Saint Mary (res.) . . . . D 5
Saint Mary (riv.) . . . . D 5
Saulteaux (riv.) . . . . C 2
Seibert (lake) . . . . E 2
Simonette (riv.) . . . . A 2
Slave (riv.) . . . . C 5
Smoky (riv.) . . . . A 2
Snake Indian (riv.) . . . . A 3
Snipe (lake) . . . . B 2
Sounding (creek) . . . . E 4
South Saskatchewan (riv.) . . . . E 4
South Wabasca (lake) . . . . D 2
Spencer (lake) . . . . E 2
Spray (mts.) . . . . C 4
Sturgeon (lake) . . . . B 2
Sullivan (lake) . . . . D 3
Swan (hills) . . . . C 2
Swan (riv.) . . . . C 2
Temple (mt.) . . . . B 4
The Twins (mt.) . . . . B 3
Thickwood (hills) . . . . D 1
Touchwood (lake) . . . . E 2
Travers (res.) . . . . D 4
Trout (mt.) . . . . C 1
Trout (riv.) . . . . C 1
Utikuma (lake) . . . . C 2
Utikuma (riv.) . . . . C 1
Utikumasis (lake) . . . . C 2
Vermilion (riv.) . . . . E 3
Wabasca (riv.) . . . . C 1
Wallace (mt.) . . . . C 2
Wapiti (riv.) . . . . A 2
Wappau (lake) . . . . E 2
Watchusk (lake) . . . . E 1
Waterton-Glacier Int'l Peace Park . . . . C 5
Waterton Lakes Nat'l Park . . . . C 5
Whitemud (riv.) . . . . A 1
Wildhay (riv.) . . . . B 3
Willmore Wilderness Prov. Park . . . . A 3
Winagami (lake) . . . . B 2
Winefred (lake) . . . . E 2
Winefred (riv.) . . . . E 2
Wolf (lake) . . . . E 2
Wolverine (riv.) . . . . B 1
Wood Buffalo Nat'l Park . . . . B 5
Yellowhead (pass) . . . . A 3
Zama (lake) . . . . A 5

*Population of metropolitan area.

AREA 255,285 sq. mi. (661,185 sq. km.)
POPULATION 2,237,724
CAPITAL Edmonton
LARGEST CITY Edmonton
HIGHEST POINT Mt. Columbia 12,294 ft. (3,747 m.)
SETTLED IN 1861
ADMITTED TO CONFEDERATION 1905
PROVINCIAL FLOWER Wild Rose

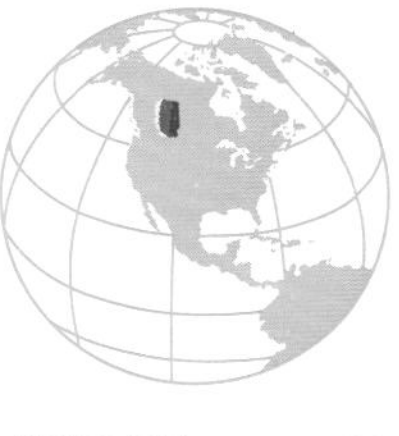

Agriculture, Industry and Resources

DOMINANT LAND USE

- Wheat
- Cereals (chiefly barley, oats)
- Cereals, Livestock
- Dairy
- Pasture Livestock
- Range Livestock
- Forests
- Nonagricultural Land

MAJOR MINERAL OCCURRENCES

- C Coal
- G Natural Gas
- Na Salt
- O Petroleum
- S Sulfur
- Water Power
- Major Industrial Areas

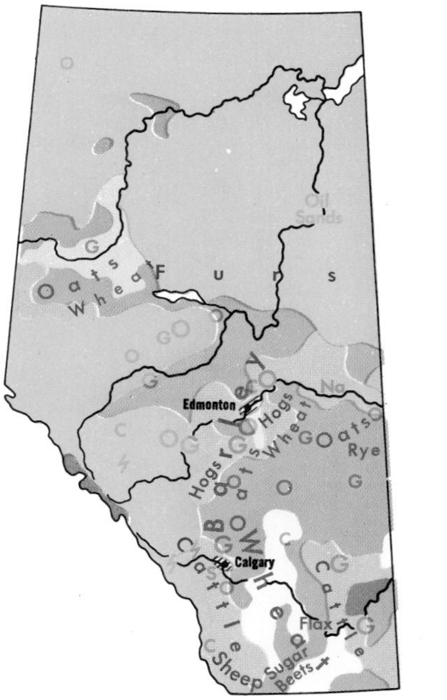

Topography

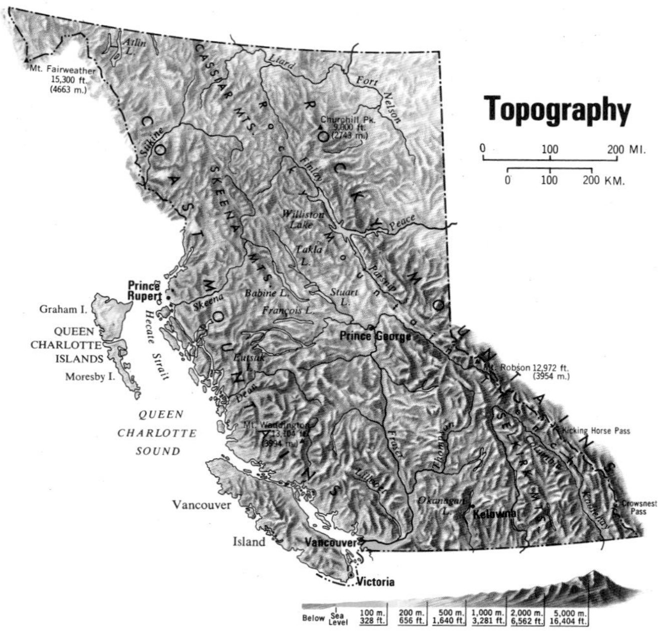

CITIES and TOWNS

Abbotsford 12,745 .... L 3
Alert Bay 626 .... D 5
Armstrong 2,683 .... H 5
Ashcroft 2,156 .... G 5
Ashton Creek 452 .... H 5
Balfour 472 .... J 5
Barlow 441 .... F 3
Barrière 1,370 .... H 4
Blueberry Creek 635 .... J 5
Blue River 384 .... H 4
Boston Bar 498 .... G 5
Bowen Island 1,125 .... K 3
Brackendale 1,719 .... F 5
Burnaby ○136,494 .... K 3
Burns Lake 1,777 .... D 3
Cache Creek 1,308 .... G 5
Campbell River 15,370 .... E 5
Canal Flats 919 .... K 5
Canyon 698 .... J 5
Cassiar 1,045 .... K 2
Castlegar 6,902 .... J 5
Cawston 785 .... H 5
Central Saanich ○9,890 .... K 3
Chase 1,777 .... H 5
Chemainus 2,069 .... J 3
Cherry Creek 450 .... G 5
Chetwynd 2,553 .... G 2
Chilliwack ○40,642 .... M 3
Clearwater 1,461 .... G 4
Clinton 804 .... G 4
Coldstream ○6,450 .... H 5
Comox 6,607 .... H 2
Coquitlam ○61,077 .... K 3
Courtenay 8,992 .... E 5
Cranbrook 15,915 .... K 5
Creston 4,190 .... J 5
Crofton 1,303 .... J 3
Cultus Lake 481 .... M 3
Cumberland 1,947 .... E 5
Dawson Creek 11,373 .... G 2
Delta ○74,692 .... K 3
Duncan 4,228 .... J 3
Elkford 3,126 .... K 5
Enderby 1,816 .... H 5
Erickson 972 .... J 5
Errington 609 .... J 3
Esquimalt ○15,870 .... K 4
Falkland 478 .... H 5
Fernie 5,444 .... K 5
Forest Grove 444 .... G 4
Fort Fraser 574 .... E 3
Fort Langley 2,326 .... L 3
Fort Nelson 3,724 .... M 2
Fort Saint James 2,284 .... E 3
Fort Saint John 13,891 .... G 2
Fraser Lake 1,543 .... E 3
Fruitvale 1,904 .... J 5
Gabriola 1,627 .... J 3
Galiano 669 .... K 3
Ganges 1,118 .... K 3
Gibsons 2,594 .... K 3
Gold River 2,225 .... D 5
Golden 3,476 .... J 4
Grand Forks 3,486 .... H 6
Granisle 1,430 .... D 3
Greenwood 856 .... H 5
Hagensborg 350 .... D 4
Harrison Hot Springs 569 .... M 3
Hatzic 1,055 .... L 3
Hazelton 393 .... D 2
Hedley 426 .... G 5
Holberg 444 .... C 5
Honeymoon Bay 474 .... J 3
Hope 3,205 .... M 3
Hornby Island 474 .... H 2
Horsefly 430 .... G 4
Houston 1,714 .... D 3
Hudson Hope 984 .... F 2
Invermere 1,969 .... J 5
Kaleden 998 .... H 5
Kamloops 64,048 .... G 5
Kaslo 854 .... J 5
Kelowna 59,196 .... H 5
Kent ○3,394 .... M 3
Keremeos 830 .... G 5
Kimberley 7,375 .... K 5
Kitimat 12,462 .... C 3
Kitsault 554 .... C 2
Kitwanga 369 .... D 2
Lac La Hache 647 .... G 4
Ladysmith 4,558 .... J 3
Lake Cowichan 2,391 .... J 3
Langley 15,124 .... L 3
Lantzville 969 .... J 3
Likely 425 .... G 4
Lillooet 1,725 .... G 5
Lion's Bay 1,078 .... K 3
Logan Lake 2,637 .... G 5
Lumby 1,266 .... H 5
Lytton 428 .... G 5
Mackenzie 5,797 .... F 2
Mackenzie ○5,890 .... F 2
Malakwa 392 .... H 5
Maple Bay 393 .... K 3
Maple Ridge ○32,232 .... L 3
Masset 1,569 .... B 3
Matsqui ○42,001 .... L 3
Mayne 546 .... K 3
McBride 641 .... G 3
Merritt 6,110 .... G 5
Midway 633 .... H 6
Mill Bay 583 .... K 3
Mission ○20,056 .... L 3
Mission City 9,948 .... L 3
Montrose 1,229 .... J 5
Nakusp 1,495 .... J 5
Nanaimo 47,069 .... J 3
Naramata 876 .... H 5
Nelson 9,143 .... J 5
New Denver 642 .... J 5
New Hazelton 792 .... D 2
New Westminster 38,550 .... K 3
Nicomen Island 360 .... L 3
Nootka .... D 5
North Cowichan ○18,210 .... J 3
North Pender Island 906 .... K 3
North Saanich ○6,117 .... K 3
North Vancouver 33,952 .... K 3
North Vancouver ○65,367 .... K 3
Oak Bay ○16,990 .... K 4
Okanagan Falls 1,030 .... H 5
Okanagan Landing 834 .... H 5
Okanagan Mission .... H 5
Old Barkerville 11 .... G 3
Oliver 1,893 .... H 5
One Hundred Mile House 1,925 .... G 4
Osoyoos 2,738 .... H 5
Oyama 430 .... H 5
Parksville 5,216 .... J 3
Peachland ○2,865 .... G 5
Penticton 23,181 .... H 5
Pitt Meadows ○6,209 .... L 3
Port Alberni 19,892 .... H 3
Port Alice 1,668 .... D 5
Port Clements 380 .... B 3
Port Coquitlam 27,535 .... L 3
Port Edward 989 .... B 3
Port Hardy ○3,778 .... D 5
Port McNeill 2,474 .... D 5
Port Moody 14,917 .... L 3
Pouce-Coupé 821 .... G 2
Powell River ○13,423 .... E 5
Prince George 67,559 .... F 3
Prince Rupert 16,197 .... B 3
Princeton 3,051 .... G 5
Qualicum Beach 2,844 .... J 3
Queen Charlotte 1,070 .... A 3
Quesnel 8,240 .... F 4
Radium Hot Springs 419 .... J 5
Revelstoke 5,544 .... J 5
Richmond ○96,154 .... K 3
Roberts Creek 926 .... J 3
Robson 1,008 .... J 5
Rossland 3,967 .... H 6
Royston 754 .... H 2
Saanich ○78,710 .... K 3
Salmo 1,169 .... J 5
Salmon Arm 1,946 .... H 5
Salmon Arm ○10,780 .... H 5
Saltair 1,356 .... J 3
Sandspit 794 .... B 3
Sayward 482 .... D 5
Sechelt 1,096 .... J 2
Shawnigan Lake 419 .... J 3
Shoreacres 555 .... J 5
Sicamous 1,057 .... H 5
Sidney 7,946 .... K 3
Slocan 351 .... J 5
Slocan Park 414 .... J 5
Smithers 4,570 .... D 3
Sointula 567 .... D 5
Sooke 852 .... J 4
Sorrento 659 .... H 5
South Hazelton 500 .... D 2
South Wellington 620 .... J 3
Spallumcheen 4,213 .... H 5
Sparwood 3,267 .... K 5
Sproat Lake 440 .... H 3
Squamish 1,590 .... F 5
Stewart ○1,456 .... C 2
Summerland ○7,473 .... G 5
Surrey ○147,138 .... K 3
Tahsis 1,739 .... D 5
Taylor 966 .... G 2
Telkwa 840 .... D 3
Terrace 8,893 .... C 3
Terrace ○10,914 .... C 3
Thornhill 4,281 .... C 3
Thrums 360 .... J 5
Tofino 705 .... E 5
Trail 9,599 .... J 6
Ucluelet 1,593 .... E 6
Union Bay 601 .... H 2
Valemount 1,130 .... H 4
Vancouver 414,281 .... K 3
Vancouver (Greater) *1,169,831 .... K 3
Vanderhoof 2,323 .... E 3
Vavenby 479 .... H 4
Vernon 19,987 .... H 5
Victoria (cap.) 64,379 .... K 4
Victoria *233,481 .... K 4
Warfield 1,969 .... J 5
Wasa 345 .... K 5
Wells 417 .... G 3
Westbank 1,271 .... H 5
West Vancouver ○35,728 .... K 3
Westwold 409 .... G 5
Whistler ○1,365 .... F 5
White Rock 13,550 .... K 3
Williams Lake 8,362 .... F 4
Wilson Creek 611 .... J 2
Windermere 611 .... K 5
Winlaw 435 .... J 5
Woss Lake 395 .... D 5
Wynndel 566 .... J 5
Yarrow 1,201 .... M 3
Youbou 965 .... J 3

OTHER FEATURES

Adams (lake) .... H 4
Adams (riv.) .... H 4
Alberni (inlet) .... H 3
Alsek (riv.) .... H 1
Aristazabal (isl.) .... C 4
Assiniboine (mt.) .... K 5
Atlin (lake) .... J 1
Azure (lake) .... G 4
Babine (lake) .... E 3
Babine (riv.) .... D 2
Banks (isl.) .... B 3
Barkley (sound) .... E 6
Beale (cape) .... E 6
Beatton (riv.) .... G 1
Bella Coola (riv.) .... D 4
Bennett, W.A.C. (dam) .... F 2
Birkenhead Lake Prov. Park .... F 5
Bowron Lake Prov. Park .... G 3
Bowser (lake) .... C 2
Brooks (pen.) .... D 5
Browning Entrance (str.) .... B 3
Bryce (mt.) .... J 4
Bugaboo Glacier Prov. Park .... J 5
Bulkley (riv.) .... D 2
Burke (chan.) .... D 4
Burnaby (isl.) .... B 4
Bute (inlet) .... E 5
Caamaño (sound) .... C 4
Calvert (isl.) .... C 4
Canim (lake) .... G 4
Canoe (riv.) .... H 4
Cariboo (mts.) .... G 3
Carpenter (lake) .... F 5
Carp Lake Prov. Park .... F 3
Cassiar (mts.) .... K 2
Castle (mt.) .... A 2
Cathedral Prov. Park .... H 5
Charlotte (lake) .... E 4
Chatham (sound) .... B 3
Chehalis (lake) .... L 3
Chilcotin (riv.) .... E 4
Chilko (lake) .... F 4
Chilko (riv.) .... E 4
Chilkoot (pass) .... J 1
Chuchi (lake) .... E 2
Churchill (peak) .... L 2
Clayoquot (sound) .... D 5
Clearwater (lake) .... G 4
Clearwater (riv.) .... G 4
Coast (mts.) .... D 3
Columbia (lake) .... K 5
Columbia (mt.) .... J 4
Columbia (riv.) .... H 4
Cook (cape) .... C 5
Cowichan (lake) .... J 3
Crowsnest (pass) .... K 5
Cypress Prov. Park .... K 3
Dean (chan.) .... D 4
Dean (riv.) .... D 4
Dease (lake) .... K 2
Dease (riv.) .... K 2
Devils Thumb (mt.) .... A 1
Dixon Entrance (chan.) .... A 3
Douglas (chan.) .... C 3
Duncan (riv.) .... J 5
Dundas (isl.) .... B 3
Elk (riv.) .... K 5
Elk Lakes Prov. Park .... K 5
Eutsuk (lake) .... D 3
Fairweather (mt.) .... H 1
Finlay (riv.) .... E 1
Fitzhugh (sound) .... D 4
Flathead (riv.) .... K 6
Flores (isl.) .... D 5
Fontas (riv.) .... M 2
Forbes (mt.) .... J 4
Fort Nelson (riv.) .... M 2
François (lake) .... D 3
Fraser (lake) .... E 3
Fraser (riv.) .... F 4
Fraser Reach (chan.) .... C 3
Galiano (isl.) .... K 3
Gardner (canal) .... C 3
Garibaldi Prov. Park .... F 5
Georgia (str.) .... J 3
Germansen (lake) .... E 2
Gil (isl.) .... C 3
Glacier Nat'l Park .... J 4
Golden Ears Prov. Park .... L 2
Gordon (riv.) .... H 3
Graham (isl.) .... A 3
Graham Reach (chan.) .... C 3
Grenville (chan.) .... C 3
Halfway (riv.) .... F 2
Hamber Prov. Park .... H 4
Harrison (lake) .... M 2
Hawkesbury (isl.) .... C 3
Hazelton (mts.) .... C 2
Hecate (str.) .... B 3
Hobson (lake) .... H 4
Homathko (riv.) .... E 4
Horsefly (lake) .... G 4

Agriculture, Industry and Resources

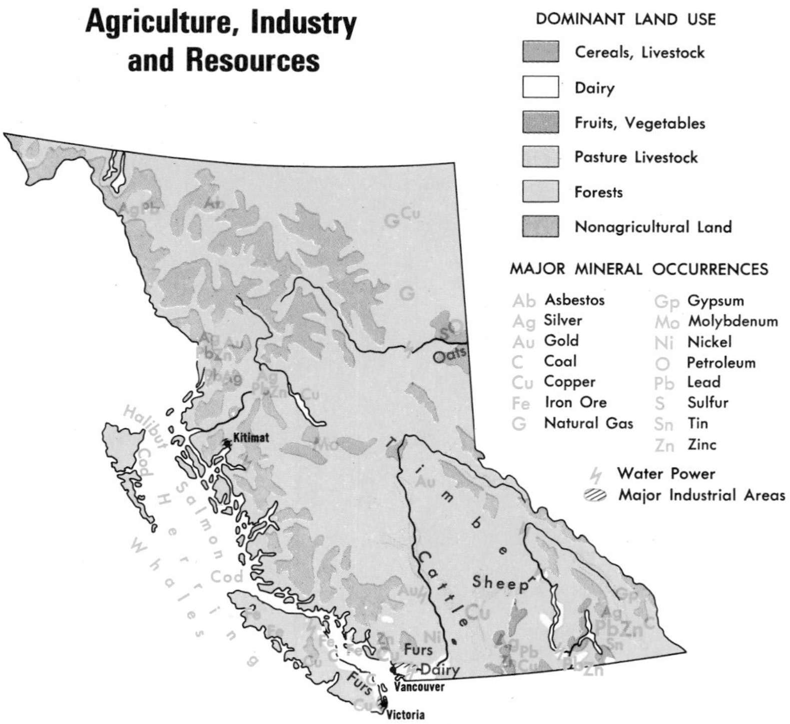

Howe (sound) . . . . . K 2
Hunter (isl.) . . . . . C 4
Inklin (riv.) . . . . . J 2
Inzana (lake) . . . . . E 3
Isaac (lake) . . . . . G 3
Iskut (riv.) . . . . . B 2
Jervis (inlet) . . . . . E 5
John Jay (mt.) . . . . . B 2
Johnstone (str.) . . . . . D 5
Juan de Fuca (str.) . . . . . J 4
Kates Needle (mt.) . . . . . A 1
Kechika (riv.) . . . . . L 2
Kenney (dam) . . . . . E 3
Kettle (riv.) . . . . . H 5
Kicking Horse (pass) . . . . . J 4
King (isl.) . . . . . D 4
Klinaklini (riv.) . . . . . E 4
Kloch (lake) . . . . . E 2
Knight (inlet) . . . . . E 5
Knox (cape) . . . . . A 3
Kokanee Glacier Prov. Park . . . J 5
Koocanusa (lake) . . . . . K 6
Kootenay (lake) . . . . . J 5
Kootenay (riv.) . . . . . K 5
Kootenay Nat'l Park . . . . . J 4
Kotcho (lake) . . . . . M 2
Kotcho (riv.) . . . . . M 2
Kunghit (isl.) . . . . . B 4
Kyuquot (sound) . . . . . D 5
Langara (isl.) . . . . . A 3
Laredo (sound) . . . . . C 4
Liard (riv.) . . . . . L 2
Lillooet (riv.) . . . . . F 5
Louise (isl.) . . . . . B 4
Lower Arrow (lake) . . . . . H 5
Lyell (isl.) . . . . . B 4
Lyell (mt.) . . . . . J 4
Mabel (lake) . . . . . H 5
Mahood (lake) . . . . . G 4
Malaspina (str.) . . . . . J 2
Manning Prov. Park . . . . . G 5
Masset (inlet) . . . . . A 3
McCauley (isl.) . . . . . B 3
McGregor (riv.) . . . . . G 3
Meziadin (lake) . . . . . C 2
Milbanke (sound) . . . . . C 4
Moberly (lake) . . . . . F 2
Monashee (mts.) . . . . . H 4
Moresby (isl.) . . . . . B 4
Morice (lake) . . . . . D 3
Morice (riv.) . . . . . D 3
Mount Assiniboine Prov. Park . K 5
Mount Edziza Prov. Park and Rec. Area . . . . . B 1
Mount Revelstoke Nat'l Park . . H 4
Mount Robson Prov. Park . . . . H 3
Muncho Lake Prov. Park . . . . L 2
Murray (riv.) . . . . . G 3
Murtle (lake) . . . . . H 4
Muskwa (riv.) . . . . . M 2
Nanika (dam) . . . . . D 3
Nass (riv.) . . . . . C 2
Nation (riv.) . . . . . F 2
Nechako (riv.) . . . . . E 3
Nitinat (lake) . . . . . H 3
Nootka (isl.) . . . . . D 5
Nootka (sound) . . . . . D 5
North Thompson (riv.) . . . . . G 4
Observatory (inlet) . . . . . C 2
Okanagan (lake) . . . . . H 5
Okanagan Mtn. Prov. Park . . . G 5
Okanogan (riv.) . . . . . H 6
Omineca (mts.) . . . . . E 2
Omineca (riv.) . . . . . E 2
Ootsa (lake) . . . . . D 3
Owikeno (lake) . . . . . D 4
Pacific Rim Nat'l Park . . . . . E 6
Parsnip (riv.) . . . . . F 3
Peace (riv.) . . . . . G 2
Pend Oreille (riv.) . . . . . J 6
Petitot (riv.) . . . . . M 2
Pinchi (lake) . . . . . E 3
Pine (riv.) . . . . . G 2
Pitt (isl.) . . . . . C 3
Pitt (lake) . . . . . L 2
Porcher (isl.) . . . . . B 3
Portland (canal) . . . . . B 2
Portland (inlet) . . . . . C 3
Price (isl.) . . . . . C 3
Princess Royal (isl.) . . . . . C 3
Principe (chan.) . . . . . C 3
Prophet (riv.) . . . . . M 2
Purcell (mts.) . . . . . J 5
Quatsino (sound) . . . . . C 5
Queen Charlotte (isls.) . . . . . B 3
Queen Charlotte (sound) . . . . . C 4
Queen Charlotte (str.) . . . . . D 5
Queens (sound) . . . . . C 4
Quesnel (lake) . . . . . G 4
Quesnel (riv.) . . . . . F 4
Rivers (inlet) . . . . . D 4
Robson (mt.) . . . . . H 3
Rocky (mts.) . . . . . F 2
Roderick (isl.) . . . . . C 4
Rose (pt.) . . . . . B 3
Saint James (cape) . . . . . B 4
Salmon (riv.) . . . . . F 3
Salmon Arm (inlet) . . . . . J 2
San Juan (riv.) . . . . . J 3
Schoen Lake Prov. Park . . . . . E 5
Scott (cape) . . . . . C 5
Scott (isls.) . . . . . C 5
Seechelt (inlet) . . . . . J 2
Seechelt (pen.) . . . . . J 2
Selkirk (mts.) . . . . . J 4
Seymour (inlet) . . . . . D 4
Sheslay (riv.) . . . . . J 2
Shuswap (lake) . . . . . H 4
Sikanni Chief (riv.) . . . . . F 1
Silver Star Prov. Park . . . . . H 5
Sir Sandford (mt.) . . . . . H 4
Skagit (riv.) . . . . . G 6
Skeena (mts.) . . . . . C 2
Skeena (riv.) . . . . . C 3
Skidegate (inlet) . . . . . B 3
Slocan (lake) . . . . . J 5
Smith (sound) . . . . . C 4
South Bentinck Arm (inlet) . . . D 4
Stave (lake) . . . . . L 3
Stephens (isl.) . . . . . B 3
Stikine (riv.) . . . . . B 1
Stone Mountain Prov. Park . . . L 2
Strathcona Prov. Park . . . . . E 5
Stuart (lake) . . . . . E 3
Sustut (riv.) . . . . . D 2
Tagish (lake) . . . . . J 1
Tahtsa (lake) . . . . . D 3
Takla (lake) . . . . . D 2
Taku (riv.) . . . . . J 2
Tatlatui (lake) . . . . . D 2
Tatlayoko (lake) . . . . . E 4
Tchentlo (lake) . . . . . E 2
Teslin (lake) . . . . . K 1
Tetachuck (lake) . . . . . E 3
Texada (isl.) . . . . . J 2
Tezzeron (lake) . . . . . E 3
Thompson (riv.) . . . . . G 5
Three Guardsmen (mt.) . . . . . H 1
Thutade (lake) . . . . . D 2
Tiedemann (mt.) . . . . . E 4
Toad (riv.) . . . . . L 2
Toba (inlet) . . . . . E 5
Tochcha (lake) . . . . . E 3
Top Of The World Prov. Park . . K 5
Trembleur (lake) . . . . . E 3
Troitsa (lake) . . . . . D 3
Tumeka (lake) . . . . . C 1
Turnagain (riv.) . . . . . K 2
Tuya (riv.) . . . . . K 2
Tweedsmuir Prov. Park . . . . . D 3
Upper Arrow (lake) . . . . . H 5
Valdes (isl.) . . . . . K 3
Vancouver (isl.) . . . . . D 5
Virago (sound) . . . . . A 3
Waddington (mt.) . . . . . E 4
Wapiti (riv.) . . . . . H 3
Wells Gray Prov. Park . . . . . H 4
West Road (riv.) . . . . . E 3
Whitesail (lake) . . . . . D 3
Williston (lake) . . . . . F 2
Work (chan.) . . . . . C 3
Yellowhead (pass) . . . . . H 4
Yoho Nat'l Park . . . . . J 4

*Population of metropolitan area.
○Population of municipality.

AREA 366,253 sq. mi. (948,596 sq. km.)
POPULATION 2,744,467
CAPITAL Victoria
LARGEST CITY Vancouver
HIGHEST POINT Mt. Fairweather 15,300 ft. (4,663 m.)
SETTLED IN 1806
ADMITTED TO CONFEDERATION 1871
PROVINCIAL FLOWER Dogwood

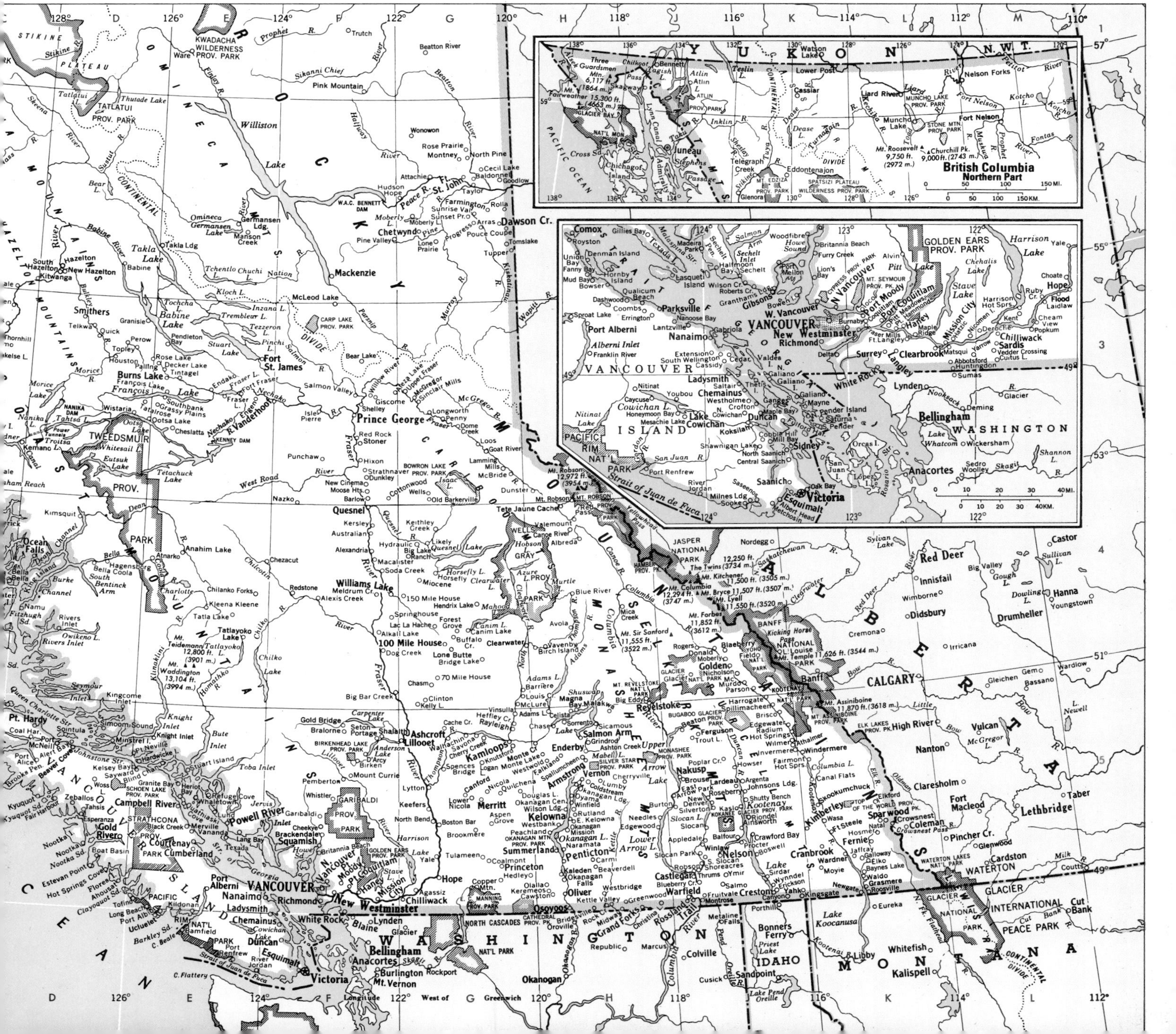

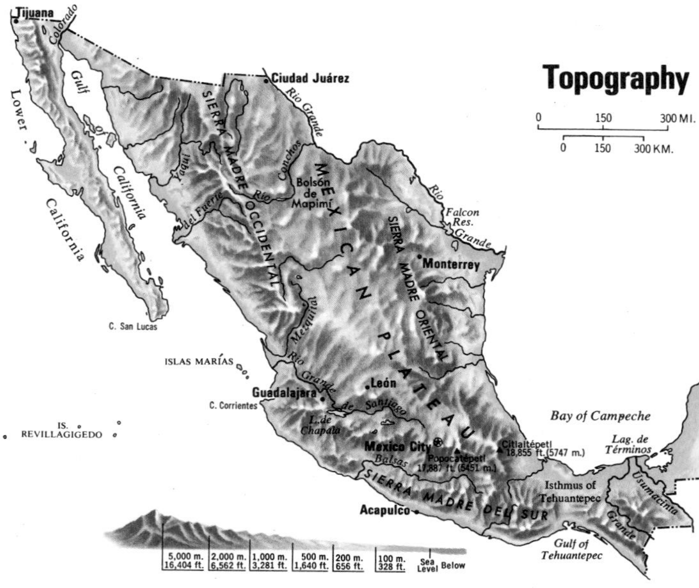

STATES

Aguascalientes 504,300 .... H6
Baja California 1,227,400 .... B1
Baja California Sur 221,000 .... C3
Campeche 371,800 .... O7
Chiapas 2,097,500 .... N8
Chihuahua 1,935,100 .... F2
Coahuila 1,561,000 .... H3
Colima 339,400 .... G7
Distrito Federal 9,377,300 .... L1
Durango 1,160,300 .... G4
Guanajuato 3,045,600 .... J6
Guerrero 2,174,200 .... J8
Hidalgo 1,518,200 .... K6
Jalisco 4,296,500 .... H6
México 7,542,300 .... K7
Michoacán 3,049,400 .... H7
Morelos 931,400 .... K7
Nayarit 729,500 .... G6
Nuevo León 2,463,500 .... K4
Oaxaca 2,517,500 .... L8
Puebla 3,285,300 .... L7
Querétaro 730,900 .... J6
Quintana Roo 209,900 .... P7
San Luis Potosí 1,669,900 .... J5
Sinaloa 1,882,200 .... F4
Sonora 1,498,100 .... D2
Tabasco 1,150,000 .... N7
Tamaulipas 1,924,900 .... K4
Tlaxcala 548,500 .... N1
Veracruz 5,263,800 .... L7
Yucatán 1,034,300 .... P6
Zacatecas 1,144,700 .... H5

CITIES and TOWNS

Acala 11,483 .... N8
Acámbaro 32,257 .... J7
Acaponeta 11,844 .... G5
Acapulco de Juárez 309,254 .... K8
Acatlán de Osorio 7,624 .... K7
Acatzingo de Hidalgo 6,905 .... N2
Acayucan 21,173 .... M8
Aconchi 1,596 .... D2
Actopan, Hidalgo 11,037 .... K6
Actopan, Veracruz 2,265 .... Q1
Agua Dulce 21,060 .... M7
Agualeguas 2,502 .... J3
Agua Prieta 20,754 .... E1
Aguascalientes 181,277 .... H6
Aguililla 5,715 .... H7
Ahome 4,182 .... E4
Ahuacatitlán 6,436 .... L1
Ahuacatlán 5,350 .... G6
Ahumada 6,466 .... F1
Ajalpan 8,238 .... L7
Alamo 9,954 .... L6
Álamos 4,269 .... E3
Aldama, Chihuahua 6,047 .... G2
Aldama, Tamaulipas 3,033 .... L5
Aljojuca 3,204 .... O1
Allende, Coahuila 11,076 .... J2
Allende, Nuevo León 9,914 .... J4
Almoloya del Río 3,714 .... K1
Altamira 6,053 .... L5
Altar 2,519 .... D1
Altepexi 6,661 .... L7
Alto Lucero 3,698 .... P1
Altotonga 6,754 .... P1
Alvarado 15,592 .... M7
Amatlán de los Reyes 3,664 .... P2
Amealco 2,960 .... K6
Ameca 21,018 .... H6
Amecameca de Juárez 16,276 .... L1
Amozoc de Mota 9,203 .... N2
Anáhuac, Chihuahua 10,886 .... F2
Anáhuac, Nuevo León 8,168 .... J3
Angostura 2,663 .... E4
Antiguo Morelos 1,569 .... K5
Apan 13,705 .... M1
Apatzingán de la
Constitución 44,849 .... H7
Apizaco 21,189 .... N1
Aquiles Serdán 2,565 .... G2
Aramberri 1,786 .... J5
Arandas 18,934 .... H6
Arcelia 10,024 .... J7
Ario de Rosales 8,774 .... J7
Arizpe 1,736 .... D1
Armería 10,616 .... G7
Arriaga 13,193 .... N8
Arteaga 5,324 .... H7
Ascensión 4,104 .... E1
Asunción Nochixtlán 3,235 .... L8
Atlixco 41,967 .... M2
Atotonilco el Alto 16,271 .... H6
Atoyac de Álvarez 8,874 .... J8
Autlán de Navarro 20,398 .... G7
Axochiapan 8,283 .... M2
Ayutla de los Libres 3,618 .... K8
Azcapotzalco 534,554 .... L1
Azoyú 3,446 .... K8
Bacadéhuachi 1,514 .... E2
Bacalar 2,121 .... P7
Bachíniva 1,809 .... F2
Bácum 2,668 .... D3
Bahía Tortugas 1,457 .... B3
Balancán de
Domínguez 3,669 .... O8
Bamoa 5,866 .... E4
Banderilla 3,488 .... P1
Baviácora 2,049 .... E2
Benjamín Hill 5,366 .... D1
Bernardino de Sahagún 12,327 .... M1
Boca del Río 2,354 .... Q2
Bolonchén de Rejón 2,342 .... O7
Buenaventura 3,924 .... F2
Burgos 673 .... K4
Cabo San Lucas 1,534 .... E5
Cacahoatán 5,079 .... N9
Cadereyta Jiménez 13,586 .... K4
Calkiní 6,870 .... O6
Calnali 3,318 .... K6
Calpulálpan 8,659 .... M1
Calvillo 6,453 .... H6
Campeche 69,506 .... O7
Cananea 17,518 .... D1
Canatlán 5,983 .... G4
Cancún 326 .... Q6
Candela 1,689 .... J3
Candelaria 1,982 .... O7
Cañitas de Felipe
Pescador 4,885 .... H5
Capulhuac de Mirafuentes 8,289 .... K1
Carbo 2,804 .... D2
Cárdenas, San Luis
Potosí 12,020 .... K6
Cárdenas, Tabasco 15,643 .... N8
Carichic 1,520 .... F2
Castaños 8,996 .... J3
Catemaco 11,786 .... M7
Ceballos 2,937 .... H3
Cedral 4,057 .... J5
Celaya 79,977 .... J6
Celestún 1,490 .... O6
Cerritos 10,421 .... J5
Cerro Azul 20,259 .... L6
Chahuites 5,218 .... M8
Chalchihuites 1,894 .... G5
Chalco de Díaz
Covarrubias 12,172 .... M1
Champotón 6,606 .... O7
Charcas 10,491 .... J5
Chetumal 23,685 .... Q7
Chiapa de Corzo 8,571 .... N8
Chiautempan 12,327 .... N1
Chietla 4,602 .... M2
Chignahuapan 3,805 .... N1
Chihuahua 327,313 .... F2
Chilapa de Álvarez 9,204 .... K8
Chilpancingo de los
Bravos 36,193 .... K8
China, Nuevo León 4,958 .... K4
Chocomán 5,114 .... P2
Choix 2,503 .... E3
Cholula de Rivadavia 15,399 .... M1
Cihuatlán 9,451 .... G7
Cintalapa de Figueroa 12,036 .... N8
Ciudad Acuña (Villa
Acuña) 30,276 .... J2
Ciudad Altamirano 8,694 .... J7
Ciudad Camargo,
Chihuahua 24,030 .... G3
Ciudad Camargo,
Tamaulipas 5,953 .... K3
Ciudad del Carmen 34,656 .... N7
Ciudad Delicias 52,446 .... G2
Ciudad del Maíz 5,241 .... K5
Ciudad de Río Grande 11,651 .... H5
Ciudad Guerrero 3,110 .... F2
Ciudad Guzmán 48,166 .... H7
Ciudad Hidalgo, Chiapas 4,105 .... N9
Ciudad Hidalgo,
Michoacán 24,692 .... J7
Ciudad Juárez 424,135 .... F1
Ciudad Lerdo 19,803 .... H4
Ciudad Madero 115,302 .... L5
Ciudad Mante 51,247 .... K5
Ciudad Mendoza 18,696 .... O2
Ciudad Miguel Alemán 11,259 .... K3
Ciudad Obregón 144,795 .... E3
Ciudad Río Bravo 39,018 .... K4
Ciudad Satélite 35,083 .... L1
Ciudad Serdán 9,581 .... O2
Ciudad Valles 47,587 .... K5
Ciudad Victoria 83,897 .... K5
Coalcomán de Matamoros 4,875 .... H7
Coatepec 21,542 .... P1
Coatetelco 5,268 .... L2
Coatzacoalcos 69,753 .... M7
Coatzingo 3,038 .... N2
Cocorit 4,478 .... E3
Colima 58,450 .... H7
Colón 3,346 .... K6
Colotlán 6,135 .... H5
Comala 5,592 .... H7
Comalcalco 14,963 .... N7
Comitán de
Domínguez 21,249 .... O8
Compostela 9,801 .... G6
Concepción del Oro 8,144 .... J4
Concordia 3,947 .... G5
Contla 7,517 .... N1
Copala 3,783 .... K8
Coquimatlán 6,212 .... G7
Córdoba 78,495 .... P2
Cosalá 2,279 .... F4
Cosamaloapan de Carpio 19,766 .... M7
Cosautlán de Carvajal 2,039 .... P1
Coscomatepec de Bravo 6,023 .... P2
Coslo 2,680 .... H5
Costa Rica 11,795 .... F4
Cotija de la Paz 9,178 .... H7
Coyoacán 339,446 .... L1
Coyotepec 8,888 .... L1
Coyuca de Benítez 6,328 .... J8
Coyuca de Catalán 2,926 .... J7
Coyutla 3,726 .... L6
Cozumel 5,858 .... Q6
Creel 2,449 .... E3
Cuatrociénagas de
Carranza 5,523 .... H3
Cuauhtémoc 26,598 .... F2
Cuautepec de Hinojosa 5,501 .... K6
Cuautitlán de Romero
Rubio 11,439 .... L1
Cuautla Morelos 13,946 .... L2
Cuencamé de Ceniceros 3,774 .... H4
Cuernavaca 239,813 .... L2
Cuicatlán 2,733 .... L8
Cuitlahuac 4,813 .... P2
Culiacán 228,001 .... F4
Cumpas 2,395 .... E1
Cunduacán 4,397 .... N7
Dimas 2,194 .... F5
Doctor Arroyo 4,290 .... K5
Dolores Hidalgo de la Independencia
Naci 16,849 .... J6
Durango 182,633 .... G1
Dzibalchén 1,917 .... P7
Dzidzantún 7,064 .... P6
Dzitbalché 4,393 .... P6
Ebano 17,489 .... K5
Ecatepec de Morelos 11,899 .... L1
Ejutla de Crespo 5,263 .... L8
Eldorado 8,115 .... E4
El Fuerte 7,179 .... E3
El Porvenir 3,030 .... G1
El Potosí 2,032 .... J4
El Salto 7,818 .... G5
El Zacatón 2,686 .... J5
Empalme 24,927 .... D2
Encarnación de Díaz 10,474 .... H6
Ensenada 77,687 .... A1
Escalón 2,998 .... G3
Escarcega 7,248 .... O7
Escuinapa de Hidalgo 16,442 .... G5
Escuintla 4,111 .... N9
Esperanza, Puebla 4,258 .... O2
Esperanza, Sonora 11,762 .... E3
Espita 5,394 .... Q6
Esqueda 1,458 .... E1
Etchojoa 4,398 .... E3
Ezequiel Montes 3,139 .... K6
Fortín de las Flores 9,358 .... P2
Francisco I. Madero 12,613 .... H4
Fresnillo de González
Echererría 44,475 .... H5
Frontera 10,066 .... N7
Galeana, Nuevo León 3,429 .... J4
General Bravo 2,894 .... K4
General Cepeda 3,486 .... J4
General Terán 5,354 .... K4
Gómez Farías 3,030 .... F2
Gómez Palacio 79,650 .... G4
González 6,440 .... K5
Guadalajara 1,478,383 .... H6
Guadalajara* 2,343,034 .... H6
Guadalupe, Nuevo León 51,899 .... K4
Guadalupe, Zacatecas 13,246 .... H5
Guadalupe Bravo 3,333 .... F1
Guadalupe Victoria,
Durango 7,931 .... H4
Guadalupe Victoria,
Puebla 3,946 .... O1
Guamúchil 17,151 .... E4
Guanajuato 36,809 .... J6
Guasave 26,080 .... E4
Guaymas 57,492 .... D3
Gustavo Díaz Ordaz 10,154 .... K3
Gutiérrez Zamora 9,099 .... L6
Halachó 4,804 .... O6
Hecelchakán 4,279 .... O6
Hermosillo 232,691 .... D2
Heroica Caborca 20,771 .... C1
Heroica Nogales 52,108 .... D1
Hidalgo, Tamaulipas 2,450 .... K4
Hidalgo del Parral
(Parral) 57,619 .... G3
Hopelchén 3,699 .... P7
Huajuapan de León 13,822 .... L8
Huamantla 15,565 .... N1
Huaquechula 2,294 .... M2
Huatabampo 18,506 .... D3
Huatusco de Chicuellar 9,501 .... P2
Huauchinango 16,826 .... L6
Huautla de Jiménez 6,132 .... L7
Huehuetlán el Chico 2,667 .... M2
Huejotzingo 8,552 .... M1
Huejutla 6,854 .... K6
Huetamo 9,333 .... J7
Hueyotlipan de Hidalgo 2,353 .... M1
Huimanguillo 7,075 .... N8
Huitzilán 3,573 .... O1
Huitzuco de los Figueroa 9,406 .... K7
Huixcolotla 4,039 .... N2
Huixtepec 5,927 .... L8
Huixtla 15,737 .... N9
Hunucmá 8,020 .... O6
Ignacio de la Llave 3,962 .... Q2
Iguala de la
Independencia 45,355 .... K7
Imuris 1,958 .... D1
Irapuato 135,596 .... J6
Isla Mujeres 2,663 .... Q6
Isla, Veracruz 8,075 .... M7
Ixmiquilpan 6,048 .... K6
Ixtapa J8
Ixtapalapa 522,095 .... L1
Ixtenco 5,035 .... N1
Ixtepec 14,025 .... M8
Ixtlán del Río 10,986 .... G6
Izamal 9,749 .... P6
Izúcar de Matamoros 21,164 .... M2
Jala 4,535 .... G6
Jalacingo 3,427 .... P1
Jalapa Enríquez 161,352 .... P1
Jalpa 9,904 .... H6
Jalpa de Méndez 4,785 .... N7
Jalpan 1,878 .... K6
Jáltipan de Morelos 15,170 .... M8
Jantetelco 2,015 .... L2
Jaumave 3,072 .... K5
Jerez de García
Salinas 20,325 .... H5
Jico 7,269 .... P1
Jilotepec de Abasolo 4,252 .... K7
Jiménez, Chihuahua 18,095 .... G3
Joachín 3,918 .... Q2
Jojutla de Juárez 14,438 .... L2
Jonacatepec 3,868 .... M2
Jonuta 2,746 .... N7
José Cardel 5,396 .... Q1
Juan Aldama 9,667 .... H4
Juchipila 6,328 .... H6
Juchitán de Zaragoza 30,218 .... M8
Kantunilkin 1,970 .... Q6
La Barca 18,055 .... H6
La Barra de Navidad 1,829 .... G7
La Concordia 3,559 .... N9
La Cruz, Sinaloa 4,218 .... F5
Lagos de Moreno 33,782 .... J6
La Huerta 4,328 .... G7
La Paz, Baja California
Sur 46,011 .... D5
La Paz, San Luis
Potosí 3,735 .... J5
La Piedad Cavadas 34,963 .... H6
Las Choapas 20,166 .... M7
Las Hadas G7
Las Nieves 2,262 .... G3
Las Rosas 7,658 .... N8
León 468,887 .... J6
Lerdo de Tejada 11,628 .... M8
Lerma 4,158 .... O7
Libres 4,830 .... O1
Linares 24,456 .... K4
Llera de Canales 3,564 .... K5
Loma Bonita 15,804 .... M7
Loreto, Baja California 2,570 .... D4
Loreto, Zacatecas 7,132 .... J5
Los Mochis 67,953 .... E4
Los Reyes de Salgado 19,452 .... H7
Macuspana 12,293 .... N8
Madera 9,759 .... F2
Magdalena de Kino 10,281 .... D1
Maltrata 5,457 .... O2
Manzanillo 20,777 .... G7
Mapastepec 5,907 .... N9
Mapimí 2,737 .... G4
Martínez de la Torre 17,203 .... L6
Mascota 5,674 .... G6
Matamoros, Coahuila 15,125 .... H4
Matamoros, Tamaulipas 165,124 .... L4
Matehuala 28,799 .... J5
Matías Romero 13,200 .... M8
Maxcanú 6,505 .... O6
Mazatlán 147,010 .... F5
Melchor Múzquiz 18,868 .... H3
Melchor Ocampo del
Balsas 4,766 .... H8
Meoquí 12,308 .... G2
Mérida 233,912 .... P6
Metepec 4,625 .... M2
Metlatonoc 1,870 .... K8
Mexicali 317,228 .... B1
Mexico City (cap.) 9,377,300 .... L1
Mexico City* 13,993,866 .... L1
Miacatlán 3,980 .... K2
Mier 5,636 .... K3
Miguel Auza 9,303 .... H4
Minatitlán 68,397 .... M8
Mineral del Monte 8,887 .... K6
Miquihuana 1,971 .... J5
Misantla 8,799 .... P1
Miahuatlán de Porfirio
Díaz 5,714 .... L8
Mocorito 3,993 .... F4
Moctezuma, San Luis
Potosí 1,734 .... J5
Moctezuma, Sonora 2,700 .... E2
Monclova 78,134 .... J3
Montemorelos 18,642 .... K4
Monterrey 1,006,221 .... J4
Monterrey* 1,923,402 .... J4
Morelia 199,099 .... J7
Morelos 4,241 .... J2
Morelos Cañada 2,288 .... O2
Moroleón 25,620 .... J6
Motozintla de Mendoza 4,682 .... N9
Motul de Felipe Carillo
Puerto 12,949 .... P6
Muna 5,491 .... P6
Naco 3,580 .... D1
Nacozari 2,976 .... E1
Nadadores 2,461 .... H3
Naica 7,190 .... G2
Namiquipa 4,875 .... F2
Nanacamilpa 6,356 .... M1
Naolinco de Victoria 4,365 .... P1
Naranjos 14,732 .... L6
Naucalpan de Juárez 9,425 .... L1
Nautla 1,935 .... L6
Nava 4,097 .... J2
Navojoa 43,817 .... E3
Navolato 12,799 .... E4
Nazas 2,881 .... G4
Netzahualcóyotl 580,436 .... L1
Nieves 3,966 .... H5
Nochistlán 8,780 .... H6
Nogales 14,254 .... P2
Nombre de Dios 3,188 .... G5
Nopalucan de la Granja 3,002 .... O1
Nueva Casas Grandes 20,023 .... F1
Nueva Ciudad Guerrero 3,300 .... K3
Nueva Italia de Ruiz 14,718 .... J7
Nueva Rosita 34,706 .... J2
Nuevo Ideal 5,252 .... G4
Nuevo Laredo 184,622 .... J3
Oaxaca de Juárez 114,948 .... L8
Ocampo, Coahuila 1,613 .... H3
Ocampo, Tamaulipas 4,801 .... K5
Ocosingo 2,946 .... O8
Ocotlán 35,361 .... H6
Ocotlán de Morelos 5,882 .... L8
Ojinaga 12,757 .... G2
Ojocaliente 7,582 .... H5
Ometepec 7,342 .... K8
Oriental 6,009 .... O1
Orizaba 105,150 .... P2
Otumba de Gómez
Farías 3,198 .... M1
Oxkutzcab 8,182 .... P6
Ozuluama 2,851 .... L6
Ozumba de Alzate 6,876 .... M1
Pachuca de Soto 83,892 .... K6
Padilla 4,581 .... K5
Palenque 2,595 .... O8
Palizada 2,332 .... O7
Palomas 2,129 .... F1

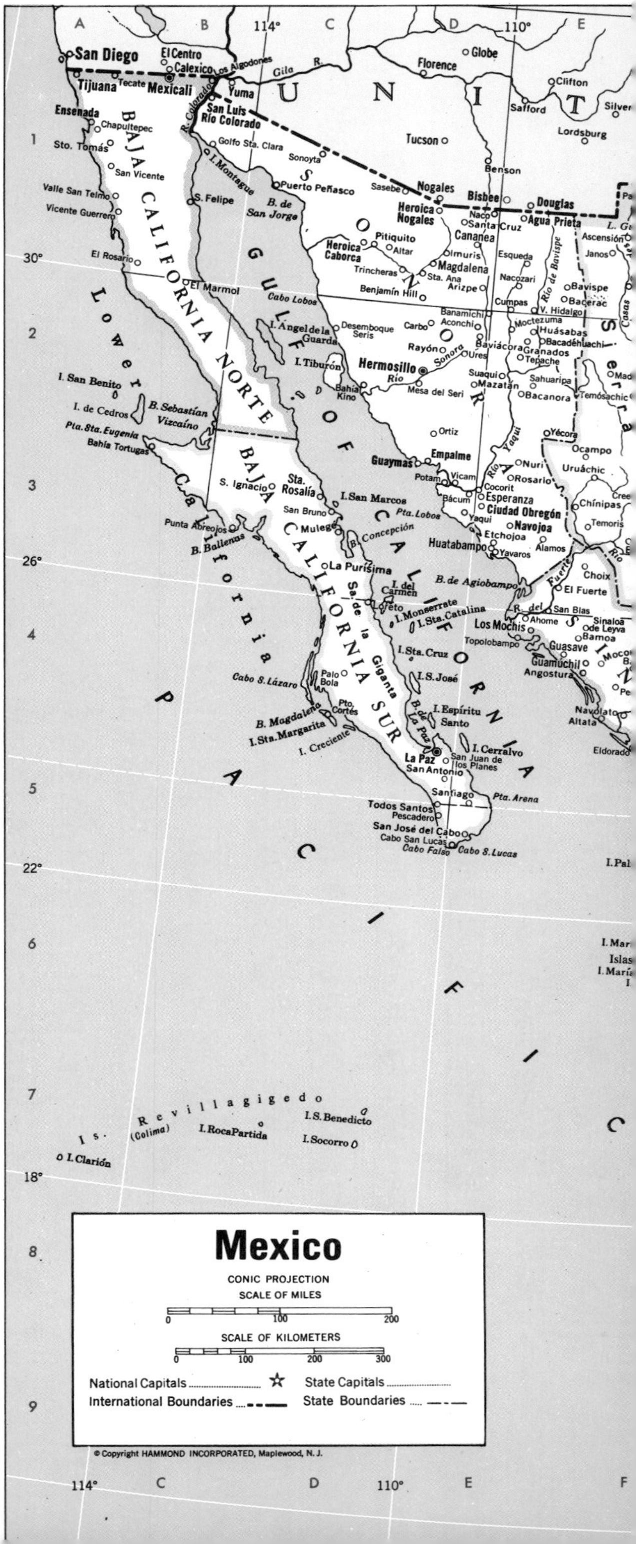

Panabá 3,056 .... P6
Pánuco 14,277 .... K6
Papanoa 3,033 .... J8
Papantla de Olarte 26,773 .... L6
Paraíso 7,561 .... N7
Parral 57,619 .... G3
Parras de la Fuente 18,207 .... H4
Paso de Ovejas 4,371 .... Q2
Pátzcuaro 17,299 .... J7
Pedro Montoya 4,563 .... K6
Pénjamo 9,245 .... J6
Peñón Blanco 2,726 .... H4
Pericos 4,445 .... F4
Perote 12,742 .... O1
Petatlán 9,419 .... J8
Peto 8,362 .... P6
Pichucalco 4,615 .... N8
Piedras Negras, Coahuila 41,033 .... J2
Piedras Negras, Veracruz 4,099 .... Q2
Pijijiapan 5,053 .... N9
Pitiquito 2,268 .... D1
Potam 2,825 .... D3
Poza Rica de Hidalgo 152,276 .... L6
Praxedis G. Guerrero 2,399 .... G1
Profesor Rafael Ramírez 5,338 .... O1
Progreso 17,518 .... P6
Puebla de Zaragoza 465,985 .... N2
Puente de Ixtla 10,435 .... K2
Puerto Ángel 1,489 .... L9
Puerto Escondido 3,845 .... L9
Puerto Juárez 100 .... Q6
Puerto Madero 1,908 .... N9
Puerto Peñasco 8,452 .... C1
Puerto Vallarta 24,155 .... G6
Purificación 3,311 .... G7
Puruándiro 9,956 .... J7
Putla de Guerrero 3,572 .... L8
Quecholac 3,374 .... O2
Querétaro 142,448 .... J6
Ramos Arizpe 6,205 .... J4
Rayón, San Luis Potosí 4,451 .... K6
Rayón, Sonora D2
Reynosa 181,646 .... K3
Rincón de Romos 8,348 .... H5
Rioverde 16,804 .... J6
Rodeo 2,584 .... G4
Rosamorada 2,635 .... G5

(continued on following page)

AREA 761,601 sq. mi. (1,972,546 sq. km.)
POPULATION 67,395,826
CAPITAL Mexico City
LARGEST CITY Mexico City
HIGHEST POINT Citlaltépetl 18,855 ft. (5,747 m.)
MONETARY UNIT Mexican peso
MAJOR LANGUAGE Spanish
MAJOR RELIGION Roman Catholicism

(continued)

Rosario, Sinaloa 10,276 G5
Rosario, Sonora 1,887 E3
Ruiz 8,954 G6
Sabancuy 1,819 O7
Sabinas 20,538 J3
Sabinas Hidalgo 17,439 J3
Sahuaripa 4,710 E2
Sahuayo de Díaz 28,727 H7
Sain Alto 3,628 H5
Salamanca 61,039 J6
Salina Cruz 22,004 M9
Salinas 7,471 J5
Saltillo 200,712 J4
Salvatierra 18,975 J6
San Andrés Tuxtla 24,267 M7
San Blas, Nayarit 3,443 G6
San Blas, Sinaloa 6,222 E3
San Buenaventura 9,188 J3
San Carlos, Coahuila 1,960 J2
San Cristóbal de las Casas 25,700 N8
San Felipe, Baja California 160 B1
San Felipe, Guanajuato 10,129 J6
San Fernando, Tamaulipas 27,656 L4
San Francisco del Oro 12,116 F3
San Francisco del Rincón 27,079 H6
San Gabriel Chilac 6,707 K7
San Ignacio, Sinaloa 1,804 F5
San Jerónimo de Juárez 5,204 J8
San José del Cabo 2,571 D5
San Juan 15,422 K6
San Juan de los Lagos 19,570 H6
San Juan Xiutetelco 3,306 O1
San Luis de la Paz 12,654 J6
San Luis del Cordero 2,203 H4
San Luis Potosí 271,123 J5
San Luis Río Colorado 49,990 B1
San Marcos 5,861 K8
San Martín de las Pirámides 4,575 M1
San Martín Texmelucan 23,355 M1
San Miguel de Allende 24,286 J6
San Nicolás de los Garza 28,803 J3
San Pedro de las Colonias 26,882 H4
San Pedro Pochutla 4,395 L9
San Rafael 8,974 M1
San Salvador el Seco 7,729 O1
Santa Ana 7,020 D1
Santa Ana Chiautempan (Chiautémpan) 12,327 N1
Santa Bárbara 16,978 F3
Santa Clara 3,449 H4
Santa María del Oro 4,231 G3
Santa María del Río 4,972 J6
Santa María del Tule 1,674 L8
Santander Jiménez 3,586 K4
Santa Rosalía 7,356 C3
Santiago Ixcuintla 17,321 G6
Santiago Jamiltepec 5,280 K8
Santiago Juxtlahuaca 2,923 K8
Santiago Miahuatlán 4,917 O2
Santiago Papasquiaro 6,636 F4
Santiago Pinotepa Nacional 9,382 K8
Santiago Tuxtla 9,426 M7
Saucillo 8,467 G2
Sayula 14,339 H7
Sayula de Alemán 4,896 M8
Seybaplaya 4,439 O7
Silao 31,825 J6
Simojovel de Allende 3,779 N8
Sinaloa de Leyva 1,998 E4
Soledad de Doblado 6,612 Q2
Soledad Díez Gutiérrez 9,622 J5
Sombrerete 11,077 H5
Sonoyta 2,463 C1
Sotuta 3,772 P6
Tabasco 3,197 H6
Tacámbaro de Codallos 9,695 J7
Tacotalpa 2,019 N8
Tala 15,744 H6
Talpa de Allende 4,264 G6
Tamazulapan del Progreso 2,870 L8
Tamazunchale 12,302 K6
Tamiahua 6,264 L6
Tampico 212,188 L5
Tamuín 7,251 K6
Tantoyuca 11,902 L6
Tapachula 60,620 N9
Taxco de Alarcón 27,089 K7
Tayoltita 2,697 G4
Teapa 6,534 N8
Tecamachalco 3,319 O2
Tecate 14,738 A1
Tecomán 31,625 H7
Tecpan de Galeana 8,095 J8
Tecuala 12,461 G5
Tehuacán 47,497 L7
Tehuantepec 16,179 M8
Tekax de Álaro Obregón 10,326 P6
Teloloapan 10,335 J7
Temax 4,915 P6
Temósachic 1,738 E2
Tenabo 3,278 P6
Tenancingo de Degollado 12,807 K7
Tenango de Río Blanco 12,302 O2
Tenosique de Pino Suárez 11,393 O8
Teocaltiche 13,745 H6
Teocelo 4,572 P1
Teotihuacán de Arista 2,238 L1
Teotitlán del Camino 3,106 L8
Tepache 1,591 E2
Tepalcingo 5,968 M2
Tepatitlán de Morelos 29,292 H6
Tepeaca 7,466 N2
Tepeapulco 7,027 M1
Tepehuanes 2,531 G4
Tepeji del Río 10,365 L1
Tepexi de Rodríguez 2,618 N2
Tepic 108,924 G6
Tepoztlán 6,851 L1
Tequixquitla 4,825 O1
Terán 5,215 N8
Terrenate 1,515 N1
Texcoco de Mora 18,044 M1
Teziutlán 23,948 O1
Tezonapa 3,506 P2
Tezontepec 2,762 M1
Ticul 14,341 P6
Tierra Blanca 22,727 L7
Tila 2,633 N8
Tijuana 363,154 A1
Tixtla de Guerrero 10,334 K8
Tizayuca 6,262 L1
Tizimín 18,343 Q6
Tlachichuca 3,721 O1
Tlacolula de Matamoros 8,300 L8
Tlacotepec de Mejiá 1,595 P1
Tlahualilo de Zaragoza 8,951 H3
Tlalancaneca 5,090 M1
Tlalixcoyan 3,211 Q2
Tlalmanalco de Velásquez 5,744 L1
Tlalnepantla de Comonfort 45,575 L1
Tlalpan 130,719 L1
Tlaltenango de Sánchez Román 7,698 H6
Tlaltizapan 6,384 L2
Tlapacoyan 13,172 P1
Tlapa de Comonfort 6,676 K8

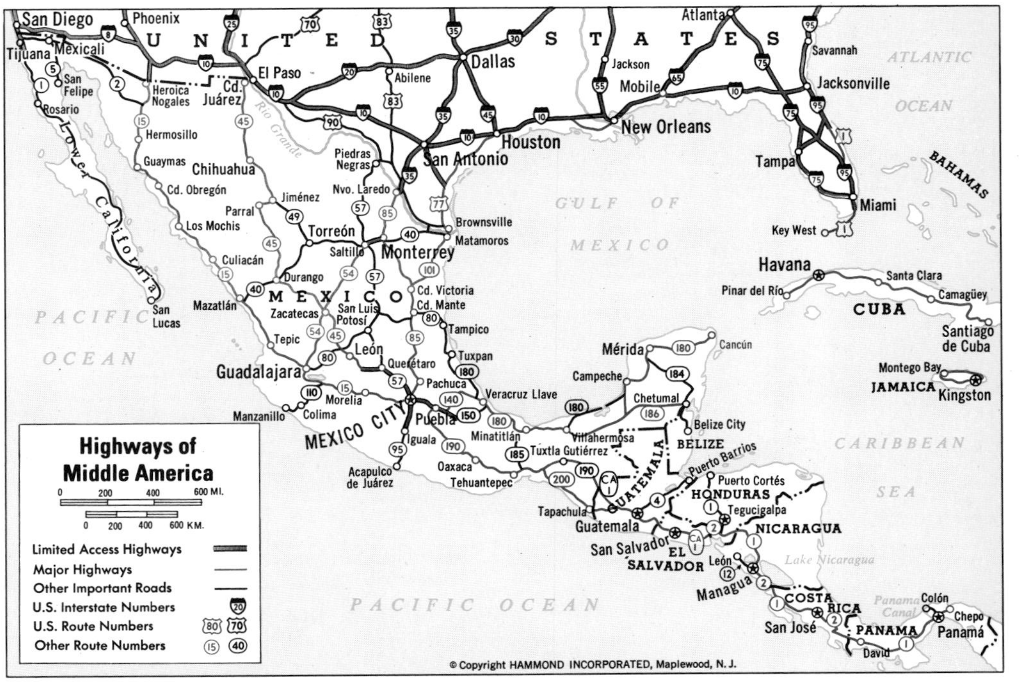

Tlaquepaque 59,760 G6
Tlatlauquitepec 4,272 O1
Tlaquiltenango 8,625 L2
Tláxcala de Xicotencatl 9,972 M1
Tlaxco 4,969 N1
Tlaxiaco 4,477 L8
Tlayacapan 3,538 L1
Tochimilco 3,190 M2
Todos Santos 2,400 D5
Toluca de Lerdo 136,092 K7
Tomatlán 2,695 G6
Tonalá 15,611 N8
Topolobampo 4,685 E4
Torreón 244,309 H4
Tula, Tamaulipas 5,407 K5
Tula de Allende 10,720 K6
Tulancingo 35,799 K7
Tulcingo del Valle 2,983 M2
Tultepec 8,321 L1
Tuxpan, Jalisco 14,693 H7
Tuxpan, Nayarit 20,322 G6
Tuxpan de Rodríguez Cano 33,901 L6
Tuxtepec 17,701 L7
Tuxtla Gutiérrez 66,851 N8
Tzucabab 4,876 P7
Umán 8,371 P6
Unión de Tula 6,399 G7
Unión Hidalgo 8,658 M8
Ures 3,681 D2
Ursulo Galván 2,637 Q1
Uruapan del Progreso 108,124 H7
Valladolid 14,663 P6
Valle de Allende 4,973 G3
Valle de Bravo 7,628 J7
Valle Hermoso 19,278 L4
Vanegas 2,042 J5
Venado 2,790 J5
Venustiano Carranza 23,624 N8
Veracruz 255,646 Q1
Vicam 4,104 D3
Vicente Guerrero, Durango 8,451 G5
Victor Rosales 7,629 H5
Viesca 2,923 H4
Villa Acuña 30,276 J2
Villa Cuauhtémoc 6,611 L5
Villa de Cos 1,850 H5
Villa de Guadelupe Hidalgo 88,537 L1
Villa Frontera 25,761 J3
Villa García 2,765 J5
Villahermosa 133,181 N8
Villa Hidalgo 2,126 E1
Villaldama 2,350 J3
Villa Matamoros 1,998 G3
Villanueva 5,895 H5
Villa Unión, Coahuila 4,058 J2
Villa Unión, Durango 4,042 H5
Villa Unión, Sinaloa 6,789 F5
Villa Vicente Guerrero 18,280 N1
Xaltocan 2,524 N1
Xicoténcatl 6,374 K5
Xicotepec de Juárez 12,656 L6
Xochihuehuetlán 3,268 K8
Xochimilco 116,493 L1
Xochitlán 3,312 N2
Yajalón 4,506 N8
Yanga 3,843 P2
Yaqui 8,061 D3
Yautepec 13,952 L2
Yavaros 1,959 E3
Yécora E2
Yecuatla 2,816 P1
Yehualtepec 2,558 O2
Zaachila 7,270 L8
Zacapoaxtla 4,527 O1
Zacapu 31,989 J7
Zacatepec 16,839 L2
Zacatecas 50,251 H5
Zacatelco 14,117 N1
Zacatlán 7,909 N1
Zacoalco de Torres 11,343 H6
Zamora de Hidalgo 5,775 H7
Zaragoza, Coahuila 6,797 J2
Zaragoza, Chihuahua 3,984 F1
Zaragoza, Puebla 4,754 O1
Zempoala 5,064 Q1
Zihuatenejo 4,879 J8
Zimatlán de Álvarez 5,746 L8
Zitácuaro 36,911 J7
Zongolica 2,378 P2
Zumpango de Ocampo 12,923 L1
Zumpango del Río 8,162 J8

OTHER FEATURES

Agiobampo (bay) E3
Aguanaval (riv.) H4
Amistad (res.) J2
Ángel de la Guarda (isl.) C2
Antigua (riv.) Q1
Arena (pt.) E5
Arenas (cay) O5
Atoyac (riv.) N2
Atoyac (riv.) Q2
Babia (riv.) J2
Bacalar (lake) P7
Ballenas (bay) C3
Balsas (riv.) J7
Banderas (bay) G6
Bavispe, Río de (riv.) E1
Blanco (riv.) Q2
Bravo (Grande) (riv.) G2
Burro (mts.) J2
California (gulf) D3
Campeche (bank) O6
Campeche (bay) N7
Candelaria (riv.) O8
Carmen (isl.) D3
Casas Grandes (riv.) F1
Catoche (cape) Q6
Cedros (isl.) B2
Cerralvo (isl.) E4
Chamela (bay) G7
Chapala (lake) H6
Chetumal (bay) P8
Chichén-Itzá (ruin) P6
Citlaltépetl (mt.) O2
Clarión (isl.) B7
Colorado (riv.) B1
Conchos (riv.) G2
Corrientes (cape) F6
Coyuca (riv.) O1
Creciente (isl.) D5
Cuitzeo (lake) J7
Delgada (pt.) L7
Dzibichaltún (ruin) P6
El Azúcar (res.) K3
Espíritu Santo (isl.) D4
Falcón (res.) K3
Falso (cape) D5
Fuerte (riv.) E3
Giganta, Sierra de la (mts.) D4
Grande (riv.) G2
Grande (riv.) N8
Grande de Santiago (riv.) G6
Grijalva (riv.) N7
Guzmán (lake) F1
Herrero (pt.) Q7
Hondo (riv.) P7
Jesús María (reef) L4
La Boquilla (res.) G3
La Paz (bay) D4
Lobos (cape) C2
Lobos (pt.) D3
Lower California (pen.) C3
Madre (lag.) L4
Madre del Sur, Sierra (mts.) K8
Madre Occidental, Sierra (mts.) F3
Madre Oriental, Sierra (mts.) J4
Magdalena (bay) C4
Maldonado (pt.) K8
Mapimí (depr.) G3
María Cleófas (isl.) F6
María Madre (isl.) F6
María Magdalena (isl.) F6
Mexico (gulf) N4
Mezquital (riv.) G5
Mita (pt.) G6
Mitla (ruin) M8
Moctezuma (riv.) K6
Monserrate (isl.) D4
Montague (isl.) B1
Muerto, Mar (lag.) N9
Nauhcampatépetl (mt.) O1
Nayarit, Sierra (mts.) G5
Nazas (riv.) G4
Nuevo, Bajo (reef) O6
Orizaba (Citlaltépetl) (mt.) O2
Palenque (ruin) O8
Palmito de la Virgen (isl.) F5
Palmito del Verde (isl.) F5
Pánuco (riv.) K5
Paricutín (vol.) H7
Pátzcuaro (lake) J7
Pérez (isl.) P5
Petacalco (bay) H8
Popocatépetl (mt.) M1
Ramos (riv.) G4
Revillagigedo (isls.) C7
Roca Partida (isl.) C7
Sabinas (riv.) J3
San Antonio (reef) L4
San Benedicto (isl.) D7
San Benito (isl.) B2
San Jorge (bay) C1
San José (isl.) D4
San Lázaro (cape) C4
San Lucas (cape) E5
San Marcos (isl.) D3
San Rafael (reef) L4
Santa Ana (reef) N7
Santa Catalina (isl.) D4
Santa Cruz (isl.) D4
Santa Eugenia (pt.) B3
Santa Margarita (isl.) C4
Santa María (lake) F1
Santa María (riv.) F1
Santiaguillo (lake) G4
Sebastián Vizcaíno (bay) B2
Socorro (isl.) D7
Sonora (riv.) D2
Superior (lag.) M9
Teacapán (inlet) F5
Tehuantepec (gulf) M9
Tehuantepec (isth.) M8
Teotihuacán (ruin) M1
Términos (lag.) O7
Tiburón (isl.) C2
Triángulo Este (isl.) N6
Triángulo Oeste (isl.) N6
Tula (riv.) L1
Urique (riv.) F3
Usumacinta (riv.) O8
Uxmal (ruins) P6
Valsequillo (res.) N2
Verde (riv.) F3
Verde (riv.) L8
Yaqui (riv.) E2

*City and suburbs.

Agriculture, Industry and Resources

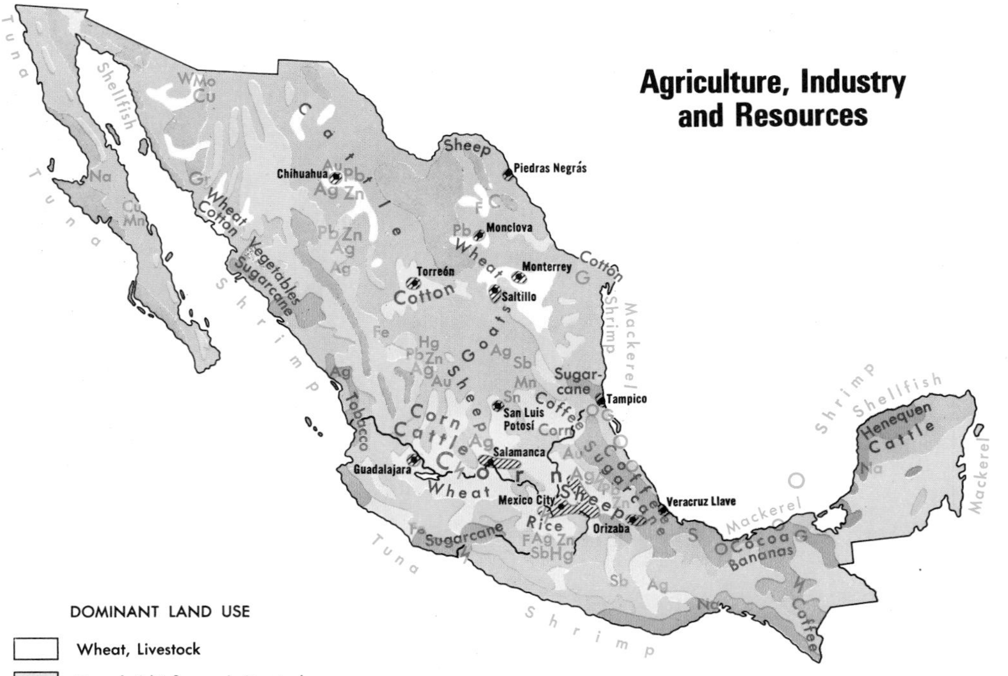

DOMINANT LAND USE

- Wheat, Livestock
- Cereals (chiefly corn), Livestock
- Diversified Tropical Cash Crops
- Cotton, Mixed Cereals
- Livestock, Limited Agriculture
- Range Livestock
- Forests
- Nonagricultural Land

- Water Power
- Major Industrial Areas

MAJOR MINERAL OCCURRENCES

Ag	Silver	G	Natural Gas	O	Petroleum
Au	Gold	Gr	Graphite	Pb	Lead
C	Coal	Hg	Mercury	S	Sulfur
Cu	Copper	Mn	Manganese	Sb	Antimony
F	Fluorspar	Mo	Molybdenum	Sn	Tin
Fe	Iron Ore	Na	Salt	W	Tungsten
				Zn	Zinc

GUATEMALA

AREA 42,042 sq. mi. (108,889 sq. km.)
POPULATION 7,262,419
CAPITAL Guatemala
LARGEST CITY Guatemala
HIGHEST POINT Tajumulco 13,845 ft. (4,220 m.)
MONETARY UNIT quetzal
MAJOR LANGUAGES Spanish, Quiché
MAJOR RELIGION Roman Catholicism

BELIZE

AREA 8,867 sq. mi. (22,966 sq. km.)
POPULATION 144,857
CAPITAL Belmopan
LARGEST CITY Belize City
HIGHEST POINT Victoria Peak 3,681 ft. (1,122 m.)
MONETARY UNIT Belize dollar
MAJOR LANGUAGES English, Spanish, Mayan
MAJOR RELIGIONS Roman Catholicism, Protestantism

EL SALVADOR

AREA 8,260 sq. mi. (21,393 sq. km.)
POPULATION 4,813,000
CAPITAL San Salvador
LARGEST CITY San Salvador
HIGHEST POINT Santa Ana 7,825 ft. (2,385 m.)
MONETARY UNIT colón
MAJOR LANGUAGE Spanish
MAJOR RELIGION Roman Catholicism

HONDURAS

AREA 43,277 sq. mi. (112,087 sq. km.)
POPULATION 3,691,000
CAPITAL Tegucigalpa
LARGEST CITY Tegucigalpa
HIGHEST POINT Las Minas 9,347 ft. (2,849 m.)
MONETARY UNIT lempira
MAJOR LANGUAGE Spanish
MAJOR RELIGION Roman Catholicism

NICARAGUA

AREA 45,698 sq. mi. (118,358 sq. km.)
POPULATION 2,703,000
CAPITAL Managua
LARGEST CITY Managua
HIGHEST POINT Cerro Mocotón 6,913 ft. (2,107 m.)
MONETARY UNIT córdoba
MAJOR LANGUAGE Spanish
MAJOR RELIGION Roman Catholicism

COSTA RICA

AREA 19,575 sq. mi. (50,700 sq. km.)
POPULATION 2,245,000
CAPITAL San José
LARGEST CITY San José
HIGHEST POINT Chirripó Grande 12,530 ft. (3,819 m.)
MONETARY UNIT colón
MAJOR LANGUAGE Spanish
MAJOR RELIGION Roman Catholicism

PANAMA

AREA 29,761 sq. mi. (77,082 sq. km.)
POPULATION 1,830,175
CAPITAL Panamá
LARGEST CITY Panamá
HIGHEST POINT Vol. Baru 11,401 ft. (3,475 m.)
MONETARY UNIT balboa
MAJOR LANGUAGE Spanish
MAJOR RELIGION Roman Catholicism

Agriculture, Industry and Resources

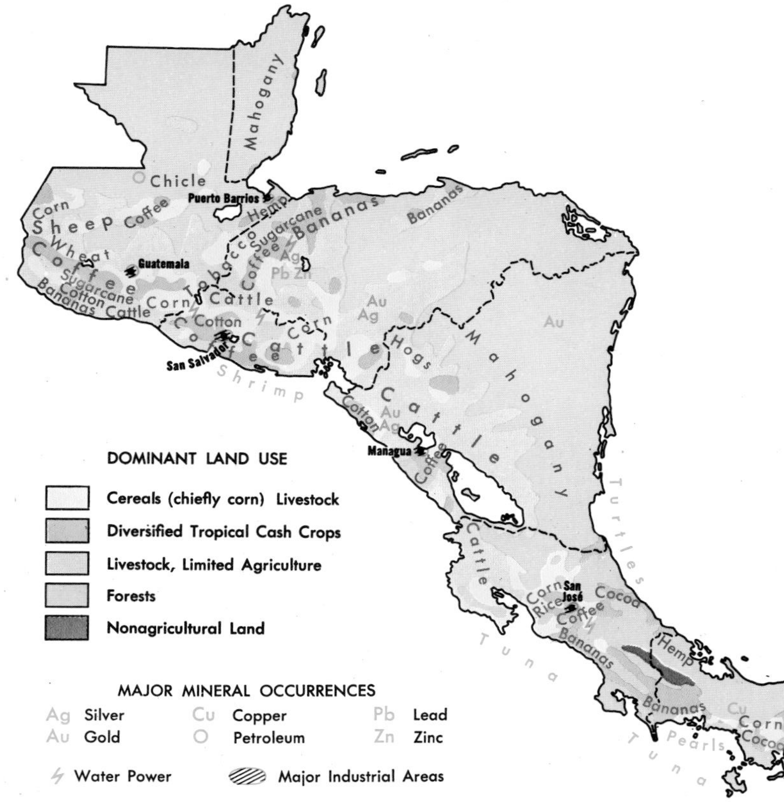

GUATEMALA

HONDURAS

BELIZE

NICARAGUA

EL SALVADOR

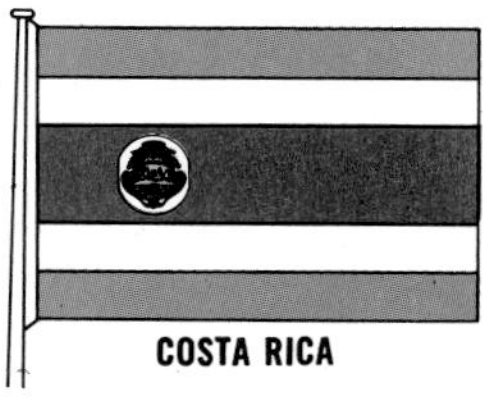
COSTA RICA

PANAMA

BELIZE

CITIES and TOWNS

Belize City 39,887 .... C2
Belize City* 50,925 .... C2
Belmopan (cap.) 2,932 .... C2
Corozal Town 6,862 .... C1
Hattieville 904 .... C2
Libertad 856 .... C1
Orange Walk Town 8,441 .... C1
Punta Gorda 2,219 .... C2
San Ignacio 5,606 .... C2
Stann Creek Town 6,627 .... C2

OTHER FEATURES

Ambergris (cay) D1
Belize (riv.) C2
Bokel (cay) D2
Glover (reef) D2
Half Moon (cay) D2
Hondo (riv.) C1
Honduras (gulf) D2
Mauger (cay) D2
New (riv.) C2
Saint Georges (cay) D2
Sarstún (riv.) C3
Turneffe (isls.) D2

COSTA RICA

CITIES and TOWNS

Alajuela 33,122 .... E6
Atenas 1,728 .... E6
Bagaces 2,129 .... E5
Boruca⊙ 1,892 .... F6
Buenos Aires⊙ 302 .... F6
Cañas 6,053 .... E5
Cartago 21,753 .... F6
Ciudad Quesada 9,754 .... E5
Esparta 4,699 .... E5
Filadelfia 2,958 .... E5
Golfito 6,962 .... F6
Grecia 8,355 .... E5
Guácimo 1,168 .... F5
Guápiles 3,524 .... F5
Heredia 22,700 .... E5
Las Juntas 1,129 .... E5
Liberia 10,802 .... E5
Limón 29,621 .... F6
Miramar 1,673 .... E5
Nicoya 7,474 .... E5
Orotina 3,170 .... E6
Palmares 3,083 .... F6
Paraíso 8,446 .... F6
Puerto Cortés 2,070 .... F6
Puntarenas 26,331 .... E6
Quepos 2,155 .... E6
San José (cap.) 215,441 .... F5
San José* 391,107 .... F5
San Marcos 917 .... E6
San Ramón 9,245 .... E5
Santa Cruz 5,777 .... E5
Santo Domingo 5,148 .... F6
Siquirres 4,361 .... F5
Turrialba 12,151 .... F6

(continued on following page)

(continued)

OTHER FEATURES

Blanca (pt.) F5
Blanco (cape) E6
Blanco (peak) F6
Burica (pt.) F6
Cahuita (pt.) F6
Caño (isl.) F6
Carreta (pt.) F6
Chirripó Grande (mt.) F6
Coronada (bay) F6
Cuilapa Miravalles (vol.) E5
Dulce (gulf) F6
Góngora (mt.) E5
Guiones (pt.) E6
Irazú (mt.) F6
Judas (pt.) E6
Llerena (pt.) F6
Matapalo (cape) F6
Nicoya (gulf) E6
Nicoya (pen.) E6
Papagayo (gulf) E5
Salinas (bay) D5
San Juan (riv.) E5
Santa Elena (cape) D5
Talamanca (range) F6
Velas (cape) D5

EL SALVADOR

CITIES and TOWNS

Acajutla 8,598 B4
Ahuachapán 17,242 B4
Atiquizaya 7,035 C3
Chalatenango 7,633 C3
Chinameca 6,303 C4
Cojutepeque 20,615 C4
Estanzuelas 2,548 C4
Ilobasco 6,572 C4
Intipucá 3,469 D4
Jucuarán 1,443 C4
La Libertad C4
La Palma 1,998 C3
La Unión 17,207 D4
Metapán 7,704 C3
Nueva San Salvador 35,106 C4
Puerto de la Concordia C4
San Francisco Gotera 4,725 C4
San Miguel 59,304 D4
San Salvador (cap.) 337,171 C4
Santa Ana 96,306 C4
Santa Rosa de Lima 5,707 D4
San Vicente 18,872 C4
Sensuntepeque 7,226 C4
Sonsonate 33,562 C4
Suchitoto 5,540 C4
Texistepeque 1,722 C3
Usulután 19,616 C4
Zacatecoluca 15,718 C4

OTHER FEATURES

Fonseca (gulf) D4
Güija (lake) C3
Lempa (riv.) C4
Remedios (pt.) B4
Santa Ana (mt.) C4

GUATEMALA

CITIES and TOWNS

Amatitlán 15,251 B3
Antigua 17,994 B3
Asunción Mita 7,477 C3
Cahabón 1,344 C3
Chajul 4,329 B3
Champerico 5,722 A3
Chichicastenango 2,635 B3
Chimaltenango 12,860 B3
Chiquimula 16,126 C3
Coatepeque 15,979 A3
Cobán 11,418 B3
Comalapa 10,980 B3
Cubulco 2,021 B3
Cuilapa 4,287 B3
Cuilco 862 B3
Dolores 973 C2
El Estor 2,324 C3
El Progreso 4,009 B3
Escuintla 33,205 B3
Flores 1,477 C2
Gualán 5,169 C3
Guatemala (cap.) 700,538 B3
Huehuetenango 12,570 B3
Ipala 3,386 C3
Iztapa 1,237 B4
Jacaltenango 4,517 B3
Jalapa 13,788 B3
Jutiapa 8,210 B3
La Gomera 2,394 B3
La Libertad 908 B2
Livingston 2,898 C3
Los Amates 1,383 C3
Masagua 1,178 B3
Mazatenango 23,285 B3
Momostenango 5,210 B3
Morales 2,113 C3
Ocós 741 A3
Panzós 1,643 C3
Puerto Barrios 22,598 C3
Quezaltenango 53,021 B3
Quezaltepeque 2,222 C3
Rabinal 4,625 B3
Retalhuleu 19,060 B3
Río Hondo 1,416 C3
Sacapulas 1,439 B3
Salamá 5,529 B3
San Andrés 1,066 B2
San Felipe 3,210 B3
San José 9,402 B4
San Luis 1,136 C2
San Luis Jilotepeque 6,055 C3
San Marcos 5,700 B3
San Martín Jilotepeque 3,770 B3
San Mateo Ixtatán 1,834 B3
San Pedro Carchá 4,465 B3
Santa Cruz del Quiché 7,651 B3
Santa Rosa de Lima 1,161 B3
Sololá 3,960 B3
Tacaná 1,280 A3
Tejutla 1,205 B3
Tikal C2
Totonicapán 8,568 B3
Zacapa 12,688 C3

OTHER FEATURES

Atitlán (lake) B3
Atitlán (vol.) B3
Azul (riv.) C2
Chixoy (riv.) B2
Güija (lake) C3
Honduras (gulf) D2
Izabal (lake) C3
Minas (mts.) C3
Motagua (riv.) C3
Pasión (riv.) B2
Petén-Itzá (lake) B2
San Pedro (riv.) B2
Sarstún (riv.) C3
Tacaná (vol.) A3
Tajumulco (vol.) B3
Tres Puntas (cape) C3
Usumacinta (riv.) B2

HONDURAS

CITIES and TOWNS

Amapala 2,274 D4
Brus Laguna 933 E3
Catacamas 9,134 E3
Cedros 917 D3
Choloma 961 C3
Choluteca 26,152 D4
Comayagua 15,941 D3
Corquín 2,629 C3
Danlí 10,825 D3
El Dulce Nombre 1,297 E3

El Paraíso, Copán 2,164 .... C3
El Paraíso, El
  Paraíso 6,709 .... D4
El Porvenir 1,076 .... D3
El Progreso 28,105 .... D3
El Triunfo 2,925 .... D4
Goascorán 996 .... D4
Gracias 2,299 .... C3
Guaimaca 3,953 .... D3
Guanaja 1,947 .... E2
Guayape 804 .... D3
Iriona 26 .... E2
Jacaleapa 1,609 .... D3
Jesús de Otoro 2,976 .... C3
Jutiapa 1,126 .... D3
Juticalpa 10,075 .... D3
La Ceiba 38,788 .... D3
La Esperanza 2,146 .... C3
La Paz 6,811 .... D3
Limón 1,704 .... E3
Manto 689 .... D3
Marcala 3,183 .... C3
Morazán 4,367 .... D3
Morocelí 1,442 .... D3
Nacaome 6,159 .... D4
Namasigüe 816 .... D4
Naranjito 2,770 .... C3
Nueva Armenia 670 .... D4
Nueva Ocotepeque 4,724 .... C3
Olanchito 7,411 .... D3
Omoa 9,161 .... C3
Pespire 1,895 .... D4
Puerto Castilla D3
Puerto Cortés 25,817 .... D2
Puerto Lempira 727 .... F3
Roatán 1,943 .... D2
Sabanagrande 1,446 .... D4
Salado D3
San Francisco 1,557 .... D3
San Francisco de la Paz 2,291 .... D3
San Juan de Flores 1,184 .... D3
San Luis 2,237 .... C3
San Marcos 2,499 .... C3
San Pedro Sula 150,991 .... C3
Santa Bárbara 5,883 .... C3
Santa Cruz de Yojoa 1,848 .... D3
Santa Rita 5,298 .... D3
Santa Rosa de Aguán 1,622 .... E2
Santa Rosa de Copán 12,413 .... C3
Siguatepeque 12,456 .... D3

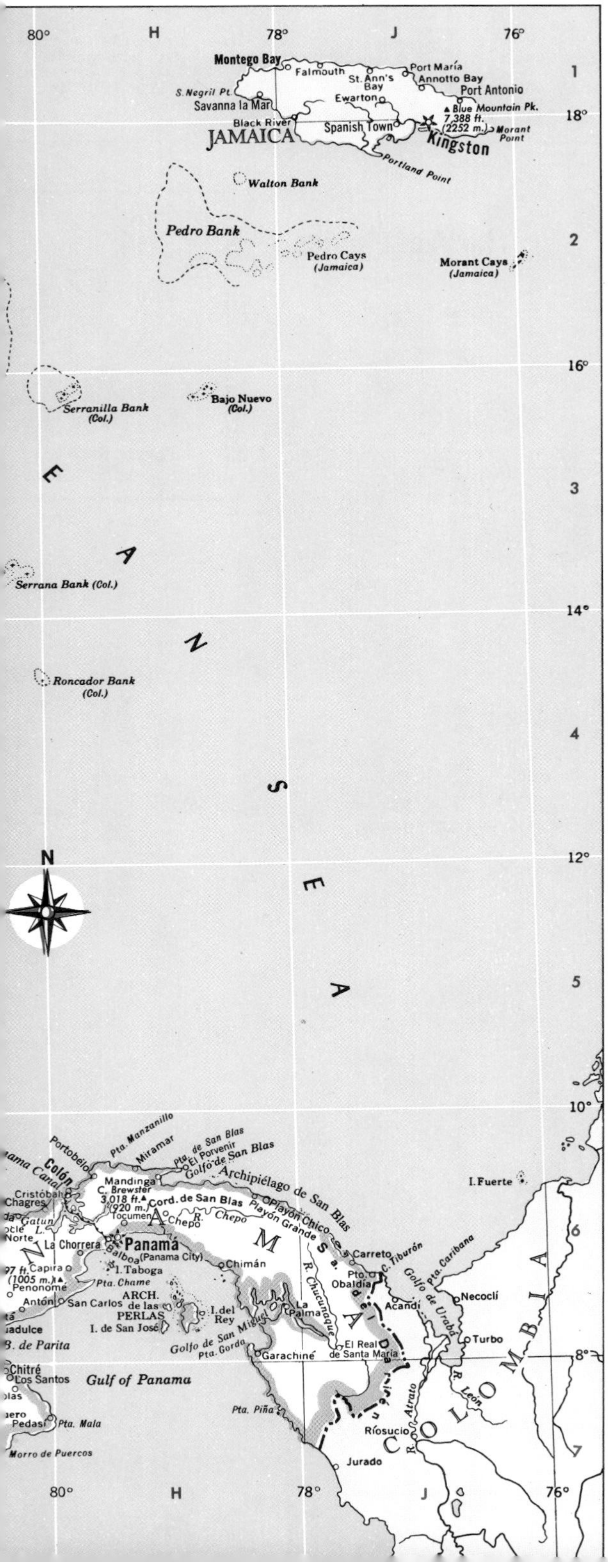

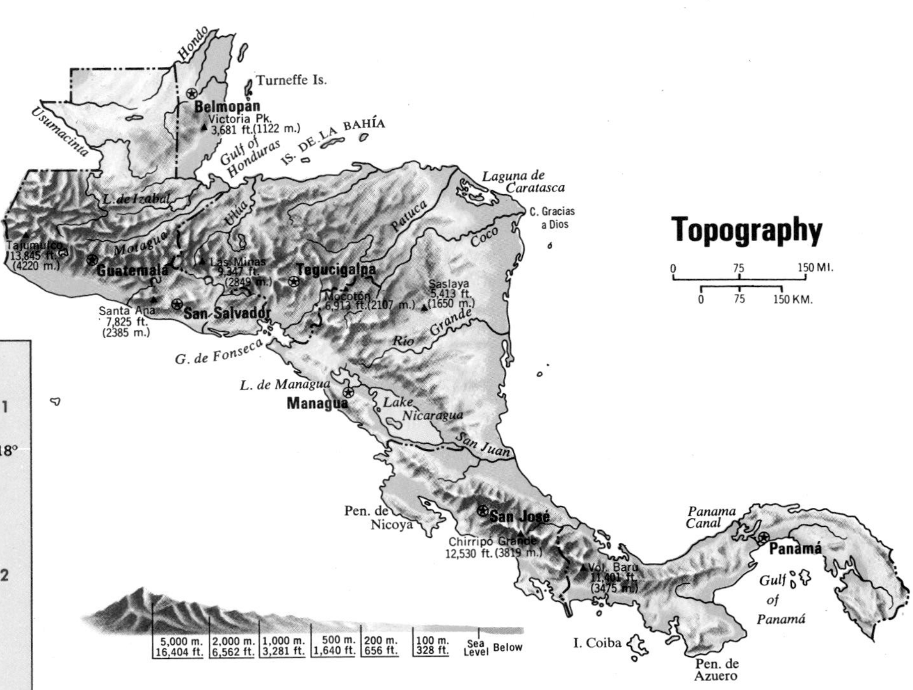

Sinuapa 831 .... C3
Sonaguera 2,264 .... D3
Sulaco 1,121 .... D3
Tegucigalpa (cap.) 273,894 .... D3
Tegucigalpa* 305,387 .... D3
Tela 19,055 .... D3
Teupasenti 2,003 .... D3
Tocoa 2,803 .... E3
Trinidad 1,598 .... C3
Trujillo 3,961 .... E3
Utila 1,177 .... D2
Villa de San Antonio 2,359 .... D3
Yorito 770 .... D3
Yoro 4,449 .... D3
Yuscarán 1,835 .... D4

OTHER FEATURES

Aguán (riv.) D3
Bahía (isls.) D2
Bonacca (Guanaja) (isl.) E2
Brus (lag.) E2
Camarón (cape) E2
Caratasca (cays) F2
Caratasca (lag.) F3
Choluteca (riv.) D4
Coco (riv.) E3
Colón (mts.) E3
Esperanza (mts.) E3
Falso (cape) F3
Fonseca (gulf) D4
Gorda (bank) F3
Guanaja (isl.) E2
Honduras (cape) E2
Honduras (gulf) D2
Patuca (pt.) E3
Patuca (riv.) E3
Paulaya (riv.) E3
Pija, Sierra de (mts.) D3
Roatán (isl.) D2
San Pablo, Sierra
  (mts.) E3
Santanilla (isls.) F2
Segovia (Coco) (riv.) E3
Sico (riv.) E3
Sulaco (riv.) D3
Swan (Santanilla) (isls.) F2
Ulúa (riv.) D3
Utila (isl.) D2
Wanks (Coco) (riv.) E3
Yojoa (lake) D3

NICARAGUA

CITIES and TOWNS

Acoyapa 2,588 .... E5
Barra de Río Grande F4
Bluefields 14,252 .... F4
Boaco 6,372 .... E4
Bonanza E4
Bragman's Bluff (Puerto
  Cabezas) 5,457 .... F3
Cabo Gracias a Dios○ 3,846 .... F3
Camoapa 4,385 .... E4
Chichigalpa 14,498 .... D4
Chinandega 30,441 .... D4
Ciudad Darío 5,304 .... D4
Condega 3,414 .... D4
Corinto 13,404 .... D4
Diriamba 10,085 .... D5
El Jícaro 1,669 .... E4
El Limón E4
El Realejo 2,229 .... D4
El Sauce 3,202 .... D4
El Viejo 8,507 .... D4
Esquipulas 2,232 .... E4
Estelí 20,222 .... D4
Granada 34,976 .... E5
Greytown (San Juan del
  Norte) 294 .... F5
Jalapa 3,633 .... E4
Jinotega 9,506 .... E4
Jinotepe 12,473 .... D5
Juigalpa 8,497 .... E4
La Cruz 150 .... E4
La Libertad 1,286 .... E4
La Paz Central 6,175 .... D4
La Paz de Oriente 957 .... E5
La Trinidad 3,548 .... D4
León 55,625 .... D4
Managua (cap.) 398,514 .... D4
Managua* 404,634 .... D4
Masatepe 6,307 .... D5
Masaya 30,753 .... D5
Matagalpa 21,385 .... E4
Mateare 1,405 .... D4
Morrito 368 .... E5
Moyogalpa 1,551 .... E5
Muy Muy 1,373 .... E4
Nagarote 7,185 .... D4
Nandaime 5,631 .... E5
Ocotal, Segovia 8,215 .... D4
Poneloya D4
Prinzapolka 8,979 .... F4
Puerto Cabezas 5,457 .... F3
Quilalí 1,245 .... E4
Rama 1,341 .... E4
Rivas 10,125 .... E5
San Carlos 2,022 .... E5
San Jorge 2,874 .... E5
San Juan del Norte 294 .... F5
San Juan del Sur 2,393 .... D5
San Miguelito 1,312 .... E5
San Rafael del Norte 1,938 .... E4
San Rafael del Sur 2,914 .... D5
San Ramón 477 .... E4
Santo Domingo 1,949 .... E4
Santo Tomás 2,309 .... E5
Siuna E4
Somotillo 1,864 .... D4
Somoto 5,847 .... D4
Telpaneca 991 .... D4
Terrabona 904 .... E4
Teustepe 1,060 .... E4
Tipitapa 5,758 .... E4
Waspán 1,246 .... E3

OTHER FEATURES

Coco (riv.) E3
Cosegüina (pt.) D4
Dariense, Cordillera (range) E4
Dipilto, Cordillera (range) D4
Escondido (riv.) F4
Fonseca (gulf) D4
Gorda (pt.) F5
Gracias a Dios (cape) F3
Grande (riv.) E4
Great Corn (isl.) F4
Huapí (mts.) E4
Isabelia, Cordillera (range) E4
King (cays) F4
Kukalaya (riv.) F4
Little Corn (isl.) F4
Maíz Grande (Great Corn)
  (isl.) F4
Maíz Pequeña (Little Corn)
  (isl.) F4
Managua (lake) E4
Miskitos (cays) F3
Monkey (pt.) F5
Mosquitos, Costa de (reg.) E4
Nicaragua (lake) E5
Ometepe (isl.) E5
Pearl (cays) F4
Perlas (pt.) F4
Prinzapolca (riv.) F4
Salinas (bay) D5
San Juan (riv.) E5
San Juan del Norte (bay) F5
Solentiname (isls.) E5
Tuma (riv.) E4
Tyra (cays) F4
Waspuk (riv.) E3
Wawa (riv.) E3
Zapatera (isl.) E5

PANAMA

CITIES and TOWNS

Aguadulce 10,659 .... G6
Alanje 866 .... F6
Almirante 4,664 .... F6
Antón 4,259 .... G6
Bajo Boquete 2,831 .... F6
Balboa 1,952 .... H6
Bocas del Toro 2,515 .... F6
Cañazas 1,526 .... G6
Capira 1,749 .... G6
Changuinola 9,528 .... F6
Chepo 4,529 .... H6
Chiriquí Grande F6
Chitré 17,156 .... G7
Coclé del Norte G6
Colón 59,832 .... H6
Cristóbal⊙ 7,959 .... G6
David 50,621 .... F6
Dolega 1,019 .... F6
El Real de Santa María 912 .... J6
Garachiné 1,116 .... H6
Gualaca 1,510 .... F6
Horconcitos 1,090 .... F6
La Chorrera 36,971 .... H6
La Concepción 10,460 .... F6
La Palma 1,634 .... H6
La Pintada 1,100 .... G6
Las Palmas 738 .... G6
Las Tablas 5,230 .... G7
Los Santos 4,644 .... G7
Mandinga 81 .... H6
Montijo 1,152 .... G6
Natá 5,603 .... G6
Nuevo Chagres 306 .... G6
Ocú 2,353 .... G7
Panamá (cap.) 388,638 .... H6
Panamá* 498,624 .... H6
Parita 1,616 .... G6
Pedasí 934 .... G7
Penonomé 7,389 .... G6
Playón Chico 1,395 .... H6
Portobelo 551 .... H6
Puerto Armuelles 12,488 .... F6
Puerto Obaldía 491 .... J6
San Francisco 990 .... G6
Santa Fe 490 .... G6
Santiago 21,809 .... G6
Soná 4,471 .... G6
Tocumen⊙ 21,745 .... H6
Tolé 1,052 .... G6
Tonosí 891 .... G7

OTHER FEATURES

Azuero (pen.) G7
Bastimentos (isl.) G6
Brewster, Cerro (mt.) H6
Burica, Punta (cape) F6
Cébaco (isl.) G7
Chepo (riv.) H6
Chiriquí (gulf) F7
Chiriquí (lag.) G6
Chucunaque (riv.) J6
Coiba, Isla de (isl.) F7
Colón, Isla de (isl.) G6
Contreras (isls.) F7
Darién (mts.) J6
Escudo de Veraguas (isl.) G6
Gatun (lake) G6
Gorda (pt.) H6
Jicarón (isl.) F7
Ladrones (isls.) F7
Manzanillo (pt.) H6
Montijo (gulf) G7
Mosquitos, Golfo de los
  (gulf) G6
Panama (gulf) H7
Pando, Cerro (mt.) F6
Parida (isl.) F6
Parita (bay) G6
Perlas (arch.) H6
Puercos, Morro de (head) H7
Rey (isl.) H6
Rincón (pt.) G6
San Blas, Golfo de (bay) H6
San Blas, Pta. de (pt.) H6
San Blas, Cordillera de
  (mts.) H6
San José (isl.) H6
San Miguel, Golfo de (bay) H6
Santiago, Cerro (mt.) G6
Secas (isls.) G7
Tabasará (mts.) G6
Taboga (isl.) H6
Tiburón (pt.) J6
Valiente (pen.) G6

*City and suburbs.
○Population of sub-district or division.
⊙Population of district.

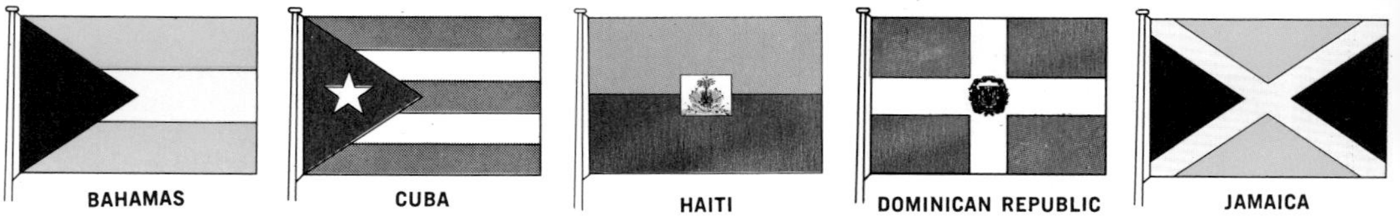

BAHAMAS

AREA 5,382 sq. mi. (13,939 sq. km.)
POPULATION 209,505
CAPITAL Nassau
LARGEST CITY Nassau
HIGHEST POINT Mt. Alvernia 206 ft. (63 m.)
MONETARY UNIT Bahamian dollar
MAJOR LANGUAGE English
MAJOR RELIGIONS Roman Catholicism, Protestantism

CUBA

AREA 44,206 sq. mi. (114,494 sq. km.)
POPULATION 9,706,369
CAPITAL Havana
LARGEST CITY Havana
HIGHEST POINT Pico Turquino 6,561 ft. (2,000 m.)
MONETARY UNIT Cuban peso
MAJOR LANGUAGE Spanish
MAJOR RELIGION Roman Catholicism

JAMAICA

AREA 4,411 sq. mi. (11,424 sq. km.)
POPULATION 2,161,000
CAPITAL Kingston
LARGEST CITY Kingston
HIGHEST POINT Blue Mountain Peak 7,402 ft. (2,256 m.)
MONETARY UNIT Jamaican dollar
MAJOR LANGUAGE English
MAJOR RELIGIONS Protestantism, Roman Catholicism

GRENADA

AREA 133 sq. mi. (344 sq. km.)
POPULATION 103,103
CAPITAL St. George's
LARGEST CITY St. George's
HIGHEST POINT Mt. St. Catherine 2,757 ft. (840 m.)
MONETARY UNIT East Caribbean dollar
MAJOR LANGUAGES English, French patois
MAJOR RELIGIONS Roman Catholicism, Protestantism

DOMINICA

AREA 290 sq. mi. (751 sq. km.)
POPULATION 74,089
CAPITAL Roseau
HIGHEST POINT Morne Diablotin 4,747 ft. (1,447 m.)
MONETARY UNIT Dominican dollar
MAJOR LANGUAGES English, French patois
MAJOR RELIGIONS Roman Catholicism, Protestantism

SAINT VINCENT AND THE GRENADINES

AREA 150 sq. mi. (388 sq. km.)
POPULATION 124,000
CAPITAL Kingstown
HIGHEST POINT Soufrière 4,000 ft. (1,219 m.)
MONETARY UNIT East Caribbean dollar
MAJOR LANGUAGE English
MAJOR RELIGIONS Protestantism, Roman Catholicism

HAITI

AREA 10,694 sq. mi. (27,697 sq. km.)
POPULATION 5,009,000
CAPITAL Port-au-Prince
LARGEST CITY Port-au-Prince
HIGHEST POINT Pic La Selle 8,793 ft. (2,680 m.)
MONETARY UNIT gourde
MAJOR LANGUAGES Creole French, French
MAJOR RELIGION Roman Catholicism

TRINIDAD AND TOBAGO

AREA 1,980 sq. mi. (5,128 sq. km.)
POPULATION 1,067,108
CAPITAL Port of Spain
LARGEST CITY Port of Spain
HIGHEST POINT Mt. Aripo 3,084 ft. (940 m.)
MONETARY UNIT Trinidad and Tobago dollar
MAJOR LANGUAGES English, Hindi
MAJOR RELIGIONS Roman Catholicism, Protestantism, Hinduism, Islam

DOMINICAN REPUBLIC

AREA 18,704 sq. mi. (48,443 sq. km.)
POPULATION 5,647,977
CAPITAL Santo Domingo
LARGEST CITY Santo Domingo
HIGHEST POINT Pico Duarte 10,417 ft. (3,175 m.)
MONETARY UNIT Dominican peso
MAJOR LANGUAGE Spanish
MAJOR RELIGION Roman Catholicism

BARBADOS

AREA 166 sq. mi. (430 sq. km.)
POPULATION 248,983
CAPITAL Bridgetown
LARGEST CITY Bridgetown
HIGHEST POINT Mt. Hillaby 1,104 ft. (336 m.)
MONETARY UNIT Barbadian dollar
MAJOR LANGUAGE English
MAJOR RELIGION Protestantism

SAINT LUCIA

AREA 238 sq. mi. (616 sq. km.)
POPULATION 115,783
CAPITAL Castries
HIGHEST POINT Mt. Gimie 3,117 ft. (950 m.)
MONETARY UNIT East Caribbean dollar
MAJOR LANGUAGES English, French patois
MAJOR RELIGIONS Roman Catholicism, Protestantism

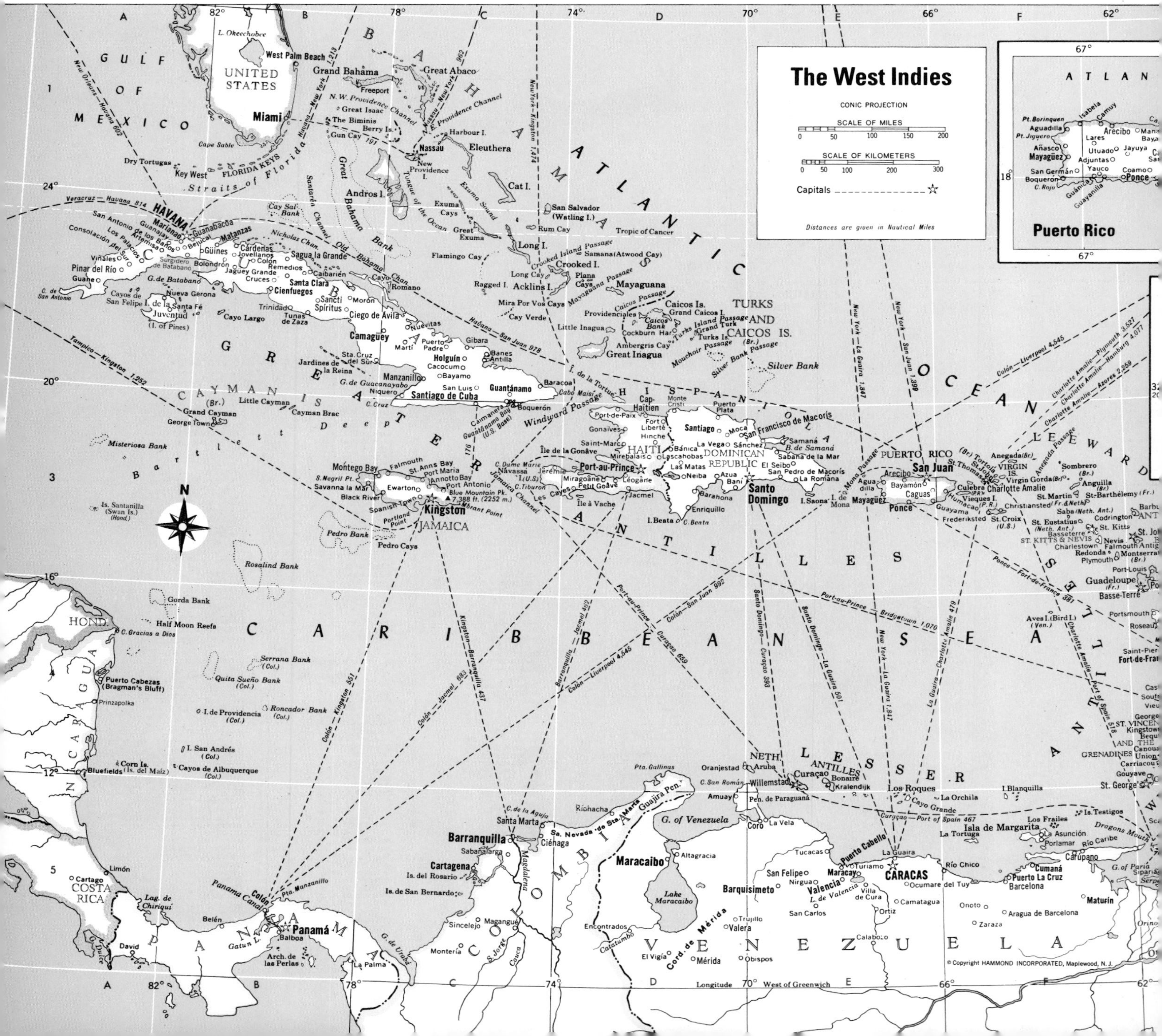

BARBADOS

TRINIDAD & TOBAGO

DOMINICA

Agriculture, Industry and Resources

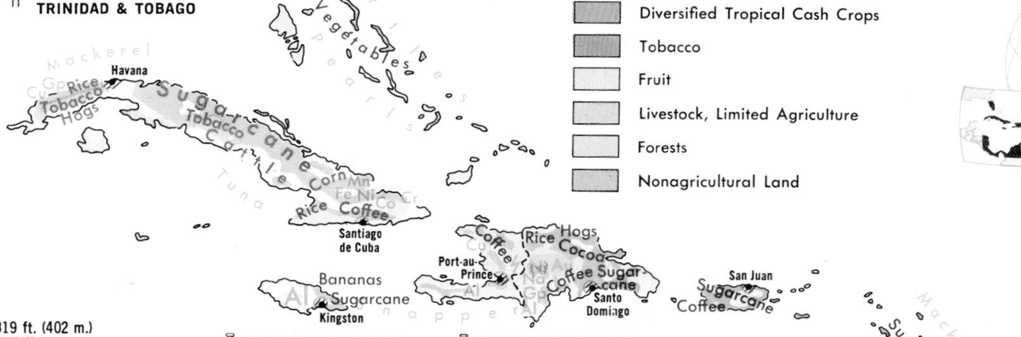

DOMINANT LAND USE

- Diversified Tropical Cash Crops
- Tobacco
- Fruit
- Livestock, Limited Agriculture
- Forests
- Nonagricultural Land

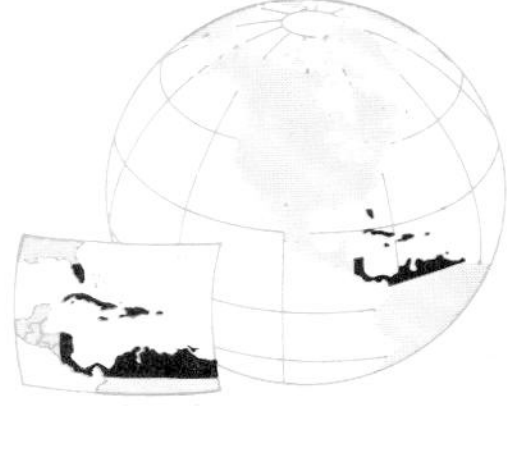

MAJOR MINERAL OCCURRENCES

- Al Bauxite
- At Asphalt
- Au Gold
- Co Cobalt
- Cr Chromium
- Cu Copper
- Fe Iron Ore
- Gp Gypsum
- Mn Manganese
- Na Salt
- Ni Nickel
- O Petroleum
- P Phosphates
- Water Power
- Major Industrial Areas

SAINT LUCIA

ST. KITTS & NEVIS

SAINT VINCENT & THE GRENADINES

GRENADA

ANTIGUA AND BARBUDA

ANTIGUA AND BARBUDA

AREA 171 sq. mi. (443 sq. km.)
POPULATION 72,000
CAPITAL St. John's
HIGHEST POINT Boggy Peak 1,319 ft. (402 m.)
MONETARY UNIT East Caribbean dollar
MAJOR LANGUAGE English
MAJOR RELIGION Protestantism

ST. KITTS & NEVIS

AREA 104 sq. mi. (269 sq. km.)
POPULATION 44,404
CAPITAL Basseterre
HIGHEST POINT Mt. Misery 4,314 ft. (1,315 m.)
MONETARY UNIT East Caribbean dollar
MAJOR LANGUAGE English
MAJOR RELIGIONS Protestantism, Roman Catholicism

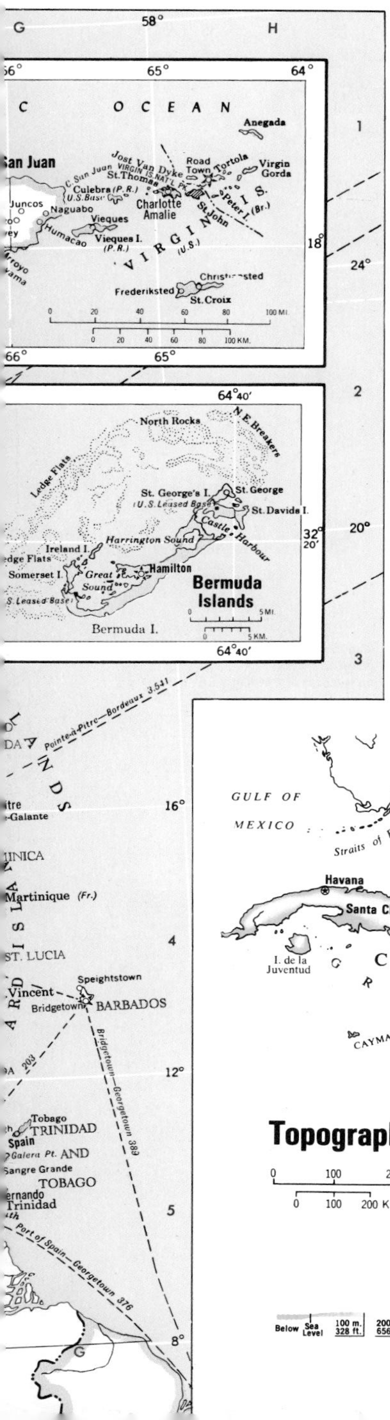

Acklins (isl.), Bahamas 616 ... C 2
Aguadilla, P. Rico 22,039 ... F 1
Andros (isl.), Bahamas 8,397 ... B 1
Anguilla (isl.) 6,519 ... F 3
Antigua and Barbuda 72,000 ... G 3
Antilles, Greater (isls.) ... B 2
Antilles, Lesser (isls.) ... E 4
Arecibo, P. Rico 48,779 ... G 1
Aruba (isl.), 55,148 ... E 4
Bahamas 209,505 ... C 1
Banes, Cuba 31,305 ... C 2
Baní, Dom. Rep. 36,705 ... D 3
Barahona, Dom. Rep. 49,334 ... D 3
Barbados 248,983 ... G 4
Barbuda (isl.), Ant. & Bar. 1,071 ... G 3
Basse-Terre (cap.), Guad. 13,397 ... F 4
Basseterre (cap.), St. Chris.-Nevis 14,725 ... F 3
Bayamo, Cuba 100,543 ... C 2
Bayamón, P. Rico 185,087 ... G 1
Bejucal, Cuba 14,300 ... A 2
Bermuda 67,761 ... G 3
Bermuda (isl.), Bermuda ... H 3
Biminis, The (isls.), Bahamas 1,432 ... B 1
Blue Mountain (peak), Jamaica ... C 3
Bonaire (isl.), Neth. Ant. 8,087 E 4
Bridgetown (cap.), Barbados 7,552 ... G 4
Caguas, P. Rico 87,214 ... G 1
Caicos (isls.), Turks & Caicos 4,008 ... D 2
Camagüey, Cuba 245,235 ... B 2
Cap-Haïtien, Haiti 46,217 ... D 3
Cárdenas, Cuba 59,500 ... B 2
Caribbean (sea) ... B 4
Carriacou (isl.), Grenada ... G 4
Castries (cap.), St. Lucia •42,770 ... G 4
Cat (isl.), Bahamas 2,143 ... C 1
Cataño, P. Rico 26,243 ... G 1
Cayman Islands 16,677 ... B 3
Charlotte Amalie (cap.), V.I. (U.S.) 11,671 ... H 1
Ciego de Ávila, Cuba 74,216 ... B 2
Cienfuegos, Cuba 102,426 ... B 2
Colón, Cuba 35,100 ... B 2
Cuba 9,706,369 ... B 2
Curaçao (isl.), Neth. Ant. 145,430 ... E 4
Dominica 74,089 ... G 4
Dominican Republic 5,647,977 ... D 3
Eleuthera (isl.), Bahamas 8,326 ... C 1
Florida (straits) ... B 1
Fort-de-France (cap.), Mart. 97,649 ... G 4
George Town (cap.), Cayman Is. 7,617 ... B 3
Gonâve (isl.), Haiti ... D 3
Gonaïves, Haiti 29,261 ... D 3
Grand Bahama (isl.), Bahamas 33,102 ... B 1
Grand Caicos, Turks & Caicos 371 ... D 2
Grand Cayman (isl.), Cayman Is. 15,000 ... B 3
Grand Turk (isl), Turks & Caicos 3,146 ... D 2
Great Abaco (isl.), Bahamas 7,324 ... C 1
Great Bahama (bank), Bahamas ... B 1
Great Exuma (isl.), Bahamas ... C 2
Grenada 103,103 ... G 4
Grenadines (isls), St. Vinc. & Grens. 8,371 ... G 4
Guadeloupe 328,400 ... F 3
Guanabacoa, Cuba 89,741 ... B 2
Guantánamo, Cuba 167,400 ... C 2
Güines, Cuba 41,600 ... B 2
Haiti 5,009,000 ... D 3
Hamilton (cap.), Bermuda 1,617 ... G 3
Harrington (sound), Bermuda ... G 3
Havana (cap.), Cuba 1,924,886 ... A 2
Hispaniola (isl.) 10,440,000 ... D 2
Holguín, Cuba 186,013 ... C 2
Ireland (isl.), Bermuda ... G 3
Jamaica 2,161,000 ... C 3
Jamaica (chan.) ... C 3
Jérémie, Haiti 17,624 ... C 3
Jovellanos, Cuba 20,900 ... B 2
Juventud (Pines) (isl.), Cuba 57,879 ... A 2
Kingston (cap.), Jamaica 106,791 ... C 3
Kingstown (cap.), St. Vinc. & Grens. 17,117 ... G 4
La Romana, Dom. Rep. 91,571 ... E 3
La Vega, Dom. Rep. 52,432 ... D 3
Leeward (isls.) ... F 3
Les Cayes, Haiti 22,065 ... C 3
Long (isl.), Bahamas ... C 2
Maisí (pt.), Cuba ... D 2
Manatí, P. Rico 17,347 ... G 1
Manzanillo, Cuba 87,500 ... C 2
Marianao, Cuba 127,563 ... A 2
Marie-Galante (isl.), Guad. 13,757 ... G 4
Martinique 328,566 ... G 4
Matanzas, Cuba 99,194 ... B 2
Mayagüez, P. Rico 82,968 ... F 1
Moca, Dom. Rep. 31,176 ... D 3
Mona (passg.) ... E 3
Mona (isl.), P. Rico ... E 3
Montego Bay, Jamaica 43,521 B 3
Montserrat 12,073 ... G 3
Morón, Cuba 40,400 ... B 2
Nassau (cap.), Bahamas 135,437 ... C 1
Navassa (isl.) ... C 3
Netherlands Antilles 246,000 ... E 4
New Providence (isl.), Bahamas 135,437 ... C 1
Nuevitas, Cuba 35,100 ... C 2
Old Bahama (chan.) ... B 2
Paria (gulf) ... G 5
Pelée (vol.), Mart. ... G 4
Peter (isl.), V.I. (Br.) ... H 1
Pinar del Río, Cuba 95,476 ... A 2
Pines (Juventud) (isl.), Cuba 57,879 ... A 2
Plymouth (cap.), Montserrat 1,623 ... F 3
Pointe-à-Pitre, Guad. 25,151 ... G 3
Ponce, P. Rico 161,739 ... F 1
Port-au-Prince (cap.), Haiti 306,053 ... D 3
Port-de-Paix, Haiti 13,913 ... D 3
Port-of-Spain (cap.), Trin. & Tob. 62,680 ... G 5
Puerto Padre, Cuba 23,200 ... C 2
Puerto Plata, Dom. Rep. 45,348 ... D 3
Puerto Rico 3,196,520 ... G 1
Redonda (isl.), Ant. & Bar. ... F 3
Road Town (cap.), V.I. (Br.) 2,200 ... H 1
Roseau (cap.), Dominica 9,968 ... G 4
Saba (isl.), Neth. Ant. 949 ... F 3
Sagua la Grande, Cuba 42,700 ... B 2
Saint-Barthélemy (isl.), Guad. 3,042 ... F 3
Saint Croix (isl.), V.I. (U.S.) 49,725 ... H 2
Saint Eustatius (isl.), Neth. Ant. 1,341 ... F 3
Saint George's (cap.), Grenada 6,463 ... F 5
Saint John (isl.), V.I. (U.S.) 2,472 ... H 1
Saint John's (cap.), Ant. & Bar. 21,814 ... G 3
Saint Kitts and Nevis 44,404 ... F 3
Saint Lucia 115,783 ... G 4
Saint Marc, Haiti 17,263 ... D 3
Saint Martin (isl.), Guad. 8,038 ... F 3
Saint Martin (Sint Maarten) (isl.), Neth. Ant. 7,435 ... F 3
Saint Thomas (isl.), V.I. (U.S.) 44,372 ... G 1
Saint Vincent and The Grenadines 124,000 ... G 4
San Antonio de los Baños, Cuba 27,600 ... A 2
Sancti Spíritus, Cuba 71,959 ... B 2
San Fernando, Trin. & Tob. 36,870 ... G 5
San Francisco de Macorís, Dom. Rep. 64,906 ... E 2
San Juan (cap.), P. Rico 424,600 ... G 1
San Pedro de Macorís, Dom. Rep. 78,562 ... E 3
San Salvador (isl.), Bahamas ... D 1
Santa Clara, Cuba 171,914 ... B 2
Santiago, Dom. Rep. 278,638 D 3
Santiago de Cuba, Cuba 345,289 ... C 3
Santo Domingo (cap.), Dom. Rep. 1,313,172 ... E 3
Serpents Mouth (passg.) ... G 5
Spanish Town, Jamaica 40,731 ... C 3
Tobago (isl.), Trin. & Tob. 38,754 ... C 3
Tortola (isl.), V.I. (Br.) 9,257 ... H 1
Tortue (Tortuga) (isl.), Haiti ... D 2
Trinidad, Cuba 32,800 ... B 2
Trinidad (isl.), Trin. & Tob. 892,317 ... G 5
Trinidad and Tobago 1,067,108 ... G 5
Turks (isls.), Turks & Caicos 3,348 ... D 2
Turks and Caicos Islands 7,436 ... D 2
Vieques (isl.), P. Rico 7,662 ... G 1
Virgin Gorda (isl.), V.I. (Br.) 1,443 ... H 1
Virgin Islands, British 11,006 ... H 1
Virgin Islands (U.S.) 96,569 ... H 1
Watling (San Salvador) (isl.), Bahamas ... C 1
Willemstad (cap.), Neth. Ant. 95,000 ... E 4
Windward (isls.) ... G 4
Windward (passg.) ... C 3
Yauco, P. Rico 14,594 ... F 1
• Population of district.

Topography

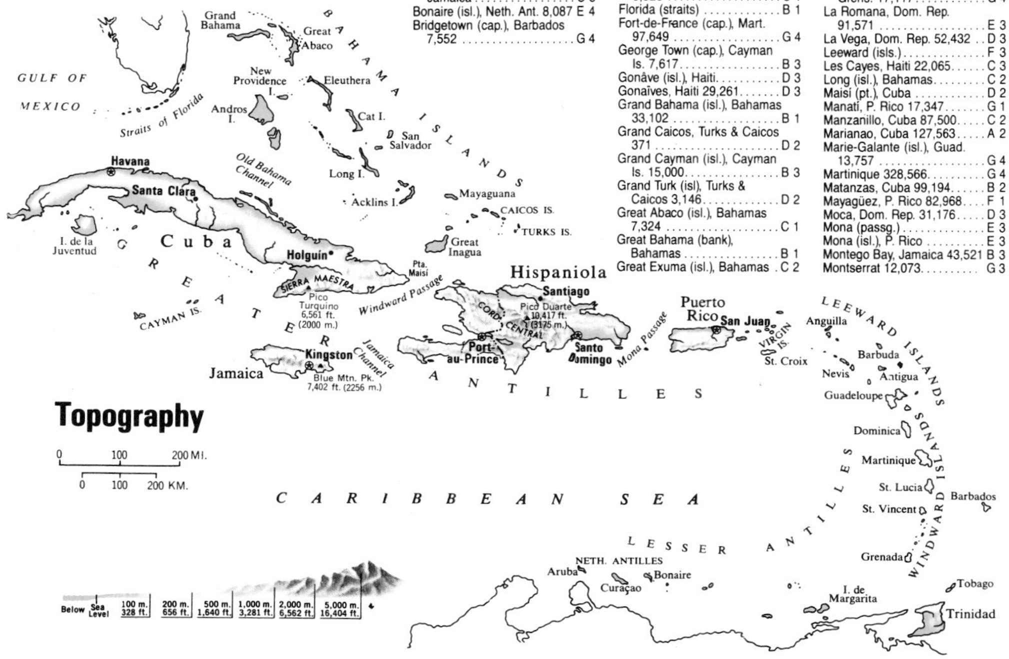

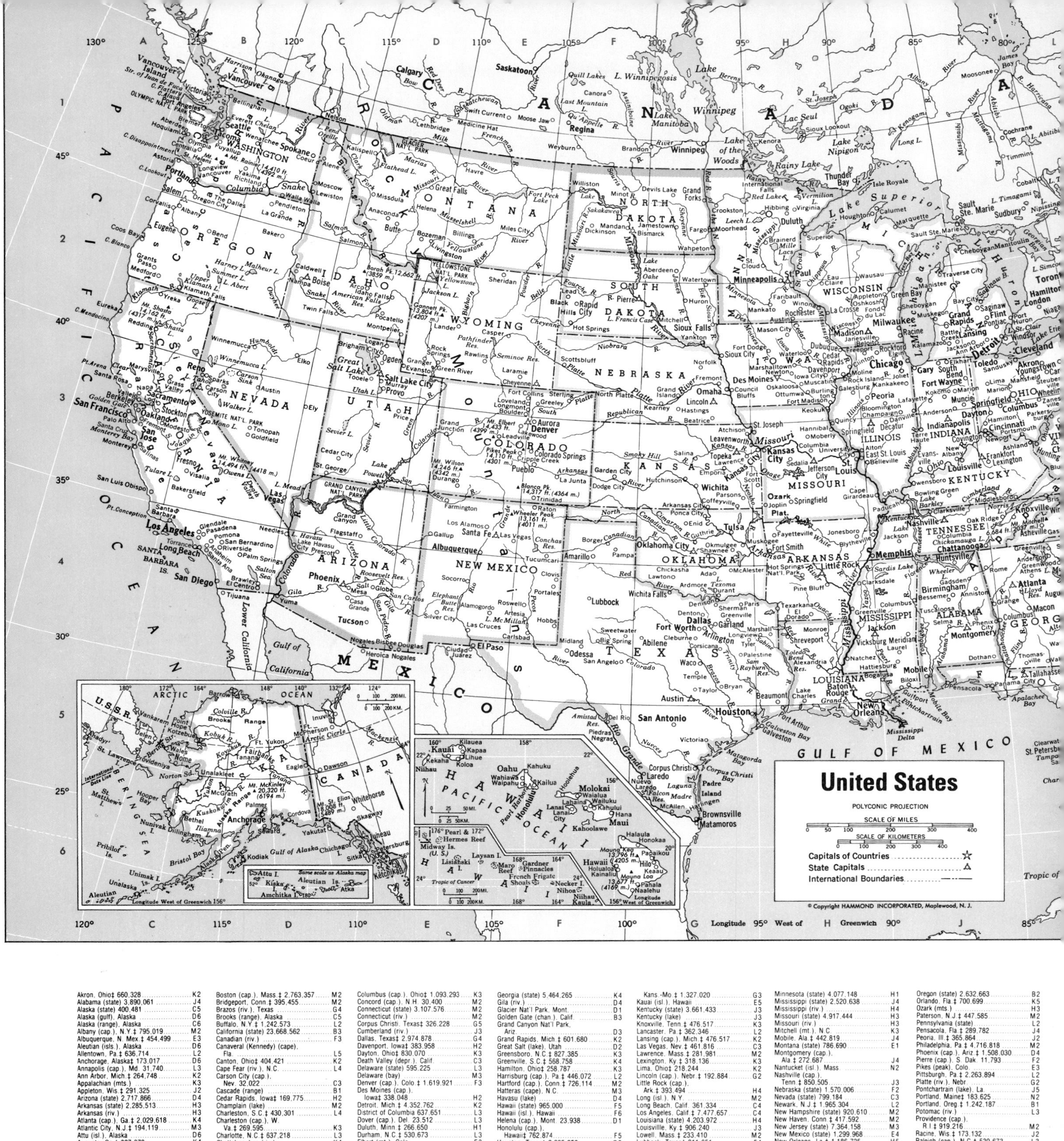

Akron, Ohio‡ 660,328 .... K2
Alabama (state) 3,890,061 .... J4
Alaska (state) 400,481 .... C5
Alaska (gulf), Alaska D6
Alaska (range), Alaska C6
Albany (cap.), N.Y.‡ 795,019 .... M2
Albuquerque, N. Mex.‡ 454,499 .... E3
Aleutian (isls.), Alaska D6
Allentown, Pa.‡ 636,714 .... L2
Anchorage, Alaska‡ 173,017 .... D6
Annapolis (cap.), Md. 31,740 .... L3
Ann Arbor, Mich.‡ 264,748 .... K2
Appalachian (mts.) K3
Appleton, Wis.‡ 291,325 .... J2
Arizona (state) 2,717,866 .... D4
Arkansas (state) 2,285,513 .... H3
Arkansas (riv.) H3
Atlanta (cap.), Ga.‡ 2,029,618 .... K4
Atlantic City, N.J.‡ 194,119 .... M3
Attu (isl.), Alaska D6
Augusta, Ga.‡ 327,372 .... K4
Augusta (cap.), Maine 21,819 .... N2
Austin (cap.), Texas‡ 536,450 .... G4
Bakersfield, Calif.‡ 403,089 .... C3
Baltimore, Md.‡ 2,174,023 .... L3
Baton Rouge (cap.),
La.‡ 493,973 .... H4
Beaumont, Texas‡ 375,497 .... H4
Bering (sea), Alaska C6
Bering (str.), Alaska C5
Bighorn (riv.) E2
Binghamton, N.Y.‡ 301,336 .... L2
Birmingham, Ala.‡ 847,360 .... J4
Bismarck (cap.), N.
Dak.‡ 79,988 .... G1
Bitterroot (range) D1
Black Hills (mts.) F2
Boise (cap.), Idaho‡ 173,076 .... C2
Borah (peak), Idaho D2
Boston (cap.), Mass.‡ 2,763,357 .... M2
Bridgeport, Conn.‡ 395,455 .... M2
Brazos (riv.), Texas G4
Brooks (range), Alaska C5
Buffalo, N.Y.‡ 1,242,573 .... L2
California (state) 23,668,562 .... B3
Canadian (riv.) F3
Canaveral (Kennedy) (cape),
Fla. L5
Canton, Ohio‡ 404,421 .... K2
Cape Fear (riv.), N.C. L4
Carson City (cap.),
Nev. 32,022 .... C3
Cascade (range) B1
Cedar Rapids, Iowa‡ 169,775 .... H2
Champlain (lake) M2
Charleston, S.C.‡ 430,301 .... L4
Charleston (cap.), W.
Va.‡ 269,595 .... K3
Charlotte, N.C.‡ 637,218 .... L3
Chattahoochee (riv.) K4
Chattanooga, Tenn.‡ 426,540 .... J3
Chesapeake (bay) L3
Cheyenne (cap.), Wyo. 47,283 .... E2
Cheyenne (riv.) F2
Chicago, Ill.‡ 7,102,328 .... J2
Cimarron (riv.) G3
Cincinnati, Ohio‡ 1,401,403 .... K3
Cleveland, Ohio‡ 1,898,720 .... K2
Coast (ranges) B2
Cod (cape), Mass. N2
Colorado (state) 2,888,834 .... E3
Colorado (riv.) D4
Colorado (riv.), Texas G4
Colorado Springs,
Colo.‡ 317,458 .... F3
Columbia (cap.), S.C.‡ 408,176 .... K4
Columbia (riv.) B1
Columbus, Ga.‡ 239,196 .... K4
Columbus (cap.), Ohio‡ 1,093,293 .... K3
Concord (cap.), N.H. 30,400 .... M2
Connecticut (state) 3,107,576 .... M2
Connecticut (riv.) M2
Corpus Christi, Texas‡ 326,228 .... G5
Cumberland (riv.) J3
Dallas, Texas‡ 2,974,878 .... G4
Davenport, Iowa‡ 383,958 .... H2
Dayton, Ohio‡ 830,070 .... K3
Death Valley (depr.), Calif. C3
Delaware (state) 595,225 .... L3
Delaware (bay) M3
Denver (cap.), Colo.‡ 1,619,921 .... F3
Des Moines (cap.),
Iowa‡ 338,048 .... H2
Detroit, Mich.‡ 4,352,762 .... K2
District of Columbia 637,651 .... L3
Dover (cap.), Del. 23,512 .... L3
Duluth, Minn.‡ 266,650 .... H1
Durham, N.C.‡ 530,673 .... L3
Elbert (mt.), Colo. E3
El Paso, Texas‡ 479,899 .... E4
Erie, Pa.‡ 279,780 .... K2
Erie (lake) K2
Eugene, Oreg.‡ 275,226 .... B2
Evansville, Ind.‡ 309,408 .... J3
Everglades, The (swamp),
Fla. K5
Fayetteville, N.C.‡ 247,160 .... L3
Flint, Mich.‡ 521,589 .... K2
Florida (state) 9,739,992 .... K5
Florida (keys), Fla. K6
Fort Smith, Ark.‡ 203,269 .... H3
Fort Wayne, Ind.‡ 382,961 .... J2
Fort Worth, Texas 385,141 .... G4
Frankfort (cap.), Ky. 25,973 .... K3
Fresno, Calif.‡ 515,013 .... C3
Galveston, Texas‡ 195,940 .... H5
Gary, Ind.‡ 642,781 .... J2
Georgia (state) 5,464,265 .... K4
Gila (riv.) D4
Glacier Nat'l Park, Mont. D1
Golden Gate (chan.), Calif. B3
Grand Canyon Nat'l Park,
Ariz. D3
Grand Rapids, Mich.‡ 601,680 .... K2
Great Salt (lake), Utah D2
Greensboro, N.C.‡ 827,385 .... K3
Greenville, S.C.‡ 568,758 .... K4
Hamilton, Ohio‡ 258,787 .... K3
Harrisburg (cap.), Pa.‡ 446,072 .... L2
Hartford (cap.), Conn.‡ 726,114 .... M2
Hatteras (cape), N.C. M3
Havasu (lake) D4
Hawaii (state) 965,000 .... F5
Hawaii (isl.), Hawaii F6
Helena (cap.), Mont. 23,938 .... D1
Honolulu (cap.),
Hawaii‡ 762,874 .... F5
Houston, Texas‡ 2,905,350 .... G5
Huntington, W. Va.‡ 311,350 .... K3
Huntsville, Ala.‡ 308,593 .... J4
Huron (lake), Mich. K2
Idaho (state) 943,935 .... D2
Illinois (state) 11,418,461 .... J3
Indiana (state) 5,490,179 .... J3
Aleutian (isls.), Alaska D6
Iowa (state) 2,913,387 .... H2
Jackson (cap.), Miss.‡ 320,425 .... J4
Jacksonville, Fla.‡ 737,519 .... K4
Jefferson City (cap.),
Mo. 33,619 .... H3
Jersey City, N.J.‡ 556,972 .... M2
Johnstown, Pa.‡ 664,506 .... L2
Juneau (cap.), Alaska 19,528 .... E6
Kalamazoo, Mich.‡ 279,192 .... J2
Kansas (state) 2,363,208 .... G3
Kansas City,
Kans.-Mo.‡ 1,327,020 .... G3
Kauai (isl.), Hawaii E5
Kentucky (state) 3,661,433 .... J3
Kentucky (lake) J3
Knoxville, Tenn.‡ 476,517 .... K3
Lancaster, Pa.‡ 362,346 .... L2
Lansing (cap.), Mich.‡ 476,517 .... K2
Las Vegas, Nev.‡ 461,816 .... C3
Lawrence, Mass.‡ 281,981 .... M2
Lexington, Ky.‡ 318,136 .... K3
Lima, Ohio‡ 218,244 .... K2
Lincoln (cap.), Nebr.‡ 192,884 .... G2
Little Rock (cap.),
Ark.‡ 393,494 .... H4
Long (isl.), N.Y. M2
Long Beach, Calif. 361,334 .... C4
Los Angeles, Calif.‡ 7,477,657 .... C4
Louisiana (state) 4,203,972 .... H4
Louisvillle, Ky.‡ 906,240 .... J3
Lowell, Mass.‡ 233,410 .... M2
Lubbock, Texas‡ 211,651 .... F4
Macon, Ga.‡ 254,623 .... K4
Madison (cap.), Wis.‡ 323,545 .... H2
Maine (state) 1,124,660 .... N1
Maryland (state) 4,216,446 .... L3
Massachusetts (state) 5,737,037 .... M2
Maui (isl.), Hawaii F5
Mauna Kea (mt.), Hawaii G6
Mauna Loa (mt.), Hawaii G6
May (cape), N.J. M3
McKinley (mt.), Alaska D5
Memphis, Tenn.‡ 912,887 .... J3
Mendocino (cape), Calif. A2
Mexico (gulf) J5
Miami, Fla.‡ 1,625,979 .... K5
Michigan (state) 9,258,344 .... J1
Michigan (lake) J2
Milwaukee, Wis.‡ 1,397,143 .... J2
Minneapolis, Minn.‡ 2,114,256 .... H1
Minnesota (state) 4,077,148 .... H1
Mississippi (state) 2,520,638 .... J4
Mississippi (riv.) H4
Missouri (state) 4,917,444 .... H3
Missouri (riv.) H3
Mitchell (mt.), N.C. K3
Mobile, Ala.‡ 442,819 .... J4
Montana (state) 786,690 .... E1
Montgomery (cap.),
Ala.‡ 272,687 .... J4
Nantucket (isl.), Mass. N2
Nashville (cap.),
Tenn.‡ 850,505 .... J3
Nebraska (state) 1,570,006 .... F2
Nevada (state) 799,184 .... C3
Newark, N.J.‡ 1,965,304 .... L2
New Hampshire (state) 920,610 .... M2
New Haven, Conn.‡ 417,592 .... M2
New Jersey (state) 7,364,158 .... M3
New Mexico (state) 1,299,968 .... E4
New Orleans, La.‡ 1,186,725 .... H5
Newport News, Va.‡ 364,449 .... L3
New York (state) 17,557,288 .... L2
New York, N.Y.‡ 9,119,737 .... M2
Norfolk, Va.‡ 806,691 .... L3
North Carolina
(state) 5,874,429 .... L3
North Dakota (state) 652,695 .... F1
Oahu (isl.), Hawaii F5
Oakland, Calif.‡ 3,252,721 .... B3
Ohio (state) 10,797,419 .... K2
Ohio (riv.) J3
Oklahoma (state) 3,025,266 .... G3
Oklahoma City (cap.),
Okla.‡ 834,088 .... G3
Olympia (cap.), Wash.‡ 124,264 .... B1
Olympic Nat'l Park, Wash. A1
Omaha, Nebr.‡ 570,399 .... G2
Ontario (lake), N.Y. L2
Oregon (state) 2,632,663 .... B2
Orlando, Fla.‡ 700,699 .... K5
Ozark (mts.) H3
Paterson, N.J.‡ 447,585 .... M2
Pennsylvania (state) L2
Pensacola, Fla.‡ 289,782 .... J4
Peoria, Ill.‡ 365,864 .... J2
Philadelphia, Pa.‡ 4,716,818 .... M2
Phoenix (cap.), Ariz.‡ 1,508,030 .... D4
Pierre (cap.), S. Dak. 11,793 .... F2
Pikes (peak), Colo. E3
Pittsburgh, Pa.‡ 2,263,894 .... L2
Platte (riv.), Nebr. G2
Pontchartrain (lake), La. J5
Portland, Maine‡ 183,625 .... N2
Portland, Oreg.‡ 1,242,187 .... B1
Potomac (riv.) L3
Providence (cap.),
R.I.‡ 919,216 .... M2
Racine, Wis.‡ 173,132 .... J2
Raleigh (cap.), N.C.‡ 530,673 .... L3
Rainier (mt.), Wash. B1
Reading, Pa.‡ 312,509 .... L2
Red (riv.) H4
Red River of the North
(riv.) G1
Rhode Island (state) 947,154 .... M2
Richmond (cap.), Va.‡ 632,015 .... L3
Rio Grande (riv.) F5
Roanoke, Va.‡ 218,244 .... K3
Rochester, N.Y.‡ 971,079 .... L2
Rockford, Ill.‡ 279,514 .... J2
Rocky (mts.) E3
Sacramento (cap.),
Calif.‡ 1,014,002 .... B3
Saginaw, Mich.‡ 224,548 .... K2
Saint Clair (lake), Mich. K2
Saint Lawrence (riv.), N.Y. N1
Saint Louis, Mo.‡ 2,355,276 .... H3

AREA 3,623,420 sq. mi. (9,384,658 sq. km.)
POPULATION 226,504,825
CAPITAL Washington
LARGEST CITY New York
HIGHEST POINT Mt. McKinley 20,320 ft. (6,194 m.)
MONETARY UNIT U.S. dollar
MAJOR LANGUAGE English
MAJOR RELIGIONS Protestantism, Roman Catholicism, Judaism

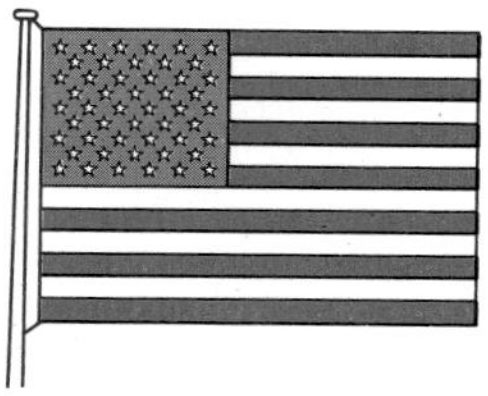

Population Distribution

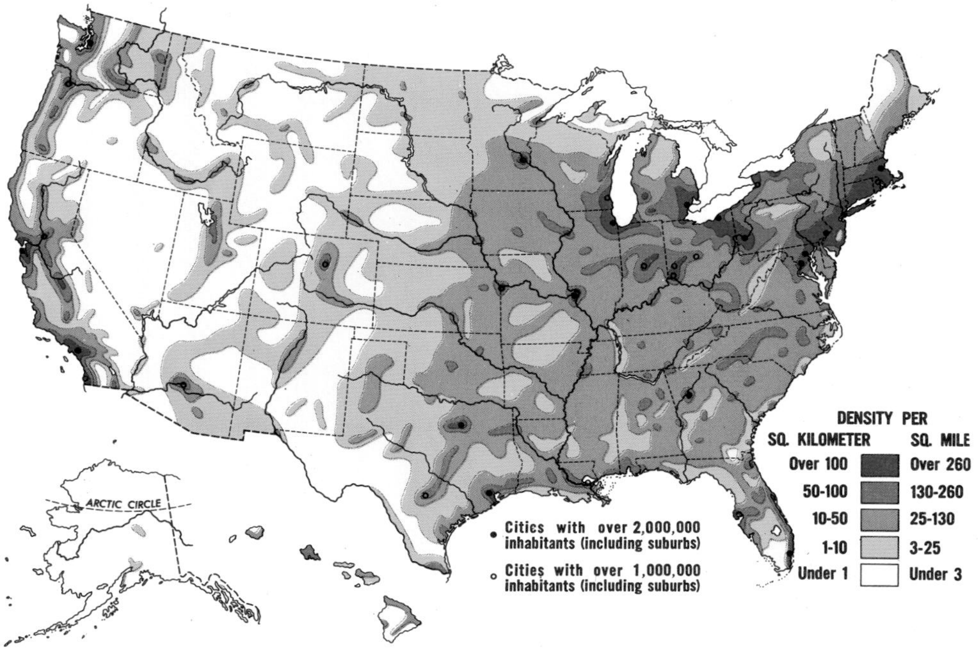

Vegetation

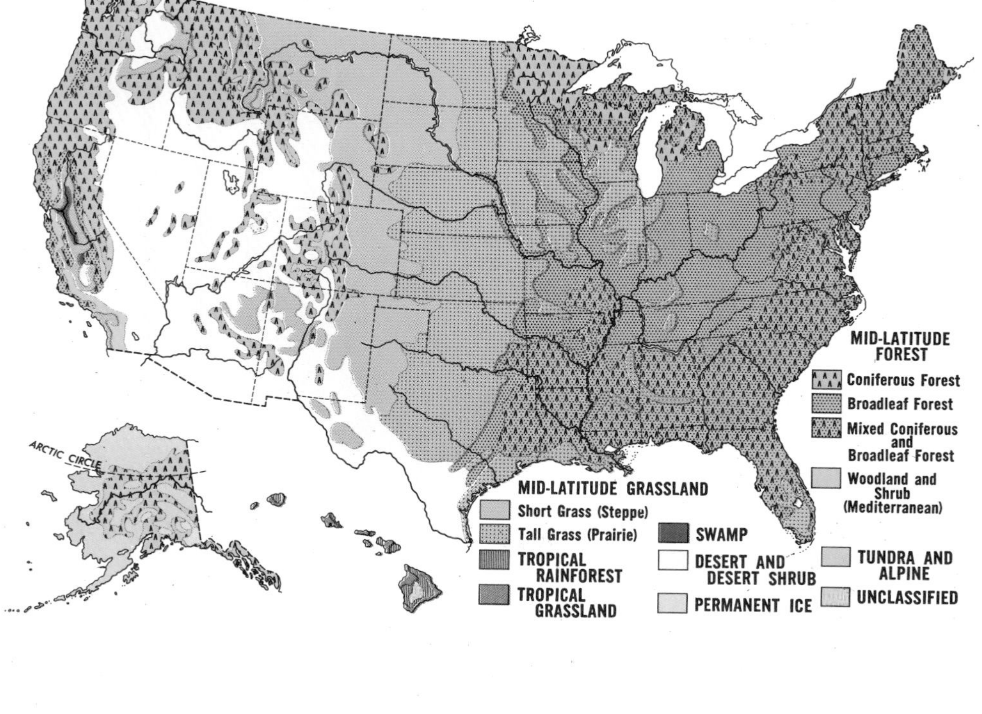

Saint Paul (cap.), Minn. 270,230 .... H1
Sakakawea (lake), N. Dak. F1
Salem (cap.), Oreg. ‡ 249,895 .... B1
Salinas, Calif. ‡ 290,444 .... B3
Salt Lake City (cap.), Utah‡ 936,255 .... D2
Salton Sea (lake), Calif. C4
San Antonio, Texas‡ 1,071,954 .... G5
San Bernardino, Calif. ‡ 1,557,080 .... C4
San Diego, Calif. ‡ 1,861,846 .... C4
San Francisco, Calif. ‡ 325,721 .... B3
San Joaquin (riv.), Calif. C3
San Jose, Calif. ‡ 1,295,071 .... B3
Santa Ana, Calif. ‡ 1,931,570 .... C4
Santa Barbara, Calif. ‡ 298,660 .... C4
Santa Fe (cap.), N. Mex. 48,899 .... E3
Savannah, Ga. ‡ 228,178 .... K4
Scranton, Pa. 88,117 .... L2
Seattle, Wash. ‡ 1,606,765 .... B1
Shasta (mt.), Calif. B2
Shreveport, La. ‡ 376,646 .... H4
Sierra Nevada (mts.) B3
Snake (riv.) C1
South Bend, Ind. ‡ 280,772 .... J2
Spokane, Wash. ‡ 341,835 .... C1
South Carolina (state) 3,119,208 .... K4
South Dakota (state) 690,178 .... F2
Springfield (cap.), Ill. ‡ 187,338 .... H3
Springfield, Mass. ‡ 530,668 .... M2
Springfield, Mo. ‡ 207,704 .... H3
Springfield, Ohio‡ 183,885 .... K2
Stockton, Calif. ‡ 347,342 .... B3
Superior (lake) J1
Syracuse, N.Y. ‡ 642,375 .... L2
Tacoma, Wash. ‡ 485,643 .... B1
Tahoe (lake) C3
Tallahassee (cap.), Fla. ‡ 159,542 .... K4
Tampa, Fla. ‡ 1,569,492 .... K5
Tennessee (state) 4,590,750 .... J3
Terre Haute, Ind. ‡ 176,583 .... J3
Texas (state) 14,228,383 .... G4
Toledo, Ohio‡ 791,599 .... K2
Topeka (cap.), Kans. ‡ 185,442 .... G3
Trenton (cap.), N.J. ‡ 307,863 .... M2
Tucson, Ariz. ‡ 531,263 .... D4
Tulsa, Okla. ‡ 689,628 .... G3
Utah (state) 1,461,037 .... D3
Utica, N.Y. ‡ 320,180 .... M2
Vermont (state) 511,456 .... M2
Virginia (state) 5,346,279 .... L3
Wabash (riv.) J3
Washington (state) 4,130,163 .... B1
Washington, D.C. (cap.), U.S. ‡ 3,060,240 .... L3
Waterbury, Conn. ‡ 228,059 .... M2
Waterloo, Iowa 75,985 .... H2
West Palm Beach, Fla. ‡ 573,125 .... K5
West Virginia (state) 1,949,644 .... K3
Wheeling, W. Va. ‡ 185,566 .... K2
Whitney (mt.), Calif. C3
Witchita, Kans. ‡ 411,313 .... G3
Wilkes-Barre, Pa. 51,551 .... L2
Wilmington, Del. ‡ 524,108 .... M3
Wisconsin (state) 4,705,335 .... J2
Woods (lake), Minn. G1
Worcester, Mass. ‡ 372,940 .... M2
Wyoming (state) 470,816 .... E2
Yellowstone Nat'l Park, Wyo. E2
York, Pa. ‡ 381,255 .... L3
Yosemite Nat'l Park, Calif. C3
Youngstown, Ohio‡ 531,350 .... K2
Yukon (riv.), Alaska C5

‡ Population of metropolitan area.

Topography

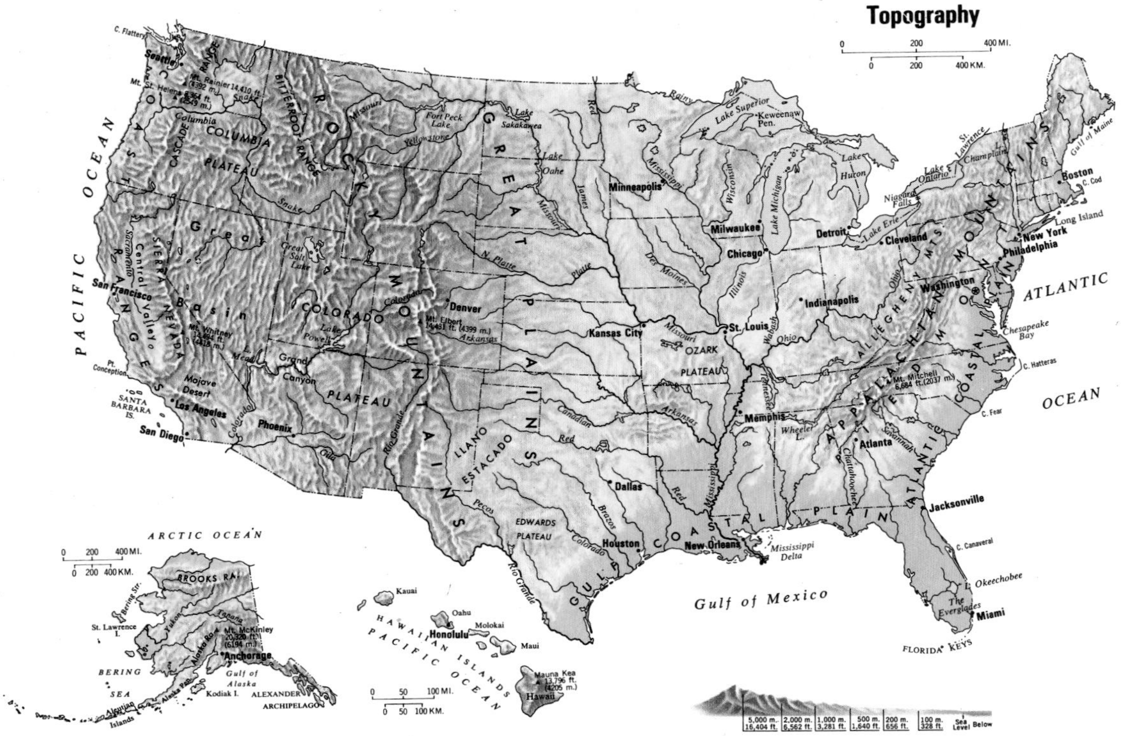

Agriculture, Industry and Resources

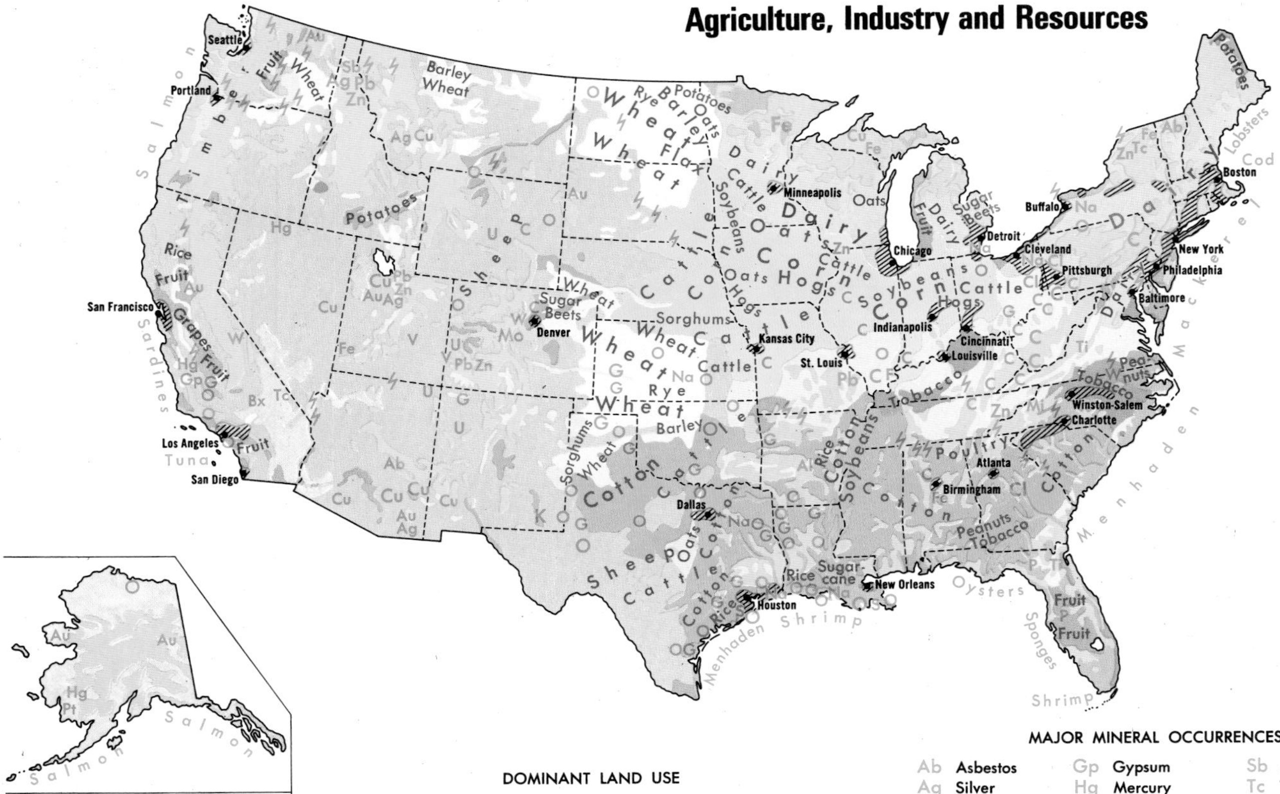

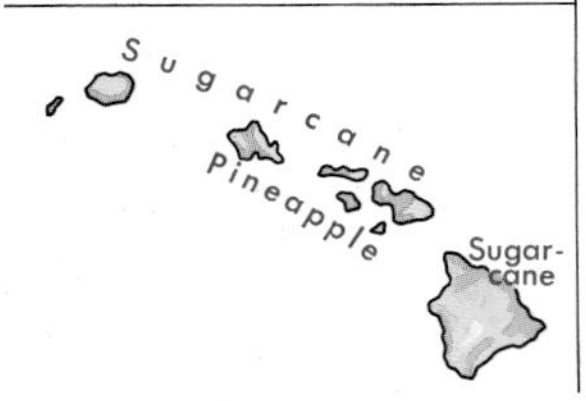

DOMINANT LAND USE

- Wheat and Small Grains
- Feed Grains and Livestock
- Dairy
- General Farming
- Cotton
- Fruit, Truck and Mixed Farming
- Tobacco and General Farming
- Special Crops and General Farming
- Range Livestock
- Forests
- Swampland
- Nonagricultural Land

MAJOR MINERAL OCCURRENCES

Ab	Asbestos	Gp	Gypsum	Sb	Antimony
Ag	Silver	Hg	Mercury	Tc	Talc
Al	Bauxite	K	Potash	Ti	Titanium
Au	Gold	Mi	Mica	U	Uranium
Bx	Borax	Mo	Molybdenum	V	Vanadium
C	Coal	Na	Salt	W	Tungsten
Cl	Clay	O	Petroleum	Zn	Zinc
Cu	Copper	P	Phosphates		
F	Fluorspar	Pb	Lead	ϟ	Water Power
Fe	Iron Ore	Pt	Platinum		Major Industrial Areas
G	Natural Gas	S	Sulfur		

Alabama
SCALE
0 5 10 20 30 40 MI.
0 5 10 20 30 40 KM.
State Capitals
County Seats
GULF OF MEXICO
TENNESSEE
FLORIDA
GEORGIA
MISSISSIPPI
Longitude E West of 30′ Greenwich F
MONTGOMERY
BIRMINGHAM
MOBILE
Huntsville
Tuscaloosa
Gadsden
Anniston
Dothan
Selma
Florence
Decatur
Pensacola
Chattanooga
Atlanta
Columbus
LAUDERDALE
LIMESTONE
MADISON
JACKSON
COLBERT
LAWRENCE
MORGAN
MARSHALL
DE KALB
FRANKLIN
MARION
WINSTON
CULLMAN
BLOUNT
ETOWAH
CHEROKEE
LAMAR
FAYETTE
WALKER
JEFFERSON
ST. CLAIR
CALHOUN
CLEBURNE
PICKENS
TUSCALOOSA
SHELBY
TALLADEGA
CLAY
RANDOLPH
GREENE
HALE
BIBB
CHILTON
COOSA
TALLAPOOSA
CHAMBERS
SUMTER
PERRY
AUTAUGA
ELMORE
LEE
MARENGO
DALLAS
LOWNDES
MONTGOMERY
MACON
RUSSELL
CHOCTAW
WILCOX
BULLOCK
BARBOUR
CLARKE
MONROE
BUTLER
CRENSHAW
PIKE
WASHINGTON
CONECUH
COVINGTON
COFFEE
DALE
HENRY
ESCAMBIA
GENEVA
HOUSTON
MOBILE
BALDWIN
MOBILE BAY
GULF ISLANDS NATIONAL SEASHORE
Tennessee-Tombigbee Waterway
Walter F. George Res. (Lake Eufaula)
Lake Martin
Lewis Smith Lake
Weiss Lake
Cheaha Mtn. 2,407 ft. (734 m.)
Copyright HAMMOND INCORPORATED, Maplewood, N. J.

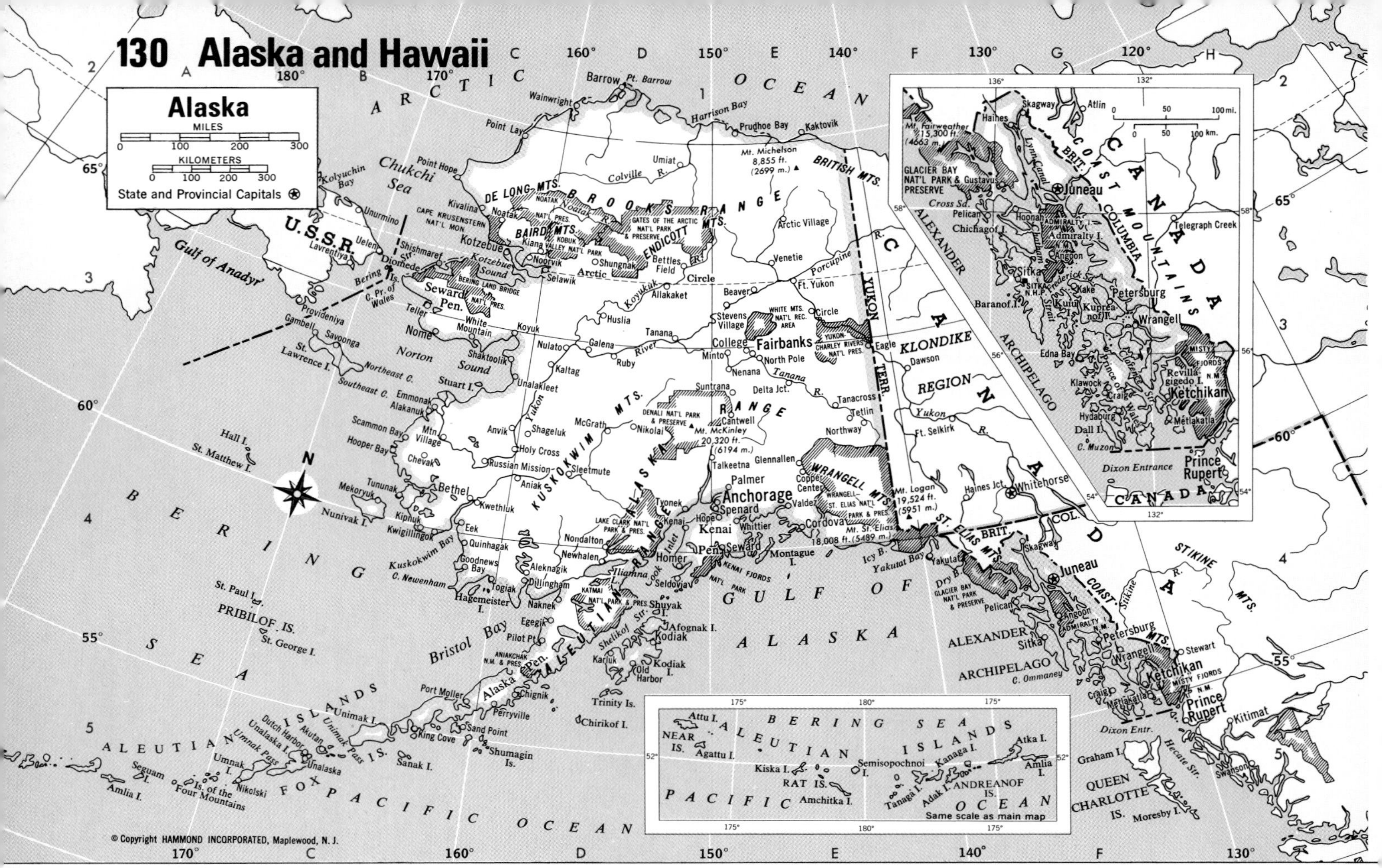
Alaska
MILES
KILOMETERS
State and Provincial Capitals
ARCTIC OCEAN
BERING SEA
GULF OF ALASKA
PACIFIC OCEAN
BROOKS RANGE
ALASKA RANGE
KUSKOKWIM MTS.
Anchorage
Fairbanks
Juneau
Nome
Kodiak
Ketchikan
Sitka
U.S.S.R.
CANADA
KLONDIKE REGION
ALEXANDER ARCHIPELAGO
ALEUTIAN ISLANDS
BERING SEA
PACIFIC OCEAN
Same scale as main map
Mt. McKinley 20,320 ft. (6194 m.)

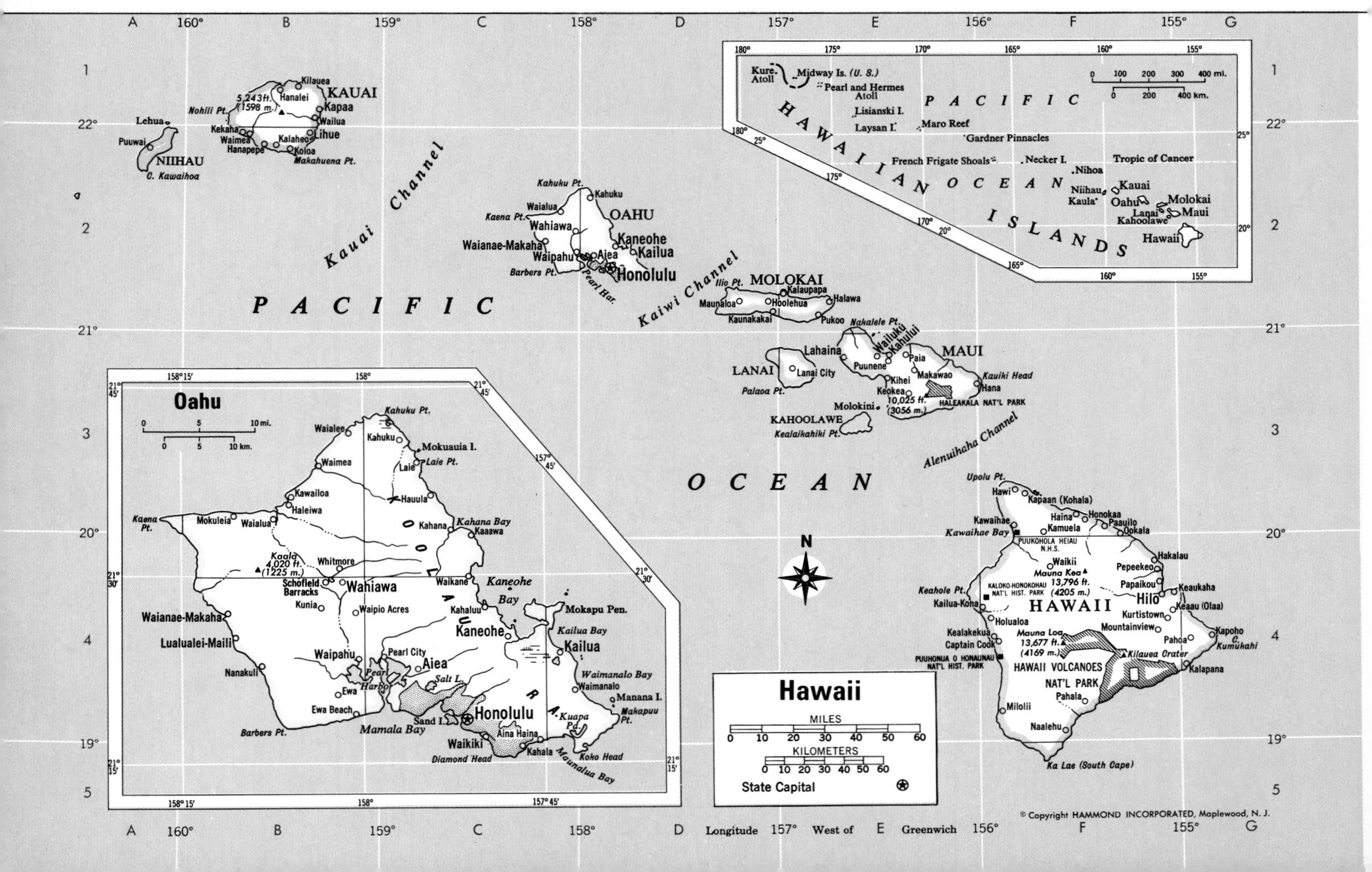
Hawaii
MILES
KILOMETERS
State Capital
Oahu
PACIFIC OCEAN
HAWAIIAN ISLANDS
Tropic of Cancer
KAUAI
NIIHAU
OAHU
MOLOKAI
LANAI
MAUI
KAHOOLAWE
HAWAII
Honolulu
Hilo
Kauai Channel
Kaiwi Channel
Alenuihaha Channel
HAWAII VOLCANOES NAT'L PARK
Mauna Kea 13,796 ft. (4205 m.)
Mauna Loa 13,677 ft. (4169 m.)
Longitude West of Greenwich

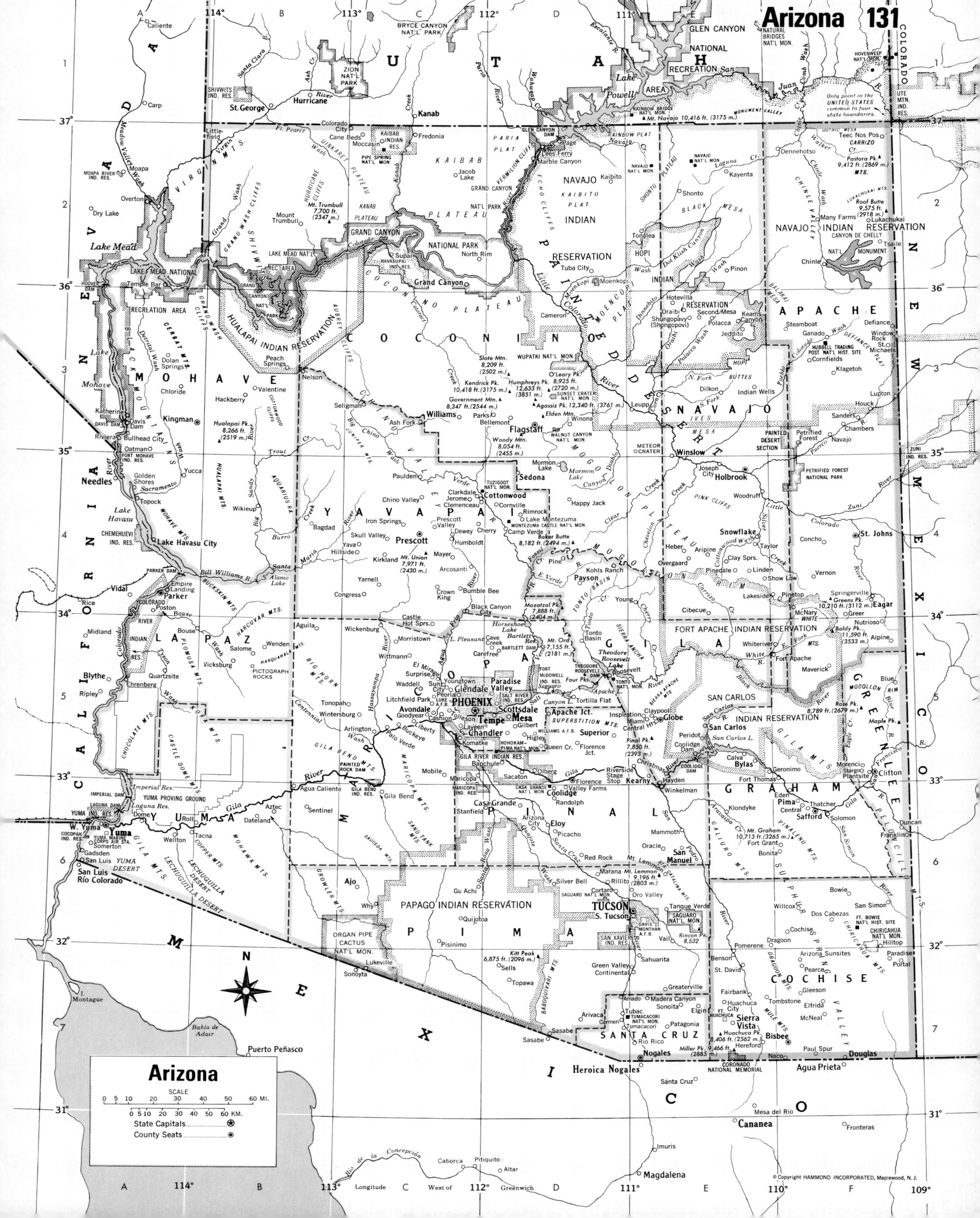
Arizona
SCALE
0 5 10 20 30 40 50 60 MI.
0 5 10 20 30 40 50 60 KM.
State Capitals
County Seats
U T A H
N E V A D A
C A L I F O R N I A
N E W M E X I C O
M E X I C O
C O L O R A D O
M O H A V E
C O C O N I N O
N A V A J O
A P A C H E
Y A V A P A I
L A P A Z
M A R I C O P A
G I L A
G R E E N L E E
G R A H A M
P I N A L
Y U M A
P I M A
S A N T A C R U Z
C O C H I S E
Only point in the UNITED STATES common to four state boundaries.
GLEN CANYON NATIONAL RECREATION AREA
Lake Powell
NAVAJO INDIAN RESERVATION
HOPI INDIAN RESERVATION
GRAND CANYON NATIONAL PARK
LAKE MEAD NATIONAL RECREATION AREA
HUALAPAI INDIAN RESERVATION
FORT APACHE INDIAN RESERVATION
SAN CARLOS INDIAN RESERVATION
PAPAGO INDIAN RESERVATION
PAINTED DESERT
PETRIFIED FOREST NATIONAL PARK
Lake Mead
Lake Mohave
Lake Havasu
PHOENIX
Tucson
Flagstaff
Prescott
Kingman
Yuma
Holbrook
St. Johns
Globe
Safford
Clifton
Florence
Nogales
Bisbee
Parker
Mesa
Tempe
Scottsdale
Glendale
Chandler
Douglas
Sierra Vista
Winslow
Williams
Sedona
Cottonwood
Page
Lake Havasu City
Needles
Blythe
Heroica Nogales
Agua Prieta
Cananea
Magdalena
Puerto Peñasco
Bahía de Adair
N
114° 113° 112° 111° 110° 109°
37° 36° 35° 34° 33° 32° 31°
Longitude West of Greenwich
A B C D E F
1 2 3 4 5 6 7
© Copyright HAMMOND INCORPORATED, Maplewood, N. J.

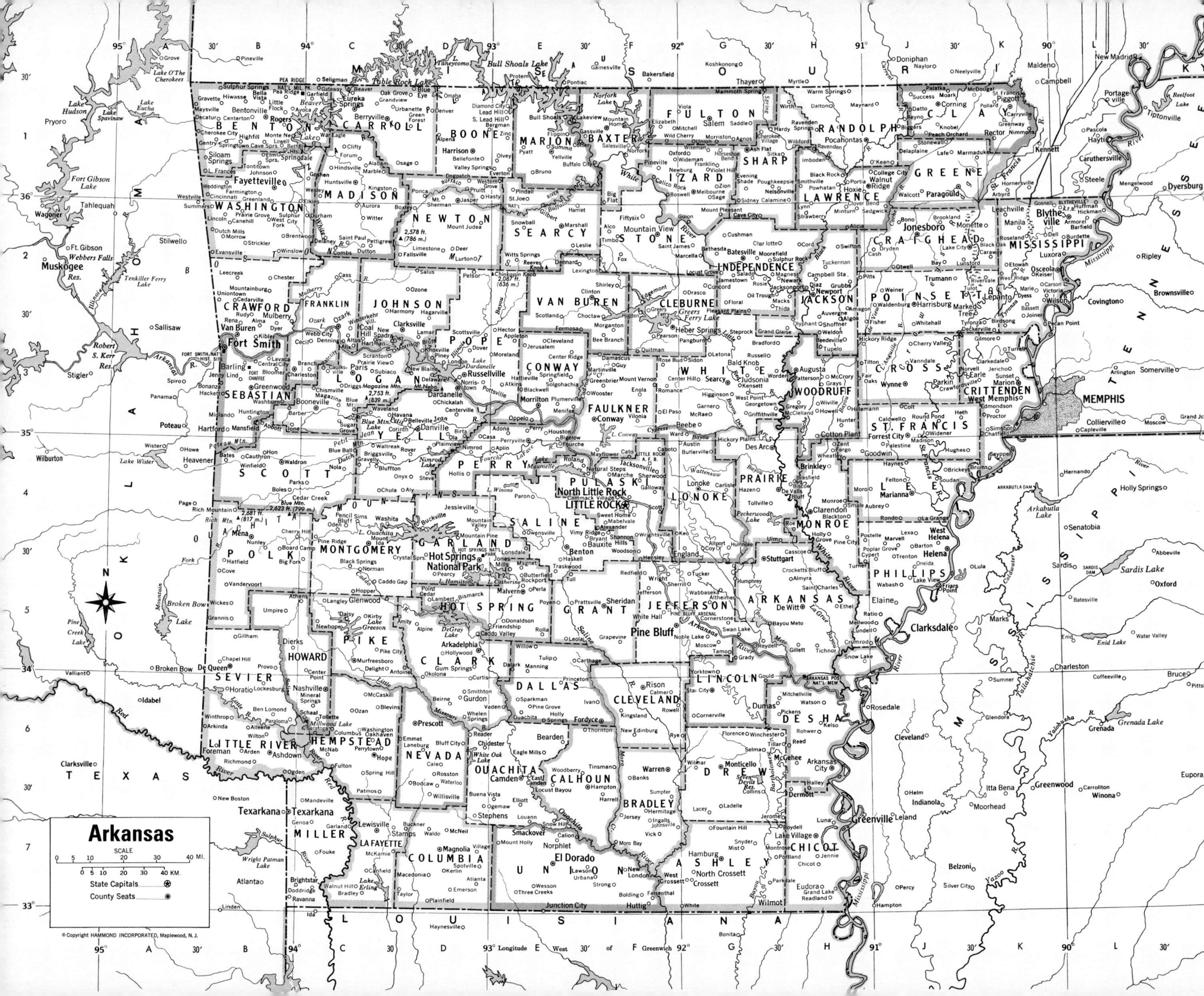
Arkansas
SCALE
0 5 10 20 30 40 MI.
0 5 10 20 30 40 KM.
State Capitals
County Seats
© Copyright HAMMOND INCORPORATED, Maplewood, N. J.
M I S S O U R I
O K L A H O M A
T E X A S
L O U I S I A N A
M I S S I S S I P P I
T E N N E S S E E
KY.
BENTON
CARROLL
BOONE
MARION
BAXTER
FULTON
RANDOLPH
CLAY
WASHINGTON
MADISON
NEWTON
SEARCY
STONE
IZARD
SHARP
LAWRENCE
GREENE
CRAIGHEAD
MISSISSIPPI
CRAWFORD
FRANKLIN
JOHNSON
POPE
VAN BUREN
CLEBURNE
INDEPENDENCE
JACKSON
POINSETT
SEBASTIAN
LOGAN
CONWAY
FAULKNER
WHITE
WOODRUFF
CROSS
CRITTENDEN
YELL
PERRY
PULASKI
LONOKE
PRAIRIE
ST. FRANCIS
SCOTT
LEE
MONROE
PHILLIPS
POLK
MONTGOMERY
GARLAND
SALINE
GRANT
JEFFERSON
ARKANSAS
HOT SPRING
SEVIER
HOWARD
PIKE
CLARK
DALLAS
CLEVELAND
LINCOLN
DESHA
LITTLE RIVER
HEMPSTEAD
NEVADA
OUACHITA
CALHOUN
BRADLEY
DREW
MILLER
LAFAYETTE
COLUMBIA
UNION
ASHLEY
CHICOT
LITTLE ROCK
North Little Rock
Fort Smith
Pine Bluff
Hot Springs National Park
MEMPHIS
93° Longitude West of Greenwich

California
SCALE
0 10 20 40 60 80 MI.
0 10 20 40 60 80 KM.
State Capitals
County Seats
Canals
San Francisco and Vicinity
Sacramento and Vicinity
Los Angeles and Vicinity
O R E G O N
N E V A D A
A R I Z O N A
M E X I C O
P A C I F I C O C E A N
Sacramento
San Francisco
Los Angeles
San Diego
Fresno
Bakersfield
Oakland
San Jose
Stockton
Lake Tahoe
Mojave Desert
Death Valley
Longitude 119° West of Greenwich 118°

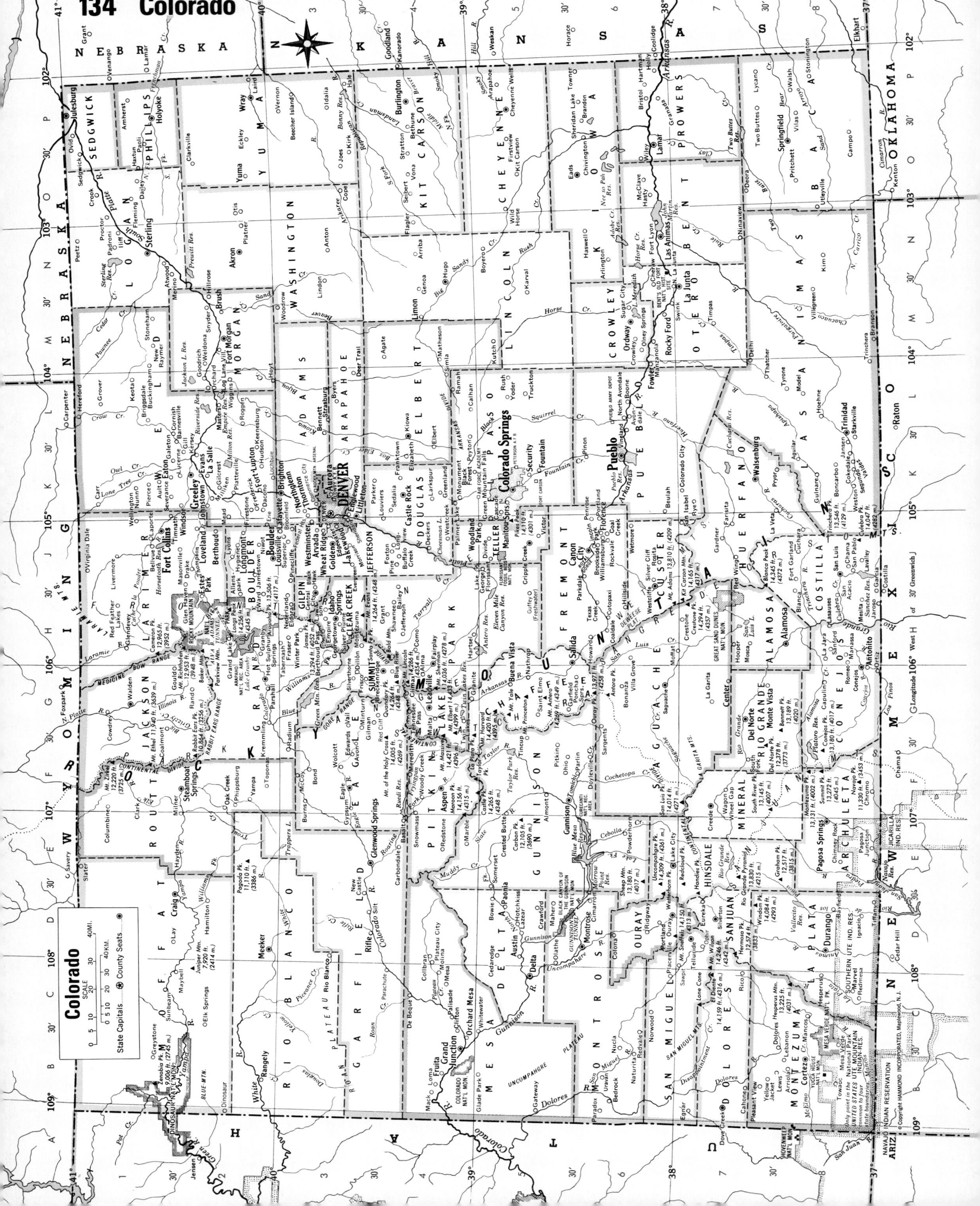
Colorado
SCALE
0 5 10 20 30 40MI.
0 5 10 20 30 40KM.
State Capitals ⊛ County Seats ◉
NEBRASKA
KANSAS
OKLAHOMA
NEW MEXICO
UTAH
WYOMING
ARIZ.
SEDGWICK
PHILLIPS
LOGAN
YUMA
WASHINGTON
MORGAN
WELD
LARIMER
JACKSON
ROUTT
MOFFAT
RIO BLANCO
GARFIELD
GRAND
EAGLE
PITKIN
LAKE
SUMMIT
CLEAR CREEK
GILPIN
BOULDER
JEFFERSON
DENVER
ADAMS
ARAPAHOE
DOUGLAS
ELBERT
LINCOLN
KIT CARSON
CHEYENNE
KIOWA
CROWLEY
OTERO
BENT
PROWERS
BACA
LAS ANIMAS
PUEBLO
EL PASO
TELLER
PARK
CHAFFEE
FREMONT
CUSTER
HUERFANO
COSTILLA
ALAMOSA
CONEJOS
RIO GRANDE
SAGUACHE
MINERAL
ARCHULETA
HINSDALE
GUNNISON
MESA
DELTA
MONTROSE
OURAY
SAN MIGUEL
DOLORES
SAN JUAN
LA PLATA
MONTEZUMA
Denver
Colorado Springs
Pueblo
Boulder
Fort Collins
Greeley
Grand Junction
Durango
Alamosa
Trinidad
Sterling
Lamar
La Junta
Leadville
Aspen
Glenwood Springs
Steamboat Springs
Gunnison
Montrose
Salida
Cañon City
Walsenburg
Limon
Burlington
Julesburg
Craig
Meeker
Rangely
Cortez
NAVAJO INDIAN RESERVATION
UTE MOUNTAIN INDIAN RES.
SOUTHERN UTE IND. RES.
JICARILLA IND. RES.
ROCKY MOUNTAIN NAT'L PARK
MESA VERDE NAT'L PK.
DINOSAUR NAT'L MON.
COLORADO NAT'L MON.
BLACK CANYON OF THE GUNNISON NAT'L MON.
GREAT SAND DUNES NAT'L MON.
CONTINENTAL DIVIDE
Longitude 106° West of Greenwich
© Copyright HAMMOND INCORPORATED, Maplewood, N.J.

Connecticut
SCALE
0 5 10 15 MI.
0 5 10 15 KM.
State Capitals ⊛
HARTFORD
SPRINGFIELD
WATERBURY
NEW HAVEN
BRIDGEPORT
STAMFORD
LITCHFIELD
HARTFORD
TOLLAND
WINDHAM
FAIRFIELD
NEW HAVEN
MIDDLESEX
NEW LONDON
MASSACHUSETTS
RHODE ISLAND
NEW YORK
LONG ISLAND SOUND
LONG ISLAND
GARDINERS BAY
ATLANTIC OCEAN
THE RACE
Mt. Frissell 2,380 ft. (725 m.)
Connecticut
Housatonic River
Naugatuck River
Quinebaug R.
Shetucket River
Thames
Farmington R.
New Britain
Meriden
Middletown
Bristol
Torrington
Danbury
Norwalk
Norwich
New London
Manchester
Stratford
Milford
West Haven
Ansonia
Derby
Shelton
Naugatuck
Willimantic
Rockville
Winsted
Putnam
Danielson
Westerly
Greenwich
Port Chester
White Plains
© Copyright HAMMOND INCORPORATED, Maplewood, N.J.

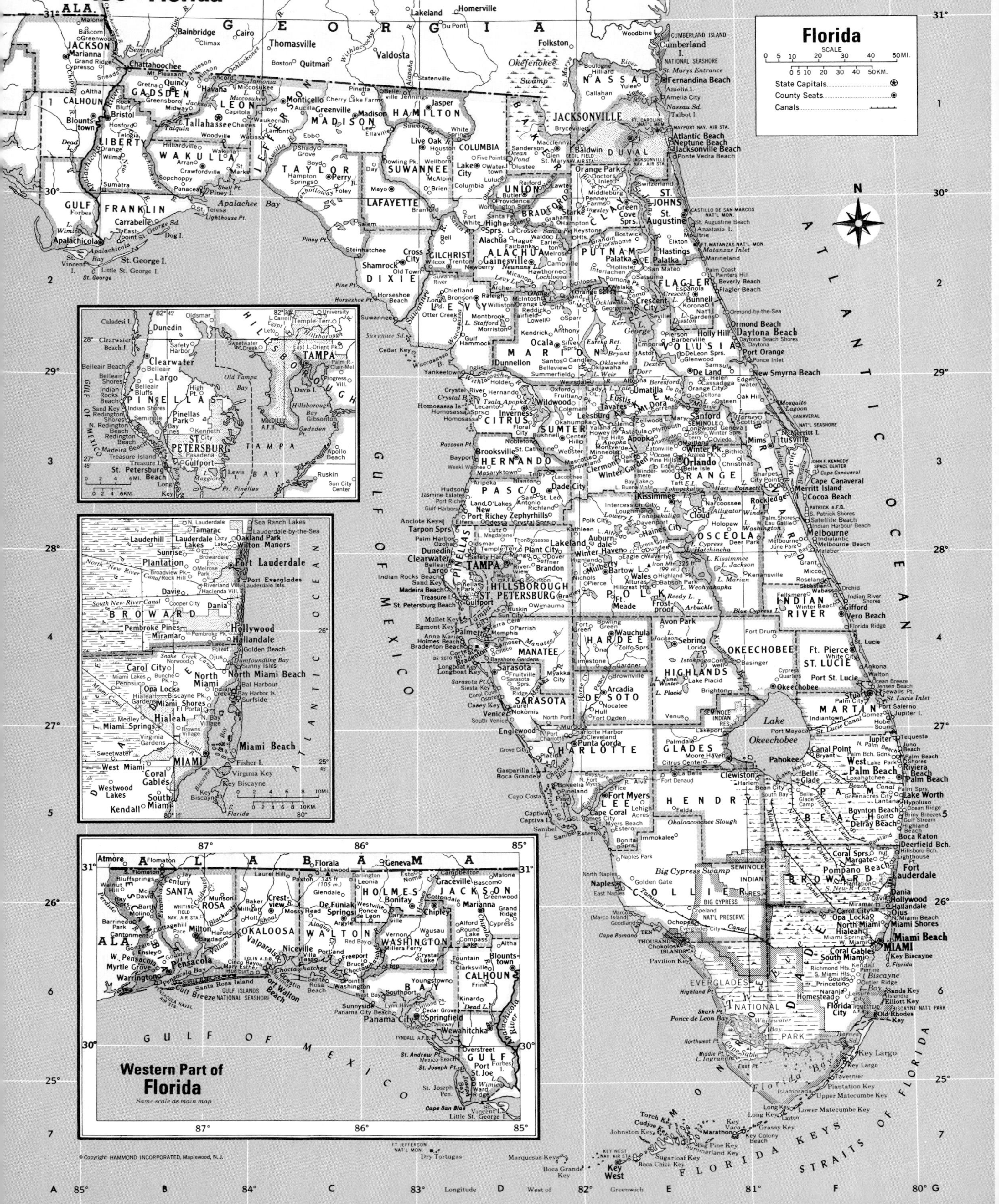
Florida
SCALE
0 5 10 20 30 40 50MI.
0 5 10 20 30 40 50KM.
State Capitals
County Seats
Canals
Western Part of
Florida
Same scale as main map
GULF OF MEXICO
ATLANTIC OCEAN
STRAITS OF FLORIDA
FLORIDA KEYS
GEORGIA
ALA.
ALABAMA
JACKSONVILLE
TAMPA
ST. PETERSBURG
MIAMI
Miami Beach
Tallahassee
Orlando
Fort Lauderdale
Hollywood
Pensacola
Panama City
Gainesville
Daytona Beach
West Palm Beach
Lake Okeechobee
EVERGLADES NATIONAL PARK
Longitude West of Greenwich

Georgia
SCALE
0 5 10 20 30 40 MI.
0 5 10 20 30 40 KM.
State Capitals
County Seats
TENNESSEE
NORTH CAROLINA
SOUTH CAROLINA
ALABAMA
FLORIDA
GULF OF MEXICO
ATLANTIC OCEAN
SEA ISLANDS
ATLANTA
Augusta
Macon
Columbus
Savannah
Albany
Athens
Valdosta
Brunswick
Tallahassee
Chattanooga
Jacksonville
Columbia
APALACHEE BAY
Longitude West of Greenwich
© Copyright HAMMOND INCORPORATED, Maplewood, N. J.

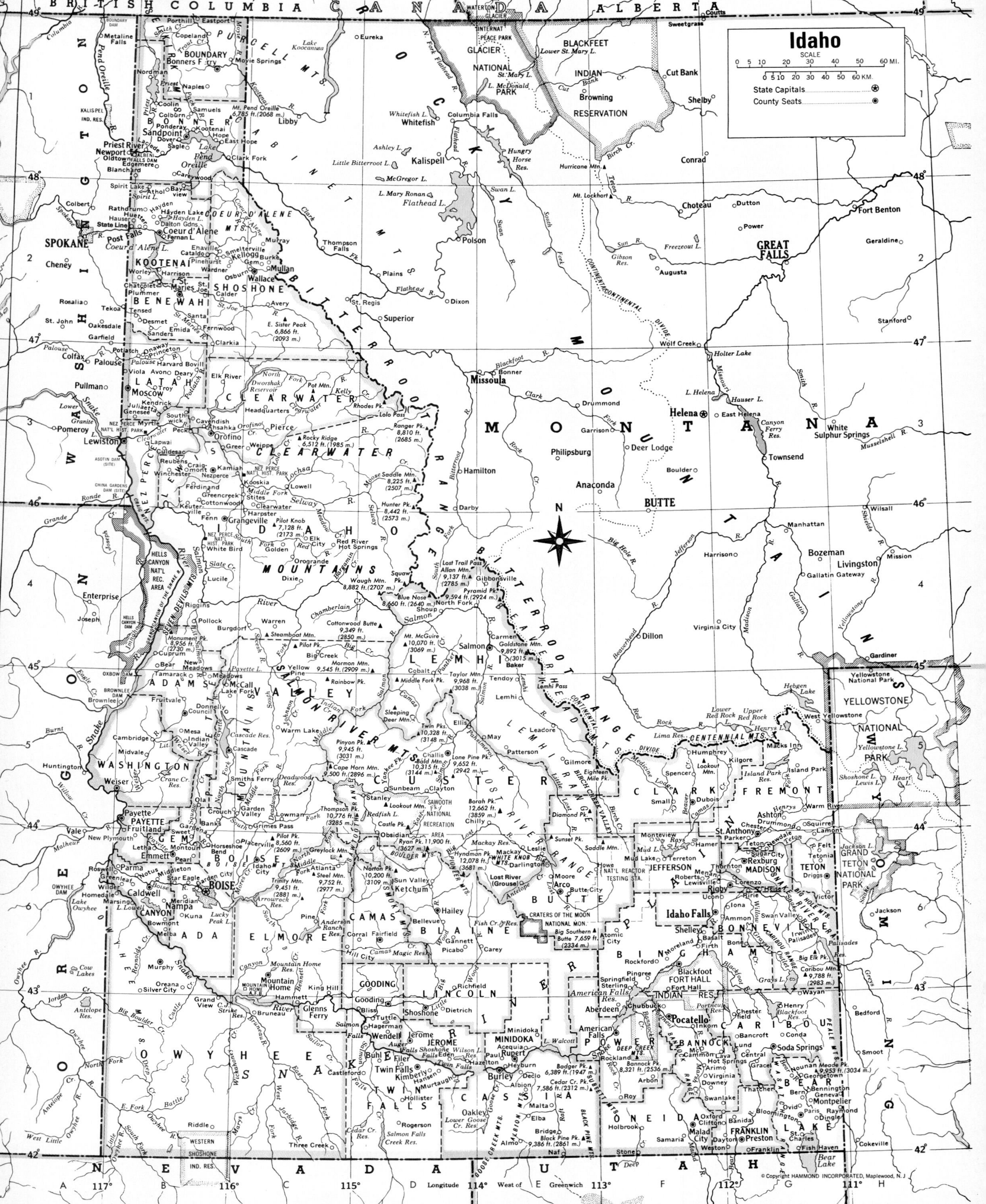
Idaho
SCALE
0 5 10 20 30 40 50 60 MI.
0 5 10 20 30 40 50 60 KM.
State Capitals
County Seats
BRITISH COLUMBIA
CANADA
ALBERTA
WASHINGTON
OREGON
NEVADA
UTAH
WYOMING
MONTANA
IDAHO
BOUNDARY
BONNER
KOOTENAI
BENEWAH
SHOSHONE
LATAH
CLEARWATER
NEZ PERCE
LEWIS
IDAHO
ADAMS
VALLEY
WASHINGTON
PAYETTE
GEM
BOISE
ADA
CANYON
ELMORE
CAMAS
BLAINE
CUSTER
LEMHI
BUTTE
CLARK
FREMONT
JEFFERSON
MADISON
TETON
BONNEVILLE
BINGHAM
BANNOCK
CARIBOU
BEAR LAKE
FRANKLIN
ONEIDA
POWER
CASSIA
TWIN FALLS
JEROME
GOODING
LINCOLN
MINIDOKA
OWYHEE
Boise
Helena
Spokane
Great Falls
Butte
Missoula
Lewiston
Coeur d'Alene
Sandpoint
Moscow
Grangeville
Salmon
Idaho Falls
Pocatello
Twin Falls
Nampa
Caldwell
Mountain Home
Ketchum
Hailey
Blackfoot
Rexburg
Burley
Rupert
BITTERROOT RANGE
SALMON RIVER MTS.
SAWTOOTH NAT'L RECREATION AREA
CRATERS OF THE MOON NATIONAL MON.
GLACIER NATIONAL PARK
YELLOWSTONE NATIONAL PARK
GRAND TETON NATIONAL PARK
HELLS CANYON NAT'L REC. AREA
NAT'L REACTOR TESTING STA.
CONTINENTAL DIVIDE
Longitude West of Greenwich
49°
48°
47°
46°
45°
44°
43°
42°
117°
116°
115°
114°
113°
112°
111°

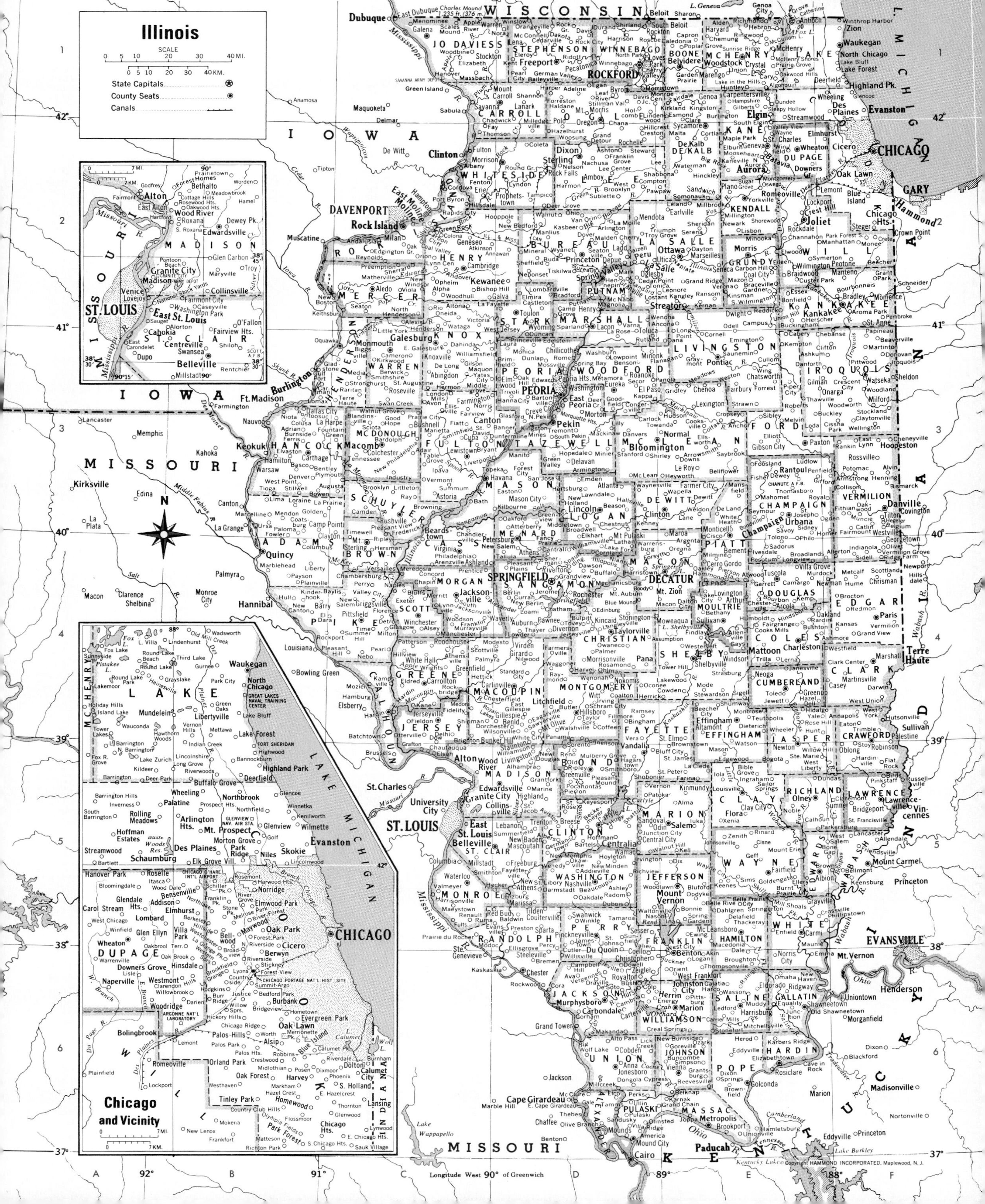
Illinois
SCALE
0 5 10 20 30 40 MI.
0 5 10 20 30 40 KM.
State Capitals
County Seats
Canals
Chicago and Vicinity
WISCONSIN
IOWA
MISSOURI
KENTUCKY
INDIANA
LAKE MICHIGAN
SPRINGFIELD
CHICAGO
ST. LOUIS
PEORIA
ROCKFORD
DAVENPORT
EVANSVILLE
GARY
Longitude West 90° of Greenwich
Copyright HAMMOND INCORPORATED, Maplewood, N. J.

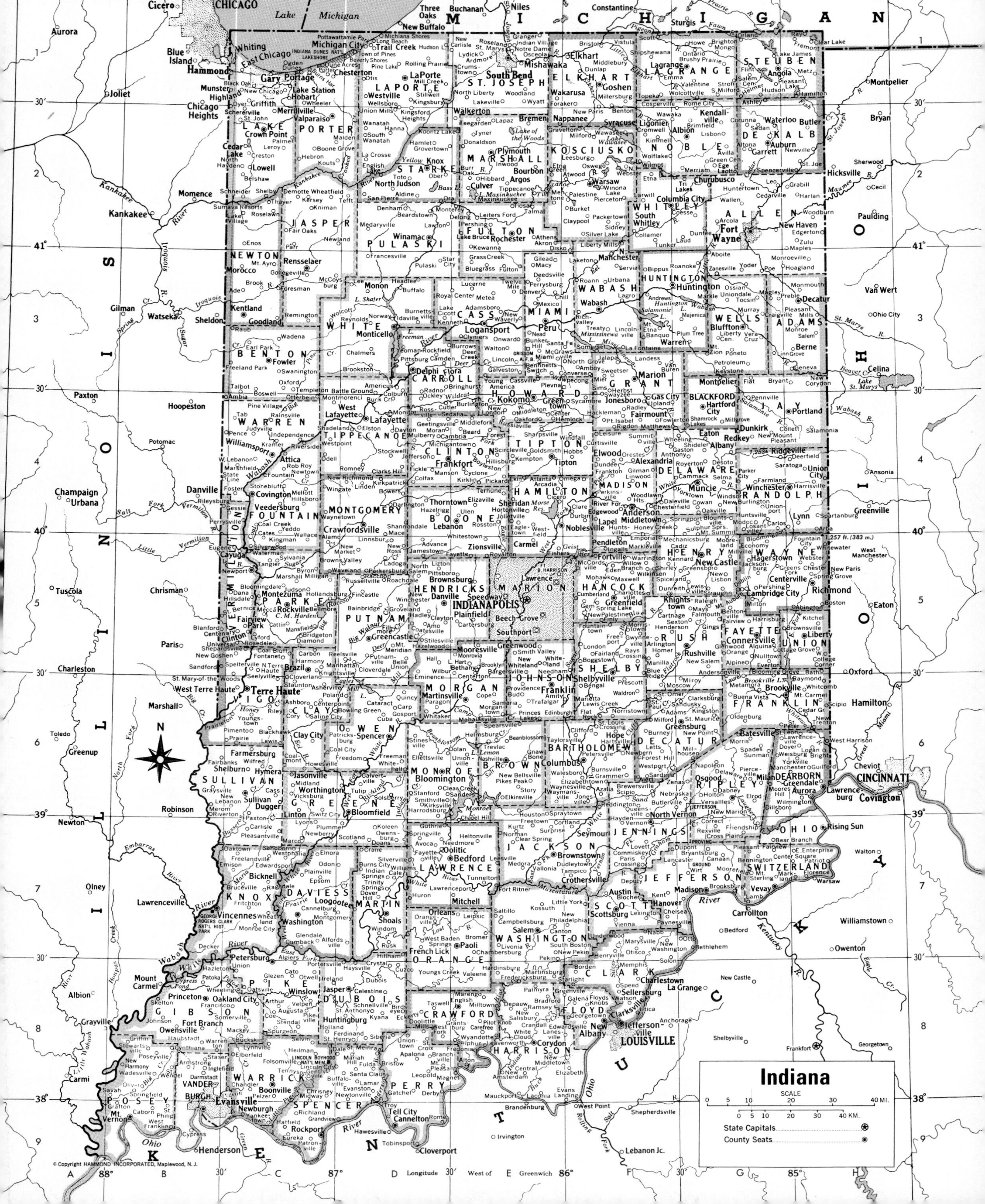
Indiana
SCALE
0 5 10 20 30 40 MI.
0 5 10 20 30 40 KM.
State Capitals
County Seats
INDIANAPOLIS
LOUISVILLE
CINCINNATI
CHICAGO
Lake Michigan
MICHIGAN
OHIO
ILLINOIS
KENTUCKY
LAKE
PORTER
LAPORTE
ST. JOSEPH
ELKHART
LAGRANGE
STEUBEN
NOBLE
DE KALB
KOSCIUSKO
MARSHALL
STARKE
JASPER
NEWTON
PULASKI
FULTON
WHITLEY
ALLEN
HUNTINGTON
WABASH
MIAMI
CASS
WHITE
BENTON
CARROLL
HOWARD
GRANT
WELLS
ADAMS
BLACKFORD
JAY
WARREN
TIPPECANOE
CLINTON
TIPTON
MADISON
DELAWARE
RANDOLPH
FOUNTAIN
MONTGOMERY
BOONE
HAMILTON
HENRY
WAYNE
VERMILLION
PARKE
PUTNAM
HENDRICKS
MARION
HANCOCK
RUSH
FAYETTE
UNION
VIGO
CLAY
MORGAN
JOHNSON
SHELBY
DECATUR
FRANKLIN
OWEN
MONROE
BROWN
BARTHOLOMEW
JENNINGS
RIPLEY
DEARBORN
OHIO
SULLIVAN
GREENE
LAWRENCE
JACKSON
JEFFERSON
SWITZERLAND
KNOX
DAVIESS
MARTIN
ORANGE
WASHINGTON
SCOTT
CLARK
FLOYD
HARRISON
CRAWFORD
DUBOIS
PIKE
GIBSON
POSEY
VANDERBURGH
WARRICK
SPENCER
PERRY
Longitude West of Greenwich

Iowa
SCALE
0 5 10 20 30 40 MI.
0 5 10 20 30 40 KM.
State Capitals
County Seats
M I N N E S O T A
SOUTH DAKOTA
N E B R A S K A
M I S S O U R I
I L L I N O I S
WISCONSIN
LYON
OSCEOLA
DICKINSON
EMMET
KOSSUTH
WINNEBAGO
WORTH
MITCHELL
HOWARD
WINNESHIEK
ALLAMAKEE
SIOUX
O'BRIEN
CLAY
PALO ALTO
HANCOCK
CERRO GORDO
FLOYD
CHICKASAW
FAYETTE
CLAYTON
PLYMOUTH
CHEROKEE
BUENA VISTA
POCAHONTAS
HUMBOLDT
WRIGHT
FRANKLIN
BUTLER
BREMER
BLACK HAWK
BUCHANAN
DELAWARE
DUBUQUE
WOODBURY
IDA
SAC
CALHOUN
WEBSTER
HAMILTON
HARDIN
GRUNDY
MONONA
CRAWFORD
CARROLL
GREENE
BOONE
STORY
MARSHALL
TAMA
BENTON
LINN
JONES
JACKSON
CLINTON
HARRISON
SHELBY
AUDUBON
GUTHRIE
DALLAS
POLK
JASPER
POWESHIEK
IOWA
JOHNSON
CEDAR
SCOTT
MUSCATINE
POTTAWATTAMIE
CASS
ADAIR
MADISON
WARREN
MARION
MAHASKA
KEOKUK
WASHINGTON
LOUISA
MILLS
MONTGOMERY
ADAMS
UNION
CLARKE
LUCAS
MONROE
WAPELLO
JEFFERSON
HENRY
DES MOINES
FREMONT
PAGE
TAYLOR
RINGGOLD
DECATUR
WAYNE
APPANOOSE
DAVIS
VAN BUREN
LEE
DES MOINES
SIOUX CITY
OMAHA
Council Bluffs
Fort Dodge
Waterloo
Cedar Falls
Dubuque
CEDAR RAPIDS
Iowa City
DAVENPORT
Rock Island
Burlington
Fort Madison
Keokuk
Ottumwa
Mason City
Ames
Marshalltown
Clinton
Muscatine
Galesburg
Albert Lea
Austin
Worthington
Fairmont
Blue Earth
Missouri
Mississippi
Des Moines
Iowa
Cedar
Longitude West of Greenwich
© Copyright HAMMOND INCORPORATED, Maplewood, N. J.

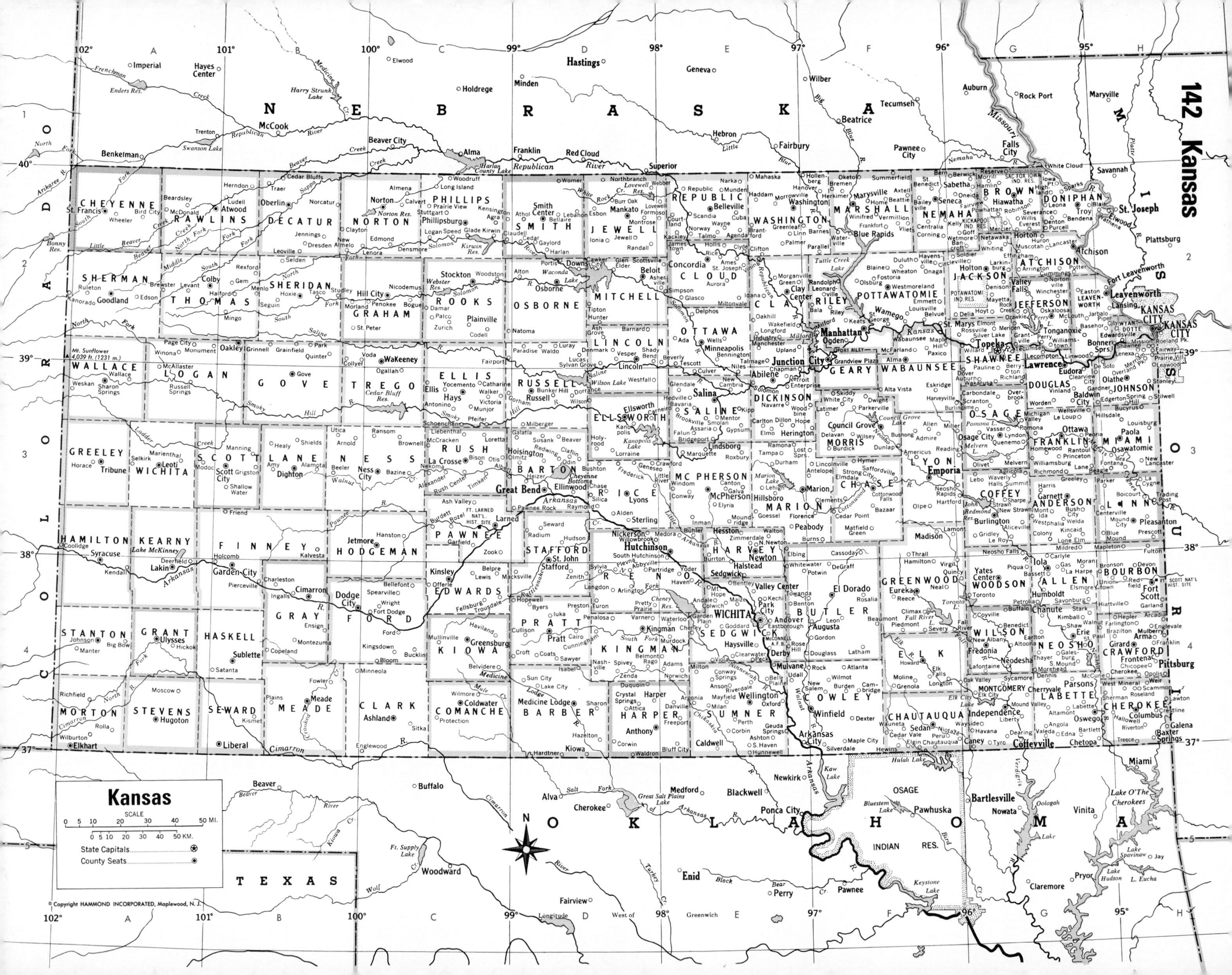
Kansas
SCALE
0 5 10 20 30 40 50 MI.
0 5 10 20 30 40 50 KM.
State Capitals
County Seats
© Copyright HAMMOND INCORPORATED, Maplewood, N. J.
NEBRASKA
COLORADO
OKLAHOMA
TEXAS
MISSOURI
CHEYENNE
RAWLINS
DECATUR
NORTON
PHILLIPS
SMITH
JEWELL
REPUBLIC
WASHINGTON
MARSHALL
NEMAHA
BROWN
DONIPHAN
SHERMAN
THOMAS
SHERIDAN
GRAHAM
ROOKS
OSBORNE
MITCHELL
CLOUD
CLAY
RILEY
POTTAWATOMIE
JACKSON
ATCHISON
JEFFERSON
LEAVENWORTH
WYANDOTTE
WALLACE
LOGAN
GOVE
TREGO
ELLIS
RUSSELL
LINCOLN
OTTAWA
DICKINSON
GEARY
WABAUNSEE
SHAWNEE
DOUGLAS
JOHNSON
GREELEY
WICHITA
SCOTT
LANE
NESS
RUSH
BARTON
ELLSWORTH
SALINE
MC PHERSON
MARION
MORRIS
CHASE
LYON
OSAGE
FRANKLIN
MIAMI
HAMILTON
KEARNY
FINNEY
HODGEMAN
PAWNEE
STAFFORD
RICE
RENO
HARVEY
BUTLER
GREENWOOD
COFFEY
ANDERSON
LINN
WOODSON
ALLEN
BOURBON
STANTON
GRANT
HASKELL
GRAY
FORD
EDWARDS
KIOWA
PRATT
KINGMAN
SEDGWICK
ELK
WILSON
NEOSHO
CRAWFORD
MORTON
STEVENS
SEWARD
MEADE
CLARK
COMANCHE
BARBER
HARPER
SUMNER
COWLEY
CHAUTAUQUA
MONTGOMERY
LABETTE
CHEROKEE

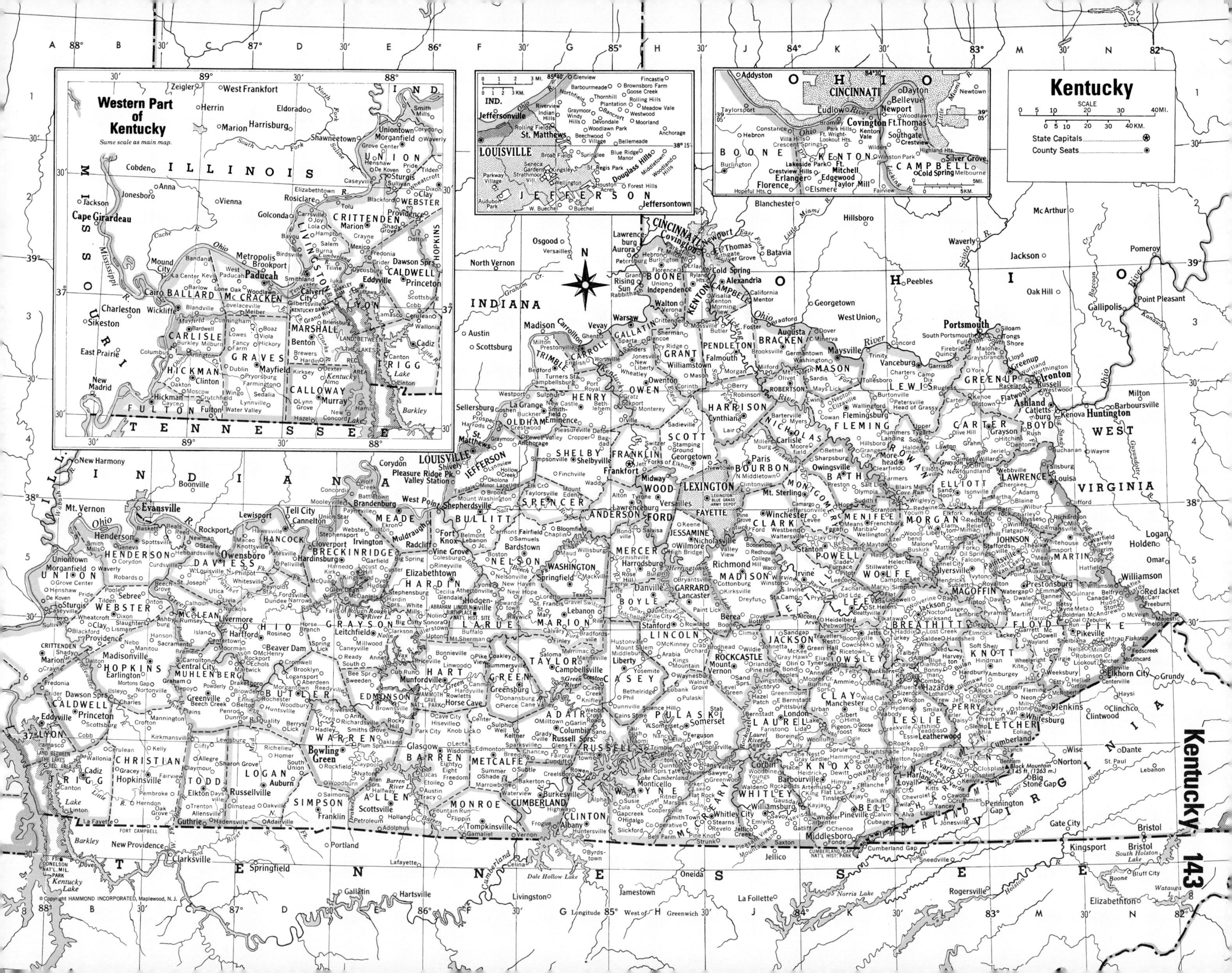
Kentucky
SCALE
0 5 10 20 30 40 MI.
0 5 10 20 30 40 KM.
State Capitals
County Seats
Western Part of Kentucky
Same scale as main map.
LOUISVILLE
CINCINNATI
ILLINOIS
INDIANA
OHIO
WEST VIRGINIA
VIRGINIA
TENNESSEE
MISSOURI
Frankfort
Lexington
Louisville
Covington
Paducah
Bowling Green
Owensboro
Ashland
© Copyright HAMMOND INCORPORATED, Maplewood, N.J.

Louisiana
SCALE
0 5 10 20 30 40 MI.
0 5 10 20 30 40 KM.
State Capitals
Parish Seats
Canals
New Orleans, Baton Rouge and Vicinity
0 5 10 15 20 MI.
0 5 10 15 20 KM.
ARKANSAS
TEXAS
MISSISSIPPI
ALABAMA
GULF OF MEXICO
Longitude 91° West of Greenwich
Delta of the Mississippi
Shreveport
Baton Rouge
New Orleans
Lake Pontchartrain
Lake Maurepas
Mobile Bay
Chandeleur Sound
Breton Sound
Atchafalaya Bay
Vermilion Bay

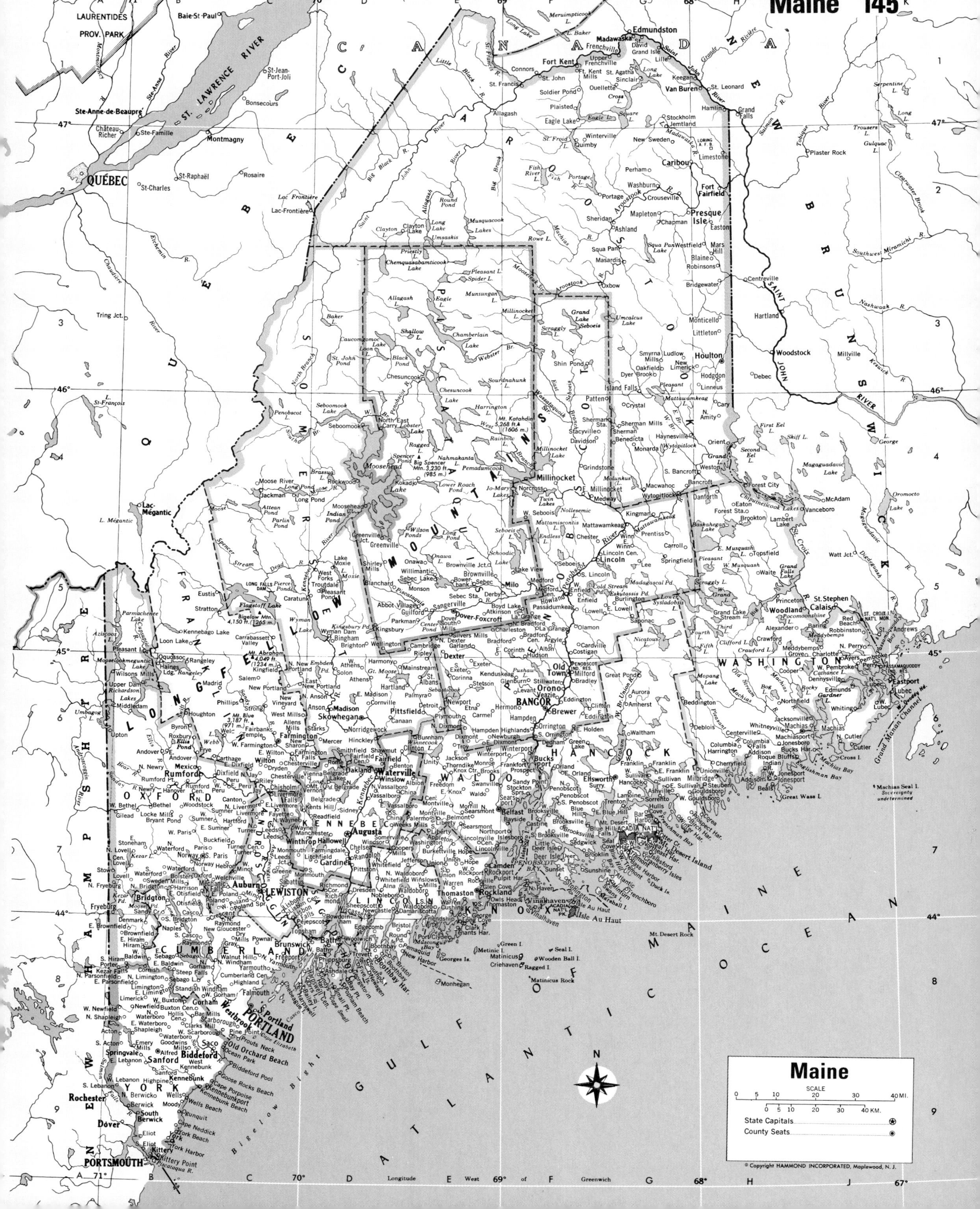
Maine
SCALE
0 5 10 20 30 40 MI.
0 5 10 20 30 40 KM.
State Capitals
County Seats
ATLANTIC OCEAN
GULF OF MAINE
Longitude West of Greenwich

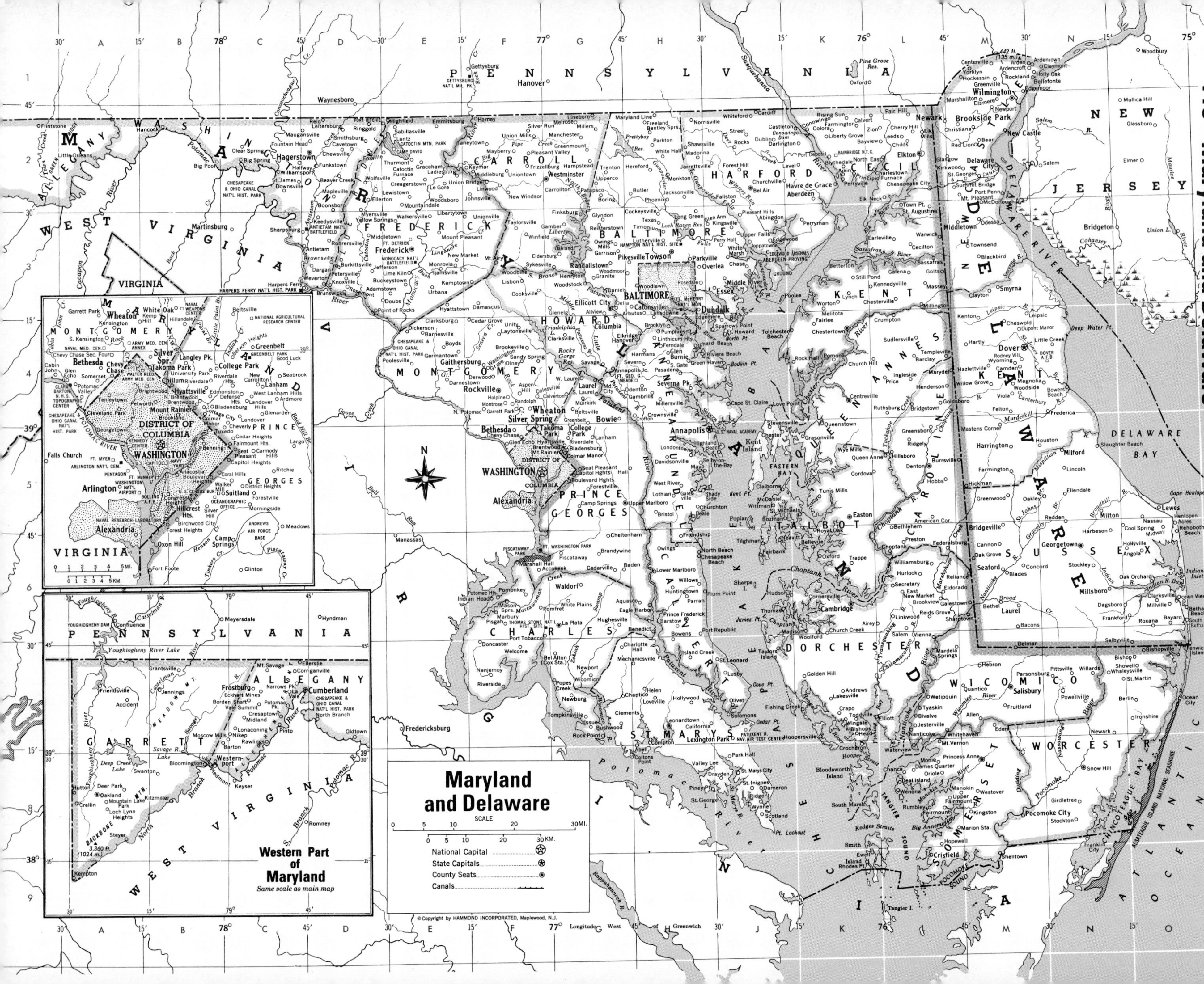

Maryland
and Delaware
SCALE
0 5 10 20 30 MI.
0 5 10 20 30 KM.
National Capital
State Capitals
County Seats
Canals
Western Part
of
Maryland
Same scale as main map
PENNSYLVANIA
WEST VIRGINIA
VIRGINIA
NEW JERSEY
MARYLAND
DELAWARE
DISTRICT OF COLUMBIA
WASHINGTON
BALTIMORE
ATLANTIC OCEAN
DELAWARE BAY
CHESAPEAKE BAY
ASSATEAGUE ISLAND NATIONAL SEASHORE
Longitude West of Greenwich

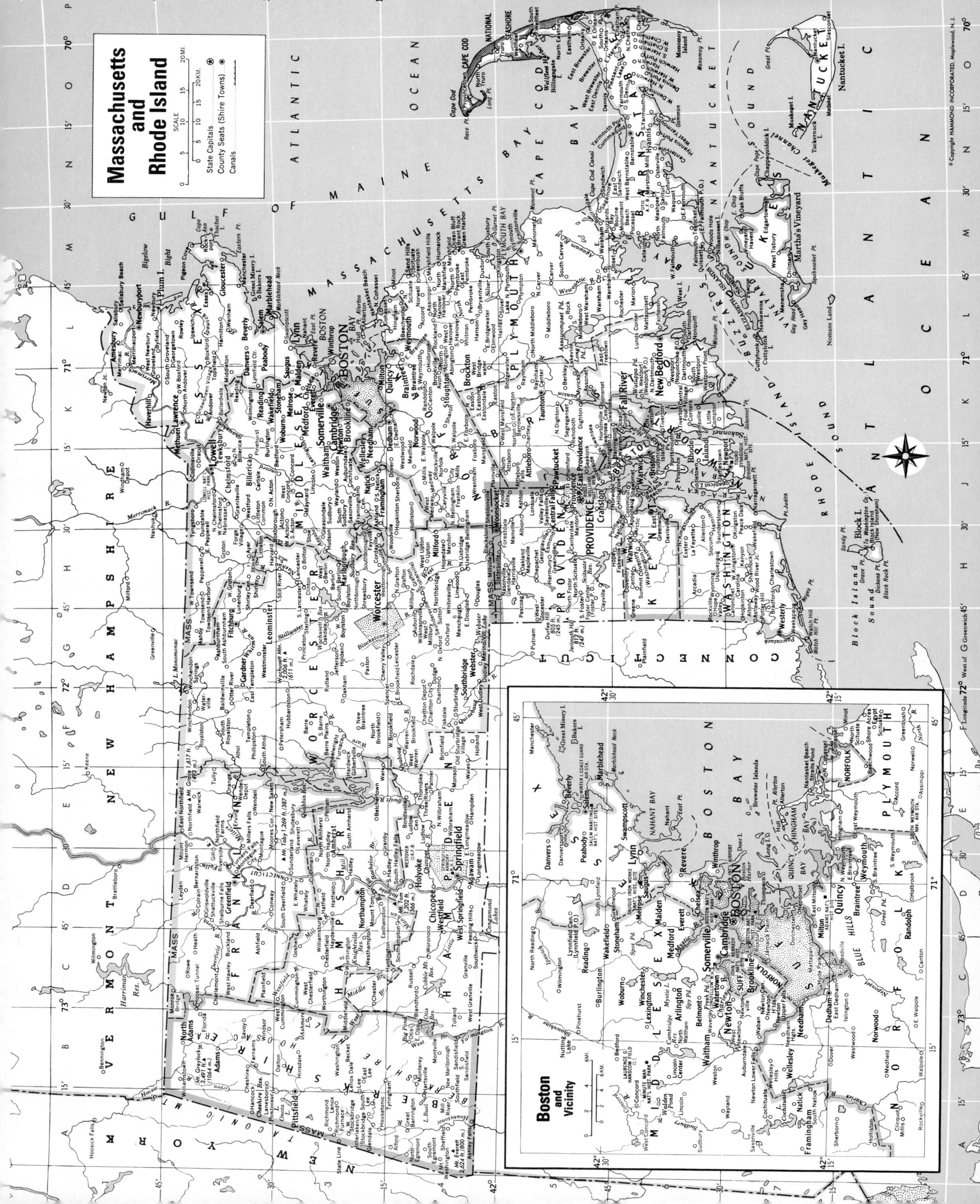
Massachusetts and Rhode Island
SCALE
0 5 10 15 20 MI.
0 5 10 15 20 KM.
State Capitals
County Seats (Shire Towns)
Canals
Boston and Vicinity
ATLANTIC OCEAN
GULF OF MAINE
MASSACHUSETTS BAY
CAPE COD BAY
NANTUCKET SOUND
RHODE ISLAND SOUND
BLOCK ISLAND SOUND
BUZZARDS BAY
BOSTON BAY
VERMONT
NEW HAMPSHIRE
NEW YORK
CONNECTICUT
BERKSHIRE
FRANKLIN
HAMPSHIRE
HAMPDEN
WORCESTER
MIDDLESEX
ESSEX
SUFFOLK
NORFOLK
BRISTOL
PLYMOUTH
BARNSTABLE
DUKES
NANTUCKET
PROVIDENCE
KENT
WASHINGTON
NEWPORT
BOSTON
PROVIDENCE
Longitude 72° West of Greenwich

Michigan
SCALE
0 5 10 20 30 40 50 MI.
0 5 10 20 30 40 50 KM.
State Capitals
County Seats
Canals
ISLE ROYALE NATIONAL PARK
L. SUPERIOR
Same scale as main map
Same scale as main map.
LAKE SUPERIOR
LAKE MICHIGAN
LAKE HURON
LAKE ERIE
LAKE ST. CLAIR
WISCONSIN
ONTARIO
INDIANA
OHIO
ILLINOIS
CANADA
KEWEENAW
HOUGHTON
BARAGA
MARQUETTE
IRON
DICKINSON
MENOMINEE
DELTA
SCHOOLCRAFT
ALGER
LUCE
CHIPPEWA
MACKINAC
ONTONAGON
GOGEBIC
EMMET
CHEBOYGAN
PRESQUE ISLE
CHARLEVOIX
ANTRIM
OTSEGO
MONTMORENCY
ALPENA
LEELANAU
GRAND TRAVERSE
KALKASKA
CRAWFORD
OSCODA
ALCONA
BENZIE
MANISTEE
WEXFORD
MISSAUKEE
ROSCOMMON
OGEMAW
IOSCO
MASON
LAKE
OSCEOLA
CLARE
GLADWIN
ARENAC
OCEANA
NEWAYGO
MECOSTA
ISABELLA
MIDLAND
BAY
HURON
MUSKEGON
MONTCALM
GRATIOT
SAGINAW
TUSCOLA
SANILAC
OTTAWA
KENT
IONIA
CLINTON
SHIAWASSEE
GENESEE
LAPEER
ST. CLAIR
ALLEGAN
BARRY
EATON
INGHAM
LIVINGSTON
OAKLAND
MACOMB
VAN BUREN
KALAMAZOO
CALHOUN
JACKSON
WASHTENAW
WAYNE
BERRIEN
CASS
ST. JOSEPH
BRANCH
HILLSDALE
LENAWEE
MONROE
Lansing
DETROIT
GRAND RAPIDS
WINDSOR
MILWAUKEE
TOLEDO
SOUTH BEND
Green Bay
North Channel
Straits of Mackinac
Saginaw Bay
Thunder Bay
POINT PELEE NAT'L PARK
PICTURED ROCKS NAT'L LAKESHORE
SLEEPING BEAR DUNES NAT'L LAKESHORE
Mt. Curwood 1,980 ft. (604 m.)
Longitude West of Greenwich
© Copyright HAMMOND INCORPORATED, Maplewood, N. J.

Minnesota
SCALE
0 5 10 20 30 40 50 MI.
0 5 10 20 30 40 50 KM.
State Capitals
County Seats
Northeastern Part of Minnesota
Same scale as main map
ONTARIO
MANITOBA
NORTH DAKOTA
SOUTH DAKOTA
WISCONSIN
IOWA
LAKE SUPERIOR
Lake of the Woods
KITTSON
ROSEAU
LAKE OF THE WOODS
MARSHALL
KOOCHICHING
PENNINGTON
RED LAKE
BELTRAMI
POLK
CLEARWATER
ITASCA
SAINT LOUIS
LAKE
COOK
NORMAN
MAHNOMEN
HUBBARD
CLAY
BECKER
CASS
CARLTON
AITKIN
CROW WING
WILKIN
OTTER TAIL
WADENA
PINE
TODD
MORRISON
MILLE LACS
KANABEC
GRANT
DOUGLAS
TRAVERSE
STEVENS
POPE
BENTON
BIG STONE
SWIFT
STEARNS
SHERBURNE
ISANTI
CHISAGO
ANOKA
KANDIYOHI
MEEKER
WRIGHT
WASHINGTON
CHIPPEWA
LAC QUI PARLE
HENNEPIN
RAMSEY
YELLOW MEDICINE
RENVILLE
MC LEOD
CARVER
SCOTT
DAKOTA
LINCOLN
LYON
REDWOOD
SIBLEY
NICOLLET
LE SUEUR
RICE
GOODHUE
WABASHA
BROWN
PIPESTONE
MURRAY
COTTONWOOD
WATONWAN
BLUE EARTH
WASECA
STEELE
DODGE
OLMSTED
WINONA
ROCK
NOBLES
JACKSON
MARTIN
FARIBAULT
FREEBORN
MOWER
FILLMORE
HOUSTON
MINNEAPOLIS
ST. PAUL
DULUTH
Superior
Rochester
St. Cloud
Moorhead
Fargo
Grand Forks
International Falls
© Copyright HAMMOND INCORPORATED, Maplewood, N. J.

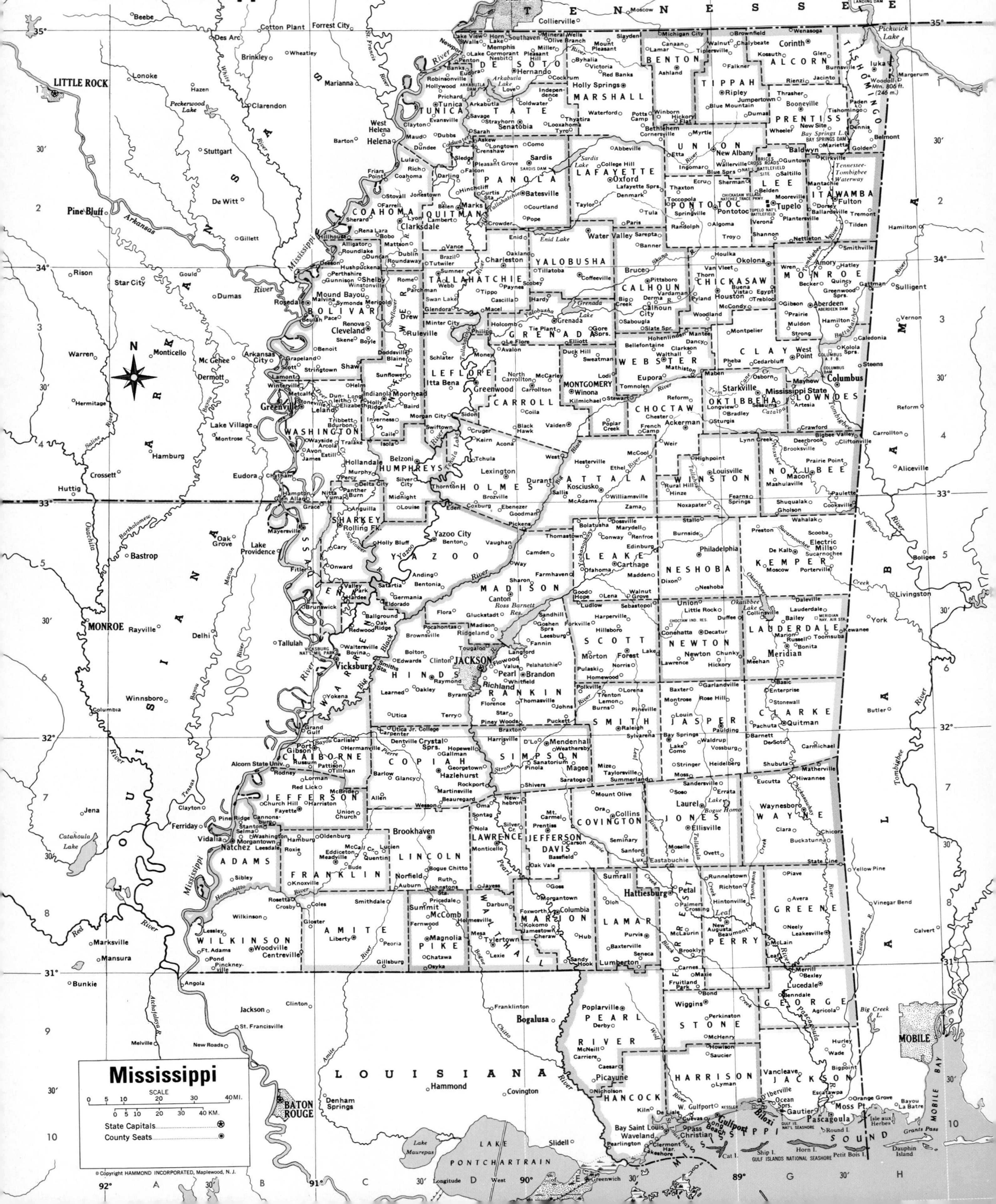
Mississippi
SCALE
0 5 10 20 30 40 MI.
0 5 10 20 30 40 KM.
State Capitals
County Seats
© Copyright HAMMOND INCORPORATED, Maplewood, N. J.
TENNESSEE
ARKANSAS
LOUISIANA
ALABAMA
MEMPHIS
LITTLE ROCK
JACKSON
BATON ROUGE
MOBILE
MONROE
Pine Bluff
Greenville
Vicksburg
Natchez
Hattiesburg
Meridian
Columbus
Tupelo
Gulfport
Biloxi
Pascagoula
LAKE PONTCHARTRAIN
MISSISSIPPI SOUND
GULF ISLANDS NATIONAL SEASHORE
MOBILE BAY
DE SOTO
MARSHALL
BENTON
TIPPAH
ALCORN
TISHOMINGO
TUNICA
TATE
PRENTISS
UNION
PANOLA
LAFAYETTE
LEE
ITAWAMBA
COAHOMA
QUITMAN
PONTOTOC
YALOBUSHA
CALHOUN
CHICKASAW
MONROE
TALLAHATCHIE
BOLIVAR
GRENADA
CLAY
SUNFLOWER
LEFLORE
CARROLL
MONTGOMERY
WEBSTER
OKTIBBEHA
LOWNDES
CHOCTAW
WASHINGTON
HUMPHREYS
HOLMES
ATTALA
WINSTON
NOXUBEE
SHARKEY
YAZOO
LEAKE
NESHOBA
KEMPER
MADISON
ISSAQUENA
WARREN
HINDS
RANKIN
SCOTT
NEWTON
LAUDERDALE
SMITH
JASPER
CLARKE
CLAIBORNE
COPIAH
SIMPSON
JEFFERSON
COVINGTON
JONES
WAYNE
ADAMS
FRANKLIN
LINCOLN
LAWRENCE
JEFFERSON DAVIS
WILKINSON
AMITE
PIKE
WALTHALL
MARION
LAMAR
FORREST
PERRY
GREENE
PEARL RIVER
STONE
GEORGE
HANCOCK
HARRISON
JACKSON

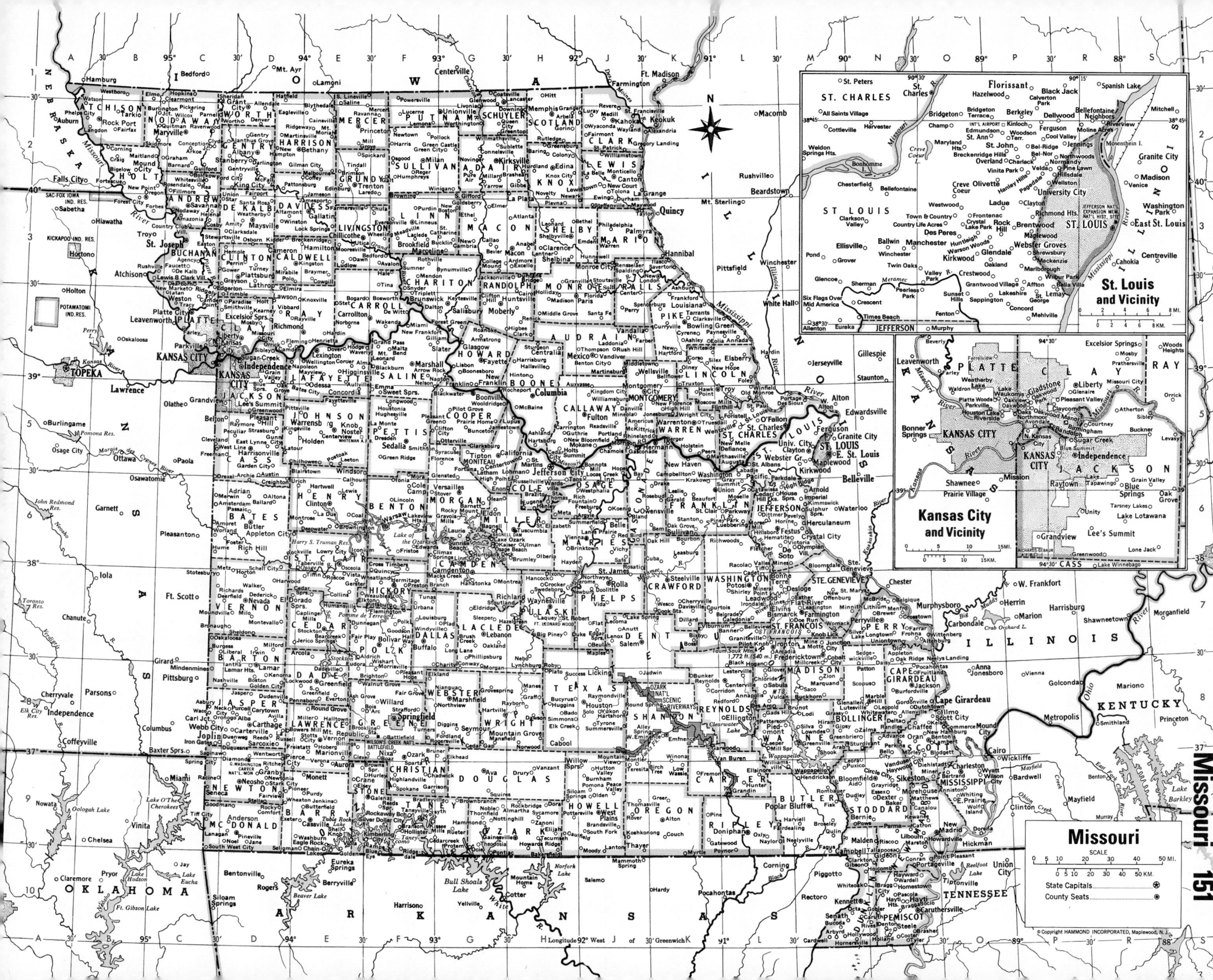
Missouri
SCALE
0 5 10 20 30 40 50 MI.
0 5 10 20 30 40 50 KM.
State Capitals
County Seats
© Copyright HAMMOND INCORPORATED, Maplewood, N.J.
St. Louis and Vicinity
Kansas City and Vicinity
0 5 10 15 MI.
0 5 10 15 KM.
0 2 4 6 8 MI.
0 2 4 6 8 KM.
IOWA
ILLINOIS
KENTUCKY
TENNESSEE
ARKANSAS
OKLAHOMA
KANSAS
NEBRASKA
Longitude 92° West of Greenwich

Montana
SCALE
0 5 10 20 40 60 80 MI.
0 5 10 20 40 60 80 KM.
State Capitals
County Seats
© Copyright HAMMOND INCORPORATED, Maplewood, N.J.
BRITISH COLUMBIA
ALBERTA
SASKATCHEWAN
CANADA
NORTH DAKOTA
S. DAKOTA
WYOMING
LINCOLN
FLATHEAD
GLACIER
TOOLE
LIBERTY
HILL
BLAINE
PHILLIPS
VALLEY
DANIELS
SHERIDAN
ROOSEVELT
SANDERS
LAKE
PONDERA
TETON
CHOUTEAU
MINERAL
MISSOULA
LEWIS AND CLARK
CASCADE
JUDITH BASIN
FERGUS
PETROLEUM
GARFIELD
MC CONE
RICHLAND
DAWSON
WIBAUX
PRAIRIE
RAVALLI
GRANITE
POWELL
MEAGHER
WHEATLAND
GOLDEN VALLEY
MUSSELSHELL
ROSEBUD
CUSTER
FALLON
DEER LODGE
SILVER BOW
JEFFERSON
BROADWATER
SWEET GRASS
STILLWATER
YELLOWSTONE
TREASURE
POWDER RIVER
CARTER
BEAVERHEAD
MADISON
GALLATIN
PARK
CARBON
BIG HORN
BLACKFEET INDIAN RESERVATION
FLATHEAD INDIAN RESERVATION
FORT BELKNAP INDIAN RES.
CROW INDIAN RESERVATION
NORTHERN CHEYENNE IND. RES.
ROCKY BOY'S IND. RES.
GLACIER NATIONAL PARK
YELLOWSTONE NATIONAL PARK
BITTERROOT RANGE
BIG BELT MTS.
BEARTOOTH RANGE
BIGHORN MTS.
CONTINENTAL DIVIDE
Longitude West of Greenwich

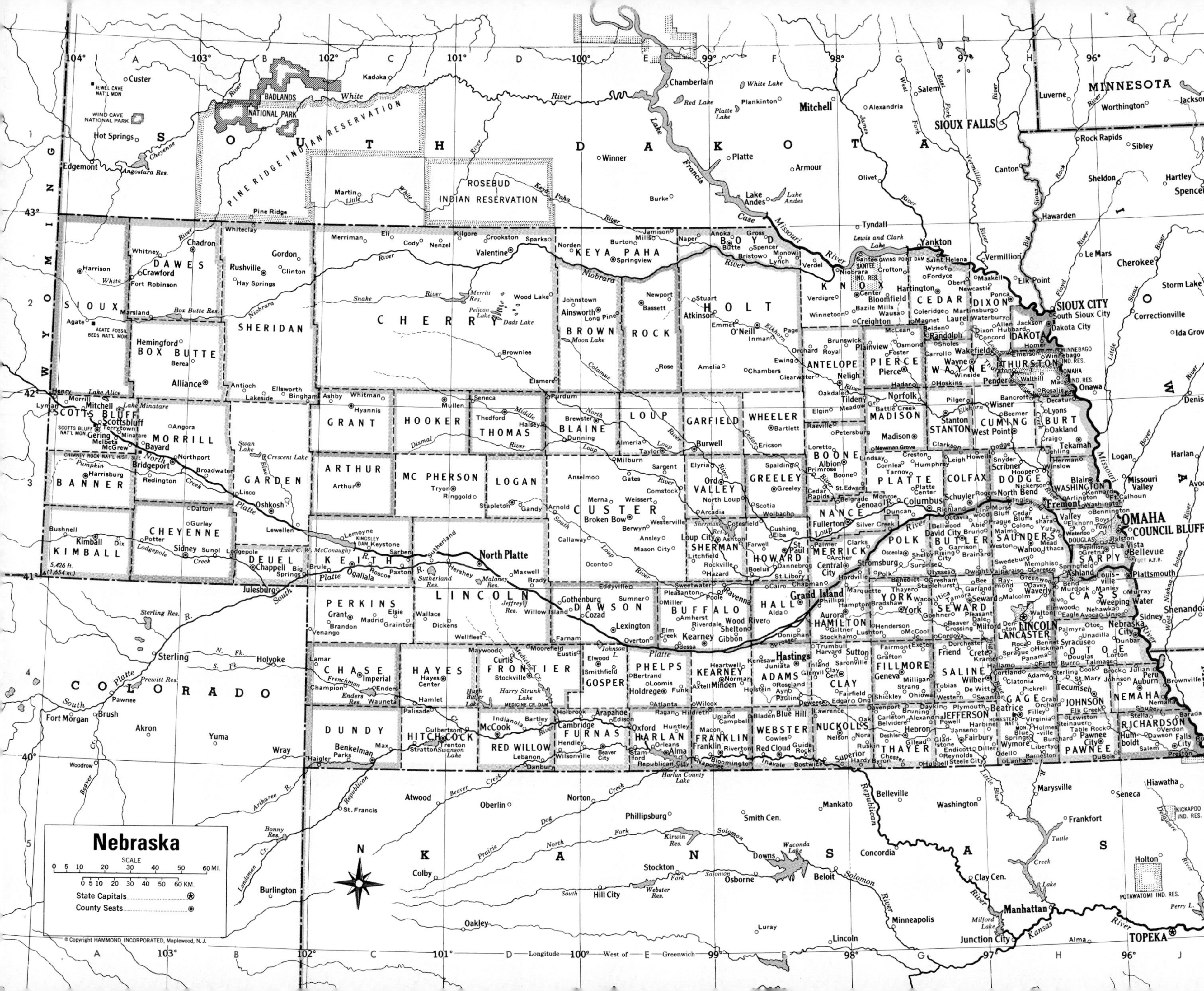
Nebraska
SCALE
0 5 10 20 30 40 50 60 MI.
0 5 10 20 30 40 50 60 KM.
State Capitals
County Seats
© Copyright HAMMOND INCORPORATED, Maplewood, N.J.
SOUTH DAKOTA
WYOMING
COLORADO
KANSAS
MISSOURI
IOWA
MINNESOTA
PINE RIDGE INDIAN RESERVATION
ROSEBUD INDIAN RESERVATION
BADLANDS NATIONAL PARK
SIOUX
DAWES
SHERIDAN
CHERRY
KEYA PAHA
BOYD
BROWN
ROCK
HOLT
KNOX
CEDAR
DIXON
DAKOTA
BOX BUTTE
SCOTTS BLUFF
MORRILL
BANNER
KIMBALL
CHEYENNE
GARDEN
DEUEL
GRANT
HOOKER
THOMAS
BLAINE
LOUP
GARFIELD
WHEELER
ANTELOPE
PIERCE
WAYNE
THURSTON
ARTHUR
MC PHERSON
LOGAN
CUSTER
VALLEY
GREELEY
BOONE
MADISON
STANTON
CUMING
BURT
PLATTE
COLFAX
DODGE
WASHINGTON
KEITH
LINCOLN
PERKINS
SHERMAN
HOWARD
NANCE
MERRICK
POLK
BUTLER
SAUNDERS
DOUGLAS
SARPY
DAWSON
BUFFALO
HALL
HAMILTON
YORK
SEWARD
LANCASTER
CASS
OTOE
CHASE
HAYES
FRONTIER
GOSPER
PHELPS
KEARNEY
ADAMS
CLAY
FILLMORE
SALINE
GAGE
JOHNSON
NEMAHA
DUNDY
HITCHCOCK
RED WILLOW
FURNAS
HARLAN
FRANKLIN
WEBSTER
NUCKOLLS
THAYER
JEFFERSON
PAWNEE
RICHARDSON
LINCOLN
OMAHA
COUNCIL BLUFFS
Grand Island
North Platte
Hastings
Kearney
Scottsbluff
Fremont
Columbus
Norfolk
Beatrice
SIOUX CITY
SIOUX FALLS
TOPEKA
Manhattan
Yankton
Mitchell
Missouri
Platte
Niobrara
Republican
Loup
Elkhorn
Longitude West of Greenwich

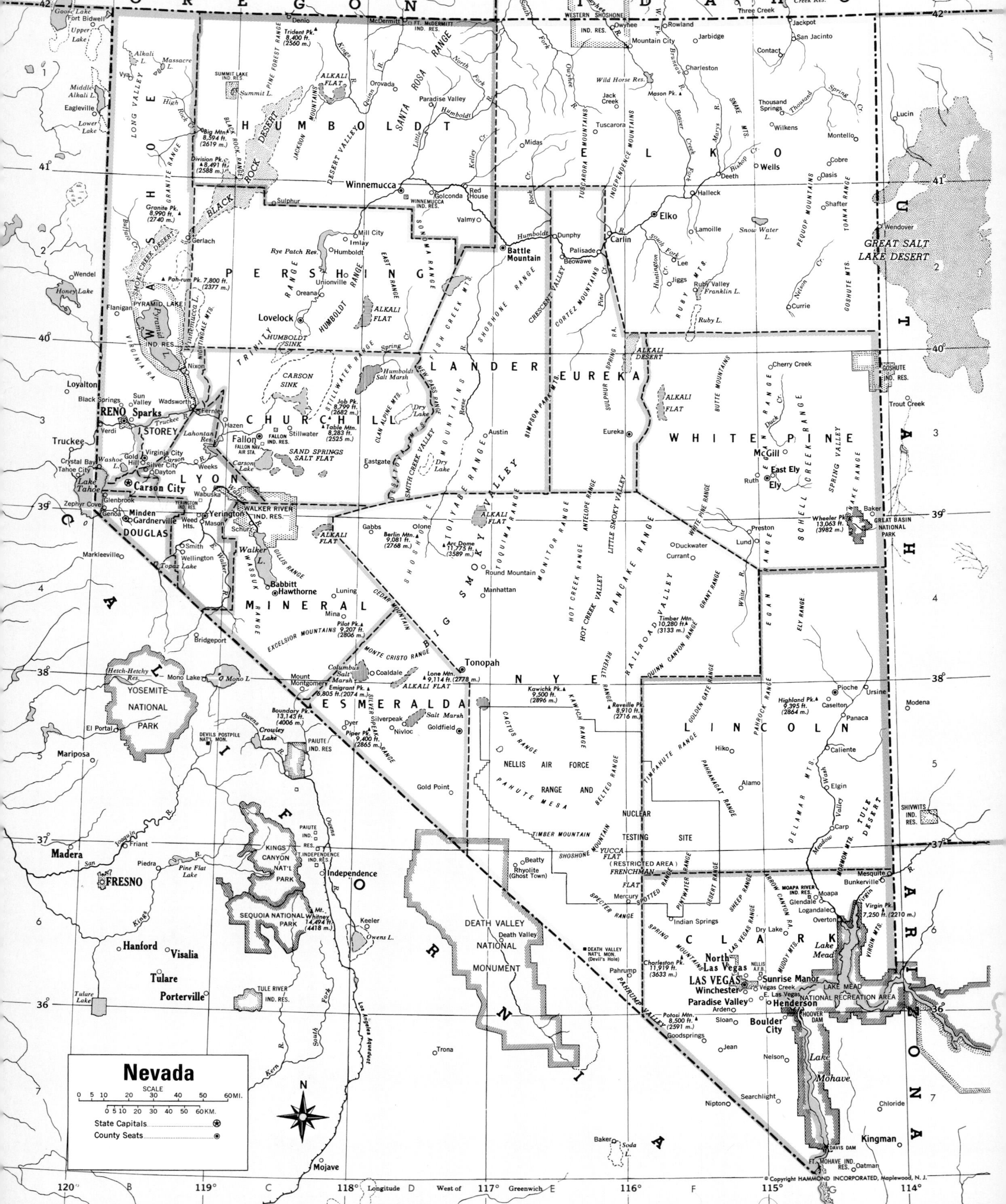
Nevada
SCALE
0 5 10 20 30 40 50 60 MI.
0 5 10 20 30 40 50 60 KM.
State Capitals
County Seats
N
OREGON
IDAHO
UTAH
ARIZONA
CALIFORNIA
HUMBOLDT
ELKO
PERSHING
LANDER
EUREKA
WHITE PINE
CHURCHILL
STOREY
LYON
DOUGLAS
MINERAL
ESMERALDA
NYE
LINCOLN
CLARK
WASHOE
CARSON CITY
RENO
Sparks
Carson City
Winnemucca
Elko
Wells
Battle Mountain
Lovelock
Fallon
Yerington
Minden
Gardnerville
Hawthorne
Babbitt
Tonopah
Goldfield
Eureka
Austin
Ely
East Ely
McGill
Pioche
Caliente
LAS VEGAS
North Las Vegas
Henderson
Boulder City
Winchester
Sunrise Manor
Paradise Valley
Mesquite
Bunkerville
Denio
McDermitt
Jackpot
Mountain City
Owyhee
Carlin
Gerlach
Lake Tahoe
Pyramid L.
Walker L.
Lake Mead
Lake Mohave
HOOVER DAM
DAVIS DAM
LAKE MEAD NATIONAL RECREATION AREA
GREAT BASIN NATIONAL PARK
Wheeler Pk. 13,063 ft. (3982 m.)
Boundary Pk. 13,143 ft. (4006 m.)
Charleston Pk. 11,919 ft. (3633 m.)
NELLIS AIR FORCE RANGE AND PAHUTE MESA
NUCLEAR TESTING SITE
BLACK ROCK DESERT
GREAT SALT LAKE DESERT
CARSON SINK
HUMBOLDT SINK
SMOKE CREEK DESERT
BIG SMOKY VALLEY
RUBY MTS.
DEATH VALLEY NATIONAL MONUMENT
YOSEMITE NATIONAL PARK
KINGS CANYON NAT'L PARK
SEQUOIA NATIONAL PARK
FRESNO
Madera
Visalia
Hanford
Tulare
Porterville
Independence
Bridgeport
Truckee
Loyalton
Kingman
Mojave
Longitude West of Greenwich
© Copyright HAMMOND INCORPORATED, Maplewood, N. J.

New Hampshire and Vermont
SCALE
0 5 10 15 20 25 MI.
0 5 10 15 20 25 KM.
State Capitals
County Seats
CANADA
QUÉBEC
NEW YORK
MASSACHUSETTS
MAINE
ATLANTIC OCEAN
Longitude 72° West of Greenwich
© Copyright HAMMOND INCORPORATED, Maplewood, N. J.

New Jersey
SCALE
0 5 10 15 20 MI.
0 5 10 15 20 KM.
State Capitals
County Seats
Canals
Copyright HAMMOND INCORPORATED, Maplewood, N. J.
Longitude 75° West of Greenwich
TRENTON
PHILADELPHIA
CAMDEN
NEW YORK
JERSEY CITY
NEWARK
ELIZABETH
PATERSON
Atlantic City
Wilmington
Chester
PENNSYLVANIA
NEW YORK
MARYLAND
DELAWARE
DELAWARE BAY
ATLANTIC OCEAN
SUSSEX
PASSAIC
BERGEN
WARREN
MORRIS
ESSEX
HUDSON
UNION
HUNTERDON
SOMERSET
MIDDLESEX
MERCER
MONMOUTH
OCEAN
BURLINGTON
CAMDEN
GLOUCESTER
SALEM
CUMBERLAND
ATLANTIC
CAPE MAY
Long Island
Staten Island
DELAWARE WATER GAP NATIONAL RECREATION AREA
High Point 1,803 ft. (550 m.)
Sandy Hook
Cape May
Barnegat Bay
Hudson River
Delaware River

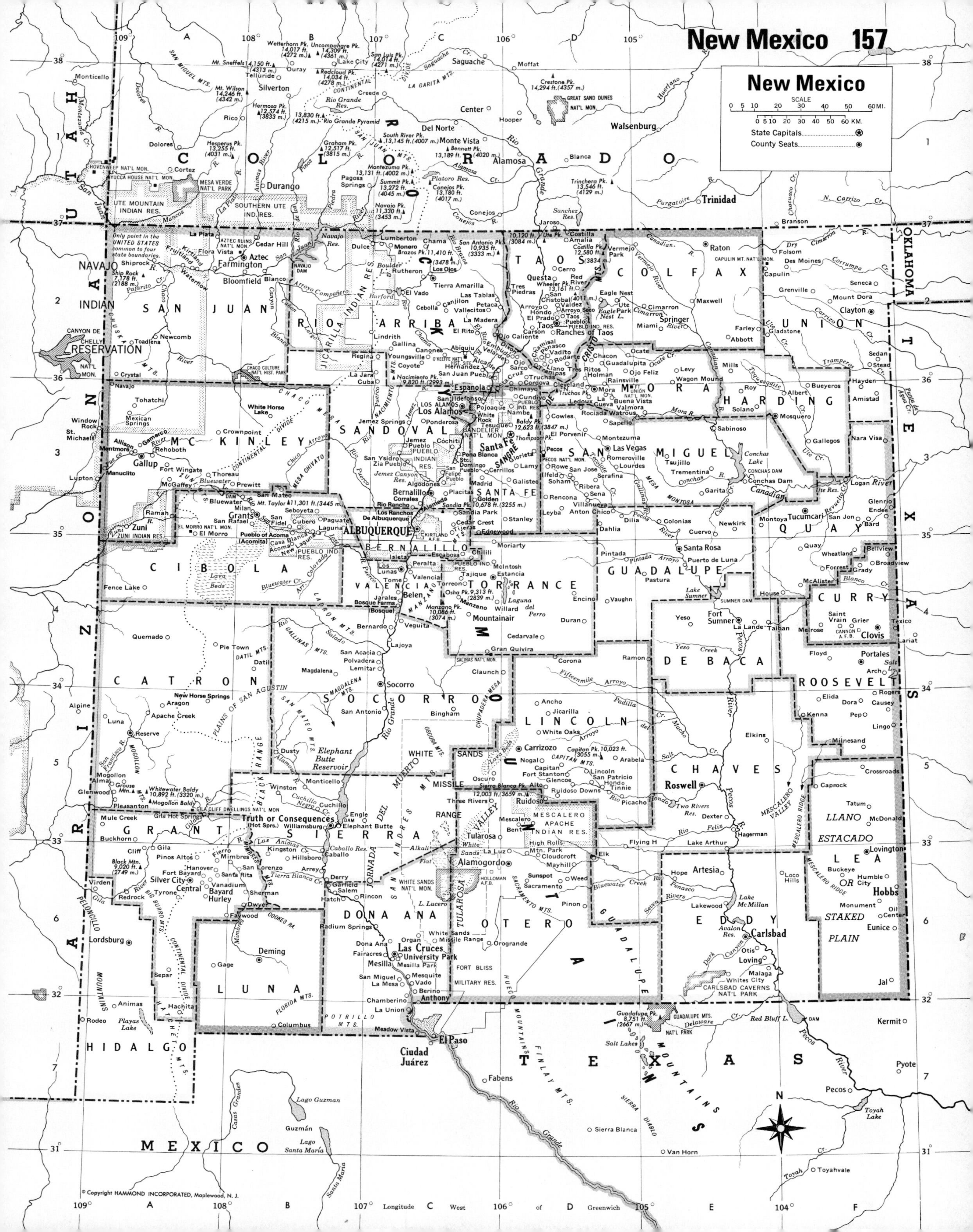
New Mexico
SCALE
0 5 10 20 30 40 50 60 MI.
0 5 10 20 30 40 50 60 KM.
State Capitals
County Seats
COLORADO
UTAH
ARIZONA
OKLAHOMA
TEXAS
MEXICO
SAN JUAN
RIO ARRIBA
TAOS
COLFAX
UNION
MC KINLEY
SANDOVAL
LOS ALAMOS
SANTA FE
MORA
HARDING
SAN MIGUEL
QUAY
CIBOLA
BERNALILLO
VALENCIA
TORRANCE
GUADALUPE
CURRY
DE BACA
ROOSEVELT
CATRON
SOCORRO
LINCOLN
CHAVES
GRANT
SIERRA
OTERO
LEA
EDDY
DONA ANA
LUNA
HIDALGO
Santa Fe
ALBUQUERQUE
Farmington
Aztec
Gallup
Grants
Raton
Clayton
Tucumcari
Clovis
Portales
Roswell
Carlsbad
Hobbs
Lovington
Las Cruces
Alamogordo
Deming
Lordsburg
Silver City
Truth or Consequences
Socorro
Las Vegas
Taos
Espanola
Los Alamos
Santa Rosa
Fort Sumner
Carrizozo
Artesia
El Paso
Ciudad Juárez
Durango
Trinidad
Alamosa
NAVAJO INDIAN RESERVATION
JICARILLA INDIAN RES.
MESCALERO APACHE INDIAN RES.
ZUNI INDIAN RES.
UTE MOUNTAIN INDIAN RES.
SOUTHERN UTE IND. RES.
WHITE SANDS NAT'L MON.
CARLSBAD CAVERNS NAT'L PARK
GREAT SAND DUNES NAT'L MON.
Rio Grande
Pecos River
Canadian R.
LLANO ESTACADO
STAKED PLAIN
PLAINS OF SAN AGUSTIN
SANGRE DE CRISTO MTS.
CONTINENTAL DIVIDE
Only point in the UNITED STATES common to four state boundaries
Longitude West of Greenwich
109° 108° 107° 106° 105° 104°
38° 37° 36° 35° 34° 33° 32° 31°
A B C D E F
1 2 3 4 5 6 7
© Copyright HAMMOND INCORPORATED, Maplewood, N. J.

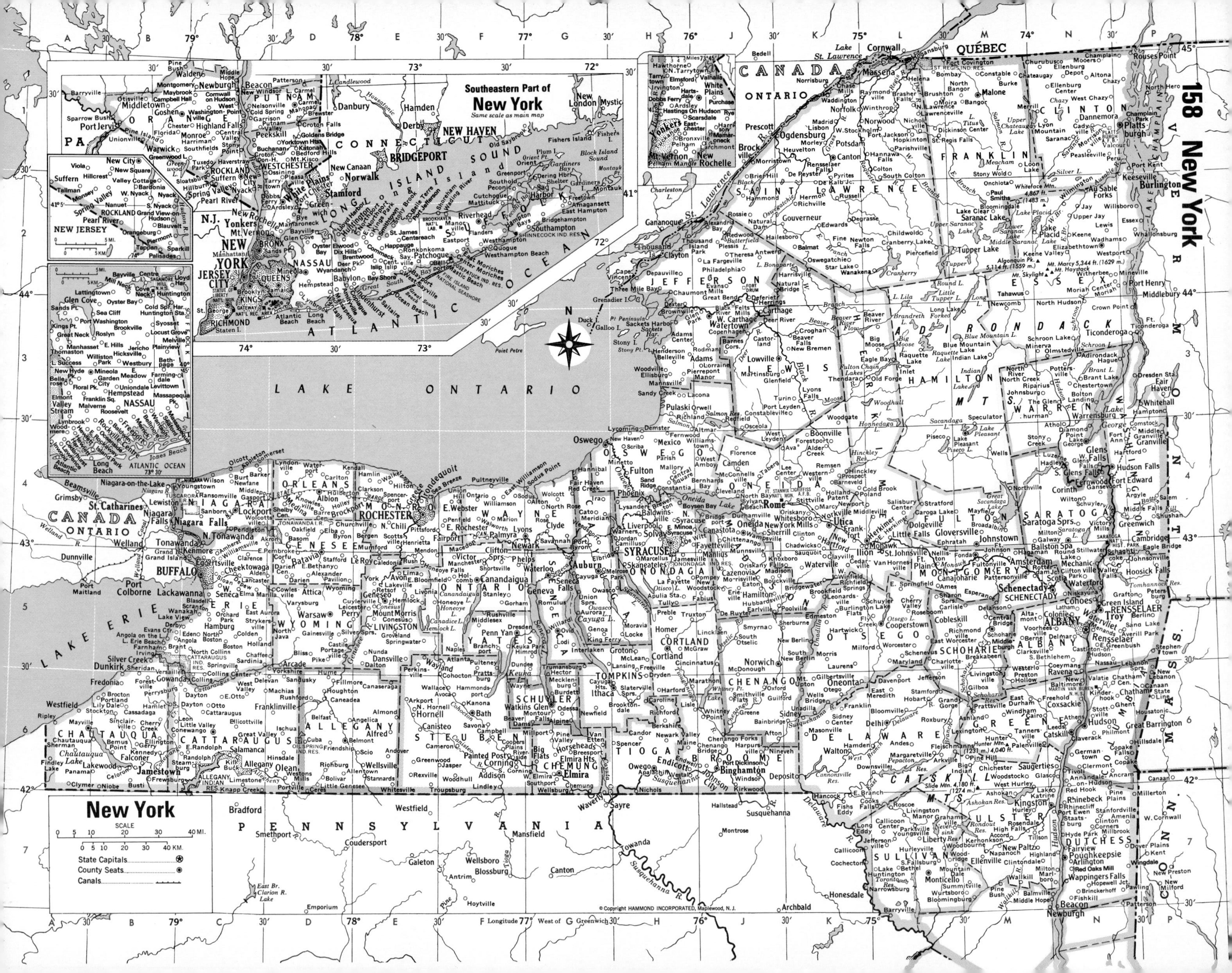
New York
SCALE
0 5 10 20 30 40 MI.
0 5 10 20 30 40 KM.
State Capitals
County Seats
Canals
Southeastern Part of
New York
Same scale as main map
LAKE ONTARIO
LAKE ERIE
ATLANTIC OCEAN
LONG ISLAND SOUND
CANADA
ONTARIO
QUÉBEC
PENNSYLVANIA
NEW JERSEY
CONNECTICUT
MASS.
VERMONT
CHAUTAUQUA
CATTARAUGUS
ALLEGANY
STEUBEN
CHEMUNG
TIOGA
BROOME
ERIE
NIAGARA
ORLEANS
GENESEE
WYOMING
LIVINGSTON
MONROE
ONTARIO
YATES
SCHUYLER
SENECA
WAYNE
CAYUGA
TOMPKINS
CORTLAND
CHENANGO
ONONDAGA
OSWEGO
MADISON
ONEIDA
JEFFERSON
LEWIS
SAINT LAWRENCE
FRANKLIN
CLINTON
ESSEX
HAMILTON
HERKIMER
WARREN
WASHINGTON
SARATOGA
FULTON
MONTGOMERY
SCHENECTADY
ALBANY
RENSSELAER
SCHOHARIE
OTSEGO
DELAWARE
GREENE
COLUMBIA
ULSTER
DUTCHESS
SULLIVAN
ORANGE
PUTNAM
ROCKLAND
WESTCHESTER
NASSAU
SUFFOLK
ADIRONDACK MTS.
CATSKILL MTS.
ALBANY
BUFFALO
ROCHESTER
SYRACUSE
UTICA
Schenectady
Binghamton
Elmira
NEW YORK
Longitude 77° West of Greenwich
© Copyright HAMMOND INCORPORATED, Maplewood, N. J.

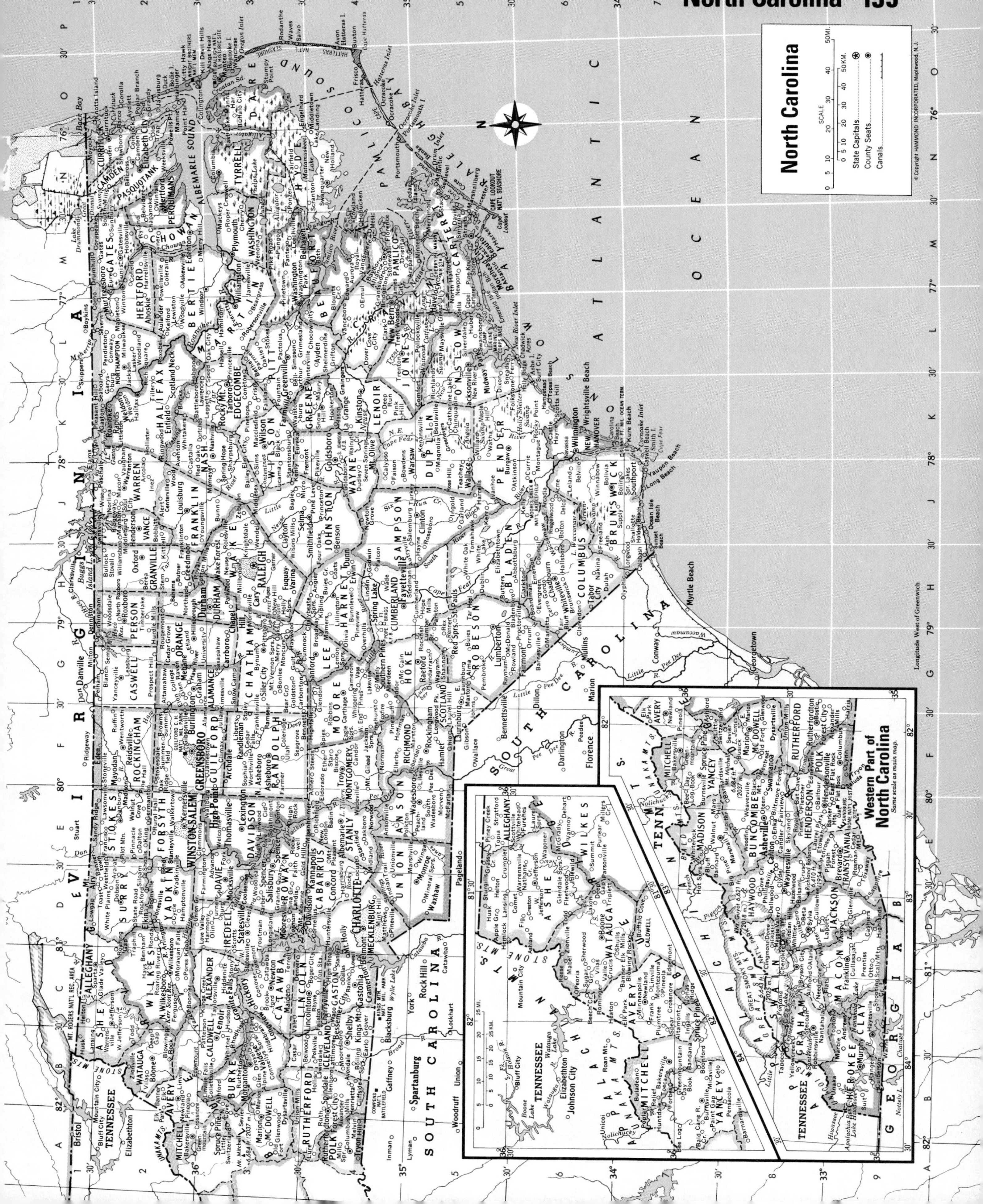
North Carolina
SCALE
0 5 10 20 30 40 50MI.
0 5 10 20 30 40 50KM.
State Capitals
County Seats
Canals
© Copyright HAMMOND INCORPORATED, Maplewood, N.J.
Western Part of
North Carolina
Same scale as main map.
Longitude West of Greenwich
V I R G I N I A
TENNESSEE
SOUTH CAROLINA
GEORGIA
A T L A N T I C
O C E A N
PAMLICO SOUND
ALBEMARLE SOUND
RALEIGH
CHARLOTTE
GREENSBORO
WINSTON-SALEM
Wilmington
Asheville
Durham
Fayetteville

North Dakota
SCALE
0 5 10 20 30 MI.
0 5 10 20 30 KM.
State Capitals
County Seats
SASKATCHEWAN
MANITOBA
MONTANA
MINNESOTA
SOUTH DAKOTA
DIVIDE
BURKE
RENVILLE
BOTTINEAU
ROLETTE
TOWNER
CAVALIER
PEMBINA
WILLIAMS
MOUNTRAIL
WARD
MCHENRY
PIERCE
BENSON
RAMSEY
WALSH
GRAND FORKS
NELSON
EDDY
WELLS
SHERIDAN
MCLEAN
MCKENZIE
FORT BERTHOLD INDIAN RESERVATION
DUNN
MERCER
OLIVER
BURLEIGH
KIDDER
STUTSMAN
FOSTER
GRIGGS
STEELE
TRAILL
BARNES
CASS
GOLDEN VALLEY
BILLINGS
STARK
MORTON
GRANT
SLOPE
HETTINGER
BOWMAN
ADAMS
SIOUX
STANDING ROCK INDIAN RESERVATION
EMMONS
LOGAN
LA MOURE
RANSOM
RICHLAND
MCINTOSH
DICKEY
SARGENT
Bismarck
Williston
Minot
Grand Forks
FARGO
Jamestown
Mandan
Dickinson
Devils Lake
Valley City
Wahpeton
Lake Sakakawea
Lake Oahe
Devils Lake
Missouri River
Theo. Roosevelt Nat'l Pk. (North Unit)
Theo. Roosevelt Nat'l Pk. (South Unit)
International Peace Garden
Turtle Mtn. Indian Res.
Fort Totten Ind. Res.
White Butte 3,506 ft. (1069 m.)
Geographical Center of North America
Longitude West of Greenwich
© Copyright HAMMOND INCORPORATED, Maplewood, N. J.

Ohio
SCALE
State Capitals
County Seats
MICHIGAN
INDIANA
PENNSYLVANIA
KENTUCKY
WEST VIRGINIA
ONTARIO
CANADA
LAKE ERIE
CLEVELAND
CINCINNATI
Columbus
Toledo
Dayton
Akron

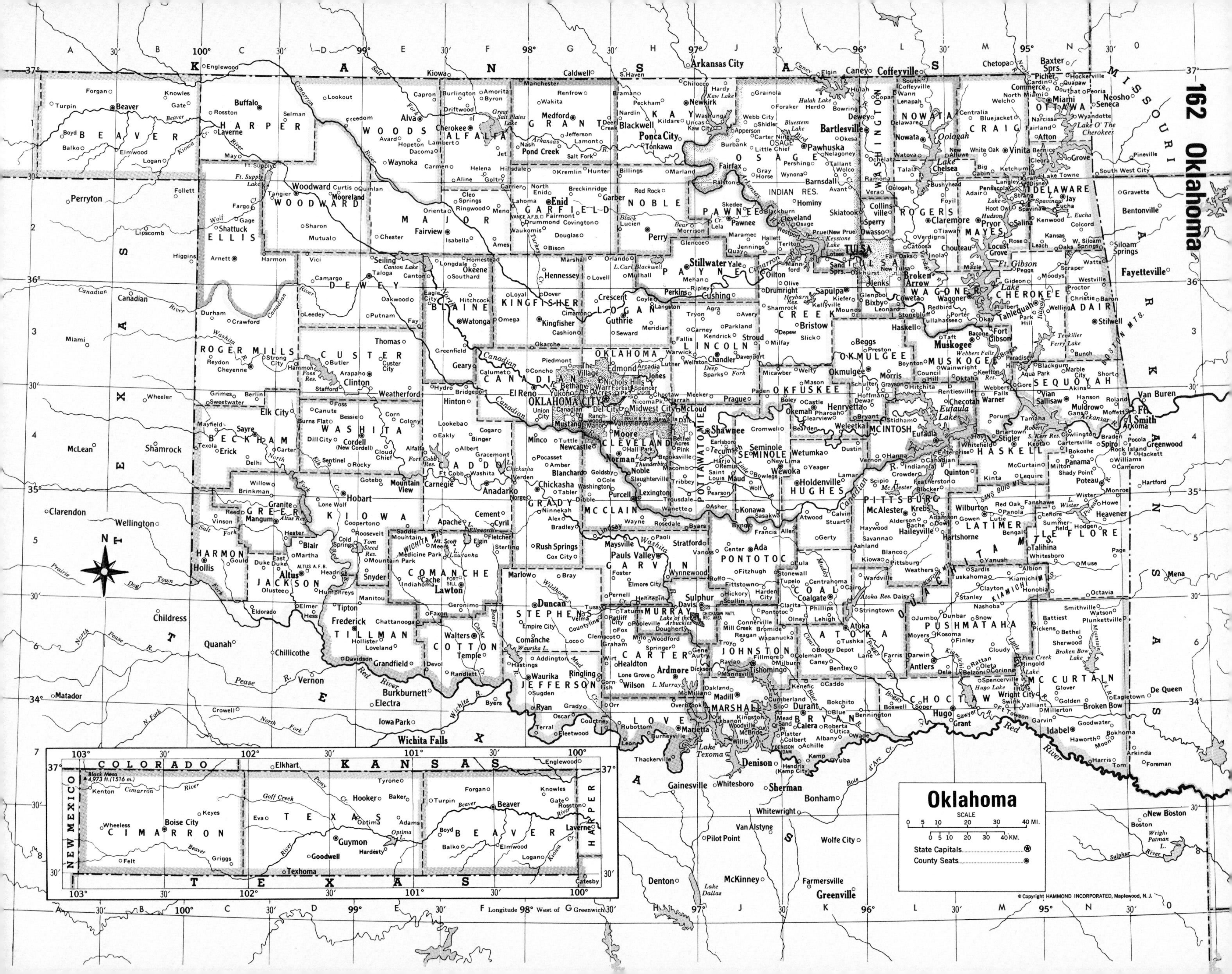

Oklahoma
SCALE
0 5 10 20 30 40 MI.
0 5 10 20 30 40 KM.
State Capitals
County Seats
© Copyright HAMMOND INCORPORATED, Maplewood, N.J.

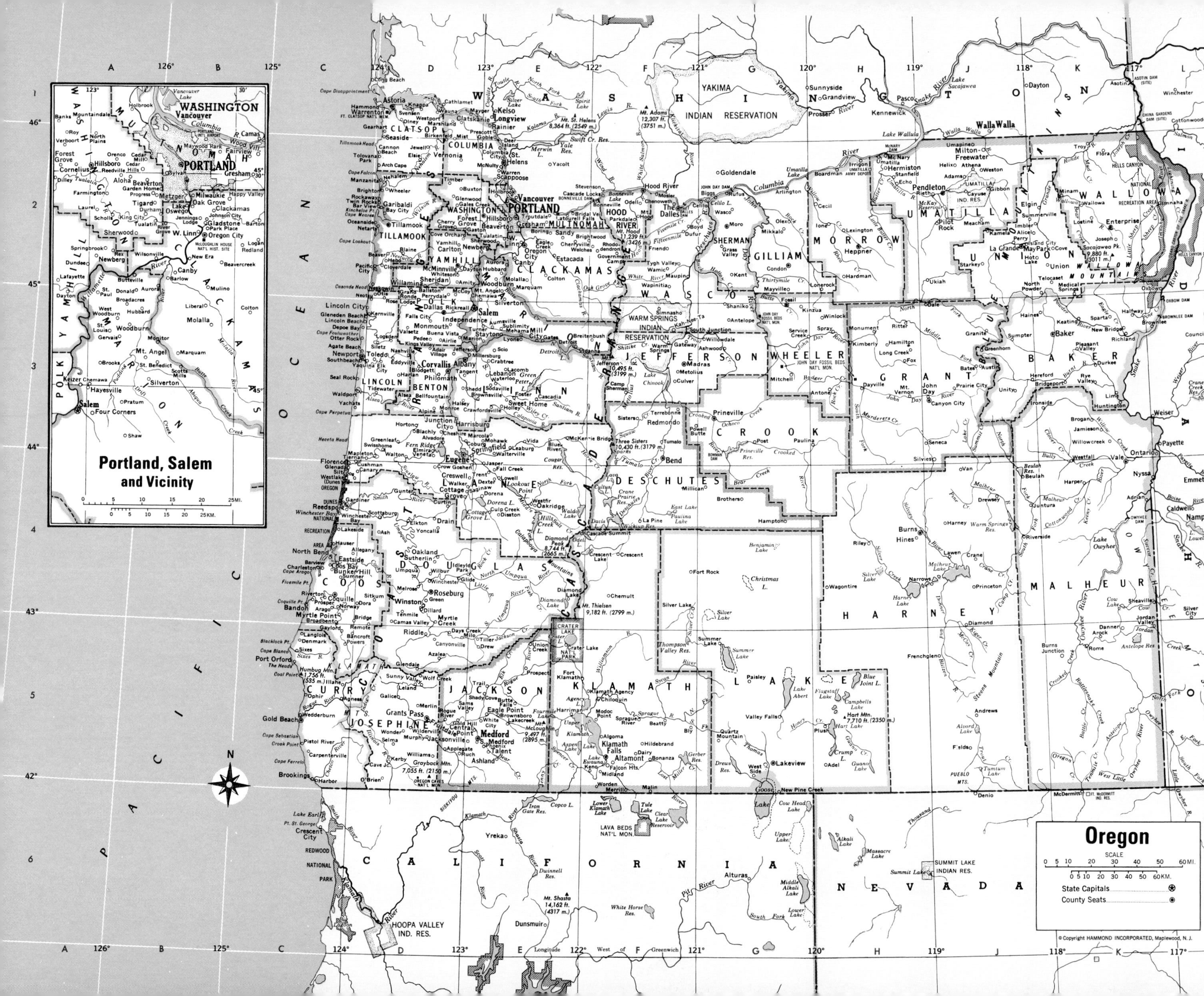
Portland, Salem and Vicinity
0 5 10 15 20 25 MI.
0 5 10 15 20 25 KM.
Oregon
SCALE
0 5 10 20 30 40 50 60 MI.
0 5 10 20 30 40 50 60 KM.
State Capitals
County Seats
© Copyright HAMMOND INCORPORATED, Maplewood, N. J.
WASHINGTON
CALIFORNIA
NEVADA
IDAHO
PACIFIC OCEAN
YAKIMA INDIAN RESERVATION
WARM SPRINGS INDIAN RESERVATION
CLATSOP
COLUMBIA
TILLAMOOK
WASHINGTON
MULTNOMAH
HOOD RIVER
YAMHILL
CLACKAMAS
POLK
MARION
LINCOLN
BENTON
LINN
LANE
WASCO
SHERMAN
GILLIAM
MORROW
UMATILLA
UNION
WALLOWA
JEFFERSON
WHEELER
GRANT
BAKER
CROOK
DESCHUTES
DOUGLAS
COOS
CURRY
JOSEPHINE
JACKSON
KLAMATH
LAKE
HARNEY
MALHEUR
PORTLAND
Salem
Eugene
Medford
Bend
Pendleton
Astoria
Klamath Falls

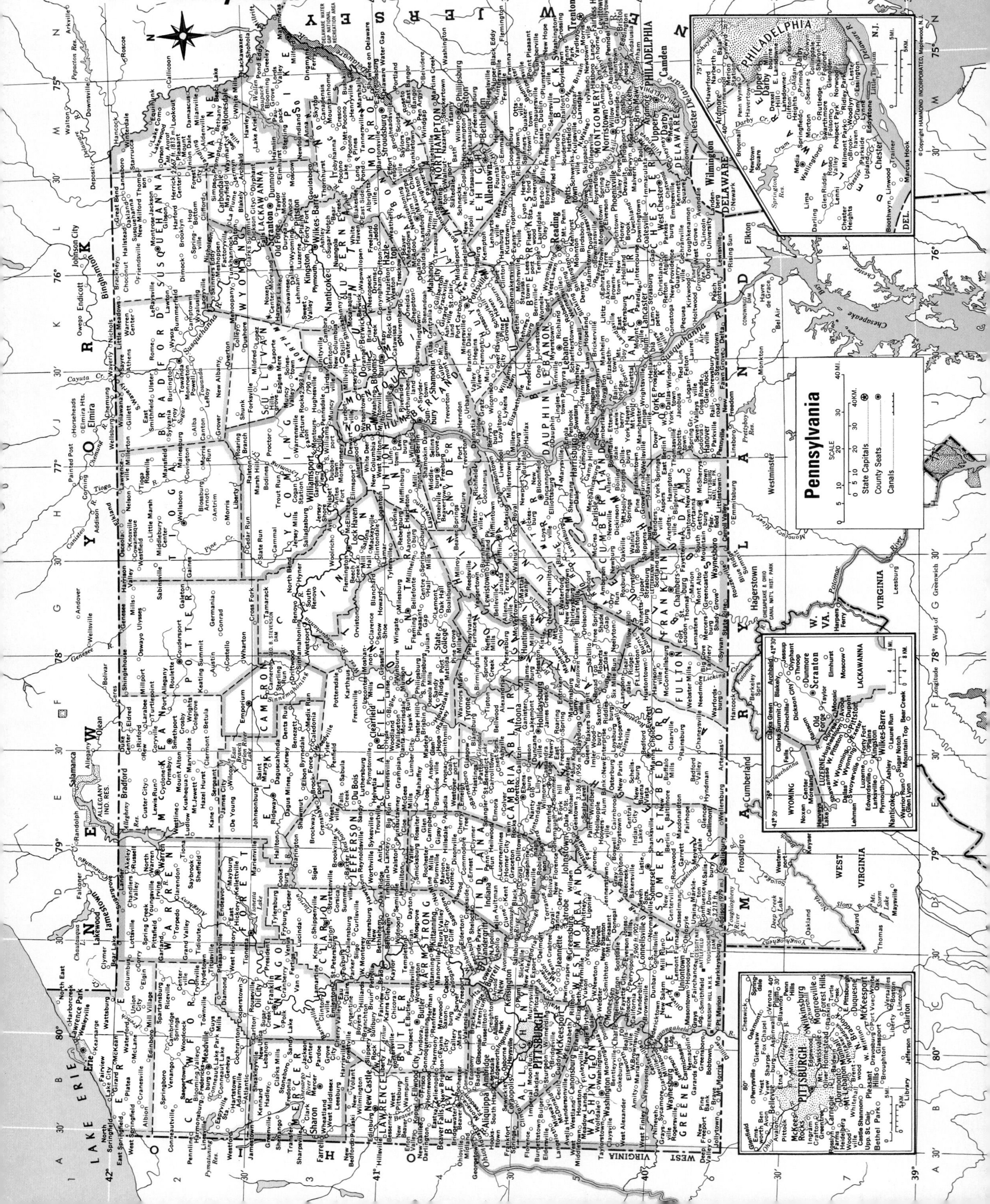

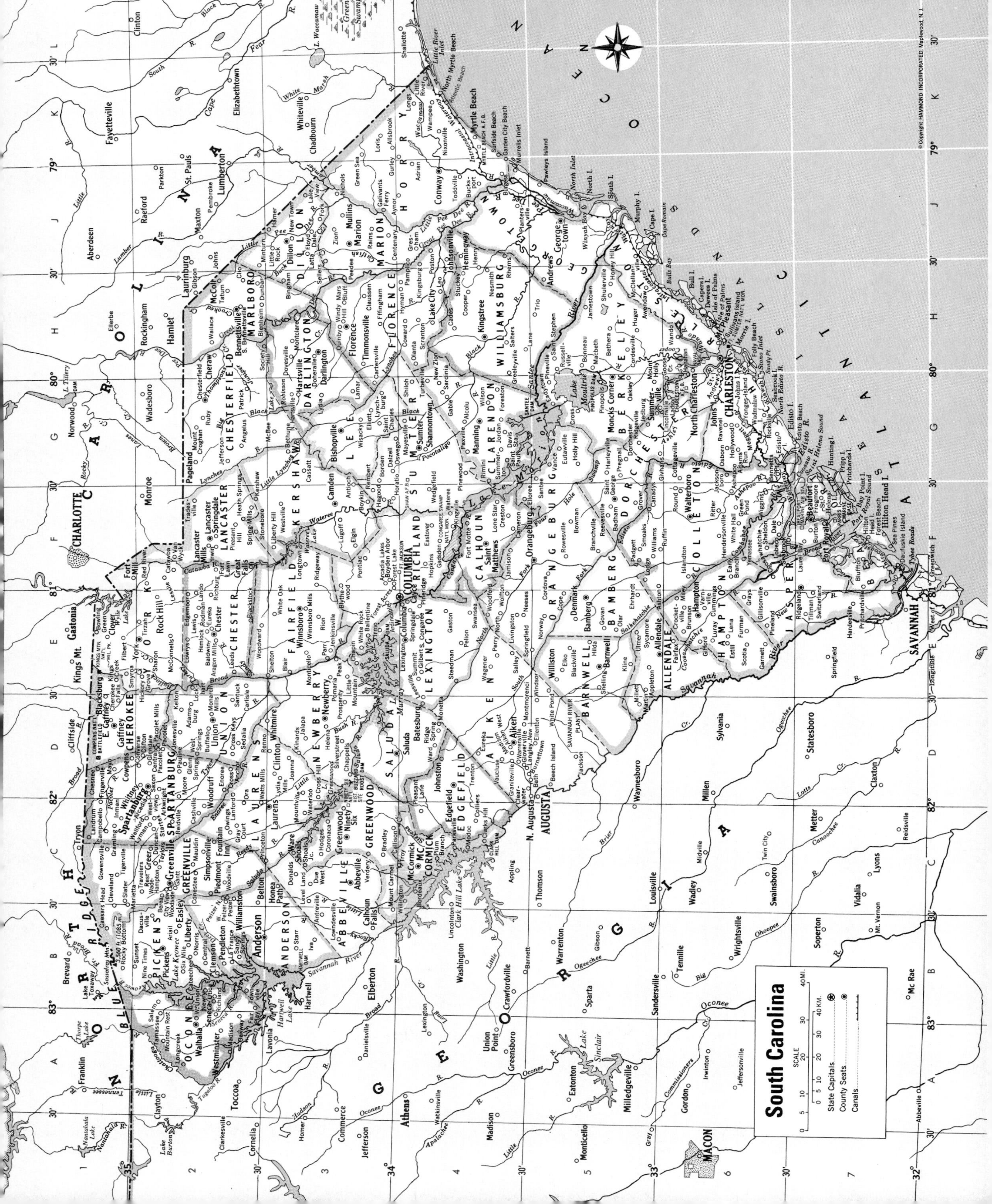
South Carolina
SCALE
0 5 10 20 30 40 MI.
0 5 10 20 30 40 KM.
State Capitals
County Seats
Canals
ATLANTIC ISLANDS
OCEAN
NORTH CAROLINA
GEORGIA
BLUE RIDGE
COLUMBIA
CHARLESTON
SAVANNAH
AUGUSTA
CHARLOTTE
MACON
Greenville
Spartanburg
Anderson
Florence
Sumter
Rock Hill
Myrtle Beach
Beaufort
Orangeburg
Aiken

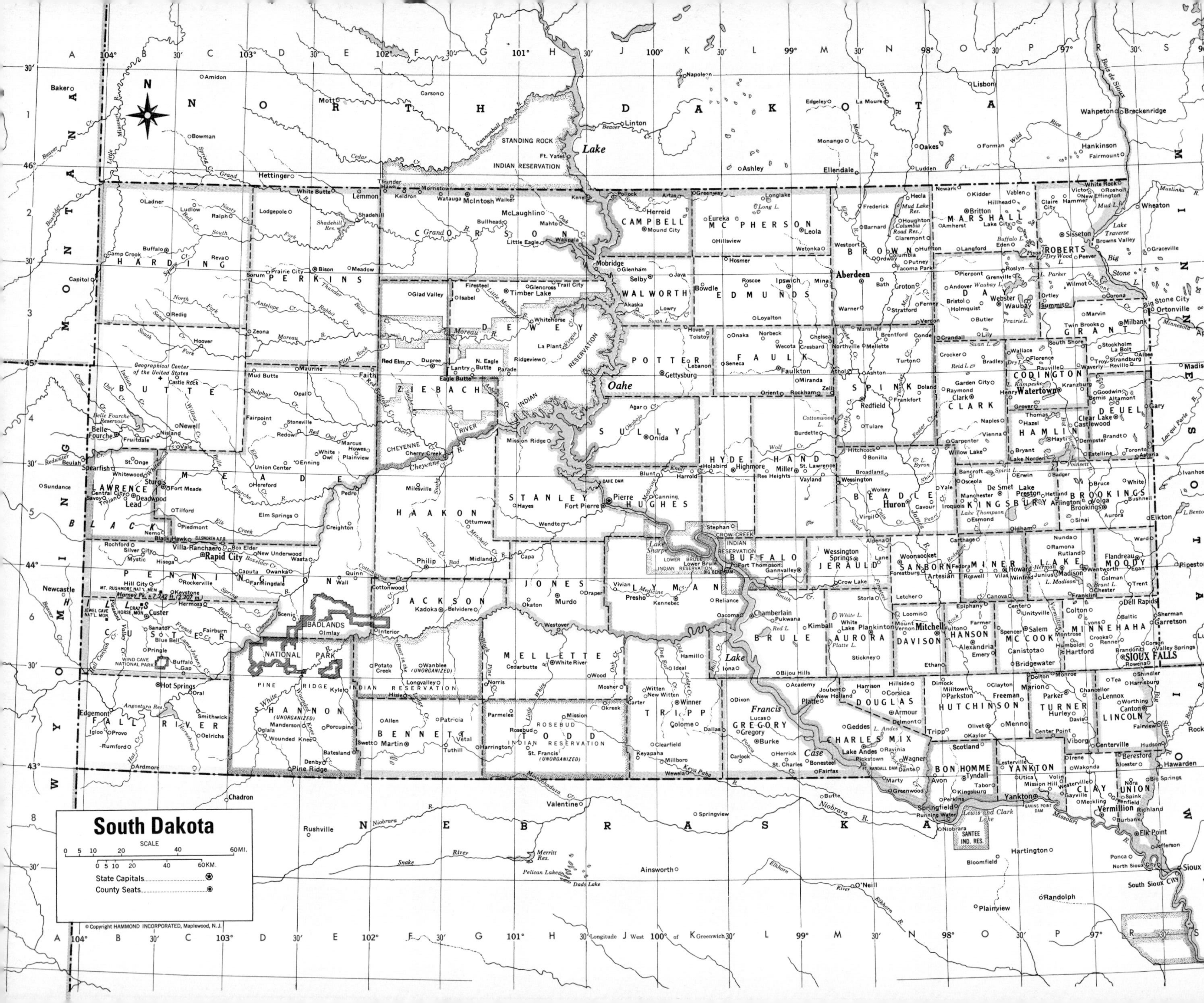
South Dakota
SCALE
0 5 10 20 40 60 MI.
0 5 10 20 40 60 KM.
State Capitals
County Seats
© Copyright HAMMOND INCORPORATED, Maplewood, N. J.
NORTH DAKOTA
NEBRASKA
MONTANA
WYOMING
MINNESOTA
IOWA
HARDING
PERKINS
CORSON
CAMPBELL
MC PHERSON
BROWN
MARSHALL
ROBERTS
BUTTE
ZIEBACH
DEWEY
WALWORTH
EDMUNDS
DAY
GRANT
POTTER
FAULK
SPINK
CLARK
CODINGTON
DEUEL
HAMLIN
LAWRENCE
MEADE
SULLY
HYDE
HAND
BEADLE
KINGSBURY
BROOKINGS
STANLEY
HUGHES
HAAKON
PENNINGTON
CUSTER
FALL RIVER
SHANNON
JACKSON
JONES
LYMAN
BUFFALO
JERAULD
SANBORN
MINER
LAKE
MOODY
MELLETTE
BENNETT
TODD
TRIPP
GREGORY
BRULE
AURORA
DAVISON
HANSON
MC COOK
MINNEHAHA
DOUGLAS
CHARLES MIX
HUTCHINSON
TURNER
LINCOLN
BON HOMME
YANKTON
CLAY
UNION
Lake Oahe
Lake Francis Case
Lewis and Clark Lake
STANDING ROCK INDIAN RESERVATION
CHEYENNE RIVER INDIAN RESERVATION
PINE RIDGE INDIAN RESERVATION
ROSEBUD INDIAN RESERVATION
BADLANDS NATIONAL PARK
WIND CAVE NATIONAL PARK
SANTEE IND. RES.
Pierre
Rapid City
Sioux Falls
Aberdeen
Huron
Watertown
Mitchell
Yankton

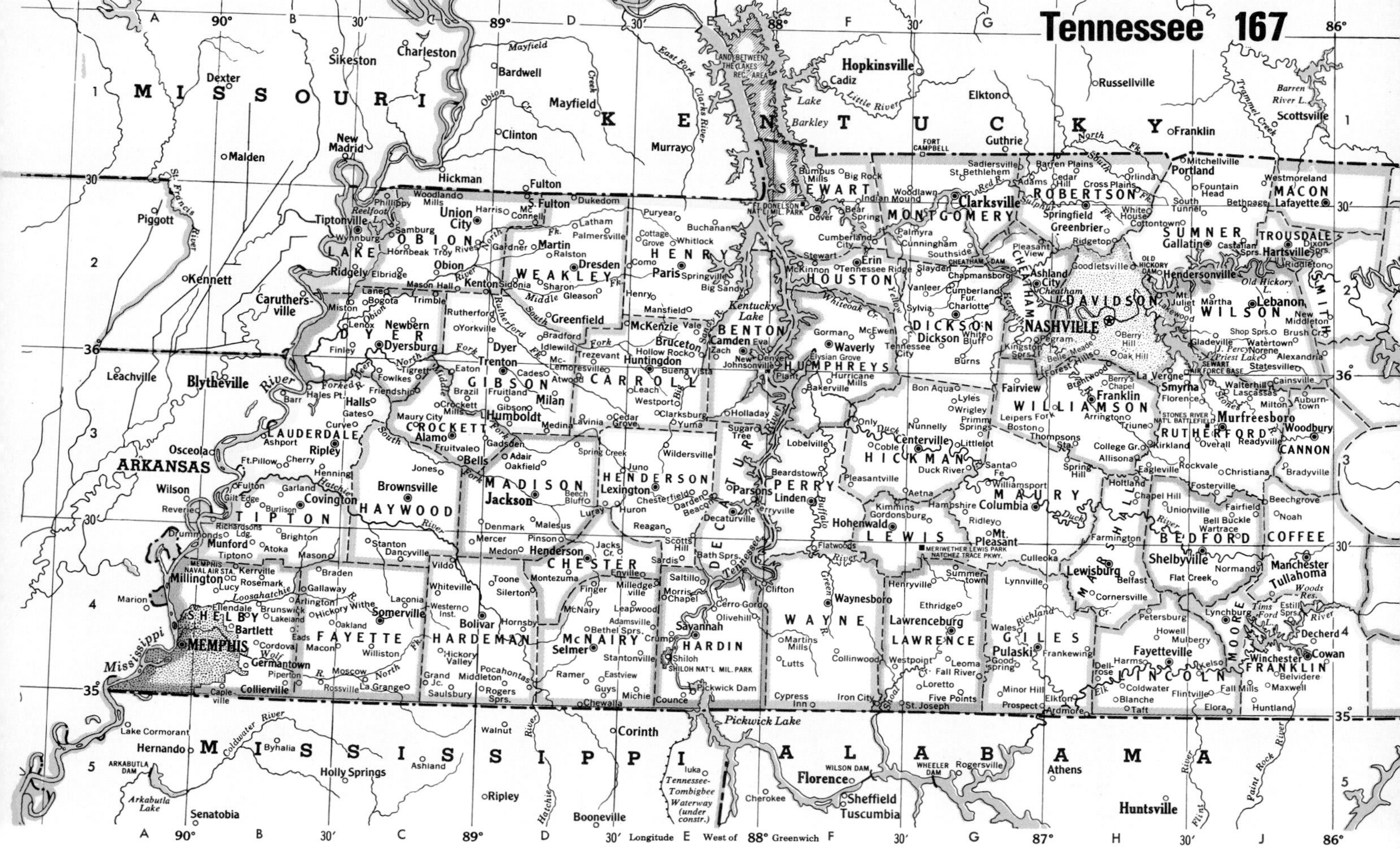
MISSOURI
KENTUCKY
ARKANSAS
MISSISSIPPI
ALABAMA
NASHVILLE
Longitude West of 88° Greenwich

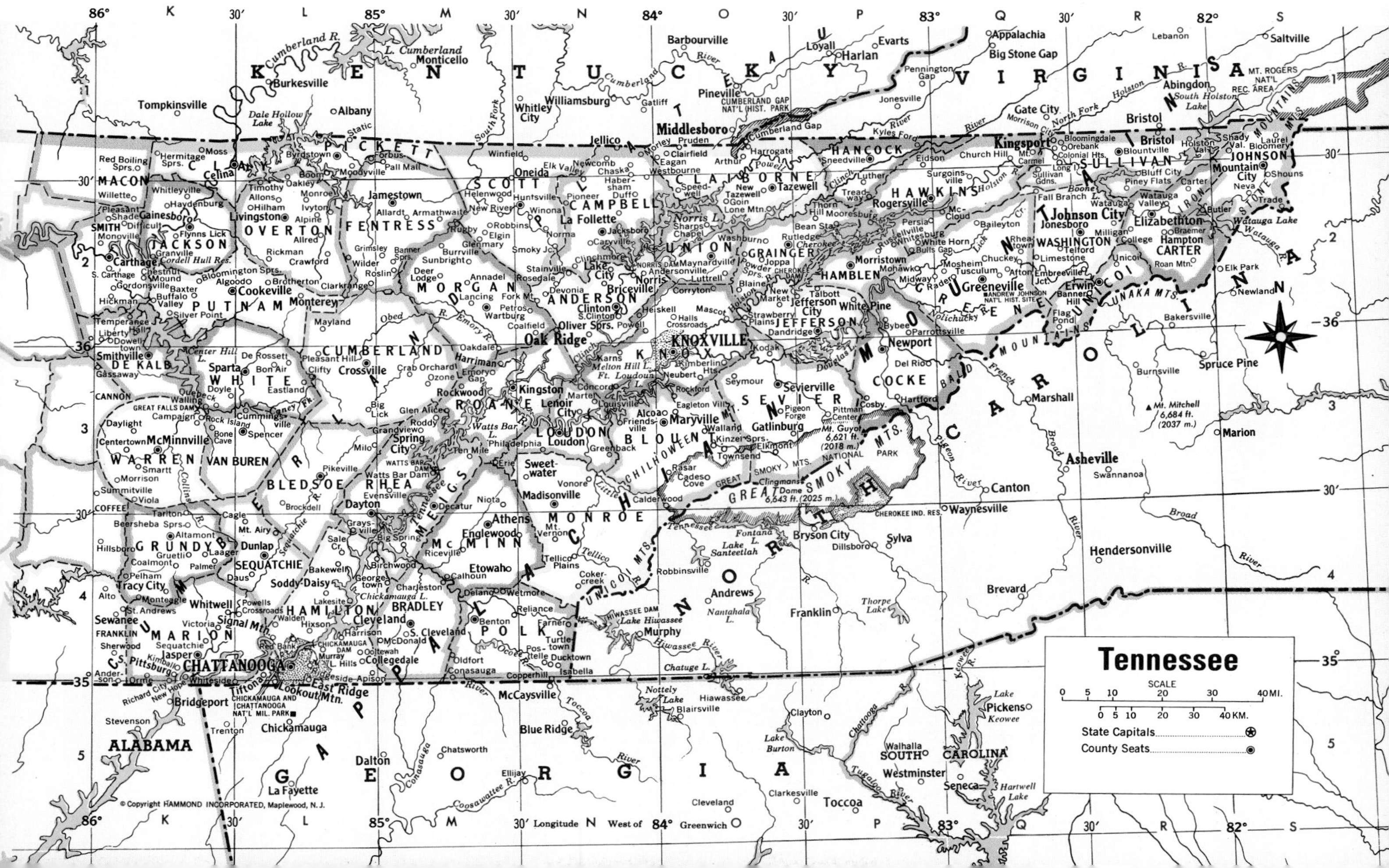
KENTUCKY
VIRGINIA
NORTH CAROLINA
GEORGIA
ALABAMA
SOUTH CAROLINA
KNOXVILLE
Tennessee
SCALE
0 5 10 20 30 40 MI.
0 5 10 20 30 40 KM.
State Capitals
County Seats
Longitude West of 84° Greenwich
© Copyright HAMMOND INCORPORATED, Maplewood, N.J.

Texas
0 20 40 60 80 100 MI.
0 20 40 60 80 100 KM.
State Capitals
County Seats
N
Western Part of Texas
Same scale as main map
MEXICO
GULF OF MEXICO
OKLAHOMA
NEW MEXICO
ARKANSAS
LOUISIANA
HOUSTON
DALLAS
FORT WORTH
SAN ANTONIO
Galveston
Austin
El Paso
Amarillo
Lubbock
Corpus Christi
Longitude 98° West of Greenwich 97°
© Copyright HAMMOND INCORPORATED, Maplewood, N.J.

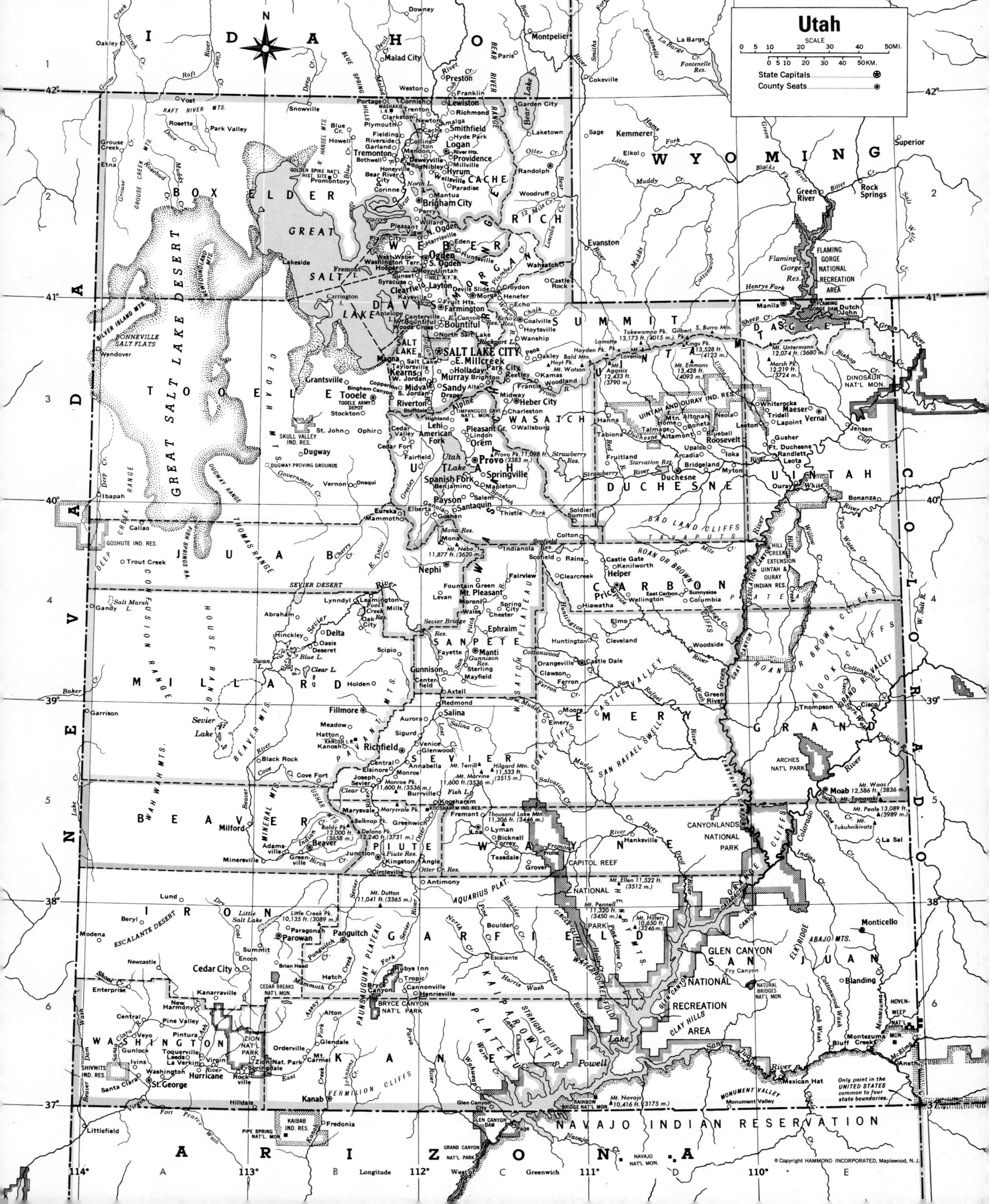
Utah
SCALE
0 5 10 20 30 40 50MI.
0 5 10 20 30 40 50KM.
State Capitals
County Seats
IDAHO
WYOMING
COLORADO
ARIZONA
NEVADA
BOX ELDER
CACHE
RICH
WEBER
MORGAN
DAVIS
SUMMIT
DAGGETT
SALT LAKE
TOOELE
WASATCH
UTAH
DUCHESNE
UINTAH
JUAB
CARBON
SANPETE
MILLARD
EMERY
GRAND
SEVIER
BEAVER
PIUTE
WAYNE
IRON
GARFIELD
SAN JUAN
WASHINGTON
KANE
GREAT SALT LAKE
GREAT SALT LAKE DESERT
SALT LAKE CITY
NAVAJO INDIAN RESERVATION
© Copyright HAMMOND INCORPORATED, Maplewood, N.J.

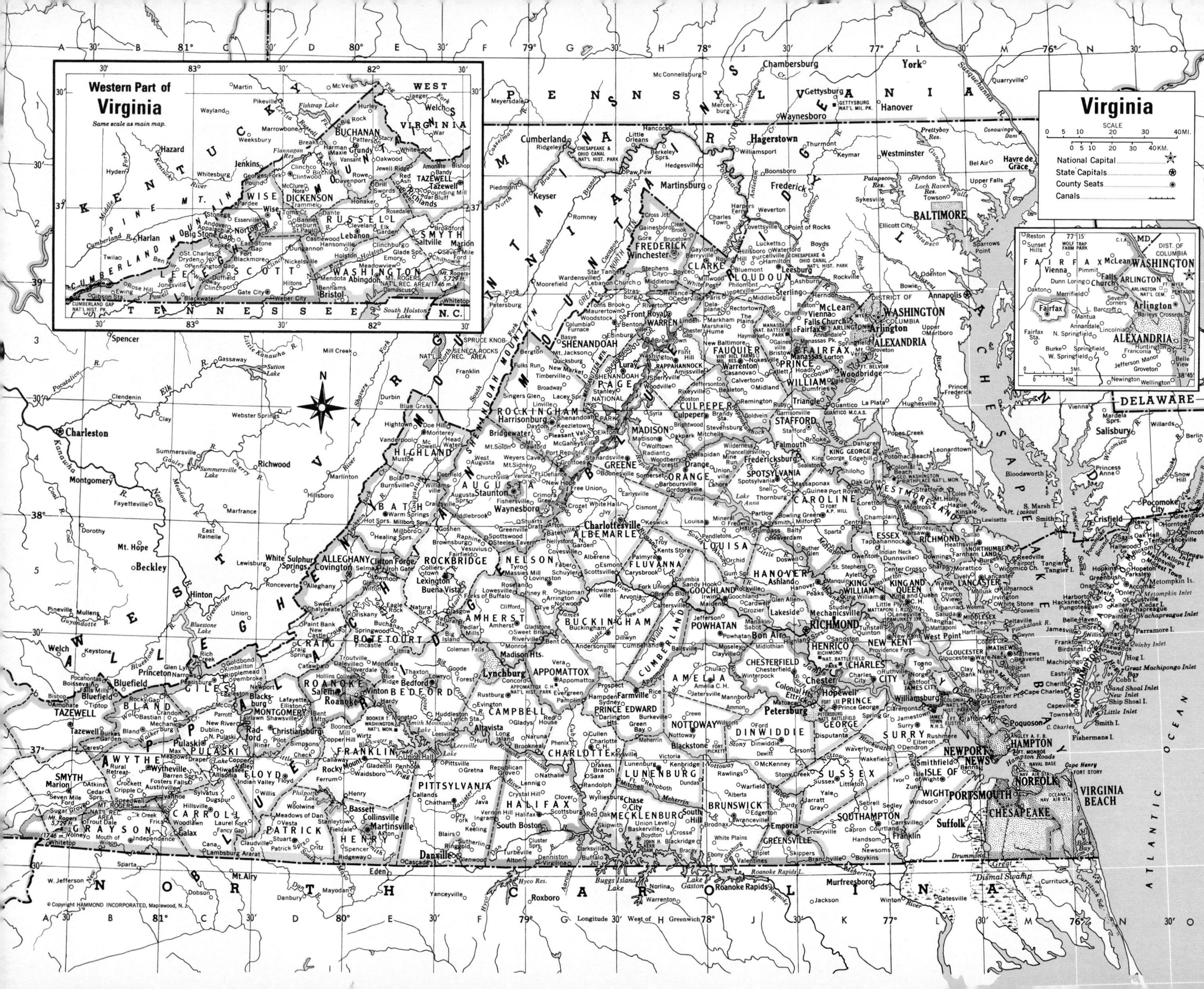
Virginia
SCALE
0 5 10 20 30 40 MI.
0 5 10 20 30 40 KM.
National Capital
State Capitals
County Seats
Canals
Western Part of Virginia
Same scale as main map.
KENTUCKY
WEST VIRGINIA
TENNESSEE
N.C.
PENNSYLVANIA
MARYLAND
DELAWARE
NORTH CAROLINA
DIST. OF COLUMBIA
WASHINGTON
Richmond
Norfolk
Virginia Beach
Chesapeake
Portsmouth
Newport News
Hampton
Alexandria
Arlington
Fairfax
Roanoke
Lynchburg
Charlottesville
Danville
Petersburg
Baltimore
Annapolis
Charleston
CHESAPEAKE BAY
ATLANTIC OCEAN
Longitude 30′ West of Greenwich 78°

Washington
SCALE
0 5 10 20 30 40 MI.
0 5 10 20 30 40 KM.
State Capitals
County Seats
PACIFIC OCEAN
BRITISH COLUMBIA
OREGON
IDAHO
CLALLAM
JEFFERSON
OLYMPIC NATIONAL PARK
GRAYS HARBOR
MASON
KITSAP
KING
PIERCE
THURSTON
PACIFIC
WAHKIAKUM
LEWIS
COWLITZ
CLARK
SKAMANIA
KLICKITAT
YAKIMA
KITTITAS
CHELAN
SNOHOMISH
SKAGIT
WHATCOM
OKANOGAN
DOUGLAS
GRANT
BENTON
FRANKLIN
ADAMS
LINCOLN
FERRY
STEVENS
PEND OREILLE
SPOKANE
WHITMAN
GARFIELD
COLUMBIA
WALLA WALLA
ASOTIN
COLVILLE INDIAN RESERVATION
YAKIMA INDIAN RESERVATION
HANFORD RESERVATION U.S. DEPT. OF ENERGY
Longitude West of Greenwich
© Copyright HAMMOND INCORPORATED, Maplewood, N. J.

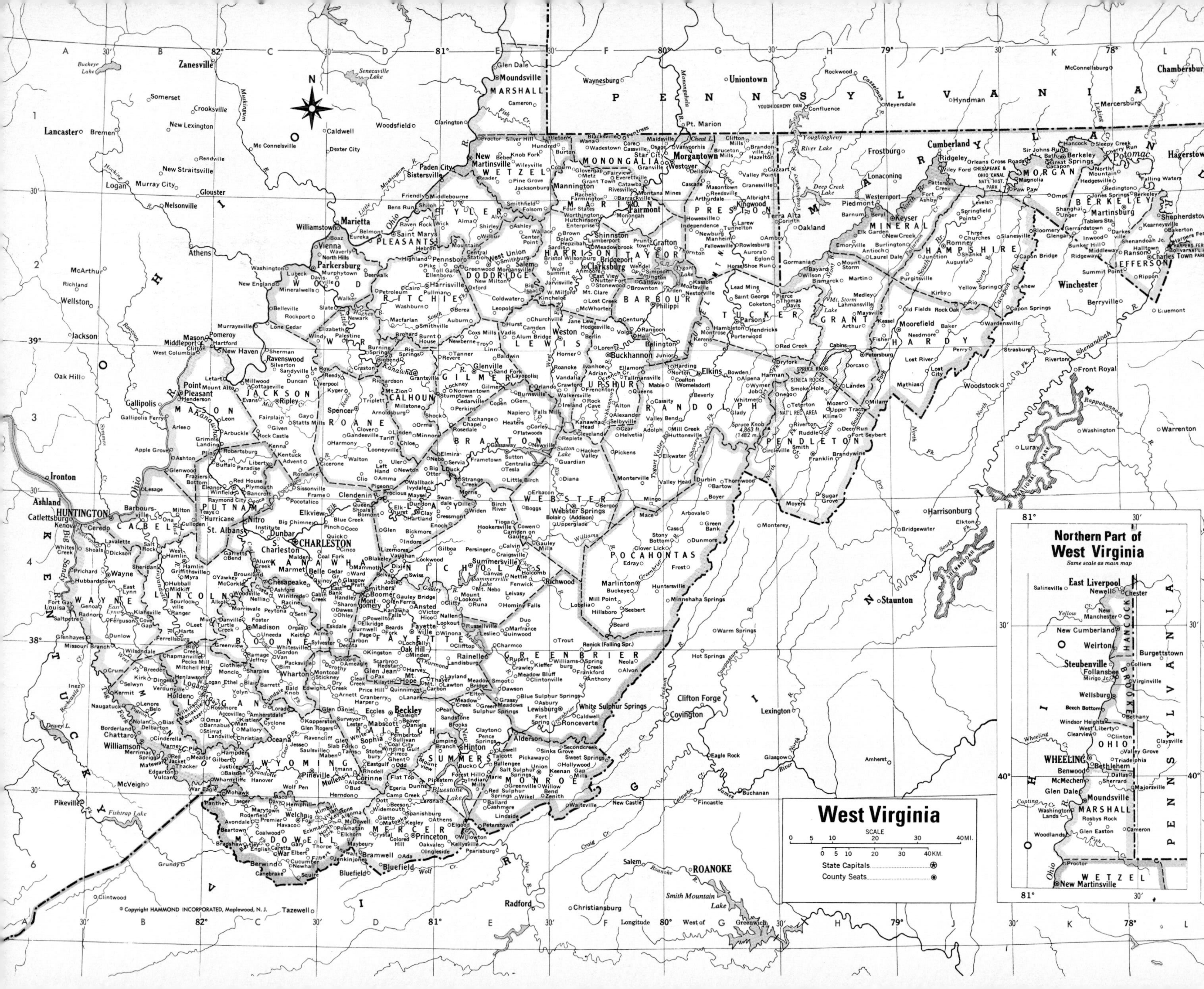
West Virginia
SCALE
0 5 10 20 30 40 MI.
0 5 10 20 30 40 KM.
State Capitals
County Seats
Northern Part of
West Virginia
Same scale as main map
© Copyright HAMMOND INCORPORATED, Maplewood, N. J.
PENNSYLVANIA
MARYLAND
OHIO
KENTUCKY
VIRGINIA
CHARLESTON
HANCOCK
BROOKE
OHIO
MARSHALL
WETZEL
TYLER
PLEASANTS
WOOD
RITCHIE
DODDRIDGE
HARRISON
TAYLOR
MARION
MONONGALIA
PRESTON
BARBOUR
TUCKER
GRANT
MINERAL
HAMPSHIRE
MORGAN
BERKELEY
JEFFERSON
HARDY
PENDLETON
RANDOLPH
UPSHUR
LEWIS
GILMER
CALHOUN
ROANE
JACKSON
MASON
PUTNAM
CABELL
WAYNE
LINCOLN
KANAWHA
CLAY
BRAXTON
WEBSTER
NICHOLAS
FAYETTE
BOONE
LOGAN
MINGO
WYOMING
RALEIGH
SUMMERS
MONROE
MERCER
McDOWELL
GREENBRIER
POCAHONTAS
WIRT
Wheeling
Huntington
Parkersburg
Morgantown
Clarksburg
Fairmont
Beckley
Bluefield
Martinsburg
Weirton
Steubenville
Cumberland
Hagerstown
Winchester
Staunton
Roanoke
Ohio R.
Potomac
Shenandoah
Monongahela
Kanawha

Wisconsin
SCALE
0 5 10 20 30 40 MI.
0 5 10 20 30 40 KM.
State Capitals
County Seats
Canals
LAKE SUPERIOR
LAKE MICHIGAN
MINNESOTA
IOWA
ILLINOIS
MICHIGAN
MADISON
MILWAUKEE
Green Bay
Duluth
Superior
La Crosse
Eau Claire
Oshkosh
Appleton
Sheboygan
Racine
Kenosha
Wausau
St. Paul
CHICAGO
Rockford
Dubuque
APOSTLE ISLANDS
Longitude West 90° of Greenwich

Wyoming
SCALE
0 5 10 20 30 40 MI.
0 5 10 20 30 40 KM.
State Capitals
County Seats
MONTANA
IDAHO
UTAH
COLORADO
NEBRASKA
SOUTH DAKOTA
YELLOWSTONE NATIONAL PARK
PARK
BIG HORN
SHERIDAN
CROOK
CAMPBELL
JOHNSON
WASHAKIE
HOT SPRINGS
TETON
WESTON
FREMONT
NATRONA
CONVERSE
NIOBRARA
SUBLETTE
LINCOLN
SWEETWATER
CARBON
ALBANY
PLATTE
GOSHEN
LARAMIE
UINTA
CHEYENNE
GREAT DIVIDE BASIN
WIND RIVER IND. RES.
CROW INDIAN RESERVATION
Longitude 107° West of Greenwich
© Copyright HAMMOND INCORPORATED, Maplewood, N. J.